THE
MICROECONOMY TODAY

FIFTEENTH EDITION

Mc
Graw
Hill
Education

The McGraw-Hill Series Economics

ESSENTIALS OF ECONOMICS

Brue, McConnell, and Flynn
Essentials of Economics
Fourth Edition

Mandel
M: Economics: The Basics
Third Edition

Schiller
Essentials of Economics
Tenth Edition

PRINCIPLES OF ECONOMICS

Asarta and Butters
Principles of Economics, Principles of Microeconomics, and Principles of Macroeconomics

Colander
Economics, Microeconomics, and Macroeconomics
Ninth Edition

Frank, Bernanke, Antonovics, and Heffetz
Principles of Economics, Principles of Microeconomics, Principles of Macroeconomics
Sixth Edition

Frank and Bernanke
Streamlined Editions: Principles of Economics, Principles of Microeconomics, Principles of Macroeconomics
Third Edition

Karlan and Morduch
Economics, Microeconomics, and Macroeconomics
Second Edition

McConnell, Brue, and Flynn
Economics, Microeconomics, and Macroeconomics
Twenty-First Edition

McConnell, Brue, and Flynn
Brief Editions: Microeconomics and Macroeconomics
Second Edition

Miller
Principles of Microeconomics
First Edition

Samuelson and Nordhaus
Economics, Microeconomics, and Macroeconomics
Nineteenth Edition

Schiller
The Economy Today, The Micro Economy Today, and The Macro Economy Today
Fifteenth Edition

Slavin
Economics, Microeconomics, and Macroeconomics
Eleventh Edition

ECONOMICS OF SOCIAL ISSUES

Guell
Issues in Economics Today
Eighth Edition

Sharp, Register, and Grimes
Economics of Social Issues
Twenty-First Edition

ECONOMETRICS

Gujarati and Porter
Basic Econometrics
Fifth Edition

Gujarati and Porter
Essentials of Econometrics
Fourth Edition

Hilmer and Hilmer
Practical Econometrics
First Edition

MANAGERIAL ECONOMICS

Baye and Prince
Managerial Economics and Business Strategy
Ninth Edition

Brickley, Smith, and Zimmerman
Managerial Economics and Organizational Architecture
Sixth Edition

Thomas and Maurice
Managerial Economics
Twelfth Edition

INTERMEDIATE ECONOMICS

Bernheim and Whinston
Microeconomics
Second Edition

Dornbusch, Fischer, and Startz
Macroeconomics
Twelfth Edition

Frank
Microeconomics and Behavior
Ninth Edition

ADVANCED ECONOMICS

Romer
Advanced Macroeconomics
Fourth Edition

MONEY AND BANKING

Cecchetti and Schoenholtz
Money, Banking, and Financial Markets
Fifth Edition

URBAN ECONOMICS

O'Sullivan
Urban Economics
Eighth Edition

LABOR ECONOMICS

Borjas
Labor Economics
Seventh Edition

McConnell, Brue, and Macpherson
Contemporary Labor Economics
Eleventh Edition

PUBLIC FINANCE

Rosen and Gayer
Public Finance
Tenth Edition

Seidman
Public Finance
First Edition

ENVIRONMENTAL ECONOMICS

Field and Field
Environmental Economics: An Introduction
Seventh Edition

INTERNATIONAL ECONOMICS

Appleyard and Field
International Economics
Eighth Edition

King and King
International Economics, Globalization, and Policy: A Reader
Fifth Edition

Pugel
International Economics
Sixteenth Edition

THE
MICROECONOMY TODAY

FIFTEENTH EDITION

Bradley R. Schiller

WITH KAREN GEBHARDT

Mc
Graw
Hill
Education

THE MICRO ECONOMY TODAY, FIFTEENTH EDITION

Published by McGraw-Hill Education, 2 Penn Plaza, New York, NY 10121. Copyright © 2019 by McGraw-Hill Education. All rights reserved. Printed in the United States of America. Previous editions © 2016, 2013, and 2010. No part of this publication may be reproduced or distributed in any form or by any means, or stored in a database or retrieval system, without the prior written consent of McGraw-Hill Education, including, but not limited to, in any network or other electronic storage or transmission, or broadcast for distance learning.

Some ancillaries, including electronic and print components, may not be available to customers outside the United States.

This book is printed on acid-free paper.

6 7 8 9 LWI 21 20

ISBN   978-1-260-10532-2
MHID   1-260-10532-6

Senior Portfolio Manager: *Katie Hoenicke*
Lead Product Developer: *Kelly Delso*
Product Developer: *Adam Huenecke*
Core Content Project Manager: *Kathryn D. Wright*
Senior Assessment Content Project Manager: *Kristin Bradley*
Media Content Project Manager: *Karen Jozefowicz*
Senior Buyer: *Laura Fuller*
Senior Designer: *Matt Diamond*
Content Licensing Specialist: *Lorraine Buczek*
Cover Image: *©The-Lightwrighter/Getty Images RF*
Compositor: *Aptara®, Inc.*

All credits appearing on page or at the end of the book are considered to be an extension of the copyright page.

Library of Congress Cataloging-in-Publication Data

Names: Schiller, Bradley R., 1943- author. | Gebhardt, Karen, author.
  Title: The micro economy today / Bradley R. Schiller, American University, emeritus, with Karen Gebhardt,
    Colorado State University.
  Description: Fifteenth Edition. | Dubuque : McGraw-Hill Education, [2019] |
    Revised edition of the authors' The micro economy today, [2016]
  Identifiers: LCCN 2017048456 | ISBN 9781260105322 (alk. paper) | ISBN 1260105326 (alk. paper)
  Subjects: LCSH: Microeconomics.
  Classification: LCC HB172 .S3625 2019 | DDC 338.5—dc23 LC record available at
    https://lccn.loc.gov/2017048456

The Internet addresses listed in the text were accurate at the time of publication. The inclusion of a website does not indicate an endorsement by the authors or McGraw-Hill Education, and McGraw-Hill Education does not guarantee the accuracy of the information presented at these sites.

Bradley R. Schiller has more than four decades of experience teaching introductory economics at American University, the University of Nevada, the University of California (Berkeley and Santa Cruz), and the University of Maryland. He has given guest lectures at more than 300 colleges ranging from Fresno, California, to Istanbul, Turkey. Dr. Schiller's unique contribution to teaching is his ability to relate basic principles to current socioeconomic problems, institutions, and public policy decisions. This perspective is evident throughout *The Micro Economy Today*.

Dr. Schiller derives this policy focus from his extensive experience as a Washington consultant. He has been a consultant to most major federal agencies, many congressional committees, and political candidates. In addition, he has evaluated scores of government programs and helped design others. His studies of poverty, discrimination, training programs, tax reform, pensions, welfare, Social Security, and lifetime wage patterns have appeared in both professional journals and popular media. Dr. Schiller is also a frequent commentator on economic policy for television and radio, and his commentary has appeared in *The Wall Street Journal, The Washington Post, The New York Times,* and *Los Angeles Times,* among other major newspapers.

Dr. Schiller received his Ph.D. from Harvard and his B.A. degree, with great distinction, from the University of California (Berkeley). His current research focus is on Cuba—its post-revolution collapse and its post-Castro prospects. On his days off, Dr. Schiller is on the tennis courts, the ski slopes, or the crystal-blue waters of Lake Tahoe.

Courtesy of Bradley R. Schiller

Dr. Karen Gebhardt is a faculty member in the Department of Economics at Colorado State University (CSU). Dr. Gebhardt has a passion for teaching economics. She regularly instructs large, introductory courses in macro- and microeconomics; small honors sections of these core principles courses; and upper-division courses in pubic finance, microeconomics, and international trade, as well as a graduate course in teaching methods.

She is an early adopter of technology in the classroom and advocates strongly for it because she sees the difference it makes in student engagement and learning. Dr. Gebhardt has taught online consistently since 2005 and coordinates the online program within the Department of Economics at CSU.

Dr. Gebhardt was the recipient of the Water Pik Excellence in Education Award in 2006 and was awarded the CSU Best Teacher Award in 2015.

Dr. Gebhardt's research interests, publications, and presentations involve the economics of human–wildlife interaction and economics and online education. Before joining CSU, she worked as an economist at the U.S. Department of Agriculture/Animal and Plant Health Inspection Service/Wildlife Services/National Wildlife Research Center, conducting research on the interactions of humans and wildlife, such as the economic effects of vampire bat–transmitted rabies in Mexico, the potential economic damage from introduction of invasive species to the Islands of Hawaii, bioeconomic modeling of the impacts of wildlife-transmitted disease, and others. In her free time, Dr. Gebhardt enjoys learning about new teaching methods that integrate technology and going rock climbing and camping in the Colorado Rockies and beyond.

Courtesy of Karen Gebhardt

The election of Donald Trump not only transformed the political landscape, but also radically altered the economic policy agenda. Trade policy became a front-page story. So did tax cuts, deregulation, and immigration policy. Sure, these issues were always on the political agenda, but they took on a greater priority with the ascension of the Trump administration. These shifting priorities require us econ professors to adapt. Students are always more interested in economics when we relate our theories to the news of the day. That means that we've got to make room in our syllabi for these rejuvenated issues.

Fortunately, *The Micro Economy Today* is exceptionally well suited for this task. From its inception, this text has been motivated by policy issues. The primary goal has been to help students understand the challenges of economic policy and the consequences of specific actions like tariffs, regulation, and tax reform. It has always provided a *balanced* discussion of these issues, allowing students to assess different perspectives on critical issues. For this edition, instructors will particularly appreciate the unique chapters that provide a solid foundation for explaining, illustrating, and assessing major Trump initiatives. Chapter 21 on international trade goes beyond the theory of comparative advantage to explain why and how some market participants seek to erect trade barriers. The unique chapter devoted to deregulation (Chapter 13) examines the rationale for government regulation of industry, the inherent trade-offs, and the consequences of (de)regulation. The same kind of insistence on critical thinking about policy issues is apparent in Chapter 14 on environmental protection.

We have two companion chapters on taxes (Chapter 19) and transfer payments (Chapter 20). The intent of these parallel chapters is to illustrate the equity vs. efficiency trade-offs that are common to both sides of the public budget. It provides a solid foundation for discussing the distributional effects of the Trump tax cuts and proposed reductions in income transfers.

No other text offers comparable, chapter-length coverage of the policy issues that have taken on a new urgency with the Trump administration. This is not a text full of fables and other abstractions; it's a text loaded with real-world applications, including the policy agenda of the Trump administration (which is explained, illustrated, and assessed—but not championed). This text makes it a lot easier for students to see the relevancy of economic principles to the front-page issues that dominate the news and political debates. It also requires critical thinking about these same economic issues and the economic concepts that underlie them. No other text comes close to this policy-driven, real-world approach. Students respond with greater interest, motivation—and even retention. If our goal is to have students understand both core economic concepts and their relevancy to the world around them, this is the text to use.

A feature titled "The Economy Tomorrow" at the end of every chapter illustrates one of the ways core economic concepts are linked to policy issues. This feature challenges students to relate the concepts they have just learned to a real-world policy problem. In the very first chapter, for example, students are forced to consider how the newly introduced concept of opportunity costs alters perspectives on "harnessing the sun," such as building more solar-power infrastructure. In Chapter 3 students are challenged to consider the deadly consequences of prohibiting the use of the market mechanism to allocate human organs.

The emphasis on real-world policy challenges is not confined to The Economy Tomorrow feature. Every chapter has an array of In the News and World View boxes that offer real-world illustrations of basic economic principles. Israel's success with its "Iron Dome" antimissile defense is a great illustration of what economists call a "public good" (Chapter 4 World View "Israel's 'Iron Dome' Frustrates Hamas"). North Korea's latest missile tests are a timely illustration of the "guns vs. butter" trade-off (Chapter 1 World View "World's

Largest Armies"). In the News "Californians Vote to Triple Cigarette Tax" in Chapter 6 on California's 2017 cigarette tax hike provides an opportunity to put the concept of price elasticity to work. You get the picture: this *is* the premier policy-driven, real-world focused introduction to economic principles.

DIFFERENTIATING FEATURES

The policy-driven focus of *The Micro Economy Today* clearly differentiates it from other principles texts. Other texts may claim real-world content, but none comes close to the empirical perspectives of this text. Beyond this unique approach, *The Micro Economy Today* offers a combination of features that no other text matches, including the following.

Markets versus Government Theme

market failure: An imperfection in the market mechanism that prevents optimal outcomes.

government failure: Government intervention that fails to improve economic outcomes.

Unique Topic Coverage

We all know there is no such thing as a pure market-driven economy and that markets operate on the fringe even in the most centralized economics. So "markets versus government" is not an all-or-nothing proposition. It is still a central theme, however, in the real world as President Trump insisted. Should the government assume *more* responsibility for managing the economy—or will *less* intervention generate better outcomes? Public opinion is clear: As the accompanying News reveals, the majority of Americans have a negative view of federal intervention. The challenge for economics instructors is to enunciate principles that help define the boundaries of public and private sector activity. When do we expect **market failure** to occur? How and why do we anticipate that government intervention might result in **government failure**? Can we get students to think critically about these central issues? *The Micro Economy Today* certainly tries, aided by scores of real-world illustrations.

The staples of introductory economics are fully covered in *The Micro Economy Today*. Beyond the core chapters, however, there is always room for additional coverage. In fact, authors reveal their uniqueness in their choice of such chapters. Those choices tend to be more abstract in competing texts, offering "extra" chapters on public choice, behavioral economics, economics of information, uncertainty, and asymmetric information. All of these are interesting and important, but they entail opportunity costs that are particularly high at the principles level. The menu in *The Micro Economy Today* is more tailored to the dimensions and issues of the world around us. Chapter 2, for example, depicts the dimensions of the U.S. economy in a comparative global framework. Where else are students

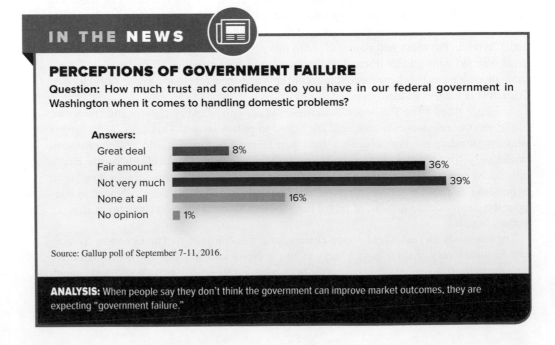

IN THE NEWS

PERCEPTIONS OF GOVERNMENT FAILURE

Question: How much trust and confidence do you have in our federal government in Washington when it comes to handling domestic problems?

Answers:
- Great deal — 8%
- Fair amount — 36%
- Not very much — 39%
- None at all — 16%
- No opinion — 1%

Source: Gallup poll of September 7-11, 2016.

ANALYSIS: When people say they don't think the government can improve market outcomes, they are expecting "government failure."

going to learn that China is *not* the world's largest economy, that U.S. workers are the most productive, or that income inequality is more severe in poor nations than rich ones?

The same emphasis on contemporary policy issues is evident throughout this edition. The parallel chapters on taxes (19) and transfers (20) underscore the central conflict between equity and efficiency concerns that impedes easy solutions to important policy questions. The comparison of the Clinton and Pence tax returns in Chapter 19 enlivens the discussion of tax "loopholes."

The extensive coverage of market structure includes *two* chapters on competition. The first (8) presents the standard, static profit maximization model for the perfectly competitive firm. The second chapter (9) adds real-world excitement. Chapter 9 focuses on market dynamics, emphasizing how competitive *forces* alter both market structures and market outcomes. The core case study takes students from the original Apple I (see the photo in Chapter 9) all the way to the iPhone 7 and iWatch. Along the way, the effects of continuous entry, exit, and innovation are highlighted. Students come away with an enhanced appreciation of how competitive markets generate superior outcomes—one of the most important insights of the micro sequence.

Also noteworthy in the micro sequence is the chapter (13) on natural monopoly. We know that natural monopoly presents unique challenges for antitrust and regulatory policy. This chapter first assesses the goal conflicts that complicate government intervention, and then reviews regulatory history and outcomes in the rail, telephone, airline, and cable industries.

Global Perspective

"Global perspective," along with "real-world" content, is promised by just about every principles author. *The Micro Economy Today* actually delivers on that promise. This is manifestly evident in the titles of Chapter 2 (global comparisons) and Chapter 23 (global poverty). The global perspective is also easy to discern in the boxed World View features embedded in every chapter. More subtle, but at least as important, is the portrayal of an open economy from the get-go. While some texts start with a closed economy—or worse still, a closed, private economy—and then add international dimensions as an afterthought, *The Micro Economy Today* depicts an open economy from start to finish. These global linkages are a vital part of any coherent explanation of micro issues (e.g., effective competition, oil prices).

WHAT'S NEW AND UNIQUE IN THIS 15TH EDITION

Every edition of *The Micro Economy Today* introduces a wealth of new content and pedagogy. This is critical for a text that prides itself on currency of policy issues, institutions, and empirical perspectives. Every page, every example, and all the data have been reviewed for currency and updated where needed. Beyond this general upgrade, this 15th edition offers the following.

28 New In the News Boxes

Price determination is illustrated in Chapter 3 with NCAA ticket scalping, price cuts on Galaxy 7 phones, and the surge in gasoline prices in the wake of Hurricane Matthew. In micro, the record-breaking Snapchat IPO highlights the role of financial markets in reallocating resources (Chapter 18). Tesla's new "gigafactory" illustrates the advantages of economies of scale (Chapter 13). Those "bikini barristers" in Everett, Washington, emphasize the importance of product differentiation in monopolistic competition (Chapter 12). And the new tariff on Canadian lumber addresses the realities of trade protection (Chapter 21).

11 New World View Boxes

Israel's deployment of its "Iron Dome" missile defense system offers a great illustration of public goods. Among the new World Views are Venezuela's increasing socialism (Chapter 23), the U.S. 2017 imposition of tariffs on Canadian lumber (Chapter 21), Heritage Foundation's 2017 global rankings on its Index of Economic Freedom (Chapter 1), and California's 2017 tax hike on cigarettes highlights the importance of price elasticity calculations.

The pricing of the iPhone 7 and iWatch highlight the central role of price elasticities (Chapter 6). And the latest OPEC deal illustrates the use of price-fixing to attain monopoly profits (Chapter 11). All In the News and World View boxes are annotated and referred to explicitly in the body of the text.

93 New Problems

As in earlier editions, the 15th edition forges explicit links between the end-of-chapter problems and the content of the chapter. Problems require students to go back into the body of the text and use data from the In the News and World View boxes, as well as from standard tables and texts. This strategy greatly improves the odds of students actually reading the boxed material and comprehending the graphs and tables.

44 New Discussion Questions

The discussion questions also require students to make use of material within the In the News boxes and the body of the text. Virtually all of the new Discussion Questions build on such in-chapter content.

5 New "Economy Tomorrow" Features

We gaze into the future of climate change and explore the methods of prospect for wider adaptation of electrical vehicles (Chapter 6) and the "War on Coal" (Chapter 14).

....

CHAPTER-BY-CHAPTER CHANGES: PURPOSE, SCOPE, AND UPDATES

Every page of this text has been subjected to review, revision, and updating. The following list gives a thumbnail sketch of the purpose, scope, and revisions of each chapter.

Chapter 1: Economics: The Core Issues introduces the core issues of What, How, and For Whom and the debate over market reliance or government regulation to resolve them. New global rankings on the extent of market reliance are highlighted. President Trump's call for cuts in space exploration and increases in defense spending highlight the guns vs. butter dilemma (opportunity cost), as does North Korea's continuing food shortage in the midst of an expensive missile program.

Chapter 2: The U.S. Economy: A Global View is intended to give students a sense of how the American economy stacks up to other nations in the world. The completely updated comparisons are organized around the core issues of What, How, and For Whom. The end-of-chapter The Economy Tomorrow feature considers the challenges of the United Nations goal for sustainable global development.

Chapter 3: Supply and Demand introduces the core elements of the market mechanism. Samsung's pricing of the Galaxy S7 illustrate the law of demand. Ticket scalping at the NCAA finals illustrates disequilibrium pricing. Supply/demand shifts are illustrated with gasoline prices in the wake of Hurricane Matthew and oil prices in the wake of Nigerian supply disruptions.

Chapter 4: The Role of Government focuses on the justifications for government intervention (market failures) and the growth of the public sector. Data on tax rates, public opinion about the role of government, state/local bond referenda, and government growth have all been updated. Israel's "Iron Dome" missile defense system is offered as a classic example of a "public good."

Chapter 5: Consumer Choice introduces the notion of consumer choice by first contrasting sociopsychiatric and economic explanations of consumer behavior. Utility theory, consumer surplus, price discrimination, and consumer choice are all discussed and illustrated. The update on LeBron James's endorsements underscores the role of advertising on consumer behavior.

Chapter 6: Elasticity explores price, income, and cross-price elasticities with the iPhone 7 launch, 2017 California tax hike on cigarettes, and consumer responses to higher gasoline prices. The role of prices in charting the future adoption of electric vehicles (EVs) is assessed in The Economy Tomorrow feature. Ten new problems provide practice in computing elasticities.

Chapter 7: The Costs of Production introduces the production function and emphasizes the relationship between productivity and cost measures. Tesla's new "gigafactory" illustrates the nature and sources of economies of scale. There are also new statistics on global competitiveness.

Chapter 8: The Competitive Firm depicts the static equilibrium behavior of the perfectly competitive firm, using the catfish industry as the core example. General Motor's temporary closure of its Detroit factories helps illustrate the differences between shutdown and exit decisions.

Chapter 9: Competitive Markets is a unique assessment of the dynamics of competitive markets—the heart and soul of market economies. The core story focuses on the evolution of the computer market, emphasizing the importance of entry, innovation, and exit to competitive outcomes. Illustrations include the tablet market, India's telecom market, and even long-run equilibrium in the catfish market.

Chapter 10: Monopoly not only examines the unique structural features of monopoly but also offers a unique, step-by-step contrast between competitive and monopoly behavior and outcomes. The American and European antitrust complaints against Google and Microsoft illustrate the nature of entry barriers and monopoly exploitation in the tech world.

Chapter 11: Oligopoly emphasizes how common oligopoly is in familiar product markets and the unique profit opportunities and coordination problems that result. OPEC's explicit price and output agreements illustrate outright price-fixing, while other industries use various entry barriers (e.g., input lockups, shelf-space rentals, distribution control, legal challenges) to thwart competition and increase profits.

Chapter 12: Monopolistic Competition stresses the differences in structure, behavior, and outcomes of this common industry category. The introduction of "Roasteries" at Starbucks and "bikini barristers" in Everett, Washington, illustrate the need for continuous product differentiation. New estimates of the dollar value of specific brands underscores the importance of brand recognition and loyalty.

Chapter 13: Natural Monopolies: (De)Regulation? goes beyond the depiction of this unique industry structure to explore the regulatory dilemmas that result. Quite simply, how can regulators compel natural monopolies to deliver the advantages of economies of scale without stifling innovation and decreasing efficiency? And how much will regulation cost? These questions are illustrated in the trucking, airline, cable, and electricity industries. The willingless of Nevada casinos to pay to escape that state's power monopoly illustrates how oppressive monopoly pricing can be.

Chapter 14: Environmental Protection is one of the world's great challenges, as the 2014 UN Climate Summit emphasized. This chapter explores the role of market incentives in environmental degradation and assesses the various policy options for inducing more eco-friendly behavior. The EPA's "war on coal," the battle over the Indian Point nuclear facility, and proposed "carbon taxes" offer timely illustrations of the theoretical and policy issues in the environmental debates.

Chapter 15: The Farm Problem just won't go away. Low price and income elasticities combine with the vagaries of weather to keep food prices volatile. The Farm Act of 2018 revisits the new price floors and subsidies designed to shelter farmers from market volatility.

Chapter 16: The Labor Market has been roiled in recent years by structural and cyclical forces. This chapter examines the underpinnings of labor demand and supply and then assesses the sources of wage inequalities. Proposals to raise the federal minimum wage are analyzed, as are the sky-high salaries of corporate CEOs.

Chapter 17: Labor Unions have lost ground in the private sector but have gained significant power in the public sector (especially in colleges and secondary schools). The parameters of collective bargaining are spelled out and then illustrated with the 2017–2021 contract for the National Basketball Association players. The 2005–2009 Silicon Valley conspiracy to hold down tech wages offers a vivid example of oligopsony power at work.

Chapter 18: Financial Markets have been front-page news since the onset of the Great Recession. This chapter emphasizes the *economic* role that stock and bond markets play in reallocating resources to new products and processes. Examples range from the financing of Columbus's New World expedition to Snapchat's $3 billion IPO in March 2017. The use of crowdfunding as a source of start-up financing is discussed.

Chapter 19: Taxes: Equity vs. Efficiency continues to be a staple of political debate. Should the "rich" pay more taxes, as President Obama urged? Or should tax rates be reduced to encourage more investment and innovation as President Trump proposed? The nature and terms of the equity/efficiency trade-off are examined, and illustrated with a comparison of the Clinton and Pence tax returns for 2015 (Trump's tax return was not available). New data on global tax rates and tax migrations are provided.

Chapter 20: Transfer Payments: Welfare and Social Security continues the discussion of equity/efficiency trade-offs, emphasizing the work disincentives inherent in all income transfer programs. New data on the redistributive impact of transfers underscores their importance for equity, and the 2017 formula for Social Security benefits highlights the efficiency concern.

Chapter 21: International Trade not only examines the theory of comparative advantage, but also investigates the opposition to free trade and the impact of trade barriers that result. The latest data on trade flows and trade balances (both aggregate and bilateral) are injected. The new U.S. tariff on Chinese steel and Canadian lumber help illustrate the winners and losers from trade barriers.

Chapter 22: International Finance explains how international exchange rates are determined and why they and the 2016–2017 collapse of the Venezuelan bolivar fluctuate. The depreciation of the Ukrainian hryvnia in the wake of Russia's invasion and the 2016–2017 collapse of the Venezuelan bolivar provide new perspectives on currency fluctuations. The loss Serena Williams incurred on her Wimbledon prize money when English voters elected to exit the EU and the pound tumbled is a nice illustration of the distributional effects of currency fluctuations.

Chapter 23: Global Poverty is receding, but billions of people remain desperately poor around the world. This chapter describes the current dimensions of global poverty and the World Bank's new (2017) antipoverty goal. Emphasis is on the importance of productivity advance and the policies that accelerate or restrain that advance. A new World View on Venezuela's economic contraction provides a relevant illustration.

EFFECTIVE PEDAGOGY

Clean, Clear Theory

Despite the abundance of real-world applications, this is at heart a *principles* text, not a compendium of issues. Good theory and interesting applications are not mutually exclusive. This is a text that wants to *teach economics,* not just increase awareness of policy issues. To that end, *The Micro Economy Today* provides a logically organized and uncluttered theoretical structure. What distinguishes this text from others on the market is that it conveys theory in a lively, student-friendly manner.

Concept Reinforcement

Student comprehension of core theory is facilitated with careful, consistent, and effective pedagogy. This distinctive pedagogy includes the following features:

Chapter Learning Objectives. Each chapter contains a set of chapter-level learning objectives. Students and professors can be confident that the organization of each chapter surrounds common themes outlined by three to five learning objectives listed on the first page of each chapter. End-of-chapter material, including the chapter summary, discussion questions, and student problem sets, is tagged to these learning objectives, as is the supplementary material, which includes the Test Bank and Instructor's Resource Manual.

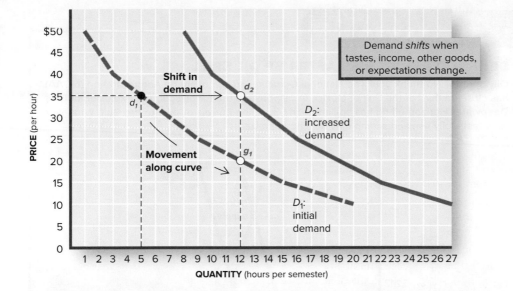

Demand *shifts* when tastes, income, other goods, or expectations change.

FIGURE 3.3

Shifts vs. Movements

A demand curve shows how a consumer responds to price changes. If the determinants of demand stay constant, the response is a *movement* along the curve to a new quantity demanded. In this case, the quantity demanded increases from 5 (point d_1), to 12 (point g_1), when price falls from $35 to $20 per hour.

If the determinants of demand *change,* the entire demand curve *shifts.* In this case, a rise in income increases demand. With more income, Tom is willing to buy 12 hours at the initial price of $35 (point d_2), not just the 5 hours he demanded before the lottery win.

	Quantity Demanded (Hours per Semester)		
	Price (per Hour)	Initial Demand	After Increase in Income
A	$50	1	8
B	45	2	9
C	40	3	10
D	35	5	12
E	30	7	14
F	25	9	16
G	20	12	19
H	15	15	22
I	10	20	27

Self-Explanatory Graphs and Tables. Graphs are *completely* labeled, colorful, and positioned on background grids. Because students often enter the principles course as graphphobics, graphs are frequently accompanied by synchronized tabular data. Every table is also annotated. This shouldn't be a product-differentiating feature, but sadly, it is. Putting a table in a text without an annotation is akin to writing a cluster of numbers on the board, then leaving the classroom without any explanation.

Reinforced Key Concepts. Key terms are defined when they first appear and, unlike in other texts, redefined as necessary in subsequent chapters. End-of-chapter discussion questions use tables, graphs, and boxed news stories from the text, reinforcing key concepts, and are linked to the chapter's learning objectives.

Boxed and Annotated Applications. In addition to the real-world applications that run through the body of the text, *The Micro Economy Today* intersperses boxed domestic (In the News) and global (World View) case studies intertextually for further understanding and reference. Although nearly every text on the market now offers boxed applications, *The Micro Economy Today*'s presentation is distinctive. First, the sheer number of In the News (60) and World View (37) boxes is unique. Second, and more important, *every* boxed application is referenced in the body of the text. Third, *every*

IN THE NEWS

SEAFOOD PRICES RISE AFTER BP OIL SPILL

Oily shrimp? No thank you! The National Oceanic and Atmospheric Administration (NOAA) has closed a third of the Gulf of Mexico in response to the BP oil spill. The explosion of BP's Deepwater Horizon oil rig has spilled nearly 5 million barrels of oil into the Gulf. Whatever their taste, oily fish and shrimp may be a health hazard.

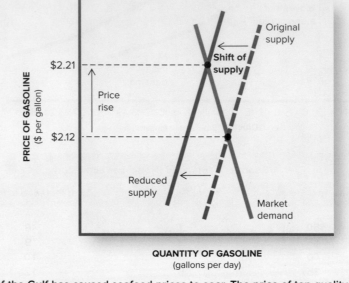

Closure of the Gulf has caused seafood prices to soar. The price of top-quality white shrimp has jumped from $3.50 a pound to $7.50 a pound. Restaurants are jacking up their prices or taking shrimp off the menu.

Source: News reports, June 2010.

ANALYSIS: When factor costs or availability worsen, the supply curve *shifts* to the left. Such leftward supply-curve shifts push prices up the market demand curve.

News and World View comes with a brief, self-contained explanation, as the accompanying example illustrates. Fourth, the News and World View boxes are the explicit subject of the end-of-chapter discussion questions and student problem set exercises. In combination, these distinctive features assure that students will actually *read* the boxed applications and discern their economic content. The Test Bank provides subsets of questions tied to the News and World View boxes so that instructors can confirm student use of this feature.

Readability The one adjective invariably used to describe *The Micro Economy Today* is "readable." Professors often express a bit of shock when they realize that students actually enjoy reading the text. (Well, not as much as a Stephen King novel, but a whole lot better than most texts they've had to plow through.) The writing style is lively and issue-focused. Unlike any other text on the market, every boxed feature, every graph, every table, and every cartoon is explained and analyzed. Every feature is also referenced in the text, so students actually learn the material rather than skipping over it. Because readability is ultimately in the eye of the beholder, you might ask a couple of students to read and compare a parallel chapter in *The Micro Economy Today* and in another text. This is a test *The Micro Economy Today* usually wins.

We firmly believe that students must *work* with key concepts in order to really learn them. Weekly homework assignments are *de rigueur* in our own classes. To facilitate homework assignments, we have prepared the student problem set at the end of each chapter. These sets include built-in numerical and graphing problems that build on the tables, graphs, and boxed material that align with each chapter's learning objectives. Grids for drawing graphs are also provided. Students cannot complete all the problems without referring to material in the chapter. This increases the odds of students actually *reading* the chapter, the tables, and the boxed applications.

The student problem set at the end of each chapter is reproduced in the online student tutorial software. This really helps students transition between the written material and online supplements. It also means that the online assignments are totally book-specific.

Student Problem Set

connect®

McGraw-Hill Connect® is a highly reliable, easy-to-use homework and learning management solution that utilizes learning science and award-winning adaptive tools to improve student results.

Homework and Adaptive Learning

- Connect's assignments help students contextualize what they've learned through application, so they can better understand the material and think critically.

- Connect will create a personalized study path customized to individual student needs through SmartBook®.

- SmartBook helps students study more efficiently by delivering an interactive reading experience through adaptive highlighting and review.

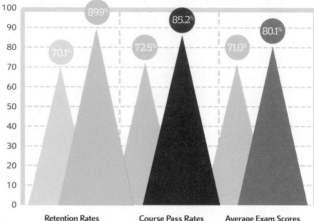

Connect's Impact on Retention Rates, Pass Rates, and Average Exam Scores

Retention Rates: 70.1%, 89.9%
Course Pass Rates: 72.5%, 85.2%
Average Exam Scores: 71.0%, 80.1%

without Connect   with Connect

Using **Connect** improves retention rates by **19.8%**, passing rates by **12.7%, and** exam scores by **9.1%.**

Over **7 billion questions** have been answered, making McGraw-Hill Education products more intelligent, reliable, and precise.

73% of instructors who use **Connect** require it; instructor satisfaction **increases** by 28% when **Connect** is required.

Quality Content and Learning Resources

- Connect content is authored by the world's best subject matter experts, and is available to your class through a simple and intuitive interface.

- The Connect eBook makes it easy for students to access their reading material on smartphones and tablets. They can study on the go and don't need internet access to use the eBook as a reference, with full functionality.

- Multimedia content such as videos, simulations, and games drive student engagement and critical thinking skills.

©McGraw-Hill Education

Robust Analytics and Reporting

©Hero Images/Getty Images RF

- Connect Insight® generates easy-to-read reports on individual students, the class as a whole, and on specific assignments.

- The Connect Insight dashboard delivers data on performance, study behavior, and effort. Instructors can quickly identify students who struggle and focus on material that the class has yet to master.

- Connect automatically grades assignments and quizzes, providing easy-to-read reports on individual and class performance.

Impact on Final Course Grade Distribution

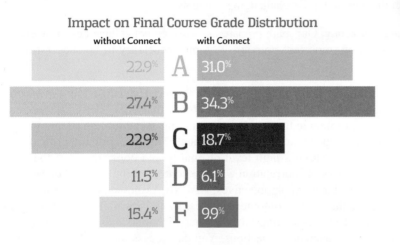

without Connect		with Connect
22.9%	A	31.0%
27.4%	B	34.3%
22.9%	C	18.7%
11.5%	D	6.1%
15.4%	F	9.9%

More students earn **As** and **Bs** when they use **Connect**.

Trusted Service and Support

- Connect integrates with your LMS to provide single sign-on and automatic syncing of grades. Integration with Blackboard®, D2L®, and Canvas also provides automatic syncing of the course calendar and assignment-level linking.

- Connect offers comprehensive service, support, and training throughout every phase of your implementation.

- If you're looking for some guidance on how to use Connect, or want to learn tips and tricks from super users, you can find tutorials as you work. Our Digital Faculty Consultants and Student Ambassadors offer insight into how to achieve the results you want with Connect.

www.mheducation.com/connect

NEW AND IMPROVED SUPPLEMENTS

The following ancillaries are available for quick download and convenient access via the Instructor Resource material available through McGraw-Hill Connect.

DIGITAL SOLUTIONS

Extensive Algorithmic and Graphing Assessment. Robust, auto-gradable question banks for each chapter now include even more questions that make use of the Connect graphing tool. More questions featuring algorithmic variations have also been added.

Interactive Graphs. This new assignable resource within Connect helps students see the relevance of subject matter by providing visual displays of real data for students to manipulate. All graphs are accompanied by assignable assessment questions and feedback to guide students through the experience of learning to read and interpret graphs and data.

Videos. New to this edition are videos that provide support for key economic topics. These short, engaging explanations are presented at the moment students may be struggling to help them connect the dots and grasp challenging concepts.

Math Preparedness Tutorials. Our math preparedness assignments have been reworked to help students refresh on important prerequisite topics necessary to be successful in economics.

Test Bank. The Test Bank has been rigorously revised for this 15th edition of *The Micro Economy Today*. Digital co-author Karen Gebhardt enlisted the help of her grad students to carefully assess *every* problem in the Test Bank, assigning each problem a letter grade and identifying errors and opportunities for improvement. This in-depth and critical assessment and revision has ensured a high level of quality and consistency of the test questions and the greatest possible correlation with the content of the text. All questions are coded according to chapter learning objectives, AACSB Assurance of Learning, and Bloom's Taxonomy guidelines. The computerized Test Bank is available in EZ Test, a flexible and easy-to-use electronic testing program that accommodates a wide range of question types, including user-created questions. You can access the test bank through McGraw-Hill Connect.

Computerized Test Bank Online. TestGen is a complete, state-of-the-art test generator and editing application software that allows instructors to quickly and easily select test items from McGraw Hill's test bank content. The instructors can then organize, edit, and customize questions and answers to rapidly generate tests for paper or online administration. Questions can include stylized text, symbols, graphics, and equations that are inserted directly into questions using built-in mathematical templates. TestGen's random generator provides the option to display different text or calculated number values each time questions are used with both quick-and-simple test creation and flexible and robust editing tools, TestGen is a complete test generator system for today's educators.

You can use our test bank software, TestGen, or Connect to easily query for learning outcomes and objectives that directly relate to the learning objectives for your course. You can then use the reporting features to aggregate student results in a similar fashion, making the collection and presentation of assurance-of-learning data simple and easy.

Assurance-of-Learning Ready

Many educational institutions today are focused on the notion of *assurance of learning,* an important element of some accreditation standards. *The Micro Economy Today* is designed specifically to support your assurance-of-learning initiatives with a simple yet powerful solution.

Each test bank question for *The Micro Economy Today* maps to a specific chapter learning outcome/objective listed in the text. You can use our test bank software, EZ Test and EZ Test Online, to easily query for learning outcomes/objectives that directly relate to the learning objectives for your course. You can then use the reporting features of EZ Test to aggregate student results in similar fashion, making the collection and presentation of assurance-of-learning data simple and easy.

AACSB Statement

McGraw-Hill Education is a proud corporate member of AACSB International. Understanding the importance and value of AACSB accreditation, *The Micro Economy Today*, 15th edition, recognizes the curricula guidelines detailed in the AACSB standards for business accreditation by connecting selected questions in the text and the test bank to the six general knowledge and skill guidelines in the AACSB standards.

The statements contained in *The Micro Economy Today*, 15th edition, are provided only as a guide for the users of this text. The AACSB leaves content coverage and assessment within the purview of individual schools, the mission of the school, and the faculty. While *The Micro Economy Today*, 15th edition, and the teaching package make no claim of any specific AACSB qualification or evaluation, we have labeled within *The Micro Economy Today*, 15th edition, labeled selected questions according to the eight general knowledge and skills areas emphasized by AACSB.

Instructor Aids

PowerPoint Presentations. Developed using Microsoft PowerPoint software, these slides are a step-by-step review of the key points in each of the book's 37 chapters. They are equally useful to the student in the classroom as lecture aids or for personal review at home or the computer lab. The slides use animation to show students how graphs build and shift.

Solutions Manual. Prepared by Karen Gebhardt, this manual provides detailed answers to the end-of-chapter questions.

Student Aids

Built-in Student Problem Set. The built-in student problem set is found at the end of every chapter of *The Micro Economy Today*. Each chapter has 8 to 10 numerical and graphing problems tied to the content of the text.

ACKNOWLEDGMENTS

This 15th edition of *The Micro Economy Today* represents a continuing commitment to disseminate the core principles of economics to a broad swath of college students. Like earlier editions, it has benefited greatly from the continuing stream of ideas and suggestions from both instructors and students. For all that feedback, I am most grateful. Among those who have contributed feedback to this and earlier editions are the following instructors:

Reviewers

Cynthia E. Abadie
Southwest Tennessee Community College

Mark Abajian
San Diego Mesa College

Steve Abid
Grand Rapids Community College

Ercument G. Aksoy
Los Angeles Valley College

Mauro Cristian Amor
Northwood University

Catalina Amuedo-Dorantes
San Diego State University

Gerald Baumgardner
Penn College

Mack A. Bean
Franklin Pierce University

Adolfo Benavides
Texas A&M University–Corpus Christi

Anoop Bhargava
Finger Lakes Community College

Joerg Bibow
Skidmore College

Eugenie Bietry
Pace University

John Bockino
Suffolk County Community College

Peter Boelman
Norco College

Walter Francis Boyle
Fayetteville Technical Community College

Amber Brown
Grand Valley State University

Don Bumpass
Sam Houston State University

Suparna Chakraborty
Baruch College, CUNY

Stephen J. Conroy
University of San Diego

Sherry L. Creswell
Kent State University

Manabendra Dasgupta
University of Alabama–Birmingham

Antony Davies
Duquesne University

Diane de Freitas
Fresno City College

Diana Denison
Red Rocks Community College

Alexander Deshkovski
North Carolina Central University

John A. Doces
Bucknell University

Ishita Edwards
Oxnard College

Eric R. Eide
Brigham Young University

Yalcin Ertekin
Trine University

Kelley L. Fallon
Owensboro Community & Technical College

Frank Garland
Tri-County Technical College

Leroy Gill
The Ohio State University

Paul Graf
Indiana University

Barnali Gupta
Miami University

Sheila Amin Gutierrez de Pineres
University of Texas–Dallas

Jonatan Jelen
City College of New York

Hyojin Jeong
Lakeland Community College

Barbara Heroy John
University of Dayton

Tim Kochanski
Portland State University

David E. Laurel
South Texas College

Raymond Lawless
Quinsigamond Community College

Richard B. Le
Cosumnes River College

Jim Lee
Texas A&M University–Corpus Christi

Sang H. Lee
Southeastern Louisiana University

Minghua Li
Franklin Pierce University

Yan Li
University of Wisconsin–Eau Claire

Paul Lockard
Black Hawk College

Rotua Lumbantobing
North Carolina State University

Paula Manns
Atlantic Cape Community College

Jeanette Milius
Iowa Western Community College

Norman C. Miller
Miami University

Stanley Robert Mitchell
McLennan Community College

Stephen K. Nodine
Tri-County Technical College

Phacharaphot Nuntramas
San Diego State University

Seth Ari Roberts
Frederick Community College

Michael J. Ryan
Western Michigan University

Craig F. Santicola
Westmoreland County Community College

Rolando A. Santos
Lakeland Community College

Theodore P. Scheinman
Mt. Hood Community College

Marilyn K. Spencer
Texas A&M University–Corpus Christi

Irina Nikolayevna Strelnikova
Red Rocks Community College

Michael Swope
Wayne County Community College

Gary Lee Taylor
South Dakota State University

Deborah L. Thorsen
Palm Beach State College

Ngoc-Bich Tran
San Jacinto College

Markland Tuttle
Sam Houston State University

Kenneth Lewis Weimer
Kellogg Community College

Selin Yalcindag
Mercyhurst College

Erik Zemljic
Kent State University

The text itself and all the accompanying supplements could not make it to the marketplace without the prodigious efforts of the production team at McGraw-Hill. In this regard, I want to extend special thanks to Adam Huenecke, who has not only managed the production process, but even tutored me in the use of the digital tools needed to produce a text today. Katie Hoenicke served once again as a valued editor of the entire project. Last but not least, I want to call out Karen Gebhardt, who is the digital co-author for this text. Karen has not only upgraded and synchronized all of the digital dimensions of our text package, but has also motivated me to check and recheck every detail of the text. She is an invaluable partner.

Let me conclude by thanking all the instructors and students who are going to use *The Micro Economy Today* as an introduction to economic principles. I will welcome any reactions (even bad ones) and suggestions you'd like to pass on for future editions.

—**Bradley R. Schiller**

CONTENTS IN BRIEF

CONTENTS

THE
MICROECONOMY
TODAY

FIFTEENTH EDITION

McGraw Hill Education

©MOF/Getty Images RF

©Kyodo via AP Images

©REUTERS/Alamy Stock Photo

©Blend Images/Getty Images RF

©Hisham F. Ibrahim/Getty Images RF

THE ECONOMIC CHALLENGE

People around the world want a better life. Whether rich or poor, everyone strives for a higher standard of living. Ultimately, the performance of the economy determines who attains that goal.

These first few chapters examine how the *limits* to output are determined and how the interplay of market forces and government intervention utilize and even expand those limits.

"The Economist in Chief"
©REUTERS/Alamy Stock Photo

CHAPTER 1

Economics: The Core Issues

LEARNING OBJECTIVES

After reading this chapter, you should know

LO1-1   What scarcity is.

LO1-2   How scarcity creates opportunity costs.

LO1-3   What the production possibilities curve represents.

LO1-4   The three core economic questions that every society must answer.

LO1-5   How market and government approaches to economic problems differ.

People understand that the president of the United States is the Commander in Chief of the armed forces. The president has the ultimate responsibility to decide when and how America's military forces will be deployed. He issues the orders that military officers must carry out. He is given credit for military successes and blame for military failures. He can't "pass the buck" down the line of command.

Less recognized is the president's role as "Economist in Chief." The president is held responsible not just for the *military* security of the United States, but for its *economic* security as well. Although he doesn't have the command powers in the economic arena that he has in the military arena, people expect him to take charge of the economy. They expect the Economist in Chief to keep the economy growing, to create jobs for everyone who wants one, and to prevent prices from rising too fast. Along the way, they expect the Economist in Chief to protect the environment, assure economic justice for all, and protect America's position in the global economy.

That is a tall order, especially in view of the president's limited constitutional powers to make economic policy decisions. The economy is also buffeted by international and natural forces that no president can control. But no matter. Voters hold the Economist in Chief responsible for economic misfortunes, whether or not he is able to single-handedly prevent them, and give him credit for economic success.

What everyone ultimately wants is a prosperous and growing economy: an economy in which people can find good jobs, enjoy rising living standards and wealth, get the education they desire, and enjoy an array of creature comforts. And we want to enjoy this good life while protecting the environment, caring for the poor, and pursuing world peace.

How are we going to get all this? Is "the economy" some sort of perpetual motion machine that will keep churning out more goods and services every year? Clearly not. During the Great Recession of 2008–2009 the economy churned out less output, eliminated jobs, and reduced living standards and wealth. A lot of college graduates had to move back home when they couldn't find jobs. What went wrong?

Even after the Great Recession ended in June 2009, economic pain persisted. The growth of the economy was agonizingly slow, and unemployment remained high for another 6 years. Was that much distress really necessary? Couldn't the Economist in Chief have fixed these problems? These questions are were debated intensely in the 2016 presidential election. Donald Trump promised "to make America great again" by creating more jobs, building more bridges and roads, strengthening the armed forces, and limiting both illegal immigration and unfair foreign competition. Voters decided to give him the opportunity to serve as Economist in Chief. Like his predecessors, President Trump's challenge has been to convert campaign promises into tangible economic results. To convert campaign promises into desirable economic outcomes requires a knowledge of what makes an economy tick. How are prices, wages, employment, and other economic outcomes actually determined? Does Wall Street run the system? How about selfish, greedy capitalists? The banks? Or maybe foreign nations? Are incompetent bureaucrats and self-serving politicians the root of our occasional woes? Who, in fact, calls the shots?

The goal of this course is to understand how the economy works. To that end, we want to determine how *markets*—the free-wheeling exchange of goods and services—shape economic outcomes—everything from the price of this text to the national unemployment rate. Then we want to examine the role that government can and does play in (re)shaping economic performance. Once we've established this foundation, we'll be in a better position to evaluate what the Economist in Chief *can* do—and what he *should* do. We'll also better understand how we can make better economic decisions for ourselves.

We'll start our inquiry with some harsh realities. In a world of unlimited resources, we could have all the goods we desired. We'd have time to do everything we wanted and enough money to buy everything we desired. We could produce enough to make everyone rich while protecting the environment and exploring the universe. The Economist in Chief could deliver everything voters asked for. Unfortunately, we don't live in that utopia: **we live in a world of limited resources.** Those limits are the root of our economic problems. They force us to make difficult decisions about how *best* to use our time, our money, and our resources. These are *economic* decisions.

In this first chapter we'll examine how the problem of limited resources arises and the kinds of choices it forces us to make. As we'll see, **three core choices confront every nation:**

- **WHAT to produce with our limited resources.**
- **HOW to produce the goods and services we select.**
- **FOR WHOM goods and services are produced—that is, who should get them.**

We also have to decide who should answer these questions. Should people take care of their own health and retirement, or should the government provide a safety net of health care and pensions? Should the government regulate airfares or let the airlines set prices? Should Microsoft decide what features get included in a computer's operating system, or should the government make that decision? Should Facebook decide what personal information is protected, or should the government make that decision? Should interest rates be set by private banks alone, or should the government try to control interest rates? The battle over *who* should answer the core questions is often as contentious as the questions themselves.

THE ECONOMY IS US

To learn how the economy works, let's start with a simple truth: *the economy is us.* "The economy" is simply an abstraction referring to the grand sum of all our production and consumption activities. What we collectively produce is what the economy produces; what we collectively consume is what the economy consumes. In this sense, the concept of "the economy" is no more difficult than the concept of "the family." If someone tells you that the Jones family has an annual income of $42,000, you know that the reference is to the collective earnings of all the Joneses. Likewise, when someone reports that the nation's income is $20 trillion per year—as it now is—we should recognize that the reference is to the grand total of everyone's income. If we work fewer hours or get paid less, both family income *and* national income decline. The "meaningless statistics" often cited in the news are just a summary of our collective market behavior.

The same relationship between individual behavior and aggregate behavior applies to specific outputs. If we as individuals insist on driving cars rather than taking public transportation, the economy will produce millions of cars each year and consume vast quantities of oil. In a slightly different way, the economy produces billions of dollars of military hardware to satisfy our desire for national defense. In each case, the output of the economy reflects the collective behavior of the 340 million individuals who participate in the U.S. economy.

We may not always be happy with the output of the economy. But we can't ignore the link between individual action and collective outcomes. If the highways are clogged and the air is polluted, we can't blame someone else for the transportation choices we made. If we're disturbed by the size of our military arsenal, we must still accept responsibility for our choices (or nonchoices, if we failed to vote). In either case, we continue to have the option of reallocating our resources. We can create a different outcome tomorrow, next month, or next year.

SCARCITY: THE CORE PROBLEM

Although we can change economic outcomes, we can't have everything we want. If you go to the mall with $20 in your pocket, you can buy only so much. The money in your pocket sets a *limit* to your spending.

The output of the entire economy is also limited. The limits in this case are set not by the amount of money in people's pockets, but by the resources available for producing goods and services. Everyone wants more housing, new schools, better transit systems, and a new car. We also want to explore space and bring safe water to the world's poor. But even a country as rich as the United States can't produce everything people want. So, like every other nation, we have to grapple with the core problem of **scarcity**—the fact that **there aren't enough resources available to satisfy all our desires.**

scarcity: Lack of enough resources to satisfy all desired uses of those resources.

Factors of Production

factors of production: Resource inputs used to produce goods and services, e.g., land, labor, capital, entrepreneurship.

The resources used to produce goods and services are called **factors of production.** *The four basic factors of production are*

- *Land.*
- *Labor.*
- *Capital.*
- *Entrepreneurship.*

These are the *inputs* needed to produce desired *outputs.* To produce this text, for example, we needed paper, printing presses, a building, and lots of labor. We also needed people with good ideas who could put it together. To produce the education you're getting in this class, we need not only a text but a classroom, a teacher, a blackboard, and maybe a computer as well. **Without factors of production, we simply can't produce anything.**

Land. The first factor of production, land, refers not just to the ground but to all natural resources. Crude oil, water, air, and minerals are all included in our concept of "land."

Labor. Labor too has several dimensions. It's not simply a question of how many bodies there are. When we speak of labor as a factor of production, we refer to the skills and abilities to produce goods and services. Hence both the quantity and the quality of human resources are included in the "labor" factor.

capital: Final goods produced for use in the production of other goods, such as equipment and structures.

Capital. The third factor of production is capital. In economics the term **capital** refers to final goods produced for use in further production. The residents of fishing villages in southern Thailand, for example, braid huge fishing nets. The sole purpose of these nets is to catch more fish. The nets themselves become a factor of production in obtaining the final goods (fish) that people desire. Thus they're regarded as *capital*. Blast furnaces used to make steel and desks used to equip offices are also capital inputs.

Entrepreneurship. The more land, labor, and capital we have, the more we can produce potential output. A farmer with 10,000 acres, 12 employees, and six tractors can grow more crops than a farmer with half those resources. But there's no guarantee that he will. The farmer with fewer resources may have better ideas about what to plant, when to irrigate, or how to harvest the crops. *It's not just a matter of what resources you have but also of how well you use them.* This is where the fourth factor of production—**entrepreneurship**—comes in. The entrepreneur is the person who sees the opportunity for new or better products and brings together the resources needed for producing them. If it weren't for entrepreneurs, Thai fishers would still be using sticks to catch fish. Without entrepreneurship, farmers would still be milking their cows by hand. If someone hadn't thought of a way to miniaturize electronic circuits, you wouldn't be able to text your friends.

entrepreneurship: The assembling of resources to produce new or improved products and technologies.

The role of entrepreneurs in economic progress is a key issue in the market versus government debate. The British economist John Maynard Keynes argued that free markets unleash the "animal spirits" of entrepreneurs, propelling innovation, technology, and growth. Critics of government regulation argue that government interference in the marketplace, however well intentioned, tends to stifle those very same animal spirits.

Limits to Output

No matter how an economy is organized, there's a limit to how much it can produce. The most evident limit is the amount of resources available for producing goods and services. One reason the United States can produce so much is that it has nearly 4 million square miles of land. Tonga, with less than 300 square miles of land, will never produce as much. The United States also has a population of more than 340 million people. That's a lot less than China (1.4 billion) but far larger than 200 other nations (Tonga has a population of less than 120,000). So an abundance of raw resources gives us the potential to produce a lot of output. But that greater production capacity isn't enough to satisfy all our desires. We're constantly scrambling for additional resources to build more houses, make better movies, and provide more health care. That imbalance between available resources and our wish list is one of the things that makes the job of Economist in Chief so difficult: He can't deliver everything people want.

The science of **economics** helps us frame these choices. In a nutshell, economics is the study of how people use scarce resources. How do you decide how much time to spend studying? How does Google decide how many workers to hire? How does Ford decide whether to use its factories to produce sport utility vehicles or sedans? What share of a nation's resources should be devoted to space exploration, the delivery of health care services, or pollution control? In every instance, **alternative ways of using scarce labor, land, and capital resources are always available, and we have to choose one use over another.**

economics: The study of how best to allocate scarce resources among competing uses.

OPPORTUNITY COSTS

Scientists have long sought to explore every dimension of space. President Kennedy initiated a lunar exploration program that successfully landed men on the moon on July 20, 1969. That only whetted the appetite for further space exploration. President George W. Bush initiated a program to land people on Mars, using the moon as a way station. Scientists believe that the biological, geophysical, and technical knowledge gained from the exploration of Mars will improve life here on Earth. But should we do it? In a world of unlimited resources the answer would be an easy "yes." But we don't live in that world.

Every time we use scarce resources in one way, we give up the opportunity to use them in other ways. If we use more resources to explore space, we have fewer resources available for producing earthly goods. The forgone earthly goods represent the **opportunity costs** of a Mars expedition. *Opportunity cost is what is given up to get*

opportunity cost: The most desired goods or services that are forgone in order to obtain something else.

something else. Even a so-called free lunch has an opportunity cost. The resources used to produce the lunch could have been used to produce something else. A trip to Mars has a much higher opportunity cost. President Obama decided those opportunity costs were too high: he scaled back the Mars programs to make more resources available for Earthly uses (like education, highway construction, and energy development). President Trump agreed. While calling space exploration "wonderful," he observed "Right now, we have bigger problems—we've got to fix our potholes." He reallocated scarce resources from space exploration to domestic infrastructure (roads, bridges, airports).

Your economics class also has an opportunity cost. The building space used for your economics class can't be used to show movies at the same time. Your professor can't lecture (produce education) and repair motorcycles simultaneously. The decision to use these scarce resources (capital, labor) for an economics class implies producing less of other goods.

Even reading this text is costly. That cost is not measured in dollars and cents. The true (economic) cost is, instead, measured in terms of some alternative activity. What would you like to be doing right now? The more time you spend reading this text, the less time you have available for other uses of your time. The opportunity cost of reading this text is the best alternative use of your scarce time. If you are missing your favorite TV show, we'd say that show is the opportunity cost of reading this text. It is what you gave up to do this assignment. Hopefully, the benefits you get from studying will outweigh that cost. Otherwise this wouldn't be the best way to use your scarce time.

Guns vs. Butter

One of the most difficult choices nations must make about resource use entails defense spending. After the September 11, 2001, terrorist attacks on the World Trade Center and Pentagon, American citizens overwhelmingly favored an increase in military spending. Even the unpopularity of the wars in Iraq and Afghanistan didn't quell the desire for more national defense. But national defense, like Mars exploration, requires the use of scarce resources; Americans wanted to feel *safe*. But there is a *cost* to assuring safety: the 1.4 million men and women who serve in the armed forces aren't available to build schools, program computers, or teach economics. Similarly, the land, labor, capital, and entrepreneurship devoted to producing military hardware aren't available for producing civilian goods. An *increase* in national defense implies more sacrifices of civilian goods and services. How many schools, hospitals, or cars are we willing to sacrifice in order to "produce" more national security? This is the "guns versus butter" dilemma that all nations confront.

PRODUCTION POSSIBILITIES

The opportunity costs implied by our every choice can be illustrated easily. Suppose a nation can produce only two goods, trucks and tanks. To keep things simple, assume that labor (workers) is the only factor of production needed to produce either good. Although other factors of production (land, machinery) are also needed in actual production, ignoring them for the moment does no harm. Assume further that we have a total of only 10 workers available per day to produce either trucks or tanks. That's a tiny work force, but it makes the math a lot easier.

Our initial problem is to determine the *limits* of output. How many trucks or tanks *can* be produced in a day with available resources (our 10 workers)?

Before going any further, notice how opportunity costs will affect the answer. If we use all 10 workers to produce trucks, no labor will be available to assemble tanks. In this case, forgone tanks would become the *opportunity cost* of a decision to employ all our resources in truck production.

We still don't know how many trucks could be produced with 10 workers or exactly how many tanks would be forgone by such a decision. To get these answers, we need more details about the production processes involved—specifically, how many workers are required to manufacture either good.

TABLE 1.1

A Production Possibilities Schedule

As long as resources are limited, their use entails an opportunity cost. In this case, resources (labor) used to produce trucks can't be used for tank assembly at the same time. Hence the forgone tanks are the opportunity cost of additional trucks. If all our resources were used to produce trucks (row *A*), no tanks could be assembled. To produce tanks, we have to reduce truck production.

	Production Options	
	Output of Trucks per Day	Output of Tanks per Day
A	5	0
B	4	2.0
C	3	3.0
D	2	3.8
E	1	4.5
F	0	5.0

production possibilities: The alternative combinations of final goods and services that could be produced in a given period with all available resources and technology.

The Production Possibilities Curve

Table 1.1 summarizes the hypothetical choices, or **production possibilities,** that we confront in this case. Suppose we wanted to produce only trucks (i.e., no tanks). Row *A* of the table shows the *maximum* number of trucks we could produce. With 10 workers available and a labor requirement of 2 workers per truck, we can manufacture a maximum of five trucks per day.

Producing five trucks per day leaves no workers available to produce tanks. Our 10 available workers are all being used to produce trucks. On row *A* of Table 1.1 we've got "butter" (trucks) but no "guns" (tanks). If we want tanks, we have to cut back on truck production. The remainder of Table 1.1 illustrates the trade-offs we confront in this simple case. By cutting truck production from five to four trucks per day (row *B*), we reduce labor use in truck production from 10 workers to 8. That leaves 2 workers available for other uses, including the production of tanks.

If we employ these remaining 2 workers to assemble tanks, we can build two tanks a day. We would then end up on row *B* of the table with four trucks and two tanks per day. What's the opportunity cost of these two tanks? It's the one additional truck (the fifth truck) that we could have produced but didn't.

As we proceed down the rows of Table 1.1, the nature of opportunity costs becomes apparent. Each additional tank built implies the loss (opportunity cost) of truck output. Likewise, every truck produced implies the loss of some tank output.

These trade-offs between truck and tank production are illustrated in the production possibilities curve of Figure 1.1. ***Each point on the production possibilities curve depicts an alternative mix of output* that could be produced.** In this case, each point represents a different combination of trucks and tanks that we could produce in a single day using all available resources (10 workers in this case).

Notice in particular how points *A* through *F* in Figure 1.1 represent the choices described in each row of Table 1.1. At point *A*, we're producing five trucks per day and no tanks. As we move down the curve from point *A* we're producing fewer trucks and more tanks. At point *B*, truck production has dropped from five to four vehicles per day while tank assembly has increased from zero to two. In other words, we've given up one truck to get two tanks assembled. The opportunity cost of those tanks is the one truck that is given up. A production possibilities curve, then, is simply a graphic summary of production possibilities, as described in Table 1.1. As such, ***the production possibilities curve illustrates two essential principles:***

- ***Scarce resources.*** There's a limit to the amount of output we can produce in a given time period with available resources and technology.
- ***Opportunity costs.*** We can obtain additional quantities of any particular good only by reducing the potential production of another good.

These principles help explain why both presidents Obama and Trump chose to devote fewer resources to space exploration. They felt the opportunity costs (reduced education, less infrastructure) were simply too high.

FIGURE 1.1

A Production Possibilities Curve

A production possibilities curve (PPC) describes the various output combinations that could be produced in a given time period with available resources and technology. It represents a menu of output choices an economy confronts.

Point *B* indicates that we could produce a *combination* of four trucks and two tanks per day. Alternatively, we could produce one less truck and a third tank by moving to point *C*.

Points *A, D, E,* and *F* illustrate still other output combinations that *could* be produced. This curve is a graphic illustration of the production possibilities schedule in Table 1.1.

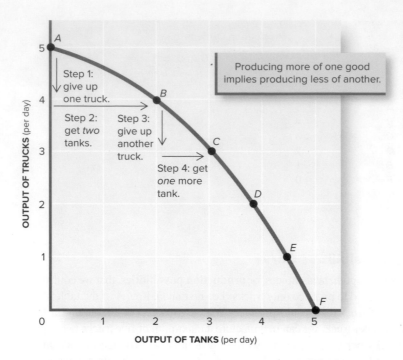

Increasing Opportunity Costs

The shape of the production possibilities curve reflects another limitation on our choices. Notice how opportunity costs increase as we move along the production possibilities curve. When we cut truck output from five to four (step 1, Figure 1.1), we get two tanks (step 2). When we cut truck production further, however (step 3), we get only one tank per truck given up (step 4). The opportunity cost of tank production is increasing. This process of increasing opportunity cost continues. By the time we give up the last truck (row *F*), tank output increases by only 0.5: we get only half a tank for the last truck given up. These increases in opportunity cost are reflected in the outward bend of the production possibilities curve.

Why do opportunity costs increase? Mostly because it's difficult to move resources from one industry to another. It's easy to transform trucks to tanks on a blackboard. In the real world, however, resources don't adapt so easily. Workers who assemble trucks may not have the right skills for tank assembly. As we continue to transfer labor from one industry to the other, we start getting fewer tanks for every truck we give up.

The difficulties entailed in transferring labor skills, capital, and entrepreneurship from one industry to another are so universal that we often speak of the *law* of *increasing opportunity cost*. This law says that we must give up ever-increasing quantities of other goods and services in order to get more of a particular good. The law isn't based solely on the limited versatility of individual workers. The *mix* of factor inputs makes a difference as well. Truck assembly requires less capital than tank assembly. In a pinch, wheels can be mounted on a truck almost completely by hand, whereas tank treads require more sophisticated machinery. As we move labor from truck assembly to tank assembly, available capital may restrict our output capabilities.

The Cost of North Korea's Military

The production possibilities curve illustrates why the core economic decision about WHAT to produce is so difficult: We can't have everything we want and, worse yet, getting more of one thing implies getting less of something else. We are forced to make difficult choices.

Consider, for example, North Korea's decision to maintain a large military. North Korea is a relatively small country: its population of 25 million ranks fiftieth in the world. Yet

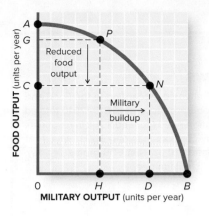

FIGURE 1.2
The Cost of War

North Korea devotes as much as 20 percent of its output to the military. The opportunity cost of this decision is reduced output of food. As the military expands from 0H to 0D, food output drops from 0G to 0C.

North Korea maintains the fourth-largest army in the world and continues to develop a nuclear weapons capability. To do so, it allocates as much as 20 percent of all its resources to feeding, clothing, and equipping its military forces. As a consequence, there aren't enough resources available to produce food. Without adequate machinery, seeds, fertilizer, or irrigation, North Korea's farmers can't produce enough food to feed the population (see World View "North Korea's Food Shortage Grows"). As Figure 1.2 illustrates, the opportunity cost of "guns" in Korea is a lot of needed "butter."

WORLD VIEW

WORLD'S LARGEST ARMIES

Rank	Country	Active Military
1	China	2,333,000
2	United States	1,492,200
3	India	1,325,000
4	North Korea	1,190,000
5	Russia	845,000
6	Pakistan	643,800
7	South Korea	630,000
8	Iran	523,000
9	Turkey	510,600
10	Vietnam	482,000

Source: U.S. Central Intelligence Agency 2017.

ANALYSIS: Nations "produce" national defense by employing land, labor, and capital in their armed forces. The opportunity cost of those "guns" are less "butter."

During World War II, the United States confronted a similar trade-off. In 1944 nearly 40 percent of all U.S. output was devoted to the military. Civilian goods were so scarce that they had to be rationed. Staples like butter, sugar, and gasoline were doled out in small quantities. Even golf balls were rationed. In North Korea, golf balls would be a luxury even without a military buildup. As the share of North Korea's output devoted to the military increased, even basic food production became more difficult. (See World View "North Korea's Food Shortage Grows.")

What is the opportunity cost of North Korea's army?

©Ed Jones/AFP/Getty Images

WORLD VIEW

NORTH KOREA'S FOOD SHORTAGE GROWS

North Korea's food shortage has taken another turn for the worse. According to the Food and Agriculture Organization and the World Food Program, food production in 2015–2016 totaled only 4.8 million tons. That's 694,000 tons less than the nation needs to feed itself. In response, the government slashed food rations from 370 grams daily per person to only 360 grams. That allocation is well below the United Nations recommendation of at least 600 grams per day. Widespread starvation continues to plague this nation of 25 million people.

Source: News accounts of 2016–2017.

ROCKET LAUNCH COST ENOUGH TO END NORTH KOREAN FOOD SHORTAGES FOR YEARS

SEOUL—North Korea's latest rocket launches cost an estimated $1.3 billion, according to an official from South Korea's Ministry of Unification. The two launches—one of which failed—cost $600 million. The launch site cost an estimated $400 million and related facilities cost around $300 million. With that much money, North Korea could have purchased 4.6 million tons of corn, a supply of corn that would have eliminated North Korea's food shortages for the next four to five years, according to the Ministry.

Source: Media reports December 2012–January 2013.

ANALYSIS: North Korea's inability to feed itself is partly due to maintaining its large army: resources used for the military aren't available for producing food.

Figure 1.3 illustrates how other nations divide available resources between military and civilian production. The $700 billion the United States now spends on national defense absorbs only 4 percent of total output. This made the opportunity costs of the post-9/11 military buildup and the wars in Iraq and Afghanistan less painful. By contrast, North Korea's commitment to military spending (20 percent) implies a very high opportunity cost.

Percentage of Output Allocated to Military

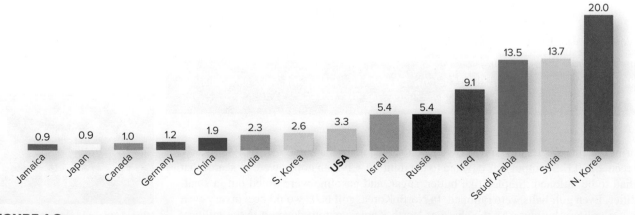

Jamaica	Japan	Canada	Germany	China	India	S. Korea	USA	Israel	Russia	Iraq	Saudi Arabia	Syria	N. Korea
0.9	0.9	1.0	1.2	1.9	2.3	2.6	3.3	5.4	5.4	9.1	13.5	13.7	20.0

FIGURE 1.3
The Military Share of Output

The share of total output allocated to the military indicates the opportunity cost of maintaining an army. North Korea has the highest cost, using one fifth of its resources for military purposes. Although China and the United States have much larger armies, their military *share* of output is much smaller.

Source: Stockholm International Peace Research Institute and U.S. Central Intelligence Agency (2015 data).

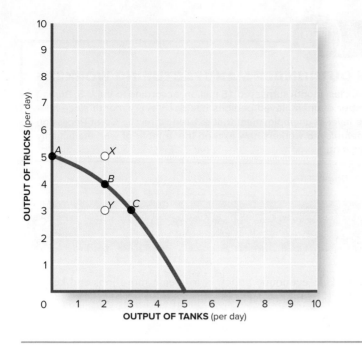

FIGURE 1.4
Points Inside and Outside the PPC Curve
Points outside the production possibilities curve (point *X*) are unattainable with available resources and technology. Points inside the PPC (point *Y*) represent the incomplete use of available resources. Only points on the PPC (*A, B, C*) represent maximum use of our production capabilities.

Efficiency

Not all of the choices on the production possibilities curve are equally desirable. They are, however, all *efficient*. **Efficiency** means squeezing *maximum* output out of available resources. Every point of the PPC satisfies this condition. Although the *mix* of output changes as we move around the production possibilities curve (Figures 1.1 and 1.2), at every point we are getting as much *total* output as physically possible. Since efficiency in production means simply getting the most from what you've got, **every point on the production possibilities curve is efficient.** At every point on the curve we are using all available resources in the best way we know how.

efficiency: Maximum output of a good from the resources used in production.

Inefficiency

There's no guarantee, of course, that we'll always use resources so efficiently. *A production possibilities curve shows* **potential** *output, not* **actual** *output.* If we're inefficient, actual output will be less than that potential. This happens. In the real world, workers sometimes loaf on the job. Or they call in sick and go to a baseball game instead of working. Managers don't always give the clearest directions or stay in touch with advancing technology. Even students sometimes fail to put forth their best effort on homework assignments. This kind of slippage can prevent us from achieving maximum production. When that happens, we end up *inside* the PPC rather than *on* it.

   Point *Y* in Figure 1.4 illustrates the consequences of inefficient production. At point *Y*, we're producing only three trucks and two tanks. This is less than our potential. We could assemble a third tank without cutting back truck production (point *C*). Or we could get an extra truck without sacrificing any tank output (point *B*). Instead we're producing *inside* the production possibilities curve at point *Y*. **Whenever we're producing inside the production possibilities curve, we are forgoing the opportunity of producing (and consuming) additional output.**

Unemployment

We can end up inside the production possibilities curve by utilizing resources inefficiently or simply by not using all available resources. This happened repeatedly in the Great Recession of 2008–2009. In October 2009, more than 15 million Americans were unemployed (see In the News "Jobless Workers Outnumber Manufacturing Workers"). These men and women were ready, willing, and available to work, but no one hired them. As a result, we were stuck *inside* the PPC, producing less output than we could have (like point

Y in Figure 1.4). The goal of U.S. economic policy is to create more jobs and keep the United States on its production possibilities curve.

Economic Growth

The challenge of getting to the production possibilities curve increases with each passing day. People are born every day. As they age, they enter the labor force as new workers. Technology, too, keeps advancing each year. These increases in available labor and technology keep pushing the producing possibilities curve outward. This **economic growth** is a good thing in the sense that it allows us to produce more goods and raise living standards. With economic growth, countries can have more guns *and* more butter (see Figure 1.5). Without economic growth, living standards decline as the population grows. This is the problem that plagues some of the world's poorest nations, where population increases every year but output often doesn't.

economic growth: An increase in output (real GDP); an expansion of production possibilities.

THREE BASIC DECISIONS

Production possibilities define the output choices that a nation confronts. From these choices every nation must make some basic decisions. As we noted at the beginning of this chapter, the three core economic questions are

- *WHAT to produce.*
- *HOW to produce.*
- *FOR WHOM to produce.*

FIGURE 1.5

Growth: Increasing Production Possibilities

A production possibilities curve is based on *available* resources and technology. If more resources or better technology becomes available, production possibilities will increase. This economic growth is illustrated by the *shift* from PP_1 to PP_2.

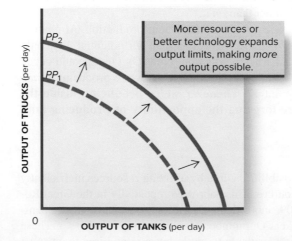

What

There are millions of points along a production possibilities curve, and each one represents a different mix of output. Unfortunately, we can choose only *one* of these points at any time. The point we choose determines what mix of output actually gets produced. That choice determines how many guns are produced, and how much butter—or how many space expeditions and how many sewage treatment facilities get built.

The production possibilities curve itself doesn't tell us which mix of output is best; it just lays out a menu of available choices. It's up to us to pick out the one and only mix of output that will be produced at a given time. This WHAT decision is a fundamental decision every nation must make.

How

Decisions must also be made about HOW to produce. Should we generate electricity by burning coal, smashing atoms, or harnessing solar power? Should we harvest ancient forests even if that destroys endangered owls or other animal species? Should we dump municipal and industrial waste into nearby rivers, or should we dispose of it in some other way? Should we use children to harvest crops and stitch clothes, or should we use only adult labor? There are lots of different ways of producing goods and services, and someone has to make a decision about which production methods to use. The HOW decision is a question not just of efficiency but of social values as well.

For Whom

After we've decided what to produce and how, we must address a third basic question: FOR WHOM? Who is going to get the output produced? Should everyone get an equal share? Should everyone wear the same clothes and drive identical cars? Should some people get to enjoy seven-course banquets while others forage in garbage cans for food scraps? How should the goods and services an economy produces be distributed? Are we satisfied with the way output is now distributed?

THE MECHANISMS OF CHOICE

Answers to the questions of WHAT, HOW, and FOR WHOM largely define an economy. But who formulates the answers? Who actually decides which goods are produced, what technologies are used, or how incomes are distributed?

The Invisible Hand of a Market Economy

Adam Smith had an answer back in 1776. In his classic work *The Wealth of Nations,* the Scottish economist Smith said the "invisible hand" determines what gets produced, how, and for whom. The invisible hand he referred to wasn't a creature from a science fiction movie but, instead, a characterization of the way markets work.

Consider the decision about how many cars to produce in the United States. Who makes that decision? There's no "auto czar" who dictates how many vehicles will be produced this year. Not even General Motors can make such a decision. Instead the *market* decides how many cars to produce. Millions of consumers signal their desire to have a car by browsing the Internet, visiting showrooms, and buying cars. Their purchases flash a green light to producers, who see the potential to earn more profits. To do so, they'll increase auto output. If consumers stop buying cars, profits will disappear. Producers will respond by reducing output, laying off workers, and even closing factories as they did during the recession of 2008–2009.

Notice how the invisible hand moves us along the production possibilities curve. If consumers demand more cars, the mix of output will include more cars and fewer of other goods. If auto production is scaled back, the displaced autoworkers will end up producing other goods and services, changing the mix of output in the opposite direction.

market mechanism: The use of market prices and sales to signal desired outputs (or resource allocations).

How does the market decide who gets this car?

©Samuel Corum/Anadolu Agency/ Getty Images

laissez faire: The doctrine of "leave it alone," of nonintervention by government in the market mechanism.

Adam Smith's invisible hand is now called the **market mechanism.** Notice that it doesn't require any direct contact between consumers and producers. Communication is indirect, transmitted by market prices and sales. Indeed, *the essential feature of the market mechanism is the price signal.* If you want something and have sufficient income, you can buy it. If enough people do the same thing, the total sales of that product will rise, and perhaps its price will as well. Producers, seeing sales and prices rise, will want to exploit this profit potential. To do so, they'll attempt to acquire a larger share of available resources and use it to produce the goods we desire. That's how the "invisible hand" works.

The market mechanism can also answer the HOW question. To maximize their profits, producers seek the lowest-cost method of producing a good. By observing prices in the marketplace, they can identify the cheapest method and adopt it.

The market mechanism can also resolve the FOR WHOM question. A market distributes goods to the highest bidder. Individuals who are willing and able to pay the most for a product tend to get it in a pure market economy. That's why someone else—not you—is driving the new Mercedes Maybach S650.

Adam Smith was so impressed with the ability of the market mechanism to answer the basic WHAT, HOW, and FOR WHOM questions that he urged government to "leave it alone" **(laissez faire). Adam Smith believed the price signals and responses of the marketplace were likely to do a better job of allocating resources than any government could.**

Government Intervention

The laissez-faire policy Adam Smith favored has always had its share of critics. The German economist Karl Marx emphasized how free markets tend to concentrate wealth and power in the hands of the few at the expense of the many. As he saw it, unfettered markets permit the capitalists (those who own the machinery and factories) to enrich themselves while the proletariat (the workers) toil long hours for subsistence wages. **Marx argued that the government not only had to intervene but had to *own* all the means of production**—the factories, the machinery, the land—in order to avoid savage inequalities. In *Das Kapital* (1867) and the revolutionary *Communist Manifesto* (1848), he laid the foundation for a communist state in which the government would be the master of economic outcomes.

The British economist John Maynard Keynes offered a less drastic solution. The market, he conceded, was pretty efficient in organizing production and building better mousetraps. However, individual producers and workers had no control over the broader economy. The cumulative actions of so many economic agents could easily tip the economy in the wrong direction. A completely unregulated market might veer off in one direction and then another as producers all rushed to increase output at the same time or throttled back production in a herdlike manner. The government, Keynes reasoned, could act like a pressure gauge, letting off excess steam or building it up as the economy needed. With the government maintaining overall balance in the economy, the market could live up to its performance expectations. While assuring a stable, full-employment environment, the government might also be able to redress excessive inequalities. **In Keynes's view, government should play an active but not all-inclusive role in managing the economy.**

Continuing Debates

These historical views shed perspective on today's political debates. The core of most debates is some variation of the WHAT, HOW, or FOR WHOM questions. Much of the debate is how these questions should be answered. Conservatives favor Adam Smith's laissez-faire approach, with minimal government interference in the markets. Liberals, by contrast, think government intervention is needed to improve market outcomes. Conservatives resist workplace regulation, price controls, and minimum wages because such interventions might impair market efficiency. Liberals argue that such interventions temper the excesses of the market and promote both equity and efficiency.

World Opinion. The debate over how best to manage the economy is not unique to the United States. **Countries around the world confront the same choice between reliance on the market and reliance on the government.** Public opinion clearly favors the market system, as World View "Market Reliance vs. Government Reliance?" documents. Yet few countries have ever relied exclusively on either the markets or the government to manage their economy.

WORLD VIEW

MARKET RELIANCE VS. GOVERNMENT RELIANCE?

A public opinion poll conducted in countries from around the world found a striking global consensus that the free market economic system is best. In all but one country polled, a majority or plurality agreed with the statement that "the free enterprise system and free market economy is the best system on which to base the future of the world."

Source: GlobeScan Toronto—London—San Francisco 2010.

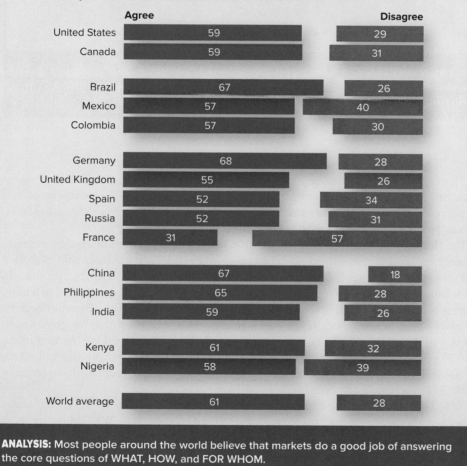

The free enterprise system and free market economy is the best system on which to base the future of the world.

	Agree	Disagree
United States	59	29
Canada	59	31
Brazil	67	26
Mexico	57	40
Colombia	57	30
Germany	68	28
United Kingdom	55	26
Spain	52	34
Russia	52	31
France	31	57
China	67	18
Philippines	65	28
India	59	26
Kenya	61	32
Nigeria	58	39
World average	61	28

ANALYSIS: Most people around the world believe that markets do a good job of answering the core questions of WHAT, HOW, and FOR WHOM.

Degrees of Market Reliance. World View "Index of Economic Freedom" categorizes nations by the extent of their actual market reliance. Hong Kong scores high on this index because its tax rates are relatively low, the public sector is comparatively small, and there

WORLD VIEW

INDEX OF ECONOMIC FREEDOM

Hong Kong ranks number one among the world's nations in economic freedom. It achieves that status with low tax rates, free-trade policies, minimal government regulation, and secure property rights. These and other economic indicators place Hong Kong at the top of the Heritage Foundation's 2017 country rankings by the degree of "economic freedom." The "most free" and the "least free" (repressed) economies on the list of 186 countries are listed here:

Greatest Economic Freedom	Least Economic Freedom
Hong Kong	North Korea
Singapore	Venezuela
New Zealand	Cuba
Switzerland	Congo
Australia	Eritrea
Estonia	Zimbabwe
Canada	Equitorial Guinea
United Arab Emirates	Timor-Leste

Source: *2017 Index of Economic Freedom,* Washington, DC: Heritage Foundation, 2017.

ANALYSIS: Nations differ in how much they rely on market signals or government intervention to shape economic outcomes. Nations that rely the least on government intervention score highest ("most free") on this Index of Economic Freedom.

are few restrictions on private investment or trade. By contrast, North Korea scores extremely low because the government owns all property, directly allocates resources, sets wages, rations food, and limits trade. In other words, Hong Kong is the most market-reliant; North Korea is the most government-reliant.

The Heritage rankings simply *describe* differences in the extent of market/government reliance across different nations. By themselves, they don't tell us which mix of market and government reliance is best. Moreover, the individual rankings change over time. In 1989 Russia began a massive transformation from a state-controlled economy to a more market-oriented economy. Some of the former Soviet republics (e.g., Estonia) became relatively free, while others (e.g., Turkmenistan) still rely on extensive government control of the economy. China has greatly expanded the role of private markets in the last 20 years, and Cuba is grudgingly moving in the same direction in fits and starts. Venezuela has moved in the opposite direction, with sharply increased government control of production and prices.

Notice that the United States is not on the World View list. Although the United States relies heavily on private markets to make WHAT, HOW, and FOR WHOM decisions, it lags behind Hong Kong, Canada, and other nations on the Heritage Index. In 2014, the United States came in 12th, down a few notches from earlier years. That modest decline was due to the increased regulation, higher taxes, and increased government spending that the Obama administration adopted in response to the Great Recession. President Trump's more market-friendly policies have reversed that move. This tug-of-war between more government regulation and more market reliance continues—in both public opinion and the U.S. Congress.

A Mixed Economy

No one advocates *complete* dependence on markets, nor *total* government control of economic resources. Neither Adam Smith's invisible hand nor the governments' very visible hand always works perfectly. As a result, *the United States, like most nations, uses a combination of market signals and government directives to direct economic outcomes.* The resulting compromises are called **mixed economies.**

The reluctance of countries around the world to rely exclusively on either market signals or government directives is due to the recognition that both mechanisms can and do fail on occasion. As we've seen, market signals are capable of answering the three core questions of WHAT, HOW, and FOR WHOM. But the answers may not be the best possible ones.

mixed economy: An economy that uses both market signals and government directives to allocate goods and resources.

Market Failure

When market signals don't give the best possible answers to the WHAT, HOW, and FOR WHOM questions, we say that the market mechanism has *failed.* Specifically, **market failure** means that the invisible hand has failed to achieve the best possible outcomes. If the market fails, we end up with the wrong (*sub*optimal) mix of output, too much unemployment, polluted air, or an inequitable distribution of income.

In a market-driven economy, for example, producers will select production methods based on cost. Cost-driven production decisions, however, may encourage a factory to spew pollution into the environment rather than to use cleaner but more expensive methods of production. The resulting pollution may be so bad that society ends up worse off as a result of the extra production. In such a case we may need government intervention to force better answers to the WHAT and HOW questions.

We could also let the market decide who gets to consume cigarettes. Anyone who had enough money to buy a pack of cigarettes would then be entitled to smoke. What if, however, children aren't experienced enough to balance the risks of smoking against the pleasures? What if nonsmokers are harmed by secondhand smoke? In this case as well, the market's answer to the FOR WHOM question might not be optimal.

market failure: An imperfection in the market mechanism that prevents optimal outcomes.

Government Failure

Government intervention might be needed to move us closer to our economic goals. If successful, the resulting mix of market signals and government directives would be an improvement over a purely market-driven economy. But government intervention may fail as well. **Government failure** occurs when government intervention fails to improve market outcomes or actually makes them worse.

Government failure often occurs in unintended ways. For example, the government may intervene to force an industry to clean up its pollution. The government's directives may impose such high costs that the industry closes factories and lays off workers. Some cutbacks in output might be appropriate, but they could also prove excessive. The government might also mandate pollution control technologies that are too expensive or even obsolete. None of this has to happen, but it might. If it does, government failure will have worsened economic outcomes.

The government might also fail if it interferes with the market's answer to the FOR WHOM question. For 50 years, communist China distributed goods by government directive, not market performance. Incomes were more equal, but uniformly low. To increase output and living standards, China turned to market incentives. As entrepreneurs responded to these incentives, living standards rose dramatically—even while inequality increased. That surge in living standards made the vast majority of Chinese believers in the power of free markets (see the World View appearing earlier in this chapter).

Excessive taxes and transfer payments can also worsen economic outcomes. If the government raises taxes on the rich to pay welfare benefits for the poor, neither the rich nor the poor may see much purpose in working. In that case, the attempt to give everybody a "fair"

government failure: Government intervention that fails to improve economic outcomes.

share of the pie might end up shrinking the size of the pie. If that happened, society could end up worse off.

Seeking Balance

None of these failures has to occur. But they might. *The challenge for any society is to minimize economic failures by selecting the appropriate balance of market signals and government directives.* This isn't an easy task. It requires that we know how markets work and why they sometimes fail. We also need to know what policy options the government has and how and when they might work.

....

WHAT ECONOMICS IS ALL ABOUT

Understanding how economies function is the basic purpose of studying economics. We seek to know how an economy is organized, how it behaves, and how successfully it achieves its basic objectives. Then, if we're lucky, we can discover better ways of attaining those same objectives.

Ends vs. Means

Economists don't formulate an economy's objectives. Instead they focus on the *means* available for achieving given *goals*. In 1978, for example, the U.S. Congress identified "full employment" as a major economic goal. Congress then directed future presidents (and their economic advisers) to formulate policies that would enable us to achieve full employment. The economist's job is to help design policies that will best achieve this and other economic goals.

The same distinction between ends and means is integral to your own life. Your *goal* (the ends) may be to achieve a specific career. The immediate question is how best to achieve that goal (the means). Should you major in economics? Take computer science? Study art history? Surely, you hope that the course choices you make will best help you attain your career goals. Economists can help select those courses based on studies of other students, their majors, and their career outcomes.

Normative vs. Positive Analysis

The distinction between ends and means is mirrored in the difference between *normative* analysis and *positive* analysis. Normative analysis incorporates subjective judgments about what *ought* to be done. Positive analysis focuses on how things might be done without subjective judgments of what is "best." The Heritage Index of Economic Freedom (World View), for example, constitutes a *positive* analysis to the extent that it objectively describes global differences in the extent of market reliance. That effort entails collecting, sorting, and ranking mountains of data. Heritage slides into *normative* analysis when it suggests that market reliance is tantamount to "economic freedom" and inherently superior to more government intervention—that markets are good and governments are bad.

Debates over the core FOR WHOM question likewise reflect both positive and normative analysis. A positive analysis would observe that the U.S. incomes are very "unequal," with the richest 20 percent of the population getting half of all income (see table in Figure 2.3). That's an observable fact—that is, positive analysis. To characterize that same distribution as "inequitable" or "unfair" is to transform (positive) fact into (normative) judgment. Economists are free, of course, to offer their judgments but must be careful to distinguish positive and normative perspectives.

macroeconomics: The study of aggregate economic behavior, of the economy as a whole.

Macro vs. Micro

The study of economics is typically divided into two parts: macroeconomics and microeconomics. **Macroeconomics** focuses on the behavior of an entire economy—the "big picture." In macroeconomics we worry about such national goals as full employment, control of inflation, and economic growth, without worrying about the well-being or behavior of specific individuals or firms. The essential concern of macroeconomics is to understand and improve the performance of the economy as a whole.

Microeconomics is concerned with the details of this big picture. In microeconomics we focus on the individuals, firms, and government agencies that actually compose the larger economy. Our interest here is in the behavior of individual economic actors. What are their goals? How can they best achieve these goals with their limited resources? How will they respond to various incentives and opportunities?

A primary concern of *macro*economics, for example, is to determine how much money, *in total,* consumers will spend on goods and services. In *micro*economics, the focus is much narrower. In micro, attention is paid to purchases of *specific* goods and services rather than just aggregated totals. Macro likewise concerns itself with the level of *total* business investment, while micro examines how *individual* businesses make their investment decisions.

Although they operate at different levels of abstraction, macro and micro are intrinsically related. Macro (aggregate) outcomes depend on micro behavior, and micro (individual) behavior is affected by macro outcomes. One can't fully understand how an economy works until one understands how all the individual participants behave. But just as you can drive a car without knowing how its engine is constructed, you can observe how an economy runs without completely disassembling it. In macroeconomics we observe that the car goes faster when the accelerator is depressed and that it slows when the brake is applied. That's all we need to know in most situations. At times, however, the car breaks down. When it does, we have to know something more about how the pedals work. This leads us into micro studies. How does each part work? Which ones can or should be fixed?

Our interest in microeconomics is motivated by more than our need to understand how the larger economy works. The "parts" of the economic engine are people. To the extent that we care about the well-being of individuals, we have a fundamental interest in microeconomic behavior and outcomes. In this regard, we examine how individual consumers and business firms seek to achieve specific goals in the marketplace. The goals aren't always related to output. Gary Becker won the 1992 Nobel Prize in Economics for demonstrating how economic principles also affect decisions to marry, to have children, to engage in criminal activities—or even to complete homework assignments in an economics class.

microeconomics: The study of individual behavior in the economy, of the components of the larger economy.

Theory vs. Reality

The economy is much too vast and complex to describe and explain in one course (or one lifetime). We need to simplify it. To do so, we focus on basic relationships, ignoring annoying details. We develop basic principles of economic behavior and then use those principles to predict and explain economic events. This means that we formulate theories, or *models,* of economic behavior and then use those theories to evaluate and design economic policy.

Our model of consumer behavior assumes, for example, that people buy less of a good when its price rises. In reality, however, people *may* buy *more* of a good at increased prices, especially if those high prices create a certain snob appeal or if prices are expected to increase still further. In predicting consumer responses to price increases, we typically ignore such possibilities by *assuming* that the price of the good in question is the *only* thing that changes. This assumption of "other things remaining equal" (unchanged) (in Latin, **ceteris paribus**) allows us to make straightforward predictions. If instead we described consumer responses to increased prices in any and all circumstances (allowing everything to change at once), every prediction would be accompanied by a book full of exceptions and qualifications. We'd look more like lawyers than economists.

ceteris paribus: The assumption of nothing else changing.

Although the assumption of *ceteris paribus* makes it easier to formulate economic theory and policy, it also increases the risk of error. If other things do change in significant ways, our predictions (and policies) may fail. But like weather forecasters, we continue to make predictions, knowing that occasional failure is inevitable. In so doing, we're motivated by the conviction that it's better to be approximately right than to be dead wrong.

Imperfect Knowledge. One last word of warning before you read further. Economics claims to be a science in pursuit of basic truths. We want to understand and explain how the economy works without getting tangled up in subjective value judgments. This may be an impossible task. First, it's not clear where the truth lies. For more than 200 years economists have been arguing about what makes the economy tick. None of the competing theories has performed spectacularly well. Indeed, few economists have successfully predicted major economic events with any consistency. Even annual forecasts of inflation, unemployment, and output are regularly in error. Worse still, never-ending arguments about what caused a major economic event continue long after it occurs. In fact, economists are still arguing over the primary causes of the Great Depression of the 1930s!

In view of all these debates and uncertainties, don't expect to learn everything there is to know about the economy today in this text or course. Our goals are more modest. We want to develop a reasonable perspective on economic behavior, an understanding of basic principles. With this foundation, you should acquire a better view of how the economy works. Daily news reports on economic events should make more sense. Congressional debates on tax and budget policies should take on more meaning. You may even develop some insights that you can apply toward running a business, planning a career, or simply managing your scarce time and money more efficiently.

THE ECONOMY TOMORROW

HARNESSING THE SUN

Is solar energy free?
©Darren Baker/Alamy Stock Photo RF

Powering our homes with solar power is an exciting prospect. Today, more than 50 percent of our electricity is generated from the burning of oil and coal. These fossil fuels pollute the air, damage the land, and, as we saw in the 2010 BP oil spill, damage marine life as well. By contrast, we don't have to burn anything to generate solar power. We just need to harness that power by absorbing it in solar panels that convert solar radiation into electricity. The U.S. Department of the Interior says solar stations built in the deserts of the southwestern states could deliver 2,300 gigawatts of energy, more than double America's entire electricity consumption.

Solar power could also be used to fuel our cars. When automakers peer into the future, they see fleets of electric cars. Those fleets will have to be continuously charged with electricity. Why not solar-powered recharging stations? Just think how much that gasoline-to-solar conversion would help clean up the air we breathe!

Opportunity Costs. It's easy to get excited about a solar-powered future. But before we jump on the solar bandwagon, we have to at least consider the costs involved. Sure, the sun's rays are free. But you need a lot of capital investment to harness that solar power. Solar panels on the roof don't come free. Nor do solar-powered electrical charging stations, solar power plants, or the electrical grids that distribute electricity to users. President Obama committed as much as $200 billion in subsidies and direct spending to accelerate the adoption of solar energy. To develop a nationwide, complete solar power infrastructure would cost *trillions* of dollars.

Remember, economists think in terms of real resources, not money. Paper money doesn't build solar panels; it takes real factors of production—land, labor, capital, and entrepreneurship. Those resources—worth trillions of dollars—could be used to produce something else. If we invested that many resources in medical technology, we might cure cancer, find an antidote for the AIDS virus, and maybe even eradicate the flu. Investing that many resources in education might make college not only more enjoyable but a lot more productive as well. To invest all those resources in solar development implies that solar development trumps all other social goals. That's a *normative* judgement that not everyone embraces. Many people worry more about their education, their homes, national defense, and the nation's infrastructure than the harm that conventional energy sources inflict on the environment. President Trump himself called President Obama's spending on solar energy a "disaster" and pushed for more development of conventional energy sources, especially natural gas and oil that are much cheaper. While his critics have lambasted President Trump for ignoring the environmental consequences of nonrenewable energy sources, the ongoing debate has highlighted a basic principle of economics: In deciding whether and how intensively to develop solar power, we have to assess opportunity costs—what goods and services we implicitly forsake in order to harness the sun.

SUMMARY

- Scarcity is a basic fact of economic life. Factors of production (land, labor, capital, entrepreneurship) are scarce in relation to our desires for goods and services. **LO1-1**
- All economic activity entails opportunity costs. Factors of production (resources) used to produce one output cannot simultaneously be used to produce something else. When we choose to produce one thing, we forsake the opportunity to produce some other good or service. **LO1-2**
- A production possibilities curve (PPC) illustrates the limits to production—the various combinations of goods and services that could be produced in a given period if all available resources and technology are used efficiently. The PPC also illustrates opportunity costs—what is given up to get more of something else. **LO1-3**
- The bent shape of the PPC reflects the law of increasing opportunity costs: Increasing quantities of any good can be obtained only by sacrificing ever-increasing quantities of other goods. **LO1-3**
- Inefficient or incomplete use of resources will fail to attain production possibilities. Additional resources or

better technologies will expand them. This is the essence of economic growth. **LO1-3**
- Every country must decide WHAT to produce, HOW to produce, and FOR WHOM to produce with its limited resources. **LO1-4**
- The study of economics focuses on the broad question of resource allocation. Macroeconomics is concerned with allocating the resources of an entire economy to achieve aggregate economic goals (e.g., full employment). Microeconomics focuses on the behavior and goals of individual market participants. **LO1-4**
- The WHAT, HOW, and FOR WHOM choices can be made by the market mechanism or by government directives. Most nations are mixed economies, using a combination of these two choice mechanisms. **LO1-5**
- Market failure exists when market signals generate suboptimal outcomes. Government failure occurs when government intervention worsens economic outcomes. The challenge for economic theory and policy is to find the mix of market signals and government directives that best fulfills our social and economic goals. **LO1-5**

Key Terms

scarcity
factors of production
capital
entrepreneurship
economics
opportunity cost

production possibilities
efficiency
economic growth
market mechanism
laissez faire
mixed economy

market failure
government failure
macroeconomics
microeconomics
ceteris paribus

Questions for Discussion

1. What opportunity costs did you incur in reading this chapter? If you read another chapter today, would your opportunity cost (per chapter) increase? Explain.   **LO1-2**

2. How much time *could* you spend on homework in a day? How much do you spend? How do you decide?   **LO1-2**

3. What's the real cost of a "free lunch" as mentioned in the discussion of "Opportunity Costs?"   **LO1-2**

4. How might a nation's production possibilities be affected by the following?   **LO1-3**
   a. New solar technology.
   b. An increase in immigration.
   c. An increase in military spending.
   d. A natural disaster.

5. What are the opportunity costs of developing wind farms to generate "clean" electricity? Should we make the investment?   **LO1-2**

6. Who would go to college in a completely private (market) college system? How does government intervention change this FOR WHOM outcome?   **LO1-4**

7. Why do people around the world have so much faith in free markets (World View "Market Reliance vs. Government Reliance?")?   **LO1-5**

8. Why did both presidents Obama and Trump reduce spending on America's space exploration program?   **LO1-2**

9. What is the connection between North Korea's missile program and its hunger problem? (World View "North Korea's Food Shortage Grows")   **LO1-2**

10. Why might more reliance on markets rather than government be desirable? When and how might it be undesirable?   **LO1-5**

11. Explain why there are limits to output and how these limits force economies to make tradeoffs.   **LO1-1**

APPENDIX

....

USING GRAPHS

Economists like to draw graphs. In fact, we didn't even make it through the first chapter without a few graphs. This appendix looks more closely at the way graphs are drawn and used. The basic purpose of a graph is to illustrate a relationship between two *variables*. Consider, for example, the relationship between grades and studying. In general, we expect that additional hours of study time will lead to higher grades. Hence we should be able to see a distinct relationship between hours of study time and grade point average.

Suppose that we actually surveyed all the students taking this course with regard to their study time and grade point averages. The resulting information can be compiled in a table such as Table A.1.

According to the table, students who don't study at all can expect an F in this course. To get a C, the average student apparently spends 8 hours a week studying. All those who study 16 hours a week end up with an A in the course.

These relationships between grades and studying can also be illustrated on a graph. Indeed, the whole purpose of a graph is to summarize numerical relationships.

We begin to construct a graph by drawing horizontal and vertical boundaries, as in Figure A.1. These boundaries are called the *axes* of the graph. On the vertical axis (often called the *y*-axis) we measure one of the variables; the other variable is measured on the horizontal axis (the *x*-axis).

In this case, we shall measure the grade point average on the vertical axis. We start at the *origin* (the intersection of the two axes) and count upward, letting the distance between horizontal lines represent half (0.5) a grade point. Each horizontal line is numbered, up to the maximum grade point average of 4.0.

The number of hours each week spent doing homework is measured on the horizontal axis. We begin at the origin again and count to the right. The *scale* (numbering) proceeds in increments of 1 hour, up to 20 hours per week.

TABLE A.1

Hypothetical Relationship of Grades to Study Time

Study Time (Hours per Week)	Grade Point Average
16	4.0 (A)
14	3.5 (B+)
12	3.0 (B)
10	2.5 (C+)
8	2.0 (C)
6	1.5 (D+)
4	1.0 (D)
2	0.5 (F+)
0	0.0 (F)

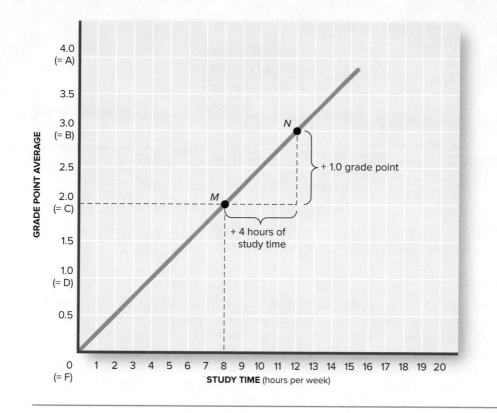

FIGURE A.1
The Relationship of Grades to Study Time

The upward (positive) slope of the curve indicates that additional studying is associated with higher grades. The average student (2.0, or C grade) studies 8 hours per week. This is indicated by point *M* on the graph.

When both axes have been labeled and measured, we can begin illustrating the relationship between study time and grades. Consider the typical student who does 8 hours of homework per week and has a 2.0 (C) grade point average. We illustrate this relationship by first locating 8 hours on the horizontal axis. We then move up from that point a distance of 2.0 grade points, to point *M*. Point *M* tells us that 8 hours of study time per week are typically associated with a 2.0 grade point average.

The rest of the information in Table A.1 is drawn (or *plotted*) on the graph the same way. To illustrate the average grade for people who study 12 hours per week, we move upward from the number 12 on the horizontal axis until we reach the height of 3.0 on the vertical axis. At that intersection, we draw another point (point *N*).

Once we've plotted the various points describing the relationship of study time to grades, we may connect them with a line or curve. This line (curve) is our summary. In this case, the line slopes upward to the right—that is, it has a *positive* slope. This slope indicates that more hours of study time are associated with *higher* grades. Were higher grades associated with *less* study time, the curve in Figure A.1 would have a *negative* slope (downward from left to right).

Slopes

The upward slope of Figure A.1 tells us that higher grades are associated with increased amounts of study time. That same curve also tells us *by how much* grades tend to rise with study time. According to point *M* in Figure A.1, the average student studies 8 hours per week and earns a C (2.0 grade point average). To earn a B (3.0 average), students apparently need to study an average of 12 hours per week (point *N*). Hence an increase of 4 hours of study time per week is associated with a 1-point increase in grade point average. This relationship between *changes* in study time and *changes* in grade point average is expressed by the steepness, or *slope,* of the graph.

The slope of any graph is calculated as

$$\text{Slope} = \frac{\text{Vertical distance between two points}}{\text{Horizontal distance between two points}}$$

In our example, the vertical distance between M and N represents a change in grade point average. The horizontal distance between these two points represents the change in study time. Hence the slope of the graph between points M and N is equal to

$$\text{Slope} = \frac{3.0 \text{ grade} - 2.0 \text{ grade}}{12 \text{ hours} - 8 \text{ hours}} = \frac{1 \text{ grade point}}{4 \text{ hours}}$$

In other words, a 4-hour increase in study time (from 8 to 12 hours) is associated with a 1-point increase in grade point average (see Figure A.1).

Shifts

The relationship between grades and studying illustrated in Figure A.1 isn't inevitable. It's simply a graphical illustration of student experiences, as revealed in our hypothetical survey. The relationship between study time and grades could be quite different.

Suppose that the university decided to raise grading standards, making it more difficult to achieve higher grades. To achieve a C, a student now would need to study 12 hours per week, not just 8 (as in Figure A.1). Whereas students could previously get a B by studying 12 hours per week, now they'd have to study 16 hours to get that grade.

Figure A.2 illustrates the new grading standards. Notice that the new curve lies to the right of the earlier curve. We say that the curve has *shifted* to reflect a change in the relationship between study time and grades. Point R indicates that 12 hours of study time now "produce" a C, not a B (point N on the old curve). Students who now study only

FIGURE A.2

A Shift

When a relationship between two variables changes, the entire curve *shifts*. In this case a tougher grading policy alters the relationship between study time and grades. To get a C, one must now study 12 hours per week (point R), not just 8 hours (point M).

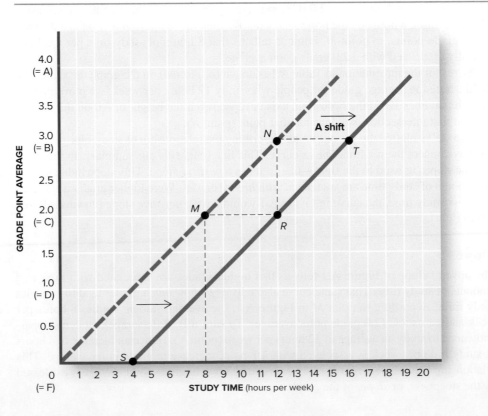

4 hours per week (point *S*) will fail. Under the old grading policy, they could have at least gotten a D. **When a curve shifts, the underlying relationship between the two variables has changed.**

A shift may also change the slope of the curve. In Figure A.2, the new grading curve is parallel to the old one; it therefore has the same slope. Under either the new grading policy or the old one, a 4-hour increase in study time leads to a 1-point increase in grades. Therefore, the slope of both curves in Figure A.2 is

$$\text{Slope} = \frac{\text{Vertical change}}{\text{Horizontal change}} = \frac{1}{4}$$

This too may change, however. Figure A.3 illustrates such a possibility. In this case, zero study time still results in an F. But now the payoff for additional studying is reduced. Now it takes 6 hours of study time to get a D (1.0 grade point), not 4 hours as before. Likewise, another 4 hours of study time (to a total of 10) raise the grade by only two-thirds of a point. It takes 6 hours to raise the grade a full point. The slope of the new line is therefore

$$\text{Slope} = \frac{\text{Vertical change}}{\text{Horizontal change}} = \frac{1}{6}$$

The new curve in Figure A.3 has a smaller slope than the original curve and so lies below it. What all this means is that it now takes a greater effort to improve your grade.

Linear vs. Nonlinear Curves

In Figures A.1–A.3 the relationship between grades and studying is represented by a straight line—that is, a *linear curve*. A distinguishing feature of linear curves is that they have the same (constant) slope throughout. In Figure A.1 it appears that *every* 4-hour

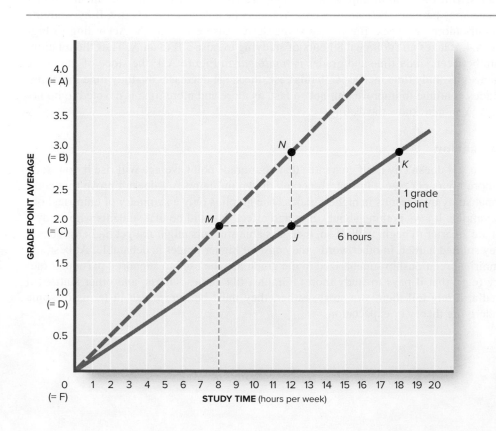

FIGURE A.3

A Change in Slope

When a curve shifts, it may change its slope as well. In this case a new grading policy makes each higher grade more difficult to reach. To raise a C to a B, for example, one must study 6 additional hours (compare points *J* and *K*). Earlier it took only 4 hours to move the grade scale up a full point. The slope of the line has declined from 0.25 (= 1 ÷ 4) to 0.17 (= 1 ÷ 6).

FIGURE A.4
A Nonlinear Relationship

Straight lines have a constant slope, implying a constant relationship between the two variables. But the relationship (and slope) may vary. In this case, it takes 6 extra hours of study to raise a C (point *W*) to a B (point *X*) but 8 extra hours to raise a B to an A (point *Y*). The slope decreases as we move up the curve.

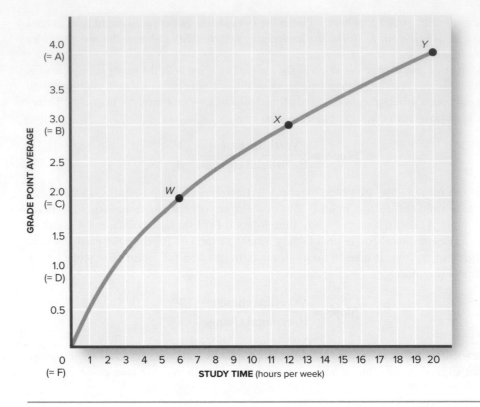

increase in study time is associated with a 1-point increase in average grades. In Figure A.3 it appears that every 6-hour increase in study time leads to a 1-point increase in grades. But the relationship between studying and grades may not be linear. Higher grades may be more difficult to attain. You may be able to raise a C to a B by studying 4 hours more per week. But it may be harder to raise a B to an A. According to Figure A.4, it takes an additional 8 hours of studying to raise a B to an A. Thus the relationship between study time and grades is *nonlinear* in Figure A.4; the slope of the curve changes as study time increases. In this case, the slope decreases as study time increases. Grades continue to improve, but not so fast, as more and more time is devoted to homework. You may know the feeling.

Causation

Figure A.4 doesn't by itself guarantee that your grade point average will rise if you study 4 more hours per week. In fact, the graph drawn in Figure A.4 doesn't prove that additional study ever results in higher grades. The graph is only a summary of empirical observations. It says nothing about cause and effect. It could be that students who study a lot are smarter to begin with. If so, then less able students might not get higher grades if they studied harder. In other words, the *cause* of higher grades is debatable. At best, the empirical relationship summarized in the graph may be used to support a particular theory (e.g., that it pays to study more). Graphs, like tables, charts, and other statistical media, rarely tell their own story; rather, they must be *interpreted* in terms of some underlying theory or expectation.

LO1-2   1. According to Table 1.1 (or Figure 1.1), what is the opportunity cost of the first truck produced?

LO1-3   2. (*a*) Compute the opportunity cost in forgone consumer goods (millions of pounds of butter) for each additional unit of military output (number of planes) produced:

Military output	0	1	2	3	4	5
Consumer goods output	100	90	75	55	30	0
Opportunity cost		—	—	—	—	—

     (*b*) As military output increases, are opportunity costs (A) increasing, (B) decreasing, or (C) remaining constant?

LO1-3   3. According to Figure 1.3, how much food production is sacrificed when North Korea moves from point *P* to point *N*?

LO1-2   4. (*a*) If the average North Korean farmer produces 1,800 pounds of food per year, what is the opportunity cost, in pounds of food, of North Korea's army (World View "World's Largest Armies")?

     (*b*) If a person needs at least 500 pounds of food per year to survive, how many people could have been fed with the forgone food output?

LO1-2   5. What is the opportunity cost (in civilian output) of a defense buildup that raises military spending from 4.0 to 4.3 percent of a $20 trillion economy?

LO1-4   6. What are the three core economic questions societies must answer?

LO1-3   7. According to the figure (similar to Figure 1.4),

     (*a*) At which point(s) is this society producing some of each type of output but producing inefficiently?

     (*b*) At which point(s) is this society producing the most output possible with the available resources and technology?

     (*c*) At which point(s) is the output combination unattainable with available resources and technology?

     (*d*) Show the change that would occur if the resources of this society increased. Label this curve PPC$_2$.

     (*e*) Show the change that would occur with a huge natural disaster that destroyed 40 percent of production capacity. Label this curve PPC$_3$.

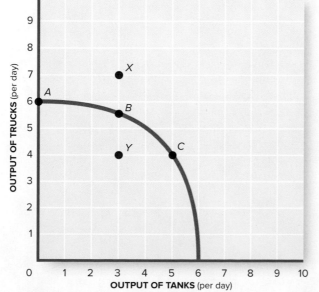

LO1-3 8. You have only 20 hours per week to use for either study time or fun time. Suppose the relationship between study time, fun time, and grades is shown in this table:

Fun time (hours per week)	20	18	14	8	0
Study time (hours per week)	0	2	6	12	20
Grade point average	*0*	*1.0*	*2.0*	*3.0*	*4.0*

(a) Draw the (linear) production possibilities curve on a graph that represents the alternative uses of your time.

(b) On the same graph, show the combination of study time and fun time that would get you a 2.0 grade average.

(c) What is the cost, in lost fun time, of raising your grade point average from 2.0 to 3.0?

LO1-5 9. According to the World View "Market Reliance vs. Government Reliance?" which nation has

(a) The highest level of faith in the market system?

(b) The lowest level of faith in the market system?

LO1-2 10. If a person literally had "nothing else to do,"

(a) What would be the opportunity cost of doing this homework?

(b) What is the likelihood of that?

LO1-1 11. According to the World View "World's Largest Armies," what percent of the total population is serving in the military in

(a) The United States (population = 340 million)?

(b) North Korea (population = 25 million)?

(c) China (population = 1.4 billion)?

LO1-2 12. The Economy Tomorrow: What are the opportunity costs of increasing the number of solar panels in use in the United States?

©Kyodo via AP Images

The U.S. Economy: A Global View

After reading this chapter, you should know

LO2-1 The relative size of the U.S. economy.

LO2-2 How the U.S. output mix has changed over time.

LO2-3 How the United States is able to produce so much output.

LO2-4 How incomes are distributed in the United States and elsewhere.

All nations must confront the central economic questions of WHAT to produce, HOW to produce, and FOR WHOM to produce it. However, the nations of the world approach these issues with vastly different production possibilities. China, Canada, the United States, Russia, and Brazil have more than *3 million* square miles of land each. All that land gives them far greater production possibilities than Dominica, Tonga, Malta, or Lichtenstein, each of which has less than 300 square miles of land. The population of China totals more than 1.4 billion people, nearly five times that of the United States, and 25,000 times the population of Greenland. Obviously these nations confront very different output choices.

In addition to vastly uneven production possibilities, the nations of the world use different mechanisms for deciding WHAT, HOW, and FOR WHOM to produce. Belarus, Romania, North Korea, and Cuba still rely heavily on central planning. By contrast, Singapore, New Zealand, Ireland, and the United States permit the market mechanism to play a dominant role in shaping economic outcomes.

With different production possibilities and mechanisms of choice, you'd expect economic outcomes to vary greatly across nations. And they do. This chapter assesses how the U.S. economy stacks up. Specifically,

- **WHAT goods and services does the United States produce?**
- **HOW is that output produced?**
- **FOR WHOM is the output produced?**

In each case, we want to see not only how the United States has answered these questions but also how America's answers compare with those of other nations.

WHAT AMERICA PRODUCES

The United States has less than 5 percent of the world's population and only 12 percent of the world's arable land, yet it produces 20 percent of the world's output.

GDP Comparisons

World View "Comparative Output (GDP)" shows how total U.S. production compares with that of other nations. Every country produces a different mix of output. So, it's impossible to compare output in purely *physical* terms (e.g., so many cars, so many fish, etc.). But we can make

COMPARATIVE OUTPUT (GDP)

The United States is by far the world's largest economy. Its annual output of goods and services is one and a half times larger than China's, three times Japan's, and more than all of the European Union's. The output of Third World countries is only a tiny fraction of U.S. output.

Source: The World Bank (Atlas method).

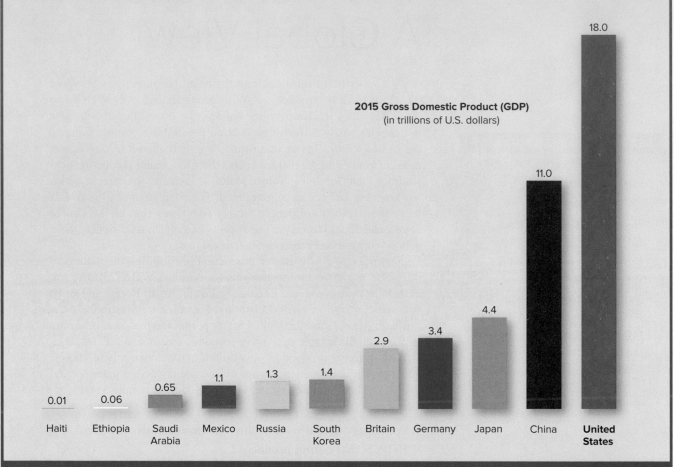

2015 Gross Domestic Product (GDP)
(in trillions of U.S. dollars)

Haiti	Ethiopia	Saudi Arabia	Mexico	Russia	South Korea	Britain	Germany	Japan	China	United States
0.01	0.06	0.65	1.1	1.3	1.4	2.9	3.4	4.4	11.0	18.0

ANALYSIS: The market value of output (GDP) is a basic measure of an economy's size. The U.S. economy is far larger than any other and accounts for more than one-fifth of the entire world's output of goods and services.

---

gross domestic product (GDP): The total market value of all final goods and services produced within a nation's borders in a given time period.

comparisons based on the *value* of output. We do this by computing the total market value of all the goods and services a nation produces in a year—what we call **gross domestic product (GDP).** In effect, GDP is the "pie" of output we bake each year.

In 2015 the U.S. economy baked a huge pie—one containing more than $18 trillion worth of goods and services. That was far more output than any other nation produced. The second-largest economy, China, produced only two-thirds that much. Japan came in third, with about a third of U.S. output. Cuba, by contrast, produced less than $90 *billion* of output, less than the state of Mississippi. Russia, which was once regarded as a superpower, produced only $1.3 trillion. The entire 27-member European Union produces less output than the United States.

Per Capita GDP. What makes the U.S. share of world output so remarkable is that we do it with so few people. The U.S. population of 340 million amounts to less than 5 percent of the world's total (7.4 billion). Yet we produce more than 20 percent of the world's output.

That means we're producing a lot of output *per person*. China, by contrast, has the opposite ratios: 20 percent of the world's population producing less than 13 percent of the world's output. So China is producing a lot of output but relatively less *per person*.

This people-based measure of economic performance is called **per capita GDP.** Per capita GDP is simply a nation's total output divided by its total population. It doesn't tell us how much any specific person gets. *Per capita GDP is an indicator of how much output the average person would get if all output were divided evenly among the population.* In effect, GDP per capita tells us how large a slice of the GDP pie the average citizen gets.

In 2015 per capita GDP in the United States was roughly $56,000. That means the average U.S. citizen could have consumed $56,000 worth of goods and services. That's a staggering amount by global standards—five times the average for the rest of the world. World View "GDP per Capita around the World" provides a global perspective on just how "rich"

per capita GDP: The dollar value of GDP divided by total population; average GDP.

WORLD VIEW

GDP PER CAPITA AROUND THE WORLD

The American standard of living is nearly five times higher than the average for the rest of the world. People in the poorest nations of the world (e.g., Haiti, Ethiopia) barely survive on per capita incomes that are a tiny fraction of U.S. standards.

Source: The World Bank.

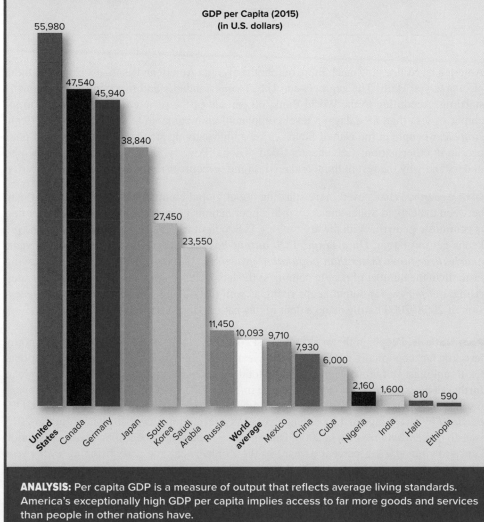

GDP per Capita (2015)
(in U.S. dollars)

Country	GDP per Capita
United States	55,980
Canada	47,540
Germany	45,940
Japan	38,840
South Korea	27,450
Saudi Arabia	23,550
Russia	11,450
World average	10,093
Mexico	9,710
China	7,930
Cuba	6,000
Nigeria	2,160
India	1,600
Haiti	810
Ethiopia	590

ANALYSIS: Per capita GDP is a measure of output that reflects average living standards. America's exceptionally high GDP per capita implies access to far more goods and services than people in other nations have.

FIGURE 2.1

U.S. Output and Population Growth since 1900

Over time, the growth of output in the United States has greatly exceeded population growth. As a consequence, GDP per capita has grown tremendously. GDP per capita was five times higher in 2000 than in 1900.

Source: U.S. Department of Labor.

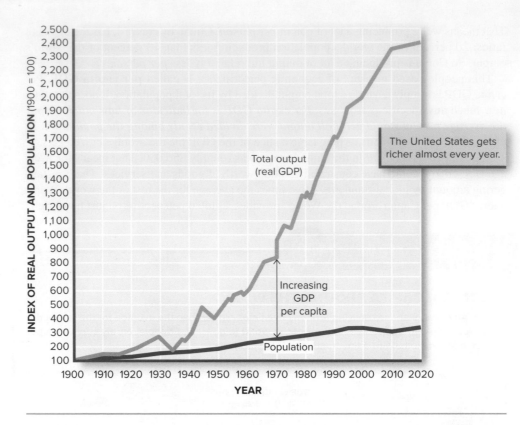

America is. Notice how much more output the average American has than a person in India or, worse yet, Haiti. The gap between U.S. living standards and those in other nations is startling. According to the World Bank, 40 percent of the people on Earth subsist on incomes of less than $3 a day—a level completely unimaginable to the average American. *Homeless* people in the United States enjoy a higher living standard than billions of poor people in other nations (see chapter titled "Global Poverty"). In this context, it's easy to understand why the rest of the world envies (and sometimes resents) America's prosperity.

GDP Growth. What's even more startling about global comparisons is that the GDP gap between the United States and the world's poor nations keeps growing. The reason for that is **economic growth.** With few exceptions, U.S. output increases nearly every year: the pie keeps getting larger. *On average, U.S. output has grown by roughly 3 percent a year, nearly three times faster than population growth (1 percent).* So the U.S. pie is growing faster than the number of people coming to the table. Hence not only does *total* output keep rising, but *per capita* output keeps rising as well (see Figure 2.1). Even the Great Recession of 2008–2009 hardly made a dent in this pattern of ever-rising incomes.

economic growth: An increase in output (real GDP); an expansion of production possibilities.

Poor Nations. People in the world's poorest countries aren't so fortunate. China's economy has grown exceptionally fast in the last 20 years, propelling it to second place in the global GDP rankings. But in many other nations total output has actually *declined* year after year, further depressing living standards. Notice in Table 2.1, for example, what's been happening in Zimbabwe. From 2000 to 2015, Zimbabwe's output of goods and services (GDP) *declined* by an average of 1.9 percent a year. As a result, total Zimbabwean output in 2015 was 40 percent *smaller* than in 2000. During those same years, the Zimbabwean population kept growing—by 1.5 percent a year. So the Zimbabwean pie was shrinking every year even as the number of people coming to the table was increasing. As a result, Zimbabwe's per capita GDP fell below $400 a year. That low level of per capita GDP left two-thirds of Zimbabwe's population undernourished.

	Average Growth Rate (2000–2015) of		
	GDP	Population	Per Capita GDP
High-income countries			
United States	1.6	0.9	0.7
Canada	1.9	1.0	0.9
Japan	0.7	0.0	0.7
France	1.1	0.6	0.5
Low-income countries			
China	10.3	0.5	9.8
Ethiopia	9.6	2.7	6.9
India	7.5	1.5	6.0
Burundi	1.0	1.6	−0.6
Haiti	1.2	1.5	−0.3
Libya	−0.5	1.1	−1.6
Zimbabwe	−1.9	1.5	−3.4

Source: The World Bank, data.worldbank.org

TABLE 2.1

GDP Growth vs. Population Growth

The relationship between GDP growth and population growth is very different in rich and poor countries. The populations of rich countries are growing very slowly, and gains in per capita GDP are easily achieved. In the poorest countries, population is still increasing rapidly, making it difficult to raise living standards. Notice how per capita incomes are *declining* in many poor countries (such as Zimbabwe, Haiti, and Libya).

The Mix of Output

Regardless of how much output a nation produces, the *mix* of output always includes both *goods* (such as cars, big-screen TVs, and potatoes) and *services* (like this economics course, visits to a doctor, or a professional baseball game). A century ago, about two-thirds of U.S. output consisted of farm goods (37 percent), manufactured goods (22 percent), and mining (9 percent). Since then, more than 25 *million* people have left the farms and taken jobs in other sectors. As a result, today's mix of output is completely reversed: ***Eighty percent of U.S. output now consists of services, not goods*** (see Figure 2.2).

The *relative* decline in goods production (manufacturing, farming) doesn't mean that we're producing *fewer* goods today than in earlier decades. Quite the contrary. While some industries such as iron and steel have shrunk, others, such as chemicals, publishing, and telecommunications equipment, have grown tremendously. The result is that manufacturing output has increased fourfold since 1950. The same kind of thing has happened in the farm sector, where output keeps rising even though agriculture's *share* of total output has declined. It's just that our output of *services* has increased so much faster.

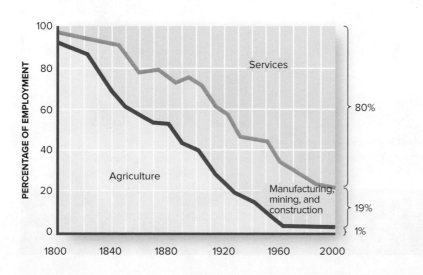

FIGURE 2.2

The Changing Mix of Output

Two hundred years ago, almost all U.S. output came from farms. Today 80 percent of output consists of services, not farm or manufactured goods.

Source: U.S. Department of Commerce.

Development Patterns. The transformation of the United States into a service economy is a reflection of our high incomes. In Ethiopia, where the most urgent concern is to keep people from starving, more than 50 percent of output still comes from the farm sector. Poor people don't have enough income to buy dental services, vacations, or even an education, so the mix of output in poor countries is weighted toward goods, not services.

HOW AMERICA PRODUCES

Regardless of how much output a nation produces, every nation ultimately depends on its resources—its **factors of production**—to produce goods and services. So *differences* in GDP must be explained in part by HOW those resources are used.

Human Capital

We've already observed that America's premier position in global GDP rankings isn't due to the number of humans within our borders. We have far fewer bodies than China or India, yet produce far more output than either of those nations. What counts for production purposes is not just the *number* of workers a nation has, but the *skills* of those workers—what we call **human capital.**

Over time, the United States has invested heavily in human capital. In 1940 only 1 out of 20 young Americans graduated from college; today more than 40 percent of young people are college graduates. High school graduation rates have jumped from 38 percent to more than 85 percent in the same period. In the poorest countries, fewer than half of youth ever *attend* high school, much less graduate (see World View "The Education Gap between Rich and Poor Nations"). As a consequence, the United Nations estimates that 1.2 billion people—a sixth of humanity—are unable to read a book or even write their own names. Without even functional literacy, such workers are doomed to low-productivity jobs. Despite low wages, they are not likely to "steal" many jobs from America's highly educated and trained workforce.

factors of production: Resource inputs used to produce goods and services, e.g., land, labor, capital, entrepreneurship.

human capital: The knowledge and skills possessed by the workforce.

WORLD VIEW

THE EDUCATION GAP BETWEEN RICH AND POOR NATIONS

Virtually all Americans attend high school and roughly 85 percent graduate. In poor countries, relatively few workers attend high school and even fewer graduate. Half the workers in the world's poorest nations are illiterate.

Source: The World Bank, WDI2016 Data Set, data.worldbank.org

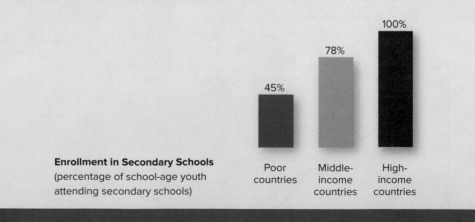

Enrollment in Secondary Schools
(percentage of school-age youth attending secondary schools)

Poor countries	Middle-income countries	High-income countries
45%	78%	100%

ANALYSIS: The high productivity of the American economy is explained in part by the quality of its labor resources. Workers in poorer, less developed countries get much less education and training.

Analysis: An abundance of capital equipment and advanced technology make American farmers and workers far more productive than workers in poor nations.

(*left*): ©McGraw-Hill Education/Barry Barker, photographer; (*right*): Source: Photo by Jeff Vanuga, USDA Natural Resources Conservation Service

Capital Stock

America has also accumulated a massive stock of capital—more than $80 *trillion* worth of machinery, factories, and buildings. As a result of all this prior investment, U.S. production tends to be very **capital-intensive.** The contrast with *labor-intensive* production in poorer countries is striking. A farmer in India still works mostly with his hands and crude implements, whereas a U.S. farmer works with computers, automated irrigation systems, and mechanized equipment (see the photos above). Russian business managers don't have the computer networks or telecommunications systems that make U.S. business so efficient. In Haiti and Ethiopia, even telephones, indoor plumbing, and dependable sources of power are scarce.

capital-intensive: Production processes that use a high ratio of capital to labor inputs.

High Productivity

When you put educated workers together with sophisticated capital equipment, you tend to get more output. This relationship largely explains why the United States has such a lead in worker **productivity**—the amount of output produced by the average worker. *American households are able to consume so much because American workers produce so much.* It's really that simple.

productivity: Output per unit of input—for example, output per labor-hour.

The huge output of the United States is thus explained not only by a wealth of resources but by their quality as well. *The high productivity of the U.S. economy results from using highly educated workers in capital-intensive production processes.*

Factor Mobility. Our continuing ability to produce the goods and services that consumers demand also depends on our agility in *reallocating* resources from one industry to another. Every year, some industries expand and others contract. Thousands of new firms start up each year, and almost as many others disappear. In the process, land, labor, capital, and entrepreneurship move from one industry to another in response to changing demands and technology. In 1975 Federal Express, Dell Computer, Staples, Oracle, and Amgen didn't exist. Walmart was still a small retailer. Starbucks was selling coffee on Seattle street corners, and the founders of Google, Facebook, and Snapchat weren't even born. Today these companies employ millions of people. These workers came from other firms and industries that weren't growing as fast.

Technological Advance. One of the forces that keeps shifting resources from one industry to another is continuing advances in technology. Advances in technology can be as sophisticated as microscopic miniaturization of electronic circuits or as simple as the reorganization of production processes. Either phenomenon increases the productivity of the workforce and potential output. ***Whenever technology advances, an economy can produce more output with existing resources;*** its **production possibilities** curve shifts outward (see Figure 1.5).

Outsourcing and Trade. The same technological advances that fuel economic growth also facilitate *global* resource use. Telecommunications has become so sophisticated and inexpensive that phone workers in India or Grenada can answer calls directed to U.S. companies. Likewise, programmers in India can work online to write computer code, develop software, or perform accounting chores for U.S. corporations. Although such "outsourcing" is often viewed as a threat to U.S. jobs, it is really another source of increased U.S. output. By outsourcing routine tasks to foreign workers, U.S. workers are able to focus on higher-value jobs. U.S. computer engineers do less routine programming and more systems design. U.S. accountants do less cost tabulation and more cost analysis. By utilizing foreign resources in the production process, U.S. workers are able to pursue their *comparative advantage* in high-skill, capital-intensive jobs. In this way, both productivity and total output increase. Although some U.S. workers suffer temporary job losses in this process, the overall economy gains.

Role of Government

In assessing HOW goods are produced and economies grow, we must also take heed of the role the government plays. As we noted in Chapter 1, the amount of economic freedom varies greatly among the 200-plus nations of the world. Moreover, the Heritage Foundation has documented a positive relationship between the degree of economic freedom and economic growth. Quite simply, when entrepreneurs are unfettered by regulation or high taxes, they are more likely to design and produce better mousetraps. When the government owns the factors of production, imposes high taxes, or tightly regulates output, there is little opportunity or incentive to design better products or pursue new technology. This is one reason why more market-reliant economies grow faster than others.

Recognizing the importance of market incentives doesn't force us to reject all government intervention. No one really advocates the complete abolition of government. On the contrary, the government plays a critical role in establishing a framework in which private businesses can operate. Among its many roles are these:

- *Providing a legal framework.* One of the most basic functions of government is to establish and enforce the rules of the game. In some bygone era maybe a person's word was sufficient to guarantee delivery or payment. Businesses today, however, rely more on written contracts. The government gives legitimacy to contracts by establishing the rules for such pacts and by enforcing their provisions. In the absence of contractual rights, few companies would be willing to ship goods without prepayment (in cash). Even the incentive to write texts would disappear if government copyright laws didn't forbid unauthorized photocopying. By establishing ownership rights, contract rights, and other rules of the game, the government lays the foundation for market transactions.
- *Protecting the environment.* The government also intervenes in the market to protect the environment. The legal contract system is designed to protect the interests of a buyer and a seller who wish to do business. What if, however, the business they contract for harms third parties? How are the interests of persons who *aren't* party to the contract to be protected?

   Numerous examples abound of how unregulated production may harm third parties. Earlier in the century, the steel mills around Pittsburgh blocked out the sun with clouds of sulfurous gases that spewed out of their furnaces. Local residents were harmed every time they inhaled. In the absence of government intervention, such side effects would be common. Decisions on how to produce would be based on costs alone, not on how the environment is affected. However, such negative **externalities**—spillover costs imposed on the broader community—affect our collective well-being. To reduce

---

production possibilities: The alternative combinations of final goods and services that could be produced in a given period with all available resources and technology.

---

externalities: Costs (or benefits) of a market activity borne by a third party; the difference between the social and private costs (benefits) of a market activity.

the external costs of production, the government limits air, water, and noise pollution and regulates environmental use.

- *Protecting consumers.* The government also uses its power to protect the interests of consumers. One way to do this is to prevent individual business firms from becoming too powerful. In the extreme case, a single firm might have a **monopoly** on the production of a specific good. As the sole producer of that good, a monopolist could dictate the price, the quality, and the quantity of the product. In such a situation, consumers would likely end up paying too much for too little.

    To protect consumers from monopoly exploitation, the government tries to prevent individual firms from dominating specific markets. Antitrust laws prohibit mergers or acquisitions that would threaten competition. The U.S. Department of Justice and the Federal Trade Commission also regulate pricing practices, advertising claims, and other behavior that might put consumers at an unfair disadvantage in product markets.

    Government also regulates the safety of many products. Consumers don't have enough expertise to assess the safety of various medicines, for example. If they rely on trial and error to determine drug safety, they might not get a second chance. To avoid this calamity, the government requires rigorous testing of new drugs, food additives, and other products.

- *Protecting labor.* The government also regulates how labor resources are used in the production process. In most poor nations, children are forced to start working at very early ages, often for minuscule wages. They often don't get the chance to go to school or to stay healthy. In Africa, 40 percent of children under age 14 work to survive or to help support their families. In the United States, child labor laws and compulsory schooling prevent minor children from being exploited. Government regulations also set standards for workplace safety, minimum wages, fringe benefits, and overtime provisions.

monopoly: A firm that produces the entire market supply of a particular good or service.

Striking a Balance

All these and other government interventions are designed to change the way resources are used. Such interventions reflect the conviction that the market alone might not always select the best possible way of producing goods and services. There's no guarantee, however, that government regulation of HOW goods are produced always makes us better off. Excessive regulation may inhibit production, raise product prices, and limit consumer choices. As noted in Chapter 1, *government* failure might replace *market* failure, leaving us no better off—possibly even worse off. This possibility underscores the importance of striking the right balance between market reliance and government regulation.

FOR WHOM AMERICA PRODUCES

As we've seen, America produces a huge quantity of output, using high-quality labor and capital resources. That leaves one basic question unanswered: FOR WHOM is all this output produced?

How many goods and services one gets largely depends on how much income one has to spend. The U.S. economy uses the market mechanism to distribute most goods and services. Those who receive the most income get the most goods. This goes a long way toward explaining why millionaires live in mansions and homeless people seek shelter in abandoned cars. This is the kind of stark inequality that fueled Karl Marx's denunciation of capitalism. Even today, people wonder how some Americans can be so rich while others are so poor.

U.S. Income Distribution

Figure 2.3 illustrates the actual distribution of income in the United States. For this illustration the entire population is sorted into five groups of equal size, ranked by income. In this depiction, all the rich people are in the top **income quintile;** the poor are in the lowest quintile. To be in the top quintile in 2015, a household needed at least $117,000 of income. All the households in the lowest quintile had incomes under $23,000.

income quintile: One-fifth of the population, rank-ordered by income (e.g., top fifth).

FIGURE 2.3

The U.S. Distribution of Income

The richest fifth of U.S. households gets half of all the income—a huge slice of the income pie. By contrast, the poorest fifth gets only a sliver.

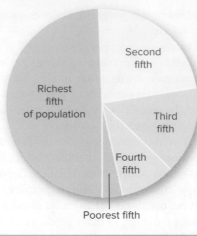

Income Quintile	2015 Income	Average Income	Share of Total Income (%)
Highest fifth	Above $117,000	$202,000	51.1
Second fifth	$72,000–117,000	$ 92,000	23.2
Third fifth	$44,000–72,000	$ 57,000	14.3
Fourth fifth	$23,000–44,000	$ 33,000	8.2
Lowest fifth	$0–23,000	$ 12,500	3.1

Source: U.S. Department of Commerce, Bureau of the Census (averages rounded to thousands of dollars; 2015 data).

The most striking feature of Figure 2.3 is how large a slice of the income pie rich people get: ***The top 20 percent (quintile) of U.S. households get half of all U.S. income.*** By contrast, the poorest 20 percent (quintile) of U.S. households get only a sliver of the income pie—about 3 percent. Those grossly unequal slices explain why nearly half of all Americans believe the nation is divided into "haves" and "have nots."

Analysis: The market distributes income (and, in turn, goods and services) according to the resources an individual owns and how well they are used. If the resulting inequalities are too great, some redistribution via government intervention may be desired.
(*left*): ©Thinkstock/Stockbyte/Getty Images RF; (*right*): ©Natalie Roeth RF

Global Inequality

As unequal as U.S. incomes are, income disparities are actually greater in many other countries. Ironically, income inequalities are often greatest in the poorest countries. The richest *tenth* of U.S. families gets 30 percent of America's income pie. The richest tenth of South Africa's families gets 51 percent of that nation's income (see World View "Income Share of the Rich"). Given the small size of South Africa's pie, the *bottom* tenth of South African families is left with mere crumbs. As we'll see in the chapter titled "Global Poverty," 40 percent of South Africa's population lives in "severe poverty," defined by the World Bank as an income of less than $3 a day.

Comparisons across countries would manifest even greater inequality. As we saw earlier, third world GDP per capita is far below U.S. levels. As a consequence, even **poor** *people in the United States receive far more goods and services than the* **average** *household in most low-income countries.*

WORLD VIEW

INCOME SHARE OF THE RICH

Inequality tends to diminish as a country develops. In poor, developing nations, the richest tenth of the population typically gets 40 to 50 percent of all income. In developed countries, the richest tenth gets 20 to 30 percent of total income.

Source: The World Bank, 2016.

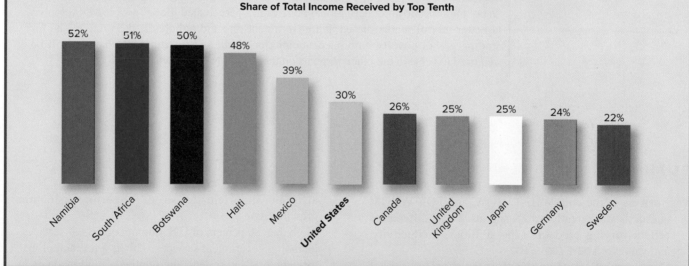

Share of Total Income Received by Top Tenth

Namibia	South Africa	Botswana	Haiti	Mexico	United States	Canada	United Kingdom	Japan	Germany	Sweden
52%	51%	50%	48%	39%	30%	26%	25%	25%	24%	22%

ANALYSIS: The FOR WHOM question is reflected in the distribution of income. Although the U.S. distribution of income is unequal, inequalities are much more severe in most poor nations.

THE ECONOMY TOMORROW

THE UNITED NATIONS AGENDA

Global answers to the basic questions of WHAT, HOW, and FOR WHOM have been shaped by market forces and government intervention. Obviously the answers aren't yet fully satisfactory.

Millions of Americans still struggle to make ends meet. Worse yet, nearly 3 *billion* people around the world live in abject poverty—with incomes of less than $3 a day. More

Continued

than a sixth of the world's population is illiterate, nearly half has no access to sanitation facilities, and a fifth is chronically malnourished.

Then there is a staggering amount of pollution, rampant inequalities, inadequate education, and insufficient health care for billions of people.

The United Nations wants us to fashion better answers for the WHAT, HOW, and FOR WHOM questions. In September 2015 the U.N. adopted a set of 17 specific goals for sustainable development and a 15-year timeline for achieving them. Ending world poverty and eliminating world hunger are the first two on the list. High on the list is also the goal of reducing inequalities across income groups, gender, and race. Protecting the environment and slowing climate change are additional goals.

Can the world meet all these goals? Perhaps. But it will take a lot of resources and even more political will. Consider just the first goal of ending global poverty.

The rich nations of the world have enough resources to wipe out global poverty. But they're not willing to give them up. People in rich nations also have aspirations: they want higher living standards in the economy tomorrow. They already enjoy more comforts than people in poor nations even dream of. But that doesn't stop them from wanting more consumer goods, better schools, improved health care, a cleaner environment, and greater economic security. So the needs of the world's poor typically get lower priority.

How about the poor nations themselves? Couldn't they do a better job of mobilizing and employing their own resources to accelerate economic growth? Governments in many poor nations are notoriously self-serving and corrupt. Private property is often at risk of confiscation and contracts hard to enforce. This discourages the kind of investment poor nations desperately need. The unwillingness of rich nations to open their markets to the exports of poor nations also puts a lid on income growth. In reality, an array of domestic and international policies has perpetuated global poverty. Developing a better mix of market-based and government-directed policies is the prerequisite for ending global poverty. Similar economic, political, and institutional changes will be required to achieve the other 16 goals on the United Nations' wish list.

SUMMARY

- Answers to the core WHAT, HOW, and FOR WHOM questions vary greatly across nations. These differences reflect varying production possibilities, productivity, and values.   **LO2-1, LO2-3, LO2-4**

- Gross domestic product (GDP) is the basic measure of how much an economy produces. The United States produces roughly $20 trillion of output per year, more than one-fifth of the world's total.   **LO2-1**

- Per capita GDP is a nation's total output divided by its population. It indicates the average standard of living. The U.S. GDP per capita is five times the world average.   **LO2-1**

- The high level of U.S. per capita GDP reflects the high productivity of U.S. workers. Abundant capital, education, technology, training, and management all contribute to high productivity. The relatively high degree of U.S. economic freedom (market reliance) is

also an important cause of superior economic growth.   **LO2-3**

- More than 80 percent of U.S. output consists of services, including government services. This is a reversal of historical ratios and reflects the relatively high incomes in the United States. Poor nations produce much higher proportions of food and manufactured goods.   **LO2-2**

- U.S. incomes are distributed very unequally, with households in the highest income class (quintile) receiving more than 10 times more income than low-income households. Incomes are even less equally distributed in most poor nations.   **LO2-4**

- The mix of output, production methods, and the income distribution continue to change. The WHAT, HOW, and FOR WHOM answers in tomorrow's economy will depend on the continuing interplay of (changing) market signals and (changing) government policy.   **LO2-2, LO2-3, LO2-4**

Key Terms

gross domestic product (GDP)
per capita GDP
economic growth
factors of production

human capital
capital-intensive
productivity
production possibilities

externalities
monopoly
income quintile

Questions for Discussion

1. Americans already enjoy living standards that far exceed world averages. Do we have enough? Should we even try to produce more? **LO2-1**

2. Why is per capita GDP so much higher in the United States than in Mexico? **LO2-3**

3. Can we continue to produce more output every year? Is there a limit? **LO2-3**

4. The U.S. farm population has shrunk by more than 25 million people since 1900. Where did all the people go? Why did they move? **LO2-2**

5. Is the relative decline in U.S. farming and manufacturing (Figure 2-2) a good thing or a bad thing? **LO2-2**

6. How many people are employed by your local or state government? What do they produce? What is the opportunity cost of that output? **LO2-1**

7. Where do growing companies like Google and Facebook get their employees? What were those workers doing before? **LO2-2**

8. Should the government try to equalize incomes more by raising taxes on the rich and giving more money to the poor? How might such redistribution affect total output and growth? **LO2-4**

9. Why are incomes so much more unequal in poor nations than in rich ones? **LO2-4**

10. How might free markets help reduce global poverty? How might they impede that goal? **LO2-3**

LO2-1 1. In 2015 the world's total output (real GDP) was roughly $80 trillion. What percent of this total was produced
    (*a*) By the three largest economies (World View "Comparative Output (GDP)")?
    (*b*) By the three smallest economies in that World View?

LO2-1 2. According to the World View "GDP per Capita around the World," how does per capita GDP in the following countries compare against America's (in percentage terms)?
    (*a*) Canada
    (*b*) China
    (*c*) Cuba

LO2-4 3. In 1980, America's GDP per capita was approximately $30,000 (measured in today's dollars). How much higher in percentage terms was America's GDP per capita in 2015 (see World View "GDP per Capita around the World")?

LO2-3 4. (*a*) How much more output does the $20 trillion U.S. economy produce when GDP increases by 1.0 percent?
    (*b*) By how much does this increase per capita income if the population is 340 million?

LO2-1 5. According to Table 2.1, how fast does total output (GDP) have to grow in order to raise per capita GDP in
    (*a*) the United States?
    (*b*) Japan?
    (*c*) Ethiopia?

LO2-3 6. (*a*) If Haiti's per capita GDP of roughly $810 were to DOUBLE every decade (an annual growth rate of 7.2 percent), what would Haiti's per capita GDP be in 50 years?
    (*b*) Compare (a) to the U.S. per capita GDP in 2015 (World View "GDP per Capita around the World)?

LO2-2 7. U.S. real gross domestic product increased from $10 trillion in 2000 to $15 trillion in 2010. During that same decade the share of manufactured goods (e.g., cars, appliances) fell from 16 percent to 12 percent. What was the dollar value of manufactured output
    (*a*) In 2000?
    (*b*) In 2010?
    (*c*) By how much did the dollar value of manufacturing output change?

LO2-4 8. Using the data in Figure 2.3,
    (*a*) Compute the average income of U.S. households.
    (*b*) If all incomes were equalized by government taxes and transfer payments, how much would the average household in each income quintile gain (via transfers) or lose (via taxes)?
        (*i*) Highest fifth
        (*ii*) Second fifth
        (*iii*) Third fifth
        (*iv*) Fourth fifth
        (*v*) Lowest fifth
    (*c*) What is the implied tax rate (i.e., tax ÷ average income) on the highest quintile?

LO2-3 9. If 150 million workers produced America's GDP in 2015 (World View "Comparative Output (GDP)"), how much output did the average worker produce?

LO2-1 10. Assuming 2016 per capita GDP growth rate is equal to the average growth rate (2000–2015) provided in Table 2.1, estimate 2016 per capita GDP for each of the following countries using data from World View "GDP per Capita around the World."
    (*a*) China
    (*b*) Canada
    (*c*) Haiti

PROBLEMS FOR CHAPTER 2 (cont'd)

LO2-2 11. Using the data from the Data Tables, calculate
    (*a*) the federal government's share of total output in 1996, 2006, and 2016.
    (*b*) the state and local government's share of total output in 1996, 2006, and 2016.

LO2-4 12. The Economy Tomorrow: How much more output per year will have to be produced in the world just to provide the 3 billion "severely" poor population with $1 more income per day?

©Blend Images/Getty Images RF

CHAPTER 3

Supply and Demand

Gasoline prices surged in early 2008, rising from $2.99 a gallon in January to $4.05 in July. Consumers were angry every time they filled up their tanks. Popular opinion blamed the "Big Oil" companies and "speculators" for the sky-high prices. They demanded that the government intervene and force prices back down. Congressional hearings were conducted, government investigations were initiated, and "excess profits" taxes on oil companies were proposed.

By the end of 2008, gasoline prices had receded. In early 2009, pump prices were back to less than $2 a gallon. No oil executives or speculators had been arrested. No congressional reports had been completed. No government indictments had been issued. Economists explained this turn of events with "supply and demand." Surging demand and limited supply had caused the price spike; slowing demand and increased supply had pushed pump prices back down. Motorists weren't entirely convinced by this explanation, but they were happy. They filled their tanks and drove off to other economic concerns.

The goal of this chapter is to explain how supply and demand really work. How do *markets* establish the price of gasoline and other products? Why do prices change so often? More broadly, how does the market mechanism decide WHAT to produce, HOW to produce, and FOR WHOM to produce? Specifically,

- **What determines the price of a good or service?**
- **How does the price of a product affect its production and consumption?**
- **Why do prices and production levels often change?**

Once we've seen how unregulated markets work, we'll observe how government intervention may alter market outcomes—for better or worse.

MARKET PARTICIPANTS

A good way to start figuring out how markets work is to see who participates in them. The answer is simple: just about every person and institution on the planet. Domestically, nearly 340 million consumers, about 25 million business firms, and tens of thousands of government agencies participate directly in the U.S. economy. Millions of international buyers and sellers also participate in U.S. markets.

Maximizing Behavior

All these market participants enter the marketplace to pursue specific goals. Consumers, for example, come with a limited amount of income to spend. Their objective is to buy the most desirable goods and services that their limited budgets will permit. We can't afford *everything* we want, so we must make *choices* about how to spend our scarce dollars. Our goal is to *maximize* the utility (satisfaction) we get from our available incomes.

Businesses also try to maximize in the marketplace. In their case, the quest is for maximum *profits.* Business profits are the difference between sales receipts and total costs. To maximize profits, business firms try to use resources efficiently in producing products that consumers desire.

The public sector also has maximizing goals. The economic purpose of government is to use available resources to serve public needs. The resources available for this purpose are limited too. Hence local, state, and federal governments must use scarce resources carefully, striving to maximize the general welfare of society. International consumers and producers pursue these same goals when participating in our markets.

Market participants sometimes lose sight of their respective goals. Consumers sometimes buy impulsively and later wish they'd used their income more wisely. Likewise, a producer may take a two-hour lunch, even at the sacrifice of maximum profits. And elected officials sometimes put their personal interests ahead of the public's interest. In all sectors of the economy, however, ***the basic goals of utility maximization, profit maximization, and welfare maximization explain most market activity.***

Specialization and Exchange

We are driven to buy and sell goods and services in the market by two simple facts. First, most of us are incapable of producing everything we want to consume. Second, even if we *could* produce all our own goods and services, it would still make sense to *specialize,* producing only one product and *trading* it for other desired goods and services.

Suppose you were capable of growing your own food, stitching your own clothes, building your own shelter, and even writing your own economics text. Even in this little utopia, it would still make sense to decide how *best* to expend your limited time and energy, relying on others to fill in the gaps. If you were *most* proficient at growing food, you would be best off spending your time farming. You could then *exchange* some of your food output for the clothes, shelter, and books you wanted. In the end, you'd be able to consume *more* goods than if you'd tried to make everything yourself.

Our economic interactions with others are thus necessitated by two constraints:

1. Our absolute inability as individuals to produce all the things we need or desire.
2. The limited amount of time, energy, and resources we have for producing those things we could make for ourselves.

Together these constraints lead us to *specialize* and interact. Most of the interactions that result take place in the market.

International Trade. The same motivations foster international trade. The United States is *capable* of producing just about everything. But we've learned that it's cheaper to import bananas from Ecuador than to grow them in hothouses in Idaho. So we *specialize* in production, exporting tractors to Ecuador in exchange for imported bananas. Both nations end up consuming more products than they could if they had to produce everything themselves. That's why *global* markets are so vital to economic prosperity.

THE CIRCULAR FLOW

Figure 3.1 summarizes the kinds of interactions that occur among market participants. Note first that the figure identifies four separate groups of participants. Domestically, the rectangle labeled "Consumers" includes all 340 million consumers in the United States. In

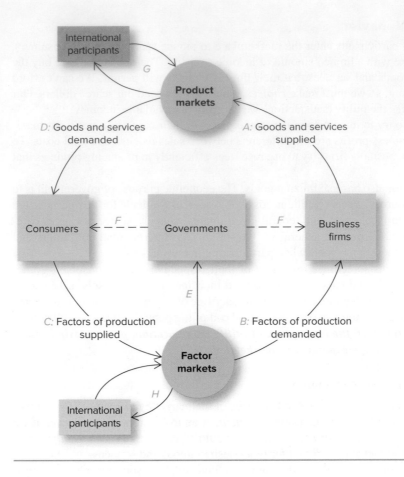

the "Business firms" box are grouped all the domestic business enterprises that buy and sell goods and services. The third participant, "Governments," includes the many separate agencies of the federal government, as well as state and local governments. Figure 3.1 also illustrates the role of global actors.

The Two Markets

The easiest way to keep track of all this activity is to distinguish two basic markets. Figure 3.1 makes this distinction by portraying separate circles for product markets and factor markets. In **factor markets,** factors of production are exchanged. Market participants buy or sell land, labor, or capital that can be used in the production process. When you go looking for work, for example, you're making a factor of production—your labor—available to producers. The producers will hire you—purchase your services in the factor market—if you're offering the skills they need at a price they're willing to pay.

Interactions within factor markets are only half the story. At the end of a hard day's work, consumers go to the grocery store (or to a virtual store online) to buy desired goods and services—that is, to buy *products*. In this context, consumers again interact with business firms, this time purchasing goods and services those firms have produced. These interactions occur in **product markets.** Foreigners also participate in the product market by supplying goods and services (imports) to the United States and buying some of our output (exports).

The government sector also supplies services (e.g., education, national defense, highways). Most government services aren't explicitly sold in product markets, however. Typically, they're delivered "free," without an explicit price (e.g., public elementary schools, highways). This doesn't mean government services are truly free, though. There's still an **opportunity cost** associated with every service the government provides. Consumers and businesses pay that cost indirectly through taxes rather than directly through market prices.

factor market: Any place where factors of production (e.g., land, labor, capital) are bought and sold.

product market: Any place where finished goods and services (products) are bought and sold.

opportunity cost: The most desired goods or services that are forgone in order to obtain something else.

In Figure 3.1, the arrow connecting product markets to consumers (*D*) emphasizes the fact that consumers, by definition, don't supply products. When individuals produce goods and services, they do so within the government or business sector. For instance, a doctor, a dentist, or an economic consultant functions in two sectors. When selling services in the market, this person is regarded as a "business"; when away from the office, he or she is regarded as a "consumer." This distinction is helpful in emphasizing that *the consumer is the final recipient of all goods and services produced.*

Locating Markets. Although we refer repeatedly to two kinds of markets in this text, it would be a little foolish to go off in search of the product and factor markets. Neither market is a single, identifiable structure. The term *market* simply refers to a place or situation where an economic exchange occurs—where a buyer and seller interact. The exchange may take place on the street, in a taxicab, over the phone, by mail, or in cyberspace. In some cases, the market used may in fact be quite distinguishable, as in the case of a Walmart store, the Chicago Commodity Exchange, or a state employment office. But whatever it looks like, *a market exists wherever and whenever an exchange takes place.*

Dollars and Exchange

Figure 3.1 neglects one critical element of market interactions: dollars. Each arrow in the figure actually has two dimensions. Consider again the arrow (*D*) linking consumers to product markets: it's drawn in only one direction because consumers, by definition, don't provide goods and services directly to product markets. But they do provide something: dollars. If you want to obtain something from a product market, you must offer to pay for it (typically with cash, check, debit or credit card). Consumers exchange dollars for goods and services in product markets.

The same kinds of exchange occur in factor markets. When you go to work, you exchange a factor of production (your labor) for income, typically a paycheck. Here again, the path connecting consumers to factor markets (*C*) really goes in two directions: one of real resources, the other of dollars. Consumers receive wages, rent, and interest for the labor, land, and capital they bring to the factor markets. Indeed, nearly *every market transaction involves an exchange of dollars for goods (in product markets) or resources (in factor markets).* Money is thus critical in facilitating market exchanges and the specialization the exchanges permit.

Supply and Demand

In every market transaction there must be a buyer and a seller. The seller is on the **supply** side of the market; the buyer is on the **demand** side. As noted earlier, we *supply* resources to the market when we look for a job—that is, when we offer our labor in exchange for income. We *demand* goods when we shop in a supermarket—that is, when we're prepared to offer dollars in exchange for something to eat. Business firms may *supply* goods and services in product markets at the same time they're *demanding* factors of production in factor markets. Whether one is on the supply side or the demand side of any particular market transaction depends on the nature of the exchange, not on the people or institutions involved.

supply: The ability and willingness to sell (produce) specific quantities of a good at alternative prices in a given time period, *ceteris paribus.*

demand: The willingness and ability to buy specific quantities of a good at alternative prices in a given time period, *ceteris paribus.*

DEMAND

To get a sense of how the demand side of market transactions works, we'll focus first on a single consumer. Then we'll aggregate to illustrate *market* demand.

Individual Demand

We can begin to understand how market forces work by looking more closely at the behavior of a single market participant. Let us start with Tom, a senior at Clearview College.

Tom has majored in everything from art history to government in his five years at Clearview. He didn't connect to any of those fields and is on the brink of academic dismissal. To make matters worse, his parents have threatened to cut him off financially unless he gets serious about his course work. By that, they mean he should enroll in courses that will lead to a job after graduation. Tom thinks he has found the perfect solution: web design. Everything associated with the Internet pays big bucks. Or at least so Tom thinks. And his parents would definitely approve. So Tom has enrolled in web design courses.

Unfortunately for Tom, he never developed computer skills. Until he got to Clearview College, he thought mastering Sony's latest alien-attack video game was the pinnacle of electronic wizardry. Tom didn't have a clue about "cookies," "wireframe," "responsive design," or the other concepts the web design instructor outlined in the first lecture.

Given his circumstances, Tom was desperate to find someone who could tutor him in web design. But desperation is not enough to secure the services of a web architect. In a market-based economy, you must also be willing to *pay* for the things you want. Specifically, *a demand exists only if someone is willing and able to pay for the good*—that is, exchange dollars for a good or service in the marketplace. Is Tom willing and able to *pay* for the web design tutoring he so obviously needs?

Let us assume that Tom has some income and is willing to spend some of it to get a tutor. With these assumptions, we can claim that Tom is a participant in the *market* for web design services; he is a potential consumer.

But how much is Tom willing to pay? Surely Tom is not prepared to exchange *all* his income for help in mastering web design. After all, Tom could use his income to buy more desirable goods and services. If he spent all his income on a web tutor, that help would have an extremely high *opportunity cost*. He would be giving up the opportunity to spend that income on things he really likes. He'd pass his web design class but have little else. It doesn't sound like a good idea.

It seems more likely that there are *limits* to the amount Tom is willing to pay for web design tutoring. These limits will be determined by how much income Tom has to spend and how many other goods and services he must forsake to pay for a tutor.

Tom also knows that his grade in web design will depend in part on how much tutoring service he buys. He can pass the course with only a few hours of design help. If he wants a better grade, however, the cost is going to escalate quickly.

Naturally, Tom wants it all: an A in web design and a ticket to higher-paying jobs. But here again the distinction between *desire* and *demand* is relevant. He may *desire* to master web design, but his actual proficiency will depend on how many hours of tutoring he is willing to *pay* for.

The Demand Schedule

We assume, then, that when Tom starts looking for a tutor he has some sense of how much money he is willing to spend. He might have in mind some sort of **demand schedule,** like that described in Figure 3.2. According to row *A* of this schedule, Tom is willing and able to buy only 1 hour of tutoring service per semester if he must pay $50 an hour. At such a high price he will learn just enough web design to pass the course.

At lower prices, Tom would behave differently. According to Figure 3.2, Tom would purchase *more* tutoring services if the price per hour were *less*. Indeed, we see from row *I* of the demand schedule that Tom is willing to purchase 20 hours per semester—the whole bag of design tricks—if the price of tutoring gets as low as $10 per hour.

Notice that the demand schedule doesn't tell us anything about *why* this consumer is willing to pay specific prices for various amounts of tutoring. Tom's expressed willingness to pay for web design tutoring may reflect a desperate need to finish a web design course, a lot of income to spend, or a relatively small desire for other goods and services. All the demand schedule tells us is what the consumer is *willing and able* to buy, for whatever reasons.

Also observe that the demand schedule doesn't tell us how many hours of design help the consumer will *actually* buy. Figure 3.2 simply states that Tom is *willing and able* to pay

demand schedule: A table showing the quantities of a good a consumer is willing and able to buy at alternative prices in a given time period, *ceteris paribus.*

Tom's Demand Schedule		
	Price of Tutoring (per Hour)	Quantity of Tutoring Demanded (Hours per Semester)
A	$50	1
B	45	2
C	40	3
D	35	5
E	30	7
F	25	9
G	20	12
H	15	15
I	10	20

The law of demand: as price falls, the quantity demanded increases.

Tom's demand curve

PRICE OF TUTORING (dollars per hour)

QUANTITY OF TUTORING DEMANDED (hours per semester)

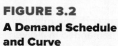

FIGURE 3.2

A Demand Schedule and Curve

A demand schedule indicates the quantities of a good a consumer is able and willing to buy at alternative prices (*ceteris paribus*). The **demand schedule** here indicates that Tom would buy 5 hours of web tutoring per semester if the price were $35 per hour (row *D*). If web tutoring were less expensive (rows *E–I*), Tom would purchase a larger quantity.

A demand curve is a graphical illustration of a demand schedule. Each point on the curve refers to a specific quantity that will be demanded at a given price. If, for example, the price of web tutoring were $35 per hour, this curve tells us the consumer would purchase 5 hours per semester (point *D*). If web tutoring cost $30 per hour, 7 hours per semester would be demanded (point *E*). Each point on the curve corresponds to a row in the schedule.

for 1 hour of tutoring per semester at $50 per hour, for 2 hours at $45 each, and so on. How much tutoring he purchases will depend on the actual price of such services in the market. Until we know that price, we cannot tell how much service will be purchased. Hence *"demand" is an expression of consumer buying intentions, of a willingness to buy, not a statement of actual purchases.*

The Demand Curve

A convenient summary of buying intentions is the **demand curve,** a graphical illustration of the demand schedule. The demand curve in Figure 3.2 tells us again that this consumer is willing to pay for only 1 hour of tutoring per semester if the price is $50 per hour (point *A*), for 2 if the price is $45 (point *B*), for 3 at $40 an hour (point *C*), and so on. Once we know what the market price of tutoring actually is, a glance at the demand curve tells us how much service this consumer will buy.

What the notion of *demand* emphasizes is that *the amount we buy of a good depends on its price.* We seldom if ever decide to buy only a certain quantity of a good at whatever price is charged. Instead we enter markets with a set of desires and a limited amount of money to spend. How much we actually buy of any particular good will depend on its price.

demand curve: A curve describing the quantities of a good a consumer is willing and able to buy at alternative prices in a given time period, *ceteris paribus.*

law of demand: The quantity of a good demanded in a given time period increases as its price falls, *ceteris paribus*.

A common feature of demand curves is their downward slope. *As the price of a good falls, people purchase more of it.* In Figure 3.2 the quantity of tutoring demanded increases (moves rightward along the horizontal axis) as the price per hour decreases (moves down the vertical axis). This inverse relationship between price and quantity is so common that we refer to it as the **law of demand.** Samsung used this law to increase sales of the Samsung Galaxy S7 in early 2016 (see In the News "Pricing the Galaxy S7").

IN THE NEWS

PRICING THE GALAXY S7

Samsung lost ground to Apple in the last round of smartphone updates. The South Korean company was determined not to let that happen again. When the Galaxy S6 was launched in April 2015, it carried a base price tag of $850. Only 10 million phones were sold in the first month, below company projections. So when Samsung launched the S7 in March 2016, it priced its phone at $750 and even offered free headsets. First-month sales for the S7 increased by 20 percent over the S6 experience.

Source: Samsung sales history.

ANALYSIS: The law of demand assured Samsung that it could increase smartphone sales by offering the phones at a lower price. That is exactly what happened.

Determinants of Demand

The demand curve in Figure 3.2 has only two dimensions—quantity demanded (on the horizontal axis) and price (on the vertical axis). This seems to imply that the amount of tutoring demanded depends only on the price of that service. This is surely not the case. A consumer's willingness and ability to buy a product at various prices depend on a variety of forces. *The determinants of market demand include*

- *Tastes* (desire for this and other goods).
- *Income* (of the consumer).
- *Other goods* (their availability and price).
- *Expectations* (for income, prices, tastes).
- *Number of buyers.*

Tom's "taste" for tutoring has nothing to do with taste buds. *Taste* is just another word for desire. In this case Tom's taste for web design services is clearly acquired. If he didn't have to pass a web design course, he would have no desire for related services and thus no demand. If he had no income, he couldn't *demand* any web design tutoring either, no matter how much he might *desire* it.

substitute goods: Goods that substitute for each other; when the price of good *x* rises, the demand for good *y* increases, *ceteris paribus*.

Other goods also affect the demand for tutoring services. Their effect depends on whether they're *substitute* goods or *complementary* goods. A **substitute good** is one that might be purchased instead of tutoring services. In Tom's simple world, pizza is a substitute for tutoring. If the price of pizza fell, Tom would use his limited income to buy more pizzas and cut back on his purchases of web tutoring. When the price of a substitute good falls, the demand for tutoring services declines.

complementary goods: Goods frequently consumed in combination; when the price of good *x* rises, the demand for good *y* falls, *ceteris paribus*.

A **complementary good** is one that's typically consumed with, rather than instead of, tutoring. If text prices or tuition rates increase, Tom might take fewer classes and demand *less* web design assistance. In this case, a price increase for a complementary good causes the demand for tutoring to decline. When Samsung cut the price of the Galaxy S7 phones (see In the News "Pricing the Galaxy S7"), it knew that the demand for Walmart wireless service (a complementary good) would increase.

Expectations also play a role in consumer decisions. If Tom expected to flunk his web design course anyway, he probably wouldn't waste any money getting tutorial help; his demand for such services would disappear. On the other hand, if he expects a web tutor to determine his college fate, he might be more willing to buy such services.

Ceteris Paribus

If demand is in fact such a multidimensional decision, how can we reduce it to only the two dimensions of price and quantity? In Chapter 1 we first encountered this ***ceteris paribus*** trick. To simplify their models of the world, economists focus on only one or two forces at a time and *assume* nothing else changes. We know a consumer's tastes, income, other goods, and expectations all affect the decision to hire a tutor. But we want to focus on the relationship between quantity demanded and price. That is, we want to know what *independent* influence price has on consumption decisions. To find out, we must isolate that one influence, price, and assume that the determinants of demand remain unchanged.

The *ceteris paribus* assumption is not as farfetched as it may seem. People's tastes, income, and expectations do not change quickly. Also, the prices and availability of other goods don't change all that fast. Hence a change in the *price* of a product may be the only factor that prompts an immediate change in quantity demanded.

The ability to predict consumer responses to a price change is important. What would happen, for example, to enrollment at your school if tuition doubled? Must we guess? Or can we use demand curves to predict how the quantity of applications will change as the price of college goes up? ***Demand curves show us how changes in market prices alter consumer behavior.*** We used the demand curve in Figure 3.2 to predict how Tom's web design ability would change at different tutorial prices. Samsung used its knowledge of consumer demand to cut Galaxy S7 prices by $100 (see In the News "Pricing the Galaxy S7").

> ***ceteris paribus:*** The assumption of nothing else changing.

Shifts in Demand

Although demand curves are useful in predicting consumer responses to market signals, they aren't infallible. The problem is that ***the determinants of demand can and do change.*** When they do, a specific demand curve may become obsolete. A ***demand curve (schedule) is valid only so long as the underlying determinants of demand remain constant.*** If the *ceteris paribus* assumption is violated—if tastes, income, other goods, or expectations change—the ability or willingness to buy will change. When this happens, the demand curve will **shift** to a new position.

Suppose, for example, that Tom won $1,000 in the state lottery. This windfall would increase his ability to pay for tutoring services. Figure 3.3 shows the effect on Tom's demand. The old demand curve, D_1, is no longer relevant. Tom's lottery winnings enable him to buy *more* tutoring at any price, as illustrated by the new demand curve, D_2. According to this new curve, lucky Tom is now willing and able to buy 12 hours per semester at the price of $35 per hour (point d_2). This is a large increase in demand; previously (before winning the lottery) he demanded only 5 hours at that price (point d_1).

With his higher income, Tom can buy more tutoring services at every price. Thus ***the entire demand curve shifts to the right when income goes up.*** Figure 3.3 illustrates both the old (pre-lottery) and the new (post-lottery) demand curves.

Income is only one of the basic determinants of demand. Changes in any of the other determinants of demand would also cause the demand curve to shift. Tom's taste for web tutoring might increase dramatically, for example, if his parents promised to buy him a new car for passing web design. In that case, he might be willing to forgo other goods and spend more of his income on tutors. ***An increase in taste (desire) also shifts the demand curve to the right.***

> **shift in demand:** A change in the quantity demanded at any (every) price.

Pizza and Politics. A similar demand shift occurs at the White House when a political crisis erupts. On an average day, White House staffers order about $300 worth of pizza from the nearby Domino's. When a crisis hits, however, staffers work well into the night and their demand for pizza soars. On the evening of the November 2016 presidential elections, White House staffers ordered more than $1,000 worth of pizza! Political analysts now use pizza deliveries to predict major White House announcements.

FIGURE 3.3
Shifts vs. Movements

A demand curve shows how a consumer responds to price changes. If the determinants of demand stay constant, the response is a *movement* along the curve to a new quantity demanded. In this case, when price falls from $35 to $20 per hour, the quantity demanded increases from 5 (point d_1), to 12 (point g_1).

If the determinants of demand *change*, the entire demand curve *shifts*. In this case, a rise in income increases demand. With more income, Tom is willing to buy 12 hours at the initial price of $35 (point d_2), not just the 5 hours he demanded before the lottery win (point d_1).

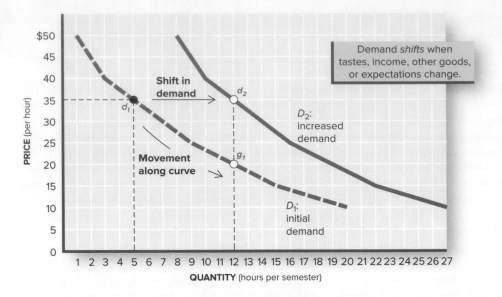

	Price (per Hour)	Quantity Demanded (Hours per Semester)	
		Initial Demand	After Increase in Income
A	$50	1	8
B	45	2	9
C	40	3	10
D	35	5	12
E	30	7	14
F	25	9	16
G	20	12	19
H	15	15	22
I	10	20	27

Movements vs. Shifts

It's important to distinguish shifts of the demand curve from movements along the demand curve. *Movements along a demand curve are a response to price changes for that good.* Such movements assume that determinants of demand are unchanged. By contrast, *shifts of the demand curve occur when the determinants of demand change.* When tastes, income, other goods, or expectations are altered, the basic relationship between price and quantity demanded is changed (shifts).

For convenience, movements along a demand curve and shifts of the demand curve have their own labels. Specifically, take care to distinguish

- *Changes in quantity demanded:* movements along a given demand curve in response to price changes of that good.
- *Changes in demand:* shifts of the demand curve due to changes in tastes, income, other goods, or expectations.

Tom's behavior in the web tutoring market will change if either the price of tutoring changes (a movement) or the underlying determinants of his demand are altered (a shift). Notice in Figure 3.3 that he ends up buying 12 hours of web tutoring if either the price of tutoring falls (to $20 per hour, leading him to point d_1) or his income increases (leading him to point d_2). Demand curves help us predict those market responses.

Market Demand

Whatever we say about demand for web design tutoring on the part of one wannabe web master, we can also say about every student at Clearview College (or, for that matter, about all consumers). Some students have no interest in web design and aren't willing to pay for related services: they don't participate in the web tutoring market. Other students want such services but don't have enough income to pay for them: they too are excluded from the web tutoring market. A large number of students, however, not only have a need (or desire) for web tutoring but also are willing and able to purchase such services.

What we start with in product markets, then, is many individual demand curves. Fortunately, it's possible to combine all the individual demand curves into a single **market demand.** The aggregation process is no more difficult than simple arithmetic. Suppose you would be willing to buy 1 hour of tutoring per semester at a price of $80 per hour. George, who is also desperate to learn web design, would buy 2 at that price; and I would buy none, since my publisher (McGraw-Hill) creates a web page for my book. What would our combined (market) demand for hours of tutoring be at that price? Collectively, we would be willing to buy a total of 3 hours of tutoring per semester if the price were $80 per hour. Our combined willingness to buy—our collective market demand—is nothing more than the sum of our individual demands. The same kind of aggregation can be performed for all consumers, leading to a summary of the total *market* demand for a specific good or service. Thus, *market demand is determined by the number of potential buyers and their respective tastes, incomes, other goods, and expectations.*

market demand: The total quantities of a good or service people are willing and able to buy at alternative prices in a given time period; the sum of individual demands.

The Market Demand Curve

Figure 3.4 provides the basic market demand schedule for a situation in which only three consumers participate in the market. It illustrates the same market situation with demand curves. The three individuals who participate in the market demand for web tutoring at Clearview College obviously differ greatly, as suggested by their respective demand schedules. Tom's demand schedule is portrayed in the first column of the table (and is identical to the one we examined in Figure 3.2). George is also desperate to acquire some job skills and is willing to pay relatively high prices for web design tutoring. His demand is summarized in the second column under Quantity Demanded in the table.

The third consumer in this market is Lisa. Lisa already knows the nuts and bolts of web design, so she isn't so desperate for tutorial services. She would like to upgrade her skills, however, especially in animation and e-commerce applications. But her limited budget precludes paying a lot for help. She will hire a tutor only if the price falls to $30 per hour. Should tutors cost less, she'd even buy quite a few hours of web design tutoring.

The differing circumstances of Tom, George, and Lisa are expressed in their individual demand schedules (Figure 3.4). To determine the *market* demand for tutoring from this information, we simply add these three separate demands. The end result of this aggregation is, first, a *market* demand schedule (last column in the table) and, second, the resultant *market* demand curve (Figure 3.4*d*). These market summaries describe the various quantities of tutoring that Clearview College students are *willing and able* to purchase each semester at various prices.

How much web tutoring will be purchased each semester? Knowing how much help Tom, George, and Lisa are willing to buy at various prices doesn't tell you how much they're *actually* going to purchase. To determine the actual consumption of web tutoring, we have to know something about prices and supplies. Which of the many different prices illustrated in Figures 3.3 and 3.4 will actually prevail? How will that price be determined?

SUPPLY

To understand how the price of web tutoring is established, we must also look at the other side of the market: the *supply* side. We need to know how many hours of tutoring services people are willing and able to *sell* at various prices—that is, the **market supply.** As on the

market supply: The total quantities of a good that sellers are willing and able to sell at alternative prices in a given time period, *ceteris paribus.*

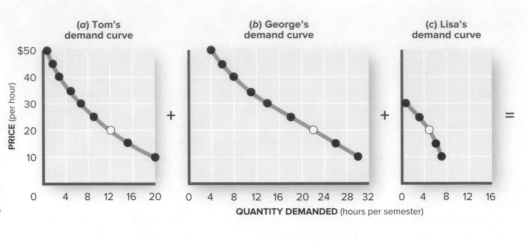

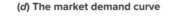

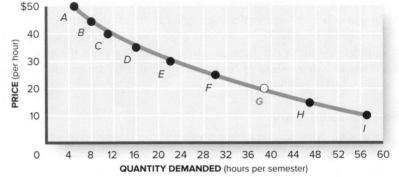

(d) The market demand curve

FIGURE 3.4

Construction of the Market Demand Curve

Market demand represents the combined demands of all market participants.

To determine the total quantity of web tutoring demanded at any given price, we add the separate demands of the individual consumers. Row *G* of this schedule indicates that a *total* quantity of 39 hours per semester will be demanded at a price of $20 per hour.

This same conclusion is reached by adding the individual demand curves, leading to point *G* on the market demand curve (see graph *d*).

	Price (per Hour)	Quantity of Tutoring Demanded (Hours per Semester)				
		Tom	+ George	+ Lisa	=	Market Demand
A	$50	1	4	0		5
B	45	2	6	0		8
C	40	3	8	0		11
D	35	5	11	0		16
E	30	7	14	1		22
F	25	9	18	3		30
G	20	12	22	5		39
H	15	15	26	6		47
I	10	20	30	7		57

demand side, the *market supply* depends on the behavior of all the individuals willing and able to supply web tutoring at some price.

Determinants of Supply

Let's return to the Clearview campus for a moment. What we need to know now is how much tutorial help people are willing and able to provide. Generally speaking, web design can be fun, but it can also be drudge work, especially when you're doing it for someone else. Hosting services like Weebly, Squarespace, and GoDaddy have made setting up a website easier and more creative. And the cloud and Wi-Fi access have made the job more convenient. But teaching someone else to design web pages is still work. So why does anyone do it? Easy answer: for the money. People offer (supply) tutoring services to earn income that they, in turn, can spend on the goods and services *they* desire.

How much money must be offered to induce web designers to do a little tutoring depends on a variety of things. The ***determinants of market supply include***

- ***Technology.***
- ***Factor costs.***
- ***Other goods.***
- ***Taxes and subsidies.***
- ***Expectations.***
- ***Number of sellers.***

The technology of web design, for example, is always getting easier and more creative. With a program like Weebly, for example, it's very easy to create a bread-and-butter web page. A continuous stream of new software programs (e.g., Wordpress, DreamWeaver) keeps stretching the possibilities for graphics, animation, interactivity, and content. These technological advances mean that web design services can be supplied more quickly and cheaply. They also make *teaching* web design easier. As a result, they induce people to supply *more* tutoring services at every price.

How much web design service is offered at any given price also depends on the cost of factors of production. If the software programs needed to create web pages are cheap (or, better yet, free), web designers can afford to charge lower prices. If the required software inputs are expensive, however, they will have to charge more for their services.

Other goods can also affect the willingness to supply web design services. If you can make more income waiting tables than you can tutoring lazy students, why would you even boot up the computer? As the prices paid for other goods and services change, they will influence people's decision about whether to offer web services.

In the real world, the decision to supply goods and services is also influenced by the long arm of Uncle Sam. Federal, state, and local governments impose taxes on income earned in the marketplace. When tax rates are high, people get to keep less of the income they earn. Once taxes start biting into paychecks, some people may conclude that tutoring is no longer worth the hassle and withdraw from the market.

Expectations are also important on the supply side of the market. If web designers expect higher prices, lower costs, or reduced taxes, they may be more willing to learn new software programs. On the other hand, if they have poor expectations about the future, they may just find something else to do.

Finally, we note that the number of potential tutors will affect the quantity of service offered for sale at various prices. If there are lots of willing tutors on campus, a lot of tutorial service will be available at reasonable prices.

All these considerations—factor costs, technology, taxes, expectations—affect the decision to offer web services at various prices. In general, we assume that web architects will be willing to provide more tutoring if the per-hour price is high and less if the price is low. In other words, there is a **law of supply** that parallels the law of demand. ***The law of supply says that larger quantities will be offered for sale at higher prices.*** Here again, the laws rest on the *ceteris paribus* assumption: the quantity supplied increases at higher prices *if* the determinants of supply are constant. ***Supply curves are upward-sloping to the right,*** as shown in Figure 3.5. Note how the *quantity supplied* jumps from 39 hours (point *d*) to 130 hours (point *h*) when the price of web service doubles (from $20 to $40 per hour).

law of supply: The quantity of a good supplied in a given time period increases as its price increases, *ceteris paribus*.

Market Supply

Figure 3.5 also illustrates how *market* supply is constructed from the supply decisions of individual sellers. In this case, only three web masters are available. Ann is willing to provide a lot of tutoring at low prices, whereas Bob requires at least $20 an hour. Carlos won't talk to students for less than $30 an hour.

By adding the quantity each tutor is willing to offer at every price, we can construct the market supply curve. Notice in Figure 3.5 how the quantity supplied to the market at $45 (point *i*)

FIGURE 3.5
Market Supply

The market supply curve indicates the *combined* sales intentions of all market participants—that is, the total quantities they are willing and able to sell at various prices.

If the price of tutoring were $45 per hour (point *i*), the *total* quantity of services supplied would be 140 hours per semester. This quantity is determined by adding the supply decisions of all individual producers. In this case, Ann supplies 93 hours, Bob supplies 33, and Carlos supplies the rest.

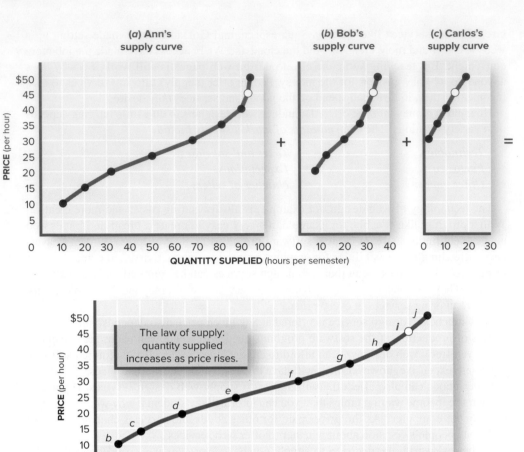

	Price per Hour	Quantity of Tutoring Supplied by					
		Ann	+	Bob	+	Carlos	=	Market
j	$50	94		35		19		148
i	45	93		33		14		140
h	40	90		30		10		130
g	35	81		27		6		114
f	30	68		20		2		90
e	25	50		12		0		62
d	20	32		7		0		39
c	15	20		0		0		20
b	10	10		0		0		10

comes from the individual efforts of Ann (93 hours), Bob (33 hours), and Carlos (14 hours). *The market supply curve is just a summary of the supply intentions of all producers.*

None of the points on the market supply curve (Figure 3.5) tells us how much web tutoring is *actually* being sold on the Clearview campus. *Market supply is an expression of sellers' intentions—an offer to sell—not a statement of actual sales.* My next-door neighbor may be willing to sell his 2004 Honda Civic for $8,000, but most likely he'll never find a buyer at that price. Nevertheless, his *willingness* to sell his car at that price is part of the *market supply* of used cars.

Shifts of Supply

As with demand, there's nothing sacred about any given set of supply intentions. Supply curves *shift* when the underlying determinants of supply change. Thus, ***it is important to distinguish***

- ***Changes in quantity supplied:*** movements along a given supply curve in response to price changes of that good.
- ***Changes in supply:*** shifts of the supply curve due to changes is technology, factor costs, other goods, taxes and subsidies, or expectations.

Our Latin friend *ceteris paribus* is once again the decisive factor. If the price of a product is the only variable changing, then we can ***track changes in quantity supplied along the supply curve.*** But if *ceteris paribus* is violated—if technology, factor costs, the profitability of producing other goods, tax rates, expectations, or the number of sellers changes—then ***changes in supply are illustrated by shifts of the supply curve.***

In the News "Gas Prices Jump in Matthew's Wake" illustrates how a supply shift pushed up gasoline prices in Florida in October 2016. Damage from Hurricane Matthew made it more difficult and expensive to supply Florida gas stations with fuel. As the market supply curve shifted to the left, the price of gasoline rose.

IN THE NEWS

GAS PRICES JUMP IN MATTHEW'S WAKE

Hurricane Matthew struck the Southeastern United States on October 6, 2016. Winds as high as 140 miles per hour and drenching rains forced thousands of people to evacuate homes in Florida, North Carolina, and Georgia.

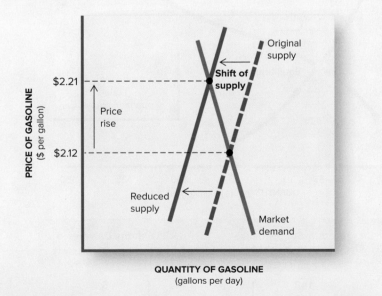

Matthew also drove the price of gasoline higher. Gasoline supplies into Florida come by tanker, then by tanker trucks to gasoline stations. Matthew damaged port facilities, flooded the roads, and destroyed highways. Gas prices rose by 9 cents to $2.21 a gallon due to the resulting leftward shift in market supply.

Source: News reports, October 2016.

ANALYSIS: When factor costs or availability worsen, the supply curve *shifts* to the left. Such leftward supply-curve shifts push prices up the market demand curve.

EQUILIBRIUM

That post-hurricane spike in gasoline prices offers some clues to how the forces of supply and demand set—and change—market prices. For a closer look at how those forces work, we'll return to Clearview College for a moment. How did supply and demand resolve the WHAT, HOW, and FOR WHOM questions in that web tutoring market?

Figure 3.6 helps answer that question by bringing together the market supply and demand curves we've already examined (Figures 3.4 and 3.5). When we put the two curves together, we see that *only one price and quantity combination is compatible with the intentions of both buyers and sellers. This equilibrium occurs at the intersection of the supply and demand curves.* Notice in Figure 3.6 where that intersection occurs—at the price of $20 and the quantity of 39 hours. So $20 is the **equilibrium price:** campus tutors will sell a total of 39 hours of tutoring per semester—the same amount that students wish to buy at that price. Those 39 hours of tutoring service will be part of WHAT is produced in the economy.

equilibrium price: The price at which the quantity of a good demanded in a given time period equals the quantity supplied.

Market Clearing

An equilibrium doesn't imply that everyone is happy with the prevailing price or quantity. Notice in Figure 3.6, for example, that some students who want to buy 60 assistance

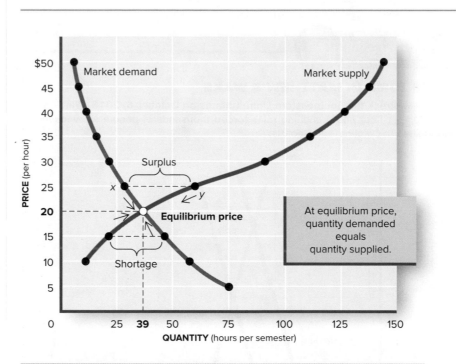

FIGURE 3.6

Equilibrium Price

The intersection of the demand and supply curves establishes the *equilibrium* price and quantity. Only at equilibrium is the quantity demanded equal to the quantity supplied. In this case, the equilibrium price is $20 per hour, and 39 hours is the equilibrium quantity.

At above-equilibrium prices, a market *surplus* exists—the quantity supplied exceeds the quantity demanded. At prices below equilibrium, a market *shortage* exists.

Price (per Hour)	Quantity Supplied (Hours per Semester)		Quantity Demanded (Hours per Semester)	
$50	148		5	
45	140		8	
40	130	Market surplus	11	Nonequilibrium prices create surpluses or shortages.
35	114		16	
30	90		22	
25	62		30	
20	39	Equilibrium	39	
15	20	Market shortage	47	
10	10		57	

services don't get any. These would-be buyers are arrayed along the demand curve *below* the equilibrium. Because the price they're *willing* to pay is less than the equilibrium price of $20, they don't get any web design help. The market's FOR WHOM answer includes only those students willing and able to pay the equilibrium price.

Likewise, some would-be sellers are frustrated by this market outcome. These wannabe tutors are arrayed along the supply curve *above* the equilibrium. Because they insist on being paid *more* than the equilibrium price of $20 per hour, they don't actually sell anything.

Although not everyone finds satisfaction in the market equilibrium, that unique outcome is efficient. ***The equilibrium price and quantity reflect a compromise between buyers and sellers. No other compromise yields a quantity demanded that's exactly equal to the quantity supplied.***

The Invisible Hand. The equilibrium price isn't determined by any single individual. Rather, it's determined by the collective behavior of many buyers and sellers, each acting out his or her own demand or supply schedule. It's this kind of impersonal price determination that gave rise to Adam Smith's characterization of the market mechanism as "the invisible hand." In attempting to explain how the **market mechanism** works, the famed 18th-century economist noted a remarkable feature of market prices. The market behaves as if some unseen force (the invisible hand) were examining each individual's supply or demand schedule and then selecting a price that assured an equilibrium. In practice, the process of price determination isn't so mysterious: it's a simple process of trial and error.

market mechanism: The use of market prices and sales to signal desired outputs (or resource allocations).

Disequilibrium: Surplus and Shortage

Market Surplus. To appreciate the power of the market mechanism, consider interference in its operation. Suppose, for example, that campus tutors banded together and agreed to charge a minimum price of $25 per hour, five dollars more than the equilibrium price. By establishing a **price floor,** a minimum price for their services, the tutors hope to increase their incomes. But they won't be fully satisfied. Figure 3.6 illustrates the consequences of this *dis*equilibrium pricing. At $25 per hour, campus tutors would be offering more than 39 hours of tutoring. How much more? Move up the market supply curve from the equilibrium price until you hit the price of $25. At that price, tutors are prepared to offer the quantity indicated by point *y*. What's wrong with that point? Students in need of tutoring aren't willing to buy that much tutoring at that price. The market demand curve tells us Tom, George, and Lisa are willing to buy only the smaller quantity indicated by point *x* at the price of $25 per hour. We have a discrepancy between the quantity suppliers want to sell and the quantity consumers want to buy. This is a *dis*equilibrium.

price floor: Lower limit set for the price of a good.

In this case, the disequilibrium creates a **market surplus:** more tutoring is being offered for sale than consumers are willing to purchase at the available price. As Figure 3.6 indicates, at a price of $25 per hour, a market surplus of 32 hours per semester exists. Under these circumstances, campus tutors would be spending many idle hours at their keyboards waiting for customers to appear. Their waiting will be in vain because the quantity of web tutoring demanded will not increase until the price of tutoring falls. That is the clear message of the demand curve. As would-be tutors get this message, they'll reduce their prices. This is the response the market mechanism signals.

market surplus: The amount by which the quantity supplied exceeds the quantity demanded at a given price; excess supply.

As sellers' asking prices decline, the quantity demanded will increase. This concept is illustrated in Figure 3.6 by the movement along the demand curve from point *x* to lower prices and greater quantity demanded. As we move down the market demand curve, the *desire* for web design help doesn't change, but the quantity people are *able and willing to buy* increases. When the price falls to $20 per hour, the quantity demanded will finally equal the quantity supplied. This is the *equilibrium* illustrated in Figure 3.6.

Market Shortage. A very different sequence of events would occur if a market shortage existed. Suppose someone were to spread the word that web tutoring services were available at only $15 per hour. Tom, George, and Lisa would be standing in line to get tutorial help, but campus web designers wouldn't be willing to supply the quantity demanded at

market shortage: The amount by which the quantity demanded exceeds the quantity supplied at a given price; excess demand.

that price. As Figure 3.6 confirms, at $15 per hour, the quantity demanded (47 hours per semester) greatly exceeds the quantity supplied (20 hours per semester). In this situation, we speak of a **market shortage**—that is, an excess of quantity demanded over quantity supplied. At a price of $15 an hour, the shortage amounts to 27 hours of tutoring services.

When a market shortage exists, not all consumer demands can be satisfied. Some people who are *willing* to buy web help at the going price ($15) won't be able to do so. To assure themselves of sufficient help, Tom, George, Lisa, or some other consumer may offer to pay a *higher* price, thus initiating a move up the demand curve in Figure 3.6. The higher prices offered will in turn induce other enterprising tutors to tutor more, thus ensuring an upward movement along the market supply curve. Notice, again, that the *desire* to tutor web design hasn't changed; only the quantity supplied has responded to a change in price. As this process continues, the quantity supplied will eventually equal the quantity demanded (39 hours in Figure 3.6).

Self-Adjusting Prices. What we observe, then, is that *whenever the market price is set above or below the equilibrium price, either a market surplus or a market shortage will emerge.* To overcome a surplus or shortage, buyers and sellers will change their behavior. Sellers will have to compete for customers by reducing prices when a market surplus exists. If a shortage exists, buyers will compete for service by offering to pay higher prices. Only at the *equilibrium* price will no further adjustments be required.

Sometimes the market price is slow to adjust, and a disequilibrium persists. This is often the case with tickets to rock concerts, football games, and other one-time events. People initially adjust their behavior by standing in ticket lines for hours, or hopping on the Internet, hoping to buy a ticket at the below-equilibrium price. The tickets are typically resold ("scalped"), however, at prices closer to equilibrium. This is a common occurrence at major college sporting events such as the Final Four basketball championships (see In the News "The Real March Madness: Ticket Prices").

IN THE NEWS

THE REAL MARCH MADNESS: TICKET PRICES

Ticket prices for Monday's NCAA championship game between the Gonzaga Bulldogs and the North Carolina Tar Heels look deceivingly cheap—only $50 according to the NCAA's official website. But don't expect to get into the University of Phoenix stadium for that paltry sum. The 80,000 seats are sold out. Scalpers are charging an average of $4,000 for front-row seats and at least one seat was sold for $18,181.80. Nosebleed seats are going for $375 apiece. It is inevitable that one team will lose on Monday night—but it won't be the scalpers.

Source: Media reports, April 2, 2017.

ANALYSIS: When tickets are sold initially at below-equilibrium prices, a market shortage is created. Scalpers resell tickets at prices closer to equilibrium, reaping a profit in the process.

Business firms can discover equilibrium prices by trial and error. If consumer purchases aren't keeping up with production, a firm may conclude that its price is above the equilibrium price. To get rid of accumulated inventory, the firm will have to lower its price. In the happier situation where consumer purchases are outpacing production, a firm might conclude that its price was a trifle too low and give it a nudge upward. In either case, the equilibrium price can be established after a few trials in the marketplace.

Changes in Equilibrium

No equilibrium price is permanent. The equilibrium price established in the Clearview College tutoring market, for example, was the unique outcome of specific demand and supply schedules. Those schedules themselves were based on our assumption of *ceteris paribus*. We assumed that the "taste" (desire) for web design assistance was given, as were consumers' incomes, the price and availability of other goods, and expectations. Any of these determinants of demand could change. When one does, the demand curve has to be redrawn. Such a shift of the demand curve will lead to a new equilibrium price and quantity. Indeed, *the equilibrium price will change whenever the supply or demand curve shifts.*

A Demand Shift. We can illustrate how equilibrium prices change by taking one last look at the Clearview College tutoring market. Our original supply and demand curves, together with the resulting equilibrium (point E_1), are depicted in Figure 3.7. Now suppose that all the professors at Clearview begin requiring class-specific web pages from each student. The increased need (desire) for web design ability will affect market demand. Tom, George, and Lisa will be willing to buy more web tutoring at every price than they were before.

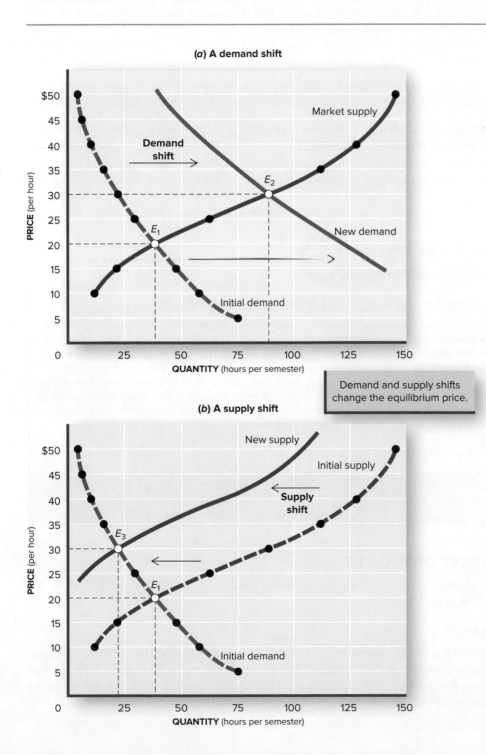

(a) A demand shift

(b) A supply shift

Demand and supply shifts change the equilibrium price.

FIGURE 3.7

Changes in Equilibrium

If demand or supply changes (shifts), market equilibrium will change as well.

Demand shift: In (*a*), the rightward shift of the demand curve illustrates an increase in demand. When demand increases, the equilibrium price rises (from E_1 to E_2).

Supply shift: In (*b*), the leftward shift of the supply curve illustrates a decrease in supply. This raises the equilibrium price to E_3.

Demand and supply curves shift only when their underlying determinants change—that is, when *ceteris paribus* is violated.

That is, the *demand* for web services has increased. We can represent this increased demand by a rightward *shift* of the market demand curve, as illustrated in Figure 3.7a.

Note that the new demand curve intersects the (unchanged) market supply curve at a new price (point E_2); the equilibrium price is now $30 per hour and 90 hours of tutoring is bought. This new equilibrium price will persist until either the demand curve or the supply curve shifts again.

A Supply Shift. Figure 3.7b illustrates a *supply* shift. The decrease (leftward shift) in supply might occur if some on-campus tutors got sick. Or approaching exams might convince would-be tutors that they have no time to spare. ***Whenever supply decreases (shifts left), price tends to rise,*** as in Figure 3.7b.

Lots of Shifts. In the real world, demand and supply curves are constantly shifting. A change in the weather can alter the supply and demand for food, vacations, and baseball games. A new product can change the demand for old products. A foreign crisis can alter the supply, demand, and price of oil (see World View "Oil Higher on Nigerian Supply Disruptions"). Look for and remember these shifts:

Type of Shift	Name	Effect on Price	Effect on Quantity
Rightward shift of demand	"Increase in demand"	Price increase	Quantity increase
Leftward shift of demand	"Decrease in demand"	Price decrease	Quantity decrease
Rightward shift of supply	"Increase in supply"	Price decrease	Quantity increase
Leftward shift of supply	"Decrease in supply"	Price increase	Quantity decrease

When you see a price change, one or more of these shifts must have occurred.

WORLD VIEW

OIL HIGHER ON NIGERIAN SUPPLY DISRUPTIONS

Nigerian militants stepped up their attacks on Nigeria's oil fields. In the last few weeks, the militants have attacked both oil production and export facilities in the Niger Delta region. The resulting supply disruptions have reduced Nigeria's oil production by as much as 750,000 barrels per day—a huge hit for a nation that produced an average of 1.9 million barrels per day in 2015.

The Nigerian supply disruptions have shown up in the price of oil in the United States and Great Britain. Spot prices in the U.S. rose yesterday by 13 cents to $49.12 per barrel for West Texas crude, reflecting tighter global supplies and concerns over continuing supply disruptions. Brent crude rose 35 cents to $47.32 per barrel.

Source: News reports of May 17, 2016.

ANALYSIS: Equilibrium prices change whenever market demand or supply curves shift. In this case, the supply curve is shifting to the left, and the equilibrium price is rising.

MARKET OUTCOMES

Notice how the market mechanism resolves the basic economic questions of WHAT, HOW, and FOR WHOM.

WHAT

The WHAT question refers to the mix of output society produces. How much web tutorial service will be included in that mix? The answer at Clearview College was 39 hours of tutoring per semester. This decision wasn't reached in a referendum, but instead in the market equilibrium (Figure 3.6). In the same way but on a larger scale, millions of consumers and a handful of auto producers decide to include 16 million or so cars and trucks in each year's mix of output. Auto manufacturers use rebates, discounts, and variable interest rates to induce consumers to buy the same quantity that auto manufacturers are producing.

HOW

The market mechanism also determines HOW goods are produced. Profit-seeking producers will strive to produce web designs and automobiles in the most efficient way. They'll use market prices to decide not only WHAT to produce but also what resources to use in the production process. If new software simplifies web design—and is priced low enough—tutors will use it. Likewise, auto manufacturers will use robots rather than humans on the assembly line if robots reduce costs and increase profits.

FOR WHOM

Finally, the invisible hand of the market will determine who gets the goods produced. At Clearview College, who got web tutoring? Only those students who were willing and able to pay $20 per hour for that service. FOR WHOM are all those automobiles produced each year? The answer is the same: those consumers who are willing and able to pay the market price for a new car.

Optimal, Not Perfect

Not everyone is happy with these answers, of course. Tom would like to pay only $10 an hour for a tutor. And some of the Clearview students don't have enough income to buy any tutoring. They think it's unfair that they have to design their own web pages while rich students can have someone else do their design work for them. Students who can't afford cars are even less happy with the market's answer to the FOR WHOM question.

Although the outcomes of the marketplace aren't perfect, they're often optimal. Optimal outcomes are the best possible given our incomes and scarce resources. Sure, we'd like everyone to have access to tutoring and to drive a new car. But there aren't enough resources available to create such a utopia. So we have to ration available tutors and cars. The market mechanism performs this rationing function. People who want to supply tutoring or build cars are free to make that choice. And consumers are free to decide how they want to spend their income. In the process, we expect market participants to make decisions that maximize their own wellbeing. If they do, then we conclude that everyone is doing as well as possible, given their available resources.

THE ECONOMY TOMORROW

DEADLY SHORTAGES: THE ORGAN TRANSPLANT MARKET

As you were reading this chapter, dozens of Americans were dying from failed organs. More than 100,000 Americans are waiting for life-saving kidneys, livers, lungs, and other vital organs. They can't wait long, however. Every day at least 20 of these organ-diseased patients die. The clock is always ticking.

Modern technology can save most of these patients. Vital organs can be transplanted, extending the life of diseased patients. How many people are saved, however, depends on how well the organ "market" works.

The Supply of Organs. The only cure for liver disease and some other organ failures is a replacement organ. More than 50 years ago, doctors discovered that they could transplant an organ from one individual to another. Since then, medical technology has advanced to the point where organ transplants are exceptionally safe and successful. The constraint on this life-saving technique is the *supply* of transplantable organs.

Continued

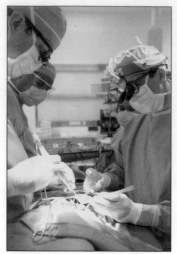

©ERproductions Ltd/Blend Images LLC RF

Although more than 2 million Americans die each year, most deaths do not create transplantable organs. Only 20,000 or so people die in circumstances—such as brain death after a car crash—that make them suitable donors for life-saving transplants. Additional kidneys can be "harvested" from live donors (we have two kidneys but can function with only one; this is not true for liver, heart, or pancreas).

You don't have to die to supply an organ. Instead you become a donor by agreeing to release your organs after death. The agreement is typically certified on a driver's license and sometimes on a bracelet or "dog tag." This allows emergency doctors to identify potential organ supplies.

People become donors for many reasons. Moral principles, religious convictions, and humanitarianism all play a role in the donation decision. It's the same with blood donations: people give blood (while alive!) because they want to help save other individuals.

Market Incentives. Monetary incentives could also play a role. When blood donations are inadequate, hospitals and medical schools *buy* blood in the marketplace. People who might not donate blood come forth to *sell* blood when a price is offered. In principle, the same incentive might increase the number of *organ* donors. If offered cash now for a postmortem organ, would the willingness to donate increase? The law of supply suggests it would. Offer $1,000 in cash for signing up, and potential donors will start lining up. Offer more, and the quantity supplied will increase further.

Zero Price Ceiling. The government doesn't permit this to happen. In 1984 Congress forbade the purchase or sale of human organs in the United States (the National Organ Transplantation Act). In part, the prohibition was rooted in moral and religious convictions. It was also motivated by equity concerns—the FOR WHOM question. If organs could be bought and sold, then the rich would have a distinct advantage in living.

The prohibition on market sales is effectively a **price ceiling** set at zero. As a consequence, the only available organs are those supplied by altruistic donors—people who are willing to supply organs at a zero price. The quantity supplied can't be increased with (illegal) price incentives. In general, *price ceilings have three predictable effects: they*

price ceiling: An upper limit imposed on the price of a good.

- *Increase the quantity demanded.*
- *Decrease the quantity supplied.*
- *Create a market shortage.*

The Deadly Shortage. Figure 3.8 illustrates the consequences of this price ceiling. At a price of zero, only the quantity q_a of "altruistic" organs is available (roughly one-third of

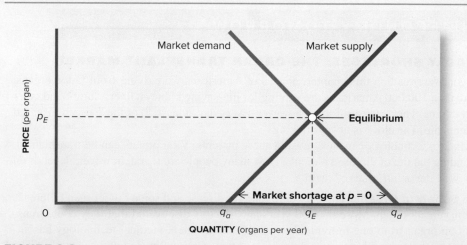

FIGURE 3.8

Organ Transplant Market

A market in human organs would deliver the quantity q_E at a price of p_E. The government-set price ceiling ($p = 0$) reduces the quantity supplied to q_a.

the potential supply). But the quantity q_d is demanded by all the organ-diseased individuals. The market shortage $q_d - q_a$ tells us how many patients will die.

Economists contend that many of these deaths are unnecessary. A University of Pennsylvania study showed that the quantity of organs supplied *doubled* when payment was offered. Without the government-set price ceiling, more organ-diseased patients would live. Figure 3.8 shows that q_E people would get transplants in a market-driven system. In the government-regulated system, only the quantity of q_a of transplants can occur.

Why does the government impose price controls that condemn more people to die? Because it feels the market unfairly distributes available organs. Only people who can afford the price p_E end up living in the market-based system—a feature regulators say is unfair. In the absence of the market mechanism, however, the government must set other rules for who gets the even smaller quantity of organs supplied. That rationing system may be unfair as well.

SUMMARY

- People participate in the marketplace by offering to buy or sell goods and services, or factors of production. Participation is motivated by the desire to maximize utility (consumers), profits (business firms), or the general welfare (government) from the limited resources each participant has.   **LO3-1, LO3-2**
- All market transactions involve the exchange of either factors of production or goods and services. Although the actual exchanges can occur anywhere, they take place in product markets or factor markets, depending on what is being exchanged.   **LO3-1, LO3-2**
- People willing and able to buy a particular good at some price are part of the market demand for that product. All those willing and able to sell that good at some price are part of the market supply. Total market demand or supply is the sum of individual demands or supplies.   **LO3-1, LO3-2**
- Supply and demand curves illustrate how the quantity demanded or supplied changes in response to a change in the price of that good, if nothing else changes *(ceteris paribus)*. Demand curves slope downward; supply curves slope upward.   **LO3-1, LO3-2**
- Determinants of market demand include the number of potential buyers and their respective tastes (desires), incomes, other goods, and expectations. If any of these

determinants changes, the demand curve shifts. Movements along a demand curve are induced only by a change in the price of that good.   **LO3-4**
- Determinants of market supply include factor costs, technology, profitability of other goods, expectations, tax rates, and number of sellers. Supply shifts when these underlying determinants change.   **LO3-4**
- The quantity of goods or resources actually exchanged in each market depends on the behavior of all buyers and sellers, as summarized in market supply and demand curves. At the point where the two curves intersect, an equilibrium price—the price at which the quantity demanded equals the quantity supplied—is established.   **LO3-3**
- A distinctive feature of the market equilibrium is that it's the only price-quantity combination acceptable to buyers and sellers alike. At higher prices, the quantity supplied is more than buyers are willing to purchase (a market surplus); at lower prices, the amount demanded exceeds the quantity supplied (a market shortage). Only the equilibrium price clears the market.   **LO3-3**
- Price ceilings are disequilibrium prices imposed on the marketplace. Such price controls create an imbalance between quantities demanded and supplied, resulting in market shortages.   **LO3-5**

Key Terms

factor market	law of demand	law of supply
product market	substitute goods	equilibrium price
opportunity cost	complementary goods	market mechanism
supply	*ceteris paribus*	price floor
demand	shift in demand	market surplus
demand schedule	market demand	market shortage
demand curve	market supply	price ceiling

Questions for Discussion

1. In our story of Tom, the student confronted with a web design assignment, we emphasized the great urgency of his desire for web tutoring. Many people would say that Tom had an "absolute need" for web help and therefore was ready to "pay anything" to get it. If this were true, what shape would his demand curve have? Why isn't this realistic?   **LO3-1**

2. Within weeks after Samsung launched its Galaxy Note 7 smartphone in August 2016, the phones started erupting into smoke and flames. How did this affect the demand for Note 7s? What determinants of demand changed?   **LO3-1**

3. With respect to the demand for college enrollment, which of the following would cause (1) a movement along the demand curve or (2) a shift of the demand curve?   **LO3-4**
   a. An increase in incomes.
   b. Lower tuition.
   c. More student loans.
   d. An increase in textbook prices.

4. Why do militant attacks in Nigeria affect the price of gasoline at U.S. gas stations? (World View "Oil Higher on Nigerian Supply Disruptions")   **LO3-5**

5. Why are scalpers able to resell tickets to the Final Four basketball games at such high prices (In the News "The Real March Madness: Ticket Prices")?   **LO3-2**

6. In Figure 3.8, why is the organ demand curve downward-sloping rather than vertical?   **LO3-1**

7. The shortage in the organ market (Figure 3.8) requires a nonmarket rationing scheme. Who should get the available (q_a) organs? Is this fairer than the market-driven distribution?   **LO3-5**

8. What would happen in the apple market if the government set a *minimum* price of $10.00 per apple? What might motivate such a policy?   **LO3-5**

9. When Hurricane Matthew struck Florida, Governor Rick Scott signed an emergency declaration outlawing "price gouging," i.e., unjustified price increases. More than 2,700 Floridians filed complaints with the State's Attorney General, most complaining about higher gasoline prices. If fully enforced, how would the governor's action have altered the market outcome depicted in In the News "Gas Prices Jump in Matthew's Wake"?   **LO3-5**

10. Is there a shortage of on-campus parking at your school? How might the shortage be resolved?   **LO3-3**

LO3-1 1. According to Figure 3.3, at what price would Tom buy 12 hours of web tutoring?
  (*a*) Without a lottery win.
  (*b*) With a lottery win.

LO3-3 2. According to Figures 3.5 and 3.6, what would the new equilibrium price of tutoring services be if Ann decided to stop tutoring?

LO3-3 3. According to In the News "The Real March Madness: Ticket Prices"
  (*a*) What was the initial price of a ticket to the NCAA finals?
  (*b*) At that price was there an equilibrium, a shortage, or a surplus?

LO3-3 4. Given the following data on gasoline supply and demand,
  (*a*) What is the equilibrium price?
  (*b*) Suppose the current price is $4. At this price, how much of a shortage or surplus exist?

Price per gallon	$5.00	$4.00	$3.00	$2.00	$1.00		$5.00	$4.00	$3.00	$2.00	$1.00
Quantity demanded (gallons per day)						Quantity supplied (gallons per day)					
Al	1	2	3	4	5	Firm A	3	3	2	2	1
Betsy	0	1	1	1	2	Firm B	7	5	3	3	2
Casey	2	2	3	3	4	Firm C	6	4	3	3	1
Daisy	1	3	4	4	6	Firm D	6	5	3	2	0
Eddie	1	2	2	3	5	Firm E	4	2	2	2	1
Market total	—	—	—	—	—	Market total	—	—	—	—	—

LO3-2 5. Illustrate using a supply and demand graph what happened to gasoline prices in In the News, "Gas Prices Jump in Matthew's Wake."
  (*a*) Which curve shifted?
  (*b*) Which direction did that curve shift (left or right)?
  (*c*) Did price increase or decrease?
  (*d*) Did quantity increase or decrease?

LO3-4 6. Illustrate using a supply and demand graph what happened to oil prices in World View "Oil Higher on Nigerian Supply Disruptions."
  (*a*) Which curve shifted?
  (*b*) Which direction did that curve shift (left or right)?
  (*c*) Did price increase or decrease?
  (*d*) Did quantity increase or decrease?

LO3-1 7. The goal of the price cut described in In the News "Pricing the Galaxy S7," was to
  (*a*) Increase supply.
  (*b*) Increase quantity supplied.
  (*c*) Increase demand.
  (*d*) Increase quantity demanded.

LO3-5 8. Which curve shifts and in which direction when the following events occur in the domestic car market?
  (*a*) The U.S. economy falls into a recession.
  (*b*) U.S. autoworkers go on strike.
  (*c*) Imported cars become more expensive.
  (*d*) The price of gasoline increases.

LO3-5 9. Use the following data to draw supply and demand curves.

Price	$ 8	7	6	5	4	3	2	1
Quantity demanded	2	3	4	5	6	7	8	9
Quantity supplied	10	9	8	7	6	5	4	3

(a) What is the equilibrium price?
(b) Suppose the current price is $7,
  (i) What kind of disequilibrium situation results?
  (ii) How large is this surplus or shortage?
(c) Suppose the current price is $3,
  (i) What disequilibrium situation results?
  (ii) How large is this surplus or shortage?
Illustrate these answers.

LO3-5 10. In Figure 3.8, when a price ceiling of zero is imposed, does
(a) The quantity of organs demanded increase?
(b) The market demand increase?
(c) The quantity of organs supplied increase?
(d) The market supply increase?
(e) The equilibrium price change?

LO3-5 11. The Economy Tomorrow: According to Figure 3.8,
(a) How many organs are supplied at a zero price?
(b) How many people die in the government-regulated economy where there is a price ceiling = $0?
(c) How many people die in the market-driven economy?

4

The Role of Government

The market has a keen ear for private wants, but a deaf ear for public needs.

—Robert Heilbroner

LEARNING OBJECTIVES

After reading this chapter, you should know

LO4-1 The nature and causes of market failure.

LO4-2 How the public sector has grown.

LO4-3 Which taxes finance state, local, and federal governments.

LO4-4 The meaning of government failure.

Markets do work: the interaction of supply and demand in product markets *does* generate goods and services. Likewise, the interaction of supply and demand in labor markets *does* yield jobs, wages, and a distribution of income. As we've observed, the market is capable of determining WHAT goods to produce, HOW, and FOR WHOM.

But are the market's answers good enough? Is the mix of output produced by unregulated markets the best possible mix? Will producers choose the production process that protects the environment? Will the market-generated distribution of income be fair enough? Will there be enough jobs for everyone who wants one?

In reality, markets don't always give us the best possible outcomes. Markets dominated by a few powerful corporations may charge excessive prices, limit output, provide poor service, or even retard technological advance. In the quest for profits, producers may sacrifice the environment for cost savings. In unfettered markets, some people may not get life-saving health care, basic education, or even adequate nutrition. When markets generate such outcomes, government intervention may be needed to ensure better answers to the WHAT, HOW, and FOR WHOM questions.

This chapter identifies the circumstances under which government intervention is desirable. To this end, we answer the following questions:

- **Under what circumstances do markets fail?**
- **How can government intervention help?**
- **How much government intervention is desirable?**

As we'll see, there's substantial agreement about how and when markets fail to give us the best WHAT, HOW, and FOR WHOM answers. But there's much less agreement about whether government intervention improves the situation. Indeed, an overwhelming majority of Americans are ambivalent about government intervention. They want the government to "fix" the mix of output, protect the environment, and ensure an adequate level of income for everyone. But voters are equally quick to blame government meddling for many of our economic woes.

MARKET FAILURE

We can visualize the potential for government intervention by focusing on the WHAT question. Our goal here is to produce the best possible mix of output with existing resources. We illustrated this goal earlier with production possibilities curves. Figure 4.1 assumes that of all the possible combinations of output we could produce, the unique combination at point X represents the most desirable one. In other words, it's the **optimal mix of output,** the one that maximizes our collective social utility. We haven't yet figured out how to pinpoint that optimal mix; we're simply using the arbitrary point X in Figure 4.1 to represent that best possible outcome.

Ideally, the **market mechanism** would lead us to point X. Price signals in the marketplace are supposed to move factors of production from one industry to another in response to consumer demands. If we demand more health care—offer to buy more at a given price—more resources (labor) will be allocated to health care services. Similarly, a fall in demand will encourage health care practitioners (doctors, nurses, and the like) to find jobs in another industry. *Changes in market prices direct resources from one industry to another, moving us along the perimeter of the production possibilities curve.*

Where will the market mechanism take us? Will it move resources around until we end up at the optimal point X? Or will it leave us at another point on the production possibilities curve with a *sub*optimal mix of output? (If point X is the *optimal,* or best possible, mix, all other output mixes must be *sub*optimal.)

We use the term **market failure** to refer to situations where the market generates imperfect (suboptimal) outcomes. If the invisible hand of the marketplace produces a mix of output that's different from the one society most desires, then it has failed. *Market failure implies that the forces of supply and demand haven't led us to the best point on the production possibilities curve.* Such a failure is illustrated by point M in Figure 4.1. Point M is assumed to be the mix of output generated by market forces. Notice that the market mix (M) doesn't represent the optimal mix, which is assumed to be at point X. We get less health care and more of other goods than are optimal. The market in this case *fails;* we get the wrong answer to the WHAT question.

Market failure opens the door for government intervention. If the market can't do the job, we need some form of *nonmarket* force to get the right answers. In terms of Figure 4.1, we need something to change the mix of output—to move us from point M (the market mix of output) to point X (the optimal mix of output). Accordingly, *market failure establishes a basis for government intervention.* We look to the government to push market outcomes closer to the ideal.

Causes of Market Failure. Because market failure is the justification for government intervention, we need to know how and when market failure occurs. *The four specific sources of market failure are*

- *Public goods.*
- *Externalities.*
- *Market power.*
- *Inequity.*

We will first examine the nature of these problems, then see why government intervention is called for in each case.

---

optimal mix of output: The most desirable combination of output attainable with existing resources, technology, and social values.

market mechanism: The use of market prices and sales to signal desired outputs (or resource allocations).

market failure: An imperfection in the market mechanism that prevents optimal outcomes.

FIGURE 4.1

Market Failure

We can produce any mix of output on the production possibilities curve. Our goal is to produce the optimal (best possible) mix of output, as represented by point X. Market forces, however, might produce another combination, like point M. In that case, the market fails—it produces a *sub*optimal mix of output.

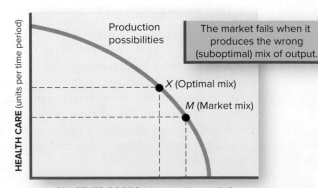

Public Goods

The market mechanism has the unique capability to signal consumer demands for various goods and services. By offering to pay for goods, we express our preferences about WHAT to produce. However, this mode of communication works efficiently only if the benefits of consuming a particular good are available only to the individuals who purchase that product.

Consider doughnuts, for example. When you eat a doughnut, you alone get the satisfaction from its sweet, greasy taste—that is, you derive a private benefit. No one else benefits from your consumption of a doughnut: The doughnut you purchase in the market is yours alone to consume; it's a **private good.** Accordingly, your decision to purchase the doughnut will be determined only by your anticipated satisfaction, your income, and your opportunity costs.

private good: A good or service whose consumption by one person excludes consumption by others.

No Exclusion. Most of the goods and services produced in the public sector are different from doughnuts—and not just because doughnuts look, taste, and smell different from "star wars" missile shields. When you buy a doughnut, you exclude others from consumption of that product. If Dunkin' Donuts sells you a particular pastry, it can't supply the same pastry to someone else. If you devour it, no one else can. In this sense, the transaction and product are completely private.

The same exclusiveness is not characteristic of national defense. If you buy a missile defense system to thwart enemy attacks, there's no way you can exclude your neighbors from the protection your system provides. Either the missile shield deters would-be attackers—like Israel's "Iron Dome" (see World View "Israel's 'Iron Dome' Frustrates Hamas")—or it doesn't. In the former case, both you and your neighbors survive happily ever after; in the latter case, we're all blown away together. In that sense, you and your neighbors consume the benefits of a missile shield *jointly*. National defense isn't a divisible service. There's no such thing as exclusive consumption here. The consumption of nuclear defenses is a communal feat, no matter who pays for them. Accordingly, national defense is regarded as a **public good** in the sense that *consumption of a public good by one person doesn't preclude consumption of the same good by another person.* By contrast, a doughnut is a private good because if I eat it, no one else can consume it.

public good: A good or service whose consumption by one person does not exclude consumption by others.

WORLD VIEW

ISRAEL'S "IRON DOME" FRUSTRATES HAMAS

The fragile peace between Israel and its Arab neighbors has broken down again. This time, though, Israel has a strategic advantage: its "Iron Dome" air defense system. The Iron Dome intercepts and destroys incoming missiles and mortars. So the hail of missiles Hamas is firing from Gaza into Israel rarely find their targets—they are destroyed in mid-air. The Israeli defense minister claims the Iron Dome is 90 percent effective in shielding population centers. Hamas has no such defense against artillery, bombs, and even ground forces dispatched by Israel into Gaza.

Source: News reports, July 20–28, 2014.

ANALYSIS: An air-defense system is a *public good*, as consumption of its services by one individual does not preclude consumption by others. Nonpayers cannot be excluded from its protection.

The Free-Rider Dilemma. The communal nature of public goods creates a dilemma. If you and I will *both* benefit from nuclear defenses, which one of us should buy the missile shield? I'd prefer that *you* buy it, thereby giving me protection at no direct cost. Hence I may profess no desire for a missile shield, secretly hoping to take a **free ride** on your

free rider: An individual who reaps direct benefits from someone else's purchase (consumption) of a public good.

Flood control is a public good.

Source: NOAA/Department of Commerce

market purchase. Unfortunately, you too have an incentive to conceal your desire for national defenses. As a consequence, neither one of us may step forward to demand a missile shield in the marketplace. We'll both end up defenseless.

Flood control is also a public good. No one in the valley wants to be flooded out. But each landowner knows that a flood control dam will protect *all* the landowners, regardless of who pays. Either the entire valley is protected or no one is. Accordingly, individual farmers and landowners may say they don't want a dam and aren't willing to pay for it. Everyone is waiting and hoping that someone else will pay for flood control. In other words, everyone wants a *free ride.* Thus, if we leave it to market forces, no one will *demand* flood control, and all the property in the valley will be washed away.

The difference between public goods and private goods rests on *technical considerations,* not political philosophy. The central question is whether we have the technical capability to exclude nonpayers. In the case of national defense or flood control, we simply don't have that capability. Even city streets have the characteristics of public goods. Although theoretically we could restrict the use of streets to those who paid to use them, a tollgate on every corner would be exceedingly expensive and impractical. Here again, joint or public consumption appears to be the only feasible alternative. As In the News "Firefighters Watch as Home Burns to the Ground" on local firefighting emphasizes, the technical capability to exclude nonpayers is the key factor in identifying "public goods."

IN THE NEWS

FIREFIGHTERS WATCH AS HOME BURNS TO THE GROUND

OBION COUNTY, Tenn.—Imagine your home catches fire, but the local fire department won't respond, then watches it burn. That's exactly what happened to a local family tonight.

A local neighborhood is furious after firefighters watched as an Obion County, Tennessee, home burned to the ground.

The homeowner, Gene Cranick, said he offered to pay whatever it would take for firefighters to put out the flames but was told it was too late. They wouldn't do anything to stop his house from burning.

©WPSD Local 6/AP Images

Each year, Obion County residents must pay $75 if they want fire protection from the city of South Fulton. But the Cranicks did not pay.

The mayor said if homeowners don't pay, they're out of luck.

This fire went on for hours because garden hoses just wouldn't put it out.

It was only when a neighbor's field caught fire, a neighbor who had paid the county fire service fee, that the department responded. Gene Cranick asked the fire chief to make an exception and save his home; the chief wouldn't.

—**Jason Hibbs**

©WPSD Local 6, Paducah, KY, September 30, 2010. Used with permission.

ANALYSIS: A product is a "public good" only if nonpayers *cannot* be excluded from its consumption. Firefighters in Tennessee proved that fire protection is not inherently a public good: they let the nonpaying homeowner's house burn down!

To the list of public goods we could add snow removal, the administration of justice (including prisons), the regulation of commerce, the conduct of foreign relations, airport security, and even Fourth of July fireworks. These services—which cost tens of *billions* of dollars and employ thousands of workers—provide benefits to everyone, no matter who pays for them. In each instance it's technically impossible or prohibitively expensive to exclude nonpayers from the services provided.

Underproduction of Public Goods. The free riders associated with public goods upset the customary practice of paying for what you get. If I can get all the national defense, flood control, and laws I want without paying for them, I'm not about to complain. I'm perfectly happy to let you pay for the services while we all consume them. Of course, you may feel the same way. Why should you pay for these services if you can consume just as much of them when your neighbors foot the whole bill? It might seem selfish not to pay your share of the cost of providing public goods. But you'd be better off in a material sense if you spent your income on doughnuts, letting others pick up the tab for public services.

Because the familiar link between paying and consuming is broken, public goods can't be peddled in the supermarket. People are reluctant to buy what they can get free. Hence, *if public goods were marketed like private goods, everyone would wait for someone else to pay.* The end result might be a total lack of public services. This is the kind of dilemma Robert Heilbroner had in mind when he spoke of the market's "deaf ear" (see the quote at the beginning of this chapter).

The production possibilities curve in Figure 4.2 illustrates the dilemma created by public goods. Suppose that point *A* represents the optimal mix of private and public goods. It's the mix of goods and services we'd select if everyone's preferences were known and reflected in production decisions. The market mechanism won't lead us to point *A*, however, because the *demand* for public goods will be hidden. If we rely on the market, nearly everyone will withhold demand for public goods, waiting for a free ride to point *A*. As a result, we'll get a smaller quantity of public goods than we really want. The market mechanism will leave us at point *B*, with few, if any, public goods. Since point *A* is assumed to be optimal, point *B* must be *suboptimal* (inferior to point *A*). The market fails: we can't rely on the market mechanism to allocate enough resources to the production of public goods, no matter how much they might be desired.

Note that we're using the term "public good" in a peculiar way. To most people, "public good" refers to any good or service the government produces. In economics, however, the meaning is much more restrictive. The term "public good" refers only to those nonexcludable goods and services that must be consumed jointly, both by those who pay for them and by those who don't. Public goods can be produced by either the government or the private sector. Private goods can be produced in either sector as well. The problem is that *the market tends to underproduce public goods and overproduce private goods.* If we want more public goods, we need a *nonmarket* force—government intervention—to get them. The government will have to force people to pay taxes, then use the tax revenues to pay for the production of national defense, flood control, snow removal, and other public goods.

Externalities

The free-rider problem associated with public goods is an important justification for government intervention. It's not the only justification, however. A second justification for

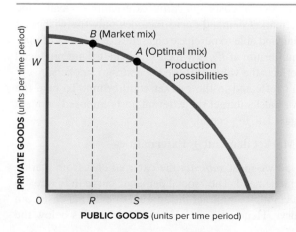

FIGURE 4.2

Underproduction of Public Goods

Suppose point *A* represents the optimal mix of output—that is, the mix of private and public goods that maximizes society's welfare. Because consumers won't demand purely public goods in the marketplace, the price mechanism won't allocate so many resources to their production. Instead the market will tend to produce a mix of output like point *B,* which includes fewer public goods (*OR*) than are optimal (*OS*).

intervention arise from the tendency of costs or benefits of some market activities to "spill over" onto third parties.

Consider the case of cigarettes. The price someone is willing to pay for a pack of cigarettes reflects the amount of satisfaction a smoker anticipates from its consumption. If that price is high enough, tobacco companies will produce the cigarettes demanded. That is how market-based price signals are supposed to work. In this case, however, the price paid isn't a satisfactory signal of the product's desirability. The smoker's pleasure is offset in part by nonsmokers' *dis*pleasure. In this case, smoke literally spills over onto other consumers, causing them discomfort, ill health, and even death (see World View "Secondhand Smoke Kills 600,000 People a Year"). Yet their loss isn't reflected in the market price: the harm caused to nonsmokers is *external* to the market price of cigarettes.

WORLD VIEW

SECONDHAND SMOKE KILLS 600,000 PEOPLE A YEAR

Secondhand smoke globally kills more than 600,000 people each year, accounting for 1 percent of all deaths worldwide.

Researchers estimate that annually secondhand smoke causes about 379,000 deaths from heart disease, 165,000 deaths from lower respiratory disease, 36,900 deaths from asthma, and 21,400 deaths from lung cancer.

©Image Source/Getty Images RF

Children account for about 165,000 of the deaths. Forty percent of children and 30 percent of adults regularly breathe in secondhand smoke.

Source: World Health Organization

ANALYSIS: The health risks imposed on nonsmokers via passive smoke represent an external cost. The market price of cigarettes doesn't reflect these costs borne by third parties.

externalities: Costs (or benefits) of a market activity borne by a third party; the difference between the social and private costs (benefits) of a market activity.

The term **externalities** refers to all costs or benefits of a market activity borne by a third party—that is, by someone other than the immediate producer or consumer. ***Whenever externalities are present, market prices aren't a valid measure of a good's value to society.*** As a consequence, the market will fail to produce the right mix of output. Specifically, ***the market will underproduce goods that yield external benefits and overproduce those that generate external costs.***

External Costs. Figure 4.3 shows how external costs—*negative* externalitites—cause the market to overproduce cigarettes. The market demand curve includes only the wishes of smokers—that is, people who are willing and able to purchase cigarettes. The forces of market demand and supply result in an equilibrium at E_M in which q_M cigarettes are produced and consumed. The market price P_M reflects the value of those cigarettes to smokers.

The well-being of *non*smokers isn't reflected in the market equilibrium. To take the *non*smokers' interests into account, we must subtract the external costs imposed on *them* from the value that *smokers* put on cigarettes. In general,

$$\text{Social demand} = \text{Market demand} \pm \text{Externalities}$$

In this case, the externality is a *cost,* so we must *subtract* the external cost from market demand to get a full accounting of social demand. The "social demand" curve in Figure 4.3 reflects this computation. To find this curve, we subtract the amount of external cost from every price on the market demand curve. Hence the social demand curve lies below the

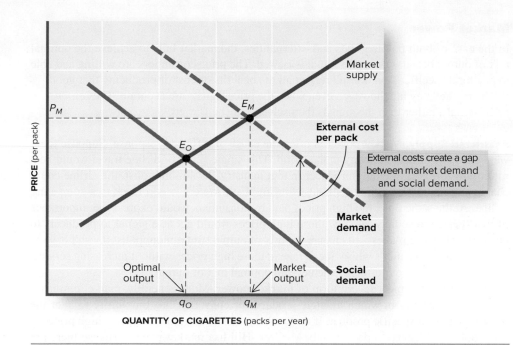

FIGURE 4.3
Externalities

The market responds to consumer demands, not externalities. Smokers demand q_M cigarettes at the equilibrium price P_M. But external costs on nonsmokers imply that the *social* demand for cigarettes is less than (below) *market* demand. The socially optimal level of output is q_O, less than the market output q_M.

market demand curve in this case. What the social demand curve tells us is how much society would be willing and able to pay for cigarettes if the preferences of *both* smokers and nonsmokers were taken into account.

The social demand curve in Figure 4.3 creates a social equilibrium at E_O. At this juncture, we see that the socially *optimal* quantity of cigarettes is q_O, not the larger market-generated level at q_M. In this sense, the market produces too many cigarettes.

Negative externalities also exist in production. A power plant that burns high-sulfur coal damages the surrounding environment. Yet the damage inflicted on neighboring people, vegetation, and buildings is external to the cost calculations of the firm. Because the cost of such pollution is not reflected in the price of electricity, the firm will tend to produce more electricity (and pollution) than is socially desirable. To reduce this imbalance, the government has to step in and change market outcomes.

External Benefits. Externalities can also be beneficial. A product may generate external *benefits* rather than external *costs*. Your college is an example. The students who attend your school benefit directly from the education they receive. That's why they (and you) are willing to pay for tuition, books, and other services. The students in attendance aren't the only beneficiaries of this educational service, however. The research that a university conducts may yield benefits for a much broader community. The values and knowledge students acquire may also be shared with family, friends, and coworkers. These benefits would all be *external* to the market transaction between a paying student and the school. Positive externalities also arise from immunizations against infectious diseases: the person getting immunized obviously benefits, but so do all the people with whom that person comes into contact. Other people (third parties) benefit when you get vaccinated.

If a product yields external benefits, the social demand is greater than the market demand. In this case, the social value of the good *exceeds* the market price (by the amount of external benefit). Accordingly, society wants *more* of the product than the market mechanism alone will produce at any given price. To get that additional output, the government may have to intervene with subsidies or other policies. We conclude then that *the market fails by*

- *Overproducing goods that have external costs.*
- *Underproducing goods that have external benefits.*

If externalities are present, the market won't produce the optimal mix of output. To get that optimal mix, we need government intervention.

Market Power

In the case of both public goods and externalities, the market fails to achieve the optimal mix of output because the price signal is flawed. The price consumers are willing and able to pay for a specific good doesn't reflect all the benefits or cost of producing that good.

The market may fail, however, even when the price signals are accurate. The *response* to price signals, rather than the signals themselves, may be flawed.

Restricted Supply. Market power is often the cause of a flawed response. Suppose there were only one airline company in the world. This single seller of airline travel would be a **monopoly**—that is, the only producer in that industry. As a monopolist, the airline could charge extremely high prices without worrying that travelers would flock to a competing airline. At the same time, the high prices paid by consumers would express the importance of that service to society. Ideally, those high prices would act as a signal to producers to build and fly more planes—to change the mix of output. But a monopolist doesn't have to cater to every consumer's whim. It can rake in those high prices without increasing service, thereby obstructing our efforts to achieve an optimal mix of output.

Monopoly is the most severe form of **market power.** More generally, market power refers to any situation in which a single producer or consumer has the ability to alter the market price of a specific product. If the publisher (McGraw-Hill) charges a high price for this book, you'll have to pay the tab. McGraw-Hill has market power because there are relatively few economics text and your professor has required you to use this one. You don't have power in the textbook market because your decision to buy or not won't alter the market price of this text. You're only one of the million students who are taking an introductory economics course this year.

The market power McGraw-Hill possesses is derived from the copyright on this text. No matter how profitable textbook sales might be, no one else is permitted to produce or sell this particular book. Patents are another common source of market power because they also preclude others from making or selling a specific product. Market power may also result from control of resources, restrictive production agreements, or efficiencies of large-scale production.

Whatever the source of market power, the direct consequence is that one or more producers attain discretionary power over the market's response to price signals. They may use that discretion to enrich themselves rather than to move the economy toward the optimal mix of output. In this case, the market will again fail to deliver the most desired goods and services.

The mandate for government intervention in this case is to prevent or dismantle concentrations of market power. That's the basic purpose of **antitrust** policy. Another option is to *regulate* market behavior. This was one of the goals of the antitrust case against Microsoft. The government was less interested in breaking Microsoft's near monopoly on operating systems than in changing the way Microsoft behaved.

In some cases, it may be economically efficient to have one large firm supply an entire market. Such a situation arises in **natural monopoly,** where a single firm can achieve economies of scale over the entire range of market output. Utility companies, local telephone service, subway systems, and cable all exhibit such scale (size) efficiencies. In these cases, a monopoly *structure* may be economically desirable. The government may have to regulate the *behavior* of a natural monopoly, however, to ensure that consumers get the benefits of that greater efficiency.

Inequity

Public goods, externalities, and market power all cause resource misallocations. Where these phenomena exist, the market mechanism will fail to produce the optimal mix of output in the best possible way.

Beyond the questions of WHAT and HOW to produce, we're also concerned about FOR WHOM output is produced. The market answers this question by distributing a larger share

---

monopoly: A firm that produces the entire market supply of a particular good or service.

market power: The ability to alter the market price of a good or service.

antitrust: Government intervention to alter market structure or prevent abuse of market power.

natural monopoly: An industry in which one firm can achieve economies of scale over the entire range of market supply.

of total output to those with the most income. Although this result may be efficient, it's not necessarily equitable. As we saw in Chapter 2, the market mechanism may enrich some people while leaving others to seek shelter in abandoned cars. If such outcomes violate our vision of equity, we may want the government to change the market-generated distribution of income.

Taxes and Transfers. The tax-and-transfer system is the principal mechanism for redistributing incomes. The idea here is to take some of the income away from those who have "too much" and give it to those whom the market has left with "too little." Taxes are levied to take back some of the income received from the market. Those tax revenues are then redistributed via transfer payments to those deemed needy, such as the poor, the aged, and the unemployed. **transfer payments** are income payments for which no goods or services are exchanged. They're used to bolster the incomes of those for whom the market itself provides too little.

Merit Goods. Often our vision of what is "too little" is defined in terms of specific goods and services. There is a widespread consensus in the United States that everyone is entitled to some minimum levels of shelter, food, and health care. These are regarded as **merit good,** in the sense that everyone merits at least some minimum provision of such goods. When the market does not distribute that minimum provision, the government is called on to fill the gaps. In this case, the income transfers take the form of *in-kind* transfers (e.g., food stamps, housing vouchers, Medicaid) rather than *cash* transfers (e.g., welfare checks, Social Security benefits).

Some people argue that we don't need the government to help the poor—that private charity alone will suffice. Unfortunately, private charity alone has never been adequate. One reason private charity doesn't suffice is the "free-rider" problem. If I contribute heavily to the poor, you benefit from safer streets (fewer muggers), a better environment (fewer slums and homeless people), and a clearer conscience (knowing that fewer people are starving). In this sense, the relief of misery is a *public* good. Were I the only taxpayer to benefit substantially from the reduction of poverty, then charity would be a private affair. As long as income support substantially benefits the public at large, then income redistribution is a *public* good, for which public funding is appropriate. This is the *economic* rationale for public income redistribution activities. To this rationale one can add such moral arguments as seem appropriate.

Macro Instability

The micro failures of the marketplace imply that we may end up at the wrong point on the production possibilities curve or inequitably distributing the output produced. There's another basic question we've swept under the rug, however. How do we get to the production possibilities curve in the first place? To reach the curve, we must utilize all available resources and technology. Can we be confident that the invisible hand of the marketplace will use all available resources? That confidence was shattered in 2008–2009 when total output contracted and **unemployment** soared. Millions of people who were willing and able to work but unable to find jobs demanded that the government intervene to increase output and create more jobs. The market had failed.

And what about prices? Price signals are a critical feature of the market mechanism. But the validity of those signals depends on some stable measure of value. What good is a doubling of salary when the price of everything you buy doubles as well? Generally, rising prices will enrich people who own property and impoverish people who rent. That's why we strive to avoid **inflation**—a situation in which the *average* price level is increasing.

Historically, the marketplace has been wracked with bouts of both unemployment and inflation. These experiences have prompted calls for government intervention at the macro level. *The goal of macro intervention is to foster economic growth—to get us on the production possibilities curve (full employment), maintain a stable price level (price stability), and increase our capacity to produce (growth).*

transfer payments: Payments to individuals for which no current goods or services are exchanged, like Social Security, welfare, and unemployment benefits.

merit good: A good or service society deems everyone is entitled to some minimal quantity of.

unemployment: The inability of labor force participants to find jobs.

inflation: An increase in the average level of prices of goods and services.

GROWTH OF GOVERNMENT

The potential micro and macro failures of the marketplace provide specific justifications for government intervention. We do need government to provide public goods, compensate for externalities, limit the excesses of market power, and redistribute incomes more fairly. We can't rely completely on a private, market-based economy to generate optimal answers to the WHAT, HOW, and FOR WHOM questions.

The question then becomes, "How well does the government respond to these needs?" We'll start answering this question by looking at what the government now does and how it has grown.

Federal Growth

Until the 1930s the federal government's role was largely limited to national defense (a public good), enforcement of a common legal system (also a public good), and provision of postal service (equity). The Great Depression of the 1930s spawned a new range of government activities, including welfare and Social Security programs (equity), minimum wage laws and workplace standards (regulation), and massive public works (public goods and externalities). In the 1950s the federal government also assumed a greater role in maintaining macroeconomic stability (macro failure), protecting the environment (externalities), and safeguarding the public's health (externalities and equity).

These increasing responsibilities have greatly increased the size of the public sector. In 1902 the federal government employed fewer than 350,000 people and spent a mere $650 *million*. Today the federal government employs nearly 4 million people and spends nearly $4 *trillion* a year.

Direct Expenditure. Figure 4.4 summarizes the growth of the public sector since 1930. Let's focus on the federal government, depicted with the orange line. Back in 1930 the federal share of total spending was close to zero. That share grew in the 1930s and sky-rocketed during World War II. Federal purchases of goods and services for the war

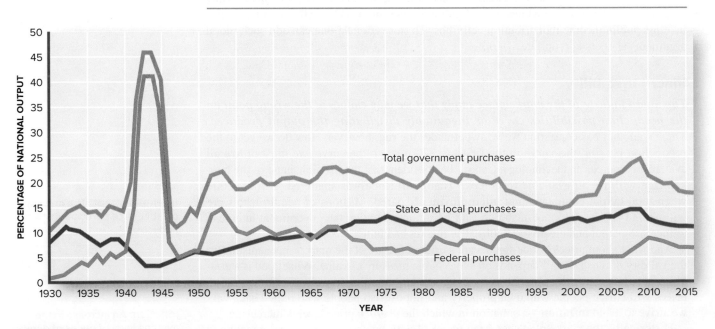

FIGURE 4.4

Government Growth

During World War II the public sector purchased nearly half of total U.S. output. Since the early 1950s the public sector share of total output has been closer to 20 percent. Within the public sector, however, there's been a major shift: state and local claims on resources have grown, while the federal share has declined significantly.

Source: U.S. Bureau of Economic Analysis.

accounted for more than 40 percent of total output during the 1943–1944 period. The federal share of total U.S. output fell abruptly after World War II, rose again during the Korean War (1950–1953), and has declined slightly since then.

The decline in the federal share of total output is somewhat at odds with most people's perception of government growth. This discrepancy is explained by two phenomena. First, people see the *absolute* size of the government growing every year. But we're focusing here on the *relative* size of the public sector. From 1950 until 2008 the public sector grew a bit more slowly than the private sector, slightly reducing its relative size. The trend was interrupted in 2008–2011, when the private sector shrank and the federal government undertook massive stimulus spending. Since then, the federal government's share of total output has hovered around 7 percent. President Trump's stepped-up spending on national defense and infrastructure has increased that share only a couple of decimal points.

Income Transfers. The federal share of output depicted in Figure 4.4 looks small (7 percent) because it doesn't include *all* federal spending. As noted above, Uncle Sam *spends* about $4 trillion a year. But the majority of that spending is for income transfers, not direct expenditure on goods and services. Figure 4.4 only counts direct expenditure on things like national defense, transportation systems, education, and other real goods—the things that are included in the WHAT outcome of the economy. By contrast, income transfers go to people who themselves decide how to spend that money—and thus what gets produced. Hence income transfers don't directly alter the mix of output. Their effect is primarily *distributional* (the FOR WHOM question), not *allocative* (the WHAT question). Were income transfers included, the relative size and growth of the federal government would be larger than Figure 4.4 depicts. This is because ***most of the growth in federal spending has come from increased income transfers, not purchases of goods and services.***

State and Local Growth

State and local spending on goods and services has followed a very different path from federal expenditure. Prior to World War II, state and local governments dominated public sector spending. During the war, however, the share of total output going to state and local governments fell, hitting a low of 3 percent in that period (Figure 4.4).

State and local spending caught up with federal spending in the mid-1960s and has exceeded it ever since. Today ***more than 80,000 state and local government entities buy much more output than Uncle Sam and employ five times as many people.*** Education is a huge expenditure at lower levels of government. Most direct state spending is on colleges; most local spending is for elementary and secondary education. The fastest-growing areas for state expenditure are prisons (public safety) and welfare. At the local level, sewage and trash services are claiming an increasing share of budgets.

TAXATION

Whatever we may think of any specific government expenditure, we must recognize one basic fact of life: we pay for government spending. We pay not just in terms of tax *dollars* but in the more fundamental form of a changed mix of output. Government expenditures on goods and services absorb factors of production that could be used to produce consumer goods. The mix of output changes toward *more* public services and *fewer* private goods and services. Resources used to produce missile shields, operate elementary schools, or journey to Mars aren't available to produce cars, houses, or restaurant meals. In real terms, ***the cost of government spending is measured by the private sector output sacrificed when the government employs scarce factors of production.***

The **opportunity cost** of public spending aren't always apparent. We don't directly hand over factors of production to the government. Instead we give the government part of our income in the form of taxes. Those dollars are then used by government agencies to buy factors of production or goods and services in the marketplace. Thus ***the primary function of taxes is to transfer command over resources (purchasing power) from the private***

opportunity cost: The most desired goods or services that are forgone in order to obtain something else.

sector to the public sector. Although the government also borrows dollars to finance its purchases, taxes are the primary source of government revenues.

Federal Taxes

As recently as 1902, much of the revenue the federal government collected came from taxes imposed on alcoholic beverages. The federal government didn't have authority to collect income taxes. As a consequence, *total* federal revenue in 1902 was only $653 million.

Income Taxes. All that changed, beginning in 1915. The Sixteenth Amendment to the U.S. Constitution, enacted in 1915, granted the federal government authority to collect *income* taxes. The government now collects more than $1.5 *trillion* in that form alone each year. Although the federal government still collects taxes on alcoholic beverages, the individual income tax has become the largest single source of government revenue (see Figure 4.5).

In theory, the federal income tax is designed to be **progressive**—that is, to take a larger *fraction* of high incomes than of low incomes. In 2017, for example, a single person with less than $9,325 of taxable income was taxed at 10 percent. People with incomes of $37,950–$91,900 confronted a 25 percent tax rate on their additional income. The marginal tax rate got as high as 39.6 percent for people earning more than $418,400 in income. Thus **people with high incomes not only pay more taxes but also pay a larger fraction of their income in taxes.**

Social Security Taxes. The second major source of federal revenue is the Social Security payroll tax. People working now transfer part of their earnings to retired workers by making "contributions" to Social Security. There's nothing voluntary about these "contributions"; they take the form of mandatory payroll deductions. In 2017, each worker paid 7.65 percent of his or her wages to Social Security, and employers contributed an equal amount. As a consequence, the government collected more than $1 trillion from this tax.

At first glance, the Social Security payroll tax looks like a **proportional tax**—that is, a tax that takes the *same* fraction of every taxpayer's income. But this isn't the case. The Social Security (FICA) tax isn't levied on every payroll dollar. Incomes above a certain ceiling ($127,200 in 2017) aren't taxed. As a result, workers with *really* high salaries turn over a smaller fraction of their incomes to Social Security than do low-wage workers. This makes the Social Security payroll tax a **regressive tax.**

Corporate Taxes. The federal government taxes the profits of corporations as well as the incomes of consumers. But there are far fewer corporations (less than 2 million) than consumers (340 million), and their profits are small in comparison to total consumer income. In 2016, the federal government collected less than $350 billion in corporate income taxes, despite the fact that it imposed a top tax rate of 35 percent on corporate profits.

progressive tax: A tax system in which tax rates rise as incomes rise.

proportional tax: A tax that levies the same rate on every dollar of income.

regressive tax: A tax system in which tax rates fall as incomes rise.

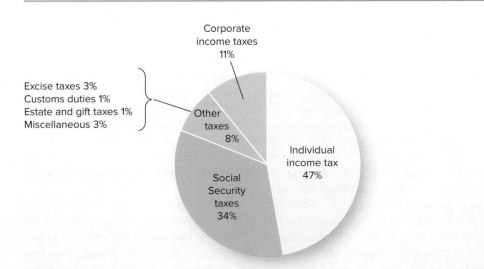

FIGURE 4.5

Federal Taxes

Taxes transfer purchasing power from the private sector to the public sector. The largest federal tax is the individual income tax. The second-largest source of federal revenue is the Social Security payroll tax.

Source: Office of Management and Budget, FY2015 data.

Corporate income taxes 11%

Excise taxes 3%
Customs duties 1%
Estate and gift taxes 1%
Miscellaneous 3%

Other taxes 8%

Individual income tax 47%

Social Security taxes 34%

Excise Taxes. The last major source of federal revenue is excise taxes. Like the early taxes on whiskey, excise taxes are sales taxes imposed on specific goods and services. The federal government taxes not only liquor ($13.50 per gallon) but also gasoline (18.4 cents per gallon), cigarettes ($1.01 per pack), air fares (7.5 percent), firearms (10–11 percent), gambling (0.25 percent), and a variety of other goods and services. Such taxes not only discourage production and consumption of these goods by raising their price and thereby reducing the quantity demanded; they also raise a substantial amount of revenue.

State and Local Revenues

Taxes. State and local governments also levy taxes on consumers and businesses. In general, cities depend heavily on property taxes, and state governments rely heavily on sales taxes. Although nearly all states and many cities also impose income taxes, effective tax rates are so low (averaging less than 2 percent of personal income) that income tax revenues are much less than sales and property tax revenues.

Like the Social Security payroll tax, state and local taxes tend to be *regressive*—that is, they take a larger share of income from the poor than from the rich. Consider a 4 percent sales tax, for example. It might appear that a uniform tax rate like this would affect all consumers equally. But people with lower incomes tend to spend most of their income on goods and services. Thus most of their income is subject to sales taxes. By contrast, a person with a high income can afford to save part of his or her income and thereby shelter it from sales taxes.

Consider a family that earns $40,000 and spends $30,000 of it on taxable goods and services. This family will pay $1,200 in sales taxes when the tax rate is 4 percent. In effect, then, they are handing over 3 percent of their *income* ($1,200 ÷ $40,000) to the state. Now consider a the family that makes only $12,000 and spends $11,500 of it for food, clothing, and shelter. That family will pay $460 in sales taxes in the same state. Their total tax is smaller, but it represents a much larger *share* (3.8 versus 3.0 percent) of their income.

Local property taxes are also regressive because poor people devote a larger portion of their incomes to housing costs. Hence a larger share of a poor family's *income* is subject to property taxes. State lotteries are also regressive for the same reason (see In the News "State Lotteries: A Tax on the Uneducated and the Poor"). Low-income players spend 1.4 percent of their incomes on lottery tickets while upper-income players devote only 0.1 percent of their income to lottery purchases.

IN THE NEWS

STATE LOTTERIES: A TAX ON THE UNEDUCATED AND THE POOR

Americans now spend over $70 billion a year on lottery tickets. That's more than we spend on sporting events, books, video games, movies, and music *combined*. That spending works out to about $640 a household.

Poor people are proportionally the biggest buyers of lottery tickets. Households with less than $25,000 of income spend $1,100 a year on lottery tickets. By contrast, households with more than $50,000 of income buy only $300 of lottery tickets each year.

Education also affects lottery spending: 2.7 percent of high school dropouts are compulsive lottery players, while only 1.1 percent of college grads play compulsively. Since lottery games are a sucker's game to start with—payouts average less than 60 percent of sales—lotteries are effectively a regressive tax on the uneducated and the poor.

Source: Research on lottery sales.

ANALYSIS: Poor people spend a larger percentage of their income on lottery tickets than do rich people. This makes lotteries a regressive source of government revenue.

FIGURE 4.6

Government Failure

When the market produces a suboptimal mix of output like point *M*, the goal of government is to move output to the social optimum (point *X*). A move to G_4 would be an improvement in the mix of output. But government intervention *may* move the economy to points G_1, G_2, or G_3—all reflecting government failure.

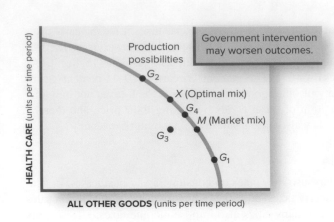

government failure: Government intervention that fails to improve economic outcomes.

GOVERNMENT FAILURE

Some government intervention in the marketplace is clearly desirable. The market mechanism can fail for a variety of reasons, leaving a laissez-faire economy short of its economic goals. But how much government intervention is desirable? Communist nations once thought that complete government control of production, consumption, and distribution decisions was the surest path to utopia. They learned the hard way that *not only markets but governments as well can fail.* In this context, **government failure** means that government intervention fails to move us closer to our economic goals.

Consider again our collective goal of producing the optimal mix of output. In Figure 4.6, this goal is again illustrated by point *X* on the production possibilities curve. Point *M* on the curve reminds us that the market may fail to generate that optimal answer to the WHAT question. This is why we want the government to intervene. We want the government to move the mix of output from point *M* to point *X*.

We have no guarantee that government intervention will yield the desired move. Government intervention might unwittingly move us to point G_1, making matters worse. Or the government might overreact, sending us to point G_2. Red tape and onerous regulation might even force us to point G_3, *inside* the production possibilities curve (with less total output than at point *M*). All those possibilities (G_1, G_2, G_3) represent government failure. **Government intervention is desirable only to the extent that it *improves* market outcomes** (e.g., G_4).

We face a similar risk when the government intervenes in the HOW and FOR WHOM questions. Regulations imposed on an industry may reduce output with little or no environmental improvements. Taxes and transfers intended to make the distribution of income fairer may actually have the opposite effect. These things won't necessarily happen, but they *could*. Even when outcomes improve, government failure may occur if the costs of government intervention exceed the benefits of an improved output mix, cleaner production methods, or a fairer distribution of income.

Perceptions of Government Failure

Taxpayers seem to have strong opinions about government failure. A 2016 poll asked people how confident they were that the federal government could successfully tackle important problems. As In the News "Perceptions of Government Failure" reveals, 70 percent of Americans don't have such confidence. In other words, they *expect* government failure.

Not surprisingly, people also feel that the federal government *wastes* their tax dollars. The average taxpayer now believes that state governments waste 42 cents out of each dollar, while the federal government wastes 51 cents out of each tax dollar!

Government "waste" implies that the public sector isn't producing as many services as it could with the resources at its disposal. Such inefficiency implies that we're producing somewhere *inside* our production possibilities curve rather than on it (e.g., point G_3 in Figure 4.6). If the government is wasting resources this way, we can't possibly be producing the optimal mix of output.

Opportunity Cost

Even if the government wasn't wasting resources, it might still be guilty of government failure. Notice in Figure 4.6 that points G_1 and G_2 are on the production possibilities curve. So resources aren't being "wasted." But those points still represent suboptimal outcomes. In reality, *the issue of government failure encompasses two distinct questions:*

- *Efficiency:* Are we getting as much service as we could from the resources we allocate to government?
- *Opportunity cost:* Are we giving up too many private sector goods in order to get those services?

When assessing government's role in the economy, *we must consider not only what governments do but also what we give up to allow them to do it.* The theory of public goods tells us only what activities are appropriate for government, not the proper *level* of such activity. National defense is clearly a proper function of the public sector. Not so clear, however, is how much the government should spend on tanks, aircraft carriers, and missile shields. The same is true of environmental protection or law enforcement.

The concept of opportunity costs puts a new perspective on the whole question of government size. *Everything the government does entails an opportunity cost.* Before we can decide how big is "too big," we must decide what we're willing to give up to support the public sector. A military force of 1.4 million men and women is "too big" from an economic perspective only if we value the forgone private production and consumption more highly than we value the added strength of our defenses. The government has gone "too far" if the highway it builds is less desired than the park and homes it replaced. In these and all cases, the assessment of bigness must come back to a comparison of what is given up with what is received. The assessment of government failure thus comes back to points on the production possibilities curve. Has the government moved us closer to the optimal mix of output (e.g., point G_4 in Figure 4.6) or not?

THE ECONOMY TOMORROW

"RIGHT"-SIZING GOVERNMENT

You don't have to be a genius to find the optimal mix of output in Figure 4.6—it's clearly marked. And Figure 4.2 clearly reveals the optimal size of the government as well. In both cases, the opportunity cost principle points to the right answer.

In practice, establishing the optimal size of the public sector isn't so easy. In fact, Gallup polls reveal that most Americans think the federal government is too big and too powerful—that we are at a point like G_2 rather than point X in Figure 4.6. Donald Trump made this perception a cornerstone of his successful campaign for the presidency in 2016. Was he right?

In principle, we should be able to answer this question. We can say with theoretical confidence that *additional public sector activity is desirable only if the benefits from that activity exceed its opportunity costs.* In other words, we compare the benefits of a public project to the value of the private goods given up to produce it. By performing this calculation repeatedly along the perimeter of the production possibilities curve, we could locate the optimal mix of output—the point at which no further increase in public sector spending activity is desirable.

Valuation Problems. Although the principles of cost–benefit analysis are simple enough, they're deceptive. How are we to measure the potential benefits of improved police services, for example? Should we estimate the number of robberies and murders prevented, calculate the worth of each, and add up the benefits? And how are we supposed to calculate the worth of a saved life? By a person's earnings? Value of assets? Number of friends? And what about the increased sense of security people have when they know the police are patrolling their neighborhood? Should this be included in the benefit calculation? Some people will attach great value to this service; others will attach little. Whose values should be the standard? Should we consult liberals or conservatives on these questions?

When we're dealing with (private) market goods and services, we can gauge the benefits of a product by the amount of money consumers are willing to pay for it. This price signal isn't available for most public services, however, because of externalities and the nonexclusive nature of pure public goods (the free-rider problem). Hence *the value (benefits) of public services must be estimated because they don't have (reliable) market prices.* This opens the door to endless political squabbles about how beneficial any particular government activity is.

The same problems arise in evaluating the government's efforts to redistribute incomes. Government transfer payments now go to retired workers, disabled people, veterans, farmers, sick people, students, pregnant women, unemployed people, poor people, and a long list of other recipients. To pay for all these transfers, the government must raise tax revenues. With so many people paying taxes and receiving transfer payments, the net effects on the distribution of income aren't easy to figure out. Yet we can't determine whether this government intervention is worth it until we know how the FOR WHOM answer was changed and what the tax-and-transfer effort cost us.

Ballot Box Economics. In practice, we rely on political mechanisms, not cost–benefit calculations, to decide what to produce in the public sector and how to redistribute incomes. *Voting mechanisms substitute for the market mechanism in allocating resources to the public sector and deciding how to use them.* Some people have even suggested that the variety and volume of public goods are determined by the most votes, just as the variety and volume of private goods are determined by the most dollars. Thus governments choose the level and mix of output (and related taxation) that seem to command the most votes.

Sometimes the link between the ballot box and output decisions is very clear and direct. State and local governments, for example, are often compelled to get voter approval before building another highway, school, housing project, or sewage plant. *Bond referenda* are direct requests by a government unit for voter approval of specific public spending projects (e.g., roads, schools). In 2016, for example, six state governments sought voter approval for $12 billion of new borrowing to finance public expenditure.

Bond referenda are more the exception than the rule. Bond referenda account for less than 1 percent of state and local expenditures (and no federal expenditures). As a consequence, voter control of public spending is typically much less direct. At best, voters get the opportunity every two years to elect Congressional representatives and every four years a president. Promises about future spending and taxes typically play a major role in those elections. But election campaigns rarely get into the details of government spending and often fail to deliver on campaign promises. So, the ballot box turns out to be a very poor substitute for the market mechanism.

Even if we had the opportunity to vote on every government spending decision, we still might not achieve the optimal mix of output. A democratic vote, for example, might yield a 51 percent majority for approval of new local highways. Should the highways then be built? The answer isn't obvious. After all, a large minority (49 percent) of the voters have stated that they don't want resources used this way. If we proceed to build the highways, we'll make those people worse off. Their loss may be greater than what proponents gain. Hence the basic dilemma is really twofold. *We don't know what the real demand for public services is, and votes alone don't reflect the intensity of individual demands.* Moreover, real-world decision making involves so many choices that a stable consensus is impossible.

Public Choice Theory. In the midst of all this complexity and uncertainty, another factor may be decisive—namely self-interest. In principle, government officials are supposed to serve the people. It doesn't take long, however, before officials realize that the public is indecisive about what it wants and takes little interest in government's day-to-day activities. With such latitude, government officials can set their own agendas. Those agendas may give higher priority to personal advancement than to the needs of the public. Agency directors may foster new programs that enlarge their mandate, enhance their visibility, and increase their prestige or income. Members of Congress may likewise pursue legislative favors like tax breaks for supporters more diligently than they pursue the general public interest. In such cases, the probability of attaining the socially optimal mix of output declines.

The theory of **public choice** emphasizes the role of self-interest in public decision making. Public choice theory essentially extends the analysis of market behavior to political behavior. Public officials are assumed to have specific personal goals (for example, power, recognition, wealth) that they'll pursue in office. *A central tenet of public choice theory is that bureaucrats are just as selfish (utility maximizing) as everyone else.*

Public choice theory provides a neat and simple explanation for public sector decision making. But critics argue that the theory provides a woefully narrow view of public servants. Some people do selflessly pursue larger, public goals, such critics argue, and ideas can overwhelm self-interest. Steven Kelman of Harvard, for example, argues that narrow self-interest can't explain the War on Poverty of the 1960s, the tax revolt of the 1970s, or the deregulation movement of the 1980s. These tidal changes in public policy reflect the power of ideas, not simple self-interest. Public choice theory tells us how many decisions about government are made; it doesn't tell us how they should be made. The "right" size of government in the economy tomorrow will depend less on self-interest and more on how much we trust *markets* to generate optimal outcomes or trust government intervention to *improve* on market failures.

public choice: Theory of public sector behavior emphasizing rational self-interest of decision makers and voters.

SUMMARY

- Government intervention in the marketplace is justified by market failure—that is, suboptimal market outcomes.   **LO4-1**
- The micro failures of the market originate in public goods, externalities, market power, and an inequitable distribution of income. These flaws deter the market from achieving the optimal mix of output or distribution of income.   **LO4-1**
- Public goods are those that can't be consumed exclusively; they're jointly consumed regardless of who pays. Because everyone seeks a free ride, no one demands public goods in the marketplace. Hence, the market underproduces public goods.   **LO4-1**
- Externalities are costs (or benefits) of a market transaction borne by a third party. Externalities create a divergence between social and private costs or benefits, causing suboptimal market outcomes. The market overproduces goods with external costs and underproduces goods with external benefits.   **LO4-1**
- Market power enables a producer to thwart market signals and maintain a suboptimal mix of output. Antitrust policy seeks to prevent or restrict market power. The government may also regulate the behavior of powerful firms.   **LO4-1**
- The market-generated distribution of income may be unfair. This inequity may prompt the government to intervene with taxes and transfer payments that redistribute incomes.   **LO4-1**
- The macro failures of the marketplace are reflected in unemployment and inflation. Government intervention is intended to achieve full employment and price stability.   **LO4-1**
- The federal government expanded greatly in the 1930s and World War II, but its share of output has shrunk in recent decades. Recent growth in federal spending has been on income transfers, not output.   **LO4-2**
- State and local governments purchase more output (11 percent of GDP) than the federal government (7 percent) and employ five times as many workers.   **LO4-2**
- Income and payroll taxes provide most federal revenues. States get most revenue from sales taxes; local governments rely on property taxes.   **LO4-3**
- Government failure occurs when intervention doesn't move toward the optimal mix of output (or income). Failure may result from outright waste (operational inefficiency) or from a misallocation of resources.   **LO4-4**
- All government activity must be evaluated in terms of its opportunity cost—that is, the *private* goods and services forgone to make resources available to the public sector.   **LO4-4**

Key Terms

optimal mix of output	monopoly	inflation
market mechanism	market power	opportunity cost
market failure	antitrust	progressive tax
private good	natural monopoly	proportional tax
public good	transfer payments	regressive tax
free rider	merit good	government failure
externalities	unemployment	public choice

Questions for Discussion

1. Why should taxpayers subsidize public colleges and universities? What external benefits are generated by higher education?   **LO4-1**
2. If Israel's "Iron Dome" (World View "Israel's 'Iron Dome' Frustrates Hamas") is so effective, why doesn't a private company produce it and sell its services directly to consumers?   **LO4-1**
3. If everyone seeks a free ride, what mix of output will be produced in Figure 4.2? Why would anyone voluntarily contribute to the purchase of public goods like flood control or snow removal?   **LO4-1**
4. Should the firefighters have saved the house in In the News "Firefighters Watch as Home Burns to the Ground"? What was the justification for their belated intervention?   **LO4-1**
5. Why might Fourth of July fireworks be considered a public good? Who should pay for them? What about airport security?   **LO4-1**
6. What is the specific market failure justification for government spending on (*a*) public universities, (*b*) health care, (*c*) trash pickup, (*d*) highways, (*e*) police, and (*f*) solar energy? Would a purely private economy produce any of these services?   **LO4-1**

7. If smoking generates external costs, should smoking simply be outlawed? How about cars that pollute?   **LO4-1**

8. The government now spends more than $700 billion a year on Social Security benefits. Why don't we leave it to individuals to save for their own retirement?   **LO4-1**

9. What government actions might cause failures like points G_1, G_2, and G_3 in Figure 4.6? Can you give examples?   **LO4-4**

10. How does Sirius Satellite deter nonsubscribers from listening to its transmissions? Does this make radio programming a private good or a public good?   **LO4-1**

11. Should the government be downsized? Which functions should be cut back? Which ones should be expanded?   **LO4-2**

12. Which taxes hit the poor hardest—those of local, state, or federal governments?   **LO4-3**

PROBLEMS FOR CHAPTER 4

LO4-1 1. In Figure 4.2, by how much is the market
    (a) Overproducing private goods?
    (b) Underproducing public goods?

LO4-1 2. (a) Use Figure 4.3 to illustrate on the accompanying production possibilities curve the optimal
      mix of output (X).

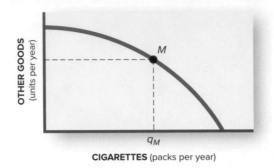

    (b) Does the optimal mix include (A) more or (B) fewer "other goods"?

LO4-1 3. Assume that the product depicted below generates external costs in consumption of $3 per unit.
    (a) What is the market price (market value) of the product?
    (b) Draw the social demand curve.
    (c) What is the socially optimal output?
    (d) By how much does the market overproduce this good?

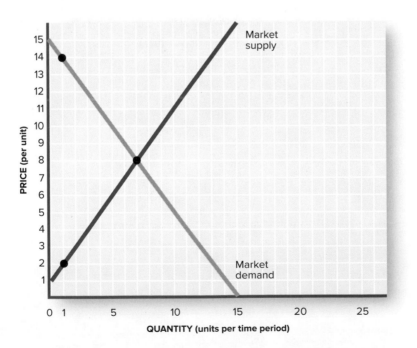

LO4-1 4. Draw market and social demand curves for the consumption of flu shots.

LO4-1 5. If the average working-age adult produces $25,000 of output per year, how much global output
    is lost as a result of adult deaths from secondhand smoke, according to In the News
    "Secondhand Smoke Kills 600,000 People a Year?" $ _____

LO4-3 6. (*a*) Assuming an 9 percent sales tax is levied on all consumption, complete the following table:

Income	Consumption	Sales Tax	Percentage of Income Paid in Taxes
$10,000	$11,000	_____	_____
20,000	20,000	_____	_____
40,000	36,000	_____	_____
80,000	60,000	_____	_____

(*b*) Is the sales tax (A) progressive or (B) regressive?

LO4-4 7. If a new home can be constructed for $150,000, what is the opportunity cost of federal defense spending, measured in terms of private housing? (Assume a defense budget of $600 billion.)

LO4-1 8. Suppose the following data represent the market demand for college education:

Tuition (per year)	$40,000	$35,000	$30,000	$25,000	$20,000	$15,000	$10,000	$5,000
Enrollment demanded (in millions per year)	1	2	3	4	5	6	7	8

(*a*) If tuition is set at $15,000, how many students will enroll?

Now suppose that society gets an external benefit of $5,000 for every enrolled student.

(*b*) Draw the social and market demand curves for this situation on the graph below.
(*c*) What is the socially optimal level of enrollment at the same tuition price of $15,000?
(*d*) If the government were to intervene and subsidize college education, how large of a subsidy is needed per student each year to achieve this optimal outcome?

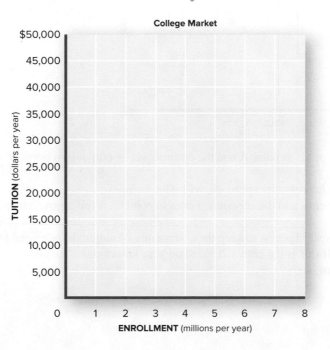

LO4-1 9. Suppose the market demand for cigarettes is given in the following table.

Price per pack	$10	$9	$8	$7	$6	$5	$4	$3
Quantity demanded (million packs per year)	2	4	6	8	10	12	14	16

Suppose further that smoking creates external costs valued at $2.00 per pack.

Graph the social and market demand curves.

If cigarettes are priced at $6 a pack,
(*a*) What is the quantity demanded in the market?
(*b*) What is the socially optimal quantity?
(*c*) If the government were to intervene and tax cigarettes, how large of a tax is needed per pack to achieve this optimal outcome?

LO4-3 10. According to In the News "State Lotteries: A Tax on the Uneducated and the Poor," what percentage of income is spent on lottery tickets by
(*a*) A low-income family with income of $20,000 per year?
(*b*) An middle-income family with income of $60,000 per year?

LO4-3 11. The Economy Tomorrow: The following production possibility curve shows the tradeoff between housing and all other goods.

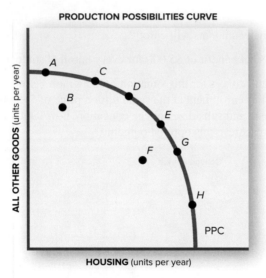

PRODUCTION POSSIBILITIES CURVE

ALL OTHER GOODS (units per year)

HOUSING (units per year)

(*a*) If the current mix of output is at point A and the optimal mix of output is at point D, does a market failure exist?
(*b*) If the government has a laissez-faire approach, will it intervene?
(*c*) If the government intervenes and the economy moves to point C, is this a government failure?
(*d*) Suppose a politician has self interest to keep the current mix of output despite need for more housing in her district. If this is the case and based on your knowledge of public choice theory, will the politician intervene?

©MOF/Getty Images RF

©Onoky/SuperStock RF

©Michele Constantini/PhotoAlto/Corbis RF

©SCPhotos/Alamy Stock Photo

PRODUCT MARKETS: THE BASICS

The prices and products we see every day emerge from decisions made by millions of individual consumers and firms. A primary objective of microeconomic theory is to explain how those decisions are made. How high a price are consumers willing to pay for the products they want? Which products will consumers actually purchase—and in what quantities? We explore these dimensions of consumer *demand* in Chapters 5 and 6. We move to the *supply* side in Chapter 7, examining the costs that businesses incur in producing the products consumers demand.

CHAPTER 5

Consumer Choice

Steve Jobs knew he had a winner with the iPhone. Every time Apple added a feature to the iPod, sales picked up. Now Jobs had a product that combined cell phone services with wireless computing and audio and video download capabilities—all accessible on a touch screen. It was sure to be a hit. The only sticky question was *price*. What price should Apple put on its new iPhone? The company's goal was to sell 10 million iPhones in the first two years of production. If it set the price low enough, it could surely do that. But Apple didn't want to give away the iPhone—it wanted to make a nice profit. Yet if it set the price *too* high, sales would fall short of its sales target. What price should it charge? Apple's pricing committee had to know how many iPhones consumers would buy at different prices. In other words, they had to know the dimensions of *consumer demand*. After considerable deliberation, they set the initial price at $499 for the 4 GB iPhone, launched in January 2007.

Apple's iPhone pricing dilemma underscores the importance of *prices* in determining consumer behavior. Consumers "want," "need," and "just have to have" a vast array of goods and services. When decision time comes, however, product *prices* often dictate what consumers will actually buy. As we observed in Chapter 3, the quantity of a product *demanded* depends on its price.

This chapter takes a closer look at how product prices affect consumer decisions. We focus on three related questions:

- **How do we decide how much of any good to buy?**
- **Why do we feel so good about our purchases?**
- **Why do we buy certain products but not others?**

The law of demand (first encountered in Chapter 3) gives us some clues for answering these questions. But we need to look beyond that law to fashion more complete answers. We need to know what forces give demand curves their downward-sloping shape. We also need to know more about how to *use* demand curves to predict consumer behavior.

DETERMINANTS OF DEMAND

In seeking explanations for consumer behavior, we have to recognize that the field of economics doesn't have all the answers. But it does offer a unique perspective that sets it apart from other fields of study.

The Sociopsychiatric Explanation

Consider first the explanations of consumer behavior offered by other fields of study. Psychiatrists and psychologists have had a virtual field

LEARNING OBJECTIVES

After reading this chapter, you should know

LO5-1 Why demand curves are downward sloping.

LO5-2 The nature and source of consumer surplus.

LO5-3 The meaning and use of price discrimination.

LO5-4 How consumers maximize utility.

day formulating such explanations. Freud was among the first to describe us humans as bundles of subconscious (and unconscious) fears, complexes, and anxieties. From a Freudian perspective, we strive for ever higher levels of consumption to satisfy basic drives for security, sex, and ego gratifications. Like the most primitive of people, we clothe and adorn ourselves in ways that assert our identity and worth. We eat and smoke too much because we need the oral gratifications and security associated with mother's breast. Oversized homes and cars give us a sense of warmth and security remembered from the womb. On the other hand, we often buy and consume some things we don't really want, just to assert our rebellious feelings against our parents (or parent substitutes). In Freud's view, it's the constant interplay of these id, ego, and superego drives that motivates us to buy, buy, buy.

Sociologists offer additional explanations for our consumption behavior. They observe our yearning to stand above the crowd, to receive recognition from the masses. For people with exceptional talents, such recognition may come easily. But for the ordinary person, recognition may depend on conspicuous consumption. A sleek car, a newer fashion, a more exotic vacation become expressions of identity that provoke recognition, even social acceptance. We strive for ever higher levels of consumption—not just to keep up with the Joneses but to surpass them.

Not *all* consumption is motivated by ego or status concerns. Some food is consumed for the sake of self-preservation, some clothing worn for warmth, and some housing built for shelter. The typical U.S. consumer has more than enough income to satisfy these basic needs, however. In today's economy, most consumers also have *discretionary* income that can be used to satisfy psychological or sociological longings. Single women are able to spend a lot of money on clothes and pets, and men spend freely on entertainment, food, and drink (see In the News "Men vs. Women: How They Spend"). Teenagers show off their affluence in purchases of electronic goods, cars, and clothes (see Figure 5.1).

IN THE NEWS

MEN VS. WOMEN: HOW THEY SPEND

Are men really different from women? If spending habits are any clue, males do differ from females. That's the conclusion one would draw from the latest Bureau of Labor Statistics (BLS) survey of consumer expenditure. Here's what the BLS found out about the spending habits of young (under age 25) men and women who are living on their own:

Common Traits

- Young men have a lot more after-tax income to spend ($15,894 per year) than do young women ($11,826).
- Both sexes spend about $21,000 per year, much more than their income. Education is one of the largest expenditures (around $3,600).
- Neither sex spends much on charity, reading, or health care.

Distinctive Traits

- Men spend twice as much more on alcoholic beverages and smoking.
- Men spend almost twice as much as women do on electronic equipment.
- Young women spend twice as much money on clothing, personal care items, and their pets.

Source: U.S. Bureau of Labor Statistics, 2014–2016, Consumer Expenditure Survey.

ANALYSIS: Consumer patterns vary by gender, age, and other characteristics. Economists try to isolate the common influences on consumer behavior.

FIGURE 5.1

Affluent Teenagers

Teenagers spend nearly $300 billion a year. Much of this spending is for cars, technology, and other durables. The percentages of U.S. teenagers owning certain items are shown here.

Industry Reports, 2015–2017

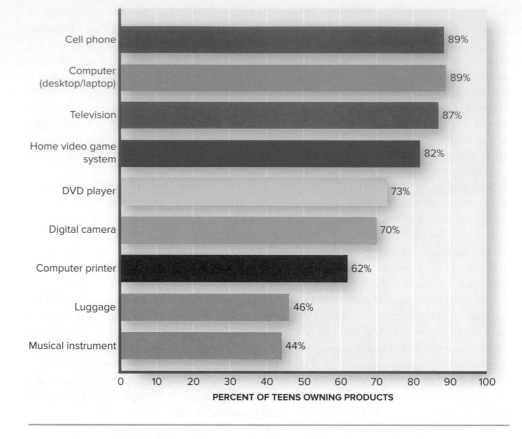

PERCENT OF TEENS OWNING PRODUCTS

The Economic Explanation

Although psychiatrists and sociologists offer intriguing explanations for our consumption patterns, their explanations fall a bit short. Sociopsychiatric theories tell us why teenagers, men, and women *desire* certain goods and services. But they don't explain which goods will actually be *purchased*. Desire is only the first step in the consumption process. To acquire goods and services, one must be willing and able to *pay* for one's wants. Producers won't give you their goods just to satisfy your Freudian desires. They want money in exchange for their goods. Hence ***prices and income are just as relevant to consumption decisions as are more basic desires and preferences.***

In explaining consumer behavior, economists focus on the *demand* for goods and services. As we observed in Chapter 3, **demand** entails the *willingness and ability to pay* for goods and services. To say that someone *demands* a particular good means that he or she will offer to *buy* it at some price(s).

demand: The willingness and ability to buy specific quantities of a good at alternative prices in a given time period, *ceteris paribus*.

Determinants of Demand. What determines a person's willingness to buy a product at some price? Economists isolate four determinants of demand. We say ***an individual's demand for a specific product is determined by these four factors:***

- *Tastes* (desire for this and other goods).
- *Income* (of the consumer).
- *Expectations* (for income, prices, tastes).
- *Other goods* (their availability and prices).

Freud might have been content to focus on tastes or desires originating in infancy. But economists go several steps further. Tastes alone do not guarantee you'll buy a specific product. Income, expectations, and the price and availability of other goods also come into play at the cash register. All four determinants of demand play a role in the purchase decision.

The remainder of this chapter examines these determinants of demand. The objective is not only to explain consumer behavior but also to predict how consumption patterns change in response to *changes* in the price of a good or to *changes* in underlying tastes, income, prices or availability of other goods, or expectations.

THE DEMAND CURVE

The starting point for an economic analysis of demand is quite simple. Economists accept consumer tastes as the outcome of sociopsychiatric and cultural influences. They don't look beneath the surface to see how those tastes originated. They don't care if your desires originated in the womb or in some TV ad. Economists want to know only how those tastes (desires) affect consumption decisions.

Utility Theory

The first observation economists make is that the more pleasure a product gives us—for whatever reason—the higher the price we're willing to pay for it. If the oral sensation of buttered popcorn at the movies really turns you on, you're likely to be willing to pay dearly for it. If, on the other hand, you have no great taste or desire for popcorn, the theater might have to give it away before you'd eat it.

Total vs. Marginal Utility. Economists use the term **utility** to refer to the expected pleasure, or satisfaction, obtained from goods and services. If you really like popcorn, we say you get a lot of utility (satisfaction) from consuming it. Pretty simple. But we then go a step further in explaining your satisfaction by distinguishing between the *total* utility you get from eating popcorn and your *marginal* utility. **Total utility** refers to the amount of satisfaction obtained from your *entire* consumption of a product. By contrast, **marginal utility** refers to the amount of satisfaction you get from consuming the *last* (i.e., "marginal") unit of a product. More generally, note that

$$\text{Marginal utility} = \frac{\text{Change in total utility}}{\text{Change in quantity}}$$

utility: The pleasure or satisfaction obtained from a good or service.

total utility: The amount of satisfaction obtained from entire consumption of a product.

marginal utility: The change in total utility obtained by consuming one additional (marginal) unit of a good or service.

Diminishing Marginal Utility. The concepts of total and marginal utility explain not only why we buy popcorn at the movies but also why we stop eating it at some point. Even people who love popcorn (i.e., derive great *total* utility from it) don't eat endless quantities of it. Why not? Presumably because the thrill diminishes with each mouthful. The first box of popcorn may bring sensual gratification, but the second or third box is likely to bring a stomachache. We express this change in perceptions by noting that the marginal utility of the first box of popcorn is higher than the additional or marginal utility derived from the second box.

The behavior of popcorn connoisseurs isn't abnormal. As a rule, the amount of additional utility we obtain from a product declines as we continue to consume it. The third slice of pizza isn't as desirable as the first, the sixth beer not as satisfying as the fifth, and so forth. Indeed, this phenomenon of diminishing marginal utility is so nearly universal that economists have fashioned a law around it. This **law of diminishing marginal utility** states that each successive unit of a good consumed yields less *additional* utility.

The law of diminishing marginal utility does *not* say that we won't like the second box of popcorn, the third pizza slice, or the sixth beer; it just says we won't like them as much as the ones we've already consumed. Time is also important here: if the first box of popcorn was eaten last year, the second box may now taste just as good. The law of diminishing marginal utility applies to short time periods.

law of diminishing marginal utility: The marginal utility of a good declines as more of it is consumed in a given time period.

The Popcorn Test. Let's put the law of diminishing marginal utility to a test—the popcorn test. The test measures how much popcorn you'd eat if it were absolutely free. To complete this test, we'll make up some numbers for total and marginal utility.

Let's start with the first box of popcorn. That first box is yummy. We'll assume an arbitrary number and say that first box delivers 20 units of utility. If we stopped there, at one box, our total utility would be 20 "utils" (units of utility).

TABLE 5.1

The Satisfaction Meter

Marginal utility refers to the pleasure we get from one more unit of a good. Although marginal utility diminishes as we consume additional units, total utility keeps rising so long as *marginal* utility is positive.

Popcorn Consumption	Marginal Utility (in Units)	Total Utility
0	0	0
First box	20	20
Second box	15	35
Third box	9	44
Fourth box	5	49
Fifth box	1	50
Sixth box	−10	40

But it's hard to stop munching on popcorn. So suppose we go for a *second* box (mini boxes, of course!). Will it taste good? If so, we say it has positive marginal utility; it adds to our pleasure.

But here's the tough question: Is the second box as satisfying as the first? Probably not. So we have to acknowledge that the marginal utility of the second box is less than the marginal utility of the first box (20 utils). Let's assume the second box adds only 15 units of pleasure.

Notice where we're at on the satisfaction meter in Table 5.1. Our total utility is now at 35 utils, based on the pleasures of the first (20 utils) and second boxes (15 utils).

We'll keep moving up the satisfaction meter so long as we continue to enjoy munching popcorn—so long as the marginal utility of the next box is positive. Sooner or later, however, another box of popcorn isn't going to look so appetizing. At some point, another handful of popcorn might even look repulsive—that is, deliver negative marginal utility. In Table 5.1 this threshold is reached with the sixth box. Notice that the marginal utility of the sixth box is *negative*—if you eat it, you'll feel *worse* than if you don't. That's why you move down the satisfaction meter of *total* utility from 50 to 40 when you consume the sixth box.

Here's the popcorn test: Would you eat that sixth box, even if it were free? Hopefully not. Once you realize that the thrill of eating popcorn diminishes with each additional box, you will stop eating it at some point.

Figure 5.2 illustrates how we get to that point. As we consume boxes 1 thru 5, we climb the utility staircase. Each step represents the marginal utility of the next box. Because

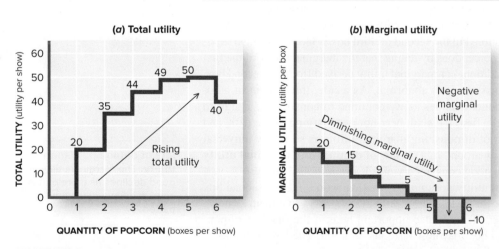

FIGURE 5.2

Total vs. Marginal Utility

The *total* utility derived from consuming a product comes from the *marginal* utilities of each successive unit. The total utility curve shows how each of the first five boxes of popcorn contributes to total utility. Note that the utility staircase is rising, but each successive step is smaller. This reflects the law of diminishing marginal utility.

The sixth box of popcorn causes the total utility steps to descend; the sixth box actually *reduces* total utility. This means that the sixth box has *negative* marginal utility.

The marginal utility curve (*b*) shows the change in total utility with each additional unit. It's derived from the total utility curve. Marginal utility here is positive but diminishing for the first five boxes.

marginal utility diminishes, each successive step gets shorter. So long as we are climbing, however, total utility is increasing. ***As long as marginal utility is positive, total utility must be increasing.***

The situation changes with the sixth box of popcorn. As we have already noted, the good sensations associated with popcorn consumption are completely forgotten by the time the sixth box arrives. Nausea and stomach cramps take over. Indeed, the sixth box is absolutely *distasteful,* as reflected in the downturn of *total* utility and the *negative* value for marginal utility. We were happier—in possession of more total utility—with only five boxes of popcorn. The sixth box—yielding *negative* marginal utility—reduces total satisfaction. This is the kind of sensation you'd probably experience if you ate six hamburgers (see the cartoon below).

Analysis: No matter how much we like a product, marginal utility is likely to diminish as we consume more of it. If marginal utility becomes *negative* (as here), total satisfaction will decrease.

Not every good ultimately reaches negative marginal utility. Yet the more general principle of diminishing marginal utility is experienced daily. That is, ***eventually additional quantities of a good yield increasingly smaller increments of satisfaction.***

Price and Quantity

Marginal utility is essentially a measure of how much we desire particular goods, our *taste.* But which ones will we buy? Clearly, we don't always buy the products we most desire. *Price* often holds us back. All too often we have to settle for goods that yield less marginal utility simply because they are available at a lower price. This explains why most people don't drive Porsches. Our desire ("taste") for a Porsche may be great, but its price is even greater. The challenge for most of us is to somehow reconcile our tastes with our bank balances.

In deciding whether to buy something, our immediate focus is typically on a single variable, namely *price.* Assume for the moment that a person's tastes, incomes, and expectations are set in stone, and that the prices of other goods are set as well. This is the ***ceteris paribus*** assumption we first encountered in Chapter 1. It doesn't mean that other influences on consumer behavior are unimportant. Rather, *ceteris paribus* simply allows us to focus on one variable at a time. In this case, we are focusing on price. What we want to know is how high a price a consumer is willing to pay for another unit of a product. This is the question Steve Jobs had to confront when Apple launched the first iPhone in 2007.

The concepts of marginal utility and *ceteris paribus* enable us to answer this question. ***The more marginal utility a product delivers, the more a consumer will be willing to pay for it.*** We also noted that marginal utility *diminishes* as increasing quantities of a product are consumed, suggesting that consumers are willing to pay progressively *less* for additional quantities of a product. The moviegoer willing to pay 50 cents for that first mouth-watering ounce

ceteris paribus: The assumption of nothing else changing.

FIGURE 5.3
An Individual's Demand Schedule and Curve

Consumers are generally willing to buy larger quantities of a good at lower prices. This demand schedule illustrates the specific quantities demanded at alternative prices. If popcorn sold for 25 cents per ounce, this consumer would buy 12 ounces per show (row *F*). At higher prices, less popcorn would be purchased.

A downward-sloping demand curve expresses the law of demand: the quantity of a good demanded increases as its price falls. Notice that points *A* through *J* on the curve correspond to the rows of the demand schedule.

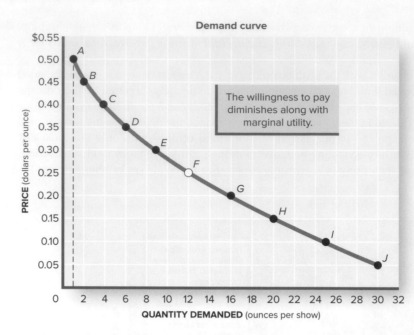

Demand curve

The willingness to pay diminishes along with marginal utility.

Demand Schedule

	Price (per Ounce)	Quantity Demanded (Ounces per Show)
A	$0.50	1
B	0.45	2
C	0.40	4
D	0.35	6
E	0.30	9
F	0.25	12
G	0.20	16
H	0.15	20
I	0.10	25
J	0.05	30

law of demand: The quantity of a good demanded in a given time period increases as its price falls, *ceteris paribus*.

demand curve: A curve describing the quantities of a good a consumer is willing and able to buy at alternative prices in a given time period, *ceteris paribus*.

market demand: The total quantities of a good or service people are willing and able to buy at alternative prices in a given time period; the sum of individual demands.

of buttered popcorn may not be willing to pay so much for a second or third ounce. The same is true for a second pizza, the sixth beer, and so forth. *Because marginal utility declines, people are willing to buy additional quantities of a good only if its price falls.* In other words, as the marginal utility of a good diminishes, so does our willingness to pay. This **law of demand** is illustrated in Figure 5.3 with the downward-sloping **demand curve.**

The law of demand and the law of diminishing marginal utility tell us nothing about why we crave popcorn or why our cravings subside. Those explanations are reserved for psychiatrists, sociologists, and physiologists. The laws of economics simply describe our market behavior.

MARKET DEMAND

Our explanation of an individual's popcorn consumption applies to all products and all consumers. As we saw in Chapter 3, the **market demand** for popcorn is just the sum of all our individual demands for that product. The market demand curve resembles an individual's demand curve but differs in two important respects. First, the units of measurement are larger: the quantities on the horizontal axis are in hundreds, thousands, or possibly millions of units, not single digits. Second, the demand curve expresses the ability and willingness to pay of thousands of consumers, not just one individual.

CONSUMER SURPLUS

The presence of so many individuals on the market demand curve has some interesting implications for both consumers and producers. To see this, let's venture into another market—say, the new car market. Let's focus on a specific car, the Porsche 918 Spyder Hybrid, a sports car with a 608 horsepower V8 engine supplemented by two electrical engines, a top speed of 211 miles per hour, and 71 miles per gallon in all-electric mode.

Lots of people crave this car. But not everyone is willing and able to buy it at the Manufacturer's Suggested Retail Price (MSRP) of $847,975. In fact, most people who *desire* the car aren't prepared to pay anywhere near that much money. Some people are, however. Indeed, some Porsche fans would pay even a *higher* price to get their hands on a 918 Spyder. And it's not just a question of who is rich enough. Remember that there are *four* determinants of an individual's demand: tastes, income, expectations, and other goods (price and availability). So a rich person with little desire for speed might not demand a Spyder at the $847,975 price. On the other hand, a real speed freak with only a modest income might be willing to borrow money, rent out the house, and sell the kids to get behind the wheel of a 918 Spyder.

You may *desire* a Porsche, but do you *demand* it?

©Sean Gallup/Getty Images

As individuals work their way through the determinants of demand, they will ultimately decide how much money they are willing to pay for a Porsche 918 Spyder. For those sorry souls who would never think of driving a Spyder, their price would be zero: they would not be part of the market demand for that car. Everyone else, however, would be deciding the *maximum* price they would be willing and able to pay for a new 918 Spyder. That decision will determine where they are positioned on the market demand curve.

Consider the positions depicted in Figure 5.4. Fred is positioned high up on the market demand curve because he is willing to pay as much as $1 million for a Spyder. Michel and Hua are also willing and able to shell out big bucks for the car. Blaise also wants a Spyder but can't or won't spend more than $650,000 to get one.

What we also see on the market demand curve is how many cars the Porsche dealer can sell at the MSRP of $847,975. At that price (point *A* on the graph), four Spyders will be demanded and therefore sold.

Fred will be particularly excited with this deal. We know that Fred would pay as much as $1 million for a 918 Spyder. But he has to pay only the $847,975 price set by the dealer. In his mind, he is getting a real bargain—getting the Spyder for a lot less money than the

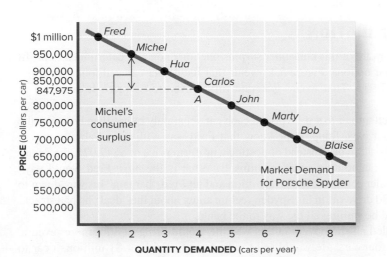

FIGURE 5.4

Consumer Surplus

A person's position on the market demand curve expresses the maximum price he or she is willing to pay. The difference between that individualized maximum price and the price paid represents "consumer surplus." At the MSRP price of $847,975, Michel would have a consumer surplus of $102,025 (= $950,000 − $847,975).

FIGURE 5.5

Total consumer surplus

Every consumer who buys a product must be willing and able to pay *at least* the prevailing price. Therefore, all consumers buying the good reap some consumer surplus. Their collective consumer surplus is represented by the shaded area in the graph.

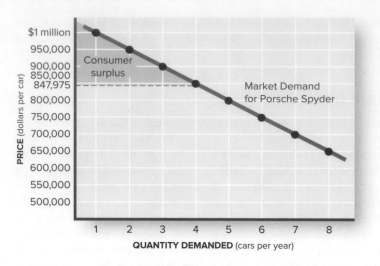

---

consumer surplus: The difference between the maximum price a person is willing to pay and the price paid.

maximum price he would be willing to pay. We call this "bargain" his **consumer surplus.** Specifically, consumer surplus is the difference between the maximum price a person is willing to pay and the price paid:

$$\text{Consumer surplus} = \text{Maximum price willing to pay} - \text{Price actually paid}$$

In Fred's case, that consumer surplus amounts to $152,025 (= $1 million − $847,975).

Michel enjoys a consumer surplus as well. Notice again in Figure 5.4 where she is on the market demand curve: she is willing to pay as much as $950,000 for a Spyder. So she enjoys a consumer surplus of $102,025 (= $950,000 − $847,975). She cannot wait to tell all her friends what a "bargain" she got.

In fact, everyone who buys a Spyder thinks she or he got a bargain! That is because *the only people who purchase a product are those whose maximum price equals or exceeds the market price*. In Figure 5.4 only the consumers at or above point A drive away in a new Spyder. Anyone *below* point A walks; John, Marty, Bob, and Blaise want a Porsche 918 Spyder but are not willing to pay $847,975 to get one.

Now you know why we love to shop. People do not buy things that are priced above their maximum price thresholds. We only buy those things priced at or below our maximum price threshold. So we are always getting some consumer surplus and bragging about the "bargains" we got. This collective consumer surplus is depicted in Figure 5.5.

PRICE DISCRIMINATION

---

total revenue: The price of a product multiplied by the quantity sold in a given time period: $p \times q$.

Car dealers are well aware of this consumer surplus phenomenon and determined to profit from it. Consider their options. Figure 5.4 reveals that the dealer can sell four cars at the posted price of $847,975. That would generate **total revenue** (= price × quantity) of $3,391,180.

But he could do better than that if he priced each car separately rather than charging the *same* price for all four cars. Suppose he knew that Fred was willing and able to pay as much as $1 million for a Spyder. Instead of posting a uniform price of $847,975, the dealer could let Fred try to negotiate a price for himself. What is the *most* Fred would pay? $1 million. So the dealer could ask for $1.2 million and let Fred "bargain" his way down to $1 million. Fred would drive off in his Spyder, feeling smug about the "deal" he had struck. And the dealer would be smiling all the way to the bank.

If the dealer handled all the buyers in this way, he would bring in a lot more revenue from the sale of his four cars. He would sell the first car to Fred for $1 million, a car to

Michel for $950,000, a car to Hua for $900,000, and one to Carlos for $850,000. His total revenue would be $3.7 million rather than the $3,391,900 he got with uniform pricing. Pretty nice deal.

What the dealer is doing here is practicing **price discrimination:** charging individual consumers different prices for the same good. In effect, the dealer is picking off consumers from their positions on the market demand curve and charging them the maximum price each is willing to pay. If successful, the dealer will eliminate all consumer surplus and maximize his own revenue.

There is nothing illegal about this kind of price discrimination. And no one gets harmed. No one paid more for a Spyder than she or he was willing to pay. And the buyers might even feel good about their negotiating skills.

Divide and Conquer. The key to the dealer's success is the ability to negotiate each price individually. There is no transparency here. Car dealers typically conduct negotiations in small cubicles, isolated from other consumers. That way the dealer can probe to discover what maximum price each individual is willing to pay. So long as that price is above the uniform price threshold ($847,975 in this case), the dealer extracts some of that consumer surplus (and increases total revenue).

Price discrimination is rampant in the auto industry, but common in many other markets as well. Next time you are on an airplane, ask your seatmates how much they paid for their tickets. Odds are that it is not the same price you paid. The airlines use a variety of techniques to "divide and conquer" airline passengers. People who must travel on short notice and with uncertain schedules pay high "unrestricted" fares. Travelers who are further down the market demand curve are singled out with advance ticketing, nonrefundable purchases, and minimum-stay restrictions. They end up paying a lower price for the same flight. That is price discrimination.

Even colleges engage in price discrimination. Your school may have a seemingly uniform price for tuition. But schools adjust that price on an individual basis with scholarships and grants. In so doing, they hope to "sell" the school to applicants with exceptional academic or athletic potential who otherwise are not willing and able to pay the posted price.

Price discrimination is most effective when consumers don't have perfect information about market prices and there are few sellers. Price discrimination is also easier to practice in markets where individual consumers make only occasional purchases (e.g., new cars, vacations, college).

price discrimination: The sale of an individual good at different prices to different consumers.

CHOOSING AMONG PRODUCTS

Our analysis of demand thus far has focused on the decision to buy a single product at varying prices. Actual consumer behavior is multidimensional, however, and therefore more complex. When we go shopping, our concern isn't limited to how much of one good to buy. Rather, we must decide *which* of many available goods to buy at their respective prices.

The presence of so many goods complicates consumption decisions. Our basic objective remains the same, however: we want to get as much satisfaction as possible from our available income. In striving for that objective, we have to recognize that the purchase of any single good means giving up the opportunity to buy more of other goods. In other words, consuming a Porsche 918 Spyder, popcorn, or any other good entails distinct **opportunity costs.**

opportunity cost: The most desired goods or services that are forgone in order to obtain something else.

Marginal Utility vs. Price

The economic explanation for consumer choice builds on the theory of marginal utility and the law of demand. Suppose you have a $10 gift card for music and video game downloads. The first proposition of consumer choice says you'll prefer the download that gives you the most satisfaction. Hardly a revolutionary proposition.

The second postulate of consumer choice takes into account market prices. Suppose you *prefer* a video game, but music downloads are cheaper. Under these circumstances, your budget may win out over your desires. There's nothing irrational about downloading a song instead of a more desirable video game when you have only a limited amount of income to spend. On the contrary, **rational behavior requires one to compare the anticipated utility of each expenditure with its price.** The smart thing to do, then, is to choose those products that promise to provide the most pleasure for the amount of income available.

Suppose your desire for a video game is *twice* as great as your desire to hear a tune. In economic terms, this means that the marginal utility of the first video game is two times that of the first music download. Which one should you download? Before hitting buttons on your smartphone, you'd better look at relative prices. What if a game costs $3 and a song costs only $1? In this case, you must pay *three* times as much for a video game that gives only *twice* as much pleasure. This isn't a good deal. You could get more utility *per dollar* by downloading music.

The same kind of principle explains why some rich people drive a Ford rather than a shiny new Porsche 918 Spyder. The marginal utility (MU) of driving a Spyder is substantially higher than the MU of driving a Ford. A nice Spyder, however, costs about 30 times as much as a basic Ford. A rich person who drives a Ford must feel that driving a Spyder is not 30 times as satisfying as driving a Ford. For such people, a Ford yields more *marginal utility per dollar spent.*

The key to utility maximization, then, isn't simply to buy the things you like best. Instead you must compare goods on the basis of their marginal utility *and* price. **To maximize utility, the consumer should choose the good that delivers the most marginal utility per dollar.**

Utility Maximization

This basic principle of consumer choice is easily illustrated. Think about spending that $10 gift card on music or game downloads, the only available choices. Your goal, as always, is to get as much pleasure as possible from this limited income. That is, you want to maximize the *total* utility attainable from the expenditure of your income. The question is how to do it. What combination of songs and games will maximize the utility you get from $10?

We've already assumed that the marginal utility (MU) of the first game is two times higher than the MU of the first song. This is reflected in the second row of Table 5.2. The MU of the first video game has set arbitrarily at 20 utils (units of utility). We don't need to know whether 20 utils is a real thrill or just a bit of amusement. Indeed, the concept of "utils" has little meaning by itself; it's only a useful basis for comparison. In this case,

TABLE 5.2

Maximizing Utility

Q: How can you get the most satisfaction (utility) from $10 if you must choose between downloading songs at $1 apiece or video games at $3 apiece?

A: By playing two games and playing four songs. See the text for explanation.

	Amount of Utility (in Units of Utility, or Utils)					
	From Music Downloads			From Game Downloads		
Quantity Consumed	Total		Marginal	Total		Marginal
0	0		—	0		—
1	10	>	10	20	>	20
2	19	>	9	38	>	18
3	27	>	8	54	>	16
4	33	>	6	66	>	12
5	38	>	5	72	>	6
6	42	>	4	73	>	1
7	45	>	3			
8	47	>	2			
9	48	>	1			
10	48	>	0			

we want to compare the MU of the first game with the MU of the first song. Hence we set the MU of the first game at 20 utils and the MU of the first song at 10 utils. The first game download is twice as satisfying as the first music download:

$$\text{MU game} = 2 \text{ MU song}$$

The remainder of Table 5.2 indicates how marginal utility diminishes with increasing consumption of a product. Look at what happens to the sound of music. The marginal utility of the first song is 10; but the MU of the second song is only 9 utils. The third song generates even less MU (= 8). You started with your favorite song; now you're working down your hits list. By the time you get to a sixth song, music downloads aren't raising your spirits much (MU = 4). By the tenth song, you're tired of music (MU = 0).

Game downloads also conform to the law of diminishing marginal utility. You start with your favorite game (MU = 20), seeking a high score. The second game is fun, too, though not quite as much (MU = 18). As you keep playing, frustration rises and marginal utility diminishes. By the time you play a sixth game your nerves are just about shot; the sixth game gives you only 1 util of marginal utility.

With these psychological insights to guide us, we can now determine how best to spend $10. What we're looking for is the combination of songs and video games that *maximizes* the total utility attainable from an expenditure of $10. We call this combination **optimal consumption**—that is, the mix of goods that yields the most utility for the available income.

We can start looking for the optimal mix of consumer purchases by assessing the utility of spending the entire $10 on video games. At $3 per play, we could buy three games. This would give us *total* utility of 54 utils (see Table 5.2). Plus we'd have enough change to download one song (MU = 10), for a grand utility total of 64 utils.

Alternatively, you could also spend the entire gift card on music downloads. With $10 to spend, you could buy 10 songs. However, this would generate only 48 utils of total utility. Hence, if you were forced to choose between *only* downloading songs or *only* playing video games, you'd pick the games.

Fortunately, we don't have to make such extreme choices. In reality, we can buy a *combination* of songs and video games. This complicates our decision making (with more choices) but permits us to attain higher levels of total satisfaction.

To reach the peak of satisfaction, consider spending your $10 in $3 dollar increments. How should you spend the first $3? If you spend it on one game, you'll get 20 utils of satisfaction. On the other hand, $3 will buy your first three music downloads. The first song has an MU of 10 and the second song adds another 9 utils to your happiness. The third song brings in another 8 utils. Hence, by spending the $3 on songs, you reap 27 utils of total utility. This is superior to the pleasure of a first game, and it's therefore your first purchase.

Having downloaded three songs, you now can spend the second $3. How should it be spent? Your choice now is that first game or a fourth, fifth, and sixth song. That first unplayed game still promises 20 utils of real pleasure. By constrast, the MU of a fourth song is 6 utils. And the MU of a fifth song is only 5 utils. Together, then, the fourth, fifth, and sixth songs will increase your total utility by 15 utils, whereas a first game will give you 20 utils. You should spend the second $3 on a game download.

The decision on how to spend the remaining four dollars is made the same way. The final choice is to purchase either a second game (MU = 18) or the fourth, fifth, and sixth songs (MU = 15). The second game offers more marginal utility and is thus the correct decision.

After working your way through these calculations, you'll end up downloading two games and four songs. Was it worth it? Do you end up with more total utility than you could have gotten from any other combination? The answer is yes. The *total* utility of two games (38 utils) and four songs (33 utils) is 71 units of utility. This is significantly better than the alternatives of spending your $10 on songs alone (total utility = 48) or three games and a song (total utility = 64). In fact, the combination of two games and four songs is the *best* one you can find. Because this combination maximizes the total utility of your income ($10), it represents *optimal consumption*.

optimal consumption: The mix of consumer purchases that maximizes the utility attainable from available income.

Utility-Maximizing Rule

Optimal consumption refers to the mix of products that maximizes total utility for the limited amount of income you have to spend. The basic approach to utility maximization is to purchase the good next that delivers the most *marginal utility per dollar*. Marginal utility per dollar is simply the MU of the good divided by its price: MU ÷ P.

From Table 5.2 we know that a first game has an MU of 20 and a price of $3. It thus delivers a marginal utility per dollar of

$$\frac{\text{MU}_{\text{first game}}}{P_{\text{game}}} = \frac{20}{\$3} = 6.67 \text{ utils per dollar}$$

On the other hand, the first song has a marginal utility of 10 and a price of $1. It offers a marginal utility per dollar of

$$\frac{\text{MU}_{\text{first song}}}{P_{\text{song}}} = \frac{10}{\$1} = 10 \text{ utils per dollar}$$

From this perspective, the first song is a better deal than the first game and should be purchased.

Optimal consumption implies that the utility-maximizing combination of goods has been found. If this is true, you can't increase your total utility by trading one good for another. All goods included in the optimal consumption mix yield the *same* marginal utility per dollar. We know we've reached maximum utility when we've satisfied the following rule:

$$\textbf{Utility-maximizing rule: } \frac{\textbf{MU}_x}{P_x} = \frac{\textbf{MU}_y}{P_y}$$

where *x* and *y* represent any two goods included in our consumption.

Rational consumer choice depends on comparisons of marginal utilities and prices. If a dollar spent on product *X* yields more marginal utility than a dollar spent on product *Y*, we should buy product *X*. To use this principle, of course, we have to know the amounts of utility obtainable from various goods and be able to perform a little arithmetic. By doing so, however, we can get the greatest satisfaction from our limited income.

Equilibrium Outcomes

All these graphs and equations make consumer choice look dull and mechanical. Economic theory seems to suggest that consumers walk through shopping malls with marginal utility tables and handheld computers. In reality, no one does this—not even your economics instructor. Yet economic theory is pretty successful in predicting consumer decisions. Consumers don't always buy the optimal mix of goods and services with their limited income. But after some trial and error, consumers adjust their behavior. What economic theory predicts is that the final choices—the *equilibrium* outcomes—will be the predicted optimal ones.

THE ECONOMY TOMORROW

CAVEAT EMPTOR

LeBron James is paid more than $50 million a year to help convince us to drink Sprite and Powerade, eat Big Macs, chew Bubblicious gum, drive a Kia, and buy Samsung TVs. Do these sponsors know something economic theory doesn't? Economists *assume* consumers know what they want and will act rationally to get the most satisfaction they can.

The companies that sponsor basketball star LeBron James don't accept that assumption. They think your tastes will follow LeBron's lead. Your perception of the marginal utility associated with LeBron-endorsed products will increase.

Advertisers now spend more than $200 *billion* per year to change our perceptions. In the United States, this spending works out to more than $600 per consumer, one of the highest per capita advertising rates in the world. Some of this advertising (including product labeling) is intended to provide information about existing products or to bring new products to our attention. A great deal of advertising, however, is also designed to exploit our senses and lack of knowledge. Recognizing that we're guilt-ridden, insecure, and sex-hungry, advertisers promise exoneration, recognition, and love; all we have to do is buy the right products.

A favorite target of advertisers is our sense of insecurity. Thousands of products are marketed in ways that appeal to our need for identity. Thousands of brand images are designed to help the consumer answer the nagging question, Who am I? The answers, of course, vary. *Playboy* magazine says, I'm a virile man of the world; Marlboro cigarettes say, I'm a rugged individualist who enjoys "man-sized flavor." Sprite says, I'll be a winner if I drink the same soda LeBron James does. And I'll be able to jump 8 feet high if I wear Nike Zoom LeBron Soldier 10 shoes.

Are Wants Created? Advertising can't be blamed for all of our foolish consumption. Even members of the most primitive tribes, uncontaminated by the seductions of advertising, adorned themselves with rings, bracelets, and pendants. Furthermore, advertising has grown to massive proportions only in the past 50 years, but consumption spending has been increasing throughout recorded history. Finally, a lot of advertising simply fails to change buying decisions. Accordingly, it's a mistake to attribute the growth or content of consumption entirely to the persuasions of advertisers.

This isn't to say that advertising has necessarily made us happier. The objective of all advertising is to alter the choices we make. Just as product images are used to attract us to particular products, so are pictures of hungry, ill-clothed children used to persuade us to give money to charity. In the same way, public relations gimmicks are employed to sway our votes for public servants. In the case of consumer products, advertising seeks to increase tastes for particular goods and services and therewith our willingness to pay. *A successful advertising campaign is one that increases the perceived marginal utility of a product, thereby* **shifting the demand curve** *for that product to the right* (see Figure 5.6). By influencing our choices in this way, advertising will affect the consumption choices we make in the economy tomorrow. Advertising alone is unlikely to affect the total *level* of consumption, however.

Is this a shoe salesman?!
©Jamie Sabau/Getty Images

shift in demand: A change in the quantity demanded at any (every) price.

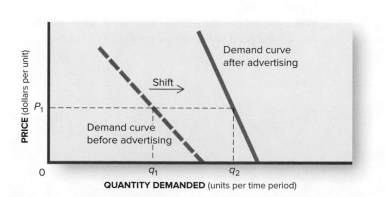

FIGURE 5.6
The Impact of Advertising on a Demand Curve

Advertising seeks to increase our taste for a particular product. If our taste (the product's perceived utility) increases, so will our willingness to buy. The resulting change in demand is reflected in a rightward shift of the demand curve, often accompanied by diminished elasticity.

SUMMARY

- Our desires for goods and services originate in the structure of personality and social dynamics and aren't explained by economic theory. Economic theory focuses on *demand*—that is, our ability and willingness to buy specific quantities of a good at various prices. **LO5-1**
- The determinants of demand include tastes (desires), income, other goods (price and availability), and expectations. **LO5-1**
- Marginal utility measures the additional satisfaction obtained from consuming one more unit of a good. The law of diminishing marginal utility says that the more of a product we consume, the smaller the increments of pleasure we tend to derive from additional units of it. This is a basis for the law of demand. **LO5-1**
- The determinants of demand establish the maximum price a consumer will pay for a good. That maximum price determines where an individual is positioned on the market demand curve. **LO5-1**
- A person will buy a product only if its price is at or below the maximum price that person is willing and able to pay. The difference between that maximum price threshold and the price paid is called "consumer surplus." **LO5-2**
- Producers can extract some or all consumer surplus by charging different prices to individuals, based on their willingness to pay—a practice called "price discrimination." **LO5-3**
- In choosing among alternative goods and services, a consumer compares the prices and anticipated satisfactions that they offer. To maximize utility with one's available income—to achieve an optimal mix of goods and services—one has to get the most utility for every dollar spent. To do so, one must choose those goods promising the most marginal utility per dollar. **LO5-4**
- Advertising seeks to change consumer tastes and thus the willingness to buy. If tastes do change, the demand curve for that product will shift. **LO5-1**

Key Terms

demand	*ceteris paribus*	total revenue
utility	law of demand	price discrimination
total utility	demand curve	opportunity cost
marginal utility	market demand	optimal consumption
law of diminishing marginal utility	consumer surplus	shift in demand

Questions for Discussion

1. What does the demand for enrollments in your college look like? What is on the axes? How do tuition, enrollment, and total revenue interact? **LO5-1**
2. If the marginal utility of pizza never diminished, how many pizzas would you eat? **LO5-1**
3. How do total and marginal utility change as you spend more time tweeting your friends? **LO5-1**
4. Can you think of any product that violates the law of diminishing marginal utility? **LO5-1**
5. How did Apple decide what price to charge for its 10-year anniversary iPhone in 2017? Could it have charged a higher price? Should it have? **LO5-1**
6. When the producer price discriminates in Figure 5.4, what happens to unit sales? Total revenue? Total profit? **LO5-3**
7. Under what circumstances could a producer extract *the entire* consumer surplus in Figure 5.5? **LO5-2**
8. How does a car dealer determine where a buyer is on the market demand curve? **LO5-3**
9. Why do airlines charge different fares for the same flight? **LO5-3**
10. When you eat out and have $25 to spend, what information do you need to maximize your utility? **LO5-4**

APPENDIX

INDIFFERENCE CURVES

A consumer's demand for any specific product is an expression of many forces. As we've observed, the actual quantity of a product demanded by a consumer varies inversely with its price. The price–quantity relationship is determined by

- *Tastes* (desire for this and other goods).
- *Income* (of the consumer).
- *Expectations* (for income, prices, tastes).
- *Other goods* (their availability and price).

Economic theory attempts to show how each of these forces affects consumer demand. Thus far, we've used two-dimensional demand curves to illustrate the basic principles of demand. We saw that, in general, a change in the price of a good causes a movement along the demand curve, whereas a change in tastes, income, expectations, or other goods shifts the entire demand curve to a new position.

We haven't looked closely at the origins of demand curves, however. We assumed that a demand curve could be developed from observations of consumer behavior, such as the number of boxes of popcorn that were purchased at various prices (Figure 5.3).

It's possible, however, to derive a demand curve without actually observing consumer behavior. In theory we can identify consumer *preferences* (tastes), then use those preferences to construct a demand curve. In this case, the demand curve is developed explicitly from known preferences rather than on the basis of market observations. The end result—the demand curve—is the same, at least so long as consumers' behavior in product markets is consistent with their preferences.

Indifference curves are a mechanism for illustrating consumer tastes. We examine their construction and use in this appendix. Indifference curves provide an explicit basis for constructing a demand curve. In addition, they are another way of viewing how consumption is affected by price, tastes, and income. Indifference curves are also a useful tool for explicitly illustrating consumer *choice*—that is, the decision to purchase one good rather than another.

Constructing an Indifference Curve

Suppose you're in an arcade and want to buy some Cokes and play video games but don't have enough money to buy enough of each. The income constraint compels you to make hard decisions. You have to consider the **marginal utility** each additional Coke or video game will provide, compare their respective prices, then make a selection. With careful introspection and good arithmetic you could select the optimal mix of Cokes and video games—that is, the combination that yields the most satisfaction (utility) for the income available. This process of identifying your **optimal consumption** was illustrated in Table 5.2 with downloads of music and video games.

Computing your optimal consumption is difficult because you must assess the marginal utility of each prospective purchase. In Table 5.2 we assumed that the marginal utility of the first music download was 10 utils, while the first game download had a marginal utility of 20. Then we had to specify the marginal utility of every additional music and game download. Can we really be so specific about our tastes?

Indifference curves require a bit less arithmetic. *Instead of trying to measure the marginal utility of each prospective purchase, we now look for combinations of goods that yield equal satisfaction.* In the arcade, this entails different combinations of Cokes and games. All we need is to determine that one particular combination of Cokes and video games is as satisfying as another. We don't have to say how many "units of pleasure" both combinations provide—it's sufficient that they're both equally satisfying.

marginal utility: The change in total utility obtained by consuming one additional (marginal) unit of a good or service.

optimal consumption: The mix of consumer purchases that maximizes the utility attainable from available income.

Combination	Cokes	Video Games
A	1	8
B	2	5
C	3	4

TABLE 5A.1

Equally Satisfying Combinations

Different combinations of two goods may be equally satisfying. In this case we assume that the combinations A, B, and C all yield equal total utility. Hence the consumer will be indifferent about which of the three combinations he or she receives.

The initial combination of 1 Coke and 8 video games is designated as combination *A* in Table 5A.1. This combination of goods yields a certain, but unspecified, level of total utility. What we want to do now is to find another combination of Cokes and games that's just as satisfying as combination *A*. Finding other combinations of equal satisfaction isn't easy, but it's at least possible. After a lot of soul searching, we decide that 2 Cokes and 5 video games would be just as satisfying as 1 Coke and 8 games.[1] This combination is designated as *B* in Table 5A.1.

Table 5A.1 also depicts a third combination of Cokes and video games that's as satisfying as the first. Combination *C* includes 3 Cokes and 4 games, a mix of consumption assumed to yield the same total utility as 1 Coke and 8 games (combination *A*).

Notice that we haven't said anything about how much pleasure combinations *A*, *B*, and *C* provide. We're simply asserting that these three combinations are *equally* satisfying.

Figure 5A.1 illustrates the information about tastes that we've assembled. Points *A*, *B*, and *C* represent the three equally satisfying combinations of Cokes and video games we've identified. By connecting these points we create an **indifference curve.** The indifference curve illustrates all combinations of two goods that are equally satisfying. A consumer would be just as happy with any combination represented on the curve, so a choice among them would be a matter of indifference.

indifference curve: A curve depicting alternative combinations of goods that yield equal satisfaction.

An Indifference Map. Not all combinations of Cokes and video games are as satisfying as combination *A*, of course. Surely 2 Cokes and 8 games would be preferred to only 1 Coke and 8 games. Indeed, ***any combination that provided more of one good and no less of the***

FIGURE 5A.1

An Indifference Curve

An indifference curve illustrates the various combinations of two goods that would provide equal satisfaction. The consumer is assumed to be indifferent to a choice between combinations *A*, *B*, and *C* (and all other points on the curve) because they all yield the same total utility.

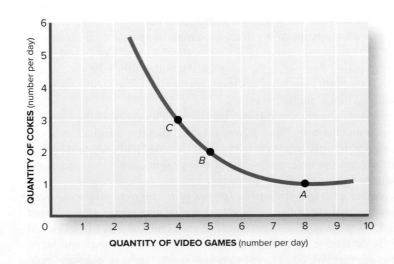

[1]The utility computations used here aren't based on Table 5.2; a different set of tastes is assumed

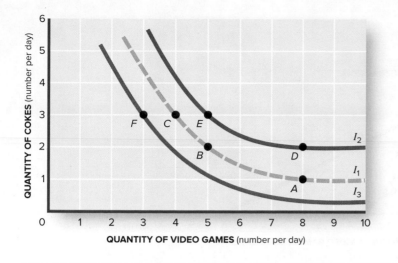

FIGURE 5A.2

An Indifference Map

All combinations of goods depicted on any given indifference curve (e.g., I_1) are equally satisfying. Other combinations are more or less satisfying, however, and thus lie on higher (I_2) or lower (I_3) indifference curves. An indifference map shows all possible levels of total utility (e.g., $I_1, I_2, I_3, \ldots, I_n$) and their respective consumption combinations.

other would be preferred. Point D in Figure 5A.2 illustrates just one such combination. Combination D must yield more total utility than combination A because it includes one more Coke and no fewer games. A consumer wouldn't be indifferent to a choice between A and D; on the contrary, combination D would be preferred.

Combination D is also preferred to combinations B and C. How do we know? Recall that combinations A, B, and C are all equally satisfying. Hence, if combination D is better than A, it must also be better than B and C. Given a choice, a consumer would select combination D (2 Cokes, 8 games) in preference to *any* combination depicted on indifference curve I_1.

There are also combinations that are as satisfying as D, of course. These possibilities are illustrated on indifference curve I_2. All these combinations are equally satisfying and must therefore be preferred to any points on indifference curve I_1. In general, *the farther the indifference curve is from the origin, the more total utility it yields.*

The curve I_3 illustrates various combinations that are less satisfying. Combination F, for example, includes 3 Cokes and 3 games. This is 1 game less than the number available in combination C. Therefore, F yields less total utility than C and isn't preferred: a consumer would rather have combination C than F. By the same logic we just used, all points on indifference curve I_3 are less satisfying than combinations on curve I_2 or I_1.

Curves 1, 2, and 3 in Figure 5A.2 are the beginnings of an **indifference map.** An indifference map depicts all the combinations of goods that would yield various levels of satisfaction. A single indifference curve, in contrast, illustrates all combinations that provide a single (equal) level of total utility.

indifference map: The set of indifference curves that depicts all possible levels of utility attainable from various combinations of goods.

Utility Maximization

We assume that all consumers strive to maximize their utility. They want as much satisfaction as they can get. In the terminology of indifference curves, this means getting to the indifference curve that's farthest from the origin. The farther one is from the origin, the greater the total utility.

Although the goal of consumers is evident, the means of achieving it isn't so clear. Higher indifference curves aren't only more satisfying, they're also more expensive. We're confronted again with the basic conflict between preferences and prices. With a limited amount of income to spend, we can't attain infinite satisfaction (the farthest indifference curve). We have to settle for less (an indifference curve closer to the origin). The question is, How do we maximize the utility attainable with our limited income?

The Budget Constraint. For starters, we have to determine how much we have to spend. Suppose for the moment that we have only $2 to spend in the arcade and that Cokes and video games are still the only objects of our consumption desires. The price of a Coke is

FIGURE 5A.3

The Budget Constraint

Consumption possibilities are limited by available income. The budget constraint illustrates this limitation. The end points of the budget constraint are equal to income divided by the price of each good. All points on the budget constraint represent affordable combinations of goods.

budget constraint: A line depicting all combinations of goods that are affordable with a given income and given prices.

50 cents; the price of a game is 25 cents. Accordingly, the maximum number of Cokes we could buy is 4 if we didn't play any video games. On the other hand, we could play as many as 8 games if we were to forsake Coke.

Figure 5A.3 depicts the limitations placed on our consumption possibilities by a finite income. The **budget constraint** illustrates all combinations of goods affordable with a given income. In this case, the outermost budget line illustrates the combinations of Cokes and video games that can be purchased with $2.

The budget line is easily drawn. The end points of the budget constraint are found by dividing one's income by the price of the good on the corresponding axis. Thus the outermost curve begins at 4 Cokes ($2 ÷ 50 cents) and ends at 8 games ($2 ÷ 25 cents). All the other points on the budget constraint represent other combinations of Cokes and video games that could be purchased with $2.

A smaller income is also illustrated in Figure 5A.3. If we had only $1 to spend, we could afford fewer Cokes and fewer games. Hence a smaller income is represented by a budget constraint that lies closer to the origin.

Optimal Consumption. With a budget constraint looming before us, the limitation on utility maximization is evident. We want to reach the highest indifference curve possible. Our limited income, however, restricts our grasp. We can go only as far as our budget constraint allows. In this context, *the objective is to reach the highest indifference curve that is compatible with our budget constraint.*

Figure 5A.4 illustrates the process of achieving optimal consumption. We start with an indifference map depicting all utility levels and product combinations. Then we impose a budget line that reflects our income. In this case, we continue to assume that Coke costs 50 cents, video games cost 25 cents, and we have $2 to spend. Hence *we can afford only those consumption combinations that are on or inside the budget line.*

Which particular combination of Cokes and video games maximizes the utility of our $2? It must be 2 Cokes and 4 video games, as reflected in point M. Notice that point M isn't only on the budget line but also touches indifference curve I_c. No other point on the budget line touches I_c or any higher indifference curve. Accordingly, I_c represents the most utility we can get for $2 and is attainable only if we consume 2 Cokes and 4 video games. Any other affordable combination yields less total utility—that is, falls on a lower indifference curve. Point G, for example, which offers 3 Cokes and 2 video games for $2, lies on the indifference curve I_b. Because I_b lies closer to the origin than I_c, point G must be less satisfying than point M. We conclude, then, that *the point of tangency between the budget constraint and an indifference curve represents optimal consumption.* It's the combination we should buy if we want to maximize the utility of our limited income.

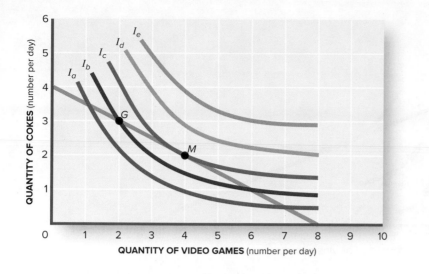

FIGURE 5A.4
Optimal Consumption

The optimal consumption combination—the one that maximizes the utility of spendable income—lies at the point where the budget line is tangent to (just touches) an indifference curve. In this case, point *M* represents the optimal mix of Cokes and video games because no other affordable combination lies on a higher indifference curve than I_c.

Marginal Utility and Price: A Digression. We earlier illustrated the utility-maximizing rule, which required a comparison of the ratios of marginal utilities to prices. Specifically, optimal consumption was represented as that combination of Cokes and video games that yielded

$$\frac{MU\ Coke}{P\ Coke} = \frac{MU\ games}{P\ games}$$

Does point *M* in Figure 5A.4 conform to this rule?

To answer this question, first rearrange the preceding equation as follows:

$$\frac{MU\ Coke}{MU\ games} = \frac{P\ Coke}{P\ games}$$

In this form, the equation says that the relative marginal utilities of Cokes and video games should equal their relative prices when consumption is optimal. In other words, if a Coke costs twice as much as a video game, then it must yield twice as much marginal utility if the consumer is to be in an optimal state. Otherwise, some substitution of Cokes for video games, or vice versa, would be desirable.

With this foundation, we can show that point *M* conforms to our earlier rule. Consider first the slope of the budget constraint, which is determined by the relative prices of Cokes and video games. In fact, *the (absolute) slope of the budget constraint equals the relative price of the two goods.* In Figure 5A.4 the slope equals the price of video games divided by the price of Cokes (25 cents ÷ 50 cents = ½). It tells us the rate at which video games can be exchanged for Cokes in the market. In this case, one video game is "worth" half a Coke.

The relative marginal utilities of the two goods are reflected in the slope of the indifference curve. Recall that the curve tells at what rate a consumer is willing to substitute one good for another, with no change in total utility. In fact, the slope of the indifference curve is called the **marginal rate of substitution.** It's equal to the relative marginal utilities of the two goods. Presumably one would be indifferent to a choice between 2 Cokes + 5 games and 3 Cokes + 4 games—as suggested in Table 5A.1—only if the third Coke were as satisfying as the fifth video game.

At the point of optimal consumption (*M*) in Figure 5A.4 the budget constraint is tangent to the indifference curve I_c, which means that the two curves must have the same slope at that point. In other words,

$$\frac{P\ games}{P\ Coke} = \frac{MU\ games}{MU\ Coke}$$

marginal rate of substitution: The rate at which a consumer is willing to exchange one good for another; the relative marginal utilities of two goods.

FIGURE 5A.5

Changing Prices

When the price of a good changes, the budget constraint shifts, and a new consumption combination must be sought. In this case, the price of video games is changing. When the price of games increases from 25 cents to 50 cents, the budget constraint shifts inward and optimal consumption moves from point *M* to point *N*.

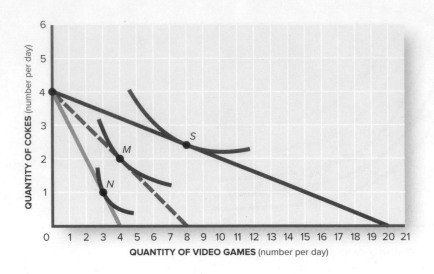

or alternatively,

$$\frac{\text{Rate of}}{\text{market exchange}} = \frac{\text{Marginal rate}}{\text{of substitution}}$$

Both indifference curves and marginal utility comparisons lead us to the same optimal mix of consumption.

Deriving the Demand Curve

We noted at the beginning of this appendix that indifference curves not only give us an alternative path to optimal consumption but also can be used to derive a demand curve. To do this, we need to consider how the optimal consumption combination changes when the price of one good is altered. We can see what happens in Figure 5A.5.

Figure 5A.5 starts with the optimal consumption attained at point *M*, with income of $2 and prices of 50 cents for a Coke and 25 cents for a video game. Now we're going to change the price of video games and observe how consumption changes.

Suppose that the price of a video game doubles, from 25 cents to 50 cents. This change will shift the budget constraint inward: our income of $2 now buys a maximum of 4 games rather than 8. Hence the lower end point of the budget constraint moves from 8 games to 4 games. ***Whenever the price of a good changes, the budget constraint shifts.***

Only one end of the budget constraint is changed in Figure 5A.5. The budget line still begins at 4 Cokes because the price of Coke is unchanged. If only one price is changed, then only one end of the budget constraint is shifted.

Because the budget constraint has shifted inward, the combination *M* is no longer attainable. Two Cokes (at 50 cents each) and 4 games (at 50 cents each) now cost more than $2. We're now forced to accept a lower level of total utility. According to Figure 5A.5, optimal consumption is now located at point *N*. This is the point of tangency between the new budget constraint and a lower indifference curve. At point *N* we consume 1 Coke and 3 video games.

Consider what has happened here. The price of video games has increased (from 25 cents to 50 cents), and the quantity of games demanded has decreased. This is the kind of relationship that demand curves describe. **Demand curves** indicate how the quantity demanded of a good changes in response to a change in its price, given a fixed income and all other things held constant. Not only does Figure 5A.5 provide the same information, it also conforms to the **law of demand:** as the price of games increases, the quantity demanded falls.

Suppose the price of video games were to fall rather than increase. Specifically, assume that the price of a game fell to 10 cents. This price reduction would shift the budget constraint farther out on the horizontal axis because as many as 20 games could then be

demand curve: A curve describing the quantities of a good a consumer is willing and able to buy at alternative prices in a given time period, *ceteris paribus*.

law of demand: The quantity of a good demanded in a given time period increases as its price falls, *ceteris paribus*.

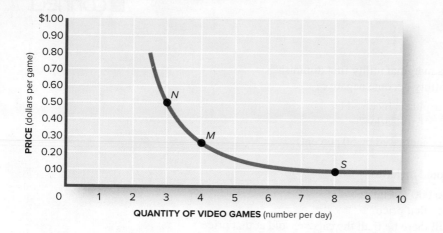

The Demand for Video Games

Figure 5A.5 shows how optimal consumption is altered when the price of video games changes. From that figure we can determine the quantity of video games demanded at alternative prices, *ceteris paribus.* That information is summarized here in the demand schedule (below) and the demand curve (above).

Point	Price (per Game)	Quantity Demanded (Games per Day)
N	50 cents	3
M	25	4
S	10	8

purchased with $2. As a result of the price reduction, we can now buy more goods and thus attain a higher level of satisfaction.

Point *S* in Figure 5A.5 indicates the optimal combination of Cokes and video games at the new video game price. At these prices, we consume 8 video games and 2.4 Cokes (we may have to share with a friend). The law of demand is again evident: when the price of video games declines, the quantity demanded increases.

The Demand Schedule and Curve. Figure 5A.6 summarizes the information we've acquired about the demand for video games. The demand schedule depicts the price–quantity relationships prevailing at optimal consumption points *N, M,* and *S* (from Figure 5A.5). The demand curve generalizes these observations to encompass other prices. What we end up with is a demand curve explicitly derived from our (assumed) knowledge of consumer tastes.

Key Terms

marginal utility
optimal consumption
indifference curve

indifference map
budget constraint
marginal rate of substitution

demand curve
law of demand

LO5-1   1. According to Table 5.1,
  (*a*) With which box of popcorn does marginal utility first diminish?
  (*b*) With which box does marginal utility become negative?

LO5-2   2. In Figure 5.4, how much consumer surplus is received by
  (*a*) Fred?   (*b*) Hua?   (*c*) Carlos?

LO5-2   3. In Figure 5.4, if Bob's maximum price increased by 50 percent,
  (*a*) Would he buy a Spyder?
  (*b*) How much consumer surplus would he have?

LO5-2   4. If the price of a Spyder drops to $700,000 in Figure 5.4,
  (*a*) How many Spyders can be sold at that price?
  (*b*) How much consumer surplus will there be if all the cars are sold at that price?
  (*c*) How much revenue will the car dealer get if he sells all the cars at
    (i)   the same price ($700,000)?
    (ii) the maximum price each buyer is willing to pay?

LO5-3   5. The following data reveal how much each consumer is willing to pay for an Alaskan cruise:

Amy	$ 900	Ed	$2,000
Bob	$1,100	Gigi	$1,300
Carol	$1,500	Hugo	$1,800
Eduardo	$ 400	Isabelle	$1,500

  (*a*) Draw the market demand for these eight consumers.
  (*b*) If the cruise costs $1,000, how many passengers will there be?
  (*c*) If the cruise costs $1,000, how much total revenue will be collected?
  (*d*) If the cruise costs $1,000, how much consumer surplus will those passengers enjoy?

LO5-4   6. Suppose movie downloads cost $2 apiece and game downloads cost $3. If the marginal utility of movie downloads at the optimal mix of consumption is 10 utils, what is the marginal utility of a game download?

LO5-1   7. Suppose the graph below depicts the demand for football tickets at Grand University.
  (*a*) If current demand is represented as Demand 2, what is total revenue at the price of $24?
  (*b*) If the price drops to $12, how many tickets would consumers purchase?
  (*c*) What is total revenue at that point?
  (*d*) If the team has a losing streak and the price is still $24, at what point do we end up?
  (*e*) What is total revenue at that point?

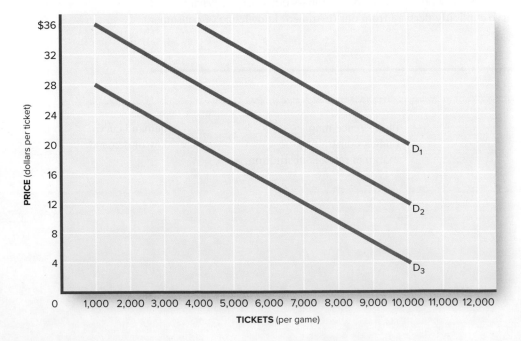

LO5-4 8. Suppose the following table reflects the total satisfaction derived from consumption of pizza slices and Pepsis. Assume that pizza costs $1 per slice and a large Pepsi costs $2. With $20 to spend, what consumption mix will maximize satisfaction?

Quantity consumed	1	2	3	4	5	6	7	8	9	10	11	12	13	14
Total units of pleasure from pizza slices	47	92	132	166	196	224	251	271	288	303	313	315	312	300
Total units of pleasure from Pepsis	111	200	272	336	386	426	452	456	444	408	340	217	92	−17

LO5-4 9. A consumer downloads 4 movies and 3 apps per week. Suppose the price is $5 per movie and $3 per app, and the marginal utility is 12 for a movie and 10 for an app.
   (*a*) Calculate marginal utility per dollar.
   (*b*) Is this optimal consumption?
   (*c*) If not, how should they change their consumption to maximize?

LO5-1 10. The Economy Tomorrow: Use the following data to illustrate the relevant demand curve:

Price	$ 10	9	8	7	6	5	4	3	2	1
Quantity	2	4	6	8	10	12	14	16	18	20

   (*a*) If the price increases from $4 to $8, by how much does the quantity demanded decline?
   (*b*) If a successful advertising campaign increases the quantity demanded at every price by 4 units,
   　　(*i*) Draw the new demand curve D_2.
   　　(*ii*) How many units are now purchased at $8?

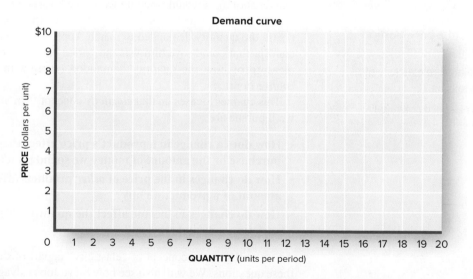

Demand curve

©Michele Constantini/PhotoAlto/Corbis RF

CHAPTER 6

Elasticity

S teve Jobs made a pricing mistake when he launched the 8 GB iPhone in June 2007. He knew all about consumer demand and its many determinants. And he could draw a downward-sloping demand curve just as well as any college economics major (even though he dropped out of Reed College after just one semester). But he overestimated the dimensions of market demand. The demand curve he drew projected that the quantity of iPhones demanded at the price of $599 would be far greater than it turned out to be. This mistake created an instant dilemma. If he kept the price of $599, iPhone sales would come in below publicized projections, and the phone would be deemed a failure. Apple's image of consistent success would be tarnished. Software writers might not develop the library of iPhone apps that would make the iPhone irresistible. So Jobs knew what he had to do: reduce the iPhone's price—fast!

But he couldn't afford to make another mistake. If he reduced the price too little, iPhone sales would still fall short of projections. If he reduced the price too much, sales would soar past production rates and market shortages would frustrate would-be buyers. On the second go-round, Steve Jobs had to pick the right price—the one that would increase the quantity demanded to match Apple's sales projections. The concept that could save him was the "price elasticity of demand"—a measure of how the quantity demanded *changes* in response to a *change* in price.

This chapter focuses on that *elasticity* concept. Among the questions we'll pursue are

- **How does a change in a product's price affect the quantity we purchase or the amount of money we spend on it?**
- **How do changes in the price of *other* products affect the amount of a product we buy?**
- **How do changes in income affect the quantity demanded of various goods and services?**

As we will see, the concept of "elasticity" is part of the answer to all these questions. We w ill also see how Steve Jobs salvaged the original iPhone with the same concept and how Apple used the concept again in 2017 to price the iPhone 8.

LEARNING OBJECTIVES

After reading this chapter, you should know

LO6-1 How to compute price elasticity of demand.

LO6-2 The relationships between price changes, price elasticity, quantity demanded, and total revenue.

LO6-3 What the cross-price elasticity of demand measures.

LO6-4 What the income elasticity of demand tells us.

LO6-5 What the elasticity of supply measures.

PRICE ELASTICITY

What Steve Jobs wanted to know in September 2007 was how much phone sales would *increase* if he *reduced* its price. The same question haunts movie theater owners. They make a big chunk of profit from the sale of popcorn, candy, and soda. People are always complaining about how expensive those snacks are. But will they buy more if prices are reduced? A *lot* more, or just a *little* more?

Like Apple, theater owners know all about the **law of demand** and the downward-sloping **demand curve.** But that law isn't greatly informative; it tells them only that the quantity demanded will increase when the price is reduced. That begs the critical question of *how much*. What the theater owner wants to know is *by how much* the quantity demanded will increase if the price is reduced. Steve Jobs wanted to know the same thing about the demand for iPhones: how many *more* iPhones would be purchased if he reduced its price?

The central question in all these decisions is the response of quantity demanded to a change in price. ***The response of consumers to a change in price is measured by the price elasticity of demand.*** Specifically, the **price elasticity of demand** refers to the *percentage* change in quantity demanded divided by the *percentage* change in price:

$$\text{Price elasticity} \atop (E) = \frac{\text{\% change in quantity demanded}}{\text{\% change in price}}$$

What would the value of price elasticity be if air travel didn't change at all when airfares were cut by 5 percent? In that case the price elasticity of demand would be

$$E = \frac{\text{\% change in quantity demanded}}{\text{\% change in price}}$$

$$= \frac{0}{5} = 0$$

But is this realistic? According to the law of demand, the quantity demanded goes up when price goes down. So we'd expect *somebody* to buy more airline tickets if fares fell by 5 percent. In a large market like air travel, we don't expect *everybody* to jump on a plane when airfares are reduced. But if *some* consumers fly more, the percentage change in quantity demanded will be larger than zero. Indeed, ***the law of demand implies that the price elasticity of demand will always be greater than zero.***

Technically, the price elasticity of demand (*E*) is a negative number since quantity demanded and price always move in opposite directions (law of demand). For simplicity, however, *E* is typically expressed in absolute terms (without the minus sign). ***The key question, then, is how much greater than zero E actually is.***

Computing Price Elasticity

To get a feel for the dimensions of elasticity, let's return to the popcorn counter at the movies that we first encountered in Chapter 5. We observed there that at a price of 45 cents an ounce the average moviegoer demands 2 ounces of popcorn per show. This is illustrated again in Figure 6.1 at point *B*. At the lower price of 40 cents per ounce (point *C*), the quantity demanded jumps to 4 ounces per show.

Percentage Change in *q*. We can summarize this response with the price elasticity of demand. To do so, we have to calculate the *percentage* changes in quantity and price. Consider the percentage change in quantity first. In this case, the change in quantity demanded is 4 ounces − 2 ounces = 2 ounces. The *percentage* change in quantity is therefore

$$\text{\% change in quantity} = \frac{2}{q}$$

law of demand: The quantity of a good demanded in a given time period increases as its price falls, *ceteris paribus.*

demand curve: A curve describing the quantities of a good a consumer is willing and able to buy at alternative prices in a given time period, *ceteris paribus.*

price elasticity of demand: The percentage change in quantity demanded divided by the percentage change in price.

How do prices affect popcorn sales?

©D. Hurst/Alamy Stock Photo RF

FIGURE 6.1

Demand and Elasticity

We know from the Law of Demand that the quantity demanded increases when price is reduced. This demand curve (identical to Figure 5.3) informs us that when the price of popcorn falls from 45 cents per ounce to 25 cents, the quantity demanded increases from 2 (point *B*) to 12 ounces per show (point *F*).

What the price elasticity of demand tells us is how much, *in percentage terms*, the quantity demanded changes in response to various price changes.

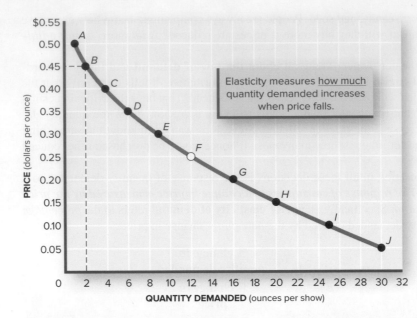

Elasticity measures how much quantity demanded increases when price falls.

	Price (per Ounce)	Quantity Demanded (Ounces per Show)
A	$0.50	1
B	0.45	2
C	0.40	4
D	0.35	6
E	0.30	9
F	0.25	12
G	0.20	16
H	0.15	20
I	0.10	25
J	0.05	30

The computational problem is to transform the denominator q into a number. Should we use the quantity of popcorn purchased *before* the price reduction—that is, $q_1 = 2$? Or should we use the quantity purchased *after* the price reduction—that is, $q_2 = 4$? The choice of denominator will have a big impact on the computed percentage change. To ensure consistency, economists prefer to use the *average* quantity in the denominator:[1]

$$\% \text{ change in quantity demanded} = \frac{\text{Change in quantity}}{\text{Average quantity}}$$

Our first task is therefore to compute the **average** quantity: the average of the first (pre–price change) and second (post–price change) quantities. The formula for this calculation is

$$\text{Average quantity} = \frac{q_1 + q_2}{2} = \frac{2 + 4}{2} = 3 \text{ ounces}$$

(3 is the average value of 2 and 4).

---

[1]This procedure is referred to as the *arc* (midpoint) elasticity of demand. If a single quantity (price) is used in the denominator, we refer to the *point* elasticity of demand.

We can now complete the calculation of the percentage change in quantity demanded. It is

$$\text{% change in quantity demanded} = \frac{\text{Change in quantity}}{\text{Average quantity}} = \frac{q_2 - q_1}{\frac{q_1 + q_2}{2}} = \frac{2}{3} = 0.667$$

Popcorn sales increased by an average of 67 percent when the price of popcorn was reduced from 45 cents to 40 cents per ounce.

Percentage Change in p. The computation of the percentage change in price is similar. We first note that the price of popcorn fell by 5 cents (40¢ − 45¢) when we move from point *B* to point *C* on the demand curve (Figure 6.1). We then compute the *average* price of popcorn in this range of the demand curve as

$$\text{Average price of popcorn} = \frac{p_1 + p_2}{2} = \frac{45¢ + 40¢}{2} = 42.5 \text{ cents}$$

This *average* is the denominator we use in calculating the percentage price change. Using these numbers, we see that the absolute value of the percentage change is

$$\text{% change in price} = \frac{\text{Change in price}}{\text{Average price}} = \frac{p_2 - p_1}{\frac{p_1 + p_2}{2}} = \frac{5}{42.5} = 0.118$$

The price of popcorn fell by 11.8 percent.

These calculations are a bit cumbersome, but they give us all the information required to compute the price elasticity of demand. In this case,

$$E = \frac{\text{% change in quantity demanded}}{\text{% change in price}} = \frac{0.667}{0.118} = 5.65$$

What we get from all these calculations is a very useful number. It says that the consumer response to a price reduction will be extremely large. Specifically, the quantity of popcorn consumed will increase 5.65 times as fast as price falls. A 1 percent reduction in price brings about a 5.65 percent increase in purchases. The theater manager can therefore boost popcorn sales greatly by lowering price a little. Steve Jobs would have been thrilled if the demand for the first iPhones had been that elastic.

Elastic vs. Inelastic Demand. We characterize the demand for various goods in one of three ways: *elastic, inelastic,* or *unitary elastic:*

- *If E is larger than 1, demand is* **elastic.** Consumer response is large relative to the change in price. This is clearly the case in the popcorn example above (*E* = 5.65).
- *If E is less than 1, demand is* **inelastic.** If demand is inelastic (*E* < 1), consumers aren't very responsive to price changes.
- *If E is equal to 1, demand is* **unitary** *elastic.* In this case, the percentage change in quantity demanded is exactly equal to the percentage change in price.

Consider the case of smoking. Many smokers claim they'd "pay anything" for a cigarette after they've run out. But would they? Would they continue to smoke just as many cigarettes if prices doubled or tripled? If so, the demand curve would be vertical (as in Figure 6.2b) rather than downward-sloping. Research suggests this is not the case: higher cigarette prices *do* curb smoking. There is at least *some* elasticity in the demand for cigarettes. But the elasticity of demand is low; Table 6.1 indicates that the price elasticity of cigarette demand is only 0.4. Since 0.4 is less than 1.0, we say that cigarette demand is inelastic. But that doesn't mean smokers are completely unresponsive to cigarette prices. If the price goes up, they will buy fewer cigarettes, but not a *lot* fewer.

FIGURE 6.2

Extremes of Elasticity

If demand were perfectly elastic ($E = \infty$), the demand curve would be *horizontal*. In that case, any increase in price (e.g., p_1 to p_2) would cause quantity demanded to fall to zero.

A *vertical* demand curve implies that an increase in price won't affect the quantity demanded. In this situation of perfectly *in*elastic ($E = 0$) demand, consumers are willing to pay *any* price to get the quantity q_1.

In reality, elasticities of demand for goods and services lie between these two extremes (obeying the law of demand).

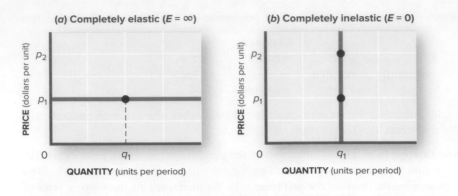

(a) Completely elastic ($E = \infty$)   *(b) Completely inelastic ($E = 0$)*

Although the average adult smoker is not very responsive to changes in cigarette prices, teen smokers apparently are. Research studies confirm that teen smoking drops by almost 7 percent when cigarette prices increase by 10 percent. Thus the price elasticity of *teen* demand for smoking is

$$E = \frac{\text{Percentage drop in quantity demanded}}{\text{Percentage increase in price}} = \frac{7\%}{10\%} = 0.7$$

Hence higher cigarette prices can be an effective policy tool for curbing teen smoking. The *tripling* of the federal excise tax on cigarettes in 2009 (from 39 cents to $1.01 per pack) raised the price of cigarettes by 13 percent and deterred 250,000 teens from smoking.

According to Table 6.1, the demand for airline travel is much more price-elastic than the demand for cigarettes. Whenever a fare cut is announced, the airlines get swamped with telephone and internet inquiries. If fares are discounted by 25 percent, the number of passengers may increase by as much as 60 percent. As Table 6.1 shows, the elasticity of airline demand is 2.4, meaning that the percentage change in quantity demanded (60 percent) will be 2.4 times larger than the price cut (25 percent).

TABLE 6.1

Elasticity Estimates

Price elasticities vary greatly. When the price of gasoline increases, consumers reduce their consumption only slightly ($E = 0.2$). When the price of fish increases, however, consumers cut back their consumption substantially ($E = 2.2$). These differences reflect the availability of immediate substitutes, the prices of the goods, and the amount of time available for changing behavior.

Product	Price Elasticity
Relatively elastic ($E > 1$)	
Airline travel, long run	2.4
Restaurant meals	2.3
Fresh fish	2.2
New cars, short run	1.2–1.5
Unitary elastic ($E = 1$)	
Private education	1.1
Radios and televisions	1.2
Shoes	0.9
Movies	0.9
Relatively inelastic ($E < 1$)	
Milk	0.6
Cigarettes	0.4
Coffee	0.3
Eggs	0.3
Gasoline, short run	0.2
Electricity (in homes)	0.1

Sources: Houthakker, Hendrick S. and Lester D. Taylor, *Consumer Demand in the United States, 1929–1970.* Cambridge: Harvard University Press, 1966; Bell, F. W., "The Pope and Price of Fish," *American Economic Review,* December 1968; Scarf, Herbert and John Shoven, *Applied General Equilibrium Analysis.* New York: Cambridge University Press, 1984; and Ward, Michael, "Product Substitutability and Competition in Long-Distance Telecommunications," *Economic Inquiry,* October 1999.

Steve Jobs was pleased to discover that the demand for iPhones was even more elastic than that. Two months after launching the 8 GB iPhone in 2007, he reduced its price from $599 to $399. Unit sales not only increased, they soared, as In the News "After iPhone Price Cut, Sales Are Up by 200 Percent" reports. Demand for the iPhone was very elastic.

©McGraw-Hill Education

IN THE NEWS

AFTER IPHONE PRICE CUT, SALES ARE UP BY 200 PERCENT

Piper Gene Munster, the person responsible for a survey dedicated to Apple in which he "found" out an estimated number of iPhones that were sold, has come up with yet another interesting theory.

According to Munster and the past-week Apple announcement about 1 million iPhones sold, the calculations take to the conclusion that after the price cut, the sales increased up to 200 percent. . . .

By Munster's reckoning, Apple and AT&T were selling an average of 9,000 iPhones a day before the price reduction, which would have put their quarterly sales at 594,000 as of September 5.

By the end of the quarter, he believes Apple will have sold a total of 1.28 million iPhones.

Source: Mobilewhack.com, September 11, 2007.

ANALYSIS: If demand is elastic, unit sales increase by a larger percentage than price declines. The demand for iPhones was highly elastic.

Determinants of Elasticity

Why are consumers so price-sensitive ($E > 1$) with some goods and not ($E < 1$) with others? To answer that, we must go back to the demand curve itself. The elasticity of demand is computed between points on a given demand curve. Hence *the price elasticity of demand is influenced by all the determinants of demand.* Four factors are particularly worth noting.

Necessities vs. Luxuries. Some goods are so critical to our everyday life that we regard them as "necessities." A hairbrush, toothpaste, and perhaps textbooks might fall into this category. Our "taste" for such goods is so strong that we can't imagine getting along without them. As a result, we don't change our consumption of "necessities" much when the price increases; *demand for necessities is relatively inelastic.*

A "luxury" good, by contrast, is something we'd *like* to have but aren't likely to buy unless our income jumps or the price declines sharply, such as vacation travel, new cars (that Porsche 918 Spyder!), and iPhones. We want them but can get by without them. That is, *demand for luxury goods is relatively elastic.*

Availability of Substitutes. Our notion of which goods are necessities is also influenced by the availability of substitute goods. The high elasticity of demand for fish (Table 6.1) reflects the fact that consumers can eat chicken, beef, or pork if fish prices rise. On the other hand, most bleary-eyed coffee drinkers can't imagine any other product that could substitute for a cup of coffee. As a consequence, when coffee prices rise, consumers don't reduce their purchases much at all. Likewise, the low elasticity of demand for gasoline reflects the fact that most cars can't run on alternative fuels . In general, *the greater the availability of substitutes, the higher the price elasticity of demand.*

The availability of substitutes frustrated California's attempt to both reduce smoking and increase tax revenues when it hiked the state tax on cigarettes from 87 cents a pack to $2.87 a pack in 2017 (see In the News "Californians Vote to Triple Cigarette Tax") Studies have shown conclusively that the price elasticity for cigarettes is low. But the demand for *California-taxed* cigarettes is much more elastic. Why? Because Californians can buy cigarettes in neighboring states, on Indian reservations, or even order them over the internet.

In New York, where the state tax is a whopping $4.35 per pack, over half of all the cigarettes smoked are smuggled in from other jurisdictions.

IN THE NEWS

CALIFORNIANS VOTE TO TRIPLE CIGARETTE TAX

Sacramento, CA—Californians voted for higher cigarette taxes. Proposition 56, passed with 63 percent of the vote, more than triples the state tax on cigarettes from 87 cents a pack to $2.87 a pack, beginning April 1, 2017.

Anti-smoking groups say the higher price will reduce smoking in the state. They foresee the proportion of smokers falling from the current 11.6 percent of the population to as low as 7.1 percent by 2020.

©Michael Hierner/Alamy Stock Photo RF

The state treasurer is also applauding the higher price, but for different reasons. According to the state's Legislature Analyst's Office (LAO), the additional $2 per pack tax will bring in $1.27–$1.61 billion a year to the state treasury.

Economists are skeptical. Californians now purchase about 800 million packs a year. if the new tax is to hit the high end of LAO's revenue estimate, Californians will have to continue smoking 800 million packs a year. Yet, the anti-smoking groups foresee a dramatic drop in smoking—as much as 30 percent. Both groups can't be right.

The Washington-based Tax Foundation also points out that the tax hike in California will greatly increase cigarette smuggling. At present, about 12 percent of cigarettes smoked in California are smuggled in from lower tax jurisdictions. The Tax Foundation says that rate will jump dramatically once the new tax is in place. That will frustrate both the State Treasurer and anti-smoking advocates.

Source: News reports, November 10, 2016.

ANALYSIS: Higher prices do discourage smoking. But smokers can obtain cigarettes from other jurisdictions when a single city or state increases its tax.

Relative Price (to Income). Another important determinant of elasticity is the price of the good in relation to a consumer's income. Airline travel and new cars are quite expensive, so even a small percentage change in their prices can have a big impact on a consumer's budget and consumption decisions. The demand for such big-ticket items tends to be elastic. By contrast, coffee is so cheap that even a large *percentage* change in price doesn't affect consumer behavior much.

Because the relative price of a good affects price elasticity, the value of E_1 *changes* along a given demand curve. At current prices the elasticity of demand for coffee is low. How would consumers behave, however, if coffee cost $5 a cup? Some people would still consume coffee. At such higher prices, however, the quantity demanded would be more sensitive to price changes. Accordingly, when we observe, as in Table 6.1, that the demand for coffee is price-inelastic, that observation applies only to the current range of prices. Were coffee prices dramatically higher, the price elasticity of demand would be higher as well. As a rule, *the price elasticity of demand declines as price moves down the demand curve.*

Time. Finally, time affects the price elasticity of demand. Car owners can't switch to electric autos every time the price of gasoline goes up. In the short run, the elasticity of demand for gasoline is quite low. With more time to adjust, however, consumers can buy more fuel-efficient cars, relocate their homes or jobs, and even switch fuels. As a

Age Group	Percent Decline in Smoking
12–17 years	5 %
18 years	4.5
19–39 years	4
40 years and older	1.5

Source: Congressional Budget Office, *Raising the Excise Tax on Cigarettes,* June 2012.

TABLE 6.2

Long-Run Price Elasticities for Cigarettes

The Congressional Budget Office (CBO) has estimated the following responses over a 10-year period to a 10 percent rise in cigarette prices.

consequence, *the long-run price elasticity of demand is higher than the short-run elasticity.* Nobel Prize–winning economist Gary Becker used the distinction between long-run and short-run elasticities to explain why a proposed increase in cigarette excise taxes wouldn't generate nearly as much revenue as President Clinton expected (see In the News "Professor Becker Rejects Clinton's Tax Math"). Table 6.2 depicts long-run price elasticities for smokers of various ages.

IN THE NEWS

PROFESSOR BECKER REJECTS CLINTON'S TAX MATH

In seeking ways to balance the federal budget, President Clinton has seized on the excise tax on cigarettes. That tax, now at 24 cents per pack, brought in around $12 billion in federal revenue last year. President Clinton says that raising that tax by $1 a pack could generate another $53 billion over the next five years.

Chicago professor and Nobel laureate Gary Becker says the president is blowing smoke. A quadrupling of the excise tax will convince a lot of smokers to quit—or at least smoke less. Because smoking is addictive, the decline in smoking won't be immediate. In the short run every 10 percent hike in the price of cigarettes will reduce consumption by only 4 percent. But in the long run, smoking will decline by about 7 percent. As a result, the tax hike will bring in only a fraction of what Clinton anticipates.

Source: Media reports, 1994.

ANALYSIS: It takes time for people to adjust their behavior to changed prices. Hence the short-run price elasticity of demand is lower than the long-run elasticity.

PRICE ELASTICITY AND TOTAL REVENUE

The concept of price elasticity refutes the popular misconception that producers charge the "highest price possible." Were that true, Steve Jobs might have initially priced the iPhone at $8,996. Except in the very rare case of completely inelastic demand, this notion makes no sense. Indeed, higher prices not only reduce unit sales, but may actually reduce total sales revenue as well.

The **total revenue** of a seller is the amount of money received from product sales. It is determined by the quantity of the product sold and the price at which it is sold:

$$\text{Total revenue} = \text{Price} \times \text{Quantity sold}$$

total revenue: The price of a product multiplied by the quantity sold in a given time period: $p \times q$.

In the movie theater example, if the price of popcorn is 40 cents per ounce and only 4 ounces are sold, total revenue equals $1.60 per show. This revenue is illustrated by the shaded rectangle in Figure 6.3. (The area of a rectangle is equal to its height [p] times its width [q].)

Now consider what happens to total revenue when the price of popcorn is increased. From the law of demand, we know that an increase in price will lead to a decrease in

FIGURE 6.3

Elasticity and Total Revenue

Total revenue is equal to the price of the product times the quantity sold. It is illustrated by the area of the rectangle formed by $p \times q$.

The shaded rectangle illustrates total revenue ($1.60) at a price of 40 cents and a quantity demanded of 4 ounces. When price is increased to 45 cents (point *B*), the rectangle and total revenue shrink (see the dashed lines) because demand is relatively elastic in that price range. Price hikes increase total revenue only if demand is inelastic.

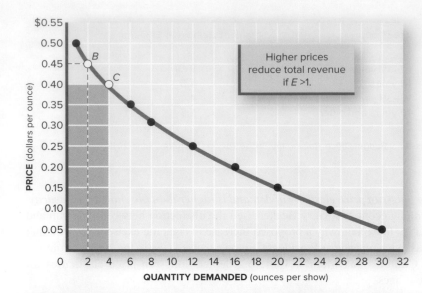

Higher prices reduce total revenue if *E* >1.

	Price	×	Quantity Demanded	=	Total Revenue
A	50¢		1		$0.50
B	45		2		0.90
C	40		4		1.60
D	35		6		2.10
E	30		8		2.40
F	25		12		3.00
G	20		16		3.20
H	15		20		3.00
I	10		25		2.50
J	5		30		1.50

quantity demanded. But what about total revenue? The change in total revenue depends on *how much* quantity demanded falls when price goes up.

Suppose we raise popcorn prices again, from 40 cents back to 45 cents. What happens to total revenue? At 40 cents per box, 4 ounces are sold (see Figure 6.3) and total revenue equals $1.60. If we increase the price to 45 cents, only 2 ounces are sold and total revenue drops to 90 cents. In this case, an *increase* in price leads to a *decrease* in total revenue. This new and smaller total revenue is illustrated by the dashed rectangle in Figure 6.3.

Price increases don't always lower total revenue. If consumer demand was relatively *inelastic* ($E < 1$), a price increase would lead to *higher* total revenue. Thus we conclude that

- *A price hike increases total revenue only if demand is inelastic (E < 1).*
- *A price hike reduces total revenue if demand is elastic (E > 1).*
- *A price hike does not change total revenue if demand is unitary elastic (E = 1).*

Table 6.3 summarizes these and other responses to price changes.

Changing Value of E. Once we know the price elasticity of demand, we can predict how consumers will respond to changing prices. We can also predict what will happen to the total revenue of the seller when the price is raised or reduced. Figure 6.4 shows how elasticity and total revenue change along a given demand curve. Demand for cigarettes is *elastic* ($E > 1$) at prices above $6 per pack but *inelastic* ($E < 1$) at lower prices.

The bottom half of Figure 6.4 shows how total revenue changes along the demand curve. At very high prices (e.g., $14 a pack), few cigarettes are sold and total revenue is low. As the price is reduced, however, the quantity demanded increases so much that total

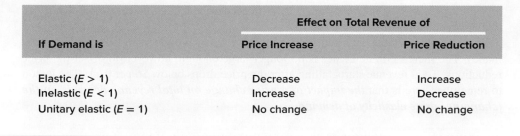

	Effect on Total Revenue of	
If Demand is	**Price Increase**	**Price Reduction**
Elastic ($E > 1$)	Decrease	Increase
Inelastic ($E < 1$)	Increase	Decrease
Unitary elastic ($E = 1$)	No change	No change

TABLE 6.3

Price Elasticity of Demand and Total Revenue

The impact of higher prices on total revenue depends on the price elasticity of demand. Higher prices result in higher total revenue only if demand is inelastic. If demand is elastic, *lower* prices result in *higher* revenues.

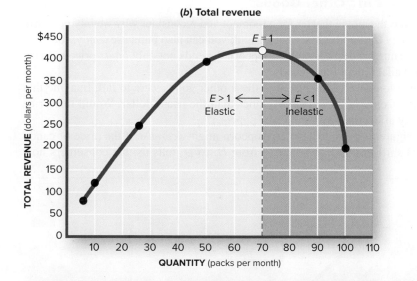

(a) The demand curve

(b) Total revenue

Price of Cigarettes	×	Quantity Demanded	=	Total Revenue	
$ 2		100		$200	Low elasticity; $E < 1$
4		90		360	(total revenue rises
6		70		420	when price increases)
8		50		400	High elasticity; $E > 1$
10		25		250	(total revenue falls
12		10		120	when price increases)
14		6		84	

FIGURE 6.4

Price Elasticity Changes along a Demand Curve

The concept of price elasticity can be used to determine whether people will spend more money on cigarettes when their price rises. The answer to this question is yes and no, depending on how high the price goes.

Notice in the table and the graphs that total revenue rises when the price of cigarettes increases from $2 to $4 a pack and again to $6. At low prices, the demand for cigarettes appears relatively inelastic: price and total revenue move in the same direction.

As the price of cigarettes continues to increase, however, total revenue starts to fall. As the price is increased from $6 to $8 a pack, total revenue drops. At higher prices, the demand for cigarettes is relatively elastic: price and total revenue move in *opposite directions*. Hence the price elasticity of demand depends on where one is on the demand curve.

revenue *increases* despite the lower price. With each price reduction from $14 down to $6, total revenue increases.

Price cuts below $6 a pack continue to increase the quantity demanded (the law of demand). The increase in unit sales is no longer large enough, however, to offset the price reductions. Total revenue starts falling after the price drops below $6 per pack. The lesson to remember here is that *the impact of a price change on total revenue depends on the (changing) price elasticity of demand.*

CROSS-PRICE ELASTICITY

The price elasticity of demand tells us how consumers will respond to a change in the price of a good under the assumption of *ceteris paribus*. But other factors do change, and consumption behavior may respond to those changes as well.

Shifts vs. Movements

We recognized this problem in Chapter 3 when we first distinguished *movements* along a demand curve from *shifts* of the demand curve. A movement along an unchanged demand curve represents consumer response to a change in the *price* of that specific good. The magnitude of that movement is expressed in the price elasticity of demand.

When the underlying determinants of demand change, the entire demand curve shifts. These shifts also alter consumer behavior. The *price* elasticity of demand is of no use in gauging these behavioral responses because it refers to price changes (movements along a constant demand curve) for that good only. Now we have to ask how consumers will respond when an underlying determinant of demand (tastes, income, other goods, or expectations) changes and the demand curve shifts.

A Change in Price of "Other Goods"

Let's sneak back into the movie theater for a moment and reconsider why we buy popcorn. Popcorn isn't the only treat at the concession stand; you can also purchase candy, soda, ice cream, and more. Thus the decision to buy popcorn depends not only on *its* price but also on the price and availability of other goods.

Suppose for the moment that the prices of these other goods were to fall. Imagine that candy bars were put on sale for a quarter, rather than the usual dollar. Would this price reduction for candy affect the consumption of popcorn?

According to Figure 6.5, the demand for popcorn might *decrease* if the price of candy fell. The leftward shift of the demand curve from D_1 to D_2 tells us that consumers now

Do soda prices affect popcorn sales?

©Fuse/Corbis via Getty Images RF

FIGURE 6.5

Substitutes and Complements

The curve D_1 represents the initial demand for popcorn, given the prices of other goods. Other prices may change, however. If a reduction in the price of another good (candy) causes a *reduction* in the demand for this good (popcorn), the two goods are *substitutes*. Popcorn demand shifts to the left (to D_2) when the price of a *substitute good* falls.

If a reduction in the price of another good (e.g., Pepsi) leads to an *increase* in the demand for this good (popcorn), the two goods are *complements*. Popcorn demand shifts to the right (to D_3) when the price of a *complementary good* falls.

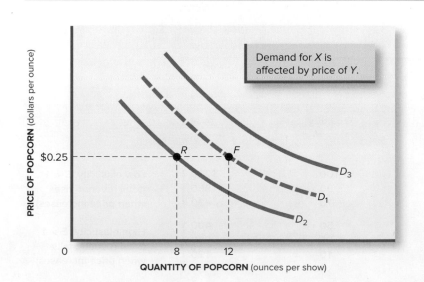

Demand for *X* is affected by price of *Y*.

demand less popcorn at every price. At 25 cents per ounce, consumers now demand only 8 ounces of popcorn (point *R*) rather than the previous 12 ounces (point *F*). In other words, a decline in the price of *candy* has caused a reduction in the demand for *popcorn*. We conclude that candy and popcorn are **substitute goods**—when the price of one declines, demand for the other falls. That is why sales of the Galaxy S5 declined so dramatically when Apple introduced the iPhone 6 and cut the price of the iPhone 5 (see In the News "Samsung Stung by Apple Moves"): iPhones and Galaxies are *substitute* goods.

substitute goods: Goods that substitute for each other; when the price of good *x* rises, the demand for good *y* increases, *ceteris paribus.*

IN THE NEWS

SAMSUNG STUNG BY APPLE MOVES

Samsung reported a staggering 20 percent drop in sales of its flagship smartphone, the Galaxy S5, for the last three months. Profits declined even more—a 49 percent collapse from last year. The reason for this collapse: Apple's introduction of its large-screen iPhone 6 and price cuts on the iPhone 5. Apple dropped the price of the 16GB iPhone 5s from $199 to $99 and the 8GB iPhone 5s from $99 to a cool $0, with contract.

Source: News reports, October 2014.

ANALYSIS: Two products are substitute goods if a price decline in one causes a decline in demand (leftward shift) for the other.

Popcorn sales would follow a very different path if the price of soda fell. People like to wash down their popcorn with soda. When soda prices fall, moviegoers actually buy *more* popcorn. Here again, *a change in the price of one good affects the demand for another good.* In this case, however, we're dealing with **complementary goods** because a decline in the price of one good causes an *increase* in the demand for the other good.

The distinction between substitute goods and complementary goods is illustrated in Figure 6.5. Note that *in the case of substitute goods the price of one good and the demand for the other move in the same direction.* (A *decrease* in candy prices causes a *decrease* in popcorn demand.) The iPhone price cut increased the demand for AT&T wireless services: iPhones and wireless services are *complementary* goods. The same iPhone price cut *reduced* the demand for Galaxys; iPhones and Galaxys are *substitute* goods.

In the case of complementary goods (e.g., Pepsi and popcorn, cream and coffee), the price of one good and the demand for the other move in opposite directions. This helps explain why U.S. consumers bought more cars in 2016 when gasoline prices were falling and fewer SUVs in 2011 when gasoline prices were rising. The concept of complementary goods also explains why the demand for online apps increases when the price of smartphones drops.

complementary goods: Goods frequently consumed in combination; when the price of good *x* rises, the demand for good *y* falls, *ceteris paribus.*

©Thinkstock/Stockbyte/Getty Images RF

Calculating Cross-Price Elasticity. The mathematical relationship between the price of one good and demand for another is summarized in yet another elasticity concept. The **cross-price elasticity of demand** is the *percentage* change in the quantity demanded of one good divided by the *percentage* change in the price of *another* good:

$$\text{Cross-price elasticity of demand} = \frac{\text{\% change in quantity demanded of good } X \text{ (at given price)}}{\text{\% change in price of good } Y}$$

cross-price elasticity of demand: Percentage change in the quantity demanded of *X* divided by the percentage change in the price of *Y*.

What has changed here is the denominator. Now the denominator refers to a change in the price of *another* good rather than the *same* good.

Think back to the impact of the iPhone price cut on Galaxy sales (see In the News "Samsung Stung by Apple Moves"). The 16GB iPhone 5s dropped in price from $199 to $99. We compute the *percentage* decline as

$$\frac{\%\ \text{change}}{\text{in iPhone price}} = \frac{\textbf{Change in price}}{\textbf{Average price}} = \frac{\$199 - \$99}{\$149} = -0.67$$

Galaxy sales *declined* by 20 percent. Hence the cross-price elasticity of demand was

$$E_x = \frac{-0.20}{-0.67} = +0.30$$

Demand for Galaxys declined by 0.30 percent for every 1 percent decline in the iPhone price. A 67 percent iPhone price cut therefore caused a 20 percent decline in Galaxy demand.

Notice that the cross-price elasticity computed here is a *positive* number (+0.30). We saw earlier that the simple (same-product) price elasticity of demand is always a negative number, so we could ignore its sign. That's not the case with cross-price elasticities. In fact, the sign of the cross-price elasticity of demand is important. *If the cross-price elasticity is positive, the two goods are substitutes; if the cross-price elasticity is negative, the two goods are complements.* Pepsi and popcorn are complements because a fall (−) in the price of one leads to an increase (+) in the demand for the other; in other words, the cross-price elasticity is negative.

INCOME ELASTICITY

Changes in the price of other goods aren't the only source of demand shifts. Each of the four determinants of demand is a potential shift factor. Suppose consumer incomes were to increase. How would popcorn consumption be affected? Figure 6.6 provides an answer. Before the change in income, consumers demanded 12 ounces of popcorn at a price of 25 cents per ounce. With more income to spend, the new demand curve (D_2) suggests that consumers will now purchase a greater quantity of popcorn at every price. The increase in income has caused a rightward shift in demand. If popcorn continues to sell for 25 cents per ounce, consumers will now buy 16 ounces per show (point *N*) rather than only 12 ounces (point *F*).

It appears that changes in income have a substantial impact on consumer demand for popcorn. The graph in Figure 6.6 doesn't tell us, however, how large the change in income was. Will a *small* increase in income cause such a shift, or does popcorn demand increase only when moviegoers have a *lot* more money to spend?

FIGURE 6.6

Income Elasticity

If income changes, the demand curve *shifts*. In this case, an increase in income enables consumers to buy more popcorn at every price. At a price of 25 cents, the quantity demanded increases from 12 ounces (point *F*) to 16 ounces (point *N*). The *income elasticity of demand* measures this response of demand to a change in income.

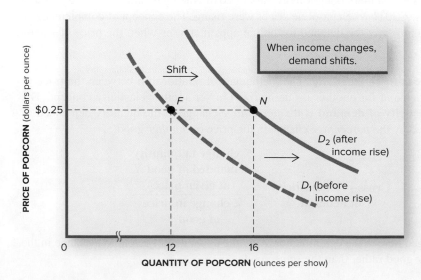

Figure 6.6 doesn't answer these questions. But a little math will. Specifically, the **income elasticity of demand** relates the *percentage* change in quantity demanded to the *percentage* change in income:

$$\text{Income elasticity of demand} = \frac{\substack{\text{\% change in} \\ \text{quantity demanded} \\ \text{(at given price)}}}{\substack{\text{\% change in} \\ \text{income}}}$$

The similarity to the price elasticity of demand is apparent. In this case, however, the denominator is *income* (a determinant of demand), not *price*.

Computing Income Elasticity. As was the case with price elasticity, we compute income elasticity with *average* values for the changes in quantity and income. Suppose that the shift in popcorn demand illustrated in Figure 6.6 occurred when income increased from $110 per week to $120 per week. We would then compute

$$\text{Income elasticity} = \frac{\dfrac{\text{Change in quantity demanded}}{\text{Average quantity}}}{\dfrac{\text{Change in income}}{\text{Average income}}}$$

$$= \frac{\dfrac{16 \text{ ounces} - 12 \text{ ounces}}{14 \text{ ounces}}}{\dfrac{\$120 - \$110}{\$115}}$$

$$= \frac{4}{14} \div \frac{10}{115}$$

$$= \frac{0.286}{0.087} = 3.29$$

Popcorn purchases are very sensitive to changes in income. When incomes rise by 8.7 percent, popcorn sales increase by a whopping 28.6 percent (that is, 8.7% × 3.29). The computed elasticity of 3.29 summarizes this relationship.

Normal vs. Inferior Goods. Demand and income don't always move in the same direction. Popcorn is a **normal good** because consumers buy more of it when their incomes rise. People actually buy *less* of some goods, however, when they have more income. With low incomes, people buy discount clothes, used textbooks, and cheap beer, and they eat at home. With more money to spend, they switch to designer clothes, new books, premium beer, and restaurant meals. The former items are called **inferior goods** because the quantity demanded *falls* when income *rises*. Similarly, when incomes *decline,* people demand *more* spaghetti, pawnbrokers, and lottery tickets. *For inferior goods, the income elasticity of demand is negative; for normal goods, it is positive.*

ELASTICITY OF SUPPLY

Sensitivity to changing prices is not just a consumer phenomenon. Producers, too, alter their behavior when prices change. We know from the **law of supply** (Chapter 3) that businesses will produce more output at higher prices. What we want to know is how much more they'll produce as prices go up. That is what the **price elasticity of supply** tells us. Like its counterpart on the demand side, the price elasticity of supply relates *percentage* changes in the quantity supplied to *percentage* changes in price:

$$\text{Price elasticity of supply} = \frac{\text{Percentage change in quantity supplied}}{\text{Percentage change in price}}$$

income elasticity of demand: Percentage change in quantity demanded divided by percentage change in income.

normal good: Good for which demand increases when income rises.

inferior good: Goods for which demand decreases when income rises.

law of supply: The quantity of a good supplied in a given time period increases as its price increases, *ceteris paribus.*

price elasticity of supply: The percentage change in quantity supplied divided by the percentage change in price.

A high price elasticity of supply means that producers are very responsive to price changes; a low elasticity implies a sluggish response. As World View "Rebounding Oil Price Spurs More Rigs" reports, U.S. oil *production* responds to changes in oil *prices*.

WORLD VIEW

REBOUNDING OIL PRICE SPURS MORE RIGS

The recent spike in the price of oil has brought more rigs on line. According to the weekly Baker Hughes count, the number of active oil rigs has jumped 60 percent since last year. When oil prices were falling, the number of active U.S. rigs fell from 2,000 in 2015 to only 480 in 2016. The latest survey, for the week of March 10, 2017 put the number at 762. Higher-cost shale producers in the Permian basin are quick to respond to higher oil prices, acting as the marginal producer. Overall, economists estimate the elasticity of oil supply at around 0.1.

Source: Media reports of March 2017.

Source: U.S. Coast Guard photo by Petty Officer 3rd Class Patrick Kelley

ANALYSIS: Higher oil prices spur additional drilling and production.

THE ECONOMY TOMORROW

WILL EVS OVERTAKE GAS GUZZLERS?

Electric cars have been a hit. Sales of battery-only (BEV) and plug-in hybrid (PHEV) electric cars have risen every year. Sales in the United States hit a record of 160,000 units in 2016. Some analysts predict that EV sales will reach 400,000 a year by 2020 and surpass 500,000 a year by 2023. One EV producer, Tesla, is completing a lithium battery factory in Nevada that will produce 500,000 batteries a year by 2020.

One of the attractions of EVs is their environmental impact. The BEVs burn no gasoline and the PHEVs burn very little. They get mileage in the range of 100-120 miles per gallon, three or four times the mileage of gasoline-powered cars. Even when the pollution associated with electricity generation is factored in, EVs do less harm to the environment than do gasoline-powered autos. In view of this positive externality, both the federal government and several states offer substantial subsidies (tax credits and purchase rebates) for EV buyers.

For all their success, however, EVs are still a tiny fraction of new car sales. The record 160,000 EVs sold in 2016 pales in comparison to the 17.5 *million* gas guzzlers sold in the United States that year. EVs got less than 1 percent of the market that year and even the most optimistic forecasts of future sales envision a market share of 2.4 percent by 2023. So, EVs aren't about to overtake the gas guzzlers (a substitute good) anytime soon.

A couple of factors will materially affect future EV sales. The first, of course, is the price of the EVs themselves. Producers are hoping that advances in battery technology will bring down the cost of batteries, the most expensive ingredient in EVs. Lower battery prices (a complimentary good) will in turn lead to lower EV prices (and more sales via the price elasticity of demand).

EV producers also have to hope that the price of gasoline (another substitute good) keeps going up. The experience of the last decade shows that high gasoline prices sway consumers' decision to buy an EV. By contrast, when gasoline prices are low, consumers ignore EVs and opt to buy SUVs and bigger cars.

EV producers also have to worry about alternative technologies. Cars powered by natural gas or fuel cells may prove to be cheaper and more efficient. Then there is the prospect of more autonomous vehicles. Autonomous vehicles must be larger than EVs in order to store all the cameras, computers, and other technology embedded in self-driving cars. As these substitute goods become more popular—especially in ride-sharing services like Lyft and Uber—the demand for EVs may wane.

Last but not least, EV producers have to worry about those government subsidies. If the federal government or individual states terminate the tax credits and purchase rebates EV buyers now enjoy, the effective price of an EV will increase by a couple of thousand dollars. That could really put a dent in EV sales in the economy tomorrow.

SUMMARY

- The price elasticity of demand (E) is a numerical measure of consumer response to a change in price, *ceteris paribus*. It equals the percentage change in quantity demanded divided by the percentage change in price. **LO6-1**
- Demand for a product is *elastic* if E is greater than 1.0 or *inelastic* if E is less than 1.0. **LO6-1**
- The degree of price elasticity depends on the price of a good relative to income, the availability of substitutes, and time. **LO6-1**
- The effect of a price change on total revenue depends on price elasticity. Total revenue and price move in the *same* direction only if demand is price-inelastic ($E < 1$). **LO6-2**
- The shape and position of any particular demand curve depend on a consumer's income, tastes, expectations,

and the price and availability of other goods. Should any of these factors change, the assumption of *ceteris paribus* will no longer hold, and the demand curve will *shift*. **LO6-3, LO6-4**

- Cross-price elasticity measures the response of demand for one good to a change in the price of another. The cross-price elasticity of demand is positive for substitute goods and negative for complementary goods. **LO6-3**
- The income elasticity of demand measures the response of demand to a change in income. If demand increases (shifts right) with income, the product is a normal good. If demand declines (shifts left) when income rises, it's an inferior good. **LO6-4**
- The price elasticity of supply is the percentage change in quantity *supplied* divided by the percentage change in price. **LO6-5**

Key Terms

law of demand	substitute goods	normal good
demand curve	complementary goods	inferior good
price elasticity of demand	cross-price elasticity of demand	law of supply
total revenue	income elasticity of demand	price elasticity of supply

Questions for Discussion

1. Is the demand for enrollments in your college price-elastic? How could you find out? **LO6-1**
2. If the price of gasoline doubled, how would consumption of (*a*) cars, (*b*) public transportation, and (*c*) resturants be affected? How quickly would these adjustments be made? **LO6-3**
3. Identify two goods each whose demand exhibits (*a*) high income elasticity, (*b*) low income elasticity, (*c*) high price elasticity, and (*d*) low price elasticity. What accounts for the differences in elasticity? **LO6-4**
4. Why does the price elasticity of demand for cigarettes differ for teenagers and adults (see Table 6.2)? **LO6-1**

5. In California, 15.7 percent of low-income households smoke but only 9.4 percent of high-income households do so. So, the burden of higher cigarette taxes (In the News "Californians Vote to Triple Cigarette Tax") falls disproportionately on the poor. Is this fair?   **LO6-2**

6. If you owned a movie theater, would you want the demand for movies to be elastic or inelastic?   **LO6-2**

7. How has the Internet affected the price elasticity of demand for air travel?   **LO6-1**

8. If the elasticity of demand for coffee is so low (Table 6.1), why doesn't Starbucks raise the price of coffee to $10 a cup?   **LO6-2**

9. Is the demand for iPhones price inelastic or elastic? Why? Is income elasticity high or low?   **LO6-4**

10. In the Economy Tomorrow section, what are the substitute goods and complementary goods that will affect future EV sales? Is the price elasticity of demand for EVs likely to be high or low?   **LO6-3**

11. Suppose that quantity supplied for a product falls by 10 percent. If the price elasticity of supply is 2, what should happen to the price of the product?   **LO6-5**

PROBLEMS FOR CHAPTER 6

LO6-1 1. What was the price elasticity of demand for iPhones in 2007 (In the News "After iPhone Price Cut, Sales Are Up by 200 Percent" and section "Computing Price Elasticity")?

LO6-1 2. According to Professor Becker (In the News "Professor Becker Rejects Clinton's Tax Math"), by how much would cigarette prices have to rise to get a 15 percent reduction in smoking in
   (*a*) one year?
   (*b*) three years?

LO6-1 3. What is the price elasticity of demand for cigarettes implied in In the News "Californians Vote to Triple Cigarette Tax" by
   (*a*) The state's legislative analyst office?
   (*b*) Anti-smoking advocates?
   If the actual price elasticity of demand for California-tax cigarettes is 0.8 (In the News "Californians Vote to Triple Cigarette Tax"),
   (*c*) By how much will the quantity demanded decrease with the new tax?
   (*d*) How much additional revenue will the state take in?

LO6-1 4. Suppose consumers buy 50 million packs of cigarettes per month at a price of $5 per pack. If a $2 tax is added to that price,
   (*a*) By what percentage does price change? (Use the midpoint formula in "Computing Price Elasticity.")
   (*b*) By what percentage will cigarette sales decline in the short run? (See Table 6.1 for a clue.)
   (*c*) According to Gary Becker, by how much will sales decline in the long run? (In the News "Professor Becker Rejects Clinton's Tax Math").

LO6-2 5. From Figure 6.1, compute
   (*a*) The price elasticity between each of the following points
   (*b*) The total revenue at each point.
   (*c*) If there is a price decrease, will total revenue increase when demand is elastic or inelastic?

	Price Elasticity		Total Revenue
Point *C* to *D*	_____	At point *C*	_____
		D	_____
H to *I*	_____	*H*	_____
		I	_____

LO6-4 6. According to the calculation in the section "Income Elasticity," by how much will popcorn sales increase if average income goes up by 8 percent?

LO6-5 7. Using the World View "Rebounding Oil Price Spurs More Rigs," calculate the price elasticity of supply between 2016 and 2017 if the price of oil increased by 20 percent in the same time period.

LO6-3 8. If the cross-price elasticity of demand between printed textbooks and e-books is +0.50,
   (*a*) Are e-books and textbooks complementary (C) or substitute (S) goods?
   (*b*) If textbook prices increase by 10 percent, by how much will e-books demand change?

LO6-1 9. Suppose that in a week the price of Greek yogurt increases from $1.25 to $1.75 per container. At the same time, the quantity of Greek yogurt demanded at a typical grocery store increases from 10,000 to 18,000 containers per month. What is the price elasticity of demand for Greek yogurt?

LO6-2 10. Use the following data to illustrate the (*a*) demand curve and (*b*) total revenue curve:

Price	$10	9	8	7	6	5	4	3	2	1
Quantity	2	4	6	8	10	12	14	16	18	20

(*a*) At what price is total revenue maximized?
(*b*) At that price, what is the elasticity of demand?

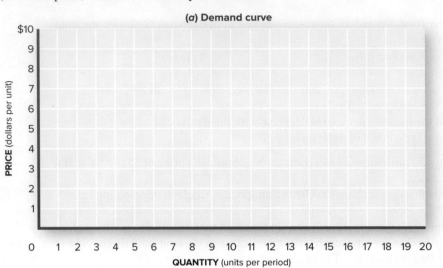

(*a*) Demand curve

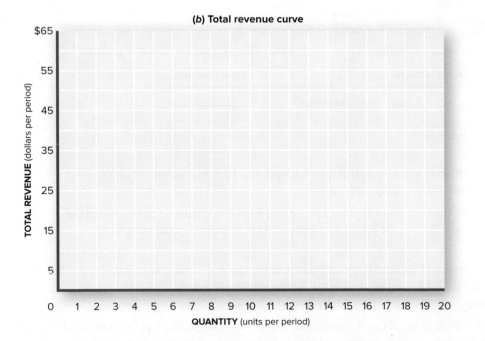

(*b*) Total revenue curve

LO6-3   11. On the graphs below, show the impact of the price reduction for iPhones, as described in In the News "Samsung Stung by Apple Moves."

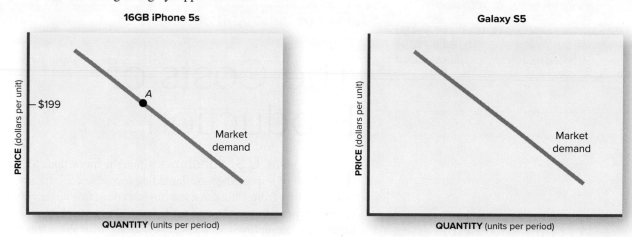

12. The Economy Tomorrow: In 2016, 160,000 electric vehicles (EVs) were sold in the United States.

LO6-1   (a) Suppose the average price of these cars was $37,000. Calculate price elasticity of demand if a $2000 tax credit caused an increase in sales by 10,000 EVs.

LO6-3   (b) Calculate cross-price elasticity if a 20% increase in the price of gasoline caused an increase in sales of EVs by 3000.

©SCPhotos/Alamy Stock Photo

CHAPTER 7

The Costs of Production

L ast year U.S. consumers bought more than $2 *trillion* worth of imported goods, including Japanese cars, Italian shoes, and toys from China. As you might expect, this angers domestic producers, who frequently end up with unsold goods, half-empty factories, and unemployed workers. They, along with President Trump, rage against the "unfair" competition from abroad, asserting that producers in India, Brazil, and China can undersell U.S. producers because workers in these countries are paid dirt-poor wages.

But lower wages don't necessarily imply lower costs. You could pay me $2 per hour to type and still end up paying a lot for typing. Truth is, I type only about 10 words a minute, with lots of misteakes. The cost of producing goods depends not only on the price of inputs (e.g., labor) but also on how much they produce. Paying $10 an hour to someone who types 90 words a minute is a lot cheaper than paying $2 an hour to someone who types only 10 words a minute.

In this chapter we begin looking at the costs of producing the goods and services that market participants demand. We confront the following questions:

- **How much output *can* a firm produce?**
- **How do the *costs* of production vary with the rate of output?**
- **Do larger firms have a cost advantage over smaller firms?**

The answers to these questions are important not only to producers facing foreign competition but to consumers as well. The costs of producing a good have a direct impact on the prices we pay at the grocery store, the mall, or even the campus bookstore.

THE PRODUCTION FUNCTION

No matter how large a business is or who owns it, all businesses confront one central fact: it costs something to produce goods. To produce corn, a farmer needs land, water, seeds, equipment, and labor. To produce fillings, a dentist needs a chair, a drill, some space, and labor. Even the production of educational services such as this economics class requires the use of labor (your teacher), land (on which the school is built), and capital (the building, blackboard, computers). In short, unless you're producing unrefined, unpackaged air, you need **factors of production**—that is, resources that can be used to produce a good or service. These factors of production provide the basic measure of economic cost. The costs of your economics class, for example, are

LEARNING OBJECTIVES

After reading this chapter, you should know

LO7-1 What the production function represents.

LO7-2 What the law of diminishing returns means.

LO7-3 How the various measures of cost relate to each other.

LO7-4 How economic and accounting costs differ.

LO7-5 What (dis)economies of scale are.

factors of production: Resource inputs used to produce goods and services, e.g., land, labor, capital, entrepreneurship.

measured by the amounts of land, labor, and capital it requires. These are *resource* costs of production.

To assess the costs of production, we must first determine how many resources are actually needed to produce a given product. You could use a lot of resources to produce a product or use just a few. What we really want to know is how *best* to produce. What's the *smallest* amount of resources needed to produce a specific product? Or we could ask the same question from a different perspective: what's the *maximum* amount of output attainable from a given quantity of resources?

The answers to these questions are reflected in the **production function,** which tells us the maximum amount of good *X* producible from various combinations of factor inputs. With one chair and one drill, a dentist can fill a *maximum* of 32 cavities per day. With two chairs, a drill, and an assistant, a dentist can fill up to 55 cavities per day.

A production function is a technological summary of our ability to produce a particular good.[1] Table 7.1 provides a partial glimpse of one such function. In this case, the output is designer jeans, as produced by Low-Rider Jeans Corporation. The essential inputs in the production of jeans are land, labor (garment workers), and capital (a factory and sewing machines). With these inputs, Low-Rider Jeans Corporation can produce and sell hip-hugging jeans to style-conscious consumers.

production function: A technological relationship expressing the maximum quantity of a good attainable from different combinations of factor inputs.

Varying Input Levels

As in all production endeavors, we want to know how much output we can produce with available resources. To make things easy, we'll assume that the factory is already built, with fixed space dimensions. The only inputs we can vary are labor (the number of garment workers per day) and additional capital (the number of sewing machines we lease per day).

In these circumstances, the quantity of jeans we can produce depends on the amount of labor and capital we employ. ***The purpose of a production function is to tell us just how much output we can produce with varying amounts of factor inputs.*** Table 7.1 provides such information for jeans production.

Consider the simplest option—that of employing no labor or capital (the upper left corner in Table 7.1). An empty factory can't produce any jeans; maximum output is zero per

Capital Input (Sewing Machines per Day)	Labor Input (Workers per Day)								
	0	1	2	3	4	5	6	7	8
	Jeans Output (Pairs per Day)								
0	0	0	0	0	0	0	0	0	0
1	0	15	34	44	48	50	51	51	47
2	0	20	46	64	72	78	81	82	80
3	0	21	50	73	83	92	99	103	103

TABLE 7.1

A Production Function

A production function tells us the maximum amount of output attainable from alternative combinations of factor inputs. This particular function tells us how many pairs of jeans we can produce in a day with a given factory and varying quantities of capital and labor. With one sewing machine, and one operator, we can produce a maximum of 15 pairs of jeans per day, as indicated in the second column of the second row. To produce more jeans, we need more labor or more capital.

[1]By contrast, the production possibilities curve discussed in Chapter 1 expresses our ability to produce various *combinations* of goods, given the use of *all* our resources. The production possibilities curve summarizes the output capacity of the entire economy. A production function describes the capacity of a single firm.

day. Even though land, capital (an empty factory), and even denim are available, some essential labor and capital inputs are missing, and jeans production is impossible.

Suppose now we employ some labor (a machine operator) but don't lease any sewing machines. Will output increase? Not according to the production function. The first row in Table 7.1 illustrates the consequences of employing labor without any capital equipment. Without sewing machines (or even needles, another form of capital), the operators can't make jeans. Maximum output remains at zero no matter how much labor is employed in this case.

The dilemma of machine operators without sewing machines illustrates a general principle of production: *the productivity of any factor of production depends on the amount of other resources available to it.* Industrious, hardworking machine operators can't make designer jeans without sewing machines.

We can increase the productivity of garment workers by providing them with machines. The production function again tells us by *how much* jeans output could increase. Suppose we leased just one machine per day. Now the second row in Table 7.1 is the relevant one. It says jeans output will remain at zero if we lease one machine but employ no labor. If we employ one machine *and* one worker, however, the jeans will start rolling out the door. Maximum output under these circumstances (row 2, column 2) is 15 pairs of jeans per day. Now we're in business!

The remaining columns in row 2 tell us how many additional jeans we can produce if we hire more workers, still leasing only one sewing machine. With one machine and two workers, maximum output rises to 34 pairs per day. If a third worker is hired, output could increase to 44 pairs.

Table 7.1 also indicates how production would increase with additional sewing machines (capital). By reading down any column of the table, you can see how more machines increase potential jeans output.

Efficiency

The production function summarized in Table 7.1 underscores the essential relationship between resource *inputs* and product *outputs*. It's also a basic introduction to economic costs. To produce 15 pairs of jeans per day, we need one sewing machine, an operator, a factory, and some denim. All these inputs make up the *resource cost* of producing jeans.

Another feature of Table 7.1 is that it conveys the *maximum* output of jeans producible from particular input combinations. The standard garment worker and sewing machine, when brought together at Low-Rider Jeans Corporation, can produce *at most* 15 pairs of jeans per day. They could also produce a lot less. Indeed, a careless cutter can waste a lot of denim. A lazy or inattentive worker won't keep the sewing machines humming. As many a producer has learned, actual output can fall far short of the limits described in the production function. Jeans output will reach the levels in Table 7.1 only if the jeans factory operates with relative **efficiency.** This requires getting maximum output from the resources used in the production process. *The production function represents maximum technical efficiency—that is, the most output attainable from any given level of factor inputs.*

We can always be inefficient, of course. This merely means getting less output than possible for the inputs we use. But this isn't a desirable situation. To a factory manager, it means less output for a given amount of input (cost). To society as a whole, inefficiency implies a waste of resources. If Low-Rider Jeans isn't producing efficiently, we're being denied some potential output. It's not only a question of having fewer jeans. We could also use the labor and capital now employed by Low-Rider Jeans to produce something else. Specifically, the **opportunity cost** of a product is measured by the most desired goods and services that could have been produced with the same resources. Hence, if jeans production isn't up to par, society is either (1) getting fewer jeans than it should for the resources devoted to jeans production or (2) giving up too many other goods and services in order to get a desired quantity of jeans.

---

productivity: Output per unit of input—for example, output per labor-hour.

efficiency: Maximum output of a good from the resources used in production.

opportunity cost: The most desired goods or services that are forgone in order to obtain something else.

Although we can always do worse than the production function suggests, we can't do better, at least not in the short run. The production function represents the *best* we can do with our current technological know-how. For the moment, at least, there's no better way to produce a specific good. As our technological and managerial capabilities increase, however, we'll attain higher levels of future productivity. These advances in our productive capability will be represented by new production functions.

Short-Run Constraints

Let's step back from the threshold of scientific advance for a moment and return to Low-Rider Jeans. Forget about possible technological breakthroughs in jeans production (e.g., electronic sewing machines or robot operators) and concentrate on the economic realities of our modest endeavor. For the present we're stuck with existing technology. In fact, all the output figures in Table 7.1 are based on the use of a specific factory. Once we've purchased or leased that factory, we've set a limit to current jeans production. When such commitments to fixed inputs (e.g., the factory) exist, we're dealing with a **short-run** production problem. If no land or capital were in place—if we could build or lease any sized factory—we'd be dealing with a *long-run* decision.

Our short-run objective is to make the best possible use of the factory we've acquired. This entails selecting the right combination of labor and capital inputs to produce jeans. To simplify the decision, we'll limit the number of sewing machines in use. If we lease only one sewing machine, then the second row in Table 7.1 is the only one we have to consider. In this case, the single sewing machine (capital) becomes another short-run constraint on the production of jeans. With a given factory and one sewing machine, the short-run rate of output depends entirely on how many workers are hired.

Figure 7.1 illustrates the short-run production function applicable to the factory with one sewing machine. As noted before, a factory with a sewing machine but no machine

short run: The period in which the quantity (and quality) of some inputs can't be changed.

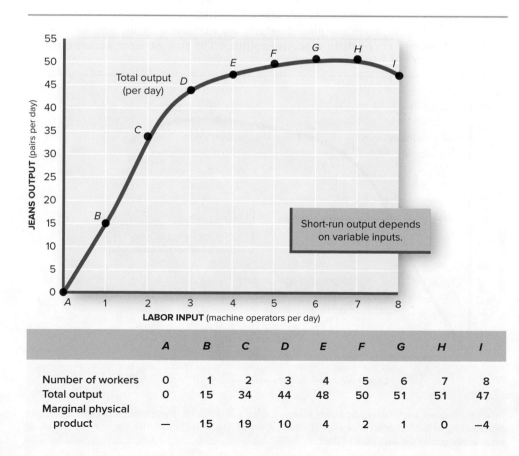

	A	B	C	D	E	F	G	H	I
Number of workers	0	1	2	3	4	5	6	7	8
Total output	0	15	34	44	48	50	51	51	47
Marginal physical product	—	15	19	10	4	2	1	0	−4

FIGURE 7.1

Short-Run Production Function

In the short run some inputs (e.g., land and capital) are fixed in quantity. Output then depends on how much of a variable input (e.g., labor) is used.

The short-run production function shows how output changes when more labor is used. This figure and the table below are based on the second (one-machine) row in Table 7.1.

operators produces no jeans. This was observed in Table 7.1 (row 1, column 0) and is now illustrated by point *A* in Figure 7.1. To get any jeans output, we need to hire some labor. In this simplified example, ***labor is the variable input that determines how much output we get from our fixed inputs (land and capital).*** By placing one worker in the factory, we can produce 15 pairs of jeans per day. This possibility is represented by point *B*. The remainder of the production function shows how jeans output changes as we employ more workers in our single-machine factory.

MARGINAL PRODUCTIVITY

The short-run production function not only defines the *limit* to output but also shows how much each worker contributes to that limit. Notice again that jeans output increases from zero (point *A* in Figure 7.2) to 15 pairs (point *B*) when the first machine operator is hired. In other words, total output *increases* by 15 pairs when we employ the first worker. This increase is called the **marginal physical product (MPP)** of that first worker—that is, the *change* in total output that results from employment of one more unit of (labor) input:

> **marginal physical product (MPP):** The change in total output associated with one additional unit of input.

$$\text{Marginal physical product (MPP)} = \frac{\text{Change in total output}}{\text{Change in input quantity}}$$

With zero workers, total output was zero. When that first worker is employed, total output increases to 15 pairs of jeans per day. The MPP of the first worker is 15 pairs of jeans.

If we employ a second operator, jeans output more than doubles, to 34 pairs per day (point *C*). The 19-pair *increase* in output represents the marginal physical product of the *second* worker.

The higher MPP of the second worker raises a question about the first. Why was the first's MPP lower? Laziness? Is the second worker faster, less distracted, or harder working?

The second worker's higher MPP isn't explained by superior talents or effort. We assume, in fact, that all "units of labor" are equal—that is, one worker is just as good as another.[2] Their different marginal products are explained by the structure of the production process, not by their respective abilities. The first garment worker not only

FIGURE 7.2

Marginal Physical Product (MPP)

Marginal physical product is the *change* in total output that results from employing one more unit of input. The *third* worker, for example, increases *total output* from 34 (point *C*) to 44 (point *D*). Hence the *marginal* output of the third worker is 10 pairs of jeans (point *d*).

What's the MPP of the fourth worker? What happens to *total* output when this worker is hired?

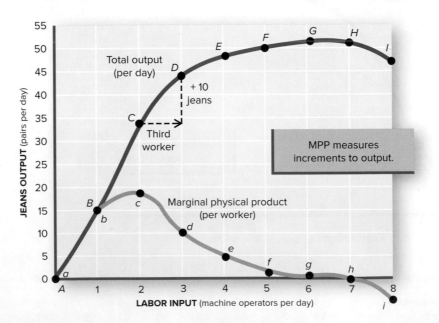

[2]In reality, garment workers do differ greatly in energy, talent, and diligence. These differences can be eliminated by measuring units of labor in *constant-quality* units. A person who works twice as hard as everyone else would count as two *quality-adjusted* units of labor.

had to sew jeans but also had to unfold bolts of denim, measure the jeans, sketch out the patterns, and cut them to approximate size. A lot of time was spent going from one task to another. Despite the worker's best efforts, this person simply couldn't do everything at once.

A second worker alleviates this situation. With two workers, less time is spent running from one task to another. While one worker is measuring and cutting, the other can continue sewing. This improved *ratio* of labor to other factors of production results in the large jump in total output. The second worker's superior MPP isn't unique to this person: it would have occurred even if we'd hired the workers in the reverse order.

Diminishing Marginal Returns

Unfortunately, total output won't keep rising so sharply as more workers are hired. Look what happens when a third worker is hired. Total jeans production continues to increase. But the increase from point *C* to point *D* in Figure 7.2 is only 10 pairs per day. Hence the third worker's MPP (10 pairs) is *less* than that of the second (19 pairs). Marginal physical product is *diminishing*. This concept is illustrated by point *d* in Figure 7.2.

What accounts for this decline in MPP? The answer lies in the ratio of labor to other factors of production. A third worker begins to crowd our facilities. We still have only one sewing machine. Two people can't sew at the same time. As a result, some time is wasted as the operators wait for their turns at the machine. Even if they split up the various jobs, there will still be some "downtime" because measuring and cutting aren't as time-consuming as sewing. Consequently, we can't make full use of a third worker. The relative scarcity of other inputs (capital and land) constrains the third worker's marginal physical product.

Resource constraints are even more evident when a fourth worker is hired. Total output increases again, but the increase this time is very small. With three workers, we got 44 pairs of jeans per day (point *D*); with four workers, we get a maximum of 48 pairs (point *E*). Thus the fourth worker's MPP is only 4 pairs of jeans. There simply aren't enough machines to make productive use of so much labor.

If a seventh worker is hired, the operators get in one another's way, argue, and waste denim. Notice in Figure 7.1 that total output doesn't increase at all when a seventh worker is hired (point *H*). The MPP of the seventh worker is zero (point *h*). Were an eighth worker hired, total output would actually *decline,* from 51 pairs (point *H*) to 47 pairs (point *I*). The eighth worker has a *negative* MPP (point *i* in Figure 7.2).

Law of Diminishing Returns. The problems of crowded facilities apply to most production processes. In the short run, a production process is characterized by a fixed amount of available land and capital. Typically, the only factor that can be varied in the short run is labor. Yet **as more labor is hired, each unit of labor has less capital and land to work with.** This is simple division: the available facilities are being shared by more and more workers. At some point, this constraint begins to pinch. When it does, marginal physical product declines. This situation is so common that it's the basis for the **law of diminishing returns,** which says that the marginal physical product of any factor of production, such as labor, will diminish at some point as more of it is used in a given production setting. Notice in Figure 7.2 how diminishing returns set in when the third worker was hired.

law of diminishing returns: The marginal physical product of a variable input declines as more of it is employed with a given quantity of other (fixed) inputs.

RESOURCE COSTS

A production function tells us how much output a firm *can* produce with its existing plant and equipment. From Figure 7.2 we know that Low-Rider Jeans *could* produce up to 51 pairs per day, employing 6 workers. But Figure 7.2 doesn't tell us how much the firm will *want* to produce. A firm *might* want to produce at capacity if the profit picture were bright enough. On the other hand, a firm might not produce *any* output if costs always exceeded sales revenue. The most desirable rate of output is the one that maximizes total

profit—the difference between total revenue and total costs. And *there is no reason to expect maximum* **profit** *to coincide with maximum* **output.**

The production function therefore is just a starting point for supply decisions. To decide how much output to produce with that function, a firm must next examine the costs of production. How fast do costs rise when output increases?

The law of diminishing returns provides a clue to how fast costs rise. *The economic cost of a product is measured by the value of the resources needed to produce it.* What we've seen here is that those resource requirements eventually increase. Each additional sewing machine operator produces fewer and fewer jeans. In effect, then, each additional pair of jeans produced uses more and more labor.

Suppose we employ one sewing machine and one operator again, for a total output of 15 pairs of jeans per day; see point *b* in Figure 7.3*a*. Now look at production from another perspective—that of *costs*. The resource costs of producing jeans are measured by how much labor is used in the production process. How much labor cost are we using at point *b* to produce one pair of jeans? We know that one worker is producing 15 pairs of jeans, so the labor input per pair of jeans must be one-fifteenth of a worker's day—that is, 0.067 unit of labor. This resource cost is illustrated by point 1/*b* in Figure 7.3*b*. All we're doing here is translating *output* data into related *input* (cost) data.

Marginal Resource Cost

The next question is, How do input costs change when output increases? As point *c* in Figure 7.3*a* reminds us, total output increases by 19 pairs when we hire a second worker. What's the implied labor cost of those *additional* 19 pairs? By dividing one worker by 19 pairs of jeans, we observe that the labor cost of that extra output is one-nineteenth, or 0.053 of a worker's day; see point 1/*c* in Figure 7.3*b*.

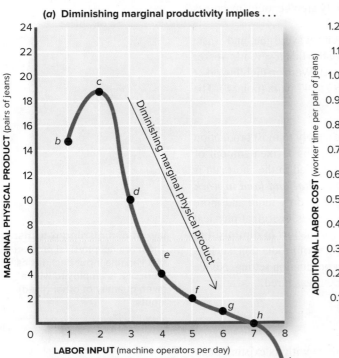

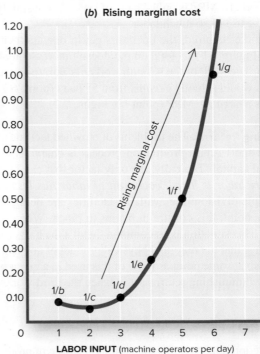

FIGURE 7.3

Falling MPP Implies Rising Marginal Cost

Marginal physical product (MPP) is the additional output obtained by employing one more unit of input. If MPP is falling, each additional unit of input is producing less additional output, which means the input cost of each unit of output is rising. The third worker's MPP is 10 pairs (point *d* in part *a*). Therefore, the labor cost of these additional jeans is approximately 1/10 unit of labor per pair (point 1/*d* in part *b*).

When we focus on the *additional* costs incurred from increasing production, we're talking about *marginal* costs. Specifically, **marginal cost (MC)** refers to the *increase* in total costs required to get one additional unit of output. More generally,

$$\frac{\text{Marginal}}{\text{cost (MC)}} = \frac{\text{Change in total cost}}{\text{Change in output}}$$

In this simple case—where labor is the only variable input—the marginal cost of the added jeans is

$$\text{Marginal cost of jeans} = \frac{\text{1 additional worker}}{\text{19 additional pairs}}$$
$$= 0.053 \text{ worker per pair}$$

The amount 0.053 of labor represents the *change* in total resource cost when we produce one *additional* pair of jeans.

Notice in Figure 7.3*b* that the marginal labor cost of jeans production declines when the second worker is hired. Marginal cost falls from 0.067 unit of labor (plus denim) per pair (point 1/*b* in Figure 7.3*b*) to only 0.053 unit of labor per pair (point 1/*c*). It costs less labor *per pair* to use two workers rather than only one. This is a reflection of the second worker's increased MPP. ***Whenever MPP is increasing, the marginal cost of producing a good must be falling.*** This is illustrated in Figure 7.3 by the upward move from *b* to *c* in part *a* and the corresponding downward move from 1/*b* to 1/*c* in part *b*.

Unfortunately, marginal physical product typically declines at some point. As it does, the marginal costs of production rise. In this sense, each additional pair of jeans becomes more expensive—we need more and more labor per pair.

Figure 7.3 illustrates this inverse relationship between MPP and marginal cost. The third worker has an MPP of 10 pairs, as illustrated by point *d*. The marginal labor input of these extra 10 pairs is thus 1 ÷ 10, or 0.10 unit of labor. In other words, one-tenth of a third worker's daily effort goes into each pair of jeans. This additional labor cost *per unit* is illustrated by 1/*d* in part *b* of the figure.

Note in Figure 7.3 how marginal physical product declines after point *c* and how marginal costs rise after point 1/*c*. This is no accident. ***If marginal physical product declines, marginal cost increases.*** Thus increasing marginal cost is as common as—and the direct result of—diminishing returns. These increasing marginal costs aren't the fault of any person or factor; they simply reflect the resource constraints found in any established production setting (i.e., existing and limited plants and equipment). In the short run, the quantity and quality of land and capital are fixed, and we can vary only their intensity of use by employing more or fewer workers. It's in this short-run context that we keep running into diminishing marginal returns and rising marginal costs.

If MPP is falling, MC must be rising. MPP and MC move in opposite directions.

DOLLAR COSTS

This entire discussion of diminishing returns and marginal costs may seem a bit alien. After all, we're interested in the costs of production, and costs are typically measured in *dollars,* not such technical notions as MPP. Jeans producers need to know how many dollars it costs to keep jeans flowing; they don't want a lecture on marginal physical product.

Jeans manufacturers don't have to study marginal physical products, or even the production function. They can confine their attention to dollar costs. The dollar costs observed, however, are directly related to the underlying production function. To understand *why* costs rise—and how they might be reduced—some understanding of the production function is necessary. In this section we translate production functions into dollar costs.

Total Cost

The **total cost** of producing a product includes the market value of *all* the resources used in its production. To determine this cost we simply identify all the resources used in production, determine their value, and then add up everything.

TABLE 7.2

The Total Costs of Production (Total Cost of Producing 15 Pairs of Jeans per Day)

The total cost of producing a good equals the market value of all the resources used in its production. In this case, the production of 15 pairs of jeans per day requires resources worth $245.

Resource Input	×	Unit Price of Input	=	Total Cost
1 factory		$100 per day		$100
1 sewing machine		20 per day		20
1 operator		80 per day		80
1.5 bolts of denim		30 per bolt		45
Total cost				$245

In the production of jeans, these resources included land, labor, and capital. Table 7.2 identifies these resources, their unit values, and the total dollar cost associated with their use. This table is based on an assumed output of 15 pairs of jeans per day, with the use of one worker and one sewing machine (point *B* in Figure 7.2). The rent on the factory is $100 per day, a sewing machine rents for $20 per day, and the wages of a garment worker are $80 per day. We'll assume Low-Rider Jeans Corporation can purchase bolts of denim for $30 apiece, with each bolt providing enough denim for 10 pairs of jeans. In other words, one-tenth of a bolt ($3 worth of material) is required for one pair of jeans. We'll ignore any other potential expenses. With these assumptions, the total cost of producing 15 pairs of jeans per day amounts to $245, as shown in Table 7.2.

Fixed Costs. Total costs will change of course as we alter the rate of production. But not *all* costs increase. In the short run, some costs don't increase at all when output is increased. These are **fixed costs** in the sense that they don't vary with the rate of output. The factory lease is an example. Once you lease a factory, you're obligated to pay for it whether or not you use it. The person who owns the factory wants $100 per day. Even if you produce no jeans, you still have to pay that rent. That's the essence of fixed costs.

fixed costs: Costs of production that don't change when the rate of output is altered, such as the cost of basic plants and equipment.

The leased sewing machine is another fixed cost. When you rent a sewing machine, you must pay the rental charge. It doesn't matter whether you use it for a few minutes or all day long—the rental charge is fixed at $20 per day.

Variable Costs. Labor costs are another story altogether. The amount of labor employed in jeans production can be varied easily. If we decide not to open the factory tomorrow, we can just tell our only worker to take the day off (without pay, of course!). We'll still have to pay rent, but we can cut back on wages. On the other hand, if we want to increase daily output, we can also hire additional workers easily and quickly. Labor is regarded as a **variable cost** in this line of work—that is, a cost that *varies* with the rate of output.

variable costs: Costs of production that change when the rate of output is altered, such as labor and material costs.

The denim itself is another variable cost. Denim not used today can be saved for tomorrow. Hence how much we spend on denim today is directly related to how many jeans we produce. In this sense, the cost of denim input varies with the rate of jeans output.

Figure 7.4 illustrates how these various costs are affected by the rate of production. On the vertical axis are the costs of production in dollars per day. Notice that the total cost of producing 15 pairs per day is still $245, as indicated by point *B*. This cost figure consists of

DOLLAR COST OF PRODUCING 15 PAIRS

Fixed costs:		
Factory rent	$100	
Sewing machine rent	20	
Subtotal		$120
Variable costs:		
Wages to labor	$ 80	
Denim	45	
Subtotal		$125
Total costs		$245

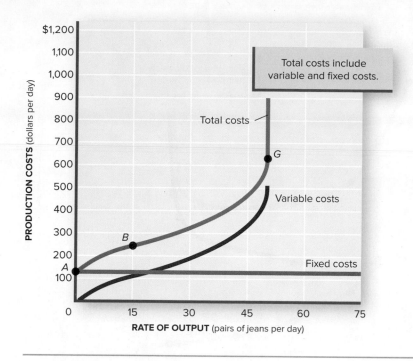

Total costs include variable and fixed costs.

PRODUCTION COSTS (dollars per day)

RATE OF OUTPUT (pairs of jeans per day)

Total costs

Variable costs

Fixed costs

FIGURE 7.4
The Cost of Jeans Production

Total cost includes both fixed and variable costs. Fixed costs must be paid even if no output is produced (point *A*). Variable costs start at zero and increase with the rate of output. The total cost of producing 15 pairs of jeans (point *B*) includes $120 in fixed costs (rent on the factory and sewing machines) and $125 in variable costs (denim and wages). Total cost rises as output increases because additional variable costs must be incurred.

In this example, the short-run capacity is equal to 51 pairs (point *G*). If still more inputs are employed, costs will rise but not total output.

If we increase the rate of output beyond these 15 pairs, total costs will rise. *How fast total costs rise depends on variable costs only,* however, since fixed costs remain at $120 per day. (Notice the horizontal fixed cost curve in Figure 7.4.)

Capacity. With one sewing machine and one factory, there's an absolute limit to daily jeans production. According to the production function in Figure 7.1, the capacity of a factory with one machine is roughly 51 pairs of jeans per day. If we try to produce more jeans than this by hiring additional workers, our total costs will rise, but our output won't. Recall that the seventh worker had a *zero* marginal physical product (Figure 7.2). In fact, we could fill the factory with garment workers and drive total costs sky-high. But the limits of space and one sewing machine don't permit output in excess of 51 pairs per day. This limit to productive capacity is represented by point *G* on the total cost curve. Further expenditure on inputs will increase production *costs* but not *output.*

Although there's no upper limit to costs, there is a lower limit. If output is reduced to zero, costs won't completely disappear. At zero output, total costs fall only to $120 per day, the level of fixed costs, as illustrated by point *A* in Figure 7.4. As before, *there's no way to avoid fixed costs in the short run.* Indeed, those fixed costs define the short run.

Average Costs

While Figure 7.4 illustrates *total* costs of production, other measures of cost are often desired. One of the most common measures of cost is average, or per-unit, cost. **Average total cost (ATC)** is simply total cost divided by the rate of output:

$$\text{Average total cost (ATC)} = \frac{\text{Total cost}}{\text{Total output}}$$

average total cost (ATC): Total cost divided by the quantity produced in a given time period.

At an output of 15 pairs of jeans per day, total costs are $245. The average cost of production is thus $16.33 per pair (= 245 ÷ 15) at this rate of output.

The average cost of production is not a constant number. On the contrary, average total cost changes with the rate of output. So, when someone cites the average cost of producing something, they must have a specific quantity of output in mind.

Figure 7.5 shows how average costs change as the rate of output varies. Row *J* of the cost schedule, for example, again indicates the fixed, variable, and total costs of producing 15

FIGURE 7.5
Average Total Costs (ATC)

Average total cost (ATC) in column 7 equals total cost (column 4) divided by the rate of output (column 1).

Since total cost includes both fixed (column 2) and variable (column 3) costs, ATC also equals AFC (column 5) plus AVC (column 6). This relationship is illustrated in the graph. The ATC of producing 15 pairs per day (point *J*) equals $16.33—the sum of AFC ($8) and AVC ($8.33).

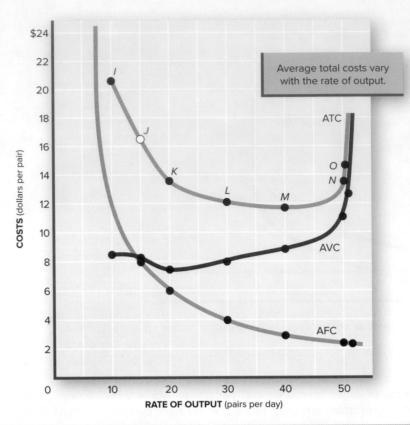

Average total costs vary with the rate of output.

	(1)	(2)		(3)		(4)	(5)		(6)		(7)
	Rate of Output	Fixed Costs	+	Variable Costs	=	Total Cost	Average Fixed Cost	+	Average Variable Cost	=	Average Total Cost
H	0	$120		$ 0		$120	—		—		—
I	10	120		85		205	$12.00		$ 8.50		$20.50
J	15	120		125		245	8.00		8.33		16.33
K	20	120		150		270	6.00		7.50		13.50
L	30	120		240		360	4.00		8.00		12.00
M	40	120		350		470	3.00		8.75		11.75
N	50	120		550		670	2.40		11.00		13.40
O	51	120		633		753	2.35		12.41		14.76

average fixed cost (AFC): Total fixed cost divided by the quantity produced in a given time period.

average variable cost (AVC): Total variable cost divided by the quantity produced in a given time period.

pairs of jeans per day. Fixed costs are still $120; variable costs are $125. Thus the total cost of producing 15 pairs per day is $245, as we saw earlier.

The rest of row *J* shows the average costs of jeans production. These figures are obtained by dividing each dollar total (columns 2, 3, and 4) by the rate of physical output (column 1). At an output rate of 15 pairs per day, **average fixed cost (AFC)** is $8 per pair, **average variable cost (AVC)** is $8.33, and *average total cost (ATC)* is $16.33. ATC, then, is simply the sum of AFC and AVC:

$$ATC = AFC + AVC$$

Falling AFC. At this relatively low rate of output, fixed costs are a large portion of total costs. The rent paid for the factory and sewing machines works out to $8 per pair ($120 ÷ 15). This high average fixed cost accounts for nearly one-half of total average costs. This suggests that it's quite expensive to lease a factory and sewing machine to produce only

15 pairs of jeans per day. To reduce average costs, we must make fuller use of our leased plant and equipment.

Notice what happens to average costs when the rate of output is increased to 20 pairs per day (row K in Figure 7.5). Average fixed costs go down to only $6 per pair. This sharp decline in AFC results from the fact that total fixed costs ($120) are now spread over more output. Even though our rent hasn't dropped, the *average* fixed cost of producing jeans has.

If we produce more than 20 pairs of jeans per day, AFC will continue to fall. Recall that

$$\text{AFC} = \frac{\text{Total fixed cost}}{\text{Total output}}$$

The numerator is fixed (at $120 in this case). But the denominator increases as output expands. Hence *any increase in output will lower average fixed cost.* This is reflected in Figure 7.5 by the constantly declining AFC curve.

As jeans output increases from 15 to 20 pairs per day, AVC falls as well. AVC includes the price of denim used in a pair of jeans and associated labor costs. The price of denim is unchanged at $3 per pair ($30 per bolt). But per-unit *labor* costs fall when output increases from 15 to 20 pairs, from $5.33 to $4.50 per pair. Thus the reduction in AVC is completely due to the greater productivity of a second worker. To get 20 pairs of jeans, we had to employ a second worker part-time. In the process, the marginal physical product of labor rose and AVC fell.

With both AFC and AVC falling, ATC must decline as well. In this case, *average* total cost falls from $16.33 per pair to $13.50. This is reflected in row K in the table as well as in point K on the ATC curve in Figure 7.5.

Rising AVC. Although AFC continues to decline as output expands, AVC doesn't keep dropping. On the contrary, AVC tends to start rising quite early in the expansion process. Look at column 6 of the table in Figure 7.5. After an initial decline, AVC starts to increase. At an output of 20 pairs, AVC is $7.50. At 30 pairs, AVC is $8.00. By the time the rate of output reaches 51 pairs per day, AVC is $12.41.

Average variable cost rises because of diminishing returns in the production process. We discussed this concept before. As output expands, each unit of labor has less land and capital to work with. Marginal physical product falls. As it does, labor costs *per pair of jeans* rise, pushing up AVC.

U-Shaped ATC. The steady decline of AFC, when combined with the typical increase in AVC, results in a U-shaped pattern for average total costs. In the early stages of output expansion, the large declines in AFC outweigh any increases in AVC. As a result, ATC tends to fall. Notice that ATC declines from $20.50 to $11.75 as output increases from 10 to 40 pairs per day. This is also illustrated in Figure 7.5 with the downward move from point I to point M.

The battle between falling AFC and rising AVC takes an irreversible turn soon thereafter. When output is increased from 40 to 50 pairs of jeans per day, AFC continues to fall (row N in the table). But the decline in AFC (−60 cents) is overshadowed by the increase in AVC (+$2.25). Once rising AVC dominates, ATC starts to increase as well. ATC increases from $11.75 to $13.40 when jeans production expands from 40 to 50 pairs per day.

This and further increases in average total costs cause the ATC curve in Figure 7.5 to start rising. *The initial dominance of falling AFC, combined with the later resurgence of rising AVC, is what gives the ATC curve its characteristic U shape.*

Minimum Average Cost. Whew! There are a lot of numbers here. It's easy to get lost in this thicket of intertwined graphs and jumble of equations. A couple of landmarks will help guide us out, however. One of those is located at the very bottom of the U-shaped average total cost curve. Point M in Figure 7.5 represents *minimum* average total costs. By producing exactly 40 pairs per day, we minimize the amount of land, labor, and capital used per pair of jeans. For Low-Rider Jeans Corporation, point M represents least-cost production—the lowest-cost jeans. For society as a whole, point M also represents the

TABLE 7.3

Resource Computation of Marginal Cost

Marginal cost refers to the value of the additional inputs needed to produce one more unit of output. To increase daily jeans output from 15 to 16 pairs, we need 0.053 unit of labor and one-tenth of a bolt of denim. These extra inputs cost $7.24.

Inputs Used to Produce 16th Pair of Jeans	×	Market Value of Input	=	Marginal Cost
0.053 unit of labor		0.053 × $80 per unit of labor		$4.24
0.1 bolt of denim		0.1 × $30 per bolt		3.00
				$7.24

lowest possible opportunity cost: at point *M,* we're minimizing the amount of resources used to produce a pair of jeans and therefore maximizing the amount of resources left over for the production of other goods and services.

As attractive as point *M* is, you shouldn't conclude that it's everyone's dream. The goal of producers is to maximize *profits.* We already noted that maximum *profits* and maximum *output* don't necessarily coincide. Now we'll see that **minimizing average total cost isn't necessarily the same thing as maximizing profit**, either.

Marginal Cost

To get a firmer grip on profit maximization, we need to introduce one last cost concept. Indeed, this last concept is probably the most important one for production. It's *marginal cost.* We encountered this concept in our discussion of resource costs, where we noted that marginal cost refers to the value of the resources needed to produce one more unit of a good. To produce *one* more pair of jeans, we need the denim itself and a very small amount of additional labor. These are the extra or added costs of increasing output by one pair of jeans per day.

To compute the *dollar* value of these marginal costs, we could determine the market price of denim and labor and then add them up. Table 7.3 provides an example. In this case, we calculate that the additional or *marginal* cost of producing a sixteenth pair of jeans is $7.24. This is how much *total* costs will increase if we decide to expand jeans output by only one pair per day (from 15 to 16).

Table 7.3 emphasizes the link between resource costs and dollar costs. However, there's a much easier way to compute marginal cost. ***Marginal cost refers to the change in total costs associated with one more unit of output.*** Accordingly, we can simply observe *total* dollar costs before and after the rate of output is increased. The difference between the two totals equals the *marginal cost* of increasing the rate of output. This technique is much easier for jeans manufacturers who don't know much about marginal resource utilization but have a sharp eye for dollar costs. It's also a lot easier for economics students, of course. But they have an obligation to understand the resource origins of marginal costs and what causes marginal costs to rise or fall. As we noted before, ***diminishing returns in production cause marginal costs to increase as the rate of output is expanded.***

Figure 7.6 shows what the marginal costs of producing jeans look like. At each output rate, marginal cost is computed as the *change* in total cost divided by the *change* in output. When output increases from 20 jeans to 30 jeans, total cost rises by $90. Dividing this change in costs by 10 (the change in output) gives us a marginal cost of $9, as illustrated by point *s.*

Increasing MC. Notice in Figure 7.6 how the marginal cost curve starts climbing upward after 20 units of output have been produced. This rise in marginal costs reflects the law of diminishing returns. As increases in output become more difficult to achieve, they also become more expensive. Each additional pair of jeans beyond 20 requires a bit more labor than the preceding pair and thus entails rising marginal cost. After output passes 40 pairs, marginal costs really shoot upward.

A Cost Summary

All these cost calculations can give you a real headache. They can also give you second thoughts about jumping into Low-Rider Jeans or any other business. There are tough

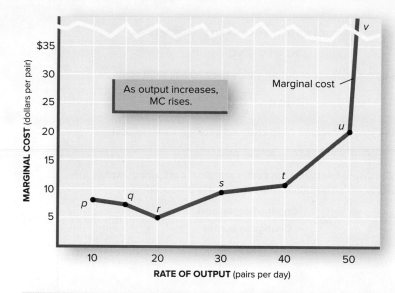

FIGURE 7.6

Marginal Costs

Marginal cost is the change in total cost that occurs when more output is produced. MC equals $\Delta TC/\Delta q$.

When diminishing returns set in, MC begins rising, as it does here after the output rate of 20 pairs per day is exceeded.

	Rate of Output	Total Cost	$\dfrac{\Delta TC}{\Delta q}$ = MC
	0	$120	—
p	10	205	$85/10 = $8.5
q	15	245	$40/5 = $8.0
r	20	270	$25/5 = $5.0
s	30	360	$90/10 = $9.0
t	40	470	$110/10 = $11.0
u	50	670	$200/10 = $20.0
v	51	753	$83/1 = $83.0

choices to be made. A given firm can produce many different rates of output, each of which entails a distinct level of costs. *The output decision has to be based not only on the capacity to produce (the production function) but also on the costs of production (the cost functions).* Only those who make the right decisions will succeed in business.

The decision-making process is made a bit easier with the glossary in Table 7.4 and the generalized cost curves in Figure 7.7. As before, we're concentrating on a short-run production process, with fixed quantities of land and capital. In this case, however, we've abandoned the Low-Rider Jeans Corporation and provided hypothetical costs for an idealized production process. The purpose of these figures is to provide a more general view of how the various cost concepts relate to each other. Note that MC, ATC, AFC, and AVC can all be computed from total costs. All we need, then, are the first two columns of the table in Figure 7.7, and we can compute and graph all the rest of the cost figures.

MC–ATC Intersection. The centerpiece of Figure 7.7 is the U-shaped ATC curve (in green). Of special significance is its relationship to marginal costs. Notice that *the MC curve intersects the ATC curve at its lowest point* (point *m*). This will always be the case. So long as the marginal cost of producing one more unit is less than the previous average cost, average costs must fall. *Thus average total costs decline as long as the marginal cost curve lies below the average cost curve,* as to the left of point *m* in Figure 7.7.

We already observed, however, that marginal costs rise as output expands, largely because additional workers reduce the amount of land and capital available to each worker (in the short run, the size of plant and equipment is fixed). Consequently, at some point (*m* in Figure 7.7) marginal costs will rise to the level of average costs.

TABLE 7.4

A Guide to Costs

A quick reference to key measures of cost.

---

average fixed cost (AFC): Total fixed cost divided by the quantity produced in a given time period.

---

average variable cost (AVC): Total variable cost divided by the quantity produced in a given time period.

Total costs of production are made up of **fixed costs** and **variable costs:**

$$TC = FC + VC$$

Dividing total costs by the quantity of output yields the **average total cost:**

$$ATC = \frac{TC}{q}$$

which also equals the sum of **average fixed cost** and **average variable cost:**

$$ATC = AFC = AVC$$

The most important measure of changes in cost is **marginal cost,** which equals the increase in total costs when an additional unit of output is produced:

$$MC = \frac{\text{Change in total cost}}{\text{Change in output}}$$

FIGURE 7.7

Basic Cost Curves

With total cost and the rate of output, all other cost concepts can be computed.

The resulting cost curves have several distinct features. The AFC curve always slopes downward. The MC curve typically rises, sometimes after a brief decline.

The ATC curve has a U shape. And the MC curve will always intersect both the ATC and AVC curves at their lowest points (*m* and *n*, respectively).

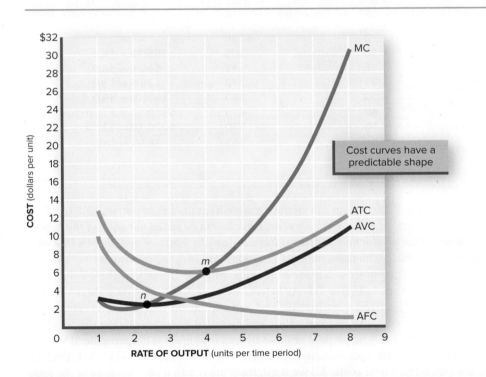

Cost curves have a predictable shape

Rate of Output	TC	MC	ATC	AFC	AVC
0	$10.00	—	—	—	—
1	13.00	$ 3.00	$13.00	$10.00	$ 3.00
2	15.00	2.00	7.50	5.00	2.50
3	19.00	4.00	6.33	3.33	3.00
4	25.00	6.00	6.25	2.50	3.75
5	34.00	9.00	6.80	2.00	4.80
6	48.00	14.00	8.00	1.67	6.33
7	68.00	20.00	9.71	1.43	8.28
8	98.00	30.00	12.25	1.25	11.00

As marginal costs continue to rise beyond point *m,* they begin to pull average costs up, giving the average cost curve its U shape. ***Average total costs increase whenever marginal costs exceed average costs.*** This is the case to the right of point *m* because the marginal cost curve always lies above the average cost curve in that part of Figure 7.7.

To visualize the relationship between marginal cost and average cost, imagine computing the average height of people entering a room. If the first person who comes through the door is six feet tall, then the average height of people entering the room is six feet at that point. But what happens to average height if the second person entering the room is only three feet tall? *Average* height declines because the last (marginal) person entering the room is shorter than the previous average. Whenever the last entrant is shorter than the average, the average must fall.

The relationship between marginal costs and average costs is also similar to that between your grade in this course and your grade point average. If your grade in economics is better (higher) than your other grades, then your overall grade point average will rise. In other words, a high *marginal* grade will pull your *average* grade up. If you don't understand this, your grade point average is likely to fall.

ECONOMIC VS. ACCOUNTING COSTS

The cost curves we observed here are based on *real* production relationships. The dollar costs we compute are a direct reflection of underlying resource costs: the land, labor, and capital used in the production process. Not everyone counts this way. On the contrary, accountants and businesspeople typically count dollar costs only and ignore any resource use that doesn't result in an explicit dollar cost.

Return to Low-Rider Jeans for a moment to see the difference. When we computed the dollar cost of producing 15 pairs of jeans per day, we noted the following resource inputs:

INPUTS	COST PER DAY
1 factory rent	$100
1 machine rent	20
1 machine operator	80
1.5 bolts of denim	45
Total cost	$245

The total value of the resources used in the production of 15 pairs of jeans was thus $245 per day. But this figure needn't conform to *actual* dollar costs. Suppose the owners of Low-Rider Jeans decided to sew jeans themselves. Then they wouldn't have to hire a worker and pay $80 per day in wages. **Explicit costs**—the *dollar* payments—would drop to $165 per day. The producers and their accountant would consider this a remarkable achievement. They might assert that the cost of producing jeans had fallen.

explicit costs: A payment made for the use of a resource.

Economic Cost

An economist would draw no such conclusions. ***The essential economic question is how many resources are used in production.*** This hasn't changed. One unit of labor is still being employed at the factory; now it's simply the owner, not a hired worker. In either case, one unit of labor is not available for the production of other goods and services. Hence society is still paying $245 for jeans, whether the owners of Low-Rider Jeans write checks in that amount or not. The only difference is that we now have an **implicit cost** rather than an explicit one. We really don't care who sews jeans—the essential point is that someone (i.e., a unit of labor) does.

The same would be true if Low-Rider Jeans owned its own factory rather than rented it. If the factory were owned rather than rented, the owners probably wouldn't write any rent checks. Hence, *accounting* costs would drop by $100 per day. But the factory would still be in use for jeans production and therefore unavailable for the production of other goods and services. The economic (resource) cost of producing 15 pairs of jeans would still be $245.

implicit cost: The value of resources used, for which no direct payment is made.

economic cost: The value of all resources used to produce a good or service; opportunity cost.

The distinction between an economic cost and an accounting cost is essentially one between resource and dollar costs. *Dollar cost* refers to the explicit dollar outlays made by a producer; it's the lifeblood of accountants. **Economic cost,** in contrast, refers to the *value* of *all* resources used in the production process; it's the lifeblood of economists. In other words, economists count costs as

$$\text{Economic cost} = \text{Explicit costs} + \text{Implicit costs}$$

As this formula suggests, *economic and accounting costs will diverge whenever any factor of production is not paid an explicit wage (or rent, etc.).*

The Cost of Homework. These distinctions between economic and accounting costs apply also to the "production" of homework. You can pay people to write term papers for you or buy them off the Internet. At large schools you can often buy lecture notes as well. But most students do their own homework so they'll learn something and not just turn in required assignments.

Doing homework is expensive, however, even if you don't pay someone to do it. The time you spend reading this chapter is valuable. You could be doing something else if you weren't reading right now. What would you be doing? That forgone activity—the best alternative use of your time—represents the economic cost of doing homework. Even if you don't pay yourself for reading this chapter, you'll still incur that *economic* cost.

LONG-RUN COSTS

We've confined our discussion thus far to short-run production costs. ***The short run is characterized by fixed costs***—a commitment to specific plants and equipment. A factory, an office building, or some other plants and equipment have been leased or purchased: we're stuck with *fixed costs.* In the short run, our objective is to make the best use of those fixed costs by choosing the appropriate rate of production.

long run: A period of time long enough for all inputs to be varied (no fixed costs).

The long run opens up a whole new range of options. In the **long run,** we have no lease or purchase commitments. We're free to start all over again with whatever scale of plants and equipment we desire and whatever technology is available. Quite simply, ***there are no fixed costs in the long run.*** Nor are there any commitments to existing technology.

That's what excited Elon Musk when he started thinking about mass-producing Tesla electric cars. Although Tesla had sold only 30,000 vehicles in its first 6 years, Musk envisioned his company selling as many as 500,000 vehicles by the year 2020. To do so, he decided he needed to get into the battery business as well. So he made plans to build a "gigafactory" of gigantic proportions to produce the lithium-ion batteries he'd need for mass production of Tesla cars (see In the News "Tesla Banks on Gigafactory"). To do so, he was willing to incur fixed costs of $4 to $5 *billion*! If and when the factory is completed, Tesla will focus on the short-run production decision of how many batteries and cars to produce from its gigafactory.

Long-Run Average Costs

The opportunities available in the long run include building a plant of any desired size, including "gigafactories." Suppose we still wanted to go into the jeans business. In the long run, we could build or lease any size factory we wanted and could lease as many sewing machines as we desired. Figure 7.8 illustrates three choices: a small factory (ATC_1), a medium-sized factory (ATC_2), and a large factory (ATC_3). All three factories have the common U-shaped average total cost curves. But there are important differences. As we observed earlier, it's very expensive to produce lots of jeans with a small factory. The ATC curve for a small factory (ATC_1) starts to head straight up at relatively low rates of output. In the long run, we'd lease or build such a factory only if we anticipated a continuing low rate of output.

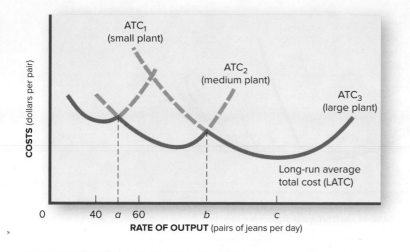

FIGURE 7.8

Long-Run Costs with Three Plant Size Options

Long-run cost possibilities are determined by all possible short-run options. In this case, there are three options of varying size (ATC$_1$, ATC$_2$, and ATC$_3$).

In the long run, we'd choose the plant that yielded the lowest average cost for any desired rate of output. The solid portions of the curves (LATC) represent these choices. The smallest factory (ATC$_1$) is best for output levels below *a*; the largest (ATC$_3$), for output rates in excess of *b*.

The ATC$_2$ curve illustrates how costs might fall if we leased or built a medium-sized factory. With a small factory, ATC becomes prohibitive at an output of 50 to 60 pairs of jeans per day. A medium-sized factory can produce these quantities at lower cost. Moreover, ATC continues to drop as jeans production increases in the medium-sized factory—at least for a while. Even a medium-sized factory must contend with resource constraints and therefore rising average costs: its ATC curve is U-shaped also.

If we expected to sell really large quantities of jeans, we'd want to build or lease a large factory. Beyond the rate of output *b,* the largest factory offers the lowest average total cost. There's a risk in leasing such a large factory, of course. If our sales don't live up to our high expectations, we'll end up with very high fixed costs and thus very expensive jeans. Look at the high average cost of producing only 60 pairs of jeans per day with the large factory (ATC$_3$).

In choosing an appropriate factory, then, we must decide how many jeans we expect to sell. Once we know our expected output, we can select the right-sized factory. It will be the one that offers the lowest ATC for that rate of output. If we expect to sell fewer jeans than *a,* we'll choose the small factory in Figure 7.8. If we expect to sell jeans at a rate between *a* and *b,* we'll select a medium-sized factory. Beyond rate *b,* we'll want the largest factory. These choices are reflected in the solid parts of the three ATC curves. The composite "curve" created by these three segments constitutes our long-run cost possibilities. ***The long-run cost curve is just a summary of our best short-run cost possibilities, using existing technology and facilities.***

We might confront more than three choices, of course. There's really no reason we couldn't build a factory to *any* desired size. In the long run, we face an infinite number of scale choices, not just three. The effect of all these choices is to smooth out the long-run cost curve. Figure 7.9 depicts the long-run curve that results. Each rate of output is most efficiently produced by some size (scale) of plant. That sized plant indicates the minimum cost of producing a particular rate of output. Its corresponding short-run ATC curve provides one point on the long-run ATC curve.

Long-Run Marginal Costs

Like all average cost curves, the long-run (LATC) curve has its own marginal cost curve. The long-run marginal cost (LMC) curve isn't a composite of short-run marginal cost curves. Rather, it's computed on the basis of the costs reflected in the long-run ATC curve itself. We won't bother to compute those costs here. Note, however, that the long-run MC curve—like all MC curves—intersects its associated average cost curve at its lowest point.

FIGURE 7.9
Long-Run Costs with Unlimited Options

If plants of all sizes can be built, short-run options are infinite. In this case, the LATC curve becomes a smooth U-shaped curve. Each point on the curve represents lowest-cost production for a plant size best suited to one rate of output. The long-run ATC curve has its own MC curve.

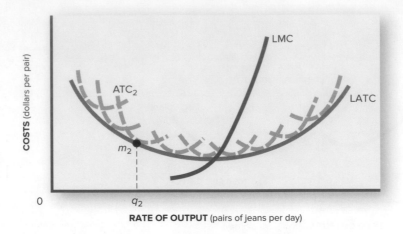

ECONOMIES OF SCALE

Figure 7.8 seems to imply that a producer must choose either a small plant or a larger one. That isn't completely true. The choice is often between one large plant or *several* small ones. Suppose the desired level of output was relatively large, as at point *c* in Figure 7.8. A single small plant (ATC_1) is clearly not up to the task. But what about using several small plants rather than one large one (ATC_3)? How would costs be affected?

Notice what happens to *minimum ATC* in Figure 7.8 when the size (scale) of the factory changes. When a medium-sized factory (ATC_2) replaces a small factory (ATC_1), minimum average cost drops (the bottom of ATC_2 is below the bottom of ATC_1). This implies that a jeans producer who wants to minimize costs should build one medium-sized factory rather than try to produce the same quantity with two small ones. **Economies of scale** exist in this situation: larger facilities reduce *minimum* average costs.

This is the kind of potential that excited Elon Musk. As he studied alternatives for building a battery factory, he saw several possibilities for bringing minimum average costs down. Innovations in manufacturing, better logistics, co-located processes, and reduced overhead could give a larger plant economies of scales that smaller plants couldn't achieve. So he decided to build a 10-million-square-foot "gigafactory" that could achieve substantial economies of scale (see In the News "Tesla Banks on Gigafactory").

economies of scale:
Reductions in minimum average costs that come about through increases in the size (scale) of plant and equipment.

IN THE NEWS

TESLA BANKS ON GIGAFACTORY

No one can say Elon Musk isn't ambitious. He wants his company, electric car maker Tesla, to get into mass production. Although Tesla sold only 200,000 cars in its first eight years, Musk wants to ramp up production to more than a million cars per year by 2020. To do so, he needs a cheap and abundant supply of lithium-ion batteries, the most expensive component in EVs. His solution? Build a "gigafactory" that will attain huge economies of scale and reduce the cost of batteries by 30 percent.

With cheaper batteries, Musk figures he can lower the price of Tesla vehicles enough to achieve a price point ($35,000) that appeals to the mass market. Tesla broke ground on its gigafactory outside Reno, Nevada in June 2014. By the beginning of 2017 it was less than 20 percent completed, with 350 workers employed. By 2020, however, Musk envisions a 1.9 million square foot factory employing 6,500 workers and producing 150 gigawatts of battery packs—enough to power 1.5 million electric vehicles. It would be the largest factory in the world, by footprint, and the second largest by volume. Now that is ambitious!

Source: News reports, January 2017.

ANALYSIS: As the size of a factory increases, it may be able to reduce the costs of doing business. Economies of scale can give a large firm a competitive advantage over smaller firms.

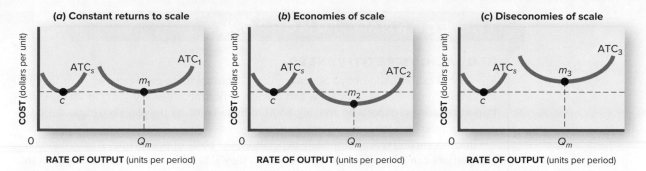

FIGURE 7.10

Economies of Scale

A lot of output (Q_m) can be produced from one large plant or many small ones. Here we contrast the average total costs associated with one small plant (ATCs) and three large plants (ATC$_1$, ATC$_2$, and ATC$_3$). If a large plant attains the same *minimum* average costs (point m_1 in part *a*) as a smaller plant (point *c*), there's no advantage to large size (scale). Many small plants can produce the same output just as cheaply. However, either economies (part *b*) or diseconomies (part *c*) of scale may exist.

Larger production facilities don't always result in cost reductions. Suppose a firm has the choice of producing the quantity Q_m from several small factories or from one large, centralized facility. Centralization may have three different impacts on costs; these are illustrated in Figure 7.10. In each illustration, we see the average total cost (ATC) curve for a typical small firm or plant and the ATC curve for a much larger plant producing the same product.

Constant Returns. Figure 7.10*a* depicts a situation in which there's no economic advantage to centralization of manufacturing operations because a large plant is no more efficient than a lot of small plants. The critical focus here is on the *minimum* average costs attainable for a given rate of output. Note that the lowest point on the smaller plant's ATC curve (point *c*) is no higher or lower than the lowest point on the larger firm's ATC curve (point m_1). Hence it would be just as cheap to produce the quantity Q_m from a multitude of small plants as it would be to produce Q_m from one large plant. Thus increasing the size (or *scale*) of individual plants won't reduce minimum average costs: this is a situation of **constant returns to scale.**

Economies of Scale. Figure 7.10*b* illustrates the situation in which a larger plant can attain a lower minimum average cost than a smaller plant. That is, economies of scale (or *increasing returns to scale*) exist. This is evident from the fact that the larger firm's ATC curve falls *below* the dashed line in the graph (m_2 is less than *c*). The greater efficiency of the large factory might come from any of several sources. This is the situation Elon Musk was counting on for his proposed gigafactory (see In the News "Tesla Banks on Gigafactory").

Diseconomies of Scale. Even though large plants may be able to achieve greater efficiencies than smaller plants, there's no guaranty that they actually will. In fact, increasing the size (scale) of a plant may actually *reduce* operating efficiency, as depicted in Figure 7.10*c*. Workers may feel alienated in a plant of massive proportions and feel little commitment to productivity. Creativity may be stifled by rigid corporate structures and off-site management. A large plant may also foster a sense of anonymity that induces workers to underperform. When these things happen, *diseconomies of scale* result. Microsoft tries to avoid such diseconomies of scale by creating autonomous cells of no more than 35 employees ("small plants") within its larger corporate structure.

In evaluating long-run options, then, we must be careful to recognize that ***efficiency and size don't necessarily go hand in hand.*** Some firms and industries may be subject to economies of scale, but others may not. Bigger isn't always better.

constant returns to scale:
Increases in plant size do not affect minimum average cost; minimum per-unit costs are identical for small plants and large plants.

THE ECONOMY TOMORROW

GLOBAL COMPETITIVENESS

From 1900 to 1970, the United States regularly exported more goods and services than it imported. Since then America has had a trade deficit nearly every year. In 2016, U.S. imports exceeded exports by roughly $500 billion. To many people, such trade deficits are a symptom that the United States can no longer compete effectively in world markets.

Global competitiveness ultimately depends on the costs of production. If international competitors can produce goods more cheaply, they'll be able to undersell U.S. goods in global markets.

Cheap Foreign Labor? Cheap labor keeps costs down in many countries. The average wage in Mexico, for example, ranges from $2 to $3 an hour, compared to more than $20 an hour in the United States. China's manufacturing workers make only $3.50 an hour. Low wages are *not,* however, a reliable measure of global competitiveness. To compete in global markets, one must produce more *output* for a given quantity of *inputs.* In other words, labor is "cheap" only if it produces a lot of output in return for the wages paid.

A worker's contribution to output is measured by *marginal physical product (MPP).* What we saw in this chapter was that *a worker's productivity (MPP) depends on the quantity and quality of other resources in the production process.* In this regard, U.S. workers have a tremendous advantage: they work with vast quantities of capital and state-of-the-art technology. They also come to the workplace with more education. Their high wages reflect this greater productivity.

Unit Labor Costs. A true measure of global competitiveness must take into account both factor costs (e.g., wages) and productivity. One such measure is **unit labor cost,** which indicates the labor cost of producing one unit of output. It's computed as

$$\text{Unit labor cost} = \frac{\text{Wage rate}}{\text{MPP}}$$

Suppose the MPP of a U.S. worker is 10 units per hour and the wage is $20 an hour. The unit labor cost would be

$$\frac{\text{Unit labor cost}}{\text{(United States)}} = \frac{\$20/\text{hour}}{10 \text{ units/hour}} = \frac{\$2/\text{unit}}{\text{of output}}$$

By contrast, assume the average worker in Mexico has an MPP of 1 unit per hour and a wage of $3 an hour. In this case, the unit labor cost would be

$$\frac{\text{Unit labor cost}}{\text{(Mexico)}} = \frac{\$3}{1} = \frac{\$3/\text{unit}}{\text{of output}}$$

According to these hypothetical examples, "cheap" Mexican labor is no bargain. Mexican labor is actually *more* costly in production despite the much lower wage rate.

Productivity Advance. What these calculations illustrate is how important productivity is for global competitiveness. If we want the United States to stay competitive in global markets, U.S. productivity must increase as fast as that in other nations.

The production function introduced in this chapter helps illustrate the essence of global competitiveness in the economy tomorrow. Until now, we've regarded a firm's production function as a technological fact of life—the *best* we could do, given our state of technological and managerial knowledge. In the real world, however, the best is always getting better. Science and technology are continuously advancing. So is our knowledge of how to organize and manage our resources. These advances keep *shifting* production functions upward: more can be produced with any given quantity of inputs. In the process, the costs of production shift downward, as illustrated in Figure 7.11 by the downward shifts of the MC and ATC curves. These downward shifts imply that we can get more of the goods and services we desire with available resources. We can also compete more effectively in global markets in the economy tomorrow.

---

unit labor cost: Hourly wage rate divided by output per labor-hour.

(a) When the production function shifts up . . .

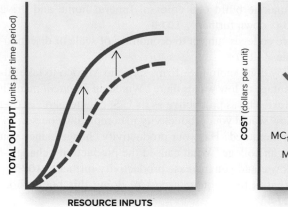

(b) Cost curves shift down

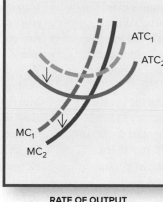

FIGURE 7.11

Improvements in Productivity Reduce Costs

Advances in technological or managerial knowledge increase our productive capability. This is reflected in upward shifts of the production function (part *a*) and downward shifts of production cost curves (part *b*).

SUMMARY

- A production function indicates the maximum amount of output that can be produced with different combinations of inputs. **LO7-1**
- In the short run, some inputs (e.g., land and capital) are fixed in quantity. Increases in (short-run) output result from more use of variable inputs (e.g., labor). **LO7-1**
- The contribution of a variable input to total output is measured by its marginal physical product (MPP). This is the amount by which *total* output increases when one more unit of the input is employed. **LO7-1**
- The MPP of a factor tends to decline as more of it is used in a given production facility. Diminishing marginal returns result from crowding more of a variable input (e.g., labor) into a production process, reducing the amount of fixed inputs *per unit* of variable input. **LO7-2**
- Marginal cost is the increase in total cost that results when output is increased by one unit. Marginal cost increases whenever marginal physical product diminishes. **LO7-3**
- Not all costs go up when the rate of output is increased. Fixed costs such as space and equipment leases don't vary with the rate of output. Only variable costs such as labor and material go up when output is increased. **LO7-3**

- Average total cost (ATC) equals total cost divided by the quantity of output produced. ATC declines when marginal cost (MC) is less than average cost and rises when MC exceeds it. The MC and ATC curves intersect at minimum ATC (the bottom of the U). That intersection represents least-cost production. **LO7-3**
- The economic costs of production include the value of *all* resources used. Accounting costs typically include only those dollar costs actually paid (explicit costs). **LO7-4**
- In the long run there are no fixed costs; the size (scale) of production can be varied. The long-run ATC curve indicates the lowest cost of producing output with facilities of appropriate size. **LO7-5**
- Economies of scale refer to reductions in *minimum* average cost attained with larger plant size (scale). If minimum ATC rises with plant size, diseconomies of scale exist. **LO7-5**
- Global competitiveness and domestic living standards depend on productivity advances. Improvements in productivity shift production functions up and push cost curves down. **LO7-1**

Key Terms

factors of production	profit	explicit cost
production function	marginal cost (MC)	implicit cost
productivity	total cost	economic cost
efficiency	fixed costs	long run
opportunity cost	variable costs	economies of scale
short run	average total cost (ATC)	constant returns to scale
marginal physical product (MPP)	average fixed cost (AFC)	unit labor cost
law of diminishing returns	average variable cost (AVC)	

Questions for Discussion

1. What are the production costs of your economics class? What are the fixed costs? The variable costs? What's the marginal cost of enrolling more students? **LO7-3**

2. Suppose all your friends offered to help wash your car. Would marginal physical product decline as more friends helped? Why or why not? **LO7-2**

3. What will happen to Tesla if it doesn't achieve the economies of scale it anticipates from its gigafactory? (See In the News "Tesla Banks on Gigafactory.") **LO7-5**

4. Owner/operators of small gas stations rarely pay themselves an hourly wage. How does this practice affect the economic cost of dispensing gasoline? **LO7-4**

5. Corporate funeral giants have replaced small family-run funeral homes in many areas, in large part because of the lower costs they achieve. What kind of economies of scale exist in the funeral business? Why doesn't someone build one colossal funeral home and drive costs down further? **LO7-5**

6. Are colleges subject to economies of scale or diseconomies? **LO7-5**

7. Why don't more U.S. firms move to Mexico to take advantage of low wages there? Would an *identical* plant in Mexico be as productive as its U.S. counterpart? **LO7-1**

8. How would your productivity in completing coursework be measured? Has your productivity changed since you began college? What caused the productivity changes? How could you increase productivity further? **LO7-1**

9. What is the economic cost of doing this homework? **LO7-4**

10. What causes unit labor costs to rise in some nations and fall in others? **LO7-3**

PROBLEMS FOR CHAPTER 7

LO7-3 1. (*a*) Complete the following cost schedule:

Rate of Output	Total Cost	Marginal Cost	Average Fixed Cost	Average Variable Cost	Average Total Cost
0	$ 600	_____	_____	_____	_____
1	800	_____	_____	_____	_____
2	1,050	_____	_____	_____	_____
3	1,400	_____	_____	_____	_____
4	1,800	_____	_____	_____	_____
5	2,300	_____	_____	_____	_____

    (*b*) Use the cost data to plot the ATC and MC curves on the accompanying graph.
    (*c*) At what output rate is ATC minimized? (Use higher rate.)

LO7-2 2. At what level of labor input in Figure 7.2 does marginal physical product
    (*a*) First diminish?
    (*b*) Become zero?
    (*c*) Turn negative?

LO7-4 3. Suppose a company incurs the following costs: labor, $600; equipment, $300; and materials, $200. The company owns the building, so it doesn't have to pay the usual $700 in rent.
    (*a*) What is the total accounting cost?
    (*b*) What is the total economic cost?
    (*c*) If the company sold the building and then leased it back, what would be the change in
        (*i*) Accounting costs?
        (*ii*) Economic costs?

LO7-2 4. Refer to the production table for jeans (Table 7.1). Suppose a firm has two sewing machines and can vary only the amount of labor input.
    (*a*) Graph the production function for jeans given the two sewing machines.
    (*b*) Compute and graph the marginal physical product curve.
    (*c*) At what amount of labor input does the law of diminishing returns first become apparent in your graph of marginal physical product?
    (*d*) Is total output still increasing when MPP begins to diminish?
    (*e*) What is the value of MPP when output no longer increases?

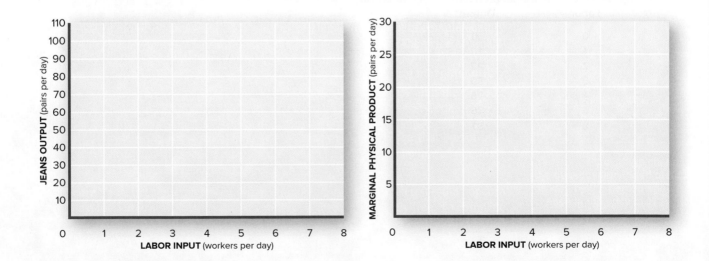

LO7-5 5. The following table indicates the average total cost of producing varying quantities of output from three different plants:

Rate of output	10	20	30	40	50	60	70	80	90	100
Average total cost										
Small firm	$ 600	$500	$400	$500	$600	$700	$800	$900	$1,000	$1,100
Medium firm	800	650	500	350	200	300	400	500	600	700
Large firm	1,000	900	800	700	600	500	400	300	400	500

(*a*) Plot the ATC curves for all three firms on the graph.

(*b*) Which plant(s) should be used to produce 40 units?

(*c*) Which plant(s) should be used to produce 100 units?

(*d*) Are there economies of scale in these plant size choices?

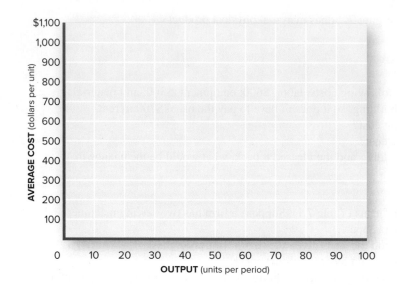

LO7-2 6. Given the following productivity information,

(*a*) Calculate marginal physical product.

(*b*) When does marginal productivity first diminish?

Labor	Output
0	0
1	10
2	22
3	30
4	36
5	38
6	37

LO7-3 7. Table 7.2 again shows the total cost of production for producing 15 pairs of jeans per day.

TABLE 7.2

The Total Costs of Production (Total Cost of Producing 15 Pairs of Jeans per Day)

The total cost of producing a good equals the market value of all the resources used in its production. In this case, the production of 15 pairs of jeans per day requires resources worth $245.

Resource Input	×	Unit Price of Input	=	Total Cost
1 factory		$100 per day		$100
1 sewing machine		20 per day		20
1 operator		80 per day		80
1.5 bolts of denim		30 per bolt		45
Total cost				$245

(*a*) Which two inputs are most likely to be fixed in the short run?
(*b*) Which two inputs are most likely to be variable in the short run?
To produce 15 pairs of jeans, calculate:
(*c*) Fixed cost
(*d*) Variable cost
(*e*) Total cost
(*f*) Average total cost

LO7-3 8. Complete the following table:

Quantity	Fixed cost	Variable cost	Total Cost
0			100
10		40	
20		100	
30	100		270
40		260	

LO7-3 9. Complete the following table:

Quantity	Total Cost	Marginal Cost	Average Variable Cost	Average Total Cost
0	20	—	—	—
1		10	10	
2				21
3		16		
4			14	
5	100			

LO7-4 10. Kanesha is an entrepreneur and has recently opened her first coffee shop, The Coffee Cat. Kanesha pays $5000 rent each month, $4800 for employee payroll, and $1200 for supplies. She was planning on selling several of her own tables and chairs on Craigslist for $1500, but instead she brought them to The Coffee Cat. Additionally, Kanesha quit working as an accountant where she was earning $52,000 per year to open up the shop. Based on this information identify:
(*a*) Explicit costs.
(*b*) Implicit costs.
Calculate annual:
(*c*) Accounting cost.
(*d*) Economic cost.

LO7-1 11. The Economy Tomorrow: Suppose the hourly wage rate is $24 in the United States and $3 in China, and productivity is 20 units per hour in the United States and 4 units per hour in China.

(*a*) What are per unit labor costs in the United States?

(*b*) What are per unit labor costs in China?

(*c*) If a company's goal is to minimize per unit labor costs, where would the production facility be located?

©Lars A. Niki RF

©David A. Barnes/Alamy Stock Photo

Source: Library of Congress Prints and Photographs Division [LC-USZ62-63968]

©McGraw-Hill Education/Andrew Resek, photographer

©McGraw-Hill Education/Jill Braaten, photographer

©MOF/Getty Images RF

MARKET STRUCTURE

Market demand curves tell us what products consumers want. And production functions tell us how much it will cost producers to supply those products. What we don't yet know is how many products will actually be supplied—or at what prices. These are *behavioral decisions,* not technological facts. Chapters 8 through 12 examine these behavioral decisions. As we'll see, the *structure* of a market—the number and size of firms in it—has a profound effect on the supply of goods and services—the quantity, quality, and price of specific goods.

©Lars A. Niki RF

CHAPTER 8

The Competitive Firm

Apple Computer would love to raise the price of downloading music from its iTunes store. It isn't likely to do so, however, because too many other firms also offer digital downloads. If Apple raises its prices, customers might sign up with another company.

Your campus bookstore may be in a better position to raise prices. On most college campuses there's only one bookstore. If the campus store increases the price of books or supplies, most of its customers (you) will have little choice but to pay the higher tab.

As we discover in this and the next few chapters, the degree of competition in product markets is a major determinant of product prices, quality, and availability. Although all firms are in business to make a profit, their profit opportunities are limited by the amount of competition they face.

This chapter begins an examination of how businesses make price and production decisions. We first explore the nature of profits and how they're computed. We then observe how one type of firm—a perfectly competitive one—can *maximize* its profits by selecting the right rate of output. The following questions are at the center of this discussion:

- **What are *profits?***
- **What are the unique characteristics of competitive firms?**
- **How much output will a competitive firm produce?**

The answers to these questions will shed more light on how the *supply* of goods and services is determined in a market economy.

THE PROFIT MOTIVE

The basic incentive for producing goods and services is the expectation of profit. *Owning* plants and equipment isn't enough. To generate a current flow of income, one must *use* the plants and equipment to produce and sell goods.

Profit is the difference between a firm's sales revenues and its total costs. It's the residual that the owners of a business receive. That profit residual may flow to the sole owner of a corner grocery store, or to the group of stockholders who collectively own a large corporation. In either case, it's the quest for profit that motivates people to own and operate a business (or a piece thereof).

Other Motivations

Profit isn't the only thing that motivates producers. Like the rest of us, producers also worry about social status and crave recognition. People

profit: The difference between total revenue and total cost.

who need to feel important, to control others, or to demonstrate achievement are likely candidates for running a business. Many small businesses are maintained by people who gave up 40-hour weeks, $50,000 incomes, and a sense of alienation in exchange for 80-hour weeks, $45,000 incomes, and a sense of identity and control.

In large corporations, the profit motive may lie even deeper below the surface. Stockholders (the owners) of large corporations rarely visit corporate headquarters. The people who manage the corporation's day-to-day business may have little or no stock in the company. Such nonowner managers may be more interested in their own jobs, salaries, and self-preservation than in the profits that accrue to the stockholding owners. If profits suffer, however, the corporation may start looking for new managers. The "bottom line" for virtually all businesses is the level of profits.

Is the Profit Motive Bad?

If it weren't possible to make a profit, few people would choose to supply goods and services. Yet the general public remains suspicious of the profit motive. As In the News "Are Profits Bad?" indicates, one out of four people thinks the profit motive is bad. An even higher percentage believes the profit motive results in *inferior* products at inflated prices. The Occupy Wall Street movement that began in September 2011 was predicated on the notion that corporate profits were a manifestation of corporate greed.

IN THE NEWS

ARE PROFITS BAD?

The following responses to a Roper survey are typical of public opinion about profits.

Agree that the. . .

Profit motive is bad—social needs are ignored in pursuit of high profits.	27%
Profit motive is good—it causes people to invest and provide monies to build plants, industries.	42%
Both (vol.)	9%
Neither (vol.)	4%
Don't know	17%

Profit system results in better products at lower prices.	39%
Profit system results in inferior products at inflated prices.	29%
Both (vol.)	8%
Neither (vol.)	5%
Don't know	19%

"'Responses to a Roper Survey," *The American Enterprise*, November–December 1993. Copyright ©1993. All rights reserved. Used with permission.

ANALYSIS: The profit motive is the primary incentive for supplying goods and services. Many consumers are distrustful of that motive, however.

As we'll see, the profit motive *can* induce business firms to pollute the environment, restrict competition, or maintain unsafe working conditions. However, ***the profit motive also encourages businesses to produce the goods and services consumers desire, at prices they're willing to pay.*** The profit motive, in fact, moves the "invisible hand" that Adam Smith said orchestrates market outcomes.

ECONOMIC VS. ACCOUNTING PROFITS

Although profits might be a necessary inducement for producers, most consumers feel that profits are too high. And that may be so in many cases. But most consumers have no idea how much profit U.S. businesses actually make. Public *perceptions* of profit are seven or eight times higher than actual profits. The typical consumer believes that 36 cents of every sales dollar goes to profits. In reality, average profit per sales dollar is closer to 5 cents.

Faulty perceptions of profits aren't confined to the general public. As surprising as it might seem, most businesses also measure their profits incorrectly.

Economic Profits

Everyone agrees that *profit represents the difference between total revenues and total costs.* Where people part ways is over the decision of what to include in total costs. Recall from Chapter 7 how economists compute costs. **Economic cost** refers to the value of *all* resources used in production, whether or not they receive an explicit payment. By contrast, most businesses count only **explicit costs**—that is, those they actually write checks for. They typically don't take into account the **implicit costs** of the labor or land and buildings they might own. As a result, they understate costs.

If businesses (and their accountants) understate true costs, they'll overstate true profits. Part of the accounting "profit" will really be compensation to unpaid land, labor, or capital used in the production process. *Whenever economic costs exceed explicit costs, observed (accounting) profits will exceed true (economic) profits.* Indeed, what appears to be an accounting profit may actually disguise an economic loss, as illustrated by the Fujishige strawberry farm once located right next to Disneyland (see In the News "The Value of Hiro's Strawberry Farm"). To determine the **economic profit** of a business, we must subtract all implicit factor costs from observed accounting profits:

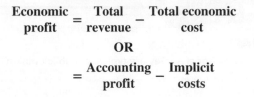

$$\text{Economic profit} = \text{Total revenue} - \text{Total economic cost}$$

$$\text{OR}$$

$$= \text{Accounting profit} - \text{Implicit costs}$$

economic cost: The value of all resources used to produce a good or service; opportunity cost.

explicit costs: A payment made for the use of a resource.

implicit cost: The value of resources used, for which no direct payment is made.

economic profit: The difference between total revenues and total economic costs.

IN THE NEWS

THE VALUE OF HIRO'S STRAWBERRY FARM

Anaheim, California—Hiroshi ("Hiro") Fujishige was a successful strawberry farmer in southern California. For more than 40 years, he maintained a 56-acre strawberry farm directly across the street from Disneyland. The Disney company repeatedly tried to convince Hiro to sell or lease his farm to Disney—offering to buy it for as much as $2 million an acre. Disney wanted the land to expand its theme park, but Hiro steadfastly refused to sell the farm he had bought for $3,500 in 1954 and on which he lived in a tiny house. For Hiro, the farm was precious, not for the profits it generated but for the security and freedom it provided. Having lost an earlier farm during the World War II internments of Japanese citizens, Hiro vowed not to give up another farm—at any price. "As long as I can make a profit from strawberries," he said, "I'll keep growing them." Which he did until he died in 1998.

Source: News reports, September 1998.

ANALYSIS: Mr. Fujishige's *accounting* profits were in stark contrast to his *economic* losses. The *implicit* costs of his time and land were enormous. After his death, Disney purchased the land for nearly $70 million and built the California Adventure Park.

Suppose, for example, that Table 8.1 accurately summarizes the revenues and costs associated with a local drugstore. Monthly sales revenues amount to $27,000. Explicit costs paid by the owner–manager include the cost of merchandise bought from producers for resale to consumers ($17,000), wages to the employees of the drugstore, rent and utilities

Total (gross) revenues per month	$27,000
less explicit costs:	
Cost of merchandise sold	$17,000
Wages to cashier, stock, and delivery help	2,500
Rent and utilities	800
Taxes	700
Total explicit costs	$21,000
Accounting profit (revenue minus explicit costs)	$ 6,000
less implicit costs:	
Wages of owner–manager, 300 hours @ $10 per hour	$ 3,000
Return on inventory investment, 10% per year on $120,000	1,000
Total implicit costs	$ 4,000
Economic profit (revenue minus *all* costs)	$ 2,000

TABLE 8.1

The Computation of Economic Profit

To calculate economic profit, we must take account of *all* costs of production. The economic costs of production include the implicit (opportunity) costs of the labor and capital a producer contributes to the production process. The accounting profits of a business take into account only explicit costs paid by the owner. Reported (accounting) profits will exceed economic profits whenever implicit costs are ignored.

paid to the landlord, and local sales and business taxes. When all these *explicit* costs are subtracted from total revenue, we're left with an *accounting profit* of $6,000 per month.

The owner–manager of the drugstore may be quite pleased with an accounting profit of $6,000 per month. He's working hard for this income, however. To keep his store running, the owner–manager is working 10 hours per day, 7 days a week. This adds up to 300 hours of labor per month. Were he to work this hard for someone else, his labor would be compensated explicitly—with a paycheck. Although he doesn't choose to pay himself this way, his labor still represents a real resource cost. To compute *economic* profit, we must subtract this implicit cost from the drugstore's accounting profits. Suppose the owner could earn $10 per hour in the best alternative job. Multiplying this wage rate ($10) by the number of hours he works in the drugstore (300), we see that the implicit cost of his labor is $3,000 per month.

The owner has also used his savings to purchase inventory for the store. He purchased the goods on his shelves for $120,000. If he had invested his savings in some other business, he could have earned a return of 10 percent per year. This forgone return represents a real cost. In this case, the implicit return (opportunity cost) on his capital investment amounts to $12,000 per year (10 percent × $120,000), or $1,000 per month.

To calculate the *economic* profit this drugstore generates, we count both explicit and implicit costs. Hence we must subtract all implicit factor payments (costs) from reported profits. The residual in this case amounts to $2,000 per month. That's the drugstore's *economic* profit.

Note that when we compute the drugstore's economic profit, we deduct the opportunity cost of the owner's capital. Specifically, we assumed that his funds would have reaped a 10 percent return somewhere else. In effect, we've assumed that a "normal" rate of return is 10 percent. This **normal profit** (the opportunity cost of capital) is an economic cost. Rather than investing in a drugstore, the owner could have earned a 10 percent return on his funds by investing in a fast-food franchise, a music store, a steel plant, or some other production activity. By choosing to invest in a drugstore instead, the owner was seeking a *higher* return on his funds—more than he could have obtained elsewhere. In other words, *economic profits represent something over and above "normal profits."*

Our treatment of "normal" returns as an economic cost leads to a startling conclusion: on average, economic profits are zero. Only firms that reap *above-average* returns can claim economic profits. This seemingly strange perspective on profits emphasizes the opportunity costs of all economic activities. *A productive activity reaps an economic profit only if it earns more than its opportunity cost.*

normal profit: The opportunity cost of capital; zero economic profit.

Entrepreneurship

Naturally, everyone in business wants to earn an economic profit. But relatively few people can stay ahead of the pack. To earn economic profits, a business must see opportunities that others have missed, discover new products, find new and better methods of production, or take above-average risks. In fact, economic profits are often regarded as a reward to entrepreneurship, the ability and willingness to take risks, to organize factors of production, and to produce something society desires.

Consider the local drugstore again. People in the neighborhood clearly want such a drugstore, as evidenced by its substantial sales revenue. But why should anyone go to the trouble and risk of starting and maintaining one? We noted that the owner–manager *could* earn $3,000 in wages by accepting a regular job plus $1,000 per month in returns on capital by investing in an "average" business. Why should he take on the added responsibilities and risk of owning and operating his own drugstore?

The inducement to take on the added responsibilities of owning and operating a business is the potential for economic profit, the extra income over and above normal factor payments. In the case of the drugstore owner, this extra income is the economic profit of $2,000 (Table 8.1). In the absence of such additional compensation, few people would want to make the extra effort required.

Risk

Don't forget, however, that the *potential* for profit is not a *guaranty* of profit. Quite the contrary. Substantial risks are attached to starting and operating a business. Tens of thousands of businesses fail every year, and still more suffer economic losses. From this perspective, profit also represents compensation for the risks incurred in owning or operating a business.

MARKET STRUCTURE

Not all businesses have an equal opportunity to earn an economic profit. The opportunity for profit may be limited by the *structure* of the industry in which the firm is engaged. One of the reasons Microsoft is such a profitable company is that it has long held a **monopoly** on computer operating systems. As the principal supplier of operating systems, Microsoft could raise software prices without losing many customers. T-shirt shops, by contrast, have to worry about all the other stores that sell similar products in the area (see In the News "Too Many Sellers: The Woes of T-Shirt Shops"). Faced with so much competition, the owner of a T-shirt shop doesn't have the power to raise prices or accumulate economic profits.

monopoly: A firm that produces the entire market supply of a particular good or service.

IN THE NEWS

TOO MANY SELLERS: THE WOES OF T-SHIRT SHOPS

Selling T-shirts is easy. People love T-shirts, especially with custom designs or logos of a special event or favorite band, product, or sports team. Consumers spend at least $15 billion a year on them. Moreover, the inventory is easy to store, doesn't spoil, and is compact. On the surface, a great business.

But there's a catch—everybody and his brother sells T-shirts. Every beach resort has dozens of T-shirt shops. And they sprout like weeds at every major sporting or concert venue. And then there are all the online sites that offer custom designs and quick delivery. So, the competition is intense. This makes it near impossible for any T-shirt shop to raise the price of its T-shirts, much less hold on to profits. The owner of a T-shirt shop in South Padre Island, Texas, lamented, "Every day you have to compete with other shops. And if you invent something new, they will copy you."

©McGraw-Hill Education

ANALYSIS: The ability to earn a profit depends on how many other firms offer similar products. A perfectly competitive firm, facing numerous rivals, has difficulty maintaining prices or profits.

FIGURE 8.1
Market Structures

The number and relative size of firms producing a good vary across industries. Market structures range from perfect competition (a great many firms producing the same good) to monopoly (only one firm). Most real-world firms are along the continuum of *imperfect* competition. Included in that range are duopoly (two firms), oligopoly (a few firms), and monopolistic competition (many firms).

Figure 8.1 illustrates various **market structures.** At one extreme is the monopoly structure in which only one firm produces the entire supply of the good. At the other extreme is **perfect competition.** In perfect competition a great many firms supply the same good.

There are relatively few monopolies or perfectly competitive firms in the real world. Most of the 30 million businesses in the United States fall between these extremes. They're more accurately characterized by gradations of *imperfect* competition—markets in which competition exists, but individual firms still retain some discretionary power over prices. In a *duopoly,* two firms supply the entire market. In an *oligopoly,* like credit card services, a handful of firms (Visa, MasterCard, American Express) dominate. In *monopolistic competition,* like fast-food restaurants, there are enough firms to ensure some competition, but not so many as to preclude some limited monopoly-type power. We examine all these market structures in later chapters, after we establish the nature of perfect competition.

market structure: The number and relative size of firms in an industry.

perfect competition: A market in which no buyer or seller has market power.

THE NATURE OF PERFECT COMPETITION

Industries can be classified by their structure—the number and relative size of the firms producing a specific good. As we'll see, the structure of an industry has a profound effect on market outcomes.

Structure

A perfectly competitive industry has several distinguishing characteristics, including

- *Many firms*—lots of firms are competing for consumer purchases.
- *Identical products*—the products of the different firms are identical, or nearly so.
- *Low entry barriers*—it's relatively easy to get into the business.

The T-shirt business has all these traits, which is why store owners have a hard time maintaining profits (see In the News "Too Many Sellers: The Woes of T-Shirt Shops").

Price Takers

Because they always have to contend with a lot of competition, T-shirt shops can't increase profits by raising T-shirt prices. More than 1 billion T-shirts are sold in the United States each year by tens of thousands of retail outlets. In such a competitive industry the many individual firms that make up the industry are all *price takers:* they take the price the market sets. A competitive firm can sell all its output at the prevailing market price. If it boosts its price above that level, consumers will shop elsewhere. In this sense, a perfectly competitive firm has no **market power**—no ability to control the market price for the good it sells.

At first glance, it might appear that all firms have market power. After all, who's to stop a T-shirt shop from raising prices? The important concept here, however, is *market* price— that is, the price at which goods are actually sold. If one shop raises its price to $15 and 40 other shops sell the same T-shirts for $10, it won't sell many shirts, and maybe none at all.

You may confront the same problem if you purchase a paper copy of this book and then try to sell it at the end of the semester. You might want to resell this textbook for $80. But

market power: The ability to alter the market price of a good or service.

you'll discover that the bookstore won't buy it at that price. With many other students offering to sell their books, the bookstore knows it doesn't have to pay the $80 you're asking. Because you don't have any market power, you have to accept the going price if you want to sell this book. You are a price taker in this market.

The same kind of powerlessness is characteristic of the small wheat farmer. Like any producer, the lone wheat farmer can increase or reduce his rate of output by making alternative production decisions. But his decision won't affect the market price of wheat.

Even the largest U.S. wheat farmers can't change the market price of wheat. The largest wheat farm produces nearly 100,000 bushels of wheat per year. But *2 billion* bushels of wheat are brought to market every year, so another 100,000 bushels simply won't be noticed. In other words, *the output of the lone farmer is so small relative to the market supply that it has no significant effect on the total quantity or price in the market.*

A distinguishing characteristic of *powerless* firms is that, individually, they can sell all the output they produce at the prevailing market price. We call all such producers **competitive firms;** they have no independent influence on market prices. *A perfectly competitive firm is one whose output is so small in relation to market volume that its output decisions have no perceptible impact on price.*

competitive firm: A firm without market power, with no ability to alter the market price of the goods it produces.

Market Demand Curves vs. Firm Demand Curves

It's important to distinguish between the market demand curve and the demand curve confronting a particular firm. T-shirt shops don't contradict the law of demand. The quantity of T-shirts purchased in the market still depends on T-shirt prices. That is, the *market* demand curve for T-shirts is still downward-sloping. A single T-shirt shop faces a *horizontal* demand curve only because its share of the market is so small that changes in its output don't disturb market equilibrium.

Collectively, though, individual firms do count. If all 40 of the T-shirt shops on South Padre Island (see In the News "Too Many Sellers: The Woes of T-Shirt Shops") were to increase shirt production at the same time, the market equilibrium would be disturbed. That is, a competitive market composed of individually powerless producers still sees a lot of action. The power here resides in the collective action of all the producers, however, not in the

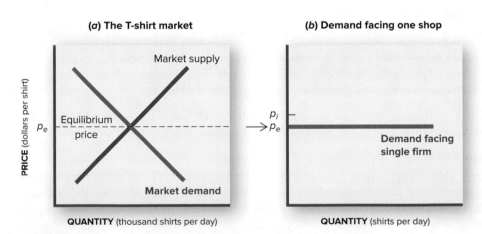

FIGURE 8.2

Market vs. Firm Demand

Consumer demand for any product is downward-sloping. The equilibrium price (p_e) of T-shirts is established by the intersection of *market* demand and *market* supply, as in the graph on the left. This market-established price is the only one at which an individual shop can sell T-shirts. If the shop owner asks a higher price (e.g., p_i in the graph on the right), no one will buy his shirts because they can buy identical T-shirts from other shops at p_e. But he can sell all his shirts at the market-set equilibrium price. The shop owner thus confronts a horizontal demand curve for his own output. (Notice the difference in market and individual shop quantities on the horizontal axes of the two graphs.)

individual action of any one. Were T-shirt production to increase so abruptly, the shirts could be sold only at lower prices, in accordance with the downward-sloping nature of the *market* demand curve. Figure 8.2 illustrates the distinction between the actions of a single producer and those of the market. Notice that

* *The market demand curve for a product is always downward-sloping (law of demand).*
* *The demand curve confronting a perfectly competitive firm is horizontal.*

THE PRODUCTION DECISION

A startling implication of Figure 8.2 is that *perfectly competitive firms don't make pricing decisions;* the *market* sets the prevailing price. All competitive firms do is *respond* to that market price. As price takers, they have only one decision to make: how much to produce. Choosing a rate of output is a firm's **production decision.** Should it produce all the output it can? Or should it produce at less than capacity?

Output and Revenues

In searching for the most desirable rate of output, focus on the distinction between total *revenue* and total *profit.* **Total revenue** is the price of the good multiplied by the quantity sold:

$$\text{Total revenue} = \text{Price} \times \text{Quantity}$$

Since a competitive firm can sell all its output at the market price (p_e), total revenue is a simple multiple of p_e. The total revenue of a T-shirt shop, for example, is the price of shirts (p_e) multiplied by the quantity sold. Figure 8.3 shows the total revenue curve that results from this multiplication. Note that *the total revenue curve of a perfectly competitive firm is an upward-sloping straight line with a slope equal to* p_e.

If a competitive firm wanted to maximize its total *revenue,* its production decision would be simple: it would always produce at capacity. Life isn't that simple, however; *the firm's goal is to maximize profits, not revenues.*

Output and Costs

To maximize profits, a firm must consider how increased production will affect *costs* as well as *revenues.* How do costs vary with the rate of output?

As we observed in Chapter 7, producers are saddled with certain costs in the **short run.** A T-shirt shop has to pay the rent every month no matter how few shirts it sells. The Low-Rider Jeans Corporation in Chapter 7 had to pay the rent on its factory and lease

production decision: The selection of the short-run rate of output (with existing plants and equipment).

total revenue: The price of a product multiplied by the quantity sold in a given time period: $p \times q$.

short run: The period in which the quantity (and quality) of some inputs can't be changed.

Price (per Shirt)	×	Quantity (Shirts per Day)	=	Total Revenue
$8		1		$ 8
8		2		16
8		3		24
8		4		32
8		5		40
8		6		48
8		7		56
8		8		64
8		9		72

FIGURE 8.3

Total Revenue

Because a competitive firm can sell all its output at the prevailing price, its total revenue curve is linear. In this case, the market (equilibrium) price of T-shirts is assumed to be $8. Hence a shop's total revenue is equal to $8 multiplied by quantity sold. Total revenue is maximized at capacity output.

FIGURE 8.4
Total Cost

Total cost increases with output. The rate of increase isn't steady, however. Typically, the rate of cost increase slows initially, then speeds up. After point *z*, diminishing returns (rising marginal costs) cause accelerating costs. These accelerating costs limit the profit potential of increased output.

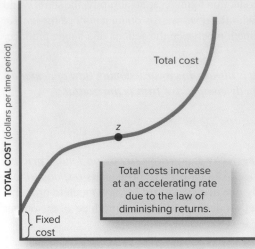

TOTAL COST (dollars per time period)

Total cost

z

Total costs increase at an accelerating rate due to the law of diminishing returns.

Fixed cost

OUTPUT (units per time period)

fixed costs: Costs of production that don't change when the rate of output is altered, such as the cost of basic plants and equipment.

variable costs: Costs of production that change when the rate of output is altered, such as labor and material costs.

marginal cost (MC): The increase in total cost associated with a one-unit increase in production.

payments on its sewing machine. These **fixed costs** are incurred even if no output is produced. Once a firm starts producing output, it incurs **variable costs** as well.

Since profits depend on the *difference* between revenues and costs, the costs of added output will determine how much profit a producer can make. Figure 8.4 illustrates a typical total cost curve. ***Total costs increase as output expands. But the rate of cost increase varies.*** Hence the total cost curve is *not* linear. At first total costs rise slowly (notice the gradually declining slope until point *z*), then they increase more quickly (the rising slope after point *z*). This S-shaped curve reflects the *law of diminishing returns.* As we first observed in Chapter 7, **marginal costs (MC)** often decline in the early stages of production and then increase as the available plants and equipment are used more intensively. These changes in marginal cost cause *total* costs to rise slowly at first, then to pick up speed as output increases.

You may suspect by now that the road to profits is not an easy one. It entails comparing ever-changing revenues with ever-changing costs. Figure 8.5 helps simplify the problem by bringing together typical total revenue and total cost curves. The total revenue line (in orange) is linear, since the price is constant. The total cost line, however, is sort of S-shaped, rising slowly at first, then much faster as marginal costs accelerate.

FIGURE 8.5
Total Profit

Profit is the *difference* between total revenue and total cost. It is represented as the vertical distance between the total revenue curve and the total cost curve. At output *h*, profit equals *r* minus *s*. The objective is to find the unique rate of output that *maximizes* profit.

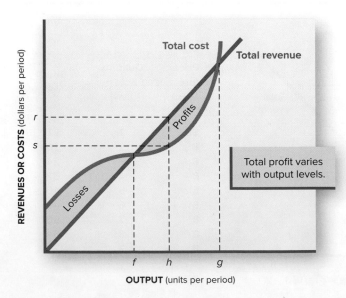

REVENUES OR COSTS (dollars per period)

Total cost

Total revenue

r

s

Profits

Losses

Total profit varies with output levels.

f   *h*   *g*

OUTPUT (units per period)

Our focus is on the *vertical distance* between the total revenue and cost curves. That vertical distance represents the *difference* between revenues and costs. Total costs in this case exceed total revenue at low rates of output (below *f*) as well as at very high rates (above *g*). The firm is profitable only at output rates between *f* and *g*.

Although all rates of output between *f* and *g* are profitable, they aren't *equally* profitable. A quick glance at Figure 8.5 confirms that the vertical distance between total revenue and total cost varies considerably within that range. ***The primary objective of the producer is to find that one particular rate of output that maximizes total profits.*** With a ruler, we could find it in Figure 8.5 by measuring the distance between the revenue and cost curves at all rates of output. In the real world, most producers need more practical guides to profit maximization.

PROFIT-MAXIMIZING RULE

The best single rule for maximizing profits in the short run is straightforward: never produce a unit of output that costs more than it brings in. By following this simple rule, a producer is likely to make the right production decision. We will see how this rule works by looking first at the revenue side of production ("what it brings in"), then at the cost side ("what it costs").

Marginal Revenue = Price

In searching for the most profitable rate of output, we need to know what an additional unit of output will bring in—that is, how much it adds to the total revenue of the firm. In general, the contribution to total revenue of an additional unit of output is called **marginal revenue (MR).** Marginal revenue is the *change* in total revenue that occurs when output is increased by one unit:

$$\text{Marginal revenue} = \frac{\text{Change in total revenue}}{\text{Change in output}}$$

To calculate marginal revenue, we compare the total revenues received before and after a one-unit increase in the rate of production; the *difference* between the two totals equals marginal revenue.

When the price of a product is constant, it's easy to compute marginal revenue. Suppose we're operating a catfish farm. Our product is catfish, sold at wholesale at the prevailing price of $13 per bushel. In this case, a one-unit increase in sales (one more bushel) increases total revenue by $13. As illustrated in Table 8.2, as long as the price of a product is constant, price and marginal revenue are the same. Hence, *for perfectly competitive firms, price equals marginal revenue.*

Marginal Cost

Keep in mind why we're breeding and selling catfish. Our goal is not to maximize *revenues* but to maximize *profits*. To gauge profits, we need to know not only the price of fish but also how much each bushel costs to produce. As we saw in Chapter 7, the added cost of producing one more unit of a good is its *marginal cost*. Figure 8.6 summarizes the marginal costs associated with the production of catfish.

marginal revenue (MR): The change in total revenue that results from a one-unit increase in the quantity sold.

Analysis: Fish farmers want to maximize profits, not the number of fish caught.
©Brian J. Skerry/National Geographic Creative

TABLE 8.2

Total and Marginal Revenue

Marginal revenue (MR) is the *change* in total revenue associated with the sale of one more unit of output. A third bushel increases total revenue from $26 to $39; MR equals $13. If the price is constant (at $13 here), marginal revenue equals price.

Quantity Sold (Bushels per Day)	×	Price (per Bushel)	=	Total Revenue (per Day)	Marginal Revenue (per Bushel)
0	×	$13	=	$ 0	—
1	×	13	=	13	$13
2	×	13	=	26	13
3	×	13	=	39	13
4	×	13	=	52	13

FIGURE 8.6
The Costs of Catfish Production

Marginal cost is the increase in total cost associated with a one-unit increase in production. When production expands from two to three units per day, total costs increase by $9 (from $22 to $31 per day). The marginal cost of the third bushel is therefore $9, as illustrated by point *D* in the graph and row *D* in the table.

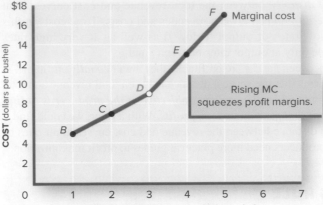

	Rate of Output (Bushels per Day)	Total Cost (per Day)	Marginal Cost (per Day)	Average Cost (per Day)
A	0	$10	—	—
B	1	15	$ 5	$15.00
C	2	22	7	11.00
D	3	31	9	10.33
E	4	44	13	11.00
F	5	61	17	12.20

The production process for catfish farming is wonderfully simple. The factory is a pond; the rate of production is the number of fish harvested from the pond per day. A farmer can alter the rate of production at will, up to the breeding capacity of the pond. As Calvin Jones, a former schoolteacher now working on a Mississippi catfish farm, says, "You raise fish. You get them out of the pond and you sell them. That's pretty much all you do. There's no genius to it."[1]

Assume that the *fixed* costs of the pond are $10 per day. The fixed costs include the rental value of the pond and the cost of electricity for keeping the pond oxygenated so the fish can breathe. These fixed costs must be paid no matter how many fish the farmer harvests.

To harvest catfish from the pond, the farmer must incur additional costs. Labor is needed to net and sort the fish. The cost of labor is *variable,* depending on how much output the farmer decides to produce. If no fish are harvested, no variable costs are incurred.

The *marginal costs* of harvesting are the additional costs incurred to harvest *one* more basket of fish. Generally, we expect marginal costs to rise as the rate of production increases. The law of diminishing returns we encountered in Chapter 7 applies to catfish farming as well. As more labor is hired, each worker has less space (pond area) and capital (access to nets, sorting trays) to work with. Accordingly, it takes a little more labor time (marginal cost) to harvest each additional fish.

Figure 8.6 illustrates these marginal costs. Notice how the MC rises as the rate of output increases. At the output rate of 4 bushels per day (point *E*), marginal cost is $13. Hence the fourth bushel *increases* total costs by $13. The fifth bushel is even more expensive, with a marginal cost of $17.

Profit-Maximizing Rate of Output

We're now in a position to make a production decision. The rule about never producing anything that adds more to cost than it brings in can now be stated in more technical terms. Since price equals marginal revenue for competitive firms, we can base the production

[1]Source: Byrd, Shelia, "Fuel, Feed Costs Crippling US Catfish Industry," Associated Press, June 22, 2008.

Price Level	Production Decision
Price > MC	Increase output
Price = MC	Maintain output (profits maximized)
Price < MC	Decrease output

TABLE 8.3

Short-Run Profit Maximization Rules for Competitive Firm

The relationship between price and marginal cost dictates short-run production decisions. For competitive firms, profits are maximized at that rate of output where price = MC.

decision on a comparison of *price* and marginal cost. ***There are only three possible scenarios for MC and price:***

- **MC > p.** We don't want to produce an additional unit of output if its MC exceeds its price. If MC exceeds price, we're spending more to produce that extra unit than we're getting back: total profits will decline if we produce it.
- **p > MC.** The opposite is true when price exceeds MC. If an extra unit brings in more revenue than it costs to produce, it is *adding* to total profit. Total profits must increase in this case. Hence a competitive firm wants to expand the rate of production whenever price exceeds MC.
- **p = MC.** Since we want to expand output when price exceeds MC and contract output if price is less than MC, the profit-maximizing rate of output is easily found. ***For perfectly competitive firms, profits are maximized at the rate of output where price equals marginal cost.*** The implications of this **profit maximization rule** are summarized in Table 8.3.

Figure 8.7 illustrates the application of our profit maximization rule in catfish farming. The prevailing wholesale price of catfish is $13 a bushel. At this price we can sell all the catfish we can produce, up to our short-run capacity. The catfish can't be sold at a higher

profit maximization rule: Produce at that rate of output where marginal revenue equals marginal cost.

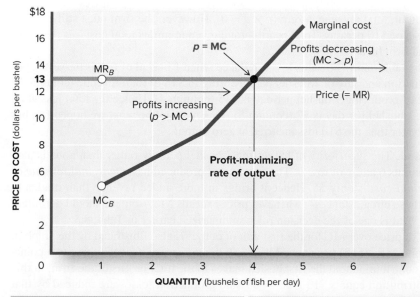

FIGURE 8.7

Maximization of Profits for a Competitive Firm

A competitive firm maximizes total profit at the output rate where MC = p. If MC is less than price, the firm can increase profits by producing more. If MC exceeds price, the firm should reduce output. In this case, profit maximization occurs at an output of 4 bushels per day.

	(1) Number of Bushels (per Day)	(2) Price	(3) Total Revenue	−	(4) Total Cost	=	(5) Total Profit	(6) Marginal Revenue	(7) Marginal Cost
A	0	$13	$ 0		$10		−$10	—	—
B	1	13	13		15		− 2	$13	$ 5
C	2	13	26		22		+ 4	13	7
D	3	13	39		31		+ 8	13	9
E	4	13	52		44		+ 8	13	13
F	5	13	65		61		+ 4	13	17

price because lots of farmers raise catfish and sell them for $13 (see In the News "The Lure of Catfish"). If we try to charge a higher price, consumers will buy their fish from other vendors. Hence we confront a horizontal demand curve at the price of $13.

IN THE NEWS

THE LURE OF CATFISH

Row-crop farmers throughout the South are taking a liking to catfish. Rising prices for catfish, combined with falling feed prices, have made the lure of catfish farming irresistible. Crop farmers are building ponds, buying aeration equipment, and breeding catfish in record numbers. Production has doubled in the last 15 years—to 340 million pounds this year—and looks to keep increasing as farmers shift from row crops to catfish.

Steve Hollingsworth, a Greensboro, Alabama farmer, now has ten ponds, each holding about 100,000 fish. He spends $18,000 a week on feed for the 1 million fish in his ponds. But he says the business is good; he takes in about $60,000 a week in sales. Crop farmers in Alabama, Mississippi, Arkansas, and Louisiana are taking the bait.

Source: Media reports, 1993.

ANALYSIS: People go into a competitive business like catfish farming to earn a profit. Once in business, they try to maximize total profits by equating price and marginal cost.

The costs of producing catfish were examined in Figure 8.6. The key concept illustrated here is marginal cost. The MC curve slopes upward in conventional fashion.

Figure 8.7 also depicts the total revenues, costs, and profits of alternative production rates. Study the table first. Notice that the firm loses $10 per day if it produces no fish (row A). At zero output, total revenue is zero ($p \times q = 0$). However, the firm must still contend with fixed costs of $10 per day. Total profit—total revenue minus total cost—is therefore *minus* $10; the firm incurs a loss.

Row *B* of the table shows how this loss is reduced when 1 bushel of fish is harvested per day. The production and sale of 1 bushel per day bring in $13 of total revenue (column 3). The total cost of producing 1 bushel per day is $15 (column 4). Hence the total loss at an output rate of 1 bushel per day is $2 (column 5). This may not be what we hoped for, but it's certainly better than the $10 loss incurred at zero output.

***p* > MC: Expand.** The superiority of harvesting 1 bushel per day rather than none is also evident in columns 6 and 7 of row *B*. The first bushel produced has a *marginal revenue* of $13. Its *marginal cost* is only $5. Hence it brings in more added revenue than it adds to costs. Under these circumstances—whenever price exceeds MC—output should definitely be expanded. That is one of the decision rules summarized earlier in Table 8.3.

The excess of price over MC for the first unit of output is also illustrated by the graph in Figure 8.7. Point MR_B ($13) lies above MC_B ($5); the *difference* between these two points measures the contribution that the first bushel makes to the total profits of the firm. In this case, that contribution equals $13 − $5 = $8, and production losses are reduced by that amount when the rate of output is increased from zero to 1 bushel per day.

As long as price exceeds MC, additional output increases total profit. Notice what happens to profits when the rate of output is increased from 1 to 2 bushels per day (row *C*). The price (MR) of the second bushel is $13; its MC is $7. Therefore it *adds* $6 to total profits. Instead of losing $2 per day, the firm is now making a profit of $4 per day.

The firm can make even more profits by expanding the rate of output further. The marginal revenue of the third bushel is $13; its marginal cost is $9 (row *D* of the table). Therefore, the third bushel makes a $4 contribution to profits.

MC = *p*: Max Profit. This firm will never make huge profits. For the fourth unit of output price and MC both equal $13. It doesn't contribute to total profits, and it doesn't subtract from them. The fourth unit of output represents the highest rate of output the

(a) Computing profits with total revenue and total cost

(b) Computing profits with price and average total cost

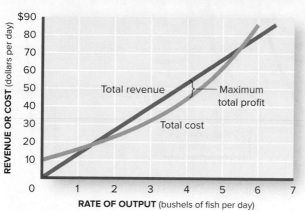

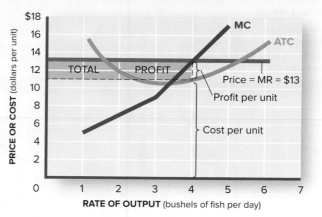

FIGURE 8.8

Alternative Views of Total Profit

Total profit can be computed as TR − TC, as in part *a*. Or it can be computed as profit *per unit* (*p* − ATC) multiplied by the quantity sold. This is illustrated in part *b* by the shaded rectangle. To find the profit-maximizing output, we could use either of these graphs or just the price and MC curves in Figure 8.7.

---

firm desires. ***At the rate of output where price = MC, total profits of the firm are maximized.***[2]

MC > *p*: Contract. Notice what happens if we expand output beyond 4 bushels per day. The price of the fifth bushel is still $13 but its MC is $17. The fifth bushel adds more to costs than to revenue. If we produce that fifth bushel, total profit will decline by $4. In Figure 8.7 the MC curve lies above the price line at all output levels in excess of 4. The lesson here is clear: ***output should not be increased if MC exceeds price.***

The correct production decision—the profit-maximizing decision—is shown in Figure 8.7 by the intersection of the price and MC curves. At this intersection, price equals MC and profits are maximized. If we produced less, we'd be giving up potential profits. If we produced more, total profits would also fall (review Table 8.3).

Adding Up Profits . . .

To reach the right production decision, we've relied on *marginal* revenues and costs. Having found the desired rate of output, however, we may want to take a closer look at the profits we are accumulating. Figure 8.8 provides two different ways of viewing our success.

with Total Revenue and Total Cost. The first view focuses on total revenues and total costs. Total profits are represented in Figure 8.8*a* by the vertical distance between the total revenue and total cost curves. This is a straightforward interpretation of our definition of total profits:

$$\text{Total profits} = \text{TR} - \text{TC}$$

The vertical distance between the TR and TC curves is maximized at the output of 4 bushels per day.

with Price and Average Cost. A second view of the same profits focuses on *average* costs and price. Total profit is equal to *average* profit per unit multiplied by the number of units produced. Profit *per unit,* in turn, is equal to price *minus* average total cost:

$$\text{Profit per unit} = p - \text{ATC}$$

---

[2]In this case, profits are the same at output levels of 3 and 4 bushels. Given the choice between the two levels, most firms will choose the higher level. By producing the extra unit of output, the firm increases its customer base. This not only denies rival firms an additional sale but also provides some additional cushion when the economy slumps. Also, corporate size may connote both prestige and power. In any case, the higher output level defines the *limit* to maximum profit production.

FIGURE 8.9
Different Goals

Businesses seek to maximize total profits, not profit per unit or total revenue. Therefore, they pursue the short-run output rate q_b, not the output rates q_a or q_c.

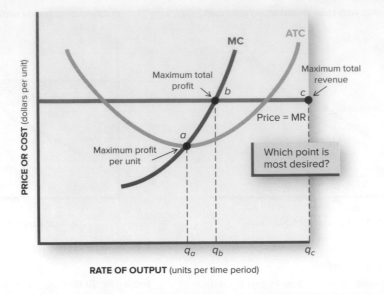

The price of catfish is illustrated in Figure 8.8*b* by the horizontal price line at $13. The average total cost of producing catfish is shown by the ATC curve. Like the ATC curve we encountered in Chapter 7, this one has a U shape. The *difference* between price and average cost—profit per unit—is illustrated by the vertical distance between the price and ATC curves. At 4 bushels per day, for example, profit per unit equals $13 − $11 = $2.

To compute *total* profits, we note that

$$\textbf{Total profits} \ = \ \textbf{Profit per unit} \times \textbf{Quantity} \ = \ (\,p - \text{ATC}\,) \times q$$

In this case, the 4 bushels generate a profit of $2 each, for a *total* profit of $8 per day. *Total* profits are illustrated in Figure 8.8*b* by the shaded rectangle. [Recall that the area of a rectangle is equal to its height (profit per unit) multiplied by its width (the quantity sold).]

Profit per unit is not only used to compute total profits but is often also of interest in its own right. Businesspeople like to cite statistics on "markups," which are a crude index to per-unit profits. However, ***the profit-maximizing producer never seeks to maximize per-unit profits. What counts is* total *profits, not the amount of profit per unit.*** This is the old $5 ice cream problem again. You might be able to maximize profit per unit if you could sell 1 cone for $5, but you would make a lot more money if you sold 100 cones at a per-unit profit of only 50 cents each.

Similarly, ***the profit-maximizing producer has no desire to produce at that rate of output where ATC is at a minimum.*** Minimum ATC does represent least-cost production. But additional units of output, even though they raise average costs, will increase total profits. This is evident in Figure 8.8; price exceeds MC for some output to the right of minimum ATC (the bottom of the U). Therefore, total profits are increasing as we increase the rate of output beyond the point of minimum average costs. Figure 8.9 illustrates the distinctions between these different markers.

THE SHUTDOWN DECISION

The rule established for short-run profit maximization doesn't guarantee any profits. By equating price and marginal cost, the competitive producer is only assured of achieving the *optimal* output. This is the best possible rate of output for the firm, given the existing market price and the (short-run) costs of production.

But what if the best possible rate of output generates a loss? What should the producer do in this case? Keep producing output? Or shut down the factory and find something else to do?

The first instinct may be to shut down the factory to stop the flow of red ink. But this isn't necessarily the wisest course of action. It may be smarter to keep operating a money-losing operation than to shut it down.

The rationale for this seemingly ill-advised course of action resides in the fixed costs of production. *Fixed costs must be paid even if all output ceases.* The firm must still pay rent on the factory and equipment even if it doesn't use these inputs. That's why we call such costs "fixed."

The persistence of fixed costs casts an entirely different light on the shutdown decision. Since fixed costs will have to be paid in any case, the question becomes: Which option creates greater losses? Does the firm lose more money by continuing to operate (and incurring a loss) or by shutting down (and incurring a loss equal to fixed costs)? In these terms, the answer becomes clear: *A firm should shut down only if the losses from continuing production exceed fixed costs.* This happens when total revenue is less than total *variable* cost.

Price vs. AVC

The shutdown decision can be made without explicit reference to fixed costs. Figure 8.10 shows how. The relationship to focus on is between the price of a good and its average *variable* cost.

The curves in Figure 8.10 represent the short-run costs and potential demand curves for catfish. As long as the price of catfish is $13 per bushel, the typical firm will produce 4 bushels a day, as determined by the intersection of the MC and MR (= price) curves (point X in part *a*). In this case, price ($13) exceeds average *total* cost ($11), and catfish farming is profitable. This is the happy situation we analyzed earlier (Figure 8.7).

The situation wouldn't look so good, however, if the market price of catfish fell to $9. Following the rule for profit maximization, the firm would be led to point Y in part *b*, where MC intersects the new demand (price) curve. At this intersection, the firm would produce 3 bushels per day. But total revenues would no longer cover total costs, as can be seen from the fact that the ATC curve now lies *above* the price line. The ATC of producing 3 bushels is $10.33 (Figure 8.6); price is $9. Hence the firm is incurring a loss of $4 per day (3 bushels at a loss of $1.33 each).

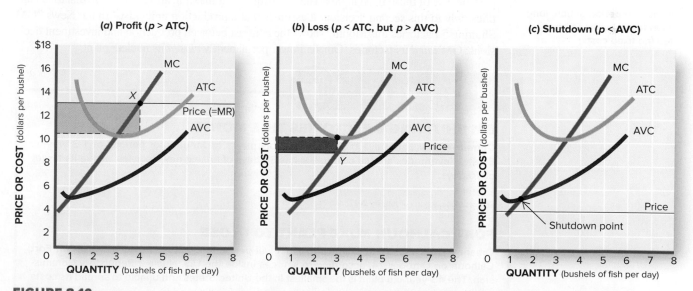

FIGURE 8.10

The Firm's Shutdown Point

A firm should cease production only if total revenue is lower than total *variable* cost. The shutdown decision may be based on a comparison of price and AVC. If the price of catfish per bushel was $13, a firm would earn a profit at point X in part *a*.

At a price of $9 (point Y in part *b*), the firm is losing money (*p* is less than ATC) but is more than covering all variable costs (*p* is greater than AVC). If the price falls to $4 per bushel, as in part *c*, output should cease (*p* is less than AVC).

Should the firm stay in business under the circumstances? The answer is yes. Recall that the catfish farmer has already dug the pond and installed equipment at a (fixed) cost of $10 per day. The producer will have to pay these fixed costs whether or not the machinery is used. Stopping production would result in a loss amounting to $10 per day. Staying in business, even when catfish prices fall to $9 each, generates a loss of only $4 a day. In this case, *where price exceeds average variable cost but not average total cost, the profit maximization rule minimizes losses.*

The Shutdown Point

If the price of catfish falls far enough, the producer may be better off ceasing production altogether. Suppose the price of catfish fell to $4 per bushel (Figure 8.10c). A price this low doesn't even cover the variable cost of producing 1 bushel per day ($5). Continued production of even 1 bushel per day would imply a total loss of $11 per day ($10 of fixed costs *plus* $1 of variable costs). Higher rates of output would lead to still greater losses. Hence the firm should shut down production, even though that action implies a loss of $10 per day. In all cases *where price doesn't cover average variable costs at any rate of output, production should cease.* Thus the **shutdown point** occurs where price is equal to minimum average *variable* cost. Any lower price will result in losses larger than fixed costs. In Figure 8.10, the shutdown point occurs at a price of $5, where the MC and AVC curves intersect.

shutdown point: The rate of output where price equals minimum AVC.

THE INVESTMENT DECISION

When a firm shuts down, it doesn't necessarily leave (exit) the industry. General Motors still produces cars even though it idled 5 of its plants in 2017 (see In the News "GM Shutting 5 Factories this Month"). *The shutdown decision is a* **short-run** *response.* It's based on the fixed costs of an established plant and the variable costs of operating it.

Ideally, a producer would never get into a money-losing business in the first place. Entry was based on an **investment decision** that the producer now regrets. *Investment decisions are* **long-run** *decisions,* however, and the firm now must pay for its bad luck or poor judgment. The investment decision entails the assumption of fixed costs (e.g., the lease of the factory); once the investment is made, the short-run production decision is designed to make the best possible use of those fixed inputs. The short-run profit maximization rule we've discussed applies only to this second decision; it assumes that a production unit exists. In the News "GM Shutting 5 Factories this Month" shows the contrast between production and investment decisions: GM *idled* its factories; Omaha Power permanently *closed* its nuclear plant.

investment decision: The decision to build, buy, or lease plants and equipment; to enter or exit an industry.

long run: A period of time long enough for all inputs to be varied (no fixed costs).

IN THE NEWS

GM SHUTTING 5 FACTORIES THIS MONTH

Detroit—GM will shut five U.S. auto assembly plants in January for periods of 1-3 weeks. Bloated inventories are the culprit: GM has 84 days of unsold new vehicles, above its target of 70 days.

Source: Media reports of January 2017.

FORT CALHOUN NUKE PLANT TO CLOSE

Omaha—The Omaha Public Power District will permanently close its nuclear plant at Fort Calhoun on October 24, according to sources inside the U.S. Nuclear Regulatory Commission. The 43-year old plant is the smallest in the United States and unable to spread its costs over enough output.

Source: Media reports of August/September 2016.

ANALYSIS: GM's decision to idle plants was a short-run *shutdown* decision; it is still in business. Omaha Power, by contrast, made a long-run decision to cease operations and *exit* a specific market.

The investment decision is of enormous importance to producers. The fixed costs that we've ignored in the production decision represent the producers' (or the stockholders') investment in the business. If they're going to avoid an economic loss, they have to generate at least enough revenue to recoup their investment—that is, the cost of (fixed) plants and equipment. Failure to do so will result in a net loss, despite allegiance to our profit-maximizing rule.

Whether fixed costs count, then, depends on the decision being made. For producers trying to decide how best to utilize the resources they've purchased or leased, fixed costs no longer enter the decision-making process. For producers deciding whether to enter business, sign a lease, or replace existing machinery and plants, fixed costs count very much. Businesspeople will proceed with an investment only if the *anticipated* profits are large enough to compensate for the effort and risk undertaken.

Long-Run Costs

When businesspeople make an investment decision, they confront not one set of cost figures but many. A plant not yet built can be designed for various rates of production and alternative technologies. In making long-run decisions, a producer isn't bound to one size of plant or to a particular mix of tools and machinery. In the long run, one can be flexible. In general, *a producer will want to build, buy, or lease a plant that's the most efficient for the anticipated rate of output.* This is the (dis)economy of scale phenomenon we discussed in the previous chapter. Once the right plant size is selected, the producer may proceed with the problem of short-run profit maximization. Once production is started, she can only hope that the investment decision was a good one and that a shutdown can be avoided.

DETERMINANTS OF SUPPLY

Whether the time frame is the short run or the long run, the central force in production decisions is the quest for profits. Producers will go into production—incur fixed costs—only if they see the potential for economic profits. Once in business, they'll expand the rate of output so long as profits are increasing. They'll shut down—cease production—when revenues don't at least cover variable costs (operating loss exceeds fixed costs).

Nearly anyone could make money with these principles if given complete information on costs and revenues. What renders the road to fortune less congested is the general absence of such complete information. In the real world, production decisions involve considerably more risk. People often don't know how much profit or loss they'll incur until it's too late to alter production decisions. Consequently, businesspeople are compelled to make a reasoned guess about prices and costs, then proceed. By way of summary, we can identify the major influences that will shape their short- and long-run decisions on how much output to supply to the market.

Short-Run Determinants

A competitive firm's short-run production decisions are dominated by marginal costs. Hence the quantity of a good supplied will be affected by all forces that alter MC. Specifically, *the determinants of a firm's supply include*

- *The price of factor inputs.*
- *Technology* (the available production function).
- *Expectations* (for costs, sales, technology).
- *Taxes and subsidies.*

Each determinant affects a producer's ability and willingness to supply output at any particular price.

The price of factor inputs determines how much the producer must pay for resources used in production. Technology determines how much output the producer will get from each unit of input. Expectations are critical because they express producers' perceptions of

FIGURE 8.11

A Competitive Firm's Short-Run Supply Curve

For competitive firms, marginal cost defines the lowest price a firm will accept for a given quantity of output. In this sense, the marginal cost curve *is* the supply curve; it tells us how quantity supplied will respond to price. At $p = \$13$, the quantity supplied is 4; at $p = \$9$, the quantity supplied is 3.

Recall, however, that the firm will shut down if price falls below minimum average variable cost. The supply curve does not exist below minimum AVC ($5 in this case).

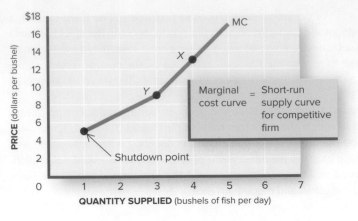

supply curve: A curve describing the quantities of a good a producer is willing and able to sell (produce) at alternative prices in a given time period, *ceteris paribus.*

what future costs, prices, sales, and profits are likely to be. And finally, taxes and subsidies may alter costs or the amount of profit a firm gets to keep.

The Short-Run Supply Curve. By using the familiar *ceteris paribus* assumption, we can isolate the effect of price on supply decisions. In other words, we can draw a short-run **supply curve** the same way we earlier constructed consumer demand curves. In this case, the forces we assume constant are input prices, technology, expectations, and taxes. The only variable we allow to change is the price of the product itself.

Figure 8.11 illustrates the response of quantity supplied to a change in price. Notice the critical role of marginal costs: *the marginal cost curve is the short-run supply curve for a competitive firm.* Recall our basic profit maximization rule. A competitive producer wants to supply a good only if its price exceeds its marginal cost. Hence marginal cost defines the lower limit for an "acceptable" price. A catfish farmer is willing and able to produce 4 bushels per day only if the price of a bushel is $13 (point X). If the price of catfish dropped to $9, the *quantity* supplied would fall to 3 (point Y). The marginal cost curve tells us what the quantity supplied would be at all other prices as well. As long as price exceeds minimum AVC (the shutdown point), the MC curve summarizes the response of a producer to price changes: it *is* the short-run supply curve of a perfectly competitive firm.

The shape of the marginal cost curve provides a basic foundation for the *law of supply.* Because marginal costs tend to rise as output expands, an increase in output makes sense only if the price of that output rises. If the price does rise, it's profitable to increase the quantity supplied.

Supply Shifts

All the forces that shape the short-run supply curve are subject to change. Factor prices change; technology changes; expectations change; and tax laws get revised. *If any determinant of supply changes, the supply curve shifts.*

An increase in wage rates, for example, would raise the marginal cost of producing catfish. This would shift the supply curve upward, making it more expensive for producers to supply larger quantities at any given price. An increase in the price of catfish feed has the same effect. Farmed catfish are fed pellets made of corn and soybean meal. Between 2010 and 2012, feed prices rose from $350 a ton to more than $450 a ton. This cost spike squeezed profit margins and forced catfish farmers to reduce production dramatically, as Figure 8.12 illustrates.

An improvement in technology would have the opposite effect. By increasing productivity, new technology lowers the marginal cost of producing a good. The supply curve shifts downward.

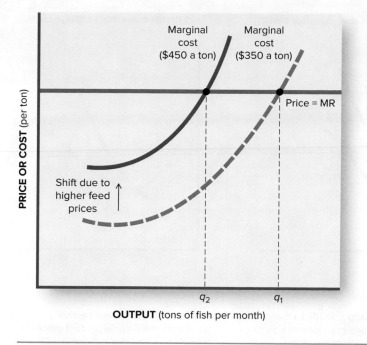

PRICE OR COST (per ton)

Marginal cost ($450 a ton)   Marginal cost ($350 a ton)

Price = MR

Shift due to higher feed prices

q_2 q_1

OUTPUT (tons of fish per month)

FIGURE 8.12
Rising MC Reduces Desired Output

An increase in feed prices (unit costs) shifts upward the marginal cost curve of a catfish farmer. That shift reduces the profit-maximizing rate of output from q_1 to q_2.

THE ECONOMY TOMORROW

TAXING BUSINESS

Changes in taxes will also alter supply behavior. But not all taxes have the same effect; some alter short-run supply behavior, whereas others affect only long-run supply decisions.

Property Taxes. Property taxes are levied by local governments on land and buildings. The tax rate is typically some small fraction (e.g., 1 percent) of total value. Hence the owner of a $10 million factory might have to pay $100,000 per year in property taxes.

Property taxes have to be paid regardless of whether the factory is used. Hence *property taxes are a fixed cost* for the firm. These additional fixed costs increase total costs and thus shift the average total cost (ATC) upward, as in Figure 8.13a.

Notice that the MC curve doesn't move when property taxes are imposed. Property taxes aren't based on the quantity of output produced. Accordingly, the production decision of the firm isn't affected by property taxes. The quantity q_1 in Figure 8.13a remains the optimal rate of output even after a property tax is introduced.

Although the optimal output remains at q_1, the profitability of the firm is reduced by the property tax. Profit per unit has been reduced by the upward shift of the ATC curve. If property taxes reduce profits too much, firms may move to a low-tax jurisdiction or another industry (investment decisions).

Payroll Taxes. Payroll taxes have very different effects on business decisions. Payroll taxes are levied on the wages paid by the firm. Employers must pay, for example, a 7.65 percent Social Security tax on the wages they pay (employees pay an identical amount). This tax is used to finance Social Security retirement benefits. Other payroll taxes are levied by federal and state governments to finance unemployment and disability benefits.

All payroll taxes add to the cost of hiring labor. In the absence of a tax, a worker might cost the firm $8 per hour. Once Social Security and other taxes are levied, the cost of labor increases to $8 plus the amount of tax. Hence $8-per-hour labor might end up costing the firm $9 or more. In other words, *payroll taxes increase marginal costs.* This is illustrated in Figure 8.13b by the upward shift of the MC curve.

Continued

(a) Property taxes affect fixed costs but not marginal costs.

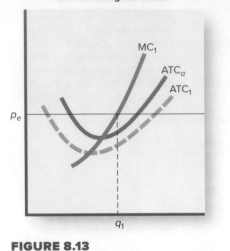

(b) Payroll taxes alter marginal costs.

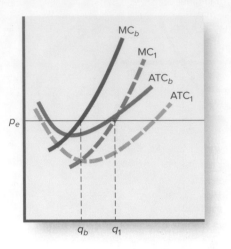

(c) Profits taxes don't change costs.

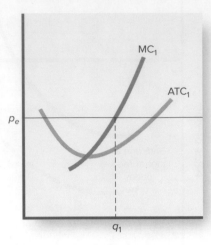

FIGURE 8.13

Impact of Taxes on Business Decisions

(a) **Property taxes** are a fixed cost for the firm. Since they don't affect marginal costs, they leave the optimal rate of output (q_1) unchanged. Property taxes raise average costs, however, and so reduce profits. Lower profits may alter investment decisions.

(b) **Payroll taxes** add directly to marginal costs and so reduce the optimal rate of output (to q_b). Payroll taxes also increase average costs and lower total and per-unit profits.

(c) **Taxes on profits** are neither a fixed cost nor a variable cost since they depend on the existence of profits. They don't affect marginal costs or price and so leave the optimal rate of output (q_1) unchanged. By reducing after-tax profits, however, such taxes lessen incentives to invest.

Notice how payroll taxes change the production decision. The new MC curve (MC_b) intersects the price line at a lower rate of output (q_b). Thus payroll taxes tend to reduce output and employment.

Profits Taxes. Taxes are also levied on the profits of a business. Such taxes are very different from either property or payroll taxes since profit taxes are paid only when profits are made. Thus they are neither a fixed cost nor a variable cost! As Figure 8.13c indicates, neither the MC nor the ATC curve moves when a profits tax is imposed. The only difference is that the firm now gets to keep less of its profits, instead "sharing" its profits with the government.

Although a profits tax has no direct effect on marginal or average costs, it does reduce the take-home (after-tax) profits of a business. This may reduce investments in new businesses. For this reason, many people urge the government to reduce corporate tax rates and so encourage increased investment. President Trump made a reduction in the corporate income tax rate a centerpiece of his economic programs.

SUMMARY

- Economic profit is the difference between total revenue and total cost. Total economic cost includes the value (opportunity cost) of *all* inputs used in production, not just those inputs for which an explicit payment is made. **LO8-1**

- A perfectly competitive firm is a *price taker*. It sells its output at the prevailing market price. It effectively confronts a horizontal demand for its output (even though the *market* demand for the product is downward-sloping). **LO8-2**

- Competitive firms don't make pricing decisions, only production decisions. **LO8-2**
- The short-run objective of a firm is to maximize profits from the operation of its existing facilities (fixed costs). For a competitive firm, the profit-maximizing output occurs at the point where marginal cost equals price (marginal revenue). **LO8-3**
- A firm may incur a loss even at the optimal rate of output. It shouldn't shut down, however, so long as price exceeds average *variable* cost. If revenues at least cover variable costs, the firm's operating loss is less than its fixed costs. **LO8-4**
- In the long run there are no fixed costs, and the firm may choose any-sized plant it wants. The decision to incur fixed costs (i.e., build, buy, or lease a plant) or to enter or exit an industry is an investment decision. **LO8-5**

- A competitive firm's supply curve is identical to its marginal cost curve (above the shutdown point at minimum average variable cost). In the short run, the quantity supplied will rise or fall with price. **LO8-6**
- The determinants of supply include the price of inputs, technology, taxes, and expectations. Should any of these determinants change, the firm's supply curve will shift. **LO8-6**
- Business taxes alter business behavior. Property taxes raise fixed costs; payroll taxes increase marginal costs. Profits taxes raise neither fixed costs nor marginal costs but diminish the take-home (after-tax) profits of a business. **LO8-6**

Key Terms

profit	perfect competition	marginal cost (MC)
economic cost	market power	marginal revenue (MR)
explicit cost	competitive firm	profit-maximization rule
implicit cost	production decision	shutdown point
economic profit	total revenue	investment decision
normal profit	short run	long run
monopoly	fixed costs	supply curve
market structure	variable costs	

Questions for Discussion

1. What economic costs will a large corporation likely overlook when computing its profits? How about the owner of a family-run business or farm? **LO8-1**
2. How can the demand curve facing a firm be horizontal if the market demand curve is downward-sloping? **LO8-2**
3. How many fish should a commercial fisher try to catch in a day? Should he catch as many as possible or return to dock before filling the boat with fish? Under what economic circumstances should he not even take the boat out? **LO8-3**
4. If a firm is incurring an economic loss, would society be better off if the firm shut down? Would the firm want to shut down? Explain. **LO8-4**
5. Why isn't the rate of output that minimizes average total cost the most profitable rate of output? **LO8-3**
6. What rate of output is appropriate for a nonprofit corporation (such as a hospital)? **LO8-3**

7. What costs did GM eliminate when it shut down its plants? (In the News "GM Shutting 5 Factories this Month") How about Omaha Power? **LO8-4**
8. What was the opportunity cost of Hiroshi Fujishige's farm? (See In the News "The Value of Hiro's Strawberry Farm") Is society better off with another Disney theme park? Explain. **LO8-1**
9. Is Apple Computer a perfectly competitive firm? **LO8-2**
10. If a perfectly competitive firm raises its price above the prevailing market rate, how much of its sales might it lose? Why? Can a competitive firm ever raise its prices? If so, when? **LO8-2**
11. Under what conditions would a firm decide to shut down in the short run but remain invested in the market in the long run? **LO8-5**
12. How does an employer-paid Social Security tax on wages affect a competitive firm's supply curve? **LO8-6**

PROBLEMS FOR CHAPTER 8

LO8-2　1. According to In the News "The Lure of Catfish,"
　　(a) How many fish did farmer Hollingsworth have in inventory?
　　(b) If each of his fish weighed 2 pounds, what percent of the market did he have?

LO8-1　2. If the owner of the Table 8.1 drugstore hired a manager for $10 an hour to take his place, how much of a change would show up in:
　　(a) Accounting profits?　　　　　(b) Economic profits?

LO8-1　3. Kanesha is an entrepreneur and has recently opened her first coffee shop, The Coffee Cat. Kanesha pays $5000 rent each month, $4800 for employee payroll, and $1200 for supplies. She was planning on selling several of her own tables and chairs on Craigslist for $1500, but instead she brought them to The Coffee Cat. Additionally, Kanesha quit working as an accountant where she was earning $52,000 per year to open up the shop. If the shop earns $180,000 in revenue this year, calculate annual:
　　(a) Accounting profit.　　　　　(b) Economic profit.

LO8-1　4. If the price of catfish fell from $13 to $7 per bushel, use Figure 8.7 to determine the
　　(a) Profit-maximizing output.　　(c) Total profit or loss.
　　(b) Profit or loss per bushel.

LO8-2　5. Complete the following cost and revenue schedules:

Quantity	Price	Total Revenue	Total Cost	Marginal Cost
0	$50	_____	$ 50	_____
1	50	_____	60	_____
2	50	_____	90	_____
3	50	_____	140	_____
4	50	_____	200	_____
5	50	_____	280	_____

PRICE OR COST (dollars per unit): $80, 70, 60, 50, 40, 30, 20, 10
QUANTITY (units per time period): 0, 1, 2, 3, 4, 5

　　(a) Graph MC and p.
　　(b) What rate of output maximizes profit?
　　(c) What is MC at that rate of output?

LO8-2　6. Complete the following cost schedules:

Quantity	0	1	2	3	4	5	6	7
Total cost	$9	$12	$16	$21	$30	$40	$52	$66
ATC	____	____	____	____	____	____	____	____
MC	—	____	____	____	____	____	____	____

Assuming the price of this product is $12, at what output rate is
　　(a) Total revenue maximized?　　(c) Profit per unit maximized?
　　(b) ATC minimized?　　　　　　(d) Total profit maximized?

LO8-3　7. Assume that the price of silk ties in a perfectly competitive market is $21 and that the typical firm confronts the following costs:

Quantity (ties per day)	0	1	2	3	4	5	6	7	8	9	10
Total cost	$10	$17	$26	$37	$50	$65	$82	$101	$122	$145	$170

　　(a) What is the profit-maximizing rate of output for the firm?
　　(b) How much profit does the firm earn at that rate of output?
　　(c) If the price of ties fell to $15, how many ties should the firm produce?
　　(d) At what price should the firm shut down?

PROBLEMS FOR CHAPTER 8 (cont'd)

LO8-6 8. Illustrate on the accompanying graph the changes to the cost curves due to
    (*a*) Higher feed prices.   (*c*) Higher worker productivity.
    (*b*) Lower wage rates.

    Does the profit-maximizing rate of output increase, decrease, or stay the same with
    (*d*) Higher feed prices?   (*f*) Higher worker productivity?
    (*e*) Lower wage rates?

LO8-4 9. Complete the following table:

Output	Total Cost	Marginal Cost	Average Total Cost	Average Variable Cost
0	$100	_____	_____	_____
5	110	_____	_____	_____
10	130	_____	_____	_____
15	170	_____	_____	_____
20	220	_____	_____	_____
25	290	_____	_____	_____
30	380	_____	_____	_____
35	490	_____	_____	_____

    According to the table above,
    (*a*) If the price is $50, how much output will the firm supply?   (*c*) At what price will the firm shut down?
    (*b*) How much profit or loss will it make?

LO8-5 10. A firm has leased plant and equipment to produce video games, which can be sold in unlimited quantities at $13 each. The following figures describe the associated costs of production:

Rate of output (per day)	0	1	2	3	4	5	6	7	8
Total cost (per day)	$50	$55	$62	$75	$96	$125	$162	$203	$248

    (*a*) How much are fixed costs?
    (*b*) Draw total revenue and cost curves on the graphs.
    (*c*) Draw the average total cost (ATC), marginal cost (MC), and demand curves of the firm.
    (*d*) What is the profit-maximizing rate of output?
    (*e*) Calculate profits or losses at this profit-maximizing rate of output.
    (*f*) How much is lost if the firm shuts down?
    (*g*) Should the firm produce or shut down in the short run?

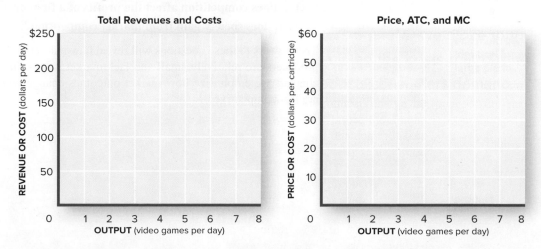

LO8-6 11. The Economy Tomorrow: Using the data from Problem 7 (at the original price of $21), determine how many ties the producer would supply if
    (*a*) A tax of $2 per tie were collected from the producer.   (*c*) Profits were taxed at 50 percent.
    (*b*) A property tax of $2 were levied.

©David A. Barnes/Alamy Stock Photo

CHAPTER 9

Competitive Markets

Catfish farmers in the South are very upset. They invested millions of dollars converting cotton farms into breeding ponds for catfish. At its peak, the catfish industry employed more than 15,000 workers and produced nearly $500 million of fish per year. But those days are long gone. First catfish farmers in the South had to contend with rising competition from Vietnamese and Chinese imports. That competition put a lid on catfish prices. Then feed prices spiked in 2010–2012, raising production costs. This combination of constrained prices and rising costs killed profits. With losses mounting, a lot of farmers got out of the catfish business, filling their ponds with dirt and planting soybeans instead (see the World View "Catfish Farmers Draining Their Ponds").

The dilemma catfish farmers find themselves in is a familiar occurrence in competitive markets. When profits look good, everybody wants to get in on the act. As more and more firms start producing the good, prices and profits tumble. This helps explain why more than 200,000 new firms are formed each year and why more than 50,000 others fail.

This chapter focuses on the behavior of competitive markets. We have three principal questions:

- **How are prices determined in competitive markets?**
- **How does competition affect the profits of a firm or industry?**
- **What does society gain from market competition?**

The answers to these questions will reveal how markets work when all producers are relatively small and lack market power. In subsequent chapters we emphasize how market outcomes change when markets are less competitive.

LEARNING OBJECTIVES

After reading this chapter, you should know

LO9-1 The market characteristics of perfect competition.

LO9-2 How prices are established in competitive markets.

LO9-3 Why long-run economic profits approach zero in competitive markets.

LO9-4 How society benefits from market competition.

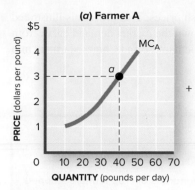
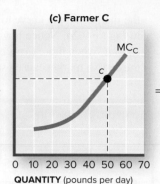
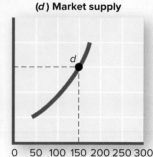

FIGURE 9.1
Competitive Market Supply

A Firm's Supply. The portion of the MC curve that lies above AVC is a competitive firm's short-run supply curve. The curve MC_A tells us that Farmer A will produce 40 pounds of catfish per day if the market price is $3 per pound.

Market Supply. To determine the *market* supply, we add up the quantities supplied at each price by every farmer. The total quantity supplied to the market at the price of $3 is 150 pounds per day ($a + b + c$). Market supply depends on the number of firms and their respective marginal costs.

THE MARKET SUPPLY CURVE

In the previous chapter we examined the supply behavior of a perfectly competitive firm. The perfectly competitive firm is a price taker. It *responds* to the market price by producing that rate of output where marginal cost equals price.

But what about the *market* supply of catfish? We need a market supply curve to determine the **equilibrium price** the individual farmer will confront. In the previous chapter we simply drew a market supply curve arbitrarily to establish a market price. Now our objective is to find out where that **market supply** curve comes from.

Like the market supply curves we first encountered in Chapter 3, we can calculate the market supply of catfish by simple addition. All we have to do is add up the quantities each of America's 1,000 catfish farmers stands ready to supply at each price. Then we'll know the total quantity of fish to be supplied to the market at that price.

Remember the critical role that **marginal cost** plays in the production decision of the competitive firm. As we saw in the previous chapter, a competitive firm will produce where $MC = p$. So, the firm's MC curve is in effect its supply curve. If we know what the MC curves of the firms in an industry look like, we can compute the *market* supply. Figure 9.1 illustrates this summation. Notice that ***the market supply curve is the sum of* the marginal cost *curves of all the firms.*** Hence whatever determines the marginal cost of a typical firm will also affect industry supply. Specifically, ***the market supply of a competitive industry is determined by***

- *The price of factor inputs.*
- *Technology.*
- *Expectations.*
- *Taxes and subsidies.*
- *The number of firms in the industry.*

Entry and Exit

If more firms enter an industry, the market supply curve will shift to the right. This is the problem confronting the catfish farmers in Mississippi (see World View "Catfish Farmers Draining Their Ponds"). It's fairly inexpensive to get into the catfish business: you can start with a pond, some breeding stock, and relatively little capital equipment. These **investment decisions** shift

equilibrium price: The price at which the quantity of a good demanded in a given time period equals the quantity supplied.

market supply: The total quantities of a good that sellers are willing and able to sell at alternative prices in a given time period, *ceteris paribus.*

marginal cost (MC): The increase in total cost associated with a one-unit increase in production.

investment decision: The decision to build, buy, or lease plants and equipment; to enter or exit an industry.

the market supply curve to the right and drive down catfish prices. This process is illustrated in Figure 9.2a. Notice how the equilibrium price slides down the market demand curve from E_1 to E_2 when more firms enter the market. The entry of Vietnamese and Chinese farmers into the catfish market caused steep declines in catfish prices.

WORLD VIEW

CATFISH FARMERS DRAINING THEIR PONDS

Catfish farming used to look good. So good, in fact, that hundreds of crop farmers stopped growing corn and soybeans, choosing instead to dig catfish ponds on their land. It was the "gold rush" for Southern farmers. Catfish production skyrocketed from 340 million pounds in 1989 to a peak of 662 million pounds in 2003.

Since then, it's been all bad news. A surge in imported catfish has sent prices for processed catfish spiraling down. At the same time, feed prices—primarily a mix of corn and soybeans—have jumped from $250 a ton in 2006 to $440 a ton this year. Dozens of catfish operators are draining their ponds in order to plant row crops.

Source: Media reports, Fall 2008.

ANALYSIS: When economic profits exist in an industry, more producers try to enter. As they do, prices and economic profits decline. When losses are incurred, firms begin to exit the industry.

If prices fall too far, profits will disappear. Indeed, profits will turn into losses if the market price falls below a farmer's minimum average total cost. When this happens, some farmers will drain their ponds and plant soybeans instead (see In the News "U.S. Catfish Industry Bleeding Finally Stops"). When they do so, they are *exiting* the catfish business and *entering* the soybean business. These exits will shift the market supply curve a bit to the left, helping to stabilize catfish prices and "stop the bleeding" in the industry.

(a) Market entry pushes price down and . . .

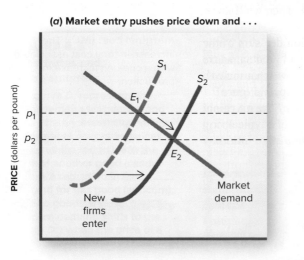

(b) Reduces profits of competitive firm.

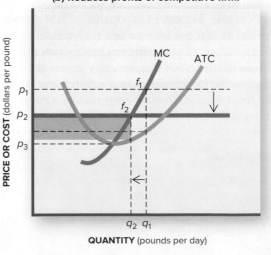

FIGURE 9.2

Market Entry

If economic profits exist in an industry, more firms will want to enter it. As they do, the market supply curve will shift to the right and cause the market price to drop from p_1 to p_2 (part a).

The lower market price, in turn, will reduce the output and profits of the typical firm. In part b, the firm's output falls from q_1 to q_2.

IN THE NEWS

U.S. CATFISH INDUSTRY BLEEDING FINALLY STOPS

Years of doom and gloom trends in the U.S. catfish industry are finally coming to an end as the industry stops losing its major companies to soybean farming.

"We've lost 50% of our farms, but I believe we've reached a point where the loss in the industry has stopped," Jack Perkins, vice president of sales and marketing for Consolidated Catfish, told *Undercurrent News*.

He estimates the industry will produce the same amount of catfish this year as it did last year, at 300 million pounds.

"Hopefully we'll see 2014 and beyond as an industry recovery time," Perkins said.

There is much to recover from, considering the past few years, [when] catfish farmers realized that converting their catfish farms to soybean farms—which is completely viable—was a better business prospect, and little by little the industry has shrunk.

Plus, staying in the industry is becoming more attractive, considering the price improvements.

Right now, prices [are] at the high level of $4 to $4.25 per pound for wholesale for fillets, which is the same price as last year at this time but a significant jump from last fall.

Stewart, Jeanine, "U.S. Catfish Industry Bleeding Finally Stops," *UnderCurrentNews,* July 3, 2013. Copyright ©2013. All rights reserved. Used with permission.

ANALYSIS: Loss-driven exits shift the market supply curve left and help stabilize prices at their long-term equilibrium, at which point net entry and exit cease.

Tendency toward Zero Profits

The profit motive drives these entry and exit decisions. Ten years ago catfish farming looked a whole lot more profitable than cotton farming. Farmers responded by flooding their cotton fields to create fish ponds; they *exited* the cotton business and *entered* the catfish industry.

The resulting shift of market supply caused the **economic profits** in catfish farming to disappear. Notice in Figure 9.2*b* how total profits for the typical firm shrink when price is driven down from p_1 to p_2. If price continued to fall, profits would shrink further. Indeed, if price declines to p_3, profits disappear.

When profits disappear (at the price p_3 in Figure 9.2*b*) there is no incentive to *enter* the industry. Were price to fall still further—below p_3—the typical catfish farmer would actually be losing money. That would motivate some farmers to *exit* the industry—planting soybeans instead of feeding fish. Eventually, price will settle at p_3, where economic profit is zero. **When economic profit disappears, entry and exit cease and the market stabilizes.** According to In the News "U.S. Catfish Industry Bleeding Finally Stops," this is exactly what has happened in the catfish industry. At this new equilibrium, catfish farmers earn only a normal (average) rate of return.

Catfish farmers would be happier, of course, if the price of catfish didn't decline to the point where economic profits disappear. But how are they going to prevent it? Keith King evidently knows all about the laws of supply and demand (see World View "Catfish Farmers Draining Their Ponds"). He would dearly like to keep all those Vietnamese and Chinese catfish out of this country. He also wishes those farmers in Maine would keep cranberries in their ponds rather than catfish. Keith would also like to get other farmers in the South to slow production a little before all the profits disappear. But King is powerless to stop the forces of a **competitive market.** He can't even afford to reduce his *own* catfish production. Even though he has 200 acres of ponds, nobody would notice the resulting drop in market supplies, and catfish prices would continue to slide. The only one affected would be King, who'd be denying himself the opportunity to share in the (dwindling) fortunes of the catfish market while they lasted.

economic profit: The difference between total revenues and total economic costs.

competitive market: A market in which no buyer or seller has market power.

King's dilemma goes a long way toward explaining why catfish farming isn't highly profitable. Whenever the profit picture looks good, everybody tries to get in on the action. This kind of pressure on prices and profits is a fundamental characteristic of competitive markets. *As long as it's easy for existing producers to expand production or for new firms to enter an industry, economic profits won't last long.*

Low Barriers to Entry

barriers to entry: Obstacles such as patents that make it difficult or impossible for would-be producers to enter a particular market.

New producers will be able to enter a profitable industry and help drive down prices and profits as long as they don't encounter significant barriers. Such **barriers to entry** may include patents, control of essential factors of production, control of distribution outlets, well-established brand loyalty, or even governmental regulation. All such barriers make it expensive, risky, or impossible for new firms to enter an industry. In the absence of such barriers, new firms can enter an industry more readily and at less risk. Not surprisingly, firms already entrenched in a profitable industry do their best to keep out newcomers by erecting barriers to entry. Unfortunately for Keith King, there are few barriers to entering the catfish business; all you need to get started is a pond and a few fish. Recall the Calvin Jones quote from Chapter 8: "You raise fish. You get them out of the pond and you sell them. There's no genius to it."

Market Characteristics of Perfect Competition

This brief review of catfish economics illustrates a few general observations about the structure, behavior, and outcomes of a competitive market:

- *Many firms.* A competitive market includes a great many firms, none of which has a significant share of total output.
- *Identical products.* Products are homogeneous. One firm's product is the same as any other firm's product.
- *Perfect information.* All buyers and sellers have complete information on available supply, demand, and prices.
- *MC = p.* All competitive firms will seek to expand output until marginal cost equals price, much as price and marginal revenue are identical for such firms.
- *Low barriers.* Barriers to enter the industry are low. If economic profits are available, more firms will enter the industry.
- *Zero economic profit.* The tendency of production and market supplies to expand when profit is high puts heavy pressures on prices and profits in competitive industries. Economic profit will approach zero in the long run as prices are driven down to the level of average production costs.

COMPETITION AT WORK: MICROCOMPUTERS

Few markets have all the characteristics just listed. That is, *few, if any, product markets are perfectly competitive.* However, many industries function much like the competitive model we sketched out. In addition to catfish farming, most other agricultural product markets are characterized by highly competitive market structures, with hundreds or even thousands of producers supplying the market. Other highly competitive, and hence not very profitable, businesses are T-shirt shops, laundromats, retail food, printing, clothing manufacturing and retailing, dry-cleaning establishments, beauty salons, and furniture. Online stockbroker services have also become highly competitive. In these markets, prices and profits are always under the threat of expanded supplies brought to market by existing or new producers.

The electronics industry offers numerous examples of how competition reduces prices and profits. Between 1972 and 1983, the price of small, handheld calculators fell from $200 to under $10. The price of digital watches fell even more dramatically, from roughly $2,000 in 1975 to under $7 in 1990. Videocassette recorders (VCRs) that sold for $2,000 in 1979 now sell for less than $30. DVD players that cost $1,500 in 1997 now sell for under $50. Cell phones that sold for $1,000 ten years ago are now given away. The same kind of competitive pressures have reduced the price of flat-screen TVs. New entrants keep bringing better TVs to market while driving prices down (see World View "Flat Panels, Thin Margins").

WORLD VIEW

FLAT PANELS, THIN MARGINS

The TVs keep getting bigger and better. Best Buy, Target, and Costco offer an almost bewildering array of TVs. The typical consumer has a difficult time deciphering the pixel counts, the varying sizes, and the myriad features of the many TV brands on display. But one thing is crystal clear: the prices keep coming down (see chart). In fact, industry experts say there is never a "right time" to buy a TV because TVs will be better and cheaper a couple of months later.

Brutal competition keeps pushing prices down and innovation up. In the last five years alone the number of LCD brands for sale in U.S. stores increased fourfold, from 26 to 102. Parts manufacturers in China, Mexico, and Taiwan make it easy to get into the industry. They will sell the needed parts to anyone—and even assemble all the pieces if asked. So, anyone with connections to big retailers can create an instant brand and get into TV retailing. At a lower price, of course.

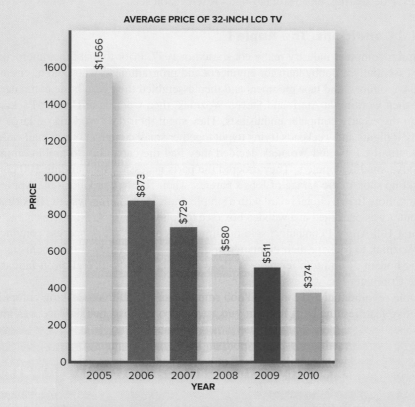

AVERAGE PRICE OF 32-INCH LCD TV

Source: Industry reports (2007–2010).

ANALYSIS: Competitive pressures compel producers of flat-panel TVs to keep improving the product and reducing prices. The lure of profits encourages firms to enter this expanding market even as prices drop.

The driving force behind all these price reductions and quality improvements is *competition.* Do you really believe the price of phone calls would be falling if only one firm supplied all telephone services? Do you think thousands of software writers would be toiling away right now if popular programs didn't generate enormous profits? Would Apple, Amazon, and Uber keep rolling out new products and services if other companies weren't always snapping at their heels?

Market Evolution

To appreciate how the process of competition works, we will examine the development of the personal computer industry. *As in other industries, the market structure of the computer industry has evolved over time. It was never a monopoly, nor was it ever perfect competition.* In its first couple of years it was dominated by only a few companies (like Apple) that were enormously successful. The high profits the early microcomputer producers obtained attracted swarms of imitators. More than 250 firms entered the microcomputer industry between 1976 and 1983 in search of high profits. The entry of so many firms transformed the industry's market structure: the industry became *more* competitive, even though not *perfectly* competitive. The increased competition pushed prices downward and improved the product. When prices and profits tumbled, scores of companies went bankrupt. They left a legacy, however, of a vastly larger market, much improved computers, and sharply lower prices.

We'll use the early experiences of the microcomputer industry to illustrate the key behavioral features of a competitive market. As we'll see, many of these competitive features are still at work in the markets for Internet services, content software, digital music, smartphones, ride sharing, cloud storage, and 4K television sets.

Initial Conditions: The Apple I

The microcomputer industry really got started in 1977. Prior to that time, microcomputers were essentially a hobby item for engineers and programmers, who bought circuits, keyboards, monitors, and tape recorders and then assembled their own basic computers. Steve Jobs, then working at Atari, and Steven Wozniak, then working at Hewlett-Packard, were among these early computer enthusiasts. They spent their days working on large systems and their nights and weekends trying to put together small computers from mail-order parts.

Eventually, Jobs and Wozniak decided they had the capability to build commercially attractive small computers. They ordered the parts necessary for building 100 computers and set up shop in the garage of Jobs's parents. Their finished product—the Apple I—was nothing more than a circuit board with a simple, built-in operating system. This first microcomputer was packaged in a wooden box (see the photo). Despite primitive characteristics, the first 100 Apple I computers sold out immediately. This quick success convinced Jobs and Wozniak to package their computers more fully—which they did by enclosing them in plastic housing—and to offer more of them for sale. Shortly thereafter, in January 1977, Apple Computer Inc. was established.

Apple revolutionized the market by offering a preassembled desktop computer with attractive features and an accessible price. The impact on the marketplace was much like

Analysis: The Apple I pictured here launched the personal computer industry in 1976. Hundreds of firms entered the industry to improve on this first preassembled microcomputer. This competition transformed the industry, the product, and prices.
©Kim Kulish/Corbis via Getty Images

that of Henry Ford's early Model T: suddenly a newfangled piece of technology came into reach of the average U.S. household, and everybody, it seemed, wanted one. The first mass-produced Apple computer—called the Apple II—was just a basic keyboard with an operating system that permitted users to write their own programs. The computer had no disk drive, no monitor, and only 4K of random access memory (RAM). Consumers had to use their TV sets as screens and audiocassettes for data storage. This primitive Apple II was priced at just under $1,300 when it debuted in June 1977. Apple was producing computers at the rate of 500 per month.

Apple didn't engineer or manufacture chips or semiconductor components. Instead it simply packaged existing components purchased from outside suppliers (much like TV brands do, see World View "Flat Panels, Thin Margins"). Hence it was easy for other companies to follow Apple's lead. Within a very brief time, other firms, such as Tandy (Radio Shack), also started to assemble computers. By the middle of 1978, the basic small computer was selling for $1,000, and industry sales were about 20,000 a month. Figure 9.3*a* depicts the initial (1978) equilibrium in the computer market, and Figure 9.3*b* illustrates the approximate costs of production for the typical computer manufacturer at that time.

The Production Decision

The short-run goal of every producer is to find the rate of output that maximizes profits. Finding this rate entails making the best possible **production decision.** In this short-run context, *each competitive firm seeks the rate of output at which marginal cost equals price.*

production decision: The selection of the short-run rate of output (with existing plants and equipment).

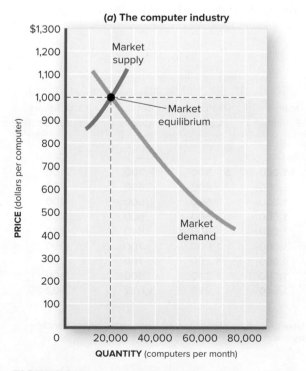

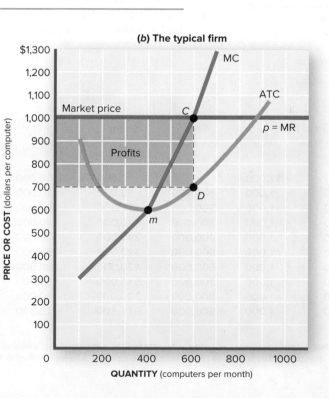

FIGURE 9.3

Initial Equilibrium in the Computer Market

(*a*) **The Industry.** In 1978 the market price of microcomputers was $1,000. This price was established by the intersection of the market supply and demand curves.

(*b*) **A Firm.** Each competitive producer in the market sought to produce computers at that rate (600 per month) where marginal cost equaled price (point *C*). Profit per computer was equal to price (point *C*) minus average total cost (point *D*). Total profits for the typical firm are indicated by the shaded rectangle.

Figure 9.3b illustrates the cost and price curves the typical computer producer confronted in 1978. As in most lines of production, the marginal costs of computer production increased with the rate of output. Marginal costs rose in part because output could be increased in the short run (with existing plants and equipment) only by crowding additional workers onto the assembly line. In 1978 Apple had only 10,000 square feet of manufacturing space. As more workers were hired, each worker had less capital and land to work with, and marginal physical product fell. The law of diminishing returns pushed marginal costs up.

The upward-sloping marginal cost curve intersected the price line at an output level of 600 computers per month (point C in Figure 9.3b). That was the profit-maximizing rate of output (MC = p) for the typical manufacturer. Manufacturing any more than 600 computers per month would raise marginal costs over price and reduce total profits. Manufacturing any fewer would be passing up an opportunity to make another buck.

Profit Calculations

Table 9.1 shows how much *profit* a typical computer manufacturer was making in 1978. As the "total profit" column indicates, the typical computer manufacturer could make a real killing in the computer market, reaping a monthly profit of $180,000 by producing and selling 600 microcomputers.

We could also calculate the computer manufacturers' profits by asking how much the manufacturers make on *each* computer and then multiplying that figure by total output:

$$\textbf{Total profit = Profit per unit} \times \textbf{Quantity sold}$$

We can compute these profits by studying the first and last columns in Table 9.1 or by using a little geometry in Figure 9.3b. In the figure, average costs (total costs divided by the rate of output) are portrayed by the **average total cost (ATC)** curve. At the output rate of

average total cost (ATC):
Total cost divided by the quantity produced in a given time period.

Output per Month	Price	Total Revenue	Total Cost	Total Profit	Marginal Revenue*	Marginal Cost*	Average Total Cost	Profit per Unit (Price Minus Average Cost)
0	$1,000	$ 0	$ 60,000	−$ 60,000	—	—	—	—
100	1,000	100,000	90,000	10,000	$1,000	$ 300	$ 900	$100
200	1,000	200,000	130,000	70,000	1,000	400	650	350
300	1,000	300,000	180,000	120,000	1,000	500	600	400
400	1,000	400,000	240,000	160,000	1,000	600	600	400
500	1,000	500,000	320,000	180,000	1,000	800	640	360
600	1,000	600,000	420,000	180,000	1,000	1,000	700	300
700	1,000	700,000	546,000	154,000	1,000	1,260	780	220
800	1,000	800,000	720,000	80,000	1,000	1,740	900	100
900	1,000	900,000	919,800	−19,800	1,000	1,998	1,022	−22

*Note that output levels are calibrated in hundreds in this example; that's why we have divided the *change* in total costs and revenues from one output level to another by 100 to calculate marginal revenue and marginal cost. Very few manufacturers deal in units of 1.

TABLE 9.1

Computer Revenues, Costs, and Profits

Producers seek that rate of output where total profit is maximized. This table illustrates the output choices the typical computer producer faced in 1978. The profit-maximizing rate of output occurred at 600 computers per month. At that rate of output, marginal cost was equal to price ($1,000), and profits were $180,000 per month.

600 (the row in white in Table 9.1), the distance between the price line ($1,000 at point *C*) and the ATC curve ($700 at point *D*) is $300, which represents the average **profit per unit.** Multiplying this figure by the number of units sold (600 per month) will give us *total* profit per month. Total profits are represented by the shaded rectangle in Figure 9.3*b* and are equal to our earlier profit figure of $180,000 per month.

profit per unit: Total profit divided by the quantity produced in a given time period; price minus average total cost.

The Lure of Profits

While gaping at the computer manufacturer's enormous profits, we should remind ourselves that those profits might not last long. Indeed, the more quick-witted among us already will have seen and heard enough to know they've discovered a good thing. And in fact, the kind of profits the early microcomputer manufacturers enjoyed attracted a lot of entrepreneurial interest. ***In competitive markets, economic profits attract new entrants.*** This is what happened in the catfish industry and also in the computer industry. Within a very short time, a whole crowd of profit maximizers entered the microcomputer industry in hot pursuit of its fabulous profits. By the end of 1980, Apple had a lot of competition, including new entrants from IBM, Xerox, Digital Equipment, Casio, Sharp, and dozens of other start-up firms.

Low Entry Barriers

A critical feature of the microcomputer market was its lack of entry barriers. A microcomputer is little more than a box containing a microprocessor "brain," which connects to a keyboard (to enter data), a memory (to store data), and a screen (to display data). Although the microprocessors that guide the computer are extremely sophisticated, they can be purchased on the open market. Thus, to enter the computer industry, all one needs is some space, some money to buy components, and some dexterity in putting parts together. Such ***low entry barriers permit new firms to enter competitive markets.*** This is what facilitated competition in the flat-screen TV market (see the World View "Flat Panels, Thin Margins"). The same low entry barriers existed in computers. According to Table 9.1, the typical producer needed only $60,000 of plant and equipment (fixed costs) to get started in the microcomputer market. Jobs and Wozniak had even less when they started making Apples in their garage.

A Shift of Market Supply

Figure 9.4 shows what happened to the computer market and the profits of the typical firm once the word got out. As more and more entrepreneurs heard how profitable computer manufacturing could be, they quickly got hold of a book on electronic circuitry, rushed to the bank, got a little financing, and set up shop. Before many months had passed, scores of new firms had started producing small computers. ***The entry of new firms shifts the market supply curve to the right.*** In Figure 9.4*a*, the supply curve shifted from S_1 to S_2. Almost as fast as a computer can calculate a profit (loss) statement, the willingness to supply increased abruptly.

But the new computer companies were in for a bit of disappointment. With so many new firms hawking microcomputers, it became increasingly difficult to make a fast buck. The downward-sloping market demand curve confirms that a greater quantity of microcomputers could be sold only if the price of computers dropped. And drop it did. The price slide began as computer manufacturers found their inventories growing and so offered price discounts to maintain sales volume. The price fell rapidly, from $1,000 in mid-1978 to $800 in early 1980.

The sliding market price squeezed the profits of each firm, causing the profit rectangle to shrink (compare Figure 9.3*b* to Figure 9.4*b*). The lower price also changed the production decision of the typical firm. The new price ($800) intersected the unchanged MC curve at the output rate of 500 computers per month (point *G* in Figure 9.4*b*). With

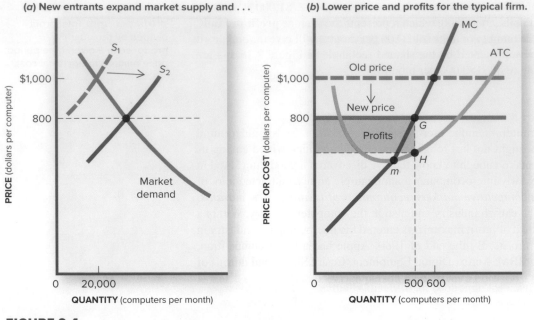

(a) New entrants expand market supply and . . .

(b) Lower price and profits for the typical firm.

FIGURE 9.4

The Competitive Price and Profit Squeeze

(a) The Industry. The economic profits in the computer industry encouraged new firms to enter the industry. As they did, the market supply curve shifted from S_1 to S_2. This rightward shift of the supply curve lowered the equilibrium price of computers.

(b) A Firm. The lower market price, in turn, forced the typical producer to reduce output to the point where MC and price were equal again (point G). At this reduced rate of output, the typical firm earned less total profit than it had earned before.

---

average production costs of $640 (Table 9.1), the firm's total profits in 1980 were only $80,000 per month [$(p - \text{ATC}) \times 500$]. Not a paltry sum, to be sure, but nothing like the fantastic fortunes pocketed earlier.

As long as an economic profit is available, it will continue to attract new entrants. Those entrepreneurs who were a little slow in absorbing the implications of Figure 9.3 eventually woke up to what was going on and tried to get in on the action, too. Even though they were a little late, they didn't want to miss the chance to cash in on the $80,000 in monthly profits still available to the typical firm. Hence the market supply curve continued to shift, and computer prices slid further, as in Figure 9.5. This process squeezed the profits of the typical firm still more, further shrinking the profit rectangle.

As long as economic profits exist in **short-run competitive equilibrium,** that equilibrium won't last. If the rate of profit obtainable in computer production is higher than that available in other industries, new firms will enter the industry. Conversely, if the short-run equilibrium is unprofitable, firms will exit the industry. Profit-maximizing entrepreneurs have a special place in their hearts for economic profits, not computers.

Price and profit declines will cease when the price of computers equals the minimum average cost of production. At that price (point *m* in Figure 9.5*b*), there's no more economic profit to be squeezed out. Firms no longer have an incentive to enter the industry, and the supply curve stops shifting. This situation represents the **long-run competitive equilibrium** for the firm and for the industry. *In long-run equilibrium, entry and exit cease, and zero economic profit (that is, normal profit) prevails* (see Figure 9.6). Table 9.2 summarizes the profit-maximizing rules that bring about this long-run equilibrium.

Once a long-run equilibrium is established, it will continue until market demand shifts or technological progress reduces the cost of computer production. In fact, that's just what happened in the computer market (and in the catfish industry, per In the News "U.S. Catfish Industry Bleeding Finally Stops").

short-run competitive equilibrium: $p = \text{MC}$.

long-run competitive equilibrium: $p = \text{MC} =$ minimum ATC.

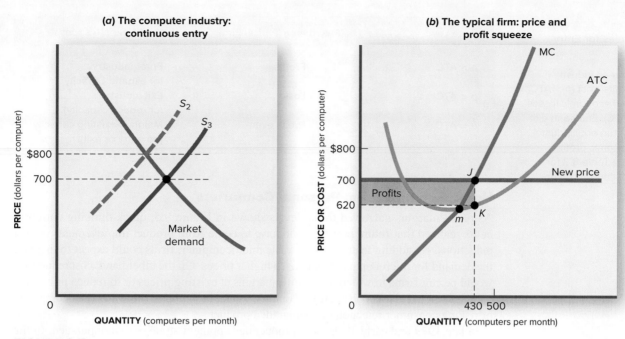

FIGURE 9.5

The Competitive Squeeze Approaching Its Limit

(*a*) **The Industry.** Even at a price of $800 per computer, economic profits attracted still more entrepreneurs, shifting the market supply curve further (*S₃*). The next short-term equilibrium occurred at a price of $700 per computer.

(*b*) **A Firm.** At this reduced market price, the typical manufacturer wanted to supply only 430 computers per month (point *J*). Total profits were much lower than they had been earlier, with fewer producers and higher prices.

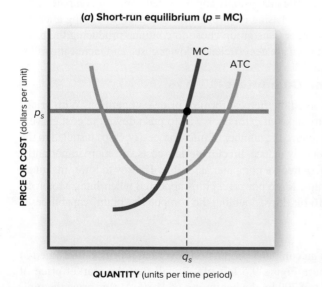

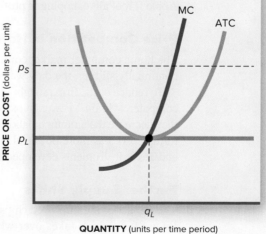

FIGURE 9.6

Short- vs. Long-Run Equilibrium for the Competitive Firm

(*a*) **Short Run.** Competitive firms strive for the rate of output at which marginal cost (MC) equals price. When they achieve that rate of output, they are in *short-run equilibrium*. Whether profitable or not, there is no incentive to alter the rate of output produced with existing (fixed) plants and equipment; it is the *best* the firm can do in the short run.

(*b*) **Long Run.** If the short-run equilibrium (*qₛ*) is profitable (*p* > ATC), other firms will want to enter the industry. As they do, market price will fall until it reaches the level of minimum ATC. In this *long-run equilibrium* (*q_L*), economic profits are zero, and nobody wants to enter or exit the industry.

TABLE 9.2

Long-Run Rules for Entry and Exit

Firms will enter an industry if economic profits exist ($p >$ ATC). They will exit if economic losses prevail ($p <$ ATC). Entry and exit cease in long-run equilibrium with zero economic profit ($p =$ ATC). (See Table 8.3 for short-run profit maximization rules.)

Price Level	Result for a Typical Firm	Market Response
$p >$ ATC	Profits	Enter industry (or expand capacity).
$p <$ ATC	Loss	Exit industry (or reduce capacity).
$p =$ ATC	Break even	Maintain existing capacity (no entry or exit).

Home Computers vs. Personal Computers

As profit margins narrowed to the levels shown in Figure 9.5, quick-thinking entrepreneurs realized that future profits would have to come from product improvements or cost reductions. By adding features to the basic microcomputer, firms could expect to increase the demand for microcomputers and fetch higher prices. On the other hand, cost reductions would permit firms to widen their profit margins at existing prices or to reduce prices and increase sales. This second strategy wouldn't require assembling more complex computers or risking consumer rejection of an upgraded product.

In late 1979 and early 1980, both product development strategies were pursued. In the process, two distinct markets were created. Microcomputers upgraded with new features came to be known as *personal* computers, or PCs. The basic unadorned computer first introduced by Apple came to be known as a *home* computer. The limited capabilities of that basic home computer greatly restricted its usefulness to simple household record keeping, games, and elementary programming.

Apple chose the personal computer route. It started enlarging the memory of the Apple II in late 1978 (from 4K to as much as 48K). It offered a monitor (produced by Sanyo) for the first time in May 1979. Shortly thereafter, Apple ceased making the basic Apple II and instead produced only upgraded versions (the Apple IIe, the IIc, and the III). Hundreds of other companies followed Apple's lead, touting increasingly sophisticated personal computers.

While one pack of entrepreneurs was chasing PC profits, another pack was going after the profits still available in home computers. This group chose to continue producing the basic Apple II lookalike, hoping to profit from greater efficiency, lower costs, and increasing sales.

Price Competition in Home Computers

The home computer market confronted the fiercest form of price competition. With prices continually sliding, the only way to make an extra buck was to push down the cost curve.

To reduce costs, firms sought to reduce the number of microprocessor chips installed in the computer's "brain." Fewer chips not only reduce direct materials costs, but more importantly, they decrease the amount of labor required for computer assembly. The key to lower manufacturing costs was more powerful chips. More powerful chips appeared when Intel, Motorola, and Texas Instruments developed 16-bit chips, doubling the computer's "brain" capabilities.

Further Supply Shifts

The impact of the improved chips on computer production costs and profits is illustrated in Figure 9.7, which takes over where Figure 9.5 left off. Recall that the market price of computers had been driven down to $700 by the beginning of 1980. At this price the typical firm maximized profits by producing 430 computers per month, as determined by the intersection of the prevailing price and MC curves (point *J* in Figure 9.7).

The only way for the firm to improve profitability at this point was to reduce costs. The new chips made such cost reductions easy. Such *technological improvements are illustrated by a downward shift of the ATC and MC curves.* Notice in Figure 9.7 how the new technology permits 430 home computers to be produced for a lower marginal cost (about $500) than previously ($700 at point *J*).

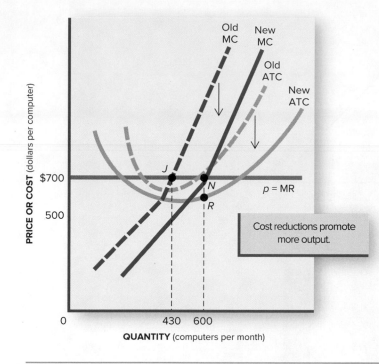

FIGURE 9.7
Lower Costs Improve Profits and Stimulate Output

The quest for profits encouraged producers to discover cheaper ways to manufacture computers. The resulting improvements lowered costs and encouraged further increases in the rate of output. The typical computer producer increased output from point *J* (where *p* = old MC) to point *N* (where *p* = new MC).

The lower cost structure increases the profitability of computer production and stimulates a further increase in production. Note in particular that the "new MC" curve intersects the price ($700) line at an output of 600 computers per month (point *N*). By contrast, the old, higher MC curve dictated a production rate of only 430 computers per month for the typical firm (point *J*) at that price. Thus existing producers suddenly had an incentive to *expand* production, and new firms had a greater incentive to *enter* the industry. The great rush into computer production was on again.

The market implications of another entrepreneurial stampede should now be obvious. As more and more firms tried to get in on the action, the market supply curve again shifted to the right. As output increased, computer prices slid further down the market demand curve.

Figure 9.8 illustrates how steeply home computer prices fell after 1980. In just over three years (December 1979 to January 1983), the price of a home computer plunged from $950 to $149. As the price plunged, so did profits. Fourth-quarter profits at Atari, for example, fell from $137 million in 1981 to only $1.2 million in 1983.

Shutdowns

That didn't stop the competitive process, however. At Texas Instruments, minimum *variable* costs were roughly $100 per computer in January 1983, so TI and other manufacturers could afford to keep producing even at lower prices. And they had little choice but to do so because if they didn't, other companies would quickly take up the slack. Industry output kept increasing despite shrinking profit margins. The increased supply pushed computer prices ever lower.

By the time computer prices reached $99 in September 1983, TI was losing $300 million per year. The company recognized then that the price would no longer even cover average variable costs. ***Once a firm is no longer able to cover variable costs, it should shut down production.*** When the price of home computers dipped below minimum average variable costs, TI had reached the **shutdown point,** and the company ceased production. At the time TI made the shutdown decision, the company had an inventory of nearly 500,000 unsold computers. To unload them, TI reduced its price to $49 (see Figure 9.8), forcing lower prices and losses on other computer firms.

shutdown point: The rate of output where price equals minimum AVC.

FIGURE 9.8
Plummeting Prices

Improved technology and fierce competition forced home computer prices down. In the span of only a few years, the price of a basic home computer fell from just under $1,000 to only $49. In the process, price fell below average variable cost, and many firms were forced to shut down.

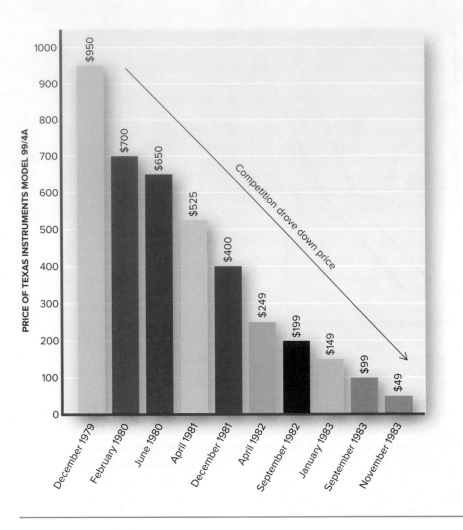

Exits

Shortly after Texas Instruments shut down its production, it got out of the home computer business altogether. Mattel, Atari, and scores of smaller companies also withdrew from the home computer market. The exit rate between 1983 and 1985 matched the entry rate of the period 1979 to 1982.

The Personal Computer Market

The same kind of price competition that characterized the home computer market eventually hit the personal computer market too. At first, competition in the PC market was largely confined to product improvements. Firms added more memory, faster microprocessors, better monitors, expanded operating systems, new applications software, and other features. New entrants into the market—Compaq in 1982; then Dell, AST, Gateway, and more—were the source of most product innovations.

The stampede of new firms and products into the PC market soon led to outright price competition too. As firms discovered that they couldn't sell all the PCs they were producing at prevailing prices, they were forced to offer price discounts. These discounts soon spread, and the slide down the demand curve accelerated.

Firms that couldn't keep up with the dual pace of improving technology and falling prices soon fell by the wayside. Scores of firms ceased production and withdrew from the industry once prices fell below minimum average variable cost. Even Apple, which had taken the "high road" to avoid price competition in home computers, was slowed by price competition.

THE COMPETITIVE PROCESS

It is now evident that consumers have reaped substantial benefits from competition in the computer market. More than 1 billion home and personal computers have been sold. Along the way, technology has made personal computers a thousand times faster than the first Apple IIs, with phenomenal increases in memory. The iMac computer introduced by Apple in 1998 made the Apple I of 1976 look prehistoric. The latest iMacs make even the 1998 model look primitive. A lot of consumers have found that computers are great for doing accounting chores, keeping records, writing papers, playing games, and accessing the Internet. Perhaps it's true that an abundance of inexpensive computers would have been produced in other market (or nonmarket) situations as well. But we can't ignore the fact that *competitive market pressures were a driving force in the spectacular growth of the computer industry.* And they still are.

Allocative Efficiency: The Right Output Mix

The squeeze on prices and profits that we've observed in the computer market is a fundamental characteristic of the competitive process. The process works as well in India (see World View "Competition Shrinks India's Phone Bills") as in the United States or elsewhere. Indeed, the **market mechanism** works best under competitive pressure. The existence of economic profits is an indication that consumers place a high value on a particular product and are willing to pay a comparatively high price to get it. The high price and profits signal this information to profit-hungry entrepreneurs, who come forward to satisfy consumer demands. Thus *high profits in a particular industry indicate that consumers want a different mix of output* (more of that industry's goods). The competitive squeeze on those same profits indicates that resources are being reallocated to produce that desired mix. In a competitive market, consumers get more of the goods they desire—and at a lower price.

iPhone 7 Plus and Apple Watch

Analysis: The evolution of personal computers from the Apple I to the latest iPhone, iPad, and Apple Watch was driven by intense competition.

©imageBROKER/Alamy Stock Photo

market mechanism: The use of market prices and sales to signal desired outputs (or resource allocations).

WORLD VIEW

COMPETITION SHRINKS INDIA'S PHONE BILLS

Ever since the Indian government opened up its telecom industry to competition in 1999, Indian consumers have seen their phone bills shrink. In 2000, the charge for making a call with a cellular phone was 16 rupees per minute (about 27 U.S. cents). By 2011, that rate had fallen to 1 paisa per second—roughly 1 cent per minute. In the same time period, the number of mobile subscribers skyrocketed from 2 million to 584 million. Today, there are 930 million cellular subscribers, making India the world's second largest mobile phone market. How did all this come about? India opened the telecom market to new entrants, reduced license fees, and lowered tariffs, encouraging dozens of firms to compete for India's telephone customers.

Source: News reports, 2011.

ANALYSIS: Competitive pressures force companies to continually improve products and cut prices.

The ability of competitive markets to allocate resources efficiently across industries originates in the way competitive prices are set. To attain the optimal mix of output, we must know the **opportunity cost** of producing different goods. A competitive market gives us the information necessary for making such choices. Why? Because competitive firms always strive to produce at the rate of output at which price equals marginal cost. Hence *the price signal the consumer gets in a competitive market is an accurate reflection of opportunity cost.* As such, it offers a reliable basis for making choices about the mix of

opportunity cost: The most desired goods or services that are forgone in order to obtain something else.

marginal cost pricing: The offer (supply) of goods at prices equal to their marginal cost.

efficiency: Maximum output of a good from the resources used in production.

output and attendant allocation of resources. In this sense, the **marginal cost pricing** characteristic of competitive markets permits society to answer the WHAT-to-produce question efficiently. The amount consumers are willing to pay for a good (its price) equals its opportunity cost (marginal cost).

Production Efficiency: Minimum Average Cost

When the competitive pressure on prices is carried to the limit, we also get the right answer to the HOW-to-produce question. Competition drives costs down to their bare minimum—the hallmark of economic **efficiency.** This was illustrated by the tendency of computer prices to be driven down to the level of *minimum* average costs. Figure 9.9 summarizes this competitive process, showing how the industry moves from short-run equilibrium (point *a*) to long-run equilibrium (point *c*). Once the long-run equilibrium has been established, society is getting the most it can from its available (scarce) resources.

Zero Economic Profit

Competitive pressures also affect the FOR WHOM question. At the limit of long-run equilibrium, all economic profit is eliminated. This doesn't mean that producers are left empty-handed, however. The zero-profit limit is rarely, if ever, reached because new products are continually being introduced, consumer demands change, and more efficient production processes are discovered. In fact, the competitive process creates strong pressures to pursue product and technological innovation. In a competitive market, the adage about the early bird getting the worm is particularly apt. As we observed in the computer market, the first ones to perceive and respond to the potential profitability of computer production were the ones who made the greatest profits.

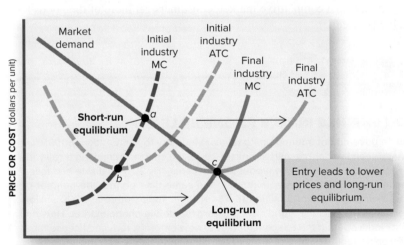

FIGURE 9.9

Summary of Competitive Process

All competitive firms seek to produce at that output where MC = *p*. Hence a competitive *industry* will produce at that rate of output where *industry* MC (the sum of all firms' MC curves) intersects market demand (point *a*).

   If economic profits exist in the industry short-run equilibrium (as they do here because price exceeds ATC at point *a*), more firms will enter the industry. As they do, the *industry* MC (supply) curve will shift to the right. The shifting MC curve will pull the *industry* ATC curve along with it. As the *industry* MC curve continues to shift rightward, the intersection of MC and ATC (point *b*) eventually will reach the demand curve at point *c*. At point *c,* MC still equals price, but no economic profits exist and entry (shifts) will cease. Point *c* will be the *long-run* equilibrium of the industry.

   If competitive pressures reduce costs (i.e., improve technology), the supply (MC) curve will shift further to the right and *down,* reducing long-run prices even more.

   Note that MC = *p* in both short- and long-run equilibrium. Notice also that equilibrium must occur on the market demand curve.

Relentless Profit Squeeze

The sequence of events common to competitive markets evolves as follows:

- High prices and profits signal consumers' demand for more output.
- Economic profit attracts new suppliers.
- The market supply curve shifts to the right.
- Prices slide down the market demand curve.
- A new equilibrium is reached at which increased quantities of the desired product are produced and its price is lower. Average costs of production are at or near a minimum, much more of the product is supplied and consumed, and economic profit approaches zero.
- Throughout the process, producers experience great pressure to keep ahead of the profit squeeze by reducing costs, a pressure that frequently results in product and technological innovation.

What is essential to remember about the competitive process is that the ***potential threat of other firms expanding production or of new firms entering the industry keeps existing firms on their toes.*** Even the most successful firm can't rest on its laurels for long. To stay in the game, competitive firms must continually update technology, improve their products, and reduce costs.

THE ECONOMY TOMORROW

$99 IPADS?

Competition didn't end with computers. Steve Jobs, the guy who started the personal computer business back in 1977, knew that. He introduced another hot consumer product in November 2001—the iPod. The iPod was the first mass-produced portable digital music player. It allowed consumers to download, store, and retrieve up to 1,000 songs. Its compact size, sleek design, and simple functionality made it an instant success: Apple was selling iPods as fast as they could be produced, piling up huge profits in the process.

So what happened? Other entrepreneurs quickly got the scent of iPod's profits. Within a matter of months, competitors were designing their own digital music players. By 2003 the "attack of the iPod clones" was in full force. Major players like Sony (MusicBox), Dell (JukeBox), Samsung (Yepp), and Creative Technology (Muvo Slim) were all bringing MP3 players to the market. Competitors were adding new features, shrinking the size, and reducing prices.

Under these circumstances, Apple could not afford to sit back and admire its profits. Steve Jobs knew he'd have to keep running to stay ahead of the MP3 player pack. He kept improving the iPod. Within 2 years Apple had three generations of iPods, each substantially better than the last. Memory capacity increased tenfold (to 10,000 songs), features were added, and the size shrank further. In less than 2.5 years, the iPod's price fell by 40 percent even while quality improved dramatically.

The same kind of unrelenting competitive dynamic has hounded Apple's iPad. The iPad wasn't the first tablet computer, but it was a huge success: 300,000 iPads were sold on the first day and 15 million in the first year. Apple reaped enormous profits.

Those profits signaled a slew of companies to enter the tablet market, seeking to get a piece of the new profit pie. More than 100 companies entered the tablet market in 2011 alone, putting enormous pressure on Apple's sales, price, and profits. Apple stayed ahead of the competitive pack by reducing price, adding new features (e.g., built-in cameras, faster processor, four speakers, live video, Bluetooth keyboard), and shrinking the tablet's size and weight (the 9.7 inch iPad Pro, March 2016). With such unrelenting competitive pressure, industry analysts predict we'll see $99 iPads in the economy tomorrow.

SUMMARY

- A perfectly competitive firm has no power to alter the market price of the product it sells. The perfectly competitive firm confronts a horizontal demand curve for its own output even though the relevant *market* demand curve is negatively sloped.   **LO9-1**
- Profit maximization induces the competitive firm to produce at that rate of output where marginal costs equal price (MC = p). This represents the short-run equilibrium of the firm.   **LO9-2**
- If profits exist in short-run equilibrium, new firms will enter the market. The resulting shift of supply will drive market prices down the market demand curve. As prices fall, the profit of the industry and its constituent firms will be squeezed.   **LO9-3**

- The limit to the competitive price and profit squeeze is reached when price is driven down to the level of minimum average total cost (MC = p = ATC). At this point (long-run equilibrium) additional output and profit will be attained only if technology is improved (lowering costs) or if market demand increases.   **LO9-3**
- Firms will shut down production if price falls below average variable cost. Firms will exit the industry if they foresee continued economic losses.   **LO9-3**
- The most distinctive thing about competitive markets is the persistent pressure they exert on prices and profits. The threat of competition is a tremendous incentive for producers to respond quickly to consumer demands and to seek more efficient means of production. In this sense, competitive markets do best what markets are supposed to do—efficiently allocate resources.   **LO9-4**

Key Terms

equilibrium price
market supply
marginal cost (MC)
investment decision
economic profit
competitive market

barriers to entry
production decision
average total cost (ATC)
profit per unit
short-run competitive equilibrium
long-run competitive equilibrium

shutdown point
market mechanism
opportunity cost
marginal cost pricing
efficiency

Questions for Discussion

1. Why would anyone want to enter a profitable industry knowing that profits would eventually be eliminated by competition?   **LO9-3**
2. Why wouldn't producers necessarily want to produce output at the lowest average cost? Under what conditions would they end up doing so?   **LO9-1**
3. What industries do you regard as being highly competitive? Can you identify any barriers to entry in those industries?   **LO9-1**
4. Why do TV prices continue to fall so much? (See World View "Flat Panels, Thin Margins.")   **LO9-2**
5. What does the "bleeding" highlighted in In the News "U.S. Catfish Industry Bleeding Finally Stops" refer to? What causes it? What cures it?   **LO9-3**

6. As the price of computers fell, what happened to their quality? How is this possible?   **LO9-4**
7. Can phone rates keep falling in India? What will cause them to rise? (See World View "Competition Shrinks India's Phone Bills.")   **LO9-4**
8. Is "long-run" equilibrium permanent? What forces might dislodge it?   **LO9-3**
9. Why don't catfish farmers raise the price of their fish and create better profits?   **LO9-2**
10. Identify two products that have either (*a*) fallen sharply in price or (*b*) gotten significantly better without price increases. How did these changes come about?   **LO9-4**
11. What happens to the factors of production that exit an industry?   **LO9-4**

PROBLEMS FOR CHAPTER 9

<img src="https://mcgrawhill.com/connect-logo.png" alt="McGraw Hill connect" />

LO9-3 1. According to World View "Competition Shrink India's Phone Bills," between 2000 and 2011 in India,
    (a) By what percentage did the price of a phone minute decline after competition emerged?
    (b) By what percentage did the quantity demanded increase?
    (c) What was the apparent price elasticity of demand?
    Note: Use the midpoint formula to compute percentage changes.

LO9-2 2. According to Table 9.1,
    (a) What were the fixed costs of production for the firm?
    (b) At what rate of output was profit per computer maximized? (Choose the highest output level.)
    (c) At what output rate was total profit maximized?

LO9-2 3. According to Figure 9.3b, if the market price for computers is $800,
    (a) What is the profit-maximizing quantity?
    (b) Calculate the profits (or losses) for this typical firm.
    (c) At this market price, will firms enter or exit the market?
    (d) Will this entry or exit cause prices to rise or fall?

LO9-1 4. Suppose the following data summarize the costs of a perfectly competitive firm:

Quantity	0	1	2	3	4	5	6	7	8
Total cost	$100	101	103	106	110	115	121	128	136

    (a) Draw the firm's MC curve on graph (a).
    (b) Draw the market supply curve on graph (b), assuming there are 8 firms identical to the one just described.
    (c) What is the equilibrium price in this market?

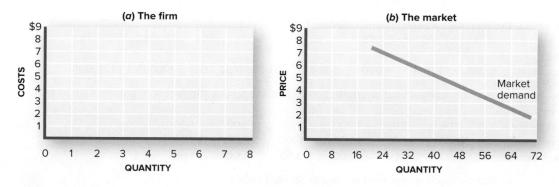

LO9-1 5. Suppose the following data describe the demand for fruit smoothies:

Price	$11	$10	$9	$8	$7	$6	$5	$4	$3	$2
Quantity demanded	7	10	13	16	19	22	25	28	31	34

Five identical, perfectly competitive firms are producing these smoothies. The cost of producing these smoothies at each firm is the following:

Quantity produced	0	1	2	3	4	5	6	7	8	9	10
Total cost	$5	$8	$10	$13	$17	$22	$28	$36	$45	$55	$67

    (a) What price will prevail in this market?
    (b) What quantity is produced?
    (c) How much profit (loss) does each firm make?
    (d) What happens to price if two more identical firms enter the market?

LO9-3 6. Suppose the typical catfish farmer was incurring an economic loss at the prevailing price p_1.
  (a) Illustrate these losses on the market and firm graphs. Include the supply and demand curves on the market graph and average total cost, marginal cost, and price in the firm graph.
  (b) Identify the price that would prevail in the long-run equilibrium.
  (c) What supply forces would raise the price to this long run equilibrium. Illustrate your answer on the graphs.

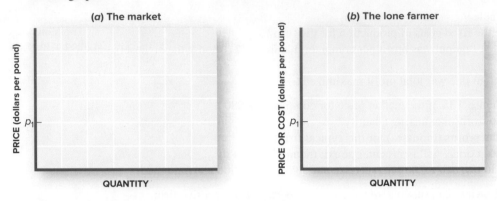

LO9-2 7. According to Table 9.1,
  (a) What was the prevailing computer price in 1978?
  (b) How much total profit did the typical firm earn?
  (c) At what price would profits have been zero?
  (d) At what price would the firm have shut down?

LO9-2 8. If a competitive firm has fixed costs of $10,000 per month and a minimum average variable cost of $28, at what price will it shutdown?

LO9-4 9. Suppose that the monthly market demand schedule for Frisbees is

Price	$8	$7	$6	$5	$4	$3	$2	$1
Quantity demanded	1,000	2,000	4,000	8,000	16,000	32,000	64,000	128,000

Suppose further that the marginal and average costs of Frisbee production for every competitive firm are

Rate of output	100	200	300	400	500	600
Marginal cost	$2.00	$3.00	$4.00	$5.00	$6.00	$7.00
Average total cost	2.00	2.50	3.00	3.50	4.00	4.50

Finally, assume that the equilibrium market price is $6 per Frisbee.
  (a) Draw the cost curves of the typical firm and identify its profit-maximizing rate of output and its total profits.
  (b) Draw the market demand curve and identify market equilibrium.
  (c) How many Frisbees are being sold?
  (d) How many (identical) firms are initially producing Frisbees?
  (e) How much profit is the typical firm making?
  (f) In view of the profits being made, more firms will enter into Frisbee production, shift the market supply curve to the right, and push price down. At what equilibrium price are all profits eliminated?
  (g) How many firms will be producing Frisbees at this long-term price?

PROBLEMS FOR CHAPTER 9 (cont'd)

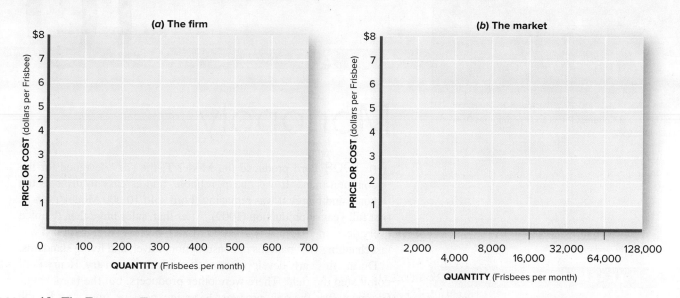

(a) The firm

PRICE OR COST (dollars per Frisbee)

QUANTITY (Frisbees per month)

(b) The market

PRICE OR COST (dollars per Frisbee)

QUANTITY (Frisbees per month)

LO9-3 10. The Economy Tomorrow: Suppose the competitive tablet market is in the long run equilibrium. If at this equilibrium, the typical firm produces 10,000 per month, total costs for this production is $4,000,000, and the minimum of the average variable costs is $75, what price will,

    (*a*) Induce entry into the market?

    (*b*) Cause firms to shut down production in the short run?

    (*c*) Result in firms exiting the market in the long run?

CHAPTER 10

Monopoly

In 1908 Ford produced the Model T, the car "designed for the common man." It was cheap, reliable, and as easy to drive as the horse and buggy it was replacing. Ford sold 10,000 Model Ts in its first full year of production (1909). After that, sales more than doubled every year. In 1913 nearly 200,000 Model Ts were sold; and Ford was fast changing U.S. patterns of consumption, travel, and living standards.

During this early development of the U.S. auto industry, Henry Ford dominated the field. There were other producers, but the Ford Motor Company was the only producer of an inexpensive "motorcar for the multitudes." In this situation, Henry Ford could dictate the price and the features of his cars. When he opened his new assembly line factory at Highland Park, he abruptly raised the Model T's price by $100—an increase of 12 percent—to help pay for the new plant. Then he decided to paint all Model Ts black. When told of consumer complaints about the lack of colors, Ford advised one of his executives in 1913, "Give them any color they want so long as it's black."[1]

Henry Ford had market power. He could dictate what color car Americans would buy. And he could raise the price of Model Ts without fear of losing all his customers. Such power is alien to competitive firms. Competitive firms are always under pressure to reduce costs, improve quality, and cater to consumer preferences.

In this chapter we examine how market structure influences market outcomes. Specifically, we examine how a market controlled by a single producer—a monopoly—behaves. We're particularly interested in the following questions:

- **What price will a monopolist charge?**
- **How much output will the monopolist produce?**
- **Are consumers better or worse off when only one firm controls an entire market?**

LEARNING OBJECTIVES

After reading this chapter, you should know

LO10-1 How a monopolist sets price and output.

LO10-2 How monopoly and competitive outcomes differ.

LO10-3 The pros and cons of monopoly.

MARKET POWER

The essence of **market power** is the ability to alter the price of a product. The catfish farmers in Chapter 9 had no such power. Because 2,000 farms were producing and selling the same good, each catfish producer had to act as a *price taker*. Each producer could sell all it wanted at the prevailing price but would lose all its customers if it tried to charge a higher price.

market power: The ability to alter the market price of a good or service.

[1] Source: Sorensen, Charles E., *My Forty Years with Ford,* New York: W. W. Norton & Co., p. 127, 1956.

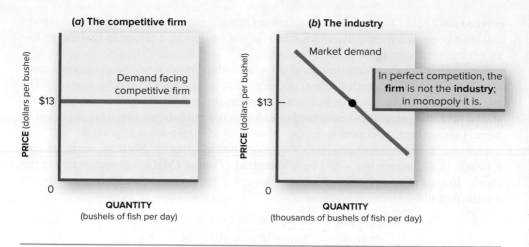

FIGURE 10.1

Firm vs. Industry Demand

A competitive firm can sell its entire output at the prevailing market price. In this sense, the firm confronts a horizontal demand curve, as in part *a*. Nevertheless, *market* demand for the product still slopes downward. The demand curve confronting the industry is illustrated in part *b*. Note the difference in the units of measurement (single bushels vs. thousands). A monopolist confronts the *industry* (market) demand curve.

The Downward-Sloping Demand Curve

Firms that have market power *can* alter the price of their output without losing all their customers. Sales volume may drop when price is increased, but the quantity demanded won't drop to zero. In other words, *firms with market power confront downward-sloping demand curves for their own output.*

The distinction between perfectly competitive (powerless) and imperfectly competitive (powerful) firms is illustrated again in Figure 10.1. Figure 10.1*a* re-creates the market situation that confronts a single catfish farmer. In Chapter 8, we assumed that the prevailing price of catfish was $13 a bushel and that a small, competitive firm could sell its entire output at this price. Hence each individual firm effectively confronted a horizontal demand curve.

We also noted earlier that catfish don't violate the law of demand. As good as catfish taste, people aren't willing to buy unlimited quantities of them at $13 a bushel. To induce consumers to buy more catfish, the market price of catfish must be reduced.

This seeming contradiction between the law of demand and the situation of the competitive firm is resolved in Figure 10.1. There are *two* relevant demand curves. The one on the left, which appears to contradict the law of demand, refers to a single competitive producer. The one on the right refers to the entire *industry,* of which the competitive producer is one very tiny part. The industry or market demand curve *does* slope downward, even though individual competitive firms are able to sell their own output at the going price.

Monopoly

An industry needn't be composed of many small firms. The entire output of catfish could be produced by a single large producer. Such a firm would be a **monopoly**—a single firm that produces the entire market supply of a good.

The emergence of a monopoly obliterates the distinction between industry demand and the demand curve facing the firm. A monopolistic firm *is* the industry. Hence there's only *one* demand curve to worry about, and that's the market (industry) demand curve, as illustrated in Figure 10.1*b*. This simplifies things: *in monopoly situations, the demand curve facing the firm is identical to the market demand curve for the product.*

monopoly: A firm that produces the entire market supply of a particular good or service.

Price and Marginal Revenue

Although monopolies simplify the geometry, they complicate the arithmetic of **profit maximization.** The basic rule for maximizing profits is unchanged—that is, produce the rate of output where marginal revenue equals marginal cost. This rule applies to *all* firms. In a competitive industry, however, this general rule was simplified. For competitive firms, marginal revenue is equal to price. Hence a competitive firm can maximize profits by producing at that rate of output where marginal cost equals *price.*

This special adaptation of the profit-maximizing rule doesn't work for a monopolist. The demand curve facing a monopolist is downward-sloping. Because of this, *marginal*

profit maximization rule: Produce at that rate of output where marginal revenue equals marginal cost.

revenue isn't equal to price for a monopolist. On the contrary, marginal revenue is always *less* than price in a monopoly, which makes it just a bit more difficult to find the profit-maximizing rate of output.

Figure 10.2 is a simple illustration of the relationship between price and marginal revenue. The monopolist can sell 1 bushel of fish per day at a price of $13. If he wants to sell a larger quantity of fish, however, he has to reduce his price. According to the demand curve shown here, the price must be lowered to $12 to sell 2 bushels per day. This reduction in price is shown by a movement along the demand curve from point *A* to point *B*.

How much additional revenue does the second bushel bring in? It's tempting to say that it brings in $12, since that's its price. **Marginal revenue (MR),** however, refers to the *change* in *total* revenue that results from a one-unit increase in output. More generally, we use the formula

$$\frac{\text{Marginal}}{\text{revenue}} = \frac{\text{Change in total revenue}}{\text{Change in quantity sold}} = \frac{\Delta \text{TR}}{\Delta q}$$

where the delta symbol Δ denotes "change in." According to this formula, the marginal revenue of the second bushel is

$$\text{MR} = \frac{\$24 - \$13}{1} = \$11.$$

Hence MR ($11) is less than price ($12) for the second bushel sold.

> **marginal revenue (MR):** The change in total revenue that results from a one-unit increase in the quantity sold.

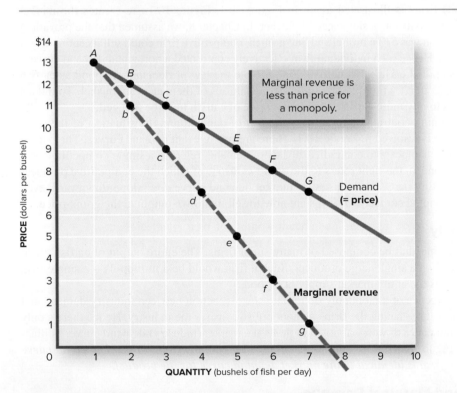

> Marginal revenue is less than price for a monopoly.

FIGURE 10.2

Price Exceeds Marginal Revenue in Monopoly

If a firm must lower its price to sell additional output, marginal revenue is less than price. If this monopoly firm wants to increase its sales from 1 to 2 bushels per day, for example, price must be reduced from $13 to $12. The marginal revenue of the second bushel is therefore only $11. This is indicated in row *B* of the table and by point *b* on the graph.

	Quantity	×	Price	=	Total Revenue	Marginal Revenue (= ΔTR ÷ Δq)
A	1		$13		$13	–
B	2		12		24	$11
C	3		11		33	9
D	4		10		40	7
E	5		9		45	5

Figure 10.2 summarizes the calculations necessary for computing MR. Row *A* of the table indicates that the total revenue resulting from one sale per day is $13. To increase sales, price must be reduced. Row *B* indicates that total revenue rises to $24 per day when fish sales double. The *increase* in total revenue resulting from the added sales is thus $11. This concept is illustrated in the last column of the table and by point *b* on the marginal revenue curve.

Notice that the MR of the second bushel ($11) is *less* than its price ($12) because both bushels are being sold for $12 apiece. In effect, the firm is giving up the opportunity to sell only 1 bushel per day at $13 to sell a larger quantity at a lower price. In this sense, the firm is sacrificing $1 of potential revenue on the first bushel to increase *total* revenue. Marginal revenue measures the change in total revenue that results.

So long as the demand curve is downward-sloping, MR will always be less than price. Compare columns 2 and 4 of the table in Figure 10.2. At each rate of output in excess of 1 bushel, marginal revenue is less than price. This is also evident in the graph: *the MR curve lies below the demand (price) curve at every point but the first.*

Profit Maximization

Although the presence of market power adds a new wrinkle, the rules of profit maximization remain the same. *Instead of looking for an intersection of marginal cost and price (as in perfect competition), we now look for the intersection of marginal cost and marginal revenue (monopoly).* This is illustrated in Figure 10.3 by the intersection of the MR and MC curves (point *d*). Looking down from that intersection, we see that the associated rate of output is 4 bushels per day. Thus 4 bushels is the profit-maximizing rate of output.

How much should the monopolist charge for these 4 bushels? Naturally, the monopolist would like to charge a very high price. But the ability to charge a high price is limited by the demand curve. If the monopolist charges $13, consumers will buy only 1 bushel, leaving 3 unsold bushels of dead fish. Not a pretty picture. As the monopolist will soon learn, *only one price is compatible with the profit-maximizing rate of output.* In this case, the price is $10. This price is found in Figure 10.3 by moving up from the quantity 4 until reaching the demand curve at point *D*. Point *D* tells us that consumers are able and willing to buy 4 bushels of fish per day only at the price of $10 each. A monopolist who tries to charge more than $10 won't be able to sell all 4 bushels.

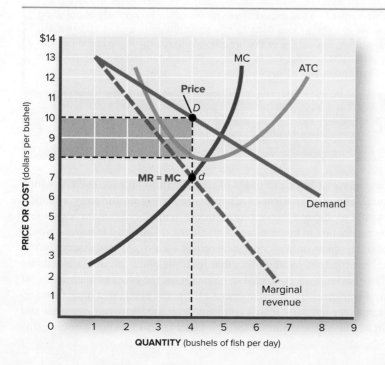

FIGURE 10.3

Profit Maximization (MR = MC)

The most profitable rate of output is indicated by the intersection of marginal revenue and marginal cost (point *d*). This intersection (MC = MR) establishes 4 bushels as the profit-maximizing rate of output. Point *D* indicates that consumers will pay $10 per bushel for this much output.

Total profits equal price ($10) minus average total cost ($8), multiplied by the quantity sold (4).

Figure 10.3 also illustrates the total profits of the catfish monopoly. To compute total profits we can first calculate profit per unit—that is, price minus *average* total cost. In this case, profit per unit is $2 at the profit-maximizing rate of output. Multiplying profit per unit by the quantity sold (4) gives us total profits of $8 per day, as illustrated by the shaded rectangle.

MARKET POWER AT WORK: THE COMPUTER MARKET REVISITED

To develop a keener appreciation for the nature of market power, we can return to the computer market of Chapter 9. The computer market wasn't perfectly competitive, but it nearly behaved as though it was. We saw how the continuing entry of new firms kept competitive pressure on computer firms to reduce costs and improve quality. In this chapter, we'll make some different assumptions about market structure. In particular, assume that a single firm, Universal Electronics, acquires an exclusive patent on the production of the microprocessors that function as the computer's "brain." This one firm is now in a position to deny potential competitors access to the basic ingredient of computers. The patent thus functions as a **barrier to entry,** to be erected or set aside at the will of Universal Electronics.

barriers to entry: Obstacles such as patents that make it difficult or impossible for would-be producers to enter a particular market.

Universal's management is familiar enough with the principles of economics (including W. C. Fields's advice about never giving a sucker an even break) to know when it's onto a good thing. It's not about to let every would-be Horatio Alger have a slice of the profit pie. Even the Russians understood this strategy during the heyday of communism. They made sure no one else could produce sable furs that could compete with their monopoly (see World View "Russia's Sable Monopoly Persists"). Let's assume that Universal Electronics is equally protective of its turf and will refuse to sell or give away any rights to its patent or the chips it produces. That is, Universal Electronics sets itself up as a computer monopoly.

WORLD VIEW

RUSSIA'S SABLE MONOPOLY PERSISTS

Ancient Greeks and Romans called the fur of the sable the "Golden Fleece." Unlike any other fur, sable is smooth in all directions, even after stroked. Living in the wilds of Siberia, the sable has always been one of Russia's most valuable exports. In 1697 Peter the Great decreed a monopoly on sable, forbidding the export of live sables or the technology of breeding them. In the 1980s Russia was selling more than 15 million sable pelts a year and reaping monopoly-type profits. Exporting live sables or the breeding technology was a crime punishable by death. The plot of the 1983 movie, *Gorky Park,* centers on the murder of three men who attempted to export live sables out of Russia.

ANALYSIS: To ward off potential competition, a monopoly must erect barriers to entry. By not letting live sables leave the country, to breed elsewhere, Russia maintained a monopoly on sable furs.

Let's also assume that Universal has a multitude of manufacturing plants, each of which is identical to the typical competitive firm in Chapter 9. This is an unlikely situation because a monopolist would probably achieve **economies of scale** by closing at least a few plants and consolidating production in larger plants. Our fictional Universal company would maintain a multitude of small plants only if constant returns to scale or actual diseconomies of scale were rampant. Nevertheless, by assuming that multiple plants are maintained, we can compare monopoly behavior with competitive behavior on the basis of identical cost structures. In particular, if Universal continues to operate the many plants that once made up the competitive home computer industry, it will confront the same short-run marginal and average cost curves already encountered in Chapter 9. Later in this chapter we relax this

economies of scale: Reductions in minimum average costs that come about through increases in the size (scale) of plant and equipment.

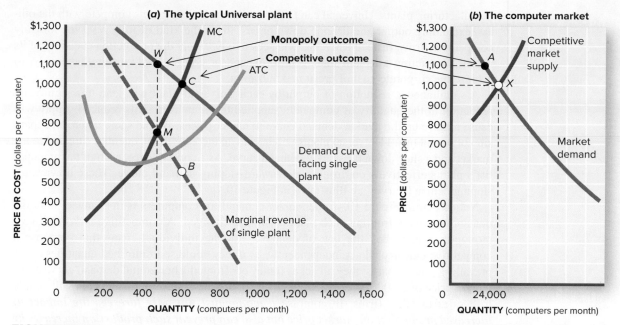

FIGURE 10.4

Initial Conditions in the Monopolized Computer Market

We assume that a monopoly firm (Universal Electronics) would confront the same costs (MC and ATC) and demand as would the competitive industry in Chapter 9. In the initial short-run equilibrium, the competitive price was $1,000 (point C), and each firm (plant) was producing 600 computers (where MC = p).

A monopolist isn't bound by the competitive market price. Instead the monopolist must contend with downward-sloping demand and marginal revenue curves. If each monopoly plant produced where MC = $1,000 (point C in part a), marginal cost (point C) would exceed marginal revenue (point B). To maximize profits, the monopolist must find that rate of output where MC = MR (point M in part a). That rate of output (475) can be sold at the higher monopoly price of $1,100 (point W in part a).

Part b illustrates the market implications of the monopolist's production decision: a reduced quantity is sold at a higher price (point A).

assumption of multiplant operations to determine whether, in the long run, a monopolist may actually lower production costs below those of a competitive industry.

Figure 10.4a re-creates the marginal costs the typical competitive firm faced in the early stages of the microcomputer boom (from Figure 9.3 and Table 9.1). We now assume that this MC curve also expresses the costs of operating one of Universal's many (identical) plants. Thus the extension of monopoly control is assumed to have no immediate effect on production costs.

The market demand for computers is also assumed to be unchanged. There's no reason why people should be less willing to buy computers now than they were when the market was competitive. Most consumers have no notion of how many firms produce a product. Even if they knew, there's no reason why their demand for the product would change. Thus Figure 10.4b expresses an unchanged market demand for computers.

Our immediate concern is to determine how Universal Electronics, as a monopolist, will respond to these unchanged demand and cost curves. Will it produce exactly as many computers as the competitive industry did? Will it sell the computers at the same price that the competitive industry did? Will it improve the product as much or as fast?

The Production Decision

Like any producer, Universal Electronics will strive to produce its output at the rate that maximizes total profits. But unlike competitive firms, Universal will explicitly take account of the fact that an increase in output will put downward pressure on computer prices. This may threaten corporate profits.

The implications of Universal's market position for the **production decision** of its many plants can be seen in the new price and marginal revenue curves imposed on each of its

production decision: The selection of the short-run rate of output (with existing plants and equipment).

manufacturing plants. Universal can't afford to let each of its plants compete with the others, expanding output and driving down prices; that's the kind of folly reserved for truly competitive firms. Instead Universal will seek to *coordinate* the production decisions of its plants, instructing all plant managers to expand or contract output simultaneously, to achieve the corporate goal of profit maximization.

A simultaneous reduction of output by each Universal plant will lead to a significant reduction in the quantity of computers supplied to the market. This reduced supply will cause a move up the market demand curve to higher prices. By the same token, an expansion of output by all Universal plants will lead to an increase in the quantity supplied to the market and a slide down the market demand curve. As a consequence, each of the monopolist's plants effectively confronts a downward-sloping demand curve. These downward-sloping demand curves are illustrated in Figure 10.4a.[2]

Notice that in Figure 10.4b the *market* demand for computers is unchanged; only the demand curve confronting each plant (firm) has changed. A competitive *industry,* like a monopoly, must obey the law of demand. But the individual firms that compose a competitive industry all act independently, *as if* they could sell unlimited quantities at the prevailing price. That is, they all act as if they confronted a horizontal demand curve at the market price of $1,000. A competitive firm that doesn't behave in this fashion will simply lose sales to other firms. In contrast, *a monopolist not only foresees the impact of increased production on market price but also can prevent such production increases by its separate plants.*

Marginal Revenue. The downward-sloping demand curve now confronting each Universal plant implies that marginal revenue no longer equals price. Notice that the marginal revenue curve in Figure 10.4a lies *below* the demand curve at every rate of output. Because marginal revenue is less than price for a monopoly, Universal's plants would no longer wish to produce up to the point where marginal cost equals price. *Only firms that confront a horizontal demand curve (perfect competitors) equate marginal cost and price.* Universal's plants must stick to the generic profit-maximizing rule about equating marginal revenue and marginal cost. Should the individual plant managers forget this rule, Universal's central management will fire them.

The output and price implications of Universal's monopoly position become apparent as we examine the new revenue and cost relationships. Recall that the equilibrium price of computers in the early stages of the home computer boom was $1,000. This equilibrium price is indicated in Figure 10.4b by the intersection of the *competitive* market supply curve with the market demand curve (point X). Each competitive *firm* produced up to the point where marginal cost (MC) equaled that price (point C in Figure 10.4a). At that point, each competitive firm was producing 600 computers a month.

Reduced Output. The emergence of Universal as a monopolist alters these production decisions. Now each Universal plant *does* have an impact on market price because its behavior is imitated simultaneously by all Universal plants. In fact, the marginal revenue associated with the 600th computer is only $575, as indicated by point B in Figure 10.4a. At this rate of output, the typical Universal plant would be operating with marginal costs ($1,000) far in excess of marginal revenues ($575). Such behavior is inconsistent with profit maximization.

The enlightened Universal plant manager will soon discover that the profit-maximizing rate of output is less than 600 computers per month. In Figure 10.4a we see that the marginal revenue and marginal cost curves intersect at point M. This MR = MC intersection occurs at an output level of only 475 computers per month. Accordingly, the typical Universal plant will want to produce *fewer* computers (475) than were produced by the typical competitive firm (600) in the early stages of the home computer boom. Recall that

---

[2]The demand and marginal revenue curves in Figure 10.4a are illustrative; they're not derived from earlier tables. As discussed here, we're assuming that the central management of Universal determines the profit-maximizing rate of output and then instructs all individual plants to produce equal shares of that output.

individual competitive firms had no incentive to engage in such production cutbacks. They couldn't alter the market supply curve or price on their own and weren't coordinated by a central management. Thus the first consequence of Universal's monopoly position is a reduction in the rate of industry output.

The Monopoly Price

The reduction in output at each Universal plant translates automatically into a decrease in the *quantity supplied* to the market. As consumers compete for this reduced market supply, they'll bid computer prices up. We can observe the increased prices in Figure 10.4 by looking at either the typical Universal plant or the computer market. Notice that in Figure 10.4*a* the price is determined by moving directly up from point *M* to the demand curve confronting the typical Universal plant. The demand curve always tells how much consumers are willing to pay for any given quantity. Hence, once we've determined the quantity that's going to be supplied (475 computers per month), we can look at the demand curve to determine the price ($1,100 at point *W*) that consumers will pay for these computers. That is,

- *The intersection of the marginal revenue and marginal cost curves establishes the profit-maximizing rate of output.*
- *The demand curve tells us how much consumers are willing to pay for that specific quantity of output.*

Figure 10.4*a* shows how Universal's monopoly position results in both reduced output and increased prices. This result is also evident in Figure 10.4*b*, where we see that a smaller quantity supplied to the market will force a move up the demand curve to the higher price of $1,100 per computer (point *A*).

Monopoly Profits

Universal's objective was and remains the maximization of profits. That it has succeeded in its effort can be confirmed by scrutinizing Figure 10.5. As you can see, the typical Universal plant ends up selling 475 computers a month at a price of $1,100 each (point *W*). The **average total cost (ATC)** of production at this rate of output is only $630 (point *K*), as was detailed in Table 9.1.

As always, we can compute total profit as

average total cost (ATC): Total cost divided by the quantity produced in a given time period.

$$\text{Total profit} = \text{Profit per unit} \times \text{Quantity sold}$$

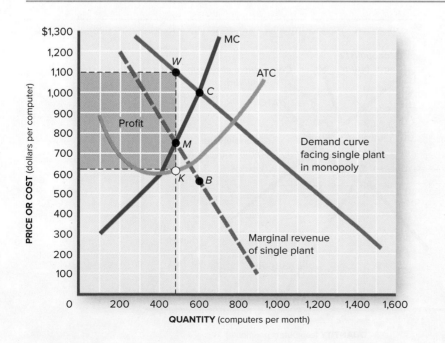

FIGURE 10.5

Monopoly Profits: The Typical Universal Plant

The profit-maximizing rate of output occurs where the marginal cost and marginal revenue curves intersect (point *M*). The demand curve indicates the price (point *W*) that consumers will pay for this much output. Total profit equals price (*W*) minus *average* total cost (*K*), multiplied by the quantity sold (475). Total profits are represented by the shaded rectangle.

In this case, we see that

$$\text{Total profit} = (\$1,100 - \$630) \times 475$$
$$= \$223,250$$

This figure significantly exceeds the monthly profit of $180,000 earned by the typical competitive firm in the early stages of the computer boom (see Table 9.1).

It's apparent from these profit figures that Universal management has learned its economic principles well. By reducing the output of each plant and raising prices a little, it has managed to increase profits. This can be seen again in Figure 10.6, which is an enlarged illustration of the *market* situation for the home computer industry. The figure translates the economics of our single-plant and competitive-firm comparison into the dimensions of the whole industry.

Figure 10.6 reaffirms that the competitive industry in Chapter 9 initially produces the quantity q_c and sells it at a price of $1,000 each. Its profits are equal to the rectangle formed by the points *R, X, U, T*. The monopolist, on the other hand, produces the smaller q_m and charges a higher price, $1,100. The monopoly firm's profits are indicated by the larger profit rectangle shaded in the figure. Thus, *a monopoly receives larger profits than a comparable competitive industry by reducing the quantity supplied and pushing prices up.* The larger profits make Universal very happy and make consumers a little sadder and wiser. Consumers are now paying more and getting less.

Barriers to Entry

The higher profits Universal Electronics attained as a result of its monopoly position aren't the end of the story. The existence of economic profit tends to bring profit-hungry entrepreneurs swarming like locusts. In the competitive computer industry of Chapter 9, the lure of high profits brought about an enormous expansion of computer output and a steep decline in computer prices. In Figure 10.6 the long-run equilibrium of a competitive industry is indicated by point *V*. What can we expect to happen in the computer market now that Universal has a monopoly position and is enjoying huge profits?

Remember that Universal is now assumed to have an exclusive patent on microprocessor chips and can use this patent as an impassable barrier to entry. Consequently, would-be competitors can swarm around Universal's profits until their wings drop off; Universal isn't about to let them in on the spoils. By locking out potential competition, Universal can prevent the surge in computer output that pushed prices down the market demand curve.

FIGURE 10.6

Monopoly Profit: The Entire Company

Total profits of the monopolist (including all plants) are illustrated by the shaded rectangle. The monopolist's total output q_m is determined by the intersection of the (industry) MR and MC curves. The price of this output is determined by the market demand curve (point *A*).

In contrast, a competitive industry would produce q_c computers in the short run and sell them at a lower price (*X*) and profit per unit (*X − U*). Those profits would attract new entrants until long-run equilibrium (point *V*) was reached. (See Figure 9.9 for a summary of competitive market equilibrium.)

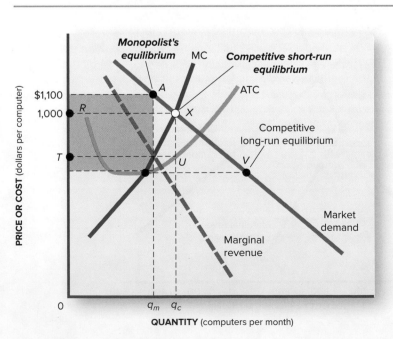

As long as Universal is able to keep out the competition, only the more affluent consumers will be able to use computers.

The same phenomenom explains why ticket prices for live concerts are so high. When Live Nation acquired Ticketmaster in 2009, it became a virtual monopolist for concert sites and ticket distribution. As In the News "Live Nation Acquires Ticketmaster" suggests, this music industry merger created a "sour note" for music fans. A monopoly has no incentive to move from point *A* in Figure 10.6, and there's no competitive pressure to force such a move. Universal may discover ways to reduce the costs of production and thus lower prices, but there's no *pressure* on it to do so, as there was in the competitive situation. Similarly, there's no *competitive pressure* on Live Nation to reduce concert prices.

IN THE NEWS

LIVE NATION ACQUIRES TICKETMASTER

The world's largest concert promoter, Live Nation, acquired the world's largest ticket distributor, Ticketmaster, creating a virtual monopoly on concert production and ticket sales. Bruce Springsteen warned back in 2009 that the merger of these two giants "would make the current ticket situation even worse for the fan than it is now" due to the increased monopoly power of the newly-created Live Nation Entertainment. A class action suit against the company charged it with "excessive and deceptive" fees, a suit the combined company settled in April 2016 by giving 50 million fans free or discounted tickets to select concerts. Fans continue to protest high prices, excessive fees, bloated parking fees, and outrageous prices for beer, hot dogs, and water. Nevertheless, Live Nation Entertainment sold 530 million tickets in 2015, generating over $7 billion in revenues.

Source: Media reports, 2009, 2016.

ANALYSIS: Control of concert sites and ticket distribution allows Live Nation Entertainment to charge monopoly prices for live concerts.

A COMPARATIVE PERSPECTIVE OF MARKET POWER

The different outcomes of the computer industry under competitive and monopoly conditions illustrate basic features of market structures. We may summarize the sequence of events that occurs in each type of market structure as follows:

COMPETITIVE INDUSTRY
- High prices and profits signal consumers' demand for more output.
- The high profits attract new suppliers.
- Production and supplies expand.
- Prices slide down the market demand curve.
- A new equilibrium is established wherein more of the desired product is produced, its price falls, average costs of production approach their minimum, and economic profits approach zero.
- Price equals marginal cost throughout the process.
- Throughout the process, there's great pressure to keep ahead of the profit squeeze by reducing costs or improving product quality.

MONOPOLY INDUSTRY
- High prices and profits signal consumers' demand for more output.
- Barriers to entry are erected to exclude potential competition.
- Production and supplies are constrained.
- Prices don't move down the market demand curve.
- No new equilibrium is established; average costs aren't necessarily at or near a minimum, and economic profits are at a maximum.
- Price exceeds marginal cost at all times.
- There's no squeeze on profits and thus no pressure to reduce costs or improve product quality.

In our discussion, we assumed that the competitive industry and the monopoly both started from the same position—an initial equilibrium in which the price of computers is $1,000. In reality, an industry may manifest concentrations of market power *before* such an equilibrium is established. That is, the sequence of events we've depicted may be altered (with step 3 occurring first, e.g.). Nevertheless, the basic distinctions between competitive and monopolistic behavior are evident.

Productivity Advances. To the extent that monopolies behave as we've discussed, they affect not just the price and output of a specific product but broader economic outcomes as well. Remember that competitive industries tend, in the long run, to produce at minimum average costs. Competitive industries also pursue cost reductions and product improvements relentlessly. These pressures tend to expand our production possibilities. No such forces are at work in the monopoly we've discussed here. Hence there's a basic tendency for monopolies to inhibit productivity advances and economic growth.

marginal cost pricing: The offer (supply) of goods at prices equal to their marginal cost.

The Mix of Output. Another important feature of competitive markets is their observed tendency toward **marginal cost pricing.** Marginal cost pricing is important to consumers because it permits rational choices among alternative goods and services. In particular, it informs consumers of the true opportunity costs of various goods, thereby allowing them to choose the mix of output that delivers the most utility with available resources. In our monopoly example, however, consumers end up getting fewer computers than they'd like, while the economy continues to produce other, less desired goods. Thus the mix of output shifted away from computers when Universal took over the industry.

The power to influence prices and product flows may have far-reaching consequences for our economic welfare. Changes in prices and product flows directly influence the level and composition of output, employment and resource allocation, the level and distribution of income, and, of course, the level and structure of prices. Hence firms that wield significant market power affect all dimensions of economic welfare.

Political Power. Market power isn't the only kind of power wielded in society, of course. Political power, for example, is a different kind of power and important in its own right. Indeed, the power to influence an election or to sway a Senate committee vote may ultimately be more important than the power to increase the price of laundry soap. Nevertheless, market power is a force that influences the way we live, the incomes we earn, and our relationships with other countries. Moreover, market power may be the basis for political power: the individual or firm with considerable market power is likely to have the necessary resources to influence an election or sway a vote on a congressional committee.

The Limits to Power

Even though market power enables a producer to manipulate market outcomes, there's a clear limit to the exercise of power. Even a monopolist can't get everything it wants. Universal, for example, would really like to sell q_m computers at a price of $1,500 each because that kind of price would bring it even greater profits. Yet, despite its monopoly position, Universal is constrained to sell that quantity of computers at the lower price of $1,100 each. Even monopolists have their little disappointments.

The ultimate limit to a monopolist's power is evident in Figure 10.6. Universal's attainment of a monopoly position allows it only one prerogative: the ability to alter the quantity of output *supplied* to the market. This is no small prerogative, but it's far from absolute power. Universal, and every other monopolist, must still contend with the market *demand* curve. Note again that the new equilibrium in Figure 10.6 occurs at a point on the *unchanged* market demand curve. In effect, *a monopolist has the opportunity to pick any point on the market demand curve and designate it as the new market equilibrium.* The point it selects will depend on its own perceptions of effort, profit, and risk (in this case point *A,* determined by the intersection of marginal revenue and marginal cost).

The ultimate constraint on the exercise of market power, then, resides in the market demand curve. How great a constraint the demand curve imposes depends largely on the **price elasticity of demand.** The greater the price elasticity of demand, the more a monopolist will be frustrated in attempts to establish both high prices and high volume. Consumers will simply reduce their purchases if price is increased. If, however, consumer demand is highly inelastic—if consumers need or want that product badly and few viable substitutes are available—the monopolist can reap tremendous profits from market power. That was clearly the case for the monopoly that produces a life-saving drug for AIDS patients (see In the News "Drugmaker Hikes Price of AIDS Drug 5,000 Percent!").

> **price elasticity of demand:** The percentage change in quantity demanded divided by the percentage change in price.

IN THE NEWS

DRUGMAKER HIKES PRICE OF AIDS DRUG 5,000 PERCENT!

Turing Pharmaceuticals hiked the price of Daraprim, a critical drug for preventing infections in people with the HIV virus, from $13.50 per capsule to $750. Turing, a pharmaceutical start-up, acquired the rights to Daraprim in August. In September, it announced a price hike of 5,000 percent. The company's CEO, Martin Shkreli, defended the price hike, saying "the companies before us were actually giving it away almost." "We need to turn profit on this drug," Shkreli told Bloomberg News. Because the cost of producing the drug is only $1 a capsule, Shkreli told his board of directors that the company could earn a cool billion dollars at the higher price.

Source: Media reports of September 2016.

ANALYSIS: If demand is inelastic, a monopolist can increase price without losing many sales.

Price Discrimination

Even in situations where the *market* demand is relatively elastic, a monopolist may be able to extract high prices. A monopolist has the power not only to raise the market price of a good (by reducing the quantity supplied) but also to charge various prices for the same good. Recall that the market demand curve reflects the combined willingness of many individuals to buy. Some of those individuals are willing to buy the good at prices higher than the market price, just as other individuals will buy only at lower prices. A monopolist may be able to increase total profits by selling each unit of the good separately, at a price each *individual* consumer is willing to pay. This practice is called **price discrimination.**

> **price discrimination:** The sale of an individual good at different prices to different consumers.

The airline industry has practiced price discrimination for many years. Basically, there are two distinct groups of travelers: business and nonbusiness travelers. Business executives must fly from one city to another on a certain day and at a particular time. They typically make flight arrangements on short notice and may have no other way to get to their destination. Nonbusiness travelers, such as people on vacation and students going home during semester break, usually have more flexible schedules. They may plan their trips weeks or months in advance and often have the option of traveling by car, bus, or train.

The different travel needs of business and vacation travelers are reflected in their respective demand curves. Business demand for air travel is less price-elastic than the demand of nonbusiness travelers. Few business executives would stop flying if airfares increased. Higher airfares would, however, discourage air travel by nonbusiness travelers.

What should airlines do in this case? Should they *raise* airfares to take advantage of the relative price inelasticity of business demand, or should they *lower* airfares to attract more nonbusiness travelers?

They should do both. In fact, they *have* done both. The airlines offer a full-fare ride, available at any time, and a discount-fare ride, available only by purchasing a ticket in advance and agreeing to some restrictions on time of departure. The advance purchase and other restrictions on discount fares effectively exclude most business travelers, who end up paying full fare. The higher full fare doesn't, however, discourage most nonbusiness travelers, who can fly at a discount. Consequently, the airlines are able to sell essentially identical units of the same good (an airplane ride) at substantially different prices to different customers. This price discrimination enables the airlines to capture the highest possible *average* price for the quantity supplied.

With *perfect* price discrimination, a monopolist would sell the product to each consumer on the demand curve at the maximum price that individual was willing to pay. If that happened, the monopolist would eliminate all **consumer surplus** and capture the extra revenue that a single price misses. Doctors, lawyers, and car dealers commonly practice this type of price discrimination.

consumer surplus: The difference between the maximum price a person is willing to pay and the price paid.

Entry Barriers

It's the lack of competitors that gives monopolists such pricing power. Accordingly, ***the preservation of monopoly power depends on keeping potential competitors out of the market.*** A monopolist doesn't want anyone else to produce an *identical* product or even a *close substitute.* To do that, a monopoly must erect and maintain barriers to market entry. Some of the entry barriers used to repel would-be competitors include:

Patents. This was the critical barrier in the mythical Universal Electronics case. A government-awarded patent gives a producer 20 years of exclusive rights to produce a particular product. Turing Pharmaceuticals used those patent rights to hike the price of Daraprim by 5,000 percent overnight (see In the News "Drugmaker Hikes Price of AIDS Drug 5,000 Percent!"): No one was producing a substitute drug. The Polaroid Corporation used its patents to keep Eastman Kodak and other potential rivals out of the market for instant development cameras. In 2007 Verizon and Sprint used broad patents to curb the growth of Vonage, the leading provider of Internet phone service.

Monopoly Franchises. The government also creates and maintains monopolies by giving a single firm the exclusive right to supply a particular good or service, even though other firms could produce it. Local cable TV stations and telephone companies are examples. Congress also bestows monopoly privileges to baseball teams and the U.S. Postal Service. Your campus bookstore may have exclusive rights to sell textbooks on campus.

Control of Key Inputs. A company may lock out competition by securing exclusive access to key inputs. Airlines need landing rights and terminal gates to compete. Oil and gas producers need pipelines to supply their products. Utility companies need transmission networks to supply consumers with electricity. Software vendors need to know the features of computer operating systems. If a single company controls these critical inputs, it can lock out potential competition. Intel was accused by the Federal Trade Commission (FTC) of trying to lock out competition by enticing computer makers with hefty discounts to use Intel chips exclusively in their computers. Microsoft was accused of using similar tactics to consolidate its monopoly position in operating systems (see the Economy Tomorrow section at the end of this chapter).

Lawsuits. In the event that competitors actually surmount other entry barriers, a monopoly may sue them out of existence. Typically, start-up firms are rich in ideas but cash poor. They need to get their products to the market quickly to generate some cash. A timely lawsuit alleging patent or copyright infringement can derail such a company by absorbing critical management, cash, and time. Long before the merits of the lawsuit are adjudicated, the company may be forced to withdraw from the market.

Acquisition. When all else fails, a monopolist may simply purchase a potential competitor. Live Nation's acquisition of Ticketmaster in 2009 (see In the News "Live Nation Acquires Ticketmaster") eliminated competition in the ticket distribution system. Mergers tend to raise consumer prices.

Economies of Scale. Last but far from least, a monopoly may persist because of economies of scale. If large firms have a substantial cost advantage over smaller firms, the smaller firms may not be able to compete. We look at this entry barrier again in a moment.

PROS AND CONS OF MARKET POWER

Despite the strong case against market power, it's conceivable that monopolies could also benefit society. One argument made for concentrations of market power is that monopolies have greater ability to pursue research and development. Another argument is that the lure of market power creates a tremendous incentive for invention and innovation. A third argument in defense of monopoly is that large companies can produce goods more efficiently than smaller firms. Finally, it's argued that even monopolies have to worry about *potential* competition and will behave accordingly.

Research and Development

In principle, monopolies are well positioned to undertake valuable research and development. First, such firms are sheltered from the constant pressure of competition. Second, they have the resources (monopoly profits) with which to carry out expensive R&D functions. The manager of a perfectly competitive firm, by contrast, has to worry about day-to-day production decisions and profit margins. As a result, she is unable to take the longer view necessary for significant research and development and couldn't afford to purchase such a view even if she could see it.

The basic problem with the R&D argument is that it says nothing about *incentives.* Although monopolists have a clear financial advantage in pursuing research and development activities, they have no clear incentive to do so. Research and development aren't necessarily required for profitable survival. In fact, research and development that make existing plants and equipment technologically obsolete run counter to a monopolist's vested interest and so may actually be suppressed (see In the News "Jury Awards $26 Million for Suppressed Technology"). In contrast, a perfectly competitive firm can't continue to make significant profits unless it stays ahead of the competition. This pressure constitutes a significant incentive to discover new products or new and cheaper ways of producing existing products.

IN THE NEWS

JURY AWARDS $26 MILLION FOR SUPPRESSED TECHNOLOGY

Two Bay Area entrepreneurs won a $25.7 million judgment in Oakland's U.S. District Court yesterday for the suppression of their energy-saving technology. In 1984, C. R. Stevens and William Alling sold to Universal Manufacturing Company a new technology that reduces the energy consumption of fluorescent lighting by 70 percent. But Universal never marketed the new technology, as it had promised. Stevens and Alling claimed that Universal suppressed their invention in order to protect its existing, less-efficient technology. The jury agreed and ordered Universal to pay $25.7 million in damages.

Source: News reports, January 10–15, 1990.

ANALYSIS: A monopoly has little incentive (no competitive pressure) to pursue R&D. In fact, R&D that threatens established products or processes may be suppressed.

Entrepreneurial Incentives

The second defense of market power uses a novel incentive argument. Every business is out to make a buck, and it's the quest for profits that keeps industries running. Thus, it's argued, even greater profit prizes will stimulate more entrepreneurial activity. Little Horatio Algers will work harder and longer if they can dream of one day possessing a whole monopoly.

The incentive argument for market power is enticing but not entirely convincing. After all, an innovator can make substantial profits in a competitive market before the competition catches up. Recall that the early birds did get the worm in the competitive computer industry (see Chapter 9), even though profit margins were later squeezed. It's not evident that the profit incentives available in a competitive industry are at all inadequate.

We must also recall the arguments about research and development efforts. A monopolist has little incentive to pursue R&D. Furthermore, entrepreneurs who might pursue product innovation or technological improvements may be dissuaded by their inability to penetrate a monopolized market. The barriers to entry that surround market power may not only keep out potential competitors but also lock out promising ideas.

Economies of Scale

A third defense of market power is the most plausible. A large firm, it's argued, can produce goods at a lower unit (average) cost than a small firm. If such *economies of scale* exist, we could attain greater efficiency (higher productivity) by permitting firms to grow to market-dominating size.

We sidestepped this argument in our story about the Universal Electronics monopoly. We explicitly assumed that Universal confronted the same production costs as the competitive industry. We simply converted each typical competitive firm into a separate plant owned and operated by Universal. Universal wasn't able to produce computers any more cheaply than its competitive counterpart, and we concerned ourselves only with the different production decisions made by competitive and monopolistic firms.

A monopoly *could,* however, attain greater cost savings. By centralizing various functions it might be able to eliminate some duplicative efforts. It might also shut down some plants and concentrate production in fewer facilities. If these kinds of efficiencies are attained, a monopoly would offer attractive resource savings.

There's no guarantee, however, of such economies of scale. As we observed in Chapter 7, increasing the size (scale) of a plant may actually *reduce* operating efficiency (see Figure 7.10). In evaluating the economies-of-scale argument for market power, then, we must recognize that *efficiency and size don't necessarily go hand in hand. Some firms and industries may be subject to economies of scale, but others won't.*

Even when economies of scale are present, there is no guarantee that consumers will benefit. The 2006 merger of Boeing and Lockheed cut the costs of rocket production by $100–150 million a year (see In the News "US FTC Enables Boeing–Lockheed 'Monopoly'"). But the Defense Department ended up paying higher prices. The Justice Department initially opposed the merger of the nation's only two satellite radio companies in 2007 for the same reason. Even though there were substantial short-run economies of scale in eliminating duplicate facilities, the Justice Department concluded that even a little competition (two firms) was better than none (a monopoly) in expanding consumer choice and keeping prices low (see In the News "A Sirius Mistake? FCC Approves XM–Sirius Merger"). Both the Justice Department and the Federal Communications Commission ultimately approved the XMSatellite–Sirius Radio merger, however, in return for their promise not to raise prices for at least three years.

natural monopoly: An industry in which one firm can achieve economies of scale over the entire range of market supply.

Natural Monopolies. Industries that exhibit economies of scale over the entire range of market output are called **natural monopolies.** In these cases, one single firm can produce the entire market supply more efficiently than any large number of (smaller) firms. As the size (scale) of the one firm increases, its minimum average costs continue to fall. These economies of scale give the one large producer a decided advantage over would-be rivals. Hence *economies of scale act as a "natural" barrier to entry.*

IN THE NEWS

US FTC ENABLES BOEING–LOCKHEED "MONOPOLY"

On 3 October 2006, the Federal Trade Commission (FTC) announced its tentative approval of merging Boeing and Lockheed Martin's space launch divisions to create the United Launch Alliance (ULA). . . . —this decision in essence creates a single-source supplier for putting US satellites on orbit.

In August 2006, Kenneth Krieg, head of acquisitions for the Pentagon, wrote to the FTC to support the proposed merger. He acknowledged that while it "will almost certainly have an adverse effect on competition, including higher prices over the long term, as well as a diminution in innovation and responsiveness," he still thought, "The national security advantages of ULA are paramount to the department's support of the transaction."

Apparently, the FTC took his recommendation to heart.

—**Victoria Samson for Center for Defense Information (CDI) November 30, 2006**

Source: Samson, Victoria, "US FTC Enables Boeing-Lockheed 'Monopoly,'" Center for Defense Information. ©2017 ETH Zurich.

ANALYSIS: Mergers eliminate duplicate facilities, thereby reducing total costs. But monopoly power permits the merged entity to retain the cost savings rather than pass them along to the consumer in the form of lower prices.

Local telephone and utility services are classic examples of natural monopoly. A single telephone or utility company can supply the market more efficiently than a large number of competing firms.

Although natural monopolies are economically desirable, they may be abused. We must ask whether and to what extent consumers are reaping some benefit from the efficiency a natural monopoly makes possible. Do consumers end up with lower prices, expanded output, and better service? Or does the monopoly keep most of the benefits for itself, in the form of higher prices and profits? Multiplex movie theaters, for example, achieve economies of scale by sharing operating and concession facilities among as many as 30 screens. But do moviegoers get lower prices for movies or popcorn? Not often. Because megamultiplex theaters tend to drive out competition, they don't have to reduce prices when costs drop.

IN THE NEWS

A SIRIUS MISTAKE? FCC APPROVES XM–SIRIUS MERGER

The Federal Communications Commission (FCC) has approved the merger of the nation's only two satellite radio companies, XM and Sirius. The merged company, called Sirius XM, will own the entire band of spectrum allocated to satellite radio. The companies said that combining their operations would cut costs by more than $150 million. In its 3-2 decision, the FCC commissioners acknowledged that the merged company would be a monopoly provider of satellite radio. But the majority argued that concessions made by the merged company—including a three-year price freeze and the guarantee of set-asides for minority and nonprofit channels—would generate consumer benefits that outweigh potential anticompetitive effects. And they noted that terrestrial radio would always be a competitor to satellite radio. The dissenting commissioners argued that programming choices would contract and subscription prices would increase after the three-year freeze ended.

Source: News reports, July 25–31, 2008.

ANALYSIS: Monopolies may enjoy economies of scale. In the long run, however, consumers may benefit more from competitive pressures to reduce costs, improve product quality, and lower prices.

Contestable Market

Governmental regulators aren't necessarily the only force keeping monopolists in line. Even though a firm may produce the entire supply of a particular product at present, it may face *potential* competition from other firms. Potential rivals may be sitting on the sidelines, watching how well the monopoly fares. If it does too well, these rivals may enter the industry, undermining the monopoly structure and profits. In such **contestable markets,** monopoly behavior may be restrained by potential competition.

contestable market: An imperfectly competitive industry subject to potential entry if prices or profits increase.

How "contestable" a market is depends not so much on its structure as on entry barriers. If entry barriers are insurmountable, would-be competitors are locked out of the market. But if entry barriers are modest, they'll be surmounted when the lure of monopoly profits is irresistible. When CNN's profits from cable news reached irresistible proportions, both domestic and foreign companies (e.g., CNBC, Fox News, Bloomberg News) decided to invade CNN's monopoly market. Since then, CNN hasn't been nearly as profitable.

Structure vs. Behavior. From the perspective of contestable markets, the whole case against monopoly is misconceived. Market *structure* per se isn't a problem; what counts is market *behavior.* If potential rivals force a monopolist to behave like a competitive firm, then monopoly imposes no cost on consumers or on society at large.

The experience with the Model T Ford illustrates the basic notion of contestable markets. At the time Henry Ford decided to increase the price of the Model T and paint them all black, the Ford Motor Company enjoyed a virtual monopoly on mass-produced cars. But potential rivals saw the profitability of offering additional colors and features such as a self-starter and left-hand drive. When rivals began producing cars in volume, Ford's market power was greatly reduced. In 1926 the Ford Motor Company tried to regain its dominant position by again supplying cars in colors other than black. By that time, however, consumers had more choices. Ford ceased production of the Model T in May 1927.

The experience with the Model T suggests that potential competition can force a monopoly to change its ways. Critics point out, however, that even contestable markets don't force a monopolist to act *exactly* like a competitive firm. There will always be a gap between competitive outcomes and those monopoly outcomes likely to entice new entry. That gap can cost consumers a lot. The absence of *existing* rivals is also likely to inhibit product and productivity improvements. From 1913 to 1926, all Model Ts were black, and consumers had few alternatives. Ford changed its behavior only after *potential* competition became *actual* competition. Even after 1927, when the Ford Motor Company could no longer act like a monopolist, it still didn't price its cars at marginal cost.

THE ECONOMY TOMORROW

MICROSOFT AND GOOGLE: BULLIES OR GENIUSES?

Ford Motor Company's experience is a useful reminder that monopolies rarely last forever. Potential competitors will always look for ways to enter a profitable market. Eventually they'll surmount entry barriers or develop substitute goods that supplant a monopolist's products.

Consumer advocates assert that we shouldn't have to wait for the invisible hand to dismantle a monopoly. They say the government should intervene to dismantle a monopoly or at least force it to change its behavior. Then consumers would get lower prices and better products a whole lot sooner.

Microsoft's dominant position in the computer industry highlights this issue. Microsoft produces the operating system (Windows) that powers 9 out of 10 personal computers. It also produces a huge share of applications software, including Internet browsers. Critics fear that this kind of monopoly power is a threat to consumers. They say Microsoft charges too much for its systems software, suppresses substitute technologies, and pushes potential competitors around. In short, Microsoft is a bully. In April 2000 a federal court accepted this argument (see In the News "Microsoft Guilty of Monopoly Abuse").

IN THE NEWS

MICROSOFT GUILTY OF MONOPOLY ABUSE

A federal judge ruled Monday that Microsoft has unfairly used its dominant position in computer operating systems to thwart competition in applications software. At the center of the case was Microsoft's practice of bundling its web browser, Internet Explorer, with its Windows operating system. Competitors charged that this practice made it difficult, if not impossible for them to sell competing web browsers (like Netscape's Navigator). They also complained that Microsoft designed its Windows operating system to render competing web browsers slow and inefficient.

Microsoft CEO Bill Gates argued that Internet Explorer and Windows were intrinsically related and should be viewed as a single product. But Microsoft sold Internet Explorer as a stand-alone product for MAC OS. Critics also charged that Microsoft forced computer manufacturers to install only Windows on new equipment, shutting the door on competing software.

U.S. District judge Thomas Penfield ruled in favor of the government, declaring that Microsoft violated the Sherman Antitrust Act by "unlawfully tying its Web browser" to its windows operating system. By "placing an oppressive thumb on the scale of competitive forces," Microsoft was guilty of abusing its dominant position in the marketplace to bully competitors, stifle competition and harm consumers.

Source: Media reports, April 4-6, 2000.

ANALYSIS: A federal court concluded that Microsoft followed the textbook script of monopoly: erecting entry barriers, suppressing innovation, and charging high prices.

To weaken Microsoft's grip on the computer market, courts in both the United States and Europe forced changes in both Microsoft's behavior and structure.

The AT&T Case. The federal government's authority to mend Microsoft's ways originates in the Sherman, the Clayton, and the Federal Trade Commission Acts. As noted in Table 10.1, these acts give the government broad **antitrust** authority to break up monopolies or compel them to change their behavior. The government used this authority in 1984 to dismantle American Telephone and Telegraph's (AT&T's) phone monopoly. AT&T then supplied 96 percent of all long-distance service and more than 80 percent of local telephone service. AT&T kept long-distance charges high and compelled consumers to purchase hardware from its own subsidiary (Western Electric). Potential competitors claimed they could supply better and cheaper services if the government ended the AT&T monopoly. After four years of antitrust litigation, AT&T agreed to (1) separate its long-distance and local services and (2) turn over the local transmission networks to new "Baby Bell" companies. Since then there has been a competitive revolution in telephone hardware, services, and pricing.

The Microsoft Case. The U.S. Department of Justice filed a similar antitrust action against Microsoft. The first accusation leveled against Microsoft was that it thwarted competitors in operating systems by erecting entry barriers such as exclusive purchase agreements with computer manufacturers. These agreements either forbade manufacturers from installing a rival operating system or made it prohibitively expensive. The second accusation against Microsoft was that it used its monopoly position in *operating* systems to gain an unfair advantage in the *applications* market. It did this by not disclosing operating features that make applications run more efficiently or by bundling software, thereby forcing consumers to accept Microsoft applications along with the operating system. When the latter occurs, consumers have little incentive to buy a

antitrust: Government intervention to alter market structure or prevent abuse of market power.

Continued

- **The Sherman Act (1890).** The Sherman Act prohibits "conspiracies in restraint of trade," including mergers, contracts, or acquisitions that threaten to monopolize an industry. Firms that violate the Sherman Act are subject to fines of up to $1 million, and their executives may be subject to imprisonment. In addition, consumers who are damaged—for example, via high prices—by a "conspiracy in restraint of trade" may recover treble damages. With this act as its principal "trustbusting" weapon, the U.S. Department of Justice has blocked attempted mergers and acquisitions, forced changes in price or output behavior, required large companies to sell some of their assets, and even sent corporate executives to jail for "conspiracies in restraint of trade."
- **The Clayton Act (1914).** The Clayton Act of 1914 was passed to outlaw specific antitrust behavior not covered by the Sherman Act. The principal aim of the act was to prevent the development of monopolies. To this end, the Clayton Act prohibited price discrimination, exclusive dealing agreements, certain types of mergers, and interlocking boards of directors among competing firms.
- **The Federal Trade Commission Act (1914).** The increased antitrust responsibilities of the federal government created the need for an agency that could study industry structures and behavior so as to identify anticompetitive practices. The Federal Trade Commission was created for this purpose in 1914.

Although the Sherman, Clayton, and FTC acts create a legal basis for government antitrust activity, they leave some basic implementation issues unanswered. What, for example, constitutes a "monopoly" in the real world? Must a company produce 100 percent of a particular good to be a threat to consumer welfare? How about 99 percent? Or even 75 percent?

And what specific monopolistic practices should be prohibited? Should we be looking for specific evidence of price gouging? Or should we focus on barriers to entry and unfair market practices?

These kinds of questions determine how and when antitrust laws will be enforced. The first question relates to the *structure* of markets, and the rest to their *behavior*.

TABLE 10.1

Antitrust Laws

The legal foundations for antitrust intervention are contained in three landmark antitrust laws.

competing product. Microsoft also prohibited computer manufacturers from displaying rival product icons on the Windows desktop. Finally, Microsoft was accused of thwarting competition by simply buying out promising rivals.

Microsoft's Defense. Bill Gates, Microsoft's chairman, scoffed at the government's charges. He contends that Microsoft dominates the computer industry only because it continues to produce the best products at attractive prices. Microsoft doesn't need to lock out potential competitors, he argues, because it can and does beat the competition with superior products. Furthermore, Gates argues, the software industry is a highly *contestable* market even if not a perfectly competitive one. So Microsoft has to behave like a competitive firm even though it supplies most of the industry's output. In short, Microsoft is a genius, not a bully. Therefore, the government should leave Microsoft alone and let the market decide who best serves consumers.

The Verdict. After nine *years* of litigation, a federal court determined that Microsoft was more of a bully than a genius. The court concluded that Microsoft not only held a monopoly position in operating systems but had abused that position in a variety of anticompetitive ways. As a result, consumers were harmed. *The real economic issue, the court asserted, was not whether Microsoft was improving its products (it was) or reducing prices (it was) but instead how much faster products would have improved and prices fallen in a more competitive market.* By limiting consumer choices and stifling competition, Microsoft had denied consumers better and cheaper information technology.

The Remedy. The trial judge suggested that Microsoft might have to be broken into two companies—an operating software company and an applications software company—to ensure enough competition. Such a *structural* remedy would have resembled the court-ordered breakup of AT&T. In November 2001, however, the U.S. Department of Justice decided to seek *behavioral* remedies only. With Windows XP about to be launched, the

Justice Department required Microsoft only to lower entry barriers for competing software applications (e.g., disclose middleware specifications, refrain from exclusive contracts, open desktops to competition). Although Microsoft reluctantly agreed to change its conduct in many ways, rivals complained that they still didn't have a fair chance of competing against the Microsoft monopoly. European regulators agreed, imposing still greater restrictions on Microsoft's business practices—particularly its continued bundling of Media Player in its operating system and confidential source code. Critics contend, however, that market *structure* is still the critical factor in determining market outcomes for the economy tomorrow.

Google a Bully? The same kind of anticompetitive concerns have been raised about Google. Google dominates the Internet search market, accounting for 87 percent of all online searches (Yahoo! has about 5 percent and Bing about 7 percent of the market). Companies pay big bucks to occupy top positions on Google search pages and to place ads in prominent locations. More than 90 percent of Google's immense profits come from paid advertising.

The core complaint against Google is that it uses its dominant search-engine position to suppress competition. Critics (including, ironically, Microsoft) say Google unfairly steers users to the company's own growing network of services (e.g., maps, travel) at the expense of rival producers. They say this harms consumers by restricting the ability of other companies to put better or cheaper products and services in front of Internet users. They contend Google reinforces its monopoly power with entry barriers such as unique key search words, long-term exclusive advertising contracts, suppression of search results for rival firms, and outright acquisitions of potential competitors. Rivals say Google is a bully. Google contends it is a genius that welcomes online competition. After a 7-year investigation (see In the News "EU Charges Google with Search Bias"), European trustbusters concluded in June 2017 that Google "denied European consumers a genuine choice of services and the full benefits of innovation." The EU imposed a record $2.7 billion fine on the company for its bullying tactics.

IN THE NEWS

EU CHARGES GOOGLE WITH SEARCH BIAS

After a five-year investigation, the European Commission has formally charged Google with "search bias." In its formal Statement of Objection, the European Union's trustbusters accuse Google of using its dominant position in Internet search to steer consumers to its own services. Google handles 90 percent of Web search in Europe. The Commission say Google "stifles competition and harms consumers" by prominently displaying ads for its own map, travel, and product services over those of rivals.

Source: Media reports, April 2015.

ANALYSIS: Does Google strengthen its dominant position in search with unfair entry barriers? Rivals say it does. Google responds that it is just a better competitor.

SUMMARY

- Market power is the ability to influence the market price of goods and services. The extreme case of market power is monopoly, a situation in which only one firm produces the entire supply of a particular product.   **LO10-1**

- The distinguishing feature of any firm with market power is the fact that the demand curve it faces is downward-sloping. In the case of monopoly, the demand curve facing the firm and the market demand curve are identical.   **LO10-1**

- The downward-sloping demand curve facing a monopolist creates a divergence between marginal revenue and price. To sell larger quantities of output, the monopolist must lower product prices. A firm without market power has no such problem.   **LO10-1**

- Like other producers, a monopolist will produce at the rate of output at which marginal revenue equals marginal cost. Because marginal revenue is always less than price in monopoly, the monopolist will produce less output than a competitive industry confronting the same market demand and costs. That reduced rate of output will be sold at higher prices in accordance with the (downward-sloping) market demand curve. **LO10-2**
- A monopoly will attain a higher level of profit than a competitive industry because of its ability to equate industry (that is, its own) marginal revenues and costs. By contrast, a competitive industry ends up equating marginal costs and price because its individual firms have no control over market supply. **LO10-2**
- Because the higher profits attained by a monopoly will attract envious entrepreneurs, barriers to entry are needed to prohibit other firms from expanding market supplies. Patents are one such barrier to entry. **LO10-2**
- The defense of market power rests on (1) the alleged ability of large firms to pursue long-term research and development, (2) the incentives implicit in the chance to attain market power, (3) the efficiency that larger firms may attain, and (4) the contestability of even monopolized markets. The first two arguments are weakened by the fact that competitive firms are under much greater pressure to innovate and can stay ahead of the profit game only if they do so. The contestability defense at best concedes some amount of monopoly exploitation. **LO10-3**
- A natural monopoly exists when one firm can produce the output of the entire industry more efficiently than can a number of small firms. This advantage is attained from economies of scale. Large firms aren't necessarily more efficient, however, because either constant returns to scale or diseconomies of scale may prevail. **LO10-3**
- Antitrust laws restrain the acquisition and abuse of monopoly power. Where barriers to entry aren't insurmountable, market forces may ultimately overcome a monopoly. **LO10-3**

Key Terms

market power	economies of scale	price discrimination
monopoly	production decision	consumer surplus
profit maximization rule	average total cost (ATC)	natural monopoly
marginal revenue (MR)	marginal cost pricing	contestable market
barriers to entry	price elasticity of demand	antitrust

Questions for Discussion

1. The objective in the game of Monopoly is to get all the property and then raise the rents. Can this power be explained with market supply and demand curves? **LO10-1**
2. According to the Federal Trade Commission (In the News "US FTC Enables Boeing–Lockheed 'Monopoly'"), how often do monopolies lead to higher prices? Why, then, did the rocket merger get approved? **LO10-1**
3. Why don't monopolists try to establish "the highest price possible," as many people allege? What would happen to sales? To profits? **LO10-1**
4. How does individualized price discrimination by car dealers affect their total revenue and profits? **LO10-1**
5. What would have happened to iPad prices and features if Apple had not faced competition from iPad clones (Chapter 23)? **LO10-2**
6. What entry barriers helped protect the following? **LO10-2**
   (a) The Russian sable monopoly (World View "Russia's Sable Monopoly Persists").
   (b) The Live Nation monopoly (In the News "Live Nation Acquires Ticketmaster").
   (c) Turing Pharmaceutical (In the News "Drugmaker Hikes Price of AIDS Drug 5,000 Percent!").
   (d) The rocket monopoly (In the News "US FTC Enables Boeing–Lockheed 'Monopoly'").
   (e) Google's search dominance (In The News "EU Charges Google with Search Bias").
7. What similarities exist between the AT&T, Microsoft, and Google antitrust cases? **LO10-3**
8. How might consumers have benefited from the merger of XM and Sirius (In the News "A Sirius Mistake? FCC Approves XM–Sirius Merger")? How might they have lost? **LO10-3**
9. How might Google's search-engine dominance harm consumers? Help them? **LO10-3**
10. Is the demand for a life-saving drug like Daraprim (In the News "Drugmaker Hikes Price of AIDS Drug 5,000 Percent!") likely to be elastic or inelastic? How does that affect the pricing decision of a monopolist? **LO10-1**

PROBLEMS FOR CHAPTER 10

LO10-1 1. Use Figure 10.3 to answer the following questions:
  (*a*) What is the highest price the monopolist could charge and still sell fish?
  (*b*) What is total revenue at that highest price?
  (*c*) What rate of output maximizes total revenue (partial unit okay)?
  (*d*) What rate of output maximizes total profit (use higher rate)?
  (*e*) What is MR at that rate of output?
  (*f*) What is the price at the profit-maximizing rate of output?

LO10-1 2. (*a*) Complete the following table:

Price	$24	$21	$18	$15	$12	$9	$6	$3
Quantity demanded	1	2	3	4	5	6	7	8
Marginal revenue	___	___	___	___	___	___	___	___

  (*b*) At what rate of output does marginal revenue turn negative?
  (*c*) If marginal cost is constant at $12, what is the profit-maximizing rate of output?
  (*d*) What price should this monopolist charge for that rate of output?

LO10-1 3. Given the following information about demand for a local utility service, graph the demand and marginal revenue curves.

Price	$ 6	5	4	3	2
Quantity demanded	20	50	90	150	210

LO10-3 Identify the barrier to entry that best matches the following news stories about monopolies:
  (*a*) In the News "US FTC Enables Boeing–Lockheed 'Monopoly.'"
  (*b*) In the News "Drugmaker Hikes Price of AIDS Drug 5,000 Percent!"
  (*c*) World View "Russia's Sable Monopoly Persists."

LO10-1 4. The following table indicates the prices various buyers are willing to pay for a MINI Cooper car:

Buyer	Maximum Price	Buyer	Maximum Price
Buyer A	$50,000	Buyer D	$20,000
Buyer B	40,000	Buyer E	10,000
Buyer C	30,000	Buyer F	0

The cost of producing the cars includes $40,000 of fixed costs and a constant marginal cost of $10,000.
  (*a*) Graph below the demand, marginal revenue, and marginal cost curves.
  (*b*) What is the profit-maximizing rate of output and price for a monopolist?
  (*c*) How much profit does the monopolist make?
  (*d*) If the monopolist can price discriminate, how many cars will he sell?
  (*e*) How much profit will he make?

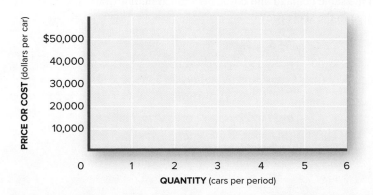

LO10-2 5. If the on-campus demand for soda is as follows:

Price (per can)	$2.00	1.75	1.50	1.25	1.00	0.75	0.50	0.25
Quantity demanded (per day)	100	90	80	70	60	50	40	30

and the marginal cost of supplying a soda is 50 cents, what price will students end up paying in
(a) A perfectly competitive market?
(b) A monopolized market?

LO10-3 6. According to the In the News "US FTC Enables Boeing–Lockheed 'Monopoly,'"
(a) What was the annual cost saving for the rocket monopoly (in $ millions)?
(b) How much of this saving did the FTC expect to be reflected in reduced rocket prices?
(c) According to economic theory, which is likely to be higher, A: the merged monopoly price; or B: the two-firm competitive price?

LO10-2 7. What was the profit per unit for the drug Daraprim (In the News "Drugmaker Hikes Price of AIDS Drug 5,000 Percent!"):
(a) Before Turing increased the price?
(b) After Turing increased the price?
(c) What barrier to entry exists in this market?

LO10-2 8. The following table summarizes the weekly sales and cost situation confronting a monopolist:

Price	Quantity Demanded	Total Revenue	Marginal Revenue	Total Cost	Marginal Cost	Average Total Cost
$22	0	_____		$ 4		_____
20	1	_____	_____	8	_____	_____
18	2	_____	_____	13	_____	_____
16	3	_____	_____	19	_____	_____
14	4	_____	_____	27	_____	_____
12	5	_____	_____	37	_____	_____
10	6	_____	_____	51	_____	_____
8	7	_____	_____	69	_____	_____

(a) Complete the table.
(b) Graph the demand, MR, and MC curves on the following graph.
(c) At what rate of output are profits maximized?
(d) What are the values of MR and MC at the profit-maximizing rate of output?
(e) What price will the firm charge?
(f) What are total profits at that output rate?
(g) If a competitive industry confronted the same demand and costs, how much output would it produce and what price would it charge in the short run?

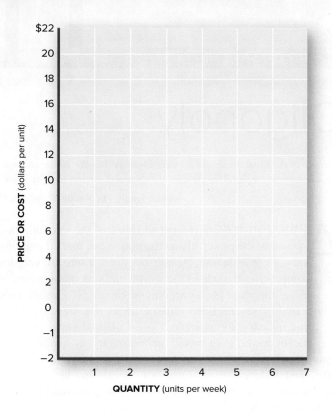

LO10-3 9. The Economy Tomorrow: Identify the market and the barrier to entry that best matches the case studies presented in The Economy Tomorrow.

    (*a*) Microsoft.

    (*b*) AT&T.

    (*c*) Google.

©McGraw-Hill Education/Andrew Resek, photographer

CHAPTER 11

Oligopoly

People of the same trade seldom meet together, but the conversation ends in a conspiracy against the public, or in some diversion to raise prices.

—**Adam Smith,** *The Wealth of Nations,* **1776**

Although it's convenient to think of the economy as composed of the powerful and the powerless, market realities don't always provide such clear distinctions. There are very few perfectly competitive markets in the world, and few monopolies. Market power is an important phenomenon nonetheless; it's just that it's typically shared by several firms rather than monopolized by one. In the soft drink industry, for example, Coca-Cola and Pepsi share tremendous market power, even though neither company qualifies as a pure monopoly. The same kind of power is shared by Kellogg, General Mills, and Ralcorp in the breakfast cereals market, and by Sony, Nintendo, and Microsoft in the video game console market. Apple Computer Inc., too, now shares power in the tablet computer market with Samsung, Lenovo, Huawei, Sony, LG, Microsoft, and other firms.

These market structures fall between the extremes of perfect competition and pure monopoly; they represent *imperfect competition.* They contain some elements of competitive rivalry but also exhibit traces of monopoly. In many cases, imperfect competitors behave much like a monopoly: restricting output, charging higher prices, and reaping greater profits than firms in a competitive market. But behavior in imperfectly competitive markets is more complicated than in a monopoly because it involves a number of decision makers (firms) rather than only one.

This chapter focuses on one form of imperfect competition: *oligopoly.* We examine the nature of decision making in this market structure and the likely impacts on prices, production, and profits. What we want to know is

- **What determines how much market power a firm has?**
- **How do firms in an oligopoly set prices and output?**
- **What problems does an oligopoly have in maintaining price and profit?**

LEARNING OBJECTIVES

After reading this chapter, you should know

LO11-1 The unique characteristics of oligopoly.

LO11-2 How oligopolies maximize profits.

LO11-3 How interdependence affects oligopolists' pricing decisions.

MARKET STRUCTURE

As we saw in Chapter 10, Microsoft is the dominant supplier of computer operating systems and Google dominates the search-engine market. As near monopolies, those companies have tremendous market power. The corner grocery store, on the other hand, must compete with other stores and has less control over prices. But even the corner grocery isn't completely powerless. If it's the only grocery within walking distance or the only one open on Sunday, it too exerts *some* influence on prices and product flows. The amount of power it possesses depends on the availability of *substitute goods*—that is, the proximity and convenience of alternative retail outlets.

Degrees of Power

Between the extremes of monopoly and perfect competition are many gradations of market power. To sort them out, we classify firms into five specific **market structures,** based on the number and relative size of firms in an industry.

> **market structure:** The number and relative size of firms in an industry.

Table 11.1 summarizes the characteristics of the five major market structures. At one extreme is the structure of *perfect competition,* the subject of Chapters 8 and 9. At the other extreme of the power spectrum is perfect *monopoly.* A perfect monopoly exists when only one firm is the exclusive supplier of a particular product. Our illustration of Universal Electronics (the imaginary computer monopolist in Chapter 10) exemplifies such a firm.

Between the two extremes of perfect competition and perfect monopoly lies most of the real world, which we call *imperfectly competitive.* **In imperfect competition, individual firms have some power in a particular product market.** *Oligopoly* refers to one of these imperfectly competitive market structures. **Oligopoly** is a situation in which only a *few* firms have a great deal of power in a product market. An oligopoly may exist because only a few firms produce a particular product or because a few firms account for most, although not all, of a product's output.

> **oligopoly:** A market in which a few firms produce all or most of the market supply of a particular good or service.

Determinants of Market Power

The number of firms in an industry is a key characteristic of market structure. The amount of market power the firms possess, however, depends on several factors. *The determinants of market power include*

- *Number of producers.*
- *Size of each firm.*
- *Barriers to entry.*
- *Availability of substitute goods.*

Characteristic	Market Structure				
	Perfect Competition	Monopolistic Competition	Oligopoly	Duopoly	Monopoly
Number of firms	Very large number	Many	Few	Two	One
Barriers to entry	None	Low	High	High	High
Market power (control over price)	None	Some	Substantial	Substantial	Substantial
Type of product	Standardized	Differentiated	Standardized or differentiated	Standardized or differentiated	Unique

TABLE 11.1

Characteristics of Market Structures

Market structure varies, depending on the number of producers, their size, barriers to entry, and the availability of substitute goods. An oligopoly is an imperfectly competitive structure in which a few firms dominate the market.

When only one or a few producers or suppliers exist, market power is automatically conferred. In addition to the number of producers, however, the size of each firm is also important. More than 600 firms supply long-distance telephone service in the United States. But just four of those firms (AT&T, Verizon, T-Mobile, and Sprint) account for 98 percent of all calls. Hence it wouldn't make sense to categorize that industry on the basis of only the number of firms; relative size is also important. The same thing is true in the beer industry. There are more than 7,000 breweries in the United States, but only four produce 80 percent of industry output (see Table 8.2).

A third and critical determinant of market power is the extent of barriers to entry. A highly successful monopoly or oligopoly arouses the envy of other profit maximizers. If it's a **contestable market,** potential rivals will seek to enter the market and share in the spoils. Should they succeed, the power of the former monopolist or oligopolists would be reduced. Accordingly, ease of entry into an industry limits the ability of a powerful firm to dictate prices and product flows. In Chapter 10 we saw how monopolies erect barriers to entry (e.g., patents) to maintain their power.

A fourth determinant of market power is the availability of substitute goods. If a monopolist or other power baron sets the price of a product too high, consumers may decide to switch to close substitutes. Thus, the price of Coors is kept in check by the price of Coke, and the price of sirloin steak is restrained by the price of chicken and pork. By the same token, a lack of available substitute products keeps the prices of insulin and AZT high.

contestable market: An imperfectly competitive industry subject to potential entry if prices or profits increase.

Measuring Market Power

Although there are many determinants of market power, most observers use just one yardstick to measure the extent of power in an industry.

Concentration Ratio. The standard measure of market power is the **concentration ratio.** This ratio tells the share of output (or combined market share) accounted for by the largest firms in an industry. Using this ratio one can readily distinguish between an industry composed of hundreds of small, relatively powerless firms and another industry also composed of hundreds of firms but dominated by a few that are large and powerful. Thus *the concentration ratio is a measure of market power that relates the size of firms to the size of the product market.*

Table 11.2 gives the concentration ratios for selected products in the United States. The standard measure used here depicts the proportion of domestic production accounted for by the largest firms, usually the four largest. As a rule of thumb, *an industry with a concentration ratio above 60 percent is considered an oligopoly.* As is apparent from the table, the supply sides of these product markets easily qualify as *oligopolies* because most of these industries' output is produced by just three or four firms. Indeed, in some markets, one single firm is so large that an outright monopoly is nearly attained. For example, 70 percent of all canned soup is produced by Campbell. Gerber produces 80 percent of all prepared baby food. And Google accounts for 87 percent of all web searches. All firms that have a market share of at least 40 percent are denoted by **boldface** type in Table 11.2.

concentration ratio: The proportion of total industry output produced by the largest firms (usually the four largest).

Firm Size. We noted before that market power isn't necessarily associated with firm size—in other words, a small firm could possess a lot of power in a relatively small market. Table 11.2, however, should be convincing testimony that we're not talking about small product markets here. Every one of the products listed enjoys a broad-based market. Even the chewing gum market (94 percent concentration ratio) rings up annual sales of $4 billion. The three oligopolists that produce video game consoles (Sony, Microsoft, Nintendo,) have 100 percent of a $25 billion market. Accordingly, for most of the firms listed in the table, market power and firm size go hand in hand. Indeed, the largest firms enjoy sales volumes that exceed the entire output of most of the *countries* in the world (see World View "Putting

Product	Largest Firms	Concentration Ratio (%)
Video game consoles	**Sony,** Microsoft, Nintendo	100%
Instant breakfast	**Carnation,** Pillsbury, Dean Foods	100
Laser eye surgery	**VISX,** Summit Technology	100
Tennis balls	**Gen Corp (Penn),** PepsiCo **(Wilson),** Dunlop, Spalding	100
Credit cards	**Visa, MasterCard, American Express,** Discover	99
Disposable diapers	**Procter & Gamble,** Kimberly-Clark, Curity, Romar Tissue Mills	99
Wireless phone service	AT&T, Verizon, T-Mobile, Sprint	98
Razor blades	**Gillette,** Warner-Lambert (Schick; Wilkinson), Bic, American Safety Razor	98
Sports drinks	**PepsiCo** (Gatorade), Coca-Cola (PowerAde), Monarch (All Sport)	98
Internet search engines	**Google,** Bing, Yahoo	98
Scientific calculators	**Texas Instruments,** Casio, Hewlett-Packard	97
Electric razors	**Norelco,** Remington, Warner-Lambert, Sunbeam	96
Sanitary napkins	**Johnson & Johnson,** Kimberly-Clark, Procter & Gamble	96
Cigarettes	**Altria,** Reynolds American, Imperial, Liggett	96
Baby food	**Gerber Products,** Beech-Nut, DelMonte	95
Batteries	**Duracell,** Eveready, Ray-O-Vac, Kodak	94
Web search ads	**Google,** Yahoo, Microsoft, AOL	94
Chewing gum	**Wm. Wrigley,** Mondelez, Hershey	94
Soft drinks	**Coca-Cola, PepsiCo,** Dr. Pepper Snapple, Cott (RC Cola)	94
Breakfast cereals	Kelloggs, General Mills, Ralcorp, PepsiCo (Quaker Oats)	92
Computer printers	**Hewlett-Packard,** Epson, Canon, Lexmark	91
Toothpaste	Colgate-Palmolive, Procter & Gamble, Church & Dwight, Beecham	91
Internet browsers	**Google,** Microsoft, Mozilla, Apple	90
Detergents	**Procter & Gamble,** Lever Bros., Dial, Colgate-Palmolive	90
Art auctions	**Sotheby's, Christie's**	90
Greeting cards	**Hallmark,** American Greetings, Gibson	88
Canned soup	**Campbell,** Progresso	85
Beer	**Anheuser-Busch,** MillerCoors, Constellation, Heineken	80

Sources: Data from Federal Trade Commission, *The Wall Street Journal, Advertising Age, Financial World, Standard & Poor's, Fortune,* and industry sources.

Note: Individual corporations with a market share of at least 40 percent are designated in **boldface.** Market shares based on selected years, 2014–2017.

TABLE 11.2

Power in U.S. Product Markets

The domestic production of many familiar products is concentrated among a few firms. These firms have substantial control over the quantity supplied to the market and thus over market price. The concentration ratio measures the share of total output produced by the largest producers in a given market.

Size in Global Perspective"). Walmart's annual revenues alone would make it the world's 23rd largest country!

Measurement Problems

A high concentration ratio or large firm size isn't the only way to achieve market power. The supply and price of a product can be altered by many firms acting in unison. Even 1,000 small producers can band together to change the quantity supplied to the market, thus exercising market power. Recall how our mythical Universal Electronics (Chapter 10) exercised market power by coordinating the production decisions of its many separate plants. Those plants could have attempted such coordination on their own even if they

WORLD VIEW

PUTTING SIZE IN GLOBAL PERSPECTIVE

The largest firms in the United States are also the dominant forces in global markets. They export products to foreign markets and produce goods abroad for sale there or to import back into the United States. In terms of size alone, these business giants rival most of the world's nations. Walmart's gross sales, for example, would make it the 23rd largest "country" in terms of national GDP.

American corporations aren't the only giants in the global markets. Volkswagen (Germany), Royal Dutch Shell (The Netherlands), and Toyota (Japan) are among the foreign giants that contest global markets.

Rank	Country or Corporation	Sales or GDP (in billions of dollars)	Rank	Country or Corporation	Sales or GDP (in billions of dollars)
1	United States	$18,036	20	Saudi Arabia	646
2	China	11,007	21	Argentina	583
3	Japan	4,383	22	Sweden	496
4	Germany	3,363	23	Walmart Stores	482
5	United Kingdom	2,858	24	Nigeria	481
6	France	2,418	25	Poland	477
7	India	2,095	26	Belgium	455
8	Italy	1,821	27	Iran	425
9	Brazil	1,774	28	Thailand	395
10	Canada	1,550	29	Norway	386
11	South Korea	1,378	30	Austria	377
12	Australia	1,339	40	Royal Dutch Shell	272
13	Russia	1,331	42	ExxonMobil	246
14	Spain	1,199	44	Volkswagon	237
15	Mexico	1,143	45	Toyota	237
16	Indonesia	862	46	Apple	234
17	The Netherlands	750	47	Finland	232
18	Turkey	718	48	Portugal	199
19	Switzerland	671			

Sources: World Bank Atlas Method, and *Fortune*'s annual ranking of the world's largest corporations, "Global 500." *Fortune* magazine, July 26, 2016.

ANALYSIS: Firm size is a determinant of market power. The size of the largest firms, as measured by total revenue, exceeds the value of total output in most of the world's 200-plus countries.

hadn't all been owned by the same corporation. Lawyers and doctors exercise this kind of power by maintaining uniform fee schedules for members of the American Bar Association (ABA) and the American Medical Association (AMA).[1] Similarly, dairy farmers act jointly through three large cooperatives (the American Milk Producers, Mid-America Dairies, and Dairymen, Inc.), which together control 50 percent of all milk production.

Finally, all the figures and corporations cited here refer to *national* markets. They don't convey the extent to which market power may be concentrated in a *local* market. In fact, many industries with low concentration ratios nationally are represented by just one or a few firms locally. Prime examples include milk, newspapers, and transportation (both public and private). For example, fewer than 60 cities in the United States have two or more independently owned daily newspapers, and nearly all those newspapers rely on only two news services (Associated Press and United Press International). Perhaps you've also noticed that most college campuses have only one bookstore. It may not be a *national* powerhouse, but it does have the power to influence what goods are available on campus and how much they cost.

[1]The courts have ruled that uniform fee schedules are illegal and that individual lawyers and doctors have the right to advertise their prices (fees). Nevertheless, a combination of inertia and self-interest has effectively maintained high fee schedules and inhibited advertising.

OLIGOPOLY BEHAVIOR

With so much market power concentrated in so few hands, it's unrealistic to expect market outcomes to resemble those of perfect competition. As we observed in Chapter 10, ***market structure affects market behavior and outcomes.*** In that chapter we focused on the contrast between monopoly and perfect competition. Now we focus on the behavior of a more common market structure: oligopoly.

To isolate the unique character of oligopoly, we'll return to the computer market. In Chapter 9 we observed that the computer market was highly competitive in its early stages, when entry barriers were low and hundreds of firms were producing similar products. In Chapter 10 we created an impassable barrier to entry (a patent on the electronic brain of the computer) that transformed the computer industry into a monopoly of Universal Electronics. Now we'll transform the industry again. This time we'll create an oligopoly by assuming that three separate firms (Universal, World, and International) all possess patent rights. The patent rights permit each firm to produce and sell all the computers it wants and to exclude all other would-be producers from the market. With these assumptions, we create three **oligopolists,** the firms that share an *oligopoly.* Our objective is to see how market outcomes would change in such a market structure.

oligopolist: One of the dominant firms in an oligopoly.

The Initial Equilibrium

As before, we'll assume that the initial conditions in the computer market are represented by a market price of $1,000 and market sales of 20,000 computers per month, as illustrated in Figure 11.1.

We'll also assume that the **market share** of each producer is accurately depicted in Table 11.3. Thus Universal Electronics is assumed to be producing 8,000 computers per month, or 40 percent of total market supply. World Computers has a market share of 32.5 percent, while International Semiconductor has only a 27.5 percent share. The assumed **concentration ratio** is therefore 100.

market share: The percentage of total market output produced by a single firm.

The Battle for Market Shares

The first thing to note about this computer oligopoly is that it's likely to exhibit great internal tension. Neither World Computers nor International Semiconductor is really happy playing second or third fiddle to Universal Electronics. Each company would like to be number one in this market. On the other hand, Universal would like a larger market share as well, particularly in view of the huge profits being made on computers. As we observed in Chapter 9, the initial equilibrium in the computer industry yielded an *average* profit of $300 per computer, and total *industry* profits of $6 million per month (20,000 × $300). Universal would love to acquire the market shares of its rivals, thereby grabbing all this industry profit for itself.

But how does an oligopolist acquire a larger market share? In a truly competitive market, a single producer could expand production at will, with no discernible impact on market

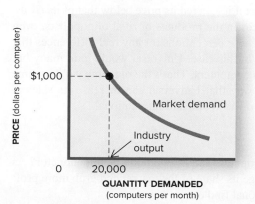

FIGURE 11.1

Initial Conditions in the Computer Market

As in Chapters 9 and 10, we assume that the initial equilibrium in the computer market occurs at a price of $1,000 and a quantity of 20,000 per month. How will an oligopoly alter these outcomes?

Producer	Output (Computers per Month)	Market Share (%)
Universal Electronics	8,000	40.0%
World Computers	6,500	32.5
International Semiconductor	5,500	27.5
Total industry output	20,000	100.0%

supply. That's not possible when there are only three firms in the market. *In an oligopoly, increased sales on the part of one firm will be noticed immediately by the other firms.*

How do we know that increased sales will be noticed so quickly? Because increased sales by one firm will have to take place either at the existing market price ($1,000) or at a lower price. Either of these two events will ring an alarm at the corporate headquarters of the other two firms.

Increased Sales at the Prevailing Market Price. Consider first the possibility of Universal Electronics increasing its sales at the going price of $1,000 per computer. We know from the demand curve in Figure 11.1 that consumers are willing to buy *only* 20,000 microcomputers per month at that price. Hence any increase in computer sales by Universal must be immediately reflected in *lower* sales by World or International. That is, *increases in the market share of one oligopolist necessarily reduce the shares of the remaining oligopolists.* If Universal were to increase its sales from 8,000 to 9,000 computers per month, the combined monthly sales of World and International would have to fall from 12,000 to 11,000 (see Table 11.3). The *quantity demanded* at $1,000 remains 20,000 computers per month (see Figure 11.1). Thus any increased sales at that price by Universal must be offset by reduced sales by its rivals.

This interaction among the market shares of the three oligopolists ensures that Universal's sales success will be noticed. It won't be necessary for World Computers or International Semiconductor to engage in industrial espionage. These firms can quickly figure out what Universal is doing simply by looking at their own (declining) sales figures.

Increased Sales at Reduced Prices. Universal could pursue a different strategy. Specifically, Universal could attempt to increase its sales by lowering the price of its computers. Reduced prices would expand total market sales, possibly enabling Universal to increase its sales without directly reducing the sales of either World or International.

But this outcome is most unlikely. If Universal lowered its price from $1,000 to, say, $900, consumers would flock to Universal Computers, and the sales of World and International would plummet. After all, we've always assumed that consumers are rational enough to want to pay the lowest possible price for any particular good. It's unlikely that consumers would continue to pay $1,000 for a World or International machine when they could get basically the same computer from Universal for only $900. If there were no difference, either perceived or real, among the computers of the three firms, a *pure* oligopoly would exist. In that case, Universal would capture the *entire* market if it lowered its price below that of its rivals.

More often, consumers perceive differences in the products of rival oligopolists, even when the products are essentially identical. These perceptions (or any real differences that may exist) create a *differentiated* oligopoly. In this case, Universal would gain many but not all customers if it reduced the price of its computers. That's the outcome we'll assume here. In either case, there simply isn't any way that Universal can increase its sales at reduced prices without causing alarms to go off at World and International.

Retaliation

So what if the alarms do go off at World Computers and International Semiconductor? As long as Universal Electronics is able to enlarge its share of the market and grab more profits, why should it care if World and International find out?

Universal *does* have something to worry about. World and International may not be content to stand by and watch their market shares and profits diminish. On the contrary, World and International are likely to take some action of their own once they discover what's going on.

There are two things World and International can do once they decide to act. In the first case, where Universal is expanding its market share at prevailing prices ($1,000), World and International can retaliate by

- Stepping up their own marketing efforts.
- Cutting prices on their computers.

Advertising. To step up their marketing efforts, World and International might increase their advertising expenditures, repackage their computers, put more sales representatives on the street, or sponsor a college homecoming week. This is the kind of behavior RC Cola used to gain market share from Coke and Pepsi (see In the News "RC Targeting Young Soda Drinkers"). Such attempts at **product differentiation** are designed to make one firm's products appear different and superior to those produced by other firms. If successful, such marketing efforts will increase RC Cola sales and market share or at least stop its rivals from grabbing larger shares.

product differentiation:
Features that make one product appear different from competing products in the same market.

IN THE NEWS

RC TARGETING YOUNG SODA DRINKERS

Tired of playing fourth fiddle to soda giants Coke, Pepsi, and Dr. Pepper, RC Cola is stepping up its advertising efforts. RC is spending $15 million to reshape the company's image as the hip alternative to "corporate colas," its characterization of Coke and Pepsi. Along with the ad blitz, RC is introducing new products, including Nehi and RC Draft, sodas designed for youthful tastes.

Some analysts are skeptical about RC's chances of success.

"Anybody in the soft drink business trying to compete with Pepsi and Coke has an uphill battle—they have huge amounts of marketing muscle, financial resources, experience and bottling agreements," said John Sicher, co-editor of *Beverage Digest,* an industry publication. "But RC's new tactics are smart. They are tossing out a bunch of beverages targeted toward younger drinkers. Against Coke and Pepsi, guerrilla warfare is the only thing that might work."

The U.S. Soda Market
Market share of soft drink makers, 2015.

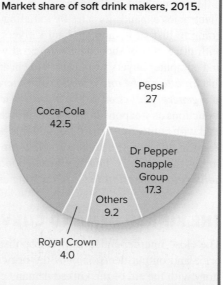

Coca-Cola 42.5
Pepsi 27
Dr Pepper Snapple Group 17.3
Others 9.2
Royal Crown 4.0

—Anthony Faiola

Source: Faiola, Anthony, "Pop Culture: RC Goes for the Youth Market," *The Washington Post*, September 14, 1995, p. D10. Copyright ©1995.

ANALYSIS: Because price competition is typically self-defeating in an oligopoly, rival firms in an oligopoly rely on advertising and product differentiation (nonprice competition) to gain market share. RC nearly doubled its market share after it launched its new marketing.

Price Cuts. An even quicker way to stop Universal from enlarging its market share is for World and International to lower the price of *their* computers. Such price reductions will destroy Universal's hopes of increasing its market share at the old price. In fact, this is the other side of a story we've already told. If the price of World and International computers drops to, say, $900, it's preposterous to assume that Universal will be able to expand its

FIGURE 11.2

Rivalry for Market Shares Threatens an Oligopoly

If oligopolists start cutting prices to capture larger market shares, they'll be behaving much like truly competitive firms. The result will be a slide down the market demand curve to lower prices, increased output, and smaller profits. In this case, the market price and quantity would move from point F to point G if rival oligopolists cut prices to gain market shares.

market share at a price of $1,000. Universal's market share will shrink if it maintains a price of $1,000 per computer after World and International drop their prices to $900. Hence the threat to Universal's market share grab is that the other two oligopolists will retaliate by reducing *their* prices. Should they carry out this threat, Universal would be forced to cut computer prices too, or accept a greatly reduced market share.

The same kind of threat exists in the second case, where we assumed that Universal Electronics expands its sales by initiating a price reduction. World and International aren't going to just sit by and applaud Universal's marketing success. They'll have to respond with price cuts of their own. Universal would then have the highest price on the market, and computer buyers would flock to cheaper substitutes. Accordingly, it's safe to conclude that *an attempt by one oligopolist to increase its market share by cutting prices will lead to a general reduction in the market price.* The three oligopolists will end up using price reductions as weapons in the battle for market shares, the kind of behavior normally associated with competitive firms. Should this behavior continue, not only will oligopoly become less fun, but it will also become less profitable as prices slide down the market demand curve (Figure 11.2). This is why *oligopolists avoid price competition and instead pursue nonprice competition* (e.g., advertising and product differentiation).

THE KINKED DEMAND CURVE

The close interdependence of oligopolists—and the limitations it imposes on individual price and output decisions—is the principal moral of this story. We can summarize the story with the aid of the kinked demand curve in Figure 11.3.

Recall that at the beginning of this oligopoly story Universal Electronics had a market share of 40 percent and was selling 8,000 computers per month at a price of $1,000 each. This output is represented by point A in Figure 11.3. The rest of the demand curve illustrates what would happen to Universal's unit sales if it changed its selling price. What we have to figure out is why this particular demand curve has such a strange "kinked" shape.

Rivals' Response to Price Reductions

Consider first what would happen to Universal's sales if it lowered the price of its computers to $900. In general, we expect a price reduction to increase sales. However, *the degree to which an oligopolist's sales increase when its price is reduced depends on the response of rival oligopolists.*

Rivals Don't Match. Suppose World and International *didn't* match Universal's price reduction. In this case, Universal would have the only low-priced computer in the market.

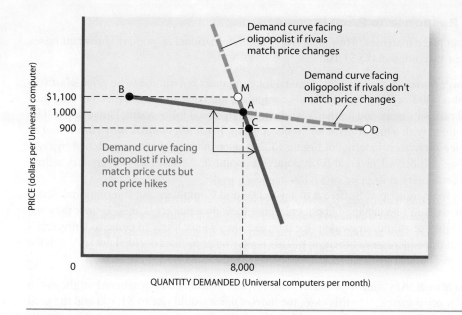

FIGURE 11.3

The Kinked Demand Curve Confronting an Oligopolist

The shape of the demand curve facing an oligopolist depends on the responses of its rivals to its price and output decisions. If rival oligopolists match price reductions but not price increases, the demand curve will be kinked.

Initially, the oligopolist is at point *A*. If it raises its price to $1,100 and its rivals don't raise their prices, it will be driven to point *B*. If its rivals match a price reduction (to $900), the oligopolist will end up at point *C*.

Consumers would flock to Universal, and sales would increase dramatically, from point *A* to point *D*.

Rivals Do Match. But point *D* is little more than a dream, as we've observed. World and International are sure to cut their prices to $900 to maintain their market shares. As a consequence, Universal's sales will expand only slightly, to point *C* rather than to point *D*. Universal's increased sales at point *C* reflect the fact that the total quantity demanded in the market has risen as the market price has fallen to $900 (see Figure 11.2). Thus, even though Universal's *market share* may not have increased, its monthly sales have.

The section of the demand curve that runs from point *A* to point *D* is unlikely to exist in an oligopolistic market. Instead *we expect rival oligopolists to match any price reductions* that Universal initiates, forcing Universal to accept the demand curve that runs from point *A* through point *C*. In the News "Rivals Match Southwest's Flash Sale" illustrates such behavior in the airline industry, where rivals were forced to match price cuts introduced by Southwest Airlines.

IN THE NEWS

RIVALS MATCH SOUTHWEST'S FLASH SALE

Rival airlines are quickly matching some—but not all—of the low fares Southwest rolled out on Tuesday as part of its 72-hour flash sale. American, United, and Jet Blue all announced fare cuts to below $100 on the short routes where Southwest is offering sale tickets. Flights between San Francisco and Los Angeles are now priced at $97, if purchased by Thursday midnight.

Source: Media reports, June 8, 2016.

DELTA ROLLS BACK FARE HIKE

Delta's fare increase didn't stick. On Tuesday Delta announced fare increases of $10–$20 per roundtrip ticket. American, United, and USAirways quickly did the same. But Southwest and Jet Blue didn't follow suit. Last night Delta started rolling back its fare hikes.

—David Koenig

Source: Media reports, April 19-22, 2012.

ANALYSIS: If rivals match price cuts but not price increases, the demand curve confronting an oligopolist will be kinked. Prices will increase only when all firms agree to raise them at the same time.

Rivals' Response to Price Increases

What about price increases? How will World and International respond if Universal raises the price of its computers to $1,100?

Rivals Don't Match. Recall that the demand for computers is assumed to be price-elastic in the neighborhood of $1,000 and that all computers are basically similar. Accordingly, if Universal raises its price and neither World nor International follows suit, Universal will be out there alone with a higher price and reduced sales. *Rival oligopolists may choose not to match price increases.* In terms of Figure 11.3, a price increase that isn't matched by rival oligopolists will drive Universal from point *A* to point *B*. At point *B*, Universal is selling very few computers at its price of $1,100 each.[2]

Is this a likely outcome? Suffice it to say that World Computers and International Semiconductor wouldn't be unhappy about enlarging their own market shares. Unless they see the desirability of an industrywide price increase, they're not likely to come to Universal's rescue with price increases of their own. This is why other airlines decided not to match the fare hikes announced by Delta (see In the News "Delta Rolls Back Fare Hike").

Rivals Do Match. Anything is possible, however, and World and International might match Universal's price increase. In this case, the *market price* would rise to $1,100 and the total quantity of computers demanded would diminish. Under such circumstances Universal's sales would diminish, too, in accordance with its (constant) share of a smaller market. This would lead us to point *M* in Figure 11.3.

Kinked Demand Curve. We may draw two conclusions from Figure 11.3:

* *The shape of the demand curve an oligopolist faces depends on the responses of its rivals to a change in the price of its own output.*
* *That demand curve will be kinked if rival oligopolists match price reductions but not price increases.*

....

GAME THEORY

The central message of the kinked demand curve is that oligopolists can't make truly independent price or output decisions. Because only a few producers participate in the market, *each oligopolist has to consider the potential responses of rivals when formulating price or output strategies.* This *strategic interaction* is the inevitable consequence of their oligopolistic position.

Uncertainty and Risk. What makes oligopoly particularly interesting is the *uncertainty* of rivals' behavior. For example, Universal *would* want to lower its prices *if* it thought its rivals wouldn't retaliate with similar price cuts. But it can't be sure of that response. Universal must instead consider the odds of its rivals not matching a price cut. If the odds are low, Universal might decide *not* to initiate a price cut. Or maybe Universal might offer price discounts to just a few select customers, hoping World and International might not notice or react to small changes in market share.

The Payoff Matrix. Table 11.4 summarizes the strategic options each oligopolist confronts. In this case, let's assume that Universal is contemplating a price cut. Its rivals have only two options: either reduce their price also or not. Hence the **payoff matrix** has only four cells, each of which refers to a possible scenario. The payoff matrix in the table summarizes the various profit consequences of each scenario. One thing should be immediately clear: *The payoff to an oligopolist's price cut depends on how its rivals respond.* Indeed, the only scenario that increases Universal's profit is one in which Universal reduces its

payoff matrix: A table showing the risks and rewards of alternative decision options.

[2]Notice again that we're assuming that Universal is able to sell some computers at a higher price (point B) than its rivals. The kinked demand curve applies primarily to differentiated oligopolies. As we'll discuss later, such differentiation may result from slight product variations, advertising, customer habits, location, friendly service, or any number of other factors. Most oligopolies exhibit some differentiation.

Universal's Options	Rivals' Actions	
	Reduce Price	Don't Reduce Price
Reduce price	Small loss for everyone	Huge gain for Universal; rivals lose
Don't reduce price	Huge loss for Universal; rivals gain	No change

TABLE 11.4

Oligopoly Payoff Matrix

The payoff to an oligopolist's price cut depends on its rivals' responses. Each oligopolist must assess the risks and rewards of each scenario before initiating a price change. Which option would you choose?

price and its rivals don't. We visualized this outcome earlier as a move from point A to point D in Figure 11.3. Note again that this scenario implies losses for Universal's two rival oligopolists.

The remaining cells in the payoff matrix show how profits change with other action/ response scenarios. One thing is evident: if Universal *doesn't* reduce prices, it can't increase profits. In fact, it might end up as the big loser if its rivals reduce *their* prices while Universal stands pat.

The option of reducing price doesn't guarantee a profit, but at least it won't ruin Universal's market share or profits. If rivals match a Universal price cut, all three oligopolists will suffer small losses.

So what should Universal do? The *collective* interests of the oligopoly are protected if no one cuts the market price. But an individual oligopolist could lose a lot if it holds the line on price when rivals reduce price. Hence each oligopolist might decide to play it safe by *initiating* a price cut.

Expected Gain (Loss). The decision to initiate a price cut boils down to an assessment of *risk*. If you thought the risk of a "first strike" was high, you'd be more inclined to reduce price. This kind of risk assessment is the foundation of game theory. You could in fact make that decision by *quantifying* the risks involved. Consider again the option of reducing price. As the first row of Table 11.4 shows, rivals can respond in one of only two ways. If they follow suit, a small loss is incurred by Universal. If they don't, there's a huge gain for Universal. To quantify the risk assessment, we need two pieces of information: (1) the size of each "payoff" and (2) the probability of its occurrence.

Suppose the "huge gain" is $1 million and the "small loss" is $20,000. What should Universal do? The huge gain looks enticing, but we now know it's not likely to h appen. But *how* unlikely is it? What if there's only a 1 percent chance of rivals not matching a price reduction? In that case, the *expected* payoff to a Universal price cut is

$$\begin{array}{l} \text{Expected payoff} \\ \text{of price cut} \end{array} = \left[\begin{array}{l} \text{Probability of} \\ \text{rival matching} \end{array} \times \begin{array}{l} \text{Loss from} \\ \text{price cut} \end{array} \right] + \left[\begin{array}{l} \text{Probability} \\ \text{of rival} \\ \text{not matching} \end{array} \times \begin{array}{l} \text{Gain} \\ \text{from} \\ \text{price cut} \end{array} \right]$$

$$= [0.99 \times -\$20,000] + [0.01 \times \$1,000,000]$$
$$= -\$19,800 + \$10,000$$
$$= -\$9,800$$

Hence it's not a good idea. Once potential payoffs and probabilities are taken into account, a unilateral price cut doesn't look promising. The odds say a unilateral price cut will result in a loss (−$9,800).

These kinds of computations underlay the Cold War games that the world's one-time superpowers played. Neither side was certain of the enemy's next move but knew a nuclear first strike could trigger retaliatory destruction. As a consequence, the United States and the former Soviet Union continually probed each other's responses but were quick to retreat from the brink whenever all-out retaliation was threatened. Oligopolists play the same kind of game on a much smaller scale, using price discounts and advertising rather than nuclear warheads as their principal weapons. The reward they receive for coexistence is the oligopoly profits that they continue to share. This reward, together with the threat of mutual destruction, leads oligopolists to limit their price rivalry. This explains why analysts predict that Coke and Pepsi price wars will be brief (see In the News "Coke Reignites Price War").

IN THE NEWS

COKE REIGNITES PRICE WAR

Coke fired the first shot again in the periodic "soda wars" with rival Pepsi, cutting the price of Coke products by as much as 7.7 percent in the third quarter. Both companies have been hurt by a continuing decline in soda sales, fueled by Millennials' turn to energy drinks, juices, and bottled water. Coke's bottom line has been hit the hardest, as 100 percent of its sales come from beverages. Pepsi has an array of snack-food products to cushion declines in soda sales. Although the soda giants prefer to use packaging, new products, and advertising to compete for sales, they have used occasional price wars in the past. With loyalty rates of 90 percent, price wars are fairly ineffective in wooing consumers from a rival brand. But Coke wants to lure "fringe" consumers back from energy drinks and fruit juices. And its willing to start another price war with Pepsi to capture some of those consumers, even if it means lower profits for both Coke and Pepsi in the short run. Analysts expect the latest price war to be short-lived.

Source: Media reports, September 2015.

ANALYSIS: Price discounting can destroy oligopoly profits. When it occurs, rival oligopolists seek to end it as quickly as possible.

This isn't to say oligopolists won't ever cut prices or use other means to gain market share. They might, given the right circumstances and certain expectations of how rivals will behave. Indeed, there are a host of different price, output, and marketing strategies an oligopolist might want to pursue. The field of **game theory** is dedicated to the study of how decisions are made when such strategic interaction exists—for example, when the outcome of a business strategy depends on the decisions rival firms make. Just as there are dozens of different moves and countermoves in a chess game, so too are there numerous strategies oligopolists might use to gain market share.

game theory: The study of decision making in situations where strategic interaction (moves and countermoves) occurs between rivals.

OLIGOPOLY VS. COMPETITION

While contemplating strategies for maximizing their *individual* profits, oligopolists are also mindful of their common interest in maximizing *joint* (industry) profits. They want to avoid behavior that destroys the very profits that they're vying for. Indeed, they might want to coordinate their behavior in a way that maximizes *industry* profits. If they do, how will market outcomes be affected?

Price and Output

Thus far we've focused on a single oligopolist's decision about whether to *change* the price of its output. But how was the initial (market) price determined? In this example, we assumed that the initial price was $1,000 per computer, the price that prevailed initially in a *competitive* market. But the market is no longer competitive. As we saw in the previous chapter, a change in industry structure will affect market outcomes. A monopolist, for example, would try to maximize *industry* profits, all of which it would keep. To do this, it

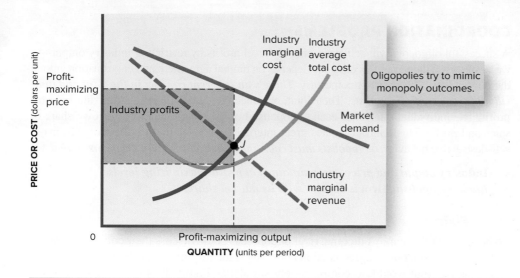

FIGURE 11.4
Maximizing Oligopoly Profits

An oligopoly strives to behave like a monopoly. Industry profits are maximized at the rate of output at which the *industry's* marginal cost equals marginal revenue (point *J*). In a monopoly, this profit all goes to one firm; in an oligopoly, it must be shared among a few firms.

In an oligopoly, the MC and ATC curves represent the combined production capabilities of several firms, rather than only one. The industry MC curve is derived by horizontally summing the MC curves of the individual firms.

would select that one rate of output where marginal revenue equals marginal cost, and it would charge whatever price consumers were willing and able to pay for that rate of output (see Figure 11.4).

An oligopoly would seek similar profits. An oligopoly is really just a *shared* monopoly. Hence *an oligopoly will want to behave like a monopoly, choosing a rate of industry output that maximizes total industry profit.*

The challenge for an oligopoly is to replicate monopoly outcomes. To do so, the firms in an oligopoly must find the monopoly price and maintain it. This is what the members of OPEC are trying to do when they meet to establish a common price for the oil they sell and agree to limit their output so as to achieve that price (see World View "Oil Spikes on OPEC Pact"). Reaching agreement requires a common view of the industry demand curve, satisfaction with respective market shares, and precise coordination.

WORLD VIEW

OIL SPIKES ON OPEC PACT

VIENNA, December 1—Oil prices spiked 14 percent, closing at a 17-month high of $51.68 a barrel on Friday. The surge in oil prices is a reaction to Wednesday's OPEC agreement to cut production for the first time since 2008. The 13 OPEC member states agreed to cut production by 1.2 million barrels a day, down from the current rate of 33.6 million barrels.

Source: Media reports, December 1–3, 2016.

ANALYSIS: An oligopoly tries to act like a shared monopoly. To maximize industry profit, the firms in an oligopoly must concur on what the monopoly price is and agree to maintain it by limiting output and allocating market shares.

Competitive industries would also like to reap monopoly-like profits. But competitive industries experience relentless pressure on profits as individual firms expand output, reduce costs, and lower prices. To maximize industry profits, competitive firms would have to band together and agree to restrict output and raise prices. If they did, though, the industry would no longer be competitive. Maximizing industry profits is easier in an oligopoly because fewer firms are involved and each is aware of its dependence on the behavior of the others.

COORDINATION PROBLEMS

A successful oligopoly will achieve monopoly-level profits by restricting industry output. As we've observed, however, this outcome depends on mutual agreement and coordination among the oligopolists. This may not come easy. *There's an inherent conflict in the joint and individual interests of oligopolists.* Their joint, or collective, interest is in maximizing industry profit. The individual interest of each oligopolist, however, is to maximize its own share of sales and profit. This conflict creates great internal tension within an oligopoly. To avoid self-destructive behavior, *oligopolists must coordinate their production decisions so that*

- Industry *output and price are maintained at profit-maximizing levels.*
- *Each oligopolistic* firm *is content with its market share.*

Price-Fixing

To bring about this happy outcome, rival oligopolists could discuss their common interests and attempt to iron out an agreement on both issues. Identifying the profit-maximizing rate of industry output would be comparatively simple, as Figure 11.4 illustrated. Once the optimal rate of output was found, the associated profit-maximizing price would be evident. The only remaining issue would be the division of industry output among the oligopolists—that is, the assignment of market shares.

The most explicit form of coordination among oligopolists is called **price-fixing**. In this case, the firms in an oligopoly explicitly agree to charge a uniform (monopoly) price. This is what the 13 OPEC member-nations do when they get together to set oil prices (see World View "Oil Spikes on OPEC Pact"). Some other examples of price-fixing include the following.

Ivy League Colleges. For more than 30 years Ivy League schools worked together to offer a uniform financial aid package for individual students, eliminating price competition. The Justice Department ordered the schools to end that practice in 1992.

Electric Generators. In 1961 General Electric and Westinghouse were convicted of fixing prices on $2 billion worth of electrical generators that they'd been selling to the Tennessee Valley Authority and commercial customers. Among the corporate executives, 7 went to prison and 23 others were put on probation. In addition, the companies were fined a total of $1.8 million and compelled to pay triple damages in excess of $500 million to their victimized customers. Nevertheless, another suit was filed against General Electric and Westinghouse in 1972, charging these same companies—still the only two U.S. manufacturers of turbine generators—with continued price-fixing.

Perfume. Thirteen companies—including Chanel, Dior, and Yves Saint Laurent—paid $55 million in penalties in 2006 for fixing prices.

Auction Commissions. Sotheby's and Christie's, who together control 90 percent of the world's art auction business, admitted in 2000 to fixing commission rates throughout the 1990s. They paid a $512 million fine when they were caught.

Laser Eye Surgery. The FTC in 2006 charged the two companies that sell the lasers used for corrective eye surgery (VISX and Summit Technology) with price-fixing that inflated the retail price of surgery by $500 per eye.

Memory Chips. In 2005 the world's largest memory chip (DRAM) manufacturers (Samsung, Micron, Infineon, Hynix) admitted to fixing prices in the $16-billion-a-year DRAM market and paid nearly $700 million in criminal fines.

Elevators. In 2007 five companies were fined $1.3 billion for fixing prices on elevators and escalators in Europe for 10 years.

e-books. In June 2015 Apple was found guilty of conspiring with five book publishers to fix the price of e-books. E-book prices on Amazon went up from $9.99 to $12.99 or $14.99. Apple paid a $450 million fine.

price-fixing: Explicit agreements among producers regarding the price(s) at which a good is to be sold.

Laundry Detergent. Colgate-Palmolive was found guilty in 2016 of conspiring with its chief rival and a retailer to fix the price of laundry detergent in Australia. The company paid an $18 million fine.

Auto Parts. Bridgestone agreed to pay a $425 million criminal fine in 2016 for conspiring with other firms to fix prices, rig bids, and allocate sales of parts to auto manufacturers in the United States.

Price Leadership

Although price-fixing agreements are still a reality in many product markets, oligopolies have discovered that they don't need *explicit* agreements to arrive at uniform prices; they can achieve the same outcome in more subtle ways. **Price leadership** rather than price-fixing will suffice. If all oligopolists in a particular product market follow the lead of one firm in raising prices, the result is the same as if they had all agreed to raise prices simultaneously. Instead of conspiring in motel rooms (as in the electrical products and soft drink cases), the firms can achieve their objective simply by reading *The Wall Street Journal* or industry publications and responding appropriately. This is apparently how Coke and Pepsi communicated their desire to end their 1997 price war (see In the News "Coke Reignites Price War").

According to the U.S. Department of Justice, the major airlines developed a highly sophisticated form of price leadership. They used their shared computer reservation systems to signal *intended* price hikes. Rival oligopolists then responded with their own *intended* price changes. Only after it was clear that all the airlines would match a planned price increase was the price hike announced. The Justice Department argued that this "electronic dialogue" was equivalent to a price-fixing conspiracy that cost consumers $1.9 billion in excessive fares. In response, the major airlines agreed to stop using the reservations system to communicate *planned* fare hikes.

price leadership: An oligopolistic pricing pattern that allows one firm to establish the (market) price for all firms in the industry.

Allocation of Market Shares

Whenever oligopolists successfully raise the price of a product, the law of demand tells us that unit sales will decline. Even in markets with highly inelastic demand *some* decrease in sales always accompanies an increase in price. When this happens in a monopolistic industry, the monopolist simply cuts back the rate of output. In an oligopoly, however, no single firm will wish to incur the whole weight of that cutback. Some form of accommodation is required by all the oligopolists.

The adjustment to the reduced sales volume can take many forms. Members of OPEC, for example, assign explicit quotas for the oil output of each member country (see World View "Oil Spikes on OPEC Pact"). Such open and explicit production-sharing agreements transform an oligopoly into a **cartel.**

Because cartels openly violate U.S. antitrust laws, American oligopolies have to be more circumspect in divvying up shared markets. A particularly novel method of allocating market shares occurred in the price-fixing case involving General Electric and Westinghouse. Agreeing to establish high prices on electric generators wasn't particularly difficult. But how would the companies decide who was to get the restricted sales? Their solution was to designate one firm as the "low" bidder for a particular phase of the moon. The "low" bidder would charge the previously agreed-upon (high) price, with the other firm offering its products at even higher prices. The "low" bidder would naturally get the sale. Each time the moon entered a new phase, the order of "low" and "high" bidders changed. Each firm got a share of the business, and the price-fixing scheme hid behind a facade of "competitive" bidding.

Such intricate systems for allocating market shares are more the exception than the rule. More often the oligopolists let the sales and output reduction be divided up according to consumer demands, intervening only when market shares are thrown markedly out of balance. At such times an oligopolist may take drastic action, such as **predatory pricing.**

cartel: A group of firms with an explicit, formal agreement to fix prices and output shares in a particular market.

predatory pricing: Temporary price reductions designed to alter market shares or drive out competition.

Predatory price cuts are temporary price reductions intended to drive out new competition or reestablish market shares. The sophisticated use of price cutting can also function as a significant barrier to entry, inhibiting potential competitors from trying to gain a foothold in the price cutter's market. In the News "Eliminating the Competition with Low Prices" describes how major airlines forced Independence Air out of their market with predatory pricing in 2006.

IN THE NEWS

ELIMINATING THE COMPETITION WITH LOW PRICES

On January 5, 2006, Independence Air ceased flying. CEO Kerry Skeen, armed with $300 million in start-up capital, had positioned Independence as a low-fare entrant at the profitable Washington, DC, Dulles airport. At its launch in June 2004, Skeen observed that the Washington, DC, area was "screaming" for low fares.

The major carriers didn't agree. United Airlines, with a hub at Dulles, slashed fares as soon as Independence took flight. The rest of the "Big Six" (Delta, American, Northwest, US Airways, Continental) did the same. The fare war kept Independence from gaining enough market share to survive. As CEO Skeen concluded, "It's a brutal industry."

The week after Independence ceased flying, the "walk-up" fare between Dulles and Atlanta jumped from $118 to $478. Other fares followed suit.

Source: "Flying Monopoly Air," *McGraw-Hill News Flash,* McGraw-Hill Education, February, 2006. ©2006.

ANALYSIS: To protect their prices and profits, oligopolists must be able to eliminate potential competition. Predatory pricing can serve that purpose.

BARRIERS TO ENTRY

If oligopolies succeed in establishing monopoly prices and profits, they'll attract the envy of would-be entrants. To keep potential competitors out of their industry, oligopolists must maintain **barriers to entry.** *Above-normal profits can't be maintained over the long run unless barriers to entry exist.* The entry barriers erected include those monopolists use (Chapter 10).

> **barriers to entry:** Obstacles such as patents that make it difficult or impossible for would-be producers to enter a particular market.

Patents

Patents are a very effective barrier to entry. Potential competitors can't set up shop until they either develop an alternative method for producing a product or receive permission from the patent holder to use the patented process. Such permission, when given, costs something, of course. In 2006 Research in Motion paid an extraordinary $612.5 million for the patent rights to produce BlackBerrys. In 2007 a federal court ordered Internet phone provider Vonage to pay $135 million and 5 percent of its future profits to its wired rivals, Verizon and Sprint. Patents and patent litigation scare off a lot of potential competition. Apple and Samsung have sued each other several times over alleged patent violations, always hoping to blunt competition.

Distribution Control

Another way of controlling the supply of a product is to take control of distribution outlets. If a firm can persuade retail outlets not to peddle anyone else's competitive wares, it will increase its market power. This control of distribution outlets can be accomplished through selective discounts, long-term supply contracts, or expensive gifts at Christmas. Recall from Chapter 10 (see In the News "Live Nation Acquires Ticketmaster") how Live Nation Entertainment locked up concert arenas and ticket distribution. According to the U.S.

Justice Department, Visa and MasterCard prevent banks that issue their credit cards from offering rival cards. Frito-Lay elbows out competing snack companies by paying high fees to "rent" shelf space in grocery stores (see In the News "Frito-Lay Eats Up Snack-Food Business"). Such up-front costs create an entry barrier for potential rivals. Even if a potential rival can come up with the up-front money, the owner of an arena or grocery store chain may not wish to anger the firm that dominates the market.

IN THE NEWS

FRITO-LAY EATS UP SNACK-FOOD BUSINESS

Anheuser-Busch is throwing in the towel on the snack-food business. The company announced it is selling off its Eagle Snacks subsidiary, after trying in vain to gain market share against Frito-Lay. Frito-Lay dominates the business, with half of all salty snack items. Competitors say Frito-Lay has secured its dominant position with shelf-space rentals in retail stores—paying as much as $40,000 a foot annually to secure prime shelf space in grocery and convenience stores. "Frito can afford it," said a regional rep for a competing company, "but we can't. It's become a real estate business." Such tactics have made Frito-Lay an invincible foe.

Source: News reports, October 1995.

ANALYSIS: Barriers to entry such as shelf-space rental and advertising enable a firm to maintain market dominance. Acquisitions also reduce competition.

New car warranties also serve as an entry barrier. The warranties typically require regular maintenance at authorized dealerships and the exclusive use of authorized parts. These provisions limit the ability of would-be competitors to provide cheaper auto parts and service. Frequent flier programs have similar effects in the airline industry.

Input Lock-Ups

Another way to deter competition is to acquire exclusive access to needed or ancillary inputs. Live Nation strengthens its power in the concert business by tying entertainers to exclusive contracts. Microsoft and Sony retain the lion's share of video console sales by contracting with developers to create games exclusively for their consoles. Apple does the same thing with applications software developers. Tesla is building a giga-factory to produce the lithium batteries that are the heart and soul of electric cars. U.S. Steel has exclusive access to coal mines it owns and operates. In all these cases, would-be competitors will find it difficult to acquire the inputs they need to produce competing products.

Mergers and Acquisition

Large and powerful firms can also limit competition by outright *acquisition*. A *merger* between two firms amounts to the same thing, although mergers often entail the creation of new corporate identities.

Perhaps the single most dramatic case of acquisition for this purpose occurred in the breakfast cereals industry. In 1946 General Foods acquired the cereal manufacturing facilities of Campbell Cereal Company, a substantial competitor. Following this acquisition, General Foods dismantled the production facilities of Campbell Cereal and shipped them off to South Africa!

Although the General Foods acquisition was more dramatic than most, acquisitions have been the most popular route to increased market power. General Motors attained a dominant share of the auto market largely by its success in merging with and acquiring two dozen independent manufacturers. In the cigarette industry, the American Tobacco

Company attained monopoly powers by absorbing 250 independent companies. Later anti-trust action (1911) split up the resultant tobacco monopoly into an oligopoly consisting of four companies, which continued to dominate the cigarette market until 2004, when R. J. Reynolds bought Brown & Williamson, leaving only three firms to dominate the cigarette industry. In 2014, Reynolds bought Lorillard, effectively creating an oligopoly (see In the News "Joe Camel Acquires Newport").

IN THE NEWS

JOE CAMEL ACQUIRES NEWPORT

In a widely anticipated move, Reynolds American, producer of best-selling brand Camel, announced yesterday that it has agreed to buy Lorillard, maker of Newport, the number 1 menthol cigarette. The $25 billion deal will combine the number 2 and number 3 cigarette manufacturers. The new company, retaining the Reynolds American name, will have 35 percent of the U.S. market, running second to Altria's 47 percent share. As part of the deal, Imperial Tobacco will purchase several of Lorillard's brands, including Blu, its popular e-cigarette, and end up with 10 percent of the market. Liggett Vector will keep 4 percent of the market. Prior to merging, Reynolds had 25 percent of the market and Lorillard had 12 percent, with Imperial at 8 percent.

Reynolds expects to cut annual costs by $800 million through eliminating overlap in sales, production, and overhead costs. Consumers worry that reduced competition will raise cigarette prices and further limit choices. The deal must win antitrust approval before it is finalized.

Source: News reports, July 15–18, 2014.

ANALYSIS: Mergers reduce competition, increase the concentration ratio, and often limit choice and raise price.

Other companies that came to dominate their product markets through mergers and acquisitions include U.S. Steel, U.S. Rubber, General Electric, United Fruit, National Biscuit Company, International Salt, and Live Nation Entertainment. Frito-Lay's 1995 acquisitions of Eagle Snacks (see In the News "Joe Camel Acquires Newport") extended its already dominant control of the chip, pretzel, and nuts markets.

Government Regulation

The government often helps companies acquire and maintain control of market supply. Patents are issued and enforced by the federal government and so represent one form of supply-restricting regulation. Barriers to international trade are another government-imposed barrier to entry. By limiting imports of everything from Chinese mushrooms to Japanese cars (see Chapter 21), the federal government reduces potential competition in U.S. product markets. Government regulation also limits *domestic* competition in many industries.

New York City also limits competition—in this case, the number of taxicabs on the streets. The maximum number of cabs was set at 11,787 in 1937 and stayed at that ceiling until 1996. The city's Taxi and Limousine Commission has since raised the ceiling to 13,605 taxis. That didn't do much to eliminate New York's perennial taxi shortage (for a population of more than 8 million people), much less reduce fares. As a result, license holders reaped monopoly-like profits for decades. A good measure of those monopoly profits was the price of the medallions that served as taxi licenses—a price that reached $1.3 million in 2014. When Uber, Lyft, and other ride-sharing services surmounted that entry barrier, the monopoly power of the medallions was shattered. In 2016, medallions were selling for as little as $250,000 and ride-sharing services had 35 percent of the market. Other states and cities are still protecting their taxi oligopolies by prohibiting Uber, Lyft, and other ride-share companies from operating.

Nonprice Competition

Producers who control market supply can enhance their power even further by establishing some influence over market demand. The primary mechanism of control is *advertising*. To the extent that a firm can convince you that its product is essential to your well-being and happiness, it has effectively shifted your demand curve. ***Advertising not only strengthens brand loyalty but also makes it expensive for new producers to enter the market.*** A new entrant must buy both production facilities and advertising outlets.

The cigarette industry is a classic case of high concentration and product differentiation. As Table 11.2 shows, the top four cigarette companies produce 96 percent of all domestic output; small, generic firms produce the rest. Together, the four cigarette companies produce well over 100 brands. To solidify brand loyalties, the cigarette industry spent more than $9 billion on advertising and promotions in 2016.

The breakfast cereal industry also uses nonprice competition to lock in consumers. Although the Federal Trade Commission has suggested that "a corn flake is a corn flake no matter who makes it," the four firms (Kellogg, General Mills, Ralcorp, and Quaker Oats) that supply more than 90 percent of all ready-to-eat breakfast cereals spend more than $500 million a year—about $1 per box!—to convince consumers otherwise.

Training

In today's technology-driven markets, early market entry can create an important barrier to later competition. Customers of computer hardware and software, for example, often become familiar with a particular system or computer package. Switching to a new product may entail significant cost, including the retraining of user staff. As a consequence, would-be competitors will find it difficult to sell their products even if they offer better quality and lower prices.

Network Economies

The widespread use of a particular product may also heighten its value to consumers, thereby making potential substitutes less viable. The utility of instant messaging—or even a telephone—depends on how many of your friends have telephones. If no one else had a phone there'd be no reason to own one. In other words, the larger the network of users, the greater the value of the product. Such network economies help explain why software developers prefer to write apps for the iPhone than applications for rival smartphones and why advertisers pay a premium to appear on Facebook.

THE ECONOMY TOMORROW

ANTITRUST ENFORCEMENT

Examples of market power at work in product markets could be extended for another 10 chapters. The few cases cited here, however, are testimony enough to the fact that market power has some influence on our lives. Market power *does* exist; market power *is* used. Although market power may result in economies of scale, the potential for abuse is evident. Market power contributes to **market failure** when it leads to resource misallocation (restricted output) or greater inequity (monopoly profits, higher prices).

market failure: An imperfection in the market mechanism that prevents optimal outcomes.

What should we do about these abuses? Should we leave it to market forces to find ways of changing industry structure and behavior? Or should the government step in to curb noncompetitive practices?

Industry Behavior. Our primary concern is the *behavior* of market participants. What ultimately counts is the quantity of goods supplied to the market, their quality, and their price. Few consumers care about the underlying *structure* of markets; what we seek are good market *outcomes*.

Continued

antitrust: Government intervention to alter market structure or prevent abuse of market power.

In principle, the government could change industry behavior without changing industry structure. We could, for example, explicitly outlaw collusive agreements and cast a wary eye on industries that regularly exhibit price leadership. We could dismantle barriers to entry and thereby promote contestable markets. We might also prohibit oligopolists from extending their market power via such mechanisms as acquisitions, excessive or deceptive advertising, and the financing of political campaigns. In fact, the existing **antitrust** laws—the Sherman Act, the Clayton Act, and the Federal Trade Commission Act (see Table 10.1)—explicitly forbid most of these practices.

There are several problems with this behavioral approach. The first limitation is scarce resources. Policing markets and penalizing noncompetitive conduct require more resources than the public sector can muster. Indeed, the firms being investigated often have more resources than the public watchdogs. The advertising expenditures of just one oligopolist, Procter & Gamble, are more than 10 times as large as the *combined* budgets of both the Justice Department's Antitrust Division and the Federal Trade Commission.

The paucity of antitrust resources is partly a reflection of public apathy. Consumers rarely think about the connection between market power and the price of the goods they buy, the wages they receive, or the way they live. As Ralph Nader discovered, "Antitrust violations are part of a phenomenon which, to the public, is too complex, too abstract, and supremely dull."[3] As a result, there's little political pressure to regulate market behavior.

The behavioral approach also suffers from the "burden-of-proof" requirement. How often will "trustbusters" catch colluding executives in the act? More often than not, the case for collusion rests on such circumstantial evidence as simultaneous price hikes, identical bids, or other market outcomes. The charge of explicit collusion is hard to prove. Even in the absence of explicit collusion, however, consumers suffer. If an oligopoly price is higher than what a competitive industry would charge, consumers get stuck with the bill whether or not the price was "rigged" by explicit collusions. The U.S. Supreme Court recognized that consumers may suffer from *tacit* collusion, even where no *explicit* collusion occurs.

Industry Structure. The concept of tacit collusion directs attention to the *structure* of an industry. It essentially says that oligopolists and monopolists will act in their own best interest. As former Supreme Court Chief Justice Earl Warren observed, "An industry which does not have a competitive structure will not have competitive behavior."[4] To expect an oligopolist to disavow profit opportunities or to ignore its interdependence with fellow oligopolists is naive. It also violates the basic motivations imputed to a market economy. As long as markets are highly concentrated, we must expect to observe oligopolistic behavior.

Judge Learned Hand used these arguments to dismantle the Aluminum Company of America (Alcoa) in 1945. Alcoa wasn't charged with any illegal *behavior*. Nevertheless, the company controlled more than 90 percent of the aluminum supplied to the market. This monopoly structure, the Supreme Court concluded, was itself a threat to the public interest.

Corporate breakups are rarely pursued today. In 2001 the Justice Department withdrew a proposal to break up Microsoft into separate systems and applications companies. The prevalent feeling today, even among antitrust practitioners, is that the powerful firms are too big and too entrenched to make deconcentration a viable policy alternative.

Objections to Antitrust. Some people think *less* antitrust enforcement is actually a good thing. The companies challenged by the public "trustbusters" protest that they're being penalized for their success. Alcoa, for example, attained a monopoly by investing heavily in a new product before anyone else recognized its value. Other firms too have captured dominant market shares by being first, best, or most efficient. Having "won" the

---

[3]Source: Green, Mark J., et al., *The Closed Enterprise System: The Report on Antitrust Enforcement*. New York, NY: Grossman, p. ix, 1972.
[4]Ibid., p. 7.

game fairly, why should they have to give up their prize? They contend that noncompetitive *behavior,* not industry *structure,* should be the only concern of antitrust enforcers.

Essentially the same argument is made for proposed mergers and acquisitions. The firms involved claim that the increased concentration will enhance productive efficiency (e.g., via economies of scale). They also argue that big firms are needed to maintain America's competitive position in international markets (which are themselves often dominated by foreign monopolies and oligopolies). Those same global markets, they contend, ensure that even highly concentrated domestic markets will be contested by international rivals.

Finally, critics of antitrust suggest that market forces themselves will ensure competitive behavior. Foreign firms and domestic entrepreneurs will stalk a monopolist's preserve. People will always be looking for ways to enter a profitable market. Monopoly or oligopoly power may slow entry but is unlikely to stop it forever. Eventually competitive forces will prevail.

Structural Guidelines: The Herfindahl-Hirshman Index. There are no easy answers. In theory, competition is valuable, but some mergers and acquisitions undoubtedly increase efficiency. Moreover, some international markets may require a minimum firm size not consistent with perfect competition. Finally, our regulatory resources are limited; not every acquisition or merger is worthy of public scrutiny.

Where would we draw the line? Can a firm hold a 22 percent market share, but not 30 percent? Are five firms too few, but six firms in an industry enough? Someone has to make those decisions. That is, *the broad mandates of the antitrust laws must be transformed into specific guidelines for government intervention.*

In 1982 the Antitrust Division of the U.S. Department of Justice adopted specific guidelines for intervention based on industry *structure* alone. They're based on an index that takes into account the market share of *each* firm rather than just the *combined* market share of the top four firms. Specifically, the **Herfindahl-Hirshman Index (HHI)** of market concentration is calculated as

$$\text{HHI} = \sum_{i=1}^{n} = \left(\frac{\text{Share of}}{\text{firm 1}}\right)^2 + \left(\frac{\text{Share of}}{\text{firm 2}}\right)^2 + \cdots + \left(\frac{\text{Share of}}{\text{firm } n}\right)^2$$

Thus a three-firm oligopoly like that described in Table 11.3 would have an HHI value of

$$\text{HHI} = (40.0)^2 + (32.5)^2 + (27.5)^2 = 3{,}412.5$$

where the numbers in parentheses indicate the market shares of the three fictional computer companies. The calculation yields an HHI value of 3,412.5.

For policy purposes, the Justice Department decided it would draw the line at 1,800. *Any merger that creates an HHI value over 1,800 will be challenged by the Justice Department.* If an industry has an HHI value between 1,000 and 1,800, the Justice Department will challenge any merger that *increases* the HHI by 100 points or more. Mergers and acquisitions in industries with an HHI value of less than 1,000 won't be challenged.

The HHI is an arbitrary but workable tool for deciding when the government should intervene to challenge mergers and acquisitions. The Justice Department reviews about 2,500 mergers a year but challenges fewer than 50.

The AT&T/T-Mobile Deal. The Justice Department's guidelines were put to the test in 2011. In March 2011 AT&T announced that it planned to purchase T-Mobile, the fourth largest wireless phone company. That acquisition would have sent the Herfindahl-Hirschmann Index through the roof. But AT&T argued that the acquisition of T-Mobile would result in economies of scale that would improve service and reduce costs. Critics said the loss of competition would raise prices and reduce phone service options. The Justice Department sided with the critics and sued in August 2011 to block the merger. AT&T abandoned the idea four months later and now competes with T-Mobile.

Herfindahl-Hirshman Index (HHI): Measure of industry concentration that accounts for number of firms and size of each.

SUMMARY

- Imperfect competition refers to markets in which individual suppliers (firms) have some independent influence on the price at which their output is sold. Examples of imperfectly competitive market structures are duopoly, oligopoly, and monopolistic competition.   **LO11-1**
- The extent of market power (control over price) depends on the number of firms in an industry, their size, barriers to entry, and the availability of substitutes.   **LO11-1**
- The concentration ratio is a measure of market power in a particular product market. It equals the share of total industry output accounted for by the largest firms, usually the top four.   **LO11-1**
- An oligopoly is a market structure in which a few firms produce all or most of a particular good or service (a concentration ratio of 60 or higher); it's essentially a shared monopoly.   **LO11-1**
- Because oligopolies involve several firms rather than only one, each firm must consider the effect of its price and output decisions on the behavior of rivals. Such firms are highly interdependent.   **LO11-3**
- Game theory attempts to identify different strategies a firm might use, taking into account the consequences of rivals' moves and countermoves.   **LO11-3**
- The kinked demand curve illustrates a pattern of strategic interaction in which rivals match a price cut but not a price hike. Such behavior reinforces the oligopolistic aversion to price competition.   **LO11-3**
- A basic conflict exists between the desire of each individual oligopolist to expand its market share and the *mutual* interest of all the oligopolists in restricting total output so as to maximize industry profits. This conflict must be resolved in some way, via either collusion or some less explicit form of agreement (such as price leadership).   **LO11-3**
- Oligopolists may use price-fixing agreements or price leadership to establish the market price. To maintain that price, the oligopolists must also agree on their respective market shares.   **LO11-3**
- To maintain economic profits, an oligopoly must erect barriers to entry. Patents are one form of barrier. Other barriers include predatory price cutting (price wars), control of distribution outlets, government regulations, advertising (product differentiation), training, and network economies. Outright acquisition and merger may also eliminate competition.   **LO11-2**
- Market power may cause market failure. The symptoms of that failure include increased prices, reduced output, and a transfer of income from the consuming public to a relatively few powerful corporations and the people who own them.   **LO11-2**
- Government intervention may focus on either market structure or market behavior. In either case, difficult decisions must be made about when and how to intervene.   **LO11-1**
- The Herfindahl-Hirshman Index is a measure of industry concentration that takes into account the number of firms and the size of each. It is used as a structural guideline to identify cases worthy of antitrust concern.   **LO11-1**

Key Terms

market structure	product differentiation	predatory pricing
oligopoly	payoff matrix	barriers to entry
contestable market	game theory	market failure
concentration ratio	price-fixing	antitrust
oligopolist	price leadership	Herfindahl-Hirshman Index (HHI)
market share	cartel	

Questions for Discussion

1. How many bookstores are on or near your campus? If there were more bookstores, how would the price of new and used books be affected?   **LO11-1**
2. What entry barriers exist in (*a*) the fast-food industry, (*b*) cable television, (*c*) the auto industry, (*d*) illegal drug trade, (*e*) potato chips, and (*f*) beauty parlors?   **LO11-1**
3. Why does RC Cola depend on advertising to gain market share? (See In the News "RC Targeting Young Soda Drinkers.") Why not offer cheaper sodas than Coke or Pepsi?   **LO11-3**
4. If an oligopolist knows rivals will match a price cut, would it ever reduce its price?   **LO11-3**
5. How might the high concentration ratio in the credit card industry (Table 11.2) affect the annual fees and interest charges for credit card services?   **LO11-2**
6. What evidence of economies of scale is cited in the proposed cigarette merger (In the News "Joe Camel

Acquires Newport")? Should the acquisition be approved? **LO11-2**

7. What reasons might rival airlines have for *not* matching Delta's fare increase? (See In the News "Delta Rolls Back Fare Hike.") **LO11-3**

8. The Ivy League schools defended their price-fixing arrangement (see Ivy League Colleges in Coordination Problems section) by arguing that their coordination assured a fair distribution of scholarship aid. Who was hurt or helped by this arrangement? **LO11-2**

9. Using the payoff matrix in Table 11.4, decide whether Universal should cut its price. What factors will influence the decision? **LO11-3**

10. Domino's and Pizza Hut hold 66 percent of the delivered-pizza market. Should antitrust action be taken? **LO11-1**

11. Why did the price of NYC taxi medallions decline so much when Uber started ride-sharing service in New York? Why are the medallions still worth $250,000? **LO11-2**

PROBLEMS FOR CHAPTER 11

LO11-1 1. According to Table 11.2, in how many markets do fewer than four firms produce at least 80 percent of total output?

LO11-2 2. According to World View "Oil Spikes on OPEC Pact,"
(a) By what percentage did the price of oil increase after OPEC's announcement?
(b) By what percentage was the quantity supplied reduced?
(c) What was the price elasticity of demand? (use the midpoint method)

LO11-2 3. According to In the News "RC Targeting Young Soda Drinkers"
(a) What is the concentration ratio in the U.S. soda market?
(b) If Dr Pepper Snapple split into two equal sized firms, what is the new concentration ratio?

LO11-2 4. (a) According to In the News "Joe Camel Acquires Newport," how many years will it take Reynolds to recoup its purchase price through cost savings?
(b) If Reynolds increases cigarette prices by 10 percent and the price elasticity of demand is 0.4, by how much will its annual revenue of $11 billion increase?

LO11-2 5. If the price of a medallion is a proxy for the profits of the NYC taxi industry, by what percentage did the industry's profits decline when Uber entered the market?

LO11-3 6. Assume an oligopolist confronts *two* possible demand curves for its own output, as illustrated here. The first (A) prevails if other oligopolists don't match price changes. The second (B) prevails if rivals *do* match price changes.

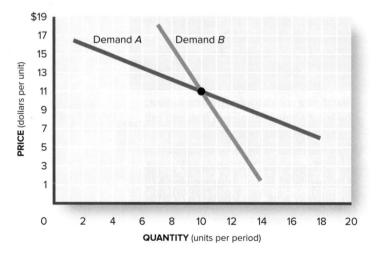

(a) By how much does quantity demanded increase if the price is reduced from $11 to $9 and
(i) Rivals match the price cut?
(ii) Rivals don't match the price cut?
(b) By how much does quantity demanded change when the price is raised from $11 to $13 and
(i) Rivals match the price hike?
(ii) Rivals don't match the price hike?

LO11-3 7. How large would the probability of a "don't match" outcome have to be to make a Universal price cut statistically worthwhile? (See expected payoff in section "Expected Gain (Loss).")

LO11-3 8. Suppose the payoff to each of four strategic interactions is as follows:

Action	Rival Response	
	Reduce Price	**Don't Reduce Price**
Reduce price	Loss = $800	Gain = $50,000
Don't reduce price	Loss = $6,000	No loss or gain

(a) If the probability of rivals matching a price reduction is 98 percent, what is the expected payoff of a price cut?

(b) If the probability of rivals reducing price when you don't reduce your price is 5 percent, what is the expected payoff of *not* reducing price?

(c) Based on your answers to (a) and (b), should the firm cut their price?

LO11-2 9. Suppose that the following schedule summarizes the sales (demand) situation confronting an oligopolist:

Price (per unit)	$20	$19	$18	$17	$16	$14	$12	$10	$ 8
Quantity demanded (units per period)	2	3	4	5	6	7	8	9	10

(a) Draw the demand and marginal revenue curves facing the firm.

(b) Identify the profit-maximizing rate of output in a situation where marginal cost is constant at $11 per unit.

LO11-2 10. What is the price elasticity of demand between points *F* and *G* in Figure 11.2 (use the midpoint method)?

LO11-1 11. The Economy Tomorrow: According to the In the News "Joe Camel Acquires Newport," what were the values of

(a) The concentration ratio in the cigarette industry
   (i)   prior to the merger?
   (ii) after the merger?

(b) The *maximum* value of the Herfindahl-Hirschman Index
   (i)   prior to the merger?
   (ii) after the merger?

(c) Which measure best reflects the increased market power?

©McGraw-Hill Education/Jill Braaten, photographer

CHAPTER 12

Monopolistic Competition

Starbucks is already the biggest coffee bar chain in the world, with roughly 25,000 locations in 70 countries, including 13,000 in the United States. And the company is determined to keep growing by setting up coffee bars in airports, department stores, and just about anywhere consumers congregate. Even if Starbucks achieves such meteoric growth, however, it will never have great market power. There are more than 15,000 other coffee bars in the United States, not to mention a million or so other places you can buy a cup of coffee (e.g., Dunkin' Donuts, McDonald's). With so many other close substitutes, the best Starbucks can hope for is a little brand loyalty. If enough consumers think of Starbucks when they get the caffeine urge, Starbucks will at least be able to charge more for coffee than a perfectly competitive firm. It won't enjoy *monopoly* profits, or even share the kind of monopoly profits *oligopolies* sometimes achieve. It may, however, be able to maintain an economic profit for many years.

Starbucks is an example of yet another market structure—*monopolistic competition.* In this chapter we focus on how such firms make price and output decisions and the market outcomes that result. Our objective is to determine

· **The unique features of monopolistic competition.**
· **How market outcomes are affected by this market structure.**
· **The long-run consequences of different market structures.**

In this chapter we'll also see why we can't escape the relentless advertising that bombards us from every angle.

STRUCTURE

As we first noted in Table 11.1, the distinguishing structural characteristic of **monopolistic competition** is that there are *many* firms in an industry. "Many" isn't an exact specification, of course. It's best understood as lying somewhere between the few that characterize oligopoly and the hordes that characterize perfect competition.

Low Concentration

A more precise way to distinguish monopolistic competition is to examine **concentration ratios.** Oligopolies have very high four-firm concentration ratios. As we saw in Chapter 11 (Table 11.2), concentration ratios of 70 to 100 percent are common in oligopolies. By contrast, there's much less concentration in monopolistic competition. A few

monopolistic competition: A market in which many firms produce similar goods or services but each maintains some independent control of its own price.

concentration ratio: The proportion of total industry output produced by the largest firms (usually the four largest).

Product	Largest Firms (Market Share)	Concentration Ratio (%)
Auto tires (replacement)	Goodyear (16%), Michelin (8%), Firestone (7.5%), General (5%)	37
Bottled water	Coca-Cola (Dasani, 9.9%), PepsiCo (Aquafina, 9.6%), Nestle (8.3%), Glaceau (7.6%)	35
Toys	Lego (12%), Mattel (11%), Hasbro (10%), Tyco (5%)	35
Casinos	MGM, Caesars, Station, Mohegan Sun	33
Coffee bars	Starbucks (15%), Caribou (6%), Peet's (4%), Coffee Beanery (3%)	28
Pizza	Pizza Hut (8.7%), Domino's (8.2%), Little Caesars (6.8%), Papa John's (4.4%)	28
Drugs	GlaxoSmithKline (5.8%), Hoechst-Marion Merrell Dow (4.4%), Merck (4.4%), American Home Products (3.8%)	18
Fast-food restaurants	McDonald's (7.3%), Subway (2.6%), Starbucks (2.27%), Wendy's (1.8%)	14

Source: Industry sources and business publications (2014–2017 data).

TABLE 12.1

Monopolistic Competition

Monopolistically competitive industries are characterized by modest concentration ratios and low entry barriers. Contrast these four-firm concentration ratios with those of oligopoly (see Table 11.2).

firms may stand above the rest, but the combined market share of the top four firms will typically be in the range of 20 to 40 percent. Hence *low concentration ratios are common in monopolistic competition.*

Starbucks has less than 15 percent of the U.S. coffee bar business and a mere 7 percent of all coffee sales. The top four coffee bar outlets (Starbucks, Caribou, The Coffee Beanery, and Peet's) have a concentration ratio of only 28 percent (see Table 12.1). Other examples of monopolistic competition include banks, radio stations, health spas, apparel stores, convenience stores, night clubs, bars, and law firms.

Defining the Market. Concentration ratios look even lower when broader concepts of the relevant market are employed. Consider Starbucks again. Table 12.1 shows its share of the U.S. coffee bar market. But other companies also sell coffee. In fact, McDonald's sells a lot more coffee than does Starbucks. So does Dunkin' Donuts. If you include these outlets, Starbucks' market share shrinks dramatically. And on a global scale, Starbucks sells a tiny fraction of the 2.4 *billion* cups of coffee consumed daily.

The same classification problem applies to McDonald's in the fast-food market. McDonald's dwarfs Starbucks in size, with 37,000 outlets in 118 countries. In the United States, it commands close to a 50 percent share of the quickie *hamburger* market. But is that the relevant market? Or should we look at the broader *fast-food* market that includes pizzas, tacos, hot dogs, and Chinese take-out? If consumers view these other food options as close substitutes for a Big Mac, then McDonald's has a lot less market power than its share of the smaller hamburger market implies. In that larger fast-food market McDonald's has a market share of only 7.3% (Table 12.1).

The same kind of consumer choice affects how we assess market power in the pizza business. Three companies have 46 percent of the pizza *delivery* business. But they compete with more than 75,000 pizzerias in the United States, as well as all the other fast-food outlets. This reduces their market shares and power.

Market Power

Although concentration rates are low in monopolistic competition, the individual firms aren't powerless. There is a *monopoly* aspect to monopolistic competition. Each producer in monopolistic competition is large enough to have some **market power.** If a perfectly competitive firm increases the price of its product, it will lose all its customers. Recall that a perfectly competitive firm confronts a horizontal demand curve for its output. Competition is less intense in monopolistic competition. *A monopolistically competitive firm confronts a downward-sloping demand curve for its output.* When Starbucks increases the price of coffee, it loses some customers, but nowhere close to all of them (see In the News "Starbucks Ups the Price of Iced Drinks"). Starbucks, like other monopolistically competitive firms, has some control over the price of its output. This is the *monopoly* dimension of monopolistic competition.

market power: The ability to alter the market price of a good or service.

IN THE NEWS

STARBUCKS UPS THE PRICE OF ICED DRINKS

Starbucks raised the price of iced coffee, frappuccinos, and other cold drinks by 10–30 cents, effective November 10. This is the second price hike this year, the company having raised the price of hot drinks by similar amounts last July. The average price of a venti mocha Frappuccino is now $4.95, up from $4.65 at most locations. While many customers took to Twitter to express their anger at another price hike, analysts see little risk for Starbucks, which maintains strong pricing power.

Source: Media reports, November 12–20, 2016.

ANALYSIS: A monopolistically competitive firm has the power to increase price unilaterally. The greater the brand loyalty, the less unit sales will decline in response.

Independent Production Decisions

In an oligopoly, a firm that increased its price would have to worry about how rivals might respond (like the airlines in Chapter 11, In the News "Rivals Match Southwest's Flash Sale"). In monopolistic competition, however, there are many more firms. As a result, *modest changes in the output or price of any single firm will have no perceptible influence on the sales of any other firm.* This relative independence results from the fact that the effects of any one firm's behavior will be spread over many other firms (rather than only two or three other firms, as in an oligopoly).

The relative independence of monopolistic competitors means that they don't have to worry about retaliatory responses to every price or output change. As a result, they confront more traditional demand curves with no kinks. Recall that the kink in the oligopolist's curve results from the likelihood that rival oligopolists will match price reductions (to preserve market shares) but not necessarily price increases (to increase their shares). In monopolistic competition, by contrast, the market shares of rival firms aren't perceptibly altered by another firm's price changes.

Low Entry Barriers

barriers to entry: Obstacles such as patents that make it difficult or impossible for would-be producers to enter a particular market.

Another characteristic of monopolistic competition is the presence of *low* **barriers to entry**—it's relatively easy to get in and out of the industry. To become a coffee vendor, all you need is boiling water, some fresh beans, and cups. You can save on rent by using a pushcart to dispense the brew, which is how Starbucks itself got started on the streets of Seattle (see the photo). Coinstar has even replaced the pushcart with bright red Rubi kiosks in grocery stores. Such unusually low entry barriers now keep Starbucks and other coffee

Low entry barriers encourage competition.
©Chris Lawrence/Alamy Stock Photo

bars on their toes. Low entry barriers also tend to push economic profits toward zero. In the pizza business more than 4,000 firms enter and exit every year. This is the *competitive* dimension of monopolistic competition.

....

BEHAVIOR

Given the unique structural characteristics of monopolistic competition, we should anticipate some distinctive behavior.

Product Differentiation

One of the most notable features of monopolistically competitive behavior is **product differentiation.** A monopolistically competitive firm is distinguished from a purely competitive firm by its downward-sloping demand curve. Individual firms in a perfectly competitive market confront horizontal demand curves because consumers view their respective products as interchangeable (virtually identical). As a result, an attempt by one firm to raise its price will drive its customers to other firms.

Brand Image. In monopolistic competition, each firm has a distinct identity—a *brand image.* Its output is perceived by consumers as being somewhat different from the output of all other firms in the industry. Nowhere is this more evident than in the fast-growing bottled water industry. Pepsi and Coke have become the leaders in the bottled water market as a result of effective marketing (see In the News "Selling 'Pure Water': A $Billion Scam?"). Although Aquafina (Pepsi) and Dasani (Coke) are just filtered municipal water, clever advertising campaigns have convinced consumers that these branded waters are different—and better—than hundreds of other bottled waters. As a result of such product differentiation, Pepsi and Coke can raise the price of their bottled waters without losing all their customers to rival firms.

> **product differentiation:** Features that make one product appear different from competing products in the same market.

IN THE NEWS

SELLING "PURE WATER": A $BILLION SCAM?

The ads for Aquafina claim it has bottled the "purest of waters," while Dasani ads assert that what it bottles is "as pure as water can get." Visual backgrounds of glacial streams and lush woodlands reinforce the image of healthy, pure water.

The reality of bottled waters is very different, however. Every drop of water in Pepsi's Aquafina and Coca-Cola's Dasani comes out of the tap, not some mountain spring or glacial melt. Yes, the two major rivals in the bottled water business do filter the tap water, but it is still tap water. In blind tastings, most consumers either prefer simple tap water or can't tell the difference between the bottled and tap options. Further, a National Resources Defense Council found that bottled (filtered) water is no safer than tap water. The Environmental Protection Agency (EPA) tightly regulates the safety of tap water, while the Food and Drug Administration (FDA) sets less stringent requirements for bottled water and often relies on self testing.

Despite the absence of any tangible benefits, consumers spend more than $15 billion on bottled water every year. They are driven in large part by the $100 million a year that Pepsi, Coca-Cola, Nestlé and other bottlers spend on ads touting their "purest of waters."

Source: News reports, 2017.

ANALYSIS: By differentiating their products, monopolistic competitors establish brand loyalty. Brand loyalty gives producers greater control over the prices of their products.

Brand Loyalty

At first blush, the demand curve facing a monopolistically competitive firm looks like the demand curve confronting a monopolist. There's a profound difference, however. In a monopoly, there are no other firms. In monopolistic competition, *each firm has a monopoly only on its brand image; it still competes with other firms offering close substitutes.* This implies that the extent of power a monopolistically competitive firm has depends on how successfully it can differentiate its product from those of other firms. The more brand loyalty a firm can establish, the less likely consumers are to switch brands when price is increased. In other words, *brand loyalty makes the demand curve facing the firm less price-elastic.*

Brand loyalty exists even when products are virtually identical. Gasoline of a given octane rating is a very standardized product. Nevertheless, most consumers regularly buy one particular brand. Because of that brand loyalty, Exxon can raise the price of its gasoline by a penny or two a gallon without losing customers to competing companies. Brand loyalty is particularly high for cigarettes, toothpaste, and even laxatives. Consumers of those products say they'd stick with their accustomed brand even if the price of a competing brand was cut by 50 percent. In other words, *brand loyalty implies low* **cross-price elasticity of demand.** Brand loyalty is less strong (and cross-price elasticity higher) for paper towels and virtually nonexistent for tomatoes.

In the computer industry, product differentiation has been used to establish brand loyalty. Although virtually all computers use identical microprocessor "brains" and operating platforms, the particular mix of functions performed on any computer can be varied, as can its appearance (packaging). Effective advertising can convince consumers that one computer is "smarter," more efficient, or more versatile than another.

Even coffee vendors go to great length to differentiate their product. Starbucks offers not just coffee, but also WiFi hot spots, mobile payments, and powermats for cordless phone charging. These features give consumers added reason to linger at Starbucks and order more coffee. In Everett, Washington, coffee vendors differentiated themselves in 2014 with "bikini baristas"—baristas attired in skimpy bikinis. Every firm is looking to establish a unique image and greater brand loyalty. If successful in any of these efforts, *each monopolistically competitive firm will establish some consumer loyalty.* With such loyalty a firm can alter its own price somewhat without fear of great changes in unit sales (quantity demanded). In other words, the demand curve facing each firm will slope downward, as in Figure 12.1.

Repurchase Rates. One measure of brand loyalty is consumers' tendency to repurchase the same brand. Nearly 8 out of 10 Apple users stick with Apple products when they upgrade smartphones, computers, or tablets. Repurchase rates are 74 percent for Dell and 72 percent for Hewlett-Packard. Starbucks also counts heavily on return customers.

---

cross-price elasticity of demand: Percentage change in the quantity demanded of *X* divided by the percentage change in the price of *Y*.

FIGURE 12.1

Short-Run Equilibrium in Monopolistic Competition

Brand loyalty makes the demand curve facing a monopolistically competitive firm downward sloping. This causes MR < price.

In the short run, a monopolistically competitive firm equates marginal revenue and marginal cost (point *K*). In this case, the firm sells the resulting output at a price (point *F*) above marginal cost. Total profits are represented by the shaded rectangle.

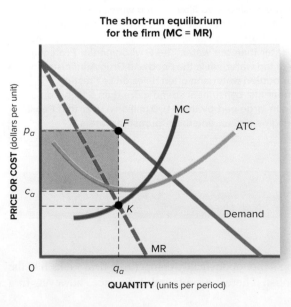

The short-run equilibrium
for the firm (MC = MR)

To maintain such brand loyalty, monopolistically competitive firms must often expand services or product offerings. Remember that entry barriers are low. In the coffee business, it was relatively easy for fast-food companies like McDonald's and Dunkin' Donuts to enter once they saw how profitable Starbucks was. When they did, Starbucks had to expand its menu to maintain its market dominance. Although menu expansion is costly, firms often decide that increased service is more cost-effective than price competition, given the low cross-price elasticity of demand in monopolistically competitive markets. In recent years, Starbucks has continued to pursue product differentiation with a new logo, instant coffee, new cup sizes (the 31-ounce "trenta"), single-serve machines, mobile payments, wine bars, and new food items.

Price Premiums. Another symptom of brand loyalty is the price differences between computer brands. Consumers are willing to pay more for an Apple, Lenovo, or Dell computer than a no-name computer with identical features. For the same reason, consumers are willing to pay more for Starbucks coffee, Ben and Jerry's ice cream, or Aquafina water, even when virtually identical products are available at lower prices.

Short-Run Price and Output

The monopolistically competitive firm's **production decision** is similar to that of a monopolist. Both types of firms confront downward-sloping demand and marginal revenue curves. To maximize profits, both seek the rate of output at which marginal revenue equals marginal cost. This short-run profit-maximizing outcome is illustrated by point K in Figure 12.1. That MC = MR intersection establishes q_a as the profit-maximizing rate of output. The demand curve indicates (point F) that q_a of output can be sold at the price of p_a. Hence the quantity–price combination q_a, p_a illustrates the short-run equilibrium of the monopolistically competitive firm.

production decision: The selection of the short-run rate of output (with existing plants and equipment).

Entry and Exit

Figure 12.1 indicates that this monopolistically competitive firm is earning an **economic profit:** price (p_a) exceeds average total cost (c_a) at the short-run rate of output. These profits are of course a welcome discovery for the firm. They also portend increased competition, however.

economic profit: The difference between total revenues and total economic costs.

Entry Effects. If firms in monopolistic competition are earning an economic profit, other firms will flock to the industry. Remember that *entry barriers are low in monopolistic competition, so new entrants can't be kept out of the market.* If they get wind of the short-run profits depicted in Figure 12.1, they'll come running.

As new firms enter the industry, supply increases and prices will be pushed down the market demand curve, just as in competitive markets. Figure 12.2a illustrates these market changes. The initial price p_1 is set by the intersection of *industry* MC and MR. Because that price generates a profit, more firms enter. This entry shifts the *industry* cost structure to the right, creating a new equilibrium price, p_2.

The impact of this entry on the firms already in the market will be different from that in competitive markets, however. As new firms enter a monopolistically competitive industry, existing firms will lose customers. This is illustrated by the leftward shift of the demand curve facing each firm, as in Figure 12.2b. Accordingly, we conclude that *when firms enter a monopolistically competitive industry,*

- *The industry cost curves shift to the right, pushing down price* (Figure 12.2a).
- *The demand curves facing individual firms shift to the left* (Figure 12.2b).

As the demand curve it faces shifts leftward, the monopolistically competitive firm will have to make a new production decision. It need not charge the same price as its rivals, however, or coordinate its output with theirs. Each monopolistically competitive firm has some independent power over its (shrinking numbers of) captive customers.

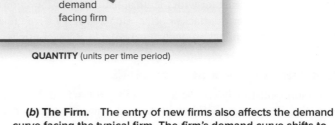

(a) Effect of entry on the industry

(b) Effect of entry on the monopolistically competitive firm

FIGURE 12.2

Market vs. Firm Effects of Entry

Barriers to entry are low in monopolistic competition. Hence new firms will enter if economic profits are available.

(a) The Market.   The entry of new firms will shift the *market* cost curves to the right, as in part *a*. This pushes the average price down the *market* demand curve.

(b) The Firm.   The entry of new firms also affects the demand curve facing the typical firm. The *firm's* demand curve shifts to the left and becomes more elastic because more close substitutes (other firms) are available

No Long-Run Profits

Although each firm has some control over its own pricing decisions, ***entry-induced leftward shifts of the demand curve facing the firm will ultimately eliminate economic profits.***

Long-Run Equilibrium. Notice in Figure 12.3 where the firm eventually ends up. In long-run equilibrium (point *G*), marginal cost is again equal to marginal revenue (at the MR = MC intersection directly below *G*). At that rate of output (q_g), however, there are no economic profits. At that output, price (p_g) is exactly equal to average total cost.

The profit-maximizing equilibrium (point *G*) occurs where the demand curve is tangent to the ATC curve. If the demand curve shifted any farther left, price would always be less than ATC and the firm would incur losses. If the demand curve were positioned farther to the right, price would exceed ATC at some rates of output. When the demand curve is *tangent* to the ATC curve, the firm's best possible outcome is to break even. At point *G* in Figure 12.3, price equals ATC and economic profit is zero.

Will a monopolistically competitive firm end up at point *G*? As long as other firms can enter the industry, the disappearance of economic profits is inevitable. Existing firms can postpone the day of reckoning by increasing their product differentiation and advertising. But rival firms will enter as long as the demand (price) line lies above ATC at some point. Firms will exit when the demand facing the firm lies to the left of and below the ATC curve. Entry and exit cease when the firm's demand curve is *tangent* to the ATC curve. Once entry and exit cease, the long-run equilibrium has been established. ***In the long run, there are no economic profits in monopolistic competition.***

Inefficiency

The zero-profit equilibrium of firms in monopolistic competition, as illustrated in Figure 12.3, differs from the perfectly competitive equilibrium. In perfect competition, long-run profits are also zero. But at that point, a competitive industry produces at the *lowest* point on the ATC curve and thus maximizes efficiency. In monopolistic competition, however, the

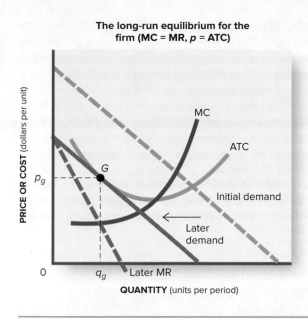

The long-run equilibrium for the firm (MC = MR, p = ATC)

FIGURE 12.3

Long-Run Equilibrium in Monopolistic Competition

In the long run, more firms enter the industry. As they do so, the demand curve facing each firm *shifts* to the left as all market shares decline. Firms still equate MR and MC. Ultimately, however, the demand curve will be tangent to the ATC curve (point *G*), at which point price equals average total cost and no economic profits exist.

demand curve facing each firm slopes downward. Hence it can't be tangent to the ATC curve at its lowest point (the bottom of the U), as in perfect competition. Instead the demand curve of a monopolistically competitive firm must touch the ATC curve on the *left* side of the U.

Note in Figure 12.3 how point *G* lies above and to the left of the bottom of the ATC curve. This long-run equilibrium occurs at an output rate that is less than the minimum-cost rate of production. In long-run equilibrium, the monopolistically competitive industry isn't producing at minimum average cost. As a consequence, *monopolistic competition tends to be less efficient in the long run than a perfectly competitive industry.*

Excess Capacity. One symptom of the inefficiencies associated with monopolistic competition is industrywide excess capacity (see In the News "Coffee Shops Seeking New Identities"). Each firm tries to gain market share by building more outlets and advertising heavily. In equilibrium, however, the typical firm is producing at a rate of output that's less than its minimum-ATC output rate. This implies that the *same* level of *industry* output could be produced at lower cost with fewer firms. If that happened, the resources used to develop that excess capacity could be used for more desired purposes.

IN THE NEWS

COFFEE SHOPS SEEKING NEW IDENTITIES

ALBANY—It's easy to get a good cup of coffee on Wolf Road. And it's getting easier.

With over 35,000 specialty coffee shops in the United States, it isn't easy to brew a profit in the coffee business anymore. To buck that trend, coffee purveyors are trying to create new niches that are less competitive. In 2015 Starbucks debuted its "Starbucks Reserve Roastery and Tasting Room," located just nine blocks up the street from its very first Seattle shop. The Roastery specializes in single-source and often rare coffees, like Peru Chontali and Rwanda Maraba (for $4–$7 a cup). Consumers can observe the in-store roasting process while viewing images of the locations the beans came from. Stumptown and Microlots are pursuing the same niche, striving to preserve profits in a saturated coffee market.

Source: Media reports, 2015–2016.

ANALYSIS: Continued entry will push economic profits to zero and leave the industry with excess capacity.

marginal cost pricing: The offer (supply) of goods at prices equal to their marginal cost.

Flawed Price Signals. The misallocation of resources that occurs in monopolistic competition is a by-product of the flawed price signal that is transmitted in imperfectly competitive markets. Because the demand curve facing a firm in monopolistic competition slopes downward, such a firm will violate the principle of **marginal cost pricing.** Specifically, it will always price its output above the level of marginal costs, just like firms in an oligopoly or monopoly. Notice in Figures 12.1 and 12.3 that price lies above marginal cost in both the short- and long-run equilibrium. As a consequence, price always exceeds the opportunity cost. Consumers respond to these flawed signals by demanding fewer goods from monopolistically competitive industries than they would otherwise. We end up with the wrong (suboptimal) mix of output and misallocated resources.

Thus *monopolistic competition results in both production inefficiency (above minimum average cost) and allocative inefficiency (wrong mix of output).* This contrasts with the model of perfect competition, which delivers both minimum average total cost and efficient (MC-based) price signals.

THE ECONOMY TOMORROW

NO CEASE-FIRE IN ADVERTISING WARS

Models of oligopoly and monopolistic competition show how industry structure affects market behavior. Of particular interest is the way different kinds of firms "compete" for sales and profits. *In truly (perfectly) competitive industries, firms compete on the basis of price.* Competitive firms win by achieving greater efficiency and offering their products at the lowest possible price.

Firms in imperfectly competitive markets don't "compete" in the same way. In oligopolies, the kink commonly found in the demand curve facing each firm inhibits price reductions. In monopolistic competition, there's also a reluctance to engage in price competition. Because each firm has its own captive market—consumers who prefer its particular brand over competing brands—price reductions by one firm won't induce many consumers to switch brands. As we noted earlier, the cross-price elasticity of demand is low in monopolistically competitive markets. Thus price reductions aren't a very effective way to increase sales or market share in monopolistic competition.

If imperfectly competitive firms don't compete on the basis of price, do they really compete at all? The answer is evident to anyone who listens to the radio, watches television, reads magazines or newspapers, clicks on the Internet, or drives on the highway. *Imperfectly competitive firms engage in nonprice competition.*

The most prominent form of *nonprice competition* is advertising. An imperfectly competitive firm typically uses advertising to enhance its own product's image, thereby increasing the size of its captive market (consumers who identify with a particular brand). The Coca-Cola Company hires rock stars to create the image that Coke is superior to other soft drinks (see In the News "The Cola Wars: It's Not All Taste"), thereby creating brand loyalty. In 2015, oligopolies and monopolistically competitive firms spent more than $200 *billion* on advertising for such purposes. Procter & Gamble alone spent $4.3 billion (see Table 12.2). P&G hopes that these expenditures shift the demand for its products (e.g., Ivory Soap, Pampers, Jif peanut butter, Crest, Tide) to the right, while perhaps making it less price-elastic as well. By contrast, perfectly competitive firms have no incentive to advertise because they can individually sell their entire output at the current market price.

A company that runs a successful advertising campaign can create enormous *goodwill* value. That value is reflected in stronger brand loyalty—as expressed in greater demand and smaller price elasticity. Often a successful brand image can be used to sell related products as well. According to World View "The Best Global Brands," the most valuable brand name in the world is Apple, whose worldwide name recognition is worth $154 *billion.*

IN THE NEWS

THE COLA WARS: IT'S NOT ALL TASTE

American consumers gulp nearly 40 million soft drinks per day. The Coca-Cola Company produces about 40 percent of those soft drinks, while Pepsi-Cola produces about 30 percent of the market supply. With nearly 70 percent of the market between them, Pepsi and Coke wage fierce battles for market share.

The major weapon in these "cola wars" is advertising. Coke spends $3.5 billion a year to convince consumers that its products are superior. Pepsi spends about $2.5 billion to win the hearts and taste buds of American consumers. The advertisements not only tout the superior taste of their respective products but also try to create a distinctive image for each cola.

The advertising apparently works. Half of all soft drink consumers profess loyalty to either Coke or Pepsi. Few of these loyalists can be persuaded to switch cola brands, even when offered lower prices for the "other" cola.

Ironically, few people can identify their favorite cola in blind taste tests. Seventy percent of the people who swore loyalty to either Coke or Pepsi picked the wrong cola in a taste test.

The moral of the story? That in imperfectly competitive markets, product *image* and *perceptions* may be as important as product quality and price in winning market shares.

ANALYSIS: Advertising is intended to create brand loyalty. Loyal consumers are likely to buy the same brand all the time, even if competitors offer nearly identical products.

From society's perspective, the resources used in advertising and other forms of non-price competition could be used instead to produce larger quantities of desired goods and services. Unless consumers are given the chance to *choose* between "more" service and lower prices, there's a presumption that nonprice competition leads to an undesirable use of our scarce resources. For example, marketing costs absorb more than a third of the price of breakfast cereal. As a result of such behavior, consumers end up with more advertising but less cereal than they would otherwise. They could, of course, save money by buying store brand or generic cereals. But they've never seen athletes or cartoon characters endorse such products. So consumers pay the higher price for branded cereals.

Models of imperfect competition imply that advertising wars between powerful corporations won't end anytime soon. As long as markets have the *structure* of oligopoly or monopolistic competition, we expect the *behavior* of nonprice competition. Advertising jingles will be as pervasive in the economy tomorrow as they are today.

Company	Ad Spending in 2015 ($ billions)
Proctor & Gamble	$4.3 billion
AT&T	3.9
General Motors	3.5
Comcast	3.4
Verizon	2.7
Ford	2.7
American Express	2.3
Fiat Chrysler	2.2
Amazon	2.2
Samsung	2.1

Source: Kantar Media

TABLE 12.2

Top 10 Advertisers

Firms with market power attempt to preserve and extend that power through advertising. A successful advertising campaign alters the demand curve facing the firm, thus increasing potential profits. Shown here are the advertising outlays of the biggest advertisers in 2015.

THE BEST GLOBAL BRANDS

For companies in almost every industry, brands are important in a way they never were before. Why? For one thing, customers for everything from soda pop to software now have a staggering number of choices. And the net can bring the full array to any computer screen with a click of the mouse. Without trusted brand names as touchstones, shopping for almost anything would be overwhelming. Meanwhile, in a global economy, corporations must reach customers in markets far from their home base. A strong brand acts as an ambassador when companies enter new markets or offer new products.

That's why companies that once measured their worth strictly in terms of tangibles such as factories, inventory, and cash have realized that a vibrant brand, with its implicit promise of quality, is an equally important asset. A brand has the power to command a premium price, increasing profits and sheltering a company from competition.

The World's 10 Most Valuable Brands

Rank	Brand	2016 Brand Value ($ billions)
1	Apple	154
2	Google	83
3	Microsoft	75
4	Coca-Cola	59
5	Facebook	53
6	Toyota	42
7	IBM	41
8	Disney	40
9	McDonald's	39
10	General Electric	38

Source: Forbes, May 2016.

ANALYSIS: Brand names are valuable economic assets and assist a firm in maintaining a base of loyal customers. These brands have worldwide recognition as a result of heavy advertising.

SUMMARY

- There are many (rather than few) firms in monopolistic competition. The concentration ratio in such industries tends to be low (20–40 percent).   **LO12-1**
- Each monopolistically competitive firm enjoys some brand loyalty. This brand loyalty, together with its relatively small market share, gives each firm a high degree of independence in price and output decisions.   **LO12-1**
- Brand loyalty is reflected in the downward-sloping demand curve facing the firm. Profits are maximized at the rate of output where MR = MC.   **LO12-3**
- The amount of market share and power a monopolistically competitive firm possesses depends on how successfully it differentiates its product from similar products. Accordingly, monopolistically competitive firms tend to devote more resources to advertising.   **LO12-2**

- The market power bestowed by brand loyalty is measured by low cross-price elasticities of demand, high repurchase rates, and price premiums.   **LO12-1**
- Low entry barriers permit new firms to enter a monopolistically competitive industry whenever economic profits exist. Such entry eliminates long-run economic profit and reduces (shifts leftward) the demand for the output of existing firms.   **LO12-4**
- Monopolistic competition results in resource misallocations (due to flawed price signals) and inefficiency (above-minimum-average cost).   **LO12-3**
- Monopolistic competition encourages nonprice competition instead of price competition. Because the resources used in nonprice competition (advertising, packaging, service, etc.) may have more desirable uses, these industry structures lead to resource misallocation.   **LO12-3**

Key Terms

monopolistic competition

concentration ratio

market power

barriers to entry

product differentiation

cross-price elasticity of demand

production decision

economic profit

marginal cost pricing

Questions for Discussion

1. What is the "pricing power" referred to in In the News "Starbucks Ups the Price of Iced Drinks"? **LO12-2**

2. Why do 4,000 new pizzerias open every year? Why do just as many close? **LO12-4**

3. Name three products each for which you have (*a*) high brand loyalty and (*b*) low brand loyalty. **LO12-2**

4. If one gas station reduces its prices, must other gas stations match the price reduction? Why or why not? **LO12-2**

5. In the News "The Cola Wars: It's Not All Taste" suggests that most consumers can't identify their favorite cola in blind taste tests. Why then do people stick with one brand? What accounts for brand loyalty in bottled water (In the News "Selling 'Pure Water': A $Billion Scam?")? **LO12-1**

6. Why would Starbucks invest $20 million in a new "Roastery" if the coffee-shop market is already saturated (In the News "Coffee Shops Seeking New Identities")? **LO12-4**

7. What happens to the demand curve facing a Starbucks shop when a Dunkin' Donuts store opens next to it? What can Starbucks do to maintain its business? **LO12-4**

8. How would our consumption of cereal change if cereal manufacturers stopped advertising? Would we be better or worse off? **LO12-3**

9. Why are people willing to pay more for Dreyer's ice cream when it has a Starbucks brand on it? **LO12-2**

10. According to World View "The Best Global Brands," what gives brand names their value? **LO12-2**

PROBLEMS FOR CHAPTER 12

LO12-1 1. What is the concentration ratio in an industry with the following market shares?

Firm A	13.2	Firm C	4.2	Firm E	2.7	Firm G	1.6
Firm B	11.4	Firm D	3.6	Firm F	2.2	Other firms	61.1

LO12-2 2. According to In the News "Starbucks Ups the Price of Iced Drinks,"
   (*a*) By what percent did Starbucks increase the price of a venti frappuccino?
   (*b*) If the price elasticity for frappuccinos is 0.2, by how much would unit sales drop?
   (*c*) After the price increase, would total revenue increase or decrease?

LO12-2 3. If Starbucks raises its price by 5 percent and McDonald's experiences a 0.4 percent increase in demand for its coffee, what is the cross-price elasticity of demand?

LO12-3 4. In Figure 12.3, at what output rate is economic profit equal to zero?

   5. (*a*) Use the accompanying graph to illustrate the short-run equilibrium of a monopolistically competitive firm.
   (*b*) At that equilibrium, what is
     (*i*) Price?   (*ii*) Output?   (*iii*) Total profit?
   (*c*) Identify the long-run equilibrium of the same firm.
   (*d*) In long-run equilibrium, what is (approximately)
     (*i*) Price?   (*ii*) Output?   (*iii*) Total profit?

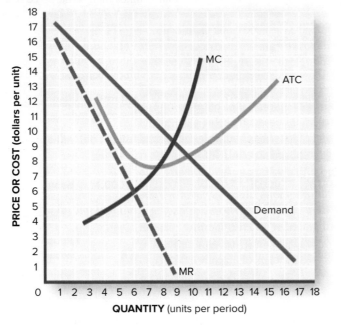

LO12-4 6. (*a*) In the *short*-run equilibrium of the previous problem, what is
     (*i*) The price of the product?
     (*ii*) The opportunity cost of producing the last unit?
   (*b*) In the *long*-run equilibrium of the previous problem, what is
     (*i*) The price of the product?
     (*ii*) The opportunity cost of producing the last unit?

LO12-4 7. On the accompanying graph, identify each of the following *market* outcomes:
  (*a*) Short-run equilibrium output in competition.
  (*b*) Long-run equilibrium output in competition.
  (*c*) Long-run equilibrium output in monopoly.
  (*d*) Long-run equilibrium output in monopolistic competition.

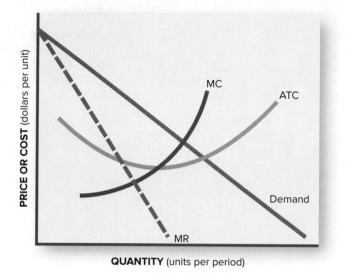

LO12-2 8. The Economy Tomorrow: On the following graph, show the effect of a successful advertising campaign on the firm's cost, demand, and marginal revenue curves.

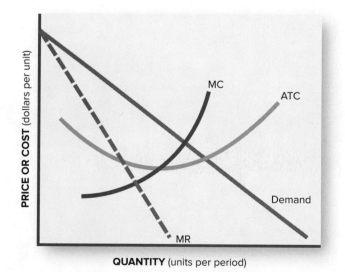

©MOF/Getty Images RF

REGULATORY ISSUES

Microeconomic theory provides insights into how prices and product flows are determined in unregulated markets. Sometimes those market outcomes are not optimal, and the government intervenes to improve them. In this section we examine government regulation of natural monopolies (Chapter 13), environmental protection (Chapter 14), and farm output and prices (Chapter 15). The goal is to determine whether and how government regulation might improve market outcomes—or possibly worsen them.

©Kevin Phillips/Stockbyte/Getty Images RF

©Alex Wong/Getty Images

©Fuse/Corbis via Getty Images RF

©Kevin Phillips/Stockbyte/Getty Images RF

Natural Monopolies: (De)Regulation?

LEARNING OBJECTIVES

After reading this chapter, you should know

LO13-1 The characteristics of natural monopoly.

LO13-2 The regulatory dilemmas posed by natural monopoly.

LO13-3 The costs associated with regulation.

LO13-4 How deregulation has fared in specific industries.

laissez faire: The doctrine of "leave it alone," of nonintervention by government in the market mechanism.

The lights went out in California in 2001—not just once but repeatedly. Offices went dark, air conditioners shut down, assembly lines stopped, and TV screens went blank. The state governor blamed power company "profiteers" for the rolling blackouts. He charged the companies with curtailing power supplies and hiking prices. He wanted *more* regulation of the power industry. Industry representatives responded that government regulation was itself responsible for throwing California into a new Dark Age. *Less* regulation, not more, would have kept the lights on, they claimed.

The battle over government regulation of the power industry quickly spread to other states. Some states that were deregulating power companies suspended the process. Other states also put (de)regulation plans on hold until they could better assess what went wrong in California. President Trump intensified the debate, asserting that excessive regulation had curbed America's energy production and eliminated thousands of jobs. He proposed a massive rollback of federal regulation.

Everyone agrees that markets sometimes fail—that unregulated markets may produce the wrong mix of output, undesirable methods of production, or an unfair distribution of income. But government intervention can fail as well. Hence we need to ask,

- **When is government regulation necessary?**
- **What form should that regulation take?**
- **When is it appropriate to deregulate an industry?**

In answering these questions we draw on economic principles as well as recent experience. This will permit us to contrast the theory of (de) regulation with reality.

ANTITRUST VS. REGULATION

A perfectly competitive market provides a model for economic efficiency. As we first observed in Chapter 3, the market mechanism can answer the basic economic questions of WHAT to produce, HOW to produce it, and FOR WHOM. Under ideal conditions, the market's answers may also be optimal—that is, the best possible outcomes. To achieve this **laissez-faire** ideal, all producers must be perfect competitors; people must have full information about tastes, costs, and prices; all costs and benefits must be reflected in market prices; and pervasive economies of scale must be absent.

In reality, these conditions are rarely, if ever, fully attained. Markets may be dominated by large and powerful producers. In wielding their power, these producers may restrict output, raise prices, stifle competition, and inhibit innovation. In other words, market power may cause **market failure,** leaving us with suboptimal market outcomes.

Behavioral Focus

As we observed in Chapter 11, the government has two options for intervention where market power prevails. It may focus on the *structure* of an industry or on its *behavior.* **Antitrust** laws cover both options: they prohibit mergers and acquisitions that reduce potential competition (structures) and forbid market practices (behavior) that are anticompetitive.

Government **regulation** has a different focus. Instead of worrying about industry structure, regulation focuses almost exclusively on *behavior.* In general, regulation seeks to change market outcomes directly by imposing specific limitations on the price, output, or investment decisions of private firms.

NATURAL MONOPOLY

Regulation is almost always the policy choice when dealing with natural monopolies. A **natural monopoly** exists when a single firm has such pervasive economies of scale that it will "naturally" dominate its industry. In natural monopoly, bigger *is* always better—at least in terms of production costs. The larger the firm, the lower its costs. Because of these scale economies, a natural monopoly can produce the products consumers want at the lowest possible price. A single cable company is more efficient than a horde of cable firms developing a maze of cable networks. The same is true of local telephone service and many utilities. In all of these cases, a single company can deliver products at lower cost than a bunch of smaller firms. Dismantling such a natural monopoly would destroy that cost advantage. A natural monopoly is therefore a potentially desirable market *structure.*

But what about behavior? Do we need to regulate natural monopolies? Even though a natural monopoly might enjoy economies of scale, it might not pass those savings along to consumers. In that case, the economies of scale don't do consumers any good, and the government might have to regulate the firm's behavior.

To determine whether regulation is desirable, we first have to determine how an *unregulated* natural monopoly will behave.

Declining ATC Curve

Figure 13.1 illustrates the unique characteristics of a natural monopoly. *The distinctive characteristic of a natural monopoly is its downward-sloping average total cost (ATC)*

market failure: An imperfection in the market mechanism that prevents optimal outcomes.

antitrust: Government intervention to alter market structure or prevent abuse of market power.

regulation: Government intervention to alter the behavior of firms—for example, in pricing, output, or advertising.

natural monopoly: An industry in which one firm can achieve economies of scale over the entire range of market supply.

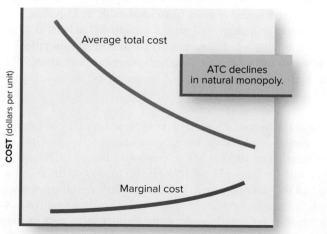

FIGURE 13.1

Declining ATC

A combination of high fixed costs and very low marginal costs generates a unique, downward-sloping ATC curve in natural monopoly. MC lies below ATC at all output levels.

curve. Because unit costs keep falling as the rate of production increases, a single large firm can underprice any smaller firm. Ultimately, it can produce all the market supply at the lowest attainable cost. In an unregulated market, such a firm will "naturally" come to dominate the industry.

High Fixed Costs. Natural monopolies typically emerge in situations where the fixed costs of production are extremely large. To supply electricity, for example, you first need to build a power source (e.g., a coal-fired plant, hydroelectric dam, or nuclear generator), then a distribution network. It's the same thing with subways and railroads: a lot of infrastructure must be constructed before anyone gets a ride. As a consequence of these high fixed costs, the *average* total cost curve starts out very high (recall that ATC = AFC + AVC).

Low Marginal Costs. Once productive capacity is built, the focus turns to *marginal costs.* In natural monopolies, marginal costs are typically low—*very low.* Supplying another kilowatt of electricity entails negligible marginal cost. Carrying one more passenger on a railroad or subway entails similarly negligible costs.

Even if marginal costs rise as production increases (the law of diminishing returns), marginal cost remains less than average total cost over the entire range of output. Notice in Figure 13.1 that *the marginal cost (MC) curve lies below the ATC curve at all rates of output for a natural monopoly.* The ATC curve never rises into its conventional U shape because marginal costs never exceed average costs. Hence there is no force to pull average total costs up, as in conventional cost structures.

The combination of high fixed costs and low (negligible) marginal costs gives the ATC curve a unique shape. The ATC curve starts out high (due to high AFC) and keeps declining as output increases (because MC < ATC at all times). *The downward-sloping ATC curve is the hallmark of a natural monopoly.*

The declining costs of a natural monopoly are of potential benefit to society. The **economies of scale** offered by a natural monopoly imply that no other market structure can supply the good as cheaply. Hence *natural monopoly is a desirable market structure.* A competitive market structure—with many smaller firms—would have higher average costs.

economies of scale: Reductions in minimum average costs that come about through increases in the size (scale) of plant and equipment.

Unregulated Behavior

Although the **structure** *of a natural monopoly may be beneficial, its* **behavior** *may leave something to be desired.* Natural monopolists have the same profit-maximizing motivations as other producers. Moreover, they have the monopoly power to achieve and maintain economic profits. Hence there's no guarantee that consumers will reap the cost-saving benefits of a natural monopoly. Critics charge that natural monopolies don't pass the cost savings along to consumers, instead keeping most of the benefits for themselves. This has been a recurrent criticism of cable TV operators: consumers have complained about high prices, poor service, and a lack of programming choices from local cable monopolies.

Figure 13.2 illustrates how we expect an unregulated natural monopolist to behave. Like all other producers, the natural monopolist will follow the **profit-maximization rule.** by producing at that rate of output where marginal revenue equals marginal cost. Point *A* in Figure 13.2 indicates that an unregulated monopoly will end up producing the quantity q_A and charging the price p_A.

profit-maximization rule: Produce at that rate of output where marginal revenue equals marginal cost.

marginal cost pricing: The offer (supply) of goods at prices equal to their marginal cost.

opportunity cost: The most desired goods or services that are forgone in order to obtain something else.

Wrong WHAT Outcome. The natural monopolist's preferred outcome isn't the most desirable one for society. This price–output combination violates the competitive principle of **marginal cost pricing.** The intersection of MC and MR at point *A* in Figure 13.2 dictates the output level q_A. At what price will that output be sold? We go up from q_A to the demand curve to find out. There we see that the monopolist will sell the quantity q_A at the price p_A. Hence, price (p_A) greatly exceeds the marginal cost of production (MC_A). As a result of this gap, consumers aren't getting accurate information about the **opportunity cost** of this product. This flawed price signal is the cause of market failure. We end up consuming less

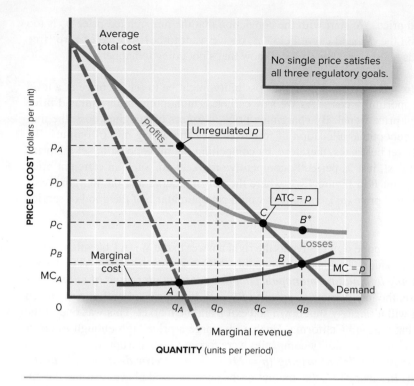

FIGURE 13.2
Natural Monopoly: Price Regulation

If unregulated, a natural monopoly will produce q_A where MR = MC (point A). And it will charge the price p_A, as determined by the demand curve for that rate of output.

Regulation designed to achieve efficient prices will seek point B, where p = MC. Still lower average costs (production efficiency) are attainable at higher rates of output (capacity), however. On the other hand, a zero-profit, zero-subsidy outcome exists only at point C.

Which price–output combination should be sought?

of this product (and more of other goods) than we would if charged its true opportunity cost. A suboptimal mix of output results.

Wrong HOW Outcome. The natural monopolist's profit-maximizing output (q_A) also fails to minimize average total cost. In a competitive industry, ATC is driven down to its minimum by relentless competition. In this case, however, reductions in ATC cease when the monopolist achieves the profit-maximizing rate of output (q_A). Were output to increase further, average total costs would fall.

Wrong FOR WHOM Outcome. Finally, notice that the higher price (p_A) associated with the monopolist's preferred output (q_A) ensures a fat profit (= per-unit profit of $p_A - p_D$ multiplied by the quantity q_A). This **economic profit** may violate our visions of equity. In 2001 millions of Californians were convinced that this kind of "profiteering" was the root of their electricity woes.

economic profit: The difference between total revenues and total economic costs.

REGULATORY OPTIONS

The suboptimal outcomes likely to emerge from a free-swinging natural monopoly prompt consumers to demand government intervention. The market alone can't overcome the natural advantage of pervasive economies of scale. (New, smaller firms would have higher average total costs and be unable to compete.) But the government could compel different outcomes. Which outcomes do we want? And how will we get them?

Price Regulation

For starters, we might consider price regulation. The natural monopolist's preferred price (p_A) is, after all, a basic cause of market failure. By regulating the firm, the government can compel a lower price. The California legislature did this in 1996 when it set a *maximum* retail price for electricity.

Setting a maximum price for the natural monopoly sounds like a simple solution. But what price should be set? As is apparent from Figure 13.2, there are lots of choices in setting a regulated price. We start with the conviction that the unregulated price p_A is too high. But where on the demand curve below p_A do we want to be? A price of zero (free electricity!) sounds really appealing, but we know that's not going to happen.

Price Efficiency ($p = MC$). A more realistic possibility might be to set the price at a level consistent with opportunity costs. As we saw earlier, a monopolist's unregulated price sends out a flawed price signal. By charging a price in excess of marginal cost, the monopolist causes a suboptimal allocation of resources (i.e., the wrong mix of output). We could improve market outcomes, therefore, by compelling the monopolist to set the price equal to marginal cost, just as perfectly competitive markets do. Such an efficient price would lead us to point B in Figure 13.2, where the demand curve and the marginal cost curve intersect. At that price (p_B), consumers would get optimal use of the good or service produced.

Subsidy. Although the price p_B will give us the right answer to the WHAT question, it will also bankrupt the producer. In a natural monopoly, MC is always less than ATC. Hence *marginal cost pricing by a natural monopolist implies a loss on every unit of output produced.* In this case, the loss per unit is equal to $B^* - B$. If confronted with the regulated price p_B, the firm will ultimately shut down and exit from the market. This was one of the many problems that plagued California. Unable to charge a price high enough to cover their costs, some of the state's utility companies were forced into bankruptcy.

If we want to require efficient pricing ($p = MC$), we must provide a subsidy to the natural monopoly. In Figure 13.2 the amount of the subsidy would have to equal the anticipated loss at q_B—that is, the quantity q_B multiplied by the per-unit loss ($B^* - B$). Such subsidies are provided to subway systems. With subsidies, local subway systems can charge fees below *average* cost and closer to *marginal* cost. These subsidized fares increase ridership, thus ensuring greater use of very expensive mass transportation systems.

Despite the advantages of this subsidized pricing strategy, taxpayers always complain about the cost of such subsidies. Taxpayers are particularly loath to provide subsidies for private companies. Hence political considerations typically preclude efficient (marginal cost) pricing, despite the economic benefits of this regulatory strategy.

Production Efficiency ($p = $ min ATC). Another option is to focus on efficient *production* rather than efficient *pricing*. Production efficiency is attained at the lowest possible average total cost. At q_B we're producing a lot of output but still have some unused capacity. Since ATC falls continuously, we could achieve still lower average costs if we increased output beyond q_B. *In a natural monopoly, production efficiency is achieved at capacity production, where ATC is at a minimum.*

Increasing output beyond q_B raises the same problems we encountered at that rate of output. At production rates in excess of q_B, ATC is always higher than price. Even MC is higher than price to the right of point B. Thus *no regulated price can induce a natural monopolist to achieve minimum average cost. A subsidy would be required to offset the market losses.*

Profit Regulation

Instead of focusing on price, why don't we focus on profits instead? Simply disallow monopoly profits like those of the unregulated monopoly (at q_A and p_A in Figure 13.2). We can achieve this result by mandating a price equal to average total cost. In Figure 13.2 this regulatory objective is achieved at point C. In this case, the rate of output is q_C and the regulated price is p_C.

Profit regulation looks appealing for two reasons. First, it eliminates the need to subsidize the monopolist. Second, it allows us to focus on profits only, thus removing the need to develop demand and cost curves. In theory, all we have to do is check the firm's annual profit-and-loss statement to confirm that it's earning a normal (average) profit. If its profits are too high, we can force the firm to reduce its price; if profits are too low, we may permit a price increase.

Bloated Costs. While beautiful in principle, profit regulation can turn ugly in practice. In particular, profit regulation can lead to bloated costs and dynamic inefficiency. *If a firm is permitted a specific profit rate (or rate of return), it has no incentive to limit costs.* On the contrary, higher costs imply higher profits. If permitted to charge 10 percent over unit costs, a monopolist may be better off with average costs of $6 rather than only $5. The higher costs translate into 60 cents of profit per unit rather than only 50 cents, even though the profit *rate* is the same. Hence there's an incentive to "pad costs." If those costs actually represent improvements in the firm's wages and salaries, executive bonuses, fringe benefits, or the work environment, then cost increases are doubly attractive to the firm and its employees. Cost efficiency is as welcome as the plague under such circumstances.

Profit regulation can also motivate a firm to inflate its costs by paying above-market prices for products purchased from an unregulated subsidiary. This was the strategy AT&T used to increase its *regulated* cost base while ringing up high profits at Western Electric, its *unregulated* subsidiary (see Chapter 10). The FCC accused Nynex (the "Baby Bell" that provided phone service in New York and New England in the 1980s) of using the same strategy to pad its profits. Nynex used its *un*regulated subsidiary (Material Enterprises Co.) to sell equipment at inflated prices to its *regulated* phone company subsidiaries (New England Telephone & Telegraph and New York Telephone). Profits in all three companies increased.

Output Regulation

Given the difficulties in regulating prices and profits, regulators may choose to regulate output instead. The natural monopolist's preferred output rate is q_A, as illustrated again in Figure 13.3. We could compel this monopolist to provide a minimum level of service in excess of q_A. This regulated minimum is designated q_D in Figure 13.3. At q_D consumers get the benefit not only of more output but also of a lower price (p_D). At q_D total monopoly profit must also be less than at q_A because q_A was the profit-maximizing rate of output.

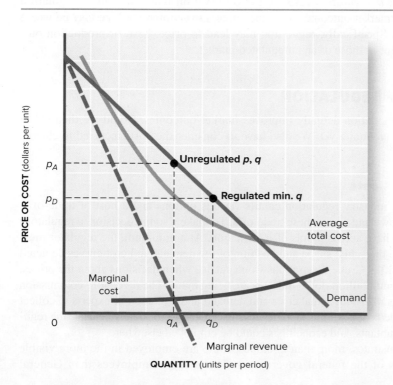

FIGURE 13.3

Minimum Service Regulation

Regulation may seek to ensure some minimal level of service. In this case, the required rate of output is arbitrarily set at q_D. Consumers are willing to pay p_D per unit for that output.

Regulated output q_D is preferable to the unregulated outcome (q_A, p_A) but may induce a decline in quality. Cost cutting is the only way to increase profits when the rate of output is fixed and price is on the demand curve.

It appears, then, that compelling any rate of output in excess of q_A can only benefit consumers. Moreover, output regulation is an easy rule to enforce.

Quality Deterioration. Unfortunately, minimum-service regulation can also cause problems. If forced to produce at the rate of q_D, the monopolist may seek to increase profits by cutting cost corners. This can be accomplished by deferring plant and equipment maintenance, reducing quality control, or otherwise lowering the quality of service. *Regulation of the quantity produced may induce a decline in quality.* Since a monopolist has no direct competition, consumers pretty much have to accept whatever quality the monopolist offers. This structural reality may explain why consumers complain so much about the services of local cable monopolies.

In addition to encouraging quality deterioration, output regulation at q_D also violates the principle of marginal cost pricing. Because an economic profit exists at q_D, equity goals may be jeopardized as well. Hence minimum service (output) regulation isn't a panacea for the regulatory dilemma. In fact, there is no panacea. *Goal conflicts are inescapable, and any regulatory rule may induce undesired producer responses.*

Imperfect Answers

The call for public regulation of natural monopolies is based on the recognition that the profit motive doesn't generate optimal outcomes in any monopoly environment. If unregulated, a natural monopolist will charge too much and produce too little. The regulatory remedy for these market failures isn't evident, however. Regulators can compel efficient prices or least-cost production only by offering a subsidy. Profit regulation is likely to induce cost-inflating responses. Output regulation is an incentive for quality deterioration. No matter which way we turn, regulatory problems result.

There's not much hope for transforming unregulated market failure into perfect regulated outcomes. In reality, regulators must choose a strategy that balances competing objectives (e.g., price efficiency and equity). A realistic goal for regulation is to *improve* market outcomes, not to *perfect* them. In the real world, *the choice isn't between imperfect markets and flawless government intervention but rather between imperfect markets and imperfect intervention.*

The argument for *deregulation* rests on the observation that government regulation sometimes worsens market outcomes. In some cases, **government failure** may be worse than market failure. Specifically, regulation may lead to price, cost, or production outcomes that are inferior to those of an unregulated market.

government failure:
Government intervention that fails to improve economic outcomes.

THE COSTS OF REGULATION

Let's *assume* that regulation actually improves market outcomes. Could we then claim regulatory success? Not quite yet. We also have to consider the *costs* incurred to change market outcomes.

Administrative Costs

As we've observed, industry regulation entails various options and a host of trade-offs. Someone must sit down and assess these trade-offs. To make a sound decision, a regulatory administration must have access to lots of information. At a minimum, the regulator must have some clue as to the actual shape and position of the demand and cost curves depicted in Figures 13.2 and 13.3. Crude illustrations won't suffice when decisions about the prices, output, or costs of a multibillion-dollar industry are being made. The regulatory commission needs volumes of details about actual costs and demand and a platoon of experts to collect and analyze the needed data. All this labor represents a real cost to society because the regulatory lawyers, accountants, and economists could be employed elsewhere.

As Table 13.1 illustrates, more than 280,000 people are employed in the more visible regulatory agencies of the federal government. That's more employees than General

Agency	Number of Employees (2018)
SOCIAL REGULATION	
Consumer Safety and Health	43,371
• Food and Drug Administration (FDA)	
• Food Safety and Inspection Service, etc.	
Homeland Security	148,152
• Transportation Security Administration (TSA)	
• Customs and Border Security	
• Immigration and Customs, etc.	
Transportation	9,300
• Federal Aviation Administration (FAA)	
• Federal Motor Carriers Safety Administration	
• Federal Railroad Administration, etc.	
Workplace	10,231
• Occupational Safety and Health Administration (OSHA)	
• Mine Safety and Health Administration	
• Employment Standards Administration, etc.	
Environment	22,554
• Environmental Protection Agency (EPA)	
• Forest and Rangeland Research	
• Fish and Wildlife Service, etc.	
ECONOMIC REGULATION	
General Business	21,668
• Patent and Trademark Office	
• Securities and Exchange Commission (SEC)	
• Federal Trade Commission (FTC), etc.	
Finance and Banking	18,234
• Federal Reserve System	
• Federal Deposit Insurance Corporation (FDIC)	
• Comptroller of the Currency, etc.	
Industry-Specific Regulation	6,482
• Agricultural Marketing Service	
• Federal Communications Commission (FCC), etc.	
Total Regulatory Employment:	**279,992**

Source: Susan Dudley and Melinda Warren, Weidenbaum Center, Washington University, July, 2017.

TABLE 13.1

Employment in Federal Regulatory Agencies

The human and capital resources the bureaucracy employs represent a real opportunity cost. The 279,992 people employed in 63 federal agencies—and tens of thousands more employed in state and local bureaucracies—could be producing other goods and services. These and other costs must be compared to the benefits of regulation.

Motors employs to build cars. On top of that, thousands more have regulatory responsibilities in smaller federal agencies and executive departments. Tens of thousands more people are employed by state and local regulatory agencies. By using all these workers to regulate private industry, we are forgoing their use in the production of desired goods and services. This is a significant economic cost.

Compliance Costs

The administrative costs of regulation focus on resources used in the public sector. By its very nature, however, regulation also changes resource use in the private sector. Regulated industries must expend resources to educate themselves about the regulations, to change their production behavior, and often to file reports with the regulatory authorities. The human and capital resources used for these purposes represent the *compliance* cost of regulation.

New rules on trucking illustrate how regulation can increase production costs. In 2013 the U.S. Department of Transportation reduced the amount of driving time permitted for interstate truckers (see In the News "Sleep Rules Raise Trucking Costs"). This rule requires freight companies to use more trucks and more labor to transport goods, thereby raising economic costs. Although the resultant gain in safety is desired, the cost of achieving that gain is not inconsequential.

IN THE NEWS

SLEEP RULES RAISE TRUCKING COSTS

The Federal Motor Carrier Safety Administration (FMCSA) now monitors the sleep hours and practices of long-haul truck drivers. As of July 1, 2013, the FMCSA insists that drivers:

- Drive no more than 11 hours a day.
- Work no more than 14 hours a day.
- Work no more than 70 hours a week.
- Take a 30-minute break in their first 8 hours of driving.
- Rest for 34 consecutive hours after completing a 70-hour week, including at least two nights between the hours of 1 and 5 a.m.

According to FMCSA, the new sleep rules will reduce chronic fatigue and related crashes, saving 19 lives per year. But the trucking industry says the new rules are too costly and even dangerous. They force drivers to sleep when they're not tired and to drive when they are tired. They also force trucks onto the road at commute times. The $700 billion industry says shipping costs will rise 2 to 6 percent, upward of $2 billion.

Source: Federal Motor Carrier Safety Administration and news reports of July 2013.

ANALYSIS: Regulations designed to improve market outcomes typically impose higher costs. The challenge is to balance benefits and costs.

Efficiency Costs

Finally, we have to consider the potential costs of changes in output. Most regulation alters the mix of output, either directly or indirectly. Ideally, regulation will always improve the mix of output. But it's possible that bad decisions, incomplete information, or faulty implementation may actually *worsen* the mix of output. If this occurs, then the loss of utility associated with an inferior mix of output imposes a further cost on society, over and above administrative and compliance costs.

Dynamic Losses. Efficiency costs may increase significantly over time. Consumer tastes change, demand and marginal revenue curves shift, costs change, and new technologies emerge. Can regulatory commissions respond to these changes as fast as the market mechanism does? If not, even optimal regulations may soon become obsolete and counterproductive. Worse still, the regulatory process itself may impede new technology, new marketing approaches, or improved production processes. These losses may be the most important. As Robert Hahn of the American Enterprise Institute observed,

> [t]he measurable costs of regulation pale against the distortions that sap the economy's dynamism. The public never sees the factories that weren't built, the new products that didn't appear, or the entrepreneurial idea that drowned in a cumbersome regulatory process.[1]

These kinds of dynamic efficiency losses are a drag on economic growth, limiting outward shifts of the production possibilities curve while perpetuating an increasingly undesired mix of output.

[1]Source: Richman, Louis S. and John Labate, "Bringing Reason to Regulation," *Fortune,* October 19, p. 94, 1992.

Balancing Benefits and Costs

The economic costs of regulation are a reminder of the "no free lunch" maxim. Although regulatory intervention may improve market outcomes, that intervention isn't without cost. The real resources used in the regulatory process could be used for other purposes. Hence, even if we could achieve perfect outcomes with enough regulation, the cost of achieving perfection might outweigh the benefits. ***Regulatory intervention must balance the anticipated improvements in market outcomes against the economic cost of regulation.*** In principle, the marginal benefit of regulation must exceed its marginal cost. If this isn't the case, then additional regulation isn't desirable, even if it would improve short-run market outcomes.

....

DEREGULATION IN PRACTICE

The push to *de*regulate is prompted by two concerns. The first concern focuses on the dynamic inefficiencies that regulation imposes, stifling innovation and rendering regulated industries less productive than desired. The other push for deregulation comes from advancing technology, which often destroys the structural basis for natural monopoly. A brief review of the resulting deregulation illustrates the impact of these forces.

Railroads

The railroad industry was the federal government's first broad regulatory target. Railroads are an example of natural monopoly, with high fixed costs and negligible marginal costs. Furthermore, there were no airports or interstate highways to compete with the railroads in 1887, when Congress created the Interstate Commerce Commission (ICC). The ICC was established to limit monopolistic exploitation of this situation while assuring a fair profit to railroad owners. The ICC established rates and routes for the railroads while limiting both entry to and exit from the industry.

With the advent of buses, trucks, subways, airplanes, and pipelines as alternative modes of transportation, railroad regulation became increasingly obsolete. Regulated cargoes, routes, and prices prevented railroads from adapting their prices or services to meet changing consumer demands. With regulation-protected routes, they also had little incentive to invest in new technologies or equipment. As a result, railroad traffic and profits declined while other transportation industries flourished.

The Railroad Revitalization and Regulatory Reform Act of 1976 was a response to this crisis. Its major goal was to reduce the scope of government regulation. Reinforced by the Staggers Rail Act of 1980, railroads were granted much greater freedom to adapt their prices and service to market demands.

Railroad companies used that flexibility to increase their share of total freight traffic. Fresh fruits and vegetables, for example, were exempted from ICC rate regulation in 1979. Railroads responded by *reducing* their rates and improving service. In the first year of deregulated rates, fruits and vegetable shipments increased more than 30 percent, a dramatic reversal of earlier trends. Deregulation of coal traffic (in 1980) and piggyback (trucks on railroad flatcars) traffic (in 1982) prompted similar turnarounds. The railroads prospered by reconfiguring routes and services, cutting operating costs, and offering lower rates. Between 1986 and 1993, the average cost of moving freight by rail dropped by 69 percent.

Not all rates have fallen. Indeed, one worrisome effect of deregulation is the increased concentration in the rail industry. After a series of mergers and acquisitions, the top four railroads (Burlington-Northern, Union Pacific, CSX, and Norfolk-Southern) now move nearly 90 percent of all rail freight—an extremely high **concentration ratio.** Moreover, these same firms hold monopoly positions on specific routes. Shippers in these captive markets pay rates 20 to 30 percent higher than in nonmonopoly routes.

concentration ratio: The proportion of total industry output produced by the largest firms (usually the four largest).

Telephone Service

The telephone industry has long been the classic example of a natural monopoly. Although enormous fixed costs are necessary to establish a telephone network, the marginal cost of an additional telephone call approaches zero. Hence it made economic sense to have a single network of telephone lines and switches rather than a maze of competing ones. Recognizing these economies of scale, Congress permitted AT&T to maintain a monopoly on both long-distance and most local telephone service for decades. To ensure that consumers would benefit from this natural monopoly, the Federal Communications Commission (FCC) regulated phone services and prices.

Once again, technology outpaced regulation. Communications satellites made it much easier and less costly for new firms to provide long-distance telephone service for decades. Moreover, the rate structure that AT&T and the Federal Communications Commission had established made long-distance service highly profitable. Accordingly, start-up firms clamored to get into the industry, and consumers petitioned for lower rates.

Long Distance. In 1982 the courts put an end to AT&T's monopoly, transforming long-distance telecommunications into a more competitive industry with more firms and less regulation. Soon thereafter more than 800 firms entered the industry, and long-distance telephone rates have dropped sharply. The quality of service also improved with fiber optic cable, advanced switching systems, cell phones, and myriad new phone line services such as fax transmissions, remote access, Internet access, texting, mobile computing, gaming, and payments. All these changes contributed to a quadrupling of long-distance telephone use in the United States.

Local Service. The deregulation of long-distance services was so spectacularly successful that observers wondered whether *local* telephone service might be deregulated as well. As competition in *long-distance* services increased, the monopoly nature of *local* rates became painfully apparent: local rates kept increasing after 1983 while long-distance rates were tumbling.

The Baby Bells that held monopolies on local service defended their high rates based on the high costs of building and maintaining transmission networks. But new technologies permitted wireless companies to offer local service if they could gain access to the monopoly networks. Congress responded in 1996. The Telecommunications Act of 1996 required the Baby Bells to grant rivals access to their transmission networks. The Baby Bells kept rivals at bay, however, by charging excessive access fees, imposing overly complex access codes, requiring unnecessary capital equipment, and raising other entry barriers. The battle for local access continues.

Airlines

The Civil Aeronautics Board (CAB) was created in 1938 to regulate airline routes and fares. From its inception, the primary concern of the CAB was to ensure a viable system of air transportation for both large and small communities. Such a system would be ensured, the CAB believed, only if a fair level of profits was maintained by entry and price regulations. Thus the focus of the CAB was on *profit* regulation.

P = ATC. To ensure fair profits, the CAB set fares in accordance with airline costs. This required the CAB to undertake intensive cost studies, based on accounting data provided by the airlines. Once the average cost of service and capital equipment was established, the CAB then set an average price that would ensure a fair rate of return (profit) (much like point *C* in Figure 13.2).

The CAB also wanted to ensure air service to smaller, less-traveled communities. Short hauls entail higher average costs and therefore justify higher fares. To avoid high fares on such routes, the CAB permitted airlines to charge prices well in excess of average costs on longer routes as long as they maintained service on shorter, unprofitable routes. This **cross-subsidization** was similar to that of the telephone industry, in which long-distance profits helped keep local telephone charges low.

To maintain this price and profit structure, the CAB had to regulate routes and limit entry into the airline industry. Otherwise, established carriers would abandon short, unprofitable

cross-subsidization: Use of high prices and profits on one product to subsidize low prices on another product.

routes, and new carriers would offer service only on more profitable routes. Unregulated entry thus threatened both cross-subsidization and the CAB's vision of a fair profit.

No Entry. The CAB was extremely effective in restricting entry into the industry. Would-be entrants had to demonstrate to the CAB that their proposed service was required by "public convenience and necessity" and was superior to that of established carriers. Established carriers could oppose a new application by demonstrating sufficient service, offering to expand their service, or claiming superior service. In view of the fact that new applicants had no airline experience, established carriers easily won the argument. From 1938 until 1977, the CAB *never* awarded a major route to a new entrant.

No Price Competition. The CAB also eliminated price competition between established carriers. The CAB fixed airfares on all routes. Airlines could reduce fares no more than 5 percent and couldn't increase them more than 10 percent without CAB approval.

Bloated Costs. Ironically, the established airlines failed to reap much profit from these high fares. Unable to compete on the basis of price, the established carriers had to engage in nonprice competition. The most costly form of nonprice competition was frequency of service. Once the CAB authorized service between any two cities, a regulated carrier could provide as many flights as desired. This enticed the regulated carriers to purchase huge fleets of planes and provide frequent departures. In the process, load factors (the percentage of seats filled with passengers) fell and average costs rose.

The regulated carriers also pursued **product differentiation** by offering special meals, first-run movies, free drinks, better service, and wider seats. This nonprice competition further inflated average costs and reduced profits.

product differentiation: Features that make one product appear different from competing products in the same market.

New Entrants. The Airline Deregulation Act of 1978 changed the structure and behavior of the airline industry. Entry regulation was effectively abandoned. With the elimination of this **barrier to entry,** the number of carriers increased greatly. Between 1978 and 1985, the number of airline companies increased from 37 to 174! The new entrants intensified competition on nearly all routes. The share of domestic markets with four or more carriers grew from 13 percent in May 1978 to 73 percent in May 1981. All those new entrants pushed airfares down sharply.

The CAB's authority over airfares ended January 1, 1983. Since then, airlines have been able to adapt their fares to market supply and demand. The CAB itself was eliminated in 1984.

barriers to entry: Obstacles such as patents that make it difficult or impossible for would-be producers to enter a particular market.

Increasing Concentration. Although airline deregulation is hailed as one of the greatest policy achievements of the 1980s, airline industry structure and behavior remain imperfect. In the competitive fray spawned by deregulation, lots of new entrants and even some established airlines went broke. Unable to match lower fares and increased service, scores of airline companies exited the industry in the period 1985–1995. In the process, a handful of major carriers increased their market share. The combined market share of the four largest carriers (American, Delta, Southwest, United) increased from 35 percent in 1985 to 60 percent in 2014. In many cases, firms gained near-monopoly power in specific hub airports. Not surprisingly, a study by the U.S. Government Accountability Office found that ticket prices are 45 to 85 percent higher on monopolized routes than on routes where at least two airlines compete.

The concentration ratio in the airline industry spiked even higher in 2013 when American Airlines merged with U.S. Airways. The merged airline became the largest U.S. carrier, and the concentration ratio jumped to 80 percent. Although U.S. Attorney General Eric Holder warned that the American/U.S. Air merger "would result in consumers paying the price—in higher fares, higher fees, and fewer choices," the Justice Department approved the merger three months after suing to block it.

Entry Barriers. To exploit their hub dominance, major carriers must keep out rivals. One of the most effective entry barriers is their ownership of landing slots. Air traffic is limited by the number of these slots, or authorized landing permits. In 1998 United Airlines controlled 82 percent of the slots at Chicago's O'Hare; Delta controls 83 percent of the slots at New York's Kennedy Airport. Smaller airlines complain that they can't get access to these slots, even when the slots aren't being used.

The Justice Department forced American and U.S. Airways to give up 52 slots at Washington, DC's Reagan airport; 17 at La Guardia; and 2 each at five other airports as a condition for approving their merger. Justice said it would make those slots available to low-cost carriers in order to create more competitive pricing situations.

When entry barriers (including slot access) are lowered, new competitors emerge and push down airfares as one would expect in a **contestable market.** A 2013 MIT study estimated that the entry of JetBlue into a new air travel market caused one-way air fares to drop an average of $32. More details on this "JetBlue effect" are noted in In the News "The JetBlue Effect."

contestable market: An imperfectly competitive industry subject to potential entry if prices or profits increase.

IN THE NEWS

THE JETBLUE EFFECT

When this carrier comes to town, fares go down, traffic goes up, and the airline ends up with a big chunk of the business.

	Change in Daily Passengers	Change in Average Fare	JetBlue Local Traffic Share
New York to Miami/Fort Lauderdale	+14%	−17% to $121.50	23.1%
New York to Los Angeles Basin	+2%	−26% to $219.31	18%
New York to Buffalo	+94%	−40% to $86.09	61.2%

Figures as of second quarter, 2003.

Data: Back Aviation Solutions.

—Wendy Zellner

Zellner, Wendy, "Is JetBlue's Flight Plan Flawed?" *Businessweek,* February 16, 2004. Copyright ©2004. All rights reserved. Used with permission.

ANALYSIS: If entry barriers are low enough, new entrants will contest a market, keeping pressure on prices and service.

Cable TV

The cable TV industry offers examples of both deregulation and *re*regulation. Up until 1986, city and county governments had the authority to franchise (approve) local cable TV operators and regulate their rates. In almost all cases, local governments franchised only one operator, thus establishing local monopolies. The monopoly structure was justified by pervasive economies of scale and the desire to avoid the cost and disruption of laying multiple cable systems. The rationale behind local regulation of cable prices (rates) was to ensure that consumers shared in the cost advantages of natural monopoly.

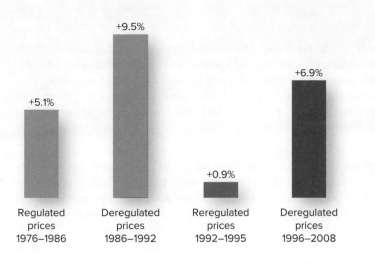

FIGURE 13.4
Annual Increase in Price of Basic Cable Service
After cable TV prices were deregulated in 1986, monthly charges moved up sharply. In 1992 Congress reregulated cable TV and prices stabilized. The Telecommunications Act of 1996 again deregulated prices and they surged, as shown in these annual averages.

Deregulation. By 1984 Congress was convinced that broadcast TV and emerging technologies (such as microwave transmissions and direct satellite broadcasts) offered sufficient competition to ensure consumers fair prices and quality service. The Cable Communications Policy Act of 1984 *de*regulated cable TV by stripping local governments of the authority to regulate prices. From 1986 to 1992, cable TV was essentially unregulated.

Soon after price regulation ended, cable companies began increasing their rates sharply. As Figure 13.4 shows, the rate of price acceleration nearly doubled after the cable industry was deregulated. Consumers also complained that local cable companies offered poor service. They demanded that Congress *re*regulate the industry.

Reregulation. In 1992 Congress responded with the Cable Television Consumer Protection and Competition Act. That act gave the Federal Communications Commission authority to reregulate cable TV rates. The FCC required cable operators to *reduce* prices by nearly 17 percent in 1993–1994. It then issued 450 pages of new rules that would limit future price increases. As Figure 13.4 illustrates, these interventions had a dramatic effect on cable prices.

While consumers applauded the new price rules, cable operators warned of unwelcome long-term effects. The rate cuts reduced cable industry revenues by nearly $4 billion between 1993 and 1995. The cable companies say they would have used that revenue to invest in improved networks and services. The cable companies also argued that increased competition from satellite transmissions and the Internet made government regulation of (wired) cable TV increasingly unnecessary.

Deregulation. Congress responded to these industry complaints by *de*regulating the cable industry again. The Telecommunications Act of 1996 mandated that rate regulation be phased out and ended completely by March 1999. Almost immediately, cable prices soared again, as Figure 13.4 shows.

Satellite Technology. The surge in cable TV prices was a boon to satellite TV providers. Satellite transmissions became a **substitute good** for cable TV—a substitute that also enjoyed pervasive economies of scale. So you suddenly had *competing* natural monopolies in a *contestable* market. Satellites won. In 1993, when cable prices were still relatively low, cable had 93 percent of the pay TV market. By 2011 the cable market share had declined to 65 percent. The high prices and profits of the cable industry ultimately spawned effective competition, first in satellite technology, then in broadband TV services (e.g., Netflix, Hulu, Blu-ray). Cable prices are still high and service below par, but at least the cable companies are now compelled by competition to improve the customer experience.

substitute goods: Goods that substitute for each other; when the price of good *x* rises, the demand for good *y* increases, *ceteris paribus*.

Electricity

The electric utility industry is the latest target for deregulation. Here again, the industry is a natural monopoly. The enormous fixed costs of a power plant and transmission network, combined with negligible marginal costs for delivering another kilowatt of electricity, give electric utilities a downward-sloping average total cost curve. The focus of government intervention was therefore on rate regulation (behavior) rather than promoting competition (structure).

Bloated Costs, High Prices. Critics of local utility monopolies complained that local rate regulation wasn't working well enough. To get higher (retail) prices, the utility companies allowed costs to rise. They also had no incentive to pursue new technologies that would reduce the costs of power generation or distribution. Big power users like steel companies complained that high electricity prices were crippling their competitive position. The only viable option for consumers was to move from a state with a high-cost power monopoly to a state with a low-cost power monopoly.

Demise of Power Plant Monopolies. Advances in transmission technology gave consumers a new choice. High-voltage transmission lines can carry power thousands of miles with negligible power loss. Utility companies used these lines to link their power grids, thereby creating backup power sources in the event of regional blackouts. In doing so, however, they created a new entry point for potential competition. Now a Kentucky power plant with surplus capacity can supply electricity to consumers in California. There's no longer any need to rely on a regional utility monopoly. At the wholesale level, utility companies have been trading electricity across state lines since 1992.

Local Distribution Monopolies. Although technology destroyed the basis for natural monopolies in power *production,* local monopolies in power *distribution* remain. Electricity reaches consumers through the wires attached to every house and business. As with TV cables, there is a natural monopoly in electricity distribution; competing wire grids would be costly and inefficient.

To deliver the benefits of competition in power *production,* rival producers must be able to access these local distribution grids. This is the same problem that has plagued competition in local telephone service. The local power companies that own the local distribution grids aren't anxious to open the wires to new competition. The central problem for electricity deregulation has been to assure wider access to local distribution grids.

California's Mistakes. The California legislature decided to resolve this problem by stripping local utility monopolies of their production capacity. By forcing utility companies to sell their power plants, California transformed its utilities into pure power *distributors.* This seemed to resolve the conflict between ownership and access to the distribution system. However, it also made California's utility companies totally dependent on third-party power producers, many of which were then out of state.

price ceiling: An upper limit imposed on the price of a good.

California also put a **price ceiling** on the *retail* price its utilities could charge. But the state had no power to control the *wholesale* price of electricity in interstate markets. When wholesale prices rose sharply in 2000, *California's utilities were trapped between rising costs and a fixed price ceiling.* Fearful of a political backlash, the governor refused to raise the retail price ceiling. As a result, some of the utility companies were forced into bankruptcy and power supplies were interrupted. The state itself entered the utility business by buying power plants and more out-of-state power supplies. In the end, Californians ended up with very expensive electricity. In Nevada, electricity prices remain high as well because the state won't allow casinos and other power users to bypass the monopoly distributor of electricity in that state unless they pay huge "exit fees" to compensate the monopoly (see In the News "Vegas Wants to Bypass Electric Monopoly").

IN THE NEWS

VEGAS WANTS TO BYPASS ELECTRIC MONOPOLY

MGM casinos in Las Vegas use more electricity to keep the neon lights bright than does the entire city of Key West, Florida. And they pay a premium price to do so. Nevada law requires residents and businesses in the state to buy their electricity from NV Energy, the monopoly power distributor in that state. Vegas casinos say they could score a jackpot by bypassing NV Energy and buying electricity directly from out-of-state power companies. With wholesale electricity priced at around 3.5 cents per kilowatt-hour and NV charging the casinos 8–9 cents per kilowatt-hour, that proposition appears to be a sure bet. In fact, MGM paid NV Energy a $86.9 million "exit fee" in 2016 for the right to stop buying electricity from that monopoly and instead buying power from a Texas power company. MGM is betting that the savings on its $600,000 per month electric bill will more than repay that fee.

Source: Media reports, October-November 2016.

ANALYSIS: A natural monopoly will want to maximize profits. If its behavior isn't regulated, consumers will end up paying the monopoly price.

THE ECONOMY TOMORROW

DEREGULATE EVERYTHING?

Deregulation of the railroad, telephone, airline, and electricity industries has yielded substantial benefits: more competition, lower prices, and improved services. Such experiences bolster the case for laissez faire. Nevertheless, we shouldn't jump to the conclusion that all regulation of business should be dismantled. All we know from experience is that the regulation of certain industries became outmoded. Changing consumer demands, new technologies, and substitute goods simply made existing regulations obsolete, even counterproductive. A combination of economic and political forces doomed them to extinction.

But were these regulations ever necessary? In the 1880s there were no viable alternatives to railroads for overland transportation. The forces of natural monopoly could easily have exploited consumers and retarded economic growth. The same was largely true for long-distance telephone service prior to the launching of communications satellites. Even the limitations on competition in trucking and banking made some sense in the depths of the Great Depression. One shouldn't conclude that regulatory intervention never made sense just because the regulations themselves later became obsolete.

Even today, most people recognize the need for regulation of many industries. The transmission networks for local telephone service and electricity delivery are still natural monopolies. The government can force owners to permit greater access. But an unregulated network owner could still extract monopoly profits through excessive prices. Hence even a deregulated industry may still require some regulation at critical entry or supply junctures. Existing regulations may not be optimal, but they probably generate better outcomes than totally unregulated monopolies.

Likewise, few people seriously propose relying on competition and the good judgment of consumers to determine the variety or quality of drugs on the market. Regulations imposed by the Food and Drug Administration restrain competition in the drug industry, raise production costs, and inhibit new technology. But they also make drugs safer. Here, as in other industries, there's a trade-off between the virtues of competition and those of regulation. ***The basic policy issue, as always, is whether the benefits of regulation exceed their administrative, compliance, and efficiency costs.*** The challenge for public policy in the economy tomorrow is to adapt regulations—or to discard them (i.e., deregulate)—as market conditions, consumer demands, or technology changes.

SUMMARY

- Antitrust and regulation are alternative options for dealing with market power. Antitrust focuses on market structure and anticompetitive practices. Regulation stipulates specific market behavior. **LO13-2**
- High fixed costs and negligible marginal costs create a downward-sloping ATC curve, the hallmark of natural monopoly. **LO13-1**
- Natural monopolies offer pervasive economies of scale. Because of this potential efficiency, a more competitive market *structure* may not be desirable. **LO13-2**
- Regulation of natural monopoly can focus on price, profit, or output *behavior*. Price regulation may require subsidies; profit regulation may induce cost escalation; and output regulation may lead to quality deterioration. These problems compel compromises and second-best solutions. **LO13-2**
- The demand for deregulation rests on the argument that the costs of regulation exceed the benefits. These costs include the opportunity costs associated with regulatory administration and compliance as well as the (dynamic) efficiency losses that result from inflexible pricing and production rules. **LO13-3**
- Deregulation of the railroad, telephone, and airline industries has been a success. In all these industries, regulation became outmoded by changing consumer demands, products, and technology. As regulation was relaxed, these industries became more competitive, output increased, and prices fell. **LO13-4**
- Recent experiences with deregulation don't imply that all regulation should end. Regulation is appropriate if market failure exists *and* if the benefits of regulation exceed the costs. As benefits and costs change, decisions about what and how to regulate must be reevaluated. **LO13-3**

Key Terms

laissez faire	profit-maximization rule	cross-subsidization
market failure	marginal cost pricing	product differentiation
antitrust	opportunity cost	barriers to entry
regulation	economic profit	contestable market
natural monopoly	government failure	substitute goods
economies of scale	concentration ratio	price ceiling

Questions for Discussion

1. Why are railroads natural monopolies? What limits their pricing power? **LO13-1**
2. New York City has limited the number of taxicabs for decades. Were taxi companies natural monopolies? What was the purpose of such regulation? Why were Uber, Lyft, and other ride-sharing companies so eager to enter the industry? **LO13-1**
3. What makes cable companies natural monopolies? How did cable profits affect the emergence of satellite transmissions? **LO13-1**
4. Given the inevitable limit on airplane landings, how should available airport slots be allocated? How would market outcomes be altered? **LO13-2**
5. Why would a profit-regulated firm want to sell itself inputs at inflated prices? Or increase wages? **LO13-3**
6. Prior to 1982, AT&T kept local phone rates low by subsidizing them from long-distance profits. Was such cross-subsidization in the public interest? Explain. **LO13-1**
7. How would you put dollar values on the benefits and costs of truck safety regulations (In the News "Sleep Rules Raise Trucking Costs")? Do benefits exceed costs? **LO13-2**
8. The Telecommunications Act of 1996 requires local phone companies to charge "reasonable" rates for transmission access. What is a "reasonable" rate? **LO13-4**
9. How could a local phone or cable company reduce service quality if forced to accept price ceilings? **LO13-2**
10. Why don't Nevada regulators allow casinos and other consumers to bypass the state's monopoly distributor of electricity? **LO13-2**

PROBLEMS FOR CHAPTER 13

LO13-1 1. Suppose a company has $400 of fixed costs and a constant marginal cost of 10 cents. What are average total costs (ATC) at
 (a) Output of 10 units?
 (b) Output of 100 units?
 (c) Output of 1,000 units?

LO13-2 2. In Figure 13.2,
 (a) How much profit does an unregulated monopolist earn?
 (b) How much profit would be earned if price efficiency ($p = MC$) were imposed?

LO13-2 3. Using the graph, identify output and price and calculate profits for
 (a) An unregulated natural monopoly.
 (b) A monopoly that is regulated according to price-efficiency ($p = MC$).
 (c) A monopoly that is required to provide a minimum service of 60.

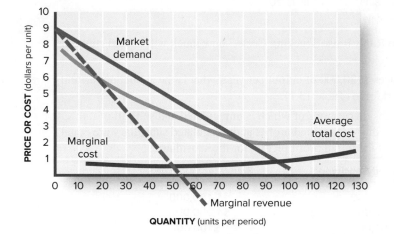

LO13-1 4. What happens to profits (or losses) when new technology reduces average total costs (shifts ATC downward in Figure 13.2) in
 (a) An unregulated natural monopoly?
 (b) A price-regulated natural monopoly without a subsidy?
 (c) A profit-regulated natural monopoly?

LO13-2 5. Suppose a natural monopolist has fixed costs of $15 and a constant marginal cost of $3. The demand for the product is as follows:

Price (per unit)	$10	$9	$8	$7	$6	$5	$4	$3	$2	$1
Quantity demanded (units per day)	0	2	4	6	8	10	12	14	16	18

Under these conditions,
 (a) What price and quantity will prevail if the monopolist isn't regulated?
 (b) What price–output combination would exist with efficient pricing ($p = MC$)?
 (c) What price–output combination would exist with profit regulation (zero economic profits)?

Illustrate your answers on the following graph:

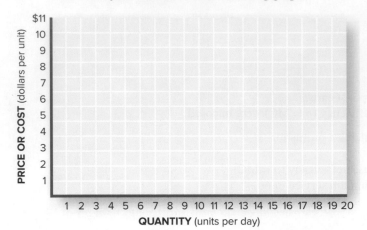

LO13-3 6. According to In the News "Sleep Rules Raise Trucking Costs," how much will annual shipping costs increase for each saved life?

LO13-3 7. If the average U.S. worker produces $120,000 of output per year, what is the annual opportunity cost of the federal regulatory workforce (Table 13.1)?

LO13-4 8. Suppose a corporation has two subsidiaries, one of which is unregulated and sells all of its output to the other, regulated subsidiary. Permitted profits at the regulated subsidiary are equal to 10 percent of total costs. Here is the initial profit picture for the subsidiaries:

	Unregulated Subsidiary	Regulated Subsidiary
Total revenue	$600,000	$1,100,000
Total costs	$400,000	$1,000,000
Total profit	$200,000	$100,000

If the unregulated subsidiary doubles its selling price and continues to sell the same quantity, what happens to profits at
(a) The unregulated subsidiary?   (b) The regulated subsidiary?

LO13-1 9. According to In the News "Vegas Wants to Bypass Electric Monopoly," if MGM's electric bill was $600,000 per month with NV Energy and its costs decrease by 60 percent in the wholesale market, how many years will it take to recoup its "exit fee"?

LO13-3 10. The Economy Tomorrow: Suppose the benefits of a regulation related to workplace safety is $10 million per year and the associated administrative costs are $200,000, compliance costs are $4 million, and efficiency costs are $5 million per year. Should deregulation occur?

©Alex Wong/Getty Images

Environmental Protection

Progress in environmental problems is impossible without a clear understanding of how the economic system works in the environment and what alternatives are available to take away the many roadblocks to environmental quality.

—**Council on Environmental Quality, First Annual Report**

What good is a clean river if you've got no jobs?

—**Steelworkers union official in Youngstown, Ohio**

Environmental protection, what they do is a disgrace; every week they come out with new regulations

—**Donald Trump, president of the United States**

A hole in the ozone layer is allowing increased ultraviolet radiation to reach the earth's surface. The hole is the result of excessive release of chlorine gases (chlorofluorocarbons, or CFCs) from air conditioners, plastic foam manufacture, industrial solvents, and aerosol spray cans such as deodorants and insecticides. The resulting damage to the stratosphere is causing skin cancer, cataracts, and immune system disorders.

Skin cancer may turn out to be one of our less serious problems. As carbon dioxide is building up in the atmosphere, it is creating a gaseous blanket around the earth that is trapping radiation and heating the atmosphere. Scientists predict that this greenhouse effect will melt the polar ice caps, raise sea levels, flood coastal areas, and turn rich croplands into deserts within 60 years.

Everyone wants a cleaner and safer environment. So why don't we stop polluting the environment with CFCs, carbon dioxide, toxic chemicals, and other waste?

Economics is part of the answer. To reduce pollution, we have to change our patterns of production and consumption. This entails economic costs, in terms of restricted consumption choices, more expensive ways of producing goods, higher prices, and jobs. Thus we have to weigh the benefits of a cleaner, safer environment against the costs of environmental protection.

Instinctively, most people don't like the idea of measuring the value of a cleaner environment in dollars and cents. But most people might also agree that spending $2 trillion to avoid a few cataracts is awfully expensive. There has to be *some* balance between the benefits of a cleaner environment and the cost of cleaning it up.

This chapter assesses our environmental problems from this economic perspective, considering three primary concerns:

- **How do (unregulated) markets encourage pollution?**
- **What are the costs of greater environmental protection?**
- **How can government policy best ensure an *optimal* environment?**

To answer these questions, we first survey the major types and sources of pollution. Then we examine the benefits and costs of environmental protection, highlighting the economic incentives that shape market behavior.

THE ENVIRONMENTAL THREAT

Water, air, and solid waste pollution, and the earth's rising temperature are at the top of the list of environmental concerns. The list is much longer, however, and very old as well. As early as A.D. 61, the statesman and philosopher Seneca was complaining about the smoky air emitted from household chimneys in Rome. Lead emissions from ancient Greek and Roman silver refineries poisoned the air in Europe and the remote Arctic. And historians are quick to remind us that open sewers running down the street were once the principal mode of urban waste disposal. Typhoid epidemics were a recurrent penalty for water pollution. So we can't say that environmental damage is a new phenomenon or that it's now worse than ever before.

But we do know more about the sources of environmental damage than our ancestors did, and we can better afford to do something about it. Our understanding of the economics of pollution has increased as well. We've come to recognize that pollution impairs health, reduces life expectancy, and thus reduces labor force activity and output. Pollution also destroys capital (such as the effects of air pollution on steel structures) and diverts resources to undesired activities (like car washes, laundry, and cleaning). Not least of all, pollution directly reduces our social welfare by denying us access to clean air, water, and beaches.

Air Pollution

Air pollution is as familiar as a smoggy horizon. But smog is only one form of air pollution.

Acid Rain. Sulfur dioxide (SO_2) is an acrid, corrosive, and poisonous gas that's created by burning high-sulfur fuels such as coal. As a contributor to acid rain, it destroys vegetation and forests. Electric utilities and industrial plants that burn high-sulfur coal or fuel oil are the prime sources of SO_2. Coal burning alone accounts for about 60 percent of all emissions of sulfur oxides. As World View "Polluted Cities" illustrates, SO_2 pollution is a serious problem not only in U.S. cities but all over the world: the air is much dirtier in Beijing, Calcutta, Tokyo, and Rome than in New York City—and virtually unbreathable in coal-mining areas like Guiyang, China.

Smog. Nitrogen oxides (NO_x), another ingredient in the formation of acid rain, are also a principal ingredient in the formation of smog. Smog not only irritates the eyes and spoils the view, but it also damages plants, trees, and human lungs. Automobile emissions account for 40 percent of urban smog. Bakeries, dry cleaners, and production of other consumer goods account for an equal amount of smog. The rest comes from electric power plants and industrial boilers.

The Greenhouse Effect. The prime villain in the greenhouse effect is the otherwise harmless carbon dioxide (CO_2) that we exhale. Unfortunately, we and nature now release so much CO_2 that the earth's oceans and vegetation can no longer absorb it all. The excess CO_2 is creating a gaseous blanket around the earth that may warm the earth to disastrous

WORLD VIEW

POLLUTED CITIES

The air in New York City may be unhealthful, but it's not nearly as polluted with sulfur dioxide (SO_2) as that in some other major cities.

©Steve Allen/Stockbyte/Getty Images RF

Source: The World Bank, *WDR2009 Data Set*.

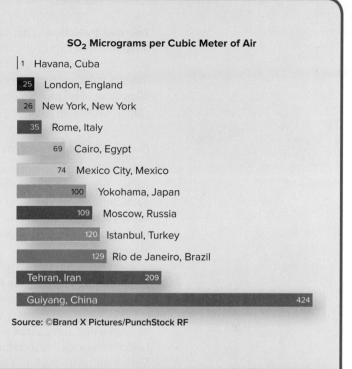

SO_2 Micrograms per Cubic Meter of Air

	City	Value
1	Havana, Cuba	
25	London, England	
26	New York, New York	
35	Rome, Italy	
69	Cairo, Egypt	
74	Mexico City, Mexico	
100	Yokohama, Japan	
109	Moscow, Russia	
120	Istanbul, Turkey	
129	Rio de Janeiro, Brazil	
	Tehran, Iran	209
	Guiyang, China	424

Source: ©Brand X Pictures/PunchStock RF

ANALYSIS: Pollution is a worldwide phenomenon with common origins and potential remedies.

levels. The burning of fossil fuels is a significant source of CO_2 buildup. The destruction of rain forests, which absorb CO_2, also contributes to the greenhouse effect.

Water Pollution

Water pollution is another environmental threat. Its effects are apparent in the contamination of drinking water, restrictions on swimming and boating, foul-smelling waterways, swarms of dead fish, and floating debris.

Organic Pollution. The most common form of water pollution occurs in the disposal of organic wastes from toilets and garbage disposals. The wastes that originate there are collected in sewer systems and ultimately discharged into the nearest waterway. The key question is whether the wastes are treated (separated and decomposed) before ultimate discharge. Sophisticated waste treatment plants can reduce organic pollution up to 99 percent. Unfortunately, only 70 percent of the U.S. population is served by a system of sewers and adequate (secondary) treatment plants. Inadequate treatment systems often result in the closure of waterways and beaches due to excessive levels of bacteria.

In addition to household wastes, our waterways must also contend with industrial wastes. More than half the volume of industrial discharge comes from just a few industries— principally paper, organic chemicals, petroleum, and steel. Finally, there are all those farm animals: the 7.5 billion chickens and 161 million cows and hogs raised each year generate 1.4 billion tons of manure (whew!). If improperly managed, that organic waste will contaminate water supplies and trigger algae blooms that can choke waterways and kill fish. Animal wastes don't cause too great a problem in Boston or New York

City, but they can wreak havoc on the water supplies of towns in California, Texas, Kansas, and Iowa.

Thermal Pollution. Thermal pollution is an increase in the temperature of waterways brought about by the discharge of steam or heated water. Heat discharges can kill fish, upset marine reproductive cycles, and accelerate biological and chemical processes in water, thereby reducing its ability to retain oxygen. Electric power plants account for more than 80 percent of all thermal discharges, with primary metal, chemical, and petroleum-refining plants accounting for nearly all the rest.

Solid Waste Pollution

Solid waste is yet another environmental threat. Solid waste pollution is apparent everywhere, from the garbage can to litter on the streets and beaches, to debris in the water, to open dumps. According to EPA estimates, we generate more than 5 billion tons of solid waste each year. This figure includes more than 30 billion bottles, 60 billion cans, 100 million tires, and millions of discarded automobiles and major appliances. Where do you think all this refuse goes?

Most solid wastes originate in agriculture (slaughter wastes, orchard prunings, harvest residues) and mining (slag heaps, mill tailings). The much smaller amount of solid waste originating in residential and commercial use is considered more dangerous, however, simply because it accumulates where people live. New York City alone generates 34,000 tons of trash a day, three times more than any other city in the world. Because it has neither the land area nor the incinerators needed for disposal, it must ship its garbage to other states. Seattle ships its trash to Oregon; Los Angeles transports its trash to the Mojave Desert; New York City sludge is dumped in west Texas; and Philadelphia ships its garbage all the way to Panama.

POLLUTION DAMAGES

Shipping garbage to Panama is an expensive answer to our waste disposal problem. But even those costs are a small fraction of the total cost of environmental damage. Much greater costs are associated with the damage to our health (labor), buildings (capital), and land. Even the little things count, like being able to enjoy a clear sunset, swim in the ocean, or just take a deep breath.

Although many people don't like to put a price on the environment, some monetary measure of environmental damage is important in decision making. Unless we value the environment above everything else, we have to establish some method of ranking the importance of environmental damage. Although it's tempting to say that clean air is priceless, *we won't get clean air, clean water, or clean beaches unless we spend resources to get them.* This economic reality suggests that we begin by determining how much cleaner air is worth to us.

Assigning Prices

In some cases, it's fairly easy to put a price on environmental damage. Scientists can measure the increase in cancer, heart attacks, and other disorders attributable to air pollution, as the EPA does for air toxins (see In the News "Air Pollution Kills"). Engineers can also measure the rate at which buildings decay or forests and lakes die. Economists can then estimate the dollar value of this damage by assessing the economic value of lives, forests, lakes, and other resources. For example, if people are willing to pay $5,000 for a cataract operation, then the avoidance of such eye damage is worth at least $5,000. Saving a tree is worth whatever the marketplace is willing to pay for the products of that tree. According to the EPA, a human life is worth $7.6 million. The EPA uses that benchmark to compute the damages due to premature deaths caused by pollution-related illnesses.

IN THE NEWS

AIR POLLUTION KILLS

Studies undertaken at Harvard's School of Public Health document how air pollution shortens life expectancies. The studies focused exclusively on airborne particulates that pollute the air—particulates that originate from vehicle traffic and smokestacks. Gaseous pollutants (sulfur and carbon dioxides, etc.) were not examined, although they, too, shorten life expectancies.

The studies' findings are dramatic: people who live in the most polluted cities (Los Angeles, Pittsburgh, St. Louis) are 15–17 percent more likely to die prematurely than those in cities with the cleanest air (Honolulu, Redding CA, Duluth MN). In the most polluted cities the decrease in life expectancy is equivalent to about one-sixth of the loss due to smoking for 25 years.

Source: National Institutes of Health.

ANALYSIS: Pollution entails real costs, as measured by impaired health, reduced life spans, and other damages.

The job of pricing environmental damage is much more difficult with intangible losses like sunsets. Nevertheless, when governmental agencies and courts are asked to assess the damages of oil spills and other accidents, they must try to inventory *all* costs, including polluted sunsets, reduced wildlife, and lost recreation opportunities. The science of computing such environmental damage is very inexact. Nevertheless, crude but reasonable procedures generate pollution-related damage estimates in the hundreds of billions of dollars per year.

Cleanup Possibilities

One of the most frustrating things about all this environmental damage is that it can be avoided. The EPA estimates that *95 percent of current air and water pollution could be eliminated by known and available technology.* Nothing very exotic is needed: just simple things like auto emission controls, smokestack cleaners, improved sewage and waste treatment facilities, and cooling towers for electric power plants. Even solid waste pollution could be reduced by comparable proportions if we used less packaging, recycled more materials, or transformed our garbage into a useful (relatively low-polluting) energy source. Why don't we do these things? Why do we continue to pollute so much?

MARKET INCENTIVES

Previous chapters emphasized how market incentives influence the behavior of individual consumers, firms, and government agencies. Incentives in the form of price reductions can be used to change consumer buying habits. Incentives in the form of high profit margins encourage production of desired goods and services. And market incentives in the form of cost differentials help allocate resources efficiently. Accordingly, we shouldn't be too surprised to learn that *market incentives play a major role in pollution behavior.*

The Production Decision

Imagine that you're the majority stockholder and manager of an electric power plant. Such plants are responsible for a significant amount of air pollution (especially sulfur dioxide and particulates) and nearly all thermal water pollution. Hence your position immediately puts you on the most-wanted list of pollution offenders. But suppose you're civic minded and would truly like to help eliminate pollution. Let's consider the alternatives.

production decision: The selection of the short-run rate of output (with existing plants and equipment).

Profit Maximization. As the owner–manager of an electric power plant, you'll strive to make a profit-maximizing **production decision.** That is, you'll seek the rate of output at which marginal revenue equals marginal cost. Let's assume that the electric power industry is still regulated by the state power commission so that the price of electricity is fixed, at least in the short run. The effect of this assumption is to render marginal revenue equal to price, thus giving us a horizontal price line, as in Figure 14.1*a*.

Figure 14.1*a* also depicts the marginal and average total costs (MC and ATC) associated with the production of electricity. By equating marginal cost (MC) to price (marginal revenue, MR), we observe (point *A*) that profit maximization occurs at an output of 1,000 kilowatt-hours per day. Total profits are illustrated by the shaded rectangle between the price line and the average total cost (ATC) curve.

The Efficiency Decision

The profits illustrated in Figure 14.1*a* are achieved in part by use of the cheapest available fuel under the boilers (which create the steam that rotates the generators). Recall that the construction of a marginal cost curve presumes some knowledge of alternative production processes. Recall too that the **efficiency decision** requires a producer to choose that production process (and its associated cost curve) that minimizes costs for any particular rate of output.

efficiency decision: The choice of a production process for any given rate of output.

Costs of Pollution Abatement. Unfortunately, the efficiency decision in this case leads to the use of high-sulfur coal, the prime villain in SO_2 and particulate pollution. Other fuels, such as low-sulfur coal, fuel oil, natural gas, and nuclear energy, cost considerably more. Were you to switch to one of them, the ATC and MC curves would both shift upward, as in Figure 14.1*b*. Under these conditions, the most profitable rate of output would be lower than before (point *B* on the graph), and total profits would decline (note the smaller profit rectangle in Figure 14.1*b*). Thus *pollution abatement can be achieved, but only at significant cost to the plant.*

The same kind of cost considerations lead the plant to engage in thermal pollution. Cool water must be run through an electric utility plant to keep the turbines from overheating. Once the water has run through the plant, it's too hot to recirculate. It must be either dumped back into the adjacent river or cooled off by being circulated through cooling

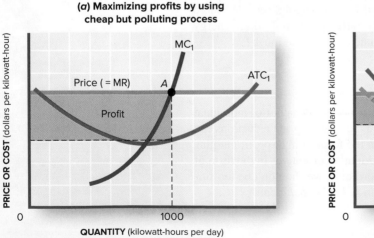

FIGURE 14.1

Profit Maximization in Electric Power Production

Production processes that control pollution may be more expensive than those that don't. If they are, the MC and ATC curves will shift upward (to MC₂ and ATC₂). At the new profit-maximizing rate of output (point *B*), output and total profit shrink. Hence a producer has an incentive to continue polluting, using cheaper technology.

towers. As you might expect, it's cheaper to simply dump the hot water in the river, as the Indian Point nuclear plant in New York does (see In the News "Cut the Power to Save the Fish?"). The fish don't like it, but they don't have to pay the construction costs associated with cooling towers.

IN THE NEWS

CUT THE POWER TO SAVE THE FISH?

Governor Andrew Cuomo has been trying to close the Indian Point nuclear plant since 2001. The governor and his environmentalist friends worry about the safety of nuclear plants and their impact on fish. The Indian Point plant sucks in 2.5 billion gallons of water out of the Hudson River every day to cool its generators. It also sucks up and kills millions of fish and larvae. More fish are killed when the heated water is returned to the river. The state's Department of Environmental Conservation (DEC) wants at least a temporary shutdown in the spawning and migration season (May 10—August 10). Better yet, they want Entergy Corp., the plant's owner, to reengineer a closed-circuit cooling system that will end the fish kills.

The DEC faces two problems. First, Entergy says it would be far too costly to reengineer the cooling system; no chance of that happening. Second, electricity consumers need the power Indian Point provides. The plant supplies 2,000 megawatts of electricity a day—about 25 percent of New York City's daily use. Although DEC promises to help find an alternative source of power, New Yorkers aren't willing to risk blackouts, brownouts, or higher electricity prices to save a few fish.

Source: News reports, April–June 2014.

ANALYSIS: When producers consider only *private* costs, they may select production processes that impose high *external* costs.

The big question here is whether you and your fellow stockholders would be willing to incur higher costs to cut down on pollution. Eliminating the water pollution emanating from the electric plant will cost a lot of money. And to whose benefit? To the people who live downstream? We don't expect profit-maximizing producers to take such concerns into account. ***The behavior of profit maximizers is guided by comparisons of revenues and costs, not by philanthropy, aesthetic concerns, or the welfare of fish.***

MARKET FAILURE: EXTERNAL COSTS

The moral of this story—and the critical factor in pollution behavior—is that ***people tend to maximize their personal welfare, balancing private benefits against private costs.*** For the electric power plant, this means making production decisions on the basis of revenues received and costs incurred. The fact that the power plant imposes costs on others, in the form of air and water pollution, is irrelevant to its profit-maximizing decisions. Those costs are *external* to the firm and don't appear on its profit-and-loss statement. Those **external costs**—or *externalities*—are no less real, but they're incurred by society at large rather than by the firm.

external costs: Costs of a market activity borne by a third party; the difference between the social and private costs of a market activity.

Externalities in Production

Whenever external costs exist, a private firm won't allocate its resources and operate its plant in such a way as to maximize social welfare. In effect, society permits the power plant the free use of valued resources—clean air and clean water. The power plant has a tremendous incentive to substitute those resources for others (such as high-priced fuel or cooling towers) in the production process. The inefficiency of such an arrangement is obvious when we recall that the function of markets is to allocate scarce resources in accordance with the consumer's expressed demands. Yet here we are, proclaiming a high value for clean air and clean water and encouraging the power plant to use up both resources by offering them at zero cost to the firm.

The inefficiency of this market arrangement can be expressed in terms of a distinction between social costs and private costs. **Social costs** are the total costs of all the resources used in a particular production activity. On the other hand, **private costs** are the resource costs incurred by the specific producer.

Ideally, a producer's private costs will encompass all the attendant social costs, and production decisions will be consistent with our social welfare. Unfortunately, this happy identity doesn't always exist, as our experience with the power plant illustrates. ***When social costs differ from private costs, external costs exist. In fact, external costs are equal to the difference between the social and private costs***:

External costs = Social costs − Private costs

When external costs are present, the market mechanism won't allocate resources efficiently. This is a case of **market failure.** The price signal confronting producers is flawed. By not conveying the full (social) cost of scarce resources, the market encourages excessive pollution. We end up with a suboptimal mix of output (too much electricity, too little clean air) and the wrong production processes.

The consequences of this market failure are illustrated in Figure 14.2, which again depicts the cost situation confronting the electric power plant. Notice that we use *two* different marginal cost curves this time. The lower one, the *private* MC curve, reflects the private costs incurred by the power plant when it operates on a profit maximization basis, using high-sulfur coal or without cooling towers. It's identical to the MC curve in Figure 14.1*a*. We now know, however, that such operations impose external costs on others in the form of air and water pollution. These external costs must be added to private marginal costs. When this is done, we get a *social* marginal cost curve that lies above the private MC curve.

To maximize profits, private firms seek the rate of output that equates private MC to MR (price). ***To maximize social welfare, we need to equate social marginal cost to marginal revenue (price).*** This social optimum occurs at point *A* in Figure 14.2 and results in output of q_s. By contrast, the firm's private profit maximization occurs at point *B*, where q_p is produced. Hence the private firm ends up producing more output than socially desired, while earning more profit and causing more pollution. As a general rule, ***if pollution costs are external, firms will produce too much of a polluting good.***

FIGURE 14.2

Market Failure

Social costs exceed private costs by the amount of external costs. Production decisions based on private costs alone will lead us to point *B*, where private MC = MR. At point *B*, the rate of output is q_p.

To maximize social welfare, we equate *social* MC and MR, as at point *A*. Only q_s of output is socially desirable. The failure of the market to convey the full costs of production keeps us from attaining this outcome.

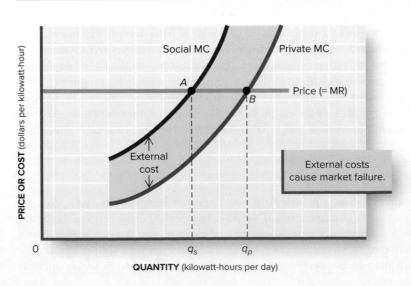

Externalities in Consumption

A divergence between private and social costs can also be observed in consumption. Consumers try to maximize their personal welfare. We buy and use more of those goods and services that yield the highest satisfaction (marginal utility) per dollar expended. By implication (and the law of demand), we tend to use more of a product if we can get it at a discount—that is, pay less than the full price. Unfortunately, the "discount" often takes the form of an external cost imposed on neighbors and friends.

Automobile driving illustrates the problem. The amount of driving one does is influenced by the price of a car and the marginal costs of driving it. People buy smaller cars and drive less when the attendant marginal costs (for instance, gasoline prices) increase substantially. But automobile use involves not only *private costs* but *external costs* as well. Auto emissions (carbon monoxide, hydrocarbons, and nitrogen oxides) are a principal cause of air pollution. In effect, automobile drivers have been able to use a valued resource, clean air, at no cost to themselves. Few motorists see any personal benefit in installing exhaust control devices because the quality of the air they breathe would be little affected by their efforts. Hence low private costs lead to excessive pollution when high social costs are dictating cleaner air.

A divergence between social and private costs can be observed even in the simplest of consumer activities, such as throwing an empty soda can out the window of your car. Hanging onto the can and later disposing of it in a trash barrel involve personal effort and thus private marginal costs. Throwing it out the window not only is more exciting but also effectively transfers the burden of disposal costs to someone else. The resulting externality ends up as roadside litter.

The same kind of divergence between private and social costs helps explain why people abandon old cars in the street rather than haul them to scrapyards. It also explains why people use vacant lots as open dumps. In all these cases, **the polluter benefits by substituting external costs for private costs.** In other words, market incentives encourage environmental damage.

REGULATORY OPTIONS

The failure of the market to include external costs in production and consumption decisions creates a basis for government intervention. As always, however, we confront a variety of policy options. We may define these options in terms of **two general strategies for environmental protection:**

- *Alter market incentives* in such a way that they discourage pollution.
- *Bypass market incentives* with some form of regulatory intervention.

Market-Based Options

Insofar as market incentives are concerned, the key to environmental protection is to eliminate the divergence between private costs and social costs. The opportunity to shift some costs onto others lies at the heart of the pollution problem. If we could somehow compel producers to *internalize* all costs—pay for both private and external costs—the divergence would disappear, along with the incentive to pollute.

Emission Charges. One possibility is to establish a system of **emission charges:** direct costs attached to the act of polluting. Suppose that we let you keep your power plant and permit you to operate it according to profit-maximizing principles. The only difference is that we no longer supply you with clean air and cool water at zero cost. From now on, we'll charge you for these scarce resources. We might, say, charge 2 cents for every gram of noxious emission discharged into the air. In addition we might charge 3 cents for every gallon of water you use, heat, and discharge back into the river.

Confronted with such emission charges, you'd have to rethink your production decision. **An emission charge increases private marginal cost and encourages lower output and**

emission charge: A fee imposed on polluters, based on the quantity of pollution.

FIGURE 14.3
Emission Fees

Emission charges can close the gap between marginal social costs and marginal private costs. Faced with an emission charge of *t*, a private producer will reduce output from q_0 to q_1. Emission charges may also induce different investment and efficiency decisions.

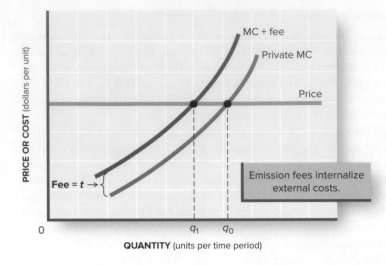

cleaner technology. Figure 14.3 illustrates this effect. Notice how the fee raises private marginal costs and induces a lower rate of (polluting) production (q_1 rather than q_0).

Once an emission fee is in place, a producer may also reevaluate the efficiency decision. Consider again the choice of fuels to be used in our fictional power plant. We earlier chose high-sulfur coal because it was the cheapest fuel available. Now, however, there's an additional cost attached to burning such fuel, in the form of an emission charge. This added cost may encourage the firm to switch to cleaner sources of energy, which would increase private marginal costs but reduce emission fees.

An emission charge might also persuade a firm to incur higher *fixed* costs. Rather than continuing to pay emission charges, it might be more economical to install scrubbers and other smokestack controls that reduce the volume of emissions. This would entail additional capital outlays for the necessary abatement equipment but might reduce variable costs (including emission charges). In this case, the fee-induced change in fixed costs might reduce pollution without any reduction in output.

The actual response of producers will depend on the relative costs involved. If emission charges are too low, it may be more profitable to continue burning and polluting with high-sulfur coal and pay a nominal fee. This is a simple pricing problem. We could set the emission price higher, prompting the behavioral responses we desire.

Economic incentives can also change consumer behavior. At one time, beverage producers imposed deposits to encourage consumers to bring bottles back so they could be used again. But producers discovered that such deposits discouraged sales and yielded little cost savings. Today returnable bottles are rarely used. One result is the inclusion of more than 30 billion glass bottles and 60 billion cans in our solid waste disposal problem. We could reverse this trend by imposing a deposit on all beverage containers. Many states do this, at least for certain cans and bottles. Such deposits internalize pollution costs for the consumer and render the throwing of a soda can out the window equivalent to throwing away money.

Some communities have also tried to reduce solid waste processing by charging a fee for each container of garbage collected. In Charlotte, Virginia, a fee of 80 cents per 32-gallon bag of garbage had a noticeable impact on consumer behavior. Economists Don Fullerton and Thomas Kinnaman observed that households reduced the weight of their garbage by 14 percent and the volume by 37 percent. As they noted, "Households somehow stomped their garbage to get more in a container and trim their garbage bill." Here again, the use of the market mechanism (higher prices) brought about the desired environmental protection.

Recycling Materials. An important bonus that emission charges offer is an increased incentive for the recycling of materials. The glass and metal in used bottles and cans can be recycled to produce new bottles and cans. Such recycling not only eliminates a lot of unsightly litter but also diminishes the need to mine new resources from the earth, a process that often involves its own environmental problems. The critical issues are once again relative costs and market incentives. *A container producer has no incentive to use recycled materials unless they offer superior cost efficiency and thus greater profits.* The largest component in the costs of recycled materials is usually the associated costs of collection and transportation. In this regard, an emission charge such as the 5-cent container deposit lowers collection costs because it motivates consumers to return all their bottles and cans to a central location.

Higher User Fees. Another market alternative is to raise the price consumers pay for scarce resources. If people used less water, we wouldn't have to build so many sewage treatment plants. In most communities, however, the price of water is so low that people use it indiscriminately. Higher water fees would encourage water conservation.

A similar logic applies to auto pollution. The cheapest way to cut down on auto pollution is to drive less. Higher gasoline prices would encourage people to use alternative transportation and drive more fuel-efficient cars. Consumers would complain, of course, about higher taxes on gasoline, but at least they'd be able to breathe cleaner air.

"Green" Taxes. Automakers don't want gasoline prices to go up; neither do consumers. So the government may have to impose *green taxes* to get the desired response. A green tax on gasoline, for example, raises the price of gasoline. The taxes not only curb auto emissions (less driving) but also create a revenue source for other pollution abatement efforts. Other nations impose far more green taxes than does the United States.

Pollution Fines. Not far removed from the concept of emission and user charges is the imposition of fines or liability for cleanup costs. In some situations, such as the April 2010 BP oil spill in the Gulf of Mexico, the pollution is so sudden and concentrated that society has little choice but to clean it up quickly. The costs for such cleanup can be imposed on the polluter, however, through appropriate fines. Such fines place the cost burden where it belongs.

Although pollution fines are inevitably imposed after the damage is done, the *expectation* of a fine can encourage more environmentally conscious behavior. To avoid a potential fine, oil companies may invest in double-hulled oil tankers and more efficient safety mechanisms on offshore oil wells. When Royal Caribbean Cruises was fined $9 million in 1998 for dumping garbage and oil from its cruise ships, the firm decided to monitor waste disposal practices more closely. In the absence of such fines, firms have little incentive to invest in environmental protection.

Tradable Pollution Permits ("Cap and Trade")

Another environmental policy option makes even greater use of market incentives. Rather than penalize firms that have already polluted, let firms *purchase* the right to continue polluting. As crazy as this policy might sound, it can be effective in limiting environmental damage.

The key to the success of pollution permits is that they're bought and sold among private firms. The system starts with a government-set standard for pollution reduction. Firms that reduce pollution by more than the standard earn pollution credits. They may then sell these credits to other firms, who are thereby relieved of cleanup chores. *The principal advantage of pollution permits is their incentive to minimize the cost of pollution control.*

To see how the permits work, suppose the policy objective is to reduce sulfur dioxide emissions by two tons. There are only two major polluters in the community: a copper smelter and an electric utility. Should each company be required to reduce its SO_2 emissions by one ton? Or can the same SO_2 reduction be achieved more cheaply with marketable pollution rights?

Reduction in Emissions (in Tons)	Marginal Cost of Pollution Abatement	
	Copper Smelter	Electric Utility
1	$200	$100
2	250	150
3	300	200

Focus on Marginal Abatement Costs. Table 14.1 depicts the assumed cost of pollution abatement at each plant. The copper smelter would have to spend $200 to achieve a one-ton reduction in SO_2 emissions. The utility can do it for only $100. Table 14.1 also indicates that the utility can attain a *second* ton of SO_2 abatement for $150. Even though its marginal cost of pollution control is increasing, the utility still has lower abatement costs than the smelter. This cost advantage creates an interesting economic opportunity.

Recall that the policy goal is to reduce emissions by two tons. The copper smelter would have to spend $200 to achieve its one-ton share of the policy target. But the utility can abate a *second* ton for $150. Accordingly, the smelter would save money by *paying* the utility for additional pollution abatement.

How much would the smelter have to pay? The utility would want at least $150 to cover its own marginal costs of additional pollution abatement. The smelter would save money at any price below $200. Accordingly, the price of this transaction would be somewhere between $150 (the utility's marginal cost of a second ton) and $200 (the smelter's marginal cost of the first ton). If they do the deal—trade pollution rights—the smelter would continue to pollute, but total SO_2 emissions would still drop by two tons (all at the electric utility). Both firms would be better off (the smelter with lower costs, the utility with more revenue).

Society also benefits from this cap-and-trade system: the social goal of pollution abatement is achieved at lower cost. Without tradable permits, the resource cost of a two-ton reduction was $300. With the cap-and-trade option, the resource cost falls to $250. So society ends up with $50 of "extra" resources to produce other desired goods and services.

At the first real auction of pollution credits, the average price paid was $156. For this price a firm could pay someone else to reduce SO_2 emissions by one ton rather than curb its own emissions. The Carolina Power and Light Company spent $11.5 *million* buying such permits.

After they first became available in 1992, tradable pollution permits ("allowances") quickly became a popular mechanism for pollution control. In 2000, 12.7 *million* sulfur dioxide allowances were traded, each covering one ton of emission reduction. The price of a permit rose sharply for several years, peaking at $1,200 a ton in 2005. A series of court rulings, however, derailed the program beginning in 2008. The key issue was whether one state could effectively transfer its pollution problems to another state via allowance trading. The courts said "no," and the SO_2 permit program ended in 2012. Nevertheless, the program demonstrated an effective and cost-efficient method for reducing pollution. Other nations now use the same cap-and-trade system to reduce CO_2 emissions.

Environmental Innovation. Pollution permits also encourage innovation in abatement technology. Entrepreneurs now have an incentive to discover cheaper methods for pollution abatement. They don't have to own a smelter or utility; they can now *sell* their pollution control expertise to the highest bidder. As the market for permits expanded, the profit opportunities for environmental engineering firms increased. This accelerated productivity and reduced the cost of pollution abatement by 25 to 34 percent. In view of these results, the European Union extended the pollution permit trading system to carbon dioxide emissions in 2005 (see World View "Paying to Pollute").

WORLD VIEW

PAYING TO POLLUTE

System Would Limit Emission, Allow Trading of Credits

It costs nothing to pump greenhouse gases into the air. . . .

That is starting to change.

Driven by fears of global warming, countries and states are trying to place a price tag on emissions of carbon dioxide, the gas considered most responsible for rising temperatures.

They are turning to a system called "cap and trade," which limits the overall amount of carbon dioxide an area or industry can emit and then lets individual companies buy and sell credits to release specific amounts of the gas.

The cap-and-trade concept is considered an alternative to strict government mandates. It tries to use market dynamics to cut pollution, allowing flexibility on emission levels—for a price. Emissions that were free in the past, regardless of their environmental cost, now would cost an amount set by the market.

In theory at least, it allows businesses that emit carbon dioxide to choose the most cost-effective way to cut their emissions. And it gives them leeway in the speed of their cuts. . . .

Europe has a carbon dioxide market up and running, with release of a ton of gas now trading at 27 euros, about $32.

—**David R. Baker**

Source: Baker, David, R., "Paying to pollute: System would limit emission, allow trading of credits," *San Francisco Chronicle*, February 19, 2006. Copyright ©2006. All rights reserved. Used with permission.

ANALYSIS: Marketable pollution permits encourage firms with more efficient pollution control technologies to overachieve, thereby earning pollution permits that can be sold to firms with more expensive pollution control technologies. Such trades reduce the *average* cost of pollution control.

Command-and-Control Options

Public policy needn't rely on tradable permits or other market incentives to achieve desired pollution abatement. The government could instead simply *require* firms to reduce pollutants by specific amounts and even specify which abatement technology must be used. This approach is often referred to as the "command-and-control" option. The government *commands* firms to reduce pollution and then *controls* the process for doing so.

The potential inefficiency of the command-and-control strategy was already revealed in Table 14.1. Had the government required *each* firm to reduce pollution by one ton, the total cost would have been $300. By allowing firms to use tradable permits, the cost of obtaining the same level of pollution abatement was only $250. The cost saving of $50 represents valuable resources that could be used to produce other desired goods and services.

Despite the superior efficiency of market-based environmental policies, the government often relies on the command-and-control approach. The Clean Air Acts of 1970 and 1990, for example, mandated not only fewer auto emissions but also specific processes such as catalytic converters and lead-free gasoline for attaining them. Specific processes and technologies are also required for toxic waste disposal and water treatment. Laws requiring the sorting and recycling of trash are other examples of process regulation.

Although such command-and-control regulation can be effective, this policy option also entails risks. By requiring all market participants to follow specific rules, the regulations may impose excessive costs on some activities and too low a constraint on others. Some communities may not need the level of sewage treatment the federal government prescribes. Individual households may not generate enough trash to make sorting and separate pickups economically sound. Some producers may have better or cheaper ways of attaining environmental standards. ***Excessive process regulation may raise the costs of*** *environmental protection and discourage cost-saving innovation.* There's also the risk of regulated processes becoming entrenched long after they are obsolete. When that happens we may end up with worse outcomes than a less regulated market would have generated— that is, **government failure.**

BALANCING BENEFITS AND COSTS

Protecting the environment entails costs as well as benefits. Installing smokestack scrubbers on factory chimneys and catalytic converters on cars requires the use of scarce resources. Taking the lead out of gasoline wears out engines faster and requires expensive changes in technology. Switching to clean fuels requires enormous investments in technology, plants, and equipment. The EPA estimates that a 10-year program to achieve national air and water standards would cost more than $1 trillion. Restoring the ozone layer, removing hazardous wastes, and cleaning up the rest of the environment would cost trillions more.

Opportunity Costs

Although cleaning up the environment is a worthwhile goal, we must remind ourselves that those resources could be used to fulfill other goals as well. The multitrillion-dollar tab would buy a lot of subways and parks or build decent homes for the poor. If we devote those resources instead to pollution abatement, we'll have to forgo other goods and services. Remember the basic principle about 'no free lunch?' Well, for the same reason there is no free environmental protection. This isn't to say that environmental goals don't deserve priority but simply to remind us that any use of our scarce resources involves an **opportunity cost.**

Fortunately, the amount of additional resources required to clean up the environment is relatively modest in comparison to our productive capacity. Over a 10-year period we'll produce more than $200 trillion of goods and services (GDP). On this basis, the environmental expenditures contemplated by present environmental policies and goals represent only 1 to 3 percent of total output.

The Optimal Rate of Pollution

Spending even a small percentage of GDP on environmental protection nevertheless entails value judgments. The **optimal rate of pollution** occurs at the point at which the opportunity costs of further pollution control equal the benefits of further reductions in pollution. *To determine the optimal rate of pollution, we need to compare the marginal social benefits of additional pollution abatement with the marginal social costs of additional pollution control expenditure.* The optimal rate of pollution is achieved when we've satisfied the following equality:

$$\begin{matrix} \text{Optimal} \\ \text{rate of} \\ \text{pollution} \end{matrix} : \begin{matrix} \text{Marginal benefit} \\ \text{of pollution} \\ \text{abatement} \end{matrix} = \begin{matrix} \text{Marginal cost} \\ \text{of pollution} \\ \text{abatement} \end{matrix}$$

This formulation is analogous to the utility-maximizing rule in consumption. If another dollar spent on pollution control yields less than a dollar of social benefits, then additional pollution control expenditure isn't desirable. In such a situation, the goods and services that would be forsaken for additional pollution control are more valued than the environmental improvements that would result.

Cost–Benefit Analysis

A 2003 White House study concluded that past efforts to clean up the air have yielded far more benefits than costs: the benefits of a 10-year (1992–2002) air pollution abatement program were five to seven times greater than its cost. Although pollution abatement has been an economic success, that doesn't mean *all* pollution controls are desirable. The focus must still be on *marginal* benefits and costs. In that context, a surprising conclusion emerges: *a totally clean environment isn't economically desirable.* The marginal benefit of achieving zero pollution is infinitesimally small. But the marginal cost of eliminating that last particle of pollution will be very high. As we weigh the marginal benefits and costs, we'll inevitably conclude that *some* pollution is cost-effective.

Mayor Bloomberg performed the same kind of analysis for New York City's recycling program. Sure, everyone thinks recycling is a good idea. But Mayor Bloomberg started looking at the cost of the recycling program and decided it didn't make economic sense (see In the News "Recycling Wastes Money"). He figured the city could use the $57 million cost of recycling for higher-priority programs, yielding greater (marginal) benefits to NYC residents.

IN THE NEWS

RECYCLING WASTES MONEY

New York City is spending $57 million a year to recycle metal, glass, and plastic. Mayor Bloomberg says that's way too much, especially when the city is cutting police and fire budgets. The mayor says the city could save a lot of money by simply sending the waste to landfills rather than recycling it. The city spends about $240 per ton to recycle waste, while the cost of sending the waste to landfills is about $130 a ton. As he sees it, "You could do a lot better things in the world with $57 million." The mayor axed the recycling program from the city's proposed 2003 budget.

M.E. Cohen

Source: News reports, March 2002.

ANALYSIS: Recycling uses scarce resources that could be employed elsewhere. The benefits of recycling may not exceed its (opportunity) costs.

Who Will Pay?

The costs of pollution control aren't distributed equally. In New York City, the cost of the recycling program is borne by those who end up with fewer city services and amenities (opportunity costs). A national pollution abatement program would target the relatively small number of economic activities—like coal-fired power plants, paper mills, steel plants—that account for the bulk of emissions and effluents. These activities will have to bear a disproportionate share of the cleanup burden.

Higher Costs. To ascertain how the burden of environmental protection will be distributed, consider first the electric power plant discussed earlier. As we observed (Figure 14.2), the plant's output will decrease if production decisions are based on social rather than private marginal costs—that is, if environmental consequences are considered. If the plant itself is compelled to pay full social costs, in the form of either compulsory investment or emission charges, its profits will be reduced. Were no other changes to take place, the burden of environmental improvements would be borne primarily by the producer.

Higher Prices. Such a scenario is unlikely, however. Rather than absorb all the costs of pollution controls themselves, producers will pass some of this burden on to their customers in the form of higher prices. Their ability to do so will depend on the extent of competition in their industry, their relative cost position in it, and the price elasticity of consumer demand. In reality, the electric power industry isn't very competitive, and its prices are still subject to government regulation. In addition, consumer demand is relatively price-inelastic. Accordingly, the profit-maximizing producer will appeal to the state or local power commission for an increase in electricity prices based on the costs of pollution control. Electric power consumers are likely to end up footing the environmental bill.

Job Losses. Workers in the impacted industry are likely to suffer as well. All of the policy options we have looked at end up reducing the production and consumption of the polluting good. That implies job losses for the affected workers. According to the government itself, environmental regulations enacted in 2011 and 2014 eliminated thousands of coal-mining jobs across the country. Although the Obama administration claimed that the resulting decline in air pollution saved thousands of lives, those displaced coal miners argued that the economic costs of the mining regulations far outweighed the environmental benefits.

THE ECONOMY TOMORROW

THE WAR ON COAL

Forget about littered beaches, smelly landfills, eye-stinging smog, and contaminated water. The really scary problem for the economy tomorrow is much more serious: some scientists say that the carbon emissions we're now spewing into the air are warming the earth's atmosphere. If the earth's temperature rises only a few degrees, they contend, polar caps will melt, continents will flood, and weather patterns will go haywire. If things get bad enough, there may not be any economy tomorrow.

The Greenhouse Effect. The earth's climate is driven by solar radiation. The energy the sun absorbs must be balanced by outgoing radiation from the earth and the atmosphere. Scientists fear that a flow imbalance is developing. Of particular concern is a buildup of carbon dioxide (CO_2) that traps heat in the earth's atmosphere, warming the planet.

The natural release of CO_2 dwarfs the emissions from human activities. But there's a concern that the steady increase in man-made CO_2 emissions—principally from burning fossil fuels like gasoline and coal—is tipping the balance.

Scientists are still debating how much the earth's temperature is likely to rise in the economy tomorrow. But the continued buildup of carbon dioxide in the atmosphere is undeniable. A 2013 United Nations study concluded with 95 percent certainty that human activity (power generation, transportation, etc.) is increasingly responsible for the rising greenhouse gas concentrations and the climate changes that accompany them.

A Global Externality. While nearly every country recognizes the threat that CO_2 emissions pose, there is less certainty about how to reduce that threat. The core problem here is that ***CO_2 emissions are a global externality.*** People don't deliberately produce CO_2 emissions. Rather, they are an unintended by-product of everyday production and consumption activities. When you drive your car, you are polluting the air not just in your immediate vicinity, but the air the entire world inhales. When a Chinese coal mine spews CO_2 into the air, it increases CO_2 concentrations over Alaska and Florida.

Because CO_2 emissions are an externality, the market will produce too much of them. As we have seen, when the market fails, the government must intervene. But with a *global* externality, no single nation can resolve the problem.

The Paris Accord. In 2014 the United Nations convened a "Climate Summit" to address the problem. After two years of deliberations among nearly 200 nations, an agreement was reached in November 2016. According to the "Paris Accord," the nations of the world agreed to limit the increase in the earth's temperature over the next decade to no more than 2 degrees Celsius. To do that, each nation agreed to pledge a specific "contribution" of CO_2 reductions. President Obama committed the United States to cutting its CO_2 emissions by 26–28 percent by 2025, compared to 2005.

Focus on Coal. Global commitments to reduce greenhouse emissions inevitably look to the coal industry. Energy production accounts for one-fourth of all global greenhouse emissions, and coal is the largest contributor in that sector. In 2015 the U.S. coal industry emitted 1.4 billion tons of CO_2, more than one fifth of the total emissions. Hence, it's virtually impossible to achieve substantial emissions reductions without curbing coal.

Recognizing the critical role of coal in CO_2 emissions, President Obama essentially declared what critics called "a war on coal" (see In the News "A 'War on Coal'?"). That "war" included a ban on coal leases on federal lands (a huge issue in Wyoming), a virtual ban on new coal-mining permits, and a Stream Protection Rule that made mountain-top mining in West Virginia nearly impossible. From 2012 to 2016 nearly 40,000 coal miners lost their jobs as coal companies closed up shop. Although not all of these job losses were due to government regulation, the majority were.

Trump's Reversal. During the 2016 presidential campaign, Donald Trump said he was "committedd to reviving America's coal mining companies, which have been hurting for too long." In his first weeks as president, Trump convinced Congress to repeal President Obama's Stream Protection Rule and repealed regulations in Obama's Clean Power Plan. In June 2017 President Trump took even more dramatic action, withdrawing the United States from the Paris Accord, arguing that its pollution-reduction goals placed an "unfair" burden on American workers while subsidizing energy development in low-income nations.

How clean (and warm) the environment is in the economy tomorrow will depend on what kind of balance is ultimately struck between the benefits of environmental protection and its associated costs. The outcome of that decision will affect the level of CO_2 concentrations in the economy tomorrow.

IN THE NEWS

A "WAR ON COAL"?

Yesterday, the Environmental Protection Agency (EPA) issued its 645-page proposal for cutting America's carbon emissions. EPA's goal is to cut CO_2 emissions by 30 percent below the level of 2005 emissions by the year 2030. This would require CO_2 emissions to drop by a staggering 1.5 billion metric tons per year in only 15 years. The Obama administration views this as a necessary contribution to the fight against global warming. They also say the proposed policy is cost-effective: U.S. health care costs will drop by $55–$93 billion per year due to 100,000 fewer asthma attacks and 2,100 few heart attacks each year. EPA estimates the annual compliance cost at $7.3–$8.8 billion.

The coal industry sees it differently. Coal provides 37 percent of America's electricity. They know the Obama administration wants to faze out the 557 certified coal plants in favor of wind, solar, and other power sources. They protest that the administration's "war on coal" will increase electricity prices, devastate coal-mining communities, threaten the electricity grid, and cost thousands of jobs.

Sources: www.epa.gov; news reports, June 2–5, 2014.

ANALYSIS: Pollution abatement is not a "free good." It requires the use of real resources and creates trade-offs among competing goals.

SUMMARY

- Air, water, and solid waste pollution impose social and economic costs. The costs of pollution include the direct damages inflicted on our health and resources, the expense of cleaning up, and the general aesthetic deterioration of the environment. **LO14-1**

- Pollution is an external cost, a cost of a market activity imposed on someone (a third party) other than the immediate producer or consumer. **LO14-1**

- Producers and consumers generally operate on the basis of private benefits and costs. A private producer or consumer has an incentive to minimize his own costs by transforming private costs into external costs. One way of making such a substitution is to pollute—to use "free" air and water rather than install pollution control equipment, or to leave the job of waste disposal to others. **LO14-1**

- Social costs are the total amount of resources used in a production or consumption process. When social costs are greater than private costs, the market's price signals are flawed. This market failure will induce people to harm the environment by using suboptimal processes and products. **LO14-1**

- One way to correct the market inefficiency created by externalities is to compel producers and consumers to internalize all (social) costs. This can be done by imposing emission charges and higher user fees. Such charges create an incentive to invest in pollution abatement equipment, recycle reusable materials, and conserve scarce elements of the environment. **LO14-2**

- Tradable pollution permits help minimize the cost of pollution control by (*a*) promoting low-cost controls to substitute for high-cost controls and (*b*) encouraging innovation in pollution control technology. **LO14-2**

- An alternative approach to cleaning up the environment is to require specific pollution controls or to prohibit specific kinds of activities. Direct regulation runs the risk of higher cost and discouraging innovations in environmental protection. **LO14-2**

- The opportunity costs of pollution abatement are the most desired goods and services given up when factors of production are used to control pollution. The optimal rate of pollution is reached when the marginal social benefits of further pollution control equal associated marginal social costs. **LO14-3**

- In addition to diverting resources, pollution control efforts alter relative prices, change the mix of output, and redistribute incomes. These outcomes cause losses for particular groups and may thus require special economic or political attention. **LO14-3**

- The greenhouse effect represents a global externality. Reducing global emissions requires consensus on optimal pollution levels (i.e., the optimal balance of pollution abatement costs and benefits) and the distribution of attendant costs. **LO14-2**

Key Terms

production decision	private costs	opportunity cost
efficiency decision	market failure	optimal rate of pollution
external cost	emission charge	
social costs	government failure	

Questions for Discussion

1. If "green" gasoline were sold for 20 cents per gallon more than "dirty" gasoline, would you buy it? How much of a premium per gallon do you think most people would pay? **LO14-1**

2. What are the *economic* costs of the externalities caused by air toxins (In the News "Air Pollution Kills"), beach closings, or thermal pollution (In the News "Cut the Power to Save the Fish?")? How would you measure their value? **LO14-1**

3. Should we try to eliminate *all* pollution? What economic considerations might favor permitting some pollution? **LO14-3**

4. Why would auto manufacturers resist higher fuel efficiency standards? How would their costs, sales, and profits be affected? **LO14-1**

5. Does anyone have an incentive to maintain auto exhaust control devices in good working order? How can we ensure that they will be maintained? Are there any costs associated with this policy? **LO14-1**

6. Should the Indian Point nuclear plant (In the News "Cut the Power to Save the Fish?") be closed? Who will benefit? Who will lose? **LO14-3**

7. What economic costs are imposed by mandatory sorting of trash (In the News "Recycling Wastes Money")? **LO14-2**

8. "The issuance of a pollution permit is just a license to destroy the environment." Do you agree? Explain. **LO14-2**

9. If a high per-bag fee were charged for garbage collection, how would consumers respond? **LO14-2**

10. Should coal mining be prohibited in order to reduce carbon emissions? **LO14-2**

11. Over 1 billion people in the world don't have access to electricity, relying mostly on fire for heat and cooking. Discuss the benefits and costs of carbon caps that limit the construction of new power plants in less developed countries. **LO14-2**

LO14-2 1. (*a*) If the Indian Point nuclear plant (In the News "Recycling Wastes Money") were charged one-tenth of a mill (0.01 cent) for every gallon of water it used, how much would it pay in annual emission fees?

        (*b*) If the cost of building and operating a closed-cycle cooling system was $100 million per year, would the plant prefer to reengineer the plant or pay the emission fees?

LO14-2 2. EPA says the value of a human life is $7.6 million, measured from birth to death. If life expectancy is 78 years, what is the value of the remaining life of an 18-year-old person?

LO14-2 3. How high would its pollution control costs have to be before a firm would "pay to pollute" a ton of carbon dioxide (World View "Paying to Pollute")?

LO14-1 4. Use the graph to answer the following questions:

        (*a*) What is the profit maximizing quantity?
             Suppose that there are external costs equal to $0.01 per kilowatt-hour.

        (*b*) Calculate the social marginal cost to produce the profit maximizing quantity.

        (*c*) What is the socially-optimal quantity?

        (*d*) How much of an emission fee should be charged to close the gap between the private and social marginal costs?

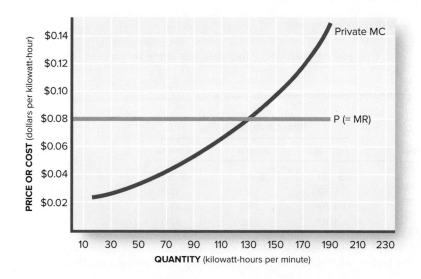

LO14-1 5. Many people pay nothing for each extra pound of garbage they create yet the garbage is a type of solid waste pollution. In view of this, we can view garbage collection as creating external benefits to society. So what's an appropriate price for garbage collection? Answer the questions based on the following graph.

        (*a*) What is the quantity of (free) garbage collection now demanded?

        (*b*) How much would be demanded if a fee of $4 per pound were charged?

        (*c*) Draw the social demand curve when an external benefit of $2 per pound exists.

        (*d*) If the marginal cost of collecting garbage were constant at $6 per pound, what would be the optimal level of garbage collection?

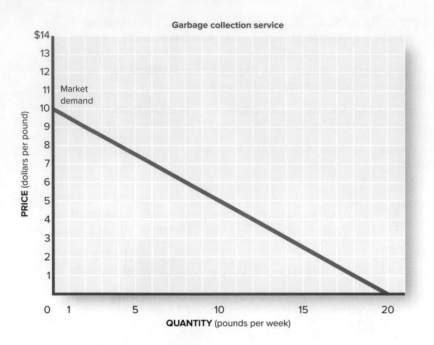

Garbage collection service

LO14-3 6. How much more per ton is New York City paying to recycle rather than just dump its garbage (In the News "Recycling Wastes Money")?

LO14-2 7. Suppose three firms confront the following costs for pollution control:

Emissions Reduction (Tons per Year)	Total Costs of Control		
	Firm A	Firm B	Firm C
1	$ 30	$ 40	$ 50
2	70	100	120
3	120	180	210
4	190	280	320

(a) If each firm must reduce emissions by one ton, how much will be spent?

(b) If the firms can trade pollution rights, what would be the cheapest way of attaining a net three-ton reduction?

(c) How much would a pollution permit trade for (price range)?

Now suppose the goal is to reduce pollution by six tons.

(d) What is the marginal cost of a second abatement ton at
   (i)   Firm A?
   (ii) Firm B?
   (iii) Firm C?

(e) If each firm must reduce emissions by two tons, how much will be spent?

(f) If the firms can trade permits, what is the cheapest way of attaining a six-ton reduction?

(g) How much will a permit cost (price change)?

LO14-3 8. The table shows the total benefits and total costs to reduce solid waste pollution in in a local river.

Quantity of Pollution Abatement (Tons of Trash Removed per Week)	Benefits	Costs
0	0	0
1	60	10
2	100	30
3	130	60
4	150	100
5	160	155
6	165	220

(a) Calculate the marginal benefits of pollution abatement.
(b) Calculate the marginal costs of pollution abatement
(c) What is the optimal level of pollution abatement?

LO14-1 9. The following cost schedule depicts the private and social costs associated with the weekly use of dicamba, a strong fertilizer that can damage nearby crops that are not genetically modified to resit the fertilizer. The sales price of dicamba is $26 per ton.

Output (in tons)	0	1	2	3	4	5	6	7	8
Total private cost	$ 5	7	13	23	37	55	77	103	133
Total social cost	$45	63	85	111	141	175	213	255	301

(a) Graph the private and social marginal costs associated with dicamba production.
(b) What is the profit-maximizing rate of output for this competitive firm?
(c) How much profit is earned at that output level?
(d) What is the socially optimal rate of output?
(e) How much profit is there at that output level?
(f) How much of a "green tax" per ton would have to be levied to induce the firm to produce the socially optimal rate of output?

LO14-3 10. The Economy Tomorrow: If health care costs are evenly divided by asthma attacks and heart attacks, what dollar value does EPA put on an asthma attack or heart attack (see In the News "A War on Coal")?

©Fuse/Corbis via Getty Images RF

CHAPTER 15

The Farm Problem

In 1996 the U.S. Congress charted a new future for U.S. farmers. No longer would they look to Washington, DC, for decisions on what crops to plant or how much farmland to leave fallow. The Freedom to Farm Act would get the government out of the farm business and let "laissez faire" dictate farm outcomes. Farmers would lose their federal subsidies but could earn as much as they wanted in the marketplace. Taxpayers loved the idea. So did most farmers, who were enjoying unusually high prices and bumper profits in 1996.

The Asian crisis that began in mid-1997 dealt farmers a severe blow. U.S. farms export 25–50 percent of all the wheat, corn, soybeans, and cotton they grow. When Asia's economies plunged into recession, those export sales evaporated. With sales, prices, and profits all declining, farmers lost their enthusiasm for the "freedom to farm"; they wanted Uncle Sam to jump back into the farm business with price and income guarantees. The U.S. Congress obliged by passing the Farm Security Act of 2001. That act not only increased farm subsidies, but also extended them to peanut farmers, hog farmers, and horse breeders. The Farm Act of 2008 spread federal subsidies to still more farmers, abandoning any notion of "free-market" agriculture. The Farm Act of 2014 continued that trend, extending subsidies to hemp and organic farmers.

This chapter examines the rationale for continuing farm subsidies and their effects on farm production, prices, and exports. In particular, we confront these questions:

- **Why do farmers need any subsidies?**
- **How do government subsidies affect farm production, prices, and incomes?**
- **Who pays for farm subsidies?**

DESTABILIZING FORCES

The agriculture industry is one of the most competitive of all U.S. industries. First, there are 2 million farms in the United States. Although some of these farms are immense—with tens of thousands of acres—no single farm has the power to affect the market supply or price of farm products. That is, individual farmers have no **market power.**

Competition in Agriculture

Competition in agriculture is maintained by low **barriers to entry.** Although farmers need large acreages, expensive farm equipment, substantial credit, hard work, and hired labor, all these resources

market power: The ability to alter the market price of a good or service.

barriers to entry: Obstacles such as patents that make it difficult or impossible for would-be producers to enter a particular market.

become affordable when farming is generating **economice profits.** When farming is profitable, existing farmers expand their farms and farmers' children are able to start new farms. It would be much harder to enter the automobile industry, the airline business, or even the farm machinery market than it would be to enter farming. Because of these low barriers to entry, economic profits don't last long in agriculture.

Given the competitive structure of U.S. agriculture, *individual farmers tend to behave like perfect competitors.* Individual farmers seek to expand their rate of output until marginal cost equals price. By following this rule, each farmer makes as much profit as possible from existing resources, prices, and technology.

Like other competitive firms, U.S. farmers can maintain economic profits only if they achieve continuing cost reductions. Above-normal profits obtained from current production techniques and prices aren't likely to last. Such economic profits will entice more people into agriculture and will stimulate greater output from existing farmers. That is exactly the kind of dilemma that confronted catfish farmers in the South and the early producers of microcomputers (Chapter 9). To stay ahead, individual farms must continue to improve their productivity.

> **economic profit:** The difference between total revenues and total economic costs.

Technological Advance

The rate of technological advance in agriculture has, in fact, been spectacular. Since 1929, the farm labor force has shrunk by two-thirds, yet farm output has increased by 80 percent. Between the early 1950s and today,

- Annual egg production has jumped from 183 to 267 eggs per laying chicken.
- Milk output has increased from 5,400 to 21,149 pounds per cow annually.
- Wheat output has increased from 17 to 56 bushels per acre.
- Corn output has jumped from 39 to 175 bushels per acre.

Farm output per labor-hour has grown even faster, having increased 10 times over in the same period. Such spectacular rates of productivity advance rival those of our most high-tech industries. These technological advances resulted from the development of higher-yielding seeds (the "green revolution"), advanced machinery (mechanical feeders and milkers), improved animal breeding (crossbreeding), improved plants (rust-resistant wheat), better land use practices (crop rotation and fertilizers), and computer-based management systems.

Inelastic Demand

In most industries, continuous increases in technology and output would be most welcome. The agricultural industry, however, confronts a long-term problem. Simply put, there's a limit to the amount of food people want to eat.

This constraint on the demand for agricultural output is reflected in the relatively inelastic demand for food. Consumers don't increase their food purchases very much when farm prices fall. The **price elasticity** of food demand is low. As a consequence, when harvests are good, farmers must reduce prices a lot to sell all that extra food. Recall the formula for the price elasticity of demand:

> **price elasticity of demand:** The percentage change in quantity demanded divided by the percentage change in price.

$$E = \frac{\text{Percentage change in quantity demanded}}{\text{Percentage change in price}}$$

Rearranging this formula gives us a guide to how far prices must fall for farmers to unload a bumper crop:

$$\frac{\text{Required percentage}}{\text{change in price}} = \frac{\text{Percentage change in quantity (harvest)}}{\text{Price elasticity of demand}}$$

FIGURE 15.1

Short-Term Instability

Changes in weather cause abrupt shifts of the food supply curve. When combined with the relatively inelastic demand for food, these supply shifts result in wide price swings. Notice how the price of grain jumps from p_1 to p_2 when bad weather reduces the harvest. If good weather follows, prices may fall to p_3.

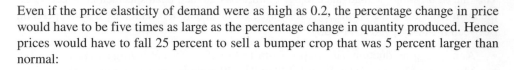

Even if the price elasticity of demand were as high as 0.2, the percentage change in price would have to be five times as large as the percentage change in quantity produced. Hence prices would have to fall 25 percent to sell a bumper crop that was 5 percent larger than normal:

$$\% \; \Delta p = \frac{0.05}{0.20} = 0.25$$

In 2016 the corn crop was 11 percent *larger* than the year before. In 2008 the corn crop *decreased* by 7 percent. As Figure 15.1 illustrates, ***with low price elasticity of demand, abrupt changes in farm output have a magnified effect on market prices.*** Between 2005 and 2017, corn prices ranged from a low of $1.96 a bushel to a high of $8.10 (see Figure 15.2). That's a *lot* of price instability.

The **income elasticity** of food demand is also low. The income elasticity of demand for food refers to the responsiveness of food demand to changes in income. Specifically,

income elasticity of demand: Percentage change in quantity demanded divided by percentage change in income.

$$\text{Income elasticity of demand} = \frac{\text{\% change in quantity demanded (at constant price)}}{\text{\% change in income}}$$

Since 1929, per capita income has quadrupled. But per capita food consumption has increased only 85 percent. Hence ***neither lower prices nor higher incomes significantly increase the quantity of food demanded.***

In the long run, then, the increasing ability of U.S. agriculture to produce food must be reconciled with very slow growth of U.S. demand for food. Over time, this implies that farm prices will fall, relative to nonfarm prices. And they have. Between the years 1910–1914 and 2009, the ratio of farm prices to nonfarm prices fell 60 percent. In the absence of government price support programs and foreign demand for U.S. farm products, farm prices would have fallen still further.

Abrupt Shifts of Supply

The long-term downtrend in (relative) farm prices is only one of the major problems confronting U.S. agriculture. The second major problem is short run. Prices of farm products are subject to abrupt short-term swings. If the weather is good, harvests are abundant. Normally, this might be a good thing. In farming, however, abundant harvests imply a severe

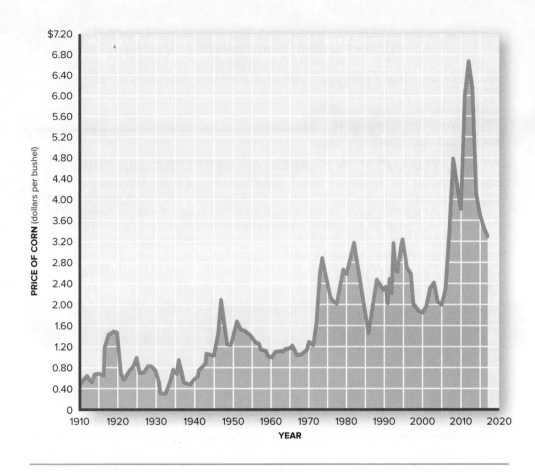

FIGURE 15.2
Unstable Corn Prices

Most agricultural prices are subject to abrupt short-term changes. Notice how corn prices rose dramatically during World Wars I and II, then fell sharply. Poor harvests in the rest of the world increased demand for U.S. food in 1973–1974. Since then prices have moved sharply in both directions.

Source: U.S. Department of Agriculture.

drop in prices. On the other hand, a late or early freeze, a drought, or an infestation by disease or insect pests can reduce harvests and push prices sharply higher (see Figure 15.1).

Response Lags. Time lags between the production decision and the resultant harvest also contribute to price instability. If prices are high one year, farmers have an incentive to increase their rate of output. In this sense, prices serve the same signaling function in agriculture as they do in nonfarm industries. What distinguishes the farmers' response is the lack of inventories and the fixed duration of the production process. In the computer industry, a larger quantity of output can be supplied to the market fairly quickly by drawing down inventories or stepping up the rate of production. In farming, supply can't respond so quickly. In the short run, the farmer can only till more land, plant additional seed, or breed more livestock. No additional food supplies will be available until a new crop or herd grows. Hence *the agricultural supply response to a change in prices is always one harvest (or breeding period) later.*

This lagged supply response intensifies short-term price swings. Suppose corn prices are exceptionally high at the end of a year because of a reduced harvest. High prices will make corn farming appear unusually profitable. Farmers will want to expand their rate of output—plant more corn acreage—to share in these high profits. But the corn won't appear on the market until the following year. By that time, there's likely to be an abundance of corn on the market, as a result of both better weather and increased corn acreage. Hence corn prices are likely to plummet. This is what happened in 2013–2014 and again in 2016–2017.

No single farmer can avoid these boom-or-bust movements of prices. Even a corn farmer who has mastered the principles of economics has little choice but to plant more corn when prices are high. If he doesn't plant additional corn, prices will fall anyway because his own production decisions don't affect market prices. By not planting additional corn, he only denies himself a share of corn market sales. *In a highly competitive market, each producer acts independently.*

Corn prices spiked to $4.20 per bushel after President Bush proposed expanded use of corn-based ethanol as an alternative fuel source. Farmers rushed to plant additional acreage (see In the News "Anticipated Surge in Harvest to Depress Corn Prices"). The 24 percent increase in production that followed pushed prices back down to $3.55 in 2009–2010 (see Figure 15.2).

IN THE NEWS

ANTICIPATED SURGE IN HARVEST TO DEPRESS CORN PRICES

WASHINGTON, D.C.—Corn prices are likely to fall again this year. The U.S. Department of Agriculture reported today that U.S. farmers planted 94 million acres of corn this season, up from last year's 88 million acres. That additional planting, combined with increased yields, will result in a harvest of 15,148 million bushels of corn, up from last year's 13,602 million bushels. Corn price futures on the New York Mercantile Exchange plunged in response to this forecast, hitting lows close to $3.00 a bushel.

Source: Media reports, February 9, 2017.

ANALYSIS: Price swings motivate farmers to alter their production. Abrupt changes in production may reverse the price movement in the next harvest, however.

THE FIRST FARM DEPRESSION, 1920–1940

The U.S. agricultural industry operated without substantial government intervention until the 1930s. In earlier decades, an expanding population, recurrent wars, and less advanced technology had helped maintain a favorable supply–demand relationship for farm products. There were frequent short-term swings in farm prices, but these were absorbed by a generally healthy farm sector. The period 1910–1919 was particularly prosperous for farmers, largely because of the expanded foreign demand for U.S. farm products by countries engaged in World War I.

The two basic problems of U.S. agriculture grew to crisis proportions after 1920. In 1919 most farm prices were at historical highs (see Figures 15.2 and 15.3). After World War I ended, however, European countries no longer demanded as much American food. U.S. exports of farm products fell from nearly $4 billion in 1919 to $1.9 billion in 1921. Farm exports were further reduced in the following years by increasing restrictions on international trade. At home, the end of the war implied an increased availability of factors of production and continuing improvement in farm technology.

FIGURE 15.3

**Farm Prices, 1910–1940
(1910–1914 = 100)**

Farm prices are less stable than nonfarm prices. During the 1930s, relative farm prices fell 50 percent. This experience was the catalyst for government price supports and other agricultural assistance programs.

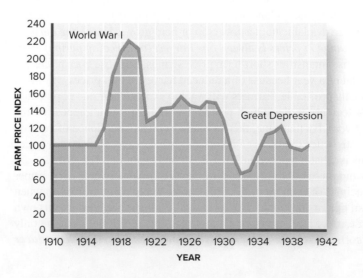

Size of Farm	Number, 1910	Percent	Number, 2002	Percent
Under 100 acres	3,691,611	58.0%	943,118	44.3%
100–499 acres	2,494,461	39.2	847,322	39.8
500–999 acres	125,295	2.0	161,552	7.6
1,000 acres and over	50,135	0.8	176,990	8.3
Total	6,361,502	100.0%	2,128,982	100.0%

Source: U.S. Department of Agriculture.

TABLE 15.1

Size Distribution of U.S. Farms, 1910 and 2002

Inelastic food demand, combined with increasing agricultural productivity, implies a declining number of farmers. Small farmers are particularly vulnerable because they don't have the resources to maintain a high rate of technological improvement. As a result, the number of small farms has declined dramatically while the number of large farms has grown.

The impact of reduced demand and increasing supply is evident in Figure 15.3. In 1919 farm prices were more than double their levels of the period 1910–1914. Prices then fell abruptly. In 1921 alone, farm prices fell nearly 40 percent.

Farm prices stabilized in the mid-1920s but resumed a steep decline in 1930. In 1932 average farm prices were 75 percent lower than they had been in 1919. At the same time, the average income per farmer from farming fell from $2,651 in 1919 to $855 in 1932.

The Great Depression hit small farmers particularly hard. They had fewer resources to withstand consecutive years of declining prices and income. Even in good times, small farmers must continually expand output and reduce costs just to maintain their incomes. Hence the Great Depression accelerated an exodus of small farmers from agriculture, a trend that continues today.

Table 15.1 shows that the number of small farms has declined dramatically. In 1910 there were 3.7 million farms under 100 acres in size. Today there are fewer than 1 million small farms. During the same period, the number of huge farms (1,000 acres or more) has more than tripled. This loss of small farmers, together with the increased mechanization of larger farms, has reduced the farm population by 23 million people since 1910.

U.S. FARM POLICY

The U.S. Congress has responded to these agricultural problems with a variety of programs. Most seek to raise and stabilize the price of farm products. Other programs seek to reduce the costs of production. When all else fails, the federal government also provides direct income support to farmers.

Price Supports

Price supports have always been the primary focus of U.S. farm policy. As early as 1926, Congress decreed that farm products should sell at a fair price. By "fair," Congress meant a price higher than the market equilibrium. The consequences of this policy are evident in Figure 15.4: *a price floor creates a* **market surplus.**

Once it set an above-equilibrium price for food, Congress had to find some way of disposing of the resultant food surplus. Initially, Congress proposed to get rid of this surplus by selling it abroad at world market prices. President Calvin Coolidge, a staunch opponent of government intervention, vetoed this legislation both times Congress passed it.

The notion of fair prices resurfaced in the Agricultural Adjustment Act of 1933. During the Great Depression farmers were going bankrupt in droves. To help them, Congress sought to restore the purchasing power of farm products to the 1909–1914 level (see Figure 15.3). The farm–nonfarm price relationships of 1909–1914 were regarded by Congress as fair and came to be known as **parity** prices. If parity prices could be restored, Congress reasoned, farm incomes would improve.

Supply Restrictions

The goal of parity pricing couldn't be attained without altering market supply and demand in some way.

market surplus: The amount by which the quantity supplied exceeds the quantity demanded at a given price; excess supply.

parity: The relative price of farm products in the period 1910–1914.

FIGURE 15.4

Fair Prices and Market Surplus

The interaction of market supply and demand establishes an equilibrium price (p_e) for any product, including food. If a higher price (p_f) is set, the quantity of food supplied (q_s) will be larger than the quantity demanded (q_d). Hence attempts to establish a "fair" (higher) price for farm products must cope with resultant market surpluses.

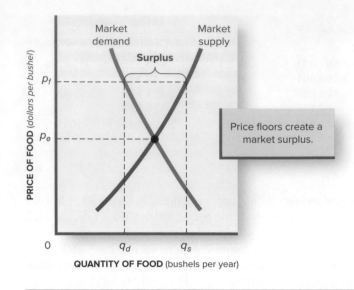

acreage set-aside: Land withdrawn from production as part of policy to increase crop prices.

Set-Asides. The easiest way to increase farm prices without creating a surplus is to reduce the production of food. Congress does this by paying farmers for voluntary reductions in crop acreage. These **acreage set-asides** shift the food supply curve to the left. In 2007 nearly 40 *million* acres of farmland—one-sixth of the nation's wheat, corn, sorghum, rice, and cotton acreage—were idled by government set-asides. If farmers didn't agree to these set-asides, they couldn't participate in the price support programs.

Dairy Termination Program. To prop up dairy prices, the federal government also started a Dairy Termination Program in 1985. This is analogous to a set-aside program. In this case, however, the government pays dairy farmers to slaughter or export dairy cattle. Between 1985 and 1987 the government paid dairy farmers more than $1 billion to "terminate" 1.6 million cows. The reduction in dairy herds boosted prices for milk and other dairy products.

Marketing Orders. The federal government also permits industry groups to limit the quantity of output brought to market. By themselves, individual farmers can't raise the market price by withholding output. If they act collectively, however, they can. If a quantity greater than authorized is actually grown, the "surplus" is disposed of by individual farmers. In the 1980s these *marketing orders* forced farmers to waste each year roughly 500 million lemons, 1 billion oranges, 70 million pounds of raisins, 70 million pounds of almonds, and millions of plums, nectarines, and other fruits. This wholesale destruction of crops gave growers market power and kept farm prices artificially high.

Import Quotas. The market supply of farm products is also limited by import restrictions. Imports of sugar, dairy products, cotton, and peanuts are severely limited by import quotas. Imports of beef are limited by "voluntary" export limits in foreign countries. Import taxes (duties) limit the foreign supply of other farm products.

Demand Distortions

While trying to limit the *supply* of farm products, the government also inflates the *demand* for selected farm products.

Government Stockpiles. An executive order signed by President Franklin Roosevelt in 1933 altered the demand for farm products. The Commodity Credit Corporation (CCC) created at that time became a buyer of last resort for selected farm products.

Commodity	Loan Rate
Corn	$1.95 per bushel
Wheat	2.94
Soybeans	5.00
Cotton (upland)	0.52 per pound
Rice	6.50 per hundredweight
Peanuts	355 per ton
Honey	0.69 per pound
Sugar (beet)	0.24 per pound

Source: U.S. Department of Agriculture (2017).

TABLE 15.2

2016–2017 Loan Rates

The Commodity Credit Corporation lends money to farmers at fixed "loan rates" that are implicit price floors. If the market price falls below the CCC loan rate, the government keeps the crop as full payment of the loan or *pays* farmers a "loan deficiency payment."

The CCC becomes a buyer of last resort through its loan programs. Farmers can borrow money from the CCC at **loan rates** set by Congress (see Table 15.2). In 2017, for example, a wheat farmer could borrow $2.94 in cash for every bushel of wheat he relinquished to the CCC. If the market price of wheat goes above $2.94, the farmer can sell the wheat in the open market, repay the CCC, and pocket the difference. If, instead, the price falls below the loan rate, the farmer can simply let the CCC keep the wheat and repay nothing. Hence, *whenever market prices are below CCC loan rates, the government ends up buying surplus crops.*

Figure 15.5 illustrates the effect of CCC price supports on individual farmers and the agricultural market. In the absence of price supports, competitive farmers would confront a horizontal demand curve at price p_e, itself determined by the intersection of market supply and demand (in part *b*). The CCC's offer to buy ("loan") unlimited quantities at a

loan rate: The implicit price paid by the government for surplus crops taken as collateral for loans to farmers.

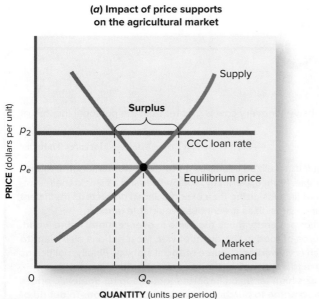

(a) Impact of price supports on the agricultural market

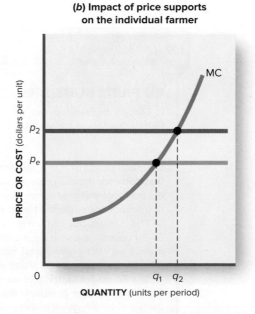

(b) Impact of price supports on the individual farmer

FIGURE 15.5

The Impact of Price Supports

In the absence of price supports, the price of farm products would be determined by the intersection of market supply and demand. In this case, the equilibrium price would be p_e, as shown in part *a*. All individual farmers would confront this price and produce up to the point where MC = p_e, as in part *b*.

Government price supports raise the price to p_2. By offering to buy (or "loan") unlimited quantities at this price, the government shifts the demand curve facing each farmer upward. Individual farmers respond by increasing their output from q_1 to q_2. As farmers increase their output, a market surplus develops.

higher price shifts the demand curve facing each farmer upward to the guaranteed price p_2. This higher price induces individual farmers to increase their rate of output from q_1 to q_2.

As farmers respond to price supports, the agriculture market is pushed out of equilibrium. At the support level p_2, more output is supplied than demanded. The market surplus created by government price supports creates an additional policy dilemma. *The market surplus induced by price supports must be eliminated in one of three ways:*

- *Government purchases* and stockpiling of surplus food.
- *Export sales.*
- *Restrictions on supply.*

Government purchases of surplus crops have led to massive stockpiles of wheat, cotton, corn, and dairy products. At one time, the excess wheat was stored in old ammunition bunkers in Nebraska and scrubbed-out oil tanks in Texas. More than 130 million pounds of surplus nonfat dry milk is now stored in limestone caverns under Kansas City. In 2017 government stockpiles of surplus farm output included 2.3 *billion* bushels of corn, 1.1 billion bushels of wheat, and 4.8 million bales of cotton.

Deficiency Payments. To keep these stockpiles from growing further, Congress amended the CCC loan program in 2001. When market prices fall below CCC loan rates (Table 15.2), farmers don't have to turn over their crops to the government. Instead the government pays them a *loan deficiency payment* equal to the *difference* between the loan rate and the market price. The farmer can then sell his crop on the open market. By dumping excess supply on the market rather than stockpiling it, this policy tends to aggravate downward price swings.

Because farm prices are artificially high in the United States, export sales are sometimes difficult. As a result, the federal government must give away lots of food to poor nations and even subsidize exports to developed nations. The United States isn't alone in this regard: the European Union maintains even higher prices and subsidies (see World View "EU Farm Subsidies").

WORLD VIEW

EU FARM SUBSIDIES

In Europe, believe it or not, the subsidy for every cow is greater than the personal income of half the people in the world.

—**Former British Prime Minister Margaret Thatcher**

U.S. farm policy isn't unique. Most industrialized countries go to even greater lengths to protect domestic agriculture. For example, France, Germany, and Switzerland all shield their farmers from international competition while subsidizing their exports. Japan protects its inefficient rice producers, while the Netherlands subsidizes greenhouse vegetable farmers.

The motivations for farm subsidies are pretty much the same in every country in the world. Every country wants a secure source of food in the event of war. Most nations also want to maintain a viable farm sector, which is viewed as a source of social stability. Finally, politicians in every country must be responsive to a well-established and vocal political constituency.

The European Union (EU) imposes high tariffs on imported food, keeping domestic prices high. The member governments also agree to purchase any surplus production. To get rid of the surplus, the governments then subsidize exports. In 2016 direct EU farm subsidies exceeded $75 billion, triple the size of U.S. farm subsidies. All this protection costs the average EU consumer more than $150 a year.

ANALYSIS: Farm subsidies are common around the world. Such subsidies alter not only domestic output decisions but international trade patterns as well.

Commodity	Reference Price
Corn	$ 3.70 per bushel
Barley	4.95
Wheat	5.50
Soybeans	8.40
Rice	14.00 per hundredweight
Peanuts	$ 535 per ton

Source: U.S. Department of Agriculture (2017).

TABLE 15.3

2014–2018 Reference Prices

Congress sets reference prices for selected commodities. If the market price falls below the reference price, a *deficiency payment* is made directly to the farmer.

Price Supports

The government's loan program is an indirect mechanism for establishing a price floor for agricultural products. In 2014, Congress reintroduced more explicit and more generous price supports. The Farm Act of 2014 set **reference prices** for major commodities. As Table 15.3 reveals, the reference price for corn is now $3.70 per bushel. If the market price for corn falls below $3.70, the government pays farmers the difference. Thus, farmers are guaranteed to get the stipulated reference prices, regardless of how abundant the national crop may be. These reference prices serve as price floors, with the same effect on output depicted in Figure 15.5.

reference price: Government-guaranteed price floor for specific agricultural commodities.

Cost Subsidies

The market surplus induced by price supports is exacerbated by cost subsidies. Irrigation water, for example, is delivered to many farmers by federally funded reclamation projects. The price farmers pay for the water is substantially below the cost of delivering it; the difference amounts to a subsidy. This water subsidy costs taxpayers more than $500 million a year. The Department of Agriculture also distributes an additional $150 million to $200 million a year to farmers to help defray the costs of fertilizer, drainage, and other production costs.

The federal government also provides basic research, insurance, marketing, grading, and inspection services to farmers at subsidized prices. All these subsidies serve to lower fixed or variable costs. Their net impact is to stimulate additional output, as illustrated in Figure 15.6.

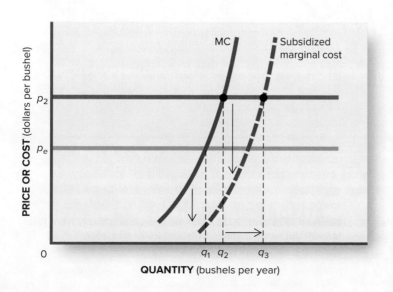

FIGURE 15.6

The Impact of Cost Subsidies

Cost subsidies lower the marginal cost of producing at any given rate of output, thereby shifting the marginal cost curve downward. The lower marginal costs make higher rates of output more profitable and thus increase output. At price p_2, lower marginal costs increase the farmer's profit-maximizing rate of output from q_2 to q_3.

CONTINUING INCOME VOLATILITY

With so many price supports, supply restrictions, cost subsidies, and income transfers, one would think that farming is a riskless and profitable business. But this hasn't been the case. Incomes remain low and unstable, especially for small farmers.

1980–1986 Depression

In fact, the entire agricultural sector experienced another setback in the 1980s. In 1980 the net income of U.S. farmers fell 42 percent. As Figure 15.7 shows, farm incomes recovered somewhat in 1981 but then resumed their steep decline in 1982. In 1983 farmers' net income was only one-third the level of 1979. This income loss was steeper than that of the Great Depression. Real farm income was actually lower in 1983 than in 1933. This second depression of farm incomes accelerated the exodus of small farmers from agriculture, severely weakened rural economies, and bankrupted many farm banks and manufacturers of farm equipment and supplies.

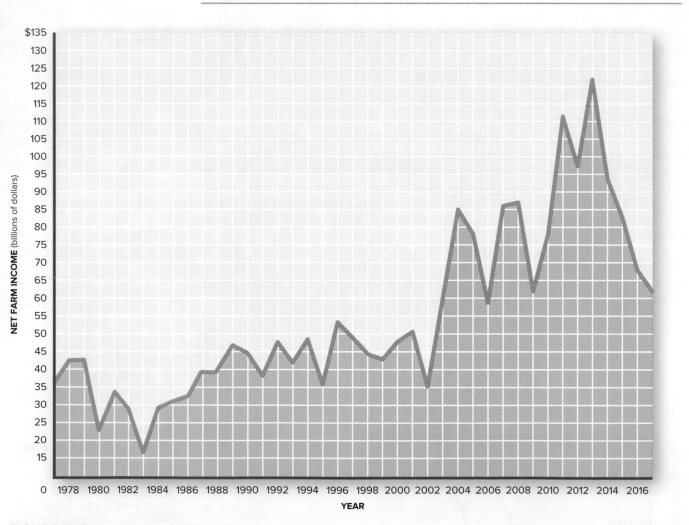

FIGURE 15.7

Net Farm Income, 1977–2017

Between 1979 and 1983 net farm income fell 64 percent. This decline was steeper than the income slide that occurred during the Great Depression (when net farm income fell 45 percent between 1929 and 1933). Farm incomes rose sharply from 1983 to 1989 but were unstable between 2007 and 2017.

Source: U.S. Department of Agriculture.

This second depression of farm incomes was not caused by abrupt price declines. Prices for farm products increased slightly between 1979 and 1983. But production costs rose much faster, led by higher fuel, fertilizer, and interest rate costs. Average farm production costs rose 30 percent between 1979 and 1983 while the average price of farm products increased only 1.5 percent. As a result, the **profit** (net income) of farmers fell abruptly.

profit: The difference between total revenue and total cost.

2008–2013 Surge

The period from 2008–2013 was a much more prosperous time for farmers. Even though the U.S. economy suffered a Great Recession in 2008–2009, American farmers did very well. A multi-year drought curtailed crop production and sent crop prices to record highs, with the price of corn exceeding $8 a bushel (see Figure 15.2). At the same time, the recession in the rest of the economy brought down the price of farm inputs. A weak dollar also helped farmers sell exports. Farm incomes peaked at $124 billion in 2013 (Figure 15.7).

Another Price Slide

As we noted earlier, high prices encourage farmers to plant more crops. That is what happened after crop prices rose to record highs in 2012–2013. Farm plantings and harvests increased significantly, driving crop prices down. The price of corn fell from over $8 a bushel in 2012 to close to $3 in 2012–2017. Weak foreign economies and a strong dollar worsened the situation further by depressing farm exports. The net result was a decline in farm incomes of roughly 50 percent between 2013 and 2017. A good thing didn't last long.

THE ECONOMY TOMORROW

FARMERS ON THE DOLE

It is apparent that farming continues to be a volatile business. Small variations in production—whether caused by the weather, global economic forces, or farmer's lagged planting responses–cause wild swings in crop prices. Furthermore, unceasing advances in agricultural technology, combined with low income and price elasticities for food, pretty much guarantee that farm prices will continue to lag behind general price inflation. Politicians also emphasize how important it is to have a secure source of food in the event of war. Given these realities, it seems certain that farmers will stay on the government dole in the economy tomorrow.

The 2018 Farm Bill. The specifics of government programs to assist farmers are spelled out in Congressional legislation. The 2014 Farm Bill eliminated direct payments to farmers and replaced them with payments based on price or revenue deficiencies. But the core system of crop subsidies was left intact.

The legal authority of the 2014 Farm Bill expires in September 2018. That will require the Congress to write a new piece of legislation, the 2018 Farm Bill. Given the recent decline in farm incomes, no one expects Congress to cut subsidy programs.

Most of the additional help farmers want lies outside the authority of the Farm Bill. Farmers are particularly angry about environmental regulations mandated by the Obama administration in 2011. Those restrictions redefine the concept of "waterways" to include ponds, creeks, and other small water accumulations, subjecting them to federal

Continued

regulation. New EPA rules also require expensive water testing, a requirement that small farmers say is very burdensome. President Trump repealed some of these regulations.

Farmers are also very concerned about immigration and trade policies. Farmers depend heavily on immigrant workers to harvest their crops. They also export as much as 30 percent of their harvests to other nations, so are hopeful that America doesn't upend international trade flows. So, the pending 2018 Farm Bill is of less concern than developments in immigration and trade.

Although farmers are sure to get continuing subsidies in the economy tomorrow, there is still a lot of opposition to these programs. Environmentalists emphasize that farming is the source of some of our worst pollution problems, especially the discharges of animal waste and other debris into waterways. They insist that if farmers are going to be subsidized, they should be required to protect the environment better. Others want stricter safeguards on food processing and safety as a condition of continuing subsidies.

Last but not least, free marketers continue to insist that the whole system of farm subsidies is inefficient and inequitable. Why do only a handful of crops (e.g., corn, wheat, sugar, honey, etc.) get subsidies while others don't? Are the prices of lemons, chickens, strawberries any less volatile than cotton or corn prices? Aren't they subject to the same internal and external forces that dictate incomes for subsidized farmers? As they see it, the current system is not only inequitable, but inefficient because it causes farmers to make uneconomical production decisions and forces the government to stockpile farm surpluses.

Despite these objections, farmers will continue on the federal dole for many years to come.

SUMMARY

- The agricultural sector has a highly competitive structure, with approximately 2 million farms. Many crops are regulated, however, by government restrictions and subsidies. **LO15-1**
- Most farm output is produced by the small percentage of large farms that enjoy economies of scale. Most small farmers rely on nonfarm employment for their income. **LO15-1**
- In a free market, farm prices tend to decline over time because of increasing productivity and low income elasticity of demand. Variations in harvests, combined with a low price elasticity of demand, make farm prices unstable. **LO15-1**
- Most of today's farm policies originated during the Great Depression in response to low farm prices and incomes. **LO15-3**

- The government uses price supports and cost subsidies to raise farm prices and profits. These policies cause resource misallocations and create market surpluses of specific commodities. **LO15-2**
- The 1996 Farm Act called for a phaseout of farm subsidies. Falling prices and incomes during 1997–2001 stalled and eventually reversed that process, as reflected in the 2008 and 2014 Farm Acts. **LO15-2**
- Farm prices and incomes continue to be highly volatile, despite government subsidy programs. **LO15-3**
- Critics demand that farmers assume more environmental responsibility in return for their subsidies. Other critics want to dismantle the whole system of farm subsidies and let farmers depend on market forces. **LO15-3**

Key Terms

market power	income elasticity of demand	loan rate
barriers to entry	market surplus	reference price
economic profit	parity	profit
price elasticity of demand	acreage set-aside	

Questions for Discussion

1. Would the U.S. economy be better off without government intervention in agriculture? Who would benefit? Who would lose? **LO15-3**

2. Are large price movements inevitable in agricultural markets? What other mechanisms might be used to limit such movement? **LO15-1**

3. Why doesn't the United States just give its crop surpluses to poor countries? What problems might such an approach create? **LO15-3**

4. Farmers can eliminate the uncertainties of fluctuating crop prices by selling their crops in futures markets (agreeing to a fixed price for crops to be delivered in the future). Who gains or loses from this practice? **LO15-2**

5. How do farmers of unsubsidized crops survive and thrive? **LO15-2**

6. You need a government permit (allotment) to grow tobacco. Who gains or loses from such regulation? **LO15-2**

7. Why are the price and income elasticities for food so low? **LO15-1**

8. How have farmers increased milk production per cow so much (see section Destabilizing Forces)? How does this affect milk prices? **LO15-1**

9. What are some of the farmers' concerns beyond what is covered in the Farm Bill? How should government best help farmers? **LO15-1**

PROBLEMS FOR CHAPTER 15

LO15-1 1. According to In the News "Anticipated Surge in Harvest to Depress Corn Prices,"
   (a) By what percent did the quantity of corn supplied increase in 2016?
   (b) If the price elasticity of demand for corn is 0.15, by how much did price decline?

LO15-1 2. If this year's harvest was greater than last year's by 12%, to sell all of the crop, how much does price have to change if the price elasticity of demand is 0.2?

LO15-1 3. According to Figure 15.2, how much did corn prices change between 2000 and 2012 in percentage terms?

LO15-2 4. The following tables show the market demand and supply for soybeans.

Price ($ per Bushel)	Quantity Demanded (Bushels per Year)	Quantity Supplied (Bushels per Year)
10	0	120
9	10	110
8	20	100
7	30	90
6	40	80
5	50	70
4	60	60
3	70	50
2	80	40
1	90	30
0	100	20

   (a) What is the equilibrium price?
   (b) What is the equilibrium quantity?
   Suppose the CCC loan rate is $5.
   (c) What is the new quantity supplied?
   (d) What is the new quantity demanded?
   (e) How much is this shortage or surplus?

LO15-2 5. Suppose the market price of corn is $1.80 per bushel.
   (a) Would a farmer sell corn to the market or to the government (CCC)? (See Table 15.2.)
   (b) If the market price rose to $2, what would the farmer do with his corn?

LO15-1 6. Suppose that consumers' incomes increase 10 percent, which results in a 0.6 percent increase in consumption of farm goods at current prices. What is the income elasticity of demand for farm goods?

LO15-3 7. Assume that the unregulated supply schedule for milk is the following:

Price (per pound)	18¢	24¢	30¢	36¢	42¢
Quantity supplied (billions of pounds per year)	43	53	63	73	83

   (a) Draw the supply and demand curves for milk, assuming that the demand for milk is perfectly inelastic (vertical) and consumers will buy 53 billion pounds of it.
   (b) What is the equilibrium price?
   Now suppose the government pays milk producers to set aside production by 20 billion pounds per year.
   (c) Draw this new supply curve that reflects the government's action.
   (d) What is the equilibrium price following the government's action?
   (e) How much more money are consumers paying for the 53 billion pounds of milk because of the higher equilibrium price?

LO15-3 8. Suppose there are 100 grain farmers, each with identical cost structures as shown in the following tables:

Production Costs (per Farm)			Demand	
Output (Bushels per Day)	Total Cost (per Day)		Price (per Bushel)	Quantity Demanded (Bushels per Day)
0	$ 5		$1	600
1	7		2	500
2	10		3	400
3	14		4	300
4	19		5	200
5	25		6	100
6	33		7	50

Under these circumstances, graph the market supply and demand.
(a) What is the equilibrium price for grain?
(b) How much grain will be produced at the equilibrium price?
(c) How much total profit will each farmer earn at that price?
(d) If the government gives farmers a cost subsidy equal to $1 a bushel, what will happen to
 (i) Output?
 (ii) Price?
 (iii) Profit?
(e) What will happen to total output if the government additionally guarantees a price of $5 per bushel?
(f) What price is required to sell this output?
(g) What is the cost to the government in d?
(h) Show your answers on the accompanying graph.

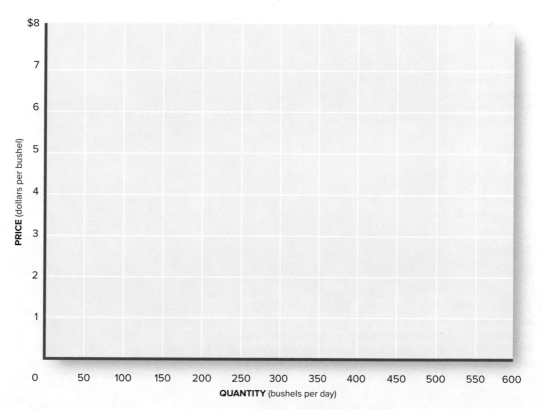

LO15-2   9. The Economy Tomorrow:

    (*a*) According to Figure 15.7, how much did farm incomes change (in percentage terms) 2008–2010?

    (*b*) If a law is passed that limits immigration, what is the predicted impact on farm incomes?

    (*c*) If subsidies are extended to agricultural products like strawberries, chickens, and lemons, what is the predicted impact on farm incomes?

©MOF/Getty Images RF

©Chattanooga Times Free Press, John Rawlston/AP Images

©Mark Richard/PhotoEdit

©Steve Allen/Stockbyte/Getty Images RF

FACTOR MARKETS: BASIC THEORY

Factor markets operate like product markets, with supply and demand interacting to determine prices and quantities. In factor markets, however, resource inputs rather than products are exchanged. Those exchanges determine the wages paid to workers and the rent, interest, and profits paid to other inputs. The micro theories presented in Chapters 16, 17, and 18 explain how those factor payments are determined.

CHAPTER 16

The Labor Market

Dwayne "The Rock" Johnson was paid $6.4 million in 2016 for starring in movies like *Fast 8* and *Central Intelligence*. LeBron James received $23 million for playing basketball and another $46 million in product endorsements (see Chapter 8). Yet the president of the United States was paid only $400,000. And the administrative assistant who typed the manuscript of this book was paid just $19,000. What accounts for these tremendous disparities in earnings?

Why does the average college graduate earn close to $60,000 while the average high school graduate earns just $30,000? Are such disparities simply a reward for enduring four years of college, or do they reflect real differences in talent?

Surely we can't hope to explain these earnings disparities on the basis of the willingness to work. After all, my administrative assistant would be more than willing to work day and night for $6.4 million per year. For that matter, so would I. Accordingly, the earnings disparities can't be attributed to differences in the quantity of labor supplied. If we're going to explain why some people earn a great deal of income while others earn very little, we must consider both the *supply* and the *demand* for labor. In this regard, the following questions arise:

- **How do people decide how much time to spend working?**
- **What determines the wage rate an employer is willing to pay?**
- **Why are some workers paid so much and others so little?**

To answer these questions, we must examine the behavior of labor *markets*.

LEARNING OBJECTIVES

After reading this chapter, you should know

LO16-1 What factors shape labor supply and demand.

LO16-2 How market wage rates are established.

LO16-3 How wage floors alter labor market outcomes.

LABOR SUPPLY

The following two ads recently appeared in the campus newspaper of a well-known university:

Will do ANYTHING for money: able-bodied liberal-minded male needs money, will work to get it. Have car. Call Josh 765-3210.

Web architect. Experienced website designer. Looking for part-time or consulting position on or off campus. Please call Danielle, ext. 0872, 9–5.

Although placed by individuals of very different talents, the ads clearly expressed Josh's and Danielle's willingness to work. Although we don't know how much money they were asking for their respective talents or whether they ever found jobs, we can be sure that they were prepared to take a job at some wage rate. Otherwise they wouldn't have paid for the ads in the "Jobs Wanted" column of their campus newspaper.

The advertised willingness to work represents a **supply of labor.** These individuals are offering to sell their time and talents to anyone who's willing to pay the right price. Their explicit offers are similar to those of anyone who looks for a job. Job seekers who check the current job openings at the student employment office, tap into Monster.com, or e-mail résumés to potential employers are demonstrating a willingness to accept employment—that is, to *supply* labor. The 4,000 people who applied for jobs at a job fair in Berlin, Germany (see World View "Thousands of Refugees Attend Job Fair") were also offering to supply labor.

> **labor supply:** The willingness and ability to work specific amounts of time at alternative wage rates in a given time period, *ceteris paribus*.

WORLD VIEW

THOUSANDS OF REFUGEES ATTEND JOB FAIR

Berlin—Over 4,000 refugees showed up at the first-ever refugee-only job fair held in Germany. 211 companies sought workers in information technology, health care, tourism, and construction. One employer noted that the job seekers displayed a "huge willingness" among the refugees to find a job—any job. The mayor noted that employment would not only help fill job vacancies in Berlin but also speed the assimilation of refugees into German life.

Source: Media reports of March 1, 2016.

ANALYSIS: The quantity of labor supplied at any given wage rate depends on the value of leisure and the desire for income. These Berlin job-seekers were all willing to supply labor.

Our first concern in this chapter is to explain these labor supply decisions. How do people decide how many hours to supply at any given wage rate? Do people try to maximize their total wages? If they did, we'd all be holding three jobs and sleeping on the commuter bus. Since most of us don't behave this way, other motives must be present.

Income vs. Leisure

The reward for working comes in two forms: (1) the intrinsic satisfaction of working and (2) a paycheck. MBA grads say they care more about the intrinsic satisfaction than the pay (see In the News "Challenging Work and Corporate Responsibility Will Lure MBA Grads"). They also get huge paychecks, however. Those big paychecks are explained in part by the quantity of labor supplied: MBA grads often end up working 60 or more hours a week. The reason people are willing to work so many hours is that they want more income.

Not working obviously has some value, too. In part, we need some nonwork time just to recuperate from working. We also want some leisure time to watch television, go to a soccer game, or enjoy other goods and services we've purchased.

The Trade-Off. Since both working and *not* working are rewarding, we have a dilemma: the more time we spend working, the more income we have but also less time to enjoy it. Working, like all activities, involves an opportunity cost: *the opportunity cost of working is the amount of leisure time that must be given up in the process.*

This inevitable trade-off between labor and leisure explains the shape of individual labor supply curves. As we work more hours, our leisure time becomes more scarce—and thus more valuable. Hence **higher wage rates are required to compensate for the increasing opportunity cost of labor** (forgone leisure). We'll work more—supply a larger quantity of

IN THE NEWS

CHALLENGING WORK AND CORPORATE RESPONSIBILITY WILL LURE MBA GRADS

STANFORD GRADUATE SCHOOL OF BUSINESS—A survey of 759 graduating MBAs at 11 top business schools reveals that the future business leaders rank corporate social responsibility high on their list of values, and they are willing to sacrifice a significant part of their salaries to find an employer whose thinking is in sync with their own.

The study by David Montgomery and Catherine Ramus of UC Santa Barbara examines the trade-offs students are willing to make when selecting a potential employer. They found that intellectual challenge ranked number one in desirable job attributes, while money and location were essentially tied for second, each roughly 80 percent as important as the most important factor.

The researchers found that the students expected to earn an average of $103,650 a year at their first job. Nearly all (97.3 percent) said they would be willing to make a financial sacrifice to work for a company that exhibited all four characteristics of social responsibility. They said they would sacrifice an average of $14,902 a year, or 14.4 percent of their expected salary.

What MBAs at Some Top Schools Earn

School	Starting Salaries in 2016
University of Pennsylvania	$155,058
Harvard	153,830
Stanford	153,553
University of Virginia	150,823
Columbia	150,229
Dartmouth	148,997
Chicago	147,475
Cornell	146,252
University of Michigan	145,926

Source: Global MBA Rankings 2016, *U.S. News & World Report*, Copyright ©2016.

Source: Stanford Graduate School of Business.

ANALYSIS: The quantity of labor supplied depends on the intrinsic satisfaction of working and the wages paid. MBA grads apparently work long hours for both high wages and job satisfaction. Would they work just as hard for *less* pay?

labor—only if offered a higher wage rate. This is reflected in the upward slope of the labor supply curve in Figure 16.1.

The upward slope of the labor supply curve is reinforced with the changing value of income. Those first few dollars earned on the job are really precious, especially if you have bills to pay. As you work and earn more, however, your most urgent needs will be satisfied. You may still want more things, but the urgency of your consumption desires is likely to diminish. Another dollar of wages doesn't mean as much. In other words, *the marginal*

FIGURE 16.1

The Supply of Labor

The quantity of any good or service offered for sale typically increases as its price rises. Labor supply responds in the same way. At the wage rate w_1, the quantity of labor supplied is q_1 (point A). At the higher wage w_2, workers are willing to work more hours per week—that is, to supply a larger quantity of labor (q_2).

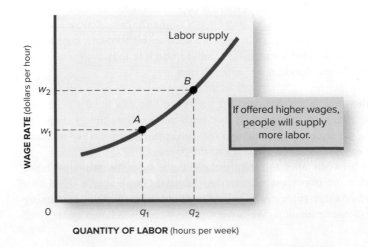

If offered higher wages, people will supply more labor.

utility of income may decline as you earn more. If this happens, you may not be willing to work more hours unless offered a still higher wage rate.

The upward slope of an individual's labor supply curve is therefore explained by the fact that as hours worked increase,

- The value of leisure time increases.
- The marginal utility of income decreases.

Money isn't necessarily the only thing that motivates people to work. People *do* turn down higher-paying jobs in favor of lower-wage jobs that they like. Many parents forgo high-wage "career" jobs to have more flexible hours and time at home. Volunteers offer their services just for the sense of contributing to their communities; they don't need a paycheck. Even MBA graduates say they're motivated more by the challenge of high-paying jobs than the money (see the previous News). But money almost always makes a difference: *People do supply more labor when offered higher wages.*

A Backward Bend?

The force that drives people up the labor supply curve is the lust for more income. Higher wages enable people to buy more goods and services. To achieve higher levels of consumption, people decide to *substitute* labor for leisure. This is the **substitution effect of higher wages.**

At some point, however, higher wages may not be so persuasive. Working added hours just to accumulate a few more toys may not seem so compelling. In fact, higher wages might create the opportunity to work *less*—without giving up any toys. Muhammad Ali once announced that he wouldn't spend an hour in the ring for less than $1 million and would box *less,* not more, as the pay for his fights exceeded $3 million. For him, the added income from one championship fight was so great that he felt he didn't have to fight more to satisfy his income and consumption desires.

A low-wage worker might also respond to higher wage rates by working *less,* not more. People receiving very low wages (such as migrant workers, household help, and babysitters) have to work really long hours just to pay the rent. The increased income made possible by higher wage rates might permit them to work *fewer* hours. These *negative* labor supply responses to increased wage rates are referred to as the **income effect of higher wages.**

The conflict between income and substitution effects shapes an individual's labor supply curve. The *substitution effect* of higher wages encourages people to work more hours. The *income effect,* on the other hand, allows them to reduce work hours without losing income. If substitution effects dominate, the labor supply curve will be upward-sloping. *If income effects outweigh substitution effects, an individual will supply **less** labor at higher wages.* This kind of reaction is illustrated by the backward-bending portion of the supply curve in Figure 16.2.

substitution effect of higher wages: An increased wage rate encourages people to work more hours (to substitute labor for leisure).

income effect of higher wages: An increased wage rate allows a person to reduce hours worked without losing income.

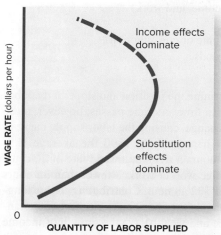

FIGURE 16.2

The Backward-Bending Supply Curve

Increases in wage rates make additional hours of work more valuable but also less necessary. Higher wage rates increase the quantity of labor supplied as long as substitution effects outweigh income effects. At the point where income effects begin to outweigh substitution effects, the labor supply curve starts to bend backward.

Backward-bending labor supply curves are more the exception than the rule. Most Americans do want more leisure. But given the choice between more leisure or more income, Americans choose added income (see World View "Your Money or Your Life"). In other words, substitution effects outweigh income effects in the U.S. labor force. This explains why Americans work such long hours despite their comparatively high incomes. Workers in Mexico and India, by contrast, appear to covet more leisure rather than more income.

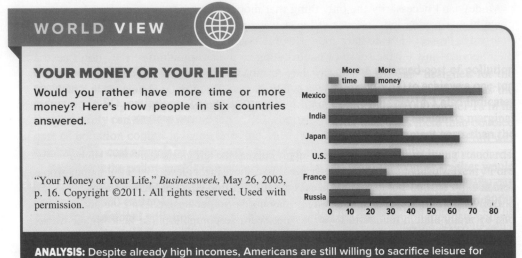

WORLD VIEW

YOUR MONEY OR YOUR LIFE

Would you rather have more time or more money? Here's how people in six countries answered.

"Your Money or Your Life," *Businessweek,* May 26, 2003, p. 16. Copyright ©2011. All rights reserved. Used with permission.

ANALYSIS: Despite already high incomes, Americans are still willing to sacrifice leisure for more income; *substitution effects* outweigh *income effects.*

market supply of labor: The total quantity of labor that workers are willing and able to supply at alternative wage rates in a given time period, *ceteris paribus.*

MARKET SUPPLY

The **market supply of labor** represents the sum of all individual labor supply decisions. Although some individuals have backward-bending supply curves, these negative responses to higher wages are swamped by positive responses from the 160 million individuals who participate in the U.S. labor market. As a result, the *market* supply curve is upward-sloping.

The upward slope of the labor supply curve doesn't imply that we'll all be working longer hours in the future. As time passes, the labor supply curve can *shift*. And it will whenever one of the underlying determinants of supply changes. ***The determinants of labor supply include***

- ***Tastes*** (for leisure, income, and work).
- ***Income and wealth.***
- ***Expectations*** (for income or consumption).
- ***Prices*** of consumer goods.
- ***Taxes.***

These shift factors determine the position and slope of the labor supply curve at any point in time. As time passes, however, these underlying determinants change, causing the labor supply curve to shift. This has evidently happened. In 1890 the average U.S. worker was employed 60 hours a week at a wage rate of 20 cents an hour. In 2016 the average worker worked fewer than 35 hours per week at a wage rate of $22 an hour. Contributing to this long-run leftward shift has been (1) the spectacular rise in living standards (a change in income and wealth), (2) the growth of income transfer programs that provide economic security when one isn't

Analysis: Monster.com brings together the supply and demand for labor.

Source: www.monster.com

working (a change in income and expectations), and (3) the increased diversity and attractiveness of leisure activities (a change in tastes and other goods).

Elasticity of Labor Supply

Despite the evident *long*-run shifts of the labor supply curve, workers still respond positively to higher wage rates in the *short* run. To measure the resulting movements along the labor supply curve, we use the familiar concept of elasticity. Specifically, the **elasticity of labor supply** is the percentage change in the quantity of labor supplied divided by the percentage change in the wage rate:

$$\text{Elasticity of labor supply} = \frac{\text{\% change in quantity of labor supplied}}{\text{\% change in wage rate}}$$

The elasticity of labor tells us how much *more* labor will be available if a higher wage is offered. If the elasticity of labor is 0.2, a 10 percent increase in wage rates will induce a 2 percent increase in the quantity of labor supplied.

The actual responsiveness of workers to a change in wage rates depends on the determinants of labor supply. Time is also important for labor supply elasticity because individuals can't always adjust their schedules or change jobs instantaneously.

> **elasticity of labor supply:** The percentage change in the quantity of labor supplied divided by the percentage change in wage rate.

Institutional Constraints

The labor supply curve and its related elasticities tell us how much time people would like to allocate to work. We must recognize, however, that people seldom have the opportunity to adjust their hours of employment at will. True, a Mark Zuckerberg or a Lady Gaga can easily choose to work more or fewer hours. Most workers, however, face more rigid choices. They must usually choose to work at a regular job for eight hours a day, five days a week, or not to work at all. Very few firms are flexible enough to accommodate a desire to work only between the hours of 11 a.m. and 3 p.m. on alternate Thursdays. Adjustments in work hours are more commonly confined to choices about overtime work or secondary jobs (moonlighting) and vacation and retirement. Families may also alter the labor supply by varying the number of family members sent into the labor force at any given time. Students, too, can often adjust their work hours. The flow of immigrants into the U.S. labor market also increases when U.S. wages rise.

LABOR DEMAND

Regardless of how many people are *willing* to work, it's up to employers to decide how many people will *actually* work. That is, there must be a **demand for labor.** What determines the number of workers employers are willing to hire at various wage rates?

> **demand for labor:** The quantities of labor employers are willing and able to hire at alternative wage rates in a given time period, *ceteris paribus.*

Derived Demand

In earlier chapters we emphasized that employers are profit maximizers. In their quest for maximum profits, firms seek the rate of output at which marginal revenue equals marginal cost. Once they've identified the profit-maximizing rate of output, firms enter factor markets to purchase the required amounts of labor, equipment, and other resources. Thus *the quantity of resources purchased by a business depends on the firm's expected sales and output.* In this sense, the demand for factors of production, including labor, is a **derived demand;** it's derived from the demand for goods and services.

Consider the plight of strawberry pickers. Strawberry pickers are paid very low wages and are employed only part of the year. But their plight can't be blamed on the greed of the strawberry growers. Strawberry growers, like most producers, would love to sell more strawberries at higher prices. If they did, the growers would hire more pickers and might even pay them higher wages. But the growers must contend with the market demand for strawberries: consumers aren't willing to buy more strawberries at higher prices. As a

> **derived demand:** The demand for labor and other factors of production results from (depends on) the demand for final goods and services produced by these factors.

consequence, the growers can't afford to hire more pickers or pay them higher wages. In contrast, information technology (IT) firms are always looking for more workers and offer very high wages to get them. This helps explain why college students who major in engineering, math, or computer science get paid a lot more than philosophy majors. IT specialists benefit from the growing demand for Internet services, while philosophy majors suffer because the search for the meaning of life is not a growth industry.

The principle of derived demand suggests that if consumers really want to improve the lot of strawberry pickers, they should eat more strawberries. An increase in the demand for strawberries will motivate growers to plant more berries and hire more labor to pick them. Until then, the plight of the pickers isn't likely to improve.

The Labor Demand Curve

The number of strawberry pickers hired by the growers isn't completely determined by the demand for strawberries. The number of pickers hired will also depend on the wage rate. That is, *the quantity of labor demanded depends on its price (the wage rate)*. In general, we expect that strawberry growers will be *willing to hire* more pickers at low wages than at higher wages. Hence the demand for labor looks very much like the demand for any good or service (see Figure 16.3).

Marginal Physical Product

The fact that the demand curve for labor slopes downward doesn't tell us what quantity of labor will be hired. Nor does it tell us what wage rate will be paid. To answer such questions, we need to know what determines the particular shape and position of the labor demand curve.

A strawberry grower will be willing to hire another picker only if that picker contributes more to output than he or she costs. Growers, as rational businesspeople, recognize that *every* sale and *every* expenditure have some impact on total profits. Hence the truly profit-maximizing grower will evaluate each picker's job application in terms of the applicant's potential contribution to profits.

Fortunately, a strawberry picker's contribution to output is easy to measure; it's the number of boxes of strawberries he or she picks. Suppose for the moment that Marvin, a college dropout with three summers of experience as a canoe instructor, is able to pick five boxes per hour. These five boxes represent Marvin's **marginal physical product (MPP)**. In other words, Marvin's MPP is the *addition* to total output that occurs when the grower hires him for an hour:

marginal physical product (MPP): The change in total output associated with one additional unit of input.

$$\text{Marginal physical product} = \frac{\text{Change in total output}}{\text{Change in quantity of labor}}$$

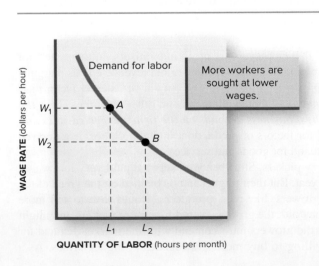

FIGURE 16.3

The Demand for Labor

The higher the wage rate, the smaller the quantity of labor demanded (*ceteris paribus*). At the wage rate W_1, only L_1 of labor is demanded. If the wage rate falls to W_2, a larger quantity of labor (L_2) will be demanded. The labor demand curve obeys the law of demand.

WAGE RATE (dollars per hour)

Demand for labor

More workers are sought at lower wages.

W_1 A

W_2 B

L_1 L_2

QUANTITY OF LABOR (hours per month)

Marginal physical product establishes an *upper* limit to the grower's willingness to pay. Clearly the grower can't afford to pay Marvin more than five boxes of strawberries for an hour's work; the grower won't pay Marvin more than he produces.

Marginal Revenue Product

Most strawberry pickers don't want to be paid in strawberries. At the end of a day in the fields, the last thing a picker wants to see is another strawberry. Marvin, like the rest of the pickers, wants to be paid in cash. To find out how much cash he might be paid, we need to know what a box of strawberries is worth. This is easy to determine. The market value of a box of strawberries is simply the price at which the grower can sell it. Thus Marvin's contribution to output can be measured by either marginal *physical* product (five boxes per hour) or the dollar *value* of that product.

The dollar value of a worker's contribution to output is called **marginal revenue product (MRP).** Marginal revenue product is the *change* in total revenue that occurs when more labor is hired:

$$\text{Marginal revenue product} = \frac{\text{Change in total revenue}}{\text{Change in quantity of labor}}$$

In Marvin's case, the "change in quantity of labor" is one extra hour of picking strawberries. The "change in total revenue" is the *value* of the extra five boxes of berries Marvin picks in that hour. If the grower can sell strawberries for $2 a box, Marvin's marginal revenue product is simply 5 boxes per hour × $2 per box, or $10 per hour.

We could have come to the same conclusion by multiplying marginal *physical* product times *price:*

$$\text{MRP} = \text{MPP} \times \rho$$

or

$$\$10 \text{ per hour} = 5 \text{ boxes per hour} \times \$2 \text{ per box}$$

In compliance with the rule about not paying anybody more than he or she contributes, the profit-maximizing grower should be willing to pay Marvin *up to* $10 an hour. In other words, ***marginal revenue product sets an upper limit to the wage rate an employer will pay.***

But what about a lower limit? Suppose the pickers aren't organized and Marvin is desperate for money. Under such circumstances, he might be willing to work—to supply labor—for only $4 an hour.

Should the grower hire Marvin for such a low wage? The profit-maximizing answer is obvious. If Marvin's marginal revenue product is $10 an hour and his wages are only $4 an hour, the grower will be eager to hire him. The difference between Marvin's marginal revenue product ($10) and his wage ($4) implies additional profits of $6 an hour. In fact, the grower will be so elated by the economics of this situation that he'll want to hire everybody he can find who's willing to work for $4 an hour. After all, if the grower can make $6 an hour by hiring Marvin, why not hire 1,000 pickers and accumulate profits at an even faster rate?

The Law of Diminishing Returns

The exploitative possibilities suggested by Marvin's picking are too good to be true. It isn't at all clear, for example, how the grower could squeeze 1,000 workers onto one acre of land and have any room left over for strawberry plants. There must be some limit to the profit-making potential of this situation.

A few moments' reflection on the absurdity of trying to employ 1,000 people to pick one acre of strawberries should be ample warning of the limits to profits here. You don't need two years of business school to recognize this. But some grasp of economics may help explain exactly why the grower's eagerness to hire additional pickers will begin to fade long before 1,000 are hired. The operative concept here is *marginal productivity.*

marginal revenue product (MRP): The change in total revenue associated with one additional unit of input.

We can measure a worker's output in *physical* terms (e.g., boxes of strawberries) or *dollar* terms (value of those boxes).

©Photodisc/Getty Images RF

Diminishing MPP. The decision to hire Marvin originated in his marginal physical product—that is, the five boxes of strawberries he can pick in an hour's time. To assess the wisdom of hiring still more pickers, we have to *consider how total output will change if additional labor is employed.* To do so, we need to keep track of marginal physical product.

Figure 16.4 shows how strawberry output changes as additional pickers are hired. Marvin picks five boxes of strawberries per hour. Total output and his marginal physical product are identical because he's initially the only picker employed. When the grower hires George, Marvin's old college roommate, we observe that the total output increases to 10 boxes per hour (point *B* in Figure 16.4). This figure represents another increase of five boxes per hour. Accordingly, we may conclude that George's *marginal physical product* is five boxes per hour, the same as Marvin's. Given such productivity, the grower will want to hire George and continue looking for more pickers.

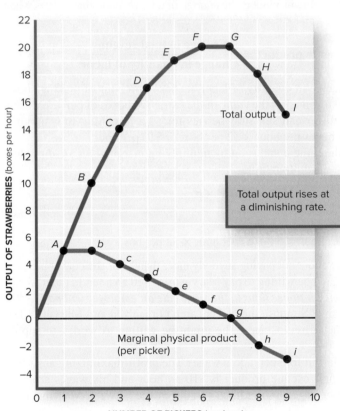

Total output

Total output rises at a diminishing rate.

Marginal physical product (per picker)

FIGURE 16.4

Diminishing Marginal Physical Product

The marginal physical product (MPP) of labor is the *increase* in total production that results when one additional worker is hired. MPP tends to fall as additional workers are hired in any given production process. This decline occurs because each worker has increasingly less of other factors (e.g., land) with which to work. When the second worker (George) is hired, total output increases from 5 to 10 boxes per hour. Hence the second worker's MPP equals 5 boxes per hour. Thereafter, capital and land constraints diminish marginal physical product.

	Number of Pickers (per Hour)	Total Strawberry Output (Boxes per Hour)	Marginal Physical Product (Boxes per Hour)
	0	0	—
A	1 (Marvin)	5	5
B	2 (George)	10	5
C	3	14	4
D	4	17	3
E	5	19	2
F	6	20	1
G	7	20	0
H	8	18	−2
I	9	15	−3

As more workers are hired, total strawberry output continues to increase but not nearly as fast. Although the later hires work just as hard, the limited availability of land and capital constrain their marginal physical product. One problem is the number of boxes. There are only a dozen boxes, and the additional pickers often have to wait for an empty box. The time spent waiting depresses marginal physical product. The worst problem is space: as additional workers are crowded onto the one-acre patch, they begin to get in one another's way. The picking process is slowed, and marginal physical product is further depressed. Note that the MPP of the fifth picker is two boxes per hour, while the MPP of the sixth picker is only one box per hour. By the time we get to the seventh picker, marginal physical product actually falls to zero because no further increases in total strawberry output take place.

Things get even worse if the grower hires still more pickers. If eight pickers are employed, total output actually *declines*. The pickers can no longer work efficiently under such crowded conditions. The MPP of the eighth worker is *negative,* no matter how ambitious or hardworking this person may be. Figure 16.4 illustrates this decline in marginal physical product, beyond point *G* on the total output curve and beyond point *g* on the MPP curve.

Our observations on strawberry production are similar to those made in most industries. In the short run, the availability of land and capital is limited by prior investment decisions. Hence additional workers must share existing facilities. As a result, *the marginal physical product of labor eventually declines as the quantity of labor employed increases.* This is the **law of diminishing returns** we first encountered in Chapter 7. It's based on the simple observation that an increasing number of workers leaves each worker with less land and capital to work with. At some point, this "crowding" causes MPP to decline.

Diminishing MRP. *As marginal physical product (MPP) diminishes, so does marginal revenue product (MRP).* As noted earlier, marginal revenue product is the increase in the *value* of total output associated with an added unit of labor (or other input). In our example, it refers to the increase in strawberry revenues associated with one additional picker and is calculated as MPP × *p*.

The decline in marginal revenue product mirrors the drop in marginal physical product. Recall that a box of strawberries sells for $2. With this price and the output statistics in Figure 16.4, we can readily calculate marginal revenue product, as summarized in Table 16.1. As the growth of output diminishes, so does marginal revenue product. Marvin's marginal revenue product of $10 an hour has fallen to $6 by the time four pickers are employed and reaches zero when seven pickers are employed.[1]

law of diminishing returns: The marginal physical product of a variable input declines as more of it is employed with a given quantity of other (fixed) inputs.

Number of Pickers (per Hour)	Total Strawberry Output (in Boxes per Hour)	×	Price of Strawberry (per Box)	=	Total Strawberry Revenue (per Hour)	Marginal Revenue Product
0	0		$2		0	—
1 (Marvin)	5		2		$10	$10
2 (George)	10		2		20	10
3	14		2		28	8
4	17		2		34	6
5	19		2		38	4
6	20		2		40	2
7	20		2		40	0
8	18		2		36	-4
9	15		2		30	-6

TABLE 16.1

Diminishing Marginal Revenue Product

Marginal revenue product (MRP) measures the change in total revenue that occurs when one additional worker is hired. At constant product prices, MRP equals MPP × price. Hence MRP declines along with MPP.

[1]Marginal revenue product would fall even faster if the price of strawberries declined as increasing quantities were supplied. We're assuming that the grower's output doesn't influence the market price of strawberries and hence that the grower is a *competitive* producer.

A FIRM'S HIRING DECISION

The tendency of marginal revenue product to diminish will cool the strawberry grower's eagerness to hire 1,000 pickers. We still don't know, however, how many pickers will be hired.

The Firm's Labor Supply

Our earlier discussion of labor supply indicated that more workers are available only at higher wage rates. But that's true only for the *market* supply. A single producer may be able to hire an unlimited number of workers at the prevailing wage rate—if the firm is perfectly competitive in the labor market. This happens when the single firm (or farm) is just a bit player in a much larger labor market. Like small firms in big product markets, it has no market power. In other words, *a firm that's a perfect competitor in the labor market can hire all the labor it wants at the prevailing market wage.*

Let's assume that the strawberry grower is so small that his hiring decisions have no effect on local wages. As far as he's concerned, there's an unlimited supply of strawberry pickers willing to work for $4 an hour. His only decision is how many of these willing pickers to hire at that wage rate.

MRP = Firm's Labor Demand

Figure 16.5 provides the answer. We already know that the grower is eager to hire pickers whose marginal revenue product exceeds their wage. He'll therefore hire at least one worker at that wage because the MRP of the first picker is $10 an hour (point *A* in Figure 16.5). A second worker will be hired as well because that picker's MRP (point *B* in Figure 16.5) also exceeds the going wage rate. In fact, *the grower will continue hiring pickers until the MRP has declined to the level of the market wage rate.* Figure 16.5 indicates that this intersection (point *C*) occurs when five pickers are employed. Accordingly the grower will be willing to hire—will *demand*—five pickers if wages are $4 an hour.

The folly of hiring more than five pickers is also apparent in Figure 16.5. The marginal revenue product of the sixth worker is only $2 an hour (point *D*). Hiring a sixth picker will cost more in wages ($4) than the picker brings in as revenue ($2). That makes no sense. The *maximum* number of pickers the grower will employ at prevailing wages is five (point *C*).

Equal Pay. The law of diminishing returns also implies that all five pickers will be paid the same wage. Once five pickers are employed, we can't say that any single picker is

FIGURE 16.5

The Marginal Revenue Product Curve Is the Labor Demand Curve

An employer is willing to pay a worker no more than the marginal revenue product. In this case, a grower would gladly hire a second worker because that worker's MRP (point *B*) exceeds the wage rate ($4). The sixth worker won't be hired at that wage rate, however, since the MRP (at point *D*) is less than $4. The MRP curve is the labor demand curve.

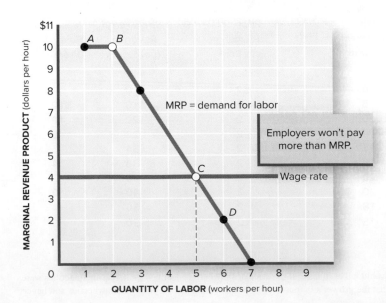

responsible for the observed decline in marginal revenue product. Marginal revenue product of labor diminishes because each worker has less capital and land to work with, not because the last worker hired is less able than the others. Accordingly, the "fifth" picker can't be identified as any particular individual. Once five pickers are hired, Marvin's MRP is no higher than any other picker's. *Each (identical) worker is worth no more than the marginal revenue product of the last worker hired, and all workers are paid the same wage rate.*

The principles of marginal revenue product apply to baseball players as well as strawberry pickers. When the Miami Marlins agreed to pay Giancarlo Stanton $325 million (see In the News "Marlins Sign Stanton to Record $325 Million Contract"), they had his MRP in mind. Not only had he led the National League in home runs and slugging, but he also caused a spike in attendance and in sales of souvenirs. If Giancarlo's bat could get the Marlins to the playoffs or World Series, total revenue would soar. The Marlins decided Giancarlo's MRP justified his extraordinary salary.

IN THE NEWS

MARLINS SIGN STANTON TO RECORD $325 MILLION CONTRACT

The Miami Marlins have signed outfielder Giancarlo Stanton to a record-breaking contract. The contract calls for Stanton to get $325 million over a 13-year period. This is the biggest amount ever paid to anyone in North American professional sports and the longest contract in baseball history. The Marlins are betting that Giancarlo (known as "Mike" prior to 2012) will propel the Marlins into National League playoffs and maybe the World Series. Last year Giancarlo led the National League with 37 home runs and a .555 slugging percentage, earning him the runner-up position in 2014's Most Valuable Player competition. He has hit some of the longest home runs in baseball history, including a 494-footer that hit the scoreboard in Coors Field.

©Jim McIsaac/Getty Images

Source: News reports, November 17–20, 2014.

ANALYSIS: Marginal revenue product measures what a worker is worth to an employer. The Miami Marlins expect a high MRP from Giancarlo Stanton.

Whatever the explanation for the disparity between the incomes of baseball players and strawberry pickers, the enormous gap between them seems awfully unfair. An obvious question then arises: Can't the number of pickers or their wages be increased?

Changes in Wage Rates

Suppose the government were to set a minimum wage for strawberry pickers at $6 an hour. At first glance this action would appear to boost the wages of pickers, who have been earning only $4 an hour. This isn't all good news for the strawberry pickers, however. *There's a trade-off between wage rates and the number of workers demanded.* If wage rates go up, growers will hire fewer pickers.

Figure 16.6a illustrates this trade-off. The grower's earlier decision to hire five pickers was based on a wage of $4 an hour (point *C*). If the wage jumps to $6 an hour, it no longer makes economic sense to keep five pickers employed. The MRP of the fifth worker is only

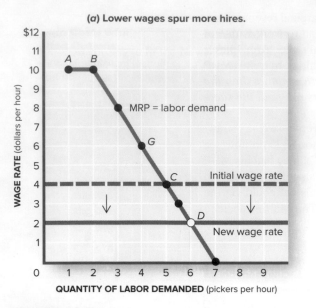

FIGURE 16.6

Incentives to Hire

(a) Lower wage   If the wage rate drops, an employer will be willing to hire more workers, *ceteris paribus*. At $4 an hour, only five pickers per hour would be demanded (point *C*). If the wage rate dropped to $2 an hour, six pickers per hour would be demanded (point *D*).

(b) Higher productivity   If the marginal revenue product of labor improves, the employer will hire a greater quantity of labor at any given wage rate. The labor demand curve will shift up (from D_1 to D_2). In this case, an increase in MRP leads the employer to hire six workers (point *E*) rather than only five workers (point *C*) at $4 per hour.

$4 an hour. The grower will respond to higher wage rates by moving up the labor demand curve to point *G*. At point *G*, only four pickers are hired, and MRP again equals the wage rate. If more workers are to be hired, the wage rate must drop.

Changes in Productivity

The downward slope of the labor demand curve doesn't doom strawberry pickers to low wages. It does emphasize, however, the inevitable link between workers' productivity and wages. *To get higher wages without sacrificing jobs, productivity (MRP) must increase.*

Suppose Marvin and his friends all enroll in a local agricultural extension course and learn new methods of strawberry picking. With these new methods, the marginal physical product of each picker increases by one box per hour. With the price of strawberries still at $2 a box, this productivity improvement implies an increase in marginal *revenue* product of $2 per worker. This change causes an upward *shift* of the labor demand (MRP) curve, as in Figure 16.6*b*.

Notice how the improvement in productivity has altered the value of strawberry pickers. The MRP of the fifth picker is now $6 an hour (point *F*) rather than $4 (point *C*). Hence the grower can now afford to pay higher wages. Or the grower could employ more pickers than before, moving from point *C* to point *E*. *Increased productivity implies that workers can get higher wages without sacrificing jobs or more employment without lowering wages.* Historically, increased productivity has been the most important source of rising wages and living standards.

Changes in Price

An increase in the price of strawberries would also help the pickers. Marginal revenue product reflects the interaction of productivity and product prices. If strawberry prices were to double, strawberry pickers would become twice as valuable, even without an increase in physical productivity. Such a change in product prices depends, however, on changes in the market supply and demand for strawberries.

MARKET EQUILIBRIUM

The principles that guide the hiring decisions of a single strawberry grower can be extended to the entire labor market. This suggests that *the market demand for labor depends on*

- *The number of employers.*
- *The marginal revenue product of labor in each firm and industry.*

Increases in either the demand for final products or the productivity of labor will tend to increase marginal revenue productivity and therewith the demand for labor.

On the supply side of the labor market we have already observed that *the market supply of labor depends on*

- *The number of available workers.*
- *Each worker's willingness to work at alternative wage rates.*

The supply decisions of workers are in turn a reflection of tastes, income, wealth, expectations, other prices, and taxes.

Equilibrium Wage

Figure 16.7 brings these market forces together. *The intersection of the market supply and demand curves establishes the* **equilibrium wage.** This is the only wage rate at which the quantity of labor supplied equals the quantity of labor demanded. Everyone who's willing and able to work for this wage will find a job.

If the labor market is perfectly competitive, all employers will be able to hire as many workers as they want at the equilibrium wage. Like our strawberry grower, every competitive firm is assumed to have no discernible effect on market wages. *Competitive employers*

equilibrium wage: The wage rate at which the quantity of labor supplied in a given time period equals the quantity of labor demanded.

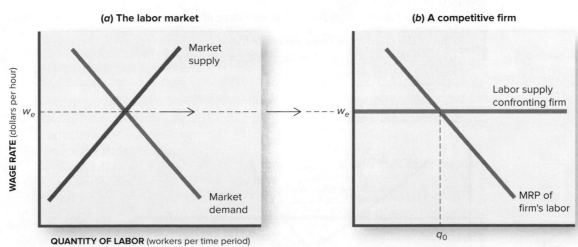

(a) The labor market   **(b) A competitive firm**

FIGURE 16.7

Equilibrium Wage

The intersection of *market* supply and demand determines the equilibrium wage in a competitive labor market. All the firms in the industry can then hire as much labor as they want at that equilibrium wage. In this case, the firm can hire all the workers

it wants at the equilibrium wage, w_e. It chooses to hire q_0 workers, as determined by their marginal revenue product within the firm.

TABLE 16.2

Minimum Wage History

The federal minimum wage has been increased periodically since first set in 1938. In 2007 Congress raised the minimum to $7.25, effective July 2009.

Date	Wage	Date	Wage
Oct. 1938	$0.25	Jan. 1978	$2.65
Oct. 1939	0.30	Jan. 1979	2.90
Oct. 1945	0.40	Jan. 1980	3.10
Jan. 1950	0.75	Jan. 1981	3.35
Mar. 1956	1.00	Apr. 1990	3.80
Sept. 1961	1.15	Apr. 1991	4.25
Sept. 1963	1.25	Oct. 1996	4.75
Feb. 1967	1.40	Sept. 1997	5.15
Feb. 1968	1.60	July 2007	5.85
May 1974	2.00	July 2008	6.55
Jan. 1975	2.10	July 2009	7.25
Jan. 1976	2.30		

act like price takers with respect to wages as well as prices. This phenomenon is also portrayed in Figure 16.7.

Minimum Wages

Some people will be unhappy with the equilibrium wage. Employers may grumble that wages are too high. Workers may complain that wages are too low. They may seek government intervention to change market outcomes. This is the goal of Congress when it establishes a legal *minimum* wage—a **price floor** in the labor market (see Table 16.2).

price floor: Lower limit set for the price of a good.

Figure 16.8 illustrates the effects of such government intervention. The market-determined equilibrium wage is W_e, and q_e workers are employed. A government-imposed minimum wage of W_M is then set, above the market equilibrium. So, what happens?

There are changes on both the supply side of the labor market and the demand side. On the supply side, the higher wage W_M encourages more low-skilled workers to seek employment; the quantity supplied *increases* from q_e to q_s. On the demand side, however, the number of available jobs *declines* from q_e to q_d. This leaves a **market surplus** at the wage W_M. As a result of the increased wage, some workers have lost jobs ($q_e - q_d$) and some new entrants fail to find employment ($q_s - q_e$). Only those workers who remain employed (q_d) benefit from the higher wage.

market surplus: The amount by which the quantity supplied exceeds the quantity demanded at a given price; excess supply.

Government-imposed wage floors thus have three distinct effects: *A legal minimum wage*

- *Reduces the quantity of labor demanded, and*
- *Increases the quantity of labor supplied, and thereby*
- *Creates a market surplus.*

FIGURE 16.8

Minimum Wage Effects

If the minimum wage exceeds the equilibrium wage, a labor surplus will result: more workers will be willing to work at that wage rate than employers will be willing to hire. Some workers will end up with higher wages, but others will end up unemployed.

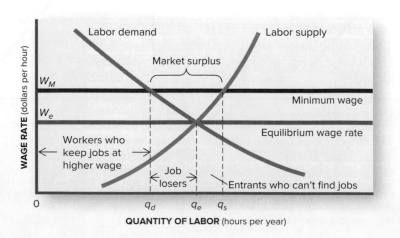

The extent of job loss resulting from a minimum wage hike is hotly debated. How many jobs are lost obviously depends on how far the minimum wage is raised above the market equilibrium.

Demand Elasticity

The elasticity of labor demand is also important. Democrats argue that labor demand is inelastic, so few jobs will be lost. Republicans assert that labor demand is elastic, so more jobs will be lost. In the early 1980s the elasticity of labor demand was found to be 0.10. Hence a 10 percent increase in the minimum wage would cause a 1 percent reduction in employment. Between 1981 and 1990, however, the minimum was stuck at $3.35 an hour while average wages increased 30 percent. By 1989 the federal minimum may have actually been *below* the equilibrium wage for low-skilled labor. When the minimum wage is below the equilibrium wage, an increase in the minimum may have little or no adverse employment effects. This appeared to be the case again in 1996. Because the federal minimum hadn't been raised for five years (see Table 16.2), the 50-cent-per-hour hike in October 1996 caused few job losses. According to Federal Reserve estimates, the 1997 wage hike may have reduced employment growth by only 100,000 to 200,000 jobs.

The same situation existed again in 2007. By then, the federal minimum of $5.15 hadn't been lifted for 10 years (Table 16.2) and had fallen below equilibrium levels (McDonald's and other fast-food outlets were paying entry wages of $6.50 and more in 2007). When Congress raised the minimum to $5.85, the legislated floor still lagged behind market wages. Further hikes, to $7.25 an hour, did cause some job losses, however. In general, *the further the minimum wage rises above the market's equilibrium wage, the greater the job loss.* That was a major source of concern when President Obama proposed raising the minimum wage again, to $10.10 an hour in 2014 (see In the News "Obama Calls for $10.10 Minimum Wage"). The Congressional Budget Office estimated that such a wage jump would eliminate 500,000 jobs, even while increasing wages for millions of workers. Since then, market wages have gone up, rendering such a hike in the minimum wage less threatening to jobs.

IN THE NEWS

OBAMA CALLS FOR $10.10 MINIMUM WAGE

Declaring that "America deserves a raise," President Obama last night called on Congress to raise the minimum wage to $10.10. The federal minimum wage has been stuck at $7.25 since 2009, and Obama said families simply can't live on such a low wage. In his State of the Union message, he urged Congress to pass a higher wage minimum this year.

Source: News reports, January 29, 2014.

ANALYSIS: A higher minimum wage encourages firms to hire fewer workers. How many jobs are lost depends on the size of the wage hike and the price elasticity of labor demand.

CHOOSING AMONG INPUTS

One of the options employers have when wage rates rise is to utilize more machinery in place of labor. In most production processes there are possibilities for substituting capital inputs for labor inputs. In the long run, there are still more possibilities for redesigning the whole production process. Given these options, how should the choice of inputs be made?

Suppose a mechanical strawberry picker can pick berries twice as fast as Marvin. Which will the grower hire, Marvin or the mechanical picker? At first it would seem that the grower would choose the mechanical picker. But the choice isn't so obvious. So far, all we know is that the mechanical picker's MPP is twice as large as Marvin's. But we haven't said anything about the *cost* of the mechanical picker.

Cost Efficiency

Suppose that a mechanical picker can be rented for $10 an hour, while Marvin is still willing to work for $4 an hour. Will this difference in hourly cost change the grower's input choice?

To determine the relative desirability of hiring Marvin or renting the mechanical picker, the grower must compare the ratio of their marginal physical products to their cost. This ratio of marginal product to cost expresses the **cost efficiency** of an input:

cost efficiency: The amount of output associated with an additional dollar spent on input; the MPP of an input divided by its price (cost).

$$\text{Cost efficiency} = \frac{\textbf{Marginal physical product of an input}}{\textbf{Cost of an input}}$$

Marvin's MPP is five boxes of strawberries per hour and his cost (wage) is $4. Thus the return on each dollar of wages paid to Marvin is

$$\text{Cost efficiency of labor} = \frac{\text{MPP}_{\text{labor}}}{\text{Cost}_{\text{labor}}} = \frac{5 \text{ boxes}}{\$4} = 1.25 \text{ boxes per \$1 of cost}$$

By contrast, the mechanical picker has an MPP of 10 boxes per hour and costs $10 per hour:

$$\begin{array}{l}\text{Cost efficiency} \\ \text{of mechanical picker}\end{array} = \frac{\text{MPP}_{\text{mechanical picker}}}{\text{Cost}_{\text{mechanical picker}}} = \frac{10 \text{ boxes}}{\$10} = 1 \text{ box per \$1 of cost}$$

These calculations indicate that Marvin is more cost-effective than the mechanical picker. From this perspective, the grower is better off hiring Marvin than renting a mechanical picker.

From the perspective of cost efficiency, the cheapness of a productive input is measured not by its price but by the amount of output it delivers for that price. Thus *the most cost-efficient factor of production is the one that produces the most output per dollar.*

The concept of cost efficiency helps explain why American firms don't move en masse to Haiti, where peasants are willing to work for as little as 80 cents an hour. Although this wage rate is far below the minimum wage in the United States, the marginal physical product of Haitian peasants is even further below American standards. American workers remain more cost-efficient than the "cheap" labor available in Haiti, making it unprofitable to **outsource** U.S. jobs. So long as U.S. workers deliver more output per dollar of wages, they will remain cost-effective in global markets.

outsourcing: The relocation of production to foreign countries.

Alternative Production Processes

Typically a producer doesn't choose between individual inputs but rather between alternative production processes. General Motors, for example, can't afford to compare the cost efficiency of each job applicant with the cost efficiency of mechanical tire mounters. Instead GM compares the relative desirability of a **production process** that is labor-intensive (uses a lot of labor) with others that are less labor-intensive. GM ignores individual differences in marginal revenue product. Nevertheless, the same principles of cost efficiency guide the decision.

production process: A specific combination of resources used to produce a good or service.

The Efficiency Decision

Let's return to the strawberry patch to see how the choice of an entire production process is made. We again assume that strawberries can be picked by either human or mechanical hands. Now, however, we assume that one ton of strawberries can be produced by only one of the three production processes described in Table 16.3. Process A is most *labor-intensive;* it uses the most labor and thus keeps more human pickers employed. By contrast, process C is *capital-intensive;* it uses the most mechanical pickers and provides the least employment to human pickers. Process B falls between these two extremes.

Input	Alternative Processes for Producing One Ton of Strawberries		
	Process A	Process B	Process C
Labor (hours)	400	270	220
Machinery (hours)	13	15	18
Land (acres)	1	1	1

TABLE 16.3

Alternative Production Processes

One ton of strawberries can be produced with varying input combinations. Which process is most efficient? What information is missing?

Which of these three production processes should the grower use? If he used labor-intensive process A, he'd be doing the pickers a real favor. But his goal is to maximize profits, so we assume he'll choose the production process that best serves this objective. That is, he'll choose the *least-cost* process to produce one ton of strawberries.

But which of the production processes in Table 16.3 is least expensive? We really can't tell on the basis of the information provided. To determine the relative cost of each process—and thus to understand the producer's choice—we must know something more about input costs. In particular, we have to know how much an hour of mechanical picking costs and how much an hour of human picking (labor) costs. Then we can determine which combination of inputs is least expensive in producing one ton of strawberries—that is, which is most *cost-efficient*. Note that we don't have to know how much the land costs because the same amount of land is used in all three production processes. Thus land costs won't affect our efficiency decision.

Suppose that strawberry pickers are still paid $4 an hour and that mechanical pickers can be rented for $10 an hour. The acre of land rents for $500 per year. With this information we can now calculate the total dollar cost of each production process and quickly determine the most cost-efficient. Table 16.4 summarizes the required calculations.

The calculations performed in Table 16.4 clearly identify process C as the least expensive way of producing one ton of strawberries. Process A entails a total cost of $2,230, whereas the capital-intensive process C costs only $1,560 to produce the same quantity of output. As a profit maximizer, the grower will choose process C, even though it implies less employment for strawberry pickers.

The choice of an appropriate production process—the decision about *how* to produce—is called the **efficiency decision.** As we've seen, a producer seeks to use the combination of resources that produces a given rate of output for the least cost. The efficiency decision requires the producer to find that particular least-cost combination.

efficiency decision: The choice of a production process for any given rate of output.

Input	Cost Calculation
Process A (labor-intensive)	
Labor	400 hours at $4 per hour = $1,600
Machinery	13 hours at $10 per hour = 130
Land	1 acre at $500 = 500
	Total cost $2,230
Process B (intermediate)	
Labor	270 hours at $4 per hour = $1,080
Machinery	15 hours at $10 per hour = 50
Land	1 acre at $500 = 500
	Total cost $1,730
Process C (capital-intensive)	
Labor	220 hours at $4 per hour = $ 880
Machinery	18 hours at $10 per hour = 180
Land	1 acre at $500 = 500
	Total cost $1,560

TABLE 16.4

The Least-Cost Combination

A producer wants to produce a given rate of output for the least cost. Choosing the least expensive production process is the efficiency decision. In this case, process C represents the most cost-efficient production process for producing one ton of strawberries.

THE ECONOMY TOMORROW

CAPPING CEO PAY

The CEO of Expedia, Dara Khosrowshahi, was paid $94.5 million in 2016 for his services. You might gasp at such a paycheck, but he thinks he deserves it. Expedia's sales increased 23 percent in 2016 to over $8 *billion* and its profits jumped more than 70 percent. By the end of the year, Expedia had more than 325,000 properties in its inventory and was taking reservations for 475 airlines and dozens of car rental companies and cruise lines.

Critics of CEO pay don't accept Khosrowshahi's explanation. They contend that Expedia revenues would have risen even without Khosrowshahi's leadership. Sales growth is a product of general economic growth, not just company management. They also assert that $94.5 million was way more than enough to secure Khosrowshahi's services; he probably would have worked just as hard for a mere $50 million.

Critics conclude that many CEO paychecks are out of line with realities of supply and demand. They want corporations to reduce CEO pay and revise the process used for setting CEO pay levels. President Obama moved in this direction by setting a pay cap of $500,000 for executives of corporations receiving government aid.

Unmeasured MRP. One of the difficulties in determining the appropriate level of CEO pay is the elusiveness of marginal revenue product. It's easy to measure the MRP of a strawberry picker or even a salesclerk. But a corporate CEO's contributions are less well defined. A CEO is supposed to provide strategic leadership and a sense of mission. These are critical to a corporation's success but hard to quantify.

Congress confronts the same problem in setting the president's pay. We noted earlier that the president of the United States is paid $400,000 a year. Can we argue that this salary represents the president's marginal revenue product? It has been estimated that the president's pay would be in the range of $38–58 million if he were paid on performance (MRP). The wage we actually pay a president is less a reflection of contribution to total output than a matter of custom. The salary also reflects the price voters believe is required to induce competent individuals to forsake private sector jobs and assume the responsibilities of the presidency. In this sense, the wage paid to the president and other public officials is set by their **opportunity wage**—that is, the wage they could earn in private industry.

opportunity wage: The highest wage an individual would earn in his or her best alternative job.

The same kinds of considerations influence the wages of college professors. The marginal revenue product of a college professor isn't easy to measure. Is it the number of students she teaches, the amount of knowledge conveyed, or something else? Confronted with such problems, most universities tend to pay college professors according to their opportunity wage—that is, the amount the professors could earn elsewhere.

Opportunity wages also help explain the difference between the wage of the CEO of Expedia and the workers who produce its products. The call center representatives at Expedia—the people who answer your calls—get paid only $12 an hour. That works out to about $25,000 a year, more than three thousand times less than Mr. Khosrowshahi's salary. How is such an enormous wage disparity possibly justified? The answer is first and foremost marginal revenue product. The people answering the phone are essential to Expedia's business, but individually they add little to total revenue per hour. Second, they are willing to work for a much lower salary because their opportunity costs are low: they aren't trained for many other jobs. By contrast, Expedia's CEO has impressive managerial skills that are in demand by many corporations; his opportunity wages are high.

Opportunity wages help explain CEO pay but don't fully justify such high pay levels. If Expedia's CEO pay is justified by opportunity wages, that means another company would be willing to pay him that much. But what would justify such high pay at another company? Would his MRP be any easier to measure? Maybe *all* CEO paychecks have been inflated.

Critics of CEO pay conclude that the process of setting CEO pay levels should be changed. All too often, executive pay scales are set by self-serving committees composed of executives of the same or similar corporations. Critics want a more independent assessment of pay scales, with nonaffiliated experts and stockholder representatives.

Some critics want to go a step further and set mandatory "caps" on CEO pay. President Clinton rejected legislated caps but convinced Congress to limit the tax deductibility of CEO pay. Any "unjustified" CEO pay in excess of $1 million a year can't be treated as a business expense but instead must be paid out of after-tax profits. This change put more pressure on corporations to examine the rationale for multimillion-dollar paychecks. President Obama wanted even stricter limits on CEO pay, especially for banks and other companies getting government "bailout" money.

If markets work efficiently, such government intervention shouldn't be necessary. Corporations that pay their CEOs excessively will end up with smaller profits than companies that pay market-based wages. Over time, "lean" companies will be more competitive than "fat" companies, and excessive pay packages will be eliminated. Legislated CEO pay caps imply that CEO labor markets aren't efficient or that the adjustment process is too slow. To forestall more government intervention in pay decisions, companies may tie executive pay more explicitly to performance (marginal revenue product) in the economy tomorrow.

SUMMARY

- The motivation to work arises from social, psychological, and economic forces. People need income to pay their bills, but they also need a sense of achievement. As a consequence, people are willing to work—to supply labor. **LO16-1**
- There's an opportunity cost involved in working—namely, the amount of leisure time one sacrifices. By the same token, the opportunity cost of not working (leisure) is the income and related consumption possibilities thereby forgone. Everyone confronts a trade-off between leisure and income. **LO16-1**
- Higher wage rates induce people to work more—that is, to substitute labor for leisure. But this substitution effect may be offset by an income effect. Higher wages also enable a person to work fewer hours with no loss of income. When income effects outweigh substitution effects, the labor supply curve bends backward. **LO16-2**
- A firm's demand for labor reflects labor's marginal revenue product. A profit-maximizing employer won't pay a worker more than the worker produces. **LO16-2**

- The marginal revenue product of labor diminishes as additional workers are employed on a particular job (the law of diminishing returns). This decline occurs because additional workers have to share existing land and capital, leaving each worker with less land and capital to work with. **LO16-2**
- A producer seeks to get the most output for every dollar spent on inputs. This means getting the highest ratio of marginal product to input price. A profit-maximizing producer will choose the most cost-efficient input (not necessarily the one with the cheapest price). **LO16-1**
- The efficiency decision involves the choice of the least-cost productive process and is also made on the basis of cost efficiency. A producer seeks the least expensive process to produce a given rate of output. **LO16-3**
- Differences in marginal revenue product are an important explanation of wage inequalities. But the difficulty of measuring MRP in some jobs leaves many wage rates to be determined by opportunity wages or other mechanisms. **LO16-3**

Key Terms

labor supply	derived demand	market surplus
substitution effect of higher wages	marginal physical product (MPP)	cost efficiency
income effect of higher wages	marginal revenue product (MRP)	outsourcing
market supply of labor	law of diminishing returns	production process
elasticity of labor supply	equilibrium wage	efficiency decision
demand for labor	price floor	opportunity wage

Questions for Discussion

1. Why are you doing this homework? What are you giving up? What utility do you expect to gain? **LO16-1**

2. Would you continue to work after winning a lottery prize of $100,000 a year for life? Would you change schools, jobs, or career objectives? What factors besides income influence work decisions? **LO16-1**

3. According to World View "Your Money or Your Life," does the substitution effect or the income effect dominate in Mexico? In Russia? Why might this be the case? **LO16-1**

4. Explain why marginal physical product would diminish as
   (*a*) More waiters are hired in a restaurant.
   (*b*) More professors are hired in the economics department.
   (*c*) More carpenters are hired to build a house. **LO16-2**

5. Is this course increasing your marginal productivity? If so, in what way? **LO16-2**

6. How might you measure the marginal revenue product of (*a*) a quarterback and (*b*) the team's coach? **LO16-2**

7. Who is hurt and who is helped by an increase in the legal minimum wage? Under what circumstances might a higher minimum *not* reduce employment? **LO16-3**

8. In 2016 the president of the University of Michigan was paid $750,000 and the football coach was paid $9 million. Does this make any sense? **LO16-2**

9. What is President Trump's opportunity cost for becoming president instead of running his businesses? How would you measure his marginal revenue product? **LO16-2**

10. The minimum wage in Mexico is less than $1 an hour. Does this make Mexican workers more cost-effective than U.S. workers? Explain. **LO16-3**

11. Why didn't President Obama set pay limits on baseball players who play in publicly funded stadiums? Why did he single out corporate executives? **LO16-2**

PROBLEMS FOR CHAPTER 16

LO16-1 1. (*a*) How many home runs did Giancarlo Stanton score in 2014? (See In the News "Marlins Sign Stanton to Record $325 Million Contract")
(*b*) If his average annual salary were based on home runs alone, how much would each home run be worth?

LO16-2 2. By what percentage did
(*a*) The federal minimum wage increase between September 1997 and July 2009? (See Table 16.2.)
(*b*) If President Obama's wage-hike proposal (In the News "Obama Calls for $10.10 Minimum Wage") were accepted, by what percentage would the federal minimum wage increase?

LO16-1 3. According to World View "Thousands of Refugees Attend Job Fair," what was the situation in the 2016 Berlin labor market?
A: Labor surplus   B: Labor shortage   C: Equilibrium

LO16-3 4. According to World View "Thousands of Refugees Attend Job Fair,"
(*a*) How many people were supplying labor?
(*b*) How many employers were demanding labor?
(*c*) Was there a surplus or shortage in this market?

LO16-3 5. (*a*) According to Figure 16.8, how many workers are unemployed at the equilibrium wage?
(*b*) How many workers are unemployed at the minimum wage?

LO16-1 6. Suppose a wage increase from $12 to $16 an hour for Expedia call center reps increases the number of daily job applicants from 42 to 58. What is the price elasticity of labor supply?

LO16-1 7. If the price of strawberries doubled, how many pickers would be hired at $4 an hour, according to Table 16.1?

LO16-3 8. Apples can be harvested by hand or machine. Handpicking yields 80 pounds per hour; mechanical pickers yield 120 pounds per hour.
(*a*) If the wage rate of human pickers is $8 an hour and the rental on a mechanical picker is $15 an hour, which is more cost-effective?
(*b*) If the wage rate increased to $12 an hour, which would be more cost-effective? _____

LO16-3 9. Assume that the following data describe labor market conditions:

Wage rate (per hour)	$3	$4	$5	$6	$7	$8	$9	$10
Labor demanded	50	45	40	35	30	25	20	15
Labor supplied	20	30	40	50	60	70	80	90

On a graph, illustrate
(*a*) The equilibrium wage.
(*b*) A government-set minimum wage of $6 per hour when the minimum wage is implemented.
(*c*) How many workers lose jobs?
(*d*) How many additional workers seek jobs?
(*e*) How many workers end up unemployed?

LO16-2 10. The following table depicts the number of grapes that can be picked in an hour with varying amounts of labor:

Number of pickers (per hour)	1	2	3	4	5	6	7	8
Output of grapes (in flats)	20	38	53	64	71	74	74	70

(a) Illustrate the supply and demand of labor for a single farmer, assuming that the local wage rate is $6 an hour and a flat of grapes sells for $2.

(b) How many pickers will be hired?

(c) If the wage rate doubles, how many pickers will be hired?

(d) If the productivity of all workers doubles, how many pickers will be hired at a wage of $12 an hour?

(e) Illustrate your answers on the following graph.

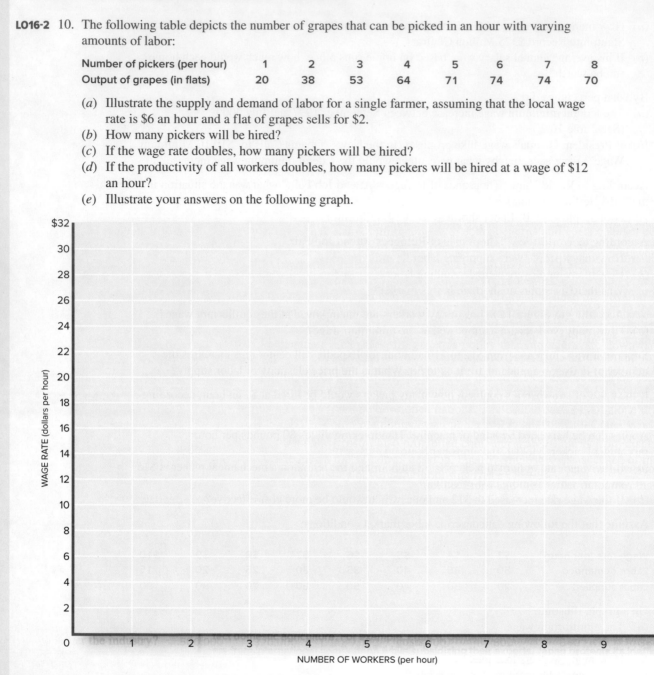

LO16-3 11. By how much would the quantity of labor demanded decrease if a minimum wage hike raised prevailing wages from $8 to $10 an hour and if the elasticity of labor demand were 0.10?

LO16-2 12. The Economy Tomorrow: If the typical Expedia call center worker is paid an annual salary of $25,000, how much higher is the CEO's annual salary in percentage terms?

©Mark Richard/PhotoEdit

CHAPTER 17

Labor Unions

The United Auto Workers Union (UAW) launched a strike against Caterpillar, Inc., in November 1991. The union wanted the manufacturer of construction machinery to increase pay, benefits, and job security. *Four years* later, Caterpillar hadn't budged; it continued to operate with replacement workers, management crews, and union members who crossed the picket line. The union finally capitulated in December 1995, sending its 8,700 members back to work with neither higher pay nor even a new contract. The union struck again in 1996 but relented after 17 months. Seven years after their first strike, the Caterpillar workers still had no contract.

To many observers, the failed UAW strike at Caterpillar climaxed a steady decline in the power of labor unions. This impression was reinforced by the failure of *public* unions in Illinois and Ohio to safeguard benefits in early 2011. But the union movement is far from dead. Labor unions are even expanding in some sectors (especially government employment). Many unions still have considerable influence on employment, wages, and working conditions. This chapter focuses on how unions acquire and use such influence. We address the following questions:

- **How do large and powerful employers affect market wages?**
- **How do labor unions alter wages and employment?**
- **What outcomes are possible from collective bargaining between management and unions?**

In the process of answering these questions, we look at the nation's most powerful unions and their actual behavior.

THE LABOR MARKET

To gauge the impact of labor market power, we must first observe how a competitive labor market sets wages and employment. On the supply side, we have all those individuals who are willing to work—to supply labor—at various wage rates. By counting the number of individuals willing to work at each and every wage rate, we can construct a *market* **labor supply** curve, as in Figure 17.1.

LEARNING OBJECTIVES

After reading this chapter, you should know

LO17-1 How unions secure higher wages.

LO17-2 The factors that affect collective bargaining outcomes.

LO17-3 How unions affect nonunion wages.

---

labor supply: The willingness and ability to work specific amounts of time at alternative wage rates in a given time period, *ceteris paribus.*

FIGURE 17.1

Competitive Equilibrium in the Labor Market

The market labor supply curve includes all persons willing to work at various wage rates. The labor demand curve tells us how many workers employers are willing to hire. In a competitive market, the intersection of the labor supply and labor demand curves (point C) determines the equilibrium wage (w_e) and employment (q_e) levels.

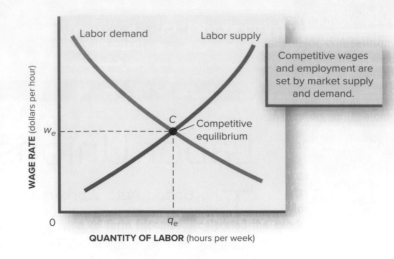

---

demand for labor: The quantities of labor employers are willing and able to hire at alternative wage rates in a given time period, *ceteris paribus*.

---

equilibrium wage: The wage rate at which the quantity of labor supplied in a given time period equals the quantity of labor demanded.

The willingness of producers (firms) to hire labor is reflected in the market labor demand curve. The curve itself is constructed by counting the number of workers each firm says it is willing and able to hire at each and every wage rate. The curve illustrates the market **demand for labor.**

Competitive Equilibrium

The intersection of the labor supply and labor demand curves (point C in Figure 17.1) reveals the **equilibrium wage** rate (w_e): the wage rate at which the quantity of labor supplied equals the quantity demanded. At this wage rate, every job seeker who's willing and able to work for the wage w_e is employed. In addition, firms are able to acquire all the labor they're willing and able to hire at that wage.

Not everyone is employed in equilibrium. Workers who demand wages in excess of w_e are unable to find jobs. By the same token, employers who refuse to pay a wage as high as w_e are unable to attract workers.

Local Labor Markets

Figure 17.1 appears to suggest that there's only *one* labor market and thus only one equilibrium wage. This is a gross oversimplification. If you were looking for a job in Tulsa, you'd have little interest in employment prospects or power configurations in New York City. You'd be more concerned about the available jobs and wages in Tulsa—that is, the condition of the *local* labor market.

Even within a particular geographical area, interest usually focuses on particular occupations and workers rather than on all the people supplying or demanding labor. If you were looking for work as a dancer, you'd have little interest in the employment situation for carpenters or dentists. Rather, you'd want to know how many nightclubs or dance troupes had job vacancies, and what wages and working conditions they offered.

The distinction among various geographical, occupational, and industrial labor markets provides a more meaningful basis for analyzing labor market power. The tremendous size of the national labor market, with more than 150 million workers, precludes anyone from acquiring control of the entire market. The largest employer in the United States (Walmart) employs less than 1 percent of the labor force. General Motors employs far fewer than that, and the top 500 industrial corporations employ less than 20 percent of all workers. The situation on the supply side is similar. The largest labor unions (National Education Association and the Service Employees International Union) each represents just 1.2 percent of all workers in the country. All unions together represent less than one out of every nine U.S. workers. This doesn't mean that particular employers or unions have no influence on our economic welfare. It does suggest, however, that **market power** *in labor markets is likely to be more effective in specific areas, occupations, and industries.*

market power: The ability to alter the market price of a good or service.

LABOR UNIONS

The immediate objective of labor unions is to alter the equilibrium wage and employment conditions in specific labor markets. ***To be successful, unions must be able to exert control over the market supply curve.***

Types of Unions

That's why workers have organized themselves along either industry or occupational craft lines. *Industrial unions* include workers in a particular industry (the United Auto Workers, for example). *Craft unions* represent workers with a particular skill (like the International Brotherhood of Electrical Workers), regardless of the industry in which they work.

The purpose of both types of labor unions is to coordinate the actions of thousands of individual workers, thereby achieving control of market supply. If a union is able to control the supply of workers in a particular industry or occupation, the union acquires a *monopoly* in that market. Like most monopolies, unions attempt to use their market power to increase their incomes.

Union Objectives

A primary objective of unions is to raise the wages of union members. In the 2012 dispute between pro hockey team owners and players, money was the sole issue. The players, who were already getting an average paycheck of $2.4 million per season, were resisting a salary cap that would restrain wages. The team owners wanted to limit total player salaries to 53–55 percent of league revenues, rather than the existing 57 percent.

An exclusive focus on wages is somewhat unusual. Union objectives also include improved working conditions, job security, and other nonwage forms of compensation, such as retirement (pension) benefits, vacation time, and health insurance. The Players Association and the National Football League have bargained about the use of artificial turf, early retirement, player fines, television revenues, game rules, the use of team doctors, drug tests, pensions, and the number of players permitted on a team. A recurring concern of the United Auto Workers is job security. Consequently, they focus on work rules that may eliminate jobs and unemployment benefits for laid-off workers.

Although union objectives tend to be as broad as the concerns of union members, we focus here on just one objective: wage rates. This isn't too great a simplification because most nonwage issues can be translated into their effective impact on wage rates. In 2016, for example, the National Basketball Association and the players' union agreed to more than a dozen different job provisions ranging from the length of time a player had to stay on the disabled list to the location of games (see In the News "NBA and Players Strike a Deal"). It was possible, however, to figure out the cost of these many provisions ($1.5 million per worker per year). Hence the "bottom line" of the compensation package could be expressed in terms of wage costs.

What we seek to determine is whether and how unions can raise effective wage rates in a specific labor market by altering the competitive equilibrium depicted in Figure 17.1. What is the source of union power and how do unions use it?

IN THE NEWS

NBA AND PLAYERS STRIKE A DEAL

The games will go on. The National Basketball Association and the players' union averted a lockout by finalizing the terms of a new contract early Thursday morning. With overflowing revenues of $10 billion per year to divvy up, neither side wanted to disrupt the season schedule. The new contract will last for five years, from 2017 to 2021. Here's what the two sides got:

The players agreed

- To take a smaller share (51 percent down from 57 percent) of total basketball income, including lucrative TV deals.
- To let the league schedule games outside the United States, provided players get compensated as much as $100,000 per game for travel and inconvenience.

The owners agreed

- To increase the minimum salary from $507,500 to $555,000 by 2019, with cost of living adjustments thereafter.
- To reduce the number of exhibition games.
- To shorten the minimum time on the disabled list from 15 days to 10 days.
- To start the season a week earlier so players can get 4 more days of rest.
- To reduce the number of back-to-back games (consecutive days).
- To shorten the length of contracts so players become free agents more often.
- To raise the payroll limit on individual teams.
- To maintain the existing limits on roster size (40 players).

Despite the reduced revenue share, the players will see fatter paychecks: the average salary is projected to increase from $8.5 million in 2016 to $10 million in the 2020–2021 season.

Source: Media reports of November-December 2016.

ANALYSIS: Labor unions bargain with management over a variety of employment conditions. Most issues, however, can be expressed in terms of their impact on wage costs.

THE POTENTIAL USE OF POWER

In a competitive labor market, each worker makes a labor supply decision on the basis of his or her own perceptions of the relative values of labor and leisure (Chapter 16). Whatever decision is made won't alter the market wage. One worker simply isn't that significant in a market composed of thousands. Once a market is unionized, however, these conditions no longer hold. A *union evaluates job offers on the basis of the collective interests of its members.* In particular, it must be concerned with the effects of increased employment on the wage rate paid to its members.

The Marginal Wage

Like all monopolists, unions have to worry about the downward slope of the demand curve. In the case of labor markets, a larger quantity of labor can be "sold" only at lower wage rates. Suppose the workers in a particular labor market confront the market labor demand schedule depicted in Figure 17.2. This schedule tells us that employers aren't willing to hire any workers at a wage rate of $6 per hour (row S) but will hire one worker per hour if the wage rate is $5 (row T). At still lower rates, the quantity of labor demanded increases; five workers per hour are demanded at a wage of $1 per hour.

An individual worker offered a wage of $1 an hour would have to decide whether such wages merited the sacrifice of an hour's leisure. But a union would evaluate the offer differently. A union must consider how the hiring of one more worker will affect the wages of all the workers.

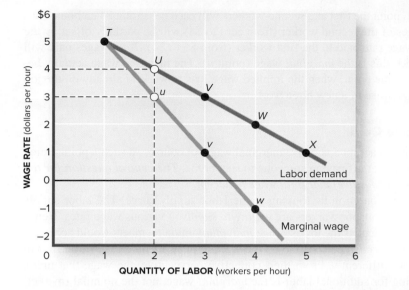

FIGURE 17.2

The Marginal Wage

The *marginal wage* is the change in *total wages* (paid to all workers) associated with the employment of an additional worker. If the wage rate is $4 per hour, only two workers will be hired (point *U*). The wage rate must fall to $3 per hour if three workers are to be hired (point *V*). In the process, *total* wages paid rise from $8 ($4 × 2 workers) to $9 ($3 × 3 workers). The *marginal* wage of the third worker is only $1 (point *v*).

The graph illustrates the relationship of the marginal wage to labor demand. The marginal wage curve lies below the labor demand curve because the marginal wage is less than the nominal wage. Compare the marginal wage (point *v*) and the nominal wage (point *V*) of the third worker.

	Wage Rate (per Hour)	×	Number of Workers Demanded (per Hour)	=	Total Wages Paid (per Hour)	Marginal Wage (per Labor-Hour)
S	$6		0		$0	
T	5		1		5	$5
U	4		2		8	3
V	3		3		9	1
W	2		4		8	−1
X	1		5		5	−3

Total Wages Paid. Notice that when four workers are hired at a wage rate of $2 an hour (row *W*), *total* wages are $8 per hour. In order for a fifth worker to be employed, the wage rate must drop to $1 an hour (row *X*). At wages of $1 per hour, the *total* wages paid to the five workers amount to only $5 per hour. Thus total wages paid to the workers actually *fall* when a fifth worker is employed. Collectively the workers would be better off sending only four people to work at the higher wage of $2 an hour and paying the fifth worker $1 an hour to stay home!

The basic mandate of a labor union is to evaluate wage and employment offers from this *collective* perspective. To do so, ***a union must distinguish the marginal wage from the market wage.*** The market wage is simply the current wage rate paid by the employer; it's the wage received by individual workers. The **marginal wage,** on the other hand, is the change in *total* wages paid (to all workers) when an additional worker is hired:

$$\text{Marginal wage} = \frac{\text{Change in total wages paid}}{\text{Change in quantity of labor employed}}$$

The distinction between marginal wages and market wages arises from the downward slope of the labor demand curve. It's analogous to the distinction we made between marginal revenue and price for monopolists in product markets. The distinction simply reflects the law of demand: if more workers are to be hired, wage rates must fall.

The impact of increased employment on marginal wages is also illustrated in Figure 17.2. According to the labor demand curve, one worker will be hired at a wage rate of $5 an hour (point *T*); two workers will be hired only if the market wage falls to $4 an hour

marginal wage: The change in total wages paid associated with a one-unit increase in the quantity of labor employed.

(point *U*), at which point the first and second workers will each be getting $4 an hour. Thus the increased wages of the second worker (from zero to $4) will be partially offset by the reduction in the wage rate paid to the first worker (from $5 to $4). *Total* wages paid will increase by only $3; this is the *marginal* wage (point *u*). The marginal wage actually becomes negative at some point, when the implied wage loss to workers already on the job begins to exceed the wage of a new hired worker.

The Union Wage Goal

A union never wants to accept a negative marginal wage, of course. At such a point, union members would be better off paying someone to stay home. ***The central question for the union is what level of (positive) marginal wage to accept.***

We can answer this question by looking at the labor supply curve. The labor supply curve tells us how much labor workers are *willing to supply* at various wage rates. Hence the labor supply curve depicts the lowest wage *individual* union members would accept. If the union adopts a *collective* perspective on the welfare of its members, however, it will view the wage offer differently. From their collective perspective, the wage that union members are getting for additional labor is the *marginal* wage, not the nominal (market) wage. Hence the marginal wage curve, not the labor demand curve, is decisive in the union's assessment of wage offers.

If the union wants to maximize the *total* welfare of its members, it will seek the level of employment that equates the marginal wage with the supply preferences of union members. In Figure 17.3, ***the intersection of the marginal wage curve with the labor supply curve identifies the desired level of employment for the union.*** This intersection occurs at point *u*, yielding total employment of two workers per hour.

The marginal wage at point *u* is $3. However, the union members will get paid an actual wage higher than that. Look up from point *u* on the marginal wage curve to point *U* on the employer's labor demand curve. Point *U* tells us that the employer is *willing to pay* a wage rate of $4 an hour to employ two workers. The union knows it can demand and get $4 an hour if it supplies only two workers to the firm.

What the union is doing here is choosing a point on the labor demand curve that the union regards as the optimal combination of wages and employment. In a competitive market, point *C* would represent the equilibrium combination of wages and employment. But the union forces employers to point *U*, thereby attaining a higher wage rate and reducing employment.

FIGURE 17.3
The Union Wage Objective

The intersection of the marginal wage and labor supply curves (point *u*) determines the union's desired employment. Employers are willing to pay a wage rate of $4 per hour for that many workers, as revealed by point *U* on the labor demand curve.

More workers (*H*) are willing to work at $4 per hour than employers demand (*U*). To maintain that wage rate, the union must exclude some workers from the market. In the absence of such power, wages would fall to the competitive equilibrium (point *C*).

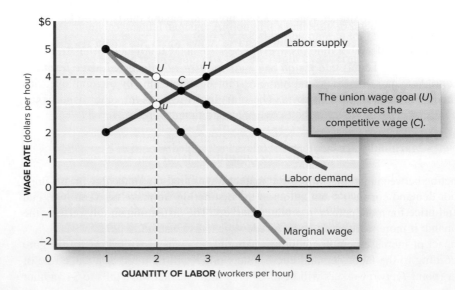

The union wage goal (*U*) exceeds the competitive wage (*C*).

Exclusion

The union's ability to maintain a wage rate of $4 an hour depends on its ability to exclude some workers from the market. Figure 17.3 reveals that three workers are willing and able to work at the union wage of $4 an hour (point *H*), whereas only two are hired (point *U*). If the additional worker were to offer his services, the wage rate would be pushed down the labor demand curve (to $3 per hour). Hence, *to maintain a noncompetitive wage, the union must be able to exercise some control over the labor supply decisions of individual workers.* The essential force here is union solidarity. Once unionized, the individual workers must agree not to compete among themselves by offering their labor at nonunion wage rates. Instead the workers must agree to withhold labor—to strike, if necessary—if wage rates are too low, and to supply labor only at the union-set wage.

Unions can solidify their control of the labor supply by establishing **union shops:** workplaces where workers must join the union within 30 days after being employed. In this way, the unions gain control of all the workers employed in a particular company or industry, thereby reducing the number of replacement workers available for employment during a strike. Stiff penalties (such as loss of seniority or pension rights) and general union solidarity ensure that only nonunion workers will "fink" or "scab"—take the job of a worker on strike.

union shop: An employment setting in which all workers must join the union within 30 days after being employed.

Replacement Workers. Even union shops, however, are subject to potential competition from substitute labor. When the UAW struck Caterpillar in 1991, the company advertised nationally for replacement workers and set up a toll-free phone line for applicants. In the midst of a recession, the company got a huge response. The resulting flow of replacement workers crippled the UAW strike. Professional baseball players faced the same problem in 1995. When the continued strike threatened a second consecutive season, the team owners started hiring new players to replace the regulars. The huge supply of aspiring ball players forced the strikers to reconsider.

Replacement workers are even more abundant in agriculture. The United Farm Workers has been trying for decades to organize California's 20,000 strawberry pickers. But the workers know that thousands of additional workers will flock to California from Mexico if they protest wages and working conditions.

THE EXTENT OF UNION POWER

The first labor unions in America were organized in the 1780s, and the first worker protests as early as 1636. Union power wasn't a significant force in labor markets, however, until the 1900s, when heavily populated commercial centers and large-scale manufacturing became common. Only then did large numbers of workers begin to view their employment situations from a common perspective.

Early Growth

The period 1916–1920 was one of particularly fast growth for labor unions, largely because of the high demand for labor resulting from World War I. All these membership gains were lost, however, when the Great Depression threw millions of people out of work. By 1933 union membership had dwindled to the levels of 1915.

As the Depression lingered on, public attitudes and government policy changed. Too many people had learned the meaning of layoffs, wage cuts, and prolonged unemployment. In 1933 the National Industrial Recovery Act (NIRA) established the right of employees to bargain collectively with their employers. When the NIRA was declared unconstitutional by the Supreme Court in 1935, its labor provisions were incorporated into a new law, the Wagner Act. With this legislative encouragement, union membership doubled between 1933 and 1937. Unions continued to gain in strength as the production needs of World War II increased the demand for labor. Figure 17.4 reflects the tremendous spurt of union activity between the depths of the Depression and the height of World War II.

FIGURE 17.4

Changing Unionization Rates

Unions grew most rapidly during the decade 1935–1945. Since that time, the growth of unions hasn't kept pace with the growth of the U.S. labor force. Most employment growth has occurred in service industries that have traditionally been nonunion.

Source: U.S. Department of Labor.

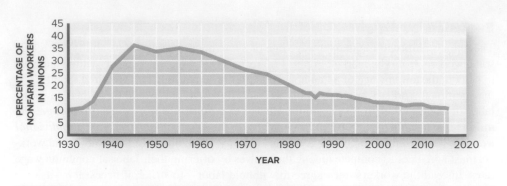

---

unionization rate: The percentage of the labor force belonging to a union.

Union Power Today

Union membership stopped increasing in the 1950s, even though the labor force kept growing. As a result, the unionized percentage of the labor force—the **unionization rate**—has been in steady decline for more than 40 years. The current unionization rate of 10.7 percent is less than a third of its post–World War II peak and far below unionization rates in other industrialized nations (see World View "Union Membership").

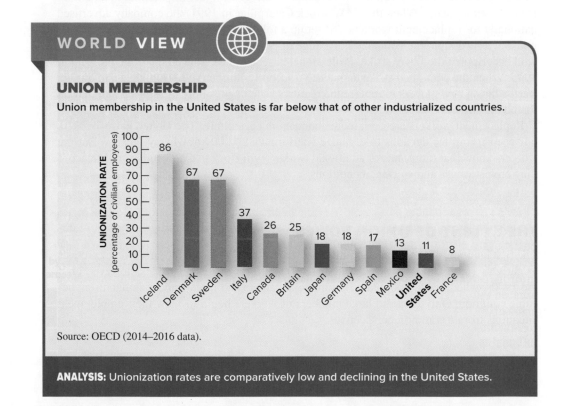

WORLD VIEW

UNION MEMBERSHIP

Union membership in the United States is far below that of other industrialized countries.

Source: OECD (2014–2016 data).

ANALYSIS: Unionization rates are comparatively low and declining in the United States.

Private vs. Public Sector Trends. The decline in the *national* unionization rate conceals two very different trends. Union representation of *private* sector workers has plunged even more sharply than Figure 17.4 suggests. In the last 10 years, the unionization rate in the private sector has fallen from 11.5 percent to only 6.4 percent. At the same time, union membership has increased sharply among teachers, government workers, and nonprofit employees. As of 2017, more than 35 percent of workers on government payrolls were union members. This concentration of unions in the public sector is evident in Figure 17.5. The trend is clear: *the old industrial unions are being supplanted by unions of service workers, especially those employed in the public sector.* Unionization is highest among public schoolteachers, including college professors.

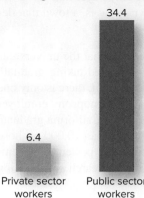

Percentage of workers in unions

34.4

6.4

Private sector
workers

Public sector
workers

FIGURE 17.5

Private vs. Public Unions

Unionization rates have declined sharply in private industry but risen in the public sector. Public sector union membership now exceeds private sector union membership.

Source: U.S. Bureau of Labor Statistics (2016 data).

Although industrial unions have been in general decline, they still possess significant pockets of market power. The Teamsters, the UAW, the United Mine Workers, the Union of Needletrades and Textile Employees, and the Food Workers all have substantial representation in their respective markets. Their strength in those specific markets, not national averages, determines their ability to alter market outcomes.

The AFL-CIO. One labor organization with a decidedly national focus is the AFL-CIO (the American Federation of Labor–Congress of Industrial Organizations). The AFL-CIO is not a separate union but a representational body of more than 50 national unions, representing 12 million workers. It doesn't represent or negotiate for any particular group of workers but focuses instead on issues of general labor interest. The AFL-CIO acts as an advocate for the labor movement and represents labor's interest in legislative areas. It's the primary vehicle for political action. In addition, the AFL-CIO may render economic assistance to member unions or to groups of workers who wish to organize.

Change to Win Coalition. The AFL-CIO's political activity upset member unions who favored more focus on traditional union interests, particularly union organizing. In September 2005 some of these unions (including teamsters, garment workers, food workers, service workers) quit the AFL-CIO and formed a new multiunion organization, the Change to Win Coalition. By 2017 the coalition included three of the largest unions, representing more than 5 million workers.

EMPLOYER POWER

The power possessed by labor unions in various occupations and industries seldom exists in a power vacuum. Power exists on the demand side of labor markets, too. The United Auto Workers confront GM, Ford, and Chrysler; the Steelworkers confront U.S. Steel and AK Steel; the Teamsters confront the Truckers' Association; the Communications Workers confront AT&T; and so on. An imbalance of power often exists on one side of the market or the other (as with, say, the Carpenters versus individual construction contractors). However, *labor markets with significant power on both sides are common.* To understand how wage rates and employment are determined in such markets, we have to assess the market power possessed by employers.

Monopsony

Power on the demand side of a market belongs to a *buyer* who can influence the market price of a good. With respect to labor markets, market power on the demand side implies the ability of a single employer to alter the market wage rate. The extreme case of such

monopsony: A market in which there's only one buyer.

power is a **monopsony,** a situation in which one employer is the only buyer in a particular market. The classic example of a monopsony is a company town—that is, a town that depends for its livelihood on the decisions of a single employer.

Graduate Assistants. Graduate teaching assistants have complained that the universities that employ them are much like company towns. Once they've started taking graduate classes at one university, it's difficult to transfer to another. As they see it, there is only one local labor market for graduate students. They complain that their monopsony employer compels them to work long hours at low wages. In 1998 University of California graduate students went out on strike to protest those conditions. In 1999 more than 10,000 of those graduate students affiliated with the United Auto Workers to gain more power. In November 2000 the National Labor Relations Board decreed that graduate research and teaching assistants are employees with the right to organize and strike.

Pro Athletes. Before 1976 professional sports teams also had monopsony power. Sports contracts prohibited pro players from moving from one team (employer) to another without permission. This gave team owners a lot of power to set wages and working conditions. That power was diluted when players got the right to be "free agents" and bargain with more than one team.

Buyer Concentration. There are many degrees of market power, and they can be defined in terms of *buyer concentration*. When buyers are many and of limited market power, the demand for resources is likely to be competitive. When only one buyer has access to a particular resource market, a monopsony exists. Between the two extremes lie the various degrees of imperfect competition, including the awkward-sounding but empirically important case of *oligopsony*. In an oligopsony, only a few firms account for most of the industry's employment.

This was pretty much the situation in Silicon Valley from 2005 to 2009 when Apple, Google, and a few other tech firms were the premier employers. They later admitted to colluding to prevent competitive bidding for programmers, systems engineers, and other tech workers. In other words, they were acting in unison to acquire monopsony powers in the hi-tech labor market (see In the News "Judge OKs $415 Million Settlement of 'No Poaching' Charges").

IN THE NEWS

JUDGE OKS $415 MILLION SETTLEMENT OF "NO POACHING" CHARGES

San Jose, CA—Federal judge Lucy Koh yesterday approved a settlement of the five-year litigation that pitted Silicon Valley workers against their corporate employers. Lawyers claimed that some of the Valley's largest employers—Apple, Google, Intel, and Adobe Systems—conspired to suppress competition for engineers and other valued tech workers. They had, it was alleged, a "no poaching" agreement to not recruit workers from each other. The effect of that agreement was to curtail competitive bidding for Valley talent, thereby holding salaries in check. The four companies agreed to pay $415 million to settle the case, which works out to about $5,800 for each of the 64,446 claimants.

Source: Media reports, September 3, 2015.

ANALYSIS: When employers agree not to bid against each other for available workers, they are behaving as an oligopsony, attempting to hold wages below competitive levels.

The Potential Use of Power

Firms with power in labor markets generally have the same objective as all other firms—to maximize profits. What distinguishes them from competitive (powerless) firms is their ability to attain and keep economic profits. In labor markets, this means using fewer workers and paying them lower wages.

The distinguishing characteristic of labor market monopsonies is that their hiring decisions influence the market wage rate. In a competitive labor market, no single employer has any direct influence on the market wage rate; each firm can hire as much labor as it needs at the prevailing wage. But a monopsonist confronts the *market* labor supply curve. As a result, any increase in the quantity of labor demanded will force the monopsonist to climb up the labor supply curve in search of additional workers. In other words, *a monopsonist can hire additional workers only if it offers a higher wage rate.*

Marginal Factor Cost. Any time the price of a resource (or product) changes as a result of a firm's purchases, a distinction between marginal cost and price must be made. Making this distinction is one of the little headaches—and potential sources of profit—of a monopsonist. For labor, we distinguish between the **marginal factor cost (MFC)** of labor and its wage rate.

Suppose that Figure 17.6 accurately describes the labor supply schedule confronting a monopsonist. It's evident that the monopsonist will have to pay a wage of at least $2 an hour if it wants any labor. But even at that wage rate (row *F* of the supply schedule), only one worker will be willing to work. If the firm wants more labor, it will have to offer higher wages.

Two things happen when the firm raises its wage offer to $3 an hour (row *G*). First, the quantity of labor supplied increases (to two workers per hour). Second, the total wages paid rise by $4. This *marginal* cost of labor is attributable to the fact that the first worker's

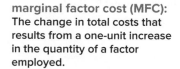

marginal factor cost (MFC): The change in total costs that results from a one-unit increase in the quantity of a factor employed.

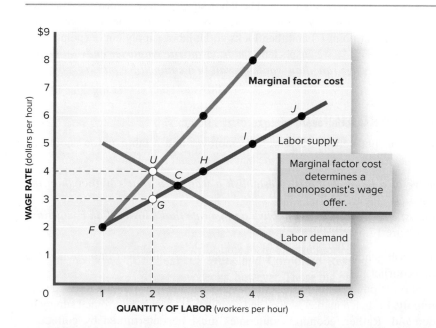

QUANTITY OF LABOR (workers per hour)

FIGURE 17.6
Marginal Factor Cost

More workers can be attracted only if the wage rate is increased. As it rises, all workers must be paid the higher wage. Consequently, the change in *total* wage costs exceeds the actual wage paid to the last worker. In the table, notice that in row *I,* for example, the marginal factor cost of the fourth worker ($8) exceeds the wage actually paid to that worker ($5). Thus the marginal factor cost curve lies above the labor supply curve.

In the graph, the intersection of the marginal factor cost and labor demand curves (point *U*) indicates the quantity of labor a monopsonist will want to hire. The labor supply curve (at point *G*) indicates the wage rate that must be paid to attract the desired number of workers. This is the monopsonist's desired wage ($3). In the absence of market power, an employer would end up at point *C* (the competitive equilibrium), paying a higher wage and employing more workers.

	Wage Rate (per Hour)	×	Quantity of Labor Supplied (Workers per Hour)	=	Total Wage Cost (per Hour)	Marginal Factor Cost (per Labor-Hour)
E	1		0		0	—
F	2		1		2	2
G	3		2		6	4
H	4		3		12	6
I	5		4		20	8
J	6		5		30	10

wages also rise when the wage rate is increased to attract additional workers. If all the workers perform the same job, the first worker will demand to be paid the new (higher) wage rate. Thus *the marginal factor cost exceeds the wage rate because additional workers can be hired only if the wage rate for all workers is increased.*

The Monopsony Firm's Goal. The marginal factor cost curve confronting this monopsonist is shown in the upper half of Figure 17.6. It starts at the bottom of the labor supply curve and rises above it. The monopsonist must now decide how many workers to hire, given the impact of its hiring decision on the market wage rate.

Remember from Chapter 16 that the labor demand curve is a reflection of labor's **marginal revenue product (MRP)**—that is, the increase in total revenue attributable to the employment of one additional worker.

As we've emphasized, the profit-maximizing producer always seeks to equalize marginal revenue and marginal cost. Accordingly, the monopsonistic employer will seek to hire the amount of labor at which the marginal revenue product of labor equals its marginal factor cost:

$$\text{Profit-maximizing level of input use} : \begin{array}{c}\text{Marginal revenue}\\\text{product of input}\\\text{(MRP)}\end{array} = \begin{array}{c}\text{Marginal factor}\\\text{cost of input}\\\text{(MFC)}\end{array}$$

In Figure 17.6, this objective is illustrated by the intersection of the marginal factor cost and labor demand curves at point *U*.

At point *U* the monopsonist is *willing to hire* two workers per hour at a wage rate of $4. But the firm doesn't have to pay this much. The labor supply curve informs us that two workers are *willing to work* for only $3 an hour. Hence the firm first decides how many workers it wants to hire (at point *U*) and then looks at the labor supply curve (point *G*) to see what it has to pay them. As we suspected, *a monopsonistic employer ends up hiring fewer workers at a lower wage rate than would prevail in a competitive market* (point *C*).

....

COLLECTIVE BARGAINING

The potential for conflict between a powerful employer and a labor union should be evident:

- *The objective of a labor union is to establish a wage rate that's* **higher** *than the competitive wage* (Figure 17.3).
- *A monopsonist employer seeks to establish a wage rate that's* **lower** *than competitive standards* (Figure 17.6).

The resultant clash generates intense bargaining that often spills over into politics, the courts, and open conflict.

The confrontation of power on both sides of the labor market is a situation referred to as **bilateral monopoly.** In such a market, wages and employment aren't determined simply by supply and demand. Rather, economic outcomes must be determined by **collective bargaining**—that is, direct negotiations between employers and labor unions for the purpose of determining wages, employment, working conditions, and related issues.

Possible Agreements

In a typical labor–business confrontation, the two sides begin by stating their preferences for equilibrium wages and employment. The *demands* laid down by the union are likely to revolve around point *U* in Figure 17.7; the *offer* enunciated by management is likely to be at point *G*.[1] Thus the boundaries of a potential settlement—a negotiated final equilibrium—are

---

[1]Even though points *U* and *G* may not be identical to the initial bargaining positions, they represent the positions of maximum attainable benefit for both sides. Points outside the demand or supply curve will be rejected out of hand by one side or the other.

marginal revenue product (MRP): The change in total revenue associated with one additional unit of input.

bilateral monopoly: A market with only one buyer (a monopsonist) and one seller (a monopolist).

collective bargaining: Direct negotiations between employers and unions to determine labor market outcomes.

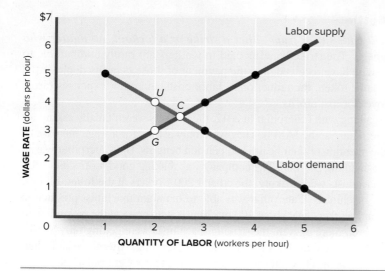

FIGURE 17.7
The Boundaries of Collective Bargaining

Firms with power in the labor market seek to establish wages and employment levels corresponding to point *G* (from Figure 17.6). Unions, on the other hand, seek to establish an equilibrium at point *U* (from Figure 17.3). The competitive equilibrium is at point *C.* The function of collective bargaining is to identify a compromise between these points—that is, to locate an equilibrium somewhere in the shaded area.

usually established at the outset of collective bargaining. In the News "Caterpillar vs. the IAM" summarizes the points of contention in the 2012 dispute between Caterpillar and the International Association of Machinists.

IN THE NEWS

CATERPILLAR VS. THE IAM
What Separates the Two Sides

	Company Proposal	Union Proposal
Wages	6-year wage freeze for 'old' employees Market-based wages for newly hired workers	Pay hike of 1.5% per year all employees
Benefits	Cut company share of health insurance premiums form 90% to 80%	Keep employee share of insurance premiums at 10%
Job security	Curtail seniority rights of individual workers	Keep seniority rights

Source: Media reports, March-April 2012.

ANALYSIS: Collective bargaining begins with a set of union demands and management offers. The outcome depends on the relative strength and tactics of the two parties.

The interesting part of collective bargaining isn't the initial bargaining positions but the negotiation of the final settlement. The speed with which a settlement is reached and the terms of the resulting compromise depend on the patience, tactics, and resources of the negotiating parties. ***The fundamental source of negotiating power for either side is its ability to withhold labor or jobs.*** The union can threaten to strike, thereby cutting off the flow of union labor to the employer. The employer can impose a lockout, thereby cutting off jobs and paychecks. The effectiveness of those threats depends on the availability of substitute workers or jobs.

The Pressure to Settle

Labor and management both suffer from either a strike or a lockout, no matter who initiates the work stoppage. The strike benefits paid to workers are rarely comparable to wages they would otherwise have received, and the payment of those benefits depletes the union treasury. By the same token, the reduction in labor costs and other expenses rarely compensates the employer for lost profits.

In the machinists' bargaining with Caterpillar in 2012, the workers weren't really asking for much (In the News "Caterpillar vs. the IAM"). They were only asking for a wage increase of 1.5 percent a year and the retention of their health and pension benefits. But Caterpillar was in an exceptionally strong bargaining position. The company was making good profits and sales were strong. Only 780 machinists were striking; the other 1,200 workers at the Joliet, Illinois, plant weren't joining the machinists. Caterpillar was able to maintain machinist production with supervisors, temporary workers, and about 100 machinists who crossed the picket line to work. To make the battle even more uneven, the striking machinists were getting only $150 a week in strike benefits from their union. They couldn't hold out for long. After three and a half months, the machinists capitulated. They returned to work on the terms Caterpillar set.

Collective bargaining isn't always so favorable to the employer. In 1998 the balance of power was reversed. Car sales were brisk, and inventories were lean. So when the UAW struck a key parts plant in June 1998, GM was under greater pressure to settle. Rather than continuing to lose more than $100 million a day in lost sales, GM relented after 54 days, accepting little more than a UAW promise not to strike again for a year and a half.

Collective bargaining isn't always so lopsided. In 2016 pro basketball teams were enjoying huge and growing revenues. Both the owners and the players recognized that a strike would be foolish. So they were very willing to make a deal that made both sides richer (In the News "NBA and Players Strike a Deal").

Hockey players weren't so fortunate. Bargaining between the players and the National Hockey League stalled completely in 2012. The owners expressed their frustration by cancelling the first three months of the 2012–2013 hockey season. That lockout cost the players $1 *billion* in lost pay and the team owners more than $200 million. Walmart used an extreme version of the lockout tactic to fend off union power: it simply shuttered its Canadian store and eliminated all the jobs (see World View "Walmart Shutters Quebec Store as Union Closes In").

WORLD VIEW

WALMART SHUTTERS QUEBEC STORE AS UNION CLOSES IN

Walmart decided to close its store in Jonquiere, Quebec, rather than give in to union demands. A majority of the store's 145 hourly employees had signed union cards, forcing Walmart to enter into negotiations with the United Food and Commercial Workers (UFCW) union. That was a turn of events Walmart was not prepared to accept. In preliminary negotiations, the union demanded better pay and new work rules. Walmart said the union's demands would force it to hire 30 more workers, which wasn't economically feasible. So Walmart, with a history of fending off unions, decided to close the Jonquiere store. Had the UFCW succeeded in unionizing that store, it would have been the first unionized Walmart in North America.

Walmart CEO H. Lee Scott Jr. defended his decision, saying, "You can't take a store that is a struggling store anyway and add a bunch of people and a bunch of work rules that cause you to even be in worse shape." The Canadian director of UFCW responded that, "Walmart is trying to send a message to the rest of their employees that if they join a union the same thing could happen to them . . ."

Source: News reports, February 9–12, 2005.

ANALYSIS: The power to lock out workers is the ultimate source of employer power in collective bargaining. Walmart chose an extreme use of that power.

Sometimes, third parties are critical to pushing for a settlement. In October 2016 the professors at 14 Pennsylvania colleges went on strike. They had been working for more than a year without a contract and wanted the state to come to terms. The state demanded 249 changes in the work rules and pay of the professors. But the faculty resisted the changes and wanted higher wages. On October 14, 2016, they went on strike, cancelling classes for more than 100,000 students. The families of the students besieged the governor, who in turn pushed for a settlement. After a three-day strike, the professors and the state settled their differences.

Because potential income losses are usually high, both labor and management try to avoid a strike or lockout if they can. In fact, **more than 90 percent of the 20,000 collective bargaining agreements negotiated each year are concluded without recourse to a strike** and often without even the explicit threat of one.

The Final Settlement

The built-in pressures for settlement help resolve collective bargaining. They don't tell us, however, what the dimensions of that final settlement will be. All we know is that the settlement will be located within the boundaries established in Figure 17.7. The relative pressures on each side will determine whether the final equilibrium is closer to the union or the management position.

The final settlement almost always necessitates hard choices on both sides. The union usually has to choose between an increase in job security and higher pay. A union must also consider how management will react in the long run to higher wages, perhaps by introducing new technology that reduces its dependence on labor. The employer has to worry whether productivity will suffer if workers are dissatisfied with their pay package.

THE IMPACT OF UNIONS

We know that unions tend to raise wage rates in individual companies, industries, and occupations. But can we be equally sure that unions have raised wages in general? If the UAW is successful in raising wages in the automobile industry, what, if anything, happens to car prices? If car prices rise in step with UAW wage rates, labor and management in the auto industry will get proportionally larger slices of the economic pie. At the same time, workers in other industries will be burdened with higher car prices.

Relative Wages

One measure of union impact is *relative* wages—the wages of union members in comparison with those of nonunion workers. As we've noted, unions seek to control the supply of labor in a particular industry or occupation. This forces the excluded workers to seek work elsewhere. As a result of this labor supply imbalance, wages tend to be higher in unionized industries than in nonunionized industries. Figure 17.8 illustrates this displacement effect.

Although the theoretical impact of union exclusionism on relative wages is clear, empirical estimates of that impact are fairly rare. We do know that union wages in general are significantly higher than nonunion wages ($1,004 versus $802 per week in 2017). But part of this differential is due to the fact that unions are more common in industries that have always been more capital-intensive and paid relatively high wages. When comparisons are made within particular industries or sectors, the differential narrows considerably. Nevertheless, there's a general consensus that unions have managed to increase their relative wages by 15 to 20 percent.

Labor's Share of Total Income

Even though unions have been successful in redistributing some income from nonunion to union workers, the question still remains whether they've increased labor's share of *total* income. The *labor share* of total income is the proportion of income received by all

(a) Unionized labor market

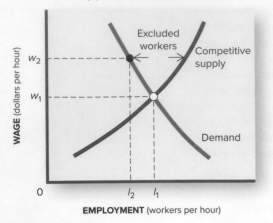

(b) Nonunionized labor market

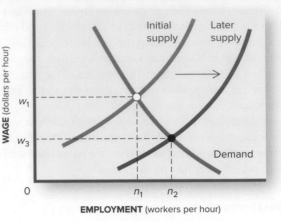

FIGURE 17.8

The Effect of Unions on Relative Wages

In the absence of unions, the average wage rate would be equal to w_1. As unions take control of the market, however, they seek to raise wage rates to w_2, in the process reducing the amount of employment in that market from l_1 to l_2. The workers displaced from the unionized market will seek work in the nonunionized market, thereby shifting the nonunion supply curve to the right. The result will be a reduction of wage rates (to w_3) in the nonunionized market. Thus union wages end up higher than nonunion wages.

workers, in contrast to the share of income received by owners of capital (the *capital share*). The labor share of total income will rise only if the gains to union workers exceed the losses to the (excluded) nonunion workers.

Evidence of unions' impact on labor's share is almost as difficult to assemble as evidence on relative wages, and for much the same reasons. Labor's share of national income has risen dramatically, from only 56 percent in 1919 to 75 percent today. But there have been tremendous changes in the mix of output during that same period. The proportion of output composed of personal services (accountants, teachers, electricians) is much larger now than it was in 1919. The labor share of income derived from personal services is and always was close to 100 percent. Accordingly, *most of the rise in labor's share of total income is due to changes in the structure of the economy rather than to unionization.*

Prices

One way firms can protect their profits in the face of rising union wages is to raise product prices. If firms raise prices along with union wages, consumers end up footing the bill. In that case, profits and the capital share of total income might not be reduced.

The ability of firms to pass along increased union wages depends on the structure of product markets as well as labor markets. If a firm has power in both markets, it's better able to protect itself in this way. There's little evidence, however, that unions have contributed significantly to general cost-push inflation.

Productivity

productivity: Output per unit of input—for example, output per labor-hour.

Unions also affect prices indirectly via changes in **productivity.** Unions bargain not only for wages but also for work rules that specify how goods should be produced. Work rules may limit the pace of production, restrict the type of jobs a particular individual can perform, or require a minimum number of workers to accomplish a certain task. A factory carpenter, for example, may not be permitted to change a lightbulb that burns out in his shop area. And the electrician who is summoned may be required to have an apprentice on all work assignments. Such restrictive work rules would make it very costly to change a burned-out lightbulb.

Not all work rules are so restrictive. In general, however, work rules are designed to protect jobs and maximize the level of employment at any given rate of output. From this perspective, work rules directly restrain productivity and thus inflate costs and prices.

Work rules may also have some beneficial effects. The added job security provided by work rules and seniority provisions tends to reduce labor turnover (quitting) and thus saves recruitment and training costs. Protective rules may also make workers more willing to learn new tasks and to train others in specific skills. Richard Freeman of Harvard asserts that unions have actually accelerated advances in productivity and economic growth.

Political Impact

Perhaps more important than any of these specific union effects is the general impact the union movement has had on our economic, social, and political institutions. Unions are a major political force in the United States. They've not only provided critical electoral and financial support for selected political candidates, but they've also fought hard for important legislation. Unions have succeeded in establishing minimum wage laws, work and safety rules, and retirement benefits. They've also actively lobbied for civil rights legislation and health and education programs. Whatever one may think of any particular union or specific union action, it's clear that our institutions and national welfare would be very different in their absence.

THE ECONOMY TOMORROW

MERGING TO SURVIVE

Unions have been in retreat for nearly a generation. As shown in Figure 17.4, the unionized share of the labor force has fallen from 35 percent in 1950 to less than 11 percent today. Even that modest share has been maintained only by the spread of unionism among public schoolteachers and other government employees. In the private sector, the unionization rate is less than 7 percent and still declining. The Teamsters, the Auto Workers, and the Steelworkers have lost more than 1 million members in the last 15 years.

The decline in unionization is explained by three phenomena. Most important is the relative decline in manufacturing, coupled with rapid growth in high-tech service industries (like computer software, accounting, and medical technology). The second force is the downsizing of major corporations and the relatively faster growth of smaller companies. These structural changes have combined to shrink the traditional employment base of labor unions.

The third cause of shrinking unionization is increased global competition. The decline of worldwide trade and investment barriers has made it easier for firms to import products from low-wage nations and even to relocate production plants. With more options, firms can more easily resist increased wage demands.

The labor union movement is fully aware of these forces and determined to resist them. To increase their power, unions are merging across craft and industry lines. In 1995 the Rubber Workers merged with the Steelworkers, the two major textile unions combined forces, and the Food Workers and Retail Clerks formed a new union. In 1999 the Grain Millers merged with the Paperworkers Union. By merging, the unions hope to increase representation, gain financial strength, and enhance their political clout. They're also seeking to broaden their appeal by organizing low-wage workers in the service industries. These efforts, together with their political strength, will help unions to play a continuing role in the economy tomorrow, even if their share of total employment continues to shrink.

SUMMARY

- Power in labor markets is the ability to alter market wage rates. Such power is most evident in local labor markets defined by geographical, occupational, or industrial boundaries. **LO17-1**
- Power on the supply side of labor markets is manifested by unions, organized along industry or craft lines. The basic function of a union is to evaluate employment offers in terms of the *collective* interest of its members. **LO17-1**
- The downward slope of the labor demand curve creates a distinction between the marginal wage and the market wage. The marginal wage is the change in *total* wages occasioned by employment of one additional worker and is less than the market wage. **LO17-1**
- Unions seek to establish that rate of employment at which the marginal wage curve intersects the labor supply curve. The desired union wage is then found on the labor demand curve at that level of employment. **LO17-1**
- Power on the demand side of labor markets is manifested in buyer concentrations such as monopsony and oligopsony. Such power is usually found among the same firms that exercise market power in product markets. **LO17-2**

- By definition, power on the demand side implies some direct influence on market wage rates; additional hiring by a monopsonist will force up the market wage rate. Hence a monopsonist must recognize a distinction between the marginal factor cost of labor and its (lower) market wage rate. **LO17-2**
- The goal of a monopsonistic employer is to hire the number of workers at which the marginal factor cost of labor equals its marginal revenue product. The employer then looks at the labor supply curve to determine the wage rate that must be paid for that number of workers. **LO17-2**
- The desire of unions to establish a wage rate that's higher than competitive wages directly opposes the desire of powerful employers to establish lower wage rates. In bilateral monopolies unions and employers engage in collective bargaining to negotiate a final settlement. **LO17-2**
- The impact of unions on the economy is difficult to measure. It appears, however, that they've increased their own relative wages and contributed to rising prices. They've also had substantial political impact. **LO17-3**

Key Terms

labor supply	union shop	bilateral monopoly
demand for labor	unionization rate	collective bargaining
equilibrium wage	monopsony	productivity
market power	marginal factor cost (MFC)	
marginal wage	marginal revenue product (MRP)	

Questions for Discussion

1. Collective bargaining sessions often start with unreasonable demands and categorical rejections. Why do unions and employers tend to begin bargaining from extreme positions? **LO17-2**
2. Does a strike for a raise of 5 cents an hour make any sense? What kinds of long-term benefits might a union gain from such a strike? **LO17-1**
3. Why do some college professors join a union? What are the advantages or disadvantages of campus unionization? **LO17-1**
4. Are large and powerful firms easier targets for union organization than small firms? Why or why not? **LO17-1**
5. Nonunionized firms tend to offer wage rates that are close to rates paid by unionized firms in the same industry. How do you explain this? **LO17-3**
6. Why are farmworkers much less successful than airplane machinists in securing higher wages? **LO17-2**

7. In 1998 teaching assistants at the University of California struck for higher wages and union recognition, something they had sought for 14 years. How might the availability of replacement workers have affected their power? **LO17-2**
8. Why did the NBA players avert a strike (In the News "NBA and Players Strike a Deal" and Collective Bargaining text) ? **LO17-2**
9. Why did Walmart choose to close its store rather than hire 30 more workers (World View "Walmart Shutters Quebec Store as Union Closes In")? **LO17-2**
10. Why do pro basketball players want team owners to limit roster size to 40 players (In the News "NBA and Players Strike a Deal")? Why would owners like larger rosters? **LO17-1**

PROBLEMS FOR CHAPTER 17

LO17-1 1. Complete the following table:

Wage rate	$14	$13	$12	$11	$10	$9	$8	$7
Quantity of labor demanded	0	5	20	50	75	95	110	120
Marginal wage	___	___	___	___	___	___	___	___

   (a) What is the marginal wage when the nominal wage is $11?

   (b) At what wage rate does the marginal wage first become negative?

LO17-1 2. Complete the following table:

Wage rate	$6	$7	$8	$9	$10	$11	$12
Quantity of labor supplied	80	120	155	180	200	210	215
Marginal factor cost	___	___	___	___	___	___	

LO17-2 3. Based on the data in Problems 1 and 2 above,

   (a) What is the competitive wage rate?

   (b) Approximately what wage will the union seek?

   (c) How many workers will the union have to exclude in order to get that wage?

LO17-2 4. At the time of the National Football League strike in 1987, the football owners made available the following data:

Source of Revenue	Total Team Revenues and Costs	
	Before the Strike	**During the Strike**
Television	$973,000	$973,000
Stadium gate	526,000	126,000
Luxury box seats	255,000	200,000
Concessions	60,000	12,000
Radio	40,000	40,000
Players' salaries and costs	854,000	230,000
Nonplayer costs (coaches' salaries)	200,000	200,000

   (a) Compute total revenues, total expenses, and profits both before and during the strike.

	Before Strike	**During Strike**
Total revenue	_____	_____
Total expense	_____	_____
Total profit	_____	_____

   (b) Who was better positioned to endure the strike? NFL owners or the players?

LO17-2 5. Suppose the following supply and demand schedules apply in a particular labor market:

Wage rate (per hour)	$4	$5	$6	$7	$8	$9	$10
Quantity of labor supplied (workers per hour)	2	3	4	5	6	7	8
Quantity of labor demanded (workers per hour)	6	5	4	3	2	1	0

Graph the relevant curves and identify the
(a) Competitive wage rate.
(b) Union wage rate.
(c) Monopsonist's wage rate.

LO17-3 6. The graphs show unionized and nonunionized labor markets.
(a) Identify a likely wage and employment outcome when the market becomes unionized on the unionized labor market graph.
(b) Show the impact of this unionization on the nonunionized labor market.

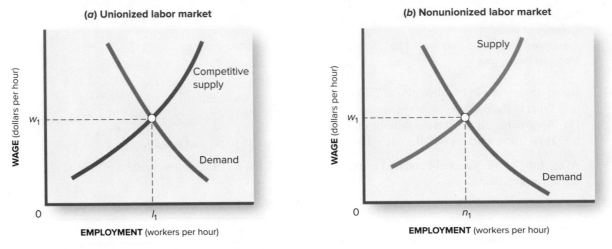

(a) Unionized labor market   (b) Nonunionized labor market

LO17-2 7. In the Silicon Valley hiring-conspiracy case (In the News "Judge OKs $415 Million Settlement of 'No Poaching' Charges"), attorneys for the 64,000 plaintiffs asked for $3 billion in damages.
(a) How much did this work out per worker?
(b) How much did the judge approve (per worker)?

LO17-2 8. In the 2012 Machinists'-Caterpillar confrontation, the workers' average pay was $26 per hour. If their demand for a 1.5% pay hike per year had been granted, what would their hourly wage have been
(a) In the following year?
(b) Three years later?
Caterpillar offered the machinists a one-time bonus of $5,000 if they didn't strike. Assuming the machinists worked an average of 2,000 hours per year, was this more or less than the wage demand the union made for
(c) The first year?
(d) The first three years?

LO17-2 9. The Economy Tomorrow: Identify if the following would likely strengthen or weaken a union membership in the United States.
(a) Increase in manufacturing.
(b) Faster growth of small companies.
(c) Increased global competition.

©Steve Allen/Stockbyte/Getty Images RF

Financial Markets

Christopher Columbus had a crazy entrepreneurial idea. He was certain he could find a new route to the Indies by sailing not east from Europe but west—around the world. Such a route, he surmised, would give Europe quicker access to the riches of the East Indies. Whoever discovered that western route could become very, very rich.

To find that route, Columbus needed ships, sailors, and tons of provisions. He couldn't afford to supply these resources himself. He needed financial backers who would put up the money. For several years he tried to convince King Ferdinand of Spain to provide the necessary funds. But the king didn't want to risk so much wealth on a single venture. Twice he turned Columbus down.

Fortunately, Genoese merchant bankers in Seville came to Columbus's rescue. Convinced that Columbus's "enterprise of the Indies" might bring back "pearls, precious stones, gold, silver, spiceries," and other valuable merchandise, they guaranteed repayment of any funds lent to Columbus. With that guarantee in hand, the Duke of Medina Sidonia, in April 1492, offered to lend 1,000 maravedis (about $5,000 in today's dollars) to Queen Isabella for the purpose of funding Columbus's expedition. With no personal financial risk, King Ferdinand then granted Columbus the funds and authority for a royal expedition.

Columbus's experience in raising funds for his expedition illustrates a critical function of financial markets—namely, the management of *risk*. This chapter examines how financial markets facilitate economic activities (like Columbus's expedition) by managing the risks of failure. Three central questions guide the discussion:

- **What is traded in financial markets?**
- **How do the financial markets affect the economic outcomes of WHAT, HOW, and FOR WHOM?**
- **Why do financial markets fluctuate so much?**

THE ROLE OF FINANCIAL MARKETS

A central question for every economy is WHAT to produce. In 1492 all available resources were employed in farming, fishing, food distribution, metalworking, and other basic services. For Columbus to pursue his quest, he needed some of those resources. To get them, he needed money to bid scarce resources from other pursuits and employ them on his expedition.

Financial Intermediaries

Entrepreneurs who don't have great personal wealth must get start-up funds from other people. There are two possibilities: either *borrow* the money or invite other people to *invest* in the new venture.

How might you pursue these options? You could ask your relatives for a loan or go door-to-door in your neighborhood seeking investors. But such direct fund-raising is costly, inefficient, and often unproductive. Columbus went hat in hand to the Spanish royal court twice, but each time he came back empty-handed.

financial intermediary: Institution (e.g., a bank or the stock market) that makes savings available to dissavers (e.g., investors).

The task of raising start-up funds is made much easier by the existence of **financial intermediaries**—institutions that steer the flow of savings to cash-strapped entrepreneurs and other investors. Funds flow into banks, pension funds, bond markets, stock markets, and other financial intermediaries from businesses, households, and government entities that have some unspent income. This pool of national savings is then passed on to entrepreneurs, expanding businesses, and other borrowers by these same institutions (see Figure 18.1).

Financial intermediaries provide several important services. They greatly reduce the cost of locating loanable funds. Their pool of savings offers a clear economy of scale compared to the alternative of door-to-door solicitations. They also reduce the cost to savers of finding suitable lending or investment opportunities. Few individuals have the time, resources, or *interest to do the searching on their own. With huge pools of amassed savings, how*ever, financial intermediaries have the incentive to acquire and analyze information about lending and investment opportunities. Hence ***financial intermediaries reduce search and information costs*** in the financial markets. In so doing, they make the allocation of resources more efficient.

Crowdfunding. Financial intermediaries come in many shapes and sizes. They are not all banks or brick-and-mortar institutions. The Internet has made door-to-door solicitations a thing of the past. Now people can disseminate their entrepreneurial ideas on a crowdfunding platform like GoFundMe, Kickstarter, or Indiegogo and hope that others like the idea enough to contribute some financing. Although **crowdfunding** has become a popular, inexpensive, and efficient method of raising start-up financing, it accounts for a tiny percentage of the funds raised by more traditional intermediaries (see In the News "Where Do Start-Ups Get Their Money?" later in the chapter).

crowdfunding: An internet-based method of raising funds from a large number of people.

FIGURE 18.1
Mobilizing Savings

The central economic function of financial markets is to channel national savings into new investment and other desired expenditure. Financial intermediaries such as banks, insurance companies, and stockbrokers help transfer purchasing power from savers to spenders.

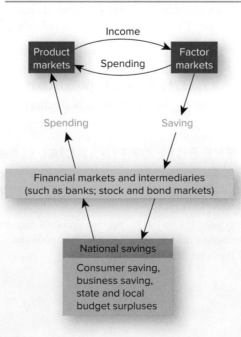

Although financial intermediaries make the job of acquiring start-up funds a lot easier, there's no guarantee that the funds needed will be acquired. First, there must be an adequate supply of funds available. Second, financial intermediaries must be convinced that they should allocate some of those funds to a project.

The Supply of Loanable Funds

As noted, the supply of loanable funds originates in the decisions of market participants to not spend all their current income. Those saving decisions are influenced by time preferences and interest rates.

Time Preferences. In deciding to *save* rather than *spend,* people effectively reallocate their spending over time. That is, people save *now* in order to spend more *later.* How much to save, then, depends partly on *time preference.* If a person doesn't give any thought to the future, she's likely to save little. If, by contrast, a person wants to buy a car, a vacation, or a house in the future, she's more inclined to save some income now.

Interest Rates. Interest rates also affect saving decisions. If interest rates are high, the future payoff to every dollar saved is greater. A higher return on savings translates into more future income for every dollar of current income saved. Hence *higher interest rates increase the quantity of available savings (loanable funds).*

Risk. In early 2009 banks in Zimbabwe were offering interest rates on savings accounts of more than 100,000 percent a year. Yet few people rushed to deposit their savings in Zimbabwean banks. Inflation was running at a rate of 230 *million* percent a year, making a 100,000 percent return look pitifully small. Further, people worried that political instability in Zimbabwe might cause the banks to fail, wiping out their savings in the process. In other words, there was a high *risk* attached to those phenomenal interest rates.

Anyone who contemplated lending funds to Columbus confronted a similar risk: the potential payoff was huge but so was the risk. That was the dilemma King Ferdinand confronted. He had enough funds to finance Columbus's expedition, but he didn't want to risk losing so much on a single venture.

Risk Management. This is why the Genoese bankers were so critical: these financial intermediaries could spread the risk of failure among many individuals. Each investor could put up just a fraction of the needed funds. No one had to put all his eggs in one basket. Once the consortium of bankers agreed to share the risks of Columbus's expedition, the venture had wings. The Genoese merchant bankers could afford to take portions of the expedition's risks because they also financed many less risky projects. By diversifying their portfolios, they could attain whatever degree of *average* risk they preferred. That is the essence of risk management.

Risk Premiums. Even though diversification permits greater risk management, lenders will want to be compensated for any above-average risks they take. Money lent to local merchants must have seemed a lot less risky than lending funds to Columbus. Thus no one would have stepped forward to finance Columbus unless promised an *above-average* return upon the expedition's success. The difference between the rates of return on a safe (certain) investment and a risky (uncertain) one is called the **risk premium.** Risk premiums compensate people who finance risky ventures that succeed. Because these ventures are risky, however, investors often lose their money in such ventures too.

Risk premiums help explain why blue-chip corporations such as Microsoft can borrow money from a bank at the low "prime" rate while ordinary consumers have to pay much higher interest rates on personal loans. Corporate loans are less risky because corporations typically have plenty of revenue and assets to cover their debts. Consumers often get overextended, however, and can't pay all their bills. As a result, there's a greater risk that consumers' loans won't be paid back. Banks charge higher interest rates on consumer loans to compensate for this risk.

risk premium: The difference in rates of return on risky (uncertain) and safe (certain) investments.

THE PRESENT VALUE OF FUTURE PROFITS

In deciding whether to assume the *risk* of supplying funds to a new venture, financial intermediaries assess the potential *rewards*. In Columbus's case, the rewards were the fabled treasures of the East Indies. Even if he found those treasures, however, the rewards would only come long after the expedition was financed. When Columbus proposed his East Indies expedition, he envisioned a round trip that would last at least six months. If he located the treasures he sought, he planned subsequent trips to acquire and transport his precious cargoes back home. Although King Ferdinand granted Columbus only one-tenth of any profits from the first expedition, Columbus had a claim on one-eighth of the profits of any subsequent voyages. Hence, even if Columbus succeeded in finding a shortcut to the East, he wouldn't generate any substantial profit for perhaps two years or more. That's a long time to wait.

Suppose for the moment that Columbus expected no profit from the first expedition but a profit of $1,000 at the end of two years from a second voyage. How much was that future profit worth to Columbus in 1492?

Time Value of Money

To assess the present value of *future* receipts, we have to consider the *time value* of money. A dollar received today is worth more than a dollar received two years from today. Why? Because a dollar received today can earn *interest*. If you have a dollar today and put it in an interest-bearing account, in two years you'll have your original dollar *plus* accumulated interest. *As long as interest-earning opportunities exist, present dollars are worth more than future dollars.*

In 1492 there were plenty of opportunities to earn interest. Indeed, the Genoese bankers were charging high interest rates on their loans and guarantees. If Columbus had had the cash, he too could have lent money to others and earned interest on his funds.

To calculate the present value of future dollars, this forgone interest must be taken into account. This computation is essentially interest accrual in reverse. *We "discount" future dollars by the opportunity cost of money*—that is, the market rate of interest.

Suppose the market rate of interest in 1492 was 10 percent. To compute the **present discounted value (PDV)** of future payment, we discount as follows:

$$\text{PDV} = \frac{\text{Future payment}_N}{(1 + \text{Interest rate})^N}$$

where N refers to the number of years into the future when a payment is to be made. If the future payment is to be made in one year, the N in the equation equals 1, and we have

$$\text{PDV} = \frac{\$1,000}{1.10}$$
$$= \$909.09$$

Hence the present discounted value of $1,000 to be paid one year from today is $909.09. If $909.09 were received today, it could earn interest. In a year's time, the $909.09 would grow to $1,000 with interest accrued at the rate of 10 percent per year.

Suppose it would have taken Columbus two years to complete his expeditions and collect his profits, rather than one year. In that case, the present value of the $1,000 payment would be lower. The N in the formula would be 2, and the present value would be

$$\text{PDV} = \frac{\$1,000}{(1.10)^2} = \frac{\$1,000}{1.21} = \$826.45$$

Hence *the longer one has to wait for a future payment, the less present value it has.*

Lottery winners often have to choose between present and future values. In July 2004, for example, Geraldine Williams, a 68-year-old housekeeper in Lowell, Massachusetts, won a $294 million MegaMillions lottery. The $294 million was payable in 26 annual

The success of Columbus's voyage was highly uncertain.

Source: Library of Congress Prints and Photographs Division [LC-USZ62-105062].

present discounted value (PDV): The value today of future payments, adjusted for interest accrual.

Years in the Future	Future Payment ($ millions)	Present Value ($ millions)
0	$ 11.3	$ 11.30
1	11.3	10.82
2	11.3	10.35
3	11.3	9.91
4	11.3	9.49
5	11.3	8.04
*	*	*
*	*	*
*	*	*
25	11.3	3.79
	$294.0	$168.0

Note: The general formula for computing present values is $PDV = \sum \dfrac{\text{Payment in year } N}{(1 + r)^N}$, where r is the prevailing rate.

TABLE 18.1

Computing Present Value

The present value of a future payment declines the longer one must wait for a payment. At an interest rate of 4.47 percent, $11.3 million payable in one year is worth only $10.82 million today. A payout of $11.3 million 25 years from now has a present value of only $3.79 million. A string of $11.3 million payments spread out over 25 years has a present value of $168 million (at 4.47 percent interest).

installments of $11.3 million. If the lucky winner wanted to get her prize sooner, she could accept an immediate but smaller payout rather than 25 future installments.

Table 18.1 shows how the lottery officials figured the present value of the $294 million prize. The first installment of $11.3 million would be paid immediately. Mrs. Williams would have had to wait one year for the second check, however. At the then-prevailing interest rate of 4.47 percent, the *present* value of that second $11.3 million check was only $10.82 million. The *last* payoff check had even less present value since it wasn't due to be paid for 25 years. With so much time for interest to accrue, that final $11.3 million payment had a present value of only $3.79 million. The calculations in Table 18.1 convinced lottery officials to offer an immediate (present) payout of only $168 million on the $294 million (future) prize. Mrs. Williams chose to take the immediate present-value sum—and wasn't too disappointed. Marvin and Mae Acosta made the same choice in July 2016, accepting $327.8 million in present value for their $528.8 million share of a $1.6 *billion* Powerball jackpot.

Interest Rate Effects

The winner would have received even *less* money had interest rates been higher. At the time Mrs. Williams won the lottery, the interest rate on bonds was 4.47 percent. Had the interest rate been higher, the discount for immediate payment would have been higher as well. Table 18.2 indicates that Mrs. Williams would have received only $107 million had the prevailing interest rate been 10 percent. What Tables 18.1 and 18.2 illustrate, then, is that *the present discounted value of a future payment declines with*

- *Higher interest rates.*
- *Longer delays in future payment.*

Uncertainty

The valuation of future payments must also consider the possibility of *non*payment. State governments are virtually certain to make promised lottery payouts, so there's little risk in accepting a promised payout of 25 annual installments. But what about the booty from Columbus's expeditions? There was great uncertainty that Columbus would ever return from his expeditions, much less bring back the "pearls, precious stones, gold, silver, and

TABLE 18.2

Higher Interest Rates Reduce Present Values

Higher interest rates reduce the *present* value of future payments. Shown here is the present discounted value of the July 2004 MegaMillions lottery prize of $294 million at different interest rates.

Interest Rate (%)	Present Discounted Value of $294 Million Lottery Prize ($ millions)
5.0%	$166.3
6.0	150.8
7.0	137.5
8.0	126.0
9.0	115.9
10.0	107.1

expected value: The probable value of a future payment, including the risk of nonpayment.

spiceries" that people coveted. Investing in those expeditions was far riskier than deferring a lottery payment.

Expected Value. Whenever an anticipated future payment is uncertain, a risk factor should be included in present value computations. This is done by calculating the **expected value** of a future payment. Suppose there was only a 50:50 chance that Columbus would bring back the goods. In that event, the expected payoff would be

$$\text{Expected value} = (1 - \text{Risk factor}) \times \text{Present discounted value}$$

With a 50:50 chance of failure, the expected value of Columbus's first-year profits would have been

$$\text{Expected value} = (1 - 0.5) \times \$909.09$$
$$= \$454.55$$

Expected values also explain why people buy more lottery tickets when the prize is larger. The odds of winning the multistate Powerball lottery are 80 *million*:1. That's about the same odds as getting struck by lightning *14 times* in the same year! So it makes almost no sense to buy a ticket. With a $16 million prize, the *undiscounted* expected value of a $1 lottery ticket is only 20 cents. When the lottery prize increases, however, the expected value of a ticket grows as well (there are still only 80 million possible combinations of numbers). When the grand prize reached $425 million in February 2014, the undiscounted expected value of a lone winning ticket jumped to more than $5. Millions of people decided that the expected value was high enough to justify buying a $1 lottery ticket. People took off from work, skipped classes, and drove across state lines to queue up for lottery tickets. When the prize is only $10 million, far fewer people buy tickets.

The Demand for Loanable Funds

People rarely borrow money to buy lottery tickets. But entrepreneurs and other market participants often use other people's funds to finance their ventures. ***How much loanable funds are demanded depends on***

- *The expected rate of return.*
- *The cost of funds.*

The higher the expected return, or the lower the cost of funds, the greater will be the amount of loanable funds demanded.

Figure 18.2 offers a general view of the loanable funds market that emerges from these considerations. From the entrepreneur's perspective, the prevailing interest rate represents the cost of funds. From the perspective of savers, the interest rate represents the payoff to savings. When interest rates rise, the quantity of funds supplied goes up and the quantity demanded goes down. The prevailing (equilibrium) interest rate is set by the intersection of these supply and demand curves.

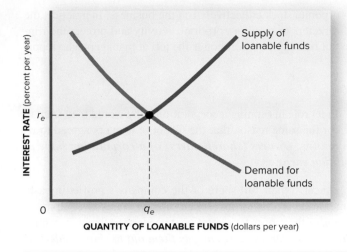

FIGURE 18.2
The Loanable Funds Market
The market rate of interest (r_e) is determined by the intersection of the curves representing supply of and demand for loanable funds. The rate of interest represents the price paid for the use of money.

THE STOCK MARKET

The concept of a loanable funds market sounds a bit alien. But the same principles of supply, demand, and risk management go a long way in explaining the action in stock markets. Suppose you had $1,000 to invest. Should you invest it all in lottery tickets that offer a multimillion-dollar payoff? Put it in a savings account that pays next to nothing? Or how about the stock market? The stock market can reward you handsomely, or it can wipe out your savings if the stocks you own tumble. Hence *stocks offer a higher average return than bank accounts but also entail greater average risk.* People who bought Amazon.com stock in May 1997 got a 1,000 percent profit on their stock in only two years. But people who bought Amazon.com stock in December 1999 lost 90 percent of their investment in even less time.

Corporate Stock

When people buy a share of stock, they're buying partial ownership of a corporation. The three legal forms of business entities are

- Corporations.
- Partnerships.
- Proprietorships.

Limited Liability. Proprietorships are businesses owned by a single individual. The owner–proprietor is entirely responsible for the business, including repayment of any debts. Members of a partnership are typically liable for all business debts and activities as well. By contrast, a **corporation** is a limited liability form of business. The corporation itself, not its individual shareholders, is responsible for all business activity and debts. As a result of this limited liability, you can own a piece of a corporation without worrying about being sued for business mishaps (like environmental damage) or nonpayment of debt. This feature significantly reduces the risk of owning corporate stock.

corporation: A business organization having a continuous existence independent of its members (owners) and power and liabilities distinct from those of its members.

Shared Ownership. The ownership of a corporation is defined in terms of stock shares. Each share of **corporate stock** represents partial ownership of the business. Apple, for example, has 5.2 *billion* shares of stock outstanding (that is, shares held by the public). Hence each share of Apple stock represents less than one-fifth of one-billionth ownership of the corporation. Potentially, this means that as many as 5.2 billion people could own the Apple Corporation. In reality, many individuals own hundreds of shares, and institutions may own thousands. Indeed, some of the largest pension funds in the United States own more than a million shares of Apple.

corporate stock: Shares of ownership in a corporation.

In principle, the owners of corporate stock collectively run the business. In practice, the shareholders select a board of directors to monitor corporate activity and protect their interests. The day-to-day business of running a corporation is the job of managers who report to the board of directors.

Stock Returns

If shareholders don't have any direct role in running a corporation, why would they want to own a piece of it? Essentially, for the same reason that the Genoese bankers agreed to finance Columbus's expedition: profits. *Owners (shareholders) of a corporation hope to share in the profits the corporation earns.*

Dividends. Shareholders rarely receive their full share of the company's profits in cash. Corporations typically use some of the profits for investment in new plants or equipment. They may also want to retain some of the profits for operational needs or unforeseen contingencies. *Corporations may choose to retain earnings or pay them out to shareholders as* **dividends.** Any profits *not* paid to shareholders are referred to as **retained earnings.** Thus

Dividends = Corporate profits − Retained earnings

In 2016 Apple paid quarterly dividends amounting to $2.28 per share for the year. But the company earned profits equal to $8.35 per share. Thus shareholders received only 27 percent of their accrued profits in dividend checks; Apple retained the remaining $6.07 per-share profit earned in 2016 for future investments.

Capital Gains. If Apple invests its retained earnings wisely, the corporation may reap even larger profits in the future. As a company grows and prospers, each share of ownership may become more valuable. This increase in value would be reflected in higher market prices for shares of Apple stock. Any increase in the value of a stock represents a **capital gain** for shareholders. Capital gains directly increase shareholder wealth.

Total Return. People who own stocks can thus get two distinct payoffs: dividends and capital gains. Together these payoffs represent the total return on stock investments. Hence *the higher the expected total return (future dividends and capital gains), the greater the desire to buy and hold stocks.* If a stock paid no dividends and had no prospects for price appreciation (capital gain), you'd probably hold your savings in a different form (such as another stock or maybe an interest-earning bank account).

Initial Public Offering

When a corporation is formed, its future sales and profits are most uncertain. When shares are first offered to the public, the seller of stock is the company itself. By *going public,* the corporation seeks to raise funds for investment and growth. A true *start-up* company may have nothing more than a good idea, a couple of dedicated employees, and big plans. To fund these plans, it sells shares of itself in an **initial public offering (IPO).** People who buy the newly issued stock are putting their savings directly into the corporation's accounts.[1] As new owners, they stand to profit from the corporation's business or take their lumps if the corporation fails.

In 2004 Google was still a relatively new company. Although the company had been in operation since 1999, search engine capacities were limited. To expand, it needed more computers, more employees, and more technology. To finance this expansion, Google needed more money. The company could have borrowed money from a bank or other financial institution, but that would have saddled the company with debt and forced it to make regular interest payments.

---

dividend: Amount of corporate profits paid out for each share of stock.

retained earnings: Amount of corporate profits not paid out in dividends.

capital gain: An increase in the market value of an asset.

initial public offering (IPO): The first issuance (sale) to the general public of stock in a corporation.

---

[1]In reality, some of the initial proceeds will go to stockbrokers and investment bankers as compensation for their services as financial intermediaries. The entrepreneur who starts the company, other company employees, and any venture capitalists who help fund the company before the public offering may also get some of the IPO receipts by selling shares they acquired before the company went public.

Rather than borrow money, Google's directors elected to sell ownership shares in the company. In August 2004 the company raised $1.7 *billion* in cash by selling 19.6 million shares for $85 per share in its initial public offering. Snap Inc., the parent company of the popular Snapchat raised even more at its initial public offering, selling 230 million shares netting the company over $3 *billion* (In the News "Snapchat IPO Nets $3 Billion").

IN THE NEWS

SNAPCHAT IPO NETS $3 BILLION

Snap Inc., the parent company of the popular disappearing messaging app "Snapchat," sold 230 million shares to the public yesterday. Snap's initial public offering (IPO) was a huge success, netting the company over $3 billion, which it said would be used for "general corporate purposes" and possible acquisitions. The company priced its shares at $17 to institutional investors. Once trading started, investors quickly pushed the shares' price up by 47% to $24.

Investors were paying a high premium for Snap. The company launched its platform for disappearing messaging in 2011, facilitating the exchange of "selfies." In 2016 there were 158 million daily active users, generating 2.5 billion "snaps" per day. But the company gets nearly all of its revenue from advertising. Revenue was up 48 percent to $405 million last year, but the company's loss widened to $515 million. The company itself warned that it faces increasing competition from the likes of Facebook's new Instagram "stories," as well as from Twitter, Apple, and Google, and may never be profitable.

Source: Media reports, March 3, 2017.

ANALYSIS: Investors had high expectations for the future growth and profits of Snapchat when they purchased the stock on the first day of trading.

Secondary Trading

Why were people eager to buy shares in Google? They certainly weren't buying the stock with expectations of high dividends. The company hadn't earned much profit in its first five years and didn't expect substantial profits for at least another few years.

P/E Ratio. In 2003 Google had earned only 41 cents of profit per share. In 2004 it would earn $1.46 per share. So people who were buying Google stock for $85 per share in August 2004 were paying a comparatively high price for relatively little profit. This can be seen by computing the **price/earnings (P/E) ratio:**

$$\text{P/E ratio} = \frac{\text{Price of stock share}}{\text{Earnings (profit) per share}}$$

For Google in 2004,

$$\text{P/E ratio} = \frac{\$85}{\$1.46} = 58.2$$

In other words, investors were paying $58.20 for every $1 of profits. That implies a rate of return of $1 \div \$58.20$, or only 1.7 percent. Compared to the interest rates banks were paying on deposit balances, Google shares didn't look like a very good buy.

Profit Expectation. People weren't buying Google stock just to get a piece of *current* profits. What made Google attractive was its *growth* potential. The company projected that revenues and profits would grow rapidly as its search capabilities expanded, more people used its services, and, most important, more advertisers clamored to get premium spots on the company's web pages. Given these expectations, investors projected that Google's profits would jump from $1.46 per share in 2004 to roughly $10 in four years. From that perspective, the *projected* P/E ratio looked cheap.

price/earnings (P/E) ratio: The price of a stock share divided by earnings (profit) per share.

Investors who wanted a piece of those future profits rushed to buy Google stock after its IPO. On the first day of trading, the share price rose from the IPO price of $85 to $100. Within a month the price rose to $120. Two years later Google's stock sold for more than $450 a share! A lot of investors racked up huge capital gains.

That post-IPO rise in Google's stock price had no direct effect on the company. A corporation reaps the proceeds of stock sales only when it sells shares to the public (the initial public offering). After the IPO, the company's stock is traded among individuals in the "after market." Virtually all the trading activity on major stock exchanges consists of such after-market sales. Mr. Dow sells his Google shares to Ms. Jones, who may later sell them to Mr. Pitt. Such *secondary* trades may take place at the New York Stock Exchange (NYSE) on Wall Street or in the computerized over-the-counter market (e.g., NASDAQ). In its earliest secondary trading, Snap Inc.'s share price soared (see In the News "Snapchat IPO Nets $3 Billion").

Market Fluctuations

The price of a stock at any moment is the outcome of supply-and-demand interactions. I wouldn't mind owning a piece of Google. But since I think the current share price is too high, I'll buy the stock only if the price falls substantially. Even though I'm not buying any Google stock now, I'm part of the *market demand*. That is, all the people who are willing and able to buy Google stock at *some* price are included in the demand curve in Figure 18.3. The cheaper the stock, the more people will want to buy it, *ceteris paribus*. The opposite is true on the supply side of the market: ever-higher prices are necessary to induce more shareholders to part with their shares.

Changing Expectations. In early 2006 investors reevaluated the profit prospects for Google and other Internet companies. Several years of experience had shown that earning profits in e-commerce wasn't so easy. Projections of advertising sales growth and future profits were sharply reduced. In two months' time Google's stock price fell from $470 to $340. Figure 18.3 illustrates how this happened. Higher perceived risk reduced the demand for Google stock and increased the willingness of existing shareholders to sell. Such *changes in expectations imply shifts in supply and demand for a company's stock.* As Figure 18.3 illustrates, these combined shifts sent Google stock plummeting.

Table 18.3 summarizes the action in Google stock on a single day. On that day 1.7 million shares of Google were bought and sold. At the end of the trading day (4 p.m. in New

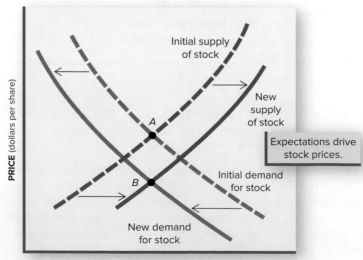

FIGURE 18.3

Worsened Expectations

The supply and demand for stocks is fueled by expectations of future profits. When investors concluded that Google's future profit potential wasn't so great demand for the stock decreased, supply increased, and the share price fell from point *A* to point *B*.

52 Weeks		Stock	Sym	Div	Yld%	P/E	Vol 100s	HI	Lo	Close	Net Chg
HI	Lo										
35.56	22.48	Intel	INTC	0.90	2.57	17.33	262790	35.20	34.74	34.98	+0.05
604.83	502.80	Google	GOOG	0	0	29.84	16910	587.52	578.98	584.77	+4.82

The information provided by this quotation includes the following:

52-Weeks Hi and Lo: The highest and lowest prices paid for a share of stock in the previous year.

Stock: The name of the corporation whose shares are being traded.

Sym: The symbol used as a shorthand description for the stock.

Div: A dividend is the amount of profit paid out by the corporation in the preceding year for each share of stock.

Yld%: The yield is the dividend paid per share divided by the price of a share.

P/E: The price of the stock (P) divided by the earnings (profit) per share (E). This indicates how much a purchaser is effectively paying for each dollar of profits.

Vol 100s: The number of shares traded in hundreds.

HI: The highest price paid for a share of stock on the previous day.

Lo: The lowest price paid for a share of stock on the previous day.

Close: The price paid in the last trade of the day as the market was closing.

Net Chg: The change in the closing price yesterday vs. the previous day's closing price.

Source: E-Trade (September 17, 2014).

TABLE 18.3

Reading Stock Quotes

The financial pages of the daily newspaper summarize the trading activity in corporate stocks. The quotation here summarizes trading in Intel and Google shares on September 17, 2014.

York City) Google shares were selling for $584.77 apiece (see "Close" in Table 18.3). Along the path to that closing equilibrium, the price had fluctuated between $578.78 ("Lo") and $587.52 ("Hi"). The stock price fluctuated even more over the preceding year: the "52-week Hi" was $604.83, while the "52-week Lo" was only $502.80. This huge range in the price of Google shares reflects the changing performance and market expectations for the company.

The Value of Information. The wide fluctuations in the price of Google stock illustrate the value of *information* in financial markets. People who paid high prices for Google shares in 2014 had optimistic expectations for the company's continued growth and share appreciation. Those who *sold* shares at high prices weren't so sure. No one *knew* what future profits would be; everyone was acting on the basis of expectations.

The evident value of information raises a question of access. Do some people have better information than others? Do they get their information fairly? Or do they have "inside" sources (such as company technicians, managers, directors) who give them preferential access to information? If so, these insiders would have an unfair advantage in the marketplace and could alter the distribution of income and wealth in their favor.

The value of information also explains the demand for information services. People pay hundreds and even thousands of dollars for newsletters, wire services, and online computer services that provide up-to-date information on companies and markets. They also pay for the services of investment bankers, advisers, and brokers to help keep them informed. These services help disseminate information quickly, thereby helping financial markets operate efficiently.

Booms and Busts. If stock markets are so efficient at computing the present value of future profits, why does the entire market make abrupt moves every so often? Fundamentally,

TABLE 18.4

Stock Market Averages

More than 1,600 stocks are listed (traded) on the New York Stock Exchange, and many times that number are traded in other stock markets. To gauge changes in so many stocks, people refer to various indexes, such as the Dow Jones Industrial Average. The Dow and similar indexes help us keep track of the market's ups and downs.

Some of the most frequently quoted indexes are

Dow Jones

Industrial Average: An arithmetic average of the prices of 30 blue-chip industrial stocks traded on the New York Stock Exchange (NYSE) and by computers of the National Association of Securities Dealers (NASD).

Transportation Average: An average of 20 transportation stocks traded on the NYSE.

Utilities Average: An average of 15 utility stocks traded on the NYSE.

S&P 500: An index compiled by Standard and Poor of 500 stocks drawn from major stock exchanges as well as over-the-counter stocks. The S&P 500 is made up of 400 industrial companies, 40 utilities, 20 transportation companies, and 40 financial institutions.

NASDAQ Composite: Index of stocks traded in the over-the-counter market among securities dealers.

New York Stock Exchange composite index: The "Big Board" index, which includes all 1,600-plus stocks traded on the NYSE.

Nikkei index: An index of 225 stocks traded on the Tokyo stock market.

the same factors that determine the price of a single stock influence the broader stock market averages as well (see Table 18.4). An increase in interest rates, for example, raises the opportunity cost of holding stocks. Hence higher interest rates should cause stock prices to fall, *ceteris paribus*. Stocks might decline even further if higher interest rates are expected to curtail investment and consumption, thus reducing future sales and profits. Such a double whammy could cause the whole stock market to tumble.

Other factors also affect the relative desirability of holding stock. Congressional budget and deficit decisions, monetary policy, consumer confidence, business investment plans, international trade patterns, and new inventions are just a few of the factors that may alter present and future profits. These ***broad changes in the economic outlook tend to push all stock prices up or down at the same time.***

Broad changes in the economic outlook, however, seldom occur overnight. Moreover, these changes are rarely of a magnitude that could precipitate a stock market boom or bust. In reality, the stock market often changes more abruptly than the economic outlook. These ***exaggerated movements in the stock market are caused by sudden and widespread changes in expectations.*** Keep in mind that the value of the stock depends on anticipated *future* profits and *expectations* for interest rates and the economic outlook. No elements of the future are certain. Instead people use present clues to try to discern the likely course of future events. In other words, ***all information must be filtered through people's expectations.***

The central role of expectations implies that the economy can change more gradually than the stock market. If, for example, interest rates rise, market participants may regard the increase as temporary or inconsequential: their expectations for the future may not change. If interest rates keep rising, however, investors may have greater doubts. At some point, the market participants may revise their expectations. Stock prices may falter, triggering an adjustment in expectations. A herding instinct may surface, sending expectations for stock prices abruptly lower.

Resource Allocations

Although it's fascinating and sometimes fun to watch stock market gyrations, we shouldn't lose sight of the *economic* role of financial markets. Columbus needed *real* resources—ships, men, equipment—for his expeditions. Five centuries later, Google also needed real resources—computers, labor, technology—to expand. To find the necessary economic resources, both Columbus and Google had to convince society to reallocate resources from other activities to their new ventures.

Financial markets facilitate resource reallocations. In Columbus's case, the Genoese bankers lent the funds that Columbus used to buy scarce resources. The funds obtained from Google's 2004 initial public offering served the same purpose. In both cases, the funds obtained in the financial markets helped change the mix of output. If the financial markets hadn't supplied the necessary funding, neither Columbus nor Google would have been able to go forth. The available resources would have been used to produce other goods.

THE BOND MARKET

The bond market is another financial mechanism for transferring the pool of national savings into the hands of would-be spenders. It operates much like the stock market. The major difference is the kind of paper traded. *In the stock market, people buy and sell shares of corporate ownership. In the bond market, people buy and sell promissory notes (IOUs).* A **bond** is simply an IOU, a written promise to repay a loan. The bond itself specifies the terms of repayment, noting both the amount of interest to be paid each year and the maturity date (the date on which the borrower is to repay the entire debt). The borrower may be a corporation (corporate bonds), a local government (municipal bonds), the federal government (Treasury bonds), or some other institution.

bond: A certificate acknowledging a debt and the amount of interest to be paid each year until repayment; an IOU.

Bond Issuance

A bond is first issued when an institution wants to borrow money. Recall the situation Google faced in 2004. The company needed additional funds to expand its Internet operations. Rather than sell equity shares in itself, Google could have *borrowed* funds. The advantage of borrowing funds rather than issuing stock is that the owners can keep control of their company. *Lenders aren't owners, but shareholders are.* The disadvantage of borrowing funds is that the company gets saddled with a repayment schedule. Lenders want to be paid back—with interest. For a new company like Google, the burden of interest payments may be too great.

Ignoring these problems momentarily, let's assume that Google decided in 2004 to borrow funds rather than sell stock in itself. To do so, it would have *issued* bonds. This simply means that it would have printed formal IOUs called bonds. Typically, each bond certificate would have a **par value** (face value) of $1,000. The bond certificate would also specify the rate of interest to be paid and the promised date of repayment. A Google bond issued in 2004, for example, might specify repayment in 10 years, with annual interest payments of $100. The individual who bought the bond from Google would lend $1,000 for 10 years and receive annual interest payments of $100. Thus *the initial bond purchaser lends funds directly to the bond issuer.* The borrower (such as Google, General Motors, or the U.S. Treasury) can then use those funds to acquire real resources. Thus *the bond market also functions as a financial intermediary, transferring available savings (wealth) to those who want to acquire more resources (invest).*

par value: The face value of a bond; the amount to be repaid when the bond is due.

As in the case of IPOs of stock, the critical issue here is the *price* of the bond. How many people are willing and able to lend funds to the company? What rate of interest will they charge?

As we observed in Figure 18.2, the quantity of loanable funds supplied depends on the interest rate. At low interest rates no one is willing to lend funds to the company. Why lend your savings to a risky venture like Google when more secure bonds and even banks pay higher interest rates? Google might not succeed and later **default** on (not pay) its obligations. Potential lenders would want to be compensated for this extra risk with above-average interest rates—that is, a risk premium. Remember that lenders don't share in any

default: Failure to make scheduled payments of interest or principal on a bond.

profits Google might earn; they get only interest payments. Hence they'd want a hefty premium to compensate them for the risk of default.

Suppose that market participants will lend the desired amount of money to Google only at 16 percent interest. In this case, Google may agree to pay an interest rate—the so-called **coupon rate**—of 16 percent to secure start-up funding of $50 million. That means Google agrees to pay $160 of interest each year for every $1,000 borrowed and to repay the entire $50 million at the end of 10 years.

coupon rate: Interest rate set for a bond at time of issuance.

Bond Trading

Once a bond has been issued, the initial lenders don't have to wait 10 years to get their money back. They can't go back to the company and demand early repayment, but they can sell their bonds to someone else. This **liquidity** is an important consideration for prospective bondholders. If a person had no choice but to wait 10 years for repayment, he or she might be less willing to buy a bond (lend funds). *By facilitating resales, the bond market increases the availability of funds to new ventures and other borrowers.* As is the case with stocks, most of the action in the bond markets consists of such after-market trades—that is, the buying and selling of bonds issued at some earlier time. The company that first issued the bonds doesn't participate in these trades.

liquidity: The ability of an asset to be converted into cash.

The portfolio decision in the bond market is motivated by the same factors that influence stock purchases. The *opportunity cost* of buying and selling bonds is the best alternative rate of return—for example, the interest rate on other bonds or money market mutual funds. *Expectations* also play a role in gauging both likely changes in opportunity costs and the ability of the borrower to redeem (pay off) the bond when it's due. *Changes in expectations or opportunity costs shift the bond supply and demand curves,* thereby altering market interest rates.

Current Yields

We've assumed that Google would have had to offer 16 percent interest to induce enough people to lend the company (buy bonds worth) $50 million for its initial operations. This was far higher than the 6 percent the U.S. Treasury was paying on its bonds (borrowed funds). This large risk premium reflected the fear that Google might not succeed and end up defaulting on it loans.

Suppose that Google actually took off. The risk of a bond default would diminish, and people would be more willing to lend it funds. This change in the availability of loanable funds is illustrated in the rightward shift of the supply curve in Figure 18.4.

According to the new supply curve in Figure 18.4, Google could now borrow $50 million at 10 percent interest (point *B*) rather than paying 16 percent (point *A*). Unfortunately,

FIGURE 18.4

Shifts in Funds Supply

If lenders decide that a company's future is less risky, they will be more willing to lend it money or hold its bonds. The resulting shift of the loanable funds supply curve reduces the current yield on a bond by raising its price.

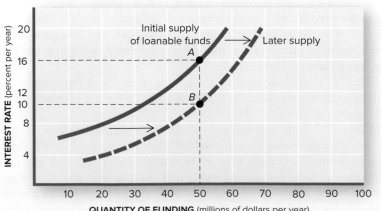

Google already borrowed the funds and is obliged to continue paying $160 per year in interest on each bond. Hence the company doesn't benefit directly from the supply shift.

The change in the equilibrium value of Google bonds must show up somewhere, however. People who hold Google bonds continue to get $160 per year in interest (16 percent of $1,000). Now there are lots of people who would be willing to lend funds to Google at that rate. These people want to hold Google bonds themselves. To get them, they'll have to buy the bonds in the market from existing bondholders. Thus the **increased willingness to lend funds is reflected in an increased demand for bonds.** This increased demand will push up the price of Google bonds. As bond prices rise, their implied effective interest rate (**current yield**) falls. Table 18.5 illustrates this relationship. Notice the phenomenal yield (50.5 percent) on GM bonds in February 2009. GM was teetering on bankruptcy back then, raising the prospect of a bond default. So prospective GM bondholders wanted a huge risk premium for buying GM bonds (they ended up losing when GM declared bankruptcy in June 2009).

current yield: The rate of return on a bond; the annual interest payment divided by the bond's price.

Changing bond prices and yields are important market signals for resource allocation. In our example, the rising price of Google's bonds reflects increased optimism for the company's sales prospects. The collective assessment of the marketplace is that web search engines will be profitable. The increase in the price of Google bonds will make it easier and less costly for the company to borrow additional funds. The reverse scenario unfolded in 2008–2009. When investors concluded that the recession was sapping corporate finances, the supply of funds to dot-coms dried up. That supply shift raised interest rates and made it more difficult for firms to borrow money for new investments.

Price of Bond	Coupon Rate (Annual Interest Payment)	Current Yield
$ 600	$150	25.0%
800	150	18.8
1,000	150	15.0
1,200	150	12.5

The annual interest payment on a bond—the "coupon rate"—is fixed at the time of issuance. Accordingly, only the market (resale) price of the bond itself can change. An increase in the price of the bond lowers its *effective* interest rate, or yield. The formula for computing the current yield on a bond is

$$\text{Current yield} = \frac{\text{Annual interest payment}}{\text{Market (resale) price of bond}}$$

Thus higher bond prices imply lower yields (effective interest rates), as confirmed in the table above. Bond prices and yields vary with changes in expectations and opportunity costs.

The newspaper quotation below shows how changing bond prices and yields are reported. This General Motors (GM) bond was issued with a coupon rate (nominal interest rate) of 8⅜ percent. Hence GM promised to pay $83.75 in interest each year until it redeemed (paid off) the $1,000 bond in the year 2033. In February 2009, however, the market price of the bond was only $160.50 ("16.50"). This created a phenomenal yield of 50.5 percent!

Bond	Current Yield	Volume	Close
GM 8⅜ 33	50.5	142	16.50

TABLE 18.5

Bond Price and Yields Move in Opposite Directions

THE ECONOMY TOMORROW

VENTURE CAPITALISTS—FINANCING TOMORROW'S PRODUCTS

One of the proven paths to high incomes and wealth is entrepreneurship. Most of the great American fortunes originated in entrepreneurial ventures, such as building railroads, mass-producing automobiles, introducing new computers, perfecting mass-merchandising techniques, or pioneering social networking sites (e.g., Facebook). These successful ventures all required more than just a great idea. To convert the original idea into actual output requires the investment of real resources.

Recall that Apple Computer started in a garage with a minimum of resources (Chapter 9). The idea of packaging a personal computer was novel, and few resources were required to demonstrate that it could be done. But Steven Jobs couldn't have become a multimillionaire by building just a few dozen computers a month. To reap huge economic profits from his idea, he needed much greater production capacity. He also needed resources for marketing the new Apples to a broader customer base. In other words, Steven Jobs needed lots of economic resources—land, labor, and capital—to convert his entrepreneurial dream into a profit-making reality.

Steven Jobs and his partner, Steve Wozniak, had few resources of their own. In fact, they'd sold Jobs's Volkswagen and Wozniak's scientific calculator to raise the finances for the first computer. To go any further, they needed financial support from others. Loans were hard to obtain since the company had no assets, no financial history, and no certainty of success. Jobs needed people who were willing to share the *risks* associated with a new venture. He found one such person in A. C. Markkula, who put up $250,000 and became a partner in the new venture. Shortly thereafter, other venture capitalists provided additional financing. With this start-up financing, Jobs was able to acquire more resources and make the Apple Computer Company a reality.

Facebook. Facebook grew from equally modest origins (Mark Zuckerberg's Harvard dorm room) back in 2004. It went from a small start-up to a national phenomenon only with the help of venture capitalists. Three venture capitalists invested $40 million, giving Facebook the resources to buy its own domain name ($200,000) and build the infrastructure that allowed it to become the premier social networking site. These are classic case studies in venture capitalism.

As In the News "Where Do Start-Ups Get Their Money?" documents, most business start-ups are created with shoestring budgets, averaging less than $20,000 (Apple and Facebook started with even less). The initial seed money typically comes from an entrepreneur's own assets or credit, with a little help from family and friends. If the idea pans out, entrepreneurs need a lot more money to develop their product. This is where venture capitalists come in. Venture capitalists provide initial funding for entrepreneurial ventures. In return for their financial backing, the venture capitalists are entitled to a share of any profits that result. If the venture fails, however, they get nothing. Thus *venture capitalists provide financial support for entrepreneurial ideas and share in the risks and rewards.* Even Christopher Columbus needed venture capitalists to fund his risky expeditions to the New World.

Venture capital is as important to the economy tomorrow as it was to Columbus. For technology and entrepreneurship to continue growing, market conditions and tax provisions must be amenable to venture capitalists.

Crowdfunding is all the rage these days but start-ups get relatively little initial capital from throngs of anonymous investors. Personal savings remain the most important source of start-up capital according to a survey of 600 business owners. initial capital averages less than $20,000. Loans from banks are the second most common source of this start-up funding, as the accompanying chart shows.

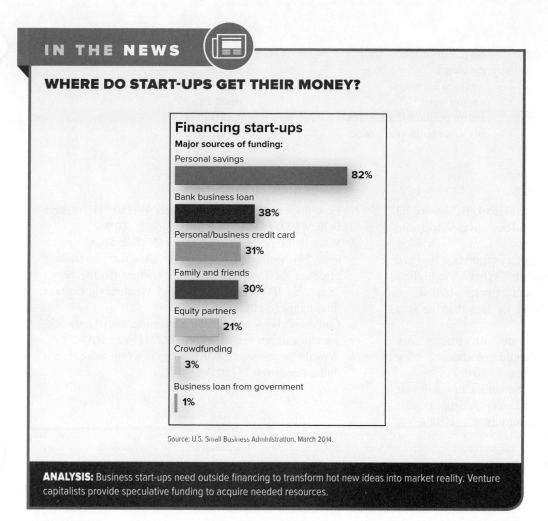

WHERE DO START-UPS GET THEIR MONEY?

Financing start-ups

Major sources of funding:

Personal savings
82%

Bank business loan
38%

Personal/business credit card
31%

Family and friends
30%

Equity partners
21%

Crowdfunding
3%

Business loan from government
1%

Source: U.S. Small Business Administration, March 2014.

ANALYSIS: Business start-ups need outside financing to transform hot new ideas into market reality. Venture capitalists provide speculative funding to acquire needed resources.

SUMMARY

- The primary economic function of financial markets is to help allocate scarce resources to desired uses. They do this by providing access to the pool of national savings for entrepreneurs, investors, and other would-be spenders. **LO18-4**
- Financial markets enable individuals to manage risk by holding different kinds of assets. Financial intermediaries also reduce the costs of information and search, thereby increasing market efficiency. **LO18-4**
- Future returns on investments must be discounted to present value. The present discounted value (PDV) of a future payment adjusts for forgone interest accrual. **LO18-1**
- Future returns are also uncertain. The *expected* value of future payments must also reflect the risk of nonpayment. **LO18-1**

- Shares of stock represent ownership in a corporation. The shares are initially issued to raise funds and are then traded on the stock exchanges. **LO18-2**
- Changes in the value of a corporation's stock reflect changing expectations and opportunity costs. Share price changes, in turn, act as market signals to direct more or fewer resources to a company. **LO18-4**
- Bonds are IOUs issued when a company (or government agency) borrows funds. After issuance, bonds are traded in the after (secondary) market. **LO18-2**
- The interest (coupon) rate on a bond is fixed at the time of issuance. The price of the bond itself, however, varies with changes in expectations (perceived risk) and opportunity cost. Yields vary inversely with bond prices. **LO18-3**

Key Terms

financial intermediary	corporate stock	bond
crowdfunding	dividend	par value
risk premium	retained earnings	default
present discounted value (PDV)	capital gain	coupon rate
expected value	initial public offering (IPO)	liquidity
corporation	price/earnings (P/E) ratio	current yield

Questions for Discussion

1. If there were no organized financial markets, how would an entrepreneur acquire resources to develop and produce a new product?   **LO18-2**

2. Why would anyone buy shares of a corporation that had no profits and paid no dividends? What's the highest price a person would pay for such a stock?   **LO18-3**

3. Why would anyone sell a bond for less than its face (par) value?   **LO18-3**

4. If you could finance a new venture with either a stock issue or bonds, which option would you choose? What are their respective (dis)advantages?   **LO18-2**

5. Why is it considered riskier to own stock in a software company than to hold U.S. Treasury savings bonds? Which asset will generate a higher return?   **LO18-4**

6. How does a successful IPO affect WHAT, HOW, and FOR WHOM the economy produces?   **LO18-2**

7. What is the price of Snap Inc.'s (NYSE: SNAP) stock today? How much has it risen or fallen from its trading price on the first day of public trading (In the News "Snapchat IPO Nets $3 Billion")? What might explain this change?   **LO18-4**

8. Could Facebook have become a premier social networking site without venture capitalists? How?   **LO18-2**

9. Why do people say "a dollar today is worth more than a dollar tomorrow"?   **LO18-1**

LO18-3   1. If an $60 stock pays a quarterly dividend of $1, what is the implied annual rate of return?

LO18-3   2. If a $24 per share stock has a P/E ratio of 16 and pays out 40 percent of its profits in dividends,
- (a) How much profit is it earning per share?
- (b) How large is its dividend?
- (c) What is the implied rate of cash return?

LO18-3   3. According to the data in Table 18.3,
- (a) How much profit per share did Google earn?
- (b) How much of that profit did it pay out in dividends?

LO18-3   4. According to the data in Table 18.3,
- (a) How much profit per share did Intel earn?
- (b) How much of that profit did it pay out in dividends?

LO18-1   5. If the market rate of interest is 5 percent, what is the present discounted value of $1,000 that will be paid in
- (a) 1 year?
- (b) 5 years?
- (c) 10 years?

LO18-1   6. What is the present discounted value of $10,000 that is to be received in 2 years if the market rate of interest is
- (a) 0 percent?
- (b) 4 percent?
- (c) 8 percent?

LO18-4   7. What was the expected return on Columbus's expedition, assuming that he had a 50 percent chance of discovering valuables worth $1 million, a 25 percent chance of bringing home only $100,000, and a 25 percent chance of sinking?

LO18-3   8. Compute the market price of the GM bonds described in Table 18.5 if the yield falls to 20 percent.

LO18-3   9. What is the current yield on a $1,000 bond with a 4 percent coupon if its market price is
- (a) $900?
- (b) $1,000?
- (c) $1,100?

LO18-4   10. How much interest accrued each day on the immediate cash payoff of the MegaMillions jackpot? (See Table 18.1.)

LO18-4   11. Illustrate with demand and supply shifts the impact of the following events on stock prices:
- (a) A federal court finds Google guilty of antitrust violations. Which way (right or left) did
  - (i) Demand shift?
  - (ii) Supply shift?
- (b) Intel announces a new and faster processor. Which way did
  - (i) Demand shift?
  - (ii) Supply shift?

PROBLEMS FOR CHAPTER 18 (cont'd)

    (*c*) Corporate executives announce that they intend to sell a large block of stock.
        Which way did
        (*i*)   Demand shift?
        (*ii*) Supply shift?
    (*d*) Google enhances its search capabilities. Which way did
        (*i*)   Demand shift?
        (*ii*) Supply shift?

LO18-2 12. Which investment has a higher rate of annual cash return? Investment A: $1,000 bond with a coupon rate of 4 percent selling for $1,200 or Investment B: $1,000 stock with a P/E ratio of 10 that pays out half its profits in dividends.

LO18-4 13. The Economy Tomorrow: What are the three most important sources of funding for financing a start-up?

©MOF/Getty Images RF

©Jeffrey Hamilton/Digital Vision/Getty Images RF

©DreamPictures/Pam Ostrow/Blend Images LLC RF

DISTRIBUTIONAL ISSUES

Of the three core questions in economics, the FOR WHOM issue is often the most contentious. Should the market decide who gets the most output? Or should the government intervene and redistribute market incomes to achieve greater equity?

Tax and transfer systems are designed to redistribute market incomes. The next two chapters survey these systems. In the process, we assess not only how effective they are in achieving greater *equity,* but also what impacts they have on *efficiency.* High taxes and generous transfer payments may blunt work incentives and so reduce the size of the pie being resliced. This creates a fundamental conflict between the goals of equity and efficiency. Chapters 19 and 20 examine this conflict.

CHAPTER 19

Taxes: Equity versus Efficiency

Insistence on carving the pie into equal slices would shrink the size of the pie. That fact poses the trade-off between economic equality and economic efficiency.

—Arthur M. Okun

Eric Schmidt was rewarded handsomely for his effort in cofounding Google in 2001. When he stepped down as CEO in 2011, Schmidt had amassed 9.2 million shares of Google stock, worth nearly $6 billion. As a parting gift, Google gave him an additional $100 million bonus when he turned the CEO job over to fellow cofounder Larry Page in January 2011. That would have been enough income to lift more than 2 million poor persons out of poverty. But Schmidt didn't share his good fortune with those people, and they remained poor.

The market mechanism generated both Schmidt's extraordinary income and that of so many poor families. Is this the way we want the basic FOR WHOM question to be settled? Should some people own vast fortunes while others seek shelter in abandoned cars? Or do the inequalities that emerge in product and factor markets violate our notions of equity? If the market's answer to the FOR WHOM question isn't right, some form of government intervention to redistribute incomes may be desired.

The tax system is the government's primary lever for redistributing income. But taxing Peter to pay Paul may affect more than just income shares. If taxed too heavily, Peter may stop producing so much. Paul, too, may work less if assured of government support. The end result may be *less* total income to share. In other words, **taxes affect production as well as distribution. This creates a potential trade-off between the goal of equity and the goal of efficiency.**

This chapter examines this equity–efficiency trade-off, with the following questions as a guide:

- **How are incomes distributed in the United States?**
- **How do taxes alter that distribution?**
- **How do taxes affect the rate and mix of output?**

After addressing these questions, we examine some proposed tax changes, including the tax cuts championed by President Trump.

WHAT IS *INCOME*?

Before examining the distribution of income in the United States, let's decide what to count as *income.* There are several possibilities.

Personal Income

The most obvious choice is **personal income (PI)**—the flow of annual income received by households before payment of personal income taxes. Personal income includes wages and salaries, corporate dividends, rent, interest, Social Security benefits, welfare payments, and any other form of money income.

Personal income isn't a complete measure of income, however. Many goods and services are distributed directly as **in-kind income** rather than through market purchases. Many poor people, for example, live in public housing and pay little or no rent. As a consequence, they receive a larger share of total output than their money incomes imply. People with low incomes also receive food stamps (now called Supplemental Nutrition Assistance Program [SNAP] vouchers) that allow them to purchase more food than their money incomes would allow.

In-kind benefits aren't limited to low-income households. Students who attend public schools and colleges consume more goods and services than they directly pay for: public education is subsidized by all taxpayers. People over age 65 also get medical services through Medicare that they don't directly pay for. Middle-class workers get noncash fringe benefits (like health insurance, paid vacations, pension contributions) that don't show up in their paychecks or on their tax returns. Even the president of the United States gets substantial in-kind benefits. President Trump doesn't pay rent at the White House and gets free food, health care, transportation, and security services. Hence his real income greatly exceeds his $400,000-a-year presidential paycheck (which he declined to take).

So long as some goods and services needn't be purchased in the marketplace, *the distribution of money income isn't synonymous with the distribution of goods and services.* This measurement problem is particularly important when comparisons are made over time. For example, the federal government officially classifies people as "poor" if their money income is below a certain threshold. By this standard, we've made no progress against poverty. The Census Bureau counted 40 million Americans as "poor" in 2016, more than it counted in 1965. In both years the Census Bureau counted only money incomes. In 1965 that approach was acceptable because little income was transferred in-kind. In 2016, however, the federal government spent $60 billion on food stamps, $50 billion on housing subsidies, and $560 billion on Medicaid. Had all this in-kind income been counted, 12 million fewer Americans would have been counted as poor in 2016. Although that would still leave a lot of people in poverty, at least more progress in eliminating poverty would be evident.

Wealth

If our ultimate concern is access to goods and services, the distribution of wealth is also important. **Wealth** refers to the market value of assets (such as houses, cars, and bank accounts) people own. Hence *wealth represents a stock of potential purchasing power; income statistics tell us only how this year's flow of purchasing power (income) is being distributed.* Accordingly, to provide a complete answer to the FOR WHOM question, we have to know how wealth, as well as income, is distributed. In general, wealth tends to be distributed much less equally than income. The Internal Revenue Service estimates that 10 percent of the adult population own 75 percent of all personal wealth in the United States but earn around 50 percent of total income.

THE SIZE DISTRIBUTION OF INCOME

Although incomes aren't a perfect measure of access to goods and services (much less happiness), they're the best single indicator of the FOR WHOM outcomes. The **size distribution of income** tells us how large a share of total personal income is received by

personal income (PI): Income received by households before payment of personal taxes.

in-kind income: Goods and services received directly, without payment, in a market transaction.

wealth: The market value of assets.

size distribution of income: The way total personal income is divided up among households or income classes.

various households, grouped by income class. Imagine for the moment that the entire population is lined up in order of income, with lowest-income recipients in front and highest-income recipients at the end of the line. We want to know how much income the people in front get in comparison with those at the back.

We first examined the size distribution of income in Chapter 2. Figure 2.3 showed that households in the lowest quintile received less than $23,000 apiece in 2015. As a group, this class received only 3.1 percent of total income, despite the fact that it included 20 percent of all households (the lowest fifth). Thus the **income share** of the people in the lowest group (3.1 percent) was much smaller than their proportion in the total population (20 percent).

Moving back to the end of the line, we observed that a household needed $117,000 to make it into the highest income class in 2015. Many families in that class made much more than $117,000—some even millions of dollars. But $117,000 was at least enough to get into the top fifth (quintile).

The top quintile ended up with half of total U.S. income and, by implication, that much of total output.

The Lorenz Curve

The size distribution of income provides the kind of information we need to determine how total income (and output) is distributed. The **Lorenz curve** is a convenient summary of that information; it is a graphic illustration of the size distribution.

Figure 19.1 is a Lorenz curve for the United States. Our lineup of individuals is on the horizontal axis, with the lowest-income earners on the left. On the vertical axis we depict the cumulative share of income received by people in our income line. Consider the lowest quintile of the distribution again. They're represented on the horizontal axis at 20 percent. If their share of income was identical to their share of population, they'd get 20 percent of total income. This would be represented by point *C* in the figure. In fact, the lowest quintile gets only 3.1 percent, as indicated by point *A*. Point *B* tells us that the *cumulative* share of income received by the lowest *three*-fifths of the population was 25.6 percent.

The really handy feature of the Lorenz curve is the way it contrasts the actual distribution of income with an absolutely equal one. If incomes were distributed equally, the first 20 percent of the people in line would be getting exactly 20 percent of all income. In that case, the Lorenz curve would run through point *C*. Indeed, the Lorenz "curve" would be a straight line along the diagonal. The actual Lorenz curve lies below the diagonal because

income share: The proportion of total income received by a particular group.

Lorenz curve: A graphic illustration of the cumulative size distribution of income; contrasts complete equality with the actual distribution of income.

FIGURE 19.1

The Lorenz Curve

The Lorenz curve illustrates the extent of income inequality. If all incomes were equal, each fifth of the population would receive one-fifth of total income. In that case, the diagonal line through point *C* would represent the cumulative size distribution of income.

In reality, incomes aren't distributed equally. Point *A*, for example, indicates that the 20 percent of the population with the lowest income receive only 3.1 percent of total income.

Source: Figure 2.3.

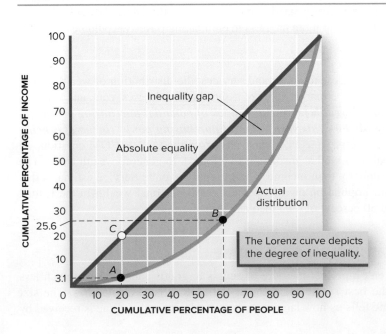

Analysis: An increase in the size of the economic pie doesn't ensure everyone a larger slice. A goal of the tax system is to attain a fairer distribution of the economic pie.

©Robert Graysmith.

our national income isn't distributed equally. In fact, the area between the diagonal and the actual Lorenz curve (the shaded area in Figure 19.1) is a convenient measure of the degree of inequality. ***The greater the area between the Lorenz curve and the diagonal, the more inequality exists.***

The visual summary of inequality the Lorenz curve provides is also expressed in a mathematical relationship. The ratio of the shaded area in Figure 19.1 to the area of the triangle formed by the diagonal is called the **Gini coefficient.** The higher the Gini coefficient, the greater the degree of inequality. Between 2000 and 2015, the Gini coefficient rose from 0.462 to 0.479. In other words, the shaded area in Figure 19.1 expanded by nearly 4 percent, indicating *increased* inequality. Although the size of the economic pie (real GDP) increased by 30 percent between 2000 and 2015, some people's slices got a lot bigger while other people saw little improvement, or even less (see the cartoon above).

> **Gini coefficient:**
> A mathematical summary of inequality based on the Lorenz curve.

The Call for Intervention

To many people, large and increasing inequality represents a form of **market failure:** the market is generating a suboptimal (unfair) answer to the FOR WHOM question. As in other instances of market failure, the government is called on to intervene. The policy lever in this case is taxes. **By levying taxes on the rich and providing transfer payments to the poor, the government *redistributes* market incomes.**

> **market failure:** An imperfection in the market mechanism that prevents optimal outcomes.

THE FEDERAL INCOME TAX

The federal income tax is designed for this redistributional purpose. Specifically, the federal income tax is designed to be **progressive**—that is, to impose higher tax *rates* on high incomes than on low ones. Progressivity is achieved by imposing increasing **marginal tax rates** on higher incomes. The *marginal* tax rate refers to the tax rate imposed on the last (marginal) dollar of income.

> **progressive tax:** A tax system in which tax rates rise as incomes rise.

> **marginal tax rate:** The tax rate imposed on the last (marginal) dollar of income.

Tax Brackets and Rates

In 2016, the tax code specified the seven tax brackets shown in Table 19.1. For an individual with less than $9,275 of taxable income, the tax rate was 10 percent. Any income in excess of $9,275 was taxed at a *higher* rate of 15 percent. If an individual's income rose above $91,150, the amount between $91,150 and $190,150 was taxed at 28 percent. Any income greater than $415,000 was taxed at 39.6 percent.

To understand the efficiency and equity effects of taxes, we must distinguish between the *marginal* tax rate and the *average* tax rate. A person who earned $420,000 taxable income in 2016 paid the 39.6 percent tax only on the income in excess of $415,050—that is, the last (marginal) $4,950. The first $9,275 was taxed at a marginal rate of only 10 percent.

TABLE 19.1

Progressive Taxes

The federal income tax is progressive because it levies higher tax rates on higher incomes. The 2016 marginal tax rate started out at 10 percent for incomes below $9,275 and rose to 39.6 percent for incomes above $415,050.

Tax Bracket	Marginal Tax Rate
$0–9,275	10%
$9,275–37,650	15
$37,650–91,150	25
$91,950–190,150	28
$190,150–413,350	33
$413,350–415,050	35
Over $415,050	39.6

Source: Internal Revenue Service (2016 tax rates for single individuals).

Here is how taxes are computed on $420,000 of income:

Marginal Tax Rate	Income		Tax
10% of	$ 9,275	=	$ 927.50
15% of	28,375	=	4,256.25
25% of	53,500	=	13,375.00
28% of	99,000	=	27,720.00
33% of	223,200	=	73,656.00
35% of	1,700	=	595.00
39.6% of	4,950	=	1,960.20
	$420,000		$122,489.95

Notice that the various marginal tax rates apply only to the income in that specific bracket. By adding up the taxes in each bracket, we get a total tax of $122,489.95. This represents only 29.2 percent of this individual's income. Hence this person had a

- *Marginal* tax rate of 39.6 percent.
- *Average* (or nominal) tax rate of 29.2 percent.

By contrast, a person with only $20,000 of taxable income would pay a *marginal* tax of only 15 percent and an *average* tax of 12.7 percent. The rationale behind this progressive system is to tax ever-larger percentages of higher incomes, thereby reducing income inequalities. **By making the *after-tax* distribution of income more equal than the *before-tax* distribution,** *progressive taxes reduce inequality.*

Efficiency Concerns

Although the redistributive intent of a progressive tax system is evident, it raises concerns about efficiency. As noted in the chapter-opening quote, attempts to reslice the pie may end up reducing the size of the pie. The central issue here is incentives. Chapter 16 emphasized that the supply of labor is motivated by the pursuit of income. If Uncle Sam takes away ever-larger chunks of income, won't that dampen the desire to work? If so, *the incentive to work more, produce more, or invest more is reduced by higher marginal tax rates.* This suggests that as marginal tax rates increase, total output shrinks, creating a basic conflict between the goals of equity (more progressive taxes) and efficiency (more output).

Tax Migration. How great the conflict is between the equity and efficiency depends on how responsive market participants are to higher tax rates. The Rolling Stones left Great Britain off their 1998–1999 world tour because the British marginal tax rate was so high. The band U2 went a step further—moving their home base from Ireland to the Netherlands to avoid paying Irish income taxes (see World View "Bono Says 'Stupid' to Pay Irish Taxes"). A 2011 study by the National Bureau of Economic Research (NBER) revealed that international soccer stars choose to live in low-tax nations even while playing for teams in high-tax nations. Many other businesses relocate to low-tax nations for the same reason.

BONO SAYS "STUPID" TO PAY IRISH TAXES

When Ireland eliminated the tax break for royalty income in 2006, the rock band U2 packed their bags and moved to the Netherlands where tax rates are much lower. The band has been subjected to criticism ever since. At the Glastonbury Festival in 2011, protesters inflated a huge banner that asked, "U pay tax 2?," which led to a violent skirmish with concert security. In interviews in 2013–2015 Bono, whose real name is Paul Hewson, has repeatedly rejected the charge that the Irish band's tax exile status is hypocritical, given its well-publicized calls for more aid to the world's poor. Bono says he doesn't have to be "stupid" about taxes; the band is just being "sensible about the way we're taxed."

Source: Media reports and interviews, 2007–2015.

ANALYSIS: High tax rates deter people from supplying resources. In this case, high taxes motivated U2 to move to another country.

Tax Elasticity of Supply. For the typical household, however, the response to higher tax rates is limited to reducing hours worked. In all cases we can summarize the response with the **tax elasticity of supply:**

$$\text{Tax elasticity of supply} = \frac{\text{\% change in quantity supplied}}{\text{\% change in tax rate}}$$

> **tax elasticity of supply:** The percentage change in quantity supplied divided by the percentage change in tax rates.

If the tax elasticity of supply were zero, there'd be no conflict between equity and efficiency. But a zero tax elasticity would also imply that people would continue to work, produce, and invest even if Uncle Sam took *all* their income in taxes. In today's range of taxes, the average household's tax elasticity of labor supply is between 0.15 and 0.30. Hence, if tax *rates* go up by 20 percent, the quantity of labor supplied would decline by 3 to 6 percent. In other words, the size of the pie being resliced would shrink by 3–6 percent. Figure 19.2 confirms that the top marginal tax rate has changed by much more than 20 percent in the past, thereby significantly altering the size of the economic pie.

Equity Concerns

As if the concern about efficiency weren't enough, critics also raise questions about how well the federal income tax promotes equity. What appears to be a fairly progressive tax in theory turns out to be a lot less progressive in practice. Hundreds of people with $1 million incomes pay no taxes. They aren't necessarily breaking any laws, just taking advantage of loopholes in the tax system.

Loopholes. The progressive *tax rates described in the tax code apply to "taxable" income, not to all income.* The so-called loopholes in the system arise from the way Congress defines taxable income. The tax laws permit one to subtract certain exemptions and deductions from gross income in computing taxable income:

$$\text{Taxable income} = \text{Gross income} - \text{Exemptions and deductions}$$

Exemptions are permitted for dependent children, spouses, old age, and disabilities. Deductions are permitted for an array of expenses, including home mortgage interest, work-related expenses, child care, depreciation of investments, interest payments, union dues, medical expenses, charitable contributions, and many other items.

The purpose of these many *itemized deductions* is to encourage specific economic activities and reduce potential hardship. The deduction for mortgage interest payments, for

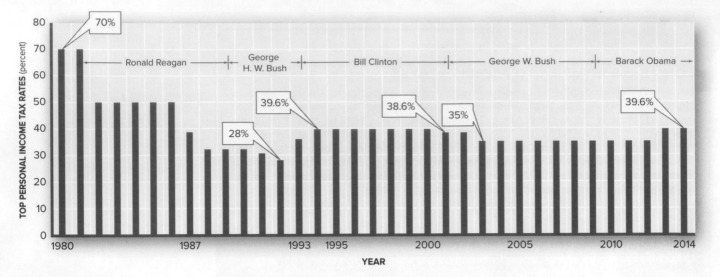

FIGURE 19.2

Changes in Marginal Tax Rates

During the past 40 years, Congress revised the federal income tax system many times. The top marginal tax rate was steadily reduced from 70 percent in 1980 to 28 percent in 1992. It was then raised in 1993–1995. The Bush tax cuts of 2001–2004 reduced marginal tax rates once more. Then President Obama increased the top marginal tax rate to 39.6 again in 2013. President Trump sought to reverse the trend again, dropping the top tax rate to 35 percent.

Source: Internal Revenue Service.

vertical equity: Principle that people with higher incomes should pay more taxes.

horizontal equity: Principle that people with equal incomes should pay equal taxes.

TABLE 19.2

Vertical Inequity

Tax exemptions and deductions create a gap between total income and *taxable* income. In this case, Mr. Jones has both a higher income and extensive deductions. He ends up with less *taxable* income than Ms. Smith and so pays less taxes. This vertical inequity is reflected in the lower effective tax rate paid by Mr. Jones (4.4 percent) than Ms. Smith (18.3 percent).

example, encourages people to buy their own homes. The deduction for medical expenses helps relieve the financial burden of illness.

Whatever the merits of specific exemptions and deductions, they create potential inequities. ***People with high incomes can avoid high taxes by claiming large exemptions and deductions.*** In fact, some people with high incomes end up paying *less* tax than people with lower incomes. This violates the principle of **vertical equity,** the progressive intent of taxing people on the basis of their ability to pay.

Table 19.2 illustrates vertical *in*equity. Mr. Jones has an income ($90,000) three times larger than Ms. Smith's ($30,000). However, Mr. Jones also has huge deductions ($70,000) that reduce his *taxable* income dramatically. In fact, Mr. Jones ends up with less *taxable* income ($20,000) than Ms. Smith ($25,000). As a result, he also ends up paying lower taxes ($4,000 vs. $5,500). How is this possible? Simply because Mr. Jones has huge itemized deductions for things like mortgage interest, charitable contributions, and the like, and Ms. Smith has nothing comparable.

The deductions that create the vertical inequity between Mr. Jones and Ms. Smith could also violate the principle of **horizontal equity**—as people with the *same* incomes end up

	Mr. Jones	Ms. Smith
1. Total income	$90,000	$30,000
2. Less exemptions and deductions	−$70,000	−$ 5,000
3. Taxable income	$20,000	$25,000
4. Tax	$ 4,000	$ 5,500
5. Nominal tax rate (= row 4 ÷ row 3)	20%	22%
6. Effective tax rate (= row 4 ÷ row 1)	4.4%	18.3%

paying different amounts of income tax. These horizontal *in*equities also contradict basic notions of fairness.

Nominal vs. Effective Tax Rates. The "loopholes" created by exemptions, deductions, and tax credits cause a distinction between gross economic income and taxable income. That distinction, in turn, requires us to distinguish between *nominal* tax rates and *effective* tax rates. The term **nominal tax rate** refers to the taxes actually paid as a percentage of *taxable* income. By contrast, the **effective tax rate** is the tax paid divided by *total* economic income without regard to exemptions, deductions, or other intricacies of the tax laws.

As Table 19.2 illustrates, someone with a gross income of $90,000 might end up with a much lower *taxable* income, thanks to various tax deductions and exemptions. Mr. Jones ended up with a taxable income of only $20,000 and a tax bill of merely $4,000. As a result, we can characterize Mr. Jones's tax burden in two ways:

nominal tax rate: Taxes paid divided by taxable income.

effective tax rate: Taxes paid divided by total income.

$$\frac{\text{Nominal}}{\text{tax rate}} = \frac{\text{Tax paid}}{\text{Taxable income}}$$

$$= \frac{\$4,000}{\$20,000} = 20 \text{ percent}$$

or alternatively,

$$\frac{\text{Effective}}{\text{tax rate}} = \frac{\text{Tax paid}}{\text{Total economic income}}$$

$$= \frac{\$4,000}{\$90,000} = 4.4 \text{ percent}$$

This huge gap between the nominal tax rate (20 percent) and the effective tax rate (4.4 percent) is a reflection of loopholes in the tax code. It's also the source of the vertical and horizontal inequities discussed earlier. Notice that Ms. Smith, with much less gross income, ends up with an effective tax rate (18.3 percent) that's more than four times higher than Mr. Jones's (4.4 percent).

In the News "Taxes: The Pences vs. The Clintons" shows how the Pences and the Clintons used these many loopholes in 2015. Mike Pence had a very modest wage back in 2015, especially in comparison to Bill and Hillary Clinton, who took in over $10 million in speaking fees. Both the Pences and the Clintons took advantage of deductions for state and

IN THE NEWS

TAXES: THE PENCES VS. THE CLINTONS

	The Pences	The Clintons
Gross Income	$115,562	$10,745,378
Deductions		
Charitable contributions	$ 8,923	$ 1,042,000
State and local taxes	6,611	1,467,501
Mortgage interest	—	41,040
Exemptions	16,000	—
Taxable Income	$ 81,492	$ 8,352,507
Income Tax	$ 8,956	$ 3,236,975

Source: Tax History.org (2015 tax returns)

ANALYSIS: Taxes are levied on *taxable* income, not total income. Various deductions and exemptions reduce taxable income and *effective* tax rates.

local taxes they paid and contributions to charity they made. Nearly all of the Clintons' $1 million charitable contributions went to their own, tax-exempt Clinton Foundation.

After all the deductions and exemptions were accounted for, the IRS recognized only a portion of their gross income as "taxable income." Only that taxable income counts for Uncle Sam. The resulting tax bills are noted in the last row of the News.

Clearly, the Clintons were among the highest income U.S. households in 2015. Their multimillion income planted them in the highest tax bracket of Table 19.1. But they didn't pay 39.6 percent of their income to Uncle Sam. Their effective tax rate was only 30.1 percent (tax paid dividend by gross income) whereas the Pences' effective tax rate was 7.7 percent. Like the Pences, the Clintons paid only a 10 percent tax on the first $9,275 of income. They then moved up the tax brackets and rates of Table 19.1 to compute their total tax bill. If there were no exemptions or deductions, the income tax bills for the Clintons would have gone up by $887,841 and the Pences would have had to pay $7,884 more.

Tax-Induced Misallocations. Tax loopholes not only foster inequity but encourage inefficiency as well. The optimal mix of output is the one that balances consumer preferences and opportunity costs. Tax loopholes, however, encourage a different mix of output. By offering preferential treatment for some activities, the tax code reduces their relative accounting cost. In so doing, ***tax preferences induce resource shifts into tax-preferred activities.*** The deduction for mortgage interest, for example, encourages people to purchase homes, thereby changing the mix of output.

These resource allocations are the explicit goal of tax preferences. The accumulation of exemptions, deductions, and credits has become so unwieldy and complex, however, that tax considerations often overwhelm economic considerations in many investment and consumption decisions. The resulting mix of output, many observers feel, is decidedly inferior to a *pure* market outcome. From this viewpoint, the federal income tax promotes both inequity and inefficiency.

A Shrinking Tax Base. Loopholes in the tax code create yet another problem. As the **tax base** gets smaller and smaller, it becomes increasingly difficult to sustain, much less increase, tax revenues. The tax arithmetic is simple:

tax base: The amount of income or property directly subject to nominal tax rates.

$$\text{Tax revenue} = \frac{\text{Average}}{\text{tax rate}} \times \frac{\text{Tax}}{\text{base}}$$

As deductions, exemptions, and credits accumulate, the tax base (taxable income) keeps shrinking. To keep tax rates low—or to reduce them further—Congress has to stop this erosion of the tax base.

The Bush Tax Cuts (2001–2010)

Tax reforms in 1986 and 1993 broadened the tax base but also raised tax rates (to a top rate of 39.6 percent). President Bush worried that those higher marginal tax rates would slow economic growth. He also felt that low-income households would gain more from faster economic growth than from progressive tax and transfer policies. After his 2000 election, he made tax *cuts* one of his highest priorities.

Reduced Marginal Rates. As Figure 19.2 illustrated, the 2001 Tax Relief Act reduced the highest marginal tax rate in three steps, to 35 percent from 39.6 percent. That act also reduced the marginal tax rate for the *lowest* income class to only 10 percent (from 15 percent). The goal of this rate cut was to increase the disposable income of low-wage workers (equity) while giving them more incentive to work (efficiency).

New "Loopholes." Aside from encouraging more *work,* President Bush also sought to encourage more *education.* The biggest incentive was a tuition tax deduction of $3,000 per year. This allows students, or their parents, to reduce their taxable income by the amount of tuition payments. In effect, Uncle Sam ends up paying part of the first $3,000 in tuition. In addition, the 2001 legislation allows people to save more money for college in tax-free accounts.

As welcome as these "loopholes" are to college students, they raise the same kind of efficiency and equity concerns as other tax preferences. If most of the students who take the tax deduction would have gone to college anyway, the deduction isn't very *efficient* in promoting education. Furthermore, most of the deductions go to middle-class families who itemize deductions. Hence the tuition deduction introduces new vertical *inequities*. Few students have protested this particular loophole, however.

The creation of this and other tax preferences raises all the same issues about equity and efficiency. ***The greater the number of loopholes, the wider the distinction between gross incomes and taxable incomes***, as the previous News reveals.

The Obama Tax Hikes

Despite his personal exposure to the highest tax rates, President Obama vowed to reverse the "Bush tax cuts for the rich." Within a month of his inauguration, Obama proposed to raise the highest marginal tax rate from 35 percent to its former 39.6 percent. He also proposed raising taxes on capital gains, dividends, and estates. Critics objected that the resultant gains in *equity* (Obama's avowed goal) would be more than offset by the loss of *efficiency*. In other words, the pie would shrink when Obama resliced it. When the economy fell into the 2008–2009 recession, President Obama agreed to table the proposed tax hikes. In 2011 he again pressed for higher marginal tax rates, however, and made it a pledge of his reelection campaign. In 2012, Congress agreed to increase the top marginal tax rate.

Trump Tax Cuts

The tax-rate pendulum swung back again with the election of Donald Trump. President Trump vowed to both simplify the tax code and reduce tax burdens as part of his broad "Make America Great Again" agenda. To that end, he proposed to reduce the number of tax brackets from seven to only three. He also proposed to limit sharply itemized deductions so as to shrink the gap between gross and taxable incomes. Last but not least, he proposed to reduce the top marginal tax rate on individuals to 35 percent from 39.6 percent. These changes were intended to make the personal income tax both more efficient and more fair.

President Trump proposed more dramatic changes for business taxes. He proposed to drop the tax rate on corporate incomes to 15 percent from 35 percent and to allow small, noncorporate businesses to enjoy the same low rate. The primary motivation for these proposals was *efficiency;* Trump believed such a dramatic drop in business taxes would spur a sharp increase in investment, and ultimately economic growth. Critics, though, worried about the *equity* implications of such tax cutting. The millions of businesses organized as partnerships and subchapter S corporations—disproportionately owned by higher income individuals—would get a windfall tax break. Congress had to grapple with these competing goals in deciding how to treat the Trump proposals.

PAYROLL, STATE, AND LOCAL TAXES

The federal income tax is only one of many taxes people must pay. For many families, in fact, the federal income tax is the smallest of many tax bills. Other tax bills come from the Social Security Administration and from state and local governments. These taxes also affect both efficiency and equity.

Sales and Property Taxes

Sales taxes are the major source of revenue for state governments. Many local governments also impose sales taxes, but most cities rely on *property taxes* for the bulk of their tax receipts. Both taxes are **regressive:** they impose higher tax rates on lower incomes.

regressive tax: A tax system in which tax rates fall as incomes rise.

TABLE 19.3

The Regressivity of Sales Taxes

A sales tax is imposed on consumer purchases. Although the sales tax itself is uniform (here at 5 percent), the taxes paid represent different proportions of high and low incomes. In this case, the low-income family's *sales tax* bill equals 4.75 percent of its *income.* The high-income family has a sales tax bill equal to only 2.86 percent of its income.

	High-Income Family	Low-Income Family
Income	$70,000	$20,000
Consumption	$40,000	$19,000
Saving	$30,000	$ 1,000
Sales tax paid (5% of consumption)	$ 2,000	$ 950
Effective tax rate (sales tax ÷ income)	2.86%	4.75%

At first glance, a 5 percent sales tax doesn't look very regressive. After all, the same 5 percent tax is imposed on virtually all goods. But we're interested in *people,* not goods and services, so **we gauge tax burdens in relation to people's incomes.** A tax is regressive if it imposes a proportionally *larger* burden on *lower* incomes.

This is exactly what a uniform sales tax does. To understand this concept, we have to look not only at how much tax is levied on each dollar of consumption but also at *what percentage of income* is spent on consumer goods.

Low-income families spend everything they've got (and sometimes more) on basic consumption. As a result, most of their income ends up subject to sales tax. By contrast, higher-income families save more. As a result, a smaller proportion of their income is subject to a sales tax. Table 19.3 illustrates this regressive feature of a sales tax. Notice that the low-income family ends up paying a larger fraction of its income (4.75 percent) than does the high-income family (2.86 percent).

Property taxes are regressive also and for the same reason. Low-income families spend a higher percentage of their incomes for shelter. A uniform property tax thus ends up taking a larger fraction of their income than it does of the incomes of high-income families.

Tax Incidence. It may sound strange to suggest that low-income families bear the brunt of property taxes. After all, the tax is imposed on the landlords who *own* property, not on people who *rent* apartments and houses. However, here again we have to distinguish between the apparent payee and the individual whose income is actually reduced by the tax. **Tax incidence** refers to the actual burden of a tax—that is, who really ends up paying it.

tax incidence: Distribution of the real burden of a tax.

In general, people who rent apartments pay higher rents as a result of property taxes. In other words, landlords pass along to tenants any property taxes they must pay. Thus to a large extent **the burden of property taxes is reflected in higher rents.** Tenants pay property taxes *indirectly* via these higher rents. The incidence of the property tax thus falls on renters in the form of higher rents, rather than on the landlords who write checks to the local tax authority.

Payroll Taxes

Payroll taxes also impose effective tax burdens quite different from their nominal appearance. Consider, for example, the Social Security payroll tax, the second-largest source of federal tax revenue (see Figure 4.5). Every worker sees a Social Security (FICA) tax taken out of his or her paycheck. The nominal tax rate on workers is 7.65 percent. But there's a catch: only wages below a legislated ceiling are taxable. In 2017, the taxable wage ceiling was $127,200. Hence a worker earning $200,000 paid no more tax than a worker earning $127,200. As a result, the effective tax *rate* (tax paid ÷ total wages) is lower for high-income workers than low- and middle-income workers. That's a *regressive* tax.

There is another problem in gauging the impact of the Social Security payroll tax. Nominally, the Social Security payroll tax consists of two parts: half paid by employees and half by employers. But do employers really pay their half? Or do they end up paying lower wages to compensate for their tax share? If so, employees end up paying *both* halves of the Social Security payroll tax.

Figure 19.3 illustrates how the tax incidence of the payroll tax is distributed. The supply of labor reflects the ability and willingness of people to work for various wage rates. Labor

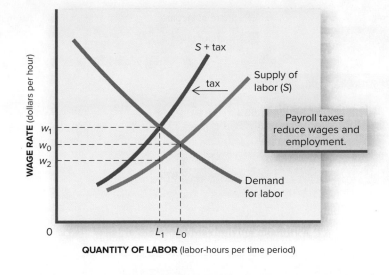

FIGURE 19.3
The Incidence of a Payroll Tax
Some portion of a payroll tax imposed on employers may actually be borne by workers. The tax raises the cost of labor and so imposes a tax-burdened supply curve (S + tax) on employers. The intersection of this tax-burdened supply curve with the labor demand curve determines a new equilibrium of employment (L_1). At that level, employers pay w_1 in wages and taxes, but workers get only w_2 in wages. The wage reduction from w_0 to w_2 is a real burden of the payroll tax, and it is borne by workers.

demand reflects the **marginal revenue product (MRP)** of labor; it sets a *limit* to the wage an employer is willing to pay.

Cost of Labor. The employer's half of the payroll tax increases the nominal cost of labor. Thus the S + tax curve lies *above* the labor supply curve. It incorporates the wages that must be paid to workers *plus* the payroll tax that must be paid to the Social Security Trust Fund. This total labor cost is the one that will determine how many workers are hired. Specifically, the intersection of the S + tax curve and the labor demand curve determines the equilibrium level of employment (L_1). The employer will pay the amount w_1 for this much labor. But part of that outlay ($w_1 - w_2$) will go to the public treasury in the form of payroll taxes. Workers will receive only w_2 in wages. This is less than they'd get in the absence of the payroll tax (compare w_0 and w_2). Thus *fewer workers are employed, and the net wage is reduced when a payroll tax is imposed.*

Tax Incidence. What Figure 19.3 reveals is how the true incidence of payroll taxes is distributed. The employer share of the Social Security tax is $w_1 - w_2$. This is the amount sent to the Social Security Administration for every hour of labor. Of this amount, the employer incurs higher labor costs ($w_1 - w_0$) and workers lose ($w_0 - w_2$) in the wage rate. Hence workers end up paying *their* share (7.65 percent) of the Social Security tax *plus* a sizable part ($w_0 - w_2$) of the employer's share ($w_1 - w_2$).

These reflections on tax incidence don't imply that payroll taxes are necessarily bad. They do emphasize, however, that *the apparent taxpayer isn't necessarily the individual who bears the real burden of a tax.*

TAXES AND INEQUALITY

The regressivity of the Social Security payroll tax and of many state and local taxes offsets most of the progressivity of the federal income tax. The top 1 percent of income recipients gets 19 percent of total income and pays 38 percent of federal income tax (see Figure 19.4). Hence the federal income tax is still progressive, despite rampant loopholes. Other federal taxes (Social Security, excise), however, reduce the tax share of the rich to only 21 percent. State and local tax incidence reduces their tax share still further.

A Proportional System

The final result is that *the tax system as a whole ends up being nearly proportional.* High-income families end up paying roughly the same percentage of their income in taxes as do

marginal revenue product (MRP): The change in total revenue associated with one additional unit of input.

FIGURE 19.4

Income Tax Shares

Despite loopholes, the federal income tax remains progressive. The richest 1 percent of households pay 38 percent of all federal income taxes, though they receive only 19 percent of all income.

Source: Internal Revenue Service (2013 data).

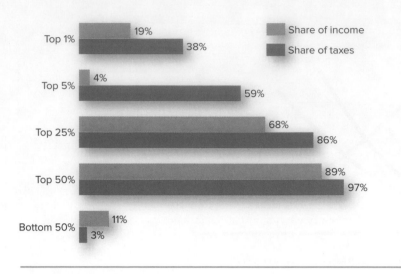

income transfers: Payments to individuals for which no current goods or services are exchanged, such as Social Security, welfare, and unemployment benefits.

government failure: Government intervention that fails to improve economic outcomes.

low-income families. The tax system does reduce inequality somewhat, but the redistributive impact is quite small.

The Impact of Transfers

The tax system tells only half the redistribution story. It tells whose income was taken away. Equally important is who gets the income the government collects. The government completes the redistribution process by *transferring* income to consumers. The **income transfers** may be explicit, as in the case of welfare benefits, Social Security payments, and unemployment insurance. Or the transfers may be indirect, as in the case of public schools, farm subsidies, and student loans. We'll look more closely at how income transfers alter the distribution of income in the next chapter.

WHAT IS *FAIR*?

To many people, the apparent ineffectiveness of the tax system in redistributing income is a mark of **government failure.** They want a much more decisive reslicing of the pie—one in which the top quintile gets a *lot* less than half the pie and the poor get more than 3.1 percent (Figure 2.3). But how much redistribution should we attempt? Rich people can rattle off as many good reasons for preserving income inequalities as poor people can recite for eliminating them.

Economists aren't uniquely qualified to overcome self-interest, much less to divine what a fair distribution of income might look like. But economists can assess some of the costs and benefits of altering the distribution of income.

The Costs of Greater Equality

The greatest potential cost of a move toward greater equality is the reduced incentives it might leave in its wake. People *are* motivated by income. In factor markets, higher wages call forth more workers and induce them to work longer hours. In fields where earnings are very high, as in the medical and legal professions, people are willing to spend many years and thousands of dollars acquiring the skills such earnings require. Could we really expect people to make such sacrifices in a market that paid everyone the same wage?

The same problem exists in product markets. The willingness of producers to supply goods and services depends on their expectation of profits. Why should they work hard and take risks to produce goods and services if their efforts won't make them any better off? If incomes were distributed equally, producers might just as well sit back and enjoy the fruits of someone else's labor.

The essential economic problem absolute income equality poses is that it breaks the market link between effort and reward. If all incomes were equal, it would no longer pay to make an above-average effort. If people stopped making such efforts, total output would decline, and we'd have less income to share (a smaller pie). Not that all high incomes are attributable to great skill or effort. Such factors as luck, market power, and family connections also influence incomes. It remains true, however, that the promise of higher income encourages work effort. Absolute income equality threatens those conditions.

The argument for preserving income inequalities is thus anchored in a concern for productivity. From this perspective, income inequalities are the driving force behind much of our production. By preserving inequalities, we not only enrich the fortunate few, but also provide incentives to take risks, invest more, and work harder. In so doing, we enlarge the economic pie, including the slices available to lower-income groups. Thus everyone is potentially better off, even if only a few end up rich. This is the rationale that keeps the top marginal tax rate in the United States below those in many other countries (see World View "Top Tax Rates").

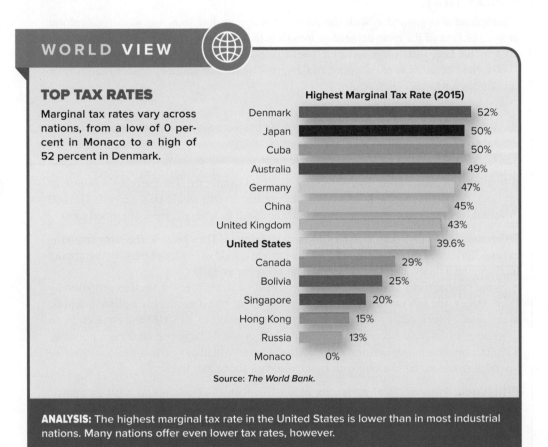

WORLD VIEW

TOP TAX RATES

Marginal tax rates vary across nations, from a low of 0 percent in Monaco to a high of 52 percent in Denmark.

Highest Marginal Tax Rate (2015)

Denmark	52%
Japan	50%
Cuba	50%
Australia	49%
Germany	47%
China	45%
United Kingdom	43%
United States	39.6%
Canada	29%
Bolivia	25%
Singapore	20%
Hong Kong	15%
Russia	13%
Monaco	0%

Source: *The World Bank.*

ANALYSIS: The highest marginal tax rate in the United States is lower than in most industrial nations. Many nations offer even lower tax rates, however.

The Benefits of Greater Equality

Although the potential benefits of inequality are impressive, *there's a trade-off between efficiency and equality.* Moreover, many people are convinced that the terms of the trade-off are exaggerated and the benefits of greater equality are ignored. These rebuttals take the form of economic and noneconomic arguments.

The economic arguments for greater equality also focus on incentives. The first argument is that the present degree of inequality is more than necessary to maintain work incentives. Upper-class incomes needn't be 15 times as large as those of the lowest-income classes; perhaps 4 times as large would do as well.

The second argument is that low-income earners might actually work harder if incomes were distributed more fairly. As matters now stand, the low-income worker sees little chance of making it big. Extremely low income can also inhibit workers' ability to work by subjecting them to poor health, malnutrition, or inadequate educational opportunities. Accordingly, some redistribution of income to the poor might improve the productivity of low-income workers and compensate for reduced productivity among the rich.

Finally, we noted that the maze of loopholes that preserves inequality also distorts economic incentives. Labor and investment decisions are influenced by tax considerations, not just economic benefits and costs. If greater equality were achieved via tax simplification, a more efficient allocation of resources might result.

THE ECONOMY TOMORROW

A FLAT TAX?

flat tax: A single-rate tax system.

Widespread dissatisfaction with the present tax system has spawned numerous reform proposals. One of the most debated proposals is to replace the current federal income tax with a **flat tax.** First proposed by Nobel Prize–winner Milton Friedman in the early 1960s, the flat tax was championed in Congress by former majority leader (and former economics professor) Dick Armey.

The key features of a flat tax include

- Replacing the current system of multiple tax brackets and rates with a single (flat) tax rate that would apply to all taxable income.
- Eliminating all deductions, credits, and most exemptions.

Simplicity. A major attraction of the flat tax is its simplicity. The current 74,608-page tax code that details all the provisions of the present system would be scrapped. The 800 different IRS tax forms now in use would be replaced by a single, postcard-sized form.

Fairness. Flat tax advocates also emphasize its fairness. They point to the rampant vertical and horizontal inequities created by the current tangle of tax loopholes. By scrapping all those deductions, the flat tax would treat everyone equally.

Some progressivity could also be preserved with a flat tax. In the version proposed by Dick Armey, the flat tax rate would be 17 percent, but one personal exemption would be maintained. Every adult would get a personal exemption of $13,100 and each child an exemption of $5,300. Accordingly, a family of four would have personal exemptions of $36,800. Hence a family earning less than that amount would pay no income tax. *Effective* tax rates would increase along with rising incomes above that threshold.

Efficiency. Proponents of a flat tax claim it enhances efficiency as well as equity. Taxpayers now spend more than a billion hours a year preparing tax returns. Legions of lobbyists, accountants, and lawyers devote their energy to tax analysis and avoidance. With a simplified flat tax, all those labor resources could be put to more productive use.

A flat tax would also change the mix of output. Consumption and investment decisions would be made on the basis of economic considerations, not tax consequences.

The Critique. As alluring as a flat tax appears, it has aroused substantial opposition. As proposed by Dick Armey, the flat tax would not apply to all income. Income on savings and investments (such as interest and dividends, capital gains) wouldn't be taxed. The purpose of that exemption would be to encourage greater saving, investment, and economic growth. At the same time, however, such a broad exemption creates a whole new set of horizontal and vertical inequities. Someone receiving $1 million in interest and dividends could escape all income taxes, while a family earning $50,000 in wages would have to pay.

Critics also object to the wholesale elimination of all deductions and credits. Many of those loopholes are expressly designed to encourage desired economic activity. The Bush tax cuts were explicitly designed to encourage education, family stability, and savings. President Obama used tax deductions and credits to encourage more use of solar power. By discarding all tax preferences, the flat tax significantly reduces the government's ability to alter the mix of output.

Finally, critics point out that the transition to a flat tax would entail a wholesale reshuffling of wealth and income. Home values would fall precipitously if the tax preference for homeownership were eliminated. That would hit the middle class particularly hard. State and local governments would have greater difficulty raising their own revenues if the federal deduction for state and local taxes were eliminated. Confronted with such consequences, many people begin to have second thoughts about the desirability of adopting a flat tax in the economy tomorrow. Taxpayers seem to like the *principle* of a flat tax more than its actual provisions.

SUMMARY

- The distribution of income largely determines access to the goods and services we produce. Wealth distribution is important for the same reason. **LO19-3**
- The size distribution of income tells us how incomes are divided up among individuals. The Lorenz curve is a graphic summary of the cumulative size distribution of income. The Gini coefficient is a mathematical summary. **LO19-3**
- Personal incomes are distributed quite unevenly in the United States. At present, the highest quintile (the top 20 percent) gets half of all cash income, and the bottom quintile gets less than 4 percent. **LO19-3**
- The trade-off between equity and efficiency is rooted in supply incentives. The tax elasticity of supply measures how the quantity of available resources (labor and capital) declines when tax rates rise. **LO19-3**
- The progressivity of the federal income tax is weakened by various loopholes (exemptions, deductions, and credits) that create a distinction between nominal and effective tax rates and cause vertical and horizontal inequities. **LO19-2**
- Marginal tax rates were reduced greatly in the 1980s and have alternately risen and fallen since. **LO19-1**

- Mildly progressive federal income taxes are offset by regressive payroll, state, and local taxes. Overall, the tax system redistributes little income; most redistribution occurs through transfer payments. **LO19-2**
- Tax incidence refers to the real burden of a tax. In many cases, reductions in wages, increases in rent, or other real income changes represent the true burden of a tax. **LO19-2**
- There is a trade-off between efficiency and equality. If all incomes are equal, there's no economic reward for superior productivity. On the other hand, a more equal distribution of incomes might increase the productivity of lower-income groups and serve important noneconomic goals as well. **LO19-3**
- A flat tax is a nominally proportional tax system. A personal exemption and the exclusion of capital income can render a flat tax progressive or regressive, however. A flat tax reduces the government's role in resource allocation (the WHAT and HOW questions). **LO19-1**

Key Terms

personal income (PI)	progressive tax	regressive tax
in-kind income	marginal tax rate	tax incidence
wealth	tax elasticity of supply	marginal revenue product (MRP)
size distribution of income	vertical equity	income transfers
income share	horizontal equity	government failure
Lorenz curve	nominal tax rate	flat tax
Gini coefficient	effective tax rate	
market failure	tax base	

Questions for Discussion

1. What goods or services do you and your family receive without directly paying for them? How do these goods affect the distribution of economic welfare? **LO19-2**

2. Why are incomes distributed so unevenly? Identify and explain three major causes of inequality. **LO19-3**

3. Do inequalities stimulate productivity? In what ways? Provide two specific examples. **LO19-3**

4. What loopholes reduced the Pences' and the Clintons' 2015 tax bill (see In the News "Taxes: The Pences vs. the Clintons")? What's the purpose of those loopholes? **LO19-1**

5. How might a flat tax affect efficiency? Fairness? **LO19-3**

6. If a new tax system encouraged more output but also created greater inequality, would it be desirable? **LO19-3**

7. If the tax elasticity of supply were zero, how high could the tax rate go before people reduced their work effort? How do families vary the quantity of labor supplied when tax rates change? **LO19-3**

8. Is a tax deduction for tuition likely to increase college enrollments? How will it affect horizontal and vertical equities? **LO19-3**

9. What share of taxes *should* the rich pay (see Figure 19.4)? Should the poor pay *any* taxes? **LO19-3**

10. How would President Trump's proposed changes in the tax system affect efficiency and equity? Should they have been adopted? **LO19-3**

LO19-1 1. How much tax did the Clintons pay in 2015 (In the News "Taxes: The Pences vs. the Clintons") on:
    (*a*) The first $9,000 of taxable income?
    (*b*) The last $9,000 of taxable income?
    How much tax did the Pences pay in 2015 on:
    (*c*) The first $9,000 of taxable income?
    (*d*) The last $9,000 of taxable income?

LO19-2 2. If there were no deduction for charitable contributions, how much more tax would the Clintons have paid in 2015 (In the News "Taxes: The Pences vs. the Clintons")?

LO19-2 3. According to In the News "Taxes: The Pences vs. the Clintons," in 2015 what was the Pences'
    (*a*) Nominal tax rate?
    (*b*) Effective tax rate?

LO19-1 4. Use Table 19.1 to compute the taxes on a taxable income of $200,000.
    (*a*) What is the marginal tax rate?
    (*b*) What is the average tax rate?

LO19-1 5. Using Table 19.1, compute the taxable income and taxes for the following taxpayers:

Taxpayer	Gross Income	Exemptions and Deductions	Taxable Income	Tax
A	$ 20,000	$ 4,000	_____	_____
B	40,000	16,000	_____	_____
C	80,000	34,000	_____	_____
D	200,000	110,000	_____	_____

Which taxpayer has
(*a*) The highest nominal tax rate?
(*b*) The highest effective tax rate?
(*c*) The highest marginal tax rate?

LO19-2 6. If the tax elasticity of supply is 0.15, by how much will the quantity supplied increase when the marginal tax rate decreases from 40 to 36 percent?

LO19-2 7. By how much might the quantity of labor supplied decrease if the tax elasticity of supply were 0.20 and the marginal tax rate increased from 35 to 45 percent?

LO19-3 8. What is the difference in the top marginal tax rate between Japan and Hong Kong (World View "Top Tax Rates")?

LO19-2 9. What percentage of income is paid in Social Security taxes by a worker with wage earnings of
    (*a*) $30,000?
    (*b*) $70,000?
    (*c*) $200,000?
    (*d*) Is this a progressive, regressive, or proportional tax?

LO19-1 10. Following are hypothetical data on the size distribution of income and wealth for each quintile (one-fifth) of a population:

Quintile	Lowest	Second	Third	Fourth	Highest
Income	5%	10%	15%	25%	45%
Wealth	2%	8%	12%	20%	58%

(a) On the a graph, draw the line of absolute equity; then draw a Lorenz curve for income, and shade the area between the two curves.

(b) In the same diagram, draw a Lorenz curve for wealth. Is the distribution of wealth more equal or less equal than the distribution of income?

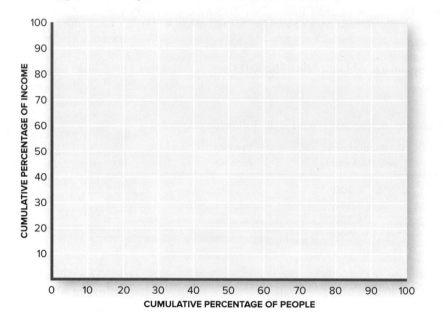

LO19-3 11. (a) On the graph shown below, draw the supply and demand for labor represented by the following data:

Wage	12	11	10	9	8	7	6	5	4	3	2	$1
Quantity of labor												
Supplied	20	17	14	12	10	8	6	5	4	3	2	1
Demanded	2	3	4	5	6	8	10	12	14	16	18	20

(b) How many workers are employed in equilibrium?

(c) What wage are they paid?

(d) Now suppose a payroll tax of $2 per worker is imposed on the employer. Draw the "supply + tax" graph that results.

(e) How many workers are now employed?

(f) Now how much is the employer paying for each worker?

(g) Now how much is each worker receiving?

For the incidence of this tax, compared to the initial equilibrium:

(h) What is the increase in the wage paid by the employer?

(i) What is the reduction in the wage received by the workers?

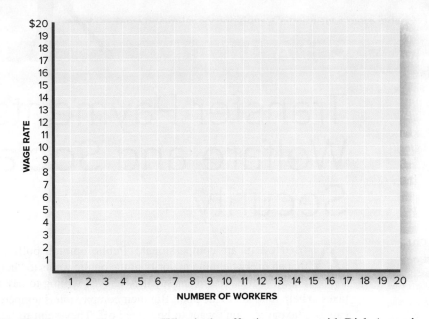

LO19-3 12. The Economy Tomorrow: What is the effective tax rate with Dick Armey's proposed flat tax for a family of four with earnings of

(a) $30,000?

(b) $50,000?

(c) $100,000?

©DreamPictures/Pam Ostrow/Blend Images LLC RF

CHAPTER 20

Transfer Payments: Welfare and Social Security

Americans are compassionate. Public opinion polls reveal that an overwhelming majority of the public wants to "help the needy." Most Americans say they're even willing to pay more taxes to help fund aid to the poor. But their compassion is tempered by caution: taxpayers don't want to be ripped off. They want to be sure their money is helping the "truly needy," not being squandered by deadbeats, drug addicts, shirkers, and "welfare queens."

The conflict between compassion and resentment affects not only welfare programs for the poor but also Social Security for the aged, unemployment insurance benefits for the jobless, and even disability benefits for injured workers. In every one of these programs, people are getting money without working. In effect, they're getting a "free ride."

The risk of providing a free ride is that some of the people who take it could have gotten by without it. As the humorist Dave Barry observed, if the government offers $1 million to people with six toes, a lot of people will try to grow a sixth toe or claim they have one. Income transfers create similar incentives: they encourage people to change their behavior in order to get a free ride.

This chapter focuses on how income transfer programs change not only the distribution of income but also work incentives and behavior. We address the following central questions:

- **How much income do income transfer programs redistribute?**
- **How are transfer benefits computed?**
- **How do transfer payments alter market behavior?**

LEARNING OBJECTIVES

After reading this chapter, you should know

LO20-1 The major income transfer programs.

LO20-2 How transfer programs affect labor supply and total output.

LO20-3 The trade-offs between equity and efficiency.

income transfers: Payments to individuals for which no current goods or services are exchanged, such as Social Security, welfare, and unemployment benefits.

MAJOR TRANSFER PROGRAMS

More than half of every dollar the federal government spends goes to **income transfers** (see Figure 4.5). That amounts to *$2.5 trillion* a year in transfer payments. Who gets all this money?

The easy answer to this question is that almost every household gets some of the transfer money. There are more than 100 federal income transfer programs. Students get tuition grants and subsidized loans. Farmers get crop assistance. Home owners get disaster relief when their homes are destroyed. Veterans get benefit checks and subsidized health care. People over age 65 get Social Security benefits and

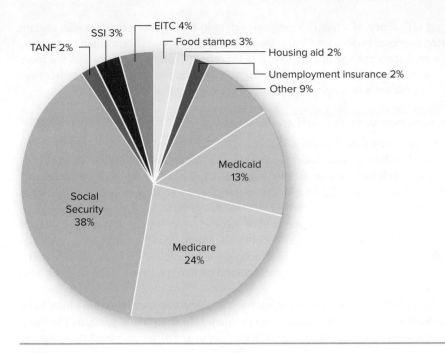

FIGURE 20.1

Income Transfer Programs

There are nearly 100 different federal income transfer programs redistributing more than $2 trillion. However, just three programs—Social Security, Medicare, and Medicaid—account for 75 percent of all transfers. Cash welfare benefits (TANF, SSI) absorb only 5 percent of all income transfers.

Source: U.S. Office of Management and Budget (FY 2016 data).

subsidized health care. And poor people get welfare checks, food stamps, and subsidized housing.

Although income transfers are widely distributed, not everyone shares equally in the tax-paid bounty. As Figure 20.1 shows, just three of the myriad transfer programs account for 75 percent of total outlays. Social Security, the largest program, alone accounts for 38 percent of the transfer budget. Medicare and Medicaid benefits absorb another 37 percent. By contrast, welfare checks account for only 4 percent of all income transfers.

Cash versus In-Kind Benefits

Income transfer doesn't always entail cash payments. The Medicare program, for example, is a health insurance subsidy program that pays hospital and doctor bills for people over age 65. The 56 million people who receive Medicare benefits don't get checks from Uncle Sam; instead Uncle Sam pays the bills for the medical *services* they receive. The same is true for the 69 million people who get Medicaid. Poor people get free health care from the Medicaid program; their benefits are paid *in-kind,* not in cash. Such programs provide **in-kind transfers**—that is, direct transfers of goods and services rather than cash. Food stamps, rent subsidies, legal aid, and subsidized school lunches are all in-kind transfer programs. By contrast, Social Security is a **cash transfer** because it mails benefit checks, not services, to recipients.

The provision of in-kind benefits rather than cash is intended to promote specific objectives. Few taxpayers object to feeding the hungry. But they bristle at the thought that welfare recipients might spend the income they receive on something potentially harmful like liquor or drugs or on nonessentials like cars or fancy clothes. To minimize that risk, taxpayers offer electronic food stamps (now called Supplemental Nutrition Assistance Program [SNAP] vouchers), not cash, thereby limiting the recipient's consumption choices. This helps reassure taxpayers that their assistance is being well spent.

Similar considerations shape the Medicare program. Taxpayers could "cash out" Medicare by simply mailing older people the $700 billion now spent on the program every year. But then some healthy older Americans would get cash they didn't need. Some sick people might not get as much money as *they* needed. Or they might choose to spend their new-found income on something other than health care. The end result would be a smaller health care gain than in-kind transfers facilitate.

in-kind transfers: Direct transfers of goods and services rather than cash, such as food stamps, Medicaid benefits, and housing subsidies.

cash transfers: Income transfers that entail direct cash payments to recipients, such as Social Security, welfare, and unemployment benefits.

target efficiency: The percentage of income transfers that go to the intended recipients and purposes.

The **target efficiency** of a transfer program refers to how well income transfers attain their intended purpose. In-kind medical transfers are more target-efficient than cash transfers because recipients can spend cash transfers for other purposes. Food stamps are more target-efficient than cash in reducing hunger for the same reason. If given cash rather than food stamps, recipients would spend less than 70 cents of each dollar on food.

Social Insurance versus Welfare

You may have noted by now that not all income transfers go to the poor. A lot of student loans go to middle-class college students. And disaster relief helps rebuild both mansions and trailer parks. Such income transfers are triggered by specific *events,* not the recipient's income. By contrast, welfare checks are *means-tested:* they go only to families with little income and few assets.

welfare programs: Means-tested income transfer programs, such as welfare and food stamps.

Welfare programs always entail some kind of income eligibility test. To receive welfare payments, a family must prove that it has too little income to fend for itself. Medicaid is an in-kind **welfare program** because only poor people are eligible for the health care benefits of that program. To get food stamps, another in-kind welfare program, a family must also pass an income test.

Social Security and Medicare aren't *welfare* programs because recipients don't have to be poor. To get Social Security or Medicare benefits you just have to be old enough. The *event* of reaching age 62 makes people eligible for Social Security retirement benefits. At age 65 everyone—whether rich or poor—gets Medicare benefits. These event-conditioned benefits are the hallmark of **social insurance programs:** they insure people against the costs of old age, illness, disability, unemployment, and other specific problems. As Figure 20.2 illustrates, *most income transfers are for social insurance programs, not welfare.*

social insurance programs: Event-conditioned income transfers intended to reduce the costs of specific problems, such as Social Security and unemployment insurance.

Transfer Goals

If the market sliced up the economic pie in a manner that society deemed fair, there would be no need for all these government-provided income transfers. Hence the mere existence of such programs implies a **market failure**—an unfair market-generated distribution of income. When the market alone slices up the pie, some people get too much and others get too little. To redress this inequity, we ask the government to play Robin Hood—taking income from the rich and giving it to the poor. Thus *the basic goal of income transfer programs is to reduce income inequalities*—to change the market's answer to the FOR WHOM question.

market failure: An imperfection in the market mechanism that prevents optimal outcomes.

Unintended Consequences

Although income transfers try to change the distribution of income in desired ways, they are not costless interventions. The Law of Unintended Consequences rears its ugly head

FIGURE 20.2

Social Insurance versus Welfare

Social insurance programs provide *event*-based transfers—for example, upon reaching age 65 or becoming unemployed or disabled. Welfare programs offer benefits only to those in need; they're *means-tested*. Social insurance transfers greatly outnumber welfare transfers.

Source: U.S. Office of Management and Budget (FY 2016 data).

WELFARE
Food stamps
TANF
SSI
Housing aid
Child nutrition
Medicaid

SOCIAL INSURANCE
Social Security
Medicare
Unemployment insurance

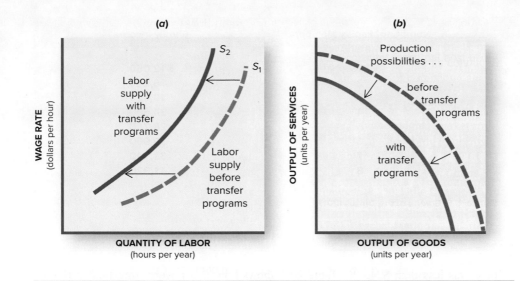

FIGURE 20.3
Reduced Labor Supply and Output

Transfer payments may induce people to supply less labor. If this happens, the supply of labor shifts to the left and the economy's production possibilities shrink. We end up with less total output.

here: *income transfers often change market behavior and outcomes in unintended (and undesired) ways.*

Reduced Output. Work incentives are a potential problem. If you can get paid for *not* working (via a transfer payment), why would you go to work? Why endure 40 hours of toil for a paycheck when you can stay home and collect a welfare check, an unemployment check, or Social Security? If the income transfers are large enough, I'll stay home too. When people reduce their **labor supply** in response to income transfers, total output will shrink. Figure 20.3 shows that *attempts to redistribute income may reduce total income.* In other words, the pie shrinks when we try to reslice it.

Undesirable Behavior. A reduction in labor supply isn't the only unintended consequence of income transfer programs. People may also change their *nonwork* behavior. Welfare benefits give a (small) incentive to women to have more children and to teen moms to establish their own households. Medicare and Medicaid encourage people to overuse health care services and neglect the associated costs. Unemployment benefits encourage workers to stay jobless longer. And as Dave Barry noted at the beginning of the chapter, disability payments encourage people to grow a sixth toe. Although the actual response to these incentives is hotly debated, the existence of the undesired incentives is unambiguous.

labor supply: The willingness and ability to work specific amounts of time at alternative wage rates in a given time period, *ceteris paribus.*

WELFARE PROGRAMS

To understand how income transfer programs change market behavior and outcomes, let's look closely at how welfare programs operate. The largest federal cash welfare program is called Temporary Aid to Needy Families (TANF). The TANF program was created by congressional welfare reforms in 1996 and replaced an earlier program (AFDC) that had operated since 1935. The new program offers states more discretion to decide who gets welfare, under what conditions, and for how long.

Benefit Determination

The first task of the TANF program is to identify potential recipients. In principle, this task is easy: find out who is poor. To do this, the federal government has established a poverty line that specifies how much cash income families of different sizes need just to buy basic necessities. In 2017, the federal government estimated that a family of four was poor if its

TABLE 20.1

Poverty Lines

The official definition of poverty relates current income to the minimal needs of a family. Poverty thresholds vary with family size. In 2017, a family of four was considered poor if it had less than $24,600 of income.

Number of Family Members	Family Income
1	$12,060
2	16,240
3	20,420
4	24,600
5	28,780
6	32,960
7	37,140
8	41,320

Source: U.S. Bureau of the Census (2017).

poverty gap: The shortfall between actual income and the poverty threshold.

income was less than $24,600. Table 20.1 shows how this poverty threshold varies by family size.

According to Table 20.1, a four-person family with $20,000 of income in 2017 would have had a **poverty gap**—the shortfall between actual income and the poverty threshold—of $4,600. The Jones family needed at least that much *additional* income to purchase what the government deems a "minimally adequate" standard of living.

So how much welfare should the government give this family? Should it give $4,600 to this family, thereby closing its poverty gap? As simple as that proposition sounds, it creates some unintended problems.

The Work Incentive Problem

Suppose we guaranteed all families enough income to reach their respective poverty line. Any family earning less than the poverty line would receive a welfare check in the amount of their poverty gap. No one would be poor.

This sounds like a simple solution to the poverty problem, but it isn't. First, people who *weren't* poor would have a strong incentive to become poor. Why try to support a family of four with a paycheck of $25,000 when you can quit and get $24,600 in welfare checks? Recall from Chapter 16 that the decision to work is a response to both the financial and psychological rewards associated with employment. People in dull, dirty, low-paying jobs get little of either. By quitting their jobs, declaring themselves poor, and accepting a guaranteed income transfer, they would gain much more leisure at little financial or psychological cost. In the process, total output would shrink (Figure 20.3).

The second potential problem affects the work behavior of people who were poor to begin with. We assumed that the Jones family was earning $20,000 before they got a welfare check. The question now is whether the welfare check will change their work behavior.

Suppose that family gets an opportunity to earn an extra $2,000 a year by working overtime. Should they seize that opportunity? Consider the effect of the higher *wages* on the family's *income*. Before working overtime, the Jones family earned

INCOME WITHOUT OVERTIME WAGES

Wages	$20,000
Welfare benefits	4,600
Total income	$24,600

If they now work overtime, their income is

INCOME WITH OVERTIME WAGES

Wages	$22,000
Welfare benefits	2,600
Total income	$24,600

Something is wrong here: although *wages* have gone up, the family's *income* hasn't. How would you like to be in this position? How would you react? Would you work overtime?

Implicit Marginal Tax Rates. The failure of income to rise with wages is the by-product of how welfare benefits were computed. *If welfare benefits are set equal to the poverty gap, every additional dollar of wages reduces welfare benefits by the same amount.* In effect, the Jones family confronts a **marginal tax rate** of 100 percent: every dollar of wages results in a lost dollar of benefits. Uncle Sam isn't literally raising the family's taxes by a dollar. By reducing benefits dollar for dollar, however, the end result is the same.

> **marginal tax rate:** The tax rate imposed on the last (marginal) dollar of income.

With a 100 percent marginal tax rate, a family can't improve its income by working more. In fact, this family might as well work *less*. As wages decline, welfare benefits increase by the same amount. Thus we end up with a conflict between compassion and work incentives. By guaranteeing a poverty-level income, we destroy the economic incentive of low-income workers to support themselves. This creates a **moral hazard** for welfare recipients; that is, we encourage undesirable behavior. The moral hazard here is the temptation not to support oneself by working—choosing welfare checks instead.

> **moral hazard:** An incentive to engage in undesirable behavior.

Less Compassion

To reduce this moral hazard, Congress and the states changed the way benefits are computed. First, they set a much lower ceiling on welfare benefits. States don't offer to close the poverty gap; instead they set a maximum benefit far below the poverty line. Hence we have this amended benefit formula:

$$\frac{\text{Welfare}}{\text{benefit}} = \frac{\text{Maximum}}{\text{benefit}} - \text{Wages}$$

In 2017, the typical state set a maximum benefit of about $9,000 for a family of four. Hence a family without any other income couldn't get enough money from welfare to stay out of poverty. As a result, *a family totally dependent on welfare is unquestionably poor.* Although the lower benefit ceiling is less compassionate, it reduces the risk of people climbing on the welfare wagon for a free ride.

More Incentives

To encourage welfare recipients to lift their own incomes above the poverty line, welfare departments made another change in the benefit formula. As we just saw, *the rate at which benefits are reduced as wages increase is the marginal tax rate.* The dollar-for-dollar benefit cuts illustrated destroyed the financial incentive to work. To give recipients more incentive to work, the marginal tax rate was cut from 100 to 67 percent. So we now have a new benefit formula:

$$\frac{\text{Welfare}}{\text{benefit}} = \frac{\text{Maximum}}{\text{benefit}} - \frac{2}{3}[\text{Wages}]$$

Figure 20.4 illustrates how this lower marginal tax rate alters the relationship of total income to wages. The black line in the figure shows the total wages Mrs. Jones could earn at $9 per hour. She could earn nothing by not working or as much as $18,000 per year by working full-time (2,000 hours per year, as depicted by point *F* in the figure).

The blue lines in the figure show what happens to her welfare benefits and total income when a 100 percent marginal tax rate is imposed. At point *A* she gets $9,000 in welfare benefits because she's not working at all. That $9,000 is also her total income because she has no wages.

Now consider what happens to the family's total income if Mrs. Jones goes to work. If she works 1,000 hours per year (essentially half-time), she could earn $9,000 (point *B*). But what would happen to her *income*? If the welfare department cuts her benefit by $1 for every dollar she earns, her benefit check slides down the blue "welfare benefits" line to point *C*, where she gets nothing from welfare. By working 1,000 hours per year, all

FIGURE 20.4

Work (Dis)Incentives

If welfare benefits are reduced dollar for dollar as wages increase, the implied marginal tax rate is 100 percent. In that case, total income remains at the benefit limit of $9,000 (point *A*) as work effort increases from 0 to 1,000 hours (point *B*). There is no incentive to work in this range.

When the marginal tax rate is reduced to 67 percent, total income starts increasing as soon as the welfare recipient starts working. At 1,000 hours of work, total income is $12,000 (point *G*).

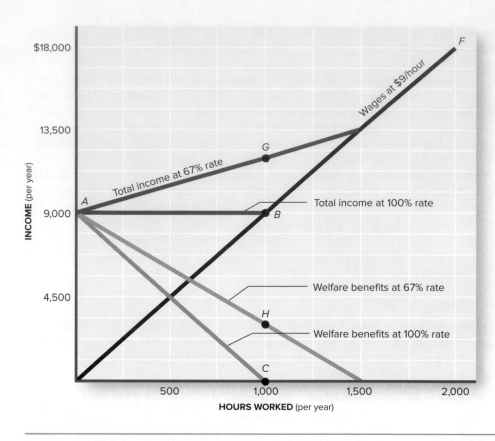

Mrs. Jones has done is replace her welfare check with a paycheck. That might make tax-payers smile, but Mrs. Jones will wonder why she bothered to go to work. With a 100 percent tax rate, her total income doesn't rise above $9,000 until she works more than 1,000 hours.

The green lines in Figure 20.4 show how work incentives improve with a lower marginal tax rate. Now welfare benefits are reduced by only 67 cents for every $1 of wages earned. As a result, total income starts rising as soon as Mrs. Jones goes to work. If she works 1,000 hours, her total income will include

Wages	$ 9,000
Welfare benefit	3,000 = $9,000 − 2/3($9,000)
Total income	$12,000

Point *G* on the graph illustrates this outcome.

Incentives versus Costs

It may be comforting to know that the Jones family can now increase its income from $9,000 when not working to $12,000 by working 1,000 hours per year. But they still face a higher marginal tax rate (67 percent) than rich people (the top marginal tax rate on federal income taxes is 39.6 percent). Why not lower their marginal tax rate even further, thus increasing both their work incentives and their total income?

Unfortunately, a reduction in the marginal tax rate would also increase welfare costs. Suppose we eliminated the marginal tax rate altogether. Then the Jones family could earn wages of $9,000 by working 1,000 hours *and* keep welfare benefits of $9,000. That would boost their total income to $18,000. Sounds great, doesn't it? But should we still be providing $9,000 in welfare payments to someone who earns $9,000 on her own? How about someone earning $20,000 or $30,000? Where should we draw the line? Clearly, *if we don't impose a marginal tax rate at some point, everyone will be eligible for welfare benefits.*

The thought of giving everyone a welfare check might sound like a great idea, but it would turn out to be incredibly expensive. In the end, we'd have to take those checks back, in the form of increased taxes, to pay for the vastly expanded program. We must recognize, then, a basic dilemma:

- *Low marginal tax rates encourage more work effort but make more people eligible for welfare.*
- *High marginal tax rates discourage work effort but make fewer people eligible for welfare.*

The conflict between work incentives and the desire to limit welfare costs and eligibility can be summarized in this simple equation:

$$\text{Breakeven level of income} = \frac{\text{Basic benefits}}{\text{Marginal tax rate}}$$

The **breakeven level of income** is the amount of income a person can earn before losing all welfare benefits. In the Joneses' case, the basic welfare benefit was $9,000 per year and the benefit reduction (marginal tax) rate was 0.67. Hence the family could earn as much as

$$\text{Breakeven level of income} = \frac{\$9,000}{0.67} \text{ per year}$$

$$= \$13,500$$

before losing all welfare benefits. Thus *low marginal tax rates encourage work but make it hard to get completely off welfare.*

If the marginal tax rate were 100 percent, as under the old welfare system, the breakeven point would be $9,000 divided by 1.00. In that case, people who earned $9,000 on their own would get no assistance from welfare. Fewer people would be eligible for welfare, but those who drew benefits would have no incentive to work. If the marginal tax rate were lowered to 0, the breakeven point would rise to infinity ($9,000 divided by 0)—and we'd all be on welfare.

As this arithmetic shows, *there's a basic conflict between work incentives (low marginal tax rates) and welfare containment (smaller welfare rolls and outlays).* We can achieve a lower breakeven level of income (less welfare eligibility) only by sacrificing low marginal tax rates or higher income floors (basic benefits). Hence welfare costs can be minimized only if we sacrifice income provision or work incentives.

Tax Elasticity of Labor Supply. The terms of the trade-off between more welfare and less work depend on how responsive people are to marginal tax rates. As we first noted in Chapter 19, the **tax elasticity of labor supply** measures the response to changes in tax rates:

$$\text{Tax elasticity of labor supply} = \frac{\% \text{ change in quantity of labor supplied}}{\% \text{ change in tax rate}}$$

If the tax elasticity of labor supply were zero, it wouldn't matter how high the marginal tax rate was: people would work for nothing (100 percent tax rate). In reality, the tax elasticity of labor supply among low-wage workers is more in the range of 0.2 to 0.3, so marginal tax rates *do* affect work effort. *So long as the tax elasticity of labor supply is greater than zero, there is a conflict between equity (more welfare) and efficiency (more work).*

Time Limits. The 1996 welfare reforms partially sidestepped this dilemma by setting time limits on welfare eligibility. TANF recipients *must* engage in some sort of employment-related activity (e.g., a job, job search, or training) within two years of first receiving benefits. There is also a five-year *lifetime* limit on welfare eligibility. States, however, can still use their own (nonfederal) funds to extend welfare benefits beyond those time limits.

breakeven level of income: The income level at which welfare eligibility ceases.

tax elasticity of labor supply: The percentage change in quantity of labor supplied divided by the percentage change in tax rates.

SOCIAL SECURITY

Like welfare programs, the Social Security program was developed to redistribute incomes. In the case of Social Security, however, *age,* not low income, is the primary determinant of eligibility. The program seeks to provide a financial prop under retirement incomes. Although Social Security is a *social insurance* program rather than a *welfare* program, it has the same kind of conflict between equity and efficiency. Here again we have to confront policy conflicts among the goals of compassion, work incentives, and program costs.

Program Features

The Social Security program is actually a mix of three separate income transfers. The main program is for retired workers, the second for survivors of deceased workers, and the third for disabled workers. Created in 1935, this combined Old Age Survivors and Disability Insurance (OASDI) program is now so large that it accounts for 40 percent of all federal income transfers. The monthly benefit checks distributed to 61 million recipients are financed with a payroll tax on workers and employers.

Retirement Age. As Figure 20.5 confirms, the retirement program is by far the largest component of OASDI. Individuals become eligible for Social Security retirement benefits when they reach certain ages. People can choose either "early" retirement (at age 62 to 64) or "normal" retirement (at age 65 to 67). Those who choose early retirement receive a smaller monthly benefit because they're expected to live longer in retirement.

For people born after 1940, the age threshold for "normal" retirement is increasing each year. By the year 2022, the age threshold for normal retirement will be age 67. This delay in benefit eligibility is intended to keep aging baby boomers working longer, thereby curtailing a surge in benefit outlays.

Progressive Benefits. Retirement benefits are based on an individual's wages. In 2017, the median Social Security retirement benefit for an individual was about $16,000. But high-wage workers could get nearly $32,000 and low-wage workers as little as $8,000 a year.

Although high-wage workers receive larger benefit checks than low-wage workers, the *ratio* of benefits to prior wages isn't constant. Instead the ***Social Security benefits formula is progressive*** because the ratio of benefits to prior wages declines as wages increase. Social Security replaces 90 percent of the first $885 of prior average monthly earnings but only 15 percent of monthly wages above $5,336 (see Table 20.2). The declining **wage replacement rate** ensures that low-wage workers receive *proportionately* greater benefits.

wage replacement rate: The percentage of base wages paid out in benefits.

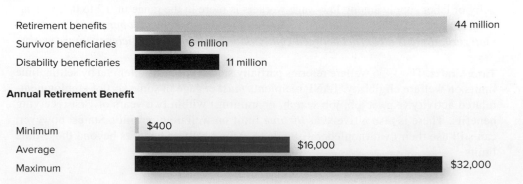

Who Pays Social Security Taxes

Payroll taxes

   7.65% paid by workers

   7.65% paid by employers

Who Gets Social Security Checks

Retirement benefits — 44 million
Survivor beneficiaries — 6 million
Disability beneficiaries — 11 million

Annual Retirement Benefit

Minimum — $400
Average — $16,000
Maximum — $32,000

FIGURE 20.5

Social Security Finances

The Social Security retirement, survivor, and disability programs are financed with payroll taxes. Most benefits go to retired workers, who get an average transfer of $16,000 per year.

Source: U.S. Social Security Administration (2017 data).

Wage Replacement Rate (%)	For Average Monthly Wages of
90%	$1–885
32	$886–5,336
15	over $5,336

Source: U.S. Social Security Administration (2017).

TABLE 20.2

Progressive Benefits

Social Security redistributes income progressively by replacing a larger share of low wages than high wages. Shown here are the wage replacement rates for 2017 (adjusted annually for inflation).

Suppose two workers are retiring. One had prior wages averaging $9,000 per month; the other had $3,000. These workers will get Social Security benefits of

High-wage worker = 0.90($885) + 0.32($4,450) + 0.15($3,665) = $2,770.25

Low-wage worker = 0.90($885) + 0.32($2,115) = $1,681.18

Notice how their relative incomes change. When working, the high-wage worker had three times more income than the low-wage worker. In retirement, however, the high-wage worker's benefits are not even two times the low-wage worker's benefits. Thus *retirement benefits end up more equally distributed than wages*. In this sense, Social Security is a *progressive* mechanism of income distribution.

The Earnings Test

In reality, a worker doesn't have to *retire* to receive Social Security benefits. But the government imposes an *earnings test* to determine how much retirement benefits an older person can collect while still working. The earnings test is similar to the formula used to compute welfare benefits. The formula establishes a maximum benefit amount and a marginal tax rate that reduces benefits as wages increase:

$$\frac{\text{Benefit}}{\text{amount}} = \frac{\text{Maximum}}{\text{award}} - 0.5(\text{Wages in excess of ceiling})$$

Consider the case of Leonard, a 62-year-old worker contemplating retirement. Suppose Leonard's wage history entitles him to a maximum award of $12,000 per year. But he wants to keep working to supplement Social Security benefits with wages. What happens to his benefits if he continues to work?

In 2017, the wage "ceiling" for workers 62 to 64 was $16,920. Hence the benefit formula was

$$\frac{\text{Benefit}}{\text{amount}} = \$12,000 - 0.5(\text{Wage} > \$16,920)$$

As a result, a person could earn as much as $16,900 and still get maximum retirement benefits ($12,000) since there would be no wage-related deduction. This would put Leonard's total income at $28,920.

The Work Disincentive

Suppose Leonard wants a bit more income than that. Can he increase his total income by working still more? Yes, but not by much. He faces the same kind of work disincentives the Jones family had when on welfare. The formula just described says benefits will drop by 50 cents for every $1 of wages earned more than $16,920. Hence *the implicit marginal tax rate is 50 percent*. Uncle Sam is effectively getting half of any wages Leonard earns in excess of $16,920 per year. Figure 20.6 illustrates this sorry state of affairs.

Notice how many hours Leonard can work before the government starts reducing his Social Security check. At a wage of $20 an hour, Leonard can work 846 hours a year (about 2 days a week) and keep all his benefits. In that case, he resides at point *C* in Figure 20.6.

FIGURE 20.6

The Social Security Earnings Test

A worker aged 62–64 can earn up to $16,920 (point *A*) without losing any Social Security benefits. At point *C*, income includes $12,000 in benefits and $16,920 in wages.

If wages increase beyond $16,920, however, Social Security benefits decline by 50 cents for every $1 earned. After point *C*, income rises only half as fast as wages.

At the breakeven point *D*, earnings are $40,920, and there are no Social Security benefits (point *B*).

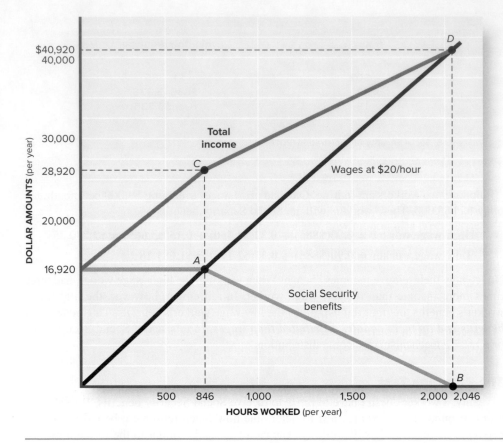

Beyond that, however, every additional hour of work brings in $20 of wages but a $10 reduction in benefits. After point *C*, his income rises *half* as fast as his wages. That's a real disincentive to work.

In reality, the marginal tax rate on Leonard's wages is even higher and the incentive to work lower. If he works, Leonard will have to pay the Social Security payroll tax (7.65 percent) as well as federal, state, and local income taxes (say, another 15 percent). These additional (explicit) taxes increase the *combined* marginal tax rate to 72.65 percent. In other words, Leonard would get to keep only 27.35 cents out of every additional dollar he earned.

Declining Labor Supply

labor force participation rate: The percentage of the working-age population working or seeking employment.

Like welfare recipients, older people are quick to realize that work no longer pays. Not surprisingly, they've exited the labor market in droves. The **labor force participation rate** measures the percentage of the population that is either employed or actively seeking a job (unemployed). Figure 20.7 shows how precipitously the labor force participation rate has declined among older Americans. This problem isn't unique to the United States. The relative size of the over-65 population is growing everywhere, and more older people are retiring earlier.

Prior to the creation of the Social Security system, most older people had to continue working until advanced age. Many "died with their boots on" because they had no other means of support. Just a generation ago, more than 75 percent of men 62 to 64 were working. Today less than 50 percent of that group is working.

Compassion, Incentives, and Cost

The primary economic cost of the Social Security program isn't the benefits it pays but the reduction in total output that occurs when workers retire early. In the absence of Social Security benefits, millions of older workers would still be on the job, contributing to the output of goods and services. When they instead retire—or simply work less—total output shrinks.

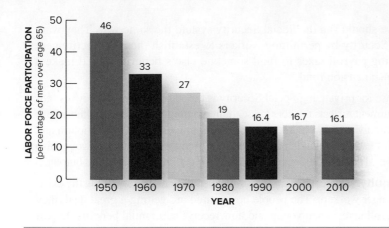

FIGURE 20.7
Declining Labor Force Participation

In the 1960s and 1970s, the eligibility age for Social Security was lowered for men and benefits were increased. This convinced an increased percentage of older men to leave the labor force and retire. In a single generation the labor force participation rate of men over age 65 was halved.

Source: U.S. Bureau of Labor Statistics.

Trade-offs. Just because the intergenerational redistribution is expensive doesn't mean we shouldn't do it. Going to college is expensive too, but you're doing it. The real economic issue is benefits versus costs. Compassion for older workers is what motivates Social Security transfers. Presumably, society gains from the more equitable distribution of income that results (a revised FOR WHOM). The economic concern is that we *balance* this gain against the implied costs.

One way of reducing the economic cost of the Social Security program would be to eliminate the earnings test. AARP (formerly known as the American Association of Retired Persons) has advocated this option for many years. If the earnings test were eliminated, the marginal tax rate on the wages of older workers would drop from 50 percent to 0. In a flash, the work disincentive would vanish, and older workers would produce more goods and services.

There's a downside to this reform, however. If the earnings test were eliminated, all older individuals would get their full retirement benefit, even if they continued to work. This would raise the budgetary cost of the program substantially. To cover that cost, payroll taxes would have to increase. Higher payroll taxes would in turn reduce supply and demand for *younger* workers. Hence the financial burden of eliminating the earnings test might actually *increase* the economic cost of Social Security.

There's also an equity issue here. Should we increase payroll taxes on younger low-income workers to give higher Social Security benefits to older workers who still command higher salaries? In 2000 Congress gave a very qualified "yes" to this question. The earnings test was eliminated for workers over age 70 and for workers who retired at "normal" age (65–67 depending on year of birth). The marginal tax rate for workers who "retire" early but continue working at ages 65–69 was also reduced to 33.3 percent. The lower earnings test and 50 percent marginal tax rate were left intact, however, for people aged 62–64, the ones for whom the retirement decision is most pressing. The *budget* cost of greater work incentives for "early retirees" (ages 62–64) was regarded as too high.

THE ECONOMY TOMORROW

PRIVATIZE SOCIAL SECURITY?

All income transfer programs entail a redistribution of income. In the case of Social Security, the redistribution is largely intergenerational: *payroll taxes levied on younger workers finance retirement benefits for older workers.* The system is financed on a pay-as-you-go basis; future benefits depend on future taxes. This is very different from private pension plans, whereby you salt away some wages while working to finance your own eventual benefits. Such private plans are *advance-funded.*

Continued

Many people say we should run the Social Security system the same way. They want to "privatize" Social Security by permitting workers to establish their own retirement plans. Instead of paying payroll taxes to fund someone else's benefits, you'd make a contribution to your *own* pension fund.

More Output. The case for privatizing Social Security is based on both efficiency and equity. The efficiency argument reflects the core laissez-faire argument that markets know best. In a privatized system, individuals would have the freedom to tailor their consumption and saving choices. The elimination of mandatory payroll taxes and the earnings test would also lessen work disincentives. People would work harder and longer, maximizing total output.

Intergenerational Equity. Advocates of privatization also note how inequitable the existing program is for younger workers. The people now retired are getting a great deal: they paid relatively low payroll taxes when young and now receive substantial benefits. In part this high payoff is due to demographics. Thirty years ago there were four workers for every retired person. As the post–World War II baby boomers retire, the ratio of workers to retirees is declining dramatically. By the year 2030, there will be only two workers for every retiree (see Figure 20.8). As a result, the tax burden on tomorrow's workers will have to be a lot higher, or the baby boomers will have to accept much lower Social Security benefits. Either way, some generation of workers will get a lot less than everyone else. If Social Security is privatized, tomorrow's workers won't have to bear such a demographic tax burden.

More Poverty. As alluring as these suggestions sound, the privatization of Social Security would foster other inequities. The primary goal of Social Security is to fend off poverty among the aged. Social Security does this in two ways: by (1) transferring income from workers to retirees and (2) redistributing income from high-wage workers to low-wage workers in retirement with progressive wage replacement rates. By contrast, a privatized system would let the market alone determine FOR WHOM goods are produced. Low-income workers and other people who saved little while working would end up poor in their golden years. In a privatized system, even some high earners and savers might end up poor if their investments turned sour. Would we turn our collective backs on these people? If not, then the government would have to intervene with *some* kind of transfer program. The real issue, therefore, may not be whether a privatized Social Security system would work but what kind of *public* transfer program we'd have to create to supplement it. Then the choice would be either (1) Social Security or (2) a privatized retirement system plus a public welfare program for the aged poor. Framed in this context, the choice for the economy tomorrow is a lot more complex.

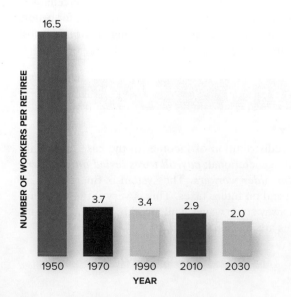

FIGURE 20.8

A Declining Tax Base

Because Social Security benefits are financed by payroll taxes, the ratio of workers to retirees is a basic measure of the program's fiscal health. That ratio has declined dramatically, and it will decline even more as the baby boomers are retiring.

Source: U.S. Social Security Administration.

SUMMARY

- Income transfers are payments for which no current goods or services are exchanged. They include both cash payments such as welfare checks and in-kind transfers such as food stamps and Medicare. **LO20-1**
- Most transfer payments come from social insurance programs that cushion the income effects of specific events, such as aging, illness, or unemployment. Welfare programs are means-tested; they pay benefits only to the poor. **LO20-1**
- The basic goal of transfer programs is to alter the market's FOR WHOM outcome. Attempts to redistribute income may, however, have the unintended effect of reducing total income. This is the core equity versus efficiency dilemma. **LO20-2**
- Welfare programs reduce work incentives in two ways. They offer some income to people who don't work at all,

and they also tax the wages of recipients who do work via offsetting benefit reductions. **LO20-2**
- The benefit reduction that occurs when wages increase is an implicit marginal tax. The higher the marginal tax rate, (1) the less the incentive to work but (2) the smaller the welfare caseload. **LO20-3**
- The Social Security retirement program creates similar work disincentives. It provides an income floor for people who don't work and imposes a high marginal tax rate on workers aged 62–64. **LO20-2**
- The core policy dilemma is to find an optimal balance between compassion (transferring more income) and incentives (keeping people at work contributing to total output). **LO20-3**

Key Terms

income transfers	social insurance programs	moral hazard
in-kind transfers	market failure	breakeven level of income
cash transfers	labor supply	tax elasticity of labor supply
target efficiency	poverty gap	wage replacement rate
welfare programs	marginal tax rate	labor force participation rate

Questions for Discussion

1. If we have to choose between compassion and incentives, which should we choose? Do the terms of the trade-off matter? **LO20-3**
2. What's so hard about guaranteeing everyone a minimal level of income support? What problems arise? **LO20-2**
3. If poor people don't want to work, should they get welfare? What about their children? **LO20-3**
4. Once someone has received TANF welfare benefits for a total of five years, he or she is permanently ineligible for more TANF benefits. Should this person receive any further assistance? How will work incentives be affected? **LO20-2**
5. In what ways do younger workers pay for Social Security benefits received by retired workers? **LO20-2**
6. Should the Social Security earnings test be eliminated? What are the benefits and costs of doing so? **LO20-2**
7. How would the distribution of income change if Social Security were privatized? **LO20-1**
8. Who pays the economic cost of Social Security? In what ways? **LO20-2**
9. Why don't we give poor people more cash welfare instead of in-kind transfers like food stamps, housing assistance, and Medicaid? **LO20-3**
10. Why is the increasing ratio of older people to younger people a problem for Social Security? Is there any way to mitigate this demographic problem? **LO20-3**

LO20-2 1. Suppose the annual welfare benefit formula is

$$\text{Benefit} = \$8000 - 0.67(\text{Wages} > \$2,000)$$

(*a*) What is the marginal tax rate on
  (*i*) The first $2,000 of wages?
  (*ii*) Wages above $2,000?
(*b*) How large is the benefit if wages equal
  (*i*) $0?
  (*ii*) $2,000?
  (*iii*) $6,000?
(*c*) What is the breakeven level of income in this case?

LO20-2 2. A welfare recipient can receive food stamps as well as cash welfare benefits. If the food stamp allotment is set as follows,

$$\text{Food stamps} = \$6,000 - 0.30(\text{Wages})$$

(*a*) How high can wages rise before all food stamps are eliminated?
(*b*) If the welfare benefit formula in Problem 1 applies, what is the *combined* marginal tax rate of both welfare and food stamps for wages above $2,000?

LO20-3 3. Draw a graph showing how benefits, total income, and wages change under the following conditions:

$$\textbf{Wage rate} = \textbf{\$10 per hour}$$

$$\textbf{Welfare benefit} = \textbf{\$5,000} - \textbf{0.5(Wages} > \textbf{\$3,000)}$$

Identify here and label on the graph the following points:
  A—welfare benefit when wages = 0   (*a*) How much is that benefit?   _____
  B—welfare benefit when wages = $10,000   (*b*) How much is that benefit?   _____
  C—breakeven level of income   (*c*) What is that income level?   _____

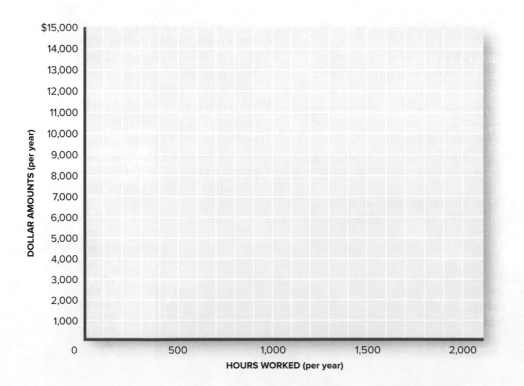

LO20-3 4. What is the breakeven level of income for Social Security as depicted in Figure 20.6?

LO20-3 5. According to the benefit formula in Table 20.2, how large will the Social Security benefit be for a worker who had prior earnings of
(*a*) $36,000 a year?
(*b*) $96,000 a year?
What is the marginal wage replacement rate for
(*c*) The $36,000-per-year worker?
(*d*) The $96,000-per-year worker?

LO20-3 6. How large a monthly Social Security check will a retiree get if her maximum benefit is $1,600 per month and she continues working for wages of $2,000 per month?

7. (*a*) On the following graph, depict the wages, income, and Social Security benefits at different hours of work for a worker aged 62–64 who earns $15 per hour and is eligible for $15,000 in Social Security benefits.
(*b*) What is the total income if the person works 1,000 hours per year?
(*c*) What is the breakeven level of income?

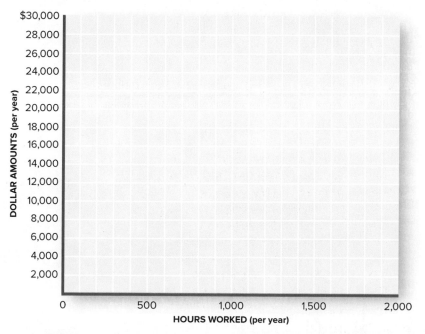

LO20-3 8. If older workers have a tax elasticity of labor supply equal to 0.20, by how much will their work activity decline when they reach the Social Security earnings test limit? (Assume *explicit* taxes of 20 percent below that limit.)

L020-1 9. Suppose the benefit formulas for various welfare programs are

> **Food stamps: $400 per month − 0.30(Wages)**
> **Housing assistance: $1,000 per month − 0.25(Wages)**
> **Cash welfare: $400 per month − 0.67(Wages above $500)**

(a) How much will someone earning $800 a month receive in
  (i) Food stamps?
  (ii) Housing assistance?
  (iii) Cash welfare?
(b) What is the cumulative marginal tax rate at
  (i) Wages under $500?
  (ii) Wages over $500?

L020-1 10. The Economy Tomorrow: Social Security tax revenue comes from taxes on current workers' wages up to a cap. Social Security benefits go out to current retirees and are based on age and past earnings. In The Economy Tomorrow, it is discussed how in the near future tax revenue will be less than the benefits paid out. Identify three ways to keep this program in balance.

©MOF/Getty Images RF

INTERNATIONAL ECONOMICS

©Ingram Publishing RF

©Don Tonge/Alamy Stock Photo

Our interactions with the rest of the world have a profound impact on the mix of output (WHAT), the methods of production (HOW), and the distribution of income (FOR WHOM). Trade and global money flows can also affect the stability of the macro economy. Chapters 21 and 22 explore the motives, the nature, and the effects of international trade and finance.

Chapter 23 examines one of the world's most urgent problems—the deprivation that afflicts nearly 3 billion people worldwide. In this last chapter, the dimensions, causes, and potential cures for global poverty are discussed.

©William West/AFP/Getty Images

CHAPTER 21

International Trade

The 2016 World Series between the Cleveland Indians and the Chicago Cubs was played with Japanese gloves, baseballs made in Costa Rica, and Mexican bats. Most of the players were wearing shoes made in Korea or China. And during the regular season, many of the games throughout the major leagues were played on artificial grass made in Taiwan. Baseball, it seems, has become something less than the "all-American" game.

Imported goods have made inroads into other activities as well. All DVDs, smartphones, and video game consoles are imported, as are most televisions, fax machines, personal computers, and iPads. Most of these imported goods could have been produced in the United States. Why did we purchase them from other countries? For that matter, why does the rest of the world buy computers, tractors, chemicals, airplanes, and wheat from us rather than produce such products for themselves? Wouldn't we all be better off relying on ourselves for the goods we consume (and the jobs we need) rather than buying and selling products in international markets? Or is there some advantage to be gained from international trade?

This chapter begins with a survey of international trade patterns— what goods and services we trade, and with whom. Then we address basic issues related to such trade:

- **What benefit, if any, do we get from international trade?**
- **How much harm do imports cause, and to whom?**
- **Should we protect ourselves from "unfair" trade by limiting imports?**

After examining the arguments for and against international trade, we draw some general conclusions about trade policy. As we'll see, international trade tends to increase *average* incomes, although it may diminish the job and income opportunities for specific industries and workers.

LEARNING OBJECTIVES

After reading this chapter, you should know

LO21-1 What comparative advantage is.

LO21-2 What the gains from trade are.

LO21-3 How trade barriers affect prices, output, and incomes.

U.S. TRADE PATTERNS

The United States is by far the largest player in global product and resource markets. In 2016 we purchased 20 percent of the world's exports and sold 15 percent of the same total.

Imports

In dollar terms, our imports in 2016 exceeded $2.7 trillion. These **imports** included the consumer items mentioned earlier as well as capital equipment, raw materials, and food. Table 21.1 represents the goods and services we purchase from foreign suppliers.

imports: Goods and services purchased from international sources.

TABLE 21.1

A U.S. Trade Sampler

The United States imports and exports a staggering array of goods and services. Shown here are the top exports and imports with various countries. Notice that we export many of the same goods we import (such as cars and computers). What's the purpose of trading goods we produce ourselves?

Country	Imports from	Exports to
Australia	Beef Alumina Autos	Airplanes Computers Auto parts
Belgium	Jewelry Cars Optical glass	Cigarettes Airplanes Diamonds
Canada	Cars Trucks Paper	Auto parts Cars Computers
China	Computers Clothes Toys	Soybeans Airplanes Cars
Germany	Cars Engines Auto parts	Airplanes Computers Cars
Japan	Cars Computers Telephones	Airplanes Computers Timber
Mexico	Cars Computers Appliances	Computers Cars Chemicals
Russia	Oil Platinum Artworks	Corn Wheat Oil seeds
South Korea	Shoes Cars Computers	Airplanes Leather Iron ingots and oxides

Source: U.S. Department of Commerce.

Although imports represent only 15 percent of total GDP, they account for larger shares of specific product markets. Coffee is a familiar example. Since virtually all coffee is imported (except for a tiny amount produced in Hawaii), Americans would have a harder time staying awake without imports. Likewise, there'd be no aluminum if we didn't import bauxite, no chrome bumpers if we didn't import chromium, no tin cans without imported tin, no smartphones, and a lot fewer computers without imported components. We couldn't even play the all-American game of baseball without imports because baseballs are no longer made in the United States.

We import *services* as well as *goods*. If you fly to Europe on Virgin Airways, you're importing transportation services. If you stay in a London hotel, you're importing lodging services. When you go to Barclay's Bank to cash traveler's checks, you're importing foreign financial services. If you go to Mexico for Spring Break, you are importing tourism services. These and other services now account for one-sixth of U.S. imports.

Exports

While we're buying goods (merchandise) and services from the rest of the world, global consumers are buying our **exports.** In 2016 we exported $1.5 trillion of *goods,* including farm products (wheat, corn, soybeans), tobacco, machinery (computers), aircraft, automobiles and auto parts, raw materials (lumber, iron ore), and chemicals (see Table 21.1

exports: Goods and services sold to foreign buyers.

for a sample of U.S. merchandise exports). We also exported $750 billion of services (movies, software licenses, tourism, engineering, financial services, etc.).

Although the United States is the world's largest exporter of goods and services, exports represent a relatively modest fraction of our total output. As World View "Export Ratios" illustrates, other nations export much larger proportions of their GDP. Belgium is one of the most export-oriented countries, with tourist services and diamond exports pushing its export ratio to an incredible 83 percent. By contrast, Afghanistan is basically a closed economy with few exports (other than opium and other drugs traded in the black market).

WORLD VIEW

EXPORT RATIOS

Very poor countries often have little to export and thus low export ratios. Saudi Arabia, by contrast, depends heavily on its oil exports. Fast-developing countries in Asia also rely on exports to enlarge their markets and raise incomes. The U.S. export ratio is low by international standards.

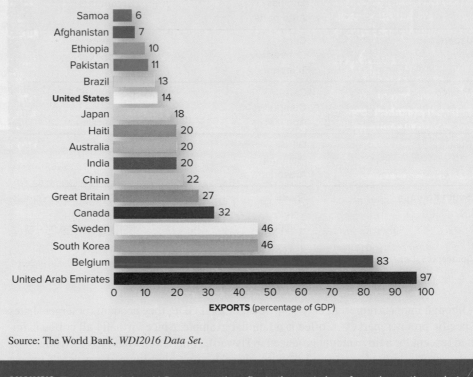

Source: The World Bank, *WDI2016 Data Set.*

ANALYSIS: The relatively low U.S. export ratio reflects the vast size of our domestic market and our relative self-sufficiency in food and resources. European nations are smaller and highly interdependent.

The low U.S. export ratio (14 percent) disguises our heavy dependence on exports in specific industries. We export 25 to 50 percent of our rice, corn, and wheat production each year, and still more of our soybeans. Clearly a decision by international consumers to stop eating U.S. agricultural products could devastate a lot of American farmers. Such companies as Boeing (planes), Caterpillar Tractor (construction and farm machinery), Weyerhaeuser (logs, lumber), Dow (chemicals), and Oracle (computer workstations) sell more than one-fourth of their output in foreign markets. McDonald's sells hamburgers to nearly 70 million people a day in 128 countries around the world; to do so, the company exports management and marketing services (as well as frozen food) from the United States. The Walt Disney Company produces the most popular TV shows in Russia and Germany, publishes Italy's best-selling weekly magazine, and has the most popular tourist attraction in

Product Category	Exports ($ billions)	Imports ($ billions)	Surplus (Deficit) ($ billions)
Merchandise	$1,460	$2,210	$(750)
Services	750	502	248
Total trade	$2,210	$2,712	$(502)

Source: U.S. Department of Commerce.

TABLE 21.2
Trade Balances

Both merchandise (goods) and services are traded between countries. The United States typically has a merchandise deficit and a services surplus. When combined, an overall trade deficit remained in 2016.

Japan (Tokyo Disneyland). The 500,000 foreign students attending U.S. universities are purchasing $5 billion of American educational services. All these activities are part of America's service exports.

Trade Balances

Although we export a lot of products, we usually have an imbalance in our trade flows. The trade balance is the difference between the value of exports and imports:

$$\text{Trade balance} = \text{Exports} - \text{Imports}$$

During 2016 we imported much more than we exported and so had a *negative* trade balance. A negative trade balance is called a **trade deficit.**

Although the overall trade balance includes both goods and services, these flows are usually reported separately, with the *merchandise* trade balance distinguished from the *services* trade balance. As Table 21.2 shows, the United States had a merchandise (goods) trade deficit of $750 billion in 2016 and a *services* trade *surplus* of $248 billion, leaving the overall trade balance in the red.

When the United States has a trade deficit with the rest of the world, other countries must have an offsetting **trade surplus.** On a global scale, imports must equal exports because every good exported by one country must be imported by another. Hence *any imbalance in America's trade must be offset by reverse imbalances elsewhere.*

Whatever the overall balance in our trade accounts, bilateral balances vary greatly. Table 21.3 shows, for example, that our 2016 aggregate trade deficit ($502 billion) incorporated huge bilateral merchandise trade deficits with China, Germany, Japan, and Mexico. In the same year, however, we had trade surpluses with Brazil, the Netherlands, Belgium, Australia, and Hong Kong.

trade deficit: The amount by which the value of imports exceeds the value of exports in a given time period (negative net exports).

trade surplus: The amount by which the value of exports exceeds the value of imports in a given time period (positive net exports).

Country	Merchandise Exports to ($ billions)	Merchandise Imports from ($ billions)	Trade Balance ($ billions)
Top Deficit Countries			
China	$115	$463	−$348
Japan	63	132	−69
Germany	49	114	−65
Mexico	231	294	−63
Canada	267	278	−11
Top Surplus Countries			
Hong Kong	$35	$ 7	+$28
The Netherlands	40	16	+24
Belgium	32	17	+15
Australia	22	10	+12
Brazil	30	26	+4

Source: U.S. Census Bureau (2016 data).

TABLE 21.3
Bilateral Trade Balances

The U.S. trade deficit is the net result of bilateral deficits and surpluses. We had huge trade deficits with China, Germany, and Japan in 2016, for example, but small trade surpluses with Brazil, the Netherlands, Belgium, Australia, and Hong Kong. International trade is *multi*national, with surpluses in some countries being offset by trade deficits elsewhere.

MOTIVATION TO TRADE

Many people wonder why we trade so much, particularly since (1) we import many of the things we also export (like computers, airplanes, cars, clothes), (2) we *could* produce many of the other things we import, and (3) we worry so much about trade imbalances. Why not just import those few things that we can't produce ourselves, and export just enough to balance that trade?

Specialization

Although it might seem strange to be importing goods we could produce ourselves, such trade is entirely rational. Our decision to trade with other countries arises from the same considerations that motivate individuals to specialize in production: satisfying their remaining needs in the marketplace. Why don't you become self-sufficient—growing all your own food, building your own shelter, and recording your own songs? Presumably because you've found that you can enjoy a much higher standard of living (and better music) by working at just one job and then buying other goods in the marketplace. When you do so, you're no longer self-sufficient. Instead you are *specializing* in production, relying on others to produce the array of goods and services you want. When countries trade goods and services, they are doing the same thing—*specializing* in production and then *trading* for other desired goods. Why do they do this? Because **specialization increases total output.**

To see how nations benefit from trade, we'll examine the production possibilities of two countries. We want to demonstrate that two countries that trade can together produce more output than they could in the absence of trade. If they can, **the gain from trade is increased world output and a higher standard of living in all trading countries.** This is the essential message of the *theory of comparative advantage.*

Production and Consumption without Trade

Consider the production and consumption possibilities of just two countries—say, the United States and France. For the sake of illustration, assume that both countries produce only two goods: bread and wine. Let's also set aside worries about the law of diminishing returns and the substitutability of resources, thus transforming the familiar **production possibilities** curve into a straight line, as in Figure 21.1.

The "curves" in Figure 21.1 suggest that the United States is capable of producing much more bread than France. With our greater abundance of labor, land, and other resources, we assume that the United States is capable of producing up to 100 zillion loaves of bread per year. To do so, we'd have to devote all our resources to that purpose. This capability is indicated by point *A* in Figure 21.1a and in row *A* of the accompanying production possibilities schedule.

France (Figure 21.1b), on the other hand, confronts a *maximum* bread production of only 15 zillion loaves per year (point *G*) because it has little available land, less fuel, and fewer potential workers.

The capacities of the two countries for wine production are 50 zillion barrels for us (point *F*) and 60 zillion for France (point *L*), largely reflecting France's greater experience in tending vines. Both countries are also capable of producing alternative *combinations* of bread and wine, as evidenced by their respective production possibilities curves (points *A–F* for the United States and *G–L* for France).

A nation that doesn't trade with other countries is called a **closed economy.** In the absence of contact with the outside world, the production possibilities curve for a closed economy also defines its **consumption possibilities.** Without imports, a country cannot consume more than it produces. Thus the only immediate issue in a closed economy is which mix of output to choose—*what* to produce and consume—out of the domestic choices available.

Assume that Americans choose point *D* on their production possibilities curve, producing and consuming 40 zillion loaves of bread and 30 zillion barrels of wine. The French, on the other hand, prefer the mix of output represented by point *I* on their production

production possibilities: The alternative combinations of final goods and services that could be produced in a given period with all available resources and technology.

closed economy: A nation that doesn't engage in international trade.

consumption possibilities: The alternative combinations of goods and services that a country could consume in a given time period.

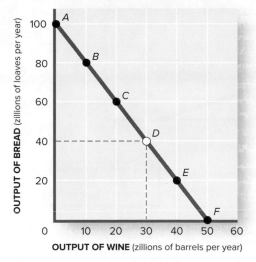

(a) U.S. production possibilities

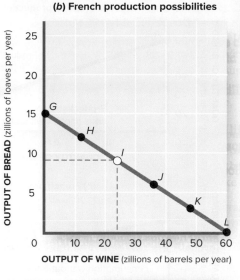

(b) French production possibilities

In a closed economy, production possibilities and consumption possibilities are identical.

FIGURE 21.1

Consumption Possibilities without Trade

In the absence of trade, a country's consumption possibilities are identical to its production possibilities. The assumed production possibilities of the United States and France are illustrated in the graphs and the corresponding schedules. Before entering into trade, the United States chose to produce and consume at point *D,* with 40 zillion loaves of bread and 30 zillion barrels of wine. France chose point *I* on its own production possibilities curve. By trading, each country hopes to increase its consumption beyond these levels.

	U.S. Production Possibilities				French Production Possibilities		
	Bread (Zillions of Loaves)	+	Wine (Zillions of Barrels)		Bread (Zillions of Loaves)	+	Wine (Zillions of Barrels)
A	100	+	0	G	15	+	0
B	80	+	10	H	12	+	12
C	60	+	20	I	9	+	24
D	40	+	30	J	6	+	36
E	20	+	40	K	3	+	48
F	0	+	50	L	0	+	60

possibilities curve. At that point they produce and consume 9 zillion loaves of bread and 24 zillion barrels of wine.

To assess the potential gain from trade, we must focus the *combined* output of the United States and France. In this case, total world output (points *D* and *I*) comes to 49 zillion loaves of bread and 54 zillion barrels of wine. What we want to know is whether world output would increase if France and the United States abandoned their isolation and started trading. Could either country, or both, consume more output by engaging in a little trade?

Production and Consumption with Trade

Because both countries are saddled with limited production possibilities, trying to eke out a little extra wine and bread from this situation might not appear very promising. Such a conclusion is unwarranted, however. Take another look at the production possibilities confronting the United States, as reproduced in Figure 21.2. Suppose the United States were to produce at point *C* rather than point *D*. At point *C* we could produce 60 zillion loaves of bread and 20 zillion barrels of wine. That combination is clearly *possible* because it lies on the production possibilities curve. We didn't choose that point earlier because we assumed the mix of output at point *D* was preferable. The mix of output at point *C could* be produced, however.

FIGURE 21.2

Consumption Possibilities with Trade

A country can increase its consumption possibilities through international trade. Each country alters its mix of domestic output to produce more of the good it produces best. As it does so, total world output increases, and each country enjoys more consumption. In this case, trade allows U.S. consumption to move from point *D* to point *N*. France moves from point *I* to point *M*.

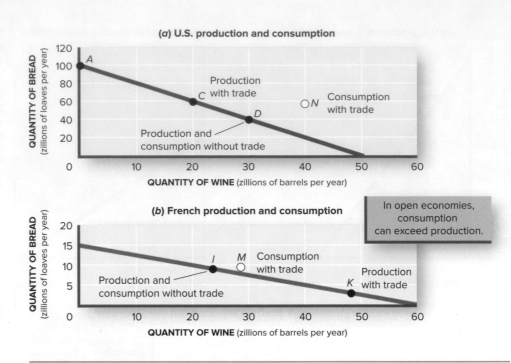

(a) U.S. production and consumption

(b) French production and consumption

In open economies, consumption can exceed production.

We could also change the mix of output in France. Assume that France moved from point *I* to point *K*, producing 48 zillion barrels of wine and only 3 zillion loaves of bread.

Two observations are now called for. The first is simply that output mixes have changed in each country. The second, and more interesting, is that total world output has *increased*. Notice how this works. When the United States and France were at points *D* and *I*, their *combined* output consisted of

A: Initial Production Choices		
	Bread (Zillions of Loaves)	**Wine** (Zillions of Barrels)
United States (at point *D*)	40	30
France (at point *I*)	9	24
Total pre-trade output	49	54

After they moved along their respective production possibilities curves to points *C* and *K*, the combined world output became

B: Revised Production Choices		
	Bread (Zillions of Loaves)	**Wine** (Zillions of Barrels)
United States (at point *C*)	60	20
France (at point *K*)	3	48
Total output with trade	63	68

Total world output has increased by 14 zillion loaves of bread and 14 zillion barrels of wine. *Just by changing the mix of output in each country, we've increased total world output.* This additional output creates the potential for making both countries better off than they were in the absence of trade.

This almost seems like a magic trick, but it isn't. Here's what happened. The United States and France weren't initially producing at points C and K before because they simply didn't want to *consume* those particular output combinations. Nevertheless, our discovery that points C and K allow us to produce *more* output suggests that everybody can consume more goods and services if we change the mix of output in each country. This is our first clue as to how specialization and trade can benefit an **open economy**—a nation that engages in international trade.

open economy: A nation that engages in international trade.

Suppose we Americans are the first to discover the potential benefits from trade. Using Figure 21.2 as our guide, we suggest to the French that they move their mix of output from point *I* to point *K*. As an incentive for making such a move, we promise to give them 6 zillion loaves of bread in exchange for 20 zillion barrels of wine. This would leave them at point *M*, with as much bread to consume as they used to have, plus an extra 4 zillion barrels of wine. At point *I* they had 9 zillion loaves of bread and 24 zillion barrels of wine. At point *M* they can have 9 zillion loaves of bread and 28 zillion barrels of wine. Thus by altering their mix of output (from point *I* to point *K*) and then trading (point *K* to point *M*), the French end up with more goods and services than they had in the beginning. Notice in particular that this new consumption possibility (point *M*) lies *outside* France's domestic production possibilities curve.

The French will be quite pleased with the extra output they get from trading. But where does this leave us? Does France's gain imply a loss for us? Or do we gain from trade as well?

Mutual Gains

As it turns out, *both* the United States and France gain by trading. The United States, too, ends up consuming a mix of output that lies outside our production possibilities curve.

Note that at point C we *produce* 60 zillion loaves of bread per year and 20 zillion barrels of wine. We then *export* 6 zillion loaves to France. This leaves us with 54 zillion loaves of bread to *consume*.

In return for our exported bread, the French give us 20 zillion barrels of wine. These imports, plus our domestic production, permit us to *consume* 40 zillion barrels of wine. Hence we end up consuming at point *N*, enjoying 54 zillion loaves of bread and 40 zillion barrels of wine. Thus by first changing our mix of output (from point *D* to point *C*), then trading (point *C* to point *N*), we end up with 14 zillion more loaves of bread and 10 zillion more barrels of wine than we started with. Time to celebrate! International trade has made us better off, too.

Table 21.4 recaps the gains from trade for both countries. Notice that U.S. imports match French exports and vice versa. Also notice how the ***trade-facilitated consumption in each country exceeds no-trade levels.***

	Production and Consumption with Trade							Production and Consumption with No Trade
	Production	+	Imports	−	Exports	=	Consumption	
United States at	Point C						Point N	Point D
Bread	60	+	0	−	6	=	54 compare	40
Wine	20	+	20	−	0	=	40	30
France at	Point K						Point M	Point I
Bread	3	+	6	−	0	=	9 compare	9
Wine	48	+	0	−	20	=	28	24

TABLE 21.4

Gains from Trade

When nations specialize in production, they can export one good and import another and end up with *more* total goods to consume than they had without trade. In this case, the United States specializes in bread production. Notice how U.S. *consumption* of both goods increases (compare total U.S. consumption of bread and wine at point *N* [with trade] to consumption at point *D* [no trade]).

All these numbers do indeed look like some kind of magic trick, but there's no sleight of hand going on here; the gains from trade are due to specialization in production. When each country goes it alone, it's a prisoner of its own production possibilities curve; it must make production decisions on the basis of its own consumption desires. When international trade is permitted, however, each country can concentrate on the exploitation of its production capabilities. *Each country produces those goods it makes best and then trades with other countries to acquire the goods it desires to consume.*

The resultant specialization increases total world output. In the process, each country is able to escape the confines of its own production possibilities curve, to reach beyond it for a larger basket of consumption goods. *When a country engages in international trade, its consumption possibilities always exceed its production possibilities.* These enhanced consumption possibilities are emphasized by the positions of points *N* and *M outside* the production possibilities curves (Figure 21.2). If it weren't possible for countries to increase their consumption by trading, there'd be no incentive for trading, and thus no trade.

PURSUIT OF COMPARATIVE ADVANTAGE

Although international trade can make everyone better off, it's not so obvious which goods should be traded, or on what terms. In our previous illustration, the United States ended up trading bread for wine in terms that were decidedly favorable to us. Why did we export bread rather than wine, and how did we end up getting such a good deal?

Opportunity Costs

comparative advantage: The ability of a country to produce a specific good at a lower opportunity cost than its trading partners.

opportunity cost: The most desired goods or services that are forgone in order to obtain something else.

The decision to export bread is based on **comparative advantage**—that is, the *relative* cost of producing different goods. Recall that we can produce a maximum of 100 zillion loaves of bread per year or 50 zillion barrels of wine. Thus the domestic **opportunity cost** of producing 100 zillion loaves of bread is the 50 zillion barrels of wine we forsake in order to devote all our resources to bread production. In fact, at every point on the U.S. production possibilities curve (Figure 21.2a), the opportunity cost of a loaf of bread is ½ barrel of wine. We're effectively paying half a barrel of wine to get a loaf of bread.

Although the cost of bread production in the United States might appear outrageous, even higher opportunity costs prevail in France. According to Figure 21.2b, the opportunity cost of producing a loaf of bread in France is a staggering 4 barrels of wine. To produce a loaf of bread, the French must use factors of production that could otherwise be used to produce 4 barrels of wine.

Comparative Advantage. A comparison of the opportunity costs prevailing in each country exposes the nature of comparative advantage. The United States has a comparative advantage in bread production because less wine has to be given up to produce bread in the United States than in France. In other words, the opportunity costs of bread production are lower in the United States than in France. *Comparative advantage refers to the relative (opportunity) costs of producing particular goods.*

A country should specialize in what it's *relatively* efficient at producing—that is, goods for which it has the lowest opportunity costs. In this case, the United States should produce bread because its opportunity cost (½ barrel of wine) is less than France's (4 barrels of wine). Were you the production manager for the whole world, you'd certainly want each country to exploit its relative abilities, thus maximizing world output. Each country can arrive at that same decision itself by comparing its own opportunity costs to those prevailing elsewhere. *World output, and thus the potential gains from trade, will be maximized when each country pursues its comparative advantage. To do so, each country*

* *Exports goods with relatively low opportunity costs.*
* *Imports goods with relatively high opportunity costs.*

That's the kind of situation depicted in Table 21.4.

Absolute Costs Don't Count

In assessing the nature of comparative advantage, notice that we needn't know anything about the actual costs involved in production. Have you seen any data suggesting how much labor, land, or capital is required to produce a loaf of bread in either France or the United States? For all you and I know, the French may be able to produce both bread and wine with fewer resources than we're using. Such an **absolute advantage** in production might exist because of their much longer experience in cultivating both grapes and wheat or simply because they have more talent.

We can envy such productivity, and even try to emulate it, but it shouldn't alter our production or trade decisions. All we really care about are *opportunity costs*—what *we* have to give up in order to get more of a desired good. If we can get a barrel of wine for less bread in trade than in production, we have a comparative advantage in producing bread. As long as we have a *comparative* advantage in bread production, we should exploit it. It doesn't matter to us whether France could produce either good with fewer resources. For that matter, even if France had an absolute advantage in *both* goods, we'd still have a *comparative* advantage in bread production, as we've already confirmed. The absolute costs of production were omitted from the previous illustration because they were irrelevant.

To clarify the distinction between absolute advantage and comparative advantage, consider this example. When Charlie Osgood joined the Willamette Warriors football team, he was the fastest runner ever to play football in Willamette. He could also throw the ball farther than most people could see. In other words, he had an *absolute advantage* in both throwing and running. Charlie would have made the greatest quarterback or the greatest end ever to play football. *Would have.* The problem was that he could play only one position at a time. Thus the Willamette coach had to play Charlie either as a quarterback or as an end. He reasoned that Charlie could throw only a bit farther than some of the other top quarterbacks but could far outdistance all the other ends. In other words, Charlie had a *comparative advantage* in running and was assigned to play as an end.

absolute advantage: The ability of a country to produce a specific good with fewer resources (per unit of output) than other countries.

TERMS OF TRADE

It definitely pays to pursue one's comparative advantage by specializing in production. It may not yet be clear, however, how we got such a good deal with France. We're clever traders; but beyond that, is there any way to determine the **terms of trade**—the quantity of good A that must be given up in exchange for good B? In our previous illustration, the terms of trade were very favorable to us; we exchanged only 6 zillion loaves of bread for 20 zillion barrels of wine (Table 21.4). The terms of trade were thus 6 loaves = 20 barrels.

terms of trade: The rate at which goods are exchanged; the amount of good A given up for good B in trade.

Limits to the Terms of Trade

The terms of trade with France were determined by our offer and France's ready acceptance. But why did France accept those terms? France was willing to accept our offer because the terms of trade permitted France to increase its wine consumption without giving up any bread consumption. Our offer of 6 loaves for 20 barrels was an improvement over France's domestic opportunity costs. France's domestic possibilities required it to give up 24 barrels of wine in order to produce 6 loaves of bread (see Figure 21.2b). Getting bread via trade was simply cheaper for France than producing bread at home. France ended up with an extra 4 zillion barrels of wine (take another look at the last two columns in Table 21.4).

Our first clue to the terms of trade, then, lies in each country's domestic opportunity costs. *A country won't trade unless the terms of trade are superior to domestic opportunities.* In our example, the opportunity cost of 1 barrel of wine in the United States is 2 loaves of bread. Accordingly, we won't *export* bread unless we get at least 1 barrel of wine in exchange for every 2 loaves of bread we ship overseas.

All countries want to gain from trade. Hence we can predict that *the terms of trade between any two countries will lie somewhere between their respective opportunity costs in production.* That is, a loaf of bread in international trade will be worth at least ½ barrel of

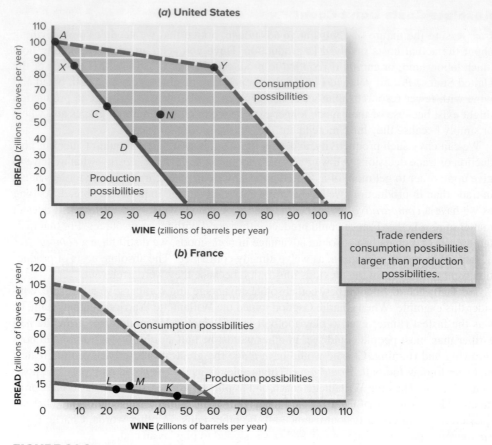

FIGURE 21.3

Searching for the Terms of Trade

Assume the United States can produce 100 zillion loaves of bread per year (point *A*). If we reduce output to only 85 zillion loaves, we could move to point *X*. At point *X* we have 7.5 zillion barrels of wine and 85 zillion loaves of bread.

Trade increases consumption possibilities. If we continued to produce 100 zillion loaves of bread, we could trade 15 zillion loaves to France in exchange for as much as 60 zillion barrels of wine. This would leave us *producing* at point *A* but *consuming* at point *Y*. At point *Y* we have more wine and no less bread than we had at point *X*. This is our motivation to trade.

A country will end up on its consumption possibilities curve only if it gets *all* the gains from trade. It will remain on its production possibilities curve only if it gets *none* of the gains from trade. The terms of trade determine how the gains from trade are distributed, and thus at what point in the shaded area each country ends up.

Note: The kink in the consumption possibilities curve at point Y occurs because France is unable to produce more than 60 zillion barrels of wine.

---

wine (the U.S. opportunity cost), but no more than 4 barrels (the French opportunity cost). In our example, the terms of trade ended up at 1 loaf = 3.33 barrels (that is, at 6 loaves = 20 barrels). This represented a very large gain for the United States and a small gain for France. Figure 21.3 illustrates this outcome and several other possibilities.

The Role of Markets and Prices

Relatively little trade is subject to such direct negotiations between countries. More often than not, the decision to import or export a particular good is left up to the market decisions of individual consumers and producers.

Individual consumers and producers aren't much impressed by such abstractions as comparative advantage. Market participants tend to focus on prices, always trying to allocate their resources in order to maximize profits or personal satisfaction. Consumers tend to buy the products that deliver the most utility per dollar of expenditure, while producers try to get the most output per dollar of cost. Everybody's looking for a bargain.

So what does this have to do with international trade? Well, suppose that Henri, an enterprising Frenchman, visited the United States before the advent of international trade. He observed that bread was relatively cheap while wine was relatively expensive—the opposite of the price relationship prevailing in France. These price comparisons brought to his mind the opportunity for making a fast euro. All he had to do was bring over some French wine and trade it in the United States for a large quantity of bread. Then he could return to France and exchange the bread for a greater quantity of wine. *Alors!* Were he to do this a few times, he'd amass substantial profits.

Henri's entrepreneurial exploits will not only enrich him but will also move each country toward its comparative advantage. The United States ends up exporting bread to France, and France ends up exporting wine to the United States, exactly as the theory of comparative advantage suggests. The activating agent isn't the Ministry of Trade and its 620 trained economists but simply one enterprising French trader. He's aided and encouraged, of course, by consumers and producers in each country. American consumers are happy to trade their bread for his wines. They thereby end up paying less for wine (in terms of bread) than they'd otherwise have to. In other words, the terms of trade Henri offers are more attractive than the prevailing (domestic) relative prices. On the other side of the Atlantic, Henri's welcome is equally warm. French consumers are able to get a better deal by trading their wine for his imported bread than by trading with the local bakers.

Even some producers are happy. The wheat farmers and bakers in the United States are eager to deal with Henri. He's willing to buy a lot of bread and even to pay a premium price for it. Indeed, bread production has become so profitable in the United States that a lot of people who used to grow and mash grapes are now growing wheat and kneading dough. This alters the mix of U.S. output in the direction of more bread, exactly as suggested in Figure 21.2*a*.

In France the opposite kind of production shift is taking place. French wheat farmers are planting more grape vines so they can take advantage of Henri's generous purchases. Thus Henri is able to lead each country in the direction of its comparative advantage while raking in a substantial profit for himself along the way.

Where the terms of trade and the volume of exports and imports end up depends partly on how good a trader Henri is. It will also depend on the behavior of the thousands of individual consumers and producers who participate in the market exchanges. In other words, trade flows depend on both the supply and the demand for bread and wine in each country. ***The terms of trade, like the price of any good, depend on the willingness of market participants to buy or sell at various prices.*** All we know for sure is that the terms of trade will end up somewhere between the limits set by each country's opportunity costs.

PROTECTIONIST PRESSURES

Although the potential gains from world trade are impressive, not everyone will be cheering at the Franco–American trade celebration. On the contrary, some people will be upset about the trade routes that Henri has established. They'll not only boycott the celebration but actively seek to discourage us from continuing to trade with France.

Microeconomic Pressures

Consider, for example, the winegrowers in western New York. Do you think they're going to be happy about Henri's entrepreneurship? Americans can now buy wine more cheaply from France than they can from New York. Before long we may hear talk about unfair foreign competition or about the greater nutritional value of American grapes (see World View "U.S. Winemakers Hurt by Imported Wine"). The New York winegrowers may also emphasize the importance of maintaining an adequate grape supply and a strong wine industry at home, just in case of terrorist attacks.

U.S. WINEMAKERS HURT BY IMPORTED WINE

American consumers are increasingly sipping imported wines. Although the domestic wine industry continues to grow at a respectable pace, imported wines are taking an increasing share of the U.S. market. Sales of domestic wines grew 5.4 percent in 2016, while sales of imports from France surged 16.1 percent, from New Zealand 15.4 percent, and Italy 6.2 percent. As the U.S. dollar continues to strengthen, domestic wine producers faced increasing price competition. They say foreign producers are also aided by unfair tax, marketing, and export subsidies that put U.S. winemakers at a disadvantage. California growers took nearly 30,000 acres out of production last year, planting almonds and avocados in the former vineyards.

Source: Media and industry reports, February 2017.

ANALYSIS: Although trade increases consumption possibilities, imports typically compete with a domestic industry. The affected industries will try to restrict imports in order to preserve their own jobs and incomes.

Import-Competing Industries. Joining with the growers will be the farmworkers and the other merchants whose livelihood depends on the New York wine industry. If they're clever enough, the growers will also get the governor of the state to join their demonstration. After all, the governor must recognize the needs of his people, and his people definitely don't include the wheat farmers in Kansas who are making a bundle from international trade, much less French vintners. New York consumers are of course benefiting from lower wine prices, but they're unlikely to demonstrate over a few cents a bottle. On the other hand, those few extra pennies translate into millions of dollars for domestic wine producers.

The wheat farmers in France are no happier about international trade than are the winegrowers in the United States. They'd dearly love to sink all those boats bringing cheap wheat from America, thereby protecting their own market position.

If we're to make sense of trade policies, then, we must recognize one central fact of life: Some producers have a vested interest in restricting international trade. In particular, ***workers and producers who compete with imported products—who work in import-competing industries—have an economic interest in restricting trade.*** This helps explain why GM, Ford, and Chrysler are unhappy about auto imports and why shoe workers in Massachusetts want to end the importation of Italian shoes. It also explains why textile producers in South Carolina think China is behaving irresponsibly when it sells cheap cotton shirts and dresses in the United States.

Export Industries. Although imports typically mean fewer jobs and less income for some domestic industries, exports represent increased jobs and income for other industries. Producers and workers in export industries gain from trade. Thus on a microeconomic level there are identifiable gainers and losers from international trade. ***Trade not only alters the mix of output but also redistributes income from import-competing industries to export industries.*** This potential redistribution is the source of political and economic friction.

Net Gain. We must be careful to note, however, that the microeconomic gains from trade are greater than the microeconomic losses. It's not simply a question of robbing Peter to enrich Paul. We must remind ourselves that consumers enjoy a higher standard of living as a result of international trade. As we saw earlier, trade increases world efficiency and total output. Accordingly, we end up slicing up a larger pie rather than just reslicing the same old smaller pie.

The gains from trade will mean little to workers who end up with a smaller slice of the (larger) pie. It's important to remember, however, that the gains from trade are large enough to make everybody better off. Whether we actually choose to distribute the gains from trade in this way is a separate question, to which we shall return shortly. Note here, however, that ***trade restrictions designed to protect specific microeconomic interests reduce the total gains from trade.*** Trade restrictions leave us with a smaller pie to split up.

Additional Pressures

Import-competing industries are the principal obstacle to expanded international trade. Selfish micro interests aren't the only source of trade restrictions, however. Other arguments are also used to restrict trade.

National Security. The national security argument for trade restrictions is twofold. We can't depend on foreign suppliers to provide us with essential defense-related goods, it is said, because that would leave us vulnerable in time of war. The machine tool industry used this argument to protect itself from imports. In 1991 the Pentagon again sided with the toolmakers, citing the need for the United States to "gear up military production quickly in case of war," a contingency that couldn't be assured if weapons manufacturers relied on imported lathes, milling machines, and other tools. After the September 11, 2001, terrorist attacks on the World Trade Center and Pentagon, U.S. farmers convinced Congress to safeguard the nation's food supply with additional subsidies. The steel industry emphasized the importance of not depending on foreign suppliers.

Dumping. Another argument against free trade arises from the practice of **dumping.** Foreign producers "dump" their goods when they sell them in the United States at prices lower than those prevailing in their own country, perhaps even below the costs of production.

dumping: The sale of goods in export markets at prices below domestic prices.

Dumping may be unfair to import-competing producers, but it isn't necessarily unwelcome to the rest of us. As long as foreign producers continue dumping, we're getting foreign products at low prices. How bad can that be? There's a legitimate worry, however. Foreign producers might hold prices down only until domestic producers are driven out of business. Then we might be compelled to pay the foreign producers higher prices for their products. In that case, dumping could consolidate market power and lead to monopoly-type pricing. The fear of dumping, then, is analogous to the fear of predatory pricing.

The potential costs of dumping are serious. It's not always easy to determine when dumping occurs, however. Those who compete with imports have an uncanny ability to associate any and all low prices with predatory dumping. The United States has used dumping *charges* to restrict imports of Chinese shrimp, furniture, lingerie, solar panels, and other products in which China has an evident comparative advantage. The Chinese have retaliated with dozens of their own dumping investigations, including the fiber optic cable case. As World View "U.S. Slaps China with Huge Anti-Dumping Tariffs" explains, such actions slow imports and protect domestic producers.

WORLD VIEW

U.S. SLAPS CHINA WITH HUGE ANTI-DUMPING TARIFFS

After a year-long investigation, the International Trade Administration yesterday announced a five-fold increase in tariffs on imported Chinese steel. The new tariff of 265.79 percent will make Chinese steel imports prohibitively expensive. This was good news for U.S. steel producers, who had asked the ITA for tariff relief, claiming that China was unfairly subsidizing its steel exports. The resultant dumping of Chinese steel had forced domestic steelmakers to close factories and eliminate 12,000 jobs they claimed. The new tariffs apply to cold-rolled flat steel that is used to manufacture appliances, cars, electric motors, containers, and in construction. Last year, over $270 million of that steel was imported from China. China's Commerce Ministry called the move "irrational" and said it would harm cooperation between the two countries.

Source: Media reports, March 2, 2016.

ANALYSIS: *Dumping* means that a foreign producer is selling exports at prices below cost or below prices in the home market, putting import-competing industries at a competitive disadvantage. *Accusations* of dumping are an effective trade barrier.

Infant Industries. Actual dumping threatens to damage already established domestic industries. Even normal import prices, however, may make it difficult or impossible for a new domestic industry to develop. Infant industries are often burdened with abnormally high start-up costs. These high costs may arise from the need to train a whole workforce and the expenses of establishing new marketing channels. With time to grow, however, an infant industry might experience substantial cost reductions and establish a comparative advantage. When this is the case, trade restrictions might help nurture an industry in its infancy. Trade restrictions are justified, however, only if there's tangible evidence that the industry can develop a comparative advantage reasonably quickly.

Improving the Terms of Trade. A final argument for restricting trade rests on how the gains from trade are distributed. As we observed, the distribution of the gains from trade depends on the terms of trade. If we were to buy fewer imports, foreign producers might lower their prices. If that happened, the terms of trade would move in our favor, and we'd end up with a larger share of the gains from trade.

One way to bring about this sequence of events is to put restrictions on imports, making it more difficult or expensive for Americans to buy foreign products. Such restrictions will reduce the volume of imports, thereby inducing foreign producers to lower their prices. Unfortunately, this strategy can easily backfire. Retaliatory restrictions on imports, each designed to improve the terms of trade, will ultimately eliminate all trade and therewith all the gains people were competing for in the first place.

BARRIERS TO TRADE

The microeconomic losses associated with imports give rise to a constant clamor for trade restrictions. People whose jobs and incomes are threatened by international trade tend to organize quickly and air their grievances. World View "Irish Farmers Block Barley Imports" depicts the efforts of barley farmers in Ireland to block imports of German barley. They wanted their government to impose restrictions on imports. More often than not, governments grant the wishes of these well-organized and well-financed special interests.

WORLD VIEW

IRISH FARMERS BLOCK BARLEY IMPORTS

Drogheda—Barley farmers blocked the unloading of imported barley at the port here. Joe Healy, president of the Irish Farmers Association, said "the future of grain farming in Ireland is at stake." With grain incomes at records lows, farmers see imports as a threat to their survival. Healy said barley imports—used in beer production—were "unnecessary" when there are plentiful supplies of "quality native grain" available. He pleaded for public support to restrict continuing barley imports.

Source: Media reports, August 24–26, 2016.

ANALYSIS: Import-competing industries cite lots of reasons for restricting trade. Their primary concern, however, is to protect their own jobs and profits.

Embargoes

embargo: A prohibition on exports or imports.

The surefire way to restrict trade is simply to eliminate it. To do so, a country need only impose an embargo on exports or imports, or both. An **embargo** is nothing more than a prohibition against trading particular goods.

In 1951 Senator Joseph McCarthy convinced the U.S. Senate to impose an embargo on Soviet mink, fox, and five other furs. He argued that such imports helped finance world communism. Senator McCarthy also represented the state of Wisconsin, where most U.S. minks are raised. The Reagan administration tried to end the fur embargo in 1987 but met with stiff congressional opposition. By then U.S. mink ranchers had developed a $120 million per year industry.

The United States has also maintained an embargo on Cuban goods since 1959, when Fidel Castro took power there. This embargo severely damaged Cuba's sugar industry and deprived American smokers of the famed Havana cigars. It also fostered the development of U.S. sugar beet and tobacco farmers, who now have a vested interest in maintaining the embargo.

Tariffs

A more frequent trade restriction is a **tariff,** a special tax imposed on imported goods. Tariffs, also called *customs duties,* were once the principal source of revenue for governments. In the 18th century, tariffs on tea, glass, wine, lead, and paper were imposed on the American colonies to provide extra revenue for the British government. The tariff on tea led to the Boston Tea Party in 1773 and gave added momentum to the American independence movement.

In modern times, tariffs have been used primarily as a means to protect specific industries from import competition. The current U.S. tariff code specifies tariffs on more than 9,000 different products—nearly 50 percent of all U.S. imports. Although the average tariff is less than 5 percent, individual tariffs vary widely. The tariff on cars, for example, is only 2.5 percent, while cotton sweaters confront a 17.8 percent tariff. As World View "U.S. Slaps China with Huge Anti-Dumping Tariffs" noted, the tariff on Chinese steel is a whopping 265.79 percent!

The attraction of tariffs to import-competing industries should be obvious. *A tariff on imported goods makes them more expensive to domestic consumers and thus less competitive with domestically produced goods.* Among familiar tariffs in effect in 2017 were 50 cents per gallon on Scotch whisky and 76 cents per gallon on imported champagne. These tariffs made American-produced spirits look relatively cheap and thus contributed to higher sales and profits for domestic distillers and grape growers. In the same manner, imported baby food is taxed at 34.6 percent, maple sugar at 9.4 percent, golf shoes at 8.5 percent, and imported sailboats at 1.5 percent. In 2009 President Obama imposed a 35 percent tariff on imported Chinese tires and a 26 percent tariff on Chinese solar panels in 2014. In 2017, President Trump announced a 24 percent tariff on Canadian lumber. In each case, domestic producers in import-competing industries gain. The losers are domestic consumers, who end up paying higher prices. The tariff on orange juice, for example, raises the price of drinking orange juice by $525 million a year. The tariff on Canadian lumber raises the price of a new home by $3,000. Tariffs also hurt foreign producers, who lose business, and world efficiency, as trade is reduced. These potential victims of trade protection rallied in 2017 to resist President Trump's proposal for a "border-adjustment tax," an across-the-board tariff, combined with a blanket export subsidy (see In the News "A Border-Adjustment Tax?").

tariff: A tax (duty) imposed on imported goods.

IN THE NEWS

A BORDER-ADJUSTMENT TAX?

When he first took office, President Trump expressed a lot of enthusiasm for a "border-adjustment" tax that would bring more jobs back to America. House Speaker Paul Ryan likes the idea as well and has made it part of the Republican's tax-reform plan. In the House version, a 20 percent tax would be imposed on all imports and U.S. exports would get a 20 percent tax subsidy. This would cut imports, promote exports, and create even more jobs at home.

Or, so the theory goes. U.S. retailers are horrified at the thought. Companies like Walmart import most of their inventory; raising the prices on that inventory by 20 percent would destroy Walmart's competitive position. Retailers point out that 97 percent of all the clothes sold in America are imported, as are 98 percent of the shoes. Higher import taxes would depress retail sales and force layoffs throughout the industry.

After meeting with retail executives last week, President Trump seemed to cool to the idea of a border-adjustment tax.

Source: Media and industry reports, February 2017.

ANALYSIS: A border-adjustment tax is a combined import tariff and export subsidy. It helps exporters but hurts importers and the consumers who purchase those goods.

"Beggar Thy Neighbor." Microeconomic interests aren't the only source of pressure for tariff protection. Imports represent leakage from the domestic circular flow and a potential loss of jobs at home. From this perspective, reducing imports looks like an easy solution to the problem of domestic unemployment. Just get people to "buy American" instead of buying imported products, so the argument goes, and domestic output and employment will surely expand. President Obama used this argument to include "buy American" rules in his 2009 stimulus package. President Trump was even more insistent about "bringing jobs home" by restricting imports and signing "buy American" orders.

Congressman Willis Hawley used this same argument in 1930. He assured his colleagues that higher tariffs would "bring about the growth and development in this country that has followed every other tariff bill, bringing as it does a new prosperity in which all people, in all sections, will increase their comforts, their enjoyment, and their happiness."[1] Congress responded by passing the Smoot-Hawley Tariff Act of 1930, which raised tariffs to an average of nearly 60 percent, effectively cutting off most imports.

Tariffs designed to expand domestic employment are more likely to fail than to succeed. If a tariff wall does stem the flow of imports, it effectively transfers the unemployment problem to other countries, a phenomenon often referred to as "beggar thy neighbor." The resultant loss of business in other countries leaves them less able to purchase our exports. The imported unemployment also creates intense political pressures for retaliatory action. That's exactly what happened in the 1930s. Other countries erected trade barriers to compensate for the effects of the Smoot-Hawley tariff. World trade subsequently fell from $60 billion in 1928 to a mere $25 billion in 1938. This trade contraction increased the severity of the Great Depression (see World View " 'Beggar-Thy-Neighbor' Policies in the 1930s").

WORLD VIEW

"BEGGAR-THY-NEIGHBOR" POLICIES IN THE 1930S

President Herbert Hoover signed the Smoot-Hawley Tariff Act on June 17, 1930, despite the pleas from 1,028 economists to veto it. The Act raised the effective tariff on imports by 50 percent between 1929 and 1932. Although designed to limit import competition and boost domestic employment, the Act triggered quick retaliation from America's trading partners:

- Spain passed the Wais tariff in July in reaction to U.S. tariffs on grapes, oranges, cork, and onions.
- Switzerland, objecting to new U.S. tariffs on watches, embroideries, and shoes, boycotted American exports.
- Italy retaliated against tariffs on hats and olive oil with high tariffs on U.S. and French automobiles in June 1930.
- Canada reacted to high duties on many food products, logs, and timber by raising tariffs threefold in August 1932.
- Australia, Cuba, France, Mexico, and New Zealand also joined in the tariff wars.

From 1930 to 1931 U.S. imports dropped 29 percent, but U.S. exports fell even more, 33 percent, and continued their collapse to a modern-day low of $2.4 billion in 1933. World trade contracted by similar proportions, spreading unemployment around the globe.

In 1934 the U.S. Congress passed the Reciprocal Trade Agreements Act to empower the president to reduce tariffs by half the 1930 rates in return for like cuts in foreign duties on U.S. goods. The "beggar-thy-neighbor" policy was dead. Since then, the nations of the world have been reducing tariffs and other trade barriers.

Source: " 'Beggar-Thy-Neighbor' Policies in the 1930s," *World Development Report 1987,* p. 139, Box 8.4.

ANALYSIS: Tariffs inflict harm on foreign producers. If foreign countries retaliate with tariffs of their own, world trade will shrink and unemployment will increase in all countries.

[1]*The New York Times,* June 15, 1930, p. 25.

The same kind of macroeconomic threat surfaced in 2009. The "buy American" provisions introduced by the Obama administration angered foreign nations that would lose export sales. When they threatened to retaliate with trade barriers of their own, President Obama had to offer reassurances about America's commitment to "free trade."

Quotas

Tariffs reduce the flow of imports by raising import prices. The same outcome can be attained more directly by imposing import **quotas,** numerical restrictions on the quantity of a particular good that may be imported. The United States limits the quantity of ice cream imported from Jamaica to 950 gallons a year. Only 1.4 million kilograms of Australian cheddar cheese and no more than 7,730 tons of Haitian sugar can be imported. Textile quotas are imposed on every country that wants to ship textiles to the U.S. market. According to the U.S. Department of State, approximately 12 percent of our imports are subject to import quotas.

quota: A limit on the quantity of a good that may be imported in a given time period.

Comparative Effects

Quotas, like all barriers to trade, reduce world efficiency and invite retaliatory action. Moreover, their impact can be even more damaging than tariffs. To see this, we may compare market outcomes in four different contexts: no trade, free trade, tariff-restricted trade, and quota-restricted trade.

No-Trade Equilibrium. Figure 21.4*a* depicts the supply-and-demand relationships that would prevail in an economy that imposed a trade *embargo* on foreign textiles. In this situation, the **equilibrium price** of textiles is completely determined by domestic demand and supply curves. The no-trade equilibrium price is p_1, and the quantity of textiles consumed is q_1.

equilibrium price: The price at which the quantity of a good demanded in a given time period equals the quantity supplied.

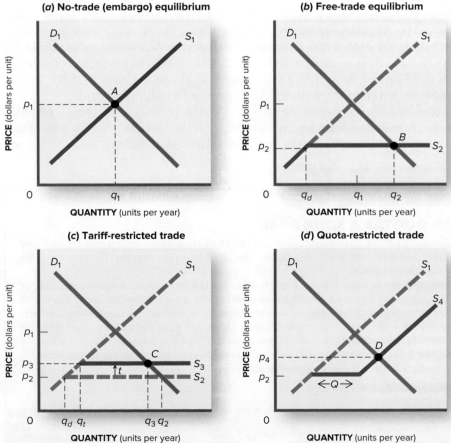

(a) No-trade (embargo) equilibrium

(b) Free-trade equilibrium

(c) Tariff-restricted trade

(d) Quota-restricted trade

FIGURE 21.4

The Impact of Trade Restrictions

In the *absence of trade,* the domestic price and sales of a good will be determined by domestic supply and demand curves (point *A* in part *a*). Once trade is permitted, the market supply curve will be altered by the availability of imports. With *free trade* and unlimited availability of imports at price p_2, a new market equilibrium will be established at world prices (point *B*).

Tariffs raise domestic prices and reduce the quantity sold (point *C*). *Quotas* put an absolute limit on imported sales and thus give domestic producers a great opportunity to raise the market price (point *D*).

Free-Trade Equilibrium. Suppose now that the embargo is lifted. The immediate effect of this decision will be a rightward shift of the market supply curve, as foreign supplies are added to domestic supplies (Figure 21.4*b*). If an unlimited quantity of textiles can be bought in world markets at a price of p_2, the new supply curve will look like S_2 (infinitely elastic at p_2). The new supply curve (S_2) intersects the old demand curve (D_1) at a new equilibrium price of p_2 and an expanded consumption of q_2. At this new equilibrium, domestic producers are supplying the quantity q_d while foreign producers are supplying the rest ($q_2 - q_d$). Comparing the new equilibrium to the old one, we see that *free trade results in reduced prices and increased consumption.*

Domestic textile producers are unhappy, of course, with their foreign competition. In the absence of trade, the domestic producers would sell more output (q_1) and get higher prices (p_1). Once trade is opened up, the willingness of foreign producers to sell unlimited quantities of textiles at the price p_2 puts a lid on domestic prices. Domestic producers hate this.

Tariff-Restricted Trade. Figure 21.4*c* illustrates what would happen to prices and sales if the United Textile Producers were successful in persuading the government to impose a tariff. Assume that the tariff raises imported textile prices from p_2 to p_3, making it more difficult for foreign producers to undersell domestic producers. Domestic production expands from q_d to q_t, imports are reduced from $q_2 - q_d$ to $q_3 - q_t$, and the market price of textiles rises. Domestic textile producers are clearly better off. So is the U.S. Treasury, which will collect increased tariff revenues. Unfortunately, domestic consumers are worse off (higher prices), as are foreign producers (reduced sales).

Quota-Restricted Trade. Now consider the impact of a textile *quota*. Suppose we eliminate tariffs but decree that imports can't exceed the quantity Q. Because the quantity of imports can never exceed Q, the supply curve is effectively shifted to the right by that amount. The new curve S_4 (Figure 21.4*d*) indicates that no imports will occur below the world price p_2 and above that price the quantity Q will be imported. Thus the *domestic* demand curve determines subsequent prices. Foreign producers are precluded from selling greater quantities as prices rise further. This outcome is in marked contrast to that of tariff-restricted trade (Figure 21.4*c*), which at least permits foreign producers to respond to rising prices. Accordingly, *quotas are a greater threat to competition than tariffs because quotas preclude additional imports at any price.* The actual quotas on textile imports raise the prices of shirts, towels, and other textile products by 58 percent. As a result, a $10 shirt ends up costing consumers $15.80. All told, U.S. consumers end up paying an extra $25 billion a year for textile products.

The sugar industry is one of the greatest beneficiaries of quota restrictions. By limiting imports to 15 percent of domestic consumption, sugar quotas keep U.S. prices artificially high (see In the News "Sugar Quotas a Sour Deal"). This costs consumers nearly $3 billion a

IN THE NEWS

SUGAR QUOTAS A SOUR DEAL

The Sugar Act of 1934 gave sugar growers a sweet treat—a quota on the amount of sugar that could be imported into the United States. The 2014 Farm Bill kept that quota in place for at least another five years.

By restricting the amount of sugar imported into the U.S., the quotas keep domestic sugar prices high— about 17 cent s a pound above world prices. That's a sweet deal for the 4,700 U.S. sugar farmers (mostly beet sugar) but a sour deal for U.S. consumers and manufacturers, who pay more for all sugar products. U.S. candy producers have cut thousands of jobs and moved manufacturing plants to Canada and elsewhere, where sugar is cheaper. Analysts estimate that 3 manufacturing jobs have been lost for every 1 sugar job saved and consumers are paying $3 billion a year in higher sugar prices.

Source: Industry and media reports, 2016–2017.

ANALYSIS: Import quotas preclude increased foreign competition when domestic prices rise. Protected domestic producers enjoy higher prices and profits while consumers pay higher prices.

year in higher prices. Candy and soda producers lose sales and profits. According to the U.S. Department of Commerce, more than 6,000 jobs have been lost in sugar-using industries (e.g., candy manufacturing) due to high sugar costs. Hershey alone closed plants in Pennsylvania, Colorado, and California and moved candy production to Canada. Foreign sugar producers (mainly in poor nations) also lose sales, profits, and jobs. Who gains? Domestic sugar producers—who, coincidentally, are highly concentrated in key electoral states like Florida.

Voluntary Restraint Agreements

A slight variant of quotas has been used in recent years. Rather than impose quotas on imports, the U.S. government asks foreign producers to "voluntarily" limit their exports. These so-called **voluntary restraint agreements** have been negotiated with producers in Japan, South Korea, Taiwan, China, the European Union, and other countries. Korea, for example, agreed to reduce its annual shoe exports to the United States from 44 million pairs to 33 million pairs. Taiwan reduced its shoe exports from 156 million pairs to 122 million pairs per year. In 2005 China agreed to slow its exports of clothing, limiting its sales growth to 8–17 percent a year. For their part, the Japanese agreed to reduce sales of color TV sets in the United States from 2.8 million to 1.75 million per year. In 2006 Mexico agreed to limit its cement exports to the United States to 3 million tons a year. In 2014 Mexico also agreed to curtail its sugar exports to the United States, forsaking its unique treaty rights to unrestricted exports.

> **voluntary restraint agreement (VRA):** An agreement to reduce the volume of trade in a specific good; a "voluntary" quota.

All these voluntary export restraints, as they're often called, represent an informal type of quota. The only difference is that they're negotiated rather than imposed. But these differences are lost on consumers, who end up paying higher prices for these goods. The voluntary limit on Japanese auto exports to the United States alone cost consumers $15.7 billion in only four years.

Nontariff Barriers

Tariffs and quotas are the most visible barriers to trade, but they're only the tip of the iceberg. Indeed, the variety of protectionist measures that have been devised is testimony to the ingenuity of the human mind. At the turn of the century, the Germans were committed to a most-favored-nation policy: a policy of extending equal treatment to all trading partners. The Germans, however, wanted to lower the tariff on cattle imports from Denmark without extending the same break to Switzerland. Such a preferential tariff would have violated the most-favored-nation policy. Accordingly, the Germans created a new and higher tariff on "brown and dappled cows reared at a level of at least 300 meters above sea level and passing at least one month in every summer at an altitude of at least 800 meters." The new tariff was, of course, applied equally to all countries. But Danish cows never climb that high, so they weren't burdened with the new tariff.

With the decline in tariffs over the last 20 years, nontariff barriers have increased. The United States uses product standards, licensing restrictions, restrictive procurement practices, and other nontariff barriers to restrict roughly 15 percent of imports. In 1999–2000 the European Union banned imports of U.S. beef, arguing that the use of hormones on U.S. ranches created a health hazard for European consumers. Although both the U.S. government and the World Trade Organization disputed that claim, the ban was a highly effective nontariff trade barrier. The United States responded by slapping 100 percent tariffs on dozens of European products.

Mexican Trucks. One of the more flagrant examples of nontariff barriers is the use of safety regulations to block Mexican trucking companies from using U.S. roads to deliver goods. The resulting trade barrier forces Mexican trucks to unload their cargoes at the U.S. border, and then reload them into U.S. (Teamster-driven) trucks for shipment to U.S. destinations. The U.S. agreed to lift that restriction in 1995, but didn't. In 2009 President Obama actually solidified the Mexican roadblock, despite the fact that Mexican trucks passed all 22 safety (nontariff) regulations the U.S. Department of Transportation had imposed. In so doing, President Obama secured more jobs for Teamster-union drivers, but raised costs for U.S. shippers and consumers and drove down sales and employment for Mexican trucking companies. Fed up with U.S. protectionism, Mexico retaliated by slapping tariffs on 90 U.S. export products (see World View "Mexico Retaliates for U.S. Trucking Roadblocks"). By early 2011, U.S. exports to Mexico of those products had declined by 81 percent. This prompted President Obama to offer Mexico a new round of negotiations, which ended in January 2015 with the U.S. declaring Mexican trucks to be safe enough to travel U.S. roads and Mexico repealing the tariffs on U.S. exports. Although Teamsters president Jim Hoffa declared that he was "outraged" by such a "rash decision," cross-border trade increased substantially.

WORLD VIEW

MEXICO RETALLIATES FOR U.S. TRUCKING ROADBLOCKS

The United States promised to open American roads to Mexican trucks back in 1995. But fierce resistance from the Teamsters Union and independent truckers has blocked access to American roads. Goods shipped from Mexico have to be transferred at the border to U.S. trucks, denying Mexican truckers fair access to U.S. deliveries. Two months ago President Obama effectively made that roadblock permanent.

Mexico retalliated on Monday with steep tariffs on 99 U.S. products exported to Mexico from 43 American states. The list includes hams, fresh apples, soups, cheese, beauty products, fresh pears, and pet food. In all, $2.4 billion worth of U.S. exports will feel the pain of lost sales.

Source: Media reports, March 2009.

ANALYSIS: Nontariff barriers like extraordinary safety requirements on Mexican trucks limit import competition and invite retaliation.

THE ECONOMY TOMORROW

POLICING WORLD TRADE

Proponents of free trade and import-competing industries are in constant conflict. Most of the time the trade policy deck seems stacked in favor of the special interests. Because import-competing firms and workers are highly concentrated, they're quick to mobilize politically. By contrast, the benefits of freer trade are less direct and spread over millions of consumers. As a consequence, the beneficiaries of freer trade are less likely to monitor trade policy—much less lobby actively to change it. Hence the political odds favor the spread of trade barriers.

Multilateral Trade Pacts. Despite these odds, the long-term trend is toward *lowering* trade barriers, thereby increasing global competition. Two forces encourage this trend. ***The principal barrier to protectionist policies is worldwide recognition of the gains from freer trade.*** Since world nations now understand that trade barriers are ultimately self-defeating, they're more willing to rise above the din of protectionist cries and dismantle trade barriers. They diffuse political opposition by creating across-the-board trade pacts that seem to spread the pain (and gain) from freer trade across a broad swath of industries. Such pacts also incorporate multiyear timetables that give affected industries time to adjust.

Trade liberalization has also been encouraged by firms that *export* products or use imported inputs in their own production. Tariffs on imported steel raise product costs for U.S.-based auto producers and construction companies. In 2007 the European Union eliminated a tariff on frozen Chinese strawberries, largely due to complaints from EU yogurt and jam producers who were incurring higher costs.

Global Pacts: GATT and WTO. The granddaddy of the multilateral, multiyear free-trade pacts was the 1947 *General Agreement on Tariffs and Trade (GATT)*. Twenty-three nations pledged to reduce trade barriers and give all GATT nations equal access to their domestic markets.

Since the first GATT pact, seven more "rounds" of negotiations have expanded the scope of GATT; 117 nations signed the 1994 pact. As a result of these GATT pacts, average tariff rates in developed countries have fallen from 40 percent in 1948 to less than 4 percent today.

WTO. The 1994 GATT pact also created the *World Trade Organization (WTO)* to enforce free-trade rules. If a nation feels its exports are being unfairly excluded from another country's market, it can file a complaint with the WTO. This is exactly what the United States did when the EU banned U.S. beef imports. The WTO ruled in favor of the United States. When the EU failed to lift its import ban, the WTO authorized the United States to impose retaliatory tariffs on European exports.

The EU turned the tables on the United States in 2003. It complained to the WTO that U.S. tariffs on imported steel violated trade rules. The WTO agreed and gave the EU permission to impose retaliatory tariffs on $2.2 billion of U.S. exports. That prompted the Bush administration to scale back the tariffs in December 2003.

In effect, the WTO is now the world's trade police force. It is empowered to cite nations that violate trade agreements and even to impose remedial action when violations persist. Why do sovereign nations give the WTO such power? Because they are all convinced that free trade is the surest route to GDP growth.

Regional Pacts. Because worldwide trade pacts are so complex, many nations have also pursued *regional* free-trade agreements.

NAFTA. In December 1992 the United States, Canada, and Mexico signed the *North American Free Trade Agreement (NAFTA)*, a 1,000-page document covering more than 9,000 products. The ultimate goal of NAFTA is to eliminate all trade barriers between these three countries. At the time of signing, intraregional tariffs averaged 11 percent in Mexico, 5 percent in Canada, and 4 percent in the United States. NAFTA requires that all tariffs among the three countries be eliminated. The pact also requires the elimination of specific nontariff barriers.

The NAFTA-initiated reduction in trade barriers substantially increased trade flows between Mexico, Canada, and the United States. It also prompted a wave of foreign investment in Mexico, where both cheap labor and NAFTA access were available. Overall, NAFTA accelerated economic growth and reduced inflationary pressures in all three nations. Some industries (like construction and apparel) suffered from the freer trade, but others (like trucking, farming, and finance) reaped huge gains (see In the News "NAFTA Reallocates Labor: Comparative Advantage at Work").

TPP. The Trans-Pacific Partnership was intended to be another regional trade pact, linking 12 nations that border the Pacific Ocean in a multi-year commitment to freer trade. After eight years of negotiations, those 12 nations signed a tentative TPP agreement in February 2016. That 2,000-page agreement called not only for reductions in tariffs and nontariff trade barriers among the member nations, but also sought greater coordination of policies on environmental protection, workers' rights, and regulatory practices. To become effective, the legislatures of the 12 nations had to ratify the agreement by February 2018. By early 2017 only one nation—Japan—had ratified the agreement. The others were aware that newly-elected President Trump had campaigned heavily against TPP and all other multilateral trade agreements. He called TPP a particularly "bad deal" and vowed to kill it. He kept that vow by officially withdrawing the United States from the TPP on his very first day of office. Henceforth, he said, he only wanted bilateral deals and deals that "put America first." Critics warned that he was ignoring the benefits of freer trade and risking the perception that America was an unreliable trading partner.

NAFTA REALLOCATES LABOR: COMPARATIVE ADVANTAGE AT WORK

More Jobs in These Industries		but . . .	Fewer Jobs in These Industries	
Agriculture	+10,600		Construction	−12,800
Metal products	+6,100		Medicine	−6,000
Electrical appliances	+5,200		Apparel	−5,900
Business services	+5,000		Lumber	−1,200
Motor vehicles	+5,000		Furniture	−400

The lowering of trade barriers between Mexico and the United States is changing the mix of output in both countries. New export opportunities create jobs in some industries while increased imports eliminate jobs in other industries. (Estimated gains and losses are during the first five years of NAFTA.)

Source: Congressional Budget Office.

ANALYSIS: The specialization encouraged by free trade creates new jobs in export but reduces employment in import-competing industries. In the process, total world output increases.

SUMMARY

- International trade permits each country to specialize in areas of relative efficiency, increasing world output. For each country, the gains from trade are reflected in consumption possibilities that exceed production possibilities. **LO21-2**
- One way to determine where comparative advantage lies is to compare the quantity of good A that must be given up in order to get a given quantity of good B from domestic production. If the same quantity of B can be obtained for less A by engaging in world trade, we have a comparative advantage in the production of good A. Comparative advantage rests on a comparison of relative opportunity costs. **LO21-1**
- The terms of trade—the rate at which goods are exchanged—are subject to the forces of international supply and demand. The terms of trade will lie somewhere between the opportunity costs of the trading partners. The terms of trade determine how the gains from trade are shared. **LO21-2**

- Resistance to trade emanates from workers and firms that must compete with imports. Even though the country as a whole stands to benefit from trade, these individuals and companies may lose jobs and incomes in the process. **LO21-3**
- Trade barriers take many forms. Embargoes are outright prohibitions against import or export of particular goods. Quotas limit the quantity of a good imported or exported. Tariffs discourage imports by making them more expensive. Other nontariff barriers make trade too costly or time-consuming. **LO21-3**
- The World Trade Organization (WTO) seeks to reduce worldwide trade barriers and enforce trade rules. Regional accords such as the North American Free Trade Agreement (NAFTA) pursue similar objectives among fewer countries. **LO21-3**

Key Terms

imports	consumption possibilities	dumping
exports	open economy	embargo
trade deficit	comparative advantage	tariff
trade surplus	opportunity cost	quota
production possibilities	absolute advantage	equilibrium price
closed economy	terms of trade	voluntary restraint agreement (VRA)

Questions for Discussion

1. Suppose a lawyer can type faster than any secretary. Should the lawyer do her own typing? Can you demonstrate the validity of your answer? **LO21-1**

2. What would be the effects of a law requiring bilateral trade balances? **LO21-2**

3. If a nation exported much of its output but imported little, would it be better or worse off? How about the reverse—that is, exporting little but importing a lot? **LO21-2**

4. How does international trade restrain the price behavior of domestic firms? **LO21-3**

5. Suppose we refused to sell goods to any country that reduced or halted its exports to us. Who would benefit and who would lose from such retaliation? **LO21-2**

6. Domestic producers often base their demands for import protection on the fact that workers in country X are paid substandard wages. Is this a valid argument for protection? **LO21-1**

7. Who, besides Chinese steel producers, was hurt by the new tariffs on Chinese imports (World View "U.S. Slaps China with Huge Anti-Dumping Tariffs")? **LO21-3**

8. According to the National Association of Home Builders, the 2017 tariff on Canadian lumber will result in the loss of 8,000 U.S. construction jobs. How does this happen? **LO21-3**

9. Who gains and who loses from nontariff barriers to Mexican trucks (World View "Mexico Retaliates for U.S. Trucking Roadblocks")? What made President Obama offer renewed negotiations? **LO21-3**

10. What are the potential benefits and risks of a border-adjustment tax? **LO21-3**

LO21-2 1. Which countries are
  (a) The two largest export markets for the United States? (See Table 21.3.)
  (b) The two biggest sources of imports?

LO21-1 2. Suppose a country can produce a maximum of 12,000 jumbo airliners or 2,000 aircraft carriers.
  (a) What is the opportunity cost of an aircraft carrier?
  (b) If another country offers to trade eight planes for one aircraft carrier, should the offer be accepted?
  (c) What is the implied "price" of the carrier in trade?

LO21-1 3. If it takes 10 farmworkers to harvest 1 ton of strawberries and 3 farmworkers to harvest 1 ton of wheat, what is the opportunity cost of 4 tons of strawberries?

LO21-2 4. Alpha and Beta, two tiny islands in the Pacific, produce pearls and pineapples. The following production possibilities schedules describe their potential output in tons per year:

Alpha		Beta	
Pearls	Pineapples	Pearls	Pineapples
0	30	0	20
2	25	10	16
4	20	20	12
6	15	30	8
8	10	40	4
10	5	45	2
12	0	50	0

  (a) Graph the production possibilities confronting each island.
  (b) What is the opportunity cost of pineapples on each island (before trade)?
  (c) Which island has a comparative advantage in pineapple production?
  (d) Which island has a comparative advantage in pearl production?
  Now suppose Alpha and Beta specialize according to its comparative advantage and trades.
  If one pearl is traded for 1.5 pineapples,
  (e) How many pearls would have to be exported to get 15 pineapples in return?
  After this trade,
  (f) What is Alpha's consumption?
  (g) What is Beta's consumption?

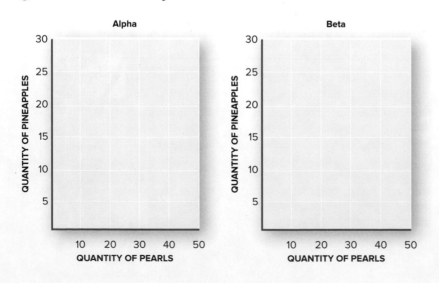

PROBLEMS FOR CHAPTER 21 (cont'd)

LO21-3 5. (*a*) How much more are U.S. consumers paying for the 12 tons of sugar they consume each year as a result of the quotas on sugar imports? (See In the News "Sugar Quotas a Sour Deal").
(*b*) How much sales revenue are foreign sugar producers losing as a result of those same quotas?

LO21-3 6. (*a*) How much was the tariff on Chinese steel imposed in 2016 (World View "U.S. Slaps China with Huge Anti-Dumping Tariffs")?
(*b*) If China was selling its steel for $50 a ton, what would that steel cost American automakers?

LO21-2 7. Suppose the two islands in Problem 4 agree that the terms of trade will be one for one and exchange 10 pearls for 10 pineapples.
(*a*) If Alpha produced 6 pearls and 15 pineapples while Beta produced 30 pearls and 8 pineapples before they decided to trade, how many pearls would each be producing after trade? Assume that the two countries specialize according to their comparative advantage.
(*b*) How much would the combined production of pineapples increase for the two islands due to specialization?
(*c*) How much would the combined production of pearls increase?
(*d*) What is the post trade consumption for each island?

LO21-3 8. Suppose the following table reflects the domestic supply and demand for Bluetooth headphones:

Price ($)	60	55	50	45	40	35	30	25
Quantity supplied (in millions per year)	8	7	6	5	4	3	2	1
Quantity demanded (in millions per year)	2	4	6	8	10	12	14	16

(*a*) Graph these market conditions and identify
  (*i*) The equilibrium price.
  (*ii*) The equilibrium quantity.
(*b*) Now suppose that foreigners enter the market, offering to sell an unlimited supply of Bluetooth headphones for $35 apiece. Illustrate and identify
  (*i*) The new market price.
  (*ii*) Domestic consumption.
  (*iii*) Domestic production.
(*c*) If a tariff of $5 per unit is imposed, what will be
  (*i*) The market price?
  (*ii*) Domestic consumption?
  (*iii*) Domestic production?
Graph your answers.

LO21-3 9. The Economy Tomorrow:
(*a*) Which regional trade pact is among Canada, the United States, and Mexico?
(*b*) Which industries have gained from this trade pact?
(*c*) Which industries have lost from this trade pact?

©Don Tonge/Alamy Stock Photo

CHAPTER 22

International Finance

Textile, furniture, and shrimp producers in the United States want China to increase the value of the yuan. They say China's undervalued currency makes Chinese exports too cheap, undercutting American firms. President Trump agreed, claiming a higher value for the Chinese currency would "bring jobs back from China."

Walmart disagrees. Walmart thinks a cheap yuan is a good thing because it keeps prices low for the *$50 billion* of toys, tools, linens, and other goods it buys from China each year. Those low import prices help Walmart keep its own prices low and its sales volume high. Walmart is also the largest employer in the United States, providing more than 1.5 million jobs.

This chapter examines how currency values affect trade patterns and ultimately the core questions of WHAT, HOW, and FOR WHOM to produce. We focus on the following questions:

- **What determines the value of one country's money compared to the value of another's?**
- **What causes the international value of currencies to change?**
- **How and why governments intervene to alter currency values?**

LEARNING OBJECTIVES

After reading this chapter, you should know

LO22-1 How the value of a currency is measured.

LO22-2 The sources of foreign exchange demand and supply.

LO22-3 How exchange rates are established.

LO22-4 How changes in exchange rates affect prices, output, and trade flows.

EXCHANGE RATES: THE GLOBAL LINK

As we saw in Chapter 21, the United States exports and imports a staggering volume of goods and services. Although we trade with nearly 200 nations around the world, we seldom give much thought to where imports come from and how we acquire them. Most of the time, all we want to know is which products are available and at what price.

Suppose you want to buy an Apple iPad. You don't have to know that iPads are manufactured in China. And you certainly don't have to fly to China to pick it up. All you have to do is drive to the nearest electronics store; or you can just "click and buy" at the Internet's virtual mall.

But you may wonder how the purchase of an imported product was so simple. Chinese companies sell their products in yuan, the currency of China. But you purchase the iPad in dollars. How is this possible?

There's a chain of distribution between your dollar purchase in the United States and the yuan-denominated sale in China. Somewhere along that chain someone has to convert your dollars into yuan. The critical question for everybody concerned is how many yuan we can get for our dollars—that is, what the **exchange rate** is. If we can get eight yuan for every dollar, the exchange rate is 8 yuan = 1 dollar. Alternatively, we could note that the price of a yuan is 12.5 U.S. cents when the exchange rate is 8 to 1. Thus *an exchange rate is the price of one currency in terms of another.*

Which currency is most valuable? It depends on exchange rates.

©Maria Toutoudaki/Getty Images RF

exchange rate: The price of one country's currency expressed in terms of another's; the domestic price of a foreign currency.

FOREIGN EXCHANGE MARKETS

Most exchange rates are determined in foreign exchange markets. Stop thinking of money as some sort of magical substance, and instead view it as a useful commodity that facilitates market exchanges. From that perspective, an exchange rate—the price of money—is subject to the same influences that determine all market prices: demand and supply.

The Demand for Dollars

When the Japanese Toshiba Corporation bought Westinghouse Electric Co. in 2006, it paid $5.4 billion. When Belgian beer maker InBev bought Anheuser-Busch (Budweiser, etc.) in 2008, it also needed dollars—more than 50 billion of them. When Fiat acquired control of Chrysler in 2011, it also needed U.S. dollars. In all three cases, the objective of the foreign investor was to acquire an American business. To attain their objectives, however, the buyers first had to buy *dollars*. The Japanese, Belgian, and Italian buyers had to exchange their own currency for American dollars.

Canadian tourists also need American dollars. Few American restaurants or hotels accept Canadian currency as payment for goods and services; they want to be paid in U.S. dollars. Accordingly, Canadian tourists must buy American dollars if they want to warm up in Florida.

Some foreign investors also buy U.S. dollars for speculative purposes. When Argentina's peso started losing value in 2012–2013, many Argentinians feared that its value would drop further and preferred to hold U.S. dollars; they *demanded* U.S. dollars. Ukrainians clamored for U.S. dollars when Russia invaded its territory in 2014. In 2017 Venezuelans were desperately trying to sell their worthless bolivars for pennies.

All these motivations give rise to a demand for U.S. dollars. Specifically, *the market demand for U.S. dollars originates in*

- *Foreign demand for American exports* (including tourism).
- *Foreign demand for American investments.*
- *Speculation.*

Governments also create a demand for dollars when they operate embassies, undertake cultural exchanges, or engage in intergovernment financial transactions.

The Supply of Dollars

The *supply* of dollars arises from similar sources. On the supply side, however, it's Americans who initiate most of the exchanges. Suppose you take a trip to Mexico. You'll need to buy Mexican pesos at some point. When you do, you'll be offering to *buy* pesos by offering to *sell* dollars. In other words, *the* **demand** *for foreign currency represents a* **supply** *of U.S. dollars.*

When Americans buy BMW cars, they also supply U.S. dollars. American consumers pay for their BMWs in dollars. Somewhere down the road, however, those dollars will be exchanged for European euros. At that exchange, dollars are being *supplied* and euros *demanded*.

American corporations demand foreign exchange too. General Motors builds cars in Germany, Coca-Cola produces Coke in China, and Exxon produces and refines oil all over the world. In nearly every such case, the U.S. firm must first build or buy some plants and equipment, using another country's factors of production. This activity requires foreign currency and thus becomes another component of our demand for foreign currency.

We may summarize these market activities by noting that *the supply of dollars originates in*

- *American demand for imports* (including tourism).
- *American investments in foreign countries.*
- *Speculation.*

As on the demand side, government intervention can also contribute to the supply of dollars.

The Value of the Dollar

Whether American consumers will choose to buy an imported BMW depends partly on what the car costs. The price tag isn't always apparent in international transactions. Remember that the German BMW producer and workers want to be paid in their own currency, the euro. Hence the *dollar* price of an imported BMW depends on two factors: (1) the German price of a BMW and (2) the *exchange rate* between U.S. dollars and euros. Specifically, the U.S. price of a BMW is

$$\frac{\text{Dollar price}}{\text{of BMW}} = \frac{\text{Euro price}}{\text{of BMW}} \times \frac{\text{Dollar price}}{\text{of euro}}$$

Suppose the BMW company is prepared to sell a German-built BMW for 100,000 euros and that the current exchange rate is 2 euros = \$1. At these rates, a BMW will cost you

$$\frac{\text{Dollar price}}{\text{of BMW}} = 100{,}000 \text{ euros} \times \frac{\$1}{2 \text{ euros}}$$

$$= \$50{,}000$$

If you're willing to pay this much for a shiny new German-built BMW, you may do so at current exchange rates.

Now suppose the exchange rate changes from 2 euros = \$1 to 1 euro = \$1. Now you're getting only 1 euro for your dollar rather than 2 euros. In other words, euros have become more expensive. *A higher dollar price for euros will raise the dollar costs of European goods.* In this case, the dollar price of a euro increases from \$0.50 to \$1. At this new exchange rate, the BMW plant in Germany is still willing to sell BMWs at 100,000 euros apiece. And German consumers continue to buy BMWs at that price. But this constant euro price now translates into a higher *dollar* price. That same BMW that you previously could buy for \$50,000 now costs you \$100,000—not because the cost of manufacturing the car in Germany went up, but simply because the exchange rate changed.

As the dollar price of a BMW rises, the number of BMWs sold in the United States will decline. As BMW sales decline, the quantity of euros demanded may decline as well. Thus the quantity of foreign currency demanded declines when the exchange rate rises because foreign goods become more expensive and imports decline. When the dollar price of European currencies actually increased in 1992, BMW decided to start producing cars in South Carolina. A year later Mercedes-Benz decided to produce cars in the United States as well. Sales of American-made BMWs and Mercedes no longer depend on the exchange rate of the U.S. dollar. But the dollar price of German-made Audis, French wine, and Italian shoes does.

The Supply Curve. These market responses suggest that the supply of dollars is upward-sloping. If the value of the dollar rises, Americans will be able to buy more euros. As a result, the dollar price of imported BMWs will decline. American consumers will respond by demanding more imports, thereby supplying a larger quantity of dollars. The supply curve in Figure 22.1 shows how the quantity of dollars supplied rises as the value of the dollar increases.

The Demand Curve. The demand for dollars can be explained in similar terms. Remember that the demand for dollars arises from the foreign demand for U.S. exports and investments. If the exchange rate moves from 2 euros = \$1 to 1 euro = \$1, the euro price of dollars falls.

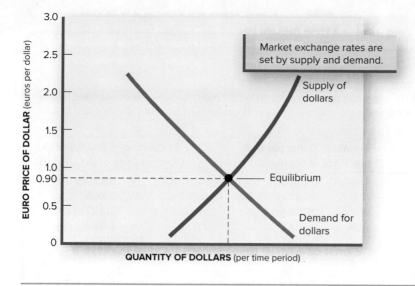

FIGURE 22.1

The Foreign Exchange Market

The foreign exchange market operates like other markets. In this case, the "good" bought and sold is dollars (foreign exchange). The price and quantity of dollars actually exchanged are determined by the intersection of market supply and demand.

As dollars become cheaper for Germans, all American exports effectively fall in price. Germans will buy more American products (including trips to Disney World) and therefore demand a greater quantity of dollars. In addition, foreign investors will perceive in a cheaper dollar the opportunity to buy U.S. stocks, businesses, and property at fire-sale prices. Accordingly, they join foreign consumers in demanding more dollars. Not all these behavioral responses will occur overnight, but they're reasonably predictable over a brief period of time.

Equilibrium

Given market demand and supply curves, we can predict the **equilibrium price** of any commodity—that is, the price at which the quantity demanded will equal the quantity supplied. This occurs in Figure 22.1 where the two curves cross. At that equilibrium, the value of the dollar (the exchange rate) is established. In this case, the euro price of the dollar turns out to be 0.90.

The value of the dollar can also be expressed in terms of other currencies. World View "Foreign Exchange Rates" displays a sampling of dollar exchange rates in March 2017. Notice how many Indonesian rupiah you could buy for $1: a dollar was worth 13,346 rupiah. By contrast, a U.S. dollar was worth only 0.94 euro. **The *average* value of the dollar is a weighted mean of the exchange rates between the U.S. dollar and all these currencies.** The value of the dollar is "high" when its foreign exchange price is above recent levels, and it is "low" when it is below recent averages.

equilibrium price: The price at which the quantity of a good demanded in a given time period equals the quantity supplied.

The Balance of Payments

The equilibrium depicted in Figure 22.1 determines not only the *price* of the dollar, but also a specific *quantity* of international transactions. Those transactions include the exports, imports, international investments, and other sources of dollar supply and demand. A summary of all those international money flows is contained in the **balance of payments**—an accounting statement of all international money flows in a given period of time.

balance of payments: A summary record of a country's international economic transactions in a given period of time.

Trade Balance. Table 22.1 depicts the U.S. balance of payments for 2016. Notice first how the millions of separate transactions are classified into a few summary measures. The trade balance is the difference between exports and imports of goods (merchandise) and services. In 2016 the United States imported more than $2.7 trillion of goods and services but exported only $2.2 trillion. This created a **trade deficit** of $501 billion. That trade deficit represents a net outflow of dollars to the rest of the world.

trade deficit: The amount by which the value of imports exceeds the value of exports in a given time period (negative net exports).

$$\text{Trade balance} = \text{Exports} - \text{Imports}$$

WORLD VIEW

FOREIGN EXCHANGE RATES

The foreign exchange midrange rates here show (a) how many U.S. dollars are needed to buy one unit of foreign currency and (b) how many units of foreign currency are needed to buy one U.S. dollar.

Country	(a) U.S. Dollar per Unit (Dollar Price of Foreign Currency)	(b) Currency per U.S. Dollar (Foreign Price of U.S. Dollar)
Brazil (real)	0.3215	3.1100
Britain (pound)	1.2411	0.8057
Canada (dollar)	0.7534	1.3273
China (yuan)	0.1456	6.8680
Indonesia (rupiah)	0.0001	13,346.92
Japan (yen)	0.0089	112.067
Mexico (peso)	0.0498	20.0869
Russia (ruble)	0.0171	58.3163
Eurozone (euro)	1.0600	0.9434
Venezuela (bolivar)	0.1000	9.9950

Source: March 2017 data from Federal Reserve Board of Governors.

ANALYSIS: The exchange rates between currencies are determined by supply and demand in foreign exchange markets. The rates reported here represent the equilibrium exchange rates on a particular day.

Current Account Balance. The current account balance is a second subtotal in Table 22.1. It includes the trade balance as well as private transfers such as wages sent home by foreign citizens working in the United States. It also includes the income flows from international investments.

$$\text{Current account balance} = \text{Trade balance} + \text{Unilateral transfers} + \text{Net investment income}$$

The current account balance is the most comprehensive summary of our trade relations. As indicated in Table 22.1, the United States had a current account deficit of $481 billion in 2016.

TABLE 22.1

The U.S. Balance of Payments

The balance of payments is a summary statement of a country's international transactions. The major components of that activity are the trade balance (merchandise exports minus merchandise imports), the current account balance (trade, services, and transfers), and the capital account balance. The net total of these balances must equal zero because the quantity of dollars paid must equal the quantity received.

Item	Amount ($ billions)
1. Merchandise exports	$1,460
2. Merchandise imports	(2,210)
3. Service exports	752
4. Service imports	(503)
Trade balance (items 1–4)	**−501**
5. Income from U.S. overseas investments	802
6. Income outflow for foreign-owned U.S. investments	(621)
7. Net transfers and pensions	(161)
Current account balance (items 1–7)	**−481**
8. U.S. capital inflow	759
9. U.S. capital outflow	−331
Capital account balance (items 8–9)	**428**
10. Statistical discrepancy	53
Net balance (items 1–10)	**0**

Source: U.S. Department of Commerce (2016 data).

Capital Account Balance. The current account deficit is offset by the capital account surplus. The capital account balance takes into consideration assets bought and sold across international borders:

$$\text{Capital account balance} = \text{Foreign purchase of U.S. assets} - \text{U.S. purchases of foreign assets}$$

As Table 22.1 shows, foreign consumers demanded $759 billion in 2016 to buy farms and factories as well as U.S. bonds, stocks, and other investments (item 8). This exceeded the flow of U.S. dollars going overseas to purchase foreign assets (item 9).

The net capital inflows were essential in financing the U.S. trade deficit (negative trade balance). As in any market, the number of dollars demanded must equal the number of dollars supplied. Thus *the capital account surplus must equal the current account deficit.* In other words, there can't be any dollars left lying around unaccounted for. Item 10 in Table 22.1 reminds us that our accounting system isn't perfect—we can't identify every transaction. Nevertheless, all the accounts must eventually "balance out":

$$\text{Net balance of payments} = \text{Current account balance} + \text{Capital account balance} = 0$$

That's the character of a market *equilibrium:* the quantity of dollars demanded equals the quantity of dollars supplied.

MARKET DYNAMICS

The interesting thing about markets isn't their character in equilibrium but the fact that prices and quantities are always changing in response to shifts in demand and supply. The U.S. demand for BMWs shifted overnight when Japan introduced a new line of sleek, competitively priced cars (e.g., Lexus). The reduced demand for BMWs shifted the supply of dollars leftward. That supply shift raised the value of the dollar vis-à-vis the euro, as illustrated in Figure 22.2. (It also increased the demand for Japanese yen, causing the yen value of the dollar to *fall.*)

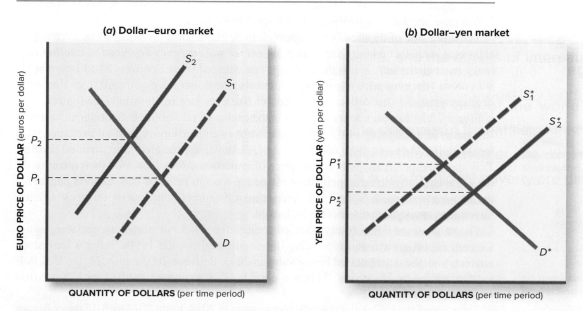

(a) Dollar–euro market

(b) Dollar–yen market

FIGURE 22.2

Shifts in Foreign Exchange Markets

When the Japanese introduced luxury autos into the United States, the American demand for German cars fell. As a consequence, the supply of dollars in the dollar–euro market (part *a*) shifted to the left and the euro value of the dollar rose.

At the same time, the increased American demand for Japanese cars shifted the dollar supply curve in the yen market (part *b*) to the right, reducing the yen price of the dollar.

FIGURE 22.3
Changing Values of U.S. Dollar

Since 1973, exchange rates have been flexible. As a result, the value of the U.S. dollar has fluctuated with international differences in inflation, interest rates, and economic growth. U.S. economic stability has given the U.S. dollar increasing value over time.

Source: Federal Reserve Board of Governors.

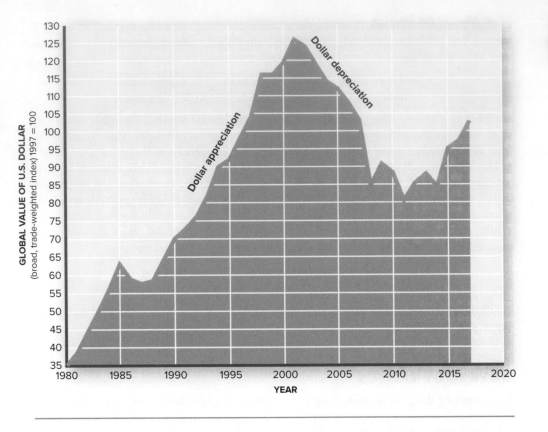

depreciation: The consumption of capital in the production process; the wearing out of plant and equipment.

appreciation: A rise in the price of one currency relative to another.

If the dollar is rising in value (appreciating), the euro must be depreciating.

Depreciation and Appreciation

Exchange rate changes have their own terminology. **Depreciation** of a currency occurs when one currency becomes cheaper in terms of another currency. In our earlier discussion of exchange rates, for example, we assumed that the exchange rate between euros and dollars changed from 2 euros = $1 to 1 euro = $1, making the euro price of a dollar cheaper. In this case, the dollar *depreciated* with respect to the euro.

The other side of depreciation is **appreciation,** an increase in value of one currency as expressed in another country's currency. ***Whenever one currency depreciates, another currency must appreciate.*** When the exchange rate changed from 2 euros = $1 to 1 euro = $1, not only did the euro price of a dollar fall, but also the dollar price of a euro rose. Hence the euro appreciated as the dollar depreciated. It's like a see-saw relationship (see figure).

Figure 22.3 illustrates actual changes in the exchange rate of the U.S. dollar since 1980. The trade-adjusted value of the U.S. dollar is the (weighted) average of all exchange rates for the dollar. Between 1980 and 1985, the U.S. dollar appreciated more than 80 percent. This appreciation greatly reduced the price of imports and thus increased their quantity. At the same time, the dollar appreciation raised the foreign price of U.S. exports and so reduced their volume. U.S. farmers, aircraft manufacturers, and tourist services suffered huge sales losses. The trade deficit ballooned.

The value of the dollar briefy reversed course after 1985 but started appreciating again, slowing export growth and increasing imports throughout the 1990s. After a long steep appreciation, the dollar started losing value in 2003. Between 2003 and 2011, the U.S. dollar depreciated by 25 percent. This was good for U.S. exporters but bad for U.S. tourists and foreign producers.

The value of the U.S. dollar reversed course again in 2014. From 2014 to 2017 the dollar appreciated by more than 20 percent. This put a lot of pressure on U.S. companies that competed with imported products. It also made winter vacations in Florida more expensive for Canadians. But Walmart loved the stronger dollar, as it made the price of the imported goods that it sells much less expensive (see World View "Who Gains, Who Loses from Strong Dollar").

WHO GAINS, WHO LOSES FROM STRONG DOLLAR

The value of the U.S. dollar has been rising since 2010. In the past 4 years, the dollar has risen by nearly 6 percent against the world's major currencies. Should we be cheering? Some of us, perhaps, but not all. Here's who in the United States wins and who loses from a strong dollar:

The winners:
Consumers of imported goods
Producers like Apple that use imported parts and equipment
Retailers like Walmart that sell imported goods
Investors in foreign stocks and production facilities
American tourists

The losers:
U.S. exporters like Boeing, Caterpillar, farmers
Import-competing industries like steel, autos, solar panels
Companies like Disney that attract foreign visitors
Companies with overseas factories and outlets

ANALYSIS: Depreciation of a nation's currency is good for that nation's exporters but bad for that nation's importers (including its tourists).

Market Forces

Exchange rates change for the same reasons that any market price changes: the underlying supply or demand (or both) has shifted. Among the more important sources of such shifts are

- **Relative income changes.** If incomes are increasing faster in country A than in country B, consumers in A will tend to spend more, thus increasing the demand for B's exports and currency. B's currency will appreciate (and A's will depreciate).
- **Relative price changes.** If domestic prices are rising rapidly in country A, consumers will seek out lower-priced imports. The demand for B's exports and currency will increase. B's currency will appreciate (and A's will depreciate).
- **Changes in product availability.** If country A experiences a disastrous wheat crop failure, it will have to increase its food imports. B's currency will appreciate.
- **Relative interest rate changes.** If interest rates rise in country A, people in country B will want to move their deposits to A. Demand for A's currency will rise and it will appreciate.
- **Speculation.** If speculators anticipate an increase in the price of A's currency, for the preceding reasons or any other, they'll begin buying it, thus pushing its price up. A's currency will appreciate.

All these various changes are taking place every minute of every day, thus keeping **foreign exchange markets** active. On an average day, more than *$4 trillion* of foreign exchange is bought and sold in the market. Significant changes occur in currency values, however, only when several of these forces move in the same direction at the same time. This is what caused the Asian crisis of 1997–1998.

foreign exchange markets: Places where foreign currencies are bought and sold.

Ukraine Crisis of 2014

Exchange values are also subject to abrupt changes when an unexpected political or natural upheaval occurs. The Russian invasion of Ukraine in early 2014 was a classic case of an external shock. Foreign exchange markets reacted quickly, sending the value of the hryvnia (Ukraine's currency) into a prolonged depreciation. The dollar value of the hryvnia plunged from 12.3 cents to 7.6 cents in a couple of months. That 40 percent depreciation in the value of the hryvnia substantially increased the cost of badly needed food, oil, and weapons imports.

Venezuelan Currency Collapse, 2016–2017

The collapse of the Venezuelan bolivar was a bit less abrupt, but no less dramatic. Hyperinflation in 2016 was eroding the value of the bolivar. People needed wads of bolivars just to buy everyday staples like bread. Worse yet, few goods were available to buy as the economy contracted. People needed US. dollars to buy goods from other countries or in the black markets. The bolivar became so worthless that the government had to increase the face value of the bolivar from a maximum of 100 to as much as 20,000 at the end of 2016. Venezuelans were desperate to buy U.S. dollars at any price. The unofficial exchange rate plummeted from 12 cents per bolivar to less than 1 cent in 2016–2017.

RESISTANCE TO EXCHANGE RATE CHANGES

Given the scope and depth of currency crises, it's easy to understand why people crave *stable* exchange rates. The resistance to exchange rate fluctuations originates in various micro- and macroeconomic interests.

Micro Interests

The microeconomic resistance to changes in the value of the dollar arises from two concerns. First, people who trade or invest in world markets want a solid basis for forecasting future costs, prices, and profits. Forecasts are always uncertain, but they're even less dependable when the value of money is subject to change. An American firm that invests $2 million in a ski factory in Sweden expects not only to make a profit on the production there but also to return that profit to the United States. If the Swedish krona depreciates sharply in the interim, however, the profits amassed in Sweden may dwindle to a mere trickle, or even a loss, when the kronor are exchanged back into dollars. The same thing happens to the top prize money at Wimbledon when the British pound depreciates (see World View "Brexit Vote Nicks Serena's Paycheck"). From this view, the uncertainty associated with fluctuating exchange rates is an unwanted burden.

WORLD VIEW

BREXIT VOTE NICKS SERENA'S PAYCHECK

Serena Williams's straight-set victory over Angelique Kerber last Saturday confirmed her position as the number-one women's player in the world. But Britain's Brexit vote took a big bite out of her paycheck. The prize for the top women's player at Wimbledon is 2 million British pounds. Before the June 23 Brexit vote, a British pound was worth $1.50, which works out to $3 million. But the decision by British voters to exit the European Union sent the value of the pound tumbling. When the market closed the day after the Brexit vote, the pound was worth only $1.31. That change in the value of the pound cut Serena's paycheck by nearly $340,000.

Source: Media reports, June 24–July 10, 2016.

©Quinn Rooney/Getty Images

ANALYSIS: Currency depreciations reduce the external value of domestic income and assets. The dollar value of the top prize at Wimbledon declined when the British pound depreciated.

Even when the direction of an exchange rate move is certain, those who stand to lose from the change are prone to resist. ***A change in the price of a country's money automatically alters the price of all its exports and imports.*** When the Russian ruble and Japanese yen depreciated in 2015–2016, for example, the dollar price of Russian and Japanese steel declined as well. This prompted U.S. steelmakers to accuse Russia and Japan of "dumping" steel. Steel companies and unions appealed to Washington to protect their sales and jobs.

Even in the country whose currency becomes cheaper, there will be opposition to exchange rate movements. When the U.S. dollar appreciates, Americans buy more foreign products. This increased U.S. demand for imports may drive up prices in other countries. In addition, foreign firms may take advantage of the reduced American competition by raising their prices. In either case, some inflation will result. The consumer's insistence that the government "do something" about rising prices may turn into a political force for "correcting" foreign exchange rates.

Macro Interests

Any microeconomic problem that becomes widespread enough can turn into a macroeconomic problem. The huge U.S. trade deficits of the 1980s effectively exported jobs to foreign nations. Although the U.S. economy expanded rapidly in 1983–1985, the unemployment rate stayed high, partly because American consumers were spending more of their income on imports.

This is the kind of scenario that prompted President Trump to castigate "currency manipulators" like China. In his view, the strong dollar of 2014–2017 was in part due to other nations keeping their currencies artificially low. Those low values encouraged American consumers to buy more imports and American businesses to build more factories abroad. He vowed "to bring jobs back to America" by imposing border taxes and subsidies (Chapter 21) that would offset the cheap price of foreign currencies.

The U.S. trade deficits are typically offset by capital account surpluses. Foreign investors participate in the U.S. economic expansion by buying land, plants, and equipment and by lending money in U.S. financial markets. These capital inflows complicate monetary policy, however, and increase U.S. foreign debt and interest costs.

U.S. a Net Debtor

The inflow of foreign investment also raised anxieties about "selling off" America. When Japanese and other foreign investors increased their purchases of farmland, factories, and real estate (e.g., Rockefeller Center), many Americans worried that foreign investors were taking control of the U.S. economy.

Fueling these fears was the dramatic change in America's international financial position. From 1914 to 1984, the United States had been a net creditor in the world economy. We owned more assets abroad than foreign investors owned in the United States. Our financial position changed in 1985. Continuing trade deficits and offsetting capital inflows transformed the United States into a net debtor in that year. Since then foreigners have owned more U.S. assets than Americans own of foreign assets.

America's debtor status can complicate domestic policy. A sudden flight from U.S. assets could severely weaken the dollar and disrupt the domestic economy. To prevent that from occurring, policymakers must consider the impact of their decisions on foreign investors. This may necessitate difficult policy choices.

There's a silver lining to this cloud, however. The inflow of foreign investment is a reflection of confidence in the U.S. economy. Foreign investors want to share in our growth and profitability. In the process, their investments (like BMW's auto plant) expand America's production possibilities and stimulate still more economic growth.

Foreign investors actually assume substantial risk when they invest in the United States. If the dollar falls, the foreign value of *their* U.S. investments will decline. Hence foreigners who've already invested in the United States have no incentive to start a flight from the dollar. On the contrary, a strong dollar protects the value of their U.S. holdings.

EXCHANGE RATE INTERVENTION

Given the potential opposition to exchange rate movements, governments often feel compelled to intervene in foreign exchange markets. The intervention is usually intended to achieve greater exchange rate stability. But such stability may itself give rise to undesirable micro- and macroeconomic effects.

Fixed Exchange Rates

One way to eliminate fluctuations in exchange rates is to fix a currency's value. The easiest way to do this is for each country to define the worth of its currency in terms of some common standard. Under a **gold standard,** each country declares that its currency is worth so much gold. In so doing, it implicitly defines the worth of its currency in terms of all other currencies that also have a fixed gold value. In 1944 the major trading nations met at Bretton Woods, New Hampshire, and agreed that each currency was worth so much gold. The value of the U.S. dollar was defined as being equal to 0.0294 ounce of gold, while the British pound was defined as being worth 0.0823 ounce of gold. Thus the exchange rate between British pounds and U.S. dollars was effectively fixed at \$1 = 0.357 pound, or 1 pound = \$2.80 (or \$2.80/0.0823 = \$1/0.0294).

Balance-of-Payments Problems. It's one thing to proclaim the worth of a country's currency; it's quite another to *maintain* the fixed rate of exchange. As we've observed, foreign exchange rates are subject to continual and often unpredictable changes in supply and demand. Hence two countries that seek to stabilize their exchange rate at some fixed value will have to somehow neutralize such foreign exchange market pressures.

Suppose the exchange rate officially established by the United States and Great Britain is equal to e_1, as illustrated in Figure 22.4. As is apparent, that particular exchange rate is consistent with the then-prevailing demand and supply conditions in the foreign exchange market (as indicated by curves D_1 and S_1).

Now suppose that Americans suddenly acquire a greater taste for British cars and start spending more income on Jaguars, Bentleys, and Mini Coopers. This increased desire for British goods will *shift* the demand for British currency from D_1 to D_2 in Figure 22.4. Were exchange rates allowed to respond to market influences, the dollar price of a British pound would rise, in this case to the rate e_2. But we've assumed that government intervention has *fixed* the exchange rate at e_1. Unfortunately, at e_1, American consumers want to buy more pounds (q_D) than the British are willing to supply (q_S). The difference between the quantity demanded and the quantity supplied in the market at the rate e_1 represents a **market shortage** of British pounds.

---

gold standard: An agreement by countries to fix the price of their currencies in terms of gold; a mechanism for fixing exchange rates.

market shortage: The amount by which the quantity demanded exceeds the quantity supplied at a given price; excess demand.

FIGURE 22.4

Fixed Rates and Market Imbalance

If exchange rates are fixed, they can't adjust to changes in market supply and demand. Suppose the exchange rate is initially fixed at e_1. When the demand for British pounds increases (shifts to the right), an excess demand for pounds emerges. More pounds are demanded (q_D) at the rate e_1 than are supplied (q_S). This causes a balance-of-payments deficit for the United States.

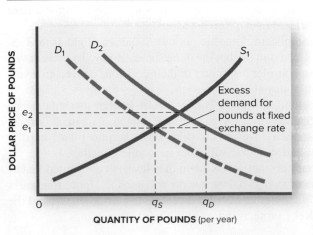

QUANTITY OF POUNDS (per year)

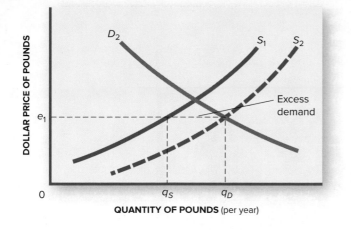

FIGURE 22.5
The Impact of Monetary Intervention

If the U.S. Treasury holds reserves of British pounds, it can use them to buy U.S. dollars in foreign exchange markets. As it does so, the supply of pounds will shift to the right, to S_2, thereby maintaining the desired exchange rate, e_1. The Bank of England could bring about the same result by offering to buy U.S. dollars with pounds (i.e., *supplying* pounds).

The excess demand for pounds implies a **balance-of-payments deficit** for the United States: more dollars are flowing out of the country than into it. The same disequilibrium represents a **balance-of-payments surplus** for Britain because its outward flow of pounds is less than its incoming flow.

Basically, there are only two solutions to balance-of-payments problems brought about by the attempt to fix exchange rates:

- Allow exchange rates to rise to e_2 (Figure 22.4), thereby eliminating the excess demand for pounds.
- Alter market supply or demand so they intersect at the fixed rate e_1.

Since fixed exchange rates were the initial objective of this intervention, only the second alternative is of immediate interest.

The Need for Reserves. One way to alter market conditions would be for someone simply to supply British pounds to American consumers. The U.S. Treasury could have accumulated a reserve of foreign currency in earlier periods. By selling some of those **foreign exchange reserves** now, the Treasury would be *supplying* British pounds, helping to offset excess demand. The rightward shift of the pound supply curve in Figure 22.5 illustrates the sale of accumulated British pounds—and related purchase of U.S. dollars—by the U.S. Treasury.

Although foreign exchange reserves can be used to fix exchange rates, such reserves may not be adequate. Indeed, Figure 22.6 should be testimony enough to the fact that today's deficit isn't always offset by tomorrow's surplus. A principal reason that fixed exchange rates didn't live up to their expectations is that the United States had balance-of-payments deficits for 22 consecutive years. This long-term deficit overwhelmed the government's stock of foreign exchange reserves.

The Role of Gold. Gold reserves are a potential substitute for foreign exchange reserves. As long as each country's money has a value defined in terms of gold, we can use gold to buy British pounds, thereby restocking our foreign exchange reserves. Or we can simply use the gold to purchase U.S. dollars in foreign exchange markets. In either case, the exchange value of the dollar will tend to rise. However, we must have **gold reserves** available for this purpose. Unfortunately, the continuing U.S. balance-of-payments deficits recorded in Figure 22.6 exceeded even the hoards of gold buried under Fort Knox. As a consequence, our gold reserves lost their credibility as a guarantor of fixed exchange rates. When it appeared that foreigners would demand more gold than the U.S. government possessed, President Nixon simply ended the link between the U.S. dollar and gold. As of August 15, 1971, the U.S. dollar had no guaranteed value.

balance-of-payments deficit: An excess demand for foreign currency at current exchange rates.

balance-of-payments surplus: An excess demand for domestic currency at current exchange rates.

foreign exchange reserves: Holdings of foreign currencies by official government agencies, usually the central bank or treasury.

gold reserves: Stocks of gold held by a government to purchase foreign exchange.

FIGURE 22.6

The U.S. Balance of Payments, 1950–1973

The United States had a balance-of-payments deficit for 22 consecutive years. During this period, the foreign exchange reserves of the U.S. Treasury were sharply reduced. Fixed exchange rates were maintained by the willingness of foreign countries to accumulate large reserves of U.S. dollars. However, neither the Treasury's reserves nor the willingness of foreigners to accumulate dollars was unlimited. In 1973 fixed exchange rates were abandoned.

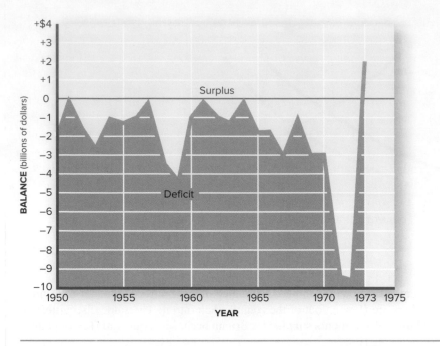

Domestic Adjustments. Government can also use fiscal, monetary, and trade policies to achieve a desired exchange rate. With respect to trade policy, *trade protection can be used to prop up fixed exchange rates.* We could eliminate the excess demand for pounds (Figure 22.4), for example, by imposing quotas and tariffs on British goods. Such trade restrictions would reduce British imports to the United States and thus the demand for British pounds. In August 1971 President Nixon imposed an emergency 10 percent surcharge on all imported goods to help reduce the payments deficit that fixed exchange rates had spawned. Such restrictions on international trade, however, violate the principle of comparative advantage and thus reduce total world output. Trade protection also invites retaliatory trade restrictions.

Fiscal policy is another way out of the imbalance. An increase in U.S. income tax rates will reduce disposable income and have a negative effect on the demand for all goods, including imports. A reduction in government spending will have similar effects. In general, *deflationary (or restrictive) policies help correct a balance-of-payments deficit by lowering domestic incomes and thus the demand for imports.*

Monetary policies in a deficit country could follow the same restrictive course. A reduction in the money supply raises interest rates. The balance of payments will benefit in two ways. The resultant slowdown in spending will reduce import demand. In addition, higher interest rates may induce international investors to move more of their funds into the deficit country. Such moves will provide immediate relief to the payments imbalance.[1] Russia tried this strategy in 1998, tripling key interest rates (to as much as 150 percent). But even that wasn't enough to restore confidence in the ruble, which kept depreciating. Within three months of the monetary policy tightening, the ruble lost half its value.

A surplus country could help solve the balance-of-payments problem. By pursuing expansionary—even inflationary—fiscal and monetary policies, a surplus country could stimulate the demand for imports. Moreover, any inflation at home will reduce the competitiveness of exports, thereby helping to restrain the inflow of foreign demand. Taken together, such efforts would help reverse an international payments imbalance.

---

[1]Before 1930, not only were foreign exchange rates fixed, but domestic monetary supplies were tied to gold stocks as well. Countries experiencing a balance-of-payments deficit were thus forced to contract their money supply, and countries experiencing a payments surplus were forced to expand their money supply by a set amount. Monetary authorities were powerless to control domestic money supplies except by erecting barriers to trade. The system was abandoned when the world economy collapsed into the Great Depression.

Even under the best of circumstances, domestic economic adjustments entail significant costs. In effect, ***domestic adjustments to payments imbalances require a deficit country to forsake full employment and a surplus country to forsake price stability***. China has had to grapple with these domestic consequences of fixing the value of its currency. The artificially low value of the yuan promoted Chinese exports and accelerated China's GDP growth. But it also created serious macro problems. To keep the value of the yuan low, the Chinese had to keep buying dollars. By 2011 China had more than $3 trillion of foreign currency reserves (see World View "The Risks of China's Foreign-Exchange Stockpile"). It paid for those dollars with yuan, adding to China's money supply. All that money stoked inflation in China. Ultimately, the Chinese government had to adopt restrictive monetary and fiscal policies to keep inflation in check. The Chinese government also had to be willing to keep accumulating U.S. dollars and other currencies.

WORLD VIEW

THE RISKS OF CHINA'S FOREIGN-EXCHANGE STOCKPILE

China's foreign-exchange stockpile topped $4 trillion this month, a sum equal to the entire value of China's equity markets. Some see this stockpile of U.S. dollars, euros, yen, and pounds as a testament to China's economic strength. But others warn of substantial risks to the Chinese economy of this foreign-exchange build-up.

The most obvious risk is a decline in the values of the U.S. dollar or U.S. Treasury bonds. About two-thirds of the stockpile consists of U.S. Treasury bonds. When U.S. interest rates start rising—as everyone expects—the market value of Treasury bonds will fall, cutting the value of China's holdings. Inflation poses an even greater risk. China must print more yuan every time exports exceed imports. The Bank of China says the money supply will grow 12–13 percent this year as a result. All that money threatens to accelerate domestic inflation, a problem that has already raised political concerns in China.

Critics say the problem originates in the undervalued yuan. Observers accuse China of intervening in the market to keep the value of the yuan artificially low. This helps drive exports, but adds to China's already gargantuan stockpile of foreign exchange.

Source: News reports, December 2014.

ANALYSIS: When a currency is deliberately undervalued, strong export demand may kindle inflation. The trade surplus that results also increases foreign exchange reserves.

As we noted earlier, President Trump has proposed yet another way to correct market imbalances. He blamed the huge trade deficit with China on the intentional manipulation of the value of the yuan by the Chinese government. He called China the "grand champion of currency manipulation" for its alleged role in keeping the value of the yuan low (essentially a fixed rate). To offset that "unfair" exchange rate, Trump proposed tariffs on all Chinese imports. That would reduce the flow of dollars to China and "bring jobs back from China." But China denies the charge and points to the fact that its dollar reserves have fallen since 2015. Observers also warn that unilateral tariffs can easily spark a trade war that hurts both nations.

There's no easy way out of this impasse. Market imbalances caused by fixed exchange rates can be corrected only with abundant supplies of foreign exchange reserves or deliberate changes in fiscal, monetary, or trade policies. At some point, it may become easier to let a currency adjust to market equilibrium.

The Euro Fix. The original 12 nations of the European Monetary Union (EMU) fixed their exchange rates in 1999. They went far beyond the kind of exchange rate fix we're discussing here. Members of the EMU *eliminated* their national currencies, making the euro the common currency of Euroland. They don't have to worry about reserve balances or domestic adjustments. However, they do have to reconcile their varied national interests to a single monetary authority, which has proven to be difficult politically in times of economic stress.

Flexible Exchange Rates

flexible exchange rates: A system in which exchange rates are permitted to vary with market supply-and-demand conditions; floating exchange rates.

Balance-of-payments problems wouldn't arise in the first place if exchange rates were allowed to respond to market forces. Under a system of **flexible exchange rates** (often called floating exchange rates), the exchange rate moves up or down to choke off any excess supply of or demand for foreign exchange. Notice again in Figure 22.4 that the exchange rate move from e_1 to e_2 prevents any excess demand from emerging. *With flexible exchange rates, the quantity of foreign exchange demanded always equals the quantity supplied,* and there's no imbalance. For the same reason, there's no need for foreign exchange reserves.

Although flexible exchange rates eliminate balance-of-payments and foreign exchange reserves problems, they don't solve all of a country's international trade problems. *Exchange rate movements associated with flexible rates alter relative prices and may disrupt import and export flows.* As noted before, depreciation of the dollar raises the price of all imported goods, contributing to domestic cost-push inflation. Also, domestic businesses that sell imported goods or use them as production inputs may suffer sales losses. On the other hand, appreciation of the dollar raises the foreign price of U.S. goods and reduces the sales of American exporters. Hence *someone is always hurt, and others are helped, by exchange rate movements.* The resistance to flexible exchange rates originates in these potential losses. Such resistance creates pressure for official intervention in foreign exchange markets or increased trade barriers.

The United States and its major trading partners abandoned fixed exchange rates in 1973. Although exchange rates are now able to fluctuate freely, it shouldn't be assumed that they necessarily undergo wild gyrations. On the contrary, experience with flexible rates since 1973 suggests that some semblance of stability is possible even when exchange rates are free to change in response to market forces.

Speculation. One force that often helps maintain stability in a flexible exchange rate system is—surprisingly—speculation. Speculators often counteract short-term changes in foreign exchange supply and demand. If a currency temporarily rises above its long-term equilibrium, speculators will move in to sell it. By selling at high prices and later buying at lower prices, speculators hope to make a profit. In the process, they also help stabilize foreign exchange rates.

Speculation isn't always stabilizing, however. Speculators may not correctly gauge the long-term equilibrium. Instead they may move "with the market" and help push exchange rates far out of kilter. This kind of destabilizing speculation sharply lowered the international value of the U.S. dollar in 1987, forcing the Reagan administration to intervene in foreign exchange markets, borrowing foreign currencies to buy U.S. dollars. In 1997 the Clinton administration intervened for the opposite purpose: stemming the rise in the U.S. dollar. The Bush administration was more willing to stay on the sidelines, letting global markets set the exchange rates for the U.S. dollar.

These kinds of interventions are intended to *narrow* rather than *eliminate* exchange rate movements. Such limited intervention in foreign exchange markets is often referred to as **managed exchange rates,** or, popularly, "dirty floats."

managed exchange rates: A system in which governments intervene in foreign exchange markets to limit but not eliminate exchange rate fluctuations; "dirty floats."

Although managed exchange rates would seem to be an ideal compromise between fixed rates and flexible rates, they can work only when some acceptable "rules of the game" and mutual trust have been established. As Sherman Maisel, a former governor of the Federal Reserve Board, put it, "Monetary systems are based on credit and faith: If these are lacking, a . . . crisis occurs."[2]

[2]Sherman Maisel, *Managing the Dollar* (New York: W. W. Norton, 1973), p. 196.

THE ECONOMY TOMORROW

CURRENCY BAILOUTS

The world has witnessed a string of currency crises, including the one in Asia during 1997–1998, the Brazilian crisis of 1999, the Argentine crisis of 2001–2002, the Greek and Portuguese crises of 2010–2012, and recurrent ruble crises in Russia. In every instance, the country in trouble pleads for external help. In most cases, a currency "bailout" is arranged, whereby global monetary authorities lend the troubled nation enough reserves (such as U.S. dollars) to defend its currency. Typically the International Monetary Fund (IMF) heads the rescue party, joined by the central banks of the strongest economies.

The Case for Bailouts. The argument for currency bailouts typically rests on the domino theory. Weakness in one currency can undermine another. This seemed to be the case during the 1997–1998 Asian crisis. After the **devaluation** of the Thai baht, global investors began worrying about currency values in other Asian nations. Choosing to be safe rather than sorry, they moved funds out of Korea, Malaysia, and the Philippines and invested in U.S. and European markets (notice in Figure 22.3 the 1997–1998 appreciation of the U.S. dollar).

The initial baht devaluation also weakened the competitive trade position of these same economies. Thai exports became cheaper, diverting export demand from other Asian nations. To prevent loss of export markets, Thailand's neighbors felt they had to devalue as well. Speculators who foresaw these effects accelerated the domino effect by selling the region's currencies.

When Brazil devalued its currency (the *real*) in January 1999, global investors worried that a "samba effect" might sweep across Latin America. The domino effect could reach across the ocean and damage U.S. and European exports as well. The Greek crisis of 2010 threatened the common currency (euro) of 28 nations. Hence, richer, more stable countries often offer a currency bailout as a form of self-defense.

The Case against Bailouts. Critics of bailouts argue that such interventions are ultimately self-defeating. They say that once a country knows for sure that currency bailouts are in the wings, it doesn't have to pursue the domestic policy adjustments that might stabilize its currency. A nation can avoid politically unpopular options such as high interest rates, tax hikes, or cutbacks in government spending. It can also turn a blind eye to trade barriers, monopoly power, lax lending policies, and other constraints on productive growth. Hence the expectation of readily available bailouts may foster the very conditions that cause currency crises.

Future Bailouts? The decision to bail out a depreciating currency isn't as simple as it appears. To minimize the ill effects of bailouts, the IMF and other institutions typically require the nation in crisis to pledge more prudent monetary, fiscal, and trade policies. Usually there's a lot of debate about what kinds of adjustments will be made—and how soon. As long as the nation in crisis is confident of an eventual bailout, however, it has a lot of bargaining power to resist policy changes. Only after the IMF finally said no to further bailouts in Greece did the Greek parliament pass austerity measures that reduced its fiscal imbalances.

> **devaluation:** An abrupt depreciation of a currency whose value was fixed or managed by the government.

SUMMARY

- Money serves the same purposes in international trade as it does in the domestic economy—namely, to facilitate specialization and market exchanges. The basic challenge of international finance is to create acceptable standards of value from the various currencies maintained by separate countries. **LO22-1**

- Exchange rates are the mechanism for translating the value of one national currency into the equivalent value of another. An exchange rate of $1 = 2$ euros means that one dollar is worth two euros in foreign exchange markets.   **LO22-1**

- Foreign currencies have value because they can be used to acquire goods and resources from other countries. Accordingly, the supply of and demand for foreign currency reflect the demands for imports and exports, for international investment, and for overseas activities of governments.   **LO22-2**

- The balance of payments summarizes a country's international transactions. Its components are the trade balance, the current account balance, and the capital account balance. The current and capital accounts must offset each other.   **LO22-2**

- The equilibrium exchange rate is subject to any and all shifts of supply and demand for foreign exchange. If relative incomes, prices, or interest rates change, the demand for foreign exchange will be affected. A depreciation is a change in market exchange rates that makes one country's currency cheaper in terms of another currency. An appreciation is the opposite kind of change.   **LO22-3**

- Changes in exchange rates are often resisted. Producers of export goods don't want their currencies to rise in value (appreciate); importers and tourists dislike it when their currencies fall in value (depreciate).   **LO22-4**

- Under a system of fixed exchange rates, changes in the supply and demand for a specific currency can't be expressed in exchange rate movements. Instead such shifts will be reflected in excess demand for or supply of that currency. Such market imbalances are referred to as balance-of-payments deficits or surpluses.   **LO22-3**

- To maintain fixed exchange rates, monetary authorities must enter the market to buy and sell foreign exchange. To do so, deficit countries must have foreign exchange reserves. In the absence of sufficient reserves, a country can maintain fixed exchange rates only if it's willing to alter basic fiscal, monetary, or trade policies.   **LO22-4**

- Flexible exchange rates eliminate balance-of-payments problems and the crises that accompany them. But complete flexibility can lead to disruptive changes. To avoid this contingency, many countries prefer to adopt managed exchange rates—that is, rates determined by the market but subject to government intervention.   **LO22-4**

Key Terms

exchange rate
equilibrium price
balance of payments
trade deficit
depreciation (currency)
appreciation

foreign exchange markets
gold standard
market shortage
balance-of-payments deficit
balance-of-payments surplus
foreign exchange reserves

gold reserves
flexible exchange rates
managed exchange rates
devaluation

Questions for Discussion

1. Why would a rise in the value of the dollar prompt U.S. manufacturers to build production plants in Mexico? **LO22-4**

2. How do changes in the value of the U.S. dollar affect foreign enrollments at U.S. colleges? **LO22-4**

3. How would rapid inflation in Canada affect U.S. tourism travel to Canada? Does it make any difference whether the exchange rate between Canadian and U.S. dollars is fixed or flexible? **LO22-3**

4. Under what conditions would a country welcome a balance-of-payments deficit? When would it *not* want a deficit? **LO22-4**

5. In what sense do fixed exchange rates permit a country to "export its inflation"? **LO22-4**

6. Why did the value of the Ukrainian hryvnia depreciate so much when Russia invaded (see section Ukraine Crisis of 2014)? **LO22-3**

7. If a nation's currency depreciates, are the reduced export prices that result "unfair"? **LO22-4**

8. How would each of these events affect the supply or demand for Japanese yen? **LO22-3**
   (a) Stronger U.S. economic growth.
   (b) A decline in Japanese interest rates.
   (c) Higher inflation in the United States.
   (d) A Japanese tsunami.

9. Who in Mexico is helped or hurt by a strong U.S. dollar? Redo World View "Who Gains, Who Loses from Strong Dollar" for Mexicans. **LO22-4**

10. Why does World View "The Risks of China's Foreign-Exchange Stockpile" say the undervalued yuan is "more bane than boom"? **LO22-4**

LO22-1 1. According to World View "Foreign Exchange Rates," which nation had
    (*a*) The cheapest currency?
    (*b*) The most expensive currency?

LO22-1 2. If a euro is worth $1.25, what is the euro price of a dollar?

LO22-3 3. How many Ukrainian hryvnia (see section Ukraine Crisis of 2014) could you buy with one U.S. dollar
    (*a*) Before the Russian invasion?
    (*b*) After the Russian invasion?

LO22-1 4. If a McDonald's Big Mac meal sold for $6.00 in March 2017, how much would it cost in the currencies of
    (*a*) Brazil?
    (*b*) Japan?
    (*c*) Indonesia?
    (See World View "Foreign Exchange Rates.")

LO22-1 5. Between 2014 and 2017, did the U.S. dollar appreciate or depreciate (see Figure 22.3)?

LO22-1 6. If a PlayStation 4 costs 30,000 yen in Japan, how much will it cost in U.S. dollars if the exchange rate is
    (*a*) 110 yen = $1?
    (*b*) 1 yen = $0.009?
    (*c*) 100 yen = $1?

LO22-1 7. Between 1990 and 2000, by how much did the dollar appreciate (Figure 22.3)?

LO22-1 8. If inflation raises U.S. prices by 2 percent and the U.S. dollar appreciates by 5 percent, by how much does the foreign price of U.S. exports change?

LO22-1 9. According to World View "Foreign Exchange Rates," what was the peso price of a euro in March 2017?

LO22-2 10. For each of the following possible events, indicate whether the global value of the U.S. dollar will rise or fall.
    (*a*) American cars become suddenly more popular abroad.
    (*b*) Inflation in the United States accelerates.
    (*c*) The United States falls into a recession.
    (*d*) Interest rates in the United States drop.
    (*e*) The United States experiences rapid increases in productivity.
    (*f*) Anticipating a return to the gold standard, Americans suddenly rush to buy gold from the two big producers, South Africa and the Soviet Union.
    (*g*) War is declared in the Middle East.
    (*h*) The stock markets in the United States collapse.

LO22-3 11. The following schedules summarize the supply and demand for trifflings, the national currency of Tricoli:

Triffling price (U.S. dollars per triffling)	0	$4	$8	$12	$16	$20	$24
Quantity demanded (per year)	40	38	36	34	32	30	28
Quantity supplied (per year)	1	11	21	31	41	51	61

Use these schedules for the following:
    (*a*) Graph the supply and demand curves.
    (*b*) Determine the equilibrium exchange rate.

(*c*) Determine the size of the excess supply or excess demand that would exist if the Tricolian government fixed the exchange rate at $22 = 1 triffling.

(*d*) Which of the following events would help reduce the payments imbalance? Which would not?

    (*i*) Domestic inflation.

    (*ii*) Foreign inflation.

    (*iii*) Slower domestic growth.

    (*iv*) Faster domestic growth.

LO22-3 12. As shown in Table 22.1, in 2016 the United States was running a current account deficit. Would the following events increase or decrease the current account deficit?

(*a*) U.S. companies, the largest investors in Switzerland, see even more promising investment opportunities there.

(*b*) The Netherlands, one of the largest foreign investors in the United States, finds U.S. investment opportunities less attractive.

(*c*) Unemployment rises and recession deepens in the United States.

LO22-3 13. The Economy Tomorrow: Show graphically the impact on the South Korean currency (won) when the Thai baht was devalued.

©William West/AFP/Getty Images

CHAPTER 23

Global Poverty

Bono, the lead singer for the rock group U2, has performed concerts around the world to raise awareness of global poverty. He doesn't have a specific agenda for eradicating poverty. He does believe, though, that greater awareness of global poverty will raise assistance levels and spawn more ideas for combating global hunger, disease, and isolation.

The dimensions of global poverty are staggering. According to the World Bank, more than a third of the world's population lacks even the barest of life's necessities. *Billions* of people are persistently malnourished, poorly sheltered, minimally clothed, and at constant risk of debilitating diseases. Life expectancies among the globally poor population still hover in the range of 40–50 years, far below the norm (70–80 years) of the rich, developed nations.

In this chapter we follow Bono's suggestion and take a closer look at global poverty. We address the following issues:

- **What income thresholds define "poverty"?**
- **How many people are poor?**
- **What actions can be taken to reduce global poverty?**

In the process of answering these questions, we get another opportunity to examine what makes economies "tick"—particularly what forces foster faster economic growth for some nations and slower economic growth for others.

AMERICAN POVERTY

Poverty, like beauty, is often in the eye of the beholder. Many Americans feel "poor" if they can't buy a new car, live in a fancy home, or take an exotic vacation. Indeed, the average American asserts that a family needs at least $58,000 a year "just to get by." With that much income, however, few people would go hungry or be forced to live in the streets.

Official Poverty Thresholds

To develop a more objective standard of poverty, the U.S. government assessed how much money a U.S. family needs to purchase a "minimally adequate" diet. Back in 1963 it concluded that $1,000 per year was needed for that purpose alone. Then it asked how much income was needed to purchase other basic necessities like housing, clothes, transportation, and so on. It figured all those *non*food necessities would cost twice as much as the food staples. So it concluded that a budget of $3,000 per year would fund a "minimally adequate" living standard for a U.S. family of four. That standard became the official **U.S. poverty threshold** in 1963.

LEARNING OBJECTIVES

After reading this chapter, you should know

LO23-1 How U.S. and global poverty are defined.

LO23-2 How many people in the world are poor.

LO23-3 What factors impede or promote poverty reduction.

---

poverty threshold (U.S.): Annual income of less than $24,600 for a family of four (2016).

Inflation Adjustments. Since 1963, prices have risen every year. As a result, the price of the poverty "basket" has risen as well. In 2017, it cost roughly $25,000 to purchase those same basic necessities for a family of four that cost only $3,000 in 1963.

Twenty-five thousand dollars might sound like a lot of money, especially if you're not paying your own rent or feeding a family. If you break the budget down, however, it doesn't look so generous. Only a third of the budget goes for food. And that portion has to feed four people. So the official U.S. poverty standard provides less than $6 per day for an individual's food. That just about covers a single Big Mac combo at McDonald's. There's no money in the poverty budget for dining out. And the implied rent money is only $800 a month (for the whole family). So the official U.S. poverty standard isn't that generous—certainly not by *American* standards (where the *average* family has an income of nearly $80,000 per year and eats outside their $250,000 home three times a week).

U.S. Poverty Count

The Census Bureau counted more than 40 million Americans as "poor" in 2016 according to the official U.S. thresholds (as adjusted for family size). This was one out of eight U.S. households, for a **poverty rate** of roughly 13 percent. According to the Census Bureau, the official U.S. poverty rate has been in a narrow range of 11–15 percent for the last 40 years.

How Poor Is U.S. "Poor"?

Many observers criticize these official U.S. poverty statistics. They say that far fewer Americans meet the government standard of poverty and even fewer are really destitute.

In-Kind Income. A major flaw in the official tally is that the government counts only *cash* income in defining poverty. Since the 1960s, however, the United States has developed an extensive system of **in-kind transfers** that augment cash incomes. Food stamps, for example, can be used just as easily as cash to purchase groceries. Medicaid and Medicare pay doctor and hospital bills, reducing the need for cash income. Government rent subsidies and public housing allow poor families to have more housing than their cash incomes would permit. These in-kind transfers allow "poor" families to enjoy a higher living standard than their cash incomes imply. Adding those transfers to cash incomes would bring the U.S. poverty count down into the 9–11 percent range.

Material Possessions. Even those families who remain "poor" after counting in-kind transfers aren't necessarily destitute. More than 40 percent of America's "poor" families own their homes, 70 percent own a car or truck, and 30 percent own at least *two* vehicles. Telephones, color TVs, dishwashers, clothes dryers, air conditioners, and microwave ovens are commonplace in America's poor households.

America's poor families themselves report few acute problems in everyday living. Fewer than 14 percent report missing a rent or mortgage payment, and fewer than 8 percent report a food deficiency. So American poverty isn't synonymous with homelessness, malnutrition, chronic illness, or even social isolation. These problems exist among America's poverty population, but they don't define American poverty.

GLOBAL POVERTY

Poverty in the rest of the world is much different from poverty in America. *American poverty is more about* **relative** *deprivation than* **absolute** *deprivation. In the rest of the world, poverty is all about* **absolute** *deprivation.*

Low Average Incomes

As a starting point for assessing global poverty, consider how *average* incomes in the rest of the world stack up against U.S. levels. By global standards, the United States is unquestionably

---

poverty rate: Percentage of the population counted as poor.

in-kind transfers: Direct transfers of goods and services rather than cash, such as food stamps, Medicaid benefits, and housing subsidies.

a very rich nation. As we observed in Chapter 2 (see World View "GDP per Capita around the World"), U.S. GDP per capita is five times larger than the world average. More than three-fourths of the world's population lives in what the World Bank calls "low-income" or "lower-middle-income" nations. In those nations the *average* income is under $4,000 a year, less than *one-tenth* of America's per capita GDP. Average incomes are lower yet in Haiti, Nigeria, Ethiopia, and other desperately poor nations. By American standards, virtually all the people in these nations would be poor. By *their* standards, no American would be poor.

World Bank Poverty Thresholds

Because national poverty lines are so diverse and culture-bound, the World Bank decided to establish a uniform standard for assessing global poverty. And it set the bar amazingly low. In fact, the World Bank regularly uses two thresholds, namely $1.90 per day for **"extreme" poverty** and a higher $3.10 per day standard for less "severe" poverty.

The World Bank thresholds are incomprehensibly low by American standards. The $1.90 standard works out to $2,774 per year for a family of four—a mere tenth of America's poverty standard. Think about it. How much could you buy for $1.90 a day? A little rice, maybe, and perhaps some milk? Certainly not a Big Mac. Not even a grande coffee at Starbucks. And part of that $1.90 would have to go for rent. Clearly this isn't going to work. Raising the World Bank standard to $3.10 per day (**severe poverty**) doesn't reach a whole lot further.

The World Bank, of course, wasn't defining "poverty" in the context of American affluence. They were instead trying to define a rock-bottom threshold of absolute poverty—a threshold of physical deprivation that people everywhere would acknowledge as the barest "minimum"—a condition of "unacceptable deprivation."

Global Poverty Counts

On the basis of household surveys in more than 100 nations, *the World Bank classifies 800 million people as being in "extreme" poverty (<$1.90/day) and 2 billion people as being in "severe" poverty (<$3.10/day).*

Figure 23.1 shows where concentrations of extreme poverty are the greatest. Concentrations of extreme poverty are alarmingly high in dozens of smaller, less developed nations like Mali, Haiti, and Zambia, where average incomes are also shockingly low. However, the greatest *number* of extremely poor people reside in the world's largest countries. China and India alone contain a third of the world's population and 40 percent of the world's extreme poverty.

Table 23.1 reveals that the distribution of severe poverty (<$3.10/day) is similar. The incidence of this higher poverty threshold is, of course, much greater. Severe poverty afflicts more than 80 percent of the population in dozens of nations and even reaches more than 90 percent of the population in some (e.g., Burundi). By contrast, less than 15 percent of the U.S. population falls below the official *American* poverty threshold, and *virtually no American household has an income below the* **global** *poverty threshold.*

extreme poverty (world): World Bank income standard of less than $1.90 per day per person (inflation adjusted).

severe poverty (world): World Bank income standard of $3.10 per day per person (inflation adjusted).

Analysis: Global poverty is defined in terms of absolute deprivation.
©Stockbyte/Getty Images RF

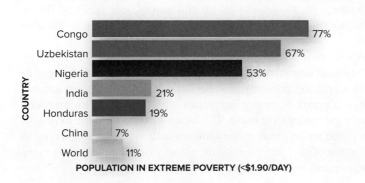

POPULATION IN EXTREME POVERTY (<$1.90/DAY)

COUNTRY:
- Congo — 77%
- Uzbekistan — 67%
- Nigeria — 53%
- India — 21%
- Honduras — 19%
- China — 7%
- World — 11%

FIGURE 23.1

Geography of Extreme Poverty

Nearly 800 million people around the world are in "extreme" poverty. In smaller, poor nations, deprivation is commonplace.

Source: The World Bank, *WDR2015-16 Data Set.*

TABLE 23.1

Population in Severe Poverty (<$3.10/day)

More than a third of the world's population has income of less than $3.10 per person per day. Such poverty is pervasive in low-income nations.

Country	Living in Severe Poverty (Percent)
Tanzania	92%
Burundi	92
Congo	91
Uzbekistan	88
Nigeria	77
Honduras	71
Bangladesh	80
Ethiopia	71
India	58
China	11
World	**30%**

Source: The World Bank, *WDR2015 Data Set.*

Social Indicators

The levels of poverty depicted in Figure 23.1 and Table 23.1 imply levels of physical and social deprivation few Americans can comprehend. Living on less than two or three dollars a day means always being hungry, malnourished, ill-clothed, dirty, and unhealthy. The problems associated with such deprivation begin even before birth. Pregnant women often fail to get enough nutrition or medical attention. In low-income countries only a third of all births are attended by a skilled health practitioner. If something goes awry, both the mother and the baby are at fatal risk. Nearly all of the children in global poverty are in a state of chronic malnutrition. At least 1 out of 10 children in low-income nations will actually die before reaching age 5. In the poorest sectors of the population, infant and child mortality rates are often two to three times higher than that. Children often remain unimmunized to preventable diseases. And AIDS is rampant among both children and adults in the poorest nations. All of these factors contribute to a frighteningly short life expectancy—less than half that in the developed nations.

Fewer than one out of two children from extremely poor households are likely to stay in school past the eighth grade. Women and minority ethnic and religious groups are often wholly excluded from educational opportunities. As a consequence, great stocks of human capital remain undeveloped: in low-income nations only one out of two women and only two out of three men are literate.

Persistent Poverty

Global poverty is not only more desperate than American poverty, but also more permanent. In India a rigid caste system still defines differential opportunities for millions of rich and poor villagers. Studies in Brazil, South Africa, Peru, and Ecuador document barriers that block access to health care, education, and jobs for children of poor families. Hence inequalities in poor nations not only are more severe than in developed nations but also tend to be more permanent.

Economic stagnation also keeps a lid on upward mobility. President John F. Kennedy observed that "a rising tide lifts all boats," referring to the power of a growing economy to raise everyone's income. In a growing economy, one person's income *gain* is not another person's *loss*. By contrast, a stagnant economy intensifies class warfare, with everyone jealously protecting whatever gains they have made. The *haves* strive to keep the *have-nots* at bay. Unfortunately, this is the reality in many low-income nations. As we observed in Chapter 2 (Table 2.1), in some of the poorest nations in the world output grows more slowly than the population, intensifying the competition for resources.

GOALS AND STRATEGIES

Global poverty is so extensive that no policy approach offers a quick solution. Even the World Bank doesn't see an end to global poverty. The United Nations set a much more modest goal back in 2000.

The UN Millennium Goals

The UN established a Millennium Poverty Goal of cutting the incidence of extreme global poverty in half by 2015 (from 30 percent in 1990 to 15 percent in 2015). That goal was attained. But that didn't significantly decrease the *number* of people in poverty. The world's population keeps growing at upward of 80–100 million people a year. In 2017, there were close to 7.4 billion people on this planet. Fifteen percent of that population would still have left more than a *billion* people in extreme global poverty. In 2015, the World Bank set a new and more ambitious goal of *eliminating* extreme poverty by 2030.

Why should we care? After all, America has its own poverty problems and a slew of other domestic concerns. So why should an American—or, for that matter, an affluent Canadian, French, or German citizen—embrace the **UN and World Bank Poverty Goal**? For starters, one might embrace the notion that a poor child in sub-Saharan Africa or Borneo is no less worthy than a poor child elsewhere. And a child's death in Bangladesh is just as tragic as a child's death in Buffalo, New York. In other words, humanitarianism is a starting point for *global* concern for poor people. Then there are pragmatic concerns. Poverty and inequality sow the seeds of social tension both within and across national borders. Poverty in other nations also limits potential markets for international trade. Last but not least, undeveloped human capital anywhere limits human creativity. For all these reasons, the World Bank feels its Poverty Goal should be universally embraced.

> **UN and World Bank Poverty Goal:** UN goal of eliminating extreme poverty by 2030.

Policy Strategies

Eliminating severe poverty around the world won't be easy. In principle, ***there are only two general approaches to global poverty reduction:***

- ***Redistribution*** of incomes within and across nations.
- ***Economic growth*** that raises average incomes.

The following sections explore the potential of these strategies for eliminating global poverty.

INCOME REDISTRIBUTION

Many people suggest that the quickest route to eliminating global poverty is simply to *redistribute* incomes and assets, both within and across countries. The potential for redistribution is often exaggerated, however, and its risks underestimated.

Within-Nation Redistribution

Take another look at those nations with the highest concentrations of extreme poverty. Nigeria is near the top of the list in Figure 23.1 and Table 23.1, with an incredible 53 percent of its population in extreme poverty and 77 percent in severe poverty. Yet the other 23 percent of the population lives fairly well, taking more than half of that nation's income. So what would happen if we somehow forced Nigeria's richest households to share that wealth? Sure, Nigeria's poorest households would be better off. But the gains wouldn't be spectacular: the *average* income in Nigeria is only $2,800 a year. Haiti, Zambia, and Madagascar also have such low *average* incomes that outright redistribution doesn't hold great hope for income gains by the poor. (See World View "Glaring Inequalities").

GLARING INEQUALITIES

Inequality tends to diminish as a country develops. In poor nations, the richest tenth of the population typically gets 40 to 50 percent of all income—sometimes even more. In developed countries, the richest tenth gets 20 to 30 percent of total income.

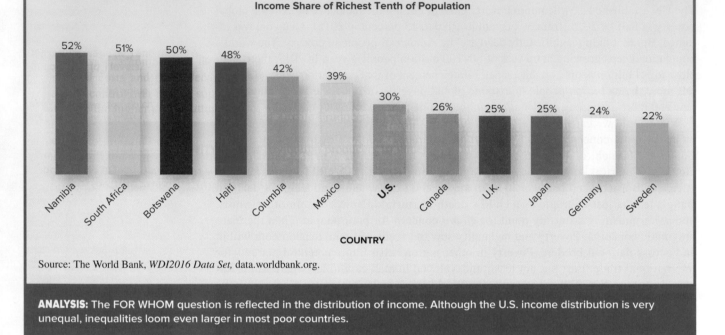

Income Share of Richest Tenth of Population

Namibia	South Africa	Botswana	Haiti	Columbia	Mexico	U.S.	Canada	U.K.	Japan	Germany	Sweden
52%	51%	50%	48%	42%	39%	30%	26%	25%	25%	24%	22%

COUNTRY

Source: The World Bank, *WDI2016 Data Set,* data.worldbank.org.

ANALYSIS: The FOR WHOM question is reflected in the distribution of income. Although the U.S. income distribution is very unequal, inequalities loom even larger in most poor countries.

Economic Risks. Then there's the downside to direct redistribution. How is the income pie going to be resliced? Will the incomes or assets of the rich be confiscated? How will underlying jobs, stocks, land, and businesses be distributed to the poor? How will *total* output (and income) be affected by the redistribution?

If savings are confiscated, people will no longer want to save and invest. If large, efficient farms are divided up into small parcels, who will manage them? After Zimbabwe confiscated and fragmented that nation's farms in 2000, its agricultural productivity plummeted and the economy collapsed. Cuba experienced the same kind of economic decline after the government seized and fragmented sugar and tobacco plantations. If the government expropriates factories, mills, farms, or businesses, who will run them? If the *rewards* to saving, investment, entrepreneurship, and management are expropriated, who will undertake these economic activities?

This is not to suggest that *no* redistribution of income or assets is appropriate. More progressive taxes and land reforms can reduce inequalities and poverty. But the potential of direct within-nation redistribution is often exaggerated. Historically, nations have often been forced to reverse land, tax, and property reforms that have slowed economic growth and reduced average incomes.

Expenditure Reallocation. In addition to directly redistributing private income and wealth, governments can also reduce poverty by reallocating direct government expenditures. As we observed in Chapter 1 (Figure 1.3), some poor nations devote a large share of output to the military. If more of those resources were channeled into schools, health services, and infrastructure, the poor would surely benefit. Governments in poor nations also tend to give priority to urban development (where the government and middle class reside), to the

Country	Total Aid ($ billions)	Percentage of Donor Total Income
United States	$ 32	0.19%
United Kingdom	18	0.70
Germany	14	0.42
France	11	0.37
Japan	12	0.19
Canada	5	0.24
Australia	5	0.31
Norway	6	1.00
Italy	4	0.19
24-Nation Total	$140	0.29%

Source: World Bank (2014 data).

TABLE 23.2
Foreign Aid

Rich nations give roughly $140–150 billion to poor nations every year. This is a tiny fraction of donor GDP, however.

neglect of rural development (where the poor reside). Redirecting more resources to rural development and core infrastructure (roads, electricity, and water) would accelerate poverty reduction.

Across-Nation Redistribution

Redistribution *across* national borders could make even bigger dents in global poverty. After all, the United States and other industrialized nations are so rich that they could transfer a lot of income to the globally poor if they chose to.

Foreign Aid. Currently developed nations give poorer nations $140–$150 billion a year in "official development assistance." That's a lot of money. But even if it were distributed exclusively to globally poor households, it would amount to only $50 per year per person.

Developed nations have set a goal of delivering more aid. The United Nations' **Millennium Aid Goal** is to raise foreign aid levels to 0.7 percent of donor-country GDP. That may not sound too ambitious, but it's a much larger flow than at present. As Table 23.2 reveals, few "rich" nations now come close to this goal. Although the United States is by far the world's largest aid donor, its aid equals only 0.19 percent of U.S. total output. For all developed nations, the aid ratio averages around 0.29 percent—just 40 percent of the UN goal.

Given the history of foreign aid, the UN goal is unlikely to be met anytime soon. But what if it were? What if foreign aid *tripled*? Would that cure global poverty? No. Tripling foreign aid would generate only $200 a year for each of the 2 billion people now in global poverty. Even that figure is optimistic, as it assumes all aid is distributed to the poor in a form (e.g., food, clothes, and medicine) that directly addresses their basic needs.

Nongovernmental Aid. Official development assistance is augmented by private charities and other nongovernmental organizations (NGOs). The Gates Foundation, for example, spends upward of $1 billion a year on health care for the globally poor, focusing on treatable diseases like malaria, tuberculosis, and HIV infection (see World View "The Way We Give"). Religious organizations operate schools and health clinics in areas of extreme poverty. The International Red Cross brings medical care, shelter, and food in emergencies.

As with official development assistance, the content of NGO aid can be as important as its level. Relatively low-cost immunizations, for example, can improve health conditions more than an expensive, high-tech health clinic can. Teaching basic literacy to a community of young children can be more effective than equipping a single high school with Internet capabilities. Distributing drought-resistant seeds to farmers can be more effective than donating advanced farm equipment (which may become useless when it needs to be repaired).

Millennium Aid Goal: United Nations goal of raising foreign aid levels to 0.7 percent of donor-country GDP.

THE WAY WE GIVE

Philanthropy Can Step In Where Market Forces Don't

One day my wife Melinda and I were reading about millions of children dying from diseases in poor countries that were eliminated in this country. . . .

Malaria has been known for a long time. In 1902, in 1907, Nobel Prizes were given for advances in understanding the malaria parasite and how it was transmitted. But here we are a hundred years later and malaria is setting new records, infecting more than 400 million people every year, and killing more than a million people every year. That's a number that's increasing every year, and every day it's more than 2,000 African children. . . .

And this would extend to tuberculosis, yellow fever, AIDS vaccine, acute diarrheal illnesses, respiratory illnesses; you know, millions of children die from these things every year, and yet the advances we have in biology have not been applied because rich countries don't have these diseases. The private sector really isn't involved in developing vaccines and medicines for these diseases because the developing countries can't buy them. . . .

And so if left to themselves, these market forces create a world, which is the situation today, where more than 90 percent of the money spent on health research is spent on those who are the healthiest. An example of that is the billion a year spent on combating baldness. That's great for some people, but perhaps it should get behind malaria in terms of its priority ranking. . . .

So philanthropy can step in where market forces are not there. . . . It can get the people who have the expertise and draw them in. It can use awards, it can use novel arrangements with private companies, it can partner with the universities. . . . And every year the platform of science that we have to do this on gets better.

—Bill Gates

Source: Gates, Bill, "Speech at The Tech Museum," Bill & Melinda Gates Foundation, November 15, 2006. ©2006.

ANALYSIS: When markets fail to provide for basic human needs, additional institutions and incentives may be needed.

ECONOMIC GROWTH

No matter how well designed foreign aid and philanthropy might be, across-nation transfers alone cannot eliminate global poverty. As Bill Gates observed, the entire endowment of the Gates Foundation would meet the health needs of the globally poor for only one year. The World Bank concurs: "Developing nations hold the keys to their prosperity; global action cannot substitute for equitable and efficient domestic policies and institutions."[1] So as important as international assistance is, it will never fully suffice.

Increasing Total Income

economic growth: An increase in output (real GDP); an expansion of production possibilities.

The "key" to ending global poverty is, of course, **economic growth.** As we've observed, *redistributing existing incomes doesn't do the job;* total *income has to increase.* This is what economic growth is all about.

Unique Needs. The generic prescription for economic growth is simple: more resources and better technology. But this growth formula takes on a new meaning in the poorest nations. Rich nations can focus on research, technology, and the spread of "brain power." Poor nations need the basics—the "bricks and mortar" elements of an economy such as water systems, roads, schools, and legal systems. Bill Gates learned this firsthand in his

[1]World Bank, *World Development Report, 2006* (Washington, DC: World Bank, 2006), p. 206.

early philanthropic efforts. In 1996 Microsoft donated a computer for a community center in Soweto, one of the poorest areas in South Africa. When he visited the center in 1997 he discovered the center had no electricity. He quickly realized that growth policy priorities for poor nations are different from those for rich nations.

Growth Potential

The potential of economic growth to reduce poverty in poor nations is impressive. The 40 nations classified as "low-income" by the World Bank have a combined output of only $600 billion. That's about twice the annual sales revenue of Walmart. "Lower-middle-income" nations like China, Brazil, Egypt, and Sri Lanka produce another $5 trillion or so of annual output. Hence every percentage point of economic growth increases total income in these combined nations by nearly $60 billion. According to the World Bank, if these nations could grow their economies by just 3.8 percent a year, that would generate an extra $280 billion of output in the first year and increasing thereafter. That "growth dividend" is twice the amount of foreign aid (Table 23.2).

China has demonstrated just how effective economic growth can be in reducing poverty. Since 1990 China has been the world's fastest-growing economy, with annual GDP growth rates routinely in the 8–10 percent range. This sensational growth has not only raised *average* incomes but has also dramatically reduced the incidence of poverty. In fact, *the observed success in reducing extreme global poverty from 30 percent in 1990 to 11 percent in 2016 is almost entirely due to the decline in Chinese poverty.* By contrast, slow economic growth in Africa, Latin America, and South Asia has *increased* their respective poverty populations.

Growth of per Capita Output

The really critical factor in reducing poverty is the relationship of output growth to population growth. China has been spectacularly successful in this regard: not only does it have one of the fastest GDP growth rates, but it also has one of the world's slowest population growth rates. As a result, its per capita output has grown by a incredible 9.6 percent a year.

Notice in Table 23.3 how slow population growth rates in high-income nations allows them to achieve ever-rising living standards. Japan is the ultimate example: with zero population growth, its pretty easy to achieve an increase in per capita income.

	Average Annual Growth Rate (2000–2015) of		
	GDP	Population	Per Capita GDP
High-income countries			
Canada	1.9	1.0	0.9
United States	1.7	0.9	0.8
Japan	0.7	0.0	0.7
France	1.1	0.6	0.5
Low-income countries			
China	10.1	0.5	9.6
India	7.5	1.5	6.0
West Bank/Gaza	3.9	2.8	1.1
Burundi	3.6	3.3	0.3
Libya	1.3	1.1	0.2
Madagascar	2.8	2.9	−0.1
Haiti	1.3	1.5	−0.2
Central African Republic	−0.1	1.8	−1.9
Zimbabwe	−1.3	1.5	−2.8

Source: The World Bank, *WDR2016 Data Set.*

TABLE 23.3

Growth Rates in Selected Countries, 2000–2015

The relationship between GDP growth and population growth is very different in rich and poor countries. The populations of rich countries are growing very slowly, and gains in per capita GDP are easily achieved. In the poorest countries, population is still increasing rapidly, making it difficult to raise living standards. Notice how per capita incomes are declining in many poor countries (such as Zimbabwe and Haiti).

Zimbabwe and the Central African Republic don't fare so well. Their output shrank every year, even while their populations were increasing. As a consequence, the average citizen had less output to consume every year: extreme poverty spread.

Investing in Human Capital

While the math of global poverty is simple, the strategies for reducing poverty and many and diverse. A common observation, however, is the need to invest more in **human capital.**

human capital: The knowledge and skills possessed by the workforce.

Education. In poor nations, the need for human capital development is evident. Only 71 percent of the population in low-income nations completes even elementary school. Even fewer people are *literate*—that is, able to read and write a short, simple statement about everyday life (e.g., "We ate rice for breakfast"). Educational deficiencies are greatest for females, who are often prevented from attending school by cultural, social, or economic concerns (see World View "The Female 'Inequality Trap'"). In Chad and Liberia, fewer than one out of six girls completes primary school. Primary school completion rates for girls are in the 25–35 percent range in most of the poor nations of sub-Saharan Africa.

WORLD VIEW

THE FEMALE "INEQUALITY TRAP"

In many poor nations, women are viewed as such a financial liability that female fetuses are aborted, female infants are killed, and female children are so neglected that they have significantly higher mortality rates. The "burden" females pose results from social norms that restrict the ability of women to earn income, accumulate wealth, or even decide their own marital status. In many of the poorest nations, women

- Have restricted property rights.
- Can't inherit wealth.
- Are prohibited or discouraged from working outside the home.
- Are prohibited or discouraged from going to school.
- Are prevented from voting.
- Are denied the right to divorce.
- Are paid less than men if they do work outside the home.
- Are often expected to bring a financial dowry to the marriage.
- May be beaten if they fail to obey their husbands.

These social practices create an "inequality trap" that keeps returns on female human capital investment low. Without adequate education or training, they can't get productive jobs. Without access to good jobs, they have no incentive to get an education or training. This kind of vicious cycle creates an inequality trap that keeps women and their communities poor.

Source: The World Bank, *World Development Report 2006,* pp. 51–54.

ANALYSIS: Denying women economic rights not only is discriminatory but reduces the amount of human capital available for economic growth.

inequality trap: Institutional barriers that impede human and physical capital investment, particularly by the poorest segments of society.

In Niger and Mali, only one out of five *teenage* girls is literate. This lack of literacy creates an **inequality trap** that restricts the employment opportunities for young women to simple, routine, manual jobs (e.g., carpet weaving and sewing). With so few skills and little education, they are destined to remain poor.

The already low levels of *average* education are compounded by unequal access to schools. Families in extreme poverty typically live in rural areas, with primitive transportation and communication facilities. *Physical* access to school itself is problematic. On top of that, the poorest families often need their children to work, either within the family or in paid employment. In Somalia, only 8 percent of poor young children attend primary schools; in Ethiopia, Yemen, and Mali, about 50 percent attend. These forces often foreclose school attendance for the poorest children.

Health. In poor nations, basic health care is also a critical dimension of human capital development. Immunizations against measles, diphtheria, and tetanus are more the exception than the rule in Somalia, Nigeria, Afghanistan, Congo, the Central African Republic, and many other poor nations. For all low-income nations taken together, the child immunization rate is only 67 percent (versus 96 percent in the United States). Access and education—not money—are the principal barriers to greater immunizations.

Water and sanitation facilities are also in short supply. The World Bank defines "adequate water access" as a protected water source of at least 20 liters per person a day within 1 kilometer of the home dwelling. We're not limited to indoor plumbing with this definition: a public water pipe a half mile from one's home is considered adequate. Yet only three out of four households in low-income nations meet even this minimum threshold of water adequacy In Afghanistan, Ethiopia, and Somalia only one out of four households has even that much water access. Access to sanitation facilities (ranging from pit latrines to flush toilets) is less common still (on average one out of three low-income-nation households). In Ethiopia only 6 percent of the population is so privileged.

When illness strikes, professional health care is hard to find. In the United States, there is one doctor for every 180 people. In Sierra Leone, there is one doctor for every 10,000 people! For low-income nations as a group, there are 2,500 people for every available doctor.

These glaring inadequacies in health conditions breed high rates of illness and death. In the United States, only 8 out of every 1,000 children die before age 5. In Angola, 260 of every 1,000 children die that young. For all low-income nations, the under-5 mortality rate is 13.5 percent (nearly one out of seven). Those children who live are commonly so malnourished (severely underweight and/or short) that they can't develop fully (another inequality trap).

AIDS takes a huge toll as well. Only 0.6 percent of the U.S. adult population has HIV. In Botswana, Lesotho, Swaziland, and Zimbabwe, more than 25 percent of the adult population is HIV-infected. As a result of these problems, life expectancies are inordinately low. In Zambia, only 16 percent of the population lives to age 65. In Botswana, life expectancy at birth is 35 years (versus 78 years in the United States). For low-income nations as a group, life expectancy is a mere 57 years.

Capital Investment

If they are ever going to eradicate poverty and its related social ills, poor nations need sharply increased capital investment in both the public and private sectors. Transportation and communications systems must be expanded and upgraded so markets can function. Capital equipment and upgraded technology must flow into both agricultural and industrial enterprises.

Internal Financing. Acquiring the capital resources needed to boost productivity and accelerate economic growth is not an easy task. Domestically, freeing up scarce resources for capital investment requires cutbacks in domestic consumption. In the 1920s Stalin used near-totalitarian powers to cut domestic consumption in Russia (by limiting output of consumer goods) and raise Russia's **investment rate** to as much as 30 percent of output. This elevated rate of investment accelerated capacity growth, but at a high cost in terms of consumer deprivation.

Other nations haven't had the power or the desire to make such a sacrifice. China spent two decades trying to raise consumption standards before it gave higher priority to investment. Once it did so, however, economic growth accelerated sharply. Unfortunately, low investment rates continue to plague other poor nations.

Pervasive poverty in poor nations sharply limits the potential for increased savings. Nevertheless, governments can encourage more saving with improved banking facilities,

Analysis: Unsafe water is a common problem for the globally poor.
©Dr. Parvinder Sethi RF

investment rate: The percentage of total output (GDP) allocated to the production of new plants, equipment, and structures.

microfinance: The granting of small ("micro"), unsecured loans to small businesses and entrepreneurs.

transparent capital markets, and education and saving incentives. And there is mounting evidence that even small dabs of financing can make a big difference. Extending a small loan that enables a poor farmer to buy improved seeds or a plow can have substantial effects on productivity. Financing small equipment or inventory for an entrepreneur can get a new business rolling. Such **microfinance** can be a critical key to escaping poverty (see World View "Muhammad Yunus: Microloans").

WORLD VIEW

MUHAMMAD YUNUS: MICROLOANS

Teach a man to fish, and he'll eat for a lifetime. But only if he can afford the fishing rod. More than 30 years ago in Bangladesh, economics Professor Muhammad Yunus recognized that millions of his countrymen were trapped in poverty because they were unable to scrape together the tiny sums they needed to buy productive essentials such as a loom, a plow, an ox, or a rod. So he gave small loans to his poor neighbors, secured by nothing more than their promise to repay.

Microcredit, as it's now known, became a macro success in 2006, reaching two huge milestones. The number of the world's poorest people with outstanding microloans—mostly in amounts of $15 to $150—was projected to reach 100 million. And Yunus, 66, shared the Nobel Peace Prize with the Grameen Bank he founded. The Nobel Committee honored his grassroots strategy as "development from below."

You know an idea's time has come when people start yanking it in directions its originator never imagined. Some, like Citigroup, are making for-profit loans, contrary to Yunus's breakeven vision. Others, like Bangladesh's BRAC, are nonprofit but have a more holistic vision than Grameen, offering health care and social services in addition to loans.

Source: "The Best Ideas," *BusinessWeek,* December 18, 2006, pp. 96–106. Used with permission of Bloomberg L.P. Copyright © 2015. All rights reserved.

ANALYSIS: Microloans focus on tiny loans to small businesses and farmers that enable them to increase output and productivity.

Some nations have also used inflation as a tool for shifting resources from consumption to investment. By financing public works projects and private investment with an increased money supply, governments can increase the inflation rate. As prices rise faster than consumer incomes, households are forced to curtail their purchases. This "inflation tax" ultimately backfires, however, when both domestic and foreign market participants lose confidence in the nation's currency. Periodic currency collapses have destabilized many South and Central American economies and governments. Inflation financing also fails to distinguish good investment ideas from bad ones.

External Financing. Given the constraints on internal financing, poor nations have to seek external funding to lift their investment rate. In fact, Columbia University economist Jeffrey Sachs has argued that external financing is not only necessary but, if generous enough, also sufficient for *eliminating* global poverty (see World View "Jeffrey Sachs: Big Money, Big Plans"). As we've observed, however, actual foreign aid flows are far below the "Big Money" threshold that Sachs envisions. Skeptics also question whether more foreign aid would really solve the problem, given the mixed results of previous foreign aid flows. They suggest that more emphasis should be placed on increasing *private* investment flows. Private investment typically entails *direct foreign investment* in new plants, equipment, and technology, or the purchase of ownership stakes in existing enterprises.

WORLD VIEW

JEFFREY SACHS: BIG MONEY, BIG PLANS

Columbia University economics professor Jeffrey Sachs has seen the ravages of poverty around the world. As director of the UN Millennium Project, he is committed to attaining the UN's goal of reducing global poverty rates by half by 2015. In fact, Professor Sachs thinks we can do even better: the complete *elimination* of extreme poverty by 2025.

How will the world do this? First, rich nations must double their foreign aid flows now, and then double them again in 10 years. Second, poor nations must develop full-scale, comprehensive plans for poverty reduction. This "shock therapy" approach must address all dimensions of the poverty problem simultaneously and quickly, sweeping all inequality traps out of the way.

Critics have called Sachs's vision utopian. They point to the spotty history of foreign aid projects and the failure of many top-down, Big Plan development initiatives. But they still applaud Sachs for mobilizing public opinion and economic resources to fight global poverty.

Source: Sachs, Jeffrey, *The End of Poverty,* New York, NY: Penguin Random House, 2006.

ANALYSIS: World poverty can't be eliminated without committing far more resources. Jeffrey Sachs favors an externally financed, comprehensive Big Plan approach.

Agricultural Development

When we think about capital investment, we tend to picture new factories, gleaming office buildings, and computerized machinery. In discussing global poverty, however, we have to remind ourselves of how dependent poor nations are on agriculture. As Figure 23.2 illustrates, nearly 60 percent of Somalia's income originates in agriculture. Agricultural shares in the range of 35–55 percent are common in the poorest nations. By contrast, only 1 percent of America's output now comes from farms.

Low Farm Productivity. What keeps poor nations so dependent on agriculture is their incredibly low **productivity.** Subsistence farmers are often forced to plow their own fields by hand with wooden plows. Irrigation systems are primitive and farm machinery is scarce or nonexistent. While high-tech U.S. farms produce nearly $80,000 of output per worker, Ugandan

productivity: Output per unit of input—for example, output per labor-hour.

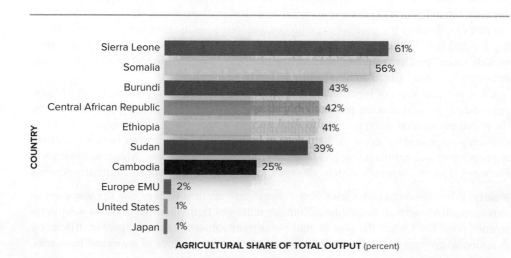

FIGURE 23.2
Agricultural Share of Output

In poor nations, agriculture accounts for a very large share of total output.

Source: The World Bank, *WDR2016 Data Set.*

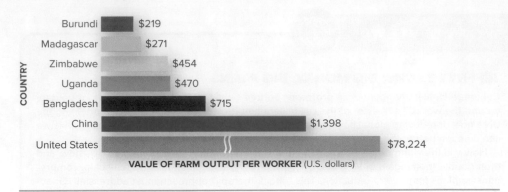

FIGURE 23.3

Low Agricultural Productivity

Farmers in poor nations suffer from low productivity. They are handicapped by low education, inferior technology, primitive infrastructure, and a lack of machinery.

Source: The World Bank, *WDR2016 Data Set*.

farms produce a shockingly low $219 of output per worker (see Figure 23.3). Farmers in Sudan produce only 683 kilograms of cereal per hectare, compared with 7,637 kilos per hectare in the United States.

To grow their economies, poor nations have to invest in agricultural development. Farm productivity has to rise beyond subsistence levels so that workers can migrate to other industries and expand production possibilities. One of the catapults to China's growth was an exponential increase in farm productivity that freed up labor for industrial production. (China now produces nearly 5,900 kilos of cereal per hectare.) To achieve greater farm productivity, poor nations need capital investment, technological know-how, and improved infrastructure.

Institutional Reform

Clearly, poor nations need a lot more investment. But more resources alone may not suffice. To attract and keep capital, **a *nation needs an institutional structure that promotes economic growth.***

Property Rights. Land, property, and contract rights have to be established before farmers will voluntarily improve their land or invest in agricultural technology. China saw how agricultural productivity jumped when it transformed government-run communal farms into local enterprises and privately managed farms, beginning in 1978. China is using the lessons of that experience to now extend ownership rights to farmers.

Entrepreneurial Incentives. Unleashing the "animal spirits" of the marketplace is also critical. People *do* respond to incentives. If farmers see the potential for profit—and the opportunity to keep that profit—they will pursue productivity gains with more vigor. To encourage that response, governments need to assure the legitimacy of profits and their fair tax treatment. In 1992 the Chinese government acknowledged the role of profits and entrepreneurship in fostering economic advancement. Before then, successful entrepreneurs ran the risk of offending the government with conspicuous consumption that highlighted growing inequalities. The government even punished some entrepreneurs and confiscated their wealth. Once "profits" were legitimized, however, entrepreneurship and foreign investment accelerated, raising China's growth rate significantly.

Cuba stopped short of legitimizing private property and profits. Although Fidel Castro periodically permitted some private enterprises (e.g., family restaurants), he always withdrew that permission when entrepreneurial ventures succeeded. As a consequence, Cuba's economy stagnated for decades. Venezuela has recently moved further in that direction, expropriating and nationalizing private enterprises (see World View "Maduro: 'Bourgeois Parasites' Thwart Growth"), thereby discouraging private investment and entrepreneurship.

Equity. What disturbed both Castro and Venezuelan President Chávez was the way capitalism intensified income inequalities. Entrepreneurs got rich while the mass of people remained poor. For Castro, the goal of equity was more important than the goal of efficiency. A nation where everyone was equally poor was preferred to a nation of haves and have-nots.

Analysis: Lack of capital, technology, and markets keeps farm productivity low.
©McGraw-Hill Education/Barry Barker, photographer

WORLD VIEW 🌐

MADURO: "BOURGEOIS PARASITES" THWART GROWTH

When he won a third presidential term in 2006, Hugo Chávez made his intentions clear. Venezuela, he said, is "heading toward socialism, and no one can prevent it." He embarked on a policy of nationalization, price controls, and a political takeover of Venezuela's central bank. Since then, the Venezuelan economy has stalled; factories, oil fields, and farms have shut down; inflation has soared; and food and energy shortages have become commonplace.

Chávez's successor, Nicolas Maduro, blames the nation's economic woes not on government policy but on the "bourgeois parasites" who have conspired to raise prices, hoard commodities, and strangle the economy. He ordered the nation's largest electronic retailer, Daka, to cut its prices in half and sent the military into its stores to enforce those price cuts. He urged Venezuelans to "leave nothing on the shelves, nothing in the warehouses" and threatened store managers with arrest if they interfered. Critics called the action "government-sanctioned looting." Maduro also levied fines and threatened jail sentences for General Motors executives who he accused of cutting back production and charging "exploitive" prices for new cars. Meanwhile, people have to wait for years to get a new car, while food, water, and energy are now being rationed because of spreading shortages.

Source: News reports, September 2014.

ANALYSIS: By restricting private ownership and market freedom, governments curb the entrepreneurship and investment that may be essential for economic development.

In many of today's poorest nations, policy interests are not so noble. A small elite often holds extraordinary political power and uses that power to protect its privileges. Greed restricts the flow of resources to the poorest segments of the population, leaving them to fend for themselves. These inequalities in power, wealth, and opportunity create inequality traps that restrain human capital development, capital investment, entrepreneurship, and ultimately economic growth.

Business Climate. To encourage capital investment and entrepreneurship, governments have to assure a secure and supportive business climate. Investors and business start-ups want to know what the rules of the game are and how they will be enforced. They also want assurances that contracts will be enforced and that debts can be collected. They want their property protected from crime and government corruption. They want minimal interference from government regulation and taxes.

As the annual surveys by the Heritage Foundation document, nations that offer a more receptive business climate grow at a faster pace. Figure 23.4 illustrates this connection. Notice that nations with the most pro-business climate (e.g., Hong Kong, Singapore, Iceland, the United States, and Denmark) enjoy living standards far superior to those in nations with hostile business climates (e.g., North Korea, Cuba, Congo, Sudan, Zimbabwe, and Myanmar). This is no accident; ***pro-business climates encourage the capital investment, the entrepreneurship, and the human capital investment that drive economic growth.***

Unfortunately, some of the poorest nations still fail to provide a pro-business environment. Figure 23.5 illustrates how specific dimensions of the business climate differ across fast-growing nations (China) and perpetually poor ones (Cambodia and Kenya). A biannual survey of 26,000 international firms elicits their views of how different government policies restrain their investment decisions. Notice how China offers a more certain policy environment, less corruption, more secure property rights, and less crime. Given these business conditions, where would you invest?

The good news about the business climate is that it doesn't require huge investments to fix. It does require, however, a lot of political capital.

FIGURE 23.4

Business Climates Affect Growth

Nations that offer more secure property rights, less regulation, and lower taxes grow faster and enjoy higher per capita incomes.

Note: Business climate in 183 nations gauged by 50 measures of government tax, regulatory, and legal policy.

2011 Index of Economic Freedom, Washington, DC: The Heritage Foundation, p. 7, 2011.

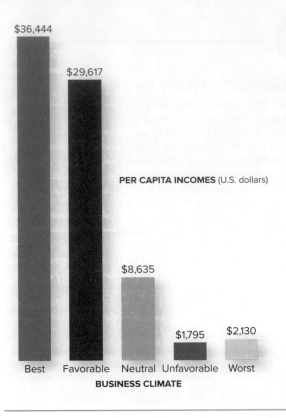

PER CAPITA INCOMES (U.S. dollars)

$36,444 — Best
$29,617 — Favorable
$8,635 — Neutral
$1,795 — Unfavorable
$2,130 — Worst

BUSINESS CLIMATE

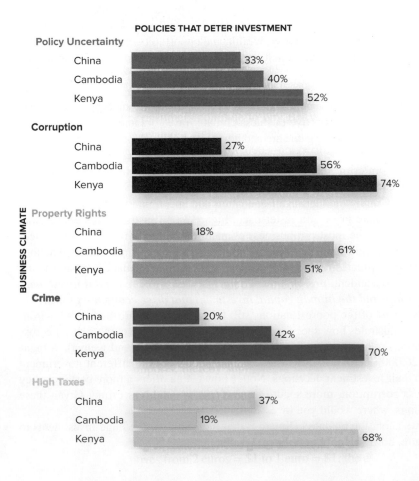

POLICIES THAT DETER INVESTMENT

Policy Uncertainty
China — 33%
Cambodia — 40%
Kenya — 52%

Corruption
China — 27%
Cambodia — 56%
Kenya — 74%

Property Rights
China — 18%
Cambodia — 61%
Kenya — 51%

Crime
China — 20%
Cambodia — 42%
Kenya — 70%

High Taxes
China — 37%
Cambodia — 19%
Kenya — 68%

BUSINESS CLIMATE

FIGURE 23.5

Investment Climate

International investors gravitate toward nations with business-friendly policies. Shown here are the percentages of international firms citing specific elements of the business climate that deter their investment in the named countries.

Source: The World Bank, *World Development Indicators 2006.*

World Trade

When it comes to political capital, poor nations have a complaint of their own. They say that rich nations lock them out of their most important markets—particularly agricultural export markets. Poor nations typically have a **comparative advantage** in the production of agricultural products. Their farm productivity may be low (see Figure 23.3), but their low labor costs keep their farm output competitive. They can't fully exploit that advantage in export markets, however. The United States, the European Union, and Japan heavily subsidize their own farmers. This keeps farm prices low in the rich nations, eliminating the cost advantage of farmers in poor nations. To further protect their own farmers from global competition, rich nations erect trade barriers to stem the inflow of Third World products. The United States, for example, enforces an **import quota** on foreign sugar. This trade barrier has fostered a high-cost, domestic beet sugar industry while denying poor nations the opportunity to sell more sugar and grow their economies faster.

Poor nations need export markets. Export sales generate the hard currency (dollars, euros, and yen) that is needed to purchase capital equipment in global markets. Export sales also allow farmers in poor nations to expand production, exploit economies of scale, and invest in improved technology. Ironically, *trade barriers in rich nations impede poor nations from pursuing the agricultural development that is a **prerequisite** for growth.* The latest round of multilateral trade negotiations dragged on forever because of the resistance of rich nations to opening their agricultural markets. Poor nations plead that "trade, not aid" is their surest path to economic growth.

comparative advantage: The ability of a country to produce a specific good at a lower opportunity cost than its trading partners.

import quota: A limit on the quantity of a good that may be imported in a given time period.

THE ECONOMY TOMORROW

UNLEASHING ENTREPRENEURSHIP

The traditional approach to economic development emphasizes the potential for government policy to reallocate resources and increase capital investment. External financing of capital investment was always at or near the top of the policy agenda (see World View "Jeffrey Sachs: Big Money, Big Plans"). This approach has been criticized for neglecting the power of people and markets.

One of the most influential critics is the Peruvian economist Hernando de Soto. When he returned to his native Peru after years of commercial success in Europe, he was struck by the dichot-

Analysis: Markets exist but struggle in poor nations.
©Lissa Harrison RF

omy in his country. The "official" economy was mired in bureaucratic red tape and stagnant. Most of the vitality of the Peruvian economy was contained in the unofficial "underground" economy. The underground economy included trade in drugs but was overwhelmingly oriented to meeting the everyday demands of Peruvian consumers and households. The underground economy wasn't hidden from view; it flourished on the streets, in outdoor markets, and in transport services. The only thing that forced this thriving economy underground was the failure of the government to recognize it and give it legitimate status. Government restrictions on prices, business activities, finance, and trade—a slew of inequality traps—forced entrepreneurs to operate "underground."

De Soto concluded that countries like Peru could grow more quickly if governments encouraged rather than suppressed these entrepreneurial resources. In his best-selling

Continued

book *The Other Path,* he urged poor countries to refocus their development policies. This "other path" entails improving the business climate by

- Reducing bureaucratic barriers to free enterprise.
- Spreading private ownership.
- Developing and enforcing legal safeguards for property, income, and wealth.
- Developing infrastructure that facilitates business activity.

Yunus's "microloans" (see World View "Muhammad Yunus: Microloans") would also fit comfortably on this other path.

De Soto's book has been translated into several languages and has encouraged market-oriented reforms in Peru, Argentina, Mexico, Russia, Vietnam, and elsewhere. In India the government is drastically reducing both regulation and taxes to pursue De Soto's other path. The basic message of his other path is that poor nations should exploit the one resource that is abundant in even the poorest countries—entrepreneurship.

SUMMARY

- Definitions of "poverty" are culturally based. Poverty in the United States is defined largely in *relative* terms, whereas global poverty is tied more to *absolute* levels of subsistence. **LO23-1**
- About 13 percent of the U.S. population (more than 40 million people) are officially counted as poor. Poor people in America suffer from *relative* deprivation, not *absolute* deprivation, as in global poverty. **LO23-1**
- Global poverty thresholds are about one-tenth of U.S. standards. "Extreme" poverty is defined as less than $1.90 per day per person; "severe" poverty is less than $3.10 per day (inflation adjusted). **LO23-1**
- 800 million people around the world are in extreme poverty; 2 billion are in severe poverty. In low-income nations global poverty rates are as high as 70–90 percent. **LO23-2**
- The United Nations' Millennium Poverty Goal is to eliminate severe poverty by 2030. **LO23-3**

- Redistribution of incomes *within* poor nations doesn't have much potential for reducing poverty, given their low *average* incomes. *Across*-nation redistributions (e.g., foreign aid) can make a small dent, however. **LO23-3**
- Economic growth is the key to global poverty reduction. Many poor nations are held back by undeveloped human capital, primitive infrastructure, and subsistence agriculture. To grow more quickly, they need to meet basic human needs (health and education), increase agricultural productivity, and encourage investment. **LO23-3**
- To move into sustained economic growth, poor nations need capital investment and institutional reforms that promote both equity and entrepreneurship. **LO23-3**
- Poor nations also need "trade, not aid"—that is, access to rich nation markets, particularly in farm products. **LO23-3**

Key Terms

poverty threshold (U.S.)	UN and World Bank Poverty Goal	investment rate
poverty rate	Millennium Aid Goal	microfinance
in-kind transfers	economic growth	productivity
extreme poverty (world)	human capital	comparative advantage
severe poverty (world)	inequality trap	import quota

Questions for Discussion

1. Why should Americans care about extreme poverty in Haiti, Ethiopia, or Bangladesh? **LO23-2**
2. If you had only $17 to spend per day (the U.S. poverty threshold), how would you spend it? What if you had only $1.90 a day (the World Bank "extreme poverty" threshold)? **LO23-1**
3. If a poor nation must choose between building an airport, some schools, or a steel plant, which one should it choose? Why? **LO23-3**
4. How do more children per family either restrain or expand income-earning potential? **LO23-3**

5. Are property rights a prerequisite for economic growth? Explain. **LO23-3**

6. How do unequal rights for women affect economic growth? **LO23-3**

7. How does microfinance alter prospects for economic growth? The distribution of political power? **LO23-3**

8. Can poor nations develop without substantial increases in agricultural productivity? (See Figure 23.2.) How? **LO23-3**

9. Would you invest in Cambodia or Kenya on the basis of the information in Figure 23.5? **LO23-3**

10. Why do economists put so much emphasis on entrepreneurship? How can poor nations encourage it? **LO23-3**

11. How do nations expect nationalization of basic industries to foster economic growth? **LO23-3**

12. If economic growth reduced poverty but widened inequalities, would it still be desirable? **LO23-3**

13. What market failure does Bill Gates (World View "The Way We Give") cite as the motivation for global philanthropy? **LO23-3**

PROBLEMS FOR CHAPTER 23

LO23-1 1. The World Bank's threshold for "extreme" poverty is $1.90 per person per day.
  (*a*) How much *annual* income does this imply for a family of four?
  (*b*) What portion of the official U.S. poverty threshold (roughly $25,000 for a family of four) is met by the World Bank's measure?

LO23-2 2. There are 2 billion people in "severe" poverty with less than $3.10 of income per day.
  (*a*) What is the maximum *combined* income of this "severely" poor population?
  (*b*) What percentage of the world's *total* income (roughly $85 trillion) does this represent?

LO23-2 3. In Namibia,
  (*a*) What percentage of total output is received by the richest 10 percent of households? (See World View "Glaring Inequalities.")
  (*b*) How much output did this share amount to in 2017, when Namibia's GDP was $15 billion?
  (*c*) With a total population of 2.5 million, what was the implied per capita income of
    (*i*) The richest 10 percent of the population?
    (*ii*) The remaining 90 percent?

LO23-3 4. (*a*) How much foreign aid did the United States provide in 2014? (See Table 23.2.)
  (*b*) How much more is required to satisfy the UN's Millennium Aid Goal if U.S. GDP was $16.8 trillion?

LO23-3 5. If the 24 industrialized nations were to satisfy the UN's Millennium Aid Goal, how much *more* foreign aid would they give annually? (See Table 23.2.)

LO23-3 6. According to Table 23.3, how many years will it take for per capita GDP to double in
  (*a*) China?
  (*b*) Libya?
  (*c*) Zimbabwe?

LO23-3 7. According to World View "The Way We Give,"
  (*a*) How much money is spent annually to combat baldness?
  (*b*) How much medical care would that money buy for each child who dies from malaria each year?

LO23-3 8. Foreign aid to poor nations amounted to $20 per year per person. What percentage did this aid cover of
  (*a*) The extreme poverty annual budget?
  (*b*) The severe poverty annual budget?

LO23-3 9. The Economy Tomorrow: Identify the four key paths identified by De Soto to improve business climate in less developed countries.

A

absolute advantage: The ability of a country to produce a specific good with fewer resources (per unit of output) than other countries.

acreage set-aside: Land withdrawn from production as part of policy to increase crop prices.

AD excess: The amount by which aggregate demand must be reduced to achieve full-employment equilibrium after allowing for price-level changes.

AD shortfall: The amount of additional aggregate demand needed to achieve full employment after allowing for price-level changes.

adjustable-rate mortgage (ARM): A mortgage (home loan) that adjusts the nominal interest rate to changing rates of inflation.

aggregate demand (AD): The total quantity of output (real GDP) demanded at alternative price levels in a given time period, *ceteris paribus*.

aggregate expenditure: The rate of total expenditure desired at alternative levels of income, *ceteris paribus*.

aggregate supply (AS): The total quantity of output (real GDP) producers are willing and able to supply at alternative price levels in a given time period, *ceteris paribus*.

antitrust: Government intervention to alter market structure or prevent abuse of market power.

appreciation: A rise in the price of one currency relative to another.

arithmetic growth: An increase in quantity by a constant amount each year.

asset: Anything having exchange value in the marketplace; wealth.

automatic stabilizer: Federal expenditure or revenue item that automatically responds countercyclically to changes in national income, like unemployment benefits and income taxes.

autonomous consumption: Consumer spending not dependent on current income.

average fixed cost (AFC): Total fixed cost divided by the quantity produced in a given time period.

average propensity to consume (APC): Total consumption in a given period divided by total disposable income.

average total cost (ATC): Total cost divided by the quantity produced in a given time period.

average variable cost (AVC): Total variable cost divided by the quantity produced in a given time period.

B

balance of payments: A summary record of a country's international economic transactions in a given period of time.

balance-of-payments deficit: An excess demand for foreign currency at current exchange rates.

balance-of-payments surplus: An excess demand for domestic currency at current exchange rates.

bank reserves: Assets held by a bank to fulfill its deposit obligations.

barriers to entry: Obstacles such as patents that make it difficult or impossible for would-be producers to enter a particular market.

barter: The direct exchange of one good for another, without the use of money.

base year: The year used for comparative analysis; the basis for indexing price changes.

bilateral monopoly: A market with only one buyer (a monopsonist) and one seller (a monopolist).

bond: A certificate acknowledging a debt and the amount of interest to be paid each year until repayment; an IOU.

bracket creep: The movement of taxpayers into higher tax brackets (rates) as nominal incomes grow.

breakeven level of income: The income level at which welfare eligibility ceases.

budget constraint: A line depicting all combinations of goods that are affordable with a given income and given prices.

budget deficit: The amount by which government spending exceeds government revenue in a given time period.

budget surplus: An excess of government revenues over government expenditures in a given time period.

business cycle: Alternating periods of economic growth and contraction.

C

capital: Final goods produced for use in the production of other goods, such as equipment and structures.

capital gain: An increase in the market value of an asset.

capital gains tax: A tax levied on the profit from the sale of property.

capital-intensive: Production processes that use a high ratio of capital to labor inputs.

cartel: A group of firms with an explicit, formal agreement to fix prices and output shares in a particular market.

cash transfers: Income transfers that entail direct cash payments to recipients, such as Social Security, welfare, and unemployment benefits.

ceteris paribus: The assumption of nothing else changing.

closed economy: A nation that doesn't engage in international trade.

collective bargaining: Direct negotiations between employers and unions to determine labor market outcomes.

comparative advantage: The ability of a country to produce a specific good at a lower opportunity cost than its trading partners.

competitive firm: A firm without market power, with no ability to alter the market price of the goods it produces.

competitive market: A market in which no buyer or seller has market power.

complementary goods: Goods frequently consumed in combination; when the price of good *x* rises, the demand for good *y* falls, *ceteris paribus*.

concentration ratio: The proportion of total industry output produced by the largest firms (usually the four largest).

constant returns to scale: Increases in plant size do not affect minimum average cost; minimum per-unit costs are identical for small plants and large plants.

Consumer Price Index (CPI): A measure (index) of changes in the average price of consumer goods and services.

consumer surplus: The difference between the maximum price a person is willing to pay and the price paid.

consumption: Expenditure by consumers on final goods and services.

consumption function: A mathematical relationship indicating the rate of desired consumer spending at various income levels.

consumption possibilities: The alternative combinations of goods and services that a country could consume in a given time period.

contestable market: An imperfectly competitive industry subject to potential entry if prices or profits increase.

core inflation rate: Changes in the CPI, excluding food and energy prices.

corporate stock: Shares of ownership in a corporation.

corporation: A business organization having a continuous existence independent of its members (owners) and power and liabilities distinct from those of its members.

cost efficiency: The amount of output associated with an additional dollar spent on input; the MPP of an input divided by its price (cost).

cost-of-living adjustment (COLA): Automatic adjustments of nominal income to the rate of inflation.

coupon rate: Interest rate set for a bond at time of issuance.

cross-price elasticity of demand: Percentage change in the quantity demanded of X divided by the percentage change in the price of Y.

cross-subsidization: Use of high prices and profits on one product to subsidize low prices on another product.

crowdfunding: The financing of a project through individual contributions from a large number of people, typically via an Internet platform.

crowding in: An increase in private sector borrowing (and spending) caused by decreased government borrowing.

crowding out: A reduction in private sector borrowing (and spending) caused by increased government borrowing.

current yield: The rate of return on a bond; the annual interest payment divided by the bond's price.

cyclical deficit: That portion of the budget deficit attributable to unemployment or inflation.

cyclical unemployment: Unemployment attributable to a lack of job vacancies—that is, to an inadequate level of aggregate demand.

D

debt ceiling: An explicit, legislated limit on the amount of outstanding national debt.

debt service: The interest required to be paid each year on outstanding debt.

default: Failure to make scheduled payments of interest or principal on a bond.

deficit ceiling: An explicit, legislated limitation on the size of the budget deficit.

deficit spending: The use of borrowed funds to finance government expenditures that exceed tax revenues.

deflation: A decrease in the average level of prices of goods and services.

demand: The willingness and ability to buy specific quantities of a good at alternative prices in a given time period, *ceteris paribus.*

demand curve: A curve describing the quantities of a good a consumer is willing and able to buy at alternative prices in a given time period, *ceteris paribus.*

demand for labor: The quantities of labor employers are willing and able to hire at alternative wage rates in a given time period, *ceteris paribus.*

demand for money: The quantities of money people are willing and able to hold at alternative interest rates, *ceteris paribus.*

demand-pull inflation: An increase in the price level initiated by excessive aggregate demand.

demand schedule: A table showing the quantities of a good a consumer is willing and able to buy at alternative prices in a given time period, *ceteris paribus.*

deposit creation: The creation of transactions deposits by bank lending.

depreciation: The consumption of capital in the production process; the wearing out of plant and equipment.

depreciation (currency): A fall in the price of one currency relative to another.

derived demand: The demand for labor and other factors of production results from (depends on) the demand for final goods and services produced by these factors.

devaluation: An abrupt depreciation of a currency whose value was fixed or managed by the government.

discount rate: The rate of interest the Federal Reserve charges for lending reserves to private banks.

discounting: Federal Reserve lending of reserves to private banks.

discouraged worker: An individual who isn't actively seeking employment but would look for or accept a job if one were available.

discretionary fiscal spending: Those elements of the federal budget not determined by past legislative or executive commitments.

disposable income (DI): After-tax income of households; personal income less personal taxes.

dissaving: Consumption expenditure in excess of disposable income; a negative saving flow.

dividend: Amount of corporate profits paid out for each share of stock.

dumping: The sale of goods in export markets at prices below domestic prices.

E

economic cost: The value of all resources used to produce a good or service; opportunity cost.

economic growth: An increase in output (real GDP); an expansion of production possibilities.

economic profit: The difference between total revenues and total economic costs.

economics: The study of how best to allocate scarce resources among competing uses.

economies of scale: Reductions in minimum average costs that come about through increases in the size (scale) of plant and equipment.

effective tax rate: Taxes paid divided by total income.

efficiency: Maximum output of a good from the resources used in production.

efficiency decision: The choice of a production process for any given rate of output.

elasticity of labor supply: The percentage change in the quantity of labor supplied divided by the percentage change in wage rate.

embargo: A prohibition on exports or imports.

emission charge: A fee imposed on polluters, based on the quantity of pollution.

employment rate: The percentage of the adult population that is employed.

employment targeting: The use of an unemployment-rate threshold (6.5 percent) to signal the need for monetary stimulus.

entrepreneurship: The assembling of resources to produce new or improved products and technologies.

equation of exchange: Money supply (M) times velocity of circulation (V) equals level of aggregate spending (P × Q).

equilibrium (macro): The combination of price level and real output that is compatible with both aggregate demand and aggregate supply.

equilibrium GDP: The value of total output (real GDP) produced at macro equilibrium (AS = AD).

equilibrium price: The price at which the quantity of a good demanded in a given time period equals the quantity supplied.

equilibrium rate of interest: The interest rate at which the quantity of money demanded in a given time period equals the quantity of money supplied.

equilibrium wage: The wage rate at which the quantity of labor supplied in a given time period equals the quantity of labor demanded.

excess reserves: Bank reserves in excess of required reserves.

exchange rate: The price of one country's currency expressed in terms of another's; the domestic price of a foreign currency.

expected value: The probable value of a future payment, including the risk of nonpayment.

expenditure equilibrium: The rate of output at which desired spending equals the value of output.

explicit costs: A payment made for the use of a resource.

exports: Goods and services sold to foreign buyers.

external costs: Costs of a market activity borne by a third party; the difference between the social and private costs of a market activity.

external debt: U.S. government debt (Treasury bonds) held by foreign households and institutions.

externalities: Costs (or benefits) of a market activity borne by a third party; the difference between the social and private costs (benefits) of a market activity.

extreme poverty (world): World Bank income standard of less than $1.90 per day per person (inflation adjusted).

F

factor market: Any place where factors of production (e.g., land, labor, capital) are bought and sold.

factors of production: Resource inputs used to produce goods and services, e.g., land, labor, capital, entrepreneurship.

federal funds rate: The interest rate for interbank reserve loans.

financial intermediary: Institution (e.g., a bank or the stock market) that makes savings available to dissavers (e.g., investors).

fine-tuning: Adjustments in economic policy designed to counteract small changes in economic outcomes; continuous responses to changing economic conditions.

fiscal policy: The use of government taxes and spending to alter macroeconomic outcomes.

fiscal restraint: Tax hikes or spending cuts intended to reduce (shift) aggregate demand.

fiscal stimulus: Tax cuts or spending hikes intended to increase (shift) aggregate demand.

fiscal year (FY): The 12-month period used for accounting purposes; begins October 1 for the federal government.

fixed costs: Costs of production that don't change when the rate of output is altered, such as the cost of basic plants and equipment.

flat tax: A single-rate tax system.

flexible exchange rates: A system in which exchange rates are permitted to vary with market supply-and-demand conditions; floating exchange rates.

foreign exchange markets: Places where foreign currencies are bought and sold.

foreign exchange reserves: Holdings of foreign currencies by official government agencies, usually the central bank or treasury.

free rider: An individual who reaps direct benefits from someone else's purchase (consumption) of a public good.

frictional unemployment: Brief periods of unemployment experienced by people moving between jobs or into the labor market.

full employment: The lowest rate of unemployment compatible with price stability, variously estimated at between 4 percent and 6 percent unemployment.

full-employment GDP: The value of total market output (real GDP) produced at full employment.

G

game theory: The study of decision making in situations where strategic interaction (moves and countermoves) occurs between rivals.

GDP deflator: A price index that refers to all goods and services included in GDP.

GDP per capita: Total GDP divided by total population; average GDP.

geometric growth: An increase in quantity by a constant proportion each year.

Gini coefficient: A mathematical summary of inequality based on the Lorenz curve.

gold reserves: Stocks of gold held by a government to purchase foreign exchange.

gold standard: An agreement by countries to fix the price of their currencies in terms of gold; a mechanism for fixing exchange rates.

government failure: Government intervention that fails to improve economic outcomes.

gross business saving: Depreciation allowances and retained earnings.

gross domestic product (GDP): The total market value of all final goods and services produced within a nation's borders in a given time period.

gross investment: Total investment expenditure in a given time period.

growth rate: Percentage change in real output from one period to another.

growth recession: A period during which real GDP grows but at a rate below the long-term trend of 3 percent.

H

Herfindahl-Hirshman Index (HHI): Measure of industry concentration that accounts for number of firms and size of each.

horizontal equity: Principle that people with equal incomes should pay equal taxes.

human capital: The knowledge and skills possessed by the workforce.

hyperinflation: Inflation rate in excess of 200 percent, lasting at least one year.

I

implicit cost: The value of resources used, for which no direct payment is made.

import quota: A limit on the quantity of a good that may be imported in a given time period.

imports: Goods and services purchased from international sources.

income effect of higher wages: An increased wage rate allows a person to reduce hours worked without losing income.

income elasticity of demand: Percentage change in quantity demanded divided by percentage change in income.

income quintile: One-fifth of the population, rank-ordered by income (e.g., top fifth).

income share: The proportion of total income received by a particular group.

income transfers: Payments to individuals for which no current goods or services are exchanged, such as Social Security, welfare, and unemployment benefits.

indifference curve: A curve depicting alternative combinations of goods that yield equal satisfaction.

indifference map: The set of indifference curves that depicts all possible levels of utility attainable from various combinations of goods.

inequality trap: Institutional barriers that impede human and physical capital investment, particularly by the poorest segments of society.

inferior good: Goods for which demand decreases when income rises.

inflation: An increase in the average level of prices of goods and services.

inflation rate: The annual percentage rate of increase in the average price level; (Price Level$_{\text{Year 2}}$ − Price Level$_{\text{Year 1}}$)/Price Level$_{\text{Year 1}}$.

inflation targeting: The use of an inflation ceiling ("target") to signal the need for monetary-policy adjustments.

inflationary flashpoint: The rate of output at which inflationary pressures intensify; the point on the AS curve where slope increases sharply.

inflationary gap: The amount by which aggregate spending at full employment exceeds full-employment output.

inflationary GDP gap: The amount by which equilibrium GDP exceeds full-employment GDP.

infrastructure: The transportation, communications, education, judicial, and other institutional systems that facilitate market exchanges.

initial public offering (IPO): The first issuance (sale) to the general public of stock in a corporation.

injection: An addition of spending to the circular flow of income.

in-kind income: Goods and services received directly, without payment, in a market transaction.

in-kind transfers: Direct transfers of goods and services rather than cash, such as food stamps, Medicaid benefits, and housing subsidies.

interest rate: The price paid for the use of money.

intermediate goods: Goods or services purchased for use as input in the production of final goods or in services.

internal debt: U.S. government debt (Treasury bonds) held by U.S. households and institutions.

investment: Expenditures on (production of) new plants, equipment, and structures (capital) in a given time period, plus changes in business inventories.

investment decision: The decision to build, buy, or lease plants and equipment; to enter or exit an industry.

investment rate: The percentage of total output (GDP) allocated to the production of new plants, equipment, and structures.

item weight: The percentage of total expenditure spent on a specific product; used to compute inflation indexes.

L

labor force: All persons over age 16 who are either working for pay or actively seeking paid employment.

labor force participation rate: The percentage of the working-age population working or seeking employment.

labor productivity: Amount of output produced by a worker in a given period of time; output per hour (or day, etc.).

labor supply: The willingness and ability to work specific amounts of time at alternative wage rates in a given time period, *ceteris paribus.*

laissez faire: The doctrine of "leave it alone," of nonintervention by government in the market mechanism.

law of demand: The quantity of a good demanded in a given time period increases as its price falls, *ceteris paribus.*

law of diminishing marginal utility: The marginal utility of a good declines as more of it is consumed in a given time period.

law of diminishing returns: The marginal physical product of a variable input declines as more of it is employed with a given quantity of other (fixed) inputs.

law of supply: The quantity of a good supplied in a given time period increases as its price increases, *ceteris paribus.*

leakage: Income not spent directly on domestic output but instead diverted from the circular flow—for example, saving, imports, taxes.

liability: An obligation to make future payment; debt.

liquidity: The ability of an asset to be converted into cash.

liquidity trap: The portion of the money demand curve that is horizontal; people are willing to hold unlimited amounts of money at some (low) interest rate.

loan rate: The implicit price paid by the government for surplus crops taken as collateral for loans to farmers.

long run: A period of time long enough for all inputs to be varied (no fixed costs).

long-run competitive equilibrium: $p = MC = $ minimum ATC.

Lorenz curve: A graphic illustration of the cumulative size distribution of income; contrasts complete equality with the actual distribution of income.

M

macroeconomics: The study of aggregate economic behavior, of the economy as a whole.

managed exchange rates: A system in which governments intervene in foreign exchange markets to limit but not eliminate exchange rate fluctuations; "dirty floats."

marginal cost (MC): The increase in total cost associated with a one-unit increase in production.

marginal cost pricing: The offer (supply) of goods at prices equal to their marginal cost.

marginal factor cost (MFC): The change in total costs that results from a one-unit increase in the quantity of a factor employed.

marginal physical product (MPP): The change in total output associated with one additional unit of input.

marginal propensity to consume (MPC): The fraction of each additional (marginal) dollar of disposable income spent on consumption; the change in consumption divided by the change in disposable income.

marginal propensity to save (MPS): The fraction of each additional (marginal) dollar of disposable income not spent on consumption; $1 - $ MPC.

marginal rate of substitution: The rate at which a consumer is willing to exchange one good for another; the relative marginal utilities of two goods.

marginal revenue (MR): The change in total revenue that results from a one-unit increase in the quantity sold.

marginal revenue product (MRP): The change in total revenue associated with one additional unit of input.

marginal tax rate: The tax rate imposed on the last (marginal) dollar of income.

marginal utility: The change in total utility obtained by consuming one additional (marginal) unit of a good or service.

marginal wage: The change in total wages paid associated with a one-unit increase in the quantity of labor employed.

market demand: The total quantities of a good or service people are willing and able to buy at alternative prices in a given time period; the sum of individual demands.

market failure: An imperfection in the market mechanism that prevents optimal outcomes.

market mechanism: The use of market prices and sales to signal desired outputs (or resource allocations).

market power: The ability to alter the market price of a good or service.

market share: The percentage of total market output produced by a single firm.

market shortage: The amount by which the quantity demanded exceeds the quantity supplied at a given price; excess demand.

market structure: The number and relative size of firms in an industry.

market supply: The total quantities of a good that sellers are willing and able to sell at alternative prices in a given time period, *ceteris paribus.*

market supply of labor: The total quantity of labor that workers are willing and able to supply at alternative wage rates in a given time period, *ceteris paribus.*

market surplus: The amount by which the quantity supplied exceeds the quantity demanded at a given price; excess supply.

merit good: A good or service society deems everyone is entitled to some minimal quantity of.

microeconomics: The study of individual behavior in the economy, of the components of the larger economy.

microfinance: The granting of small ("micro"), unsecured loans to small businesses and entrepreneurs.

Millennium Aid Goal: United Nations goal of raising foreign aid levels to 0.7 percent of donor-country GDP.

misery index: The sum of inflation and unemployment rates.

mixed economy: An economy that uses both market signals and government directives to allocate goods and resources.

monetary policy: The use of money and credit controls to influence macroeconomic outcomes.

money: Anything generally accepted as a medium of exchange.

money illusion: The use of nominal dollars rather than real dollars to gauge changes in one's income or wealth.

money multiplier: The number of deposit (loan) dollars that the banking system can create from $1 of excess reserves; equal to 1 ÷ required reserve ratio.

money supply (M1): Currency held by the public, plus balances in transactions accounts.

money supply (M2): M1 plus balances in most savings accounts and money market funds.

monopolistic competition: A market in which many firms produce similar goods or services but each maintains some independent control of its own price.

monopoly: A firm that produces the entire market supply of a particular good or service.

monopsony: A market in which there's only one buyer.

moral hazard: An incentive to engage in undesirable behavior.

multiplier: The multiple by which an initial change in aggregate spending will alter total expenditure after an infinite number of spending cycles; 1/(1 − MPC).

N

national debt: Accumulated debt of the federal government.

national income (NI): Total income earned by current factors of production: GDP less depreciation and indirect business taxes, plus net foreign factor income.

national income accounting: The measurement of aggregate economic activity, particularly national income and its components.

natural monopoly: An industry in which one firm can achieve economies of scale over the entire range of market supply.

natural rate of unemployment: The long-term rate of unemployment determined by structural forces in labor and product markets.

net domestic product (NDP): GDP less depreciation.

net exports: The value of exports minus the value of imports: $(X − M)$.

net investment: Gross investment less depreciation.

nominal GDP: The value of final output produced in a given period, measured in the prices of that period (current prices).

nominal income: The amount of money income received in a given time period, measured in current dollars.

nominal tax rate: Taxes paid divided by taxable income.

normal good: Good for which demand increases when income rises.

normal profit: The opportunity cost of capital; zero economic profit.

O

Okun's law: One percent more unemployment is estimated to equal 2 percent less output.

oligopolist: One of the dominant firms in an oligopoly.

oligopoly: A market in which a few firms produce all or most of the market supply of a particular good or service.

open economy: A nation that engages in international trade.

open market operations: Federal Reserve purchases and sales of government bonds for the purpose of altering bank reserves.

opportunity cost: The most desired goods or services that are forgone in order to obtain something else.

opportunity wage: The highest wage an individual would earn in his or her best alternative job.

optimal consumption: The mix of consumer purchases that maximizes the utility attainable from available income.

optimal mix of output: The most desirable combination of output attainable with existing resources, technology, and social values.

optimal rate of pollution: The rate of pollution that occurs when the marginal social benefit of pollution control equals its marginal social cost.

outsourcing: The relocation of production to foreign countries.

P

par value: The face value of a bond; the amount to be repaid when the bond is due.

parity: The relative price of farm products in the period 1910–1914.

payoff matrix: A table showing the risks and rewards of alternative decision options.

per capita GDP: The dollar value of GDP divided by total population; average GDP.

perfect competition: A market in which no buyer or seller has market power.

personal income (PI): Income received by households before payment of personal taxes.

Phillips curve: A historical (inverse) relationship between the rate of unemployment and the rate of inflation; commonly expresses a trade-off between the two.

portfolio decision: The choice of how (where) to hold idle funds.

poverty gap: The shortfall between actual income and the poverty threshold.

poverty rate: Percentage of the population counted as poor.

poverty threshold (U.S.): Annual income of less than $24,600 for a family of four (2016).

precautionary demand for money: Money held for unexpected market transactions or for emergencies.

predatory pricing: Temporary price reductions designed to alter market shares or drive out competition.

present discounted value (PDV): The value today of future payments, adjusted for interest accrual.

price ceiling: An upper limit imposed on the price of a good.

price discrimination: The sale of an individual good at different prices to different consumers.

price/earnings (P/E) ratio: The price of a stock share divided by earnings (profit) per share.

price elasticity of demand: The percentage change in quantity demanded divided by the percentage change in price.

price elasticity of supply: The percentage change in quantity supplied divided by the percentage change in price.

price-fixing: Explicit agreements among producers regarding the price(s) at which a good is to be sold.

price floor: Lower limit set for the price of a good.

price leadership: An oligopolistic pricing pattern that allows one firm to establish the (market) price for all firms in the industry.

price stability: The absence of significant changes in the average price level; officially defined as a rate of inflation of less than 3 percent.

private costs: The costs of an economic activity directly borne by the immediate producer or consumer (excluding externalities).

private good: A good or service whose consumption by one person excludes consumption by others.

product differentiation: Features that make one product appear different from competing products in the same market.

product market: Any place where finished goods and services (products) are bought and sold.

production decision: The selection of the short-run rate of output (with existing plants and equipment).

production function: A technological relationship expressing the maximum quantity of a good attainable from different combinations of factor inputs.

production possibilities: The alternative combinations of final goods and services that could be produced in a given period with all available resources and technology.

production process: A specific combination of resources used to produce a good or service.

productivity: Output per unit of input—for example, output per labor-hour.

profit: The difference between total revenue and total cost.

profit-maximization rule: Produce at that rate of output where marginal revenue equals marginal cost.

profit per unit: Total profit divided by the quantity produced in a given time period; price minus average total cost.

progressive tax: A tax system in which tax rates rise as incomes rise.

proportional tax: A tax that levies the same rate on every dollar of income.

public choice: Theory of public sector behavior emphasizing rational self-interest of decision makers and voters.

public good: A good or service whose consumption by one person does not exclude consumption by others.

Q

quota: A limit on the quantity of a good that may be imported in a given time period.

R

rational expectations: Hypothesis that people's spending decisions are based on all available information, including the anticipated effects of government intervention.

real GDP: The value of final output produced in a given period, adjusted for changing prices.

real income: Income in constant dollars; nominal income adjusted for inflation.

real interest rate: The nominal interest rate minus the anticipated inflation rate.

recession: A decline in total output (real GDP) for two or more consecutive quarters.

recessionary gap: The amount by which aggregate spending at full employment falls short of full-employment output.

recessionary GDP gap: The amount by which equilibrium GDP falls short of full-employment GDP.

reference price: Government-guaranteed price floor for specific agricultural commodities.

refinancing: The issuance of new debt in payment of debt issued earlier.

regressive tax: A tax system in which tax rates fall as incomes rise.

regulation: Government intervention to alter the behavior of firms—for example, in pricing, output, or advertising.

relative price: The price of one good in comparison with the price of other goods.

required reserves: The minimum amount of reserves a bank is required to hold; equal to required reserve ratio times transactions deposits.

reserve ratio: The ratio of a bank's reserves to its total transactions deposits.

retained earnings: Amount of corporate profits not paid out in dividends.

risk premium: The difference in rates of return on risky (uncertain) and safe (certain) investments.

S

saving: That part of disposable income not spent on current consumption; disposable income less consumption.

Say's law: Supply creates its own demand.

scarcity: Lack of enough resources to satisfy all desired uses of those resources.

seasonal unemployment: Unemployment due to seasonal changes in employment or labor supply.

severe poverty (world): World Bank income standard of $3.10 per day per person (inflation adjusted).

shift in demand: A change in the quantity demanded at any (every) price.

short run: The period in which the quantity (and quality) of some inputs can't be changed.

short-run competitive equilibrium: $p = \text{MC}$.

shutdown point: The rate of output where price equals minimum AVC.

size distribution of income: The way total personal income is divided up among households or income classes.

social costs: The full resource costs of an economic activity, including externalities.

social insurance programs: Event-conditioned income transfers intended to reduce the costs of specific problems, such as Social Security and unemployment insurance.

speculative demand for money: Money held for speculative purposes, for later financial opportunities.

stagflation: The simultaneous occurrence of substantial unemployment and inflation.

structural deficit: Federal revenues at full employment minus expenditures at full employment under prevailing fiscal policy.

structural unemployment: Unemployment caused by a mismatch between the skills (or location) of job seekers and the requirements (or location) of available jobs.

substitute goods: Goods that substitute for each other; when the price of good x rises,

the demand for good y increases, *ceteris paribus*.

substitution effect of higher wages: An increased wage rate encourages people to work more hours (to substitute labor for leisure).

supply: The ability and willingness to sell (produce) specific quantities of a good at alternative prices in a given time period, *ceteris paribus*.

supply curve: A curve describing the quantities of a good a producer is willing and able to sell (produce) at alternative prices in a given time period, *ceteris paribus*.

supply-side policy: The use of tax incentives, (de)regulation, and other mechanisms to increase the ability and willingness to produce goods and services.

T

T-accounts: The accounting ledgers used by banks to track assets and liabilities.

target efficiency: The percentage of income transfers that go to the intended recipients and purposes.

tariff: A tax (duty) imposed on imported goods.

tax base: The amount of income or property directly subject to nominal tax rates.

tax elasticity of labor supply: The percentage change in quantity of labor supplied divided by the percentage change in tax rates.

tax elasticity of supply: The percentage change in quantity supplied divided by the percentage change in tax rates.

tax incidence: Distribution of the real burden of a tax.

tax rebate: A lump-sum refund of taxes paid.

terms of trade: The rate at which goods are exchanged; the amount of good A given up for good B in trade.

total cost: The market value of all resources used to produce a good or service.

total revenue: The price of a product multiplied by the quantity sold in a given time period: $p \times q$.

total utility: The amount of satisfaction obtained from entire consumption of a product.

trade deficit: The amount by which the value of imports exceeds the value of exports in a given time period (negative net exports).

trade surplus: The amount by which the value of exports exceeds the value of imports in a given time period (positive net exports).

transactions account: A bank account that permits direct payment to a third party—for example, with a check or debit card.

transactions demand for money: Money held for the purpose of making everyday market purchases.

transfer payments: Payments to individuals for which no current goods or services are exchanged, like Social Security, welfare, and unemployment benefits.

Treasury bonds: Promissory notes (IOUs) issued by the U.S. Treasury.

U

UN and World Bank Poverty Goal: UN goal of eliminating extreme poverty by 2030.

underemployment: People seeking full-time paid employment who work only part-time or are employed at jobs below their capability.

unemployment: The inability of labor force participants to find jobs.

unemployment rate: The proportion of the labor force that is unemployed.

union shop: An employment setting in which all workers must join the union within 30 days after being employed.

unionization rate: The percentage of the labor force belonging to a union.

unit labor cost: Hourly wage rate divided by output per labor-hour.

utility: The pleasure or satisfaction obtained from a good or service.

V

value added: The increase in the market value of a product that takes place at each stage of the production process.

variable costs: Costs of production that change when the rate of output is altered, such as labor and material costs.

velocity of money (V)**:** The number of times per year, on average, that a dollar is used to purchase final goods and services; $PQ \div M$.

vertical equity: Principle that people with higher incomes should pay more taxes.

voluntary restraint agreement (VRA): An agreement to reduce the volume of trade in a specific good; a "voluntary" quota.

W

wage replacement rate: The percentage of base wages paid out in benefits.

wealth: The market value of assets.

wealth effect: A change in consumer spending caused by a change in the value of owned assets.

welfare programs: Means-tested income transfer programs, such as welfare and food stamps.

Y

yield: The rate of return on a bond; the annual interest payment divided by the bond's price.

Note: **Bold** page numbers indicate definitions; page numbers followed by *n* indicate material in notes.

HOUSEHOLD POVERTY STATUS, 1990–2015

Year	All	White		Black	Hispanic	Asian
	Number (in millions) and Percent of Persons in Poverty					
2015	43,123 (13.5)	17,786	(9.1)	10,020 (24.1)	12,133 (21.4)	2,078 (11.4)
2014	46,657 (14.8)	19,652	(10.1)	10,755 (26.2)	13,104 (23.6)	2,137 (12.0)
2013	45,318 (14.5)	18,796	(9.6)	11,041 (27.2)	12,744 (23.5)	1,785 (10.5)
2012	46,496 (15.0)	18,940	(9.7)	10,911 (27.2)	13,616 (25.6)	1,921 (11.7)
2011	46,247 (15.0)	19,171	(9.8)	10,929 (27.6)	13,244 (25.3)	1,973 (12.3)
2010	46,180 (15.1)	19,599	(9.9)	10,675 (27.4)	13,243 (26.6)	1,729 (12.1)
2009	43,569 (14.3)	18,530	(9.4)	9,944 (25.8)	12,350 (25.3)	1,746 (12.5)
2008	39,829 (13.2)	17,024	(8.6)	9,379 (24.7)	10,987 (23.2)	1,576 (11.8)
2007	37,276	16,032	(8.2)	9,237 (24.5)	9,890 (21.5)	1,349 (10.2)
2006	36,460	16,013	(8.2)	9,048 (24.3)	9,243 (20.6)	1,353 (10.3)
2005	36,950 (12.6)	16,227	(8.3)	9,168 (24.8)	9,368 (21.8)	1,402 (11.1)
2004	37,040 (12.7)	16,908	(8.7)	9,014 (24.7)	9,122 (21.9)	1,201 (9.8)
2003	35,861 (12.5)	15,902	(8.2)	8,781 (24.4)	9,051 (22.5)	1,401 (11.8)
2002	34,570 (12.1)	15,567	(8.0)	8,602 (24.1)	8,555 (21.8)	1,161 (10.1)
2001	32,907 (11.7)	15,271	(7.8)	8,136 (22.7)	7,997 (21.4)	1,275 (10.2)
2000	31,581 (11.3)	14,366	(7.4)	7,982 (22.5)	7,747 (21.5)	1,258 (9.9)
1999	32,791 (11.9)	14,735	(7.7)	8,441 (23.6)	7,876 (22.7)	1,285 (10.7)
1998	34,476 (12.7)	15,799	(8.2)	9,091 (26.1)	8,070 (25.6)	1,360 (12.5)
1997	35,574 (13.3)	16,491	(8.6)	9,116 (26.5)	8,308 (27.1)	1,468 (14.0)
1996	36,529 (13.7)	16,462	(8.6)	9,694 (28.4)	8,697 (29.4)	1,454 (14.5)
1995	36,425 (13.8)	16,267	(8.5)	9,872 (29.3)	8,574 (30.3)	1,411 (14.6)
1994	38,059 (14.5)	18,110	(9.4)	10,196 (30.6)	8,416 (30.7)	974 (14.6)
1993	39,265 (15.1)	18,882	(9.9)	10,877 (33.1)	8,126 (30.6)	1,134 (15.3)
1992	38,014 (14.8)	18,202	(9.6)	10,827 (33.4)	7,592 (29.6)	985 (12.7)
1991	35,708 (14.2)	17,741	(9.4)	10,242 (32.7)	6,339 (28.7)	996 (13.8)
1990	33,585 (13.5)	16,622	(8.8)	9,837 (31.9)	6,006 (28.1)	858 (12.2)

Source: U.S. Bureau of the Census.

HOUSEHOLD INCOME, 1990–2015

Year	Income (in 2015 dollars)		Mean Income, by Race			
	Median	Mean	White	Black	Hispanic	Asian
2015	56,516	79,263	85,585	54,352	63,612	105,417
2014	53,718	75,825	82,560	51,289	57,600	97,674
2013	52,850	73,915	80,731	50,499	55,602	92,343
2012	52,666	73,577	80,359	49,280	55,148	94,354
2011	52,751	73,431	80,161	49,801	55,172	90,258
2010	53,568	73,262	79,721	48,873	55,871	91,952
2009	54,988	75,093	80,908	50,867	57,697	100,318
2008	55,376	75,325	81,575	51,226	56,773	94,877
2007	57,423	77,286	83,657	53,306	58,103	97,187
2006	56,663	78,257	84,340	53,049	59,454	103,793
2005	56,224	76,878	83,261	51,525	57,210	97,210
2004	55,629	75,871	81,884	50,985	57,565	96,012
2003	55,823	76,118	82,330	51,716	57,305	90,172
2002	55,871	76,217	81,833	52,712	59,136	92,283
2001	56,531	77,924	83,595	52,542	59,416	97,939
2000	57,790	78,634	84,032	53,920	60,526	100,189
1999	57,909	77,889	83,366	54,730	57,474	95,889
1998	56,510	75,359	81,299	49,613	55,631	87,498
1997	54,506	73,193	78,897	48,552	52,853	86,741
1996	53,407	70,909	75,954	48,844	51,169	85,089
1995	52,664	69,451	74,575	46,983	48,221	85,355
1994	51,065	68,268	73,092	46,309	49,986	83,191
1993	50,478	66,938	71,783	43,996	48,944	81,183
1992	50,725	64,309	68,920	42,138	47,721	77,571
1991	51,145	64,380	68,538	42,516	49,016	78,567
1990	52,684	65,810	69,981	43,660	49.216	81,661

Source: U.S. Census Bureau.

PRODUCTIVITY AND RELATED DATA, BUSINESS SECTOR 1980–2016 (2009 = 100)

Year	Output per Hour	Output	Hours Worked	Unit Labor Costs	Hourly Compensation	Real Hourly Compensation
1980	53.4	41.8	78.3	54.5	29.1	72.1
1981	54.6	43.0	78.9	58.3	31.8	72.1
1982	54.1	41.7	77.1	63.1	34.2	73.0
1983	56.1	44.0	78.4	63.6	35.7	73.1
1984	57.7	47.9	83.0	64.6	37.3	73.4
1985	59.0	50.1	85.0	66.4	39.2	74.5
1986	60.7	52.0	85.6	68.2	41.4	77.3
1987	61.0	53.8	88.2	70.4	43.0	77.7
1988	61.9	56.1	90.6	73.1	45.2	78.9
1989	62.6	58.3	93.0	74.4	46.6	77.9
1990	64.0	59.2	92.5	77.5	49.6	79.0
1991	65.2	58.9	90.3	79.8	52.1	80.0
1992	68.1	61.4	90.1	81.0	55.2	82.6
1993	68.2	63.1	92.6	82.1	56.0	81.8
1994	68.7	66.2	96.3	82.2	56.5	80.9
1995	69.0	68.3	98.9	83.5	57.6	80.5
1996	71.0	71.4	100.5	84.4	60.0	81.7
1997	72.4	75.2	103.9	85.9	62.2	82.9
1998	74.6	79.1	106.0	88.2	65.9	86.6
1999	77.2	83.5	108.1	89.0	68.8	88.6
2000	79.9	87.3	109.2	92.4	73.8	92.0
2001	82.1	87.8	107.0	94.0	77.2	93.6
2002	85.6	89.4	104.4	92.2	78.9	94.1
2003	88.9	92.3	103.7	92.1	81.9	95.5
2004	91.7	96.4	105.1	93.4	85.7	97.3
2005	93.7	100.1	106.8	94.8	88.8	97.6
2006	94.6	103.2	109.1	97.5	92.3	98.2
2007	96.0	105.4	109.8	100.4	96.4	99.7
2008	96.8	104.2	107.6	102.2	98.9	98.6
2009	100.0	100.0	100.0	100.0	100.0	100.0
2010	103.2	103.1	99.8	98.6	101.8	100.2
2011	103.3	105.3	101.9	100.6	104.0	99.2
2012	104.2	108.6	104.1	102.6	106.9	99.9
2013	105.5	111.5	105.7	102.7	108.4	99.8
2014	105.4	114.3	108.4	105.4	111.2	100.8
2015	106.2	117.8	110.7	107.5	114.5	103.6
2016	106.5	119.8	112.3	110.4	117.7	105.2

Source: U.S. Bureau of Labor Statistics.

STOCK PRICES AND YIELDS, 1980–2016

Year	Common Stock Prices	Common Stock Yields		10-Year Treasury Bond (to yield)
	Dow Jones Industrial Average (year end)	Dividend-Price Ratio	Price Earnings Ratio	
1980	964	5.26	9.16	11.46
1981	875	5.20	7.98	13.91
1982	1047	5.81	11.13	13.00
1983	1253	4.40	11.76	11.10
1984	1212	4.64	10.05	12.44
1985	1547	4.25	14.46	10.62
1986	1896	3.49	16.72	7.68
1987	1939	3.08	14.12	8.39
1988	2169	3.64	11.69	8.85
1989	2753	3.45	15.45	8.49
1990	2634	3.61	15.47	8.55
1991	3169	3.24	26.12	7.86
1992	3301	2.99	22.82	7.01
1993	3154	2.78	21.32	5.87
1994	3834	2.82	15.01	7.09
1995	5117	2.56	18.14	6.57
1996	6448	2.19	19.13	6.44
1997	7908	1.77	24.43	6.35
1998	9181	1.49	32.60	5.26
1999	11,497	1.25	30.50	5.65
2000	10,287	1.15	26.41	6.03
2001	10,022	1.32	46.50	5.02
2002	8,342	1.61	31.89	4.61
2003	10,454	1.77	22.81	4.01
2004	10,283	1.72	20.20	4.27
2005	10,718	1.83	17.85	4.29
2006	12,463	1.87	17.40	4.80
2007	13,265	1.86	17.36	4.63
2008	8,776	2.37	21.46	3.66
2009	10,428	2.40	20.91	3.26
2010	11,518	1.98	20.70	3.22
2011	12,218	2.13	16.30	2.78
2012	13,104	2.20	14.87	1.80
2013	16,577	1.94	17.03	2.35
2014	17,165	1.92	20.02	1.88
2015	16,466	2.11	22.18	2.09
2016	19,864	2.03	25.54	2.43

Source: U.S. Bureau of Economic Analysis.

CORPORATE PROFITS WITH INVENTORY VALUATION AND CAPITAL CONSUMPTION ADJUSTMENTS, 1980–2016 (billions of dollars)

Year	Corporate Profits with Inventory Valuation and Capital Consumption Adjustments	Taxes on Corporate Income	Corporate Profits after Tax with Inventory Valuation and Capital Consumption Adjustments		
			Total	Net Dividends	Undistributed Profits with Inventory Valuation and Capital Consumption Adjustments
1980	201	87	114	64	50
1981	226	84	142	74	68
1982	210	66	143	78	65
1983	264	81	184	83	100
1984	319	98	221	91	130
1985	330	99	231	98	133
1986	319	110	210	106	104
1987	369	130	238	112	126
1988	433	142	291	130	161
1989	427	146	280	158	123
1990	438	145	292	169	123
1991	451	139	313	181	132
1992	479	149	331	188	143
1993	542	171	371	203	168
1994	600	194	407	285	172
1995	697	219	478	254	224
1996	786	232	554	298	257
1997	868	246	622	334	288
1998	802	248	553	352	202
1999	851	259	593	337	255
2000	818	265	553	378	175
2001	767	204	563	371	192
2002	886	193	694	399	294
2003	993	243	750	425	325
2004	1,231	300	924	540	384
2005	1,448	399	1,034	577	457
2006	1,669	475	1,200	702	498
2007	1,511	446	1,065	795	271
2008	1,263	308	954	798	157
2009	1,758	255	1,003	719	284
2010	1,800	411	1,389	737	652
2011	1,816	379	1,438	704	734
2012	2,023	455	1,568	857	711
2013	2,107	474	1,633	960	673
2014	2,152	533	1,619	971	649
2015	2,088	554	1,534	971	563
2016	2,086	543	1,543	968	575

Source: U.S. Bureau of Economic Analysis.

detected. How does this occur? It is thought that long-term stress causes changes in the energy fields and chakras that over time repattern themselves and begin to affect the cells of the body. Depending on the severity of the repatterning, illness and disease can occur. By addressing the stressors, one is able to fix or heal any changes made in the energy field or chakras.

Humans as Multidimensional Beings

This concept of energy fields and chakras intermixing contributes to humans being multidimensional. In other words, you are made up of more than just your parts. You not only contain energy, but you are energy that is constantly changing. The body uses energy to perform its functions: for nerves to stimulate muscles, the beating of the heart, lungs to exchange air, cells to digest nutrients, and the creation of an idea. There is nothing in the body that is not involved in some form of energy. When the normal energy flow is interrupted or destroyed, the body is unable to function to its fullest capacity, and illness, disease, and disability can develop. When all of the energy workings cease, death occurs.

Nevertheless, quantum physics has shown us that energy cannot be destroyed. Thus, when we die, it is just the physical part of ourselves that dies. The energy that aided us in our physical form transforms and is released into the environment; therefore, one does not die—the physical body is just transformed.

Touch is Powerful

With this discussion of the energy systems of the body, you can see that a touch is not just a simple physical act. Something happens human to human, human to animal, human to plant, and animal to animal when touch occurs. This exchange of energy affects not only the one receiving the touch, but also the one giving the touch.

KEY POINT

One of the most important aspects of touch is its intention.

There are neutral touches, such as tapping someone on the arm to get their attention. In addition, there are those touches out of anger that are meant to hurt someone, like a slap or kick. Then there are the loving touches of a hug or caress. The intention is what differentiates.

The way to obtain the power of touch for healing is through a centered heart. This is done in several ways. It occurs spontaneously for couples in love or in the love that a parent

---

they all have a slightly different belief or philosophy, they share the common denominator of touch.

Energy as a Component of Touch

There is considerable discussion today about *energy*. People state, "I don't have any energy today," "I feel energized," or " I have a lot of energy." You may have experienced these feelings and know that there is a difference between having high and low energy. After listening to an uplifting speech and hearing the thunderous applause, one may say the room was "energized" or "electrified." What is this energy that we are talking about?

REFLECTION

Do you have sensitivity to your body's energy? Are there particular experiences or people that seem to energize you and others that drain your energy?

The terms for energy date back to the older traditions of ancient cultures. Every society had a term for the life force. For some cultures, caring for this energy influenced health and wellness; by blocking or disrupting energy, disease or death could result. Other societies merely referred to it in reference to religious or spiritual beliefs. For examples of these terms, see Exhibit 14-2.

EXHIBIT 14-2   Cultural Names for Energy

Culture	Energy name
Aborigine	Arunquiltha
Ancient Egypt	Ankh
Ancient Greece	Pneuma
China	Chi (Qi)
General usage	Life force
India	Prana
Japan	Ki
Polynesia	Mana
United States	Bioenergy, biomagnetism, subtle energy

The Role of Chi

The Chinese culture has used the idea of energy for thousands of years through the philosophy of *chi (qi)*, or life force, which is an energetic substance that flows from the environment into the body. The chi flows through the body by means of 12 pairs of meridians (energy pathways to provide life-nourishing and sustaining energy). The organs of the body are affected by the pairs of meridians. There needs to be a balance of chi flowing through each side of the paired meridian in order for balance to occur and health to be attained and/or maintained.

Science is beginning to get a better understanding of this energy, what it is, and how it functions. Some researchers have developed machinery to try to detect this energy. Although success has been limited for some, others have been more successful.

KEY POINT

Motoyama, a Japanese researcher, developed a machine to assist in the detection of meridian lines within the tissues of humans. He found that these meridians do exist and that an energy flow, he calls *ki*, travels through the body. Motoyama states that a center in the brain controls the movement of ki.[8] In addition, these meridians feed the different organ systems of the body. By using his machine, called the *AMI machine*, he has been able to detect strong correlations between meridians that have energy imbalances to organs systems, which have diseases present. His machine is being used in the research of Parkinson's disease at the Bob Hope Parkinson Research Institute in Florida.

The Energy Fields or Auras

In addition to the seven chakras (see Chapter 20 for an explanation of chakras), there exist seven layers of energy fields, or auric fields, around the body. These energy fields surround all living and nonliving matter. Science has begun to study and explain these fields over the last several years. The science of physics has done the most extensive work in explaining energy fields. Through Newtonian physics, field theory, and Einstein's theory of relativity, a better understanding of how energy works has been acquired, but it is quantum physics that has really helped explain the characteristics and behaviors of energy. Since then, many scientists have begun looking at things as a *hologram* (a multidimensional piece of something whole). The discussion of specifics is beyond this chapter; however, it is intended to show that science is now rethinking some of its early and persistent cause and effect notions.

One way energy fields have been viewed is through *Kirlian photography*, which was created in the 1940s by a Russian researcher, Semyon Kirlian. By using this form of photography,

he was able to measure changes in the energy fields of living systems. He found that cancer causes significant changes in the electromagnetic field around the body. One of the best known experiments is that of the Phantom Leaf Effect, whereby a portion of a leaf was cut away and Kirlian photography done on the amputated leaf. Amazingly, the leaf still appeared whole with an energy field present in the form and space of the cutaway portion.

In other important work, a Japanese researcher named Motoyama, has developed a number of electrode devices to measure the human energy field at various distances from the body.[9] Thus, it is now possible to measure the excess or lack of energy around the body and determine a person's health status. Future technology advances may allow a body to be scanned and the beginnings of disease detected before symptoms appear in the physical body. In fact, a new CT scan is being used for this very reason to detect early onset of heart disease and cancer.

Where exactly are these fields, however? As stated previously, there are seven energy fields that are generally accepted by most energy workers. Each field corresponds to a specific chakra, for example, the first energy field with the first chakra and so on; however, the fields lay one on top of another yet do not interfere with each other's functions. These fields interconnect yet maintain their own separateness.

KEY POINT

Energy fields of the body work similar to a television. When you change channels, you get a different picture. All of the pictures do not end up on the same channel, but they do come through one television set. Likewise, when listening to a radio, you change stations to hear different music, but you still have one radio. The same idea works for the energy fields of the body.

When two people interact, their energy fields connect and they can pick up information about each other. For example, you are riding on an elevator, and a stranger gets on. You do not say anything to the person, but you feel safe and secure. At another floor, a second person gets on. Immediately you feel uncomfortable with this person even though you have not spoken to him either. What is occurring is the intermixing of energy fields, which is giving you subconscious information about these people. It has nothing to do with what they are wearing or how they look.

One of the leading causes of illness in our society is stress, yet stress is not internal. Stress originates outside the body and works its way inward through the energy fields and chakras. It is a well-known fact that long-term stress can weaken the immune system's response and cause heart attacks, high blood pressure, and depression. Of course, there are physical evidences for each of these, but the process starts long before any physical evidence is feels toward a child. One can feel the heart open and a strong connection to the other, even when the other person is not physically present. Another way to obtain this power is through the *intention* of helping someone. This can be spontaneous as in an accident or planned as in changing someone's wound dressing after surgery.

A third way is through inner focus and awareness in order to become calm and in a state of balance. You probably have experienced times when you are not in balance. Things around you are chaotic—you stumble and cannot seem to get anything done. Yet, in a state of balance you are able to accomplish many tasks regardless of what goes on around you.

KEY POINT

Belly breathing, sounds, and imagery can be used to help you center and focus.

You can learn to have a centered heart using several methods, one of which is belly breathing. Taking slow breaths in through the nose and out through the mouth allows you to become present in the moment. By having a rhythmic pattern of breathing, you become still and calm. In addition, belly breathing can help reduce your stress. To belly breathe, move your belly or abdomen outward on inspiration (the in breath) and retract inward on expiration (the out breath). Counting numbers during the in breath and out breath, along with belly breathing, helps quiet the mind and focus the awareness inward.

Another method of becoming more self aware is through the use of sound. By focusing on a sound externally, like the sound of a bell chime, or one that is self-created, like *om*, you may be able to quickly focus and center. Some people find it easy to learn how to center by listening to quiet music, whether it be classical music, jazz, nature sounds set to music, religious music, or new age music. There is no one type of music that is perfect for all people. Generally, it is whatever you need to listen to in order to help you attain a sense of focus.

Imagery also can be used to center. The mind is a powerful tool and can be used to create a center of focus. The exercise in Exhibit 14-3 is an example of a way to use imagery to focus.

With practice, you will be able to get into a centered state within a few seconds by using your breath, a sound, or imagery. You can combine any of these and see what works best for you. These techniques can be used in conjunction with touch healing or as a method to reduce stress at any time.

REFLECTION

When providing assistance or care to another person, do you give the person your undivided attention? Do you need to adopt a technique to help you get into a centered state?

EXHIBIT 14-3   Using Imagery to Center or Focus

1. First, find a quiet place to sit without distractions. Loosen clothes if necessary. Sit upright with back supported, feet flat on the ground, and hands in a comfortable position on your lap or the arms of a chair.

2. Close your eyes, and begin to breathe in through your nose allowing your stomach to move outward. Then exhale slowly, allowing your stomach to retract naturally. Try to have the in breath equal the out breath and let this become a cycle. If you have difficulty, just keep practicing. There is no wrong way to do this.

3. Imagine your feet on the ground growing roots downward through the floor, like a tree. With each breath, allow the roots to move further and further into the earth until it reaches the center of the earth. Feel the warmth of the earth on your roots.

4. Using your breath, have the warmth move upward through the roots and into your feet. Feel the warmth. Continue moving this energy higher into your legs, hips, back, and stomach, into your chest and shoulders, your neck, your face, your head, and out the top of your head up to the sky.

5. Imagine a ball of white light way above your head shining downward. Using your breath, help this light come down and touch the top of your head. You may feel some pressure or heaviness on your head. This is normal.

6. Now using the breath, allow this white light to move through the center of your body, out the base of your spine, and down your legs, through your feet and into your roots. Let the energy go down your roots to the center of the earth.

7. Leaving these images there, focus on your heart center in the middle of your chest. Imagine a pink, light, fluffy ball of light like cotton candy. With each breath, allow the ball to become bigger and bigger. Feel how warm and light this is.

8. Imagine a white or pink light coming from your heart center and running down your arms into your hands and fingers. Some of the sensations you may feel are warm, cold, tingly, prickly, vibrating, or any other sensation special to you. You may not even feel anything at all. It doesn't matter, just know it is there.

9. You are now centered. At this point, you can stay in this state and just enjoy it, or if there is someone who you are going to do touch healing on, open your eyes and begin.

The Practice of Touch

While centering is one of the most important aspects to any touch healing, intuition is another one. Intuition often is a heartfelt feeling of certainty. All people have intuition but may ignore it or not identify it as such. At one point or another, many people have said, "I knew that would happen." Some people can tell who is on the other end of the phone before or at the moment it rings. Others know when loved ones are in trouble or hurt. This is intuition. It is something often used in touch healing in order to allow for the best outcome for that person. You just seem to know where to place your hands.

KEY POINT

Intuition is the internal knowing of something, often without any external or visible means of proving its existence. One just knows.

When you get a burn on your finger, the first reaction is to pull away from the source of the burn and the second to place your hand over the spot that is burned. The covering hand helps reduce the pain. You know what to do. You do not even think about it. This is intuition.

The same thing happens in touch healing. Of course there are many distinct techniques one can learn step by step, but often this is not necessary. If you allow yourself to follow your intuition, you will know where to place your hands. It may be on the body in a specific area. It may be out in the field away from the body. You may use one hand, two hands together, or two hands in different places. Sometimes your hand may start to do a movement over an area for no particular reason. You may feel things while your hands are placed on the body or off the body, such as temperature, texture, vibration, density, or contour (shape). Just let go and allow the energy of touch to work. You do not need to do anything else, and when it is time to finish, you will just know to stop.

If the power of touch sounds easy, that is because it is. As long as you prevent yourself from thinking about what you are doing and allow the centered heart and energy to do its work, it happens naturally. The centered heart, with the intention of healing, is the greatest gift you can give anyone, including yourself. The energy used to help someone else benefits you, too. It is like you are a hose watering flowers. The flowers receive the water to drink and live and the hose stays wet inside; both benefit.

The way to master touch healing is to practice, practice, practice. In addition, many schools and programs teach the various forms of touch healing for those interested in learning more specific techniques. For more information on various programs, see Exhibit 14-4.

The power of touch is a natural gift, ready to be developed. Some people are using it without knowing what they are really accomplishing. They just *know* it is a good thing. Others recognize this ability and use it help others heal and feel better, and some are afraid of the power their touch has on others. Just know that whenever touch is used with a centered heart and the intention to heal or help, it will not hurt anyone. It is a wonderful, loving act you are able to share with others or do for yourself. Touch has a powerful capacity to heal through a centered heart filled with love.

EXHIBIT 14-4 Educational Programs for Touch Healers

Healing Touch International, Inc.
12477 W. Cedar Drive, Suite 202
Lakewood, Colorado 80228
303-989-7982
E-mail: HTIheal@aol.com
http://healingtouch.net

Nurse Healers and Professional Associates Therapeutic Touch
11250-8 Roger Bacon Drive, Suite 8
Reston, Virginia 20190
703-234-4149
http://www.therapeutic-touch.org

International Center for Reiki Training
21421 Hilltop St. Unit #28
Southfield, Michigan 48034
800-332-8112
http://www.reiki.org

Cautions

As therapeutic and comforting as touch may be, it must be appreciated that not everyone will welcome touch or touch therapies. Culture influences may cause people to be uncomfortable being touched by a stranger or to believe it is inappropriate for a person to be touched by a member of the opposite sex who is not a spouse. Some people have opposition to touch therapies because of their faith. For example, Christians who believe that the only spirit one should call on is Jesus Christ may be uncomfortable with a practitioner who channels energy from an unknown source. Sensitivity to different reactions to touch is warranted. It is beneficial for a practitioner to explain the procedure/process to an individual and obtain consent before initiating touch therapy. Consumers also should explore the spiritual foundation for any touch therapy used to assure it is compatible with personal belief systems.

Summary

All major religions have used some form of laying on of hands for healing, as have most ancient cultures. Therapeutic touch, healing touch, and Reiki are practices in which energy from one person transfer to another to stimulate healing. Other touch therapies include acupressure, craniosacral therapy, polarity, chakra balancing, neuromuscular release, Rolfing, Trager, massage, and reflexology. To obtain the most healing benefit from touch, one needs to have an intention to do good for the person being touched, have a centered heart, and be focused and aware. Self-awareness can be enhanced through belly breathing, focusing on a sound, and the use of imagery. Practice and experience enhance skill in using touch for healing.

References

1. Graham, R., Litt, F., & Irwin, W. (1998). *Healing from the Heart*. Winfield, BC, Canada: Wood Lake Books Publishing, p. 41.
2. Sayre-Adams, J., & Wright, S. (1995). *The Theory and Practice of Therapeutic Touch*. New York: Churchill Livingstone, p. 3.
3. Graham, R., Litt, F., & Irwin, W. (1998). *Healing from the Heart*. Winfield, BC, Canada: Wood Lake Books Publishing, pp. 48–49.
4. Graham, R., Litt, F., & Irwin, W. (1998). *Healing from the Heart*. Winfield, BC, Canada: Wood Lake Books Publishing, pp. 43–44.
5. Krieger, D. (1992). *The Therapeutic Touch: How to Use Your Hands to Help or Heal*. New York: Simon & Schuster, p. 15.
6. Ehrenreich, B., & English, D. (1973). *Witches, Midwives and Nurses: A History of Women Healers*. New York: The Feminist Press, pp. 6–14.
7. Krieger, D. (1992). *The Therapeutic Touch: How to Use Your Hands to Help or Heal*. New York: Simon & Schuster, pp. 4–8.
8. Motoyama, H. (1981). *A biophysical elucidation of the Meridian and Ki-Energy. International Association for Religion and Parapsychology, 7*(1):1981.
9. Motoyama, H. (2003). *Theories of the Chakras*. Wheaton, IL: Theosophical Publishing House, p. 257.

Suggested Reading

Aufenthie, J. (2006). Healing touch. In Yuan, C., Bieber, E. J., & Bauer, B. A. (eds.). *Textbook of Complementary and Alternative Medicine*, 2nd ed. London: Informa Healthcare.

Courcey, K. (2001). Investigating therapeutic touch. *Nurse Practitioner Forum, 26*(11):12–15.

Engle, V., & Graney, M. (2000). Biobehavioral effects of therapeutic touch. *Journal of Nursing Scholarship, 32*(3):287–289.

Halcon, L. (2002). Reiki. In Snyder, M., & Lindquist, R. (eds.). *Complementary/Alternative Therapies in Nursing*. New York: Springer, pp. 197–203.

Hurwitz, W. (2001). Energy Medicine. In Micozzi, M. (ed.). *Fundamentals of Complementary and Alternative Medicine*. New York: Churchill Livingstone.

Kunz, D., & Kreiger, D. (2004). *The Spiritual Dimension of Therapeutic Touch*. Rochester, VT: Bear & Co.

Mentgen, J. (2001). Healing touch. *Nursing Clinics of North America: Holistic Nursing Care, 36*(1):142–145.

O'Mathuna, D. (2000). Evidence-based practice and review of therapeutic touch. *Journal of Nursing Scholarship, 32*(3):277–279.

Paul, N. L. (2006). *Reiki for Dummies*. Indianapolis, IN: Wiley & Sons.

Stein, D. (2007). *Essential Reiki Teaching Manual*. Berkeley, CA: Crossing Press.

Chapter 15

Taking Life Lightly: Humor, the Great Alternative

OBJECTIVES

This chapter should enable you to

· Define gelotology

· List at least six physiological effects of laughter

· Identify positive from negative humor

· List at least three ways to develop a comic vision

· Describe at least four strategies for adding humor to work and home

Humor adds perspective to life, altering our perception of a potentially negative incident and providing preventive maintenance against the strain of hard times in personal and professional relationships.

KEY POINT

Laughter is the shortest distance between two people.

A humorous perspective about life helps you to deal with stressors in life, from minor irritation to life-threatening illness. Humor can alter the perception of a situation by changing the expectation of a negative result. A man was upset and taking it out on coworkers. A friend thought to query, "What's the matter, John, did you have nails for breakfast?" This quip got John's attention. He realized he was bringing other problems to work and was able to laugh at himself. The nurse leader on a busy hospital unit would walk down the hall wearing a pair of huge sunglasses when staff was rushing and stressed. This was the sign to take a deep breath, have a good laugh, and start again. One long-term patient would tell her, "Lois, get the glasses. We need them today."

Humor and a playful attitude can build relationships at home and at work and prevent negative reactions in stressful times. In an atmosphere of general goodwill, where no one

237

is expected to be perfect at all times, tough times become more manageable. The mother who can make a game out of power outages by roasting hot dogs in the fireplace models a positive coping strategy for unexpected inconveniences. The manager who organizes a baby picture contest for staff mobilizes positive energy, provides something to look forward to at work, and humanizes team members.

Health Benefits of Humor

Gelotology is the study of the physiological effects of humor and laughter. This body of knowledge tells us that humor and laughter benefits us in many of the following ways.

- Stimulation of the production of catecholamines and hormones, which enhance feelings of well-being and pain tolerance
- A decrease in anxiety
- An increase in endorphins (natural narcotic-like substances produced in the brain)
- An increase in cardiac and respiratory rates
- Enhancement of metabolism
- An improvement of muscle tone
- Perception of the relief of stress and tension with increased relaxation, which may last up to 45 minutes following laughter[1]
- Increased numbers of natural killer cells, which fight viral infections of cells and some cancer cells
- Increased T cells (T lymphocytes) that fight infection
- Increased antibody immunoglobulin A, which fights upper-respiratory infections
- Increased gamma interferon, which helps activate the immune system[2]

Laughter exercises the breathing muscles, benefits the cardiovascular system by increasing oxygenation, and promotes relaxation. Laughter helps control pain by distracting one's attention, reducing tension, and changing or reframing one's perspective. During episodes of laughter the blood pressure increases, but then it lowers below the initial rate. Dr. William Fry, a researcher of the physiology of laughter has called laughter "internal jogging," giving our internal organs a workout.

Studies have shown that laughter can help in fighting the negative effects of stress. For example, in a study at Loma Linda University School of Medicine, blood samples were drawn after subjects were shown humor videos. Results were compared with those of a control group. The mirthful experience appeared to reduce serum cortisol, dopac, epinephrine, and growth hormone. These changes are related to the reversal of the neuroendocrine and classical stress hormone response.

KEY POINT

In times of stress, the adrenal glands release corticosteroids, which are converted to cortisol in the blood. Increased levels of cortisol can suppress the immune system. If laughter reduces serum cortisol, it may diminish the chemical effects of stress on the immune system.

Hospitals, long-term care facilities, hospices, and rehabilitation centers have implemented humor programs with a humor cart or designated room equipped with humorous audiocassettes, videos, games, and toys.

KEY POINT

Attention to the role of laughter and healing was profoundly increased when author Norman Cousins shared his personal experience. Trying to cope with pain from the inflammatory disease ankylosing spondylitis, Cousins watched reruns of *Candid Camera* and old Marx Brothers films and had people read humorous material to him. He found that 10 minutes of belly laughter gave him 2 hours of pain-free sleep. Blood studies of his sedimentation rate (a measure of the inflammatory response), which were drawn after his laughter therapy, showed a cumulative positive effect. He had reasoned that if being in a bad mood makes people feel worse, perhaps, being in a good mood would make him feel better![3]

Positive versus Negative Humor

Not all humor is positive. Have you ever been on the receiving end of negative humor? Perhaps someone got a laugh at your expense. You feel hurt and angry and do not see anything funny about the situation. To make matters worse, your reaction may be met with "can't you take a joke?" making it seem that you are the one with a problem.

REFLECTION

Negative humor ridicules, belittles, and distances people. It can be sexist, racist, or embarrassing. Have you been the victim of negative humor? If so, how did it make you feel?

Positive humor intends to bring people closer together. It is associated with hope, love, and closeness. It is a gentle banter, not a caustic, sarcastic barb. It is timely and adds perspective.

Consider three criteria for positive uses of humor. Ask yourself these questions:

1. Is the timing right for this quip? When someone is in the middle of a crisis or is in great pain, humor might not be appreciated even though you have often swapped one-liners.

2. Is the other person receptive to humor? Does this person already use humor to cope? Some people do not seem to have or value a sense of humor.

3. Is the content acceptable? Is it in good taste? Does it make light of self, rather than others? Jokes that could help relieve tension in a closely knit work group could be seen as insensitive to outsiders who do not understand the commitment of the group to the service it provides.[4]

Develop Your Comic Vision

Sometimes being able to laugh at life and at yourself relieves tension. Consider the mental self-talk that can alter the interpretation of minor irritants in life. How about remembering with a smile, the one-liner from the children's story, *The Little Engine That Could*:[5] "I think I can, I think I can," instead of ruminating over such lines as, "I can't do this. It's too hard. It isn't fair"? Begin to collect one-liners of your own to share. How about this one?

New clinical studies show there aren't any answers.

ANONYMOUS

How do you develop your comic vision (see Exhibit 15-1)? If you think you have no sense of humor or just want more joy in your life, try planning to have fun, looking for humor in your life, and exposing yourself to humorous stories and other resources. Taking time to read the cartoons along with the front page will help you reframe your day.

Joel Goodman, founder of the Humor Project in New York,[6] talks about aikido humor, humor that uses the momentum of the situation to "roll with the punches." Aikido is a form of martial arts that uses the principle of nonresistance rather than pushing forward; it looks like a flowing dance. Goodman exemplified this with the story of an elementary school teacher. Precisely at 10 A.M., while the teacher had her back turned writing on the blackboard, all of the students knocked their books from their desks onto the floor. The teacher turned around, looked at the clock, said, "Oh, sorry. I'm late" and swept the books off her desk, too.

Think of things you can use to add a light touch (see Exhibit 15-2). Add colorful confetti, available for all occasions, to letters or memos. Give out stickers at home or at work when someone does something right or just needs a boost. Use a noisemaker to get people's attention when chairing a meeting. The element of surprise can be effective in changing the mood. This is positive humor—when the sound is not an irritating one and is used playfully.

EXHIBIT 15-1   Developing Your Comic Vision

1. Start with yourself. Laugh at yourself. Give yourself permission to be human. If you trip, laugh out loud.

2. Read the comics and political cartoons in newspapers as examples of comic vision. Look at local newspapers when you travel to get the community perspective and learn about regional humor.

3. Start an album with cartoons that track current work issues and encourage all team members to contribute.

4. Attend funny movies and comedy clubs. Rent classic comedy videos.

5. Listen to humorous audiocassettes on the way to work to begin your day looking for humor.

6. Collect humorous one-liners that are inside jokes with your work team.

7. Experiment with building a humor kit at work. Start with a few items and encourage participation and a feeling of ownership.

8. Laugh with others for what they do, at the incongruities in life in which we all share.

9. Pay attention to your own self-talk. Replace negative thoughts with positive ones. Focus on being someone others find pleasant company.

10. Share your comic vision to make other people laugh. Laughter is contagious and adds much needed joy in all our lives.

Copyright © Julia Balzer Riley RN, Mn, (2000). Humor and Health, home study, AKH Consultant, Inc., Orange Park, Florida. Used with permission.

It is negative humor if it is used to interrupt someone who is speaking and embarrasses the person. Use toys and props to facilitate teams and to teach important content such as customer service.[7] Take a new look at garage sales and your children's cast-off toys. Take a field trip to a toy store or magic shop for props to add to your kit. Purchase inexpensive toys in quantity to use as incentives at work and at home.

KEY POINT

He who laughs, lasts!

ANONYMOUS

EXHIBIT 15-2   Building a Humor Kit

Collect these items to use at work or school. Put them in a tote bag or box for easy access by all.

· Bubbles—small bottles, bubble bottles on necklaces, or wands that make giant bubbles. Take a bubble break to give yourself and others a laugh, and to appreciate the small wonders in life.

· Whistles for stress relief

· Funny hats

· Clown noses and other wild noses

· Funny books, audiotapes, videotapes

· Cartoons collected in a photo album or for display on bulletin boards

· Children's games—wooden paddle and ball, pick-up sticks, coloring books and crayons—ahh, that smell! Splurge and get the box of 64 with the sharpener—they even have bigger boxes now!

· A laughter box

· A big teddy bear when a hug is needed

· Lapel buttons with funny one-liners

· A magic wand

· Be on the lookout for funny things. Sources include toy stores, clown supply stores, party stores, Halloween and other seasonal displays, souvenir shops, teacher/school supply stores, your children's discards, and garage sales.

· Bubble gum for a brief bubble-blowing contest for staff stress relief

Copyright © Julia Balzer Riley, RN, MN, (1996). Used with permission.

Plan to Laugh

If humor helps you stay healthy, how can you build it into your daily life? Be open to humor and actively pursue it. Remembering jokes and delivering a powerful punch line can be part of a rich sense of humor, but reading jokes or funny greeting cards can do wonders to stimulate laughter, too.

REFLECTION

How long has it been since you have laughed out loud?

Electronic communication can help you find a steady source of laughter. Subscribe to a list of jokes. Find a humor buddy online or be one. Remember that not every sense of humor is alike. Try to open yourself to a variety of kinds of humor to see what tickles your funny bone. *PUNs . . . Please Forgive Me* (Exhibit 15-3) offers examples of puns circulated via electronic mail (e-mail). A *pun* is a playful use of words, using words with different meanings that sound alike or similar. It is the stretching that makes these examples funny. If you groan when you read this, consider the comic relief this can offer on a tough day. *OXYMORONS . . . Be on the Alert for More* (Exhibit 15-4) gives examples of oxymorons, also shared via email. An *oxymoron* is an amusing contradiction in language. Trying to construct puns or recognize oxymorons is good practice for creative thinking.

Plan to Play

Evidence of play and toys is found as far back as relics of human existence in ruins of Egypt, Babylonia, China, and Aztec civilizations. Humor can shift our mental paradigms in prob-

---

Exhibit 15-3   PUNS . . . Please Forgive Me

Middle Age: When actions creak louder than words

Egotist: One who is me-deep in conversation

Income tax: Capital punishment

Archeologist: A man whose career lies in ruins

California smog test: Can UCLA?

Two Eskimos sitting in a kayak were chilly, but when they lit a fire in the craft, it sank—proving once and for all that you can't have your kayak and heat it, too.

Two boll weevils grew up in South Carolina. One went to Hollywood and became a famous actor. The other stayed behind in the cotton fields and never amounted to much. The second one, naturally, became known as the lesser of two weevils.

A mystic refused his dentist's Novocain during root canal work. He wanted to transcend dental medication.

A woman has twins and gives them up for adoption. One of them goes to a family in Egypt and is named "Amal." The other goes to a family in Spain; they name him "Juan." Years later, Juan sends a picture of himself to his mom. Upon receiving the picture, she tells her husband that she wishes she also had a picture of Amal. Her husband responds, "But they are twins—if you've seen Juan, you've seen Amal."

EXHIBIT 15-4   OXYMORONS . . . Be on the Alert for More

Act naturally

Clearly misunderstood

Alone together

Airline food

Found missing

Resident alien

Genuine imitation

Almost exactly

Legally drunk

Small crowd

Taped live

Plastic glasses

Working vacation

Jumbo shrimp

And the number one listing . . . Microsoft Works (a little computer humor)

---

lem solving to stimulate creative thinking. To be more open to creativity, plan to play. Put leisure activities on your calendar. Take time to just be and not do; lie on the ground and look at the clouds, fly a kite, take a break to play several games of Solitaire when you have computer fatigue. See Exhibit 15-5 to get you thinking playfully. This is quite a task for some grown-ups! Take some time now to generate your own list. Ask friends and family members to add to the list. Contract to do one thing just for fun within the next two weeks and develop a plan for increasing the play in your life (see Exhibit 15-6).

Humor and Play at Work

Do you know someone at work who always sees the funny side of life? Think of the popularity of Dilbert cartoons. How may Farside cartoons have surfaced in the workplace? Do you have an employee picnic with games? Do you decorate for holidays? Do you celebrate birthdays? How do you feel reading this if your workplace includes such activities? What if

---

EXHIBIT 15-5 Plan to Play

1. Find someone to take the children on an outing and have the house to yourself.

2. Go to a museum, a play, or a concert.

3. Look through a catalog and circle all of the things that you would buy if you could.

4. Buy a lottery ticket and fantasize how you would spend the winnings.

5. Just move. Turn on music you like and move with the rhythm. You do not have to know how to dance.

6. Go to a travel agency and get some brochures.

7. Go bowling or play miniature golf.

8. Go get an ice cream cone.

9. Take a novel. Go to a restaurant. Order a drink, and sit and read.

10. Bake bread or prepare your childhood comfort food.

11. Call a local recreation department and sign up for a class.

12. Find a new recipe. Buy the ingredients. Prepare it, and invite someone to join you for dinner.

---

it does not? Some settings do not seem to lend themselves to such formalized play; nevertheless, staff members appreciate comic relief in meetings. Consider activities that might actually help people to look forward to coming to work (see Exhibit 15-7).

KEY POINT

A light touch at work can help staff build team spirit—they who laugh together stay together, manage stress, and tap their creativity.

Humor at Home

We take ourselves and our lives so seriously. We need to be perfect and expect others to have a positive attitude at all times and to appreciate our efforts. A helpful principle to remember is that whatever behavior a person offers at any given time is usually the best that he or she can do. We all have grumpy times. Give some thought to the last time you were able to laugh at yourself. Consider how much more peaceful life would be if we could lighten up (see Exhibit 15-8).

EXHIBIT 15-6   A Playful Plan of Self-Care

Just for fun I can . . .

1. _____
2. _____
3. _____
4. _____
5. _____
6. _____
7. _____
8. _____
9. _____
10. _____
11. _____
12. _____
13. _____
14. _____
15. _____
16. _____
17. _____
18. _____
19. _____
20. _____

I, _____ , promise to

    print your name

_____

    one fun thing I will do

by _____ .

    2 weeks from today

_____

    signature

Copyright © Julia Balzer Riley, RN, MN, (2000). Used with permission.

EXHIBIT 15-7   Humor at Work . . . We Need It

1. Remember to greet staff in person and on the telephone with a smile. Share a joke.
2. Post cartoons that make light of shared concerns at work.
3. Buy a bottle of bubbles. Start building a humor kit for the office.
4. Collect funny Post-it notes and use them with staff. Use stickers and gold stars.
5. Organize a fun activity at work, such as a staff baby picture contest, a pumpkin-carving contest at Halloween, a bowling night, or a funny movie night.

Work on keeping a positive attitude. Here are some tips to help keep a positive attitude:

· Focus on positive thoughts, such as "I'm full of energy" and "Today is a good day."

· Imagine good things happening to you. If you are trying to lose weight, picture yourself at your ideal weight.

· Stop looking for the negatives or the flaws in situations and people.

· Find the humor in a difficult situation.

· Smile. A study showed that using all your facial muscles in a smile can put you in a more cheerful mood.

· Exercise and keep active to keep up the flow of endorphins, a hormone that elevates mood.

· Just do it. . . . Eat right and take care of your body to feel better.

EXHIBIT 15-8   Humor at Home

· Try sharing moments of laughter.
· Learn to laugh at your own seriousness.
· Forgive yourself and others.
· Remember that we do not always have to understand each other or even like each other all of the time.
· Lighten up!
· Agree to disagree.
· Do not try to be so perfect, and do not expect it of others.
· Add a little humor by intention. Go do something just for fun—get a life.

> **REFLECTION**
>
> What measures do you use to promote a positive attitude in yourself? List a few ways that you can improve this.

Be an Ambassador for Humor

As you search for ways to be healthy, to tap into the power of the mind–body–spirit connection, some strategies intuitively feel right. If you are lucky enough to have a sense of humor, a comic vision . . . share it; the world needs you! If humor does not come easily, pursue it. Take life lightly. Humor is a great alternative.

Summary

Gelotology, the study of the physiology of laughter, reveals that laughter produces many physiological effects, including stimulation of the production of catecholamines, a decrease in anxiety, an increase in heart and respiratory rate, an increase in endorphins, an enhancement of metabolism, improvement of muscle tone, an increase in natural killer cells, and relief from stress. There are many practical ways that healthcare professionals can implement humor appropriately into healthcare settings; doing so is therapeutic and beneficial to health and healing. In addition, incorporating humor into daily life and work also is an important self-care measure for healthcare professionals.

References

1. Sullivan, J. L., & Deane, D. M. (1988). Humor and health. *Journal of Gerontological Nursing, 14*(1):20–24.
2. Klein, A. (2008). Who says humor heals. Retrieved August 5, 2008 from www.allenklein.com/articles/whosays.htm
3. Cousins, N. (1979). *Anatomy of an Illness as Perceived by the Patient*. New York: WW Norton.
4. Riley, J. B. (2003). *Humor at Work*. Ellenton, FL: Constant Source Seminars.
5. Piper, W. (1978). *The Little Engine That Could*. New York: Grosset & Dunlap.
6. *The Humor Project*. Retrieved from http://www.humorproject.com
7. Riley, J. B. (2003). *Customer Service from A to Z . . . Making the Connection*. Albuquerque, NM: Hartman Publishers.

Humor and Health Resources

Association for Applied and Therapeutic Humor
www.AATH.org

The Humor Project
www.humorproject.com

Part III

Taking Charge of Challenges to the Mind, Body, and Spirit

Chapter 16

Understanding the Hidden Meaning of Symptoms

OBJECTIVES

This chapter should enable you to

- List at least six early warning signs of health problems
- Discuss lessons that can be learned by the choices people make
- Describe the meanings that symptoms can have

Recognizing warning signs is easy when driving a car. The yellow sign with the curved black arrow communicates clearly that the road ahead has a curve and that the driver needs to slow down and pay attention. If this warning sign is observed and the driver gives complete attention, the curve in the road makes the journey more interesting. If the warning sign is ignored, the driver could be forced to pay attention to a car accident, a much less pleasant diversion on the journey.

When people experience good health, they feel alive, trusting, enthusiastic, and full of expectation. When health is threatened, warning signs can develop that alert them to "watch the curve in the road." A short list of early warning signs of health problems could include the following:

- A lack of physical vitality
- Symptoms of illness (e.g., pain, rash, abnormal function, shortness of breath, irregular heartbeat, weight loss, discoloration)
- A feeling of isolation or loneliness
- Frequent accidents
- Poor relationships with family, friends, or coworkers
- An inability to concentrate or solve problems
- An absence of meaning in life; feelings of hopelessness
- Having "enough" by the world's standards, but not feeling satisfied

These warning signs first appear as whispers, but if ignored, they may become shouts. A whisper may be a toothache that ignored becomes the shout of an abscess, or a sore knee that unattended gives out and causes you to slip and break a bone. It may be the whisper of a spouse who is unhappy with your behavior and eventually disrupts your life with the shout of a divorce.

REFLECTION

Would you have the same attention to a whispered message from your own body that you would to an unusual sound from your car?

Purposes of Warning Signs

Warning signs provide feedback for people to pay attention to the way they are living so that their energies will not be diverted to unnecessary complications, expense, and hardship. They remind that "a stitch in time saves nine."

KEY POINT

Warning signs can offer important feedback about life choices that affect health.

Warning signs also teach people how to recognize their choices. They do not spell out exactly what people should do, but they give hints as to what a wise decision would be in a particular situation. The warning signs attempt to help people learn how to be healthy and protect themselves. For instance, working out to stay physically fit is a wonderful way to stay healthy; however, if people try to initiate the same exercise program at age 60 that was used at age 20, they may find themselves frustrated, dreading exercise time, and perhaps injured—warning signs that their exercise program needs to be adjusted. Warning signs can help individuals to recognize safe limits.

Good Health as a Process

When taking an automobile journey, people usually have some idea of where they are going and when they will arrive at their destination. What about health? How will they know when they have achieved a satisfactory level of health?

Some people have conceived of health as a continuum from 0–100%, in which 0% is severe sickness and debilitation and 100% is a perfect, disease-free state. This perspective does not account for the quality of life, nor does a continuum model address the rewards experienced through living. Individuals can have meaningful, satisfying lives even in the presence of physical illness. Many people living with chronic illnesses hold the view that they may have *xyz* disease, but *xyz* disease does not have them. A continuum does not account for this feeling of well-being or enthusiasm for living in the presence of an illness. A continuum does not account for the synergy of the physical, mental, emotional, and spiritual aspects of health. Furthermore, a continuum presupposes that death is bad and, by implication, that old age is something to be avoided.

KEY POINT

Health involves possessing a greater understanding of self. It means that a person feels at peace, whole, alive, and trusting and that each day is faced with expectation and enthusiasm.

Good health is better conceived of as a process rather than a continuum. What is a process? The *American Heritage Dictionary* defines process as "a series of actions, changes, or functions bringing about a result"—for example, the process of digestion and the process of obtaining a driver's license. Health can be conceived as the process by which people become more aware of themselves. Health, as a process, means that people recognize their level of well-being and acknowledge their ability to respond to their current level of well-being. After this part of the process is completed, they will then proceed to either forgive themselves and/or others and change what they need to change or accept the circumstances in which they find themselves and continue to act in ways that will help them achieve a high level of well-being. Sometimes, people learn to achieve good health by experiencing poor health. If one has always known good health, a person may not be aware of what elements make up this experience of well-being nor is he or she likely to be aware of how these elements are related. For example, if your computer is working, you may have little interest in what makes it work, but as soon as you cannot access your e-mail, you are calling tech support to find out how to fix the problem. After help is at hand, some people will want to learn more about what caused the problem and how they may be able to fix it in the future without having to call tech support, whereas other people may only be interested in having tech support tell them what to do to fix the current problem. Both approaches are valuable because they result in your e-mail being accessible. Likewise, the process of health may lead to a problem being fixed, or it may lead to the problem being fixed and also a greater understanding of what constitutes well-being and what behaviors are likely to sustain it.

If people want to take a vacation and tour the temples of ancient Egypt, they typically hope to enjoy good health on the trip. Good *enough* health may be defined in this case as the ability to walk short distances in the hot sun. To achieve their goal of physical endurance, they may engage in the behaviors of eating well, exercising, and getting enough rest. These behaviors dynamically interact to produce the experience of physical endurance and health good enough to accomplish their goal of walking short distances in the hot sun. Each time they make choices about food, exercise, and rest, they have the potential to learn more about themselves, such as which attitudes and behaviors support their goal of physical endurance and which do not. They may also become more confident in their ability to recognize choices that result in a feeling of well-being. As individuals make decisions to support their goals, they feel "at one" with themselves. Health is the process of learning how to achieve this sense of wholeness. Health is recognizing, acknowledging, accepting, and continuing the behaviors that lead to a sense of well-being, peace, and wholeness.

People can also learn about themselves by making choices and engaging in behaviors that do not support their goals. When this occurs, people feel separated from themselves and conflicted. Health is then the process of recognizing, acknowledging, forgiving, and changing the behaviors that lead us to a sense of separation.

REFLECTION

Choices made about your health can give insight into values, courage and commitment, strengths and weaknesses, creativity and patience. What do your health-related choices say about you?

In the process of making bad decisions, there are lessons as well. Here people can touch a part of self that feels cut off. It is a piece of self that is demanding expression and will most likely sabotage them until they either give it their attention or unhappily pay attention to it.

How people choose to give attention and expression to that which seems to be at odds with their goals of good health may, in fact, teach them more about health than their good choices. Forgiveness can be learned and practiced in the presence of bad decisions. Forgiveness has incredible power to help individuals feel whole and at peace. When people practice forgiving themselves, they find it is only a short step to feeling the forgiveness presented to them as a gift from their creator.

Warning signs are messages of conflicting choices that call for people to make single-minded decisions. When they shrink from the opportunity to examine their choices or see where they have made conflicting decisions, people pass up an opportunity to learn more about themselves. Likewise, when they expect someone else to "fix" them, they forfeit an opportunity to reflect upon their choices, make decisions, and learn. Reflection leads to greater self-awareness.

REFLECTION

In what ways does the healthcare system foster consumers' attitudes that someone else needs to fix their health problems?

Warning Signs as Opportunities

Warning signs present at least two opportunities: to ask for help and to have the chance to allow more love into life. In order to ask for help and in order to allow more love into their lives, individuals must recognize the warning signs that are speaking to them; they are in the driver's seat and hold the power; therefore, it makes sense to set aside the temptation to cast blame on self or others for the current situation. The driver is not going to manage a curve in the road by closing his eyes and chanting, "I'm a terrible driver, I shouldn't have started on this journey." Rather, full attention must be given to managing the present reality.

When traveling in a car, it would seem rather silly to say, "These yellow signs are distracting my attention from the enjoyment of this trip." If people resent a warning or blame someone else for their experiences, they are being equally absurd and missing the point of a sign that was meant to be of help.

Where does the process of health lead? How will a person know when he or she has arrived at the destination? What is the health destination? The destination is unique for each person. For some, it can be facing death with the assurance that life has been satisfying and meaningful. For others, the experience of health comes in those special and discrete moments when peace with self, others, and God is achieved. For others, health comes in those magic moments when the joy of living is experienced. This view of health does not concern itself with the physical symptoms of an illness because the presence of a disease does not necessarily mean one is not healthy.

KEY POINT

The experience of a physical illness can awaken one to the experience of health, healing, and wholeness.

Symptoms as Teachers

Physical symptoms can be teaching tools to help people learn how to bring more vitality to living and allow more love into their lives. It is possible to learn without experiencing problems, but if problems unfold, then it is a challenge to use them as learning experiences. The presence or absence of physical symptoms may offer feedback about how alive people feel and how trusting, how enthusiastic, and how much expectation they hold. Symptoms can warn people of imbalances and problems that involve more than the body parts in which they are manifested.

REFLECTION

Symptoms are private and personal messages to you, coded in metaphor. They speak to your uniqueness. How do frequent symptoms that you experience speak to your uniqueness?

In the attempt to decode warning signs, a person may turn to other people—friends, family, and healthcare practitioners—for help. These other people may assist in decoding the messages, but the final interpretation is the person's alone.

These coded messages have the power to bring about change when they are assigned meaning. Decoding the metaphor of a warning sign will have limited power to affect change if it is handled in a cookbook manner that does not resonate with the individual. Take for example a problem with your teeth. This problem has many potential interpretations that may have little to do with dental health. It may mean you are afraid to bite into (take on) something, that you are reluctant to chew (reflect) on something, or that you have bitten off more than you can chew. The correct interpretation of the metaphor can only be known by the person experiencing the symptom. It may be helpful to have others suggest possible interpretations of the metaphor. Their suggestions will stimulate you to think, and thinking may promote an insight that, without their suggestion, you may have missed. The power of the metaphor to create change occurs only when the interpretation resonates with you and creates that "aha" feeling.

Warning signs will have different meanings at different times along the life journey. This is not intended to make life more difficult. Life is not a textbook experience. Understanding the variety of possible meanings enables people to learn about themselves more fully and deeply. Furthermore, the many possible interpretations provide the opportunity to choose the specific meaning of a symptom. For example, you have lost a front tooth, and while waiting to see the dentist, you reflect on this event. You begin to see a metaphor, and it strikes you that you must be experiencing difficulty "biting into something" or "taking a bite." You could think this: "This is another example of how I'm doomed to have one problem after another," or you could think "This dental problem is an example of how I do not pay ample attention to small matters that eventually accumulate into big problems for me. I need to seek help to do the tasks of daily living that need my attention and action." It is expected that a person would respond to a tooth problem by visiting the dentist; however, the tooth problem holds other meaning. The metaphor, if used, can lead to even greater self-knowledge and change. When you manage the physical symptom on more than the surface level (the dentist) and seek to work with the metaphor, you have an opportunity to heal on more than just the physical level. In fact, it may be that the physical symptom will not change, but that change will occur on a more profound level, bringing greater happiness, growth, and satisfaction than you could ever experience by simply treating the physical symptom.

> **KEY POINT**
>
> When physical symptoms are addressed on more than the surface level and the other meanings they hold in life are explored, people have an opportunity to heal beyond the physical level.

Summary

Symptoms involving the mind, body, and spirit can indicate the presence of a health problem. They are warning signs that offer feedback as to the way one is living and lifestyle and health-related choices. Rather than treat or mask their symptoms, people can achieve higher levels of holistic health by exploring their deeper meaning and choosing attitudes and behaviors that will foster health and healing.

Suggested Reading

Bauby, J. (2007). *The Diving Bell and the Butterfly*. New York: Vintage International.

Burkhardt, M. A., & Nagai-Jacobson, M. G. (2002). *Spirituality: Living Our Connectedness*. Albany, NY: Delmar, Thomson Learning.

Duff, K. (2000). *The Alchemy of Illness*. New York: Random House.

Frank, A. W. (1997). *The Wounded Storyteller: Body, Illness, and Ethics*. Chicago: University of Chicago Press.

McSherry, W. (2006). *Spirituality in Nursing Practice: An Interactive Approach*. New York: Churchill Livingstone.

Morris, D. B. (2000). *Illness and Culture in the Postmodern Age*. Berkeley, CA; University of California Press.

Sacks, O. (1998). *A Leg to Stand On*. New York: Touchstone Books.

Chapter 17

Working in Partnership with Your Health Practitioner: Advocating for Yourself

OBJECTIVES

This chapter should enable you to

· List three responsibilities that consumers have when meeting with their health practitioner

· Describe a consumer's responsibilities when diagnosed with a medical problem, hospitalized, and when facing surgery

· List at least five questions to ask of health insurance plans

· Describe at least six factors to evaluate in a primary healthcare practitioner

A *partnership* implies an active relationship of give and take with a mutual respect between the parties. Of the various partnerships that you may experience in your life, your partnership with your healthcare provider is among the more important ones that you can develop. Yesterday's model of blind obedience and dependency on one's physician or other healthcare provider is no longer appropriate or desirable. People have a right to be informed, to have a variety of healthcare options (conventional and complementary/alternative) made available to them, and to make decisions that are right for them—not only medically, but also emotionally, spiritually, and financially. They also have the responsibility to take an active role in their health care, educate themselves about health matters, and equip themselves with the necessary information to make sound healthcare decisions. They must be responsible advocates for themselves.

Responsibilities When Seeking Health Care

Choosing a Healthcare Practitioner

Because the relationship with a healthcare practitioner is an important one that should function with the same harmony as a good marriage, people need to choose a primary healthcare practitioner with whom they can communicate. They must feel free to ask questions and expect to get responses they understand.

When making an appointment, if people think they will need more time than usual to talk things over, they should let the office know in advance. The response to this request could offer insight into the type of relationship that can be expected with the healthcare provider. For example, if you ask that you be scheduled for a longer visit because there are some complementary therapies that you want to review with the physician as soon as possible and you are told, "Sorry, the doctor only can only spend 10 minutes with each patient," you may need to assess whether this is the best source for your primary care.

It is helpful for people to write a list of health concerns or questions that they want to discuss before the appointment. They can include information about symptoms, such as when the symptoms started, what they feel like, whether they are constant, or whether they come and go. Records that are kept, such as blood-sugar levels, daily blood pressure, dietary history, and mood changes, should be taken to the appointment. It is important for people to tell their practitioners personal information—even if it feels uncomfortable to do so. Any allergies or reactions experienced in the past to any medicines or foods need to be discussed. Health practitioners need to know as much as possible about their clients.

KEY POINT

People need to prepare for visits to their healthcare practitioners by writing down health history, medications used, symptoms, and other pertinent information that can be shared with the practitioner.

It is helpful for people to compile a written list of the medicines and supplements that are taken, including those that do not require a prescription, such as over-the-counter pain relievers, laxatives, vitamins, herbs, flower essences, or eye drops. Also helpful is a list of the names of other healthcare practitioners visited, including physicians, chiropractors, acupuncturists, massage therapists, nutritionists, and herbalists. People should supply each of their healthcare practitioners with this information. It is useful for people to be open about their reasons for seeing other healthcare practitioners and the care they are receiving from them. If a healthcare practitioner does not agree with what is being done, it is useful for people to listen to the reasons. All of the facts can be evaluated and decisions made to stay with this practitioner or change to one who is more supportive. Practitioners need to be given permission to contact each other for clarification when necessary.

KEY POINT

It is wise for people to keep their own health file that records their medicines, treatments, surgeries, hospitalizations, and visits to all practitioners.

People should take a notepad to appointments and take notes when given instructions. Most individuals only remember a portion of what they are told, and if anxious, they could forget most of the information. In some circumstances, it could be helpful to bring along someone to help ask questions, clarify, and remember responses.

When Diagnosed With a Medical Condition

If diagnosed with a medical condition, people need to ask about the causes. Often improvements can be made if the reasons are understood. It is beneficial for people to ask for guidelines as to symptoms that should be reported: For example, if the temperature is over what degree? If the discharge is what color? If the stools are loose for how long? If the coughing persists for how many days? If the pain is not relieved by what time? Healthcare practitioners may have printed information about conditions (e.g., diabetes fact sheets) that can be given to take home; if not, people should ask where more information can be obtained. People need to be knowledgeable about their conditions. They need to be informed about the tests that are ordered (see Exhibit 17-1).

KEY POINT

It is useful for copies of diagnostic tests to be requested and kept in a personal health record.

It is important for people to learn about the available treatments for their conditions. Some of the questions that need to be answered when treatments are ordered are listed in Exhibit 17-2. People also can check out information in their libraries or on the Internet. Discussing the issue with friends or relatives who are nurses or other healthcare practitioners is beneficial.

EXHIBIT 17-1 Questions to Ask When Tests Are Recommended

Why is the test needed?

Does the test require any special preparation?

What are the side effects and risks?

When can the results be expected and how are they obtained?

Will additional testing be required at a later date?

Does my insurance cover this test?

What are the alternatives to this test?

EXHIBIT 17-2   Questions to Ask When Treatments Are Ordered

When should treatment start?

How long will the treatment be needed?

What are the benefits of the treatment, and how successful is it usually?

What are the risks and side effects associated with the treatment?

What are the alternatives to this treatment?

What is the cost of the treatment?

After the visit, people need to follow up. Questions should be phoned or e-mailed to the healthcare practitioner. If symptoms worsen or people have problems with what they are asked to do, they need to contact the practitioner. If tests are ordered, arrangements should be made at the laboratory or other offices to get them done. If tests were completed and people have not been informed of the outcome, they need to call for test results. Some healthcare practitioners' offices call patients to see how everything is going, but in most instances, it is up to the individual to do the follow-up.

REFLECTION

How much responsibility do you assume for your personal health care? Do you ask the right questions, demand answers, take action when you think you are not being heard, and follow up as needed? If you do, what has caused you to develop these skills? If you do not, what prohibits you from doing so?

When Hospitalized

Everyone needs to know the physician in charge of their care. This may seem like a ridiculous statement; however, this may be an issue when people go into the hospital for a surgical procedure and have an existing medical problem or several health-related issues. Different doctors may be responsible for different aspects of care. It can be particularly difficult in a teaching hospital where there are several medical residents writing orders. People need to make sure all health professionals know their health history. It is smart for people to keep a brief summary (just a short page) of their condition and health history at the bedside. It cannot be assumed that each doctor or resident knows everything about the history. Very likely, they do not.

KEY POINT

Protection from errors during hospitalization can be increased when a summary of personal health history is kept by the bedside.

When people have questions about procedures or a medicine and the answer is "your doctor ordered it," they need to ask which doctor. If they do not understand the purpose or did not receive an adequate explanation, they are wise to politely refuse. They are not being difficult or uncooperative patients but, rather, informed and responsible patients participating in their own care. They are within their rights to ask their primary doctor to give an explanation. If illness prevents someone from taking on this total responsibility, he or she can ask a family member or friend to be an advocate (see Exhibit 17-3).

It is helpful for people to learn the names of the hospital staff who do anything to or for them. By having their notebooks handy, they can write down staff names and positions,

---

EXHIBIT 17-3   "The Doctor Ordered It. . . ."

An example of what can happen when the only response to your question is "the doctor ordered it" is what happened to a patient who had just gone through a surgical procedure in the hospital to prepare her for kidney dialysis treatments. Early one morning the nurse came in to do a finger stick for a drop of blood. The patient accepted this, assuming that blood tests may be needed. The nurse came in again before lunch to repeat the procedure, and the patient asked, "Why are you sticking me again?" The reply was simply, "The doctor ordered it."

Her daughter, a registered nurse, came to visit later in the day just as the nurse was about to do yet another finger stick. Knowing that this type of testing was typically done for persons with diabetes and that her mother was not diabetic, the daughter asked, "Why are you checking her blood sugar? Is it high?"

"The doctor ordered it," came the reply.

"Well, before you do it, please tell me her blood-sugar level."

With this, the patient said. "Blood sugar! I'm not a diabetic, I don't want you to do this."

The family later learned that one day her blood-sugar level was 147 mg, a little high, but not alarming considering that she was receiving intravenous fluids with dextrose (sugar water). An intern had ordered the test.

When the patient told her primary medical doctor he remarked, "The intern was being overly cautious. I'll write an order that they need to check with me before ordering any more tests."

This situation caused the patient unnecessary worry, discomfort, and expense.

whether it is the nurse assistant who is responsible for bathing assistance or the anesthesiologist who assists with surgery.

When Surgery Is Recommended

There is information that needs to be considered in order to make an informed decision about surgery. First, people need to ask the doctor the purpose of the procedure. Sometimes surgery is not the only answer to a medical problem. Nonsurgical treatments, such as a change in diet, special exercises, acupuncture treatments, herbs, or other nonconventional treatments might help just as well or better. The benefits and risks of these other choices need to be discussed. Individuals can research these on their own.

KEY POINT

One approach when surgery is recommended is watchful waiting, in which the doctor and patient monitor the problem to see if it gets better or worse. If it gets worse, surgery may be needed fairly soon. If it gets better, surgery may be able to be postponed, perhaps indefinitely.

There should be a clear understanding of how the proposed operation relates to the diagnosis. It is reasonable for people to ask why a particular surgeon was chosen. When they meet with the surgeon, people should ask for an explanation of the surgical procedure in detail. They should find out if there are different ways of doing the operation and why the surgeon has chosen the particular procedure. One way may require more extensive surgery than another one and a longer recovery period.

It is important that people know what they will gain by having the operation and how long the benefits are likely to last. For some procedures, the benefits may last only a short time with a need for a second operation at a later date. For other procedures, the benefits may last a lifetime. Published information about the outcomes of the procedure can be reviewed. Because all operations carry some risk, people need to weigh the benefits of the operation against the risks of complications or side effects.

KEY POINT

Surgeons should be asked about possible complications and side effects of the surgery. *Complications* are unplanned events, such as infection, too much bleeding, reaction to anesthesia, or accidental injury. Some people have an increased risk of complications because of other medical conditions. *Side effects* are anticipated occurrences, such as swelling and some soreness at the incision site.

Pain almost always occurs with surgery. People should ask how much pain can be expected and what the doctors and nurses will do to reduce the pain. Individuals may want to discuss how staff will respond if they want to use nonconventional, alternative methods of pain control. Controlling the pain helps people to be more comfortable while they heal, get well faster, and improves the results of their operation.

It is useful for individuals to find out whether the surgeon agrees to their own treatment plans during and after the surgery. For example, what does the physician think about a plan to take higher doses of vitamins and minerals before surgery to promote healing afterward? Will the hospital permit music or guided imagery tapes during the surgery? Can a therapeutic touch practitioner offer treatments after surgery? All desires and suggestions should be openly discussed.

Getting other opinions from a different surgeon and healthcare practitioner of choice is a very good way to make sure having the operation is the best alternative. When people seek second opinions, they can spare themselves unnecessary duplicative testing by obtaining a copy of their records from the first doctor.

Anesthesia is used so that surgery can be performed without unnecessary pain. People should ask to meet with the anesthesiologist to learn about his or her qualifications. The anesthesiologist can explain whether the operation calls for local, regional, or general anesthesia and why this form of anesthesia is recommended for the procedure. Questions about expected side effects and risks of having anesthesia should be asked. Some hospitals are using acupuncture as an adjunct to anesthesia, and this may be requested if appropriate.

If surgery is agreed on, people need to ask if the operation will be done in the hospital or in an outpatient setting. If the doctor recommends inpatient surgery for a procedure that is usually done as outpatient surgery, or just the opposite, the reason should be examined because it is important to be in the most appropriate place for the operation. Until recently, most surgery was performed on an inpatient basis and patients stayed in the hospital for one or more days. Today, many surgeries are done on an outpatient basis in a doctor's office, a special surgical center, or a day surgery unit of a hospital.

People should ask how long they will be in the hospital. The surgeon can describe how people can expect to feel and what they will be able to do or not do the first few days, weeks, or months after surgery. Before discharge, individuals should find out what kinds of supplies, equipment, and any other help they will need when they go home. Knowing what to expect can help them better prepare and cope with recovery. They should ask when they can start regular exercise again and return to work. People do not want to do anything that will slow down the recovery process. Lifting a 10-pound bag of onions may not seem to be too much a week after surgery, but it could be.

Choosing a Health Insurance Plan

Selecting a health plan to cover themselves and their families is an important decision many people make every year. Health insurance varies greatly, and thus, to avoid surprises, it is important for people to find out exactly what their insurance plan covers. Does it allow for

---

EXHIBIT 17-4   Questions to Ask of a Health Insurance Plan

· What benefits and services are covered?

· Is my current doctor in the network?

· How does the plan work?

· How much will it cost me?

· Does the plan have programs in place to assist me in managing chronic conditions?

· Is it evident that qualified healthcare professionals make decisions about medical treatments and services provided to plan members?

· How will I get needed emergency services and procedures that ensure I will get the level of care needed?

· Is the information about member services, benefits, rights, and responsibilities clearly stated?

· Is there easy access to primary care and behavioral health care (mental health services)?

· Does the plan include alternative approaches?

· How prompt are decisions made about coverage of medical treatments and services?

· Are there clear communications from the health plan to members and doctors about reasons for denying medical treatments or services and about the process for appealing decisions to deny treatment or services?

---

any alternative approaches? Many policies now cover acupuncture, and some cover nutrition counseling, massage, and other forms of body work. People need to be informed. Some questions worth asking are offered in Exhibit 17-4.

Health insurance coverage for surgery can vary, and there may be some costs individuals will have to pay. Many health insurance plans require patients to get a second opinion before they have certain nonemergency or elective operations. Even if a plan does not require a second opinion, people may still ask to have one. Before having a test, procedure, or operation, it is advisable for people to call their insurance plan to find out how much of these costs it will pay and how much they will have to pay themselves. They also may be billed by the hospital for inpatient or outpatient care, any doctor who visited, the anesthesiologist, and others providing care related to the operation.

KEY POINT

People should do their homework to assure that they are not surprised by unexpected bills.

The Agency for Health Care Policy and Research, within the Department of Health and Human Services, has excellent information on choosing quality health care. The National Committee for Quality Assurance, a nonprofit accrediting agency, has a Health Plan Report Card that shows consumers how well managed health plans are doing (see the resources at the end of the chapter).

How to Get Quality Care

From the Primary Healthcare Practitioner

People must decide what they want and need in a healthcare practitioner. What is most important to them in working in partnership? Internists and family physicians are the two largest groups of primary healthcare practitioners for adults. Many women see obstetricians/gynecologists for some, or all, of their primary care needs. Pediatricians and family practitioners are primary healthcare practitioners for many children.

REFLECTION

What do you look for in a healthcare practitioner?

Nurse practitioners, certified nurse midwives, and physician assistants are trained to deliver many aspects of primary care. Physician assistants must practice in partnership with doctors. Nurse practitioners and certified nurse midwives can work independently in some states, but not others. Some people may choose an acupuncturist, chiropractor, or naturopath for their health maintenance and consult with the medical doctor when hospitalization or special tests are needed.

There are minimum requirements to look for in any practitioner (see Exhibit 17-5). Is the primary healthcare practitioner listening with full attention and not distracted with other things going on? Does the practitioner answer questions without impatience? When a client calls the office with a concern, do the staff members respond, or do they refer it to the practitioner? Does the practitioner return calls? Does the entire staff treat clients with respect? Does the receptionist or billing person answer all questions and assist in a courteous way if help is needed?

KEY POINT

Staff members are an extension of the primary healthcare practitioner, and their attitude and actions often reflect those of their boss.

EXHIBIT 17-5   Characteristics to Look for in a Primary Healthcare Practitioner

Look for someone who:

· Listens to you

· Explains things clearly

· Encourages you to ask questions

· Treats you with respect

· Understands the language that you are most comfortable speaking (or has someone in the office who does)

· Takes steps to help you prevent illness

· Is rated or certified to give quality care

· Has the training and experience that meets your needs

· Has privileges at the hospital of your choice

· Participates in your health plan, unless you choose to pay out of pocket

---

What role does prevention have in the plan for health care? Does the practitioner offer advice about a healthful diet, exercise, adequate sleep, addictive behaviors, and how to prevent minor illnesses?

Does the practitioner have additional certification and/or experience (e.g., board certified, licensed)? There are organizations that certify people in many different specialties and modalities. Is the person knowledgeable about alternative treatments or willing to listen to the search for alternative/complementary treatments? Does the practitioner have privileges at the hospital that you wish to use?

If they are already enrolled in a health plan, people's choices may be limited to doctors and healthcare practitioners who participate in the plan. If they have a choice of plans, individuals may want to first think about whom they would like to use. Then they may be able to choose a plan that fits their preferences.

When Surgery Is Recommended

It is important for people to check their surgeons' qualifications. One way to reduce the risks associated with surgery is to choose a surgeon who has been thoroughly trained to do the procedure and has plenty of experience doing it. Surgeons can be asked about their recent record of successes and complications with a procedure. If they are more comfortable, people can discuss the topic of a surgeon's qualifications with their primary healthcare practitioner or do their own research.

People undergoing surgery will want to know that their surgeon is experienced and qualified to perform the operation. Many surgeons have taken special training and passed exams given by a national board of surgeons. People should ask whether their surgeon is board certified in surgery. Some surgeons also have the letters *FACS* after their name, which means they are Fellows of the American College of Surgeons and have passed a review by surgeons of their surgical practices. To check out qualifications, people can contact the American Board of Medical Specialists or Administrators in Medicine (see the resources at the end of the chapter).

From a Complementary/Alternative Modality Practitioner

Complementary/alternative modality (CAM) covers a broad range of healing philosophies, approaches, and therapies that conventional medicine does not commonly use or make available. People use CAM treatments in a variety of ways. Therapies may be used alone as an alternative to conventional treatment. They may also be used in addition to, or in combination with, conventional methods, in what is referred to as an *integrative approach*. Many CAM therapies are called holistic, which generally means they consider the whole person, including physical, mental, emotional, and spiritual aspects. Many are reviewed in this book. Some useful sources of information are the National Institutes of Health, National Center for Complementary and Alternative Medicine, American Holistic Nurses Association, and Natural Healers (see the resources at the end of the chapter).

Most often people learn about these modalities and the therapists as referrals from friends. Today, people can go on the Internet, search for the particular modality, and find most anything they want to know. Schools often have a listing of their graduates, which can serve as a referral source. The telephone book yellow pages can be explored for alternative medicine. Primary healthcare practitioners can be good referral sources, too. Many chiropractors are knowledgeable about alternative treatments. Friends who are nurses can also be asked for ideas.

How do people know whether these therapies and practitioners are appropriate for them? They can check to see whether the practitioner has had training and experience. Practitioners can be asked for referrals of other clients. People should look for the same qualities as they would for any healthcare practitioner—and more. Are they holistic in their practice? Do they consider mind, body, and spirit when planning treatment? Do they explain what they are doing? Have they trained at a licensed school? Do they have certification or state licensing for what they do? It is useful for people to check the credentials of practitioners. Practitioners can be asked whether their therapy has been used to treat conditions similar to the ones for which treatment is sought, whether there are any side effects or cautions in using this particular therapy, and whether they can they share research to support the treatment or product they use (for more information see Chapter 21).

> **KEY POINT**
>
> Many CAM therapies are available for health maintenance, prevention, and treatment of illness. It is the individual's responsibility to learn about and choose the ones that are appropriate for his or her condition.

Working in partnership with their healthcare practitioners gives people the tools that they need to get the quality health care they deserve. It takes work and being alert and proactive, not just accepting everything they are told. By being active participants, people increase their chances of getting the best health care available.

Summary

When meeting with a healthcare practitioner, consumers have responsibilities, including preparing for the visit, informing the practitioner of medications and supplements used and other practitioners seen, and remembering instructions in detail. When diagnosed with a medical condition, consumers need to ask about the cause, symptoms, and guidelines for treatment.

Asking questions about procedures, medications, and the staff are important during a hospitalization. When facing surgery, consumers need to ask about alternatives, benefits, and risks of surgery, as well as expected pain, where the surgery will be done, and anticipated time for recovery.

A variety of questions need to be asked when considering a health insurance plan, including benefits covered, how the plan works, cost, how decisions are made, and whether one's current practitioners are in the network.

When evaluating a primary healthcare practitioner, consumers should consider whether the practitioner listens, explains things clearly, encourages questions, treats them with respect, speaks the same language, takes steps to prevent illness, is certified, has privileges at the hospital of their choice, and participates in their insurance plan.

By being active participants and informed consumers of their health care, people can maximize the quality of care they receive and reduce risks.

Suggested Reading

Benner, P. (2003). Enhancing patient advocacy and social ethics. *American Journal of Critical Care*, *12*(4):374–375.

Clark, C. C. (2003). *American Holistic Nurses Association Guide to Common Chronic Conditions: Self-Care Options to Complement Your Doctor's Advice*. Hoboken, NJ: John Wiley & Sons.

Ekegren, K. (2000). We are all advocates. *Journal of the Society of Pediatric Nursing*, *5*(2):100–102.

Ford, S., Schofield, T., & Hope, T. (2003). What are the ingredients for a successful evidence-based patient choice consultation? A qualitative study. *Society of Science and Medicine, 56*(3):589–602.

Greggs-McQuilkin, D. (2002). Nurses have the power to be advocates. *Medical Surgical Nursing, 11*(6):265, 309.

Henderson, S. (2003). Power imbalance between nurses and patients: a potential inhibitor of partnership in care. *Journal of Clinical Nursing, 12*(4):501–508.

Hyland, D. (2002). An exploration of the relationship between patient autonomy and patient advocacy: implications for nursing practice. *Nursing Ethics, 9*(5):472–482.

Penson, R. T. (2001). Complementary, alternative, integrative, or unconventional medicine? *Oncologist, 6*(5):463–473.

Roter, D. L., & Hall, J. A. (2006) *Doctors Talking with Patients/Patients Talking with Doctors: Improving Communication in Medical Visits*, 2nd ed. Westport, CT: Praeger.

Strax, T. E. (2003). Consumer, advocate, provider: a paradox requiring a new identity paradigm. *Archives of Physical Medicine and Rehabilitation, 84*(7):943–945.

Resources

Administrators in Medicine
www.docboard.org

Information on doctors in many states is available from state medical board directors.

Agency for Healthcare Research and Quality
2101 E. Jefferson St., Suite 501
Rockville, MD 20852
301-594-6662
www.ahrq.gov

Your Guide to Choosing Quality Health Care is based on research about the information people want and need when making decisions about health plans, doctors, treatments, hospitals, and long-term care.

American Board of Medical Specialties
800-776-2378
www.certifieddoctor.org

This site can tell you whether the doctor is board certified. *Certified* means that the doctor has completed a training program in a specialty and has passed an exam (board) to assess his or her knowledge, skills, and experience to provide quality patient care in that specialty.

American Holistic Nurses Association
800-278-2462
www.ahna.org

The American Holistic Nurses Association has a directory of members with additional training in various modalities.

American Medical Association
American Medical Association Chicago Headquarters
515 N. State Street
Chicago, IL 60610
312-464-5000
800-665-2882
www.ama-assn.org

"Physician Select" information is available on training, specialties, and board certification about many licensed doctors in the United States.

Joint Commission on Accreditation of Healthcare Organizations
One Renaissance Boulevard
Oakbrook Terrace, IL 60181
630-792-5000
www.jcaho.org

The Joint Commission evaluates and accredits nearly 20,000 healthcare organizations and programs in the United States. An independent, not-for-profit organization, the Joint Commission is the nation's predominant standards-setting and accrediting body in health care.

National Center for Complementary or Alternative Medicine
P.O. Box 8218
Silver Spring, MD 20907-8218
888-644-6226
www.nccam.nih.gov

Focuses on evaluating the safety and efficacy of widely used natural products, such as herbal remedies and nutritional and food supplements; supporting pharmacological studies to determine the potential interactive effects of CAM products with standard treatment medications; and evaluating CAM practices.

The National Committee for Quality Assurance
Health Plan Accreditation
2000 L Street, NW, Suite 500
Washington, D.C. 20036
202-955-3500
www.ncqa.org

This is an accrediting agency that gives standardized, objective information about the quality of managed-care organizations, managed behavioral healthcare organizations, credentials verification organizations, and physician organizations.

Natural Healers
www.naturalhealers.com

This Web site describes many complementary and alternative therapies and gives a list of schools in the United States and Canada that teach the various disciplines. Schools often have lists of graduates who are practitioners in your area.

National Institutes of Health
Bethesda, MD 20892
301-496-4000
www.nih.gov/niams/healthinfo/library

This is a place to start to find information on any medical topic, resources, research, and self-help groups.

National Library of Medicine
www.nlm.nih.gov/medlineplus/patientissues

This site has useful topics on a variety of issues effecting patients.

U.S. Department of Health and Human Services
200 Independence Ave.
Washington, D.C. 20201
877-696-6775
www.healthfinder.gov

free guides to reliable health information.

Chapter 18

Menopause: Time of the Wise Woman

OBJECTIVES

This chapter should enable you to

- Describe the three seasons of a woman's life
- Discuss how menopause is a sacred journey
- Define menopause
- List the three types of estrogen produced by the ovaries
- Describe what is meant by a natural hormone
- List a multistep approach to assisting women in menopausal transition years
- Describe at least six factors that can trigger hot flashes

Imagine a time long, long ago, when cycles of life were celebrated. There were ceremonies celebrating the cycles of the sun and the moon, the cycles of planting and harvesting, the cycles of seasonal change, and the cycles of birth and death, marriages, and rites of passage. The cycles of our lives were honored and celebrated as necessary transitions and initiations. People knew how to stay connected to their spirit and to that which had meaning in their lives.

REFLECTION

Do you know how to call in your spirit? Do you know how to connect to the deepest part of your soul? Do you know what your soul yearns for? Do you know what has heart and meaning for you?

Menopause is the time that helps women to answer these questions. The physiological, emotional, and spiritual changes that take place direct women's hearts, souls, and spirits. If they do not pay attention, their bodies and emotions call out to them—sometimes whispering gently, sometimes yelling to get noticed.

We must get back to remembering our roots. Remembering means to reconnect, to put our members back together, to put all the pieces of ourselves back together again.

Remembering our roots reminds us to reconnect to what keeps us centered and balanced in our lives. We can also reconnect to the plants that have nurtured women for centuries.

KEY POINT

Women are reminded to honor the different seasons of their lives:

The time of the maiden: of innocence, joy, playfulness, passions

The time of the mother: of unconditional loving, giving, and creativity

The time of the crone: of achieving the crowning glory of the wisdom of age

All of these seasons evoke celebration in honor of these transitions.

Many cultures have rites of puberty for males and females, honoring the transition into adulthood. There are trials, challenges, and initiations that evoke honor, integrity, courage, and moral character. Individuals then are welcomed into society as important and contributing members, often being given new names that honor special characteristics or individual traits. They are launched into their lives with a supportive send-off and expected to live as responsible members of the community. As their lives progress, there is another initiation when these people become elders. Respect is shown to these individuals, honoring the wisdom that they have gleaned from living life and life's experiences. The wisdom is honored and cherished, for it is passed down through generations, ensuring the future survival of the community. It is considered imperative to pass one's knowledge to others. It is not customary to keep it to oneself.

Many of the experiences that build wisdom were gathered from mistakes along the way—wisdom does not come easy. To take what life gives you and turn it into wisdom requires courage and fortitude. As with any initiation, this does not occur overnight. It requires patience, endurance, and intention, and a willingness to step outside your comfort zone. The courage to forge ahead in the midst of bodily changes can bring a new relationship with your body, that of a much deeper connection.

KEY POINT

If ever there is a time for a woman to tune into her spiritual nature, it is during menopause. If by that time she has not discovered her spiritual essence, her spirit will call upon her to start listening.

Menopause as a Sacred Journey

How does this idealistic philosophy translate into our Western culture? For the most part, gray-haired men become more distinguished with age. Gray-haired women are encouraged to dye their hair, use wrinkle-reducing creams, consider cosmetic surgery, and hide any signs of aging whatsoever. Many women approach aging with dread, feeling like they are unappreciated and fearing they will be useless and discarded.

A more holistic approach to menopause is to view this as a sacred journey on one of life's rivers. It is an initiation into wisdom and creativity that takes time, preparedness, courage, fortitude, patience, and support. The river must be approached with respect, for you cannot predict what nature has in store for you throughout the journey. As you embark with anticipation, you do not know what will be waiting for you at the mouth of the river. You may start in peaceful waters but may face big rapids ahead. Sometimes you get caught in an eddy and need to sit in the stillness for awhile. At times, you have to weather the storm on *terra firma*.

Because menopause is such an important and vital transition in a woman's life, it is meaningful to approach it as a time of celebration rather than a time of dread. Perhaps it is this dreaded anticipation that causes women to approach the menopausal transition with more fear and trepidation, which causes more intense symptoms. That is unknown; however, now, more than ever, women have many more options available to them so that they can embark on the menopausal journey with knowledge and many hormonal and herbal preparations that will facilitate this wondrous and sacred passage.

Taking Charge

The first thing a menopausal woman must consider is her goals. Are they to relieve symptoms, such as hot flashes, night sweats, insomnia, or vaginal dryness? Are they to have future protection against osteoporosis and heart disease? A combination? She must reflect deeply on this to make her decision. She can use her wise-woman intuition combined with true medical facts and then choose her intention. After she decides, she needs to surround herself with a healing team. One aspect of this is finding health professionals that will support her decisions and provide information to keep her informed of new options. She needs to learn about nutritious foods to nurture her body. Keeping her body balanced with massage therapies or energy therapies could prove helpful, as could seeking a spiritual mentor. She will find it beneficial, if she is not already doing so, to exercise with a friend. She can start her own circle of women who can gather monthly to support one another. Keeping company with people who energize, not drain her, will prove to be therapeutic. With a healing team, a woman can realize that she does not have to walk this path alone.

REFLECTION

As you go through life passages, who will make up your healing team to offer support, guidance, and assistance?

The Energetics of Healing

Most indigenous cultures have a word in their language that means *energy flow through the body*. The Chinese call it *chi*. The Japanese call it *ki*. In India it is called *prana*. The English language, unfortunately, lacks a word that translates into energy flow. Most other cultures are aware of the energy centers in our bodies and how to keep the energy flowing to maintain harmony and balance and to prevent disease. There are several energy systems in the body, including energy fields, energy meridians, and energy centers called *chakras*. You can learn how to look at your body in an energetic way and keep your energy centers strong (see Healing Touch International, listed under the resources section, for classes pertaining to energy healing). Menopause is a perfect time for a woman to start observing her own energy flow and to commit to a way of life that promotes balanced energy in her body and mind. Everyone has a personal and individual energy makeup or blueprint. That is why certain things work for some people and do not work for others. The woman needs to begin looking at things energetically. She needs to learn to trust her body's inner wisdom to find medicines, herbs, and approaches that work for her individually. Finding her own balance is another example of the wise-woman way.

The Art of Mindfulness

There is a spiritual practice termed *mindfulness*, which teaches to be always present, centered, and observant in each thought that you have and in each action that you take. Mindfulness is a perfect practice during the transition of menopause. If a woman can be mindful of what is happening with each different emotion or symptom that she experiences, then she can observe the effects of different substances and situations that may trigger symptoms. When she knows what triggers a symptom, then she can modify it. It is important for a woman to learn to be mindful of her body during this phase. She can start tuning in to her body's natural rhythms so that she will know when it needs rest, when it needs nourishing foods, when it needs quiet, when it needs play and laughter. If she believes that menopause directs her toward self-growth, then if she is mindful, she can see the connections more clearly and gain wonderful insights.

The Art of Healing

Healing is different from curing. The word *healing* means wholeness. Each individual has a unique energy matrix that defines wholeness. Menopause is a time for discovering and connecting to that which brings a woman closer to wholeness. Only her own inner wisdom ultimately knows what that is. During menopause, she is remembering—bringing mind, body, and spirit together to be more whole. This can be done with the use of herbs, foods, friends, exercise, quiet time, and nature. By reflecting in the quiet and the stillness, a woman will know what she needs for her own personal wholeness and healing.

KEY POINT

A new wholeness of mind, body, and spirit can be realized during menopause.

Defining Menopause

The medical definition of menopause is the absence of periods for 12 months in a row. Some experts define it as no periods for 6 months in a row, whereas others say if you are having menopausal symptoms unrelated to other medical pathology, then that constitutes menopause. The average age to experience menopause in the United States is age 52.

KEY POINT

Sixty million women will be experiencing the menopausal journey by the year 2020. Women's health programs that address the holistic needs of this population will need to expand.

Some blood tests can be used to confirm menopause, especially thyroid-stimulating hormone (TSH) and follicle-stimulating hormone (FSH) levels (see Exhibit 18-1). It is important to rule out underlying thyroid disease by getting a TSH level, as some of the symptoms can be similar to menopause. FSH is elevated in menopause, and thus, measuring the level can be a useful diagnostic measure.

Saliva can be tested instead of blood to obtain hormone levels (see Aeron Life Cycles in the resources section). This is equally reliable as blood tests, and less expensive, and therefore useful for people who may not have health insurance.

Estrogen

Estrogen, which is produced in the ovaries, adrenal glands, and fat cells, is involved in many functions. Increasingly, research reveals new insights into the effects of estrogen; researchers are finding more estrogen receptors in the body than were originally considered. There are estrogen receptors in the skin, the brain, the heart, the bones, the genitourinary tract, and

---

Exhibit 18-1   Follicle-Stimulating Hormone

FSH is produced in the pituitary gland. Through a feedback loop system, it sends a message to the ovaries each month to stimulate ovulation. In the perimenopausal and menopausal years, there is a gradual decline in estrogen production. When the pituitary gland notices that there is less estrogen being produced in the ovaries, it produces more FSH in an effort to get the ovaries to respond by producing more estrogen. As this feedback loop continues, FSH levels start rising. A normal FSH level is under 20 mLU/mL. Many infertility specialists claim that it is difficult to conceive with FSH levels greater than 12. Some experts feel that an FSH level of greater than 20, with accompanying symptoms, defines menopause. Other experts feel that a true menopausal level of FSH is more like 90 or greater and that FSH levels between 20 and 90 are considered resistant ovary syndrome, where the woman has declining levels of estrogen, but may get a period every few months.

---

the intestines. When estrogen levels decline in menopause, it affects all these organ systems. Through much research since the 1930s and through medical evaluation, doctors began advising estrogen replacement in the 1950s. It was believed that after menopause estrogen replacement helped to protect against heart disease, osteoporosis, colon cancer, vaginal atrophy, and urethral and bladder atrophy. It was suggested that estrogen helped to keep skin supple, keep our teeth strong, and help our brains stay healthy, even preventing Alzheimer's disease; however, the benefits of estrogen replacement were found to be overshadowed by the risks when the results of the *Women's Health Initiative* study began to show that women who took oral estrogen with progesterone therapy showed increased risks for breast cancer, coronary heart disease, and venous thromboembolism.[1] Many women, frightened by these findings, ceased using estrogen. Although estrogen is no longer seen as the cure for all of the negative consequences of aging, it now is viewed as having a place for short-term use in the relief of menopausal symptoms.

KEY POINT

Five times as many women die of heart disease and osteoporosis than breast cancer. Heart disease causes as many deaths each year as the next eight leading causes combined. Approximately 240,000 women die of heart attacks each year. Women are more likely to die of a first heart attack than men. The American Heart Association claims that woman's lifetime risk of heart attack is one in two (see Exhibit 18-2).

Twenty-eight million Americans, mostly women, have osteoporosis. Osteoporosis causes more dangerous effects than one would think. Osteoporosis leads to 1.5 million fractures

EXHIBIT 18-2   Heart Disease and Women

Risks for Heart Disease

· Natural menopause occurring before age 40

· Menopause induced by surgery or illness before age 45

· Previous diagnosis of heart disease or hypertension

· Family history of heart disease especially heart attack prior to age 50

· Bulk of body fat is in upper body/waist

· Smoking

· Poor diet—low in nutrients, high fat, frequent fast foods

· Physically inactive

· No passion for life

· Inability to express anger; unresolved anger and grief

· Social isolation; limited community support

How to Strengthen Your Heart

· Exercise 3 to 5 times per week for 30–40 minutes

· Eat a high-nutrient diet, rich in whole grains, green leafy vegetables, low-fat protein, low sugar

· Keep your heart emotionally strong by expressing feelings

· Learn the art of forgiveness (yourself and others)

· Practice the art of the four-chambered heart

   1. Be full hearted. Do not do anything half heartedly.

   2. Be open hearted. Open yourself to receiving as well as giving.

   3. Be strong hearted. Let go of fear.

   4. Be clear hearted. Set a clear intention.

· Herbal support

   1. Garlic

   2. Onions

   3. Motherwort tincture

   4. Cardiovascular support tonic—hawthorne (leaf, flower, berry), motherwort, ginger, and passionflower

each year, according to the National Osteoporosis Foundation. One out of three women older than age 50 will develop vertebral fractures. Half of the women who develop a hip fracture from osteoporosis never leave the hospital because of ensuing complications. A woman's risk of developing a hip fracture is equal to her combined risk of breast, uterine, and cervical cancer (see Exhibit 18-3). The increased risk for developing osteoporosis caused

---

EXHIBIT 18-3   Osteoporosis: Identifying and Reducing Risks

Risks for Osteoporosis

· Surgical or abrupt menopause
· Menopause
· Strong family history of osteoporosis
· Caucasian or Asian heritage
· Small body frame/slender build
· High caffeine intake
· Smoking
· High intake of phosphates from cola drinks
· Carbonated beverages
· Frequent antacids
· Low-calcium diet
· Alcoholic beverages
· High exercise/low body fat ratio/infrequent periods as seen in athletes
· Infrequent periods
· Premature gray hair

Ways to Prevent Osteoporosis

· Regular weight-bearing exercise
· High-calcium diet (including steamed leafy greens, such as kale, dandelion, mustard greens, collards, kelp, and hijiki seaweed)
· Nourishing high-calcium and mineral teas, vinegars, herbal tinctures (including nettles, alfalfa, raspberry, oatstraw, horsetail, dandelion, and red clover)
· Soy foods
· Decreased use of alcohol, caffeine, soda pop, and antacids
· No smoking
· Care to prevent accidents and injuries
· Osteoporosis screening
· Calcium, magnesium, zinc, and vitamin D supplements

by declining estrogen levels caused many women to consider hormonal replacement therapy, but there are safer options for women to consider (see Exhibit 18-3).

The ovaries produce three types of estrogen—estrone, estradiol, and estriol. Estrone (E1) was the first estrogen discovered and is very potent. This potency is attributed to many of the more intense side effects when taking it, such as breast tenderness, nausea, and headache. Estrone is possibly the estrogen most linked to an increase in breast cancer. Estradiol (E2) is the primary estrogen produced by the ovary. Estriol (E3) is the principle estrogen produced in pregnancy. It is a weak form of estrogen and has not been used much in the past because it was more difficult to formulate a high enough dose in the laboratory. Recent research is showing that estriol may be protective against breast cancer and that formulary pharmacies are making it more available now than in the past.

Options

After a woman is determined to be in menopause or has severe menopause-related symptoms that she wants to treat, she must then decide on a regimen. If she still has an intact uterus, adding estrogen can cause a buildup of the uterine lining (or endometrial lining). This buildup is called *hyperplasia* and can lead to an increased risk of uterine cancer. Adding a progestin component prevents uterine hyperplasia; therefore, if a woman takes estrogen and has a uterus, it is advised that she also take a progesterone supplement. The progesterone component often causes more intolerable side effects, such as headaches, mood swings, and irritability, which cause some women to stop taking hormone supplements. Currently, there are other, more natural progestin options, with fewer side effects.

There are many types of hormone replacement options, which is good news for women. Energetically, each woman has a unique energy blueprint; therefore, regimens work differently for each woman. Using her intuition, together with sound medical advice, will allow a woman to find a regimen that works for her.

REFLECTION

Some women are willing to assume the increased risk for cancer and heart disease in order to obtain the benefits from hormonal replacement therapy. They claim that they are more concerned with feeling and looking their best today than with the possible risks they may face in the future. How does this coincide with your beliefs and values? What has influenced your personal beliefs and values concerning this type of view?

Natural versus Synthetic Hormones

Natural refers to that which is identical to what the body produces, not the characteristic of the source of the medication or hormone. To truly be natural, a substance would have to be extracted from the human body. When a medication is derived from a plant source, it is not naturally identical to what the human produces, although you could say it came from a natural source.

For a pharmaceutical company to obtain a patent for a drug, it cannot be human identical (bioidentical); therefore, a molecule in the substance must be changed to make it slightly different from what the body produces. This change in molecular structure is very minor and formulated to work almost identically to what the body would naturally produce. The patenting of a drug is what provides exclusive rights and profits to offset the cost of research and development of the drug.

When Premarin, the first synthetic estrogen, was developed, it was derived from pregnant women's urine, which is high in estrone estrogen. During the postdepression years, it became difficult to control quality in the process of obtaining the urine. For example, people other than pregnant women would submit their urine in efforts to earn some money. This led the company to begin obtaining the urine from pregnant female horses because it was close in equivalency to human urine. The company changed the name to Premarin (pregnant mare's urine). In essence, Premarin is very natural, but it is mainly comprised of estrone, which is very potent and can cause many side effects. Also, the slight difference in molecular structure of synthetic hormones compared with natural, human-identical hormones, may account for the minor side effects.

KEY POINT

Several years ago, private, individual pharmacies began formulating their own hormones to be human identical (bioidentical). Initially, these hormones were quite expensive, but now there are many more "formulary pharmacies," and the cost has decreased. Insurance companies frequently pay for synthetic hormones, but not natural hormones.

The medical research that showed estrogen replacement helpful in preventing heart disease and osteoporosis was done using synthetic hormones. There is no medical research that proves that the bioidentical hormones protect the bones and heart. Menopause symptoms may go away with the human-identical hormones, but there is no assurance the bones and heart are staying healthy. Tests such as bone-density screens and treadmill tests can evaluate the condition of the bones and heart.

Hormonal Replacement

Oral estrogens are taken daily in varying dosages, which can take a lot of juggling. It can take several weeks or more to find just the right dosage, and thus, women need to be advised not to become discouraged or give up. It can take some time to find the right dosage for an individual, and thus, women need to be encouraged to stay in communication with their healthcare providers so that dosages can be adjusted as needed.

There are many different types of regimens for hormone replacement. If a woman has a uterus, she must use estrogen plus a progestin. Estrogen is taken daily; the progestin component is either taken daily in a smaller dose or cyclically for 12 days each month at a higher dose. If she uses a cyclic regimen, a woman generally will have a withdrawal bleed or period each month. If she does not have a uterus, she only needs to take the estrogen component. The progestin component has been the one that usually causes the most adverse side effects such as mood swings, irritability, bloating, and headaches. Examples of synthetic and natural hormones are shown in Exhibit 18-4.

EXHIBIT 18-4   Examples of Natural and Synthetic Hormonal Replacements

Oral Estrogens

- Conjugated equine estrogen (Premarin 0.3 mg, 0.625 mg, 0.9 mg, 1.25 mg, 2.5 mg daily)
- Esterified estrogen (Estratab, Menest 0.3 mg, 0.625 mg, 1.25 mg, 2.5 mg)
- Estropipate (estrone) (Ogen 0.625 mg, 1.25 mg, 2.5 mg, 5.0 mg, Ortho-est 0.625 mg, 1.25 mg)
- Estradiol (Estrace 0.5 mg, 1 mg, 2 mg)

Transdermal Estrogens

Placed on skin and changed once or twice weekly. The hormone is absorbed through the skin, which bypasses the liver metabolism.

- Estradiol (Alora, Vivelle, Climara, Estraderm)

Intravaginal Ring

Inserted into vagina for 90 days then removed and replaced.

- Estradiol (Estring 2 mg)

Vaginal Creams

Generally use 1/2 applicator in vagina 2–3 times per week as needed.

- Estradiol (Estrace vaginal cream)
- Conjugated estrogen (Premarin vaginal cream)
- Estropipate (Ogen vaginal cream)
- Dinestrol (Ortho Dinestrol vaginal cream)

(continues)

EXHIBIT 18-4   Examples of Natural and Synthetic Hormonal Replacements *(continued)*

Progestins

Oral Progestins

· Medroxyprogesterone acetate (Provera, Cycrin, Amen)

· Micronized progesterone (Prometrium)

· Norethindrone Acetate (Aygestin)

Synthetic Combinations of Estrogen and Progestin

· Conjugated estrogen with Medroxyprogesterone acetate:

  ("Prempro" = Premarin 0.625 mg with Cycrin 2.5 mg,

  "Premphase" = Premarin 0.625 mg with Cycrin 5.0 mg)

· Ethinyl Estradiol (5 mcg) with Norethindrone Acetate (1 mg) daily ("Femhrt")

· Estradiol (1 mg) with Norgestimate (0.09 mg) "OrthoPrefest"

Natural (Bio-Identical) Hormones from Formulary Pharmacies

Estrogens

    ORAL: Bi-est (80% Estriol, 20% Estradiol)

        Tri-est (80% Estriol, 10% Estradiol, 10% Estrone)

    VAGINAL: Estriol or Estradiol cream

Progestins

· Oral-micronized progesterone 100 mg once or twice daily

· Prometrium 100 or 200 mg at bedtime (Peanut oil base—do not use if allergic to peanuts)

KEY POINT

Not too long ago, menopausal women were told that soy products were beneficial and would alleviate their symptoms. The soybean contains the isoflavones, genistein, and diazein, which are plant estrogens (phytoestrogens) containing weak estrogenic activity. Isoflavones are found in many plants and legumes, such as lentils, chickpeas, cashews, and others, but are highly concentrated in soybeans. Recent research has challenged the value of soy for menopause as soy failed to show effectiveness as compared with a placebo. There also is concern that soy can cause a multiplication of breast cells and perhaps increase the risk for breast cancer.

Multistep Approach

A multistep approach can prove helpful to women in the menopausal transition years, consisting of

- Herbs
- Physical exercise
- Essential oils and aromatherapy
- Breathing techniques, meditation, journaling, self-care techniques

Herbs

The wise-woman approach focuses on a nourishing and nurturing approach. The phase of menopause can be used by a woman to become more in tune with her body, her surroundings, and her attitude on how she wants to live the next phase of her life. The focus is on finding a balance in her life that supports health, vitality, harmony, and joy. Menopause is seen as a celebration. The work of childbearing and child rearing is approaching its close, lending time for joyful expression of a woman's true essence. As her children are growing and becoming adults, a woman can direct her energies to things that support her own continued growth.

KEY POINT

Menopause can move a woman toward more outward expression in the world and, at the same time, toward becoming more introspective.

The herbal approach allows a woman to rediscover the ways of nourishing, nurturing, and replenishing her body and spirit. It can be very gratifying for a woman to begin to learn about these wondrous plants that have been growing alongside us for centuries. Herbs can be important allies for her as she takes time to observe the plants, smell their fragrances, sit with them to discover their medicine, bask in the beauty of their colors and textures. She will find certain plants call to her and resonate with her own energy vibration. These will be her healing herbs. Classes on herbs and herbal medicine can help one to become more knowledgeable so that herbs can be used wisely.

Several herbs have been shown to be effective in controlling symptoms associated with menopause. Among these are chaste tree berries, black cohosh, and licorice root (if a person has high blood pressure licorice root should not be used). Nourishing and balancing teas made of alfalfa, nettles, oatstraw, horsetail, rosehips, red clover, and licorice root can increase a sense of well-being in menopausal women (see the resources section for sources of herbal preparations). These herbs are high in minerals and calcium for nourishing, toning, and balancing. They provide minerals to keep bones strong and nourish the liver and adrenal glands.

Drinking a cup of tea containing these herbs in the afternoon seems to balance the blood sugar and helps give an energy boost. It can be suggested that the woman make a big pot of several quarts and keep a week's supply in the refrigerator. These teas can be consumed hot or cold, and stevia or succanat can be added to sweeten. It can be put in a thermos to carry throughout the day, using it as a reminder to nurture and nourish oneself. The resource list at the end of this chapter offers information on making these teas.

KEY POINT

Tea making can be used as a ritual for the menopausal woman. She can choose a beautiful teapot and mug that reflects her unique personality. As she drinks the tea, she can pay attention to the color, the aroma, the flavor, and the temperature, visualizing that it is nourishing all the organs of her body as she drinks it, bringing her vitality and health.

Physical Exercise

Do not underestimate the importance of exercise. Frequent physical exercise is imperative to moving through this transition with ease and health. Because people are no longer working in the fields, hauling wood and water, or being active as part of a day's work, physical exercise is needed to maintain hormonal balance and produce endorphins that help with well-being.

A woman should find some kind of movement that she enjoys and commit to moving at least 4 times a week for at least 30–40 minutes. It takes 3 weeks at least to feel the effects of beginning to exercise again. It will not work to binge exercise. A woman should not go more than 72 hours without moving. It is useful for a woman to find the kind of movement that she enjoys, such as dancing, gardening, walking, or swimming. Yoga and T'ai Chi are excellent. Almost all community recreation centers have adult exercise classes, including water classes if there is a pool. There are lots of hiking or cycling clubs that offer all types of activities. Walking is free and easy. The woman can take mindful meditation walks where she will notice all of her surroundings and how they are changing with the seasons. This is a good way to smell the flowers and destress.

REFLECTION

Do you engage in some kind of movement for at least 30 to 40 minutes, 4 to 5 times a week? If not, what prevents you from doing so, and what can you do to change this?

A woman will notice immense differences in how she feels if she keeps her commitment to exercise. If she does not enjoy any type of physical activity, she could find benefit in joining a movement class that interests her from a community education center and commit to it for at least six weeks. Often, she will end up liking it, even if she did not think she would. Exercising with a buddy can help. Of course, any weight-bearing exercise will be of additional value in helping to keep bones strong, but initially, the woman should be advised to start with something that interests her. To prevent osteoporosis, a weight-bearing exercise program must be added to the program.

Essential Oils

Many different essential oils work very well to help emotional well-being. The woman should find ones that seem to call to her and experiment with ones that suit her best. Lavender is always good for calming. She can place it on her pillow to help her sleep or put a few drops on her forehead or temples to help ease tension. It is nice to place lavender drops in the bath, too.

Clary sage is another good oil during menopause (consider the name—the sage-ing of the wise woman). Orange, jasmine, and ylang ylang can evoke beauty and creativity and can also be uplifting. For more information on the use of essential oils, please see Chapter 23.

Breathing Techniques, Meditation, Journaling, Self-Care

Another important step is for the woman to add a disciplined, self-care program that helps her stay centered, focused, and destressed. Learning how to switch to deep, abdominal breathing instead of shallow chest breathing, helps oxygenate the body to give her more energy (a technique for belly breathing is described in Chapter 4).

Meditation techniques are good life tools that will be invaluable throughout the rest of an individual's life. Simple meditation techniques can be done in an instant, and they energize for hours. Meditation can be simply looking at a sunset or a flower or washing the dishes in a mindful manner—it does not necessarily have to be a formal meditation practice. Many books and classes are available to help in developing techniques that work for each lifestyle (see the section on the art of self-care later in this chapter).

Managing Specific Symptoms

Using a multistep approach as the basic foundation, a woman can add specific herbal remedies and other measures to manage individual symptoms. Some specific suggestions are provided here.

Hot Flashes

Several herbs could prove useful for hot flashes:

- Black cohosh: normalizes estrogen levels
- Motherwort: good women's herb, cools flashes, relaxes nervous tension

- Chickweed: cooling, mild diuretic; helps with water retention
- Sage: cooling to hot emotions (especially anger); cools night sweats
- Hops: calms; promotes relaxation
- American ginseng: helps nervous system; strengthens adrenal glands; destresses

These can be used singularly, or a woman can create combinations of her own. A cool flash formula tincture containing these herbs is available commercially.

Night Sweats

Some of the triggers for night sweats include stress, sugar, alcohol, lack of exercise, and spicy foods. Reducing these can improve night sweats.

Remifemin is a standardized black cohosh extract in tablet form that can prove helpful. It is long-acting and can last well through the night. (Black cohosh is in danger of being overharvested and poached. People need to be mindful and knowledgeable about the products purchased and make pertinent inquiries as to the source of the companies' herbs.)

Some of the herbs used for insomnia can prove useful also (see discussion later here).

Insomnia

The woman should identify potential triggers to insomnia, which include caffeine, alcohol, sugar, Nutrasweet or aspartame, lack of exercise, emotional stress, and worry. Some women have reported problems with insomnia if they have any sugar or caffeine after 3:00 P.M. (especially ice cream, candy, or sweet desserts).

Singularly or in combination, the following herbs can help relax the nervous system, while being safe, gentle, and without morning grogginess:

- Valerian root: sedating effects
- Hops: relieves tension, anxiety, restlessness
- Skullcap: decreases nervous tension and anxiety; relaxes muscles
- Passionflower: sedates; antispasmodic

Journaling is a good tool for insomnia. It is helpful for a woman to journal what she did during the day, what her thoughts and feelings were, any frustrations or joys, and so forth. Journaling is a good daily practice for self-nurturing (see Exhibit 18-5). Several good books are listed in the bibliography to offer some good journaling techniques, and it could also be useful to take a class on journaling.

Do not forget that daily physical exercise is important in promoting good sleep patterns.

Calming essential oils and hot baths help relax nervous tension and anxiety. Suggest that the woman try lavender, geranium, ylang ylang, and clary sage as essential oils to place externally on her skin, on pillows or sheets, or in bath water.

EXHIBIT 18-5   Free Association Writing: Guidelines to Offer Women

Thirty minutes before bedtime, take your herbal sleep tincture and then sit down with a pen, paper, and a timer. Set the timer for 5 minutes. Then begin writing all of the things on your mind. Write down words or phrases of what you are thinking. Think of all the things you did that day and all the things you have to do tomorrow or later in the week. Free associate all the words that come to you. For instance, you may think that tomorrow you have a meeting where you need to bring a potluck item. That reminds you that you need to go to the grocery store, which reminds you that you should buy a card for your friend who is in the hospital while you are in the store. That reminds you that you should call your friend's mother to see how she is doing and whether she needs any help. You also remember that you have to find your notes from the last meeting and so forth. Keep writing all the things you think of until the timer goes off. Ideally, you should be done writing at least 30 seconds before the timer goes off and that you have to think really hard of what other things are on your mind to write about. If you are still writing furiously when the timer goes off, then extend the timer to 7, 8, or even 10 minutes. This exercise helps clear your mind of extraneous thoughts and worries, which in turn helps your mind relax. This relaxation helps prevent the mind chatter that sometimes makes it difficult to fall asleep or that awakens you in the night.

The spiritual state could affect a woman's sleep patterns. She should ask herself questions such as these: What is my spiritual connection? How do I create mindfulness and centeredness? How do I nurture myself? She should be encouraged to be open to asking some hard questions. Insomnia may not only be an adjustment to hormonal and physical changes, but also a signal that her spirit is calling out to her. When she does not listen to the stillness and misses her spirit calling, her spirit may awaken her at night to get her attention.

Decreased Libido

During menopause, the fluctuating hormone levels can cause changes in libido. Some women experience an increased sex drive, whereas others experience a decrease. When women are under stress, libido is one of the first things affected. In our fast-paced society and with all the many things women do in a day, making love is sometimes the last thing on their minds.

Some herbs will enhance libido, and some women report good results with hormonal therapies as well; however, other factors need to be examined. In a quiet and reflective state, the woman can ask her body's inner wisdom to speak its truth. She needs to be willing to hear the truth and answer some tough questions. Is she truly in a relationship that supports her as the person she truly is? Does the love she gives out return to her in the way she desires? Is she around people that love, support, and energize her, or does she feel drained by them? Does she get the companionship that she desires? Does she receive the communication from her partner that she wishes for? Is she too fatigued? Does her body need a deep rest?

High stress can cause the adrenal glands to work overtime. This leaves a person feeling depleted, with no extra energy for expressing sexuality. Some herbs help to strengthen the adrenal glands (e.g., American ginseng), which in turn may increase libido; however, herbs do not take the place of rest, sleep, and stress-reduction strategies that offer the adrenal glands a chance to recover.

REFLECTION

What do you notice about the way your energy and stress levels affect your libido?

Vaginal Dryness

Vaginal dryness can be attributed to the decreased estrogen affects on vaginal and vulvar tissue. The vulvar and vaginal tissue becomes thinner and atrophies. This can cause irritation and discomfort, painful intercourse, and contribute to urinary incontinence. This can be treated by oral hormone replacement and/or prescription estrogen cream that is applied to the vulvar and vaginal tissue. The estrogen cream is available as a synthetic hormone or as a bioidentical hormone.

The herbal options include creams and salves that are soothing and healing to vaginal tissue and mucus membranes. There are also moisture-enhancing teas and tinctures available. Salves can be made from marshmallow root, calendula blossom, and licorice root. It is common to find a calendula-comfrey cream or gel in health food stores. These herbs help promote nourished, well-lubricated, and supple vaginal and urethral tissues. These salves can be used daily at first and then weekly—as often as needed to provide relief.

Triggers to Hot Flashes

You have probably already heard this expression: "It's not a hot flash. It's a power surge." This may arise from the energy principle that hot flashes signify a rewiring of our nervous system towards intuition. Some energy theorists believe that hot flashes are an actual energy release. It may be a release of toxins or a type of cleansing and clearing. If a woman notices that hot flashes usually occur after an exposure to an intense substance, then this theory makes sense.

Declining estrogen levels cause vasomotor symptoms, such as hot flashes, but there may be other triggers. If a woman tunes in to her body and identifies these triggers, sometimes she can modify her experience of hot flashes. It is good for her to observe keenly and to

---

KEY POINT

In the United States, approximately 60–70% of women experience hot flashes. In other countries, there is much less reported experience of hot flashes: 30% in Canadian women, 17% in Navajo women, 9% in Japanese women, and 0% in Mayan women. It is not certain whether the hot flashes are not reported or whether they are actually not experienced or not deemed uncomfortable. Many indigenous cultures, such as the Mayan, do not have a word in their language that translates into hot flash

---

keep a diary of her symptoms to identify her own personal triggers. Common triggers to hot flashes are as follows.

Sugar

The effects that sugar and refined carbohydrates have on causing hot flashes and PMS, such as symptoms of mood swings, headaches, fatigue and low energy, anxiety and restlessness, insomnia, and breast tenderness cannot be emphasized enough. If a woman became a Sherlock Holmes for a few weeks and analyzed her sugar intake and her body's response, chances are that she would notice a connection. One way to identify this is to eliminate all sugar and wheat for three weeks and then gradually add them back in, in moderate amounts. This can be an extremely difficult undertaking for many people. It takes a lot of preparation, but the rewards at the end are worth it. People who have done this often notice an unbelievable increase in energy, as if a cloud or veil has lifted. They have increased mental clarity and alertness. There also tends to be some weight loss, which is a benefit that many would welcome!

Sometimes a little sugar or wheat products, especially ingested in the afternoon or later, can cause night sweats and insomnia. It is very common to experience hot flashes and night sweats after a special evening going out to dinner, where a woman may have a little wine, pasta, dessert, or richer foods that she may not normally eat.

Spicy or Hot Foods

Some spicy foods, such as curry, hot peppers, or cayenne can trigger hot flashes or night sweats. The woman needs to observe her own personal response to hot, spicy foods.

Alcohol

Although a glass of wine or beer may be relaxing and calming, alcohol breaks down into sugars and also can be a trigger for hot flashes. The woman's personal response to alcohol needs to be observed.

Aspartame or Nutrasweet

It is important to read labels, as these chemical sugar substitutes can be found in more products than realized and can worsen menopausal symptoms.

Stress

Stressors are different in everyone. Identify your own stressors and pay attention to them. Are they signaling that you need to honor your wise-woman ways and your intuition? Are they signaling you to be more gentle with yourself or more nurturing? Oftentimes, it is the frequent little things that cause the most stress, not the big disasters. Reflect on the hot flash you just had. Was there a message in it for you?

Chronic Sleep Deprivation

New studies are showing that Americans are chronically sleep deprived. Adults actually need about 8 hours of sleep each night, especially in our fast-paced society. A lack of sleep places extra stress on the adrenal glands that are already depleted during menopause. This is also a paradox, because during menopause women are awakened at night due to hot flashes or night sweats, and their sleep is disrupted often; therefore, it is difficult to obtain a restful night's sleep. Keeping a consistent sleep schedule by going to sleep and awakening at the same times each day, together with some herbs that help promote sleep, will sometimes help establish a better sleep pattern.

Anxiety and Worry

It is difficult to let go of worries and trust and go with the flow. If a woman has a worry, she can either take action to relieve it or let it go. She must consider whether it is worth worrying about. A woman can allow a hot flash to help her keep in tune with what worries are important to her. For example, if a woman is worried about a medical symptom, she must recognize that action is needed and get it evaluated. In anxiety-producing situations, deep-breathing techniques can help her to get through, as can learning techniques to help her stay centered, calm, and detached from the outcome.

Anger

The relative increase in testosterone in relation to the declining levels of estrogen can cause more aggression or assertiveness, which can make a woman feel out of control. Women say they become quick to anger, and they do not like that feeling. Some women say that after they have reflected on the situation they realized that their anger may have been legitimate, but that it was out of proportion, and they wish they could have controlled it better. A woman may benefit by asking herself this: Is this anger so intense because I have been silent for too long, and now cannot hold it in any longer? Do I really need something to help me temper this anger so that I can be more balanced and not so out of control? Often, when women begin a nourishing self-care program, including herbs or hormones, the anger and ensuing hot flashes diminish.

The Art of Self-Care

Woman's nature is to give and they tend to give a lot; therefore, it is imperative that women also learn how to receive. The more you give, the more it is necessary to receive also, for then you can be replenished to give again. This is the true art of recycling.

REFLECTION

The more you give, the more you need to receive in order to pass the giving around the circle. Does what you give balance with what you receive?

When someone offers something to us, it is a gift to them for us to receive it. This may need to be reinforced to women as they are encouraged to receive as part of their own nurturing. Women who have been other-oriented for most of their lives may find it hard to receive and care for self. They may be receptive if it is put in the perspective that they can help others much more if they are energized and not depleted.

Each individual must develop her own self-care model that energizes and supports her and then make a disciplined commitment to integrate it into her daily life. Some suggestions that can be offered to women are presented in Exhibit 18-6.

The Celebration

It is important to honor the transitions in life and mark one's changing seasons with ritual. A woman can create her own ritual or ceremony to acknowledge and celebrate the wisewoman she has become. She can invite a small circle of women or include special family, friends, and children, give gratitude, sing a song, light candles, share stories, and give blessings. A shared feast can follow the ceremony. A woman can use her own inner wisdom, intuition, and creativity to make her ceremony a special one.

Indigenous cultures look at life in a circle. We are all equal because we are all equidistant from the center or the source. We all travel the circle through the seasons of our lives, and we all pass in each other's footsteps at some point on the wheel. We must remember that we do not travel the circle alone. We are all connected, all related. Women need to reach out to each other, knowing that they all share the energy of their heart connections. When they have times of doubt or despair, they can call on the energy of the worldwide circle of women that will uplift their spirits and give them hope. When they have moments of joy and bliss, they should send it out to others. At midlife, women can learn to walk the path

EXHIBIT 18-6 Self-care Hints to Nourish and Energize You

- Give gratitude to your body every day. While you are taking a shower, allow the water to flow over every body part, mindfully acknowledging how it serves you, and be grateful that this day you are healthy.

- Scan your body energetically and notice areas of tension or discomfort that may need your nurturing attention.

- Embrace humor. Add levity every day. Smile and laugh often.

- Have music in your life in some way.

- Allow your creativity to flow: Sing a song, bake a cake, or paint a picture. Start by doing easy and simple things first.

- Search to find your passion and allow it to unfold.

- Find a connection to your spiritual essence, whatever that may be.

- Allow quiet time often (for reflection and basking in the stillness). Discover how much quiet time you need and honor that. Create a healing space in your home or outdoors where you can go to be quiet.

- Spend time with nature, mindfully drinking in your surroundings to nurture and replenish you.

- Create rituals to mark the passing of time or the special events in your life.

- Share a connectedness with others. Surround yourself with friends that are loving, supportive, stimulating, and energizing.

- Learn to care without rescuing or enabling.

- Honor your own body rhythms for rest, work, and play. Practice selfacceptance.

- Be open to possibilities and be willing to step outside your comfort zone to try new things or new attitudes. A trusted friend can help lend clarity if you are unsure.

- Be open to receiving and be willing to ask for help. Human nature causes you to want to give and help others. There are people around you that want to reach out and all they need is to be asked. Your gift back to them is allowing yourself to receive from them.

- Check in. If someone or something fires up your emotions negatively sit with it and ask yourself, is the problem the issue of is it the way I am reacting to the issue?

- Be open to looking at your own issues and past patterns, and be wiling to make changes that may move you towards a higher level of awareness and communication. Menopause is a time to claim your power and sometimes stand your ground over things that you have tolerated for way too long. However, remember that being in power is walking the path of the heart.

of the heart, using the gifts of the wise woman: compassion, understanding, and unconditional love.

Summary

Menopause is defined as the absence of menstruation for 12 consecutive months. This is a significant event for women, not only because of the physiological challenges that are present, but because it happens at a time when they can take stock of many aspects of their life. From this standpoint, menopause is viewed as a sacred journey into wisdom and creativity.

A multistep approach is useful for women as they face the menopause transition. Useful strategies include the use of herbs, essential oils, and exercise and self-care techniques. Women should try to identify triggers for hot flashes, which could include sugar, spicy foods, alcohol, artificial sweeteners, stress, chronic sleep deprivation, anxiety, and anger. Individualized plans are essential to address each woman's unique needs.

Menopause can be used as a time to launch new self-care behaviors that allow women to nurture themselves and receive from others. New experiences and opportunities are possible.

References

1. Writing Group for the Women's Health Initiative Investigators. (2002). Risks and benefits of estrogen plus progestin in healthy postmenopausal women: principal results from the Women's Health Initiative Randomized Controlled Trial. *Journal of the American Medical Association*, *288*:321–333.

Suggested Reading

Borysenko, J. (1998). *A Woman's Book of Life: The Biology, Psychology, and Spirituality of the Feminine Life Cycle*. New York: Riverhead Books.

Crooks, R. L., & Baur, K. (2007). *Our Sexuality*. New York: Wadsworth Publishing.

Esposito, N. (2005). Agenda dissonance: immigrant Hispanic women's and providers' assumptions and expectations for menopause healthcare. *Clinical Nursing Research*, *14*(1):32–56.

Hall, L., Callister, L. C., & Matsumura, G. (2007). Meanings of menopause: cultural influences on perception and management of menopause. *Journal of Holistic Nursing*, *25*(2):106–118.

Jones, M. L., Eichenwald, T., & Hall, N. W. (2007). *Menopause for Dummies*. Hoboken, NJ: Wiley Publishing.

Klaiber, E. L. (2001). *Hormones and the Mind. A Woman's Guide to Enhancing Mood, Memory, and Sexual Vitality*. New York: HarperCollins Publishers.

Lesser, J., Hughes, S., & Kumar, S. (2007). Sexual dysfunction in the older woman: complex medical, psychiatric illnesses should be considered in evaluation and management. *Geriatrics*, *60*(8):18–21.

Lock, M. (2005). Cross-cultural vasomotor symptom reporting: conceptual and methodogical issues. *Menopause: The Journal of the North American Menopause Society*, *12*:239–241.

McCall, K., & Meston, C. (2007). Differences between pre- and postmenopausal women in cues for sexual desire. *Journal of Sexual Medicine*, 4(2):364–371.

Northrup, C. (2006). *The Wisdom of Menopause: Creating Physical and Emotional Health and Healing During the Change*. New York: Bantam books.

Writing Group for the Women's Health Initiative Investigators. (2002). Risks and benefits of estrogen plus progestin in healthy postmenopausal women. *Journal of the American Medical Association*, 288:321–333.

Resources

Bio-identical (Natural) Hormones
To find a pharmacy in your area, contact International Academy of Compounding Pharmacies.

www.iacprx.org

800-631-7900

Organizations

American Menopause Foundation
350 Fifth Ave, #2822
New York, New York 10118
212-714-2398
www.americanmenopause.org

HERS Foundation (Hysterectomy Education Resources and Service)
422 Bryn Mawr Ave.
Bala Cynwyd, PA 19004
215-667-7757
www.hersfoundation.org

Saliva Hormone Testing
Aeron Life Cycles
1933 Davis St., #310
San Leandro, CA 94457
800-631-7900
www.aeron.com

Chapter 19

Addiction: Diseases of Fear, Shame, and Guilt

OBJECTIVES

This chapter should enable you to

- Describe what is meant by an addiction
- List at least five types of addictions
- Discuss at least five significant areas that can be affected by addictions
- Describe at least three characteristics of persons with addictions
- Describe four measures that can aid in healing the body of the addict

Addictions are among the most common diseases in the United States. An estimated 20% of our population lives with the pain of being addicted to something. Each person who is an addict affects about 10 other people who experience pain, stress, fear, shame, and guilt just as the addict does.

Clearly, addictions of all sorts are major problems in our society. The magnitude of alcohol addiction is seen in the statement of William C. Menninger, MD, who said, "If alcoholism were a communicable disease a national emergency would be declared."[1] We have lived to see that epidemic with a myriad of related abuse problems across the United States. Other addictions, such as gambling or exercise, appear more subtle but cause many of the same problems.

Scenarios of Addictions

The following are scenarios of a variety of addictions:

- They must gamble no matter what the costs. A loss of home, "maxed out" credit cards, risky loans, and threats on their lives do not stop them.
- They are driven to the next new sexual conquest in spite of the risk of HIV and AIDS, hepatitis, and loss of their marriages and children.
- They must eat and vomit even though they weigh 90 pounds and have painful dental problems from stomach acid damaging their teeth when they vomit. Addi-

tionally, they just got out of the hospital because of cardiac problems and electrolyte imbalances in their blood.

· They must eat the whole container of food (usually not vegetables, but ice cream, cookies, chips, etc.). It happens in secret especially if their weight is more than 250 pounds.

· They need the cocaine to complete some important work task, but they cannot get the sustained high anymore. Their heart hurts while their nose runs and bleeds.

· They drive drunk for the seventh time since their last DUI and lose their driver's license.

· Their best friends died in an automobile accident last year after they used a lot of drugs and marijuana. They continue to grow their own pot.

· They worked 90 hours again this week and missed their youngest child's birthday. They just have to get that promotion.

· The collection of newspapers and important magazines are a fire hazard. The cats (17 of them) cause waste that is a health hazard. Things are getting moldy and smelling. The addict is getting sick. The Department of Health threatens to condemn the home.

· They must run another 15 miles today even though they have not menstruated for more than 12 months. It does not matter that it is 10 P.M. If they hurry, they can do it before midnight.

These scenarios depict some extreme late-stage addictive behaviors. Before people get to this stage, a nonjudgmental health risk appraisal with hopeful feedback can start the healing process.

REFLECTION

Was there anyone in your family who had an addiction? How did that impact that person and the rest of the family? How did the family address this issue with the person?

Definition of Addictions

Addictions are behaviors people do repeatedly that result in problems in one or more major areas of their lives. All addictions are the result of attempts to relieve or control feelings of anxiety, vulnerability, and anger. They are related to problems with impulse control and self-esteem. The repetitious behaviors that constitute an addiction include misuse, overuse, and abuse of alcohol, food, work, sex, shopping, smoking, money, internet, power, relationships, exercise, drugs (prescription, nonprescription, and "street" drugs), and collections of "stuff" (papers, memorabilia, guns, etc.). You probably could add a few more to the list of things that are used addictively to escape facing a feeling.

KEY POINT

Significant areas that potentially are affected by addictions include the following:

· Physical and mental health (e.g., accidents, depression, etc.)
· Spirituality: loss of hope, belief, and peace; isolation from supports; anger at God, creator, supreme being
· Relationships: family, mate (partner), parents, children, and friends
· Work: poor performance; overachievement; poor working relationships; attendance problems; workaholism
· Legal: litigation, DUI, violence, stealing, tax evasion, sexually acting out
· Financial: loss of income/savings; living in guilt, fear, and shame over spending

---

Prognosis for Persons with Addictions and Their Families

The prognosis may look bleak and appalling, but it is not. Early identification, education, and intervention can lead to prevention of part or all of the problems noted previously. Intermediate and late interventions can reduce the severest symptoms of the addiction-related diseases and problems. Later in this chapter, assessment and intervention are addressed. These techniques help to reduce the inevitable destruction. Thus, the prognosis can be excellent when specific steps are followed and there is support for all who are directly involved.

Who Are Persons with Addictions?

At the very least, 1 of every 10 people suffers with some type of addiction. People with addictions are represented in all strata of society. Everyone is at risk. Persons with addictions are presidents, teenagers, generals, nuns, homeless individuals, grandmothers, rabbis, doctors, nurses, accountants, "skid row" people, pilots, school dropouts, valedictorians, and beauty queens. The types of people who become addicted are not determined by social status, income, education, ethnicity, gender, or any other demographic characteristic.

Are people with addictions bad? No, although they sometimes do very bad things. Most persons with addictions do not know why they repeat actions that keep hurting themselves and others. At first, many do not really think they have a problem. They believe they can cut back on their behaviors whenever they desire. They repeatedly try to stop the addiction and often succeed in exercising some control although the problem remains. As the behavior begins to bother others, they may make promises to stop; however, there comes a point when they cannot control the outcomes of their addictive behaviors. Unfortunately, they do not know how to break the pattern.

Next, people with addictions may feel fear, shame, and guilt. They want to stop, but the urges are out of their control. Some may not want to stop because they cannot conceive living without the habit that they believe allows them to function. If they muster a super-human effort and manage to stop acting out the addiction, they suffer severe anxiety and pain. With drugs, alcohol, gambling, and food addictions, there can be tremendous physical pain, as well as anxiety and emotional devastation.

KEY POINT

Withdrawal symptoms from some addictions can include insomnia, headaches, extreme irritability, anxiety, upset stomach, sweating, and chills.

Finally, people with addictions lose all hope, suffer guilt, lie in their shame, and hide themselves in constant fear (beginning paranoia). Prison, chronic illnesses, financial ruin, suicide attempts, and death are frequently the final results of untreated addictions.

Those with an addiction cannot imagine life without the escape and feelings of relief that their addiction gives them. Most of the people with addictions have a need to escape from some emotion that is not at a conscious level.

Persons who have loved ones who have addictions suffer many feelings, too. Families, friends, and the people with addictions themselves need compassion, love, support, and information to recover their lives. It is possible. People need to know they are not alone and that there is hope. People with an addiction are not bad, worthless, and hopeless; rather, they are sick. Since 1957 the American Medical Association recognized alcoholism as a disease. The *Diagnostic and Statistical Manual IV*, a guide for identifying mental illnesses and their characteristics, lists various addictions as diseases. These listings are helpful because they acknowledge many addictions as treatable conditions.

Commonalities Among Addictions

There are similarities among many addictions. Most people with an addiction contributed significantly to the development of their problems, which can cause society to have limited sympathy for them; however, just as many people with heart disease have contributed to the development of their illnesses because of lifestyle choices they have made. People who stray from the special diets they follow knowing they are putting their lives in jeopardy contribute to their medical problems, just as much as persons who abuse alcohol and drugs. Nevertheless, society considers people with traditional medical diagnoses as legitimately needing help and care despite their responsibility for causing their problems. There is less support and sensitivity for those who are addicted.

KEY POINT

People with addictions deserve reasonable help and support just as any person with a disease. They are sick people who need help and healing desperately. People in their lives also need healing because loving and living with an addict makes people close to them hurt and sick, too.

Help, Hope, Healing, and Health

How can you help persons with addictions and yourself if you have relationships with them? There are risk factors and risk patterns associated with the development of addictions. Identification of those patterns and the persons at risk is ideal. You can use a health risk appraisal questionnaire such as the Efinger Addictions Risk Survey (EARS) to identify persons at risk (see Exhibit 19-1). Please feel free to make copies for future use.

The EARS asks questions that are nonoffensive to most people. The survey includes topics that are common experiences and assigns a score to the degree the experience affects the person. It does not appear as invasive or judgmental like many other surveys and screening tests. For example, the traditional alcohol surveys ask questions about alcohol use that are likely to cause an alcoholic to deny or outright lie. In typical nursing and health assessments, the questions evoke an underestimation of drinking, smoking, and sexual behaviors. These surveys encourage the people with addictions to lie to health professionals and to feel guilt and fear.

People should not be made to feel guilty about their addictions; it is the only way they know how to cope with life. With a risk assessment of behaviors and thought patterns, they can be helped to identify the patterns of behaving and thinking that are leading them to addictions that are hurting, damaging, and eventually going to destroy their lives. They can be shown new patterns of living, behaving, and thinking that will help them to live more comfortably with less anger, victimization, and fear. They can be given hope that they can live happier and more serene, courageous lives without their addictions and avoidance of feelings. The new patterns can be applied to dealing with all addictions because they all have some common sources of feelings that result in the damaging behaviors. It is clear that the early addictive behaviors are often effective in coping with anxiety, anger, and other uncomfortable events. The intermediate addictive behaviors can have both effective and

Exhibit 19-1 EARS

Efinger Addictions Risk Survey (EARS)

1. Various stresses and losses occur at all stages of our lives. Please check Column A if any of these losses or stresses occurred or are occurring in your life. Please check Column B if the item checked in Column A still causes you emotional pain.

Column A	Stresses, losses, and feelings	Column B
Yes, I had or have this stress/loss.	Check the left column if you have or had these stresses or losses. Check the right column if it still causes you pain	Yes, still causes me some pain.
	Feelings of shyness as a child	
	Felt other children were favored	
	Frequent illnesses as a child	
	Feelings of aggression	
	Addicted mate	
	More than two "panic" or anxiety attacks	
	Few friends I can count on for help	
	Bothered or worried about addicted parent	
	Can't count on spiritual advisor; minister, priest, rabbi, or other	
	When I need help, I'm uncomfortable asking for it	
	Insomnia	
	Death of a pet	
	Guilt in some areas of life: religion, sexual activities, parenting	
Total:	Add column A and B	Total:

Total of Columns A and B_____

Indicator: Early risk 10–13

Intermediate risk 14–19

Late risk 20–23

Probable addictions 24–26

(continues)

Exhibit 19-1   EARS *(continued)*

2. When you have leisure time, how often do you have these feelings or reactions? Please check the box in the column that applies to you. Answer the questions as you would in a normal week. For example, do not respond as you would when you are on vacation.

Feelings or reactions to your leisure time	2 Never	2 Almost never	3 Some- times	4 Often	5 Most of the time
Tired					
Do not want to exercise					
Bored					
Anxious or "uptight"					
Want to shop					
Want to gamble					
Want to make love					
Want to have a drink					
Lonely					
Column totals: **Multiply by:**	X 1	X 2	X 3	X 4	X 5
TOTALS					

Total of:

Column 1 _____

Column 2 _____

Column 3 _____

Column 4 _____

Column 5 _____

TOTAL of 5 columns   _____

Total scores

Addiction indicators:

Early risk	24–27
Intermediate risk	28–34
Late or high risk	35–39
Probable addiction	40–45

(continues)

EXHIBIT 19-1   EARS *(continued)*

Please check the column that most applies to the frequency you have these feelings or do the following behaviors.

Behavior or feelings you may experience.	Almost always	Fre-quently	Some-times	Almost never
3. How often do you wear a seat belt?	1	2	3	4
4. How often do you feel overwhelmed?	4	3	2	1
5. How often do you feel the need for some help to change a low or sad mood?	4	3	2	1
6. How often do you do a creative activity?	1	2	3	4
7. How often do you worry about your family or being alone?	4	3	2	1
8. How often do you worry about your past?	4	3	2	1
9. How often do you worry about criticism by others?	4	3	2	1
10. How often do you feel guilty about some behavior?	4	3	2	1
11. How often are you annoyed by criticism of what you do?	4	3	2	1
12. How often do you feel grief over a loss or death of someone?	4	3	2	1
13. How often do you wish you could tell your parents, mate, or family what they've done to hurt you?	4	3	2	1
14. How often are you fearful about the results of something you've done?	4	3	2	1
15. How often have you had legal problems?	4	3	2	1
16. How often do you feel compelled to do something you really wish you didn't do?	4	3	2	1
17. How often are you lonely?	4	3	2	1
18. How often have you had a problem enjoying sexual activity?	4	3	2	1
Add the numbers in the boxes you checked.				

(continues)

EXHIBIT 19-1   EARS *(continued)*

Behavior or feelings you may experience.	Almost always	Fre-quently	Some-times	Almost never
Enter the **totals** from the previous page in the appropriate columns.				
19. How often do you feel compelled to control you anger or resentments?	4	3	2	1
20. How often are you concerned about your job performance or other responsibilities?	4	3	2	1
Totals of the numbers in the boxes you checked.				

Add each of the columns' totals _____

_____

_____

_____

TOTAL _____

Addiction indicators:	Total Scores
Early risk	40–45
Intermediate risk	46–54
Late or high risk	55–64
Probable addiction	65–76

painful, damaging results. The late behaviors have ineffective results. There is no relief at this stage for those with an addiction. They are obsessed prisoners of their addictions.

Recognizing these stages of early, intermediate, and late addictive behaviors provides hope that help can be given at earlier stages. Earlier help and hope leads to quicker healing.

Denial

Denial is a strong barrier to seeking help, hope, and healing. Denial exists for the addict, as well as for the loved ones because of the fear, shame, and guilt associated with every addiction. Gentleness, acceptance, promotion of self-esteem, and recognition of pain when communicating with an addict helps to reduce denial. When family members or healers provide compassion to an addict, they enhance treatment effectiveness and provide an opening to reduce denial.

KEY POINT

The addict's denial must be confronted.

The need for denial causes an addict to try to manipulate others. Open, compassionate confrontations and interventions are necessary in helping the addict consider beginning any type of healing and recovery process. Confronting and risking the anger of the addict may save his or her life. At times it is hard for family and traditional healers to be compassionate. Many stereotypes exist that influence feelings toward someone who has caused turmoil and pain to self and others by his or her addictions.

At this stage, a noncaring attitude directed toward the addict by family and friends is common. Some parents may wish their drug-addicted child were dead. Some people who have lost a child to addiction or an accident grieve and start their own addictions to sexual activities, excessive shopping, work, controlling another child, religion, and secret things that they often feel too ashamed to share.

EARS

EARS is a health risk appraisal survey for addictions. It can help identify those at risk for addictions at an early stage of their disease (see Exhibit 19-1). When the risks are identified, there can be interventions, education, motivation, and reduction of the horrendous costs of addictions to the persons, their families, and society. Risk identification provides information about where the problems may be. It gives a focus for the most effective counseling, education, and support interventions to reduce the progression of the risks to addictions. It appears that if the major areas of pain, fear, shame, and guilt vulnerability can be addressed first and ameliorated, a person with an addition may be more amenable to change, to attending therapy, and to be motivated to work on his or her problems.

Discussion of Risk Scores

The EARS scores are divided into early, intermediate, late, and probable addiction risk scores. There is flexibility in the scoring. The scores serve as a general framework to assess addictions risk.

Early Risk Indicators

Early risk indicators are events or predictors that occur in childhood or adolescence that reflect behaviors and attitudes characteristic of persons who later became people with addictions. Feelings of shyness as a child are one of the earliest indicators. This could be reflected through low self-esteem or other uneasy feelings when dealing with people. Some of these children have been abused and are fearful and insecure. They often have experienced a nonsupportive environment at home or school. Frequent illnesses experienced by a child set a pattern of thinking that medications or drugs can fix everything. The child may feel different from classmates and friends, and they become isolated and lonely. A lack of coping skills to deal with loss can be reflected through the unresolved death of a pet. In fact, any of the responses in Question 1 that are checked as still causing pain are risk indicators. The more items that still cause pain, the greater the risk.

Question 3, regarding almost never wearing seat belts, is an early risk indicator. Perhaps it reflects the rebellion a potential addict feels toward society. This could also indicate lack of self-care or a subtle self-destructive attitude. It also represents an effort to be in control of how rules are applied in the life of a person with an addiction. Research supports this behavior as an early risk. The number of close relatives who have a serious addiction problem should also be analyzed. The genetic component of addictions and depression are major early warning risks.

Intermediate Risk Indicators

Intermediate risk indicators are predictors that occur in childhood, adolescence, and early adulthood that reflect behaviors and attitudes that are characteristic of persons who later became people with addictions. Being very reluctant to ask for help, rarely asking for help, and having few people to count on are intermediate risk indicators. Not viewing leisure time positively is a precursor to serious risk.

KEY POINT

People with addictions often feel anxious or uptight, frequently bored, tired, lazy, and lonely when faced with leisure time. The need to avoid the quiet time alone reflects their discomfort with inner feelings and thoughts.

Feelings of isolation are a common experience. Persistent guilt, insomnia, panic attacks, and not feeling spiritually connected are serious patterns of intermediate risks. Unresolved pain related to the loss or death of a person is not an unusual experience when people receive no help with grieving; however, when this feeling is added to the other patterns of feelings and behaviors, the person is at risk.

Late Risk Indicators

Late risk indicators are predictors and stresses that affect healthy functioning of the person's spiritual, mental, physical, and economic life. All of the risk indicators already mentioned can be found to a greater degree in the late risk indicators. When Questions 4,

7, 8, 9, and 10 to 20 are primarily marked "almost always," late risk for addiction is strongly present. The degree of risk is related to the higher scores. For example, when there is a lack of any creative activity, and the "almost never" column is marked, the risk score increases.

Driving while under the influence of drugs or alcohol is a serious late risk that leads to legal problems. That behavior and other problems in legal, financial, work, or intimate relations are patterns that approach the strongest late risk indicator category.

Probable Diagnosis of an Addiction

The scores for many of the risk indicators listed previously will be higher when there is a probable diagnosis of an addiction. In addition, there may be arrests, serious illnesses, admissions to the hospital (greater than two related to the addiction), and suicidal feelings. These require immediate attention by their healthcare providers and family members.

Treatment Modalities and an Essential Paradigm Shift

The medical model of addictions management has not had a successful record of arresting and healing these diseases. A paradigm (worldview) shift toward a holistic approach is essential to access the healing tools and energy to begin effective treatment and healing. We only need a small window of hope to access a spiritual connection to the vast energy of love, compassion, and acceptance to start the healing for the addict and those involved.

KEY POINT

Medications, therapy, supervision, and support groups, such as the anonymous groups for narcotics (NA), alcoholics (AA), gamblers (GA), overeaters (OA), and so forth, have a role in holistic healing, but treatment methods must go beyond those common resources. Holistic treatment addresses the mind, body, and spirit.

Holistic Approach to Healing Using Feedback on Risk Factors

The areas of risk identified by the EARS can be individually addressed using a holistic approach. Most of the stresses and fears (work, relationships, etc.) can be decreased through use of imagery and progressive relaxation.

All transitions and changes are stressful. Planning relaxing activities for the period of time between the completion of employment activities and the start of home responsibilities can reduce stress. This is a time when people feel anxious and addictive thoughts strongly enter their minds. Simple strategies, such as clarification of job description and responsibilities, can reduce work-related stress. Reducing interruptions at work and home when involved in tasks requiring concentration can decrease irritability and stress.

Anxiety (panic) attacks are instant triggers for addictions. The thoughts with the emotional and bodily responses during an anxiety attack feel life-threatening. Seeking help is essential.

KEY POINT

A strategy that can help control an anxiety attack is to slow down breathing, look up, focus on an object, and repeat, "These feelings are terrifying, but they are not dangerous. I will not be harmed." This action seems very simple, yet it works to get people through the panic. A thought, even a prayer, can interrupt the body's responses.

Support groups for losses, illnesses, and painful life events can be healing experiences for many people. People with addictions feel acceptance and hope with the knowledge that they are not alone as they experience the group support. Sometimes the groups may be spiritual or religious in orientation.

Coping skills, assertiveness, conflict resolution, and crisis-management techniques increase the comfort of daily living. With these capabilities people can interrupt the cycle of victimization and vulnerability leading to addictions.

The identified risk factors lead to specific treatment strategies. The education, interventions, and treatments include integration of mind, body, and spirit approaches to healing.

Healing the Mind

Addictions create alterations in optimal brain chemistry. Abnormal neurotransmitters (chemicals that help send impulses through the nerves) of the brain can cause and perpetuate addictions. Healing the mind is essential to permanently heal addictions and restore normal brain chemistry.

KEY POINT

A neurotransmitter can be thought of as a brain messenger.

A diet rich in vitamins, amino acids (proteins), essential fatty acids, and minerals needs to be integrated into daily living. Some food supplements help the brain manufacture chemicals like the neurotransmitter norepinephrine that boosts energy and mood; examples of these supplements include:

- · *Glutamine,* which has been successfully used to reduce alcohol cravings in early recovery
- · *Tyrosine,* which is an important building block for norepinephrine
- · *Tryptophan,* which is a precursor for serotonin. Foods high in tryptophan are popcorn, turkey, chicken, and dairy products.
- · Serotonin, another neurotransmitter, that creates a calm, relaxed state and promotes sleep. The absence of sufficient serotonin is a trigger for addictions.

Hypoglycemia (low blood sugar) can cause depression, anxiety, panic attacks, and mood swings leading to increased addictions. Another neurotransmitter, histamine, regulates mood and energy. High levels of histamine cause the mind to race and lead to obsessive–compulsive thoughts and behaviors. Methionine, an amino acid, reduces the impact of histamine on the brain.

The mind has habits of thought that are responses to physical imbalances. Blocked energy (*chi* or *qi* or *life energy*) causes imbalances in the brain. The blockages occur throughout the body and affect the mind in harmful ways. Disturbances in brain chemistry can be reduced by helping the person to alter negative thoughts through therapy, prayer, meditation, and other modalities. Next, the body must be integrated into the holistic approach to healing.

Healing the Body

The body has many systems that affect all other aspects of healing. In turn, the body is affected by the mind, spirit, and the energies within and without. Touch and movement have key roles in healing addictions.

Massage

Touch is a gesture of support. When someone touches, respects, and cares for the body of a person with an addiction, the addict is aided to reconnect physically and center emotionally. These are important healing steps because avoiding problems and dissociating from the body are common among people with addictions. The person is more connected to his or her body and able to discuss and come to terms with his or her addiction.

Massage has a powerful impact on the body, releasing endorphins, substances that have a mood-enhancing effect. Self-massage of hands and ears helps to reduce cravings. The ear has pressure points that stimulate the body's natural pain relievers.

Full-body massage releases tension and blocked energy. Loosening the tight muscles sends the body messages to cut down on the production of stress hormones. Massage also moves lymphatic fluid through the body. This movement of fluid assists in the body's natural cleansing processes and enhances immune response. Acupressure can help people deal with stress, depression, anger, and the issues underlying their addictions.

Hatha Yoga

Hatha yoga simulates the parasympathetic nervous system and removes tension from all major muscle groups. Yoga helps the addict to become more physically aware, leading to greater mental self-awareness. Eventually, as peaceful body responses are developed, the addict becomes sensitive to how his or her behavior can change. The person experiences the ability to feel better without their addictions. The connection between mind and body heals in an integrated way.

Acupuncture

The use of acupuncture reduces cravings and unblocks energy (*chi* or *qi*). The body feels better, and there is a release of the healing neurotransmitters. It restores harmony in the body. These results are related to the skill of the practitioner.

Other Body-Healing Therapies

Dance therapy, shiatsu, Ta'i Chi Ch'uan, reflexology, aromatherapy, chiropracty, acupuncture, qigong, therapeutic touch, and healing touch are major complementary therapies. Some other treatments include homeopathy, hypnotherapy, herbals, biofeedback, and music therapy (see Chapter 21 for additional alternative therapies that could prove useful).

Healing the Spirit

Spiritual healing encompasses the removal of grudges, negative views of self, and compassion for self and others. Forgiveness, making amends, and acceptance of self and others promote spiritual love and healing. These practices also remove the fear, shame, and guilt that are characteristic of addictions.

KEY POINT

People with addictions need support and a spiritual awakening to acknowledge that total healing is possible for them.

Healing the spirit is a wonderful experience for people with addictions. People with addictions have lost focus and are unaware of their own identities and purposes. They become disconnected from the purpose of their creative energy, their inherent goodness, and ability to love and be loved. With support and guidance through the process, people with addictions may experience relief from their compulsions in a brief time frame. The willingness to heal opens the channels for healing to occur. The process is a personal empowering journey. From its deepest perspective, an unresolved longing causes addictions. This awareness is a message that opens the heart and soul of a person with an addiction to see that he or she has lost his or her way. All addictions have a common source. If only the obvious addiction is addressed, the cause will remain, and there is the risk that when one addiction pattern starts to diminish another will start to take over. This happens because the sources of the addictions have not been identified, addressed, and healed. The new addiction's role is the same as the old addiction's role; therefore, if patterns of behavior and the needs for the patterns are identified, then intervention, education, support, and prevention can be implemented.

REFLECTION

In *For Whom the Bell Tolls*, Ernest Hemingway stated that, "We become stronger at our broken places." How have you seen this occur in your own life?

Summary

Addictions are behaviors people do repeatedly that result in problems in one or more areas of their lives. People can be addicted to gambling, drugs, alcohol, sex, eating, work, collecting, or exercise. Health, spiritual, relationship, work, legal, and financial problems can result from addictions. Those with an addiction may not believe that they have a problem, feel shame, live in fear, experience guilt, and lose hope. The body of the addict can be healed using measures such as a good diet, supplements, massage, yoga, acupuncture, and other body-healing therapies. Forgiveness, making amends, and acceptance of self and others are important aspects of healing the spirit of the person who has an addiction.

References

1. Federation of American Hospitals. (1981). Alcoholism and the increasing role of the hospital. *Federation of American Hospitals Review, 14*:4.

Suggested Reading

Beattie, M. (2001). *Codependent No More and Beyond Codependency*. New York: MJF Books.

Carnes, P. (2001). *Out of the Shadows: Understanding Sexual Addiction*, 3rd ed. Center City, MN: Hazelden.

Carnes, P. (2005). *Facing the Shadow: Starting Sexual and Relationship Recovery*, 2nd ed. Carefree, AZ: Gentle Path Press.

Claude-Pierre, P. (1998). *The Secret Language of Eating Disorders: The Revolutionary New Approach to Understanding and Curing Anorexia and Bulimia*. New York: Times Books.

Durham, M. (2003). *Painkillers and Tranquilizers*. Chicago: Heinemann Library.

Hausenblas, H., & Fallon, E. (2002). Relationship among body image, exercise behavior, and exercise dependence symptoms. *International Journal of Eating Disorders, 32*(2):179–185.

Lee, S. G. (2000). *Light in the Darkness: A Guide to Recovery from Addiction: A Physician Talks Openly About His Own Addiction to Sex*. Newport News, VA: Five Star Publications.

Schwartz, J., & Beyette, B. (2005). *Brain Lock: Free Yourself from Obsessive-Compulsive Behavior: A Four-Step Self-Treatment Method to Change Your Brain Chemistry*. New York: HarperCollins.

West, M. (2000). *An Investigation of Pattern Manifestations in Substance Abuse-Impaired Nurses*. Chester, PA: Widener University.

West, M. (2002). Early risk indicators of substance abuse among nurses. *Journal of Nursing Scholarship, 34*(2):187–193.

Wright, J. (2003). *There Must Be More to This: Finding More Life, Love, and Meaning by Overcoming Your Soft Addictions*. New York: Broadway Books.

Internet Resources

AddictionSearch.com
www.addictionsearch.com

Eating Disorder Recovery Center
www.addictions.net

National Institute on Alcohol Abuse and Alcoholism
www.niaaa.nih.gov

National Institute on Drug Abuse
www.nida.nih.gov

Web of Addictions
www.well.com/user/woa

Chapter 20

Symptoms and Chakras

OBJECTIVES

This chapter should enable you to

· Describe the characteristics and purposes of chakras

· List the names and locations of the seven main chakras of the body

· Describe a symptom of imbalance or dysfunction for each of the seven chakras

Chakras

Chakra is a Sanskrit word for spinning vortices, or wheels, of energy. Many ancient systems of belief have this understanding of energy in and around the body with entry points located at distinct places along the body. The chakras are like the input valves for the body to receive nourishing energy from the universe around it and output valves to help release or transfer energy. The energy received is transformed into useable energy for the body; however, the chakras also extend outward to affect everything and everyone. It is thought to be vital to the health of all aspects of the body—physical, emotional, mental, and spiritual—that the chakras be open, flowing, and healthy.

From a physical standpoint, the energy received through the chakras affect the hormones, the organ systems, and the cellular functions of the body. Each chakra has been associated with a particular nerve plexus (group of nerve endings) or endocrine system (organs of the body that secrete necessary hormones for health and well-being). The chakras receive energy from outside of the body and transform it internally to stimulate some form of hormonal gland response or nervous system response, which in turn affects the entire body.[1]

KEY POINT

The chakras are vortices of energy that receive nourishing energy from the universe and send out energy from the body. They have distinct names, often described for the area of the body over which they reside.

There seems to be a general acceptance of the existence of seven main chakras of the body (see Figure 20-1):

First: *root chakra* comes downward from the base of the spine.

Second: *sacral chakra* is a pair of chakras located just below the umbilicus (belly button) on the front and lower back portion of the body.

Figure 20-1   Chakras

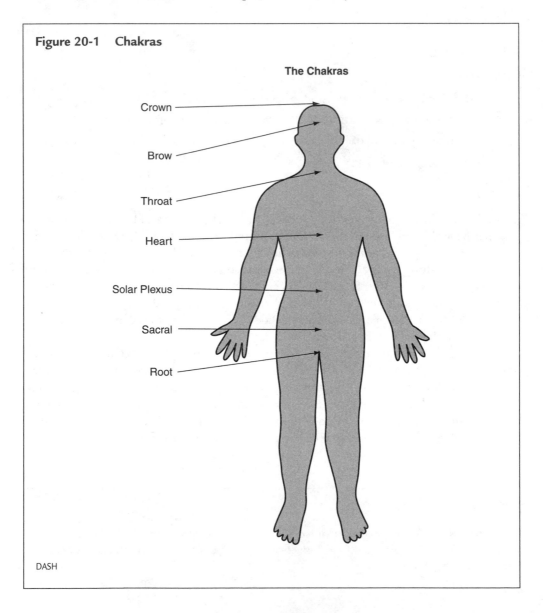

The Chakras

- Crown
- Brow
- Throat
- Heart
- Solar Plexus
- Sacral
- Root

DASH

Third: *solar plexus chakra* is a pair of chakras located where the ribs form a "v" on the front of the body and the middle of the back of the body.

Fourth: *heart chakra* is a pair of chakras located between the breasts and between the shoulder blades.

Fifth: *throat chakra* is a pair of chakras located at the point of the Adam's apple in the neck and the curve of the neck on the back of the body.

Sixth: *brow chakra* is a pair of chakras located in the middle of the forehead on the face and directly behind on the back of the head.

Seventh: *crown chakra* is a single chakra located on the top of the head.

These seven make up the chakras of the physical body. Some believe there are more chakras that affect the nonphysical portion of our existence.[2]

The crown chakra and the root chakra are the only two without a corresponding pair. The five central chakras exist on the front of the body and the back of the body. The main channel of energy exists from the top of the head, or crown, to the base of the spine. All chakras meet in this channel and connect with each other through nadi. *Nadi* are fine threads of energy that help connect the pairs of chakras to the main channel of energy through the body and to each other. In this way, all of the chakras are connected together and can affect each other.

The Root Chakra

In the yogic tradition, the root chakra is called *muladhara*, or the manifestation of life energy. The center relates to the lower portion of the body—hips, legs, and feet—and to the functions of movement and elimination.

In addition to the physical aspect, this chakra relates to feeling secure in the world, feeling grounded to the earth, and the will to survive. It deals with the sense of joy and vitality. The root chakra governs the adrenal glands, which are responsible for secreting hormones that, in frightening situations, help one to be more alert and escape danger if necessary. If the chakra is not balanced or unhealthy from prolonged stress, problems such as high blood pressure and anxiety can be seen. One often feels a sense of lacking presence, of not being here, or low on physical energy. In persons with HIV/AIDS and cancer, this chakra is said to be severely damaged or nonfunctioning.

KEY POINT

Energy can be seen through color and heard through sound. The vibrational energy of the root chakra is associated with the color red (the slowest vibration on the color spectrum) and the sound of bumble bees. It can also be related to the first sound "Do" in the scale "Do-Ray-Me-Fa-So-La-Ti-Do."

The Sacral Chakra

This chakra is known as the *svadhisthana chakra* in yogic tradition and is related to the life force and vital body energy. The reproductive organs and the lower abdomen are affected by this chakra, especially the gonads (endocrine organs of sexuality and reproduction). Nutrients and the absorption of fluids through the intestine are also related to this chakra. The color vibration that relates to this chakra is orange and the sound is the one of a flute or the sound "Ray."

Psychologically, this chakra deals with feelings and emotions. It also relates to the expression of sexuality and desires, pleasures, and feelings about reproduction. Relationships will occur easily and fall into place when the sacral chakra works properly.

KEY POINT

Creativity or the desire to create another human being or other things is greatly affected by the sacral chakra.

When imbalanced or nonfunctioning, the sacral chakra will cause problems with emotions, feelings of sexuality, or the ability to reproduce or create. If energy is deficient to this chakra, one may feel a lack of emotions or flat. There may be a tendency to avoid emotions altogether. Some may have problems feeling passionate about anything or anyone. If the chakra is overactive, it is believed that one may experience mood swings or be very emotional. Another possibility is the need for constant pleasurable stimulation.

The Solar Plexus

The third chakra, or solar plexus, is also known as the *manipura* and is associated with one's own power, strength, and ego identity. It also centers around the issues of the will to think, control, exert authority, display aggression, and warmth, as well as the physical components of digestion and metabolism. With this chakra intact, one has the ability to start things and see them through to completion. The color associated with this chakra is lemon yellow and the sound is of the stringed instruments, such as the violin, or the sound "Me."

Physically, imbalances or malfunctioning of this chakra can lead to obesity (being overweight), diabetes (elevated blood sugar), hypoglycemia (low blood sugar), heartburn, gallbladder problems (stones or infection), and stomach ulcers. Most of us have felt the "pit in the stomach" when someone verbally or physically attacks us. In fact, one may feel nauseous or even vomit. Our stomach "gets into knots" when we get nervous or fearful, and things are out of our control.

Emotionally, one feels timid or dominating when there is an imbalance. There can be feelings of anger and rage that sit within this chakra. Some persons who are passive-aggressive (act disinterested, but are really angry inside) have imbalances in this chakra. A lack of self-worth or a hidden sense of shame is often found within this chakra. A healthy outlet is one of assertiveness or being able to state your needs and feelings freely and clearly while respecting others and yourself.

The Heart Chakra

This chakra, in the Indian tradition, is called the *anahata* and is the center of love. It has the qualities of loving self and others, harmony, compassion, openness, giving, peace, and grace. The heart chakra is called the transformation center because at the heart level one begins to deal with his or her spiritual side. Whereas the first three chakras dealt with the physical, emotional, and mental components of the self, the heart center speaks to the soul. It is through this chakra we experience the feeling of unconditional love or the deep love for others. This love is of a pure or spiritual kind of caring. The heart chakra is felt open when one cries tears of happiness or joy or in those instances where the heart strings are pulled. The color associated with the heart is emerald green, and the sound is of bells or "Fa."

The heart, circulation, and respiratory systems are related to this center on the physical plane. Imbalances can be seen through physical problems, such as heart disease, high blood pressure, poor circulation, angina (chest pain), asthma, emphysema, bronchitis, or pneumonia. Without a properly functioning heart and lungs, life is not possible and death will result.

Psychologically, imbalances in the heart can leave one feeling self-hatred or lacking self-esteem. One may avoid interpersonal relationships for fear of being hurt or unloved. Some choose isolation to avoid this pain. Others may have suffered from neglect, abandonment, or abuse. Grief weighs heavy on the heart and, if left unresolved, can create many problems. Some choose to give their hearts away, leaving very little for themselves, therefore feeling very empty and lonely.

Forgiveness is not necessarily letting others off the hook but releasing the anger and hurt you experienced from the action. Forgiveness of the self is one of the hardest things to do because we tend not to feel worthy of it. By showing compassion to ourselves, we are able to show compassion to others better. Forgiveness and the release of old grudges help the heart energy to expand.

REFLECTION

Is there anything that you have done for which you are unable to forgive yourself? What prevents you from offering or receiving this forgiveness from yourself?

The Throat Chakra

The center of creative energy, the throat chakra, is also called the *vishuddha*. It deals with issues surrounding communication and expression. By using the voice, one is able to create sounds of speech or song to express oneself. This connection to others by sound allows you to reveal who you are. The throat chakra relates to the neck, esophagus, throat, mouth, and ears. The sound of wind blowing through trees or the note "So" is associated with this chakra. It resonates to the vibration color of turquoise or light blue. Some describe it as an electric blue.

Physically, a healthy throat chakra is one revealing a clear voice that communicates thoughts, feelings, and ideas concisely. If the chakra is unbalanced, one may speak softly or with a hoarseness. Having a "frog in the throat" or "choking" on words are descriptions of the free flow of speech being impeded. Other symptoms of imbalance are knots in the neck muscles, tight throats, and clenched jaws.

Emotionally, people need to express themselves and their talents, knowledge, and ideas. Hindering this expression may reflect a poor self-esteem or identify family patterns that suppressed the individual's need to create or communicate. Grief can become locked here when emotions are not released through words or tears. Anger and stress can inflame the temporomandibular joint (in front of the ears) with teeth gnashing and grinding at night.

One way of opening this chakra is through sound—speaking, singing, chanting, or toning. By opening your mouth and emitting sound, the vibration clears the throat and it becomes stronger. Additionally, the throat chakra is the communicator from the heart to the soul. It allows us to "sing to our heart's content" and allow music to "soothe the soul." It lets us speak from our heart and make sounds reflecting our emotions. Silence can be used to actively listen to others or their surroundings. By actively listening, one can learn to communicate more effectively by hearing exactly what the other is saying.

The Brow Chakra

This chakra, known as the *ajna center*, is also called the third eye. It is associated with the pituitary gland, which controls most of the hormonal functions of the body. The brow chakra relates to memory, dreams, intuition, imagination, visualization, insight, and psychic perception. This chakra is all about seeing, within and without. The color associated with the brow chakra is deep indigo blue or deep purple. The sound of "La" or waves crashing on the beach help with this center.

KEY POINT

Physically, the brow chakra relates to the eyes, brain, nose, and head. Any imbalance will result in problems with these organs.

Sinusitis, headaches, and poor vision may be seen as imbalances in this chakra. From an emotional standpoint, the brow chakra deals with compassion of putting oneself in another's shoes, being sensitive to the needs of others, and a sense of humor. Mentally, recognizing patterns helps people predict that which will occur next in addition to providing insight into their behaviors. Remembering recent events, long-term events, and even past lives is encoded within this chakra. Stored images that can be seen like a movie in one's head allow one to view the same scenario again or replay it, making changes to produce a different outcome. Dreams are another mental component of the brow chakra, whether they are daydreams or those occurring in sleep. The symbology of dreams provides a great deal of insight to feelings, thoughts, and desires.

Imbalances with the brow chakra may be seen with hallucinations, delusions, nightmares, and misguided thinking. Some people may be insensitive to others' needs either deliberately or simply by not having observed them. These are the people who just do not seem to take the hint for whatever you are trying to tell them. Others are not able to see what is in front of them; they are blinded by inaccurate thinking.

The Crown Chakra

The seventh chakra or crown chakra is called the *sahasrara* center in yogic tradition. It is often called the spiritual center or center of connection to the oneness of the universe. The crown chakra relates to the divinity of self and our connection to a higher source however one defines it. The crown chakra also relates to intelligence, thought, consciousness, and information. An alignment to a Higher Power is seen through this center. It is associated with the color white or lavender and the sound "om" or "Ti." The pineal gland is an endocrine gland that is not well understood. Its purpose is to deal with the body's rhythms and timing.

KEY POINT

The crown chakra is the one with the highest energy vibration of the physical body.

There does not seem to be much dysfunction with this center on the physical level. Some people with imbalances may experience a sense of disconnection, a "holier-than-thou" thinking, or rigid belief system of thinking. These people can be described as having their heads in the clouds or being "spacey."

The crown chakra is the center of our connection to the oneness of the universe. It allows people to define who they are in relation to the universe and to experience their higher selves as whole. It is where they connect to the Higher Power and experience the oneness with all of creation in peace and grace.

Putting It All Together

An understanding of what the various chakras represent and symptoms associated with their imbalances can provide important information as to the status of the mind, body, and spirit. It can be helpful for people to consider whether certain physical symptoms that they experience on a regular basis are related to emotions that are blocking a chakra. For example, problems with weight control or chronic upset stomach could be associated with feeling a sense of low self-worth or unexpressed anger. Learning to be assertive in expressing feelings in a healthy manner could improve the physical symptoms. Meditating and thinking of the color associated with the specific chakra that is expressing itself as imbalanced could prove useful. Also, healers who work with the energy fields, such as healing touch practitioners, can assist in balancing the chakras.

Summary

Chakra is a Sanskrit word for spinning vortices of energy. Chakras transform energy from the universe into useable energy for the body. In turn, chakras send out energy from the body to the universe. The seven main chakras of the body are the crown, brow, throat, heart, solar plexus, sacral, and root. The names often refer to the area of the body over which they reside. Specific symptoms can be manifested when there is imbalance or dysfunction of a chakra. Changing thought patterns, working with an energy therapist, and using specific sounds and meditating on colors associated with the chakra are some of the ways that chakras can be balanced and symptoms improved.

References

1. Gerber, R. (2001). *A Practical Guide to Vibrational Medicine: Energy Healing and Spiritual Transformation*. New York: HarperCollins.
2. Gerber, R. (2001). *A Practical Guide to Vibrational Medicine: Energy Healing and Spiritual Transformation*. New York: HarperCollins, p. 128.

Suggested Readings

Buhlman, W. (1999). *Chakra Technique and the Vibrational Technique*. Chatsworth, CA: Spiritual Adventures.

Lee, I. (2002). *Healing Chakra: Light to Awaken My Soul*. Mesa, AZ: Healing Society, Inc.

Mercier, P. (2007). *The Chakra Bible: the Definitive Guide to Chakra Energy*. New York: Sterling Publishing Co.

Pond, D. (1999). *Chakras for Beginners: A Guide to Balancing Your Chakra Energy*. St. Paul, MN: Llewellyn Publications.

Wauters, A. (1997). *Chakras and Their Archetypes: Uniting Energy Awareness and Spiritual Growth*. Berkeley, CA: Crossing Press.

Wauters, A. (2002). *The Book of Chakras: Discover the Hidden Forces Within You*. Haupauge, NY: Barrons Educational Series.

Chapter 21

Safe Use of Complementary Therapies

OBJECTIVES

This chapter should enable you to

- List three factors that have stimulated Americans' interest in complementary therapies
- Discuss at least three philosophical differences between holistic and conventional approaches
- Describe the role of self-awareness in health and healing
- List at least five questions that should be asked to guide the decision to use a complementary therapy
- Describe the five major categories of complementary therapies
- Describe the alternative systems of medical practice of traditional Chinese medicine, acupuncture, homeopathy, Ayurvedic medicine, and naturopathy
- Describe the manual healing methods of chiropractic, craniosacral therapy, energy medicine/healing, massage therapy, Trager approach, Feldenkrais method, and Alexander therapy
- Describe the mind–body therapies of meditation/relaxation, biofeedback, guided imagery, hypnotherapy, yoga, and T'ai Chi
- Give an example of a pharmacologic and biologic treatment
- Describe herbal medicine

Complementary therapies have been used for centuries throughout the world; however, it has been primarily since the 1990s that their use has soared in the United States. It was during that decade that the landmark study by David Eisenberg and his colleagues, published in the prestigious *New England Journal of Medicine*, revealed that one-third of Americans were using alternative therapies—a figure that has continued to grow since that study.[1] By the turn of the century, Americans were spending over $27 billion annually for complementary and alternative therapies, most of which was out of pocket. To say this caught the medical community's attention would be an understatement!

Many factors have contributed to the growing use of complementary therapies. The interest in preventive health has stimulated individuals to explore practices and products that they can use independently, and many complementary therapies, such as meditation and dietary modifications, fit the bill. Growing reports of adverse drug reactions and other complications from conventional medical care have led people to explore natural means to manage illness. The personalized attention provided by practitioners of complementary therapies offers people a superior experience to the abbreviated and often impersonal office visits and hospital stays. Furthermore, research proving the benefits of complementary therapies is growing by the day.

The heightened attention to complementary therapies also has created much confusion regarding the safety of using many of these therapies. Questions such as these emerge: Why and when is it appropriate to use these therapies? Are these therapies consistent with my health beliefs, my spiritual beliefs? How do I choose a practitioner or a therapy? Above all, are these therapies right for me?

Mystery and what seems to be a strange language surround many complementary treatments. Even the terminology used to describe these types of therapies is confusing. These therapies were first called (and continue to be called) *alternative therapies*. This term does not fit for many because it creates an either/or choice situation. Because it is felt by many that these therapies can be used in conjunction with Western medical treatments, the word *complementary* conveyed a clearer meaning. Clarifying even more the joint use of several methods of treatment at the same time, use of the term *integrative* has evolved.

Terms such as *holistic* and *natural* are frequently used to describe complementary therapies. *Allopathic* is a word that describes western conventional medicine. Some feel that using the term *traditional medicine* to describe today's practice of medicine is incorrect. It is felt by many that *traditional* indicates the use of a treatment since the beginning of time and, therefore, *conventional* better describes the present use of western medical treatments.

KEY POINT

The evolution of terms used in describing complementary therapies is most evident in the changed name of the division of the National Institute of Health (NIH) that investigates and researches these types of practices and products. First established as the Office of Alternative Therapies, in 1998, it became the National Center for Complementary and Alternative Medicine. Along with the name change has been an increase in its annual budget for research of these therapies.

History

Many complementary therapies originated from ancient and non-Western healing traditions, many of which have their roots in spiritually-based healthcare systems. These systems use such measures as prayer, meditation, drumming, storytelling, and mythology to help people in their search for wholeness by allowing them to experience sacred moments in their lives. Spirituality is not in itself religion, but it underlies and enhances all world religions. It is also seen as a drive to become a complete, balanced person and is believed by many to be related to intuition, creativity, and motivation.[2] Most ancient and non-Western cultures express healing as being in balance and harmony.

Holistic Health Beliefs

Today the word *holistic* is being used freely, and yet many of the basic concepts that underlie its true meaning are not understood or fully embraced by those using it. The most basic of these concepts is the concept of wholeness. Many ancient healing traditions have as a belief that wellness exists when there is balance of the physical, emotional, mental, and spiritual components of our being. Your physical body has an innate physical tendency to work toward equilibrium or homeostasis. It has a built-in potential to maintain physical health or optimal function of all body systems and a complex natural ability to repair itself and overcome illness. In the quest for balance emotionally, you strive to feel and express your entire range of human emotions freely and appropriately. Mentally, you seek a sense of self-worth, accomplishment, and positive self-identity. Spiritually, you seek a connectedness to others and to a Higher Power or Divine Source. This balanced state is seen as wellness in a holistic approach to health care. Illness is considered an imbalance of these components.

KEY POINT

Holistic health is the balance among your physical, emotional, mental, and spiritual components.

Healing is seen as an ongoing, lifelong process, and when viewed in a positive manner, it is seen as a continual journey of self-discovery. All healing is self-healing, and conventional (Western) medical treatments and complementary treatments help by creating an environment that supports your attempt to balance the components of your beingness. Nevertheless, some philosophical differences exist between the holistic and conventional (Western) medical approaches:

- The holistic approach to healing seeks the root cause of the problem (the source of the imbalance) and tries to re-establish a balance of mind, body, and spirit, whereas conventional medical approaches are more disease-oriented and focus more on removing or managing signs and symptoms of physical illness.

- In Western medical approaches, people have been conditioned to turn over the responsibility of healing to the healthcare provider; however, participation in one's own healing process is a key component of a holistic approach to health care. Being a passive recipient or expecting others to fix a problem independent of your efforts is inconsistent with the holistic caring process. This belief in seeking balance or healing is carried out in partnership. The person and the care provider have complementary responsibilities. Learning how to partner is a very important concept that conventional medicine, until recently, has not strongly emphasized.

- Another element of the holistic approach to health care is the requirement of self-care. The care and nurturing of all aspects of one's self supports a healthier balance and results in more productivity and a fuller participation in the life experience.

- A holistic orientation to health recognizes the interconnectedness of the mind, body, and spirit. If any aspect of yourself is not attended to and nurtured, it cannot function to its capacity; this will have a detrimental effect on the other components of your health. Imbalances are identified and addressed before they become disease processes.

Self-awareness then becomes paramount in this dance between balance and imbalance of the mind, body, and spirit. This self-awareness is supported and/or learned through many of the complementary therapies. Many of the therapies can precipitate an awareness of emotions as well as a physical awareness. It may have been the physical complaint that directs a person to seek the therapy, but the awareness of an emotional component may surface in the process. Knowing this is of importance when seeking complementary therapies. This is also the reason that these therapies are referred to as holistic: They involve all aspects of the person. Recognition and choosing to act on this self-awareness is part of the personal healing process.

REFLECTION

How do you react when you experience headaches, indigestion, and other symptoms? Do you quickly try to eliminate them with medications, or do you first take time to understand the underlying causes so that you can prevent them in the future?

Acute and Chronic Illness

Pharmacological and technological advancements have equipped conventional medicine to handle acute conditions effectively and efficiently. Heart attacks can be halted, shattered bones mended, and infections eliminated. Unfortunately, as medical technology has increased, the caring components of medical care seem to have shrunk. Hospital stays and office visits are shorter; healthcare providers seldom have ample time to learn about the whole person or to teach and empower the person for self-care. For these reasons, conventional medicine is less successful at managing chronic conditions than at treating acute illnesses.

KEY POINT

Less than 25% of the healthcare dollar in the United States today is spent on prevention and acute care; the balance is spent on the management of chronic conditions.

Persons with chronic conditions are increasingly integrating complementary therapies into their medical care. They find that complementary practitioners invest more time in getting to understand their clients, encourage an active provider–client partnership, empower clients for self-care, promote healthy lifestyle practices, and tend to see the whole person rather than merely treat the symptoms.[3]

Self-Awareness: Body Wisdom

The journey toward self-awareness like anything else begins with the first step, and a beginning point is physical body awareness. Physical body awareness appears to be a foreign concept in Western society today, as most people have been taught to deny, ignore, or push through early signs the body may express. Self-awareness is a major developmental pearl that provides key information that influences choices in making informed decisions when choosing a therapy that is most appropriate and/or safe at any given point in time.

KEY POINT

Self-awareness enables one to make informed decisions.

As body awareness develops, awareness of feelings and thoughts follows. This knowledge and understanding leads to inward focusing. Inward focus and awareness protects and guides in many ways. Most of us have been directly taught by our parents, teachers, and others how to get around our weaknesses and imbalances. We tend to ignore body messages until they scream so loudly that we finally are incapacitated and forced to stop and take notice.

Befriending and listening to the body is a lifelong process that continues to be refined as more attention is paid to it. Paying attention leads to learning the body's wisdom versus overriding it. Learning how to recognize this wisdom increases personal knowledge and with this knowledge comes personal power—power to be in greater control of knowing the best choice to help the body regain or move toward balanced health.

Self-awareness feeds into self-responsibility in a holistic approach to maintaining wellness. Rather than following the pattern of expecting others to provide information of what is best, self-awareness provides the ingredient of self-involvement in illness prevention. This journey of exploration and self-discovery can be fascinating and removes the image of the body as foreign territory. This voyage begins with small steps and requires notation of results obtained. This tuning into the body, instead of tuning out, allows the body to be worked with in a cooperative way.

Self-awareness better equips a person in making an initial choice of which complementary therapy to experience and provides information after receiving the therapy. Paying attention to the physical, mental, and emotional responses after receiving a treatment is invaluable in making future treatment decisions. Were the reasons for choosing a particular therapy satisfied? In what way? For how long? What new information was obtained about the body and the mind? This information allows for the choice to continue an old pattern of ignoring the messages received, or paying attention, learning, and deciding to make new informed choices.

KEY POINT

Paying attention to their physical, mental, and emotional responses helps people to determine what is best for their health rather than relying on the decisions of others.

The continued evolution of this self-awareness can become very powerful and self-empowering. Becoming more involved allows for greater participation in decision making in health care or wellness choices. This gentler, friendlier approach to body–mind maintenance allows for less fault-finding with the body, less rushing ahead without willpower, and less blindness to personal weaknesses. Self-awareness and self-acceptance are major components that propel a person on the journey toward a more balanced mind, body, and spirit and establish a more personal feeling of control of life in general.

Selecting a Therapy

Deciding to use a complementary/alternative therapy (CAT) requires much consideration and forethought. In order to be safe and appropriate many questions need to be asked.

KEY POINT

If a person desires to use CATs, he or she must be committed to being an active participant in regaining and/or maintaining health.

A major consideration is how to work effectively with a primary healthcare provider. Is conventional medical care required to monitor a particular medical condition? If so, developing a partnership with the conventional healthcare provider is crucial. Cooperation by the provider and the person seeking CAT is essential. For proper assessment of treatment effects, if combining conventional medicine and CAT, the conventional healthcare provider needs to be informed. Clear baseline assessment information of current symptoms or concerns is needed. The person must be prepared to keep a diary of information to assist in evaluating CAT results. Decisions need to be made regarding the safety of combined therapies or the impact of postponing conventional medical care while using CAT. Agreements need to be reached regarding follow-up visits with the western medical care provider, if necessary, during or after receiving CAT. Some suggestions for using CAT safely are listed in Exhibit 21-1.

EXHIBIT 21-1   Suggestions for Safely Using CATs

· Know your reason for choosing CAT. Is it out of frustration with experiences of Western conventional medicine? Increasing awareness of other cultures' approaches to health and illness? A desire for wellness or to explore a wholeness approach to health? Friends' positive experiences that have aroused your curiosity?

· Use CAT under the supervision of a qualified doctor if you have a serious medical illness.

· Understand and establish your goals in using CAT.

· Beware of mixing and matching conventional and CATs on your own.

· Do your homework and gather information; do not rely merely on testimonies of persons who have used a therapy.

· Avoid the more is better fallacy.

· If something sounds too good to be true, it generally is.

· Keep an open mind, and use the best of conventional medicine and CAT.

· Ask questions of practitioners before selecting their therapy, such as the following:

  · What is it?

  · How does it work?

  · What health conditions respond best to this CAT?

  · When is it best to use it/not use it?

  · What should I expect?

  · What are the possible harmful effects?

  · What is the cost and length of a session?

  · How long must I use the therapy/receive treatment?

  · What information and resources are available to help me learn about this CAT?

  · Do you need to be licensed or certified to practice this CAT? If so, are you?

  · What professional organizations can be contacted to get information about practitioners of this CAT?

Choosing a Practitioner

Deciding which therapy to receive is part of the process, but deciding which provider will deliver that therapy requires just as much serious thought and investigation. There are some important steps in selecting a treatment specialist.

First, people need to be urged to take their time. They should gather names of practitioners by contacting professional organizations, ask for recommendations from people they respect, and check local directories. After a few practitioners are identified, they can be called and asked questions regarding education, experience, and credentials/certification. Some therapies require degrees, whereas others require training with specific criteria. People need to beware of any pressure or claims about cures. A brochure can be requested, as can the names of some of the practitioners' clients who can be contacted for references. State licensing boards can provide information about standards that practitioners need to meet.

The information collected needs to be reviewed. People need to assess their own comfort level with the qualifications (educational background/licensing/certification), or lack of, and the practitioner's manners in interacting with them. They may want a consultation visit. During this visit, they should be clear about their goals, review the goals with the practitioner, discuss organizing a treatment plan, and inquire about side effects and/or adverse reactions. Also, people need to remember to budget their time and expenses appropriately to attain their goals.

After an initial session, reevaluating is helpful. People need to understand that it is their decision to continue the sessions or not: They are in charge. They should consider the practitioner's professionalism, willingness to answer questions, ability to listen, understanding of concerns, and their overall feelings of ease with this provider. People need to trust their judgment and confidence in the practitioner's skills and degree of healing relationship established.

REFLECTION

Have you ever received care from a healthcare practitioner who did not treat you with respect or listen to your concerns? How did this influence your ability to feel in charge of your care? How can you avoid behaving in the same manner when you care for others?

Common Complementary and Alternative Therapies

Now that the basic information influencing choices of approaches has been discussed, it is time to take a closer look at some specific choices. There are a variety of ways of categorizing CAT therapies. Some common categories and alternative and complementary approaches will be discussed are as follows:

- Alternative systems of medical practice, including traditional Chinese medicine, acupuncture, homeopathy, ayurvedic, and naturopathy

- Manual healing therapies, including chiropractic, osteopathy/craniosacral therapy, energy therapy/energy medicine, bodywork therapy, such as massage therapy, movement therapy (Trager approach, Feldenkrais method, and Alexander therapy)

- Mind–body therapies, including meditation/relaxation, biofeedback, guided imagery, hypnotherapy, yoga, T'ai Chi

- Pharmacologic/biologic treatments, including aromatherapy, vitamins, minerals, other supplements

- Botanical medicine/herbal medicine

Some therapies overlap into several categories. For example, T'ai Chi and yoga can be categorized under both movement and mind–body therapies.

Alternative Systems of Medical Practice

Traditional Chinese Medicine

What It Is

Traditional Chinese medicine (TCM) is a complex and sophisticated ancient system of health rooted in Chinese culture that has been passed down from generation to generation. TCM approaches the person as a whole and sees mind, body, and spirit as interrelated elements that are intertwined with nature and the universe. It embraces many theories, methods, and approaches and emphasizes prevention. Some of the basic principles inherent in TCM are listed in Exhibit 21-2.

How It Works

Diagnostic approaches are based on identifying patterns of disharmony or imbalance and consist of the following:

- Examination or assessment of the voice, pulse, and respiration
- Observation of overall appearance, eyes, skin, and tongue
- Questioning about functions of the whole person (both physical and emotional)

The patterns determined by this investigative process are the basis on which the treatment plan is made. Treatments then are focused on restoring or maintaining harmony and balance of the chi's flow.

Various therapies may be prescribed to treat patterns of disharmony. Some of these therapies are diet; herbal remedies; massage; acupuncture (insertion of very fine needles at

---

EXHIBIT 21-2   Basic Principles Inherent in Traditional Chinese Medicine

· Qi (chi) is believed to be the vital life force or invisible flow of energy that circulates through specific pathways in plants, animals, and people and are called meridians, which are necessary to maintain life

· Yin and yang, which is the interaction of opposing forces and seen as complementary aspects

· Five phases theory of fire, earth, metal, water, and wood

· Five seasons of summer, autumn, winter, spring, and late summer

· View of mind, body, and spirit as the three vital treasures

---

specific points on the body to stimulate and balance energy flow); acupressure, consisting of the application of finger pressure over specific points to also stimulate the flow of chi; moxibustion, or the burning of a special herb (mugwort) over acupuncture points in order to stimulate the energy flow through the energy channels; and qigong (pronounced *chee-gong*), involving low-impact stretches, abdominal breathing, meditation, and visualization, and/or possibly T'ai Chi (pronounced *tie-chee*), which is a form of movement meditation designed to unite body and mind, improve muscle tone, and encourage relaxation. Individualized plans determine the number of sessions prescribed for any of these forms of treatment.

Acupuncture

What It Is

As already mentioned, acupuncture is one of the treatment methods used in TCM. Acupuncture is used to unblock the pathways (meridians or channels) at specific juncture points through which the chi or life force flows. The theory is that disease or illness results from the blockage or obstructions of the pathways, therefore clearing the blockages allows the chi to run freely through the meridians and restores health.

Archeologists have traced the use of acupuncture as far back as the Stone Age. Americans began to take note in 1972, after President Richard Nixon visited China. It was during that trip that a news reporter developed appendicitis and acupuncture was used during his emergency appendectomy. The reporter wrote of this event and stimulated much interest and many visits by Western physicians to observe the use of acupuncture in China. The NIH has demonstrated the effectiveness of acupuncture for pain management after dental surgery and for controlling nausea and vomiting in pregnancy, after chemotherapy, and after surgery.

How It Works

It has been determined that acupuncture stimulates physical responses, such as changing brain activity, blood chemistry, endocrine functions, blood pressure, heart rate, and immune system response. More specifically, medical research has shown that acupuncture can regulate blood cell counts, trigger endorphin production, and control blood pressure.

Acupuncture needles are sometimes inserted and removed immediately, and at other times, they are allowed to remain in place for a period of time. Sensations described as rushing, warmth, or tingling are experienced. As the immune system is stimulated, a sense of well-being is experienced. Acupuncture is used both to maintain health and to treat illness or pain.

What It Helps

The World Health Organization (WHO) has described more than 100 different health conditions that acupuncture can treat. Much positive research has supported the use of acupuncture in the treatment of alcohol and drug addiction.

Words of Wisdom/Cautions

One of the biggest advantages of the use of acupuncture is the lack of harmful side effects. A feeling of lightheadedness or euphoria after a treatment has been reported, which is stabilized by a few minutes of rest.

Homeopathy

What It Is

Homeopathy is a system of medical practice that is based on the principle that "like cures like." It is a therapeutic system that assists self-healing by giving small doses of remedies prepared from plant, animal, and mineral substances. This system uses diluted (the more diluted the better) portions or remedies to cure symptoms of disease. The remedies encourage the body to eliminate symptoms by encouraging the symptoms to run their course instead of suppressing them. Symptoms are considered signals as the body works to restore natural balance. During this process of self-healing, the immune system is stimulated, healing is accelerated, and the body is strengthened.

Dr. Samuel Hahnemann (1755–1843), a German physician, is known as the father of homeopathy. He became familiar with the ancient "Law of Similars," which states that a substance that would cause illness or a set of uncomfortable symptoms when taken in large amounts by a healthy person, could accelerate healing if taken in minuscule amounts by a sick person.

In the 1830s, homeopathy was used in most of Europe, Russia, Latin America, and the United States. It appealed to the well educated and affluent—including the British Royal

Family. In 1880, homeopathic medical colleges were in most major cities, and by 1900, homeopaths were recognized as legitimate physicians. After the Civil War, medicine changed, and by 1914, the American Medical Association (AMA) controlled the standard for medical education and rejected homeopathy. By 1970, homeopaths became almost nonexistent; however, interest in natural remedies and concern over the growing incidence of adverse drug reactions has stirred a new interest in homeopathy.

How It Works

Remedies of healing compounds are made through a process of serial dilution. One single drop of a plant substance is mixed with 100 drops of water and shaken. This mixture is called C. One drop of that solution is then mixed with another 100 drops and shaken. This is repeated and the number of repetitions indicates the number placed before the C. For instance, the process repeated 30 times would be called a 30C dilution. During this process each dilution actually becomes higher in potency.

KEY POINT

The more dilute a homeopathic remedy is, the higher is its potency.

It is not clearly understood how homeopathic remedies work, but there are a number of theories. One theory is the hologram theory—meaning no matter how many dilutions occur a complete essence of the substance remains. Another theory is that the "water has memory"—meaning the original substance leaves an imprint of itself on the water molecules.

Homeopaths believe everyone expresses illness and heals in unique ways. This differs greatly from conventional western medicine, which lumps symptoms into categories and believes that everyone with the same disease can be treated in the same way.

Diagnostic methods in homeopathy work toward obtaining a composite picture of a person, taking into consideration the physical, emotional, and mental aspects. A person is encouraged to tell his or her story while the homeopath observes many things, including dress, posture, tone of voice, and rate of speech. Homeopathic practitioners refer clients to conventional medical physicians for drugs and surgery when appropriate. The focus is on how a person is expressing a particular problem or condition so that an individualized plan can be made for treatment. Homeopathic practitioners will determine the remedy that can most closely mimic the sick person's pattern of symptoms.

There are two types of homeopathic approaches for treatment: classical and nonclassical. A classical homeopath will prescribe a single remedy for a specific problem after determining a symptom picture and matching it to an individual's constitution. The nonclassical approach would be trying to match a symptom to a remedy without having the detailed individualized information about the person with the symptom(s).

What It Helps

Homeopathic remedies benefit arthritis, pain, anxiety, muscular aches and pains, asthma, sinusitis, allergies, headaches, acute infection, skin disorders, circulatory disorders, infant and childhood illnesses, digestive problems, pregnant and lactating women, endocrine imbalances, and cardiovascular problems.

Words of Wisdom/Cautions

There could be the potential for using remedies to treat serious conditions instead of seeking appropriate conventional care. This is especially true if someone is trying to self-treat an illness.

Because symptoms can get worse before they get better, it may be hard to determine whether a remedy is working or whether a side effect requiring immediate Western medical attention is occurring.

Dosages are different from conventional Western medicines; therefore, it would be better to seek the advice of a qualified homeopath rather than using an over-the-counter remedy.

Homeopathy can be used for minor acute care, but it is best to become informed by seeking a group study program instead of trying over-the-counter remedies or reading related literature.

Ayurvedic Medicine

What It Is

Ayurveda is a sophisticated ancient healing system derived from Hindu and Indian culture and practiced in India for 4000 years. It is a way of life, a philosophy of living, which supports the belief in the interconnectedness of mind, body, and spirit and of the individual to the environment. It teaches and emphasizes individual responsibility in becoming an active participant in maintaining healthy body systems. The focus is on prevention and regaining good health.

KEY POINT

Ayurveda means science of life. In Sanskrit, *Ayur* means life, and *Veda* means knowledge.

Ayurveda views individuals as composed of five elements: earth, water, fire, air, and space. Ayurvedic philosophy holds that there are three basic operating principles or *doshas* that govern the function of health. It is believed that a person is born with a particular dosha (body type) or combination of doshas and that the basic constitution is expressed through this body type. There is also a belief that the mind has a powerful influence on the body; therefore, a major role for a person is to become aware of the positive and negative thought patterns that support or destroy health.

How It Works

By assessing an individual's physical and emotional makeup, food and environmental preferences, and lifestyle, a particular dosha or body type is determined. Knowing the specific elements that make up this dosha along with basic patterns, 24-hour cycles, seasons, and stages of life associated with each of the doshas, a particular health plan is developed.

Some diagnostic methods used are detailed history-taking through questioning (family, interpersonal relationships, and job situation), pulse diagnosis, tongue diagnosis, and other observational skills (eyes, nails, and urine).

A treatment plan's goal is to help a person arrive at a lifestyle that results in a balance of body and mind for optimum health. Treatment suggestions may include a combination of the following:

- Nutritional suggestions, including the six tastes that are important to include in every meal (sweet, sour, salty, pungent, bitter, and astringent)
- Herbs (which are classified according to the six tastes)
- Exercise (specific for each dosha/body type)
- Breathing exercises (called *pranayama*)
- Meditation exercises (to help develop moment-to-moment awareness and cleansing of the body)
- Massage (marma therapy)
- Aromatherapy (to help balance body functions, emotions, and memories)
- Music (certain tones or rhythms to be used at certain times of the day)
- Purification technique called *panchakarma* (that includes five procedures or therapies to be experienced over the course of one week)

What It Helps

In addition to being appropriate for a wide range of physical and emotional illnesses, Ayurveda benefits anyone who is interested in optimum health.

Words of Wisdom/Cautions

Physical side effects are rare, although there may be occasional side effects from certain Ayurvedic herbs. It is always best to seek advice from a practitioner who is experienced or who has been educated in the Ayurvedic principles.

Naturopathy

What It Is

Naturopathic medicine grew out of the 19th century medical system and was given its name by Dr. John Scheel in 1895 and was formalized by Benedict Lust in 1902. It was popular in the early 1900s, but with the development of antibiotics and vaccines in the 1940s and 1950s that popularity declined. It was not until the 1970s that interest was renewed.

Naturopathy is a way of life, viewing health as more than the absence of disease. It looks at symptoms as signs of the body eliminating toxins and believes that a person should be treated as a whole, looking at physical, psychological, emotional, and genetic factors. A naturopath's emphasis is on finding and treating the cause (not just symptoms), self-responsibility, education, health maintenance, and disease prevention. The basic belief is that the body has the ability to heal itself and an innate ability to maintain health, and thus, any treatment focuses on a combination of natural healing methods that strengthen the body's natural abilities. Techniques and approaches are used that do no harm and support and restore harmony within the body.

A practice is generally built around two or more therapeutic approaches such as traditional Chinese medicine or acupuncture, clinical nutrition, counseling, dietary and lifestyle modifications, exercise, herbal medicine, homeopathy, hydrotherapy, or osteopathy.

Training for a doctor of naturopathic medicine (ND) varies from a 4-year graduate level education within a naturopathic medical college to training from a correspondence school.

How It Works

As the primary role of a naturopath is as an educator, recommendations and encouragement for self-responsibility for health are offered and the person must make a commitment to change. The first visit involves a medical history with detailed assessment of lifestyle habits, diet, occupation, family dynamics, emotional state, and environmental and genetic influences. Diagnostic procedures, such as laboratory testing and X-rays may be used and if specialized care, surgery, or hospitalization is warranted referral is made to other healthcare professionals as appropriate. Naturopaths prefer the least invasive intervention and do not do emergency care, although some may practice natural childbirth. Naturopaths pay attention to a person's individuality and susceptibility to disease.

What It Helps

There is unlimited potential for most health conditions to respond to this type of approach.

Words of Wisdom/Cautions

Natural therapies are less likely to cause complications, but choose the practitioner who knows his or her limitations with any of the approaches practiced.

Manual Healing Methods

Chiropractic

What It Is

History tells us that the use of manipulation as a healing technique was used as early as 2700 B.C. by the Chinese. The Greeks (in 1500 B.C.) and Hippocrates (460 B.C.) also used spinal manipulation to cure dysfunctions of the body.

Daniel Palmer founded chiropractic in the Midwest in 1895, and it is now the fourth largest health profession in the United States. Palmer believed that all body functions were regulated by the nervous system and that because nerves originate in the spine any displacement of vertebrae could disrupt nerve transmission (which he called subluxation). He hypothesized that almost all disease is caused by vertebral misalignment; therefore, spine manipulation could treat all disease. Today the theory has changed to what is being called intervertebral motion dysfunction. The key factor in this theory involves the loss of mobility of facet joints in the spine.

KEY POINT

Chiropractors believe that a strong agile and aligned spine is the key to good health.

How It Works

The spine is made up of 24 bones called vertebrae with discs of cartilage cushioning between each vertebra. The spinal cord runs through the middle of the vertebrae with many nerves branching off through channels in the vertebrae. Chiropractors believe that injury or poor posture can result in pressure on the spinal cord from misaligned vertebrae and that this can lead to illness and painful movement.

The chiropractor identifies and corrects the misalignments through manipulation, which are called adjustments. Muscle work is also incorporated as muscles attach and support the spine. Manipulation and muscle work can be done by hand and/or assisted by special treatment tables, application of heat or cold, or ultrasound. Some chiropractic physicians also advise about nutrition and exercise. The first visit includes a detailed medical history and examination of the spine. Sometimes X-rays of the spine are also obtained. The findings are reviewed by the chiropractor, and a plan is established with a suggested number of follow-up treatments.

What It Helps

Chiropractic is useful for lower-back syndromes, muscle spasms, mid-back conditions, sports-related injuries, neck syndromes, whiplash and accident-related injuries, headaches, arthritic conditions, carpal tunnel syndrome, shoulder conditions, and sciatica.

Words of Wisdom/Cautions

With a conscientious, professionally trained chiropractor there are few side effects, however, some soreness may be experienced for a few days after a spinal adjustment and occasionally symptoms may get worse. Manipulations are contraindicated in persons with osteoporosis and advanced degenerative joint disease as these might be worsened by spinal adjustment.

Craniosacral Therapy

What It Is

The basic theory behind craniosacral therapy is that an unimpeded cerebrospinal fluid flow is the key to optimum health. Craniosacral therapy was developed in the early 1900s and is an offshoot of osteopathy and chiropractic.

William Sutherland, an osteopathic physician, developed craniosacral therapy, which at that time was called cranial osteopathy. He believed that the bones of the skull were movable and that they move rhythmically in response to production of cerebrospinal fluid in the ventricles of the brain. This belief contradicts the teachings of anatomy in Western medicine, which holds the bones of the skull fuse together at two years of age and are no longer movable after this point in the physical development of the body.

Craniosacral therapists also believe that by realigning the bones of the skull, free circulation of the cerebrospinal fluid is restored, and strains and stresses of the meninges (that surround the brain and spinal cord) are removed, which allows the entire body to return to good health. William Sutherland researched his theory over 20 years and documented physical and emotional reactions to compression on the cranial bones.

Craniosacral therapy was further advanced by John Upledger who performed scientific studies at Michigan State University from 1975–1983. His findings validated craniosacral therapy's capability to help evaluate and treat dysfunction and pain. The Upledger Institute in Palm Beach Gardens, Florida trains practitioners in this discipline.

How It Works

Trained practitioners palpate the craniosacral rhythm by placing their hands on the cranium (skull) and sensing imbalances. This approach is painless as the practitioner uses gentle touch (less than the weight of a nickel) to sense the imbalances in the rhythm and stabilize it. Recipients report a release of tension and a state of deep relaxation and peace. Practitioners work in a quiet setting and use no needles, oils, or mechanical devices. They take a medical history, observe, and question about any symptoms. As with other alternative therapies, a person may experience a brief period of worsening symptoms after treatment (usually for only 24–48 hours) as the body adapts to the changes that occurred during the session.

What It Helps

It helps anxiety, headaches, central nervous system disorders, neck and back pain, chronic ear infections, chronic fatigue, motor coordination difficulties, facial pain, temporomandibular joint dysfunction, and sinusitis.

Words of Wisdom/Cautions

As with any integrative therapy, use with the exclusion of Western medical advice is not recommended.

Energy Medicine/Healing

What It Is

Energy medicine and energy healing are called *hands-on healing* and *hand-mediated biofield therapies*. Energy field theory (biofield theory) is based on quantum physics law. These laws recognize matter as energy and hold that all living things generate vibrational fields. Validation of the existence of human energy fields is beginning to emerge through research studies.

KEY POINT

In energy healing, subtle energy is seen as the core of life and the central force in healing.

Therapeutic Touch is one of these techniques and was developed by Dolores Krieger, a nursing professor at New York University, and Dora Kunz, a healer from Canada, in the 1970s. The concept of universal life force is central to these forms of therapy—like *qi* (pronounced chee) is in traditional Chinese medicine and acupuncture. Two other therapies that use hands to alter energy fields and assist in the healing process are *Healing Touch* and *Reiki*. Healing Touch was developed for healthcare professionals by Janet Mentgen, a nurse from Denver, Colorado, and includes a varied collection of energy techniques. Reiki is an ancient Buddhist practice that was rediscovered by Dr. Usui, a Japanese physician, through ancient Tibetan texts. A Japanese-American woman who studied with Dr. Usui later introduced Reiki in the United States.

These modern interpretations of ancient practices should not be confused with faith healing, as they are not practiced within a religious context. The goal of this form of healing is to accelerate the personal-healing process at all levels of mind, body, and spirit. These forms of treatment are not meant for diagnosing nor are they to replace conventional medicine or surgery.

Each technique has a process that is learned through training, reading, and practice. Therapeutic Touch can be learned through short courses. Healing Touch is learned through various levels of training over a period of 2 to 3 years, and criteria must be met for certification as a practitioner. Reiki is learned from a Reiki Master and includes two degrees that can be learned in weekend courses. The Master degree takes longer study and a mentorship.

KEY POINT

Although conventional scientific medicine has no evidence to support the existence of human energy fields, many of the diagnostic instruments used for diagnosis and treatment of disease are energy-medicine devices. Examples of these devices that measure electromagnetic frequencies are electrocardiogram, electroencephalogram, electromyogram, ultrasound, and magnetic resonance imaging. It is these electromagnetic frequencies or energy fields that skilled energy healers/practitioners literally feel and work with to create repatterning.

How It Works

These therapies are based on the belief that health exists when there is an abundance of energy flowing without obstruction throughout a person and between the person and his or her environment. Energy therapists help individuals create an environment that supports this self-healing. This is in essence what happens when a person interacts in a caring relationship. Healing may occur on the physical, emotional, mental, or spiritual levels as this process works with the whole person.

Practitioners center themselves in preparation for a treatment session so that they are consciously present for the client. Their focus is completely on the person receiving the treatment without any preoccupation or thought process in any other direction. Practitioners assess the energy field, clear and balance it through hand movements, and/or direct energy in a specific region of the body. The end result expressed by most people after receiving a session of energy healing is extremely deep relaxation. Reiki involves a similar process and helps restore balance to a person's energy field.

What It Helps

Research supports the use of energy healing to relieve pain, anxiety, stress, and tension and to accelerate wound healing and to help maintain health and a feeling of well-being. There are unlimited uses for these therapies when provided by a trained practitioner.

Words of Wisdom/Cautions

Always be concerned about claims of curing, and know the credentials of the practitioner offering the treatment.

Massage Therapy

What It Is

Massage is the third most common form of alternative treatment in the United States after relaxation techniques and chiropractic. It consists of the therapeutic practice of kneading or manipulating soft tissue and muscles with the intent of increasing health and well-being and assisting the body in healing.

There are many different types of massage, such as lymphatic massage, sports massage, Swedish massage, shiatsu massage, myofascial release, trigger point massage, Thai massage, and infant massage. A form of deep tissue massage that is known as structural integration is called rolfing. This system works deeply into muscle tissue and fascia to stretch and release patterns of tension and rigidity and to return the body to a state of correct alignment.

How It Works

Besides stretching and loosening muscle and connective tissue, massage also

- Improves blood flow and the flow of lymph throughout the body
- Speeds the metabolism of waste products
- Promotes the circulation of oxygen and nutrients to cells and tissues
- Stimulates the release of endorphins and serotonin in the brain and nervous system

---

KEY POINT

Massage can be seen as a form of communication from the therapist that brings comfort, gentleness, connection, trust, and peace.

What It Helps

Massage is good for health maintenance as well as an adjunct to healing. Many conditions may benefit from massage, such as chronic pain, fluid retention, circulatory problems, fatigue, muscle tension and spasms, anxiety and stress, muscle strain or sprain, and insomnia.

Words of Wisdom/Cautions

There are a few contraindications that will be screened by the therapist when taking a medical history at the first visit. This is a reason for choosing a well-trained and qualified massage therapist. Ask for credentials.

Bodywork—Movement Therapy

The Trager Approach

What It Is

In the 1920s, a physician, Milton Trager, developed a method of passive gentle movements with traction and rotation of extremities to help reeducate muscles and joints. Through this method, muscle tightness is relieved without pain, and the end result is a sense of freedom, flexibility, and lightness.

How It Works

Through smooth joint movements and gentle rhythmic rocking of body parts, communication is made with the nerves that control muscle movement to release and reorganize old patterns of tension, pain, and muscle restriction. A session lasts 60 to 90 minutes, and after a session, instructions are given for a series of simple movements (called *mentastics*) to help maintain the results of the treatment. Deep relaxation of mind and body is also promoted during these movements.

What It Helps

It helps chronic pain, severe disability, muscle spasms, fibromyalgia, temporomandibular pain, headaches, plus many other neuromuscular disorders.

Words of Wisdom/Cautions

With a trained practitioner, harmful side effects do not exist.

Feldenkrais Method

What It Is

Feldenkrais teaches a person how to alter the way the body is held and moved. It is a gentle method of bodywork that involves movement. Moshe Feldenkrais developed this method after suffering a knee injury. He studied and combined principles of anatomy, physiology, biomechanics, and psychology and integrated this knowledge with his own awareness of proper movement.

How It Works

By developing awareness of body movement patterns and changing them through specific exercises, flexibility, coordination, and range of motion improve. Through instruction, a teacher guides a person through a series of movements, such as bending, walking, and reaching. These movements can help reduce stress and pain and improve self-image. It is believed these movements access the central nervous system. There are two types of sessions: (1) a set of movement lessons learned with a group called awareness through movement and (2) individual hands-on sessions called functional integration. The results benefit mind and emotion, as well as the physical body.

KEY POINT

Feldenkrais teaches a person to be aware of the way the body moves and to use proper movement.

What It Helps

Feldenkrais helps with strokes, arthritis, bursitis, back pain, spinal cord injury, cerebral palsy, multiple sclerosis, digestive difficulties, respiratory difficulties, musculoskeletal difficulties, and concentration problems.

Words of Wisdom/Cautions

There are no known side effects or unsafe conditions when provided by a trained practitioner.

The Alexander Therapy

What It Is

Alexander therapy is an educational process that identifies poor posture habits and teaches conscious control of movements that underlie better body mechanics. Frederick Mathias Alexander, an Australian actor who lost his voice while performing, developed this therapy. Discouraged by only temporary relief from medical treatments, he began studying how posture affected his voice. After 9 years of study and perfecting his technique, he began to train others.

How It Works

Alexander therapy teaches simple exercises to improve balance, posture, and coordination. It is done with gentle hands-on guidance and verbal instruction. It results in release of excess tension in the body, lengthens the spine, and creates greater flexibility in movement.

What It Helps

Many conditions that result from poor posture can be greatly helped. This technique is taught in many drama and music universities throughout the world.

Words of Wisdom/Cautions

This is safe therapy when performed by a credentialed therapist.

Mind–Body Therapies

Meditation/Relaxation

What It Is

Relaxation involves practices that shut down the fight or flight response of the body and settles the mind. Meditation is an ancient art of focused attention and is a practice to help the body reach a relaxed state. Relaxation has been found to reduce stress, which leads to many physical and mental health benefits. Herbert Benson, MD, from Harvard, researched meditation and documented its many benefits is his book titled *The Relaxation Response*.[4]

KEY POINT

Some of the benefits of reduced stress include decreased heart rate, breathing rate, blood pressure, and brain waves; improved mood; increased awareness; and spiritual calm.

How It Works

Two forms of meditation are *concentrative meditation* and *mindfulness meditation*. The former involves focusing on a sound, an image, or one's own breathing. By doing this process, a person reaches a state of calm and deepens attention and awareness. The latter form of meditation brings full awareness in the present moment. Mindfulness meditation teaches one to not allow outside distraction to interrupt focus on the present moment. This helps a person to slow down, become more relaxed, and have more insight into what is occurring in the immediate moment.

What It Helps

It helps with unlimited usage for physical symptoms, anxiety reduction, increased energy level, and increased sense of well-being.

Words of Wisdom/Cautions

Occasionally negative emotions or thoughts can surface indicating a need for referral for further professional consultation.

Biofeedback

What It Is

Biofeedback is a process of learned control of physical responses of the body. Through this therapy a person develops a deeper awareness and voluntary control over physical processes.

KEY POINT

With biofeedback, a person learns to use thought processes to control bodily processes.

How It Works

Through the use of instruments, a person is trained to relax and monitor changes through certain feedback devices. Meditation, relaxation, and visualization techniques are taught, and these techniques ultimately teach psychological control over physical processes.

What It Helps

It helps tension headaches, chronic pain, anxiety, asthma, and high blood pressure.

Words of Wisdom/Cautions

This is a harmless technique. Some Christian clients may be concerned about leaving the mind open to demonic influences during meditation; this concern should be explored before recommending this practice so as not to cause spiritual distress.

Guided Imagery

What It Is

Guided imagery is a mind–body technique that helps a person use imagination to relieve symptoms, heal disease, or promote relaxation. It is based on the belief that the mind and body are interconnected and work together in the healing process.

How It Works

A person can use guided imagery alone or be led by a practitioner. Sessions can last 10–30 minutes. Different imaging is used as a person is guided through the process. A quiet place is needed, free from distractions. Numerous studies have demonstrated physiologic and biochemical changes.

What It Helps

Almost any medical situation can benefit from guided imagery, especially if problem solving, relaxation, decision making, or symptom relief is useful. It is used frequently to prepare for surgery and to speed recovery after surgery. It can be used to enhance the immune system, reduce stress, and to induce a sense of well-being.

Words of Wisdom/Cautions

This is a harmless healing technique. This technique may reduce the need for medications, but medications should not be adjusted or stopped without first checking with a primary healthcare professional.

Hypnotherapy

What It Is

Hypnotherapy is a state of focused concentration or relaxation that is guided by a therapist. In this state, a person is open to suggestion.

Hypnosis dates back to ancient China and Egypt and was even included as part of surgical procedures. In the 18th century, Franz Mesmer, an Austrian physician, was known for a process of inducing trance states in people and is credited with introducing hypnotism into medicine. The term mesmerize was used to describe his process.

A surgeon, James Braid, developed the technique further in the mid-19th century and used it for pain control and as anesthesia in surgery; however, because over the years Vaudeville performers, magicians, and others exploited it, hypnosis became associated with superstition, quackery, and evil. It was not until 1958, when Milton Erickson, an American psychotherapist, demonstrated how psychosomatic symptoms could be resolved with hypnotherapy that the AMA finally accepted hypnotherapy.

How It Works

In a trance state, a state between sleep and waking, which is called an *alpha state*, a person is very relaxed. It is like awakening in the morning and not being fully conscious or fully connected with the surroundings. In this state, a person is very receptive to suggestions from a therapist. Everyone is unique in his or her receptivity to entering into a guided trance state. No one can enter this state by force, and in this state, there is full awareness of everything that is happening. In this hypnotic state, past events can be more easily remembered, and trauma and anxiety around such events can be resolved. When this happens, past events no longer affect present behavior negatively.

What It Helps

Hypnotherapy is a therapeutic tool that can be very helpful in managing many situations, including fears, anxiety, chronic pain, addictions, poor self-control, low self-esteem, and behavioral problems.

Words of Wisdom/Cautions

Situations that interfere with hypnotherapy are extreme fear, religious objections, skepticism, inability to trust the therapist, and inability to relax. Hypnotherapy is not suitable when there are serious psychiatric conditions.

Yoga

What It Is

Yoga uses stretching, breathing, body postures, and relaxation/meditation to restore and promote good mental and physical health. It has been practiced in India for thousands of years and, although it was introduced in the United States in the1890s, it did not become popular until the 1960s. The goal of yoga is to create balance between movement and stillness, which is said to be the state of a healthy body. Postures require little movement, but require mental concentration. Originally yoga was developed as part of a spiritual belief system, but our Western culture primarily uses it as a health practice for improved flexibility, strength, relaxation, and physical fitness.

KEY POINT

Yoga consists of breathing exercises, various stretching postures, and meditation.

How It Works

There are many styles of yoga, and most are performed in a class. Yoga consists of breathing exercises and various postures or poses (*asanas*) that promote stretching and toning. There are beginning, intermediate, and advanced stages of practices within the various styles of yoga. Each posture has specific benefits, and each session usually ends with some form of a relaxation exercise or meditation. People have been known to practice yoga well into their 80s.

What It Helps

Yoga helps with headaches, asthma, back pain, sciatica, insomnia, balance, coordination, circulation, concentration, flexibility, endurance, physical strength, range of motion, and immunity.

Words of Wisdom/Cautions

Certain positions can cause muscle injury if the body is forced into those positions. Knowing personal limitations and consistent practice are important keys to obtaining the most benefit from yoga.

T'ai Chi

What It Is

T'ai Chi is a discipline that has been practiced in China for centuries. It is a form of slow-moving exercise that assists in uniting the mind–body connection. It is a martial art form that has been described as *meditation in motion*. It combines physical movement, breathing, and meditation to bring about relaxation and a feeling of well-being. There are various styles of T'ai Chi, and some involve up to 108 different movements and postures. Much concentration and discipline is required, and it takes time to learn the proper motion and coordination. People of all ages and physical capabilities can practice the art form, and it develops endurance, and flexibility, decreases fatigue, and improves overall physical health.

How It Works

The Chinese believe T'ai Chi helps to increase the flow of *qi* (chi or universal life force) circulating throughout the body. The movements are learned in rhythmic coordinated patterns that slowly flow from one series of movements into another. Focus is placed on breath and the body's motion, which in turn rejuvenates, stretches, strengthens, releases tension, opens points, and calms and quiets the mind at the same time. The slow turning, twisting, and stretching allow every part of the body to be exercised without strain.

What It Helps

T'ai Chi helps with high blood pressure, nervous disorders, immune system, balance, stress-related disorders, circulation, panic attacks, concentration, insomnia, muscle tone, dizziness, internal organs, fibromyalgia, and spine and back problems.

Words of Wisdom/Cautions

There should be no ill effects from doing T'ai Chi. To prevent falls, it is important to assure that people have sufficient balance to stand and change positions during the movements.

Pharmacologic and Biologic Treatments

Aromatherapy

What It Is

Aromatherapy, an offshoot of herbal medicine, is the therapeutic inhalation or application of essential oils distilled from plants. It is a pharmacologic treatment because the chemicals found in the essential oils are absorbed by the body and result in specific effects. The benefits are either physical or mental/emotional or both.

How It Works

Essential oils stimulate the release of neurotransmitters in the brain. The sense of smell connects with the part of the brain that controls the autonomic (involuntary) nervous system. The resulting effects are calming, pain reducing, stimulating, sedating, or euphoric. These oils can also be applied to the skin through the use of carrier oils or lotions. Many have antibacterial, antiviral, antifungal, and anti-inflammatory and antiseptic properties. Oils placed on the skin are absorbed and enter the circulatory system and intercellular fluid. Inhaled oil attaches to oxygen molecules and circulate throughout the body. These oils are able to penetrate cell walls and transport oxygen and nutrients to the cell (see Chapter 23 for more information).

KEY POINT

Essential oils are very potent and are obtained through steam-distillation of various parts of plants (leaves, flowers, blossoms, fruits, bark, gum, and bulbs) and grasses.

What It Helps

Essential oils help with anxiety, headaches, depression, arthritis, fatigue, bronchitis, pain, bruises, sinusitis, colic, nausea, hormonal imbalance, indigestion, muscle strain, skin conditions, and many other conditions/symptoms.

Words of Wisdom/Cautions

There are many cautions with these very powerful essential oils.

- Use oils according to direction.
- Use only diluted oils—use in a carrier oil or lotion.
- Test for allergic reactions.
- Know what you are using.
- Use oils only from reputable companies.
- Store oils in a cool place.
- Keep away from children.
- Never apply oils to eyes.
- Some oils should never be taken internally (eucalyptus, hyssop, mugwort leaf, thuja, pennyroyal, sage, or wormwood).

Herbal Medicine

What It Is

Besides a way to accent flavor in foods, herbs and plants have been used by many cultures to treat illness for thousands of years. Herbal medicine is also called *botanical medicine* or *phytotherapy* (phyto means plant). Herbs are used as prevention, as well as for treating illnesses. Many drugs are derived from plants; however, most of the ingredients in today's drugs are chemicals. Medicinal uses of herbs and plants come from different parts of a plant. Some examples are leaves, flowers, stems, seeds, berries, bark, fruit, and roots depending on the plant and its specific use.

KEY POINT

Herbal medicine is used as a main form of healing in about 80% of the world.

Conventional medicine's approach to using plants is to pinpoint the active ingredient in the plant and extract it rather than use the whole plant. It is believed by many herbalists and other traditional healing systems (such as traditional Chinese medicine and Ayurvedic medicine) that isolating and using a specific ingredient may reduce the healing power of the plant and also possibly remove the built-in buffers that protect against side effects. This is based on the belief that active ingredients in plants work together synergistically. This means that the action of two or more plant ingredients working together produces an effect that cannot be produced with the individual extracted ingredient alone.

KEY POINT

Herbs are prepared in many different forms: teas, infusions, decoctions, tinctures, extracts, tablets, capsules, injections, oils, creams, and ointments.

How It Works

Herbs have classifications according to their effects on a person just like Western drugs. Classifications are adaptogenic, antihelmintic, anti-inflammatory, antimicrobial, antispasmodic, astringent, bitters, carminative, demulcent, diuretic, expectorant, hepatic, hypotensive, laxative, nervine, stimulant, and tonic. It is important to work with a knowledgeable practitioner in order to have guidance in selection both from the standpoint of the proper herb for the proper condition and also in selecting the right purity and potency of the herb. It is very important to use herbal preparations from a source that uses standardized dosages to guarantee the correct amount of herb in each batch produced. It is important to have guidance for the length of usage of an herb and whether it is being used as a tonic (prevention) or as a treatment.

Much research is being carried out presently that is allowing for a greater understanding of safe usage, especially in combination with Western medications. The information is changing almost daily (for more information, see Chapter 22).

What It Helps

Herbs are helpful for a wide range of illnesses frequently treated by Western medicines; however, knowing how to use them safely alone or in combination requires monitoring by a knowledgeable person. Herbs provide vitamins and nutrients that enhance wellness, and thus, they are very effective as preventative agents.

If an informed practitioner is not available for guidance, then a reliable resource that provides detailed information and safety measures is a must.

Words of Wisdom/Cautions

Infants, children, and pregnant women or women attempting pregnancy need special cautions and need to always seek supervision of any herbal usage. Likewise, anyone with chronic or serious illness or anyone using Western medications needs to inform and seek the guidance of a knowledgeable healthcare professional. Taking responsibility for becoming informed about herbs helps with the safe use of herbal preparations; however, seeking the advice of a professional herbalist is the greatest safety.

Remembering to inform your healthcare provider when seeking medical care is also of prime importance, especially if any Western medicine is prescribed. This will help prevent any side effects from any potential drug–herbal interactions that could occur because of incompatibility.

Today there are many options available in the quest to maintain or regain health and wellness. Being prepared to make appropriate individual choices regarding these options requires considerable thought and a thorough investigation. This investigation leads to an understanding of the concepts of wholeness (the inseparableness of mind/body/spirit) and insights into personal health beliefs. This investigation also leads to greater knowledge of self-awareness, self-responsibility, and self-nurturance and provides a clearer vision of personal needs and more personal power in developing a partnership with the healthcare provider.

A broader view of health allows for the realization that optimum health is a lifelong journey rather than an ultimate state of being. The goal of this journey is the maintenance of balance between health and illness. The attempt at maintaining this balance is thwarted with many challenges and choices. What is the extent of your personal knowledge of your health and wellness status? Is there a need to consult with a conventional medical health care provider if you choose to integrate a complementary therapy in your journey? What do you know about the origin, today's use, and safety of a specific non-Western medical therapy? Is it safe to combine the use of conventional and complementary healthcare therapies? Is the practitioner of choice knowledgeable and appropriately educated and trained? Will there be communication between your providers if necessary? In directing your own health care, these are but a few of the questions that need to be addressed. Selection of an appropriate complementary therapy requires much consideration, and the information provided here is offered as beginning guidance and assistance along the journey of self-discovery and balanced health.

Summary

Americans have shown a growing interest in complementary therapies because they are concerned about preventive health, adverse drug reactions, and personalized care offered by complementary practitioners. Although new to many Americans, many complementary therapies originated from ancient and non-Western healing traditions that have been used in other parts of the world for centuries.

Holistic care is not the same as complementary or alternative therapies. Holistic care implies a balance and harmony among mind, body, and spirit. It assumes that individuals take an active role in achieving maximum wellness. Although people can use complementary or alternative therapies as part of holistic care, the use of these therapies does not guarantee holism.

The five major categories of complementary therapies are: alternative systems of medical practice, manual healing therapies, mind–body therapies, pharmacologic/biologic treatments, and botanical/herbal medicine. Complementary therapies need to be used wisely. To use complementary therapies safely, people need to gather information to base decisions on facts, establish goals, and keep an open mind. They need to ask questions before using a complementary therapy, including these: What conditions respond best to it? How does it work? What should be expected? How long must it be used, and what are the harmful effects?

References

1. Eisenberg, D. (1998). Advising patients who seek alternative medical therapies. *The Integrated Medical Consult, 1*(1):4–5.
2. Fontaine, K. L. (2000). *Healing Practices: Alternative Therapies for Nursing*. Upper Saddle River, New Jersey: Prentice Hall.
3. Eliopoulos, C. (1999). *Integrating Conventional and Alternative Therapies: Holistic Care for Chronic Conditions*. St. Louis: Mosby, Inc.
4. Benson, H. (1975). *The Relaxation Response*. New York: Morrow.

Suggested Reading

Carlson, L. K. (2002). Reimbursement of complementary and alternative medicine by managed care and insurance providers. *Alternative Therapies in Health and Medicine, 8*(1):38–49.

Cerrato, P. L. (2001). Complementary therapies update. *RN, 61*(6):549–552.

Chopra, D. (2001). *Perfect Health, The Complete Mind/Body Guide.* New York: Random House.

Decker, G. (1999). *An Introduction to Complementary and Alternative Therapies.* Pittsburgh, PA: Oncology Nursing Press, Inc.

Earthlink, Inc. (2000). Alternative healthcare: is it the right alternative for you? *Blink, June/July,* p. 27.

Eisenberg, D. M. (1997). Advising patients who seek alternative medical therapies. *Annals of Internal Medicine, 127*(1):61–69.

Huebscher, R., & Shuler, P. A. (2003). *Natural, Alternative, and Complementary Health Care Practices.* St. Louis: Mosby.

Kirskey, K. M., Goodroad, B. K., Kemppainen, J. K., et al. (2002). Complementary therapy use in persons with HIV/AIDS. *Journal of Holistic Nursing, 20*(3):250–263.

Krohn, J., & Taylor, F. A. (2002). *Finding the Right Treatment. Modern and Alternative Medicine: A Comprehensive Reference Guide That Will Help You Get the Best of Both Worlds.* Point Roberts, WA: Hartley & Marks Publishers.

McCaleb, R. S., Leigh E., & Morien, K. (2000). *The Encyclopedia of Popular Herbs: Your Complete Guide to the Leading Medicinal Plants.* Roseville, CA: Prima Publishing.

McGovern, K., Lockhart, A., Malay, P., et al. (eds.). (2003). *Nurse's Handbook of Alternative and Complementary Therapies,* 2nd ed. Philadelphia: Lippincott Williams & Wilkins.

Olshansky, E. (2000). *Integrated Women's Health: Holistic Approaches for Comprehensive Care.* Gaithersburg, MD: Aspen Publications.

Skinner, S. E. (2001). *An Introduction to Homeopathic Medicine in Primary Care.* Gaithersburg, MD: Aspen Publishers, Inc.

Smith, D.W., Arnstein, P., Rosa, K. C., & Wells-Felderman, C. (2002). Effects of integrating therapeutic touch into a cognitive behavioral pain treatment program. *Journal of Holistic Nursing, 20*(4):367–387.

Stephenson, N. L. N., & Dalton, J. (2003). Using reflexology for pain management. *Journal of Holistic Nursing, 21*(2):179–191.

Strovier, A. L., & Carpenter, J. E. (2006). *Introduction to Alternative and Complementary Therapies.* Philadelphia: Haworth Press.

Trivieri, L., and Anderson, J. W. (eds.). (2002). *Alternative Medicine: The Definitive Guide,* 2nd ed. Berkeley, CA: Celestial Arts.

Young, J. (2007). *Complementary Medicine for Dummies.* New York: IDG Books Worldwide, Inc.

Resources

Alternative Systems of Medical Practice

Acupuncture

Acupuncture and Oriental Medicine Alliance
6405 43rd Avenue Ct., NW, Suite B
Greg Harbor, WA 98335
253-851-6896
www.aomalliance.org

American Academy of Medical Acupuncture
4929 Wilshire Blvd., Suite 428
Los Angeles, CA 90036
800-721-2177
www.medicalacupuncture.org

American Association of Acupuncture and Oriental Medicine
5530 Wisconsin Avenue, Suite 1210
Chevy Chase, MD 20815
888-500-7999
www.aaom.org

Ayurvedic Medicine

Ayurvedic Institute
11311 Menaul NE, Suite A
Albuquerque, NM 87112
505-291-9698
www.ayurveda.com

Homeopathy

National Center For Homeopathy
801 N. Fairfax Street, Suite 306
Alexandria, VA 22314
703-548-7790
www.homeopathic.org

North American Society of Homeopathy
1122 E. Pike Street, Suite 1122
Seattle, WA 98122
206-720-7000
www.homeopathy.org

Naturopathy

American Association of Naturopathic Physicians
3201 New Mexico Avenue NW, Suite 350
Washington, DC 20016
866-538-2267
www.naturopathic.org

Bodywork—Movement Therapy

The Alexander Therapy

American Society for the Alexander Technique
P.O. Box 60008
Florence, MA 01062
800-473-0620
www.alexandertech.com

The Feldenkrais Method

Feldenkrais Guild of North America
3611 SW Hood Avenue, Suite 100
Portland, OR 97239
800-775-2118
www.feldenkrais.com

The Trager Approach

Trager International
24800 Chagrin Blvd., Suite 205
Beachwood, OH 44122
216-896-9383
www.trager.com

Manual Healing Methods

Chiropractic

American Chiropractic Association
1701 Clarendon Blvd.
Arlington, VA 22209
800-637-6244
www.amerchiro.org

Federation of Chiropractic Licensing Boards
901 54th Avenue, Suite 101
Greely, CO 80634
970-356-3500
www.fclb.org

World Chiropractic Alliance
2950 N. Dobson, Suite 1
Chandler, AZ 85224
800-347-1011
www.worldchiropracticalliance.org

Craniosacral Therapy

Upledger Institute
11211 Prosperity Farms Road
Palm Beach Garden, FL 33410
561-622-4706
www.upledger.com

Energy Medicine/Healing

American Holistic Nurses Association
P.O. Box 2130
Flagstaff, AZ 86003
800-278-2462
www.ahna.org

Colorado Center for Healing Touch
12477 W. Cedar Drive, Suite 206
Lakewood, CO 80228
303-989-0581
www.healingtouch.net

Nurse Healers Professional Associates
3760 South Highland Drive, Suite 429
Salt Lake City, Utah 84106
801-273-3390
www.therapeutic-touch.org

International Society for the Study of Subtle Energies and Energy Medicine
11005 Ralston Road, Suite 100D
Arvada, CO 80004
303-278-2228
www.issseem.org

Reiki Training International
P.O. Box 2765
Indianapolis, IN 46206
800-506-1144

International Center for Reiki Training
21421 Hilltop St., Suite 28
Southfield, MI 48034
800-332-8112
www.reiki.org

Massage Therapy

American Massage Therapy Association
820 Davis Street, Suite 100
Evanston, IL 60201
847-864-0123
www.amtamassage.org

Associated Bodywork and Massage Professionals
800-458-2267
www.abmp.com

Massage Bodywork Resource Center
www.massageresource.com

Mind–Body Therapies

Biofeedback

Association of Applied Psychophysiology and Biofeedback and
Biofeedback Certification Institute
10200 West 44th Avenue, Suite 304
Wheat Ridge, CO 80033-2840
800-477-8892
www.aapb.org

Guided Imagery

Academy for Guided Imagery
30765 Pacific Coast Highway, Suite 369
Malibu, CA 90265
800-726-2070
www.interactiveimagery.com

Nurse Certificate Program in Imagery
Beyond Ordinary Nursing
P.O. Box 8177
Foster City, CA 94404
www.imageryrn.com

Hypnotherapy

American Board of Hypnotherapy
2002 E. McFadden Avenue, Suite 100
Santa Ana, CA 92705
800-872-9996
www.hypnosis.com

American Society of Clinical Hypnosis
140 N. Bloomingdale Road
Bloomingdale, IL 60108
630-980-4740
www.asch.net

Society for Clinical Hypnosis
128-A Kings Park Drive
Liverpool, NY 13090
315-652-7299
www.hypnosis-research.org

Meditation/Relaxation

American Meditation Institute
60 Garner Road
Averill Park, NY 12018
518-674-8714
www.americanmeditation.org

The Stress Reduction Clinic
Department of Medicine
University of Massachusetts Medical Center
45 Lake Avenue North
Worcester, MA 01655
508-856-1616
www.umassmed.edu/behavmed/clinical.cfm

The Center for Mind-Body Medicine
5225 Connecticut Avenue, NW, Suite 414
Washington, DC 20015
202-966-7338
www.cmbm.org

Tai Chi

Classic Tai Chi
Synerchi Publishing
P.O. Box 165
Penfield, NY 14526
www.classictaichi.com

Yoga

American Yoga Association
P.O. Box 19986
Sarasota, FL 34236
800-226-5859
www.americanyogaassociation.org

Yoga Alliance
122 W. Lancaster Avenue, Suite 204
Reading, PA 19607
877-964-2255
www.yogaalliance.org

Yoga Science Research Foundation
1228 Daisy Lane
East Lansing, MI 48823
517-351-3056
www.yogasite.com

Pharmacologic and Biologic Treatments

Aromatherapy

Institute of Aromatherapy
Aromatherapy Consultant Program
3108 Route 10 West
Denville, NJ 07834
973-989-1999
www.instituteofaromatherapy.com

National Association for Holistic Aromatherapy
4509 Interlake Avenue North, Suite 233
Seattle, WA 98103
206-547-2164
www.naha.org

The Institute of Integrative Aromatherapy
P.O. Box 18
Issaquah, WA 98027
877-363-3422
425-557-0805 (Office and Fax)
www.aroma-rn.com

Herbal Medicine

Herb Research Foundation
4140 15th Street
Boulder, CO 80304
800-748-2617
303-449-2265
www.herbs.org

American Botanical Council
6200 Manor Road
Austin, TX 78723
512-926-2345
www.herbalgram.org

American Herbalist Guild
1931 Gaddis Road
Canton, OH 30115
770-751-6021
www.americanherbalistsguild.com

Chapter 22

Herbal Remedies

OBJECTIVES

This chapter should enable you to

- Define *phytochemical*
- Discuss the actions of a tonic, an adaptogen, and an immune stimulant
- List at least eight forms in which an herb can be used
- Describe three precautions to observe when wildcrafting herbs
- Discuss precautions when using herbs with children
- Describe the common use and cautions of at least five popular herbs

Advances in medical technology have given us antibiotics, laser surgery, and organ transplants that have changed the face of health care; however, this mushrooming of technology has come at a cost, including new risks and the insidious belief that healthcare professionals and technology are the sources of health and healing.

We have not always looked to technology for solutions to health problems. There was a time when our ancestors were very aware of and connected to the healing power of nature. It was a natural part of human existence. Unfortunately, much of this information has been lost or ignored. Throughout the last century, in our quest for modern technology, we thought that we might be able to improve on nature.

A change is taking place, however, in which we are rediscovering that one needs to venture no further than the kitchen spice cabinet, backyard garden, or nearest woods to discover the abundance of herbs that can be readily used to influence human health and well-being. Indeed, we are literally surrounded by a bounty of medicinally charged leaves, flowers, seeds, barks, and roots. We are learning of the healing power of nature. Common garden weeds, such as St. John's Wort, and garden perennials, such as echinacea, are offering natural ways to improve health and treat illnesses. Many benefits can be found in developing a relationship with plants.

Employing the use of herbs from a holistic perspective is the best way to maximize their healing potential. This means using herbs in a way that addresses the whole person—mind/body/spirit—within the dynamic environment as opposed to just trying to control, suppress, or alleviate symptoms. It is important to incorporate the appropriate herbs into a larger effort of care that includes other lifestyle decisions and factors, such as nutrition, exercise, and stress reduction (much of which has been addressed in other chapters of this book).

KEY POINT

Rather than control specific symptoms, herbal therapy, when used holistically, considers the needs of the whole person: mind, body, and spirit.

Historical Uses of Herbs and Folklore

Let us take a quick look at where herbs have fit into the history of medicine. In the United States, an untold amount of information from millennia of cultural plant medicine use by indigenous people has been lost in just a few generations (see Exhibit 22-1). Fortunately, other countries and cultures have, to varying degrees, protected centuries of experiential data and records of plant use and effectiveness.

What remains quite valid about our history with plants is the fact that we have co-evolved with them through the ages, creating a very special and unique relationship. Plants contain most of the substances that are vital to our health, but not only in the form of vitamins, minerals, and enzymes. They also contain hormones and compounds that stimulate our body to produce chemical messengers known as neurotransmitters that are responsible for major communication systems within our bodies. There is a myriad of materials known as *phytochemicals* (plant chemicals), and science seems to be uncovering, on a daily basis, new active ingredients and information regarding our health connections with plants. These phytochemicals occur in plants in mind-boggling numbers and combinations. They exist in delicate balances, buffering, strengthening each other, and creating synergy within the plants.

EXHIBIT 22-1   Wisdom of the Ancients

One particularly interesting remnant of an ancient system of herbal use is referred to as the Doctrine of Signatures. This system suggested that the physical characteristics of the plant indicated its function or action. In other words, the color, shape, or appearance of the plant signified how it could be used. For example, a plant with a thick yellow root would indicate use for liver problems or red stems for blood conditions. This explanation is an oversimplification of a very intricate, insightful system of which too little information has survived to make it relevant or safe for use today; however, it is evidence of the tremendous depth of understanding and relationship people the world over once had with their environment.

KEY POINT

Synergy is the combined and/or cooperative action of individual parts that allows the total effect to be greater than the sum of their individual effects.

Phytochemicals are stored by the plants in concert with the sun, soil, air, and water, and they exist as a product and service of the plants' own healthy growth, function, and reproduction. Because of our co-evolution, they also occur in forms that our bodies can, for the most part, readily digest, assimilate, and use for maintaining vital and healthy function. Yes, there is still a lot of research to be done, but while science continues to unravel the mysteries, we can begin to reacquaint ourselves with and take advantage of the wealth of knowledge handed down to us by our ancestors. Today, 80% of the world's population still relies on plants as part of their primary health care. This percentage is not just a reflection of less developed countries—it includes those with advanced concepts of health care such as Germany and China where the systems recognize the undeniable benefits of integrating both modern conventional technology and traditional wisdom. (The scope of this subject extends far beyond what can be addressed in this chapter. For those interested in learning more about the history of herbal medicine, please refer to the Suggested Reading list at the end of the chapter.)

REFLECTION

What has been your attitude about the medicinal use of plants? Have you believed herbal medicine to be quaint folklore or legitimate therapy that just has not yet been proven in the laboratory? How does this influence your use of these products?

Phytochemicals' Actions on the Body

Now that we know that individual plants contain hundreds, maybe thousands, of different phytochemicals in varying combinations, it is important to also develop a sense of how they work in our bodies and how those actions differ from synthetic pharmaceuticals. Foremost, the very reason most of our modern drugs came to be was to provide a particular action: to do one thing and do it with authority. This is generally achieved through potent blocking, suppressing, and overriding mechanisms in the body. As a result, we have many very powerful and effective drugs at our disposal; however, along with their power comes a

---

Exhibit 22-2   Actions of Herbs

Tonic: an action nourishing to tissues or organ systems, such as with hawthorn for the heart

Adaptogen: the action of helping regain normal function in the presence of stress such as Siberian ginseng

Immune stimulant: stimulating the immune system to recognize and mount a fight against illness inducing invaders, such as with echinacea

---

ponderous incidence of side effects even when properly taken. Recently published research documents complications from improperly prescribed and used pharmaceuticals as the fourth leading cause of death in this country. Herbs, on the other hand, with their warehouse of constituents, often do a variety of things at once on different levels (see Exhibit 22-2); they support, strengthen, and balance our systems.

Herbs provide as important a role in helping to maintain good health as they do treating the symptoms and underlying causes of disease. In addition, many herbalists feel the range of influence on specific situations can be increased by combining a number of herbs and creating a formula or compound. The goal is to address different body tissues, thereby strengthening the overall effect of the remedy. For example, someone with premenstrual syndrome could use a formula that may include dandelion leaf to relieve symptoms of fluid retention, black cohosh to ease cramping, and chaste tree to help rebalance hormones and alleviate anxiety. Thus, depending on how deep a relationship you would like, becoming familiar with some of the known plant phytochemicals and their actions would give you an added advantage in choosing the herbs that would be most effective in a given situation and avoid possible side effects or conflicts with other herbs or treatments.

Getting Started

In getting started, it is important to familiarize yourself with the different forms in which herbs are available and their advantages and disadvantages. From the holistic perspective, the form of herb is just as important a consideration as the type of herb. If it is a tea and the person does not "do teas," it is not of much use. Most of us are used to taking our medicines in the form of a pill; however, this is not the only way, nor is it always the best or most effective method. Remember that a pill is a form that must first be digested before the medicine it contains can be absorbed, assimilated, and used. This is a process that is often compromised when someone is dealing with an illness. Teas and tinctures are in liquid form, and thus, they are more readily available to the body to absorb. Also, there is an entire science involving the solubility of phytochemicals in different solutions, some releasing their properties more readily in alcohol, others in water.

KEY POINT

Herbal remedies can be used in many forms, such as extracts, teas, infusions, decoctions, tinctures, capsules, compresses, poultices, liniments, salves, or ointments.

Most herbal remedies at some point in their creation, unless you just eat them fresh or dried in an unaltered state, involve an extraction process. Extracts are made by separating the active constituents (phytochemicals) from the inactive ones (which may include sugars, starch, etc.) with the use of a solvent. This concentrates the active ingredients, which can then be kept as fluid (known as a liquid extract) or condensed and dried into a powder (referred to as powdered extract, which can then be put into capsules or made into tablets). A more potent form of the herb is created by these processes and is generally more effective for dealing with health imbalances than simply eating fresh or raw dried herbs.

Tea is a liquid extract, with water being the solvent. This a great way to get your daily medicine, particularly tonic herbs, that nourish the body's various tissues and systems, especially when taken over a period of weeks or months—it also does not seem much like medicine. A cup of tea is a thoughtful thing to do for yourself or someone else, providing you the opportunity to add your own caring intention to the preparation. Relatively speaking, it is often the least expensive way to take your medicine.

There are two methods of tea making: infusion and decoction. An *infusion* is a gentle form of preparation designed to preserve the valuable nutrients and essential oils and is used to prepare the more delicate parts of plants—leaves, flowers, and fresh berries. Generally speaking, the herbs are placed in a covered container and steeped in freshly boiled water for 10–30 minutes. The proportions used will vary depending whether the herbs are fresh or dried, usually 1 teaspoon dried or 2 teaspoons fresh to 1 cup of water or 1 ounce of dried herb (roughly 2 ounces of fresh) to 1 quart of water. The second method, *decoction*, is used for harder parts of the plant (roots, bark, and seeds), which are gently simmered for 15 minutes to an hour. There are some wonderful books that extol the virtues of medicinal teas that include tried and true recipes to make it easy. Supplies are readily available at most health food stores, in ready-to-steep bags or as loose bulk herbs to custom blend to your needs and desires. For those interested, there is little that can be more gratifying than growing, picking, and using some herbs of your own, and it is fairly easy; however, teas may not be for everyone. They do take time and space, can be cumbersome to travel with, and may not appeal to some taste buds, although most herbalists will tell you that the tasting of the herb can be a very important part of the healing relationship. Additionally, there are some phytochemicals that are not water soluble (meaning that they are not accessible to water extraction).

There are health situations when forms other than teas are more appropriate. In these cases, other liquid extracts can be used such as tinctures, which will vary depending on the solvent used—generally *alcohol, vinegar, or glycerin*. Again, these preparations are made by the active ingredients literally being pulled out of the plant into the solution; the solvent then acts as a preservative. Of the three types of solvents, food-grade alcohol is most often used as it is the strongest and provides the longest shelf life, up to 3 years or longer; however, regardless of the type of solvent used, all tinctures are easy to carry and are readily absorbed by the body's digestive process. Some people object to the taste of alcohol tinctures (even though most can be concealed in juice or tea), and there are situations when even small amounts of alcohol are undesirable. The extracts made with glycerin are nonalcoholic and sweet-tasting (and thus child-friendly), but are considerably weaker in potency than the alcohol extracts. Likewise, vinegar extracts are not as potent as alcohol tinctures and not readily available commercially, but there are those who feel that vinegar, especially apple-cider vinegar, adds healing properties of its own. When using tinctures, follow specific manufacturers' recommendations for dosage.

Capsules may contain crushed, dried herbs or the more concentrated powdered extract. The size of the capsule will determine the dose of the unaltered dried herb, with the standard "double 00" capsules holding 500 mg. If the contents are powdered extract, the strength will be higher. This is one compelling reason why it is so important to develop the habit of reading labels, and thus, you know as clearly as possible what exactly you are getting (see Table 22-1).

External forms of herbal medicines also are extremely effective, and with many possible variations in form and content, they can be useful in a wide array of situations. For example, an infusion or decoction of echinacea or goldenseal can be used as a gargle to ease the inflammation of a sore throat. A compress is made by soaking a soft cloth in a warm or cool tea made with the appropriate herb and applied to an injury, sore, or wound to speed healing. A poultice is similar, but the herb itself is applied to the skin. This could be as quick and simple as crushing a fresh plantain leaf and pressing it to a bug bite or sting to bring relief, or as specific as mixing a combination of herbs, say garlic, mustard, and onions, wrapping them in gauze and securing them over the chest to break up the congestion of a cold. Herbal tea bags make a handy poultice (wet thoroughly and bandage where needed). Yet another very effective way to use a tea is as an herbal steam inhalation, breathing in the medicinal steam to lessen the inflammation, irritation, and discomfort of sinus infections or head colds. This also is a great idea to add to your routine to prevent illness, as many herbs that are used this way are antiviral and antibacterial, with the steam helping to keep the mucous membranes in top condition to fend off infection causing bugs.

Liniments are tinctures that are used only externally. Because the alcohol that they contain is usually the isopropyl (rubbing) type, a liniment absorbs quickly on the skin, carrying the medicine into the tissues. Salves and ointments are semisolid preparations designed for application to the skin using oil-base substances or beeswax with dried herbs.

TABLE 22-1 Points to Consider in Regard to Standardized Extracts and Whole Plant Products

Standardized Extract	Whole Plant Products
· Highly purified standard amount of specific constituents	· Can confirm active constituents present at a certain level
· Nonsynthetic powerful medicine	· Does not interfere with the natural synergistic balance of nature's intent
· Some herbs have organ-specific activities and indications	· Promotes traditional or holistic approach; prevention and nutrition
· Insures proper identification of plants	· Some variations in concentration of components depending on growing conditions
· Promotes more allopathic approach of treating symptoms	
· Clinical testing and research data are available	· Record of thousands of years of use and efficacy
· Evidence of increased incidence of side effects	· Less expensive than standardized extracts
· May lose all other activity, but targeted effect	· Solvents and preservatives typically include alcohol, vinegar, water, and glycerin
· Solvents such as hexane are involved in the extraction process; solvent residues can be liver toxins	
· Takes plant constituents out of context; perpetuates the idea that we can outsmart or improve on nature	

Note: It stands to (holistic) reason to determine what will serve the individual best in each situation. Perhaps employing standardized extract in more acute cases and relying on whole plants for the majority of health needs involving nutrition, prevention, and tonification (tonics). The important issue is having access to and being able to use what works best for the individual in a given scenario.

They are not meant to blend into the skin but to form a protective outer layer that holds the medicine in place and prolongs the time that the herbs remain moist. (Included in the Suggested Readings are books that go into great detail about making your own remedies, some providing extremely helpful illustrations of each step and pictures of commonly used herbs. In addition there is a list of suppliers for finding needed materials.)

Cultivating Herbal Wisdom

After you have made the decision to incorporate herbal medicine as part of your holistic health approach, some general guidelines and tips can help make your relationship with plants rewarding and safe. Become familiar with a few herbs. A single herb can offer multiple health benefits, and thus, you may find most of your herbal needs can be met from a few plants. Attend one of the increasingly available classes and workshops. To locate courses and events, check with local health food stores, wellness centers, and universities. Also, the American Herbalists Guild and the American Botanical Council (listed in the resources section) are great organizations to check with regarding educational programs.

When deciding where to buy herbs, try to purchase locally and organically grown produce when possible. Become attuned to looking for sustainably harvested products (plants that are collected in an ecologically and environmentally conscious manner). This may require a little investigation but is well worth the effort. Search for reputable companies, particularly those with the reputation of being in the business for more reasons than just making a profit. The quality of the medicine will be enhanced by the social consciousness and good intentions of the company producing it.

Some precautions are needed when gathering your own herbs from the wild (*wildcrafting*). First, be absolutely sure that you properly identify the plant, as there are many examples of different plants that resemble each other very closely, some of them being very toxic. Be aware of the potential for chemical/pesticide contamination where you pick. For instance, do not pick along busy roads where the plants are exposed to many different pollutants from auto exhaust to detergent-laden runoff. Also, know plants well enough to avoid picking them if they are endangered species. All of these precautions can be disregarded if you are in a position to grow some herbs on your own. There are some books listed at the end of this chapter to help you do that.

For best results when using herbs, be consistent, and take them in the recommended amounts and with the recommended frequency. If taking something long term (as a tonic), it is a good idea to omit the herb at regular intervals: for instance, 5 days on/2 days off or 1 month on/1 week off—the individual situation and the herb used will help determine the schedule.

When treating a specific condition, avoid starting herbs that are generally promoted as good for the condition without some assessment. Consider how you feel and what may have contributed to or precipitated the situation. Do not ignore symptoms or delay seeking the most appropriate care or therapy. If you have a known problem, consult with a healthcare practitioner, especially if you are taking other medications. The ideal approach in these situations is to work with an experienced professional herbalist. If you do not know of one, try contacting the American Herbalists Guild to see whether there is a member in your area. In lieu of an herb-savvy healthcare professional, the safest way to proceed is with one herb at a time.

> **KEY POINT**
>
> Remember that the term *natural* does not necessarily mean *safe!*

You will do well to remember that herbs are medicines and need to be used appropriately and correctly. It is important to know the dosage range and understand that a higher dose does not necessarily mean greater effectiveness. Also, in regard to safety, you must consider individual allergies and sensitivities, particularly if taking an herb for the first time start with a low dose (perhaps half the recommended dose) and work up to a standard dose over a couple days.

> **KEY POINT**
>
> When using herbs with children particular attention must be paid to dose. A general rule is to use half the adult dose for children ages 7 to 12 years and one-quarter of the dose for children less than 7 years of age. Of course, the same guidelines of safety must be applied, as are considerations for the specific situation and individual child. Using herbs with infants should only be done with the guidance of a healthcare practitioner.

Be aware that there are definitely situations when the use of specific herbs is inappropriate and contraindicated (should be avoided), as they may give rise to side effects or complicate the situation. This is particularly true during pregnancy and breastfeeding. Although there seems to be information released daily regarding drug/drug and food/drug interactions. To date, relatively little is known about interactions between synthetic pharmaceuticals and herbs. Until more research is available, use common sense and check several reliable resources, including the practitioner who prescribed the medication. Healthcare providers need to be kept aware of all medicines, herbs, remedies, and supplements that are being taken by their patients. A growing number of pharmacists are becoming more knowledgeable about herbs, and many have access to computer databases that can help alert people to possible undesirable interactions to avoid side effects. The literature shows that most problems related to using herbs arise from misuse, allergic reactions, or improper combining with pharmaceuticals, all of which can be avoided by taking the responsibility to use herbs wisely, thoughtfully, and with respect for the abundance of health that they offer.

The following pages list some of the more popular and useful herbs readily available, along with a combination of information gathered from time-tested experience and what modern science has validated. This information is by no means all-encompassing but is offered as a place to begin.

Quick Review of Some Popular Herbs

Burdock (*Arctium lappa*)

Family: Compositae

Other names: Beggars buttons, cockle buttons, cocklebur, burr seed, hardock

Habitat: Open fields, roadsides, and waste places

Parts used: Root and seed

Common uses: Blood cleanser/purifier (alternative)

Cautions: Do not take during pregnancy. It may cause dermatitis in sensitive individuals. It can affect blood sugar in people with diabetes and produces diuretic effect in some people. Antibiotics and medications taken to treat gout, cancer, or HIV may interact with burdock.

Burdock is a large biannual plant growing up to 6 feet tall with huge leaves and a deep taproot that can reach 30 feet in length. Small purple flowers appear at the top of a single stalk in late spring of the second year and mature into seed heads, which readily stick to almost anything they touch. These are also known as beggars buttons because they were once used to fasten clothing together. The concept of Velcro is based on the sticky nature of burdock seed heads.

In Japan, the long taproot is known as *Gobo* and is used for food. Fresh, young roots can be sliced and added to a stir-fry or soup to make a nutritious meal. In general, it is an important tonic herb, which is considered gentle and nourishing. Traditionally, burdock root has been used as a blood purifier because of its ability to support the body's function in elimination of waste products via the liver. Herbalists use the root as a mild diuretic (increasing fluid elimination through the kidneys) and to promote sweating during some illnesses. A *decoction* of the root or tincture of the seeds can be used for dry skin disorders, such as eczema and psoriasis. Additionally, some cases of acne respond to treatment with burdock.

A root poultice or oil infusion of leaves can be applied to skin sores and leg ulcers. A compress made with a strong decoction will help treat topical fungal infections.

Black Cohosh (*Cimicifuga racemosa*)

Family: Ranunculaceae

Other names: Black snake root, fairy candles, bugbane

Habitat: Densely shaded, deciduous woods

Parts used: Dried root and rhizome

Common uses: General anti-inflammatory, menopausal symptoms, menstrual cramps, antispasmodic, sedative

Cautions: Large doses (over 2 teaspoons) may cause headache. Do not use during pregnancy or while nursing. Take with food to avoid stomach irritation with long-term use.

Black cohosh is a perennial plant that often reaches 6 feet in height and produces a rather showy spike of white flowers in mid-summer. It is a spectacular site when the sunlight filters down though the woodland canopy and strikes individual "candles" setting them aglow. This herb was greatly valued by Native Americans as a remedy for joint pain. It is often used as part of a formula (in combination with other herbs) to reduce inflammation of joints and soft tissues. This is an action people have found useful in easing the discomfort of some forms of arthritis, bursitis, and fibromyalgia. It is also has been thought to have a role in normalizing to the female reproductive system, providing relief of uterine pain and decreasing menopausal symptoms, such as hot flashes and anxiety; however, research results concerning its effectiveness are mixed. Because black cohosh can reduce spasms, it can be an aid in treating whooping cough and relaxing tense muscles. Black cohosh can also be used as a tincture or a decoction.

Calendula (*Calendula officinalis*)

Family: Compositae

Other names: Pot marigold

Habitat: Mediterranean area, however, it can be cultivated in any good garden soil.

Parts used: Flower petals

Common uses: Topically for healing skin and mucous membranes, internally for stomach ulcers, fevers, and menstrual cramps

Cautions: Do not take during pregnancy or when breastfeeding.

This bright yellow member of the marigold family is native to the Mediterranean region and lacks the strong smell of its more familiar nonmedicinal cousin. Almost anyone can easily grow calendula in a sunny location.

Calendula's anti-inflammatory and wound-healing properties make it a very useful herb. As an ointment, it can be applied to bruises, cuts, and scrapes. In the form of a tincture, it is a wonderful mouth rinse for red, irritated gums, gingivitis, and pyorrhea. A tea can be used as an aid in healing mouth tissues after oral surgery, as well as treating a sore throat or mouth ulcers. Just gargle and rinse. A poultice or compress can be applied to varicose veins and bruises. A tea or glycerite tincture used topically can help with healing bedsores. Although calendula is considered a mild remedy, it is effective as a tea to soothe unpleasant conditions like stomach ulcers. Externally, it can often reduce the effects of eruptions, such as measles or shingles. For day-to-day use, calendula cream makes skin feel soft and silky. In the form of a lotion, it is an excellent beauty aid for cleansing and soothing the skin.

Chasteberry (*Vitex agnus-castus*)

Family: Verbenaceae

Other names: Chaste tree, monk's pepper, hemp tree

Habitat: Mediterranean region of Asia

Parts used: Fruit

Common uses: Female tonic, kidney tonic, and thyroid tonic

Cautions: Chasteberry may affect certain hormone levels. Women who are pregnant or taking birth control pills or who have a hormone-sensitive condition (such as breast cancer) should not use chasteberry. Do not take during pregnancy or while breastfeeding. It may cause *urticaria* (itching). Because chasteberry may affect the dopamine system in the brain, people taking dopamine-related medications, such as selegiline, amantadine, and levodopa should avoid using chasteberry.

Chasteberry is a deciduous shrub growing up to 10 feet high with flower spikes made up of dense, showy clusters of pale, lilac blue flowers. In folklore, the plant was given the name of *monk's pepper* because of the alleged use of the fruit in monasteries for its ability to reduce male libido.

As a female tonic, chasteberry has been used to reduce common symptoms associated with imbalances of the menstrual cycle and menopause. It is believed to work through the female pituitary gland, which is responsible for the secretion of the hormones that regulate the ovaries. Because of this mechanism of action, it is a primary herb in helping menopausal symptoms, such as hot flashes and mood swings. Although some small studies support the benefit of this herb, additional scientific studies are needed to draw conclusive results. Chasteberry can be safely taken for months at a time with intermittent breaks to check if it is still needed.

Chasteberry can be used as a tea or a tincture.

Cinnamon (*Cinnamomum zeylanicum*)

Family: Lauraceae

Other names: Cassia

Habitat: Tropical Asia

Common uses: Antiviral, antibacterial, analgesic (pain relieving), mild digestive disorders and intestinal cramping in children and adults, flatulence, circulatory stimulant

Parts used: Bark

Cautions: Do not use with active stomach ulcers or during pregnancy. Some individuals may be sensitive and develop contact irritation.

Cinnamon is an evergreen with dense, leathery leaves that grows 30 to 40 feet tall. It is a tropical tree native to China. Cinnamon is used as both a food and a medicine. Although widely known for adding a pleasing, mellow flavor to desserts and ethnic foods, it is very safe as a medicine for children and adults. As a tea for nausea, vomiting, and motion sickness, it is pleasant and soothing.

Ground cinnamon can reduce diarrhea, especially if mixed in applesauce, because applesauce contains pectin, which helps bind the bowels. Cinnamon also possesses antibacterial properties.

Cinnamon can be ingested as fresh spice with foods or in capsules.

Cayenne (*Capsicum annum*)

Family: Solanaceae

Other names: Hot pepper, red pepper

Habitat: Tender annual can be cultivated in any good garden soil

Common uses: Stimulate circulation, aid in nerve pain, anti-inflammatory

Parts used: Dry, ground pods without seeds

Caution: Do not use the seeds (as they can be too irritating). Use with caution during pregnancy. Do not use on broken or injured skin. Avoid getting capsicum in the eyes. Some individuals may develop sensitivity to both internal and external applications. Using capsaicin cream on the skin may increase the risk of cough associated with angiotensin-converting enzyme inhibitors. Capsaicin may decrease the effectiveness of aspirin to relieve pain and may increase the risk of bleeding associated with aspirin. Capsaicin may increase the risk of bleeding associated with certain blood-thinning medications. It is not recommended to take capsicum for more than 2 days at a time.

Cayenne is popular as a condiment for food, especially in Asian, Mexican, and Indian cuisines. Recently, it has gained popularity in contemporary medicine as a topical cream to reduce nerve pain and to reduce itching and inflammation associated with psoriasis. It has been shown effective in treating mild frostbite, muscle tension, rheumatism, and chronic lumbago (lower back pain) by increasing circulation. Administering capsaicin via the nose seems to help relieve cluster headaches; this should be done by a trained professional.

Internal uses include stimulating the appetite and the prevention of atherosclerosis (plaque buildup in the arteries). Cayenne is available in capsule form, which helps in avoiding its hot, spicy sensation. Many topical ointments are available over the counter. Always follow the manufacturer's directions.

Dandelion (*Taraxacum officinale*)

Family: Compositae

Other names: Piss-a-bed, teeth of the lion, *Dent de' Leon*

Habitat: Lawns, meadows, and roadsides

Parts used: Whole plant, leaves, flowers, roots, stem

Common uses: Blood tonic, diuretic, digestive bitter, stimulates the liver

Cautions: Do not collect from sprayed lawns or roadsides.

This ubiquitous little weed, which is the bane of many homeowners, is indeed a wonderful tonic and medicine, with every part having uses. The leaves are a rich source of calcium, magnesium, sodium, zinc, manganese, copper, iron, phosphorus, and vitamins C and D. It is so nutritious that it made the top of the list in a Japanese vegetable survey of the world's most nutrient-dense plants! The golden yellow flowers are high in flavonoids and antioxidants, and a good way to use them is in savory spring biscuits or salads. The tender young leaves are also good steamed, sautéed, or raw in salads. The leaves as a medicine are a gentle, potassium-sparing (will not deplete the body of vital potassium) diuretic, making it useful in some types of congestive heart failure, high blood pressure, and water retention related to premenstrual syndrome. It is believed to support and strengthen liver function while reducing liver congestion and enhancing the flow of bile and that dandelion's bitter action stimulates digestion, absorption of nutrients, and elimination of wastes. These are some of the reasons that the dandelion was usually one of the plants used to make traditional spring tonics. Despite the long-term use of the herb, there is limited evidence supporting this. After a long sedentary winter eating heavy foods, people took advantage of the freshly sprouting herbs around them to effect their own internal spring cleaning.

Seek the advice of your practitioner or medical doctor if your symptoms include pain or the whites of your eyes are yellow.

Dong Quai (*Angelica sinensis*)

Family: Umbelliferae

Other names: Tang kwei (there are a variety of spellings and pronunciations)

Habitat: China

Common uses: Premenstrual syndrome, menopause, balancing female hormones, anemia, heart and circulatory tonic, antispasmodic

Parts used: Root

Caution: Individuals who have mid-cycle spotting or menstrual flooding should not take dong quai. Do not take during pregnancy.

This is a small, fern-leafed, aromatic plant that is native to China. Dong quai is a much revered traditional Chinese tonic herb and can be found in many oriental grocery stores. The roots, which are the parts used, are often sliced and incorporated in soups and stews. In the West, it is used as a circulatory stimulant and as a laxative in older people. It has been promoted to help nourish women with long menstrual cycles, bloating, and heavy bleeding with associated weakness, mild anemia (because of its significant iron content), and menopausal symptoms of hot flashes, skin crawling, and vaginal dryness. Although

Dong quai has many historical and theoretical uses based on animal studies, there is little human evidence supporting the effects of Dong quai for any condition. Most of the available clinical studies have either been poorly designed or reported insignificant results. Also, most have examined combination formulas containing multiple ingredients in addition to Dong quai, making it difficult to determine which ingredient may cause certain effects.

Dong quai can be added to any soup by placing the roots in a cheesecloth bag and removing it before serving. This herb can also be taken as a tea or tincture.

Echinacea (*Echinacea angustifolia, prupurea, or pallida*)

Family: Compositae

Other names: Purple coneflower

Habitat: Prairies, meadows; is easily cultivated

Parts used: Root, whole flowering head

Common uses: Immune system stimulant, anti-inflammatory, antibacterial

Cautions: Do not use with autoimmune diseases, such as lupus, some forms of arthritis, or AIDS. Because it stimulates the immune system, it has the potential of causing a flare-up. People with allergies to ragweed, chrysanthemums, marigolds, and daisies may have allergic reactions to echinacea.

Echinacea once grew in abundance on the Great Plains. Native Americans used this plant for medicinal purposes long before White settlers arrived on the shores of North America. It is now grown commercially with tons being exported to Europe annually. It has also become a common garden perennial, growing well in most sunny, dry locations and attracting butterflies.

Many people know echinacea as the immune herb. It has been used to prevent a cold or flu or shorten the duration and severity of symptoms, although research supporting this has yielded mixed views. A tincture is an effective way to take this herb for this purpose. Be aware that a good quality preparation will make the inside of the mouth tingle for a short period of time. The most appropriate and effective use is on exposure to a bacterial or viral infection or at the first signs of the same. The strategy most people find effective is to use the tincture, taking one or two droppers full every 2 to 3 hours as long as symptoms exist (or a couple of days), four times a day for another 2 to 3 days.

A less well-known use for echinacea is as a topical treatment for skin infections, such as boils, carbuncles, and bug bites. For this purpose, a strong tea or tincture can be applied as a compress. A tea may also serve as a mouthwash or gargle for gingivitis or inflamed sore throat.

Garlic (*Allium sativium*)

Family: Allium

Other names: Stinking rose

Habitat: Any good garden soil

Parts used: Individual cloves from the bulb

Common uses: Heart tonic, blood thinner, lung infections, lower cholesterol, lower blood pressure

Cautions: Do not take medicinal amounts of garlic if you are on blood thinners (such as Coumadin) or high daily doses of vitamin E without medical advice. Discontinue at least 1 week before any surgical procedure, to avoid prolonged bleeding. Garlic has been found to interfere with the effectiveness of saquinavir, a drug used to treat HIV infection. Its effect on other drugs has not been well studied.

Garlic was cultivated over 5000 years ago. It is sometimes know as the stinking rose because of its acrid smell when sliced or chopped. Garlic is rich in germanium, which is a powerful antioxidant, and sulfur, which can reduce the risk of stomach, lung, and bowel cancers. In World War I and World War II, garlic was used as a wound dressing because of its strong antibacterial and antiviral properties.

Garlic is both a food and a medicine as many herbs are—adding to the wisdom "let your medicine be your food and your food be your medicine." The activity of garlic makes it good for preventing atherosclerosis (buildup of plaque in the veins and arteries); although some evidence indicates that taking garlic can slightly lower blood cholesterol levels, studies done by the National Center for Complementary and Alternative Medicine have not drawn the same conclusions. It also acts as a mild blood thinner and can help lower blood lipids (cholesterol).

Garlic possesses potent antimicrobial (antibacterial, antiviral, and antifungal) activity, but it is best used fresh and uncooked for this purpose. Because the medicinal volatile oils are excreted through the lungs, it is useful for respiratory infections, such as colds and bronchitis. The suggested dose is to crush two to three raw cloves (the small sections of the garlic bulb) four times a day.

Because garlic can be unpleasant if taken straight, mixing it with a little honey, yogurt, or applesauce is very helpful. Try chopping the clove and placing it on a spoon. Do not chew it, but wash it down with water (like a pill). This method can help reduce the taste and residual odor. Also, raw garlic can be delicious and medicinal eaten in the form of pesto or grated over pasta. Because of the high levels of volatile oil compounds, garlic can be irritating to the stomach lining despite taking it with food. If irritation occurs, discontinue use for a period of time then restart at a small dose.

A great variety of commercial products are available, manufactured to minimize the odor and other less desirable effects. Some of these have been the subject of research for their effects on cholesterol and blood pressure and are quite effective; however, for the antimicrobial action and cost effectiveness, fresh organically grown garlic is still the best bet.

Ginkgo (*Ginkgo biloba*)

Family: Ginkgoaceae

Other names: Maidenhair tree

Habitat: Native to China

Common uses: Improve circulation

Parts used: Leaves

Caution: Some individuals may have allergic reactions. Ginkgo dilates blood vessels; therefore, individuals who have fragile blood vessels and a tendency to bleed easily should not take ginkgo. Those with a history of stroke-related aneurysm (bleeding as opposed to blood clot) should avoid ginkgo as should those on blood-thinning therapies, such as Coumadin. Uncooked ginkgo seeds contain a chemical known as ginkgotoxin, which can cause seizures. Consuming large quantities of seeds over time can cause death.

Ginkgo trees are among the oldest living plants in the world. Their survival is partly explained by the fact that they were considered sacred trees by the Chinese and therefore protected. Recently, cultivated trees have proven to be one of the finest specimen trees for inner cities, thriving undeterred by pests and pollution. These are usually the trees you see growing out of cracks in the sidewalk.

Ginkgo is one of the most researched herbs in the world. It has many uses, but most people know ginkgo as the memory herb. It is believed to help if poor memory is caused by insufficient blood flow to the brain. Increased circulation to the brain may help dementia (memory loss and confusion often in old age), Alzheimer's disease, vertigo (dizziness, lightheadedness), disorientation (confusion), and tinnitus (ringing in the ears). Some promising results have been seen in studies, but larger, well-designed research studies are needed.

The National Center for Complementary and Alternative Medicine is funding research that includes studies on ginkgo for other conditions for which it has been used, including asthma, symptoms of multiple sclerosis, vascular function (intermittent claudication), cognitive decline, sexual dysfunction caused by antidepressants, and insulin resistance.

Take tinctures as recommended by the manufacturer for up to 2 to 3 months before evaluating improvement. Because of the blood-thinning potential of ginkgo, consult your practitioner or herbalist before self-treatment.

Ginseng (American ginseng [*P. quinquefolius L.*], Asian/Chinese/Korean ginseng [*Panax ginseng*], Siberian ginseng [*Eleutherococcus senticosus*])

Family: Araliaceae

Other names: Ginseng

Habitat: Siberia, China, Northern Korea

Parts used: Root bark

Common uses: Normalize body systems, help in adapting to stress (adaptogen)

Cautions: Breast tenderness in some normally menstruating women. Some individuals may develop high blood pressure and should discontinue use; individuals with hypertension should not use. Occasionally, headaches and nervousness have been reported with ginseng use.

Siberian ginseng is a relative of American and Chinese ginsengs. It was first studied in Russia for its effects on productivity of factory workers and was shown to increase productivity and reduce the incidence of disease. In studies among athletes, endurance, speed, and stamina were increased, and recovery time was shorter.

Siberian ginseng is used as a tonic remedy for people who are stressed out, overworked, and burning the candle at both ends. It is milder and less stimulating than American ginseng and greatly valued for its ability to help the body adapt to and handle stress.

Ginseng appears to have antioxidant effects that may benefit people with heart disorders. Although additional research is needed in this area, some studies suggest that ginseng also reduces oxidation of low-density lipoprotein (LDL or "bad") cholesterol and brain tissue. Several studies suggest ginseng may lower blood sugar levels in patients with type 2 diabetes before and after meals.

It can be taken as a tea or tincture for up to 3 months at a time. Then take a break and re-evaluate how you are feeling.

Goldenseal (*Hydrastis canadensis*)

Family: Ranunculaceae

Other names: Yellow root

Habitat: Deciduous woodlands (endangered species)

Common uses: Antibacterial, anti-inflammatory, antifungal

Part used: Rhizome and root

Caution: Should not be used by women who are pregnant or breastfeeding or with infants and small children. Do not exceed the recommended dose. It is not meant for long-term use.

Goldenseal is native to deciduous woodlands of North America. Overcollection and misuse have made it an endangered species. Although it can be cultivated, it is a slow and tricky process. Fortunately, there are other herbs that contain some of the same powerful constituents as goldenseal.

Clinical studies on a compound found in goldenseal, berberine, suggest that the compound may be beneficial for certain infections—such as those that cause some types of diarrhea, as well as some eye infections; however, goldenseal preparations contain only a small amount of berberine, and thus, it is difficult to extend the evidence about the effectiveness of berberine to goldenseal. Goldenseal may be wasted on systemic (distributed by the blood stream) diseases. It will not help with general malaise, fever, or aches and pains. Other herbs, such as echinacea, are better suited for helping to fight the flu or a cold. Suggested and appropriate uses for goldenseal include urinary tract infections, gastritis, and athlete's foot. It is a very strong herb, and a little goes a long way.

Use a tea for nasal wash, eyewash (sterile tea solution) for conjunctivitis, and as a mouth rinse for gum disease, infection, or sore throat. When preparing an eyewash, carefully strain the tea through a coffee filter then reheat to sterilize. Cool to room temperature for use.

Lemon Balm (*Melissa officinalis*)

Family: Laminacea

Other names: Sweet Mary, honey plant, cure-all, dropsy plant, Melissa

Habitat: Native to the Mediterranean region and western Asia. Lemon balm will grow vigorously in average soil in temperate climates; it is a common garden herb.

Common uses: Antibacterial, antiviral, antidepressant, nervine (calms nervousness), insomnia

Parts used: Fresh leaves are preferred; dry leaves can be used.

Caution: Few studies have investigated the safety and effectiveness of lemon balm alone, except for topical use.

Lemon balm is a mild, aromatic, tasty, and effective remedy. It can be safely used to settle digestive problems. Several studies have found that lemon balm combined with other calming herbs (such as valerian, hops, chamomile) helps reduce anxiety and promote sleep. It has been know for centuries as the gladdening herb. Just sniffing fresh lemon balm can lift one's spirits. The crushed leaves, when rubbed on the skin, are used as a repellant for mosquitoes. A poultice or compress (made by soaking a cloth in a strong tea) can be used to ease the discomfort of herpes lesions or shingles.

For cold sores, mix a few drops of lemon balm essential oil with 2 to 3 tablespoons of glycerin and dab on the sore.

Licorice Root (*Glycyrrhiza glabra*)

Family: Leguminosae

Other names: Sweet root

Habitat: Southeastern Europe and western Asia

Common uses: Gastric irritation, tonic, expectorant (helps remove secretions from the chest), anti-inflammatory

Parts used: Root

Caution: Licorice should be avoided by individuals with high blood pressure, kidney disease, and edema. Large amounts over time can cause sodium retention and potassium depletion. Pregnant women should avoid using licorice as a supplement or consuming large amounts of licorice as food, as some research suggests it could increase the risk of preterm labor.

This perennial member of the pea family has long been cultivated for its flavorful root. Licorice has been a popular ingredient in candy and to disguise the unpleasant taste of other medicine. It is an integral part of traditional Chinese medicine and is used to balance other herbs used in a formula. Although traditionally used to relieve gastric irritation and stomach ulcers, research supporting this is inconclusive at this time.

Milk Thistle (*Silybum marianum*)

Family: Compositae

Other names: St. Mary's thistle

Habitat: Originated in Europe but will grow in any temperate climate (can become a noxious weed)

Common uses: Liver tonic, liver protectant, stimulating breast milk production

Parts used: Leaves, seeds

Caution: Do not take during pregnancy. Can cause mild diarrhea in large doses.

Milk thistle is a stout, hardy, invasive, annual plant. It can grow to up to 3 feet high, sporting dark green, scallop-edged spiny leaves with white streaks. The petals of the solitary purple flowers end in sharp spines. Although the leaves and seeds both have medicinal value, the seed contains the highest amount of the active component *sylibin*, which is credited with the ability to protect the liver from the damage caused by many drugs, including chemotherapy. There have been some studies of milk thistle on liver disease in humans, but these have been small. Some promising data have been reported, but study results at this time are mixed. The National Center for Complementary and Alternative Medicine is studying milk thistle's benefits for chronic hepatitis C and nonalcoholic steatohepatitis (liver disease that occurs in people who drink little or no alcohol). The National Cancer Institute and the National Institute of Nursing Research are also studying milk thistle for cancer prevention and to treat complications in HIV patients.

Silybum marianum was named milk thistle because of the traditional use of a tea from the leaves to stimulate milk production in nursing mothers. The leaves also enhance digestion.

For therapeutic purposes, standardized extracts (tinctures and freeze-dried extracts) are probably most appropriate because of the high concentration of active constituents that are most soluble in alcohol.

Plantain (*Plantago major, lanceolata*)

Family: Plantaginacea

Other names: White man's foot

Habitat: Common weed of lawns, gardens, and meadows

Common uses: Topical and internal antibacterial, anti-inflammatory, demulcent (soothing) coughs, wound healing, insect bites and stings, seed can be used as a bulk laxative

Parts used: Leaves, roots, seeds

Caution: Do not collect plantain from contaminated areas or sprayed lawns. Some individuals may be allergic to plantain.

The Native Americans named plantain white man's foot because it appeared to sprout up in the footsteps of the white settlers as they moved west. It is now common throughout most of the United States. The dark green, glossy, ribbed leaves radiate from the ground. Beneath the earth are the short, dense, radiating, brown roots. The flowers and seeds form at the top of tall stalks.

A poultice of the leaves of the plant has been used effectively for insect or spider bites and bee stings. In an emergency, plantain can be gathered from a lawn or meadow, chewed up, and applied directly onto the bite or sting; it is then covered and kept it in place for 1 to 2 hours. The pain and swelling will quickly diminish. This remedy often works better than over-the-counter pharmaceuticals. A poultice can also be applied to cuts, scrapes, and burns to aid in healing. Plantain leaf tea or juice (combine with tomato, carrot, or vegetable juice) is an effective way to soothe the symptoms of gastritis, irritable bowel, or colitis and relieve the discomfort from urinary tract infections. A tea of the leaf or root is also a mild, soothing expectorant (facilitates removal of secretions from the lungs), which makes it useful for treating bronchitis and lung congestion. The seeds are a rich source of zinc and psyllium, which is a popular bulk laxative.

Rosemary (*Rosmarinus officinalis*)

Family: Labiatae

Other names: Dew of the Sea

Habitat: Native to the Mediterranean region, will grow in any average garden soil.

Common uses: Antimicrobial, dyspepsia, rheumatism, moth repellant, some types of headache, memory aid, antioxidant, digestive aid

Parts used: Leaves

Caution: Do not use in medicinal amounts during pregnancy. Rosemary leaves are quite safe, but the essential oil should be used with caution because of its potency.

Rosemary is a native of the Middle East and around the Mediterranean Sea. From afar, it looks like green sea foam on the face of the cliffs by the sea, hence its name "dew of the sea." It is easy to grow in average garden soil but is not winter hardy. It can be grown indoors, but it is temperamental and does not like to dry out.

This herb is excellent on roasted potatoes and with lamb and other foods, but as a medicine, the crushed leaves possess potent antimicrobial activity (kills bacteria and virus), which is due to the high content of volatile oils. During World War II, rosemary leaves and juniper berries were burned in hospitals as a disinfectant.

For gas, nausea, and biliousness, take as a tea or tincture. To stimulate circulation, soothe aches, and relieve rheumatic pain, make a strong tea and add it to bath water, or make a warm compress and apply over affected areas. This is a good herb to use in steam inhalations for prevention or treatment of colds.

Saw Palmetto (*Seranoa repens*)

Family: Palmaceae

Other names: Seronna serrulata, sabal

Habitat: Subtropical sandy soil

Common uses: Tonic for male and female reproductive organs, respiratory system, irritable bladder

Parts used: Berry

Caution: No known side effects when used as recommended. Some men using saw palmetto report difficulty with erections, testicular discomfort, breast tenderness or enlargement, and changes in sexual desire. Men or women taking hormonal medications (such as finasteride/Proscar/Propecia or birth control pills) or who have hormone-sensitive conditions should use caution. Saw palmetto may increase the risk of bleeding when taken with drugs that increase the risk of bleeding, such as aspirin, anticoagulants (blood thinners) such as warfarin (Coumadin) or heparin, antiplatelet drugs such as clopidogrel (Plavix), and nonsteroidal anti-inflammatory drugs such as ibuprofen (Motrin, Advil) or naproxen (Naprosyn, Aleve).

Saw palmetto is also known as Spanish sword because its long slender leaves, which radiate from the ground and have sharp serrated edges that can rip clothing and skin. This can make collecting the berries a challenge. Writings suggest that the berries smell and taste like rotten cheese. Because of this and the added fact that many of the activities are not released in water, its use as a tea is undesirable.

Numerous human trials report that saw palmetto improves symptoms of benign prostatic hypertrophy such as nighttime urination, urinary flow, and overall quality of life, although it may not greatly reduce the size of the prostate. It is best taken as a liquid or powdered alcohol extract as the active properties are not water soluble.

St. John's Wort (*Hypericum perforatum*)

Family: Guttiferae

Other names: Hardhay, amber, goatweed, klamath weed, tipton weed

Habitat: Open fields, roadsides

Common uses: Antidepressant, anti-anxiety

Parts used: Flowers and buds

Caution: The most common side effects of St. John's wort include dry mouth, dizziness, diarrhea, nausea, increased sensitivity to sunlight, and fatigue. There has been much discussion and controversy regarding occurrences of side effects related to combining St. John's Wort with pharmaceutical antidepressants. A common-sense approach is to check with your healthcare practitioner before combining any herb and drug.

This stout little plant has come to be known as the depression herb, and it has been the subject of substantial research and clinical trials. Studies suggest that St. John's wort is of minimal benefit in treating major depression. A study co-funded by the National Center for Complementary and Alternative Medicine found that St. John's wort was no more effective than placebo in treating major depression of moderate severity. Some scientific evidence shows that St. John's wort is useful for milder forms of depression.

Thyme (*Thymus vulgaris*)

Family: Laminacea

Other names: Garden thyme

Habitat: Native to the Mediterranean region, northern Africa, and parts of Asia. It can be grown in average garden soil in a sunny location.

Common uses: Antibacterial, antiviral, expectorant (helping to remove secretions) of colds and bronchitis, antifungal

Parts used: Leaves

Caution: Avoid large amounts with hypothyroidism.

Although research on its therapeutic value is scant, thyme has been widely used for centuries as both a culinary and medicinal herb. This perennial shrub can be easily grown in a sheltered spot in the garden.

A strong tea of thyme should be considered to help eliminate mucus congestion, coughs, or sore throat associated with a cold or flu. A soothing cough medicine can be made by steeping dried thyme in honey. Tea can also be used as a gargle to ease or prevent a sore throat. Add a strong tea to bath water to soothe and deodorize the skin. A steam inhalation is effective for sinus congestion.

Sage (*Salvia officinalis*)

Family: Laminacea

Habitat: Mediterranean region; can be grown in average garden soil

Common uses: Antiseptic, astringent, antispasmodic, antioxidant, antiviral, antibacterial

Parts used: Leaves

Caution: Do not take during pregnancy.

This beautiful, woody perennial makes a nice addition to any herb garden. It likes a sheltered, sunny location and will withstand moderately cold, snowy winters.

Historically, sage was associated with longevity and mortality. Native Americans used it topically for skin conditions and baths. The astringent, antiseptic qualities of sage make it an ideal gargle for sore throats, gingivitis, or bleeding gums in the form of a tea. A tea is also a good way to make a digestive tonic and to relieve night sweats during menopause or reduce excessive perspiration.

Brew a strong tea for making a compress to soothe slow-healing wounds. Add honey to an infusion for sore throat or cough and take over 1 to 3 days. For colds and sinus congestion, use a steam inhalation to dry up excessive secretions and postnasal drip.

Yarrow (*Achillea millefolium*)

Family: Compositae

Other names: Soldier's wound wort, thousand weed, staunchweed, sanguinary, milfoil

Habitat: Temperate regions of North America and Europe

Common uses: Styptic, anti-inflammatory

Parts used: Flower heads

Caution: Some individual's skin my be sensitive; avoid during pregnancy.

Yarrow is a hardy, rampant grower and easily crowds out more delicate plants. Thus, you may want to confine it to its own section of the garden. It likes a hot, sunny location and is not fussy about rich soil, but will not tolerate wet roots.

Archeologists have identified fossils of yarrow pollen in Neanderthal burial caves of 60,000 years ago. It was used as a styptic 3000 years ago to stop bleeding from wounds suffered in the Trojan War. Native American tribes used this herb for skin sores and wounds, and it was included in the medical supplies issued during the American Civil War.

Yarrow is best known for its ability to stop bleeding and to reduce inflammation. A tea can be useful for irritable bowel syndrome and gastrointestinal complaints in general. It may be useful in alleviating the symptoms of bladder infections or as an aid to treat hemoptysis (coughing up blood).

A poultice can be placed directly onto bleeding cuts and wounds to stop bleeding.

Summary

Phytochemicals are chemicals that occur in plants. Herbs can have therapeutic effects in the body, some of which include tonics, which are nourishing, adaptogens, which help the body regain normal function in the presence of stress, and immune stimulants, which enhance the immune system's ability to fight an illness.

Herbal remedies can be used in the form of an extract, tea, infusion, decoction, tincture, capsule, compress, poultice, liniment, salve, or ointment.

When wildcrafting herbs, caution must be taken to identify the plant properly, assure that there is no contamination from pesticides or other chemicals, and avoid picking endangered species.

Children require lower doses of herbs. Herbs should not be used with infants unless guided by a healthcare practitioner.

Each herb has unique uses and cautions. It is important that individuals become knowledgeable of herbs they intend to use to determine appropriateness for the given condition, dosage, and safety issues.

Suggested Reading

Agency for Healthcare Research and Quality. Garlic: Effects on Cardiovascular Risks and Disease, Protective Effects Against Cancer, and Clinical Adverse Effects. Retrieved August 1, 2008 from ahrq.gov/clinic/epcsums/garlicsum.htm

Avins, A. L., & Bent, S. (2006). Saw palmetto and lower urinary tract symptoms: what is the latest evidence? *Current Urology Report, 7*(4):260–265.

Basch, E., Bent, S., Foppa, I, et al. (2006). Marigold (*Calendula officinalis*): an evidence-based systematic review by the Natural Standard Research Collaboration. *Journal of Herbal Pharmacotherapy, 6*(3–4):135–159.

Bent, S., Kane, C., Shinohara, K., et al. (2006). Saw palmetto for benign prostatic hyperplasia. *New England Journal of Medicine, 354*(6):557–566.

Ladas, E., Kroll, D.J., & Kelly, K.M. (2005). Milk thistle (*Silybum marianum*). In: Coates, P., Blackman, M., Cragg, G., Levine, M., Moss, J., White, J. et al., eds. *Encyclopedia of Dietary Supplements*. New York: Marcel Dekker, pp. 467–482.

Duke, J. A. (2003). *The Green Pharmacy*. Emmaus, PA: Rodale Books.

Gaby, A. R. (2006). Natural remedies for Herpes simplex. *Alternative Medicine Review*, 11(2):93–101.

Gagnier, J. J., van Tulder, M., Berman, B., & Bombardier, C. (2006). Herbal medicine for low back pain. *Cochrane Database System Review, 19*(2):CD004504.

Gardner, C. D., Lawson, L. D., Block, E., et al. (2007). Effect of raw garlic vs. commercial garlic supplements on plasma lipid concentrations in adults with moderate hypercholesterolemia: a randomized clinical trial. *Archives of Internal Medicine, 167*(4):346–353.

Gruenwald, J., Brendler, T., & Jaenicke, C. (eds.). (2007). *PDR for Herbal Medicines*. Montvale, NJ: Medical Economics Company.

Hobbs, C. (2006). *Herbal Remedies for Dummies*. Foster City, CA: IDG Books Worldwide, Inc.

Kasper, S., Anghelescu, I. G., Szegedi, A, et al. (2006). Superior efficacy of St. John's wort extract WS 5570 compared to placebo in patients with major depression: a randomized, double-blind, placebo-controlled, multi-center trial. *BMC Medicine*, 4(1):14.

Kennedy, D. O., Little, W., Haskell, C. F., & Scholey, A. B. (2006). Anxiolytic effects of a combination of Melissa officinalis and Valeriana officinalis during laboratory induced stress. *Phytotherapy Research, 20*(2):96–102.

Ody, P. (2000). *The Complete Medicinal Herbal.* New York: DK Publishing, Inc.

Solomon, P. R., Adams, F., Silver, A., et al. (2002). Ginkgo for memory enhancement: a randomized controlled trial. *Journal of the American Medical Association, 288*(7):835–840.

Winston, D. (2003). *Herbal Therapeutics: Specific Indications for Herbs and Herbal Formulas.* Broadway, NJ: Herbal Therapeutics Research Library.

Resources

Organizations

American Botanical Council
P.O. Box 201660
Austin, TX 78720
Phone 515-331-8868; fax 512-331-1924
www.herbalgram.org

American Herbalists Guild
P.O. Box 70
Boulder, CO 80302
Phone 435-722-8434; fax 435-722-8452
www.americanherbalistsguild.com

Herb Research Foundation
4140 15th St.
Boulder, CO 80304
Phone (303) 449-2265; fax (303) 449-7849
www.herbs.org

Office of Dietary Supplements
National Institutes of Health
Bethesda, MD 20892
http://ods.od.nih.gov

Chapter 23

Aromatherapy: Common Scents

OBJECTIVES

This chapter should enable you to

· Define *aromatherapy*

· Describe the method of extraction that makes an essential oil pure

· List the four basic types of aromatherapy

· Describe four methods of using aromatherapy

· Describe the use of aromatherapy for at least five different health problems

· List at least 10 precautions or contraindications with the use of aromatherapy

Aromatherapy refers to the therapeutic use of essential oils. This branch of herbal medicine is often misunderstood and maligned; even its name is a bit of a misnomer. Contrary to popular belief, aromatherapy is not a new therapy, but part of one of the oldest therapies, as herbal medicine dates back 6000 years. Aromatic plants have been used by many countries, including India, China, North and South America, Greece, the Middle East, Australia, New Zealand, and Europe. According to the World Health Organization (WHO), today, more than 85% of the world population still relies on herbal medicine, and many of the herbs are aromatic.

The renaissance of modern aromatherapy appeared in France just before World War II. (This was around the time the first antibiotics were used.) A physician named Jean Valnet, a chemist named Maurice Gattefosse, and a surgical assistant by the name of Marguerite Maury were key figures in the rediscovery of this ancient art of healing. It is fascinating that they did not use aromatherapy for its nice smell, nor did they use it for stress reduction—two of the most popular ways aromatherapy is used today. Instead, they used it clinically, as they would use any natural medicine, to help wounds heal, fight infections, and to improve skin texture. This clinical approach to aromatherapy has survived in France, and many physicians still use essential oils as an alternative or enhancement to antibiotics today. In France, as in Germany, the use of plants medicinally (*phytomedicine*), including aromatherapy, is seen as an extension of orthodox medicine.

> **KEY POINT**
>
> Aromatherapy is viewed as such an integral part of medicine in Germany that doctors and nurses there are tested in the use of essential oils in order to become licensed.

Aromatherapy does not just mean using aromas. The real definition of *aromatherapy* is *the therapeutic use of essential oils*. Perhaps we should add *the controlled therapeutic use* as essential oils are not toys, but powerful tools that can help you stay healthy. Real essential oils are either steam distillates or expressed extracts from aromatic plants. Many of them have familiar smells, such as lavender, rose, and rosemary; however, things are not quite as simple as they seem at first glance.

Essential oils are highly volatile droplets created by a plant itself to help ward off infection (bacterial, fungal, or viral), to regulate growth and hormones, and to mend damaged tissues of the plant. These tiny reservoirs of plant medicine are stored in the plant's veins, glands, or sacs, and when they are broken by being crushed or rubbed, the essential oil is released along with the aroma. Lavender has a minimal scent until the flowering head is gently rubbed between two fingers. Some plants store large amounts of essential oils—some store very little. This, along with the difficulty of harvesting the essential oils, dictates the price. For example, more than 100 kilograms of fresh rose petals are needed to produce 60 grams of essential oils. (This means that rose is one of the most expensive essential oils on the market today, and also one of the most frequently adulterated!)

There are a few important things to know about essential oils before you start using them for your health and well-being. These are the method of extraction, the botanical name (for clear identification, see Exhibit 23-1), methods of application, safety, storage, and contraindications.

Extraction

The method of extraction is crucial, as only steam-distilled or expressed extracts can legitimately be called essential oils. These two methods produce a pure product with no additional solvent or impurity. A bottle of essential oils should state that the contents are pure essential oils: steam distilled or expressed. (Only the peel from citrus plants, such as mandarin, lime, or lemon produce an expressed oil.)

> **KEY POINT**
>
> Many of the essential oils on the market are solvents extracted using petrochemicals. These hexane-based residues may cause allergic or sensitive reactions.

EXHIBIT 23-1   Essential Oils Mentioned in This Chapter and Their Botanical Names

Aniseed	Pimpinella anisum
Basil	Ocimum basilicum
Chamomile German	Matricaria recutita
Chamomile Roman	Chamomelum nobile
Clary sage	Salvia sclarea
Coriander seed	Coriandrum sativum
Eucalyptus	Eucalyptus globulus
Fennel	Foeniculum vulgare
Geranium	Pelargonium graveolens
Ginger	Zingeber officinale
Hyssop	Hyssopus officinalis
Lavender True	Lavandula officinalis
Lemongrass	Cymbopogon citratus
Neroli	Citrus aurantium var amara
Palmarosa	Cymbopogon martini
Parlsey	Petroselinum sativum
Pennyroyal	Mentha pulegium
Peppermint	Mentha piperita
Rose	Rosa damascena
Rosewood	Aniba rosaeodora
Sage	Salvia officinalis
Sandalwood	Santalum album
Tarragon	Artemesia dracunculus
Wintergreen	Gaultheria procumbens
Ylang ylang	Cananga odorata

Identification

There can be *many* different species of the same plant. For example, the genus (or surname) of thyme is *thymus*, but there are more than 60 different species or varieties of thyme, each with different therapeutic effects. (There are 3 different species of lavender and 600 different species of eucalyptus.) It is very important to know the full botanical name of a plant

---

EXHIBIT 23-2   Aromatherapy Journals

Aromatherapy Journal
www.naha.org

Aromatherapy Today
www.aromatherapytoday.com

International Journal of Clinical Aromatherapy
www.ijca.net

---

so that you can use it correctly. (At the end of this chapter, there is a list of safe essential oils to use. It gives both the botanical name and common name.) Do not buy anything that is labeled *lavender oil*, as you will have no way of knowing what you are buying. Which lavender is it? One lavender is a soothing, calming sedative oil exceptional for burns, but another lavender is a stimulant and expectorant (helps you cough up mucus and will not help you sleep or soothe your burns). You need to ask the following questions: Is it a true essential oil? How has it been extracted?

The simplest way to ensure that you are buying the real thing is to look in one of the professional journals (see Exhibit 23-2) and ask for an order form from one of the advertised suppliers. If they do not list the botanical name, method of extraction, country of origin, and part of the plant, then you cannot be certain of what they are selling.

Essential oils are common ingredients in the pharmaceutical, perfume, and food industries and, as such, are commonly used by most of the population on a daily basis. Pure essential oils rarely produce an allergic effect, unlike their synthetic cousins; however, many products on the market have been extended with synthetic fragrances and can cause a reaction.

How It Works

As mentioned, the term *aromatherapy* refers to the therapeutic use of essential oils that are the volatile organic constituents of plants. Essential oils are thought to work at psychological, physiological, and cellular levels; this means they can affect our body, our mind, and all of the delicate links in-between. The effects of aroma can be rapid, and sometimes just thinking about a scent can be as powerful as the actual scent itself. Take a moment to think of your favorite flower. Then think about an odor that makes you feel nauseated. The effects of an aroma can be relaxing or stimulating depending on the previous experience of the individual (called the *learned memory*), as well as the actual chemical makeup of the essential oils used.

KEY POINT

Aromatherapy should not be used as a replacement for medical treatment. It is a complementary therapy and is most useful when integrated with conventional medicine.

How Scents Affect You

Olfaction

Essential oils are composed of many different chemical components or molecules. These different chemical components travel via the nose to the olfactory bulb. Nerve impulses travel to the limbic system of the brain, the oldest part of our brain. There the aroma is processed. The limbic part of our brain contains an organ called the *amygdala*. This is the organ that governs your emotional response. Valium is thought to have a calming, sedative effect on the amygdala; lavandula angustifolia (true lavender) has a similar effect. The limbic system also contains another organ called the *hippocampus*. This organ is involved in the formation and retrieval of explicit memories. This is why an aroma can trigger memories that may have lain dormant for years.

REFLECTION

Does the scent of cinnamon buns baking, honeysuckle, or a particular cologne trigger specific memories for you? Can you recall unique scents associated with people or places you have known in the past? What are these?

The effect of scents on the brain has been mapped using computer-generated graphics. These brain electrical activity maps indicate how subjects, linked to an electroencephalogram, rated different odors presented to them. These maps have shown that scents can have a psychological effect even when the aroma is below the level of human awareness.

KEY POINT

The loss of the sense of smell is called *anosmia*; however, even in a person who has lost the sense of smell, if the olfactory nerve is intact, the chemicals in the aroma will still be able to travel to the limbic part of the brain and have a therapeutic effect.

Absorption Through the Skin

Essential oils are absorbed through the skin through diffusion, in much the same way as medicines administered in patches. The two layers of the skin—the dermis and fat layers—act as a reservoir before the components within the essential oils reach the bloodstream. There is some evidence that massage or hot water enhances the absorption of at least some of the essential oil's components. Essential oils, because they are *lipophilic* (attracted to fat), can be stored in the fatty areas of the body and can pass through the blood–brain barrier.

Who Uses Aromatherapy?

Aromatherapy is commonly practiced in England, France, Germany, Switzerland, Sweden, Australia, New Zealand, and Japan. It is beginning to grow in use in the United States. Many nurses and other health professionals are receiving training in aromatherapy to enhance their care. In France, medical doctors and pharmacists use aromatherapy as part of conventional medicine, often for the control of infection.

Types of Aromatherapy

There are four basic types of aromatherapy:

1. Esthetic: Used purely for pleasure, such as in candles and soaps
2. Holistic: Used for general stress
3. Environmental fragrancing: Used to manipulate mood or enhance sales
4. Clinical: Used for specific therapeutic outcomes that are measurable

Methods of Using Aromatherapy

Essential oils can be absorbed by the body in one of three ways:

1. Inhalation: 1–5 drops undiluted—without touch
2. Through the skin: 1%–12% diluted in a carrier oil, used with compresses or massage—via touch
3. Orally: 1–2 drops, which is considered aromatic medicine, requiring the training of a primary care provider who has prescribing privileges

Inhalation

Direct inhalation means an essential oil is directly targeted to the person: 1 to 5 drops on a tissue (or floated on hot water in a bowl) and inhaled for 5–10 minutes.

Indirect inhalation includes the use of burners, nebulizers, and vaporizers that can use heat generated by battery or electricity and may or may not include the use of water. Larger portable aroma systems are available to control the release of essential oils on a commercial scale into rooms up to 1500 square feet. This is similar to environmental fragrancing (using synthetics), which is common practice in hotels and department stores, and can be useful for mood enhancement and stress reduction.

Baths

Essential oils can be used in baths by dissolving 4–6 drops of essential oil into a teaspoon of milk or salt. Essential oils do not dissolve in water and would float on the top giving an uneven treatment. You then can relax in the bath for 10 minutes.

Compresses

To prepare a compress, add 4–6 drops of essential oil to warm water. Soak a soft cotton cloth in the mixture, wring it out, and apply to the affected area (contusion or abrasion). Cover the external surface with food plastic wrap to maintain moisture, cover with a towel, and keep in place for 4 hours.

Touch

Aromatherapy is often used in a gentle massage or the *m* technique. Use 1–12% essential oils diluted in a teaspoonful (5 ml) of cold-pressed vegetable oil, cream, or gel. Gentle friction and hot water enhances absorption of essential oils through the skin into the blood stream. The amount of essential oils absorbed from an aromatherapy massage will normally be 0.025 to 0.1 ml: approximately 0.5 to 2 drops.

Aromatherapy and Women's Health

Aromatherapy, which involves the senses of smell and touch, is possibly the most feminine of complementary therapies and is ideally suited to women and their health concerns. (Maybe this is why so many trained aromatherapists are women!)

KEY POINT

As aromatherapy is one of the most nurturing therapies, it is hardly surprising that many nurses throughout the world are learning to use aromatherapy as an enhancement to their nursing care. Aromatherapy began its nursing debut in England, in geriatric care, when Helen Passant brought it first to the attention of the nursing community in Oxford. She used aromatherapy in the ward and reduced the ward's drug bill by one-third. The hospital immediately responded by reducing her budget by one-third!

Almost every aspect of a woman's life can be enhanced by aromatherapy. It should be noted that although most essential oils have no affect on orthodox medication, some essential oils can augment or diminish the effects of certain medications. Following are some women's health problems that can be successfully addressed with aromatherapy.

Problems with the Menstrual Cycle

The menstrual cycle is delicately balanced. Hormones, specifically estrogen, are easily thrown out of balance by stress, illness, poor diet, or overwork. *Pelargonium graveolens* (geranium) has been used for generations to balance the female hormonal system. This species of geranium acts on the adrenal cortex that regulates the endocrine system and therefore affects the menstrual cycle.

Premenstrual tension, irregular periods, and painful periods can be greatly helped by aromatherapy. Add three drops of geranium to a teaspoon of vegetable oil. The vegetable oil should be cold pressed and not one used for cooking. Gently massage into the lower abdomen and lumbar (lower back) areas. For optimum results, apply morning and evening. For very painful menstrual periods, add 1–2 drops of high-altitude *Lavandula angustifolia* (true lavender) and *Chamaemelum nobile* (Roman chamomile) to enhance the antispasmodic effect. Geranium may also encourage regular ovulation.

Menopausal Problems

Pelargonium graveolens (geranium) may be particularly useful during menopause as an adrenal regulator when estrogen supplies begin to dry up. A disruption in the supply of estrogen can lead to irritability, mood swings, and hot flashes. This essential oil is also excellent for mature, dry skin, and thread veins that can accompany menopause. Add 3–5 drops of geranium to a teaspoon of evening Primrose oil. Rub anywhere on the body, or add 5 drops to a bath and soak for 10 minutes. *Foeniculum vulgare dulce* (sweet fennel), *Salvia sclarea* (sage), and *Pimpinella anisum* (aniseed) all contain a molecule similar to estradiol—the female hormone—and can be very beneficial at menopause also.

Hot flashes can be helped with a spritzer of geranium, clary sage, and peppermint. To make a spritzer, add 6 drops of each oil to 10 fluid ounces of water and shake vigorously before spraying the face and neck. Keep eyes closed while spraying.

Infertility

Where there is no physical reason why a woman cannot conceive, often the underlying reason can be one of tension. Trying to become pregnant can be emotionally draining, and the longer it takes the more stressful it can become. *Salvia sclaria* (clary sage) related to *Salvia officinalis* (common sage) can help a woman relax. Clary sage contains an alcohol (sclareol), which is similar in molecular form to estradiol. As well as having an estrogen-like effect, clary sage is very relaxing and antispasmodic (it contains 75% linalyl acetate, an ester).

Morning Sickness

Early morning nausea and vomiting often occurs during the first 3 months of pregnancy, although it can sometimes last the whole 9 months. Nausea can be greatly alleviated with a brief inhalation of *Zingiber officinale*, (ginger), or *Mentha piperita* (peppermint). Always remember that only 1 or 2 drops on a handkerchief is necessary, and you can repeat it whenever the need arises. Do not use more than 2 drops of either essential oil at a time, as more may exacerbate the nausea, not alleviate it. The inhalation of either ginger or peppermint for nausea during pregnancy is a soothing and safe practice. Aromatherapy is not particularly advocated during the first 3 months of pregnancy, as essential oils do cross the placenta; however, many expectant mothers like to relax in an aromatic bath and the majority of essential oils will have no detrimental effect when used in this gentle way. Aromatherapy can be used during the remainder of pregnancy, but use caution. Certain essential oils can also be safely used during labor. (Please refer to the books listed in the resource's list for guidance.)

Breastfeeding, Engorged Breasts, and Sore Nipples

Foeniculum vulgare (fennel), which mimics estrogen, has a good-milk producing action, which can help mothers who breastfeed. Fennel also has a soothing decongestant effect on engorged breasts, which will be a relief to those in the early stages of feeding. Apply 1–2 drops diluted in a carrier oil to the breasts, avoiding the nipple area, twice a day. Wash area immediately before feeding. As fennel is a gentle laxative, the baby may have looser stools.

KEY POINT

Because of their phytoestrogenic effect, sage, fennel, and aniseed are contraindicated in persons with cancer when the tumor is estrogen dependent.

Both *Matricaria recutita* (German chamomile) and *Chamaemelum nobile* (Roman chamomile) are used in some European commercial brands of ointment available for sore nipples. Both chamomiles are useful for swelling and congestion. Apply a diluted solution in a carrier oil (1 drop per 5 ml) after each feeding, and be sure to wash off any residual solution before the next feeding. *Lavandula angustifolia* (true lavender) is another useful essential oil for sore nipples, as this lavender has recognized properties that enhance healing.

Postpartum Blues

Postpartum blues or just down in the dumps? Aromatherapy can lift spirits and ease those moments when a mother feels that she cannot cope with yet another dirty diaper. *Citrus*

Aurantium ssp bergamia (bergamot) and *Melissa officinalis* (true Melissa) are ideal essential oils to make the day just a little brighter. Melissa is difficult to obtain unadulterated; however, there are some companies with integrity, and the real stuff can work miracles! It is used by putting 1–3 drops on a handkerchief and breathing deeply. Bergamot should not be used topically before sunbathing or using a sun bed, as this could result in skin photosensitivity and, in some cases, burns.

Vaginal Infections

Yeast infection, anaerobic vaginitis, and trichomonas vaginal yeast infection, caused by *Candida albicans*, is a common nuisance factor in many women's lives. Sometimes the yeast infection may be a side effect of antibiotic treatment, and it can occur during pregnancy or after an illness. When it does occur, vaginal yeast infection is messy, uncomfortable, and embarrassing. Some forms are now resistant to many of the conventional preparations; however, one essential oil, called tea tree, can help eradicate this fungal infection in only a few days. Make sure you have the correct essential oil, as tea tree is the common name of many different types of plants. The right tea tree is called *Melaleuca alternifolia CT terpineol*. There is another *Melaleuca alternifolia* that contains much higher percentages of terpineol, an oxide, which can produce discomfort when applied to the skin or mucous membrane. Put a teaspoon of carrier oil onto a saucer. Add 2–3 drops of essential oil and mix with a clean finger. Take a tampon, remove the applicator, and roll the tampon in the mixture until all the mixture has been absorbed. Insert the tampon into the vagina.

The tampon should be changed three times a day. Each time soak a new tampon in a fresh dilution of carrier oil with 2 to 3 drops of tea tree. The tampon needs to be kept in the vagina overnight. Commonly, tea tree will remove vaginal yeast infection in 3 days, regardless of how long the person has had the infection. This form of treatment is also very effective against anaerobic vaginitis and trichomonas. Incidentally, recent research in both Australia and Great Britain has shown this to be effective against methicillin-resistant *Staphylococcus aureus*, which is endemic in many hospitals.

Cystitis

Inflammation of the bladder can be due to infection, but this is not always the case. Cystitis can plague some unfortunate women for much of their lives, bringing pain and misery and taking a high toll on intimate relationships. Although many factors contribute to cystitis, such as tight clothing, insufficient fluid intake, and a diet of high sugar and refined food, stress does play an important role. Specific essential oils can help this condition. Choose an antispasmodic essential oil, which also has a strong antibiotic action, such as *Juniperus communis var erecta* (juniper), *Cymbopogon citratus* (West Indian lemongrass); which contains myrcene is very effective as a peripheral analgesic, or *Origanum marjorana* (sweet marjoram). Apply 1–2 drops diluted in a teaspoon of cold-pressed vegetable oil to the lower abdomen and lower back (kidney area). Repeat up to 4 times a day while the attack lasts, and remember to drink at least 2 liters of water a day. Drinking cranberry juice can also help in the initial stages of cystitis.

Aromatherapy for Common Complaints

Here are some essential oils that can be used for common complaints that typically are self-medicated. When using essential oils on the skin (topically), use 1–5 drops diluted in a teaspoon of carrier oil. When inhaling the essential oil, inhale 1–2 drops on a cotton ball, or add 1 to 2 drops to a basin of steaming hot water (method of application: I = inhalation, T = topical).

Psychological

Insomnia: lavender, ylang ylang, clary sage, frankincense, neroli (I, T)

Depression: bergamot, basil, lavender, geranium, neroli, angelica, rose, melissa (I, T)

Stress and anxiety: lavender, frankincense, Roman chamomile, mandarin, angelica, rose (I, T)

Anorexia: rose, neroli, lemon, fennel (I, T)

Withdrawal from substance abuse: helichrysum, angelica, rose (T)

REFLECTION

How do different scents affect your moods? How can you intentionally use this to enhance your health and well-being?

Pain Relief

Migraine: peppermint, lavender (T)

Osteoarthritis: eucalyptus, black pepper, ginger, spike lavender, Roman chamomile, rosemary, myrrh (T)

Rheumatoid arthritis: German chamomile, lavender, peppermint, frankincense (T)

Lower back pain: Roman chamomile, black pepper, eucalyptus, lemongrass, rosemary, lavender, sweet marjoram (T)

Cramps: Roman chamomile, clary sage, lavender, sweet marjoram (T)

General aches and pains: rosemary, lavender, lemongrass, clary sage, black pepper, lemon eucalyptus, spike lavender

Women's Problems

Menopausal symptoms: clary sage, sage, fennel, aniseed, geranium, rose, cypress (I, T)

Menstrual cramping: Roman chamomile, lavender, clary sage (T)

Premenstrual syndrome; infertility with no physiological cause: clary sage, sage, fennel, aniseed, geranium, rose (T)

Blood Pressure

Borderline high blood pressure (not on medication): ylang ylang, true lavender

Low blood pressure (can be caused by some antidepressants): rosemary

Urinary

Cystitis: tea tree, palma rosa (T, especially sitz bath)

Water retention: juniper, cypress, fennel (T)

Digestive

Irritable bowel syndrome: Roman chamomile, clary sage, mandarin, cardamom, peppermint, mandarin, fennel, lavender

Constipation: fennel, black pepper (T)

Indigestion: peppermint, ginger (I)

Infections

Bacterial (MRSA, VRSA): tea tree (I, T)

Other bacteria (depends on bacteria): eucalyptus, naiouli, sweet marjoram, oregano, tarragon, savory, German chamomile, thyme, manuka (I, T)

Viral: ravansara, palma rosa, lemon, Melissa, rose, bergamot (I, T)

Fungal: lemongrass, black pepper, holy basil, clove, cajuput, caraway (T) geranium, tea tree—particularly good for toenail fungus (apply twice daily undiluted for 3 months to nail bed)

Respiratory

Bronchitis: ravansara, euc globlulus, euc smithi, tea tree, spike lavender (I)

Sinusitis: euc globulus, lavender, spike lavender, rosemary (I)

Mild asthma: lavender, clary sage, Roman chamomile (I; patch test on arm first)

Skin Problems

Mild acne: tea tree, juniper, cypress, naiouli (T)

Mild psoriasis: lavender, German chamomile (T)

Diabetic ulcers: lavender, frankincense, myrrh (T)

Chemotherapy Side Effects

Nausea: peppermint, ginger, mandarin (I)

Postradiation burns: lavender, German chamomile with Tamanu carrier oil (T)

Muscular

Sports injuries: spike lavender, rosemary, sweet marjoram, black pepper, lemongrass, frankincense (T)

Children

Irritability: mandarin, lavender, Roman chamomile, rose (I, T)

Colic: Roman chamomile, mandarin (T; gently massed to the abdomen)

Diaper rash: lavender, German chamomile (T)

Sleep problems: lavender, rose, mandarin, ylang ylang

Autism (to aid with social interaction): rose, mandarin, lavender, sweet marjoram, clary sage, *Pinus sylvestris*

Geriatric Care

Memory loss: rosemary, rose, eucalyptus, peppermint, bergamot (T, I)

Dry flaky skin: geranium, frankincense, oil of evening primrose carrier oil (T)

Alzheimer's disease: rosemary, lavender, pine, frankincense, rose (I)

End-of-Life Care: Pain Relief

Spiritual: rose, angelica, frankincense

Physical: lavender, peppermint, lavender, lemongrass, rosemary

Emotional: geranium, pine, sandalwood

Relaxation: lavender, clary sage, mandarin, frankincense, ylang ylang

Bed sores: lavender, tea tree, sweet marjoram, frankincense

Care of the Dying

Rites of passage: choose selection of patient's favorite aromas or frankincense or rose

Bereavement: rose, sandalwood, patchouli, angelica

Actions

The pharmacologically active components in essential oils work at psychological, physical, and cellular levels. Essential oils are absorbed rapidly through the skin—some essential oils are now being used to help the dermal penetration of orthodox medication. Essential oils are lipotrophic and are excreted through respiration, kidneys, and skin.

KEY POINT

Because essential oils can produce physiological and psychological effects, inquiry into their use should be made during every assessment.

Risks and Safety

Most essential oils have been tested by the food and beverage industry, as many essential oils are used as flavorings. Other research has been carried out by the perfume industry. Most of the commonly used essential oils in aromatherapy have generally been regarded as safe.

Aromatherapy is a very safe complementary therapy if it is used within recognized guidelines. Avoid use with people with atopic eczema. Some essential oils have caused dermal sensitivity—mostly through impure extracts. Generally, essential oils that are high in esters and alcohols tend to be gentle in their action and the most safe to use. Essential oils that are high in phenols tend to be more aggressive and should not be used over long periods of time. There is a list of banned or contraindicated essential oils to guide the novice (see Exhibit 23-3). Do not administer essential oils orally unless trained in this method.

Herbs can interact with medications. Some precautions are listed in Exhibit 23-4. Additional warnings to heed are as follows:

· Sage, clary sage, fennel, and aniseed should be avoided with estrogen-dependent tumors
· Hyssop should be avoided in pregnancy
· Rosemary should be avoided in high blood pressure
· Hyssop should be avoided with those prone to seizures
· Cinnamon may cause dermal irritation
· Bergamot may cause dermal irritation or burns when used with sun beds or sunshine

EXHIBIT 23-3   Contraindicated Essential Oils

Common Name	Botanical Name
Basil (exotic)	Ocimum basilicum
Birch	Betula lenta
Boldo	Peumus boldus
Buchu	Agothosma betulina
Cade	Juniperus oxycedrus
Calamus	Acorus clamus var angustatus
Camphor (brown)	Cinnamomum camphora
Camphor (yellow)	Cinnamomum camphora
Cassia	Cinnamomum cassia
Cinnamon bark	Cinnamomum zeylanicum
Costus	Saussurea costus
Elecampane	Inula helenium
Horseradish	Armoracia rusticana
Melaleuca	Melaleuca bracteata
Mustard	Brassica nigra
Pennyroyal	Mentha pulegium
Ravensara	Ravensara anisata
Sage (dalmation)	Salvia officinalis
Sassafras	Sassafras albidum
Tansy	Tanacetum vulgare
Tarragon*	Artemesia dracunculus
Thuja	Thuja occidentalis
Verbena*	Lippia citriadora (Aloysia triphylla)
Wintergreen	Gaultheria procumbens
Wormseed	Chenopodium ambrosiodes var anthelminticum
Wormwood	Artemesia absinthium

* Somewhat controversial. Many aromatherapists use tarragon and verbena.

EXHIBIT 23-4   Drug Interaction with Aromatherapy

1. Avoid when using homeopathic remedies; strong aromas like peppermint and eucalyptus can negate homeopathic remedies.

2. Avoid chamomile if allergic to ragweed.

3. Eucalyptus globulus and cananga odorata may affect the absorption of 5-fluorouracil, a drug commonly used in chemotherapy.

4. Terpinenol (a component of some essential oils) may decrease the narcotic effect of pentobarbital—mainly when used orally.

5. Cymbopogon citratus (West Indian lemongrass) can increase the effects of morphine (according to studies in rats and when given orally).

6. Peppermint may negate quinidine in atrial fibrillation.

7. Lavender may increase the effect of barbiturates.

8. The effect of tranquilizers, anticonvulsants, and antihistamines may be slightly enhanced by sedative essential oils.

Pregnancy and Lactation

Use caution during the first trimester. Although many women do use essential oils success-fully and safely during their pregnancies, it is suggested that some essential oils should be avoided altogether, although the data are based on taking the essential oils orally, not inhal-ing or applying them topically. These include sage, pennyroyal, camphor, parsley, tarragon, wintergreen, juniper, hyssop, and basil. The following are thought to be safe in pregnancy: cardamom, chamomile (Roman and German), clary sage, coriander seed, geranium, ginger, lavender, neroli, palmarosa, patchouli, petitgrain, rose, rosewood, and sandalwood.

Warnings/Contraindications/Precautions When Using Essential Oils

- Do not take by mouth (unless guided by a person trained in aromatic medicine and preferably someone with prescriptive license).
- Do not touch your eyes with essential oils. If essential oils get into eyes, rinse out with milk or carrier oil (essential oils do not dissolve in water) and then water.
- Store away from fire or naked flame, as essential oils are highly volatile and highly flammable.
- Store in a cool place out of sunlight, in colored glass—amber or blue. Store expen-sive essential oils in refrigerator.

- Many essential oils stain clothing—beware!
- Do not use essential oils undiluted on the skin.
- Keep away from children and pets.
- Only use essential oils from reputable suppliers who can supply the correct botanical name, place of origin, part of plant used, method of extraction, and batch number when possible. *Lavender oil* means absolutely nothing!
- Always close the container immediately.
- Use extra care during early pregnancy.
- Use extra care with people receiving chemotherapy.
- Be aware of which essential oils are photosensitive, for example, bergamot.
- Avoid use with individuals who have severe asthma or multiple allergies.

Adverse Reactions

There have been some rare cases of adverse skin reactions caused by sensitivity. The majority of cases were from extracts that contained residual petrochemicals. People with multiple allergies are more likely to be sensitive to aromas. Bergamot used in conjunction with sunshine or tanning beds can result in skin damage, ranging from redness to full thickness burns.

Administration

Essential oils can be used topically or inhaled. One to five drops of essential oils are diluted in 5 cc (a teaspoon) cold-pressed vegetable oil, such as sweet almond oil for topical application. Some French doctors trained in aromatic medicine give essential oils (diluted in carrier oil) orally in gelatin capsules to treat infections. For topical applications, use every 4 hours. For inhalation, inhale for 10 minutes as necessary. Use touch methods such as massage or the *m* technique when appropriate. Simple stress management can be incorporated into the every day regime with the use of baths and foot soaks, vaporizers, and sprays.

Self-Help versus Professional

Aromatherapy can be self-applied for stress management, but for more clinical uses, it is better to have some training and knowledge of the chemistry and extraction methods. Many essential oils are sold under their common names. *Origanum marjorana* (sweet marjoram) is an excellent essential oil for insomnia; however, *thymus mastichina* (Spanish marjoram) is frequently sold as marjoram, but it is not a marjoram and certainly will not help insomnia. *Lavandula angustifolia* and *lavandula latifolia* are both sold as lavender. Angustifolia has sedative and antispasmodic properties: latifolia is a stimulant and expectorant.

The field of aromatherapy is vast. It can be fun to use essential oils in your home everyday just for the pleasure they give. They can make your home smell more welcoming. They can help your stress level, calm you down, and many other things, as listed previously; however, if you wish to use essential oils for clinical conditions, such as a chronic health problem, it is best to visit a professional trained in clinical aromatherapy.

KEY POINT

Currently, there is no recognized national certification and no governing body for aromatherapy, but the steering committee for Educational Standards in Aromatherapy in the United States has established the Aromatherapy Registration Board, a nonprofit entity that is responsible for administering a national exam. This exam is not clinically based. Graduates have RA (registered aromatherapist) after their names. The largest professional body for aromatherapists is the National Association of Holistic Aromatherapy. Currently, there are no requirements to become certified or accredited, and training can range from one weekend to several years. For a clinical aromatherapist who is also a licensed health professional, look for CCAP (certified clinical aromatherapy practitioner) after his or her name.

Aromatherapy is misunderstood because it is so broad; however, it encompasses many facets from pleasure through pain to infection, and it is not limited to scented candles and potpourri. Commercial use of the word *aromatherapy* to boost sales of products, such as shampoos, has confused the public. In fact, few if any cosmetic or pharmaceutical products currently include essential oils—they use synthetic fragrances as they are much cheaper; however, essential oils have been used safely for thousands of years. Aromatherapy used on a daily basis can be a useful component of healthy living.

Summary

Aromatherapy implies the therapeutic use of essential oils. Individuals can obtain the therapeutic effects of oils by inhaling them or absorbing them through the skin through baths, compresses, or touch; oils can be orally administered, but this must be done only by a trained professional. There are four basic types of aromatherapy: esthetic, holistic, environmental, and clinical. Special precautions must be considered when using aromatherapy. Essential oils are specific in their effects and must be selected based on their therapeutic benefit for the intended use and appropriateness for the specific individual.

Suggested Reading

Buckle, J. (2000). The *m* Technique. *Massage and Bodywork, 2*:52–65.
Buckle, J. (2001). The role of aromatherapy in nursing care. *Nursing Clinics of North America, 36*(1):57–71.

Buckle, J. (2003). *Clinical Aromatherapy Essential Oils in Practice*. London: Churchill Livingstone.

Clark, S. (2008). *Essential chemistry for Aromatherapy*. New York: Churchill Livingstone.

Cooksley, V. (2008). Aromatherapy research and practice. *AHNA Beginnings, 28*(3): 22–23.

Keville, K., & Green, M. (2008). *Aromatherapy: A Complete Guide to the Healing Art*. New York: Crossings Press.

Price, S., Price, L., & Daniel, P. (2006). *Aromatherapy for Health Professionals*. New York: Churchill Livingstone.

Schnaubelt, K. (1998). *Advanced Aromatherapy*. Rochester, VT: Healing Arts Press.

Schnaubelt, K. (1999). *Medical Aromatherapy: Healing with Essential Oils*. Berkeley, CA: Frog, Ltd.

Shutes, J., & Weaver, C. (2007). *Aromatherapy for Bodyworkers*. New York: Prentice Hall.

Smith, L. (2003). *Healing Oils, Healing Hands*. Avada, CO: HTSM Press.

Suskind, P. (1987). *Perfume: The Story of a Murderer*. New York: Penguin.

Tisserand, R. (2004). *The Art of Aromatherapy*. Vermont: Healing Arts Press.

Valnet, J. (1990). *The Practice of Aromatherapy*. Vermont: Healing Arts Press.

Worwood, S., & Worwood, V. A. (2003). *Essential Aromatherapy*. Novato, CA: New World Press.

Worwood, V. A. (2003). *The Complete Book of Essential Oils and Aromatherapy*. Novato, CA: New World Press.

Worwood, V. A. (2006). *Aromatherapy for the Soul*. Novato, CA: New World Press.

Resources

International Aromatherapy Association
www.internationalaromatherapyassociation.com

National Association for Holistic Aromatherapy
www.naha.org

Chapter 24

Effective Use of Homeopathic Remedies

OBJECTIVE

This chapter should enable you to

· Define a homeopathic remedy

· Describe the three laws of cure

· List three recommendations for storing homeopathic remedies

· List five suggestions for handling and administering the remedies

· List at least six substances that can reduce or eliminate the effects of a homeopathic remedy

Consumers are becoming increasingly frustrated with health practitioners' traditional approaches that rely heavily on prescribed medications or allopathic drugs. Taking prescription drugs often leads to the development of undesirable side effects. Reports in the United States indicate that there were more than 100,000 deaths and over 2 million injuries related to adverse reactions from prescription medications that were Food and Drug Agency (FDA)–approved drugs.[1] In addition to adverse effects, drugs often do little to correct the underlying condition, but instead, merely control symptoms. Not surprisingly, people are exploring natural products to manage health conditions and homeopathic remedies are among the more popular products that have caught consumers' attention.

Principles of Homeopathy: Actions of Homeopathic Remedies

The roots of the word *homeopathy* come from two Greek words: *homios*, which means *like*, and *pathos*, which means *suffering*. Homeopathy in modern society is described as treating *like with like*.

The science of homeopathy was discovered in the early 1800s by Dr. Samuel Hahnemann (1755–1843), a physician and chemist, who published, *The Organon of Medicine*. It describes in depth the philosophical perspective of homeopathy.

KEY POINT

The basic premise underlying the science of homeopathy is that the body's own healing process is activated to cure illnesses naturally. Specifically, the remedies stimulate and increase the vital force (often referred to as the life force) and restore balance to it, facilitating the body's innate healing ability. The vital force is the energy responsible for the health status of the body and for coordinating its defense against illness. If this vital force is disturbed because of environmental factors, lifestyle, inadequate nutrition, or lack of exercise, illness or unexpected, undesirable symptoms can occur.

Homeopathy is based on the theory that illness emerges as a result of a disturbance of the body's vital force, causing an imbalance in the energy within a person. The individual reacts emotionally, mentally, and physically. Each homeopathic remedy has several characteristics that influence specific symptoms and illnesses because of the imbalance.

The effects of homeopathy on the healing process within the human body was identified by Constantine Hering (1800–1880), who became known as the "Father of Homeopathy" in America and who was also the founder of the first schools and hospitals in which homeopathy was taught throughout the United States. He established the laws of cure, which are often referred to as "Hering's Laws" (see Exhibit 24-1). These were based on his observations of how healing occurs.

EXHIBIT 24-1   Hering's Laws of Cure

Healing takes place from the top to the bottom. Any symptom or ailment associated with the head area heals first, before the symptoms in the feet. Another illustration is that the symptoms disappear first from the shoulders, then the elbow, and then down the arm.

Healing takes place from inside to outside. This law refers to the fact that the symptoms will be relieved from the more centrally located organs before the extremities are improved.

Healing occurs from the most important organs to the least important organs. The symptoms move from the major or vital organs to the less vital or minor ones. Symptoms associated with any conditions of the heart will disappear first before symptoms associated with the intestines.

Symptoms disappear in reverse order of their appearance, with emotions improving first and then the physical symptoms. An example of this law is the instance in which a person who has been struggling with chronic fatigue for several months develops flu or a cold. The symptoms related to the flu or cold will disappear before the chronic fatigue symptoms clear. The healing process occurs in the reverse order to the onset of the symptoms.[7]

According to Hering's Laws, a person's health seems to get worse before it improves. In these cases in which the individuals may experience an initial worsening of their symptoms, their status will be followed by improvement and relief. This so-called worsening is often known as a *healing crisis* that signals the body's increased activity toward healing and usually passes quickly. The homeopathic practitioner refers to this worsening of symptoms as an aggravation. It is viewed as a sign that the remedy is working and has affected the vital force.[2]

In essence, it is essential that a person who uses homeopathic remedies understands the action of the remedies. The homeopathic effects on the body are different than what one expects from the use of traditional medicines, especially prescription drugs.

Homeopathic Remedies

Homeopathic remedies produce a therapeutic effect on symptoms, health conditions, and illnesses. For example, homeotherapeutic remedies are beneficial for a variety of ailments, such as digestive problems, neck stiffness, headaches, ear infections, respiratory problems, flu, motion sickness, women's health, men's health, allergies, emotional upsets, depression, anxiety, and hyperactivity.

Panos, a homeopathic physician, recommended 10 essential remedies for homeopathic first aid, as shown in Exhibit 24-2.[3] The general purpose of homeopathic first aid is to calm the mind, relieve pain, and help the body to heal itself.

REFLECTION

Do the laws of cure make sense to you? Can you think of illnesses you experienced that followed these laws?

Types, Safety, and Effectiveness of Remedies

Oral homeopathic remedies are available in several forms. The most common ones are pellets (most preferably those formed as tiny beads), tablets of soft consistency, and liquids. Some individuals prefer pellets and tablets to liquids because the dose in the tablets is predetermined and uniform. Other types of homeopathic remedies are suppositories, ointments, creams, and gels.

Homeopathic remedies have a history of effectiveness and safety without side effects. One main characteristic of homeopathic remedies is that they are nontoxic. Toxicity, a vital issue in health care, generally refers to a poisonous substance that causes an unhealthy environment within the person, leading to physiological or psychological problems, that is,

EXHIBIT 24-2 Homeopathic First Aid: The 10 Essential/Basic Remedies

Remedy
(Official name/common name)

Indications

Aconite

Aconite (Monkshood)

* early states of swelling and/or rapid swelling
* symptoms of colds—fever, chills

Apis mellifica

Apis (Honeybee)

* bee stings and other insect bites
* inflammation, rash, and allergic reactions
* swelling
* sore throat

Arnica montana

Arnica (Leopard's bane)

* serious or extensive sprains, strains, and bruises
* muscle soreness/tiredness
* external pain
* head scrapes and cuts
* itching from insect bites

Arsenicum album

Arsenicum (Arsenic)

* shock
* upset stomach
* vomiting
* food poisoning
* diarrhea
* restlessness, anxiety, and exhaustion

Belladonna

Belladonna (Deadly nightshade)

* sore throats, coughs, headaches, and earaches,
* colds, and flu
* high fever
* pulsation—pulse labored pulse
* redness—red, hot face

Gelsemium sempervirens

Gelsemium (Yellow jasmine)

* Apprehension
* flus, and head colds
* tension headaches
* apathy
* visual symptoms

(continues)

EXHIBIT 24-2   Homeopathic First Aid *(continued)*

Ipecacuanha

Ipecacuanha (Ipecac root)

* nausea and vomiting
* nosebleeds
* cold, sweaty
* gasping for air
* convulsive cough with nausea

Ledum palustre

Ledum (Marsh tea)

* minor puncture wounds
* bites and stings
* eye injuries
* ankle sprains

Nux vomica

Nux vomica (Poison nut)

* upset stomach (hangover)
* irritable
* impatient

Rhus toxicodendron

Rhus tox (Poison ivy)

* red swollen, intense itchy blisters
* stiffness
* sprains, and strains
* muscle pain

Ruta graveolens

Ruta (Rue)

* sprains, bruised tendons, and sore bones
* injuries and trauma

Source: Panos, M. & Heimlich, J. (1981). *Homeopathic Medicine at Home*. Los Angeles, CA: Jeremy P. Tarcher.

---

unpleasant, aggravating symptoms or illness. An imbalance in the immune system contributes to toxicity.

KEY POINT

There are no known adverse side effects from using homeopathic remedies and no known drug interaction risks between homeopathic remedies and conventional medications.

For effectiveness, homeopathic remedies must be chosen carefully on the basis of known information, as well as the correct usage and handling of the remedy. If the remedies are used incorrectly or handled improperly, the remedies may have only a superficial effect on the symptoms or illness or no effect at all.

Guidelines for Using Homeopathic Remedies

Whenever the client takes homeopathic remedies, certain guidelines must be followed for effectiveness of these natural products in alleviating symptoms and various health conditions.

Storing the Remedies

It is strongly recommended that the suggestions outlined herewith be followed for storing homeopathic remedies because improper storage may interfere with the effectiveness of the substance. If these remedies are properly stored and handled, they maintain their strength for years.

- Keep homeopathic remedies in their original containers. Avoid transferring the remedies to another bottle as this helps prevent any contamination.
- Secure the container tops of the remedies tightly; this prevents moisture from forming.
- Keep homeopathic remedies in a cool, dry, dark place away from humidity and out of direct sunlight and extremes of temperature (e.g., higher than 100°F). These factors may cause the remedies to lose their potency.
- Store the remedies away from any strong, pungent-smelling substances, such as perfume, camphor products, mothballs, and strong aromatic compounds found in various products, including mint foods and aromatic oils. It is believed that all of these substances act as an antidote and interfere with the effectiveness of the homeopathic therapy.
- Store homeopathic remedies out of the reach of children.

Handling the Remedies

Careful handling of homeopathic remedies, particularly those in liquid or tablet form, is very important.

- The homeopathic remedies (pellets and tablets) or the bottle dropper of the liquid remedies should be handled as little as possible because this is a source of contamination that may reduce the effectiveness of the product.
- When you pour the remedy, gently tip the pellets or tablets into the lid of the bottle or onto a clean, dry teaspoon. If any of the tablets have fallen out onto the floor or anywhere else or are unused, do not put the tablets back into the container as this will contaminate the stock. Discard the tablets.

Administering the Remedies

Following specific recommendations for taking homeopathic remedies will provide the best results of these natural-healing substances.

- The environment of the mouth should be in its natural condition. That is, the homeopathic remedies should not be taken within 20 minutes before or after eating, brushing one's teeth, or drinking anything other than water. It is important to take the solid dosage forms of homeopathic remedies when the mouth is empty and clear of any food or beverages because these other substances in the mouth may decrease the absorption and effectiveness of the remedy.

- When using homeopathic remedies, it is best to eliminate the use of certain spicy foods and strong smelling foods, including garlic, any form of caffeine, camphor, mints, toiletries, and medications (aspirin, laxatives, etc.) during this time, as these substances may counteract the effects of the homeopathic remedies (see Exhibit 24-3).

- The use of tobacco should be avoided. Nicotine may alter the response of the body to homeopathic remedies.

- Read the label on the specific homeopathic remedy. Pay attention to what is stated. Note the ingredients and amounts.

- Follow the dosage instructions on the container or as instructed by your health-care practitioner.

- Take the homeopathic dose on an empty stomach. This is essential because gastric juices and digestive processes can destroy or inactivate the remedy.

- Place the solid forms (pellets or tablets) under the tongue (sublingually) and dissolve gradually without chewing or any tongue movement. The remedies are absorbed into the buccal lining of the mouth. This in turn allows the remedies to go directly to the point of action, bypassing the stomach, intestines, and liver.

- Place the drops (liquid) under the tongue in amounts ranging from 1–10 drops. (Follow the dosage on the label or use as suggested by the healthcare practitioner.)

- A general rule would be to start with 5 drops and then after 1 week increase to 10 drops; however, there is an exception to this rule. In the case of sensitivities, the dosage amount is reduced. The healthcare practitioner may recommend starting with 1 or 2 drops and increasing the dosage by a drop each week until 10 drops is reached.

- Finally, the homeopathic remedies should be taken only for as long as one needs them. As soon as positive results are observed, the homeopathic remedies should be discontinued.

EXHIBIT 24-3 **Common Substances That Reduce the Effects of Homeopathic Remedies**

Ingredient	Product
Alcohol	Liquor
Caffeine	Chocolate
	Coffee
	Cola (soda)
	Tea
Camphor	Chapstick
	Deep-heat ointments (Tiger Balm)
	Lip salves
Eucalyptus	Candy, cough drops
	Cough mixtures
	Karvol capsules
	Tiger Balm
	Vick's products
Menthol	Candy, cough drops
	Cough mixtures
	Fisherman's Friend
	Nasal drops
	Tiger Balm
	Vick's products
	Mint flavors (peppermint, wintergreen)
	Mouthwash
	Toothpaste
Tobacco	Cigarettes

Compiled from Lockie, A., & Geddes, N. (2000). *Natural Health Complete Guide to Homeopathy*, 2nd ed. New York: Dorling Kindersley.

Summary

The main action of homeopathic remedies is to stimulate the vital force that is central to health. They energize the vital force within the body to help eliminate undesirable symptoms or illnesses. Using these natural remedies also helps to maintain a healthy, balanced immune system. Recommendations should be followed regarding storage, handling, and the correct taking of the remedies for their effectiveness and maintaining its potency. Homeopathic remedies are considered extremely safe, effective, nontoxic, and helpful in alleviating symptoms in helping the body heal itself. They can contribute to a greater sense of well-being, energy, and an overall improved resistance to illness.

References

1. Paulozzi, L. (2008). Trends in unintentional drug overdose deaths. Testimony before the Senate Judiciary Subcommittee on Crime and Drugs, March 12, 2008. Department of Health and Human Services, http://www.hhs.gov/asl/testify/2008/03/t20080312b.html
2. Lockie, A., & Geddes, N. (2000). *Natural Health Complete Guide to Homeopathy*, 2nd ed. New York: Dorling Kindersley.
3. Panos, M., & Heimlich, J. (1996). *Homeopathic Medicine at Home*. Los Angeles: Jeremy P. Tarcher.

Suggested Reading

Cummings, S., & Ullman, D. (2004). *Everybody's Guide to Homeopathic Medicines*. New York, Penguin.
Hammond, C. (1995). *The Complete Family Guide to Homeopathy*. New York: Penguin Studio.
Herhoff, A. (2000). *Homeopathic Remedies*. Garden City, NY: Avery Publishing Group.
Lockie, A. (1993). *The Family Guide to Homeopathy: Symptoms and Natural Solutions*. New York: Fireside.
Lockie, A. (2001). *Homeopathy Handbook*. New York: Dorling Kindersley.
McCabe, V. (2000). *Practical Homeopathy*. New York: St. Martin's Griffin.
Monte, T. (1997). *The Complete Guide to Natural Healing*. New York: Perigee Book.
Reichenberg-Ullman, J. (1994). *The Patients' Guide to Homeopathic Medicine*. Edmonds, WA: Picnic Point Press.
Reichenberg-Ullman, J. (2000). *Whole Woman Homeopathy*. Roseville, CA: Prima Health.
Reiter, R. (2003). *Healing Without Medication*. North Bergen, NJ: Basic Health Publications, Inc.
Schmukler, A. (2006). *Homeopathy: An A to Z Home Handbook*. Woodbury, MN: Llewellyn Press.
Shalts, E. (2006). *Easy Homeopathy*. New York: McGraw Hill.
Skinner, S. (2001). *An Introduction to Homeopathic Medicine in Primary Care*. Gaithersburg, MD: Aspen Publications.
Sollars, D. (2001). *The Complete Idiot's Guide to Homeopathy*. Indianapolis, IN: Alpha Books.
Ullman, D. (2002). *The Consumer's Guide to Homeopathy*. New York: Jeremy P. Tarcher/Putnam.
Ullman, R., & Reichenberg-Ullman, J. (1997). *Homeopathic Self-Care, The Quick and Easy Guide for the Whole Family*. Rocklin, CA: Prima Publishing.
Vithoulkas, G. (1980). *The Science of Homeopathy*. New York: Grove Press.

Resources

ABC Homeopathy
http://abchomeopathy.com

Homeopathy Home
www.homeopathyhome.com

National Center for Homeopathy
http://www.homeopathic.org

North American Society of Homeopaths
www.homeopathy.org

Chapter 25

Medication Wisdom

OBJECTIVES

This chapter should enable you to

· Describe medication-related information that is significant for healthcare providers to review and discuss with consumers

· Distinguish between medication side effects and adverse drug reactions

· List eight common undesirable consumer behaviors with prescription medications

· Describe specific interventions the healthcare provider can use to help patients resolve issues related to obtaining prescription medications

Throughout history, people have exerted self-control over the selection and use of healing agents, including medicines. The interest in selection and use of medications continues to be important to consumers. People want to know specifically about the medications they are taking, how medications work, their potential side effects, possible and potential interactions with other medications, and how the medications will impact their functional status.

KEY POINT

There are more than 100,000 nonprescription and 40,000 prescription products purchased each year in the United States. Forty-five percent of all Americans are using at least one prescription drug.[1]

Consumer Issues Related to Prescription Medications

The ultimate goal of taking medication is to enhance one's health state or level of functioning. The desired outcome is to obtain the maximum benefit with minimal side effects and little or no toxicity. Each person has a unique and individual body composition. Because of each person's unique biochemical composition, no two individuals will respond

TABLE 25-1   **Essential Information to Know When Using a Medication**

· Name (brand and generic)

· Use

· How to administer

· Side effects

· Adverse reactions

· Storage and handling

· Special precautions

· Interactions with other medications, foods, and supplements

· What to do if there are missed doses

to a medication in exactly the same way. Table 25-1 depicts general, essential information the consumer needs to have when taking any medication.

Name of the Medication

Medications have both a generic and a trade name. This information is essential for people to know for each of their prescribed medications. The trade (brand) name of the medication is the drug name as it is available from pharmaceutical manufacturers. Pharmacists, unless otherwise indicated, can substitute an equivalent generic drug without prescriber approval, and in many cases, this will pass on significant cost savings to consumers. In some cases, however, only the trade (brand) name medication can be dispensed if the prescription specifies "Dispense as Written." Consumers need to be educated that although generic products are considered to be pharmaceutically equivalent to the trade (brand) name counterparts, not all are therapeutically the same. This could ultimately result in failed therapy because of ineffectiveness of a medication.

Use of the Medication

Consumers need to know the purpose for each medication they use (e.g., to treat inner ear infection, lower blood pressure, eliminate fluids). This can be particularly important, as there can be situations where the pharmacist cannot accurately read the handwriting on the prescription. Many medication names are spelled very similarly, and there could be serious consequences if the wrong medication is given. (An example of two medications that easily could be confused is Celebrex, used to treat musculoskeletal conditions, and Celexa, used for treatment of depressive disorders.) By knowing the name and purpose of their prescribed drugs, consumers can detect errors and spare themselves complications.

> **REFLECTION**
>
> Do you know the names, purposes, side effects, and adverse effects for every medication you use?

How to Administer the Medication

Healthcare providers need to educate consumers to know the correct dosage of their medications, routes of administration, and any other important information. There are several routes for administration of prescribed medications. The most common routes for home medication administration are oral, rectal, topical, eardrops (otic), eye drops (ophthalmic), subcutaneous injection (sub-Q), intranasal, inhaled, and intramuscular injections (IM). Failure to take prescribed medication via the correct route could result in outcomes ranging from insignificant consequence to death. An example of incorrectly administering a medication could be instilling eye drops in the ear. In this case, the patient outcome will most likely not be life threatening (although not receiving the needed medication could have effects for the eye). An example of serious potential harm might be administering a medication intended for topical (skin) administration orally.

Administration of the correct dosage at the specified intervals is important. Not taking enough of the drug or skipping doses could reduce the benefit and leave the health problem with inadequate treatment. On the other hand, taking doses that exceed the prescribed amount or taking drugs more frequently than prescribed could cause damage to body organs and serious complications. Consideration also must be given to the existence of conditions, such as liver or kidney disease, that could affect the metabolism and excretion of drugs. Dosage adjustments would be warranted in these situations.

Side Effects of the Medication

Medication side effects are responses that can occur with medications. Although side effects result in patient discomfort or cause concern, they usually are not life threatening. An example of a side effect would be the onset of nausea after taking an antibiotic on an empty stomach.

Side effects may or may not require that a medication be stopped. The consumer must be educated in awareness and recognition of potential and actual side effects in the event that they occur. Healthcare providers need to inform consumers of the side effects that should be reported. Together, the healthcare provider and consumer can discuss the situation and make an informed decision about whether to stop the medication and whether the side effects warrant intervention.

Adverse Reactions to the Medication

In addition to medication side effects, consumers must be aware of potential adverse drug reactions (ADRs). ADRs have been studied in hospitalized patients, and it has been estimated that there are approximately 2 million ADRs annually in the United States, resulting in ADRs being the fourth leading cause of death.[2] ADRs can be severe adverse reactions and toxic effects that can result in loss of life or permanent impairment and loss of functioning. ADRs require prompt intervention by healthcare providers because without emergent care some ADRs could result in death within minutes.

KEY POINT

Adverse drug reactions demand speedy attention. A person taking a new medication who develops tightness in the throat or difficulty breathing, indicative of a life-threatening ADR known as anaphylaxis, could die within a short time without intervention.

Storage and Handling of the Medication

Consumers require specific information on medication storage and handling. Improper storage or handling decomposition of biochemical ingredients can result in decreased potency or efficacy. Detailed, specific medication storage and handling instructions should be provided with each medication prescribed. Examples of frequently asked questions regarding storage and handling are as follows: "Does this medication need to be refrigerated?" "Can I travel with this medication?" "How long is the medication good if I store it?" Medication labels contain specific details on storage and handling, but can be difficult to read for some older or sight-impaired persons. Special considerations would be in order in these situations to assist consumers with needed storage and handling information.

Special Medication Precautions

Nearly every prescription medication has some unique precautions, making it essential for consumers to be aware of times when a medication should or should not be used. These special precautions also help to alert the healthcare provider that the consumer should be under close surveillance when using the drug. Healthcare providers need to discuss the risks and benefits of taking a medication with consumers prior to prescribing any medication.

Older adults, young children, and pregnant women are at increased risk for harmful medication effects as a result of their physiological differences. Children's medication dosages must be carefully and accurately calculated according to age, weight, level of growth and development, and height. Older adults have an increased risk of ADRs because they do not metabolize nor excrete medications as easily as younger people because of age-related changes. Pregnant women are at increased risk of teratogenicity or harm to the unborn fetus with many medications. Healthcare providers should discuss risks and benefits of medications prescribed during pregnancy with the obstetrician and document the outcome of the conversation in the health record.

Interactions with Other Medications

Drug-to-drug interactions are a significant concern for consumers and healthcare providers. Consumers are using more and more over-the-counter medications, as well as herbal and nontraditional medicinal products. There can be interactions with or contraindications for certain foods with over-the-counter medications, herbal, and nontraditional therapies they may be using. The likelihood of drug-to-drug interaction occurrence is increased because of the complex biochemical composition of the many products now available. As the number of medications a person takes increases, there is a commensurate increase in the likelihood of an interaction. Drug-to-drug interactions can range from relatively benign or not harmful to life threatening. An example of a possible food contraindication would be that when taking Coumadin (a blood thinner), green, leafy vegetables (such as lettuce, cabbage, or brussel sprouts) should be avoided, as these vegetables counter the desired effects of the drug.

Missed Dose of Medication

It is always advisable for the consumer to call the healthcare provider if a dose of medication is missed. This is a situation that may occur because the consumer simply forgot to take their medicine, or perhaps he or she was too ill to take it. An example would be a person with diabetes who has intractable nausea and vomiting and does not know whether or not to take their morning insulin. The healthcare provider can review the situation and advise accordingly.

Common Consumer Medication Mistakes and How to Avoid Them

Healthcare providers must emphasize to consumers the need to take medications precisely as prescribed. Consumers can increase medication safety and efficacy by following five fundamental principles of medication administration each time a medication is taken:

1. Right drug
2. Right dose
3. Right route

4. Right time

5. Right person

Consumers often engage in several common undesirable behaviors with respect to medications. These behaviors are quite common and need to be addressed by the health-care provider on each patient encounter. Table 25-2 depicts eight common undesirable consumer behaviors that frequently occur with prescribed medications.

Saving Unused Medication for Oneself or Others for Future Illness

Using medications that have remained from a date far in the past or prescribed for some-one else is never advised. Medications are prescribed in a dosage that is necessary to treat a specific condition for a particular person at the given time. Prescriptions for the treatment of acute conditions, like infections, need to be fully consumed until the condition is completely resolved. People can develop a flare-up of an inadequately treated infection or resistance to certain pathogens by not completing the medication as prescribed, subjecting themselves to new risks.

Forgetting to Get the Prescription Refilled

It has become common for people to get medications filled via direct mail order. This can add to the problem of forgetting to refill a prescription or to refill it in time to avoid missed medication doses. It is not advisable to miss even one medication dose, as this can cause potentially serious or life-threatening harm. Many medications are used for the control of long-term, chronic conditions, such as heart disease, hypertension, or diabetes, and miss-

---

TABLE 25-2   Common Undesirable Behaviors to Avoid When Taking Medications

1. Saving unused medication for oneself or others for future illness

2. Forgetting to get the prescription refilled

3. Not finishing medications as prescribed because symptoms are relieved

4. Forgetting to take the medicine at the prescribed times

5. Not taking the medication as directed

6. Stopping or not filling the prescription because of cost

7. Sharing medications

8. Taking over-the-counter or nonconventional remedies without informing the healthcare provider

ing even one dose can result in undesirable or harmful effects. An example would be a person who takes the medication, Lanoxin (digoxin). Digoxin affects the contractility of the heart. Missing even one dose of digoxin can result in heart failure, a potentially life-threatening situation.

KEY POINT

When using mail-order services to fill prescriptions, people need to be careful to allow adequate time for ordering refills to assure that they do not run out of their existing supply before the new supply arrives.

It is especially important to give the mail order pharmacy prescriptions ample time to process the order. In the event that a person runs out of a drug, it could prove useful to check with the healthcare provider to see whether any medication samples are available to use until the shipment arrives. If the provider does not have samples, then the person must request a written prescription for a few doses, enough to last until their shipment arrives. In the majority of cases, the individual will most likely have to pay for these interim prescriptions, as many insurers do not. It is also important to note that many third-party insurers often will not pay for more than 90 days on a prescription, requiring the consumer to return to the primary healthcare practitioner to get a new prescription.

Not Finishing Medications as Prescribed Because a Person Feels Better

Prematurely discontinuing a medication is a common behavior that can result in potentially life-threatening situations later on. For example, in the case of *Beta hemolytic streptococcus*, the most frequent cause of strep throat, the bacteria may not be completely eradicated even though a person feels better and the symptoms are essentially resolved. These medications are usually prescribed for a full 10 days of therapy in order to eradicate the causative organism completely. When antibiotic therapy is suboptimal, the organism can become resistant to the treatment for future events, or the organism can grow in other areas of the body, such as the heart valves. This organism could then harm the heart valves resulting in abnormal leaking of blood back into the heart chambers and result in impaired circulation or damaged heart valve leaflets.

Forgetting to Take the Medication at Designated Times

Frequently, a person forgets to take a dose of medication. In some cases, the dose may be taken as soon as one remembers, if there are no special indications, such as taking it with or between meals. If the missed dose is close to the time of the next scheduled dose, the healthcare provider most likely will advise the person to take the missed dose and resume the usual schedule. The consumer should not double up or take an extra dose, as this can result in a variety of potential outcomes, depending on the medication and potential side effects. An example is a missed a dose of penicillin; attempting to double the dose to make up the missed dose often results in gastrointestinal upset, such as nausea, diarrhea, or severe stomach cramping.

Not Taking the Medication as Directed

Medications need to be taken specifically as prescribed. This is a very important consideration because many medications are designed biochemically to work in certain environments. For example, if the medication is to be taken 1 hour before meals and is consumed with a meal, its absorption could be affected and the drug may not achieve its intended purpose. Many medications should not be taken with milk or other dairy products. If this is the situation, it will be specified on the medication administration sheet and on the label of the medication container. There can be quite serious, even life-threatening consequences if directions are not adhered to as specified.

Stopping or Not Filling a Medication Prescription Because a Person Cannot Pay for It

There are reasons for medications to be prescribed; therefore, not filling prescriptions has consequences. When the healthcare practitioner prescribes the medication, it is always helpful for people to ask for an estimate of what the prescription will cost. Although the provider may not be able to give exact figures, some information regarding the approximate cost of the medication should be available. In other cases, the healthcare provider may ask that a pharmacy be called to obtain the price. If this is a prescription for a new medication and the consumer is just starting it, especially if it is a very new and expensive medication where there is no generic, less expensive equivalent, it is useful to ask the healthcare practitioner whether she or he has samples available; this can spare the cost of filling the full prescription only to discover that one cannot tolerate the drug. There is nothing more frustrating than spending a large amount of money on a medication that does not agree with the consumer and produces so many side effects that the person cannot take it. If the provider wants the consumer to have the medication but has no samples and the consumer cannot afford the medication, the consumer can try to contact a hospital social worker or community resource person for assistance. There may be a community agency that assists in these purchases—and there are also some medication programs for those who cannot pay through some of the pharmaceutical companies that cover some medication prescriptions.

The bottom line is that consumers should *never do without a medication if they cannot afford it*. Healthcare providers need to consider this issue when recommending medications.

REFLECTION

Some people complain about the cost of medications and other healthcare expenses while not hesitating to spend money on expensive restaurant dinners, manicures, theater tickets, and other nonessentials. Why do you think they hold such attitudes?

Sharing Medications

Giving medication to anyone other than the person for whom it was prescribed unfortunately does occur and this practice carries many significant risks. Using someone else's medications can mask symptoms, resulting in improper diagnosis and treatment of life-threatening disorders. It also can result in microbial resistance to organisms.

Taking Over-the-Counter or Nonconventional Products Without Informing the Health Care Provider

As previously stated, there can be potentially lethal or life-threatening interactions between medications and food substances. It is crucial that people share all information regarding over-the-counter, herbal, or nonconventional (complementary or alternative) therapies with their healthcare providers at each visit. In turn, providers need to make a practice of inquiring about the addition of an over-the-counter or nontraditional treatment with each client visit. Health records should reflect this information to provide continuity of care by all providers. An example of the importance of sharing this information involves the use of green tea preparations, which can enhance the potency of Coumadin, an agent used to thin the blood. If the herbal substance enhances the effect of the medication, the person may experience a life-threatening hemorrhage, such as in the brain, and die as a result of cerebral hemorrhage.

Suggested Times for Taking Scheduled Medications

All prescribed medications include specificity regarding the frequency of administration. Table 25-3 depicts common abbreviations and meanings for medication administration, suggested times for the common medication administration schedules, and special considerations. These abbreviations are of Latin origin.

Strategies to Assess Medications' Effectiveness

Most pharmacies now provide informational pamphlets with prescriptions. This information usually provides detailed written information ranging from medication dosing to

TABLE 25-3 Common Abbreviations and Related Information for Medications

Common Abbreviation	Meaning	Suggested Times for Taking the Medication	Special Considerations
ac	Must be taken before meals in order for it to be effective and to do what it is supposed to do	Take the medication 30 minutes before the scheduled or planned mealtime.	If the medication is skipped, take it 30 minutes before the meal; wait at least 2 hours after the meal to take the medication.
bid	Must be taken two times a day	Suggested times for taking the medication should reflect a person's lifestyle for ease of compliance. For example, if one arises at 6 a.m., the medication can be taken at 7 a.m. and 4 p.m. The two times a day dosing is usually spaced approximately 8 hours apart.	If one dose is forgotten, take it as soon as remembered and resume the regular schedule the following day. Do not double up and take two doses at one time.
tid	Must be taken three times a day	Try to incorporate these three times into individual lifestyle if possible to take the medication on time. Space the medications across the day so that doses are not taken close together. For example, if one awakens at 6 a.m., the drug could be taken at 7 a.m., 3 p.m., and 10 p.m. (These sample times are approximately 8 hours apart.)	If one dose is forgotten, take it as soon as remembered and resume the regular schedule the following day. Do not double up and take two doses at one time.

(continues)

TABLE 25-3   Common Abbreviations and Related Information for Medications *(continued)*

Common Abbreviation	Meaning	Suggested Times for Taking the Medication	Special Considerations
qid	Must be taken four times a day	Suggested times for a four times a day dosing would be 9 a.m., 1 p.m., 6 p.m., and 9 p.m. There can be individual variance and adjustment of this suggested schedule to fit individual lifestyles. It is not recommended to double doses to catch up in the event of a missed dose.	If one dose is forgotten, take it as soon as remembered and resume the regular schedule the following day. Do not double up and take two doses at one time.
hs	Must be taken at bedtime	The suggested time for a bedtime dose is 9 or 10 p.m.; however, if one retires earlier or later individual adjustment can be made.	None
qd	Must be taken once a day	This dosing regimen is usually flexible and accommodates the person's individual lifestyle. Most persons take the medication for daily dosing at 8 or 9 a.m.	It is important to take the medication at the same time each day in order not to forget to take it or to mistakenly repeat administration. Choose a consistent time that will increase the likelihood of remembering, such as with breakfast.

TABLE 25-4   Specific Tips to Insure Medication Effectiveness and Optimize Therapeutic Effects

· Always take medication specifically as prescribed

· Take the medication at the time it is prescribed

· Take the medication in the dose that is prescribed

· Do not skip medication doses

· Do not double up on the medication if a dose is missed

· Notify the primary care provider who prescribed the medication of any symptoms experienced whether they are suspected or known to be related to the medication

· Immediately report to the healthcare provider any unusual feelings or events immediately, such as swelling in any part of the body, joint aching, heart palpitations, or unusual fatigue

potential side effects. Consumers should be certain to obtain this information on any prescription that is filled. In addition, many pharmacists now provide individual counseling for each consumer. If consumers opt not to have medication counseling, they may be asked to sign a waiver to that effect. Medication information provided with each prescription includes medication purpose, potential side effects and ADRs, special precautions when taking the medication, and food/drug interactions. Medication information provided by pharmacies also includes specific tips to insure the prescription medication will be effective (see Table 25-4).

Summary

Consumers use more than 100,000 nonprescription and 40,000 prescription drugs annually. All of these products, although beneficial in many ways, can carry serious risks if used improperly. Consumers and their healthcare providers need to be in partnership in assuring safe drug use.

Consumers need to be informed users of all medications to assure safety. They need to be knowledgeable about the generic and brand names, intended use, administration, side effects, adverse reactions, storage, handling, precautions, and interactions related to each drug they use.

Common mistakes that must be avoided include saving unused medications for future use, using someone else's drugs, running out of medications because of a failure to get refills in time, discontinuing the medication prematurely, forgetting to take the drug, not taking the drug as directed, and using other drugs or over-the-counter remedies without the healthcare provider's knowledge.

Informed medication use is an important part of self-care. Consumers can seek information from pharmacists who fill prescriptions to enhance their knowledge.

References

1. National Center for Health Statistics. (2007).Table 96, Age-adjusted cancer incidence rates for selected cancer sites, by sex, race, and Hispanic origin: United States, selected geographic areas, selected years 1990–2004.
2. U.S. Food and Drug Administration, Center for Drug Evaluation and Research, (2008). Preventable Adverse Drug Reactions. Retrieved August 1, 2008 from http://www.fda.gov/CDER/DRUG/drugReactions/default.htm

Suggested Readings

Griffith, H. W., & Moore, S. (2008). *Complete Guide to Prescription and Nonprescription Drugs*. New York: Penguin Group.

Karch, A. M. (2008). *Lippincott's Nursing Drug Guide*. Philadelphia: Lippincott.

Lippincott. (2008). *Drug Facts and Comparisons*. Philadelphia, PA: Lippincott.

Medwatch. Retrieved from http://www.drugintel.com/public/medwatch/

Silverman, H. M. (2008). *The Pill Book*. New York: Bantam.

Resources

Drugs.com
www.drugs.com

Drugs, Supplements, and Herbal Information

Medline Plus
http://www.nlm.nih.gov/medlineplus/druginformation.html

RxList
www.rxlist.com/script/main/hp.asp

Chapter 26

Surviving Caregiving

OBJECTIVES

This chapter should enable you to

- · Define the terms *sandwich generation* and *club sandwiches*
- · Discuss the many roles caregivers can fill
- · List at least two major instructions provided in an advance directive
- · Discuss the difference between a delirium and a dementia
- · Describe at least two ways that caregivers' burdens can be relieved

There has been a tremendous increase in the number of aging Americans causing a graying of the population. The fact that growing numbers of people can expect to survive to later years than their grandparents is wonderful news, but it does create major challenges. These challenges can affect people very directly, either in terms of the human and financial resources needed to meet their own needs as they age or the care they will have to provide to the older adults in their lives.

> **KEY POINT**
>
> In the early 1900s, life expectancy was age 47 and only about 4% of the population lived to age 65 or older. Now in the 21st century, life expectancy is over 77 years, with nearly 13% of the population 65 years or older. The fastest growing segment within the older age group is those over the age of 85 years. It will become more commonplace to see people reaching their 100th birthday.

Sandwich Generation

In the early 90s, the term *sandwich generation* was coined. This term appropriately described the way that it feels to be caught in the middle: responsible for the care of both parents and children at the same period of time. For centuries, family members took care of each other, and thus, this certainly is not a recent development. The important differences now, however, are that so many more people are surviving much longer, primarily because of new medications and advances of technology in health care; rather than a few years, care of an elder relative can span several decades. Also noteworthy is the fact that few families have the luxury of having a stay-at-home parent, as most women are employed outside the home. The combined stressors, both internal and external, often contribute to feelings of alienation within families instead of enjoyment in relationships.

Increasingly, what can be termed *club sandwiches* is being added to the menu of family profiles. A club sandwich refers to a caregiver who is providing support and assistance to a parent, a child, as well as a grandchild. There are, however, a variety of club sandwiches. Sometimes the grandparent may become the primary care provider. The reasons for this are many. With approximately 50%–60% of marriages ending in divorce, some grandparents are faced with assisting their single-parent children with the demands of raising children. Others are handed their new obligations because their adult children became involved in drugs, alcohol abuse, or other unhealthy lifestyles that prevented them from raising their own children. Whatever the forerunner, the fact remains that many families are struggling with caregiver issues and need information and assistance.

KEY POINT

Caregiving wears many faces and includes a variety of tasks and responsibilities.

Many Faces of Caregiving

Providing daily personal care or supervision to a parent can be demanding and overwhelming; however, caregiving often entails more than physical care. One's presence—being there for a parent—can be a significant factor in preserving emotional well-being. An example of a situation that may require intervention is the vulnerable time when one's parents are attempting to make a sometimes difficult adjustment to retirement. The opportunities of retirement, although perhaps envied by many, are often accompanied by loss and role confusion.

KEY POINT

If you consider the fact that a person may have worked in a job for decades and then one day is no longer required to perform that role, it is easy to understand how emotional upheaval may occur in retirement, especially if the individual has not prepared for this change.

Adult children may assist their parents to recognize their continued value during the time of transition to retirement. It is also a time when children can be instrumental in assisting their parents to navigate the healthcare system. Older parents may be very concerned about their ability to pay for their health care with a limited income. The complexity of Medicare billing also is worrisome to many. There have been so many changes in the healthcare delivery system that clarification and advocacy are often the most supportive activities that children can provide for their parents. Being available to accompany them to doctors' visits and helping them to make some very difficult healthcare decisions can be valuable ways children can help their parents in late life.

As one ages, chronic health problems become more common. These chronic conditions (e.g., hypertension and other cardiac diseases, arthritis, diabetes, and gastrointestinal disturbances) can interfere with the quality of life and ultimately disrupt a person's function. Often these conditions may necessitate more frequent visits to healthcare providers. Many older people have never challenged a physician's diagnosis or requested a second opinion. They may be fearful of offending their doctors by asking questions. Adult children can help their parents to be assertive in this most important aspect of decision making. Frequently, making the right choice means preventing unnecessary discomfort and decline in function, which could accompany inappropriate treatments.

KEY POINT

Any declines in function that can be prevented will help to preserve independence and enhance quality of life, as well as reduce caregiving responsibilities.

Advance Directives

To help assure that appropriate care is provided and that informed decisions are made, discussions and thoughtful planning should be done well in advance of when needed. These issues can be addressed in a document called an *advance directive* or *living will.*

KEY POINT

An advance directive provides specific instructions on the treatment people want or do not want to have in the event they are not capable of expressing their opinions. This document also names a person who is authorized to make healthcare decisions for matters not specifically described in the document.

Preparation of an advance directive is extremely beneficial. This is frequently a topic of discussion at senior meetings and senior centers; however, if one's parents have not yet completed this document, they should be encouraged or assisted in this process. A copy of an advance directive is usually available from a healthcare provider or area agency on aging office.

The decision of naming a health care representative—someone who can make decisions regarding treatments if an individual is unable to do for himself or herself—is sometimes a difficult one for an older adult to make. It is vital that permission be obtained from the person who will be named as proxy healthcare representative. Also, the physician, hospital, perhaps an attorney, and other interested family members should have a copy of the advance directive, in addition to the named representative. The original should remain in a safe place with important papers.

Financial Considerations

Assisting parents or other older relatives to establish a financial system to prevent financial chaos or hardship is another useful action. Often older adults are the victims of scams. In their attempt to handle situations independently, they frequently become easy prey to unscrupulous predators. After they have sustained significant loss, they may conceal the facts and bear their shame with a mask of depression. They may be fearful that they will be considered incompetent; therefore, they may never come forward or even share the information with people who could assist them to recoup their losses. Putting some financial safety checks in place early on often helps to prevent loss and provides a good record-keeping mechanism for a future accounting. These records may be necessary to justify financial eligibility for a state or federal assistance program or to verify appropriate distribution of funds, which sometimes becomes a significant issue even within close-knit families.

KEY POINT

It is possible that early caregiving interventions can be so natural and subtle that you may not even realize that you are doing anything that resembles taking care of another.

Financial issues that may be difficult to discuss should not be avoided but rather brought to awareness and addressed before a crisis or disability occurs. Critical topics, those of financial consequence as well as those of advance directives, end-of-life issues, healthcare proxy, and guardianships are too important to wait until a court makes the decisions for individuals and their loved ones.

REFLECTION

Have you and your older relatives discussed issues pertaining to their finances and health care in the event that they are incapacitated by illness or disability? If you have, what were some of the emotional issues that you had to confront? If you have not, what are the issues preventing this discussion and how can you address them?

Age-Related Changes

Many changes occur with age. People develop into more complex physical, psychological, and spiritual beings with a greater understanding of life, having experienced many unique situations. On the down side, aging usually brings negative changes in all of the senses. Vision is frequently compromised by such conditions as aging, macular degeneration, cataracts, or *presbyopia* (blurring of vision up close due to changes in the lens). Hearing may deteriorate and limit the tones that can be heard, with the lower tones being the most audible. This condition, known as *presbycusis*, causes people to miss large portions of conversation because certain letters sound muffled. Often older adults hesitate to obtain or use hearing aids because the aids can be distracting, difficult to adjust to, or emphasize the fact that they are getting old.

KEY POINT

Sometimes presbycusis can cause people to give inappropriate responses because they misinterpret speech. Others mistakenly may view them as being confused or having early dementia.

Diminished sense of smell and taste may lead to nutritional problems, social isolation, and unsafe conditions in the home. Common reasons for visits to the emergency room for older adults are dehydration, electrolyte imbalance, malnutrition, and falls. These conditions sometimes can be prevented by frequent contact with family, friends, and others who can make visits and identify problems early. In some communities, a friendly visitor service is provided by church groups or gatekeeper programs. The postal service as well as utility companies (gas/electric/telephone/cable) often train their employees to look for signs that indicate a customer may need assistance. In many communities, older persons can receive Meals on Wheels or daily lunches through senior centers. With funding from the Older Americans Act (OAA), seniors can be transported to local sites where nutritious meals, social stimulation, and interaction await them. Coordinators of these programs are usually aware of significant changes in their members and can intervene before unsafe conditions develop or provide rapid assistance through Adult Protective Services personnel if a senior becomes unable to make independent decisions any longer.

Changes in tactile (touch) sensations cause difficulty feeling heat, cold, pain, and pressure, which increases the risk of personal injury. Sometimes fear of being injured by temperature extremes, the discomfort of feeling chilled, and the fear of falling in the bathtub or shower interfere with bathing and personal care needs. This can be most distressing to family or others who attempt to provide care; however, that in the older person, there is a process where their skin becomes drier than when they were younger. Unless there is incontinence or it is necessary to remove other irritants from the skin, a shower or bath twice a week will suffice for hygienic needs.

Perhaps the most distressing alterations are the cognitive changes, which are increasingly common with advanced age. Age-related changes in cerebral function can result in slower reaction time and increased time to learn new information, as well as greater potential for attention to be distracted. These events, coupled with the sensory changes already mentioned, and the stress of everyday living can create memory difficulties. Memory loss, significant personality changes, confusion, or changes in intellectual abilities are not normal consequences of aging. If an older adult is experiencing what is thought to be unusual changes in cognitive function, a comprehensive geriatric assessment is a wonderful means to identify the source of the problem. Some causes of memory problems that can be detected in a comprehensive geriatric assessment include delirium, depression, and dementia.

KEY POINT

A *delirium* is a change in mental function with a rapid onset that usually can be treated and corrected. Some possible causes are infections, low blood pressure, dehydration, and side effects from medications. A *dementia* is a deterioration in mental function that has a slow, subtle onset. Some possible causes include Alzheimer's disease, AIDS, and alcoholism. The losses sustained cannot be regained.

Although a dementia is not able to be reversed, there have been tremendous strides in new medications that delay further impairment. These medications are most successful when begun at an early stage of the disease. The longer function can be maintained, the longer one will be able to remain independent. When memory impairment or other cognitive changes are present, it is essential that the individual obtain a comprehensive assessment. Typically, this assessment consists of a series of visits to a geriatrician, an advanced practice geriatric nurse, and a geriatric social worker. Included in the examination are blood tests that assess complete blood count, folic acid, thyroid function, and electrolyte imbalances. There also is radiological imaging of the brain. Sufficient testing is done to assure that the memory changes are not the result of a severe depression. After all other disease processes are ruled out, a diagnosis can be established and appropriate treatment prescribed. The goal of this therapy is to help the individual maintain function as long as possible.

REFLECTION

How would your life be affected if a parent developed a dementia? What plans for that person would you believe to be necessary?

Function versus Diagnosis

Despite having their diagnoses, most people with chronic conditions are able to do quite well. Function is a key indicator for a caregiver to use to assess how the person is doing, which includes the present state of wellness/illness and the potential for the person to increase or decrease independence. Changes in function can be clues of changes in the status of a disease or the presence of new factors that require intervention. For example, if your mother was walking 100 feet unassisted last week and today she is huffing and puffing at 20 feet, something has occurred that should be immediately addressed with her healthcare provider.

Because of the numerous changes that take place throughout the body with age, physical diseases are more difficult to detect. It is very common for an older person to have an unusual response to illness. Signs and symptoms may be diminished, absent, or vary significantly from what one would observe in a younger individual. An example of this is delirium (acute onset of confusion), which may occur in older persons when they develop infections, such as urinary tract infections. In younger persons, there usually are signs and symptoms that would indicate the urinary tract infection, such as pain on urination, fever, and frequent urination. These symptoms may be absent in older adults, and instead, they may experience an acute episode or a general feeling of being run down.

KEY POINT

It is important for older adults and their caregivers to establish relationships with healthcare providers who are knowledgeable about geriatric medicine, sensitive to older adults, and aware of caregiver issues.

Medications

Medications afford many people not only more years to their lives, but add a higher quality of life to those years; however, medications can create a new host of problems. Every drug carries a risk of side effects and interactions with other drugs, herbs, and food. There is the chance that a medication may be indiscriminately used to manage a symptom when a nonpharmacologic approach could suffice. Side effects of drugs can be missed or attributed to another problem; worse still, another drug can be ordered to manage the side effects of the drug.

KEY POINT

Drug toxicity is an important consideration in caregiving to older adults. Because medications are absorbed, metabolized, and excreted very differently in the older person, a skilled geriatric professional is needed to assure safe drug prescription and management.

It is beneficial for caregivers to maintain a list of all prescriptions, over-the-counter medications, and dietary supplements that the individual is using. This list should accompany the individual to all visits to healthcare providers.

To assist the individual with self-administration of medications, the caregiver can develop a charting system whereby the person checks off the times medications are taken or use a multiday container in which several days' supply of medications can be prepoured (these are available at pharmacies or medical supply stores).

Becoming a Caregiver

Families have their own unique manner of selecting who will be the designated caregiver. Statistically, it will be a woman (about 75%)—a wife, daughter, or daughter-in-law.

KEY POINT

Despite the difficulties and complexities of family life today, most older adults are cared for in the home by family and friends.

Although many people perceive a caregiving responsibility as a burden, it can prove to be a special experience. Much can be discovered through the caregiving process when it is manifested as an act of love. It allows the caregiver the opportunity for intimacy and to heal relationships. Caregivers also can learn much about themselves—their talents, strengths, and weaknesses. Sometimes they can gain new direction in their lives or at least awareness of the relationship between themselves and others, especially those in their families. Positive family relationships and traditions can be strengthened. The act of caregiving can serve as an important lesson on values to younger members of the family.

This is not to minimize the stress and sacrifice involved with caregiving. There is usually significant effort and frustrations that may be endured while providing care. Caregiving can result in financial strain, fewer social opportunities, inconvenience in living arrangements, and reduced personal space. Career opportunities are frequently lost by caregivers, and this can have great impact on someone who is torn between climbing that corporate ladder and being the dutiful daughter or son. If a caregiver attempts to perform all caregiving responsibilities unassisted, it can be a very trying and difficult road.

Finding Help

When care is needed for a short time, as with a terminal illness, there may be sufficient help available among family and friends; however, when an illness is chronic and the need for caregiving extends for years, support and assistance may wane. Alternative arrangements for help from outside the family become crucial. There are organizations that assist people who are in need of caregiving and their caregivers that can be found through local information and referral services. Churches often have ministries that can provide assistance; a network of interfaith volunteer caregivers is available to assist those who desire help through faith communities (see the resources listing). Nonprofit organizations that assist people with specific conditions (e.g., Alzheimer's Disease and Related Disorders Association, Multiple Sclerosis Society) can also provide valuable assistance.

KEY POINT

The local office of the Area Agency on Aging can provide assistance in locating resources within your community. You can contact your local library for information and referral assistance.

Support Groups

A wonderful resource available for caregivers is special support groups that address issues of people dealing with caregiving. Information as well as successful techniques in handling complex situations is often shared at these informal meetings. There is a special bond that develops between members who share their unique stories that hold aspects to which many others in the group can relate.

An important message that surfaces in support groups is that caregivers have rights, too. Some caregivers need to be given permission to take care of themselves. Somewhere along the road they may have put their own self-care needs on the back burner. They may need to be encouraged to maintain their self-esteem and emotional balance.

There can be valuable exchanges between those who are experiencing the daily challenges of caring for loved ones who may be difficult or deteriorating very rapidly. Suggestions on the most workable method of handling a situation can save another group member hours of aggravation and frustration.

KEY POINT

There sometimes is the problem of who will stay with the dependent individual while the caregiver goes to a support group meeting. The group facilitator may have suggestions to help with this.

Caregiver support groups are an efficient, economical, user-friendly way of gaining access to a very complicated social and healthcare services maze. To obtain information about a local caregiver support group, meeting time, and place, call a nearby hospital's community education department or the local Agency on Aging. If they do not host the meetings themselves, they will be able to offer assistance in finding them. Searching the Internet by using the condition a person has (e.g., Alzheimer's disease, multiple sclerosis) often leads to information about local support groups and resources (see the Resources section at the end of this chapter).

Planning

To provide caregiving duties efficiently, a plan should be established with the input of the person who is receiving the care when possible. The plan will identify what the person needs and details on the caregiving arrangements (who will do what and when). Sometimes the person who is the recipient of the care may be a very private person or very demanding and have a specific idea of the assistance desired; the desired conditions may be unrealistic or unreasonable. The caregiver needs to be kind yet firm about setting limits. Too often, guilt or fear of displeasing the sick person leaves the caregiver a victim of never saying "no," which can lead to caregiver burnout.

Caregiving can be a full-time job, yet often it must be combined with many other household responsibilities and/or a paid job. It is important that the caregiver does not exceed realistic limits, but reaches for help to family, friends, professionals, or community resources. If other family members are unable to provide hands-on assistance, they can be asked to contribute financially to the purchase of services that can ease the caregiving burden. Respite from caregiving responsibilities is something that should be incorporated into the plan. Often a professional can assist the caregiver in obtaining respite services.

KEY POINT

Respite is a break from caregiving duties. It can be for several hours a week or several weeks a year. Respite can be achieved from a home health aide companion coming into the home or the ill person attending adult day care services or briefly staying at an assisted-living residence, at a nursing facility, or with another relative. The important point is that the caregiver receives a break from daily caregiving or duties and is able to return to responsibilities refreshed, renewed, healthy, and in good spirits. When burnout is not addressed and respite care is not arranged, the caregiver is at risk for illness.

Stresses of Caregiving

Caregiver stress is not only something that one experiences in the day-to-day, hands-on care of a loved one. This stress can exceed all boundaries and distance. Long-distance caregiving can be extremely difficult and challenging. With many families spread across the nation and around the world, caregiving has taken on a whole new appearance. Previously, families remained in close proximity, and there were family members who did not work outside the home. The care of young children and the aged was considered a normal family responsibility. There were few "old peoples' homes," as they were called, in which to place an older person. The conditions of most of those facilities were very poor, causing them to be the dread of older persons. Many families committed never to put their loved ones in such a place. Although the conditions of today's long-term care facilities are significantly improved over those of the past, many families continue to be reluctant to seek institutional care for a loved one and experience tremendous guilt when there is no alternative but to do so.

Long-Distance Caregiving

Family lifestyles have changed, and often both parents work outside the home. With some families separated by thousands of miles, family visits may be rare. Telephone calls, pictures, and even e-mails have taken the place of Sunday and holiday gatherings for many extended families. Although only about 5% of the senior population live in nursing homes, many older adults have moved to a more supportive environment. Assisted-living residences, continuing-care retirement communities, and adult communities have become increasingly common residences for elders. Most older adults no longer expect their children to provide for their daily care.

Many adult children who do not live in close proximity to their parents may not know that there is a problem with their parents until they receive a crisis telephone call; they may be ill-prepared to handle that emergency. They may have never discussed advanced directives, healthcare proxy, and other important issues with their parents, yet they may be facing some difficult decisions that have to be made. Decisions may need to be based on second-hand information (e.g., what a parent's friend recalls her desires to be regarding life-sustaining treatments).

KEY POINT

Every state has local Area Agency on Aging offices provided under the OAA, Title III. They frequently are excellent providers of information and referral, and are able to make the task of long distance caregiving easier. In some states, the Area Agency on Aging is the center for one-stop shopping for all issues that involve the older adult.

There is another group of professionals who have assisted many long-distance caregivers: geriatric care managers. This group of professionals is located throughout the United States. Their role is complex and varied. They are advocates for their clients, liaisons to clients' families, and supporters of their clients' well-being. They perform assessments, develop care plans, arrange for services, supervise auxiliary personnel, and serve as surrogate families. An additional function that is provided by many geriatric care managers is that of family or individual counseling. Many geriatric care managers are self-employed professionals, usually nurses or social workers. Some of them are part of larger corporations or affiliations, such as hospitals, Catholic Charities, or Jewish Family Services. There is a fee for their services, usually determined on an hourly basis The cost of services varies and can be quite expensive, but these care managers are able to deliver high-quality service and peace of mind that can be invaluable for long distance caregivers. More information about care managers can be obtained from their national office: National Association of Geriatric Care Managers at www.caremanager.org.

KEY POINT

The Family Medical Leave Act entitles employees to as much as 12 weeks of unpaid leave for the care of a family member.

Being Proactive

Caregivers can face significant change and loss. There is an alteration of roles, and frequently their entire lives are greatly affected. They may find themselves in the position of parenting their parents. Such lifestyle changes may result in them, as the caregivers, displaying adaptive behaviors that could include denial, excessive physical complaints, rigidity or stubbornness, an overly critical attitude, selective memory, or regression. They also could experience exhaustion, loneliness, depression, anger, or guilt. These behavioral manifestations sometimes cause them to experience the additional loss of friends, coworkers, and other support systems at a time when they most need this support. It is important for caregivers to recognize negative feelings toward their responsibilities and perhaps toward the individuals for whom they are providing care. It could prove very helpful for them to ask themselves the questions shown in Exhibit 26-1 to help identify red flags for problems.

After answering the questions in Exhibit 26-1, caregivers should consider discussing the "yes" responses with family and friends who form their support system and asking

---

EXHIBIT 26-1   Self-Assessment of Caregiver Stress

____ There are many days that I wonder if my life is worth living.

____ The care recipient requires care and attention that exceed my abilities.

____ I am often overwhelmed by my responsibilities.

____ My spouse and children feel that I am neglecting their needs.

____ I often do not sleep or eat properly.

____ There is little to no opportunity for me to exercise or engage in recreation.

____ I have postponed taking care of my own health needs because of the caregiving demands.

____ I often argue or have conflicts with the care recipient.

____ Sometimes I have thoughts of harming the care recipient.

____ I worry about what will happen to the care recipient if something happens to me.

____ My health is suffering.

____ There is little time or space for me to have personal private time.

____ It has become difficult for me to have a social life.

____ I have become resentful of other family members who do not provide assistance.

____ The care recipient takes me for granted.

____ Caregiving is creating financial hardship for me and/or my family.

____ I'm feeling guilty that my best does not seem good enough.

for advice and assistance in finding ways to change the situation. Options could include these:

- Calling a family meeting to assign or encourage additional family support
- Negotiating expectations and limitations with the care recipient
- Contacting outside community resources to come into the home and assist with care
- Finding someone to listen
- Scheduling time off
- Joining a support group
- Seeking counseling
- Exploring assisted living or nursing home care

It is far wiser to develop strategies to avoid having caregiver stress lead to negative consequences for all parties involved.

Summary

As more people are reaching their senior years and living longer once they do, their risk of becoming disabled and dependent on others increases. For most of these people, care will be provided by family members. This can present many challenges for the care recipients and the caregivers.

Caregivers can fill many roles, such as providing supervision, personal care, guidance in navigating the healthcare system, assistance with decision making, and support.

Often, caregivers have to juggle caregiving responsibilities with other family and work demands. Many people are caught between the care of their children and the care of their parents, leading to them being referred to as the *sandwich generation*. The term *club sandwich* is being added to family profiles to include caregivers who are providing care to their parents, children, and grandchildren.

It is important for caregivers to help their family members consider financial and health plans in the event that the dependent family members are incapable of making decisions and performing functions independently. An advance directive is one means to plan for future events; it provides instructions on treatment desired in the event people cannot express their opinions at a later date, and the person authorized to make healthcare decisions for them.

A variety of age-related changes can affect older individuals' abilities to function independently and engage in self-care. Furthermore, aging changes can alter the presentation of symptoms. It is important for caregivers to understand age-related changes to differentiate normal from abnormal findings.

Caregivers can lighten their burdens by planning care, seeking help with caregiving, participating in support group, and preventing and managing stress.

Suggested Reading

Acton, G. J., and Miller, E. W. (2003). Spirituality in caregivers of family members with dementia. *Journal of Holistic Nursing, 21*(2):117–130.

Blair, P. D. (2005). *The Next Fifty Years. A Guide for Women Midlife and Beyond.* Charlottesville, VA: Hampton Roads Publishing Company.

Calo-oy, S. (2004). *The Caregiver's Guide to Dealing with Guilt.* San Antonio, TX: Orchard Publications.

Dodds, M. (2006). *A Catholic Guide to Caring for Your Older Parent.* Chicago, IL: Loyola Press.

Farran, C. J. (2001). Family caregiver intervention research: where have we been? Where are we going? *Journal of Gerontological Nursing, 27*(7):38–45.

Larrimore, K. L. (2003). Alzheimer disease support group characteristics: a comparison of caregivers. *Geriatric Nursing, 24*(1):32–35.

Lerner, H. (2002). *The Dance of Connection.* New York: Quill.

Lilly, M. L., Richards, B. S., & Buckwater, K. C. (2003). Friends and social support in dementia caregiving: assessment and intervention. *Journal of Gerontological Nursing, 29*(1):29–36.

Logue, R. M. (2003). Maintaining family connectedness in long-term care: an advanced practice approach to family-centered nursing homes. *Journal of Gerontological Nursing, 29*(6):24–31.

McCall, J. B. (2000). *Grief Education for Caregivers of the Elderly.* New York: Haworth Pastoral Press.

McCullough, D. (2008). *My Mother, Your Mother: Embracing "Slow Medicine," the Compassionate Approach to Caring for Your Aging Loved Ones.* New York: HarperCollins.

Meyer, M. M., & Derr, P. (2007). *The Comfort of Home: A Step-by-Step Guide for Caregivers.* Portland, OR: CareTrust Publications LLC.

Moore, S. L., Metcalf, B., & Schow, E. (2000). Aging and meaning in life: examining the concept. *Geriatric Nursing, 21*(1), 27–29.

Ostwald, S. K., Hepburn, K. W., & Burns, T. (2003). Training family caregivers of patients with dementia: a structured workshop approach. *Journal of Gerontological Nursing, 29*(1):37–44.

Winters, S. (2003). Alzheimer disease from a child's perspective. *Geriatric Nursing, 24*(1):36–39.

Resources

Family Caregiver Alliance
690 Market Street, Dept. P, Suite 600
San Francisco, CA 94104
www.caregiver.org

National Council on Family Relations
3989 Central Avenue NE, Suite 550
Minneapolis, MN 55420
612-781-9331
www.ncfr.com

National Eldercare Locator
1112 16th Street NW, Suite 100
Washington, DC 20036
800-677-1116
www.eldercare.gov

Resources

A variety of resources exist to provide guidance and assistance in living a healthy, balanced life, and the savvy consumer needs to be equipped to use them. Some tips for developing a personal resource list—state, national, and international resources and important Internet sites, which address both conventional and complementary/alternative therapies—are offered in this chapter.

Tips for Developing a Personal Resource File

There is wisdom in having resources on hand before they are needed. This is similar to preparing for the proverbial rainy day or buying the hurricane shutters before the storm hits. Resources help people find information, and information offers more control of one's life. Here are some hints that can be beneficial to healthcare professionals and their clients.

- Purchase an accordion file that offers plenty of room for expansion. You can organize your resource file in any way that makes sense to you. One idea would be to divide the file into four sections: (1) local, (2) state, (3) national, and (4) international. This personal resource file can help to organize information you may need and enhance your self-care ability. There is value in having information when you face an actual health challenge or even before a challenge to your health occurs.

- Remember that information can come from a variety of sources. The trick is to be able to collect the information as soon as it is found and save it for when it is needed. Some places that you can find information are (1) friends who have had positive experiences with healthcare providers (keeper list), as well as less than adequate experiences (I will have to think about it), (2) local newspapers, (3) special television programs that offer current information about a variety of topics (be sure to jot down the highlights of what was said), (4) your local library, (5) workshops and seminars in your community, (6) books, (7) journals, and (8) the Internet.

Special Guidelines for the Internet

- Do not assume that just because it is labeled "medical advice" that it is "good advice." It is wise to check with a trusted healthcare provider before you take any remedies or discontinue prescribed medications or treatments.

- Always tab down to the end of the web page to see whether the Web site is updated on a monthly basis. This will at least let you know that the information is current. Try more than one Web site pertaining to the topic.

- Recognize that commercial sites are just that. They are on the Web to capture your business. A more reliable source of information would come from a medical center; a university hospital; a college of nursing, medicine, physical therapy, social work, pharmacy, chiropractic, naturopathy, traditional Chinese medicine) or Ayurvedic; or a government health agency. A simple rule of thumb is this: certification and accreditation = highest standards.

- It is necessary to ask yourself these questions when visiting sites:
  - Is there any chance that the information that I am downloading is biased?
  - Is the information being shared for the greater good of all individuals?
  - Whose benefit does it serve?
  - Is the information based on opinion only and not referenced from current professional (nursing, medical, social work, pharmacological, complementary, and naturopathic) resources?

- Know that it is important for people to make sense of the information gathered so that they can discuss it with their healthcare providers for clarification. Clients can be guided to form questions, such as these:
  - "Doctor or nurse, "I found this on the Internet, it's about my condition and I want to know more about how this can help me."
  - "This condition is being helped by _____. What is being done in our area?"
  - "I'd like to try _____. How does this affect the medicine I am taking now?"
  - "I trust the treatment you and I agreed upon, but have an interest in trying something different as well. Can I use both of these approaches together?"

Local Resources

Tips For Finding Local Resources

- The American Holistic Nurses' Association has networks throughout the country. Call the national number, 800-278-AHNA, for information. This would be a valuable resource and well worth your effort to find out about what is happening at your local level. Meetings are open to members of the community who value holism in their lives.

- Always consider local healthcare information talent. Most communities have a community college or university that has a college or school of nursing, medicine, social work, physical therapy, dentistry, massage, acupuncture, or allied health, whose faculty may be excellent resources. These potentially valuable resources can be tapped by doing the following:

1. Call the main number of the area you need (e.g., department of nursing).

2. Identify yourself as an individual in the community.

3. State your need (e.g., "I am interested in talking to someone on your faculty who knows about _____. I'd appreciate his or her ideas.")

4. Leave a message so that faculty can get in touch with you.

- Do not be intimidated if you have had little involvement with a college or university. The faculty often is eager to assist and enjoy the opportunity to put their knowledge to good use.

- Many individuals in the community experience similar issues/concerns and thus come together in support groups. Check local newspapers for health sections or community meeting announcements that list support group meetings. Even if you are not in need of a support group at present, it could be helpful to cut this information out and place it in your personal resource file for future reference.

  - Do not forget the weekly columns on "You and Your Health" or "Pharmacology News." Become a resource finder.

- Libraries are rich resources not only for the books and journals they contain, but also for the workshops and printed material that are made available to the general public. Librarians can be a valuable guide to resources on the Internet, as well as reference material in their holdings and in other libraries.

  - Do not forget that DVDs are available on health-related content.

- You probably have great resources at your fingertips that you may be overlooking: telephone directories. Directories typically have listings for community resources. Also, depending on your interest, simply look for a local agency (e.g., American Cancer Society or American Heart Association). Let the agency know specifically what your needs are (e.g., literature, schedule of classes).

Tips For Finding Local Resources on the Internet

- Go to your favorite search engine (e.g., Google, Search.com, Mama.com, Metacrawler, Dogpile, Healthfinder.gov), and type in the query that best describes your needs. An example would be "Palm Beach County, Arthritis Resources" or "Bucks County, Area Agency on Aging."

- Any time that you are looking for resources at the local level, try typing in the county where you live. This provides a more specific, local search. The reverse also may hold true. If you are not able to locate your needs at the local level, you may need to start more globally and then work your way to the local level. An example might be looking for resources for American Cancer Society and then linking until you find local resources.

· Please be patient! Consider yourself a detective who is looking for clues for resources to help you. It is worth the effort!

State Resources

Tips for Finding State Resources

· Check the state health department for your area of interest (e.g., AIDS Administration, Department of Mental Health, Nursing Home Licensing and Certification). State health departments also have divisions that license and monitor the practice of various professionals, such as nursing, medicine, nursing home administrators, dentists, acupuncturists, and massage therapists.

Tips for Finding State Resources on the Internet

· Go to your favorite search engine as you did in your local search (e.g., Dogpile, Google, Mama, Metacrawler, Healthfinder.gov), and type in the query that best describes what it is you are looking for. An example would be New York State, Licensed Acupuncturists, or Oregon, Naturopaths. This should lead you to information pertinent to your state.

· Also consider the various state agencies that may lead you to the information that you need. An example would be Michigan, Department of Health, or Florida, AIDS resources.

· Think about the hospitals in your state that are major medical centers. An example of this would be Texas, Baylor University or Philadelphia, Jefferson University. This may open up information for you that you never suspected were available to the consumer. Another way of getting information about your major medical centers would be to type in the state and the term: Arizona, medical centers or Alabama, health resources.

· Keep trying, and with patience, you will find that the Internet can offer rich resources.

National Resources

National Institutes/Centers

National Institutes of Health
http://www.nih.gov/health

This is a large resource for government agencies. This site has valuable publications that are free or at low cost.

National Cancer Institute
Building 31, Room 10A18
Bethesda, MD 20205
800-492-6600
www.nci.nih.gov

National Center for Complementary and Alternative Medicine of NIH
http://nccam.nih.gov
This is a valuable clearinghouse for information.

National Heart, Lung, and Blood Institute
P.O. Box 30105
Bethesda, MD 20824-0105
301-592-8573
http://www.nhlbi.nih.gov

National Dissemination Center for Children with Disabilities
P.O. Box 1492
Washington, DC 20013
800-695-0285
www.nichcy.org

National Institute on Aging
Building 31, Room 5C27
31 Center Drive, MSC 2292
Bethesda, MD 20892
301-496-1752
www.nia.nih.gov

National Institute on Alcohol Abuse and Alcoholism
301-443-3860
www.niaaa.nih.gov

National Institute of Arthritis and Musculoskeletal and Skin Diseases
301-495-4484
www.niams.nih.gov

National Institute of Child Health and Human Development
P.O. Box 3006
Rockville, MD 20847

800-370-2943
www.nichd.nih.gov

National Institute of Dental and Craniofacial Research
Building 45, Room 4AS19
45 Center Drive
Bethesda, MD 20892-6400
301-496-4261
www.nidcr.nih.gov

National Institute of Diabetes and Digestive and Kidney Diseases
Building 31, Room 9A04
31 Center Drive, MSC 2560
Bethesda, MD 20892-2560
301-654-3327
www.niddk.nih.gov

U.S. Center for Disease Control and Prevention
www.cdc.gov

U.S. Environmental Protection Agency
Ariel Rios Building
1200 Pennsylvania Avenue, NW
Washington, DC 20460
www.epa.gov

Warren Grant Magnuson Clinical Center
Clinical Center, NIH
Building 10, Room B1S234
Bethesda, MD 20892-1078
301-496-3311
www.cc.nih.gov

Requests can be made for Clinical Center nutrition education materials.

National and Professional Organizations

Academy for Guided Imagery
P.O. Box 2070
Mill Valley, CA 94942
800-726-2070
www.interactiveimagery.com

Alzheimer's Disease and Related Disorders Association
225 North Michigan Ave., Suite 1700
Chicago, IL 60601-7633
800-272-3900
www.alz.org

American Academy of Pain Management
13947 Mono Way #A
Sonora, CA 95370
209-533-9744
www.aapainmanage.org

American Association of Acupuncture and Oriental Medicine
1925 West County Road B2
Roseville, MN 55113
651-631-0204
www.aaaom.org

American Heart Association
800-242-8721
www.americanheart.org

American Association of Kidney Patients
3505 E. Frontage Rd Ste 315
Tampa, FL 33607
800-749-2257
www.aakp.org

American Association of Naturopathic Physicians
3201 New Mexico Ave., NW Ste 350
Washington, DC 20016
800-538-2267
www.naturopathic.org

American Botanical Council
6200 Manor Rd.
Austin, TX 78723
512-926-4900
www.herbalgram.org

American Chiropractic Association
1701 Clarendon Blvd.

Arlington, VA 22209
703-276-8800
www.amerchiro.org

American College of Hyperbaric Medicine
2476 Bolsover
Box 130
Houston, TX 77005
713-528-0657
www.hyperbaricmedicine.org

American Council on Exercise
4851 Paramount Dr.
San Diego, CA 92123
858-279-8227
www.acefitness.org

American Diabetes Association, National Call Center
1701 North Beauregard St.
Alexandria, VA 22311
800-342-2383
www.diabetes.org

American Holistic Nurses' Association
P.O. Box 2130
Flagstaff, AZ 86003
800-278-AHNA
www.ahna.org

American Holistic Medical Association
12101 Menaul Blvd. NE, Suite C
Albuquerque, NM 87112
505-292-7788
www.holisticmedicine.org

American Liver Foundation
75 Maiden Lane, Suite 603
New York, NY 10038
800-465-4837
www.liverfoundation.org

American Lung Association
61 Broadway, 6th floor

New York, NY 10006
212-315-8700
www.lungusa.org

American Massage Therapy Association
820 Davis Street, Suite 100
Evanston, IL 60201-4444
847-684-0123
www.amtamassage.org

Arthritis Foundation
1314 Spring Street NW
Atlanta, GA 30309
800-283-7800
www.arthritis.org

Asthma Hotline
800-222-LUNG

Ayurvedic Institute
11311 Menaul NE
Albuquerque, NM 87112
505-291-9698
www.ayurveda.com

Colorado Center for Healing Touch
12477 W. Cedar Dr., Suite 206
Lakewood, CO 80228
303-989-0581
www.healingtouch.net

Lighthouse National Center for Vision and Aging
111 East 59th Street
New York, NY 10022
800-829-0500
www.lighthouse.org

Multiple Sclerosis Association of America
706 Haddonfield Road
Cherry Hill, NJ 08002
800-532-7667
www.msaa.com

National Association for the Deaf
814 Thayer Avenue
Silver Spring, MD 20910
301-587-1789
www.nad.org

National Center for Homeopathy
801 North Fairfax, Suite 306
Alexandria, VA 22314
703-548-7790
www.homeopathic.org

National Hospice and Palliative Care Organization
1700 Diagonal Rd., Suite 625
Alexandria, VA 22314
703-837-1500
www.nho.org

National Osteoporosis Foundation
1232 22nd Street NW
Washington, DC 20037-1292
202-223-2226
www.nof.org

National Parkinson's Disease Foundation
1501 NW 9th Avenue
Bob Hope Road
Miami, FL 33136
800-327-4545
www.parkinson.org

National Stroke Association
9707 E. Easter Lane
Englewood, CO 80112
800-STROKES
www.stroke.org

North American Vegetarian Society
P.O. Box 72
Dolgeville, NY 13329
518-568-7970
www.navs-online.org

Nurse Healers Professional Associates, Inc.
3760 South Highland Drive, Suite 429
Salt Lake City, UT 84106
801-273-3399
www.therapeutic-touch.org

United Ostomy Association
19772 MacArthur Blvd., #200
Irvine, CA 92612-2405
800-826-0826
www.uoa.org

Web Sites Related to Health Care Information

ACTIS (Clinical Trials for HIV/AIDS)
800-TRIALS-A
www.actis.org

Adult Children of Alcoholics Worldwide Services
Organizationwww.recovery.org/acoa/acoa.html
Al-Anon Family Group Headquarters
www.al-anon-alateen.org

Anxiety Disorders Association of America
www.adaa.org

Association for Applied Psychophysiology and Biofeedback
www.aapb.org

Bioport
http://bioport.com
This has links to medical news sites, research sites, and medical universities.

CenterWatch
www.centerwatch.com
This is a resource for clinical trials on various diseases, a summary of research, and numbers to contact.

Health on the Net
www.hon.ch/home.html
This searches for available information/resources.

Healthfinder
www.healthfinder.gov

This is a gateway site sponsored that is by the government with links to more than 1400 health sites.

Healthy People 2010
www.health.gov/healthypeople

This is a national health initiative coordinated by the Office of Disease Prevention and Health Promotion and the U.S. Department of Health and Human Services. It looks at health issues for the next decade.

Journal of the American Medical Association
www.jama-assn.org

This is a valuable resource for consumers—access to the "patient page."

Medhunt
www.hon.ch/medhunt

This is a medical search engine.

Medscape
www.medscape.com

This is a gateway to reviewed information from reputable medical journals.

National Council on Family Relations
www.ncfr.com

National Library of Medicine
www.nlm.nih.gov

This offers access to the world's largest biomedical library.

Pharm Info Net
www.pharminfo.com

This has information about medications.

Prostate Cancer Resource Network
www.hmri.com

Self-Help Group Sourcebook Online
http://mentalhelp.net/selfhelp/

This is an online directory of thousands of medical and mental health support organizations around the world.

International Resources

Global Alliance for Women's Health
www.gawh.org

International Association of Yoga Therapists
P.O. Box 426
Manton, CA 96059
530-474-5700
www.iayt.org

MEL: International Health Resources
http://mel.lib.us/health/healthinternational.html

World Health Organization
www.who.int
This is a resource for issues around the globe.

U.C. Berkeley, Public Health Library
International Health Resources
www.lib.berkeley.edu/PUBL/Inthealth.html

UN Aids Organization
www.unaids.org
This is a global source for HIV/AIDS information.

Index